P9-EKR-301

East Coast Australia

Cairns & the
Daintree Rainforest
p438

Townsville to
Mission Beach
p417

Whitsunday Coast
p395

Capricorn Coast & the
Southern Reef Islands
p381

Fraser Island & the
Fraser Coast p361

Noosa & the
Sunshine Coast p338

Brisbane & Around
p279

The Gold Coast
p321

Byron Bay &
North Coast NSW
p133

Sydney & the
Central Coast p50

Melbourne &
Coastal Victoria
p200

Canberra &
South Coast NSW
p150

CALGARY PUBLIC LIBRARY

NOV   2017

Andy Symington, Kate Armstrong, Cristian Bonetto, Peter Dragicevich,
Paul Harding, Trent Holden, Kate Morgan, Charles Rawlings-Way,
Tamara Sheward, Tom Spurling, Donna Wheeler

Contents

PLAN YOUR TRIP

ON THE ROAD

KANGAROO POINT,
BRISBANE P281

FRASER ISLAND P375

SYDNEY HARBOUR
BRIDGE P52

WALTER BIBIKOW / GETTY IMAGES ©

PISAPHOTOGRAPHY / SHUTTERSTOCK ©

ODAIR FALEÇO / 500PX ©

Contents

GREAT BARRIER REEF P488

PORT CAMPBELL
NATIONAL PARK P259

KANGAROOS IN
CANBERRA P174

Contents

STOCKPERT CHILD 004 / GETTY IMAGES ©

DAINTREE NATIONAL PARK P471

MELBOURNE P200

Welcome to East Coast Australia

Pack your bags: Australia's east coast is road-tripping nirvana, with picture-perfect beaches, rainforests, hip cities and the Great Barrier Reef.

Into the Wild

Strung out for more than 18,000km end to end, Australia's east coast is a rippling ribbon of beaches and rampant wildlife. Offshore, the astonishing Great Barrier Reef is a 2000km-long hyper-coloured haven for tropical marine life. Also here are hundreds of islands, from craggy nature reserves to palm-studded paradises. Fringing the land are brilliant beaches, with Australia's best surf breaks peeling into the shore. Inland are bewitching national parks with lush rainforests, jagged peaks and native critters that rate from cuddle-worthy (koalas) to photogenic (Ulysses butterflies) and downright fearsome (saltwater crocs).

Action Stations

Traversing the east coast is an exercise in, well...exercise! The sun is shining and fit-looking locals are outdoors – jogging, swimming, surfing, cycling, kayaking, snorkelling, hiking... Why not join in? Get underwater on the Great Barrier Reef, the most photogenic submarine landscape on earth. Rampage down some white-water rapids, kayak across a lagoon, or set sail through a tropical archipelago. Move your shoes up a mountain, through a national park or alongside a rushing river. Or just head for the beach, where the locals let it all hang out.

City Scenes

Home to Indigenous Australians for millennia, Australia's east coast is also where modern Australia kicked off. The first European settlement was in Sydney, and the city remains a honey-pot lure for anyone looking for a good time. Sassy and ambitious yet unpretentious, Sydneysiders eat, drink, shop and party with hedonistic abandon. To the south, Melbourne is Australia's arts and coffee capital – a bookish, Euro-tinged town with a bohemian soul. Wrapped around river bends, boom-town Brisbane is a glam patchwork of inner-city neighbourhoods. And don't forget Australia's capital, Canberra – so much more than a political filing cabinet!

Eat, Drink & Celebrate

Australia's big east-coast cities offer rich culinary experiences, with fantastic cafes, sprawling food markets and world-class restaurants. After dark, moody wine bars, student-filled speakeasies and boisterous Aussie pubs provide plenty of excuses to bend an elbow and maybe watch a bit of football. Beyond the cities, foodie delights range from fish and chips straight off the fishing boats, to cheese producers, small-town bakeries and degustation dinners, paired perfectly with luscious wines from the Mornington Peninsula or Hunter and Yarra Valleys.

Why I Love East Coast Australia

By Charles Rawlings-Way, Writer

Growing up in a chilly southern Australian town, the lure of the east coast, with its *Endless Summer* beaches and throbbing cities, was ever-present. Melbourne enticed with its book-shops, bars, Carlton Football Club and urban soul; Sydney lured with city-slicker cool and warm waves in which to attempt to surf. Towns such as Byron Bay, Noosa and Port Douglas held near-mythical status, demanding to be explored at the first opportunity. And I haven't stopped exploring since! South–north or north–south, travelling the east coast is Australia's essential road trip.

For more about our writers, see p527

Above: Sydney skyline and the Sydney Harbour Bridge (p52)

East Coast Australia

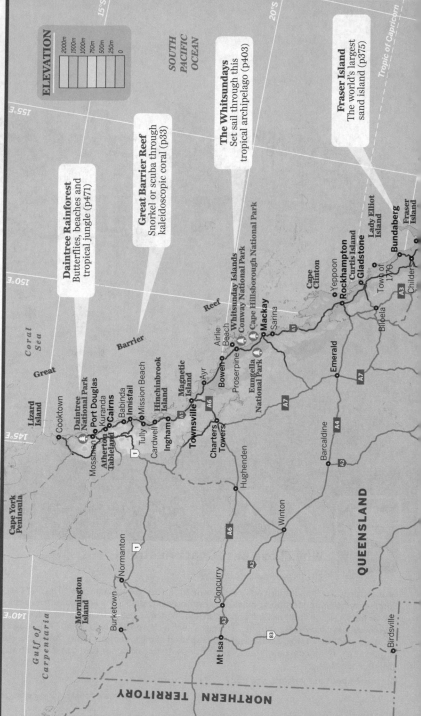

Daintree Rainforest
Butterflies, beaches and tropical jungle (p471)

Great Barrier Reef
Snorkel or scuba through kaleidoscopic coral (p33)

The Whitsundays
Set sail through this tropical archipelago (p403)

Fraser Island
The world's largest sand island (p375)

ELEVATION

2000m
1500m
1000m
750m
500m
250m
0

400 km
200 miles

SOUTH PACIFIC OCEAN

Coral Sea

Gulf of Carpentaria

QUEENSLAND

NORTHERN TERRITORY

Cape York Peninsula

Mornington Island

Great Barrier Reef

Cooktown
Lizard Island
Daintree National Park
Mossman
Port Douglas
Kuranda
Cairns
Atherton Tableland
Babinda
Innisfail
Mission Beach
Tully
Cardwell
Ingham
Hinchinbrook Island
Magnetic Island
Townsville
Ayr
Charters Towers
Hughenden
Bowen
Proserpine
Airlie Beach
Whitsunday Islands
Conway National Park
Cape Hillsborough National Park
Eungella National Park
Mackay
Sarina
Emerald
Barcaldine
Winton
Cloncurry
Mt Isa
Birdsville
Normanton
Burketown

Cape Clinton
Yeppoon
Rockhampton
Curtis Island
Gladstone
Cape Clinton
Town of 1770
Biloela
Childers
Lady Elliot Island
Bundaberg
Fraser Island

Tropic of Capricorn

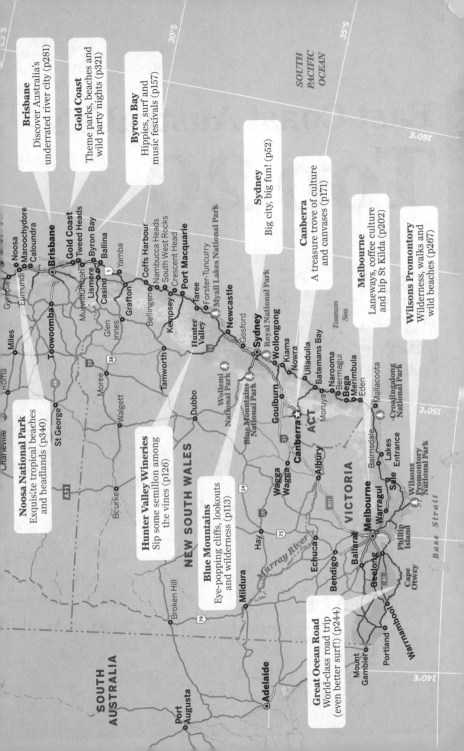

Brisbane
Discover Australia's underrated river city (p281)

Gold Coast
Theme parks, beaches and wild party nights (p321)

Byron Bay
Hippies, surf and music festivals (p157)

Sydney
Big city, big fun! (p52)

Canberra
A treasure trove of culture and canvases (p171)

Melbourne
Laneways, coffee culture and hip St Kilda (p202)

Wilsons Promontory
Wilderness, walks and wild beaches (p267)

Noosa National Park
Exquisite tropical beaches and headlands (p340)

Hunter Valley Wineries
Sip some semillon among the vines (p126)

NEW SOUTH WALES

Blue Mountains
Eye-popping cliffs, lookouts and wilderness (p113)

Great Ocean Road
World-class road trip (even better surf!) (p244)

SOUTH AUSTRALIA

VICTORIA

SOUTH PACIFIC OCEAN

Tasman Sea

Bass Strait

30°S

35°S

160°E

150°E

140°E

East Coast Australia's
Top 20

Sydney

1 The big-ticket sights are all in Sydney (p50) – the Sydney Opera House, the Rocks and Sydney Harbour Bridge top most people's lists – but to really catch Sydney's vibe, spend a day at the beach. Stakeout a patch of sand at Bondi Beach, lather yourself in sunscreen and plunge into the surf; or hop on a harbour ferry from Circular Quay to Manly for a swim, a surf or a walk along the sea-sprayed promenade to Shelly Beach. *Ahhh,* this is the life! Left: Bondi Beach (p65)

Great Barrier Reef

2 The Great Barrier Reef (p33) lives up to its reputation. Stretching more than 2000km along the Queensland coastline, it's a complex ecosystem populated with dazzling coral, languid sea turtles, gliding rays, timid reef sharks and 1500 species of colourful tropical fish. Whether you dive on it, snorkel over it, explore it via scenic flight or glass-bottom boat, linger in an island resort or camp on a remote coral-fringed atoll, this vivid undersea kingdom and its 900 coral-fringed islands is unforgettable.

2

Sailing the Whitsunday Islands

3 You can hop around an entire archipelago of tropical islands in this seafaring life and never find anywhere with the sheer tropical beauty of the Whitsundays (p403). Travellers of all monetary persuasions launch yachts from party town Airlie Beach and drift between these lush green isles in a slow search for paradise (you'll probably find it in more than one place). Wish you were here?

Daintree Rainforest

4 Lush green rainforest tumbles towards brilliant white-sand coastline in the ancient, World Heritage–listed Daintree Rainforest (p471). This extraordinary wonderland is home to 3000-or-so plant species, including fan palms, ferns and mangroves – you'll be enveloped by birdsong, the buzz of insects and the constant commentary of frogs. Continue exploring on wildlife-spotting tours, mountain treks, interpretive boardwalks, tropical-fruit orchard tours, canopy walks, 4WD trips, horse rides, kayak trips and cruises. Bottom: Mossman River

Indigenous Far North Queensland

5 The human history of Far North Queensland is as dramatic as its natural surrounds. Indigenous people have called the region's rainforests and beaches home for more than 40,000 years, and a boom in Aboriginal-led tours (p471) and experiences makes it easier than ever for visitors to see it all through native eyes. Throw a spear, make a boomerang, sample bush tucker, interpret rock art, go on a rainforest walk, or dig the didgeridoo: a world of new – yet incredibly old – adventures awaits.

Byron Bay

6 Australia's most easterly point, Byron Bay (p157; Byron to its mates) is one of the enduring icons of Australian culture. Families on school holidays, surfers and sunseekers from around the globe gather here, drawn by fabulous restaurants, a laid-back ethos, surf beaches and an astonishing range of activities. This is one of the most beautiful stretches of coast in the country and, although it's markedly upmarket these days, the town's hippie vibe will put a smile on your dial.

Melbourne's Laneways

7 Once the sole domain of garbage bins, rats, drug addicts and adult cinemas, the maze-like bluestone laneways threading through downtown Melbourne (p214) have been transformed into city hot spots. Home to some of the best street art in the world, here you can discover secret Banksy and local artists' works, the city's swankiest basement restaurants, divey rock bars and secret stairways leading up to rooftop cocktail bars. Top: Degraves St (p214)

Blue Mountains

8 Jusy a few hours from Sydney, the views from Katoomba's Echo Point and Blackheath's Govetts Leap in the Blue Mountains (p113) are so good that you'll find yourself pushing to the front of the crowd then pushing your camera's memory card to the limit. After the photo shoot, hike a trail into the magnificent Jamison Valley or Grose Valley, accompanied by the scent of eucalyptus oil, a fine mist of which issues from the dense tree canopy and gives these World Heritage–listed mountains their name. Bottom: Echo Point, Blue Mountains (p117)

HOLGER METTE / GETTY IMAGES ©

AUSTRALIAN SCENICS / GETTY IMAGES ©

Noosa National Park

9 Cloaking the headland beside the stylish resort town of Noosa itself, Noosa National Park (p340) features a string of perfect bays fringed with sand and pandanus trees. Surfers come here for the long, rolling waves; walkers make the trip for the unspoiled natural vibes. Lovely hiking trails crisscross the park: and on the scenic coastal trails you might spy sleepy koalas in the trees and dolphins swimming off the rocky headland.

Fraser Island

10 Fraser Island (p375) is an ecological wonderland created by drifting sand, where wild dingoes roam free and lush rainforest grows on sand. It's a primal island utopia, home to a profusion of wildlife, including the purest strain of dingo in Australia. The best way to explore the island is in a 4WD – cruising up the beaches and bouncing along sandy inland tracks. Tropical rainforest, pristine freshwater pools and beach camping under the stars will bring you back to nature.

Hunter Valley Wineries

11 Picture this: a glassfronted pavilion overlooking gently rolling hills covered with row after row of grape-heavy vines. Inside, you're sipping a glass of golden-hued sémillon and pondering a delectable lunch menu of top-quality local produce. Make your choice, settle back, slide into a glass of earthy shiraz and thoroughly enjoy your meal. It's the stuff of which travel memories are made, and all of this could be yours in New South Wales' premier wine district, the Hunter Valley (p126).

Great Ocean Road

12 Jutting out of turbulent waters, the Twelve Apostles on the Great Ocean Road (p244) are one of Victoria's defining sights, but it's the getting-there road trip that doubles their impact. Take it slow along roads that curl beside Bass Strait beaches, then whip inland through rainforest and quaint little towns. Great Ocean Road doesn't stop at the Twelve Apostles: further along is maritime treasure Port Fairy and hidden Cape Bridgewater. For the ultimate in slow travel, hike the Great Ocean Walk from Apollo Bay to the Apostles. Top: Twelve Apostles, Port Campbell National Park (p259)

Brisbane

13 Forget the nasty gossip. Once considered little more than a provincial sidekick to Sydney and Melbourne, Brisbane (p279) has reinvented itself as one of Asia Pacific's hippest hubs. No longer happy to settle for 261 days of sunshine a year, Queensland's new and improved capital is smashing it on the cultural front, with an ever-expanding booty of ambitious street art and galleries, boutique bookshops, secret cocktail bars and award-winning microbreweries. The result: big-city Australian cool with a laid-back, subtropical twist.

Wildlife Watching

14 Head to Phillip Island (p242), southeast of Melbourne, for a parade of adorable little penguins and fur seals cavorting along the rocky shore, or into tropical Far North Queensland for otherworldly cassowaries and dinosaur-like crocodiles. In between, you'll find a panoply of extraordinary animals found nowhere else on earth: koalas, kangaroos, wombats and adorable platypuses. There's also great whale watching along the coast in season (May to November), plus the omni-present laughter of kookaburras.

Canberra

15 Though Canberra (p171) is only a century old, Australia's purpose-built capital has always been preoccupied with history. So it's not surprising that the major drawcards here are lavishly endowed museums and galleries that focus on recounting and interpreting the national narrative. Institutions such as the National Gallery of Australia, National Museum of Australia, National Portrait Gallery and Australian War Memorial offer visitors a fascinating insight into the country's history and culture. Bottom: Australian Parliament House (p173), Canberra

ALASTAIR POLLOCK PHOTOGRAPHY / GETTY IMAGES ©

RICHARD I'ANSON / GETTY IMAGES ©

Montague Island

16 Montague Island (p193) is one of wild Australia's most under-rated destinations. Offshore from Narooma, bald, boulder-strewn Montague is a haven for nesting seabirds, including a mere 10,000 little penguins. Indigenous sacred sites, an unusual granite lighthouse, refurbished cottage accommodation and guided eco-tours set Montague apart from the mainland by more than the 9km boat ride it takes to get there. Diving (spot some grey nurse sharks!), seal watching and occasional pods of passing whales all add to the island's appeal.

Sydney After Dark

17 Sydney's hip beaches and scenic harbour get all the press, but for many it's after dark when the city really wakes up (p96). You can find your tribe amid stylish lounges, buzzing nightclubs, old-fashioned pubs and indie- rock bars scattered around town...or sidestep the crowds stage-side at an underground jazz club or a low-key wine bar overlooking the water. There are also art-gallery bars, grassy backyard lounges, restaurants with hidden dance floors, mod-Asian watering holes... Get into it! Bottom left: Sydney Opera House (p52) and Opera Bar (p96)

Wilsons Promontory

18 Wilsons Promontory (p268; aka 'Wilson's Prom', or just 'The Prom') is heaven for bushwalkers, wildlife watchers, surfers and photographers. The scenery here is out of this world: even a short detour from the park base at Tidal River will access swathes of white-sand beaches and bays. But with more than 80km of marked walking trails, the best of the Prom requires some leg work. Serious hikers should tackle the three-day Great Prom Walk, staying a night in gloriously isolated lighthouse keepers' cottages.

Lady Elliot Island

19 This ecofriendly resort island (p387) is one of the loveliest and most peaceful places to experience the Great Barrier Reef. Snorkel straight off Lady Elliot's white sands – the living reef that surrounds the tiny coral cay is teeming with tropical fish, turtles and the island's resident manta rays. At hatching time (January to April) you can see baby turtles scamper across the sand, and humpback whales pass by from June to October. Getting to the island, with a scenic flight over the turquoise reef-filled waters, is equally memorable.

Bridge Climbing

20 Vertigo not an issue? Make a bee-line for Sydney's iconic Harbour Bridge or Brisbane's Story Bridge and scale their steely heights. Once only the domain of bridge painters and trespassing daredevils (including one of our authors, who shall remain nameless), Sydney's big arch can now be tackled by anyone on a BridgeClimb (p77), Story Bridge Adventure Climb is a newer experience, but no less mesmerising. And it's not just about the sublime city views – the bridges themselves are amazing structures!

19

20

Need to Know

For more information, see Survival Guide (p499)

Currency
Australian dollar ($)

Language
English

Visas
All visitors to Australia need a visa. New Zealand visitors are granted a visa on arrival. All other passport holders must apply for a visa. Apply online through the Department of Immigration and Border Protection (p509).

Money
ATMs widely available. Credit cards accepted at most hotels, restaurants and shops.

Mobile Phones
Buy a starter kit, which may include a phone or just a SIM card (under $10) and a prepaid charge card at airport mobile-phone shops or outlets in cities.

Time
Australia's east coast is on Australian Eastern Standard Time (AEST), which is GMT/UCT plus 10 hours.

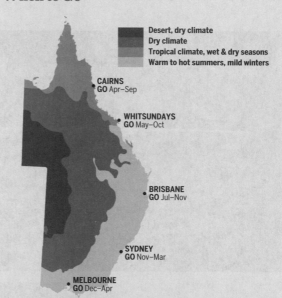

When to Go

Desert, dry climate
Dry climate
Tropical climate, wet & dry seasons
Warm to hot summers, mild winters

CAIRNS
GO Apr–Sep

WHITSUNDAYS
GO May–Oct

BRISBANE
GO Jul–Nov

SYDNEY
GO Nov–Mar

MELBOURNE
GO Dec–Apr

High Season (Dec–Feb)
➡ Summertime: hot and humid up north, warm and dry down south.

➡ Prices rise 25% for big-city accommodation.

➡ Low season in the tropical north; unsafe swimming north of Agnes Water from November to May (jellyfish).

Shoulder (Sep–Nov & Mar–May)
➡ Warm sun, clear skies, shorter queues.

➡ Spring flowers (October); autumn colours in Victoria (April).

➡ Local business people not yet stressed by summer crowds.

Low Season (Jun–Aug)
➡ Cool rainy days and off-season accommodation prices down south.

➡ Tropical high season: mild days, low humidity, pricey beds.

➡ Good visibility on the Great Barrier Reef.

Useful Websites

Lonely Planet (www.lonely
planet.com/australia) Destination information, hotel bookings,
traveller forum and more.

Tourism Australia (www.aus
tralia.com) Government tourism
site with loads of visitor info.

Queensland Tourism
(www.queenslandholidays.com.
au) Queensland coverage.

Visit NSW (www.visitnsw.com)
New South Wales information.

Visit Victoria (www.visitvictoria.
com) Victoria's official site.

Coastalwatch (www.coastal
watch.com) Surf reports and
cams.

Important Numbers

Country code	☑61
International access code	☑0011
Emergency (ambulance, fire, police)	☑000
Directory assistance	☑1223
Area codes	Vic ☑03, NSW & ACT ☑02, Qld ☑07

Exchange Rates

Canada	C$1	$1.00
Euro zone	€1	$1.40
Japan	¥100	$1.21
New Zealand	NZ$1	$0.95
UK	UK£1	$1.63
USA	US$1	$1.30

For current exchange rates, see
www.xe.com.

Daily Costs
Budget: Less than $150

➡ Hostel dorm bed: $25–35

➡ Double room in a hostel:
$80–100

➡ Budget pizza or pasta meal:
$15–20

➡ Short bus or tram ride: $4

Midrange: $150–300

➡ Double room in a motel or
B&B: $130–250

➡ Breakfast or lunch in a cafe:
$20–30

➡ Car hire per day: from $35

➡ Short taxi ride: $25

Top End: More than $300

➡ Double room in a top-end
hotel: from $250

➡ Three-course meal in a
classy restaurant: from $80

➡ Adventure activities: sailing
the Whitsundays from $300
per night, diving course $650

➡ Domestic flight Sydney to
Melbourne: from $100

Opening Hours

Business hours vary from state
to state, but use the following
as a guide:

Banks 9.30am–4pm Monday to
Thursday, to 5pm Friday

Bars 4pm–late

Cafes 7am–5pm

Nightclubs 10pm–4am Thursday to Saturday

Post Offices 9am–5pm Monday
to Friday; some also 9am–noon
Saturday

Pubs 11am–midnight

Restaurants Noon–2.30pm and
6pm–9pm

Shops 9am–5pm Monday to
Saturday

Supermarkets 7am–8pm

Arriving in Australia

Sydney Airport (p511) Airport
Link trains to central Sydney
every 10 minutes, 5am to
12.14am. Prebooked shuttle
buses service city hotels. A taxi
into the city costs $25 to $50
(30 minutes).

Melbourne Airport (p511)
SkyBus services (24 hours)
to central Melbourne every
10 to 30 minutes. A taxi into
the city costs around $40 (25
minutes).

Brisbane Airport (p511)
Airtrain trains to central Brisbane every 15 to 30 minutes,
5am to 10pm. Prebooked shuttle
buses service city hotels. A taxi
into the city costs $50 to $60
(25 minutes).

Getting Around

Australia's east coast is over
3000km long! Getting from A to
B requires some thought.

Car Travel at your own tempo,
explore remote areas and visit
regions with no public transport.
Hire cars in major towns; drive
on the left.

Plane Fast-track your holiday:
affordable, frequent, fast inter-
nal flights. Carbon-offset flights
if you're feeling guilty.

Bus Reliable, frequent long-
haul services around the
country (not always cheaper
than flying)

Train Slow, expensive,
infrequent...but the scenery
is great! Opt for a sleeper
carriage rather than an
'overnighter' seat if you want to
actually sleep.

For much more on
getting around,
see p511

PLAN YOUR TRIP NEED TO KNOW

If You Like...

Beaches

Bondi Beach Essential Sydney: carve up the surf or laze around and peoplewatch. (p65)

Wilsons Promontory Victoria's premier coastal wilderness, with deserted beaches. (p268)

Fraser Island The world's largest sand island is basically one big beach. (p375)

Whitehaven Beach The jewel of the Whitsundays, with powdery white sand and gin-clear waters. (p413)

Cape Tribulation The rainforest sweeps down to smooch the reef at empty stretches of sand. (p473)

The Spit A long, wild stretch of pristine Gold Coast sand and dunes, beyond the high-rises and the crowds. (p327)

Four Mile Beach Take a stinger-safe swim at Port Douglas, or go for a four-mile beachcomb. (p465)

Clarkes Beach Iconic strip of Byron Bay sand – at low tide you can walk to the lighthouse. (p163)

Yeppoon A long stretch of Queensland sand where locals and Rockhampton folk come to cool off. (p390)

Rose Bay One of little Bowen's best bays. Sit on the sand and eat a mango. (p414)

Indigenous Culture

Aboriginal Heritage Tour Learn about Gadigal culture and traditional medicinal and food plants in Sydney's Botanic Gardens. (p52)

Koorie Heritage Trust A great place to discover southeastern Aboriginal culture, in Melbourne. (p203)

Kuku-Yalanji Dreamtime Walks Walks through Queensland's Mossman Gorge with knowledgable Indigenous guides. (p471)

Ingan Tours Aboriginal-operated rainforest tours in tropical north Queensland. (p432)

Tjapukai Aboriginal Cultural Park Interactive tours and vibrant performances in Cairns by local Tjapukai people. (p443)

Worimi Conservation Lands Discover ancient Worimi shell middens near Stockton Bight. (p135)

Gallery of Modern Art This must-see Brisbane gallery includes a significant collection of fibre art from contemporary Indigenous artists. (p285)

Conway National Park Explore forested hillsides and isolated beaches near Airlie Beach, once the hunting grounds of the Giru Dala people. (p411)

Wildlife Encounters

Phillip Island Penguins The world's largest little penguin colony; catch them at sunset marching up from the sea. (p242)

Whale watching in Eden In season (July to November) you can spy whales offshore anywhere from Eden right up to the Great Barrier Reef. (p198)

Lone Pine Koala Sanctuary Have a one-on-one experience with a soft, furry marsupial just outside Brisbane. (p289)

Ben Boyd National Park Muddle-headed wombats aplenty at this rambling national park near Eden. (p199)

Montague Island Spy some seals, seabirds and penguins offshore from Narooma. (p193)

Hartley's Crocodile Adventures Come face to toothy snout with a prehistoric predator near Port Douglas. (p458)

Kuranda Koala Gardens Birds, bats, butterflies and – of course – koalas await at Kuranda near Cairns. (p459)

Noosa National Park Koalas, dolphins and seasonal whales are easy to spot at this highly accessible pocket of green. (p340)

Fraser Island The wild dingoes here are the purest of breed in Australia. (p375)

Wildlife Habitat Port Douglas See some koalas, kangaroos, crocs, lorikeets and cassowaries in natural habitats. (p465)

Islands

Montague Island Seabirds, little penguins, fur seals...plus revamped lighthouse accommodation. What's not to like? (p193)

Cockatoo Island Amazing Sydney Harbour isle with a dazzling history. (p68)

Fraser Island Rev up your 4WD: the world's largest sand island has giant sand dunes, freshwater lakes and rampant wildlife. (p375)

Whitsundays Book into a resort, or jump aboard a yacht and explore as many of these amazing islands as you can. (p403)

Lady Elliot Island Ringed by the Great Barrier Reef and reachable by light aircraft – the perfect place to play castaway. (p373)

Lizard Island Pitch a tent or check into the plush resort on this far-north island. (p473)

Top: Aboriginal man, Tjapukai Aboriginal Cultural Park (p443)
Bottom: Wilsons Promontory (p267)

Month by Month

January

January yawns into action as Australia recovers from its Christmas hangover, but then everyone realises, 'Hey, it's summer!'. Heat and humidity along the coast; monsoonal rains up north.

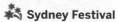 **Sydney Festival**

'It's big' says the promo material. Indeed, sprawling over three summer weeks, the Sydney Festival, a fab affiliation of music, dance, talks, theatre and visual arts – much of it free and family-focused – is an artistic behemoth. (p78)

☆ **Australian Open**

Held at Melbourne Park in late January, the Australian Open draws tennis fanatics from around the planet as the world's best duke it out on the courts. Invariably it's baking hot. (p215)

Australia Day

Australia Day is the nation's 'birthday' – when the First Fleet landed on 26 January 1788. Expect picnics, barbecues, fireworks and, increasingly, nationalistic chest beating. In less mood to celebrate are Indigenous Australians, who refer to it as 'Invasion Day'.

February

February is usually Australia's warmest month: hot and sticky up north as the wet season continues, but divine in Victoria. Everywhere else, locals go back to work, to the beach or to the cricket.

Sydney Gay & Lesbian Mardi Gras

Mardi Gras is a two-week-long arts festival running deep into March and culminating in a flamboyant parade along Sydney's Oxford St that attracts 300,000 spectators. Gyms empty out and waxing emporiums tally their profits. After-party tickets are gold. (p506)

March

Heat and humidity ease down south – crowds dissipate and resort prices drop. Meanwhile, high temps and general irritability prevail in the north. Harvest time in the vineyards.

☆ **Australian Formula One Grand Prix**

Melbourne's normally tranquil Albert Park explodes with four days of Formula One rev-head action in late March. The 5.3km street circuit around the lake is known for its smooth, fast surface. (p211)

April

Autumn brings golden colours to Victoria and cooler, mild temperatures to New South Wales. Up north it's the end of the wet season: smiling faces and warm, pleasant weather. Pricey Easter accommodation.

☆ Byron Bay Bluesfest

Music erupts over the Easter weekend when 20,000 festivalgoers swamp Byron Bay to hear blues-and-roots bands from all over the world (Ben Harper, Neil Young, Bonnie Raitt). Held on Tyagarah Tea Tree Farm, 11km north of Byron. Some folks camp. (p158)

May

Days grow noticeably cooler down south; beach days are unlikely anywhere south of the Gold Coast. You can find good deals on accommodation all around.

✯ Biennale of Sydney

Held in even-numbered years between March and June, Sydney's Biennale showcases the work of hundreds of contemporary artists and is the country's largest visual-arts event. Expect tours, talks, screenings and cutting-edge exhibitions. Most events are free. (p79)

✗ Noosa Food & Wine

One of Australia's best regional culinary fests, with cooking demonstrations, wine tastings, cheese exhibits, feasting on gourmet fare and live concerts at night. Over three days in mid-May. (p342)

✯ Sydney Writers' Festival

Books, words, books full of words... For one week in May, the Sydney Writers' Festival hosts 300-plus novelists, essayists, poets, historians and philosophers – from Australia and beyond – who read their work, run workshops and host edifying panel discussions. (p79)

☆ Whale Watching

Between May and November along the southeastern Australian coast, migrating southern right and humpback whales come close to shore to feed, breed and calve. See them at Eden (NSW) and Warrnambool (Victoria) and Hervey Bay and North Stradbroke Island (Queensland).

June

The south shivers into winter, while tourist season kicks into high gear in the warm, clear tropical north with stinger-free beaches. Migrating whales cavort off the coast (until November).

✯ Vivid Sydney

Immersive light installations and projections in the city, plus performances from local and international musicians, and public talks and debates with leading global creative thinkers; held over 18 days from late May.

✯ Sydney Film Festival

Held (mostly) at the State Theatre, this excellent film festival screens art-house gems from Australia and the world. (p79)

☆ State of Origin Series

Rugby league fanatics consider this series of three matches between Queensland and New South Wales the pinnacle of the game. The final match is held in July.

July

Pubs with open fires, cosy coffee shops and empty beaches down south; packed markets, tours and accommodation up north. Bring warm clothes for anywhere south of Brisbane. Don't miss 'MIFF'.

☆ Melbourne International Film Festival

As wildly popular as Toronto and Cannes, the Melbourne International Film Festival has been running since 1952 – tickets sell like piping-hot chestnuts. Myriad short films, feature-length spectaculars and documentaries flicker across inner-city screens. (p216)

☆ Splendour in the Grass

A splendid alt-rock music festival in Byron Bay, Splendour draws the big names from around Australia and overseas for three days in late July (winter, so the grass can get a tad muddy). (p158)

August

August is when southerners, sick of winter's grey-sky drear, head to Queensland for some sun. A good time to explore Far North Queensland before things start to heat up again.

Cairns Festival

Running for two weeks from late August into September, the massive art-and-culture Cairns Festival delivers a stellar program of music, theatre, dance, comedy, film, Indigenous art and public exhibitions. Lots of outdoor events. (p447)

Gympie Music Muster

We like both kinds of music: country *and* western! The Gympie Music Muster is a charity-based music event, with more boots and banjos than seems plausible. Bring your tent. (p371)

September

Winter ends and spring returns, bringing wildflowers and brighter spirits in the south. Weather generally remains mild across the country. Football finishes and the spring horse-racing carnival begins.

Australian Football League Grand Final

The pinnacle of the AFL season is this high-flying spectacle in Melbourne, watched (on TV) by millions. At half-time everyone's neighbourhood BBQ moves into the local park for a little amateur kick-to-kick. (p215)

Brisbane Festival

One of Australia's largest, most diverse arts fiestas, the Brisbane Festival runs for 22 days in September. An impressive schedule includes concerts, plays, dance and fringe events. It finishes off with 'Riverfire', an elaborate

fireworks show over the Brisbane River. (p295)

Floriade

Floriade is a florid display of spring flowers in Canberra running from mid-September until mid-October. Locals shake off the winter chills with a look at some blooms. (p175)

October

The weather avoids extremes everywhere: a good time to go camping or hit some vineyards. After the football and before the cricket, sports fans twiddle their thumbs.

Melbourne Festival

This annual arts festival offers some of the best of opera, theatre, dance and visual arts from around Australia and the world. It starts in early October and runs through to early November. (p216)

November

Northern beaches may close due to 'stingers' – jellyfish in the shallows north of Agnes Water. The surf-lifesaving season flexes its muscles on beaches everywhere.

Melbourne Cup

On the first Tuesday in November, Australia's (if not the world's) premier horse race chews up the Melbourne turf. The whole country does actually pause to watch the 'race that stops a nation'. (p215)

Airlie Beach Music Festival

The Airlie Beach Music Festival entails three days of letting it all hang out in the famous party town, with loads of live tunes to rock out to. (p407)

December

Ring the bell, school's out! Holidays begin a week or two before Christmas. Cities are packed with shoppers and the weather is hot. Up north, monsoon season is underway: afternoon thunderstorms bring pelting rain.

Sydney to Hobart Yacht Race

Pack a picnic and join the Boxing Day (26 December) crowds along Sydney's waterfront to watch the start of the Sydney to Hobart, the world's most arduous open-ocean yacht race (628 nautical miles!). (p79)

Woodford Folk Festival

On the Sunshine Coast, the Woodford Folk Festival stages a diverse collection of performers playing folk sounds from across the globe. Runs from 27 December to 1 January. (p358)

Sydney Harbour Fireworks

A fantastic way to ring in the new year: join the crowds overlooking the harbour as the Sydney Harbour Fireworks light up the night sky. There's a family display at 9pm; the main event erupts at midnight. (p79)

Itineraries

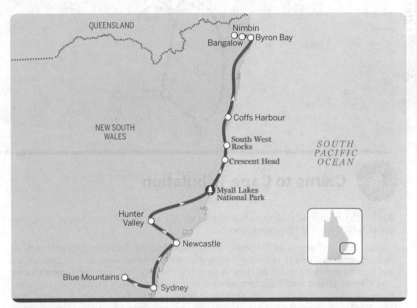

QUEENSLAND

Nimbin
Bangalow
Byron Bay

NEW SOUTH
WALES

Coffs Harbour

South West
Rocks

Crescent Head

SOUTH
PACIFIC
OCEAN

Myall Lakes
National Park

Hunter
Valley

Newcastle

Blue Mountains

Sydney

Sydney to Byron Bay

Mountains, cities, wine, beaches and quirky towns: this road trip is an Australian classic.

Kick-start your tour in **Sydney**, checking out the big-ticket sights, seeing Bondi Beach, bar hopping, shopping and shuffling between restaurants. Don't miss the seaside Bondi to Coogee Clifftop Walk. Dart inland to explore the **Blue Mountains**, with misty Katoomba's cache of art deco architecture and the amazing Three Sisters lookout. Alternatively, a couple of days shunting around the **Hawkesbury River** on a houseboat is a sure-fire stress remedy.

Next stop is the the arts- and surf-loving city of **Newcastle**. Thirsty? Detour inland to the hedonistic vineyards of the **Hunter Valley** (super semillon). Back on the coast, explore the pristine beaches of **Myall Lakes National Park**.

Northern New South Wales (NSW) basks in subtropical glory. Surf the excellent breaks at **Crescent Head** and splash around in the sea at photogenic **South West Rocks**. At **Coffs Harbour**, the very kitsch Big Banana awaits your appreciation. Further north, **Byron Bay** is inescapable – a chilled-out beach town where surfers, hipsters and hippies share the sands. Meditating in Byron's verdant hinterland is the alt-stoner haven of **Nimbin** and affluent, laid-back **Bangalow** – both worthy day trips.

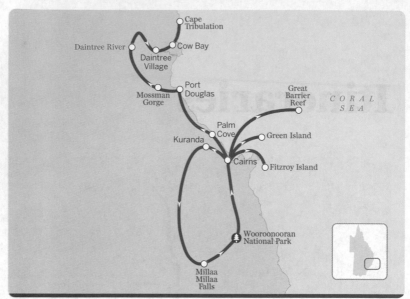

Cairns to Cape Tribulation

Far North Queensland is like nowhere else on earth – a dizzying array of coral reefs, tropical atolls, rainforests and interesting towns.

Australia's reef-diving capital and gateway to the Daintree Rainforest, **Cairns** is an obligatory east-coast destination. Spend a few days pinballing between botanic gardens, hip restaurants and buzzy watering holes. A short hop offshore, reef-trimmed **Green Island** and **Fitzroy Island** have verdant vegetation and lovely beaches, without too many folks competing for patches of sand. Further afield, a snorkelling or dive trip to the **Great Barrier Reef** is an essential east-coast experience, or plan a few days on a live-aboard expedition to Cod Hole (Lizard Island), one of Australia's best dive spots.

Next up, head inland on a gondola cableway or scenic railway to **Kuranda** for rainforest walks and a wander around the town's famous markets. If you have your own wheels you can explore further: swing by the picturesque **Millaa Millaa Falls** and take a rainforest hike in spectacular **Wooroonooran National Park**.

Back at sea level, treat yourself to a night in a plush resort at **Palm Cove**, just north of Cairns. An hour further north is **Port Douglas**, an up-tempo holiday hub with fab eateries, bars and a beaut beach. It's also a popular base for boat trips to the outer reef. Next stop is **Mossman Gorge**, where lush lowland rainforest surrounds the photogenic Mossman River. Take a guided walk and cool off in a waterhole.

Further north is the **Daintree River**, where you can go on a crocodile-spotting cruise then stop for lunch at the low-key **Daintree Village**. Afterwards, cross by vehicle ferry to the northern side of the river. From here continue driving north (easy does it – this is cassowary country!) to the Daintree Discovery Centre – a great place to learn about this magnificent jungle wilderness. The beach at nearby (and rather agriculturally named) **Cow Bay** is perfect for a few hours of beachcombing among the seashells and driftwood.

Last stop on your tropical tour is **Cape Tribulation**, a magnificent natural partnership between rainforest and reef. Spend a few nights taking in the splendour at one of the camping or backpacker places nooked into the rainforest.

Top: Fan Palms, Cape Tribulation (p472)

Bottom: Helicopter flight over the Great Barrier Reef (p33)

WILL GRAY / GETTY IMAGES ©

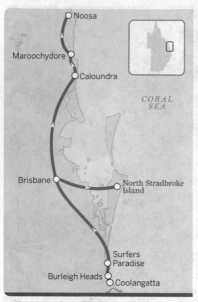

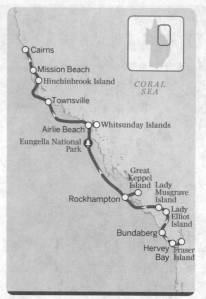

5 DAYS — South Queensland Coast

Check out Queensland's big smoke, and the sun-baked Gold and Sunshine Coasts to the south and north.

Brisbane delivers plenty of surprises. Don't miss the arty Gallery of Modern Art and Brisbane Powerhouse on the riverbanks. Check out raffish West End, ever-changing Fortitude Valley, and side-by-side Teneriffe and Newstead with their emerging crop of hip eateries, breweries and live-music venues.

Just an hour to the south, the Gold Coast exhibits the flip side of Queensland's soul: beachy, brassy and boozy. The hub of the action here is **Surfers Paradise**, with its palpable after-dark sexiness and theme parks. More relaxed and surf-centric are **Burleigh Heads** just to the south, and **Coolangatta** on the NSW border.

If time is your *amigo*, tack on a few days roaming the beaches on **North Stradbroke Island** in Moreton Bay. Otherwise, truck north to the Sunshine Coast towns of up-and-coming **Caloundra** and unpretentious **Maroochydore**. Another half-hour north is **Noosa**, a classy resort town with sublime beaches, a lush national park and a string of top-flight restaurants.

12 DAYS — Hervey Bay to Cairns

Track north along the central section of Queensland's eastern seaboard, with plenty of islands to visit en route.

Two hours north of Noosa is amiable **Hervey Bay**, from where you can explore the huge dunes and crystalline lakes on **Fraser Island**. Not far north, sip Australia's favourite rum in **Bundaberg**.

Sample Queensland's coral wonders at **Lady Musgrave Island** or **Lady Elliot Island**, then don a big hat and devour a steak at 'beef city' **Rockhampton**. Offshore, unwind for a few days on the trails and beaches on **Great Keppel Island** – pure tropical-beach bliss.

Spot a platypus in **Eungella National Park** then wheel into buzzy **Airlie Beach**, gateway to the azure waters and powdery white-sand beaches of the **Whitsunday Islands**.

Vibrant **Townsville** is next. Don't miss hiking the Thorsborne Trail on magnificent **Hinchinbrook Island**. Recover at super-chilled **Mission Beach**, where the rainforest meets the sea. End your trip in touristy **Cairns** – with a trip to the Great Barrier Reef and a seafood feast.

3 DAYS Melbourne & the Great Ocean Road

Dip into east-coast Australia's deep south, exploring hip Melbourne and the gorgeous Great Ocean Road.

Melbourne has enough to entertain for months – bars, galleries, live music, shopping, AFL football...but the Great Ocean Road: a classic Aussie road trip beckons.

Start in the surfing mecca of **Torquay** and check the swell at **Bells Beach**, then head to family-focused **Anglesea** for a surf lesson and a riverside picnic. **Aireys Inlet** is next: tour the lighthouse, then spend the night in the surprisingly cosmopolitan resort town of **Lorne**.

West of here, the Great Ocean Road gets wiggly and scenic, winding between the sea and the rainforest-clad Otway Ranges. Wind down in the artsy fishing town of **Apollo Bay**, then swing by **Cape Otway** to see some koalas and the lighthouse.

Next up is Port Campbell National Park and its famed **Twelve Apostles**. Count them from the cliff tops, then spend a night in **Port Campbell**. Scan for whales along the **Warrnambool** coast, then continue west to rather Irish-feeling **Port Fairy**. If there's time, visit tiny **Cape Bridgewater**.

10 DAYS Melbourne to Sydney

This coastal run offers lots of wilderness, bookended by Australia's biggest cities.

Kick off in savvy **Melbourne** before exploring **Phillip Island**, where penguins, seals and surfers frolic. Next stop is **Wilsons Promontory** with its fab bushwalks and beaches. Truck northeast through the the Gippsland Lakes district to **Mallacoota**, a low-key Victorian seaside town.

Entering warmer south-coast NSW, sleepy **Eden** is famed for whale watching. Don't miss historic, picture-perfect **Central Tilba**. Continue to **Narooma**, with its pretty beaches and solid surf. From here, ferry out to **Montague Island**. Tracking north, detour inland to Australian capital **Canberra** to see Parliament House.

Back on the coast, **Jervis Bay** offers white-sand beaches, dolphins and national parks. Heading north, zip through **Kiama**, then **Wollongong** to the elevated Grand Pacific Drive. South of Sydney are the dramatic cliffs of **Royal National Park**.

Welcome to **Sydney**. Tour the Sydney Opera House, catch a harbour ferry and dunk yourself in Bondi Beach waves. Leave time for the awe-inspiring **Blue Mountains**.

BAN PHOTOGRAPHY / 500PX ©

Top: The Gold Coast (p321)

Bottom: Cape Byron Lighthouse (p157)

Plan Your Trip
Your Reef Trip

The Great Barrier Reef, stretching over 2000km from just south of the Tropic of Capricorn (near Gladstone) to just south of Papua New Guinea, is the most extensive reef system in the world. There are numerous ways to experience this magnificent spectacle. Diving and snorkelling are the best methods of getting close to the menagerie of marine life and dazzling corals. You can also surround yourself with fabulous tropical fish without getting wet on a semi-submersible or a glass-bottomed boat, or see the macro perspective on a scenic flight.

When to Go

High season on the reef is from June to December. The best overall underwater visibility is from August to January.

From December to March, **northern Queensland** (north of Townsville) has its wet season, bringing oppressive heat and abundant rainfall (it's cooler from July to September). Stinger (jellyfish) season is between November and May; most reef operators offer Lycra stinger suits to snorkellers and divers, or bring your own.

Anytime is generally good to visit the **Whitsundays**. Winter (June to August) can be pleasantly warm, but you will occasionally need a jumper. South of the Whitsundays, summer (December to March) is hot and humid.

Southern and central Queensland experience mild winters (June to August) – pleasant enough for diving or snorkelling in a wetsuit.

Picking Your Spot

There are many popular and remarkable spots from which to access the 'GBR', but bear in mind that individual areas change over time, depending on the weather or recent damage.

Best for...

Wildlife

Sea turtles around Lady Elliot Island or Heron Island. (p373)

Looking for reef sharks and rays while kayaking off Green Island. (p455)

Spotting wild koalas on Magnetic Island. (p424)

Snorkelling

Getting underwater at Knuckle, Hardy and Fitzroy Reefs. (p33)

Offshore at Magnetic Island (p424) or the Whitsunday Islands (p189).

Views from Above

Scenic chopper or plane rides from Cairns (p236) or the Whitsunday Islands (p395).

Skydiving over Airlie Beach. (p405)

Sailing

Sailing from Airlie Beach through the Whitsunday Islands. (p406)

Exploring Agincourt Reef from Port Douglas. (p466)

Mainland Gateways

There are several mainland gateways to the reef, all offering slightly different experiences and activities. Here's a brief overview, ordered from south to north.

Agnes Water & Town of 1770 Small towns and good choices if you want to escape the crowds. Tours head to Fitzroy Reef Lagoon, one of the most pristine sections of the reef, where visitor numbers are still limited. The lagoon is excellent for snorkelling, but also spectacular viewed from the boat.

Gladstone A bigger town but still a relatively small gateway. It's an excellent choice for avid divers and snorkellers, being the closest access point to the southern or Capricorn reef islands and innumerable cays, including Lady Elliot Island.

Airlie Beach A small town with a full rack of sailing outfits. The big attraction here is spending two or more days aboard a boat and seeing some of the Whitsunday Islands' fringing coral reefs. Whether you're a five- or no-star traveller, there'll be a tour to match your budget.

Townsville Renowned among divers. Whether you're learning or experienced, a four- or five-night diving safari around the numerous islands and pockets of the reef is a great choice. Kelso Reef and the wreck of the SS *Yongala* are teeming with marine life. There are also a couple of day-trip options on glass-bottomed boats, but for more choice you're better off heading to Cairns. The gigantic Reef HQ Aquarium is also here.

Mission Beach Closer to the reef than any other gateway destination, this small town offers a few boat and diving tours to sections of the outer reef. The choice isn't huge, but neither are the crowds.

Cairns The main launching pad for reef tours, with a staggering number of operators offering everything from relatively inexpensive day trips on large boats to intimate five-day luxury charters. Tours cover a wide section of the reef, with some operators going as far north as Lizard Island. Inexpensive tours are likely to travel to inner, less pristine reefs. Scenic flights also operate out of Cairns.

Port Douglas A swanky resort town and a gateway to the Low Isles and Agincourt Reef, an outer ribbon reef featuring crystal-clear water and stunning corals. Diving, snorkelling and cruising trips tend to be classier, pricier and less crowded than in Cairns. You can also take a scenic flight from here.

Cooktown Close to Lizard Island, but most tour operators here shut down between November and May for the wet season.

Islands

Speckled throughout the reef is a profusion of islands and cays that offer some of the most stunning access. Here is a list of some of the best islands, travelling from south to north.

Lady Elliot Island The coral cay here is twitcher heaven, with 57 resident bird species. Sea turtles also nest here and it's possibly the best spot on the reef to see manta rays. It's also a famed diving location. There's a resort here, but you can also visit Lady Elliot on a day trip from Bundaberg.

Heron Island A tiny, tranquil coral cay sitting amid a huge spread of reef. It's a diving mecca, but the snorkelling is also good and it's possible to do a reef walk from here. Heron is a nesting ground for green and loggerhead turtles and home to 30 bird species. The sole resort on the island charges accordingly.

Hamilton Island The big daddy of the Whitsundays, Hamilton is a sprawling, family-friendly resort laden with infrastructure. While the atmosphere isn't exactly intimate, there's a wealth of tours going to the outer reef. It's also a good place to see patches of the reef that can't be explored from the mainland.

Hook Island An outer Whitsunday island surrounded by fringing reefs. There's excellent swimming and snorkelling here, and the island's sizeable bulk provides plenty of good bushwalking. There's affordable accommodation on Hook and it's easily accessed from Airlie Beach, making it a top choice for those on a modest budget.

Orpheus Island A national park and one of the reef's most exclusive, tranquil and romantic hideaways. Orpheus is particularly good for snorkelling – you can step right off the beach and be surrounded by colourful marine life. Clusters of fringing reefs also provide plenty of diving opportunities.

Green Island Another of the reef's true coral cays. The fringing reefs here are considered to be among the most beautiful surrounding any island, and the diving and snorkelling are spectacular. Covered in dense rainforest, the entire island is national park. Bird life is abundant. Accessible as a day trip from Cairns.

Lizard Island Remote, rugged and the perfect place to escape civilisation, Lizard has a ring of talcum-white beaches, remarkably blue water and few visitors. It's home to the Cod Hole, arguably Australia's best-known dive site, where you can swim with docile potato cod weighing as much as 60kg. Accommodation here has no grey areas: it's either five-star luxury or bush camping.

Reef Highlights

0 ——— 200 km
0 ——— 100 miles

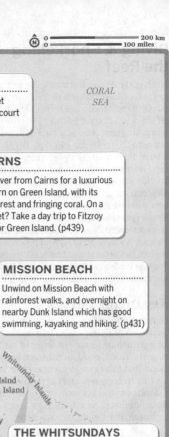

PORT DOUGLAS

Book yourself onto an upmarket catamaran day-trip out to Agincourt Reef. (p463)

CAIRNS

Hop over from Cairns for a luxurious sojourn on Green Island, with its rainforest and fringing coral. On a budget? Take a day trip to Fitzroy and/or Green Island. (p439)

MISSION BEACH

Unwind on Mission Beach with rainforest walks, and overnight on nearby Dunk Island which has good swimming, kayaking and hiking. (p431)

TOWNSVILLE

In Townsville, visit the excellent Reef HQ Aquarium for a dry-land reef encounter. If you're an experienced diver, book a trip on a live-aboard boat to dive the SS *Yongala* wreck. And don't miss the koalas on Magnetic Island. (p419)

THE WHITSUNDAYS

From party-prone Airlie Beach, explore some white-sand Whitsundays beaches and encircling coral reefs via a tour or sailing cruise. (p403)

TOWN OF 1770

Head to the Town of 1770 and day-trip out to Lady Musgrave Island for semisubmersible coral-viewing, plus snorkelling or diving in the definitive blue lagoon. (p383)

CORAL SEA

Lizard Island

Cooktown

PORT DOUGLAS
Green Island
Fitzroy Island
CAIRNS
Innisfail
Tully
MISSION BEACH
Dunk Island
Hinchinbrook Island
Ingham
Magnetic Island
TOWNSVILLE
Charters Towers
Bowen
Airlie Beach
Hamilton Islnd
Lindeman Island
Mackay

GREAT BARRIER REEF

Whitsunday Islands

Tropic of Capricorn
Great Keppel Island
Rockhampton
Emerald
Gladstone
TOWN OF 1770
Bundaberg
Fraser Island
Hervey Bay
Maryborough
Miles
Noosa

Diving & Snorkelling the Reef

Much of the diving and snorkelling on the reef is boat-based, although there are some excellent reefs accessible by walking straight off the beach of some islands. Free use of snorkelling gear is usually part of any day cruise to the reef – you can typically fit in around three hours of underwater wandering. Overnight or liveaboard trips obviously provide a more in-depth experience and greater coverage of the reefs. If you don't have a diving certificate, many operators offer the option of an introductory dive, where an experienced diver conducts an underwater tour. A lesson in safety and procedure is given beforehand and you don't require a five-day Professional Association of Diving Instructors (PADI) course or a 'buddy'.

Key Diving Details

Your last dive should be completed 24 hours before flying – even in a balloon or for a parachute jump – in order to minimise the risk of residual nitrogen in the blood that can cause decompression injury. It's fine to dive soon after arriving by air.

Find out whether your insurance policy classifies diving as a dangerous-sport exclusion. For a nominal annual fee, the Divers Alert Network (www.diversalertnetwork.org) provides insurance for medical or evacuation services required in the event of a diving accident. DAN's hotline for emergencies is ☎+1 919 684 9111.

Visibility for coastal areas is 1m to 3m, whereas several kilometres offshore visibility is 8m to 15m. The outer edge of the reef has visibility of 20m to 35m and the Coral Sea has visibility of 50m and beyond.

In the north, the water is warm all year round, from around 24°C to 30°C. Going south it gradually gets cooler, dropping to a low of 20°C in winter.

Top Reef Dive Spots

The Great Barrier Reef is home to some of the world's best diving sites. Here are a few of our favourite spots to get you started:

SS Yongala A sunken shipwreck that has been home to a vivid marine community for more than 90 years.

Cod Hole Go nose-to-nose with a potato cod.

Heron Island Join a crowd of colourful fish straight off the beach.

Lady Elliot Island With 19 highly regarded dive sites.

Wheeler Reef Massive variety of marine life, plus a great spot for night dives.

MAKING A POSITIVE CONTRIBUTION TO THE REEF

The Great Barrier Reef is incredibly fragile and it's worth taking some time to educate yourself on responsible practices while you're there.

➡ No matter where you visit, take all litter with you – even biodegradable material such as apple cores – and dispose of it back on the mainland.

➡ It is an offence to damage or remove coral in the marine park.

➡ If you touch or walk on coral you'll damage it and get some nasty cuts.

➡ Don't touch or harass marine animals.

➡ If you have a boat, be aware of the rules in relation to anchoring around the reef, including 'no anchoring areas' to avoid coral damage.

➡ If you're diving, check that you are weighted correctly before entering the water and keep your buoyancy control well away from the reef. Ensure that equipment such as secondary regulators and gauges aren't dragging over the reef.

➡ If you're snorkelling (especially if you're a beginner), practise your technique away from coral until you've mastered control in the water.

➡ Hire a wetsuit rather than slathering on sunscreen, which can damage the reef.

➡ Watch where your fins are – try not to stir up sediment or disturb coral.

➡ Do not enter the water near a dugong, whether you're swimming or diving.

➡ Note that there are limits on the amount and types of shells that you can collect.

TOP SNORKELLING SITES

Some nondivers may wonder if it's really worth going to the Great Barrier Reef 'just to snorkel'. The answer is a resounding yes! Much of the rich, colourful coral lies just underneath the surface (coral needs bright sunlight to flourish) and is easily viewed by snorkellers. Here's a round-up of some top snorkelling sites.

➡ Fitzroy Reef Lagoon (Town of 1770)

➡ Heron Island (Capricorn Coast)

➡ Keppel Island (Capricorn Coast)

➡ Lady Elliot Island (Capricorn Coast)

➡ Lady Musgrave Island (Capricorn Coast)

➡ Hook Island (Whitsundays)

➡ Hayman Island (Whitsundays)

➡ Border Island (Whitsundays)

➡ Lizard Island (Cairns)

➡ Hardy Reef (Whitsundays)

➡ Knuckle Reef (Whitsundays)

➡ Michaelmas Reef (Cairns)

➡ Hastings Reef (Cairns)

➡ Norman Reef (Cairns)

➡ Saxon Reef (Cairns)

➡ Opal Reef (Port Douglas)

➡ Agincourt Reef (Port Douglas)

➡ Mackay Reef (Port Douglas)

Boat Excursions

Unless you're staying on a coral-fringed island, you'll need to join a boat excursion to experience the reef's real beauty. Day trips leave from many places along the coast, as well as from island resorts, and typically include the use of snorkelling gear, snacks and a buffet lunch, with scuba diving an optional extra. On some boats, naturalists or marine biologists give talks on the reef's ecology.

Boat trips vary dramatically in passenger numbers, type of vessel and quality – which is reflected in the price – so get all the details before committing. When selecting a tour, consider the vessel (motorised catamaran or sailing ship), the number of passengers (from six to 400), what extras are offered and the destination. The outer reefs are usually more pristine. Inner reefs often show signs of damage from humans and coral-eating crown-of-thorns starfish. Coral bleaching is a major issue in far northern sections of the reef.

Many boats have underwater cameras for hire, although you'll save money by hiring these on land (or using your own waterproof camera or underwater housing). Some boats also have professional photographers on board who will dive and take high-quality shots of you in action.

Liveaboards

If you're eager to do as much diving as possible, a liveaboard is an excellent option as you'll do three dives per day, plus some night dives, all in more remote parts of the Great Barrier Reef. Trip lengths vary from one to 12 nights. The three-day/three-night voyages, which allow up to 11 dives (nine day and two night dives), are the most common.

It's worth checking out the various options as some boats offer specialist itineraries, following marine life and events such as minke whales or coral spawning, or offer trips to less-visited spots like the far northern reefs, Pompey Complex, Coral Sea Reefs or Swain Reefs.

It's recommended to go with operators who are Dive Queensland (www.dive-queensland.com.au) members: this ensures they follow a minimum set of guidelines. Ideally, they'll also be accredited by Ecotourism Australia (www.ecotourism.org.au).

REEF RESOURCES
....

Dive Queensland www.dive-queens
land.com.au

Tourism Queensland www.queens
landholidays.com.au

**Great Barrier Reef Marine Park
Authority** www.gbrmpa.gov.au

**Department of National Parks,
Sport & Racing** www.nprsr.qld.gov.au

Australian Bureau of Meteorology
www.bom.gov.au

Popular departure points for liveaboard dive vessels, along with the locales they visit are:

Bundaberg The Bunker Island group, including Lady Musgrave and Lady Elliot Islands, possibly Fitzroy, Llewellyn and the rarely visited Boult Reefs or Hoskyn and Fairfax Islands.

Town of 1770 Bunker Island group.

Gladstone Swains and Bunker Island group.

Mackay Lihou Reef and the Coral Sea.

Airlie Beach The Whitsundays, Knuckle Reef and Hardy Reef.

Townsville SS *Yongala* wreck, plus canyons of Wheeler Reef and Keeper Reef.

Cairns Cod Hole, Ribbon Reefs, the Coral Sea and possibly far northern reefs.

Port Douglas Osprey Reef, Cod Hole, Ribbon Reefs, Coral Sea and possibly the far northern reefs.

Dive Courses

In Queensland, there are numerous places where you can learn to dive, take a refresher course or improve your skills. Courses here are generally of a high standard, and all schools teach either PADI or Scuba Schools International (SSI) qualifications. Which certification you choose isn't as important as choosing a good instructor, so be sure to seek recommendations and meet with the instructor before committing to a program.

One of the most popular places to learn is Cairns, where you can choose between courses for the budget-minded (four-day courses cost between $520 and $765) that combine pool training and reef dives, to longer, more intensive courses that include reef diving on a liveaboard (five-day courses, including three-day/two-night liveaboard, cost between $800 and $1000).

Other places where you can learn to dive, and then head out on the reef, include Bundaberg, Mission Beach, Townsville, Airlie Beach, Hamilton Island, Magnetic Island and Port Douglas.

Camping on the Great Barrier Reef

Pitching a tent on an island is a hugely fun and affordable way to experience the Great Barrier Reef. Campers enjoy an idyllic tropical setting at a fraction of the cost of the five-star island resort down the road. Campsite facilities range from extremely basic (read: nothing) to fairly flash, with showers, flush toilets, interpretive signage and picnic tables. Most islands are remote, so ensure you're adequately prepared for medical and general emergencies.

Wherever you stay, you'll need to be self-sufficient, bringing your own food and drinking water (5L per day per person is recommended). Weather can prevent planned pick-ups, so have enough supplies to last an extra few days in case you get stranded.

Camp only in designated areas, keep to marked trails and take out all that you brought in. Fires are banned, so you'll need a gas stove or similar. National park camping permits must be booked in advance online through the Queensland government's Department of National Parks, Sport & Racing (p36). Here are our top camping picks:

Whitsunday Islands Nearly a dozen beautifully sited camping areas, scattered on the islands of Hook, Whitsunday and Henning.

Capricornia Cays Camping available on three separate coral cays – Masthead Island, North West Island and Lady Musgrave Island, a fantastic, uninhabited island with a maximum limit of 40 campers.

Dunk Island Easy to get to, with good swimming, kayaking and hiking.

Fitzroy Island Resort and national park with walking trails through bush, and coral off the beaches.

Frankland Islands Coral-fringed islands with white-sand beaches off Cairns.

Lizard Island Eye-popping beaches magnificent coral and abundant wildlife; visitors mostly arrive by plane.

Humpback whale, Hervey Bay (p363)

Plan Your Trip
East Coast Australia Outdoors

With a cavalcade of ancient rainforests, islands and craggy ranges, plus the amazing Great Barrier Reef, the east coast is tailor-made for outdoor action. Scuba diving and snorkelling are daily indulgences, while the surfing here is world-class. There's also sailing and kayaking to be had, and loads of other watery pursuits. Back on dry land you can launch into a hike, go mountain biking or rock climbing. For an adrenaline rush, try abseiling, bungee jumping or skydiving.

Best For...

Wildlife Spotting

➡ Fur seals and penguins on Montague Island

➡ Whales off Eden and Hervey Bay

➡ Koalas at Cape Otway and Magnetic Island

➡ Cassowaries in the Daintree Rainforest and Mission Beach

➡ Crocodiles in the Daintree River (on cruises from Daintree Village)

Daredevils

➡ Canyoning in the Blue Mountains

➡ Rock climbing at Mt Arapiles

➡ Skydiving over Mission Beach

➡ Bungee jumping in Cairns

➡ White-water rafting on the Tully River

On Land

Hiking

The east coast is laced with brilliant bushwalks (hikes) of every length, standard and difficulty. Coastal and hinterland national parks and state forests, many easily accessible from the cities, provide some of the best opportunities.

Where to Walk

In Victoria, for coastal treks, head down to Wilsons Promontory National Park in Gippsland, with marked trails from Tidal River and Telegraph Saddle that can take anywhere from a few hours to a couple of days. Expect squeaky white sands and clean aquamarine waters, untouched bushland and beautiful coastal vistas. Further east, and almost tipping over into New South Wales (NSW), Croajingolong National Park, near Mallacoota in East Gippsland, offers rugged inland treks and easier coastal walks past historic lighthouses and over sand dunes. The Great Ocean Road coast also offers some sublime coastal bushwalking.

Prime NSW hiking terrain includes the Blue Mountains, Ku-ring-gai Chase National Park and Royal National Park. The excellent Great North Walk heads from Sydney to Newcastle. If you'd rather mix a surf and a soy latte in with your hike, within Sydney itself are the brilliant semiurban Bondi to Coogee Clifftop Walk and Manly Scenic Walkway.

Prime spots in Queensland include Hinchinbrook Island, Springbrook National Park and D'Aguilar Range National Park. For peak baggers, Wooroonooran National Park, south of Cairns, contains Queensland's highest peak, the eccentrically named Mt Bartle Frere (1622m).

Resources

The *Take a Walk* series (www.takeawalk. com.au) includes titles covering the Blue Mountains, southeast Queensland, southern NSW and Victoria's national parks.

Bushwalking clubs and information:

Brisbane Bushwalkers www.brisbanebush walkers.org.au

Bushwalking NSW www.bushwalkingnsw.org.au

Bushwalking Queensland www.bushwalking queensland.org.au

Bushwalking Victoria www.bushwalkingvictoria. org.au

Cairns Bushwalkers Club www.cairnsbush walkers.org.au

Tablelands Bushwalking Club www.tablelands bushwalking.org

Cycling & Mountain Biking

Cyclists along the east coast have access to plenty of routes and can go touring for days or weekends, or even tackle multiweek trips. The landscape is (mostly) not mountainous, and the sun is often shining. Or you can just rent a bike for a few hours and wheel around a city.

GREAT WALKS OF QUEENSLAND

The Great Walks of Queensland is a $16.5-million project that has created a world-class set of 10 walking tracks. For complete track descriptions, maps and campsite bookings, visit www.nprsr.qld.gov.au/experiences/ great-walks.

Rates charged by rental outfits for road or mountain bikes range from $15 to $20 per hour and $30 to $50 per day. Security deposits range from $50 to $200, depending on the rental period. See www.bicycles.net.au for links to state and territory cycling organisations.

Wildlife Watching

Native wildlife is one of Australia's top selling points. National parks along the east coast are the best places to meet the residents, although many species are nocturnal (bring a torch). Australia is also a birdwatching nirvana, with a wide variety of habitats and species, particularly water birds. Most Aussies will be utterly surprised to learn that Canberra, in the Australian Capital Territory (ACT), has the richest bird life of any Australian capital city.

In NSW there are 120 bird species in Dorrigo National Park, while Border Ranges National Park is home to a quarter of all of Australia's bird species. Koalas arc a dime a dozen around Port Macquarie.

In Victoria, Wilsons Promontory National Park teems with wildlife (wombats sometimes seem to outnumber people), and don't miss the penguins on Phillip Island.

In Queensland, Cape Tribulation is the place for birds; Magnetic Island for koalas; Fraser Island for dingoes; Hervey Bay for whales; Heron Island and Mon Repos near Bundaberg for sea turtles; and the Daintree Rainforest for crocodiles and cassowaries.

Abseiling, Canyoning & Rock Climbing

NSW's Blue Mountains, especially around Katoomba, are fantastic for rock climbing, abseiling (rappelling) and canyoning, with numerous professional outfits able to set you up with equipment, training and climbing trips. In western Victoria, rock-climbing attracts climbers and boulderers from around the world.

On the Water

Going to an east coast beach isn't just about sun, sand and wading ankle deep in the water – there are plenty of more active pursuits. Other than the key ones,

Surfer, Bells Beach (p251)

you can also try jet skiing in Cairns, Southport on the Gold Coast, Caloundra, Airlie Beach and in Batemans Bay; and parasailing on Sydney Harbour, Victoria's Mornington Peninsula, and in Queensland at Cairns, Rainbow Beach and the Gold Coast beaches. Try stand-up paddleboarding in NSW at Manly and Cronulla in Sydney, Jervis Bay and Newcastle; in Queensland at Noosa and on the Gold Coast; and in Victoria on the Mornington Peninsula and at Melbourne's St Kilda.

Surfing

The southern half of the east coast is jam-packed with sandy surf beaches and point breaks. North of Agnes Water in Queensland, the Great Barrier Reef shields the coast from the ocean swells. If you're keen to learn, you'll find plenty of good waves, board hire and lessons available – notably in Sydney and Byron Bay in NSW, the Gold Coast and Noosa in Queensland, and along the Great Ocean Road in Victoria. Two-hour lessons cost around $60.

In Queensland and much of NSW you can get away with wearing board shorts and a 'rashie', but Victoria's chilly water

MXYDAYS / GETTY IMAGES ©

Snorkelling in the Great Barrier Reef (p33)

will have even the hardiest of surfers reaching for their wetsuit. A full-length, up-to-7mm-thick wetsuit is the norm.

The Best Breaks

The east coast is one long *Endless Summer*, with myriad surf breaks peeling into the shore. Our picks:

New South Wales

➡ Bondi Beach

➡ Byron Bay

➡ Crescent Head

Queensland

➡ The Superbank

➡ Burleigh Heads

➡ North Stradbroke Island

Victoria

➡ Torquay (Bells Beach) and numerous spots along the Great Ocean Road

➡ Point Leo, Flinders, Rye and Portsea

➡ Phillip Island (Woolami Beach)

Diving & Snorkelling

Even if the Great Barrier Reef wasn't just off the east coast, the diving and snorkelling here would still be world-class. Coral reefs, rich marine life (temperate, subtropical and tropical species) and hundreds of shipwrecks paint an enticing underwater picture.

Diving is generally possible year-round, although in Queensland avoid the wet season (December to March), when floods can impair visibility and stingers (jellyfish) are present (November to May, north of Agnes Water).

Diving Courses

Every major town along the east coast has a dive school, but standards vary – do some research before signing up. Budget outfits tend to focus on shore dives; pricier outfits sometimes run multiday live-aboard boat tours. Multiday Professional Association of Diving Instructors (PADI) Open-Water courses cost anywhere from $520 to $770; one-off introductory dives cost between $120 and $520.

Cycling in Brisbane (p281)

Byron Bay, Coffs Harbour, Port Stephens and Jervis Bay. In Queensland head for Mission Beach, Magnetic Island, Noosa and the Whitsundays. In Victoria you can kayak around Melbourne itself (on the Yarra River), plus there are operators running trips around Apollo Bay, Phillip Island, Wilsons Promontory and Gippsland. Two-hour paddles cost around $70.

Sailing

Sailing is the second most popular ocean activity (after surfing) on Australia's east coast. It has its own affluent marina culture and its own migratory patterns: during the winter, the yachties sail north, following the warmer weather.

Where to Sail

In NSW, Sydney Harbour and boats are inextricably and historically intertwined – this is one of the world's great nautical cities. The easiest way to get out there is on a ferry: hop a ride to Manly or Balmain and see the sea. There are also harbour cruises and yacht charters available. Beyond Sydney, Port Stephens, Jervis Bay and Ballina are busy sailing centres.

In Queensland, the postcard-perfect Whitsunday Islands are magical for a sail. You can join a full- or multiday cruise, or charter your own craft in Airlie Beach. You can also explore the Great Barrier Reef and some of the islands off the Far North Queensland coast on board a chartered boat or cruise from Cairns or Port Douglas.

In Victoria, city-based yachties gravitate to the sailing clubs around Port Phillip Bay. Other popular boating areas include the sprawling Gippsland Lakes and Mallacoota Inlet near the NSW border.

For certified divers, renting gear and going on a two-tank day dive generally costs between $180 and $250. You can also hire mask, snorkel and fins from a dive shop for around $30 to $50.

Where to Dive

In NSW you can dive all along the coast, including Sydney, Byron Bay, Jervis Bay, Coffs Harbour and Narooma. With the Great Barrier Reef a day trip offshore, Queensland is paradise for divers: most diving and snorkelling trips set sail from Cairns and Port Douglas. You can also organise dive trips at North Stradbroke Island, Moreton Island, Mooloolaba, Rainbow Beach and Bundaberg. In Victoria try Port Campbell on the Great Ocean Road and Bunurong Marine Park in Gippsland.

Kayaking & Canoeing

Kayaks and canoes let you paddle into otherwise inaccessible areas, poking your nose into dense mangroves and estuaries, river gorges, secluded island beaches and remote wilderness inlets. In NSW you can kayak on Sydney Harbour and at

---

AQUATIC HIGHLIGHTS

➡ Diving and snorkelling on the Great Barrier Reef

➡ Surfing at Bondi Beach, Byron Bay, Bells Beach or Noosa

➡ Sailing the Whitsunday Islands

➡ Kayaking at North Stradbroke Island

➡ Catching a ferry on Sydney Harbour

CHAY TALANON / SHUTTERSTOCK ©

Top: Sydney's skyline and harbour (p52)

Bottom: Grand Canyon Walk (p119), Blue Mountains

Regions at a Glance

Sydney & the Central Coast

Beaches
Food
Wilderness

Perfect Surf

Sydney's surf beaches are outstanding. Bondi is the name on everyone's lips, but the waves here get crowded. Head south to Maroubra or Cronulla, or to the Northern Beaches for a bit more elbow room.

Modern Australian

The term 'Modern Australian' (aka 'Mod Oz') is starting to sound a little dated, but this pan-Pacific fusion of styles and ingredients is still the name of Sydney's culinary game. Serve it up with a harbour view and you've got a winning combo.

National Parks

This region has some of the best national parks in Australia. Around Sydney there's Royal National Park, with fab walks and beaches; and waterways and wildlife in Ku-ring-gai Chase National Park.

p50

Byron Bay & North Coast NSW

Nightlife
Surfing
Small Towns

Drinking in Byron

Byron Bay has bars and pubs for every day of the week, be it beer barns, live-music pubs or classy wine bars. Just name your poison!

North-Coast Surf

The water is warm, and perfect point breaks are rolling in at legendary north-coast surf spots such as the Pass in Byron Bay and Lennox Head.

Nimbin & Bangalow

A short detour into the Byron Bay hinterland unveils some beaut small towns. Wander through the smoke haze in hippie Nimbin, or have a pub lunch in upmarket (but unpretentious) Bangalow.

p133

Canberra & South Coast NSW

History & Culture
Beaches
Politics

Canberra Museum Scene

Spend culture-soaked days exploring Canberra's National Gallery, with its magnificent Indigenous art, the National Museum, the War Memorial and the National Portrait Gallery.

South-Coast Beaches

Track south of Sydney into southern NSW, where you'll find impressive stretches of wide white sand, with reliable surf and (best of all) barely a footprint to be seen.

Parliament House

Attend Question Time at Australia's amazing grass-topped Parliament House, pay a visit to Old Parliament House and check out the Museum of Australian Democracy.

p169

Melbourne & Coastal Victoria

Bushwalking
Food
Beaches

Hiking Wilsons Prom

Wilsons Promontory National Park – mainland Australia's southernmost point – offers everything from short jaunts along the beach to multiday circuits covering most of the peninsula.

Eating in Melbourne

Melbourne is a foodie's paradise: produce markets, eat streets, arty cafes and restaurants, all infused with the ebullient multiculturalism that defines this southern city.

Great Ocean Road

The water is chilly, but this stretch of coast hosts some of the prettiest beaches in the country, from the big breaks at Bells Beach to Lorne's gentle bay and the swells around Wye River and Port Campbell.

p200

Brisbane & Around

Cafes
Neighbourhoods
Nightlife

Coffee Culture

Brisbane is hot and humid, but that doesn't mean the locals can't enjoy a steaming cup of java. Cool cafes abound, well supplied by a clutch of quality local bean roasters.

Inner-City Hip

Brisbane is a tight-knit web of distinct neighbourhoods. Check out the bohemian West End and postindustrial Newstead and Teneriffe, with their ever-growing number of on-point cafes, brew-bars and music rooms.

Small-Bar Scene

It's taken a while, but Brisbane has joined in on the Australia-wide boom in small speakeasies, down laneways and behind compact shopfronts across town.

p279

The Gold Coast

Surfing
Nightlife
National Parks

Surfers Paradise

The beach here is one of the best places in Australia to learn to surf, or head for the more challenging breaks around Burleigh Heads and Kirra.

Clubs, Pubs & Bars

All along the Gold Coast, from the throbbing clubs in Surfers Paradise to the surfside pubs and surf-lifesaving clubs in Coolangatta, you'll never be far from a cold après-surf beer (or tequila, champagne or poolside daiquiri).

Hinterland Greenery

Ascend into the Gold Coast hinterland to discover some brilliant national parks: Springbrook, Lamington and Tamborine feature waterfallls, hikes and constant native birdsong.

p321

Noosa & the Sunshine Coast

Surfing
Food
Nature

Sunshine Coast Surf

The relaxed surfer ethos of the Sunshine Coast permeates the backstreets, with surf shops aplenty and reliable breaks and warm waves right along the coast.

Noosa Dining Scene

You know you're *really* on holiday when choosing where to have breakfast, lunch and dinner is the most important item on the agenda. Welcome to Noosa!

Noosa National Park

Bathed by the South Pacific, with photogenic beaches reaching up to hillsides awash with dense subtropical bush – accessible Noosa National Park is perfect for bushwalking, swimming or just chilling out in the sun.

p338

Fraser Island & the Fraser Coast

Islands
Marine Life
Small Towns

Fraser Island

Sandy Fraser Island hosts a unique subtropical ecosystem that's pretty darn close to paradise. A day tour merely whets the appetite; camp overnight and wish upon 1000 shooting stars.

Whale Watching

Off Hervey Bay, migrating humpback whales breach, blow and tail slap. Controversy shrouds the whale-watching business worldwide, but eco-accredited tours give these amazing creatures the space they need.

Rainbow Beach & Childers

One on the coast and one inland, these two little towns are absolute beauties: Rainbow Beach for its magnificent cliffs, and Childers for its country vibe and historic architecture.

p361

Capricorn Coast & the Southern Reef Islands

Diving & Snorkelling
Islands
Accessible Outback

Southern Reef Encounters

From the Town of 1770, book a snorkelling cruise out to the reef or a bunk on a live-aboard dive vessel. Or base yourself on an island for full immersion in this technicolour underwater world.

Lady Elliot Island

Tiny, coral-ringed Lady Elliot is superb for snorkelling, with reefs directly off the beach. The resort is eco-attuned, and the flight here is a scenic tour in itself.

Rockhampton

Just 40km from the coast, Australia's 'beef capital' gives visitors a taste of the bush, with buckin' broncos and big hats. Further west, cattle-station stays offer full immersion into outback livin'.

p381

Whitsunday Coast

Islands
Sailing
Nightlife

The Whitsundays

With 74 tropical beauties to choose from, the Whitsunday Islands archipelago is truly remarkable. There are plenty of ways to experience the islands: bushwalking, kayaking or just lounging around on a yacht.

Island Hopping

The translucent seas around the Whitsundays would seem incomplete without the snow-white billows of sails in the picture. Climb aboard a yacht and find your perfect island.

Airlie Beach

The main jumping-off point for trips around the Whitsundays, Airlie Beach is a party town full of party people. Join the thirsty throngs in the bars after dark.

p395

Townsville to Mission Beach

Coastline
Nature
Architecture

Beaut Beaches

Between Townsville's palm-shaded Strand and Flying Fish Point near Innisfail is a stretch of coastline that shelters vast, sandy expanses, from Mission Beach to intimate coves like Etty Bay.

National Parks

Hiking, camping, swimming and picnicking opportunities abound, while flightless, prehistoric-looking cassowaries roaming the rainforest. Top picks include bushwalking paradise Hinchinbrook Island and Paluma Range National Park.

Historic Buildings

See the gold-rush era streetscapes of Charters Towers, beautiful 19th-century buildings in Townsville and the many art deco edifices in Innisfail.

p417

Great Barrier Reef

Marine Life
Diving & Snorkelling
Islands

Coral & Fish

Believe the hype: the World Heritage–listed Great Barrier Reef is home to an absolutely mind-blowing spectrum of colourful coral and fish of all shapes, sizes and demeanours.

Reef Day Trips

Don't delay – book yourself onto a diving or snorkelling trip to explore the reef. Cairns and Port Douglas offer multiple operators that can take you there for the day (or longer).

Castaway Cays

Play castaway for a day: studded along the 2000km spine of the reef are myriad sandy cays, islands and atolls, most with no one else on them.

p415

Cairns & the Daintree Rainforest

Nightlife
Food
Indigenous Culture

Cairns After Dark

There are so many backpackers and tourists in Cairns, it's sometimes hard to spot a local. You can usually find one or two in the city's boisterous pubs and bars.

Regional Produce

Many of the Atherton Tableland's farms, orchards and plantations can be visited on tours. Or simply taste the good stuff at regional restaurants.

Daintree Tours

Several Aboriginal-led tour companies can take you on a cultural journey through the timeless Daintree Rainforest, offering insights into its rich Indigenous heritage.

p438

On the Road

Sydney &
the Central Coast

Best Places to Eat

➡ Quay (p85)

➡ Sepia (p87)

➡ Subo (p130)

➡ Mr Wong (p86)

➡ Muse Restaurant (p124)

➡ Bourke Street Bakery (p91)

Best Places to Sleep

➡ ADGE Boutique Apartment Hotel (p83)

➡ Sydney Harbour YHA (p79)

➡ Ovolo 1888 (p81)

➡ Tonic (p124)

➡ Greens of Leura (p117)

Why Go?

Chances are Sydney will be your introduction to Australia's east coast and there simply isn't a better one. The city's spectacular harbour setting, sun-kissed beaches and sophisticated sheen make it unique in Australia, and its outdoorsy population endows it with a confident charm that every city yearns for but few achieve.

It would be reasonable to assume that the areas surrounding Sydney would be content to bask in the reflected and undeniably golden glow of the metropolis, but that's not the case. Each has its own delights. The Blue Mountains offer magnificent bush-clad vistas and opportunities to snuggle in front of log fires; Newcastle has surf beaches in profusion; and the Hunter Valley has leafy country roads scattered with producers of fine wine, chocolate and cheese. All three are home to world-class restaurants that rival even those in the big smoke.

When to Go
Sydney

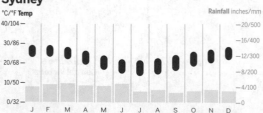

Jan The year kicks off with a spectacular fireworks display over Sydney Harbour.

Mar Sydney's summer party season culminates with the Gay & Lesbian Mardi Gras.

Jul Enjoy wood fires, wine and winter menus in the Blue Mountains and Hunter Valley.

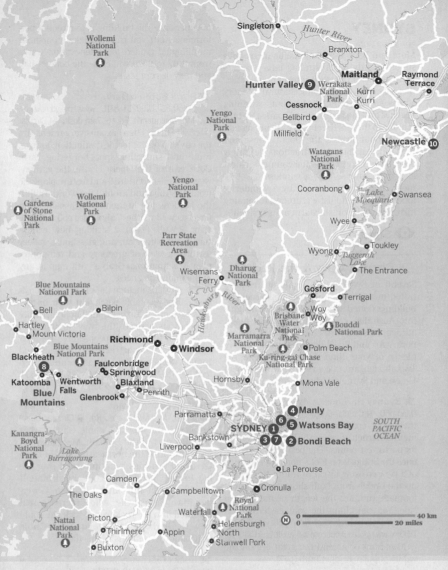

Sydney & the Central Coast Highlights

1 Sydney Opera House (p52) Coming face to face with the symbol of the city.

2 Bondi Beach (p65) Whiling away the day on the golden sands.

3 Porteño (p91) Eating in the gastronomic heartland.

4 Manly Scenic Walkway (p75) Walking between headlands and beaches.

5 Watsons Bay (p68) Catching a ferry and spending an afternoon exploring.

6 Taronga Zoo (p68) Meeting Australia's weird and wonderful native fauna.

7 White Rabbit (p69) Expanding your mind at Sydney's top art gallery.

8 Blue Mountains (p119) Exploring the eucalyptus-scented valleys on a spectacular bushwalk.

9 Hunter Valley (p121) Indulging yourself on a gourmet break, with boutique accommodation, fine food and excellent wines.

10 Newcastle (p129) Enjoying a leisurely post-surf breakfast at one of the city's excellent cafes.

SYDNEY

POP 5.1 MILLION / ☑02

More laid back than any major metropolis should rightly be, Australia's largest settlement is one of the great international cities. Blessed with outstanding natural scenery across its magnificent harbour, stunning beaches and glorious national parks, Sydney is home to three of the country's major icons – the Harbour Bridge, the Opera House and Bondi Beach. But the attractions definitely don't stop there. This is the country's oldest and most diverse city, a sun-kissed settlement that is characterised by a wonderful food culture, hedonistic attitudes, intriguing history and the brash charm of its residents.

◉ Sights

◎ Circular Quay & the Rocks

Several of Sydney's key sights are concentrated in this area. Museums and venerable buildings dotted about the Rocks give insights into Australia's colonial history, while major attractions such as the Museum of Contemporary Art and Royal Botanic Garden deserve plenty of your time. The indisputable Big Two, though, are, of course, the Sydney Opera House and Sydney Harbour Bridge.

★ **Sydney Harbour Bridge**   BRIDGE
(Map p60; ☒ Circular Quay) Sydneysiders adore their giant 'coathanger'. Opened in 1932, this majestic structure spans the harbour at one of its narrowest points. The best way to experience the bridge is on foot – don't expect much of a view crossing by car or train. Stairs climb up the bridge from both shores, leading to a footpath running the length of the eastern side. You can climb the southeastern pylon to the **Pylon Lookout** (Map p60; ☑02-9240 1100; www.pylonlookout.com.au; adult/child $15/10; ☺10am-5pm) or ascend the great arc on the wildly popular BridgeClimb (p77).

★ **Sydney Opera House**   NOTABLE BUILDING
(Map p60; ☑02-9250 7777; www.sydneyoperahouse.com; Bennelong Point; tours adult/child $37/20; ☺tours 9am-5pm; ☒ Circular Quay) Designed by Danish architect Jørn Utzon, this World Heritage–listed building is Australia's most recognisable landmark. Visually referencing a yacht's billowing white sails, it's a soaring, commanding presence on the harbour. The complex comprises five performance spaces where dance, concerts, opera and theatre are staged. The best way to experience the building is to attend a performance, but you can also take a one-hour multilingual guided tour. Renovation works from 2017 to 2019 will close the concert hall and may disrupt visits.

★ **Royal Botanic Garden**   GARDENS
(Map p60; ☑02-9231 8111; www.rbgsyd.nsw.gov.au; Mrs Macquaries Rd; ☺7am-dusk; ☒ Circular Quay) ✈ FREE These expansive gardens are the city's favourite picnic destination, jogging route and snuggling spot. Bordering Farm Cove, east of the Opera House, the gardens were established in 1816 and feature plant life from Australia and around the world. Within the gardens are hothouses with palms and ferns as well as the **Calyx** (Map p60; ☺10am-4pm; ☒ Martin Place), a striking new exhibition space whose curving glasshouse gallery features a wall of greenery and temporary plant-y exhibitions. Grab a park map at any of the main entrances.

The gardens include the site of the colony's first paltry vegetable patch, but their history goes back much further than that; long before the convicts arrived, this was an initiation ground for the Gadigal people. Free 1½-hour guided walks depart at 10.30am daily and 1pm on weekdays. Book ahead for an **Aboriginal Heritage Tour** (Map p56; ☑02-9231 8134; adult $39; ☺10am Wed, Fri & Sat).

Mrs Macquaries Point   PARK
(Map p56; Mrs Macquaries Rd; ☒ Circular Quay) Adjoining the Royal Botanic Gardens but officially part of the Domain, Mrs Macquaries Point forms the northeastern tip of Farm Cove and provides beautiful views over the bay to the Opera House and city skyline. It was named in 1810 after Elizabeth, Governor Macquarie's wife, who ordered a seat chiselled into the rock from which she could view the harbour. **Mrs Macquarie's Chair**, as it's known, remains to this day.

★ **Rocks Discovery Museum**   MUSEUM
(Map p60; ☑02-9240 8680; www.therocks.com; Kendall Lane; ☺10am-5pm; ☒ Circular Quay) FREE Divided into four chronological displays – Warrane (pre-1788), Colony (1788–1820), Port (1820–1900) and Transformations (1900 to the present) – this small, excellent museum, tucked away down a Rocks laneway, digs deep into the area's history and leads you on an artefact-rich tour. Sensitive attention is given to the Rocks' original inhabitants, the Gadigal (Cadigal) people, and there are interesting tales of early colonial characters.

SYDNEY IN...

Two Days

Start your first day by getting a train to Milsons Point and walking back to the Rocks across the **Harbour Bridge** (p52). Then explore the Rocks area, delving into all the narrow lanes. Next, follow the harbour past the **Opera House** (p52) to the **Royal Botanic Garden** (p52) and on to the **Art Gallery of NSW** (p57). That night, enjoy a performance at the **Opera House** (p105) or check out the action in Chinatown or Darlinghurst. Next day, it's time to spend the day soaking up the sun and scene at Bondi – be sure to take the cliff-top walk to Coogee and then make your way back to Bondi for a sunset dinner at **Icebergs Dining Room** (p93).

Four Days

On day three, board a ferry and sail through the harbour to Manly, where you can swim at the beach or follow the **Manly Scenic Walkway** (p75). That night, head to Surry Hills for drinks and dinner. On day four, learn about Sydney's convict heritage at the **Hyde Park Barracks Museum** (p57) and then spend the afternoon shopping in Paddington or Newtown.

One Week

With a week, you can spare a couple of days to visit the majestic Blue Mountains, fitting in a full day of bushwalking before rewarding yourself with a gourmet dinner. Back in Sydney, explore **Watsons Bay** (p68), **Darling Harbour** (p59) and **Taronga Zoo** (p68).

★**Sydney Observatory** OBSERVATORY
(Map p60; ☑02-9217 0111; http://maas.museum/sydney-observatory; 1003 Upper Fort St; ☺10am-5pm; ꙰ Circular Quay) FREE Built in the 1850s, Sydney's copper-domed, Italianate sandstone observatory squats atop pretty **Observatory Hill**, overlooking the harbour. Inside is a collection of vintage apparatus, including Australia's oldest working telescope (1874), as well as background on Australian astronomy and transits of Venus. Also on offer are entertaining tours (adult/child $10/8), which include a planetarium show. Bookings are essential for night-time stargazing sessions (adult/child $22/17), which run Monday to Saturday, and Aboriginal sky storytelling sessions (adult/child $18/12). All tours are great for kids.

★**Walsh Bay** WATERFRONT
(Map p60; www.walshbaysydney.com.au; Hickson Rd; ☐324, 325, 998, ꙰ Wynyard) This section of Dawes Point waterfront was Sydney's busiest before the advent of container shipping and the construction of new port facilities at Botany Bay. The last decade has seen the Federation-era wharves here gentrified beyond belief, morphing into luxury hotels, apartments, theatre spaces, power-boat marinas, cafes and restaurants. It's a picturesque place to stroll, combining the wharves and harbour views here with nearby Barangaroo Park.

Barangaroo Reserve PARK
(Map p60; www.barangaroo.com; Hickson Rd; ☺24hr; ☐324, 325, ꙰ Circular Quay) Part of Barangaroo, the major redevelopment project of what was a commercial port, this park sits on a headland with wonderful harbour perspectives. It only opened in 2015, so still looks a bit bare in parts as the native trees and plants have got some growing to do among the quarried sandstone blocks. A lift connecting the park's three levels is good for weary legs. There is underground parking and a cultural space to come.

Museum of Contemporary Art GALLERY
(MCA; Map p60; ☑02-9245 2400; www.mca.com.au; 140 George St; ☺10am-5pm Fri-Wed, to 9pm Thu; ꙰ Circular Quay) FREE By the harbour, the MCA is a showcase for Australian and international contemporary art, with a rotating permanent collection and temporary exhibitions. Aboriginal art often features prominently. The Gotham City–style art-deco building has had a modern gallery space grafted on to it, the highlight of which is the rooftop cafe, a stunning spot for a bite or drink with views. There are free guided tours daily, with several languages available.

Susannah Place Museum MUSEUM
(Map p60; ☑02-9241 1893; www.sydneyliving museums.com.au; 58-64 Gloucester St; adult/child $12/8; ☺tours 2pm, 3pm & 4pm; ꙰ Circular Quay)

Sydney Harbour

← NORTH

Taronga Zoo
Even if you've hired a car, the best way to reach this excellent zoo is by ferry. Zip to the top in a cable car then wind your way back down to the wharf.

Manly

North Head

South Head

Georges Head

Camp Cove

Chowder Head

Balmoral Beach

Hunters Bay

Middle Head

Taronga Zoo

Manly
Catch a ferry to Manly to explore the outer harbour. Stroll to the beach, drink at the wharf and make sure you're well positioned on your return journey for any photos you missed earlier.

Little Sirius Cove

Mosman Bay

Kirribilli
Unless the prime minister or governor-general invite you into their homes for tea, the best views you'll get of Kirribilli House and Admiralty House are from the water. Keep your eyes peeled.

Cremorne Point

Neutral Bay

Kirribilli House

Kirribilli

Admiralty House

Sydney Harbour Bridge

North Sydney Olympic Pool

Luna Park

Sydney Harbour Bridge
As you pass by the bridge, keep an eye out for the hardy souls trudging along the top on their bridge climb. Head here at sunrise or sunset for golden harbour views.

TOP TIP
Don't forget that the harbour continues west of the bridge. Back up a Manly trip with a river ferry service.

Watsons Bay

Imagine Watsons Bay as the isolated fishing village it once was as you pull into its sheltered wharf. Stroll around South Head for views up the harbour and over ocean-battered cliffs.

Fort Denison

Known as Pinchgut, this fortified speck was once a place of fearsome punishment. The bodies of executed convicts were left to hang here as a grisly warning to all; the local Aborigines were horrified.

DINOZZAVER/SHUTTERSTOCK ©

FERRIES

Circular Quay is the hub for state-run Sydney Ferries; nine separate routes leave from here, journeying to 38 different wharves.

Watsons Bay

Macquarie Lighthouse

Vaucluse Bay

Shark Bay

Rose Bay

Shark Island

Point Piper

Bradleys Head

Double Bay

Darling Point

Clark Island

Garden Island

Naval Base

Elizabeth Bay

Fort Denison

Mrs Macquaries Point

Potts Point

Woolloomooloo Finger Wharf

Sydney Opera House

Government House

Farm Cove

Royal Botanic Garden

Circular Quay

The Rocks

Sydney Opera House

You can clamber all over it and walk around it, but nothing beats the perspective you get as your ferry glides past the Opera House's dazzling sails. Have your camera at the ready.

Circular Quay

Circular Quay has been at the centre of Sydney life since the First Fleet dropped anchor here in 1788. Book your ferry ticket, check the indicator boards for the correct pier and get on board.

Sydney

Lane Cove
National Park

CHATSWOOD

Chatswood

NORTH
BALGOWLAH

CASTLE COVE

Ku-ring-gai Chase
National Park (15km)

SEAFORTH

Manly Rd

CASTLECRAG

CLONTARF

Clontarf
Beach

WILLOUGHBY

Middle

Artarmon

Epping Rd

Gore Hill Fwy

NORTHBRIDGE

LANE
COVE

NAREMBURN

Long Bay

Spit Rd

BALMORAL

Pacific Hwy

CAMMERAY

Hunters
Bay

RIVERVIEW

St Leonards

CROWS
NEST

CREMORNE

Military Rd

Bradleys Head Rd

MOSMAN

GREENWICH

Falcon St

Wollstonecraft

NEUTRAL
BAY

Chowder
Bay

LONGUEVILLE

Lane Cove River

Waverton

Taylors
Bay

WOOLWICH

North Sydney

Taronga 4
Zoo

Milsons Point

Mosman
Bay

Robertsons
Point

Bradleys
Head

Balls
Head

McMahons
Point

Kirribilli

Spectacle
Island

Snails Bay

BIRCHGROVE

Sydney Harbour
(Port Jackson)

BALMAIN

See Central Sydney
Map (p60)

Mrs Macquaries
Point

Clarke
Island

BALMAIN
EAST

See Darling Harbour &
Pyrmont Map (p64)

POINT
PIPER

Balmain Rd

PYRMONT

Rozelle Bay

See Haymarket
& Chinatown
Map (p62)

See Kings Cross,
Darlinghurst &
Woolloomooloo
Map (p66)

DOUBLE
BAY

Jubilee
Park

ULTIMO

Lilyfield

GLEBE

See Newtown Map (p74)

Edgecliff

ANNANDALE

Blue
Mountains
(90km)

See Surry Hills
Map (p70)

See Paddington &
Woollahra Map (p72)

Bondi
Junction

Stanmore

BONDI
JUNCTION

WAVERLEY

Queens
Park

St Peters

Green
Square

Centennial
Park

ST PETERS

WATERLOO
ZETLAND

Sydenham

ALEXANDRIA

KENSINGTON

RANDWICK

Bourke St

Botany Rd

Australian
Golf Club

COOGEE

TEMPE

Princes Hwy

University
of NSW

Coogee Bay Rd

Anzac Pde

MASCOT

Mascot

Gardeners Rd

ROSEBERY

Sydney
(3km)

KINGSFORD

Mahon Pool (2.4km)

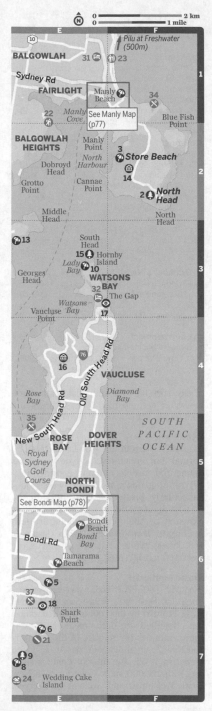

Dating from 1844, this diminutive terrace of four houses and a shop selling historical wares is a fascinating time capsule of life in the Rocks since colonial times. After you watch a short film about the people who lived here, a guide will take you through the claustrophobic homes, which are decorated to reflect different periods in their histories. The visit lasts an hour. It's worth ringing to book at weekends.

◉ City Centre & Haymarket

★**Art Gallery of NSW** GALLERY
(Map p66; ☑1800 679 278; www.artgallery.nsw. gov.au; Art Gallery Rd; ◷10am-5pm Thu-Tue, to 10pm Wed; ◲441, ◲St James) FREE With its neoclassical Greek frontage and modern rear end, this much-loved institution plays a prominent and gregarious role in Sydney society. Blockbuster international touring exhibitions arrive regularly and there's an outstanding permanent collection of Australian art, including a substantial Indigenous section. The gallery also plays host to lectures, concerts, screenings, celebrity talks and children's activities. A range of free guided tours is offered on different themes and in various languages; enquire at the desk or check the website.

Hyde Park Barracks Museum MUSEUM
(Map p60; ☑02-8239 2311; www.sydneyliving museums.com.au; Queens Sq, Macquarie St; adult/child $12/8; ◷10am-5pm; ◲St James) Convict architect Francis Greenway designed this squarish, decorously Georgian structure (1819) as convict quarters. Fifty thousand men and boys sentenced to transportation passed through here in 30 years. It later became an immigration depot, a women's asylum and a law court. These days it's a fascinating museum, focusing on the barracks' history and the archaeological efforts that helped reveal it. On the top floor, hammocks are strung out as they would have been in the day. Entry includes a good audio guide.

Museum of Sydney MUSEUM
(MoS; Map p60; ☑02-9251 5988; www.sydney livingmuseums.com.au; cnr Phillip & Bridge Sts; adult/child $12/8; ◷10am-5pm; ◲Circular Quay) Built on the site of Sydney's first Government House, the MoS is a fragmented, storytelling museum, which uses installations to explore the city's history. The area's long Indigenous past is highlighted, plus there's interesting coverage of the early days of contact between

Sydney

the Gadigal and the colonists. Key figures in Sydney's planning and architecture are brought to life, while there's a good section on the First Fleet itself, with scale models.

Martin Place SQUARE
(Map p60; ® Wynyard, ® Martin Place) Studded with imposing edifices, long, lean Martin Place was closed to traffic in 1971, forming a terraced pedestrian mall complete with fountains and areas for public gatherings. It's the closest thing to a main civic square that Sydney has.

Sydney Tower Eye TOWER
(Map p60; ☑ 1800 258 693; www.sydneytower eye.com.au; level 5, Westfield Sydney, 188 Pitt St; adult/child $26.50/17, Skywalk $70/49; ⊙ 9am-9.30pm May-Sep, to 10pm Oct-Apr; ® St James) The 309m-tall Sydney Tower (finished in 1981 and still known as Centrepoint by many Sydney-siders) offers unbeatable 360-degree views from the observation level 250m up – and even better ones for the daredevils braving the Skywalk on its roof. The visit starts with the 4D Experience – a short 3D film giving you a bird's-eye view (a parakeet's to be exact)

of city, surf, harbour and what lies beneath the water, accompanied by mist sprays and bubbles; it's actually pretty darn cool.

Hyde Park PARK
(Map p62; Elizabeth St; ® St James, Museum) Formal but much-loved Hyde Park has manicured gardens and a tree-formed tunnel running down its spine, which looks particularly pretty at night, illuminated by fairy lights. The park's northern end is crowned by the richly symbolic art-deco **Archibald Memorial Fountain** (Map p60; ® St James), while at the other end is the Anzac Memorial (p58).

Anzac Memorial MEMORIAL
(Map p62; ☑ 02-9267 7668; www.anzacmemorial. nsw.gov.au; Hyde Park; ⊙ 9am-5pm; ® Museum) FREE Fronted by the Pool of Remembrance, this dignified art-deco memorial (1934) commemorates the soldiers of the Australia and New Zealand Army Corps (Anzacs) who served in WWI. The interior dome is studded with 120,000 stars – one for each New South Welshman and -woman who served. These twinkle above Rayner Hoff's poignant

sculpture *Sacrifice*. A major project is adding a new Hall of Service, to feature names and soil samples of all the NSW places of origin of WWI soldiers.

Queen Victoria Building HISTORIC BUILDING
(QVB; Map p60; ☑02-9264 9209; www.qvb.com.au; 455 George St; tours $15; ⊙9am-6pm Mon-Wed, Fri & Sat, 9am-9pm Thu, 11am-5pm Sun; ⊠Town Hall) Unbelievably, this High Victorian Gothic masterpiece (1898) was repeatedly slated for demolition before it was restored in the mid-1980s. Occupying an entire city block on the site of the city's first markets, the QVB is a Venetian Romanesque-inspired temple to the gods of retail.

★Chinatown AREA
(Map p62; www.sydney-chinatown.info; ⊠Paddy's Markets, ⊠Town Hall) With a discordant soundtrack of blaring Canto pop, Dixon St is the heart of Chinatown: a narrow, shady pedestrian mall with a string of restaurants and insistent spruikers. The ornate dragon gates *(paifang)* at either end have fake bamboo tiles, golden Chinese calligraphy and ornamental lions to keep evil spirits at bay. Chinatown is a fabulous eating district, which effectively extends for several blocks north and south of here, and segues into Koreatown and Thaitown to the east.

◎ Darling Harbour & Pyrmont

Unashamedly tourist-focused, Darling Harbour will do its best to tempt you to its shoreline bars and restaurants with fireworks displays and a sprinkling of glitz.

The eastern side unfurls three strips of bars and restaurants at Cockle Bay, King Street Wharf and the new South Barangaroo development. On its western flank, Pyrmont, though it appears to be sinking under the weight of its casino and motorway flyovers, still has a historic feel in parts, and strolling its harbourside wharves is a real pleasure.

★Australian National Maritime Museum MUSEUM
(Map p64; ☑02-9298 3777; www.anmm.gov.au; 2 Murray St; permanent collection free, temporary exhibitions adult/child $20/free; ⊙9.30am-5pm, to 6pm Jan; ♿; ⊠Pyrmont Bay) **FREE** Beneath a soaring roof, the Maritime Museum sails through Australia's inextricable relationship with the sea. Exhibitions range from Indigenous canoes to surf culture, immigration to the navy. The worthwhile 'big ticket' (adult/child $30/18) includes entry to some of the vessels moored outside, including the atmospheric submarine HMAS *Onslow* and the destroyer HMAS *Vampire*. The high-production-value short film *Action Stations* sets the mood with a re-creation of a mission event from each vessel. Excellent free guided tours explain each vessel's features.

★Chinese Garden of Friendship GARDENS
(Map p62; ☑02-9240 8888; www.chinesegarden.com.au; Harbour St; adult/child $6/3; ⊙9.30am-5pm Apr-Sep, 9.30am-5.30pm Oct-Mar; ⊠Town Hall) Built according to Taoist principles, the Chinese Garden of Friendship is usually an oasis of tranquillity – although construction noise from Darling Harbour's

SYDNEY & THE CENTRAL COAST SYDNEY

SYDNEY FOR CHILDREN

With boundless natural attractions and relaxed, outdoor living, Sydney is great for kids.

The calm waters of the harbour beaches are tops for youngsters, and most of Sydney's surf beaches have saltwater ocean pools, such as the spectacular **Bondi Icebergs** (p75). Or make a summer's day of it at **Wet'n'Wild** (p73). Most surf schools also cater for kids and have special holiday packages.

At Darling Harbour there's **Wild Life Sydney** (p61) and the **Sydney Aquarium** (p61) plus the fascinating **Maritime Museum** (p59) and its excellent collection of boats and ships. The intriguing collection of the **Powerhouse Museum** (p69) is also (for now) close by. Across town, the **Australian Museum** (p63) is a real hit with the younger crowd, especially its excellent dinosaur exhibition.

A certain winner is the ferry ride to the excellent **Taronga Zoo** (p68), or combine a trip to Manly with a visit to the penguins at the **Sea Life Sanctuary** (p71). Across the Harbour Bridge from the centre, **Luna Park** (p69) has been thrilling kids for over 80 years.

Little astronomers might want to do some stargazing or see the Time Ball drop at the very kid-focused **Sydney Observatory** (p53).

Central Sydney, The Rocks & Circular Quay

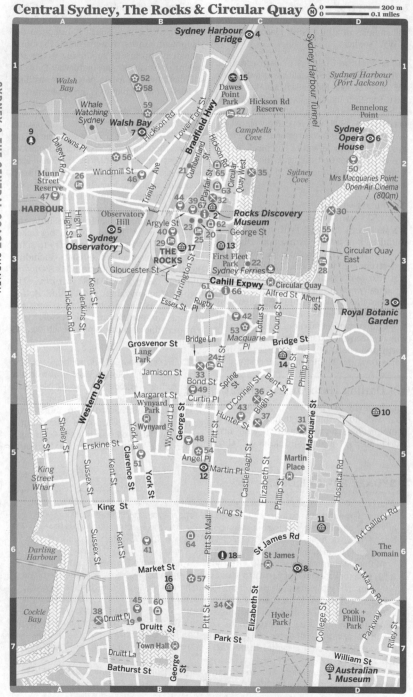

Central Sydney, The Rocks & Circular Quay

redevelopment can intrude from time to time. Designed by architects from Guangzhou (Sydney's sister city) for Australia's bicentenary in 1988, the garden interweaves pavilions, waterfalls, lakes, paths and lush plant life. There's also a teahouse.

★ **Sydney Sea Life Aquarium** AQUARIUM
(Map p64; ☑02-8251 7800; www.sydneyaquarium. com.au; Aquarium Pier; adult/child $40/28; ☺9.30am-6pm Mon-Thu, to 7pm Fri-Sun & school holidays, last entry 1hr earlier; ☒Town Hall) ☚ As well as regular wall-mounted tanks and

ground-level enclosures, this impressive complex has two large pools that you can walk through, safely enclosed in Perspex tunnels, as an intimidating array of sharks and rays pass overhead. Other highlights include a pair of dugongs, clownfish (howdy Nemo), platypuses, moon jellyfish (in a disco-lit tube), sea dragons and the swoon-worthy finale: the two-million-litre Great Barrier Reef tank.

Wild Life Sydney Zoo ZOO
(Map p64; ☑02-9333 9245; www.wildlifesydney. com.au; Aquarium Pier; adult/child $40/28;

Haymarket & Chinatown

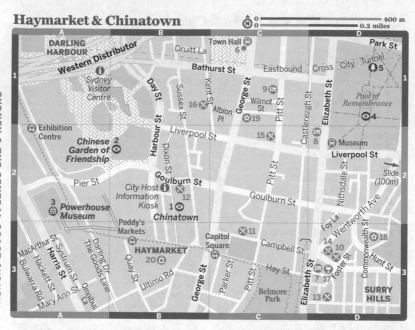

Haymarket & Chinatown

⊙9.30am-5pm Apr-Sep, to 7pm Oct-Mar, last entry 1hr before close; 🚇 Town Hall) Complementing its sister and neighbour, Sea Life, this large complex houses an impressive collection of Australian native reptiles, butterflies, spiders, snakes and mammals (including kangaroos and koalas). The nocturnal section is particularly good, bringing out the extrovert in the quolls, potoroos, echidnas and possums. As interesting as Wild Life is, it's not a patch on Taronga Zoo. Still, it's worth considering as part of a combo with Sea Life, or if you're short on time. Tickets are cheaper online.

The Star   CASINO

(Map p64; ☑ 02-9777 9000; www.star.com.au; 80 Pyrmont St, Pyrmont; ⊙24hr; 🚋 The Star) Sydney's first casino complex includes hotels, high-profile restaurants, bars, a nightclub, an excellent food court, a light-rail station and the kind of high-end shops that will ensure that, in the unlikely event that you do happen to strike it big, a large proportion of your winnings will remain within the building.

★ Sydney Fish Market   MARKET
(Map p64; ☑ 02-9004 1108; www.sydneyfish market.com.au; Bank St; ☺ 7am-4pm; ☒ Fish Market) This piscatorial precinct on Blackwattle Bay shifts over 15 million kilograms of seafood annually, and has retail outlets, restaurants, a sushi bar, an oyster bar, and a highly regarded cooking school. Chefs, locals and overfed seagulls haggle over mud crabs, Balmain bugs, lobsters and slabs of salmon at the daily fish auction, which kicks off at 5.30am weekdays. Check it out on a behind-the-scenes tour (adult/child $35/10).

◉ Kings Cross & Potts Point
Traditionally Sydney's seedy red-light zone, the Cross has changed markedly in recent years. Lockout laws have killed the late-night bar life, and major building programs have accelerated gentrification in this so-close-to-the-city district. The area's blend of backpackers and quirky locals is still enticing though, and its leafy streets and good eateries make for surprisingly pleasant daytime meanders. Below, by the water, the old sailors' district of Woolloomooloo is a great spot for glitzy wharf restaurants or a handful of pubs of some character.

★ Elizabeth Bay House   HISTORIC BUILDING
(Map p66; ☑ 02-9356 3022; www.sydneyliving museums.com.au; 7 Onslow Ave, Elizabeth Bay; adult/child $12/8; ☺ 11am-4pm Fri-Sun; ☒ Kings Cross) Now dwarfed by 20th-century apartments, Colonial Secretary Alexander Macleay's elegant Greek Revival mansion was one of the finest houses in the colony when it was completed in 1839. The architectural highlight is an exquisite oval saloon with a curved and cantilevered staircase. There are lovely views over the harbour from the upstairs rooms. Drop down to the twin cellars for an introductory audiovisual with a weird beginning.

Woolloomooloo Wharf   HISTORIC BUILDING
(The Finger Wharf; Map p56; Cowper Wharf Roadway, Woolloomooloo; ☒ 311, ☒ Kings Cross) A former wool and cargo dock, this beautiful Edwardian wharf faced oblivion for decades before a 2½-year demolition-workers' green ban on the site in the late 1980s saved it. It received a huge sprucing up in the late 1990s and has emerged as one of Sydney's most exclusive eating, sleeping and marina addresses.

◉ Surry Hills & Darlinghurst
Sydney's hippest and gayest neighbourhood is also home to its most interesting dining and bar scene. The plane trees and up-and-down of increasingly chic Surry Hills merge into the terraces of vibrant Darlinghurst. They are pleasant, leafy districts appealingly close to the centre.

★ Australian Museum   MUSEUM
(Map p60; ☑ 02-9320 6000; www.australian museum.net.au; 6 College St, Darlinghurst; adult/child $15/free; ☺ 9.30am-5pm; ☒ Museum) Under an ongoing process of modernisation, this museum, established just 40 years after the First Fleet dropped anchor, is doing a brilliant job of it. A standout is the Indigenous Australians section, covering Aboriginal history and spirituality, from Dreaming stories to videos of the Freedom Rides of the 1960s. The stuffed animal gallery of the natural history section manages to keep it relevant, while the excellent dinosaur gallery features the enormous Jobaria as well as local bruisers like Muttaburrasaurus.

There are also interesting displays on extinct megafauna (giant wombats – simultaneously cuddly and terrifying), current Australian creatures, a kids section and more. We're looking forward to the new Long Gallery exhibition, due to open in October 2017, focusing on 100 objects and 100 key people from Australia's past, and new Oceania galleries that will incorporate the colourful Pacific Island collection.

Don't miss heading up to the cafe, which has brilliant views of St Mary's Cathedral and down to Woolloomooloo.

★ Brett Whiteley Studio   GALLERY
(Map p70; ☑ 02-9225 1881; www.artgallery.nsw. gov.au/brett-whiteley-studio; 2 Raper St, Surry Hills; ☺ 10am-4pm Fri-Sun; ☒ Central) FREE Acclaimed local artist Brett Whiteley (1939–1992) lived fast and without restraint. His hard-to-find studio (look for the signs on Devonshire St) has been preserved as a gallery for some of his best work. Pride of place goes to his astonishing *Alchemy*, a giant multi-panel extravaganza that could absorb you for hours with its broad themes, intricate details and humorous asides. The studio room upstairs also gives great insight into the character of this masterful draughtsman and off-the-wall genius.

Darling Harbour & Pyrmont

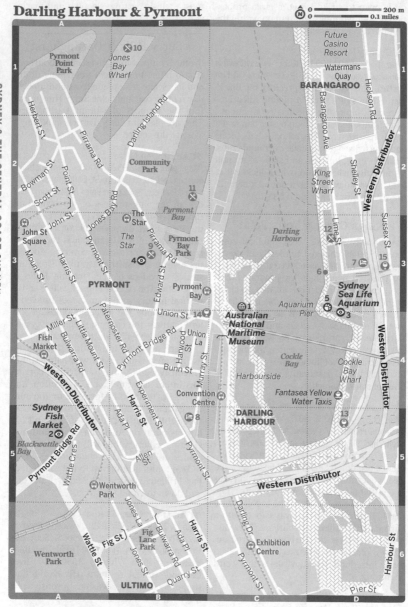

Sydney Jewish Museum MUSEUM
(Map p66; ☎02-9360 7999; www.sydneyjewish
museum.com.au; 148 Darlinghurst Rd, Darlinghurst;
adult/child $10/7; ☺1-4pm Mon-Thu, noon-2pm
Fri, 10am-4pm Sun; ☒Kings Cross) This museum examines Australian Jewish history,
culture and tradition, from the time of the
First Fleet (which included 16 known Jews),
to the immediate aftermath of WWII (when
Australia became home to the greatest number of Holocaust survivors per capita, after
Israel), to the present day. The centrepiece

Darling Harbour & Pyrmont

is a new permanent exhibition on the Holocaust, with sobering personal testimonies; another examines the role of Jews in Australia's military, while temporary exhibitions are always excellent. There's a kosher cafe upstairs.

◉ Paddington & Centennial Park

A byword for eastern-suburbs elegance, this band of suburbs is distinctly well-heeled – and in Paddington's case, they're probably Manolo Blahniks. This is still Sydney's fashion and art heartland, full of pretty corners and eye-catching boutiques.

Centennial Park   PARK
(Map p72; ☎02-9339 6699; www.centennialpark
lands.com.au; Oxford St, Centennial Park; ㉣Bondi
Junction) Scratched out of the sand in 1888 in grand Victorian style, Sydney's biggest park is a rambling 189-hectare expanse full of horse riders, joggers, cyclists and in-line skaters. During summer the Moonlight Cinema (p105) attracts the crowds.

◉ Bondi, Coogee & the Eastern Beaches

Sydney sheds its suit and tie, ditches the strappy heels and chills out in the eastern beaches. Beach after golden-sand beach, alternating with sheer sandstone cliffs, are the classic vistas of this beautiful, laid-back and egalitarian stretch of the city.

★**Bondi Beach**   BEACH
(Map p78; Campbell Pde, Bondi Beach; ㉣333, 380-2) Definitively Sydney, Bondi is one of the world's great beaches: ocean and land collide, the Pacific arrives in great foaming swells, and all people are equal, as democratic as sand. It's the closest ocean beach to the city centre (8km away), has consistently good (though crowded) waves, and is great for a rough-and-tumble swim (the average water temperature is a considerate 21°C). If the sea's angry, try the child-friendly saltwater sea baths at either end of the beach.

◉ Sydney Harbourside

Stretching inland from the heads for 20km until it morphs into the Parramatta River, the harbour has shaped the local psyche for millennia, and today it's the city's sparkling playground. Its inlets, beaches, islands and shorefront parks provide endless swimming, sailing, picnicking and walking opportunities. It's a jewel you can never tire of.

Vaucluse House   HISTORIC BUILDING
(Map p56; ☎02-9388 7922; www.sydneyliving
museums.com.au; Wentworth Rd, Vaucluse; adult/
child $12/8; ☉10am-4pm Wed-Sun; ㉣325) Construction of this imposing, turreted specimen of Gothic Australiana, set amid 10 hectares of lush gardens, commenced in 1805, but the house was tinkered with into the 1860s. Atmospheric, and decorated with beautiful European period pieces, the house offers visitors a rare glimpse into early Sydney colonial life, as lived by the well-to-do. The history of the Wentworths, who occupied it, is fascinating, and helpful guides give great background on them. In the grounds is a popular tearoom.

Kings Cross, Darlinghurst & Woolloomooloo

0 — 0.2 miles
0 — 400 m

Sydney Harbour (Port Jackson)

Elizabeth Bay Rd

Beare Park

Rushcutters Bay

RUSHCUTTERS BAY

Rushcutters Bay Park

Elizabeth Bay

Ithaca Rd

Evans Rd

Waratah St

Billyard Ave

Arthur McElhone Reserve

2 Elizabeth Bay House

Onslow Ave

John Armstrong Reserve

Onslow Pl

Greenknowe Ave

ELIZABETH BAY

Lawrence Hargrave Park

St Luke's Hospital

Roslyn Gdns

Macleay St

Crick Ave

Manning St

Macleay St

22 🍴

9 ℹ️

15 🍴 **11** 🛏️

Mcdonald La

Challis Ave

Rockwall Cres

Rockwall La

POTTS POINT

Embarkation Park

Tusculum La

Hughes Pl

Orwell La

Orwell St

20 🍴

5 ℹ️

16 ℹ️

Springfield Ave

Hughes La

Earl St

Earl Pl

Tlankelly La

Darlinghurst Rd

City Host Information Kiosk

KINGS CROSS

19 🍴

Roslyn St

Kellett Pl

14 🍴

Ward Ave

7 🍴

Bayswater Rd

8 🍴

Goderich La

Kings Cross Rd

Pennys La

Woolloomooloo Bay

Cowper Wharf Rdwy

13 🍴 **10** 🛏️

16 ⛲

Bland St

Victoria St

Brougham St

McElhone St

Dowling St

Nicholson St

Best St

Kings Cross Ⓜ️

32 🍴

17 🍴

Victoria St

Brougham St

McElhone St

Dowling St

Brougham La

24 ℹ️

Royal Botanic Gardens (150m)

Art Gallery Rd

1 Art Gallery of NSW

The Domain

Bourke St

Wilson St

Forbes St

Plunkett St

Harmer St

Stephen St

27 🍴 ℹ️

Judge Pl

Cross St

Forbes St

WOOLLOOMOOLOO

Cathedral St

Talbot Pl

Corfu St

Judge La

William La

Dowling St

Farrell Ave

Premier La

St Peters La

St Peters St

Wisdom La

Rosella La

St Marys Rd

Cathedral St

St John Young Cres

Crown St

Cook + Phillip Park

Parkway

Broughton La

Turner La

Faucett La

Palmer St

Turner St

Faucett St

Robinson St

Sutton St

Kennedy St

Cathedral St

Egan Pl

Eastbound Cross City Tunnel
William St
Westbound Cross City Tunnel
William St

Barnett La

Yurong La

25 🛏️

Crown St

Yurong St

Riley St

Stream St

Stanley St

Australian Museum (200m)

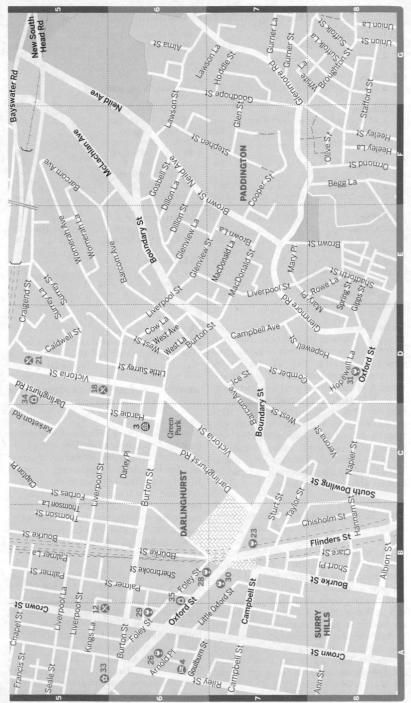

Kings Cross, Darlinghurst & Woolloomooloo

Watsons Bay AREA
(Map p56; ⊠ Watsons Bay) Watsons Bay, east of the city centre and north of Bondi, was once a small fishing village, as evidenced by the tiny heritage cottages that pepper the suburb's narrow streets (and now cost a fortune). While you're here, tradition demands that you sit in the beer garden at the Watsons Bay Hotel at sunset and watch the sun dissolve behind the disembodied Harbour Bridge, jutting up above Bradley's Head.

On the ocean side, The Gap is a dramatic cliff-top lookout where proposals and suicides happen with similar frequency.

South Head NATIONAL PARK
(Map p56; www.nationalparks.nsw.gov.au; Cliff St, Watsons Bay; ⊙ 5am-10pm; ⊠ Watsons Bay) At the northern end of Camp Cove, the South Head Heritage Trail kicks off, leading into a section of Sydney Harbour National Park distinguished by harbour views and crashing surf. It passes old fortifications and a path heading down to **Lady Bay** (Map p56; Cliff St, Watsons Bay; ⊠ Watsons Bay), before continuing on to the candy-striped Hornby Lighthouse and the sandstone Lightkeepers' Cottages (1858). Between April and November, look out to sea to where the whale-watching boats have congregated and you'll often see cetaceans.

McMahons Point VIEWPOINT
(Map p56; ⊠ McMahons Point) Is there a better view of the Bridge and the Opera House than from the wharf at this point, a short hop by ferry northwest of the centre? It's all unfolded before you and is a stunning spot to be when the sun is setting.

Cockatoo Island ISLAND
(Map p56; ☑ 02-8969 2100; www.cockatooisland. gov.au; ⊠ Cockatoo Island) Studded with photogenic industrial relics, convict architecture and art installations, fascinating Cockatoo Island (Wareamah) opened to the public in 2007 and now has regular ferry services, a campground, rental accommodation, a cafe and a bar. Information boards and audio guides ($5) explain the island's time as a prison, a shipyard and a naval base.

★ Taronga Zoo ZOO
(Map p56; ☑ 02-9969 2777; www.taronga.org.au; Bradleys Head Rd, Mosman; adult/child $46/26; ⊙ 9.30am-5pm Sep-Apr, 9.30am-4.30pm May-Aug; ⊞; ⊒ 247, ⊠ Taronga Zoo) ⬤ A 12-minute ferry ride from Circular Quay, this bushy harbour hillside is full of kangaroos, koalas and similarly hirsute Australians, plus numerous imported guests. The zoo's critters have million-dollar harbour views, but seem blissfully unaware of the privilege. Encouragingly, Taronga sets benchmarks in animal

care and welfare. Highlights include the nocturnal platypus habitat, the Great Southern Oceans section and the Asian elephant display. Feedings and encounters happen throughout the day, while in summer, twilight concerts jazz things up (see www.twilightattaronga.org.au).

Luna Park   AMUSEMENT PARK
(Map p56; ☏ 02-9922 6644; www.lunapark sydney.com; 1 Olympic Dr, Milsons Point; ⊗ 11am-10pm Fri & Sat, 10am-6pm Sun, 11am-4pm Mon; 🚊 Milsons Point) **FREE** A sinister chip-toothed clown face (50 times life-sized) forms the entrance to this old-fashioned amusement park overlooking Sydney Harbour. It's one of several 1930s features, including the Coney Island funhouse, a pretty carousel and the nausea-inducing rotor. You can purchase a two-ride pass ($20), or buy a height-based unlimited-ride pass (adults $52, kids $22 to $45, cheaper if purchased online). Hours are complex, and extended during school and public holidays. It also functions as a concert venue.

◉ Newtown & the Inner West

The bohemian sweep of the inner west is an array of suburbs packed with great places to eat and drink. The quiet streets of Glebe and louder Newtown, grouped around the University of Sydney, are the most well-known of these tightly packed suburbs, but Enmore, Marrickville, Summer Hill, Petersham and more are all worth investigating. All the essential hang-outs for students – bookshops, cafes and pubs – are present in abundance, but the Inner West is a lifestyle choice for a whole swathe of Sydney society.

★ Powerhouse Museum   MUSEUM
(Museum of Applied Arts & Sciences (MAAS); Map p62; ☏ 02-9217 0111; www.powerhousemuseum. com; 500 Harris St, Ultimo; adult/child $15/8; ⊗ 10am-5pm; 🚼; 🚊 Exhibition Centre) A short walk from Darling Harbour, this cavernous science and design museum whirs away inside the former power station for Sydney's defunct, original tram network. The collection and temporary exhibitions cover everything from robots and life on Mars to steam trains to climate change to atoms to fashion, industrial design and avant-garde art installations. There are great options for kids of all ages but it's equally intriguing for adults. Grab a map of the museum once you're inside. Disabled access is good.

The Powerhouse is due to move to a new location in Parramatta that is set to be completed in 2022.

★ White Rabbit   GALLERY
(Map p74; www.whiterabbitcollection.org; 30 Balfour St, Chippendale; ⊗ 10am-5pm Wed-Sun, closed Feb & Aug; 🚊 Redfern) **FREE** If you're an art lover or a bit of a Mad Hatter, this particular rabbit hole will leave you grinning like a Cheshire Cat. There are so many works in this private collection of cutting-edge, contemporary Chinese art that only a fraction can be displayed at one time. Who knew the People's Republic was turning out work that was so edgy, funny, sexy and idiosyncratic? It's probably Sydney's best contemporary art gallery.

Central Park   AREA
(Map p74; www.centralparksydney.com; Broadway; ⊗ 10am-8pm; 🚊 Central) Occupying the site of an old brewery, this major residential and shopping development is a striking sight.

ⓘ DISCOUNT PASSES

Sydney Museums Pass (www.sydneylivingmuseums.com.au; adult/child $24/16) Allows a single visit to 12 museums in and around Sydney, including the Museum of Sydney, Hyde Park Barracks, Justice & Police Museum and Susannah Place. It's valid for a month and available at each of the participating museums. It costs the same as two regular museum visits.

Ultimate Sydney Pass (adult/child $99/70) Provides access to the high-profile, costly attractions operated by British-based Merlin Entertainment: Sydney Tower Eye (including the Skywalk), Sydney Sea Life Aquarium, Wild Life Sydney Zoo, Madame Tussauds and Manly Sea Life Sanctuary. It's available from each of the venues, but is often considerably cheaper online through the venue websites. If you plan on visiting only some of these attractions, discounted Sydney Attractions Passes are available in any combination you desire.

Surry Hills

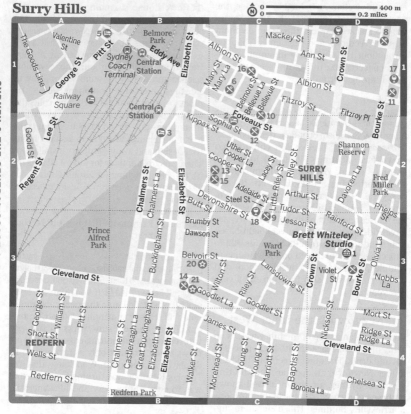

Surry Hills

Most impressive is Jean Nouvel's award-winning, vertical-garden-covered tower, **One Central Park**. The cantilevered platform high above has been designed to reflect sunlight onto the greenery below. Its lower floors have plenty of food options, ping pong, shops, a supermarket and gallery spaces, while adjacent Kensington St and Spice Alley (p94) offer further gastronomic pleasure. Two new Norman Foster–designed apartment towers, Duo, are under construction.

★ Nicholson Museum
MUSEUM

(Map p74; ☑ 02-9351 2812; www.sydney.edu.au/museums; University Pl, University of Sydney; ⊙ 10am-4.30pm Mon-Fri, noon-4pm 1st Sat of month; 🚇 412, 413, 436, 438-40, 461, 480, 483, M10) FREE
Within the University of Sydney's quadrangle, this is one of the city's great under-the-radar attractions. Combining modern ideas with ancient artefacts, it's an intriguing collection of Greek, Roman, Cypriot, Egyptian and Western Asian antiquities. Attic vases and Egyptian mummies take their place alongside themed cross-cultural displays, plus there's a fabulous Pompeii made from Lego that features toga-clad citizens alongside the likes of Pink Floyd rocking the amphitheatre. The museum is to be incorporated into the new **Chau Chak Wing Museum** (Map p74; ☑ 02-9351 2222) by 2019.

◉ Manly

With both a harbour side and a glorious ocean beach, Manly is Sydney's only ferry destination with surf. Capping off the harbour with scrappy charm, it's a place worth visiting for the ferry ride alone. The surf's good, there are appealing contemporary bars and eateries and, as the gateway to the Northern Beaches, it makes a popular base for the board-riding brigade.

★ Manly Beach
BEACH

(Map p77; 🚢 Manly) Sydney's second most famous beach stretches for nearly two golden kilometres, lined by Norfolk Island pines and scrappy midrise apartment blocks. The southern end of the beach, nearest The Corso, is known as South Steyne, with North Steyne in the centre and Queenscliff at the northern end; each has its own surf lifesaving club.

Manly Sea Life Sanctuary
AQUARIUM

(Map p77; ☑ 1800 199 742; www.manlysealifesanctuary.com.au; West Esplanade; adult/child $25/17; ⊙ 9.30am-5pm; 🚢 Manly) Not the place to come if you're on your way to Manly Beach for a surf. Underwater glass tubes enable you to become alarmingly intimate with 3m grey nurse sharks. Reckon they're not hungry? **Shark Dive Xtreme** (Map p77; ☑ 1800 199 742; dives from $299; ⊙ Fri-Wed) enables you to enter their world. Upstairs, the residents of the penguin enclosure have lawless amounts of fun.

LOCAL KNOWLEDGE

RIDING THE 389

A good introduction to Sydney's eastern suburbs is a ride on the 389 bus, as it generally avoids major roads in favour of smaller suburban streets. Catch it near the Maritime Museum (p59) and take in the Pyrmont harbour foreshore in a long loop that eventually brings you into the city centre across Darling Harbour. Crossing the city from west to east, it zigzags its way through characterful Darlinghurst streets before cruising the prettiest parts of upmarket Paddington. After a dose of urban ugliness at Bondi Junction bus interchange, it then approaches Bondi Beach via the interesting back streets, ending up at North Bondi with the beach just down the hill ahead of you.

★ Store Beach
BEACH

(Map p56; ⊙ dawn-dusk) A hidden jewel on North Head, magical Store Beach can only be reached by kayak or boat. It's a fairy-penguin breeding ground, so access is prohibited from dusk, when the birds waddle in.

★ North Head
NATIONAL PARK

(Map p56; North Head Scenic Dr, Manly; 🚇 135) About 3km south of Manly, spectacular, chunky North Head offers dramatic cliffs, lookouts and sweeping views of the ocean, the harbour and the city; hire a bike and go exploring.

North Head is believed to have been used as a ceremonial site by the native Camaraigal people. These days, most of the headland is part of Sydney Harbour National Park.

The 9km, four-hour Manly Scenic Walkway (p75) loops around the park; pick up a brochure from the visitor centre. Also here is the historic **Quarantine Station** (Q Station; Map p56; ☑ 02-9466 1551; www.quarantinestation.com.au; ⊙ museum 10am-4pm Sun-Thu, to 8pm Fri & Sat; 🚇 135) FREE.

◉ Northern Beaches

Wilder and harder to get to than Sydney's eastern strands, the Northern Beaches are a must-see, especially for surfers. Although you'll most likely approach them as a day trip, they're very much a part of the city, with the suburbs pushing right up to the water's edge. Some neighbourhoods are more

Paddington & Woollahra

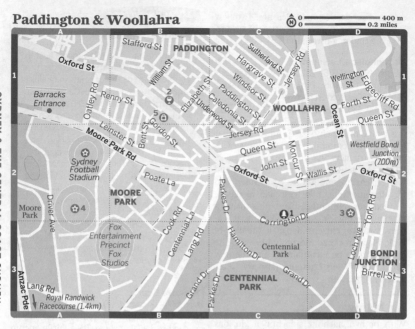

Paddington & Woollahra

ritzy than others, but what they all have in common is a devotion to the beach.

Palm Beach　　　　　　　　　　　BEACH
(Ocean Rd, Palm Beach; 🚌 L90, 190) Long, lovely Palm Beach is a meniscus of bliss, famous as the setting for cheesy TV soap *Home & Away*. The 1881 Barrenjoey Lighthouse (p72) punctuates the northern tip of the headland in an annexe of Ku-ring-gai Chase National Park. The suburb Palm Beach has two sides, the magnificent ocean beach, and a pleasant strip on Pittwater, where the calmer strands are good for young kids. From here you can get ferries to other picturesque Pittwater destinations.

Barrenjoey Lighthouse　　LIGHTHOUSE
(📞02-9451 3479; www.nationalparks.nsw.gov.au; Palm Beach; 🚌L90, 190) This historic sandstone lighthouse (1881) sits at the northern tip of the Northern Beaches in an annexe of Ku-ring-gai Chase National Park. You've got two route options, shorter stairs or a winding track, for the steep hike to the top (no toilets!), but the majestic views across Pittwater and down the peninsula are worth the effort. On Sundays short tours run half-hourly from 11am to 3pm; no need to book. The top is also a good spot for a bit of whale watching.

Avalon　　　　　　　　　　　　　BEACH
(Barrenjoey Rd, Avalon; 🚌L88, L90, 188-190) Caught in a sandy '70s time warp, Avalon is the mythical Australian beach you always dreamt of but could never find. Challenging surf and sloping, gold-tangerine sand have a boutique headland for a backdrop. There's a sea pool at the southern end. Good cheap eating options abound in the streets behind.

⊙ Parramatta

The district of Parramatta, 23km west of central Sydney, was founded in 1788 by Governor Phillip, who needed a place to grow grain to supply the colony. The Indigenous Darug people named it Burramatta for the plentiful eels that are still the symbol and nickname of Parramatta's famous rugby league team.

Parramatta is an important commercial and administrative centre, with an ambitious development program to grow it into a real alternative to the CBD. Originally a separate city, it now is roughly the geographical midpoint of Sydney's immense urban sprawl.

Experiment Farm Cottage   HISTORIC BUILDING
(☑ 02-9635 5655; www.nationaltrust.org.au; 9 Ruse St, Harris Park; adult/child $9/4; ⊗ 10.30am-3.30pm Wed-Sun; ⓡ Harris Park) This colonial bungalow stands on the site of Australia's first official land grant. In 1789 Governor Phillip allocated 12 hectares to emancipated convict James Ruse as an experiment to see how long it would take Ruse to wean himself off government supplies. The experiment was a success, and Ruse became Australia's first private farmer. He sold the land to surgeon John Harris, who built this house around 1835. It's furnished in period style with lovely early-colonial furniture.

Entrance is by very informative guided tour; the last one begins at 3pm.

Elizabeth Farm   HISTORIC BUILDING
(☑ 02-9635 9488; www.sydneylivingmuseums.com.au; 70 Alice St, Rosehill; adult/child $12/8; ⊗ 10am-4pm Wed-Sun; ⓡ Rosehill) Elizabeth Farm contains part of Australia's oldest surviving European home (1793), built by renegade pastoralist and rum trader John Macarthur. Heralded as the founder of Australia's wool industry, Macarthur was a ruthless capitalist whose politicking made him immensely wealthy and a thorn in the side of successive governors. The pretty homestead is now a hands-on museum where you can recline on the reproduction furniture and thumb voyeuristically through Elizabeth Macarthur's letters.

Old Government House   HISTORIC BUILDING
(☑ 02-9635 8149; www.nationaltrust.org.au; Parramatta Park, Parramatta; ⊗ 10am-4pm Tue-Sun; ⓡ Parramatta) The country residence of the early governors, this elegant Georgian Palladian building is now a preciously maintained museum furnished with original colonial furniture. It dates from 1799, making it the oldest remaining public building in Australia. Temporary exhibitions add to the building's interest and there's a vine-draped courtyard restaurant. The park itself is great, a pretty riverside community space with a democratic feel.

⊙ Outlying Areas

Lane Cove National Park   NATIONAL PARK
(www.nationalparks.nsw.gov.au; Lady Game Dr, Chatswood West; per car $8; ⊗ 9am-6pm; ⓡ North Ryde) This 601-hectare park, surrounded by North Shore suburbia, is a great place to stretch out on some middle-sized bushwalks. It's home to dozens of critters, including some endangered owls and toads. If you visit in spring, the water dragons will be getting horny and the native orchids and lilies will be flowering.

Wet'n'Wild Sydney   AMUSEMENT PARK
(☑ 13 33 86; www.wetnwildsydney.com.au; 427 Reservoir Rd, Prospect; over/under 110cm tall $80/70; ⊗ Sep-Apr, hours & days vary; ⓐ; ⓡ shuttle from Parramatta Station) The famous Gold Coast theme park has opened in Sydney with more than 40 slides, including a 360-degree loop slide that hits speeds of up to 60km/h. At the heart of the park is Australia's largest wave pool.

🏃 Activities

Cycling

Manly Bike Tours   CYCLING
(Map p77; ☑ 02-8005 7368; www.manlybiketours.com.au; Belgrave St, Manly; hire per hr/day from $16/33; ⊗ 9am-6pm Oct-Mar, 9am-5pm Apr-Sep; ⓐ Manly) ⌁ Hires bikes and provides maps and suggested routes for self-guided tours. There's a big variety of bikes available and it's right across from the ferry wharf. It's got lockers for you to store gear while you ride.

Diving

Dive Centre Bondi   DIVING
(Map p78; ☑ 02-9369 3855; www.divebondi.com.au; 198 Bondi Rd, Bondi; ⊗ 9am-6pm Mon-Fri, 8am-6pm Sat & Sun; ⓡ 333) Friendly and professional, this centre offers guided dives from shore ($155 for two) or boat ($185 for two) as well as equipment hire. It is PADI certified and offers dive courses (including $395 Open Water, $495 Advanced).

Gordons Bay Underwater Nature Trail   DIVING
(Map p56; www.gordonsbayscubadivingclub.com; Victory St, Clovelly; ⓡ 339) Accessed from

Newtown

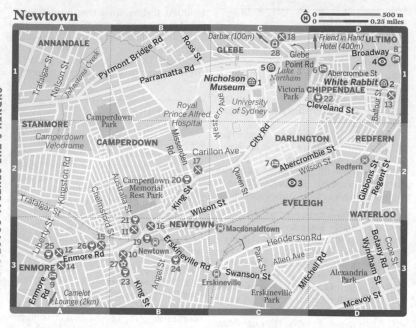

Newtown

◎ Top Sights
1 Nicholson Museum	C1
2 White Rabbit	D1

◎ Sights
3 Carriageworks	C2
4 Central Park	D1
5 Chau Chak Wing Museum	C1

🛏 Sleeping
6 Mad Monkey Backpackers	D1
7 Mandelbaum House	C2
8 Old Clare Hotel	D1
9 Tara Guest House	A3

✕ Eating
10 3 Olives	B3
11 Black Star Pastry	B3
12 Cow & the Moon	A3
13 Ester	D1
14 Faheem Fast Food	A3
Spice Alley	(see 8)
15 Stinking Bishops	A3

16 Thai Pothong	B3
17 Thanh Binh	B2
18 Wedge	C1

🍷 Drinking & Nightlife
19 Bank Hotel	B3
20 Corridor	B2
21 Courthouse Hotel	B3
22 Duck Inn	D1
23 Earl's Juke Joint	B3
24 Imperial Hotel	B3
25 Sly Fox	A3
26 Young Henry's	A3

✪ Entertainment
27 Newtown Social Club	B3

🛍 Shopping
Carriageworks Farmers Market	(see 3)
28 Glebe Markets	C1
Gleebooks	(see 18)

beyond the car park just south of Clovelly Beach, this is a 500m underwater chain guiding divers around reefs, sand flats and kelp forests.

Kayaking

Sydney Harbour Kayaks　　　KAYAKING
(Map p56; ☎02-9960 4590; www.sydneyharbour kayaks.com.au; Smiths Boat Shed, 81 Parriwi Rd, Mosman; ⊙9am-5pm Mon-Fri, 7.30am-5pm Sat & Sun;

173-180) Rents kayaks (from $20 per hour) and stand-up paddleboards (from $25), and leads excellent four-hour ecotours ($125) from near the Spit Bridge.

Surfing

Sydney has been synonymous with surfing ever since the Beach Boys effused about 'Australia's Narrabeen' in 'Surfin' USA' (Narrabeen is one of Sydney's northern beaches). For updates on what's breaking where, see www.coastal watch.com, www.surf-forecast.com, www. magicseaweed.com or www.realsurf.com.

★ Let's Go Surfing   SURFING
(Map p78; ☑ 02-9365 1800; www.letsgosurfing.com. au; 128 Ramsgate Ave, North Bondi; board & wetsuit hire 1hr/2hr/day/week $25/30/50/200; ⊙ 9am-5pm; 🚊 380-2) North Bondi is a great place to learn to surf, and this well-established surf school offers lessons catering to practically everyone. There are classes for grommets aged seven to 16 (1½ hours, $49) and adults (two hours, $110, women-only classes available), or you can book a private tutor (1½ hours, $195/284 for one/two people). Prices drop outside summer.

Manly Surf School   SURFING
(Map p56; ☑ 02-9932 7000; www.manlysurf school.com; North Steyne Surf Club, Manly; 🚊 139, 🚢 Manly) Reliable and well-established, this offers two-hour surf lessons year-round (adult/child $70/55), as well as private tuition. It's a fair bit cheaper if you book a multi-class package. Also runs surf safaris up to the Northern Beaches, including two lessons, lunch, gear and city pick-ups ($120).

Swimming

Fancy a dip? Sydney has sheltered harbour beaches, saltwater beach rock pools, more than 100 public pools and crazy surf. Always swim between the flags on lifesaver-patrolled beaches, and avoid swimming in the ocean for a day and in the harbour for three days after heavy rains. Many outdoor pools close at the end of April for the cooler months and reopen in early October.

Bondi Icebergs Pool   SWIMMING
(Map p78; ☑ 02-9130 4804; www.icebergs.com.au; 1 Notts Ave; adult/child $6.50/4.50; ⊙ 6am-6.30pm Mon-Wed & Fri, 6.30am-6.30pm Sat & Sun; 🚊 333, 380) Sydney's most famous pool commands the best view in Bondi and has a cute little cafe. It's a saltwater pool that's regularly doused by the bigger breakers. There's a more

sheltered pool for kids. It closes on Thursdays so they can clean the seaweed out again.

Murray Rose Pool   SWIMMING
(Redleaf Pool; Map p56; 536 New South Head Rd, Double Bay; 🚊 324-326, 🚢 Double Bay) **FREE** Not really a pool at all, family-friendly Murray Rose (named after a champion Olympic swimmer) is a large, shark-netted enclosure that is one of the harbour's best swimming spots. As the closest swimming spot to the city, it attracts an urbane cross-section of inner-eastern locals. A boardwalk runs around the top of the shark net, and there are two sought-after floating pontoons.

Walking

While exploring the harbour by ferry is a must, walking its foreshore is also a highlight of a visit to the city. There are numerous routes, which switch between dedicated harbourside paths, sections along beaches and stretches on quiet suburban roads. The website www.walkingcoastalsydney.com.au is a great resource for planning your own excursion, with downloadable brochures and maps.

★ Manly Scenic Walkway   WALKING
(Map p56; www.manly.nsw.gov.au; 🚢 Manly) This epic walk has two major components: the 10km western stretch between Manly and Spit Bridge, and the 9.5km eastern loop around North Head. Either download a map or pick one up from the information centre near the wharf.

★ Bondi to Coogee Clifftop Walk   WALKING
The sensational 6km Bondi to Coogee Clifftop Walk leads south from Bondi Beach along the cliff tops to Coogee via Tamarama, Bronte and Clovelly, interweaving panoramic views, beaches, sea baths, waterside parks and plaques recounting local Aboriginal stories.

Parramatta River Walk   WALKING
There's no better way to explore this part of Sydney than by walking along the Parramatta River. There's a path on both the north and south sides of the river in Parramatta itself, and plenty of birdlife in places. You could head towards Sydney, or go upstream and discover Lake Parramatta. The excellent resources on www.walkingcoastalsydney. com.au are helpful for planning.

☞ Tours

Boat Tours
There's a wide range of harbour cruises available, from paddle steamers to maxi

yachts. If you're pinching pennies, take the return ferry trip to Manly and consider yourself very clever.

★ Whale Watching Sydney   WILDLIFE

(Map p60; ☑02-9583 1199; www.whalewatchingsydney.com.au; ☺mid-May–early Dec) Humpback and southern right whales habitually shunt up and down the Sydney coastline, sometimes venturing into the harbour. Between mid-May and December, WWS runs three-hour (adult/child $97/60) or 2½-hour ($60/40) tours beyond the Heads. For a faster ride that also offers a more intimate whale experience, there are two-hour jet-boat expeditions ($65/45).

Boats depart from Jetty 6, Circular Quay or from Cockle Bay Wharf, Darling Harbour.

Captain Cook Cruises   CRUISE

(Map p60; ☑02-9206 1111; www.captaincook.com.au; Wharf 6, Circular Quay; ⓡCircular Quay) As well as ritzy lunch and dinner cruises and whale watching, this crew offers an aquatic version of a hop-on, hop-off bus tour, stopping at Watsons Bay, Taronga Zoo, Fort Denison, Garden Island, Shark Island, Manly, Circular Quay, Luna Park and Darling Harbour. It costs $45/25 per adult/child and includes some commentary.

Harbour Jet   BOATING

(Map p64; ☑1300 887 373; www.harbourjet.com; King Street Wharf 9; adult/child from $80/50; ⓢDarling Harbour) One of several jet-boat operators (Sydney Jet, Oz Jet Boating, Thunder Jet – take your pick), these guys run a 35- or 50-minute white-knuckle ride with spins, fishtails and 75km/h power stops that'll test how long it's been since you had breakfast.

Bike Tours

Bonza Bike Tours   CYCLING

(Map p60; ☑02-9247 8800; www.bonzabiketours.com; 30 Harrington St; ☺office 9am-5pm; ⓡCircular Quay) These bike boffins run a 2½-hour Sydney Highlights tour (adult/child $79/99) and a four-hour Sydney Classic tour ($119/99). Other tours include the Harbour Bridge and Manly. It also hires bikes (per hour/half-day/day/week $10/19/29/125).

BlueBananas   CYCLING

(Map p60; ☑0422 213 574; www.bluebananas.com.au; 281 Clarence St; ⓡTown Hall) Take some of the puff out of a guided cycling tour on an electric bike. Options include the 1½-hour Bike the Bridge tour ($59) and the 2½-hour Sydney City Tour ($99). The office is in a little arcade of shops.

DON'T MISS

KU-RING-GAI CHASE

Spectacular 14,928-hectare **Ku-ring-gai Chase National Park** (☑02-9472 8949; www.nationalparks.nsw.gov.au; Bobbin Head Rd, North Turramurra; per car per day $12, landing fee by boat adult/child $3/2; ⓡMt Colah), 24km from the city centre, forms Sydney's northern boundary. It's a classic mix of sandstone, bushland and water vistas, taking in over 100km of coastline along the southern edge of Broken Bay, where it heads into the Hawkesbury River.

Ku-ring-gai takes its name from its original inhabitants, the Guringai people, who were all but wiped out just after colonisation through violence at the hands of British settlers and introduced disease. It's well worth reading Kate Grenville's Booker-nominated *The Secret River* for an engrossing but harrowing telling of this story.

Remnants of Aboriginal life are visible today thanks to the preservation of more than 800 sites, including rock paintings, middens and cave art. To learn more, enter the park through the Mt Colah entrance and visit the **Kalkari Discovery Centre** (☑02-9472 9300; Ku-ring-gai Chase Rd, Mt Colah; ☺9am-5pm), which has displays and videos on Australian fauna and Aboriginal culture.

Elevated park sections offer glorious water views over Cowan Creek, Broken Bay and Pittwater. The view from West Head across Pittwater to Barrenjoey Lighthouse is a winner. This whole section of the park is a fabulous wilderness with sensational views all around. Tracks drop down to perfect little coves.

If you are arriving by car, enter the park off Pacific Hwy, Mt Colah; Bobbin Head Rd, North Turramurra; or, for the West Head, Cottage Point and Pittwater section, McCarrs Creek Rd, Terrey Hills. You can also reach the latter section by ferry from Palm Beach.

Manly

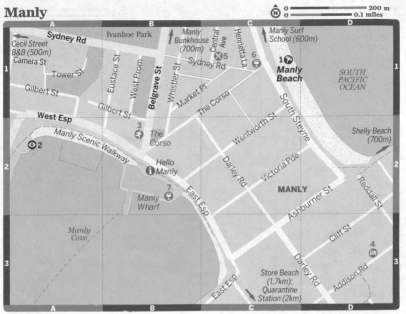

Walking Tours

Sydney Architecture Walks WALKING
(☎0403 888 390; www.sydneyarchitecture.org;
adult walks $49-59, cycle incl bike $120) These
bright young archi-buffs run two 3½-hour
cycling tours and five themed two-hour
walking tours (The City; Utzon and the
Sydney Opera House; Harbourings; Art,
Place and Landscape; and Modern Sydney).
There's an excellent focus on explaining
modern architectural principles and urban
design. It's cheaper if you book in advance.

The Rocks Walking Tours WALKING
(Map p60; ☎02-9247 6678; www.rockswalking
tours.com.au; Shop 4a, cnr Argyle & Harrington Sts;
adult/child/family $28/12/68; ☺10.30am & 1.30pm;
🚉Circular Quay) Two daily 90-minute tours
through the historic Rocks, with plenty of
tales and interesting minutiae. The office is in
a shopping arcade; you can book online too.

I'm Free WALKING
(Map p62; ☎0405 515 654; www.imfree.com.au;
483 George St; ☺10.30am & 2.30pm; 🚉Town Hall)
FREE Departing twice daily from the square
off George St between the Town Hall and St
Andrew's Cathedral (no bookings taken –
just show up), these highly rated three-hour
tours are nominally free but are run by enthusiastic young guides for tips. The route

Manly

takes in the Rocks, Circular Quay, Martin
Place, Pitt St and Hyde Park.

Other Tours

★**BridgeClimb** WALKING
(Map p60; ☎02-8274 7777; www.bridgeclimb.com;
3 Cumberland St; adult $248-383; child $168-273;
🚉Circular Quay) Don headset, safety cord and
a dandy grey jumpsuit and you'll be ready to
embark on an exhilarating climb to the top of

Bondi

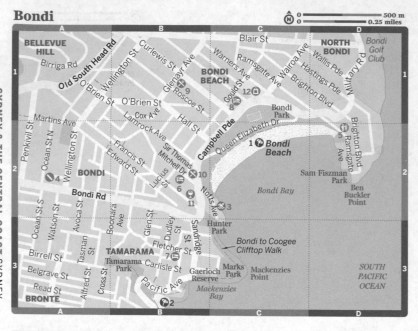

Bondi

Top Sights
1 Bondi Beach...C2

Sights
2 Tamarama Beach....................................B3

Activities, Courses & Tours
3 Bondi Icebergs Pool..............................C2
4 Dive Centre Bondi..................................A2
5 Let's Go Surfing......................................D2

Sleeping
6 Bondi Beach House B2

Sleeping
7 Bondi Beachouse YHA...........................B3
8 QT Bondi..C1

Eating
Icebergs Dining Room.....................(see 3)
9 Lox, Stock & Barrel................................B1
10 Trio...B2

Drinking & Nightlife
11 Anchor..B2

Shopping
12 Bondi Markets...C1

Sydney's famous harbour bridge. The priciest climbs are at dawn and sunset. A cheaper, 90-minute 'sampler' climb (heading only halfway up) is available, as is an 'express climb', which ascends to the top via a faster route.

★☆ Festivals & Events

★ Sydney Festival   CULTURAL
(www.sydneyfestival.org.au; ⊙ Jan) Sydney's premier arts and culture festival showcases three weeks of music, theatre and visual art.

Chinese New Year   CULTURAL
(www.sydneychinesenewyear.com) Seventeen-day, Chinatown-based festival featuring food, fire-

works, dragon dancers and dragon-boat races to see in the lunar new year. Actual dates vary slightly, but it's always in late January and early February.

★ Tropfest   FILM
(www.tropfest.org.au) The world's largest short-film festival is enjoyed from picnic blankets in Parramatta Park on one day in early February.

★ Sydney Gay &
Lesbian Mardi Gras   LGBT
(www.mardigras.org.au; ⊙ Feb-Mar) A two-week cultural and entertainment festival culminating in the world-famous massive parade and party on the first Saturday in March.

Sydney Royal Easter Show FAIR
(www.eastershow.com.au) Ostensibly an agricultural show, this wonderful Sydney tradition is a two-week fiesta of carnival rides, kiddie-centric show bags and sugary horrors. Crowds are massive.

Biennale of Sydney CULTURAL
(www.biennaleofsydney.com.au) High-profile festival of art and ideas held between March and June in even-numbered years.

★ **Sydney Writers' Festival** LITERATURE
(www.swf.org.au; ☉ May) The country's preeminent literary shindig is held over a week in May, in various prime locations around the central city.

Vivid Sydney CULTURAL
(www.vividsydney.com) Immersive light installations and projections in the city, plus performances from local and international musicians, and public talks and debates with leading global creative thinkers; held over 18 days from late May.

★ **Sydney Film Festival** FILM
(www.sff.org.au; ☉ Jun) Held (mostly) at the magnificent **State Theatre** (Map p60; ☑ 02-9373 6655; www.statetheatre.com.au; 49 Market St; ☒ Town Hall), this excellent, highly regarded film festival screens art-house gems from Australia and around the world.

Sydney to Hobart Yacht Race SPORTS
(www.rolexsydneyhobart.com; ☉ Dec) On 26 December Sydney Harbour is a sight to behold as hundreds of boats crowd its waters to farewell the yachts competing in this gruelling race.

★ **New Year's Eve** FIREWORKS
(www.sydneynewyearseve.com; ☉ 31 Dec) The biggest party of the year, with flamboyant firework displays on the harbour. There's a family-friendly display at 9pm then the main event at midnight. There are also any number of other events on and around the harbour. There's a variety of regulated zones to watch the fireworks from, some ticketed, some alcohol-free.

🛏 Sleeping

There are hotels scattered throughout Sydney, but you'll find the international chains with all their bells and whistles in Circular Quay and the city centre. The suburbs and beaches host a diverse bunch of boutique escapes, ranging from heritage-listed terrace houses right through to sleek apa.. and beach bungalows.

Nearly all hotels operate flexible pric.. so be sure to book your stay well in advance for the best rates.

🛏 Circular Quay & the Rocks

★ **Sydney Harbour YHA** HOSTEL $$
(Map p60; ☑ 02-8272 0900; www.yha.com. au; 110 Cumberland St; dm $55-75, d $200-240; ❂❄@☎; ☒ Circular Quay) ✈ Any qualms about the unhostel-like prices will be shelved the moment you head up to the ample rooftop space of this sprawling, modern hostel and see the superb views of Circular Quay. All of the spacious rooms, including the dorms, have en suites and there are a host of sustainability initiatives in place.

Lord Nelson Brewery Hotel PUB $$
(Map p60; ☑ 02-9251 4044; www.lordnelson brewery.com; 19 Kent St; r $180-200; ❂❄☎; ☒ Circular Quay) Built in 1836, this atmospheric sandstone pub has a tidy set of upstairs rooms, with exposed stone walls and dormer windows with harbour glimpses. Most of the eight light-filled rooms have en suites; there's also one with a private exterior bathroom. The downstairs microbrewery is a welcoming place for a pint and a meal. Rates include continental breakfast.

★ **Harbour Rocks** BOUTIQUE HOTEL $$$
(Map p60; ☑ 02-8220 9999; www.harbour rocks.com.au; 34 Harrington Street; r $300-550; ❂❄@☎; ☒ Circular Quay) This deluxe boutique hotel on the site of Sydney's first hospital has undergone a chic and sympathetic transformation from colonial warehouse and workers' cottages to a series of New York loft–style rooms, with high ceilings, distressed brick and elegant furnishings. It maintains a historic feel, offers relaxed personable service and has a great little garden balcony terrace.

Pullman Quay Grand
Sydney Harbour APARTMENT $$$
(Map p60; ☑ 02-9256 4000; www.pullman quaygrandsydneyharbour.com; 61 Macquarie St; apt $450-800; ℗❂❄@☎✉; ☒ Circular Quay) With the Opera House as its neighbour, the building known locally as 'The Toaster' has a scorching-hot location. These well-designed contemporary apartments, large and well-equipped, set you in Sydney's glitzy heart, encircled by top restaurants, cocktail bars and that attention-seeking harbour. The small

...alk
...to Coogee
...p Trail

START BONDI BEACH
END COOGEE BEACH
LENGTH 6KM; TWO TO THREE HOURS

Sydney's most famous and most popular walk, this coastal path really shouldn't be missed. Both ends are well connected to bus routes, as are most points in between should you feel too hot and bothered to continue – although a cooling dip at any of the beaches en route should cure that (pack your swimmers). There's little shade on this track, so make sure you dive into a tub of sunscreen before setting out. A hat's also a good idea.

Starting at iconic ❶ **Bondi Beach** (p65), take the stairs up the south end to Notts Ave, passing above the glistening ❷ **Icebergs** (p75) pool complex. Step onto the cliff-top trail at the end of Notts Ave.

Walking south, the sandstone cliffs and grinding Pacific Ocean couldn't be more spectacular (watch for dolphins, whales and surfers). Small but perfectly formed ❸ **Tamarama** has a deep reach of sand that is totally disproportionate to its width.

Descend from the cliff tops onto ❹ **Bronte Beach**. Take a dip, lay out a picnic under the Norfolk Island pines or head to a cafe for a caffeine hit. After your break, pick up the path on the southern side of the beach.

Some famous Australians are among the subterranean denizens of the amazing cliff-edge ❺ **Waverley Cemetery**. On a clear winter's day this is a prime vantage point for whale-watchers.

Pass the locals enjoying a beer or a game of lawn bowls at the Clovelly Bowling Club, then breeze past the cockatoos and canoodling lovers in ❻ **Burrows Park** to sheltered ❼ **Clovelly Beach**.

Follow the footpath up through the car park, along Cliffbrook Pde, then down the steps to the upturned dinghies lining ❽ **Gordons Bay** (p73), one of Sydney's best shore-dive spots.

The trail continues past ❾ **Dolphin Point**, which offers great ocean views, then lands you smack-bang on glorious ❿ **Coogee Beach**. Swagger into the Coogee Bay Hotel and toast your efforts with a cold beverage.

number of rooms and blend of residents and visitors gives it a quiet ambience away from its lively bar Hacienda.

Park Hyatt
HOTEL $$$

(Map p60; ☑02-9256 1234; www.sydney.park.hyatt.com; 7 Hickson Rd; r $1150-1600; P☀❋@❖❆; ☒Circular Quay) At Sydney's most expensive hotel the impeccable service levels and facilities are second to none. With full frontal views across Circular Quay, you can catch all the action from your bed, balcony or bathtub. From the rooftop pool you feel you can almost touch the Harbour Bridge. And with 24-hour butler service for all, it's not like you need to be anywhere else.

City Centre & Haymarket

★Railway Square YHA
HOSTEL $

(Map p70; ☑02-9281 9666; www.yha.com.au; 8-10 Lee St; dm $39-52, d from $142, without bathroom from $132; ❋@❖❆; ☒Central) A lovely piece of industrial renovation has converted Central station's former parcel shed into a really appealing hostel, in a great location but away from the bustle. Dorms with corrugated roofs and underfloor-heated bathrooms are spotless; some are actually in converted train carriages. There's a cafe and laundry facilities, plus the pool was being upgraded at time of research.

Sydney Central YHA
HOSTEL $

(Map p70; ☑02-9218 9000; www.yha.com.au; 11 Rawson Pl; dm $44-55, d from $150, without bathroom from $130; P❋@❖❆; ☒Central) ✚ Close to Central station, this 1913 heritage-listed monolith is the mother of all Sydney YHA properties. The renovated hostel includes everything from a travel agency to an in-house cinema. The rooms are brightly painted and the kitchens are great but the highlight is sweating it out in the sauna, then cooling off in the rooftop pool. There's a 10% HI discount.

Hyde Park Inn
HOTEL $$

(Map p62; ☑02-9264 6001; www.hydeparkinn.com.au; 271 Elizabeth St; r $198-286; P☀❋❖; ☒Museum) Right on the park, this relaxed place offers brightly decorated studio rooms with kitchenettes, deluxe rooms with balconies and full kitchens, and some two-bedroom apartments. All have flat-screen TVs with cable access and some have microwaves and kitchenettes. Breakfast and parking is included in the rate, making it great value for central Sydney.

★QT Sydney
BOUTIQUE HOTEL $$$

(Map p60; ☑02-8262 0000; www.qtsydney.com.au; 49 Market St; r $350-450; P☀❋@❖; ☒Town Hall) Fun, sexy and relaxed, this ultra-theatrical, effortlessly cool hotel is located in the historic State Theatre. Art-deco eccentricity is complemented by quirky extras in the rooms, which are distinct and decorated with real style and flair; there's a definite wow factor. There's also a luxurious spa plus a bar and grill operated by one of the city's most fashionable restaurateurs.

Establishment Hotel
BOUTIQUE HOTEL $$$

(Map p60; ☑02-9240 3100; www.merivale.com.au; 5 Bridge Lane; r $350-500; ❋@❖; ☒Wynyard) In a discreet laneway, this designer boutique hotel in a refurbished 19th-century warehouse invokes Asia with its incense aromas and dark-wood fittings. There are two principal room styles: 'light', all white-and-tan contemporary colouring; and sexier 'dark', with wooden floorboards and a nocturnal feel. Decadent nights out are assured with a posse of the company's acclaimed bars and restaurants right around you.

Primus Hotel Sydney
HOTEL $$$

(Map p62; ☑02-8027 8000; www.primushotelsydney.com; 339 Pitt St; r $290-380; P☀❋❖❆; ☒Town Hall) In the former Water Board building, this slick conversion has a magnificent lobby space with red pillars and glorious art-deco details. There's space to spare here, with wide corridors and ample, commodious rooms; excellent service is a noteworthy feature. Though the pool itself is tiny, the deck surrounding it is a fabulous spot that may open to the public.

Darling Harbour & Pyrmont

★Ovolo 1888
BOUTIQUE HOTEL $$$

(Map p64; ☑02-8586 1888; www.ovolohotels.com; 139 Murray St; shoebox d $239-299, d $299-349; ❋@❖; ☒Convention Centre) In a heritage-listed wool store, this stylish gem combines industrial minimalism with the warmth of ironbark wood beams, luxury appointments and engaged staff. Rooms range from the aptly named shoebox to airy lofts and attic suites with harbour views. The minibar is complimentary. Book direct to enjoy free drinks and canapes at happy hour.

Adina Apartment Hotel Sydney Harbourside
APARTMENT $$$

(Map p64; ☑02-9249 7000; www.adinahotels.com.au; 55 Shelley St; apt $229-500; P❋❖❆;

⚏ Darling Harbour) Heaven is a swish, spacious apartment where people clean up after you. That's exactly what happens at this low-rise development just off King St Wharf. All apartments have kitchens, and all but the studios have laundry facilities and balconies. They are all very spacious, and there's a great atrium pool and gym area.

🛏 Kings Cross & Potts Point

★ Blue Parrot Backpackers HOSTEL $
(Map p66; ☑ 02-9356 4888; www.blueparrot. com.au; 87 Macleay St, Potts Point; dm $39-45; ⊛ @ 🐾 🏊; ⊠ Kings Cross) If Polly wanted a cracker of a hostel she'd head to this brilliant, colourful spot run with real enthusiasm by a pair of sisters. It's a personal experience that feels more like a share house (but much cleaner!). There's a great back courtyard and high-ceilinged dorms with good bunks and mattresses. Movies, Playstation and a barbecue add points. For 18- to 35-year-olds.

Eva's Backpackers HOSTEL $
(Map p66; ☑ 02-9358 2185; www.evasbackpackers. com.au; 6-8 Orwell St, Kings Cross; dm $34-40, d $97-107; ⊛ ❄ @ 🐾; ⊠ Kings Cross) Likeable Eva's is a long-time favourite and a secure, clean welcoming hostel that belies the building's intriguingly shady history. The great roof terrace has a super view of the city skyline and there's a new common-kitchen area being built up there in 2017, along with a major renovation of bathrooms and dorms that should leave it looking very spruce.

Kings Cross Backpackers HOSTEL $
(Map p66; ☑ 02-8705 3761; www.kingscross backpackers.com.au; 79 Bayswater Rd, Kings Cross; dm $35-43; ⊛ ❄ @ 🐾; ⊠ Kings Cross) Nicely set in a quieter part of the Cross, this is a well-run place with renovated air-conditioned, clean dorms that sleep four to 12 and come with lockers and under-bed storage. The downstairs kitchen-lounge and sweet roof terrace are the places to hang out. Security is good and the price is fair. Breakfast is included, but it's a couple of blocks away.

Macleay APARTMENT $$
(Map p66; ☑ 02-9357 7755; www.themacleay.com; 28 Macleay St, Elizabeth Bay; r $180-250; P ⊛ ❄ @ 🐾🏊; ⊠ Kings Cross) At the posh end of Kings Cross, surrounded by fabulous restaurants, is this understated place. The studios are a little faded but all have small kitchenettes and there's a laundry on each floor. An added plus is the rooftop pool and gym. Staff are welcoming and helpful; ask for a room on a higher floor for city and harbour views.

Hotel 59 B&B $$
(Map p66; ☑ 02-9360 5900; www.hotel59.com.au; 59 Bayswater Rd, Kings Cross; s $105, d $135-145; ⊛ ❄ 🐾; ⊠ Kings Cross) With just nine simple, spotless comfortable rooms, family-run Hotel 59 offers great bang for your buck on the quiet but still very convenient part of Bayswater Rd. The owners are genuinely helpful and attentive and the cafe downstairs does whopping cooked breakfasts (included in the price) for those barbarous Kings Cross hangovers.

★ Ovolo Hotel Woolloomooloo HOTEL $$$
(Map p66; ☑ 02-9331 9000; www.ovolohotels. com; 6 Cowper Wharf Roadway, Woolloomooloo; r $400-700; P ⊛ ❄ @ 🐾; 🖵 311, ⊠ Kings Cross) Superbly set in Woolloomooloo Wharf, this excellent smart-casual hotel has extremely friendly young staff and a very likeable set of features. 'Superoo' rooms are mostly either road-facing or skylit, so for water views upgrade to a deluxe, facing east, or city, facing west. It's ultra-characterful with long corridors, industrial machinery and unusually shaped, artfully designed rooms, some split-level. A Sydney standout.

Simpsons of Potts Point BOUTIQUE HOTEL $$$
(Map p66; ☑ 02-9356 2199; www.simpsonshotel. com; 8 Challis Ave, Potts Point; r $255-355; P ⊛ ❄ @ 🐾; ⊠ Kings Cross) At the quiet end of a busy cafe strip, this 1892 villa has been affectionately restored with decorative flourishes of yesteryear. The interior is a stunner, with art, elegance and cosy luxury right through the handsome public areas and dozen guest rooms. The downstairs lounge is perfect for a game of chess and a complimentary sherry. Service is personalised and highly competent.

🛏 Surry Hills & Darlinghurst

★ Bounce HOSTEL $
(Map p70; ☑ 02-9281 2222; www.bouncehotel.com. au; 28 Chalmers St, Surry Hills; dm $40-48, d $149-159; ⊛ ❄ @ 🐾; ⊠ Central) 🚲 Right by Central, this hostel offers boutique budget accommodation. Dorms (various configurations) are modern and very spacious, with extra-large lockers. Private rooms are hotel-quality; it's a value-packed option. The place is really well run, catering to the needs of the party crew and those who want a quieter stay. The huge

kitchen is a plus and the fabulous roof terrace is a show-stealer. Top marks.

Big Hostel HOSTEL $
(Map p62; ☑02-9281 6030; www.bighostel. com; 212 Elizabeth St, Surry Hills; dm $32-36, s/d $89/110; ⊖❄@�; ⏸Central) A great, no-frills hostel experience with a rooftop terrace and a crowded but decent communal area and kitchen. Dorms do the job, with lockers, high ceilings and enough space. The four-bed ones cost a little more but have a bathroom and small TV. The price is good for central Sydney too. Continental breakfast is included. Wi-fi is free downstairs only.

57 Hotel HOTEL $$
(Map p70; ☑02-9011 5757; www.57hotel.com.au; 57 Foveaux St, Surry Hills; s $219-299, d $229-449; ⊖❄�; ⏸Central) Converted from a technical college, this hotel goes to town on modish grey, black and chocolate colouring. Rooms vary widely, from the extremely compact shoebox twins to large, light king-bedded rooms on the corners of the building. We love the doggie towel rails. Free coffee and morning pastries in the lobby lounge are great for a quick breakfast on the hoof.

⭐**ADGE Boutique Apartment Hotel** APARTMENT $$$
(Map p66; ☑02-8093 9888; www.adgehotel. com.au; 222 Riley St, Surry Hills; apt $400-800; P⊖❄�; 🖵333, 380) Modern, catchy and bold, ADGE puts a clever, upbeat twist on the ubiquitous serviced apartment experience. The idiosyncratic but extremely comfortable two-bedroom apartments have gloriously striped liquorice-allsort carpets, floor-to-ceiling windows, quality kitchens with Smeg fridge and appealing balconies. Little extras, including a welcome drink and turn-down service, add points. It's an ideal urban experience and great value for two couples.

🛌 Bondi, Coogee & the Eastern Beaches

Bondi Beachouse YHA HOSTEL $
(Map p78; ☑02-9365 2088; www.yha.com.au; 63 Fletcher St, Tamarama; dm $33-37, tw & d without bathroom $90, d/f $110/180; ⊖�; 🖵361) Perched on a hillside between Bondi and Tamarama Beaches, this 95-bed art-deco hostel is the best in Bondi. Dorms sleep four to eight and come with wooden floors and spacious lockers; some of the private rooms have ocean views – all are clean and well maintained. Facilities include a cinema

SYDNEY & THE CENTRAL COAST SYDNEY

THE HOSTEL SCENE

Sydney's hostels range from the sublime to the sublimely grotty. A clump of flashpacker-style blocks encircling Central station have raised the bar, offering en suites, air-conditioning, rooftop decks and, in one case, a pool. Private rooms in such places are often on par with midrange hotels – and in many cases the prices aren't all that different either. You'll find smaller, cheaper hostels in Kings Cross (still the backpacker capital). Many hostels have weekly rates and some have specific areas for long-stayers.

room, spacious common areas, a courtyard barbecue and a rooftop deck with top views.

Bondi Beach House GUESTHOUSE $$
(Map p78; ☑02-9300 0369; www.bondibeach house.com.au; 28 Sir Thomas Mitchell Rd, Bondi Beach; s $130, d $195-320; P⊖❄�; 🖵380-2) In a tranquil pocket behind Campbell Pde, this charming place offers a homely atmosphere with rustic-chic furnishings and a well-equipped communal kitchen. Though only a two-minute walk from the beach, you may well be tempted to stay in all day – the courtyard and terrace are great spots for relaxing, and the breezily arty rooms are conducive to long sleep-ins.

Dive Hotel BOUTIQUE HOTEL $$
(Map p56; ☑02-9665 5538; www.divehotel.com. au; 234 Arden St, Coogee; r $210-380; P⊖❄@�❄; 🖵372-374) In a cracking location right across the road from the beach, this relaxed, family-run affair is thankfully very inaccurately named. Simple, likeable contemporary rooms come with fridge, microwave and small stylish bathrooms fitted out with mosaic tiles and stainless steel sinks. Sociable continental buffet breakfast in an appealing indoor-outdoor area is a highlight, as are the personable owners and their friendly dogs.

⭐**QT Bondi** APARTMENT $$$
(Map p78; ☑02-8362 3900; www.qtbondi.com.au; 6 Beach Rd, Bondi Beach; apt $399-720; P⊖❄�❄; 🖵333, 380-2) Colourful, chic and appropriately beachy, this newish apartment hotel is steps from the beach and offers a very appealing combination of facilities, location and attitude. All the rooms and suites

are exceedingly spacious, with light-coloured furniture and an airy feel. King Deluxe and above have balconies, but there are no ocean views here. All rooms have kitchenette, bathtub and laundry facilities.

Sydney Harbourside

★Cockatoo Island   CAMPGROUND $

(Map p56; ☑02-8969 2111; www.cockatoo island.gov.au; camp sites from $45, 2-bed tents $150-175, apt from $250, houses from $595; 🛜; 🌊Cockatoo Island) Waking up on an island in the middle of the harbour is an extraordinary Sydney experience. Bring your own tent (or just sleeping bags) or 'glamp' in a two-person tent complete with a double bed on the water's edge. Non-campers will enjoy the elegant houses and apartments. For self-caterers, there's a well-equipped camp kitchen; for everyone else, there are two cafes and bars.

Note that you can't take alcohol onto the island unless you are staying in one of the houses.

Watsons Bay
Boutique Hotel   BOUTIQUE HOTEL $$

(Map p56; ☑02-9337 5444; www.watsonsbayhotel. com.au; 10 Marine Pde, Watsons Bay; r $259-559; P🐕❄🛜; 🌊Watsons Bay) The ferry pulls up to the doorstep of this chic, Hampton's-inspired hotel in a charming beachside hamlet. Expect luxuries such as crisp linen, trendy bathroom accessories and slick glassed-in en suites. The hotel's multilevel Beach Club hums on weekends, and noise can be an issue despite double glazing. Rates include breakfast.

Glenferrie Lodge   GUESTHOUSE $$

(Map p56; ☑02-9955 1685; www.glenferrie lodge.com; 12a Carabella St, Kirribilli; s/d without bathroom $88/128, d $152; P🐕@🛜🐕) 🍃 Set in a grand 19th-century house in a peaceful Kirribilli location very close to the ferry (or a pleasant stroll to the city across the bridge), this lodge offers excellent Sydney value for its modern rooms, most of which share gym-style bathrooms. It's a sizeable, slightly chaotically run complex with a kitchen-cafe area and a garden with a playground. If you book direct, breakfast is included.

Newtown & the Inner West

Mad Monkey Backpackers   HOSTEL $

(Map p74; ☑02-8705 3762; www.madmonkey broadway.com.au; 20 City Rd, Chippendale; dm $38-48; ❄🛜; 🖵412, 413, 422, 423, 🚊Central)

There's a lot to like about this friendly, well-equipped hostel in a top location. Dorms are tight but have very decent mattresses, while bathrooms are above average with hairdryers and straighteners on hand. There's a guaranteed social life with party buses and free entry to major Saturday nightclubs, plus free comfort food to aid recovery the next day. Breakfast and Netflix included.

Mandelbaum House   GUESTHOUSE $

(Map p74; ☑02-9692 5200; www.mandelbaum. usyd.edu.au; 385 Abercrombie St, Darlington; s/d without bathroom $75/98, d/apt $135/170; ⏱late Nov–mid-Feb; P🐕❄@🛜; 🚊Redfern) 🍃 One of the University of Sydney's residential colleges, this sweet spot makes a great place to stay in summer. It's a small, genuinely friendly place with a personal welcome, a not-for-profit ethos and a range of comfortable rooms, some of which share excellent bathrooms. The location is great for exploring the cafe and bar scene of Redfern and Newtown.

★Tara Guest House   B&B $$

(Map p74; ☑02-9519 4809; www.taraguesthouse. com.au; 13 Edgeware Rd, Enmore; d with/without bathroom $225/195; 🐕🛜; 🖵426) A couple who engages with and really appreciates their guests have created a wonderful place here in a character-packed 1880 house. The striking rooms are luminous, soaring spaces with fabulous features. Avant-garde nude art adds character, while Oscar the dog, free airport transfers and gourmet communal breakfasts are other highlights. Standout hospitality makes this one of Sydney's best options.

★Forsyth Bed & Breakfast   B&B $$

(Map p56; ☑02-9552 2110; www.forsythbnb.com; 3 Forsyth St, Glebe; d $195-235; 🐕❄🛜; 🖵431, 🌊Glebe) This boutique hideaway in a lovely part of Glebe is an enticing spot with just two stunning designer rooms: modern, uncluttered and graced with well-chosen art. Rozelle has a lovely balcony and spacious en suite, while Asian-inflected Blackwattle has a tiny bathroom and its own sitting room. The owner provides faultless hospitality, solicitous advice and quality breakfasts in the Japanese-inspired garden.

Old Clare Hotel   BOUTIQUE HOTEL $$$

(Map p74; ☑02-8277 8277; www.theoldclarehotel. com.au; 1 Kensington St, Chippendale; r $300-600; P🐕❄🛜🐕❄; 🚊Central) A sensitive brewery-office conversion is now a 62-room hotel in a primo Chippendale location. Rooms are well back from noisy Broadway, and high-ceilinged and easy-on-the-eye, with artful bespoke details such as the lamps made of salvaged toolshed paraphernalia. Superior categories are appreciably larger but the cheapest rooms still have king beds, attractive amenities and a good sense of space.

Manly

Manly Bunkhouse HOSTEL **$**
(Map p56; ☑ 02-9976 0472; www.bunkhouse.com. au; 35 Pine St, Manly; dm $42, d $105; ☐ ⊝ @ ☎; ▣ 151, 158, 169, ☱ Manly) An easy walk from the beach, this laid-back hostel in a nice old house has a distinct surf vibe. High-ceilinged, en-suite dorms have plenty of room to move and lots of storage space, making them popular with long-termers. The renovated private rooms also have bathrooms and are a good deal. There's a great backyard with BBQ and funky paintings on the walls.

101 Addison Road B&B **$$**
(Map p77; ☑ 02-9977 6216; www.bb-manly.com; 101 Addison Rd, Manly; r $165-200; ☐ ⊝ ☎; ☱ Manly) This sumptuously decorated 1880s cottage is perched on a quiet street close to the beach and ferry wharf. Two rooms are available but the delightful host only takes one booking at a time (from one to four people) – meaning you'll have free rein of the antique-strewn accommodation, including a private lounge with a grand piano and open fire.

✖ Eating

Sydney's cuisine rivals that of any great world city. Sydney truly celebrates Australia's place on the Pacific Rim, marrying the freshest local ingredients with the flavours of Asia, the Americas and, of course, its colonial past.

Sydney's top restaurants are properly pricey, but eating out needn't be expensive. There are plenty of ethnic eateries where you can grab a cheap, zingy pizza or a bowl of noodles. Cafes are a good bet for a solid, often adventurous and usually reasonably priced meal. And the numerous BYO (bring your own wine) restaurants offer a substantially cheaper eating experience; the Inner West is brimful of them.

✖ Circular Quay & the Rocks

The charismatic back lanes of the Rocks are dotted with little eateries, from 24-hour pancake joints to white-linen palaces. Around the horseshoe from the Harbour Bridge to the Opera House you'll find dozens of upmarket restaurants, all with winning water views. It should come as no surprise that this most touristy of precincts is also the priciest. If at all possible, budget for at least one night where you can throw on your glad rags and let Sydney's showiness seduce you.

★ Fine Food Store CAFE **$**
(Map p60; ☑ 02-9252 1196; www.finefoodstore. com; cnr Mill Lane & Kendall Lane; light meals $9-15; ☉ 7am-4.30pm Mon-Sat, 7.30am-4.30pm Sun; ☎ ☑; ▣ Circular Quay) The Rocks sometimes seems all pubs, so it's a delight to find this tucked-away contemporary cafe that works for a sightseeing stopover or a better, cheaper breakfast than your hotel. Staff are genuinely welcoming, make very respectable coffee, and offer delicious panini, sandwiches and other breakfast and lunch fare. The outside tables on this narrow lane are the spot to be.

★ Quay MODERN AUSTRALIAN **$$$**
(Map p60; ☑ 02-9251 5600; www.quay.com.au; L3, Overseas Passenger Terminal; 4/8 courses $175/235; ☉ 6-9.30pm Mon-Thu, noon-1.30pm & 6-9.30pm Fri-Sun; ▣ Circular Quay) Quay is shamelessly guilty of breaking the rule that good views make for bad food. Chef Peter Gilmore never rests on his laurels, consistently delivering the exquisitely crafted, adventurous cuisine that has landed Quay on the prestigious World's Best Restaurants list. And the view? Like dining in a postcard. Book online well in advance, but it's always worth phoning just in case.

Aria MODERN AUSTRALIAN **$$$**
(Map p60; ☑ 02-9240 2255; www.ariarestaurant. com; 1 Macquarie St; 2-/3-/4-course dinner $115/145/170, degustation $205; ☉ noon-2.15pm & 5.30-10.30pm Mon-Fri, noon-1.45pm & 5-10.30pm Sat, noon-2.15pm & 5.30-8.30pm Sun; ▣ Circular Quay) Aria is a star in Sydney's fine-dining firmament, an award-winning combination of chef Matt Moran's stellar dishes, Opera House views, a stylishly renovated interior and faultless service. A pre- and post-theatre à la carte menu is available before 7pm and after 10pm, perfect for a special meal before or after a special night at the Opera House (one/two/three courses $55/90/110).

✖ City Centre & Haymarket

Without harbour views, Sydney's central-city restaurants tend to be discreet, upmarket spots – perfect for secret handshakes over million-dollar deals. Some have beaten geography by perching themselves atop towers. Chinatown is your best bet for a cheap, satisfying meal – especially after midnight. Chinese food dominates, but you'll also find superb Vietnamese, Malaysian, Korean and Thai. There's also a Little Korea along Pitt St near Liverpool St; and Thaitown on Campbell St.

Mamak
MALAYSIAN $

(Map p62; ☑02-9211 1668; www.mamak.com.au; 15 Goulburn St; mains $6-17; ⏱11.30am-2.30pm & 5.30-10pm Mon-Thu, to 1am Fri, 11.30am-1am Sat, to 10pm Sun; ☑; ☒Town Hall) Get here early (from 5.30pm) if you want to score a table without queuing, because this eat-and-run Malaysian joint is one of the most popular cheapies in the city. The satays are cooked over charcoal and are particularly delicious when accompanied by a flaky golden roti.

★ Mr Wong
CHINESE $$

(Map p60; ☑02-9240 3000; www.merivale.com.au/mrwong; 3 Bridge Lane; mains $26-38; ⏱noon-3pm & 5.30-11pm Mon-Wed, noon-3pm & 5.30pm-midnight Thu & Fri, 10.30am-3pm & 5.30pm-midnight Sat, 10.30am-3pm & 5.30-10pm Sun; ☎☑; ☒Wynyard) Classy but comfortable in an attractive low-lit space on a CBD laneway, this has exposed-brick colonial warehouse chic and a huge team of staff and hanging ducks in the open kitchen.

FOOD COURTS

Though they aren't necessarily visible from the street, Sydney's CBD is absolutely riddled with food courts, which can be great places for a budget meal, especially at lunchtime. Look for them in shopping centres and major office towers. Some worthwhile ones are in Westfield Sydney, in Australia Sq, in the nearby Hunter Connection (downstairs and upstairs), at the north end underground in the QVB, between George and Pitt Sts north of Liverpool St, in World Sq and in the Sussex Centre.

Most of these places open Monday to Friday lunchtimes only. Sushi places tend to start discounting that day's fare in the mid-afternoon. Around 3.30pm on a Friday, nearly all places are offering bargain takeaway boxes: you can get a big feed for $5.

Lunchtime dim sum offerings bristle with flavour and the 'textured' chicken and jellyfish salad is a mouth-freshening sensation. Mains such as crispy pork hock are sinfully sticky, while Peking duck rolls are legendary.

An impressive wine list and attentive, sassy service seals the deal.

★ Restaurant Hubert
FRENCH $$

(Map p60; ☑02-9232 0881; www.restauranthubert.com; 15 Bligh St; dishes $15-42; ⏱5pm-1am Mon-Sat; ☒Martin Place) The memorable descent into the sexy old-time ambience plunges you straight from suity Sydney to some 1930s cocktail movie. Delicious French fare comes in old-fashioned portions – think terrine, black pudding or duck plus a few more avant-garde creations. Candlelit tables and a long whisky-backed counter provide seating. There are no bookings for small groups so wait it out in the bar area.

★ Azuma
JAPANESE $$

(Map p60; ☑02-9222 9960; www.azuma.com.au; Level 1, Chifley Plaza, Hunter St; mains $22-48; ⏱noon-2.30pm & 6-10pm Mon-Fri, 6-10pm Sat; ☒Martin Place) Tucked away upstairs in Chifley Plaza, this is one of Sydney's finest Japanese restaurants. Sushi and sashimi are of stellar quality and too pretty to eat – almost. Other options include sukiyaki and hot-pot DIY dishes and an excellent tasting menu ($110 per person). It's a great place to get acquainted with high-class modern Japanese fare. It also has some moreish sake by the carafe.

★ Pablo & Rusty's
CAFE $$

(Map p60; ☑02-9283 9543; www.pabloandrustys.com.au; 161 Castlereagh St; light meals $10-25; ⏱6.30am-5pm Mon-Fri, 8am-3pm Sat; ☎☑; ☒Town Hall) One of central Sydney's best cafes, this place is always buzzy. The inviting wood-and-brick decor and seriously good coffee (several single origins available daily) is complemented by a range of appealing breakfast and lunch specials ranging from sandwiches to wholesome Mediterranean- and Asian-influenced combos such as tuna poke with brown rice or lychee and ginger tapioca.

Chat Thai
THAI $$

(Map p62; ☑02-9211 1808; www.chatthai.com.au; 20 Campbell St; mains $10-20; ⏱10am-2am; ☑; ☒Capitol Square, ☒Central) Cooler than your average Thai joint, this Thaitown linchpin is so popular that a list is posted outside for you to affix your name to should you want a table. Expat Thais flock here for the dishes that don't make it onto your average suburban Thai restaurant menu – particularly the more unusual sweets.

Sydney Madang
KOREAN $$

(Map p62; ☑02-9264 7010; 371a Pitt St; mains $13-23; ⊙11.30am-2am; ☐Museum) Down a teensy Little Korea lane is this backdoor gem – an authentic BBQ joint that's low on interior charisma but high on quality and quantity. Noisy, cramped and chaotic, yes, but the chilli seafood soup will have you coming back.

★Sepia
JAPANESE, FUSION $$$

(Map p60; ☑02-9283 1990; www.sepia restaurant.com.au; 201 Sussex St; degustation $215, matching wines $135; ⊙noon-3pm Fri & Sat, 6-10pm Tue-Sat; ☐Town Hall) A Japanese sensibility permeates the boundary-pushing menu at what is sometimes said to be Australia's best restaurant, while molecular cuisine and the forage ethos play their part in the creation and presentation of the stunning morsels. Sensational seafood and exquisite bursts of flavour make the palate sing. The atmosphere is plush, low-lit and fairly formal; there's also a wine bar.

★Tetsuya's
FRENCH, JAPANESE $$$

(Map p62; ☑02-9267 2900; www.tetsuyas.com; 529 Kent St; degustation $230, matching wines $110; ⊙5.30-10pm Tue-Fri, noon-3pm & 5.30-10pm Sat; ☐Town Hall) Concealed in a villa behind a historic cottage amid the high-rises, this extraordinary restaurant is for those seeking a culinary journey rather than a simple stuffed belly. Settle in for 10-plus courses of French- and Japanese-inflected food from the creative genius of Japanese-born Tetsuya Wakuda. It's all great, but the seafood is sublime. Book way ahead.

★Rockpool Bar & Grill
STEAK $$$

(Map p60; ☑02-8078 1900; www.rockpool.com; 66 Hunter St; mains $45-59, bar mains $18-32; ⊙noon-3pm & 6-11pm Mon-Fri, 6-11pm Sat, 5.30-10.30pm Sun; ☐Martin Place) You'll feel like a 1930s Manhattan stockbroker when you dine at this sleek operation in the art-deco City Mutual Building. The bar is famous for its dry-aged, full-blood Wagyu burger (make sure you order a side of the hand-cut fat chips), but carnivores will be equally enamoured with the succulent steaks, stews and fish dishes served in the grill.

✖ Darling Harbour & Pyrmont

Rows of restaurants line Darling Harbour, many of them pairing their sea views with seafood. Most are pricey tourist-driven affairs that are good but not outstanding. The Star has sought to assert itself as a fine-dining mecca, luring many a gifted restaurateur. There are some truly excellent restaurants here, but the shopping-mall atmosphere won't be for everyone. On the wharves in Pyrmont are a couple of excellent restaurants.

Adriano Zumbo
SWEETS $

(Map p64; www.zumbo.com.au; the Star, 80 Pyrmont St; 6 zumbarons $16.50; ⊙11am-10pm Mon, to 11pm Tue-Thu, to midnight Fri & Sat, to 9pm Sun; ☐The Star) The man who introduced Sydney to the macaron keeps indulging his Willy Wonka fantasies in this open shop in the Star complex, where baked treats are artfully displayed. The macarons (or zumbarons, as they're known here), tarts, pastries and cakes are as astonishing to look at as they are to eat. It's just outside the Lyric Theatre.

The Malaya
MALAYSIAN $$

(Map p64; ☑02-9279 1170; www.themalaya.com. au; 39 Lime St; mains $24-36; ⊙noon-3pm & 6-10pm Mon-Fri, noon-3pm & 5.30-10pm Sat, 5.30-10pm Sun; ☎🍴; ☐Darling Harbour) There's something really life-affirming about quality Malaysian cooking, and what you get here is certainly that. Dishes bursting with flavour and spice make it a very authentic experience, while fabulous views over Darling Harbour (fireworks on Saturday nights) add romance. The atmosphere is a very Sydney blend of upmarket and casual. À la carte is better than the set menu.

★LuMi
ITALIAN $$$

(Map p64; ☑02-9571 1999; www.lumidining.com; 56 Pirrama Rd, Pyrmont; 8 courses $115, 3-/5-course lunches Fri & Sat $55/75; ⊙6.30-10.30pm Wed & Thu, noon-2.30pm & 6-10.30pm Fri & Sat, noon-2.30pm & 6.30-10.30pm Sun; ☎; ☐Pyrmont Bay) This wharf spot sits right alongside the bobbing boats, though views aren't quite knock-me-down. Hidden but just steps from Darling Harbour and the Star, it offers casual competence and strikingly innovative Italian-Japanese fusion cuisine. The degustation is a tour de force, with memorable creations including extraordinary pasta dishes. The open kitchen is always entertaining, service is smart and both wine and sake lists are great.

Sydney's Beaches

Whether you join the procession of the bronzed and the beautiful at Bondi, or surreptitiously slink into a deserted nook hidden within Sydney Harbour National Park, the beach is an essential part of the Sydney experience.

In the mid-1990s an enthusiastic business-woman obtained a concession to rent loungers on Tamarama Beach and offer waiter service. Needless to say, it didn't last long. Even at what was considered at the time to be Sydney's most glamorous beach, nobody was interested in that kind of malarkey.

For Australians, going to the beach is all about rolling out a towel on the sand with a minimum of fuss. And they're certainly not prepared to pay for the privilege.

Sandy-toed ice-cream vendors are acceptable; martini luggers are not. In summer one of the more unusual sights is the little ice-cream boat pulling up to Lady Bay (and other harbour beaches) and a polite queue of nude gentlemen forming to purchase their icy poles.

Surf lifesavers have a hallowed place in the culture and you'd do well to heed their instructions, not least of all because they're likely to be in your best interest. It's not coincidental that the spark for racist riots in Cronulla a few years back was an attack on this oh-so-Australian institution.

Ocean Pools

If you have children or shark paranoia, or surf just isn't your thing, you'll be pleased to hear that Sydney's blessed with a string of 40 man-made ocean pools up and down the coast, most of them free. Some, like

1. Bondi Beach (p65)
2. Mahon Rock Pool
3. Surfer at Tamarama Beach

Mahon Pool (www.randwick.nsw.gov.au; Marine Pde, Maroubra; 376-377) **FREE**, are what are known as bogey holes – natural-looking rock pools where you can safely splash about and snorkel. Others are more like swimming pools; Bondi's Icebergs (p102) is a good example of this kind. They normally close a day a week so they can clean the seaweed out.

Harbour Beaches & Pools

The pick of Sydney's harbour beaches include Camp Cove and Lady Bay near South Head (the latter of which is mainly a gay nude beach), Shark Beach at Nielsen Park in Vaucluse, and Balmoral Beach on the north shore. Also popular are the netted swimming enclosures at Cremorne Point on the North Shore and Murray Rose Pool near Double Bay. There are plenty of little gems that even locals would be hard pressed to find, including Parsley Bay and Milk Beach right in the heart of residential Vaucluse.

Beaches by Neighbourhood

Sydney Harbour Lots of hidden coves and secret sandy spots; the best are out near the Heads and around Mosman.

Eastern Beaches High cliffs frame a string of surf beaches, with excellent coffee and cold beer just a short stumble away.

Northern Beaches A steady succession of magical surf beaches stretching 30km north from Manly to Palm Beach.

Flying Fish
SEAFOOD $$$

(Map p64; ☑02-9518 6677; www.flyingfish.com.au; Jones Bay Wharf; mains $40-50; ⊘6-10.30pm Mon, noon-2.30pm & 6-10.30pm Tue-Sat, noon-2.30pm Sun; ☒The Star) On a lovely Pyrmont wharf, this is everything a seafood restaurant should be, with crisp white tablecloths to stain with crustacean juice, gleaming glasses and water views. Romance and city lights work their magic here, aided by excellent food and an indulgent cocktail list. It also has the coolest toilets in town – the clear-glass stalls frost over when you close the door.

Kings Cross & Potts Point

Room 10
CAFE $

(Map p66; ☑02-8318 0454; www.facebook.com/room10espresso; 10 Llankelly Pl, Kings Cross; mains $8-14; ⊘7am-4pm Mon-Fri, 8am-4pm Sat & Sun; ☑☑; ☒Kings Cross) Genuinely warm and welcoming, this tiny cafe is the sort of place where staff know all the locals by name. The coffee is delicious and the food's limited to sandwiches, salads and such – tasty and uncomplicated. Watch them make it in front of you as you sit at impossibly tiny tables or do some people-watching on this lovable laneway.

Piccolo Bar
CAFE $

(Map p66; ☑02-9368 1356; www.piccolobar.com.au; 6 Roslyn St, Kings Cross; light meals $5-10; ⊘8am-2.30pm Mon-Fri; ☎; ☒Kings Cross) A surviving slice of the old bohemian Cross, this tiny cafe hasn't changed much in over 60 years. The walls are covered in movie-star memorabilia, and Vittorio Bianchi still serves up strong coffee, omelettes and abrasive charm, as he's done for over 40 years.

Harry's Cafe de Wheels
FAST FOOD $

(Map p66; ☑02-9357 3074; www.harryscafedewheels.com.au; Cowper Wharf Roadway, Woolloomooloo; pies $5-8; ⊘8.30am-2am Mon & Tue, 8.30am-3am Wed & Thu, 8.30am-4am Fri, 9am-4am Sat, 9am-1am Sun; ☐311, ☒Kings Cross) Open since 1938 (except for a few years when founder Harry 'Tiger' Edwards was on active service), Harry's has been serving meat pies to everyone from Pamela Anderson to Frank Sinatra and Colonel Sanders. You can't leave without trying a Tiger: a hot meat pie with sloppy peas, mashed potato, gravy and tomato sauce.

★ Yellow
VEGETARIAN $$

(Map p66; ☑02-9332 2344; www.yellowsydney.com.au; 57 Macleay St, Potts Point; degustation menu $70; ⊘6-11pm Mon-Fri, 8am-3pm & 6-11pm Sat & Sun; ☑; ☒Kings Cross) Once a sunflower-yellow symbol of all things Bohemian, this former artists' residence is now a top-notch contemporary vegetarian restaurant. Dishes are prepared with real panache, and exquisitely presented. The tasting menus (including a vegan one) take the Sydney non-meat scene to new levels. Weekend brunch is also a highlight, as is the wine list.

Farmhouse
MODERN AUSTRALIAN $$

(Map p66; ☑0448 413 791; www.farmhousekingscross.com.au; 4/40 Bayswater Rd, Kings Cross; set menu $60; ⊘sittings 6.30pm & 8.30pm Wed-Sat, 2pm & 6.30pm Sun; ☒Kings Cross) Occupying a space between restaurant and supper club, this narrow sliver of a place has a tiny kitchen and a charming host. Diners sit at one long table and eat a set menu that features uncomplicated, delicious dishes from high-quality produce. There are good wines and a buzzy, fun atmosphere. Prebooking is essential.

Fratelli Paradiso
ITALIAN $$

(Map p66; ☑02-9357 1744; www.fratelliparadiso.com; 12-16 Challis Ave, Potts Point; breakfast $12-14, mains $22-38; ⊘7am-11pm Mon-Sat, to 10pm Sun; ☒Kings Cross) This underlit trattoria has them queuing at the door (especially on weekends). The intimate room showcases seasonal Italian dishes cooked with Mediterranean zing. Lots of busy black-clad waiters, lots of Italian chatter, lots of oversized sunglasses. No bookings.

China Doll
ASIAN $$$

(Map p66; ☑02-9380 6744; www.chinadoll.com.au; 4/6 Cowper Wharf Roadway, Woolloomooloo; mains $35-54; ⊘noon-3pm & 6-10.30pm; ☐311, ☒Kings Cross) Gaze over the Woolloomooloo marina and city skyline as you tuck into deliciously inventive dishes drawing inspiration from all over Asia. The setting is memorable, but the food keeps up, with delicious textures and flavour combinations. Plates are designed to be shared, although waiters can arrange half-serves for solo diners.

Surry Hills & Darlinghurst

Scruffy Surry Hills' transformation into Sydney's foodie nirvana means that it's an ever-changing array of wonderful eateries inhabiting surprising nooks amid terrace houses and former warehouses, with new places opening all the time.

★ **Bourke Street Bakery** BAKERY $
(Map p70; 02-9699 1011; www.bourkestreet
bakery.com.au; 633 Bourke St, Surry Hills; items
$5-14; 7am-6pm Mon-Fri, to 5pm Sat & Sun;
; 301, Central) Queuing outside this
teensy bakery is an essential Surry Hills
experience. It sells a tempting selection of
pastries, cakes, bread and sandwiches, along
with sausage rolls that are near legendary in
these parts. There are a few tables inside but
on a fine day you're better off on the street.

★ **Le Monde** CAFE $
(Map p70; 02-9211 3568; www.lemondecafe.
com.au; 83 Foveaux St, Surry Hills; dishes $10-16;
6.30am-4pm Mon-Fri, 7am-2pm Sat; ; Central) Some of Sydney's best breakfasts are
served between the demure dark wooden
walls of this small street-side cafe. Top-notch
coffee and a terrific selection of tea will gear
you up to face the world, while dishes such
as truffled poached eggs or confit pork belly
make it worth walking up the hill for.

Reuben Hills CAFE $
(Map p70; 02-9211 5556; www.reubenhills.
com.au; 61 Albion St; mains $9-22; 7am-4pm
Mon-Sat, 7.30am-4pm Sun; ; Central) An
industrial fitout and Latin American menu
await here at Reuben Hills (aka hipster
central), set in a terrace and its former garage. Fantastic single-origin coffee and fried
chicken, but the eggs, tacos and *baleadas*
(Honduran tortillas) are no slouches, either.

Messina ICE CREAM $
(Map p66; 02-9331 1588; www.gelatomessina.
com; 241 Victoria St; 1/2/3 scoops $4.80/6.80/8.80;
noon-11pm Sun-Thu, to 11.30pm Fri & Sat; ;
Kings Cross) Join the queues of people who
look like they never eat ice cream at the counter of Sydney's most popular gelato shop.
Clearly even the beautiful people can't resist
quirky flavours such as figs in marsala and
salted caramel. It's all delicious, and there are
several dairy-free options. The attached dessert bar serves sundaes.

Spice I Am THAI $
(Map p62; 02-9280 0928; www.spiceiam.
com; 90 Wentworth Ave, Surry Hills; mains $15-
20; 11.30am-3.30pm & 5-10pm Tue-Sun;
; Central) Once the preserve of expat
Thais, this little red-hot chilli pepper now
has queues out the door. No wonder, as
everything we've tried from the 70-plus dishes on the menu is superfragrant and super-
spicy. It's been so successful that it's opened
the upmarket version in **Darlinghurst** (Map

p66; 02-9332 2445; 296-300 Victoria St, Darlinghurst; mains $19-22; 5.30-10.30pm Mon-Wed,
11.30am-3.30pm & 5.30-10.30pm Thu-Sun; ;
Kings Cross). The sign is very unobtrusive
so it's easy to walk past: don't.

Nada's LEBANESE $
(Map p70; 02-9690 1289; 270 Cleveland St, Surry Hills; dishes $8-16; noon-3pm & 5.30-10pm
Wed-Mon, 5.30-10pm Tue; ; 372, Central)
There are swisher Lebanese restaurants
around, but for a no-frills delicious feed at
a very fair price, it's hard to beat this old
family-run favourite. The set meal at $29
a head is a bargain; just don't fill up too
much on the bread and dips or you won't
manage the sizeable chunks of Turkish delight at the end.

★ **Porteño** ARGENTINE $$
(Map p70; 02-8399 1440; www.porteno.com.
au; 50 Holt St, Surry Hills; sharing plates $20-50;
6pm-midnight Tue-Sat; Central) In a new lo-
cation, this upbeat and deservedly acclaimed
Argentine restaurant is a great place to eat.
The 'animal of the day' is slow-roasted for
eight hours before the doors even open and
is always delicious. Other highlights include
the homemade chorizo and morcilla, but
lighter touches are also in evidence, so it's
not all meat-feast. There's a decent Argentine
wine list too.

★ **Dead Ringer** TAPAS $$
(Map p70; 02-9331 3560; http://deadringer.
wtf; 413 Bourke St, Surry Hills; dishes $18-33;
5pm-midnight Mon-Fri, noon-midnight Sat & Sun;
; 333, 380) This charcoal-fronted terrace
is a haven of quality eating and drinking in
a laid-back format. Barstool it or grab an
outdoor table and graze on the short menu
that changes slightly daily and runs from
bar snacks through tapas to mains. Though
well-presented, the food's all about flavour
combinations rather than airy artistry.
There's always something interesting by the
glass to accompany.

★ **Gratia & Folonomo** CAFE, FUSION $$
(Map p70; 02-8034 3818; www.gratia.org.au; 370
Bourke St, Surry Hills; cafe dishes $12-21, restaurant
mains $21-34; 8am-3pm & 6-10.30pm; ;
374, 397, 399) Not-for-profit eateries of-
ten score higher on good intentions than
cooking, but this is the real deal. A great cafe,
Gratia, with genuinely friendly staff and a
pleasant, light feel, does juices and eclectic
brunchy fare, while the restaurant part, Fo-
lonomo (from 'for love not money') serves

brilliant modern Australian fare. All profits go to charitable organisations, which diners can help choose. Applause.

There's a gallery space upstairs too, and they actively help and train refugees.

Chaco
JAPANESE $$

(Map p66; ☑02-9007 8352; www.chacobar.com. au; 238 Crown St, Darlinghurst; skewers €4-7; ⊙ ramen 5.30-9pm Mon, noon-2pm Wed-Sun, yakitori 6-10pm Tue-Sat; ☒Museum) This little place has a simple, effortless Japanese cool and some seriously good food. The ramen are good, and there are very succulent gyoza and delicious meatball sticks to dip in egg. The yakitori skewers are available Tuesday to Saturday nights and are a highlight, bursting with flavour. Don't be afraid to try the more unusual ones...

Malabar
SOUTH INDIAN $$

(Map p66; ☑02-9332 1755; www.malabar cuisine.com.au; 274 Victoria St, Darlinghurst; mains $22-26; ⊙5.30-10.30pm Mon & Tue, noon-2.30pm & 5.30-10.30pm Wed-Sun; ☑; ☒Kings Cross) Delicious dosas, piquant Goan curries and the soft seductive tastes of India's south make this sizeable, well-established Darlinghurst restaurant a standout. The open kitchen and decor, with large black-and-white photos adorning the walls, add atmosphere. Owner and staff are very genial and will guide you through the substantial menu. You can BYO wine.

Muum Maam
THAI $$

(Map p70; ☑02-9318 0881; www.muummaam. com.au; 50 Holt St, Surry Hills; lunch dishes $14-16, dinner mains $24-32; ⊙11.30am-3pm & 6-10pm Mon-Fri, 6-10pm Sat; ☑; ☒Central) Packing a punch for the eyes and tastebuds, this is a buzzy spot beloved of those creative types who work hereabouts. It has a double identity that really works, with a food cart doling out lunch specials before the open kitchen turns to more serious, lavishly presented Thai creations in the evening. There's a big communal table but you can also go solo.

Bar H
ASIAN $$

(Map p62; ☑02-9280 1980; www.barhsurryhills. com; 80 Campbell St, Surry Hills; dishes $14-42; ⊙6-10pm Mon-Thu, to midnight Fri & Sat; ☒Central) Marrying Chinese and Japanese dishes with native Australian bush ingredients, this sexy, shiny, black-walled corner eatery is completely unique and extremely impressive. Dishes range considerably in size and

are designed to be shared; confer with your waiter about quantities. There's a $68 tasting menu that offers a fine experience of the quality and diversity on offer.

Single O
CAFE $$

(Single Origin Roasters; Map p62; ☑02-9211 0665; www.singleo.com.au; 60-64 Reservoir St, Surry Hills; mains $14-21; ⊙6.30am-4pm Mon-Fri, 7.30am-3pm Sat; ☞☑; ☒Central) ✿ Unshaven graphic designers roll cigarettes at little outdoor tables in the bricky hollows of deepest Surry Hills, while inside impassioned, bouncing-off-the-walls caffeine fiends prepare their beloved brews, along with a tasty selection of cafe fare. Something of a trendsetter a few years back, this place still does coffee as good as anywhere in Sydney. The hole-in-the-wall alongside does takeaways.

El Loco
MEXICAN $$

(Excelsior Hotel; Map p70; ☑02-9240 3000; www.merivale.com.au/elloco; 64 Foveaux St, Surry Hills; mains $10-18; ⊙noon-midnight Mon-Thu, to 3am Fri & Sat, to 10pm Sun; ☞☑; ☒Central) As much as we lament the passing of live rock at the Excelsior Hotel, we have to admit that the hip, colourful Mexican cantina that's taken over the band room is pretty darn cool. The food's tasty, inventive, and, at $6 per taco, fantastic value. The party kicks on till late on weekends with DJs in a social, fun atmosphere.

Devonshire
MODERN EUROPEAN $$$

(Map p70; ☑02-9698 9427; www.thedevonshire. com.au; 204 Devonshire St, Surry Hills; degustation $95, matching wines $55, mains $37; ⊙noon-2.30pm Fri, 6-10pm Tue-Sat; ☒Central) It's a long way from a two-Michelin-starred Mayfair restaurant to grungy old Devonshire St for chef Jeremy Bentley, although cuisinewise, perhaps not as far as you'd think. His food is simply extraordinary – complex, precisely presented and full of flavour. And while there's white linen on the tables, the atmosphere isn't the least bit starchy.

Bodega
TAPAS $$$

(Map p70; ☑02-9212 7766; www.bodega tapas.com; 216 Commonwealth St; tapas $12-24, share plates $22-30; ⊙noon-2pm Fri, 6-10pm Tue-Sat; ☒Central) The coolest progeny of Sydney's tapas explosion, Bodega has a casual vibe, good-lookin' staff and a funky matador mural. Dishes vary widely in size and price and are very loosely rooted in Central American and Spanish cuisine.

Wash 'em down with Spanish and South American wine, sherry, port or beer, and plenty of Latin gusto.

✗ Bondi, Coogee & the Eastern Beaches

Lox, Stock & Barrel   CAFE, JEWISH $
(Map p78; ☑02-9300 0368; www.loxstockand barrel.com.au; 140 Glenayr Ave, Bondi Beach; breakfast & lunch dishes $10-22, dinner $18-29; ◷7am-3.30pm Sun-Tue, 7am-3.30pm & 6-10pm Wed & Thu, 7am-3.30pm & 6-11pm Fri & Sat; ☎☑📶; ▢389) Stare down the barrel of a smoking hot bagel and ask yourself one question: Wagyu corned-beef Reuben, or homemade pastrami and Russian coleslaw? In the evening the menu sets its sights on steak, lamb shoulder and slow-roasted eggplant. It's always busy, even on a wet Monday.

Three Blue Ducks   CAFE $$
(Map p56; ☑02-9389 0010; www.threeblueducks. com; 141-143 Macpherson St, Bronte; breakfast $14-22, lunch $20-32, dinner $28-38; ◷6.30am-2.30pm Sun-Tue, 6.30am-2.30pm & 5-11pm Wed-Sat; ☎☑; ▢378) 🕊 These ducks are a fair waddle from the water, but that doesn't stop queues forming outside the graffiti-covered walls for weekend breakfasts across two seating areas. The adventurous chefs have a strong commitment to using local, organic and fair-trade food whenever possible.

Trio   CAFE $$
(Map p78; ☑02-9365 6044; www.triocafe.com. au; 56 Campbell Pde, Bondi Beach; dishes $18-27; ◷7am-3pm Mon-Fri, 7.30am-3.30pm Sat & Sun; ☎☑; ▢333, 380-2) Brunch in Bondi has become de rigueur in Sydney in recent years, and this friendly, unpretentious cafe is one of the top spots to do it. The menu covers several global influences, from Mexican chilaquiles to Middle Eastern shakshouka via some Italian bruschetta. It's a great way to start a day by the sea.

Icebergs Dining Room   ITALIAN $$$
(Map p78; ☑02-9365 9000; www.idrb.com; 1 Notts Ave, Bondi; mains $46-52; ◷noon-3pm & 6.30-11pm Tue-Sun; ▢333, 380) 🕊 Poised above the famous Icebergs swimming pool, Icebergs' views sweep across the Bondi Beach arc to the sea. Inside, bow-tied waiters deliver fresh, sustainably sourced seafood and steaks cooked with élan. There's also an elegant cocktail bar. In the same building, the Icebergs club has a bistro and bar with simpler, cheaper fare.

✗ Sydney Harbourside

Riverview Hotel & Dining   MODERN AUSTRALIAN $$
(Map p56; ☑02-9810 1151; www.theriverview hotel.com.au; 29 Birchgrove Rd, Balmain; bar mains $20-32, restaurant mains $36-52; ◷bar meals noon-9pm, restaurant 6-9pm Mon-Thu, noon-2.30pm & 6-9pm Fri-Sun; ☎; 🚢Balmain) Foodies flock here to try the excellent fish dishes and nose-to-tail meat creations in the elegant upstairs dining room, while locals are equally keen on the pizzas served in the downstairs bar. It's a lovely pub in itself, with hanging baskets and a characterful interior.

Dunbar House   CAFE $$
(Map p56; ☑02-9337 1226; www.dunbarhouse. com.au; 9 Marine Pde, Watsons Bay; breakfast $12-18, lunch $18-27; ◷8am-3.30pm; 🚢Watsons Bay) This meticulously restored 1830s mansion is a gorgeous spot for brunch, particularly if you can score one of the harbour-view tables on the verandah. Bookings are recommended on weekends. It's named after a famous 19th-century shipwreck that occurred near here.

Catalina   MODERN AUSTRALIAN $$$
(Map p56; ☑02-9371 0555; www.catalinarose bay.com.au; Lyne Park, Rose Bay; mains $49-52; ◷noon-3pm & 6-10.30pm Mon-Sat, noon-3pm Sun; 🚢Rose Bay) Named after the flying boats that were based here, this excellent Rose Bay restaurant has marvellous views, a buzzy eastern suburbs vibe and an impressive wine list. With this location, you expect some seafood on the menu, and it doesn't disappoint. Quality offerings are sourced from around the country, but meaty options are available, with roast suckling pig a speciality.

Doyles on the Beach   SEAFOOD $$$
(Map p56; ☑02-9337 2007; www.doyles.com. au; 11 Marine Pde, Watsons Bay; mains $40-50; ◷noon-3pm & 5.30-8.30pm Mon-Thu, to 9pm Fri, noon-4pm & 5.30-9pm Sat, noon-4pm & 5.30-8.30pm Sun; 🚢Watsons Bay) There may well be better places for seafood, but few can compete with Doyles' location or its history – this restaurant first opened in 1885. Catching the harbour ferry to Watsons Bay for a seafood lunch is a quintessential Sydney experience. If the prices make you think twice, grab fish 'n' chips ($13 to $20) from its takeaway outlet at the ferry wharf.

✕ Newtown & the Inner West

Newtown's King St and Enmore Rd are among the city's most diverse eat streets, with Thai restaurants sitting alongside Vietnamese, Greek, Lebanese and Mexican, but the scene is replicated on a smaller scale in nearly every inner west suburb. And when it comes to coffee culture, all roads point this way too.

Wedge
CAFE $

(Map p74; ☑02-9660 3313; www.the wedgeglebe.com; cnr Cowper St & Glebe Point Rd; light meals $8-18; ☉7am-4pm Mon-Sat, 8am-3pm Sun; 🛜🍴; 🚋Glebe) Cut a corridor out of the side of a building, open it to the street and add artful industrial decor and you have the Wedge, which is wowing Glebe with its delicious single-origin espressos and cold brews as well as delicious, artfully presented breakfasts, sandwiches and lunch specials. The quality and atmosphere are great, but it's popular, so lingering feels selfish.

Black Star Pastry
BAKERY $

(Map p74; ☑02-9557 8656; www.blackstar pastry.com.au; 277 Australia St, Newtown; snacks $4-10; ☉7am-5pm; 🍴; 🚋Newtown) Wise folks follow the black star to pay homage to excellent coffee, a large selection of sweet things and a few very good savoury things (gourmet pies and the like). There are only a couple of tables; it's more a snack-and-run or picnic-in-the-park kind of place. Prepare to queue.

Cow & the Moon
ICE CREAM $

(Map p74; ☑02-9557 4255; 181 Enmore Rd; small gelati $5.50; ☉8.30am-10.30pm Sun-Thu, 8.30am-11.30pm Fri & Sat; 🛜🍴👶; 🚋Newtown) Forget the diet and slink into this cool corner cafe, where an array of sinful truffles and tasty tarts beckons seductively. Ignore them and head straight for the world's best gelato – the title this humble little place won in 2014 at the Gelato World Tour title in Rimini, Italy. There's decent coffee too.

Faheem Fast Food
PAKISTANI $

(Map p74; ☑02-9550 4850; www.faheem fastfood.com.au; 194 Enmore Rd; dishes $12-14; ☉5pm-midnight Mon-Fri, noon-midnight Sat & Sun; 🍴; 🚌426) This Enmore Rd stalwart offers a totally no-frills dining atmosphere but very tasty and authentic curry and tandoori options served until late. Its Haleem lentil and beef curry is memorably tasty, while the brain *nihari* is another standout, and not as challenging as it sounds.

Spice Alley
ASIAN $

(Map p74; www.kensingtonstreet.com.au; Kensington St, Chippendale; dishes $8-16; ☉11am-9.30pm; 🍴; 🚋Central) This little laneway off Kensington St by Central Park serving street-foody dishes from several different Asian cuisines. Grab your noodles, dumplings or pork belly and fight for a stool. Quality is reasonable rather than spectacular, but prices are low and it's fun. It's cashless: pay by card or load up a prepay card from the drinks booth.

★Thanh Binh
VIETNAMESE $$

(Map p74; ☑02-9557 1175; www.thanhbinh.com. au; 111 King St; mains $18-28; ☉5-11pm Mon-Fri, noon-11pm Sat & Sun; 🍴; 🚋Macdonaldtown) This old Vietnamese favourite isn't top of the trendmeter any more, but it should be for its wide range of consistently delicious dishes. Favourites are soft-shell crab on papaya salad or sinful pork belly and quail eggs in stock. Other dishes get you launching into a wrapping, rolling, dipping and feasting frenzy. Service is always friendly.

3 Olives
GREEK $$

(Map p74; ☑02-9557 7754; 365 King St, Newtown; mains $24-27, meze dishes $13-16; ☉5.30pm-midnight Wed-Sun; 🚋Newtown) There's something very life-affirming about a good Greek restaurant, and this family-run taberna ticks all the boxes. The decor is restrained, with olive-coloured walls, but there's nothing restrained about the portions or aromas: mounds of perfectly textured BBQ octopus, big chunks of melt-in-the-mouth lamb kleftiko, warm flatbread, hearty meatballs and more-ish olives. It's an excellent celebration of traditional eating.

Timbah
TAPAS $$

(Map p56; ☑02-9571 7005; www.timbahwine bar.com.au; 375 Glebe Point Rd, entrance on Forsyth St; tapas $12-17; ☉5.30-9pm Tue-Thu, 5pm-9.30pm Fri, 4.30-9.30pm Sat; 🚋Glebe) 🍷 Quite a way down Glebe Point Rd is an excellent independent bottleshop; turn right to find this convivial wine bar it runs downstairs. There's always something interesting available by the glass, and staff are open to cracking something on demand. Food is tasty, with Australian native flavours and homegrown herbs. The bar is open for drinks from 4pm and also opens Sundays.

Thai Pothong THAI $$
(Map p74; ☑02-9550 6277; www.thaipothong.com.
au; 294 King St, Newtown; mains $18-31; ⊙noon-
3pm daily, plus 6-10.30pm Mon-Thu, 6-11pm Fri
& Sat, 5.30-10pm Sun; ℙ🖉; ⋒Newtown) The
menu at this crowd-pleasing restaurant is
full of long-time favourites and people still
queue for them. The army of staff are effi-
cient and friendly, and the food reliably ex-
cellent. Top choice is a window seat to watch
the Newtowners pass by. If you pay cash, you
get a discount, paid in a local currency only
redeemable in the gift shop.

Stinking Bishops CHEESE $$
(Map p74; ☑02-9007 7754; www.thestinkingbish
ops.com; 63 Enmore Rd, Newtown; 2-/3-/4-cheese
boards $21/29/37; ⊙5-10pm Tue & Wed, 11am-10pm
Thu-Sat, 11am-6pm Sun; 🖉; ⋒Newtown) A pun-
gent array of artisanal cheeses is the raison
d'être of this popular shop and eatery. Choose
the varieties you want, pick a wine or craft
beer to accompany, and off you go. There
are also very tasty charcuterie boards. All its
wares are sourced from small producers and
available to take home too.

Tramsheds Harold Park FOOD HALL
(Map p56; ☑02-8398 5695; www.tramsheds
haroldpark.com.au; Maxwell Rd, Glebe; ⊙7am-10pm;
🗶🛜; ⋒Jubilee Park) Sydney's latest foodie
hangout is this refurbished centenarian brick
tram depot at the northern end of Glebe. It's
a handsome redevelopment with provedores,
a supermarket and a selection of modern-
thinking eateries, including one specialising
in fresh pasta, another in organic meats, a
sustainable fish restaurant, a contemporary
Middle Eastern, a Spanishy tapas place from
the Bodega team and Messina gelati.

★**Ester** MODERN AUSTRALIAN $$$
(Map p74; ☑02-8068 8279; www.ester-
restaurant.com.au; 46/52 Meagher St; mains
$32-49; ⊙6-10pm Mon-Thu, noon-3pm & 6-11pm
Fri, 6-11pm Sat, noon-5pm Sun; 🖉; ⋒Redfern)
Ester breaks the trend for hip eateries by
accepting bookings, but in other respects it
exemplifies Sydney's contemporary dining
scene: informal but not sloppy; innovative
without being overly gimmicky; hip, but
never try-hard. Influences straddle conti-
nents and dishes are made to be shared. If
humanly possible, make room for dessert.

★**Boathouse on
Blackwattle Bay** SEAFOOD $$$
(Map p56; ☑02-9518 9011; www.boathouse.net.
au; 123 Ferry Rd, Glebe; mains $42-48; ⊙6-10pm

Tue-Thu, noon-3pm & 6-11pm Fri-Sun; ⋒Glebe)
The best restaurant in Glebe, and one of the
best seafood restaurants in Sydney. Offerings range from oysters so fresh you'd think
you shucked them yourself, to a snapper pie
that'll go straight to the top of your favour-
ite-dish list. The views over the bay and Anzac Bridge are stunning. Arrive by water taxi
for maximum effect.

Glebe Point Diner MODERN AUSTRALIAN $$$
(Map p56; ☑02-9660 2646; www.glebepoint
diner.com.au; 407 Glebe Point Rd; mains $29-48;
⊙6-10pm Mon & Tue, noon-3pm & 6-10pm Wed &
Thu, noon-3pm & 5.30-11pm Fri & Sat, noon-3pm
Sun; ⋒Jubilee Park) A sensational neigh-
bourhood diner, where only the best local
produce is used and everything – from the
home-baked bread and hand-churned
butter to the nougat finale – is made from
scratch. The food is creative and comforting
at the same time: a rare combination. The
menu changes regularly and is backed up by
blackboard specials.

✕ Manly

Jah Bar TAPAS $$
(Map p77; ☑02-9977 4449; www.jahbar.com.au;
Shop 7, 9-15 Central Ave, Manly; tapas $14-22; ⊙5-
11pm Tue-Thu, noon-11pm Fri & Sat, noon-10pm Sun;
🛜; ⋒Manly) With indoor tables squeezed
around the large open kitchen and a small
courtyard area, it pays to book ahead here. A
breezy array of tapas has shot off at tangents
from their Spanish and Mexican ancestors
and are really delicious – the raw fish crispy
tacos have appealing zing, the calamari
bursts with spicy flavours and the scallops
with braised pork cheek are sensational.
Service is very engaged.

Boathouse Shelly Beach CAFE $$
(Map p56; ☑02-9934 9977; www.theboathousesb.
com.au; 1 Marine Pde, Manly; kiosk mains $12-19,
restaurant mains $18-29; ⊙7am-4pm Mon-Sat,
7am-8pm Sun; 🛜🖉) This sweet little spot on
picturesque Shelly Beach makes a top venue
for breakfast juices, brunches, fish 'n' chips,
oysters or daily fish specials, served either
in the restaurant section or from the kiosk.

★**Pilu at Freshwater** SARDINIAN $$$
(☑02-9938 3331; www.pilu.com.au; Moore
Rd, Freshwater; 3/5/7 courses $95/110/125;
⊙noon-2.30pm Tue-Sun, plus 6-11pm Tue-Sat;
⋒139) Housed within a heritage-listed
beach house overlooking the ocean, this
multi-award-winning Sardinian restaurant

serves specialities such as oven-roasted suckling pig and traditional flatbread. Your best bet is to plump for the tasting menu (from $105) and thereby eliminate any possible order envy. There are some excellent wines on offer here, beautifully decanted and served.

✖ Northern Beaches

Boathouse Palm Beach CAFE $$
(📋 02-9974 5440; www.theboathousepb.com.au; Governor Phillip Park, Palm Beach; mains $17-29; ⊘ 7am-4pm; 🛜📋; 🚇 L90, 190) Sit on the large timber deck facing Pittwater or grab a table on the lawn out front – either option is alluring at Palm Beach's most popular cafe. The food (try the legendary fish and chips or the vibrant salads) is nearly as impressive as the views, and that's really saying something.

★ Jonah's MODERN AUSTRALIAN $$$
(📋 02-9974 5599; www.jonahs.com.au; 69 Bynya Rd, Whale Beach; 2/3/4 courses $88/115/130; ⊘ 7.30-9am, noon-2.30pm & 6.30-11pm; 🛜; 🚇 L90, 190) On the hill above Whale Beach, luxurious Jonah's has fabulous perspectives over the ocean. The food is easy on the eye too, with immaculate presentation and excellent fish dishes. For the ultimate Sydney indulgence, take a seaplane from Rose Bay, order the seafood platter for two, and stay overnight in one of the ocean-view rooms ($499 per person, including dinner and breakfast).

🍷 Drinking & Nightlife

In a city where rum was once the main currency, it's little wonder that drinking plays a big part in the Sydney social scene – whether it's knocking back some tinnies at the beach, schmoozing after work or warming up for a night on the town. Sydney offers plenty of choice in drinking establishments, from the flashy to the trashy.

🍷 Circular Quay & the Rocks

★ Glenmore PUB
(Map p60; 📋 02-9247 4794; www.theglenmore.com. au; 96 Cumberland St; ⊘ 10am-midnight Sun-Thu, to 1am Fri & Sat; 🛜; 🚇 Circular Quay) Downstairs it's a predictably nice old Rocks pub, but head up to the rooftop and the views are beyond fabulous: Opera House (until a cruise ship docks), harbour and city skyline all present and accounted for. It gets rammed up here on

the weekends, with DJs, good food and plenty of wine by the glass. The food's decent too.

★ Hero of Waterloo PUB
(Map p60; 📋 02-9252 4553; www.heroofwater loo.com.au; 81 Lower Fort St; ⊘ 10am-11.30pm Mon-Wed, 10am-midnight Thu-Sat, 10am-10pm Sun; 🚇 Circular Quay) Enter this rough-hewn 1843 sandstone pub to meet some locals, chat up the Irish bar staff and grab an earful of the swing, folk and Celtic bands (Friday to Sunday). Downstairs is a dungeon where, in days gone by, drinkers would sleep off a heavy night before being shanghaied to the high seas via a tunnel leading straight to the harbour.

★ Opera Bar BAR
(Map p60; 📋 02-9247 1666; www.operabar. com.au; lower concourse, Sydney Opera House; ⊘ 9am-midnight Sun-Thu, 9am-1am Fri & Sat; 🚇 Circular Quay) Right on the harbour with the Opera House on one side and the Harbour Bridge on the other, this perfectly positioned terrace manages a very Sydney marriage of the laid-back and the sophisticated. It's an iconic spot for visitors and locals alike. There's live music or DJs most nights and a decent selection of food (dishes $12 to $28).

Hotel Palisade PUB
(Map p60; 📋 02-9018 0123; www.hotelpalisade. com; 35 Bettington St; ⊘ noon-midnight Mon-Fri, 11am-midnight Sat & Sun; 🛜; 🚇 Circular Quay) Reopened with hipster flair, this historic Millers Point pub preserves its tea-coloured tiles, faded brick and nostalgia-tinted downstairs bar. On top of the venerable building, however, there's a shiny new glass section with super bridge views, pricey drinks and posh food. It often fills up or books out, but there's a less glitzy, more comfy perch on the little 4th-floor balcony.

Bulletin Place COCKTAIL BAR
(Map p60; www.bulletinplace.com; 10 Bulletin Pl; ⊘ 4pm-midnight Mon-Wed, 4pm-1am Thu-Sat, 4-10pm Sun; 🚇 Circular Quay) A discreet entrance on this little street of cafes and bars conceals the staircase up to one of Sydney's most talked-about cocktail bars. Personable, down-to-earth staff shake up great daily creations that are high on zinginess and freshness and low on frippery. It's a small space, so get there early. Cocktails are about 20 bucks each.

AT THE DOOR

Sydney's bouncers are often strict, arbitrary and immune to logic. They are usually contracted by outside security firms so have no problem in turning away business. Being questioned and searched every time you want a drink after 8pm on a weekend can definitely take the edge off a Sydney night out.

➡ It is against the law to serve people who are intoxicated and you won't be admitted to a venue if you appear drunk. Expect to be questioned about how much you've had to drink that night: it's more to see if you're slurring your words than actual interest.

➡ If security staff suspect that you're under the legal drinking age (18), you'll be asked to present photo ID with proof of your age. Some bars scan ID for everyone entering.

➡ Some gay bars have a 'no open-toed shoes' policy, ostensibly for safety (to avoid broken glass), but sometimes invoked to keep straight women out.

➡ Some pubs have smoking areas, but you aren't allowed to take food into that area – even if you're happy to do so.

Australian Hotel
PUB

(Map p60; ☑ 02-9247 2229; www.australian heritagehotel.com; 100 Cumberland St; ⊙ 11am-midnight; 🛜; 🚊 Circular Quay) With its wide verandah shading lots of outdoor seating, this handsome early-20th-century pub is a favoured pitstop for a cleansing ale; they were doing microbrewed beer here long before it became trendy and have a great selection. The kitchen also does a nice line in gourmet pizzas ($18 to $28), including ever-popular toppings of kangaroo, emu and crocodile.

Lord Nelson Brewery Hotel
BREWERY

(Map p60; ☑ 02-9251 4044; 19 Kent St; ⊙ 11am-11pm Mon-Sat, noon-10pm Sun; 🚊 Circular Quay) Built in 1836 and converted into a pub in 1841, this atmospheric sandstone boozer is one of three claiming to be Sydney's oldest (all using slightly different criteria). The on-site brewery cooks up its own natural ales (try the Old Admiral). A pint of dark, stout-y Nelson's Blood is a fine way to partake.

Argyle
BAR

(Map p60; ☑ 02-9247 5500; www.theargylerocks. com; 18 Argyle St; ⊙ 11am-midnight Sun-Wed, to 3am Thu-Sat; 🚊 Circular Quay) This mammoth conglomeration of five bars is spread through the historic sandstone Argyle Stores buildings, including a cobblestone courtyard and underground cellars resonating with DJ beats. The decor ranges from rococo couches to white extruded plastic tables, all offset with kooky chandeliers and moody lighting. During the day the courtyard is a pleasant place for a drink or a spot of lunch.

🍸 City Centre & Haymarket

The city centre has long been known for upmarket, after-work booze rooms, none of which you would describe as cosy locals. Much more interesting is the wide network of 'small bars', which are speakeasy-style places lurking in the most unlikely back alleys and basements.

Most small bars were subject to a midnight closure, but a trial allowing them to open until 2am was due to begin at the time of writing, so expect some opening hours to extend.

★ Frankie's Pizza
BAR

(Map p60; www.frankiespizzabytheslice.com; 50 Hunter St; ⊙ 4pm-3am Sun-Thu, noon-3am Fri & Sat; 🛜; 🚊 Martin Place) Descend the stairs and you'll think you're in a 1970s pizzeria, complete with plastic grapevines, snapshots covering the walls and tasty pizza slices ($6). But open the nondescript door in the corner and an indie wonderland reveals itself. Bands play here at least four nights a week (join them on Tuesdays for live karaoke) and there's another bar hidden below.

★ Uncle Ming's
COCKTAIL BAR

(Map p60; www.unclemings.com.au; 55 York St; ⊙ noon-midnight Mon-Fri, 4pm-midnight Sat; 🚊 Wynyard) We love the dark romantic opium-den atmosphere of this small bar secreted away in a basement by a shirt shop. It's an atmospheric spot for anything from a quick beer before jumping on a train at Wynyard to a leisurely exploration of the cocktail menu. It also does an excellent line in dumplings and usually has very welcoming bar staff.

SYDNEY & THE CENTRAL COAST SYDNEY

Grandma's
COCKTAIL BAR

(Map p60; ✆02-9264 3004; www.grandmas barsydney.com; basement, 275 Clarence St; ☺3pm-midnight Mon-Fri, 5pm-1am Sat; ☒Town Hall) Billing itself as a 'retrosexual haven of cosmopolitan kitsch and faded granny glamour', Grandma's hits the mark. A stag's head greets you on the stairs and ushers you into a tiny subterranean world of parrot wallpaper and tiki cocktails. It's very quirky, and very relaxed and casual for a CBD venue. Toasted sandwiches provide sustenance. Look for it behind the Fender shop.

Baxter Inn
BAR

(Map p60; www.thebaxterinn.com; 152-156 Clarence St; ☺4pm-1am Mon-Sat; ☒Town Hall) Yes, it really is down that dark lane and through that unmarked door (there are two easily spotted bars on this courtyard, but this is through a door to your right). Whisky's the main poison and the friendly bar staff really know their stuff. There's an elegant speakeasy atmosphere and a mighty impressive choir of bottles behind the bar.

O Bar
COCKTAIL BAR

(Map p60; ✆02-9247 9777; www.obardining. com.au; Level 47, Australia Square, 264 George St; ☺5pm-late Sat-Thu, noon-late Fri; ☎; ☒Wynyard) The cocktails at this 47th-floor revolving bar aren't cheap, but they're still substantially cheaper than admission to Sydney Tower – and it's considerably more glamorous. The views are truly wonderful; get up there shortly after opening time, and kick back to enjoy the sunset and transition into night.

Ivy
BAR, CLUB

(Map p60; ✆02-9254 8100; www.merivale.com/ ivy; L1, 330 George St; ☺noon-late Mon-Fri, 6.30pm-3.30am Sat; ☎; ☒Wynyard) Hidden down a lane off George St, Ivy is the HQ of the all-pervading Merivale Group. It's a fashionable complex of bars, restaurants... even a swimming pool. It's also Sydney's most hyped venue; expect lengthy queues of suburban kids teetering on unfeasibly high heels, waiting to shed $40 on a Saturday for entry to Sydney's hottest club night, Pacha.

At other times, the main club space is Palings, a good bar and popular eatery, with Thai street food on the menu alongside steaks, grilled fish, salads and other well-prepared meals. It's a buzzy, open space that's good for leisurely lunch once the office crowd disperses around 2pm.

Slip Inn & Chinese Laundry
PUB, CLUB

(Map p64; ✆02-8295 9999; www.merivale.com. au/chineselaundry; 111 Sussex St; club $20-30; ☺11am-late Mon-Fri, 4pm-late Sat, Chinese Laundry 9pm-3am Fri & Sat; ☎; ☒Wynyard) Slip in to this warren of moody rooms on the edge of Darling Harbour and bump hips with the kids. There are bars, pool tables, a beer garden and Mexican food, courtesy of El Loco. On Friday and Saturday nights the bass cranks up at the long-running attached Chinese Laundry nightclub, accessed via Slip St below.

🍸 Darling Harbour & Pyrmont

Home
BAR, CLUB

(Map p64; www.homesydney.com; 1 Wheat Rd, Cockle Bay Wharf; ☺club 9pm-late Thu-Sat; ☎; ☒Town Hall) Welcome to the pleasuredome: a three-level, 2100-capacity timber and glass 'prow' that's home to a dance floor, countless bars, outdoor balconies, and sonics that make other clubs sound like transistor radios. You can catch live music most nights at the attached Tokio Hotel bar downstairs (www.tokiohotellive.com.au), and the club is normally open Thursday to Saturday, and often features big-name DJs.

LOCKOUT LAWS

In an effort to cut down on alcohol-fuelled violence, tough licensing laws have been introduced to a large area of the central city bounded by the Rocks, Circular Quay, Woolloomooloo, Kings Cross, Darlinghurst, Haymarket and the eastern shores of Darling Harbour.

Within this zone, licensed venues are not permitted to admit people after 1.30am. However, if you arrive before then, the venue is permitted to continue serving you alcohol until 3am, or 3.30am in the case of venues with live entertainment, which you can enter until 2am. This latter amendment was announced in late 2016 after widespread protest from the public and industry over the severity of the laws. The change was too little, too late for many venues, which had already closed down.

Pyrmont Bridge Hotel   PUB
(Map p64; ☑02-9660 6996; www.pyrmont bridgehotel.com; 96 Union St; ⊙24hr; 🛜; 🚊Pyrmont Bay) Standing like a guardian of tradition at the entrance to Pyrmont, this solid centenarian pub is a bastion of no-frills Sydney drinking culture. With an island bar and rooftop terrace, there are plenty of handsome features; there's also lots of character and regular live music. But its biggest selling point is its 24-hour license...the CBD lockout zone ends a few metres away.

In practice, they usually close for an hour or two around 5am so they can hose the place down and begin again.

🍷 Kings Cross & Potts Point

Traditionally Sydney's premier party precinct, this neighbourhood has had the life sucked out of it by the central Sydney licensing laws introduced in 2014. Most of the late-night clubs have closed. On the upside, the streets look less like a war zone in the wee hours. Woolloomooloo has some great old pubs near the water.

★ **Old Fitzroy Hotel**   PUB
(Map p66; ☑02-9356 3848; www.oldfitzroy.com. au; 129 Dowling St, Woolloomooloo; ⊙11am-midnight Mon-Fri, noon-midnight Sat, 3-10pm Sun; 🛜; 🚊Kings Cross) Islington meets Melbourne in the backstreets of Woolloomooloo: this totally unpretentious **theatre pub** (Map p66; www.oldfitztheatre.com) is also a decent old-fashioned boozer in its own right, with a great variety of beers on tap and a convivial welcome. Prop up the bar, grab a seat at a streetside table or head upstairs to the bistro, pool table and couches.

Kings Cross Hotel   PUB
(Map p66; ☑02-9331 9900; www.kingscross hotel.com.au; 244-248 William St, Kings Cross; ⊙noon-1am Sun-Thu, to 3am Fri & Sat; 🛜; 🚊Kings Cross) This grand old brick building guards the entrance to the Cross and is one of the area's best pubs, with several levels of boozy entertainment. The balcony bar is a very pleasant spot for lunch, while the rooftop that opens weekend evenings has the drawcard vistas. Saturdays are good, with DJs on all levels.

World Bar   BAR, CLUB
(Map p66; ☑02-9357 7700; www.theworldbar.com; 24 Bayswater Rd, Kings Cross; ⊙2pm-midnight Sun & Mon, 2pm-3am Tue-Sat; 🛜; 🚊Kings Cross) 🏮 World Bar (a reformed bordello) is an unpre-tentious grungy club with three floors to lure in the backpackers and cheap drinks to loosen things up. DJs play indie, hip hop, power pop and house nightly. Wednesday (The Wall) and Saturday (Cakes) are the big nights. In the earlier evening, it's a pleasant place for a quiet drink on the foliage-rich verandah.

🍷 Surry Hills & Darlinghurst

Once upon a time this neighbourhood was known for its grungy live-music pubs and high-octane gay scene. Many of the music venues have subsequently been converted into chic bar-restaurants and the gay bars have eased up on the gas, but this area still contains some of Sydney's best nightspots. You just have to look harder to find them. The 'small bar' phenomenon has taken off here, with many of Sydney's best lurking down the most unlikely lanes.

★ **Love, Tilly Devine**   WINE BAR
(Map p66; ☑02-9326 9297; www.lovetilly devine.com; 91 Crown Lane, Darlinghurst; ⊙5pm-midnight Mon-Sat, 5-10pm Sun; 🚊Museum) This split-level laneway bar is pretty compact, but the wine list certainly isn't. It's an extraordinary document, with some exceptionally well-chosen wines and a mission to get people away from their tried-and-tested favourites and explore. Take a friend and crack open a leisurely bottle of something.

★ **Wild Rover**   BAR
(Map p62; ☑02-9280 2235; www.thewildrover.com. au; 75 Campbell St, Surry Hills; ⊙4pm-midnight Mon-Sat; 🚊Central) Look for the unsigned wide door and enter this supremely cool brick-lined speakeasy, where a big range of craft beer is served in chrome steins and jungle animals peer benevolently from the green walls. The upstairs bar opens for trivia and live bands.

★ **Shakespeare Hotel**   PUB
(Map p70; ☑02-9319 6883; www.shake spearehotel.com.au; 200 Devonshire St, Surry Hills; ⊙10am-midnight Mon-Sat, 11am-10pm Sun; 🚊Central) This is a classic Sydney pub (1879) with art nouveau tiled walls, skuzzy carpet, the horses on the TV and cheap bar meals. There are plenty of cosy hidey-holes upstairs and a cast of local characters. It's a proper convivial all-welcome place that's the antithesis of the more gentrified Surry Hills drinking establishments.

Beresford Hotel
PUB

(Map p70; ☑02-9240 3000; www.merivale.
au/thebereesfordhotel; 354 Bourke St, Surry Hills;
⊘noon-1am; ☐ 374, 397, 399) The well-polished
tiles of the facade and interior are a real
feature at this elegantly refurbished historic
pub. It's a popular pre-club venue for an upmarket mixed crowd at weekends but makes
for a quieter retreat midweek. The front bar
is as handsome as they come; out the back is
one of the area's best beer gardens, while upstairs is a schmick live-music and club space.

Shady Pines Saloon
BAR

(Map p66; ☑0405 624 944; www.shadypines
saloon.com; shop 4, 256 Crown St, Darlinghurst;
⊘4pm-midnight; ☒Museum) With no sign or
street number on the door and entry via a
shady back lane (look for the white door before Bikram Yoga on Foley St), this subterranean honky-tonk bar caters to the urban
boho. Sip whisky and rye with the good ole
hipster boys amid Western memorabilia and
taxidermy.

Winery
WINE BAR

(Map p70; ☑02-9331 0833; www.thekey
stonegroup.com.au; 285a Crown St, Surry Hills;
⊘noon-midnight; ☜; ☒Central) Beautifully situated back from the road in the leafy grounds
of a historic water reservoir, this oasis serves
dozens of wines by the glass to the swankier
Surry Hills set. Sit for a while and you'll notice all kinds of kitsch touches lurking in the
greenery: headless statues, upside-down par-
rots, iron koalas. It's a very fun, boisterous
scene on weekend afternoons.

Midnight Shift
GAY, CLUB

(The Shift; Map p66; ☑02-9358 3848; www.the
midnightshift.com.au; 91 Oxford St, Darlinghurst;
⊘noon-1am Sun-Thu, noon-3am Fri & Sat; ☒Mu-
seum) The grand dame of the Oxford St gay
scene, known for its lavish drag productions,
has been forced into something of a change
of identity by the lockout laws. The downstairs bar is much improved and appeals for
early-in-the-night drinks; the upstairs club,
which charges an entrance fee some nights,
can still get seriously tits-to-the-wind.

Stonewall Hotel
GAY, BAR

(Map p66; ☑02-9360 1963; www.stonewallhotel.
com; 175 Oxford St, Darlinghurst; ⊘noon-3am;
☐333,380) Nicknamed 'Stonehenge' by those
who think it's archaic, Stonewall has three
levels of bars and dance floors, and attracts
a younger crowd. Cabaret, karaoke and quiz

nights spice things up; Wednesday's Male-
box is an inventive way to bag yourself a boy.

Arq
GAY, CLUB

(Map p66; ☑02-9380 8700; www.arqsydney.com.
au; 16 Flinders St, Darlinghurst; ⊘9pm-3am Thu-
Sun; ☐333, 380) If Noah had to fill his Arq
with groovy gay clubbers, he'd head here
with a big net and some tranquillisers. This
flash megaclub has a cocktail bar, a recovery
room and two dance floors with high-energy
house, drag shows and a hyperactive smoke
machine.

🍷 Paddington & Centennial Park

Paddington
BAR

(Map p72; ☑02-9240 3000; www.merivale.com.
au/thepaddington; 384 Oxford St, Paddington;
⊘noon-midnight Mon-Thu, noon-3am Fri & Sat,
noon-10pm Sun; ☜; ☐333, 380) There's a new
kick to Paddington's weekend nightlife, and
this bar-restaurant is a key player. Drinks
and service are excellent, while succulent
chickens spinning on the rotisserie provide
a simple but very high class eating choice.
The design, all white tiles, distressed brick
and black-and-white photos of ancestors
brandishing haunches of meat, deliberately
recalls a butcher's shop, a little cynically, as
it wasn't one.

Unicorn
PUB

(Map p66; www.theunicornhotel.com.au; 106 Oxford St, Paddington; ⊘11am-midnight Sun, 11am-
1am Mon & Tue, 11am-3am Wed-Sat; ☜; ☐333,
380) This spacious art-deco pub is casual
and unpretentious, a fine place to sink a few
craft beers, sip some Australian wines or try
out the pool table atop a Persian-style rug.
Burgers are the highlight of the OK eating
offerings. There's a cosy downstairs bistro
and small beer garden off it. More than the
sum of its parts.

🍷 Bondi, Coogee & the Eastern Beaches

★ Coogee Pavilion
BAR

(Map p56; ☑02-9240 3000; www.merivale.
com.au/coogeepavilion; 169 Dolphin St, Coogee;
⊘7.30am-midnight; ☜⑭; ☐372-374) With
numerous indoor and outdoor bars, a kids'
play area and a glorious adults-only rooftop, this vast complex has brought a touch
of inner-city glam to Coogee. Built in 1887,
the building originally housed an aquarium

and swimming pools. Now, space, light and white wood give a breezy feel. Great eating options run from Mediterranean-inspired bar food to fish 'n' chips and sashimi.

Anchor
BAR

(Map p78; ☑02-8084 3145; www.anchor barbondi.com; 8 Campbell Pde, Bondi Beach; ⊘5pm-midnight Tue-Fri, 12.30pm-midnight Sat & Sun; ☎; ☐333, 380-382) Surfers, backpackers and the local cool kids slurp down icy margaritas at this bustling bar at the south end of the strip. It sports a dark-wood nautical-piratey feel and is also a great spot for a late snack. The two-hour happy hour from 5pm weekdays is a great way to start the post-surf debrief.

Coogee Bay Hotel
PUB

(Map p56; ☑02-9665 0000; www.coogeebayhotel. com.au; 253 Coogee Bay Rd, Coogee; ⊘7am-4am Mon-Sat, to midnight Sun; ☎; ☐372-374) This enormous, rambling, rowdy complex packs in the backpackers for live music, open-mic nights, comedy and big-screen sports in the beaut beer garden, sports bar and Selina's nightclub. Sit on a stool at the window overlooking the beach and sip on a cold one.

🍷 Sydney Harbourside

★Sheaf
PUB

(Golden Sheaf Hotel; Map p56; ☑02-9327 5877; www.thesheaf.com.au; 429 New South Head Rd, Double Bay; ⊘10am-1am Mon-Wed, to 2am Thu-Sat, to midnight Sun; ☎; ☐324-327, ☒Double Bay, ☒Edgecliff) A cracking pub, especially at weekends when it thrums with life all day, this is a real eastern suburbs favourite whose recent makeover has only enhanced it. The beer garden is among Sydney's best: large, with good wines by the glass, heaters, evening entertainment and solid food (all day from Friday to Sunday). Lots of other spaces mean there's something for all.

★Watsons Bay Beach Club
PUB

(Map p56; ☑02-9337 5444; www.watsonsbayhotel.com.au; 1 Military Rd, Watsons Bay; ⊘10am-midnight Mon-Sat, to 10pm Sun; ☒Watsons Bay) One of the great pleasures in life is languishing in the rowdy beer garden of the

---

LGBT SYDNEY

LGBT folk have migrated to Oz's Emerald City from all over Australia, New Zealand and the world, adding to a community that is visible, vibrant and an integral part of the city's social fabric. Partly because of that integration, partly because of smartphone apps facilitating contact, and partly because of lockout laws (p98), the gay nightlife scene has died off substantially. But the action's still going on and Sydney is indisputably one of the world's great queer cities.

The famous **Sydney Gay & Lesbian Mardi Gras** (p78) is now the biggest annual tourist-attracting date on the Australian calendar. While the straights focus on the parade, the gay and lesbian community throws itself wholeheartedly into the entire festival, including the blitzkrieg of partying that surrounds it. There's no better time for the gay traveller to visit Sydney than the two-week lead-up to the parade and party, held on the first Saturday in March.

Darlinghurst and Newtown have traditionally been the gayest neighbourhoods, although all of the inner suburbs have a higher-than-average proportion of gay and lesbian residents. Most of the gay venues are on the Darlinghurst section of Oxford St, with classic spots like the **Stonewall** (p100), **Midnight Shift** (p100), **Palms** (Map p66; ☑02-9357 4166; 124 Oxford St, Darlinghurst; ⊘8pm-midnight Thu & Sun, to 3am Fri & Sat; ☐333, 380) and, around the corner, **Arq** (p100). However, some of the best events are held at mixed pubs, such as the **Sly Fox** (Map p74; ☑02-9557 2917; www.slyfox.sydney; 199 Enmore Rd, Enmore; ⊘2pm-midnight Sun & Tue, to 3am Wed & Thu, to 6am Fri & Sat; ☒Newtown) and the legendary Sunday afternoon session at the **Beresford** (p100).

Beach scenes include the north end of Bondi, **Lady Bay** (p68), a pretty nudist beach tucked under South Head, **Obelisk** (Map p56; Chowder Bay Rd; ☐244); a secluded nude beach with a bush hinterland; and **Murray Rose Pool** (p75), another harbour beach. Women-only **McIvers Baths** (Map p56; www.randwick.nsw.gov.au; Beach St, Coogee; donation 20c; ⊘sunrise-sunset; ☐372-374) is extremely popuar with the Sapphic set.

Free gay and lesbian media includes *LOTL* (www.lotl.com), the *Star Observer* (www. starobserver.com.au) and *SX* (www.gaynewsnetwork.com.au).

ALFONSO FERNANDEZ / SHUTTERSTOCK ©

VIVALAPOCK / BUDGET TRAVEL ©

1. Queen Victoria Building (p59)
Shop in style at this High Victorian Gothic masterpiece, which now boasts nearly 200 shops.

2. Sydney Opera House (p52)
Book tickets to a dance, music or theatre performance to experience this remarkable building up close.

3. Bondi Icebergs Pool (p75)
For a natural saltwater wave pool, head to this Bondi institution.

4. Sydney cityscape (p52)
Sydney's privileged position on the stunning NSW coast makes it Australia's most photogenic city.

SUPERJOSEPH / SHUTTERSTOCK ©

Watsons Bay Hotel, mere metres from the ferry wharf, after a day at the beach. It goes off here at weekends, with food options and a rowdy good time had by all. Stay to watch the sun go down over the city.

Newtown & the Inner West

★ Courthouse Hotel
PUB

(Map p74; ☑02-9519 8273; 202 Australia St; ☺10am-midnight Mon-Sat, to 10pm Sun; ☒Newtown) A block back from the King St fray, the 150-year-old Courthouse is one of Newtown's best pubs, the kind of place where everyone from pool-playing goth lesbians to magistrates can have a beer and feel right at home. It packs out for Sydney Swans games. The beer garden is one of Sydney's best: spacious, sheltered and cheerful, with decent pub food available.

★ Young Henry's
BREWERY

(Map p74; ☑02-9519 0048; www.younghenrys. com; 76 Wilford St, Newtown; ☺noon-7pm Mon-Fri, 10am-7pm Sat, 11am-7pm Sun; ☒Newtown) Conviviality is assured in this craft brewery bar, where the beer is as fresh as you'll get. Basically, it's filled a bit of warehouse with high tables, a loud stereo system and a counter to serve its delicious beer, opened the roller door and filled it with happy locals. It doesn't do eats, but there's a different food truck option outside each weekend.

★ Earl's Juke Joint
BAR

(Map p74; www.facebook.com/earlsjukejoint; 407 King St, Newtown; ☺4pm-midnight; ☒Newtown) The current it-bar of the minute, swinging Earl's serves craft beers and killer cocktails to the Newtown hiperati. It's hidden behind the down-at-heel facade of the butcher's shop it used to be, but once in, you're in swinging New Orleans, with a bar as long as the Mississippi.

Duck Inn
PUB

(Map p74; ☑02-9319 4415; www.theduckinn pubandkitchen.com; 74 Rose St, Chippendale; ☺11am-11pm Mon-Sat, noon-10pm Sun; �🛜; ☐422, 423, 426, ☒Redfern) What Chippendale does best is a real feeling of neighbourhood despite its proximity to central Sydney. This backstreet pub takes food and drink seriously but is as convivial as they come, spacious with a comfortable buzz and sociable beer garden. There's an interesting, changing selection of tap beers, 18 wines

by the glass and a nice line in shared roast platters: try the duck.

Corridor
COCKTAIL BAR

(Map p74; ☑0405 671 002; www.corridor bar.com.au; 153a King St; ☺5pm-midnight Mon, 4pm-midnight Tue-Thu, 3pm-midnight Fri & Sat, 3-10pm Sun; ☒Macdonaldtown) The name exaggerates this bar's skinniness, but not by much. Downstairs the bartenders serve old-fashioned cocktails and some zingy, fruity ones – the passionfruit mojito is a great palate-cleanser – and a good range of wine, while upstairs there's interesting art (for sale) and a tiny deck. There's live music some nights.

Bank Hotel
PUB

(Map p74; ☑02-8568 1900; www.bankhotel.com. au; 324 King St; ☺11am-1am Mon-Wed, 11am-2am Thu, 11am-4am Fri & Sat, 11am-midnight Sun; 🛜; ☒Newtown) The Bank didn't always sport the artful heritage-wood look that it has now but has consistently been a Newtown classic in its central railway-side position. Its large retractable-roofed beer garden at the back is a highlight, as is the craft beer bar above it, which always has interesting guest ales on tap. Food is based around Mexican-style barbecue options.

Lockout laws in the CBD have increased the Bank's popularity markedly, so prepare to queue on Friday and Saturday night.

Imperial Hotel
GAY & LESBIAN

(Map p74; ☑02-9516 1766; www.imperialsydney. com.au; 35 Erskineville Rd, Erskineville; admission free-$15; ☺3pm-midnight Sun, Wed & Thu, to 5am Fri & Sat; ☒Erskineville) The art-deco Imperial is legendary as the starting point for *The Adventures of Priscilla, Queen of the Desert*. The front bar is a lively place for pool-shooting and cruising, with the action shifting to the cellar club late on a Saturday night. But it's in the cabaret bar that the legacy of Priscilla is kept alive.

Manly

★ Manly Wharf Hotel
PUB

(Map p77; ☑02-9977 1266; www.manlywharf hotel.com.au; East Esplanade, Manly; ☺11.30am-midnight Mon-Fri, 11am-midnight Sat, 11am-10pm Sun; 🛜🍴; 🛥Manly) Just along the wharf from the ferry, this remodelled pub is all glass and water vistas, with loads of seating so you've a good chance of grabbing a share of the view. It's a perfect spot for sunny afternoon beers. There's good pub food, too (mains $18 to $26), with pizzas, fried fish and succulent rotisserie chicken all worthwhile.

Hotel Steyne
PUB

(Map p77; ☑ 02-9977 4977; www.hotelsteyne.com. au; 75 The Corso, Manly; ◷ 9am-2am Mon-Sat, to midnight Sun; ⊗; ⌖ Manly) With something for everyone, the Steyne is a Manly classic that's big enough to get lost in: it's like a village of its own with various bars and eating areas around the sociable central courtyard, which goes loud and late most nights. The rum-focused Moonshine bar has a balcony with beach views.

🍷 Northern Beaches

Newport
PUB

(Newport Arms Hotel; ☑ 02-9997 4900; www. merivale.com.au/thenewport; cnr Beaconsfield & Kalinya Sts, Newport; ◷ 11am-midnight Mon-Sat, 11am-11pm Sun; ⊗ ♿; ⌖ 187-190) This legendary Northern Beaches pub actually overlooks not the ocean but the Pittwater side, with bobbing boats and quiet strands the outlook. It's an absolutely enormous complex, with acres of appealing outdoor seating, several bars, good food, table tennis and all sorts of stuff going on. It's a great, family-friendly place to while away a sunny afternoon.

⭐ Entertainment

Take Sydney at face value and it's tempting to unfairly stereotype its good citizens as shallow and a little narcissistic. But take a closer look: the arts scene is thriving, sophisticated and progressive – it's not a complete accident that Sydney's definitive icon is an opera house!

Cinema

⭐ Golden Age Cinema & Bar
CINEMA

(Map p62; ☑ 02-9211 1556; www.ourgoldenage. com.au; 80 Commonwealth St, Surry Hills; tickets $20; ◷ 4pm-midnight Wed-Fri, 2.30pm-midnight Sat & Sun; ⌖ Central) In what was once the Sydney HQ of Paramount pictures, a heart-warming small cinema has taken over the former screening room downstairs. It shows old favourites, art-house classics and a few recherché gems. There's a great small bar here too; it's a fabulous place for a night out. The separate cafe at ground level is an attractive coffee-stop too.

Moonlight Cinema
CINEMA

(Map p72; www.moonlight.com.au; Belvedere Amphitheatre, cnr Loch & Broome Aves, Centennial Park; adult/child $19/14.50; ◷ sunset Dec-Mar; ⌖ Bondi Junction) Take a picnic and join the bats under the stars in magnificent Centennial Park; enter via the Woollahra Gate on Oxford St. A mix of new-release blockbuster, art-house and classic films is screened.

OpenAir Cinema
CINEMA

(Map p56; www.stgeorgeopenair.com.au; Mrs Macquaries Rd; tickets $38; ◷ Jan & Feb; ⌖ Circular Quay) Right on the harbour, the outdoor three-storey screen here comes with surround sound, sunsets, skyline and swanky food and wine. Most tickets are purchased in advance, but a limited number go on sale at the door each night at 6.30pm; check the website for details.

Dendy Opera Quays
CINEMA

(Map p60; ☑ 02-9247 3800; www.dendy.com.au; 2 Circular Quay East; adult/child $20/14; ◷ sessions 9.30am-9.30pm; ⌖ Circular Quay) When the harbour glare and squawking seagulls get too much, follow the scent of popcorn into the dark folds of this plush cinema. Screening first-run, independent world films, it's augmented by friendly attendants and a cafe-bar.

Classical Music

⭐ Sydney Opera House
PERFORMING ARTS

(Map p60; ☑ 02-9250 7777; www.sydneyopera house.com; Bennelong Point; ⌖ Circular Quay) The glamorous jewel at the heart of Australian performance, Sydney's famous Opera House has five main stages. Opera may have star billing, but it's also an important venue for theatre, dance and classical concerts, while big-name bands sometimes rock the forecourt. Renovation works will close the concert hall from 2017 to 2019, and may disrupt other performances.

⭐ City Recital Hall
CLASSICAL MUSIC

(Map p60; ☑ 02-8256 2222; www.cityrecitalhall. com; 2 Angel Pl; ◷ box office 9am-5pm Mon-Fri; ⌖ Wynyard) Based on the classic configuration of the 19th-century European concert hall, this custom-built 1200-seat venue boasts near-perfect acoustics. Catch top-flight companies such as Musica Viva, the Australian Brandenburg Orchestra and the Australian Chamber Orchestra here.

Dance

Bangarra Dance Theatre
DANCE

(Map p60; ☑ 02-9251 5333; www.bangarra.com. au; Pier 4/5, 15 Hickson Rd; ⌖ 324, 325, 998, ⌖ Circular Quay) Bangarra is hailed as Australia's

> **ⓘ THE MAIN BOOKING WEBSITES**
> ....
> Moshtix (☑1300 438 849; www.moshtix.com.au)
> Ticketek (☑132 849; www.ticketek.com.au)
> Ticketmaster (☑136 100; www.ticketmaster.com.au)

finest Aboriginal performance company. Artistic director Stephen Page conjures a fusion of contemporary themes, Indigenous traditions and Western technique. When not touring internationally, the company performs at the Opera House or at its own small theatre in Walsh Bay.

Sydney Dance Company   DANCE
(SDC; Map p60; ☑02-9221 4811; www.sydneydancecompany.com; Pier 4/5, 15 Hickson Rd; ▣324, 325, 998, ▣Circular Quay) Australia's number-one contemporary-dance company has been staging wildly modern, sexy, sometimes shocking works for nearly 40 years. Performances are usually held across the street at the **Roslyn Packer Theatre** (Map p60; ☑02-9250 1999; www.roslynpackertheatre.com.au; 22 Hickson Rd; ▣324, 325, 998), or at **Carriageworks** (Map p74; ☑02-8571 9099; www.carriageworks.com.au; 245 Wilson St, Eveleigh; ⊙10am-6pm; ▣Redfern) **FREE**.

Live Music

★**Metro Theatre**   LIVE MUSIC
(Map p62; ☑02-9550 3666; www.metrotheatre.com.au; 624 George St; ▣Town Hall) The Metro is easily Sydney's best venue for catching local and alternative international acts in intimate, well-ventilated, easy-seeing comfort. Other offerings include comedy, cabaret and dance parties.

Oxford Art Factory   LIVE MUSIC
(Map p66; ☑02-9332 3711; www.oxfordartfactory.com; 38-46 Oxford St, Darlinghurst; ▣Museum) Indie kids party against an arty backdrop at this two-room multipurpose venue modelled on Andy Warhol's NYC creative base. There's a gallery, a bar and a performance space that often hosts international acts and DJs. Check the website for what's on.

Venue 505   LIVE MUSIC
(Map p70; ☑0419 294 755; www.venue505.com; 280 Cleveland St, Surry Hills; ⊙doors open 6pm Mon-Sat; ▣372, ▣Central) Focusing on jazz, roots, reggae, funk, gypsy and Latin music,

this small, relaxed venue is artist-run and thoughtfully programmed. The space features comfortable couches and murals by a local artist. It does pasta, pizza and share plates so you can munch along to the music.

Newtown Social Club   LIVE MUSIC
(Map p74; ☑02-9550 3974; www.newtownsocialclub.com; 387 King St, Newtown; ⊙7pm-midnight Tue-Thu, noon-2am Fri & Sat, noon-10pm Sun; 🚻; ▣Newtown) The legendary Sandringham Hotel (aka the 'Sando', where God used to drink, according to local band The Whitlams) may have changed names but if anything it has heightened its commitment to live music. Gigs range from local bands on the make to indie luminaries such as Gruff Rhys and Stephen Malkmus.

Basement   LIVE MUSIC
(Map p60; ☑02-9251 2797; www.thebasement.com.au; 7 Macquarie Pl; tickets $5-80; ⊙noon-1am; ▣Circular Quay) Once solely a jazz venue, the Basement now hosts international and local musicians working in many disciplines and genres. Dinner-and-show tickets net you a table by the stage, guaranteeing a better view than the standing-only area by the bar. The upstairs bar is a decent spot for a beer with the after-work crowd.

Spectator Sport

★**Sydney Cricket Ground**   SPECTATOR SPORT
(SCG; Map p72; ☑02-9360 6601; www.sydneycricketground.com.au; Driver Ave, Moore Park; ▣373-377) During the cricket season (October to March), the stately SCG is the venue for sparsely attended interstate cricket matches (featuring the NSW Blues), and sell-out international five-day Test, one-day and 20/20 limited-over matches. As the cricket season ends, the Australian Rules (AFL) season starts, and the stadium becomes a blur of red-and-white-clad Sydney Swans (www.sydneyswans.com.au) fans.

The atmosphere for international cricket and Swans games is excellent. Book via Ticketek.

Sydney Football Stadium   SPECTATOR SPORT
(Allianz Stadium; Map p72; ☑02-9360 6601; www.sydneycricketground.com.au; Moore Park Rd, Moore Park; ▣373-377) It's now officially named after an insurance company, but these naming rights change periodically, so we'll stick with the untainted-by-sponsorship moniker for this elegant 45,500-capacity stadium. It's home to local heroes the Sydney Roosters rugby league team (www.roosters.com.

au), the NSW Waratahs rugby union team (www.waratahs.com.au) and the Sydney FC A-league football (soccer) team (www.sydneyfc.com).

All of these teams have passionate fans (possibly the most vocal are the crazies in the Roosters' 'chook pen'), so a home game can be a lot of fun. Book through Ticketek.

Royal Randwick Racecourse HORSE RACING
(Map p56; ☑02-9663 8400; www.australianturfclub.com.au; Alison Rd, Randwick; ☐339) The action at Sydney's most famous racecourse peaks in April with several high-profile races, including the $4 million Queen Elizabeth Stakes; check the online calendar for race days, which are normally every second Saturday. It's always a fun day out, with Sydney fashion on show. On race days, special shuttle buses run from Chalmers St outside of Central station.

Theatre

★ **Belvoir St Theatre** THEATRE
(Map p70; ☑02-9699 3444; www.belvoir.com.au; 25 Belvoir St, Surry Hills; ☐372, ☐Central) In a quiet corner of Surry Hills, this intimate venue, with two small stages, is the home of an often-experimental and consistently excellent theatre company that specialises in quality Australian drama. It often commissions new works and is a vital cog in the Sydney theatre scene.

Sydney Theatre Company THEATRE
(STC; Map p60; ☑02-9250 1777; www.sydneytheatre.com.au; Pier 4/5, 15 Hickson Rd; ⊙box office 9am-7.30pm Mon, 9am-8.30pm Tue-Fri, 11am-8.30pm Sat, 2hr before show Sun; ☐324, 325, 998, ☐Circular Quay) Established in 1978, the STC is Sydney theatre's top dog and has played an important part in the careers of many famous Australian actors (especially Cate Blanchett, who was co-artistic director from 2008 to 2013). You can book tours of the company's Wharf and Roslyn Packer Theatres ($10). Performances are also staged at the Opera House.

The Wharf Theatre's bar is great, too; well worth a stop even without a show.

🔒 **Shopping**

Sydney's city centre is brimming over with department, chain and international fashion stores and arcades – shopping here is about as fast and furious as Australia gets. Paddington is the place for art and fashion, while new and secondhand boutiques

around Newtown and Surry Hills cater to a hipper, more alternative crowd. Double Bay, Mosman and Balmain are a bit more 'mother of the bride', and if you're chasing bargains, head to Chinatown or the Alexandria factory outlets.

Newtown and Glebe have the lion's share of book and record stores. For surf gear, head to Bondi or Manly. Woollahra, Newtown (around St Peters station) and Surry Hills are good for antiques. For souvenirs – from exquisite opals to tacky T-shirts – try the Rocks, Circular Quay and Darling Harbour.

Artery ART
(Map p66; ☑02-9380 8234; www.artery.com.au; 221 Darlinghurst Rd, Darlinghurst; ⊙10am-6pm Mon-Fri, 10am-4pm Sat & Sun; ☐Kings Cross) Step into a world of mesmerising dots and swirls at this small gallery devoted to Aboriginal art. Artery's motto is 'ethical, contemporary, affordable', and while large canvases by more established artists cost in the thousands, small, unstretched canvases start at around $35.

Gannon House Gallery ART
(Map p60; ☑02-9251 4474; www.gannonhousegallery.com; 45 Argyle St; ⊙10am-6pm; ☐Circular Quay) Specialising in contemporary Australian and Aboriginal art, Gannon House purchases works directly from artists and Aboriginal communities. You'll find the work of prominent artists such as Gloria Petyarre here, alongside lesser-known names. There are always some striking and wonderful pieces.

Makery ARTS & CRAFTS
(Map p66; ☑0419 606 724; www.work-shop.com.au; 106 Oxford St, Darlinghurst; ⊙10.30am-6.30pm Tue-Fri, 10am-5pm Sat, 11am-4pm Sun; ☐333, 380) 🖊 This ample corner space is an innovative idea that lets local artisans and designers sell their products in a single space. There's

> ℹ️ **WHAT'S ON LISTINGS**
>
> **Sydney Morning Herald** Friday's 'Shortlist' section, also online at www.smh.com.au.
>
> **What's On Sydney** (www.whatsonsydney.com)
>
> **What's On City of Sydney** (http://whatson.cityofsydney.nsw.gov.au)
>
> **Time Out Sydney** (www.timeout.com/sydney)

WORTH A TRIP

SYDNEY SPECTATOR SPORTS

Sydneysiders are sports crazy. Getting to a match is a great way to absorb some local culture and atmosphere.

Rugby League

Rugby League Sydney's all-consuming passion is rugby league, a superfast, supermacho game with a frenzied atmosphere for spectators. The **National Rugby League** (NRL; www.nrl.com) comp runs from March to October, climaxing in the sell-out Grand Final at ANZ Stadium. You can catch games every weekend during the season, played at the home grounds of Sydney's various tribes. The easiest ground to access is the 45,500-seat Sydney Football Stadium (p106), home of the Sydney Roosters. Tickets start around $25 via www.tickets.nrl.com.

Rugby Union

Union (www.rugby.com.au), despite its punishing physical component, has a more upper-class rep than rugby league and a less fanatical following in Sydney. The annual southern hemisphere Rugby Championship (formerly the Tri-Nations) between Australia's Wallabies, New Zealand's All Blacks, South Africa's Springboks and Argentina's Pumas provokes plenty of passion – particularly the matches against New Zealand, which determine the holders of the ultimate symbol of trans-Tasman rivalry, the Bledisloe Cup (the Aussies haven't won it since 2002). In the SuperRugby competition, the NSW Waratahs bang heads with other teams from Australia, New Zealand, Argentina, Japan and South Africa. Most big matches are at **ANZ Stadium** (☑02-8765 2300; www.anzstadium.com.au; Olympic Blvd; tours adult/child $29/19; ☺tours 11am, 1pm & 3pm daily, gantry 9am Fri-Wed; ☒Olympic Park).

AFL

See the Sydney Swans in their red and white splendour from March to September at the Sydney Cricket Ground (p106) or ANZ Stadium at Sydney Olympic Park. Sydney's other team, the Greater Western Sydney Giants, play most home games at another stadium in the Olympic Park complex. Tickets start at around $25, available via www.afl.com.au.

Soccer

The A-League bucks convention, playing games from late August to February rather than through the depths of winter. Sydney FC (www.sydneyfc.com) won the championship in 2006 and 2010. The newer Western Sydney Wanderers haven't won a grand final yet but landed an even bigger prize in 2014, the Asian Champions League. The W-League is the parallel women's equivalent, and is garnering rapidly increasing support. The same two Sydney clubs participate.

Cricket

Major international test, one-day and T20 matches take place at the Sydney Cricket Ground (p106) in summer. New South Wales play sparsely supported four-day Sheffield Shield matches here and at other Sydney grounds, while the all-action **Big Bash** (www.bigbash.com.au) draws huge crowds.

an excellent range of everything from jewellery to candles to clothing; it's always worth a browse.

★**Abbey's**　　　　　　　BOOKS
(Map p60; ☑02-9264 3111; www.abbeys.com.au; 131 York St; ☺8.30am-6pm Mon-Wed & Fri, 8.30am-8pm Thu, 9am-5pm Sat, 10am-5pm Sun; ☒Town Hall) Easily central Sydney's best bookshop,

Abbey's has many strengths. It's good on social sciences and has excellent resources for language learning, including a great selection of foreign films on DVD. There's also a big sci-fi and fantasy section.

★**Carriageworks Farmers Market**　MARKET
(Map p74; http://carriageworks.com.au; Carriageworks, 245 Wilson St, Eveleigh; ☺8am-1pm Sat;

Redfern) 🍴 Over 70 regular stallholders sell their goodies at Sydney's best farmers market, held in a heritage-listed railway workshop. Food and coffee stands do a brisk business and vegetables, fruit, meat and seafood from all over the state are sold in a convivial atmosphere.

★**Queen Victoria Building** SHOPPING CENTRE
(QVB; Map p60; 02-9265 6800; www.qvb.com.au; 455 George St; ⊙9am-6pm Mon-Wed, Fri & Sat, 9am-9pm Thu, 11am-5pm Sun; Town Hall) The magnificent QVB takes up a whole block and boasts nearly 200 shops on five levels. It's a High Victorian Gothic masterpiece – without doubt Sydney's most beautiful shopping centre.

★**Strand Arcade** SHOPPING CENTRE
(Map p60; www.strandarcade.com.au; 412 George St; ⊙9am-5.30pm Mon-Wed & Fri, 9am-9pm Thu, 9am-4pm Sat, 11am-4pm Sun; Town Hall) Constructed in 1891, the Strand rivals the QVB in the ornateness stakes. The three floors of designer fashions, Australiana and old-world coffee shops will make your short-cut through here considerably longer. Some of the top Australian designers have stores here.

★**Australian Wine Centre** WINE
(Map p60; 02-9247 2755; www.australianwinecentre.com; Goldfields House, 1 Alfred St; ⊙10am-7pm Sun & Mon, 9.30am-8pm Tue-Thu & Sat, 9.30am-9pm Fri; Circular Quay) This multilingual basement store is packed with quality Australian wine, beer and spirits. Despite its location, it's no tourist trap: smaller producers are well represented, along with a staggering range of prestigious Penfolds Grange wines and other bottle-aged gems. International shipping can be arranged.

Gleebooks BOOKS
(Map p74; 02-9660 2333; www.gleebooks.com.au; 49 Glebe Point Rd, Glebe; ⊙9am-7pm Sun-Wed, to 9pm Thu-Sat; Glebe) One of Sydney's best bookshops, Gleebooks' aisles are full of politics, arts and general fiction, and staff really know their stuff. Check its calendar for author talks and book launches.

Opal Minded JEWELLERY
(Map p60; 02-9247 9885; www.opalminded.com; 55 George St; ⊙9am-6.30pm; Circular Quay) This shop in the Rocks is one of several spots around here where you can stock up on the opal, that quintessential piece of Aussie bling. The quality and service are both excellent here.

Paddington Markets MARKET
(Map p72; 02-9331 2923; www.paddingtonmarkets.com.au; 395 Oxford St, Paddington; ⊙10am-4pm Sat; 333, 380) Originating in the 1970s, when they were drenched in the scent of patchouli oil, these markets are considerably more mainstream these days. They're still worth exploring for their new and vintage clothing, crafts and jewellery. Expect a crush.

Glebe Markets MARKET
(Map p74; www.glebemarkets.com.au; Glebe Public School, cnr Glebe Point Rd & Derby Pl; ⊙10am-4pm Sat; 431, 433, Glebe) The best of the west; Sydney's dreadlocked, shoeless, inner-city contingent beats a course to this crowded hippy-ish market. There are some great handcrafts and design on sale, as well as an inclusive, community atmosphere.

The Rocks Markets MARKET
(Map p60; www.therocks.com; George St; ⊙9am-3pm Fri, 10am-5pm Sat & Sun; Circular Quay) Under a long white canopy, the stalls at this sizeable weekend market are a focus for tourists, but there's not too much koala tat at all, and some excellent handicrafts. It's a good place to shop for gifts for the folks back home. It takes up the top end of George St, and winds through to Argyle St, where there are food options.

The Friday 'Foodies Market' offers more tasty treats.

Bondi Markets MARKET
(Map p78; www.bondimarkets.com.au; Bondi Beach Public School, Campbell Pde, Bondi Beach; ⊙9am-1pm Sat, 10am-4pm Sun; 380-382) On Sundays, when the kids are at the beach, their school fills up with Bondi characters rummaging through tie-dyed secondhand clothes, original fashion, books, beads, earrings, aromatherapy oils, candles, old records and more. There's a farmers market here on Saturdays.

Paddy's Markets MARKET
(Map p62; www.paddysmarkets.com.au; 9-13 Hay St; ⊙10am-6pm Wed-Sun; Paddy's Markets, Central) Cavernous, 1000-stall Paddy's is the Sydney equivalent of Istanbul's Grand Bazaar, but swap the hookahs and carpets for mobile-phone covers, Eminem T-shirts and cheap sneakers. Pick up a VB singlet for Uncle Bruce or wander the aisles in capitalist awe.

Red Eye Records MUSIC
(Map p60; 02-9267 7440; www.redeye.com.au; 143 York St; ⊙9am-6pm Mon-Wed, Fri & Sat, 9am-9pm Thu, 10am-5pm Sun; Town Hall) Partners of music freaks beware: don't let them descend the stairs into this shop unless you are prepared for a lengthy delay. The shelves are stocked with an irresistible collection of new, classic, rare and collectable LPs, CDs, crass rock T-shirts, books, posters and music DVDs.

Westfield Sydney MALL
(Map p60; www.westfield.com.au/sydney; 188 Pitt St Mall; ⊙9.30am-6.30pm Mon-Wed, Fri & Sat, 9.30am-9pm Thu, 10am-6pm Sun; ; St James) The city's most glamorous shopping mall is a bafflingly large complex gobbling up Sydney Tower and a fair chunk of Pitt St Mall. The 5th-floor food court is close to Sydney's best.

ℹ Information

EMERGENCY
Call 000 in all emergencies.

MEDICAL SERVICES
Kings Cross Clinic (02-9358 3066; www. kingscrossclinic.com.au; 13 Springfield Ave, Kings Cross; ⊙9am-1pm & 2.30-6pm Mon-Fri, 10am-1pm Sat; Kings Cross) General and travel-related medical services.

Royal Prince Alfred Hospital (RPA; 02-9515 6111; www.slhd.nsw.gov.au/rpa; Missenden Rd, Camperdown; 412)

St Vincent's Hospital (02-8382 1111; www. svhs.org.au; 390 Victoria St, Darlinghurst; Kings Cross)

POST
Australia Post (13 76 78; www.auspost.com. au) Has branches throughout the city.

TOURIST INFORMATION
City Host Information Kiosk (Map p60; www. cityofsydney.nsw.gov.au; cnr Pitt & Alfred Sts; ⊙9am-5pm; Circular Quay)

City Host Information Kiosk (Map p62; www. cityofsydney.nsw.gov.au; Dixon St; ⊙11am-5pm; Town Hall) Under a pagoda-style roof in the heart of Chinatown.

City Host Information Kiosk (Map p66; www. cityofsydney.nsw.gov.au; cnr Darlinghurst Rd & Springfield Ave, Kings Cross; ⊙9am-5pm; Kings Cross)

Hello Manly (Map p77; 02-9976 1430; www. hellomanly.com.au; East Esplanade, Manly; ⊙9am-5pm Mon-Fri, 10am-4pm Sat & Sun; Manly) This helpful visitors centre, just outside the ferry wharf and alongside the bus interchange, has free pamphlets covering the Manly Scenic Walkway (p75) and other Manly attractions, plus loads of local bus information. Staff can book a variety of tours, including quick 20-minute walking tours of Manly ($5).

Parramatta Heritage & Visitor Information Centre (02-8839 3311; www.discoverpar ramatta.com; 346a Church St, Parramatta; ⊙9am-5pm; Parramatta) Knowledgeable staff will point you in the right direction with loads of brochures, info on access for visitors with impaired mobility, and details on local Aboriginal cultural sites. They run free walking tours on Tuesdays and Fridays; phone to book.

Sydney Visitor Centre (Map p60; 02-8273 0000; www.sydney.com; cnr Argyle & Playfair Sts; ⊙9.30am-5.30pm; Circular Quay) In the heart of the Rocks, this branch has a wide range of brochures, and staff can book accommodation, tours and attractions.

Sydney Visitor Centre (Map p62; 02-8273 0000; www.sydney.com; Palm Grove, Darling Harbour; ⊙9.30am-5.30pm; Town Hall) Under the highway overpass, this branch has a wide range of brochures and events guides, and staff can book accommodation, tours and attractions. You will likely find it moved to a temporary location nearby while a major new Darling Harbour development is built on this site.

ℹ Getting There & Away

AIR
The vast majority of visitors to Sydney arrive at **Sydney Airport** (p511), 10km south of the city centre. It's Australia's busiest airport, handling flights from all over the country and the world. The international (T1) and domestic (T2 and T3) terminals are 4km apart on either side of the runway. Numerous airlines fly here from destinations throughout Australia, Asia, Oceania, Europe (with a stopover), North America and elsewhere.

Airlines
Virgin Australia (13 67 89; www.virgin australia.com), **Qantas** (13 13 13; www. qantas.com.au), **Tigerair** (1300 174 266; https://tigerair.com.au) and Qantas' budget alternative, **Jetstar** (131 538; www.jetstar. com), run frequent flights to and from other Australia capitals. **Regional Express** (REX; 13 17 13; www.rex.com.au), **AirLink** (02-6884 2435; www.airlinkairlines.com.au) and **FlyPelican** (02-4965 0111; www.flypelican. com.au) connect smaller centres.

For international airlines, see www.sydneyair port.com.au (click on 'Flight Information').

BUS
Long-distance coaches arrive at **Sydney Coach Terminal** (Map p70; 02-9281 9366;

www.sydneycoachterminal.com.au; Eddy Ave; ⊘8am-6pm, from 6am summer; ⓡCentral), underneath Central station. There's a tour desk here, internet terminals and same-day bag storage. From here you can walk along Eddy Ave for the suburban trains or turn left onto Pitt St for the major bus stop on Railway Sq.

Firefly (☑1300 730 740; www.fireflyexpress. com.au) Runs Sydney to Melbourne and on to Adelaide.

Greyhound (☑1300 473 946; www.greyhound. com.au) Has the most extensive nationwide network.

Murrays (☑13 22 51; www.murrays.com.au) Runs from Canberra to Sydney and the South Coast.

Port Stephens Coaches (☑02-4982 2940; www.pscoaches.com.au) Coaches to Newcastle and Nelson Bay.

Premier Motor Service (☑133 410; www. premierms.com.au) Runs Cairns to Eden, via Brisbane, Gold Coast and Sydney.

TRAIN

Trains chug into Sydney's Central station from as far north as Brisbane (13½ hours), and as far south as Melbourne (11½ hours).

NSW TrainLink (☑13 22 32; www.nswtrainlink. info) The government-owned train network, connecting Sydney to Canberra, Melbourne, Griffith, Broken Hill, Dubbo, Moree, Armidale and Brisbane.

Sydney Trains (☑13 15 00; www.sydneytrains. info) Connects Sydney with the Blue Mountains, South Coast and Central Coast.

❶ Getting Around

TO/FROM THE AIRPORT
Bus

Service from the airport is limited to the 400 route between Burwood and Bondi Junction (55 minutes), which departs roughly every 20 minutes.

Shuttle

Airport shuttles head to hotels and hostels in the city centre, and some reach surrounding suburbs and beach destinations. Operators include **KST Airporter** (☑02-8339 0155; www. kst.com.au; airport to CBD adult/child $17/12), **Airport Shuttle North** (☑02-9997 7767; www.asntransfers.com; to Manly 1/2/3 people $41/51/61) and **Manly Express** (☑02-8068 8473; www.manlyexpress.com.au; airport to Manly 1/2/3 people $40/55/65).

Taxi

Fares from the airport are approximately $45 to $55 to the city centre, $55 to $65 to North Sydney and $90 to $100 to Manly.

Train

Trains from both the domestic and international terminals, connecting into the main train network, are run by **Airport Link** (www.airportlink. com.au; adult/child $13.40/12 plus normal rail fare; ⊘5am-11.45pm, extended on Fri & Sat night). They're frequent (every 10 minutes), quick (13 minutes to Central) and easy to use, but airport tickets are charged at a hefty premium. If there are a few of you, it's cheaper to catch a cab. The cheapest alternative is to catch the bus to Rockdale station (route 400, 12 minutes) and then catch the regular train to Central (15 minutes).

CAR & MOTORCYCLE

Avoid driving in central Sydney if you can: there's a confusing one-way street system, parking's elusive and expensive (even at hotels), and parking inspectors, tolls and tow-away zones proliferate. Conversely, a car is handy for accessing Sydney's outer reaches (particularly the beaches) and for day trips.

Car Hire

Car-rental prices vary depending on season and demand. Read the small print to check age restrictions, exactly what your insurance covers and where you can take the car.

If you take a small car for a few days, you can hope to find deals around the $25 a day mark.

The big players have airport desks and city offices (mostly around William St, Darlinghurst). Local companies also compete on rates and quality.

For motorbike hire, try **Bikescape** (☑02-8123 0917; www.bikescape.com.au; cnr Parramatta Rd & Young St, Annandale; tours from $195; ⓡStanmore).

Car-rental companies:

Ace Rentals (☑02-9222 2595; www.acerental cars.com.au)

Avis (☑02-9246 4600; www.avis.com.au; 200 William St, Woolloomooloo; ⊘7.30am-6pm; ⓡKings Cross)

Bayswater Car Rental (☑02-9360 3622; www.bayswatercarrental.com.au; 180 William St, Woolloomooloo; ⊘7am-6.30pm Mon-Fri, 8am-3.30pm Sat, 9am-3.30pm Sun; ⓡKings Cross)

Budget (☑02-8255 9600; www.budget.com.au; 93 William St, Darlinghurst; ⊘7.30am-5.45pm Mon-Fri, to 3.45pm Sat & Sun; ⓡKings Cross)

Europcar (☑02-8255 9050; www.europcar. com.au)

Hertz (☑02-9360 6621; www.hertz.com.au; 65 William St, Darlinghurst; ⊘7.30am-5.30pm Mon-Fri, 8am-1pm Sat & Sun; ⓡSt James)

Jucy Rentals (☑1800 150 850; www.jucy. com.au)

Thrifty (☑ 02-8374 6177; www.thrifty.com.au; 85 William St, Darlinghurst; ⊙7.30am-5.30pm Mon-Fri, 7.30-11.30am Sat & Sun; ☒ Kings Cross)

Toll Roads

There are hefty tolls on most of Sydney's motorways and major links (including the Harbour Bridge, Harbour Tunnel, Cross City Tunnel and Eastern Distributor). The tolling system is electronic, meaning that it's up to you to organise an electronic tag or visitors' pass through any of the following websites: www.roam.com.au, www.roamexpress.com.au, www.tollpay.com.au or www.myetoll.com.au. Note that most car-hire companies can supply e-tags.

Vehicle Purchase

Sydney Travellers Car Market (☑ 02-9331 4361; www.sydneytravellerscarmarket.com. au; Level 2, Kings Cross Car Park, Ward Ave, Kings Cross; ⊙10am-5pm Mon-Sat; ☒ Kings Cross) In a car park, this is a useful forum for travellers looking to buy and sell vehicles for Australian road trips.

PUBLIC TRANSPORT

Sydneysiders love to complain about their public transport system, but visitors should find it surprisingly easy to navigate. The train system is the linchpin, with lines radiating out from Central station. Ferries head all around the harbour and up the river to Parramatta; light rail is useful for Pyrmont and Glebe; and buses are particularly useful for getting to the beaches.

Transport NSW (☑ 131 500; www.transportnsw.info) is the body that coordinates all of the state-run bus, ferry, train and light-rail services. You'll find a useful journey planner on its website.

The TripView app is very useful for real-time public transport info and journey planning.

Bus

Sydney Buses (☑ 131 500; www.sydney buses.info) has an extensive network, operating from around 5am to midnight, when less frequent NightRide services commence.

Bus routes starting with an X indicate limited-stop express routes; those with an L have limited stops.

There are several bus hubs in the city centre; these include Wynyard Park by Wynyard train station, Railway Square by Central train station, the QVB close to Town Hall station, and Circular Quay by the ferry and train stop of the same name.

Use your Opal card to ride buses; tap on when you board, and remember to tap off when you alight, or you'll be charged maximum fare.

Ferry

Most **Sydney Ferries** (Map p60; ☑ 131 500; www.transportnsw.info) operate between 6am and midnight. The standard Opal Card single fare for most harbour destinations is $5.74; ferries to Manly, Sydney Olympic Park and Parramatta cost $7.18.

Private company **Manly Fast Ferry** (☑ 02-9583 1199; www.manlyfastferry.com.au; adult one-way off-peak/peak $8.70/7.80) offers boats that blast from Circular Quay to Manly in 18 minutes.

Light Rail

➡ Trams run between Central station and Dulwich Hill, stopping at Chinatown, Darling Harbour, The Star casino, Sydney Fish Market, Glebe and Leichhardt en route.

OPAL CARD

Sydney's public transport network now runs on a smartcard system called Opal (www. opal.com.au).

The card can be obtained (for free) and loaded with credit (minimum $10) at numerous newsagencies and convenience stores across Sydney. When commencing a journey you'll need to touch the card to an electronic reader, which are located at the train station gates, near the doors of buses and light rail carriages, and at the ferry wharves. You then need to touch a reader when you complete your journey so that the system can deduct the correct fare. You get a discount when transferring between services, after a certain number of journeys in the week, and daily charges are capped at $15 ($2.50 on Sundays). You can use the Opal card at the airport train stations, but none of the aforementioned bonuses apply.

You can still buy single tickets (Opal single trip tickets) from machines at train stations, ferry wharves and light rail stops, or from the bus driver. These are more expensive than the same fare using the Opal card, so there's not much point unless you don't think you'll use $10 worth during your Sydney stay.

You can purchase a child/youth Opal card for those aged four to 15 years; they travel half-price. For student and pensioner discount Opal cards, you have to apply online.

→ Opal card fares cost $2.10 for a short journey and $3.50 for a longer one.

→ A second light rail line is being built and is due to open in 2019. It will run from Circular Quay down a now car-free George St right through the city centre to Central station, then veer east through Surry Hills, head past the SCG and Sydney Football Stadium and on to Kingsford, with a branch veering to Randwick.

Train

Sydney Trains (p111) has a large suburban railway web with relatively frequent services, although there are no lines to the northern or eastern beaches.

Trains run from around 5am to midnight – check timetables for your line. They run a little later at weekends. Trains are replaced by NightRide buses in the small hours. These mostly leave from Town Hall station or Central station.

Trains are significantly more expensive at peak hours, which are from 7am to 9am and 4pm to 6.30pm, Monday to Friday.

A short one-way trip costs $3.38 with an Opal card, or $2.36 off-peak.

TAXI

Metered taxis are easy to flag down in the central city and inner suburbs, except at changeover times (3pm and 3am).

Fares are regulated, so all companies charge the same. Flagfall is $3.60, with a $2.50 'night owl surcharge' after 10pm on a Friday and Saturday until 6am the following morning. After that the fare is $2.19 per kilometre, with an additional surcharge of 20% between 10pm and 6am nightly. There's also a $2.50 fee for bookings.

The ride-sharing app Uber operates in Sydney and is very popular. Other apps such as GoCatch offer ride-sharing and normal taxi bookings; which can be very handy on busy evenings.

For more on Sydney's taxis, see www.nswtaxi. org.au.

Major taxi companies:

Legion Cabs (✆13 14 51; www.legioncabs. com.au)

Premier Cabs (✆13 10 17; www.premiercabs. com.au)

RSL Cabs (✆02-9581 1111; www.rslcabs. com.au)

Silver Service (✆133 100; www.silverservice. com.au)

Taxis Combined (✆133 300; www.taxiscom bined.com.au)

WATER TAXI

Water taxis are a fast way to shunt around the harbour (Circular Quay to Watsons Bay in as little as 15 minutes). Companies will quote on any pick-up point within the harbour and the river, including private jetties, islands and other boats. All have a quote generator on their websites. It's much better value for groups than couples.

Fantasea Yellow Water Taxis (Map p64; ✆1800 326 822; www.yellowwatertaxis.com.au; Cockle Bay Wharf; ☉7.30am-10pm, prebooking required for service outside these hours) Set price for up to four passengers, then $10 per person for additional people. Sample fares from King Street Wharf: to Manly for $195, Cockatoo Island $100, Watsons Bay $135. There are shared services for closer destinations, which include Taronga Zoo ($30), the Fish Market ($25), Fort Denison ($25) and Luna Park ($15).

AROUND SYDNEY

Blue Mountains

With stunning natural beauty, the World Heritage region of the Blue Mountains is an Australian highlight. The slate-coloured haze that gives the mountains their name comes from a fine mist of oil exuded by the huge eucalypts that form a dense canopy across the landscape of deep, often inaccessible valleys and chiselled sandstone outcrops.

The foothills begin 65km inland from Sydney, rising to an 1100m-high sandstone plateau riddled with valleys eroded into the stone. There are eight connected conservation areas in the region, offering truly fantastic scenery, excellent bushwalks (hikes), Aboriginal engravings and all the canyons and cliffs you could ask for.

Although it's possible to day-trip from Sydney, consider staying a night (or longer) so you can explore the towns, do at least one bushwalk and eat at some of the excellent restaurants. The hills can be surprisingly cool throughout the year, so bring warm clothes.

🏃 Activities

The mountains are a popular cycling destination, with many people taking their bikes on the train to Woodford and then cycling downhill to Glenbrook, a ride of two to three hours. Cycling maps are available from the visitor centres.

Blue Mountains
Adventure Company   ADVENTURE
(✆02-4782 1271; www.bmac.com.au; 84a Bathurst Rd; abseiling from $150, canyoning $230, bushwalk-

Blue Mountains

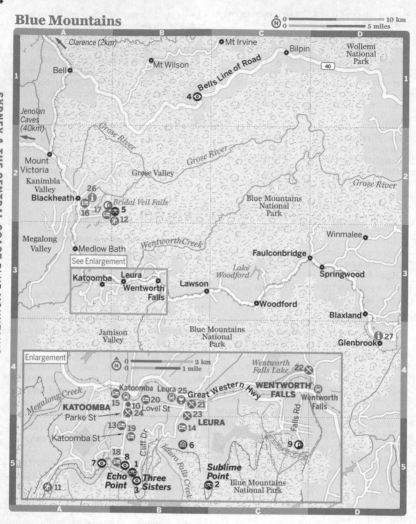

ing from $30) Located opposite Katoomba station, this set-up offers abseiling, canyoning, combinations of the two, bushwalking and rock climbing.

River Deep Mountain High ADVENTURE
(☑02-4782 6109; www.rdmh.com.au; abseiling $165-230, canyoning $230) ✎ A professional outfit rigorous about comfort and safety, these guys offer abseiling, canyoning and a combination of the two. Other options include a range of hiking and mountain-biking tours.

☞ Tours

Blue Mountains Explorer Bus BUS
(☑1300 300 915; www.explorerbus.com.au; 283 Bathurst Rd; adult/child $44/22; ⊙departures 9.45am-4.45pm) Significantly better than its average city equivalents, this is a useful way to get around the most popular Blue Mountains attractions. It offers hop-on, hop-off service on a Katoomba–Leura loop and also has a route taking in Wentworth Falls. Buses leave from Katoomba station every 30 to 60 minutes and feature entertaining live commentary. Various packages include admission to attractions.

Trolley Tours   BUS
(☑02-4782 7999; www.trolleytours.com.au; 76 Bathurst St; adult/child $25/15) This company runs a hop-on, hop-off bus barely disguised as a trolley, looping around 29 stops in Katoomba and Leura. The same company, located opposite Katoomba station, runs buses to the Jenolan Caves (p120) and various combination packages.

Festivals & Events

Yulefest   CHRISTMAS
(www.yulefest.com) These Christmas-style celebrations between June and August are held in hotels and restaurants across the region. While you can't expect snow and reindeer, it's as wintry as things get in this part of Australia.

Sleeping

There's a good range of accommodation in the Blue Mountains, but book ahead during winter and for Friday and Saturday nights. Leafy Leura is your best bet for romance, while Blackheath is a good base for hikers; Katoomba is more built-up, although it does have excellent hostels.

Caravan parks dot the area, and there are bush campsites in the parks; some free. The tourist offices have a comprehensive list.

ⓘ Information

For more information on the national parks (including walking and camping), contact the **NPWS Visitors Centre** at **Blackheath** (p120), about 2.5km off the Great Western Hwy and 10km north of Katoomba.

There are information centres on the Great Western Hwy at **Glenbrook** (☑1300 653 408; www.bluemountainscitytourism.com.au; Great Western Hwy; ⊙8.30am-4pm Mon-Sat, to 3pm Sun; ⊛) and at Echo Point in **Katoomba** (p119). Both can provide plenty of information and will book accommodation, tours and attractions.

ⓘ Getting There & Away

Trains (☑13 15 00; www.sydneytrains.info) run hourly from Sydney's Central Station to Katoomba and beyond via a string of Blue Mountains towns. The journey takes two hours to Katoomba and costs $8.30 on an Opal card.

To reach the Blue Mountains by road, leave Sydney via Parramatta Rd. At Strathfield detour onto the toll-free M4, which becomes the Great Western Hwy west of Penrith and takes you to all of the Blue Mountains towns. It takes approximately 1½ hours to drive from central Sydney to Katoomba. A scenic alternative is the Bells Line of Road.

WORTH A TRIP

BELLS LINE OF ROAD

This stretch of road between North Richmond and Lithgow is the most scenic route across the Blue Mountains and is highly recommended if you have your own transport. It's far quieter than the highway and offers bountiful views.

Bilpin, at the base of the mountains, is known for its apple orchards. The Bilpin Markets are held at the district hall every Saturday from 10am to noon.

Midway between Bilpin and Bell, the **Blue Mountains Botanic Garden Mount Tomah** (☑ 02-4567 3000; www.rbgsyd.nsw.gov.au; ⊙ 9am-5.30pm Mon-Fri, 9.30am-5.30pm Sat & Sun) 🌿 **FREE** is a cool-climate annexe of Sydney's Royal Botanic Garden where native plants cuddle up to exotic species, including some magnificent rhododendrons.

To access Bells Line from central Sydney, head over the Harbour Bridge and take the M2 and then the M7 (both have tolls). Exit at Richmond Rd, which becomes Black-town Rd, then Lennox Rd, then (after a short dog-leg) Kurrajong Rd and finally Bells Line of Road.

ℹ️ Getting Around

There are limited local bus services run by **Blue Mountains Bus** (☑ 02-4751 1077; www.bmbc. com.au), but it's often easiest to get the train between towns. In Katoomba and Leura, two competing hop-on, hop-off bus services are a good way to get around the main sights with little fuss, but walking between most of them isn't too burdensome either.

Wentworth Falls

As you head into the town of Wentworth Falls, you'll get your first real taste of Blue Mountains scenery: views to the south open out across the majestic Jamison Valley. The village itself is pleasant for a short potter along the main street.

◉ Sights

Wentworth Falls Reserve   WATERFALL, PARK
(Falls Rd; 🚉 Wentworth Falls) The falls that lend the town its name launch a plume of spray over a 300m drop. This is the starting point of several walking tracks, which delve into the sublime Valley of the Waters, with wa-terfalls, gorges, woodlands and rainforests. Be sure to stretch your legs along the 1km return to Princes Rock, which offers ex-cellent views of Wentworth Falls and the Jamison Valley. The reserve is 2.5km from Wentworth Falls station on the other side of the highway.

🍴 Eating

Nineteen23   MODERN AUSTRALIAN $$$
(☑ 0488 361 923; www.nineteen23.com.au; 1 Lake St; mains $30-40; ⊙ 6-10pm Thu & Fri, noon-3pm & 6-10pm Sat & Sun; 🐾📶) Wearing its 1920s

ambience with aplomb, this elegant dining room is a favourite with loved-up couples happy to gaze into each other's eyes over a lengthy degustation. While the food isn't particularly experimental, it's beautifully cooked and bursting with flavour. There's also upmarket B&B and self-catering accom-modation here.

Leura

Leura is the Blue Mountains' prettiest town, fashioned around undulating streets, well-tended gardens and sweeping Victorian verandahs. Leura Mall, the tree-lined main street, offers rows of country craft stores and cafes for the daily tourist influx. Leura adjoins Katoomba, slightly higher into the range.

◉ Sights

★Sublime Point   VIEWPOINT
(Sublime Point Rd) Southeast of Leura, this sharp, triangular outcrop narrows to a dra-matic lookout with sheer cliffs on each side. It's much, much quieter than Katoomba's more famous Echo Point, and on sunny days cloud shadows dance across the vast blue valley below.

**Leuralla NSW Toy &
Railway Museum**   MUSEUM, GARDENS
(☑ 02-4784 1169; www.toyandrailwaymuseum.com. au; 36 Olympian Pde; adult/child $15/5, gardens only $10/5; ⊙ 10am-5pm) The striking art deco man-sion that was once home to HV 'Doc' Evatt, the third president of the UN General Assem-bly, is jam-packed with an incredible array of collectables – from grumpy Edwardian baby

dolls to *Dr Who* figurines to a rare set of Nazi propaganda toys. Railway memorabilia is scattered throughout the handsome gardens.

🛏 Sleeping

★ Greens of Leura
B&B $$

(☑ 02-4784 3241; www.thegreensleura.com.au; 24-26 Grose St; r $175-220; P ♿ 🛜) On a quiet street parallel to the Mall, this pretty centenarian house set in a lovely garden offers genuine hospitality and five rooms named after British literary figures. All are individually decorated; some have four-poster beds and spas. There's a great lounge with attached courtyard. Rates include breakfast as well as afternoon tea with sparkling wine and other goodies.

★ Broomelea
B&B $$

(☑ 02-4784 2940; www.broomelea.com.au; 273 Leura Mall; r $175-225; P ♿ @ 🛜) A consummately romantic Blue Mountains B&B, this fine Edwardian house offers a cheery welcome, four-poster beds, lovely gardens, a great verandah, an open fire and a snug lounge. There's also a self-contained cottage for families and plenty of other comforts. There's a two-night minimum stay at weekends.

🍴 Eating & Drinking

Leura Garage
MEDITERRANEAN $$

(☑ 02-4784 3391; www.leuragarage.com.au; 84 Railway Pde; dishes $15-29; ⊗ noon-9pm or later; 🛜) In case you were in any doubt that this hip cafe-bar was once a garage, the suspended mufflers and stacks of old tyres press the point. At dinner the menu shifts gears to rustic shared plates served on wooden slabs, including deli-treat-laden pizza.

Silk's Brasserie
MODERN AUSTRALIAN $$$

(☑ 02-4784 2534; www.silksleura.com; 128 Leura Mall; 2-/3-course dinner midweek $59/69, weekends $65/75; ⊗ noon-3pm & 6-10pm) A warm welcome awaits at Leura's long-standing fine diner. Despite its contemporary approach, it's a brasserie at heart, so the serves are generous and flavoursome. It's a comfortable space, its chessboard tiles and parchment-coloured walls creating an inviting semiformal atmosphere. Make sure you save room for the decadent desserts.

Alexandra Hotel
PUB

(☑ 02-4782 4422; www.alexandrahotel.com.au; 62 Great Western Hwy; ⊗ 10am-10pm Sun-Thu, to midnight Fri & Sat; 🛜) On the main road, the Alex is a gem of an old pub, with lots of character. Join the locals at the pool table or listening to DJs and live bands on the weekend. There's also a more-than-decent line in pub food.

Katoomba

Swirling, otherworldly mists, steep streets lined with art deco buildings, astonishing valley views, and a quirky miscellany of restaurants, buskers, artists, bawdy pubs and classy hotels – Katoomba, the biggest town in the mountains, manages to be bohemian and bourgeois, embracing and distant all at once. It's got a great selection of accommodation and is a logical base, particularly if you're on a budget or travelling by public transport.

⊙ Sights & Activities

★ Echo Point
VIEWPOINT

(Echo Point Rd) Echo Point's cliff-top viewing platform offers a magical prospect of the area's most essential sight, a rocky trio called the **Three Sisters**. Warning: the point draws vast, serenity-spoiling tourist gaggles, their idling buses farting fumes into the mountain air – arrive early or late to avoid them. The surrounding parking is expensive, so park a few streets back and walk. There's a tourist office (p119) here.

Scenic World
CABLE CAR

(☑ 02-4780 0200; www.scenicworld.com.au; cnr Violet St & Cliff Dr; adult/child $39/21; ⊗ 9am-5pm) This long-time favourite, the Blue Mountains' most touristy attraction, offers spectacular views. Ride the glass-floored Skyway gondola across the gorge and then ride the vertiginously steep Scenic Railway, billed as the steepest railway in the world, down the 52-degree incline to the Jamison Valley floor. From here you can wander a 2.5km forest boardwalk (or hike the 12km, six-hour-return track to the Ruined Castle rock formation) before catching a cable car back up the slope.

The 686 bus stops at Echo Point and here, and this is on both the hop-on, hop-off bus routes, but it's only a 2.5km walk from Echo Point, and quite a pleasant one too.

Waradah Aboriginal Centre
CULTURAL CENTRE

(☑ 02-4782 1979; www.waradahaboriginalcentre.com.au; 33-37 Echo Point Rd; show adult/child $20/15; ⊗ 9am-5pm) This gallery and shop displays some exceptional examples of

Aboriginal art alongside tourist tat such as painted boomerangs and didgeridoos. However, the main reason to visit is to catch one of the 15-minute shows. Held throughout the day, they provide an interesting and good-humoured introduction to Indigenous culture.

★ **Golden Stairs Walk** HIKING
(Glenraphael Dr) If you have your own transport, you can tackle the Golden Stairs Walk, a less congested route down to the Ruined Castle (a famous rock formation) than the track leading from Scenic World (p117). It's a steep, exhilarating trail leading down into the valley (about 8km, five hours return). Take plenty of water.

To get there, continue along Cliff Dr from Scenic World for 1km and look for Glenraphael Dr on your left. It quickly becomes rough and unsealed. Watch out for the signs to the Golden Stairs on the left after a couple of kilometres.

🛏 Sleeping

No 14 HOSTEL $
(☑02-4782 7104; www.no14.com.au; 14 Lovel St; dm $28, r with/without bathroom $79/69; ⊜@☎) Resembling a cheery share house, this small hostel has a friendly vibe, colourful bedding and helpful managers. There's no TV, so guests tend to talk to actually each other. A basic breakfast is included. The verandah deck is a top spot to chill out.

Flying Fox HOSTEL $
(☑02-4782 4226; www.theflyingfox.com.au; 190 Bathurst Rd; camp sites per person $21, dm $32, r $82-84; P⊜☎) 🍃 The owners are travellers at heart and have endowed this hostel with an endearing home-away-from-home feel. There's no party scene here – just mulled wine and Tim Tams in the lounge, free breakfasts and a weekly pasta night. Dorms are high-ceilinged and spacious; private rooms are pleasant and a decent deal. The garden has spaces to pitch tents and a nice outlook.

★ **Blue Mountains YHA** HOSTEL $$
(☑02-4782 1416; www.yha.com.au; 207 Katoomba St; dm $32-37, d with/without bathroom $134/119; P⊜@☎) Behind the austere brick exterior of this popular 200-bed hostel are dorms and family rooms that are comfortable, light filled and spotlessly clean. Facilities include a lounge (with an open fire), a pool

table, an excellent communal kitchen and an outdoor space with BBQ. Staff can book activities and tours for you. HI discounts apply.

Lurline House B&B $$
(☑02-4782 4609; www.lurlinehouse.com.au; 122 Lurline St; r $160-200; P⊜❄☎) Handsome, spacious rooms with four-poster beds and dark wood furniture are true to the Federation features of this sizeable, excellently run guesthouse. Other rooms come with spa bath, and there's a lounge where guests can help themselves to fruit or drinks. Rooms are immaculately presented, but it's a cheerful, laid-back place. Breakfast is an impressive event, with an open kitchen.

Lilianfels HOTEL $$$
(☑02-4780 1200; www.lilianfels.com.au; 5-19 Lilianfels Ave; r $330-525; P⊜❄@☎☀☎) Very close to Echo Point and enjoying spectacular views, this luxury resort has 85 rooms, the region's top-rated restaurant (Darley's; dinner Tuesday to Sunday, three courses $125) and an array of facilities including a spa, heated indoor and outdoor pools, a tennis court, a billiards/games room, a library and a gym. Rooms come in a variety of categories; some have excellent vistas. Decor is classically plush.

🍴 Eating

True to the Bean CAFE $
(☑0438 396 761; www.facebook.com/truetothebean; 123 Katoomba St; waffles $3-6; ☉6.30am-4pm Mon-Sat, 8am-4pm Sun; ☎☑) The Sydney obsession with single-estate coffee has made its way to Katoomba's main drag in the form of this tiny espresso bar. There's a small but sweet selection of food, with the likes of bircher muesli, baked potatoes and waffles. In good old milk-bar style, it also does a variety of shakes in unusual flavours.

Station Bar & Woodfired Pizza PIZZA $$
(☑02-4782 4782; www.stationbar.com.au; 287 Bathurst Rd; pizzas $18-26; ☉noon-midnight; ☎) Bringing visitors and locals together, this is an upbeat space that combines three happy things – craft beer, pizza and live music – in a very likeable space next to the train station. It only does pizzas (plus a couple of salads), but they're delicious, with offbeat gourmet toppings. The compact trackside courtyard is great for a summer pint in good company.

> ### DON'T MISS
>
> ## BLUE MOUNTAINS BUSHWALKING
>
> For tips on walks to suit your level of experience and fitness, call the National Parks' Blue Mountains Heritage Centre (p120) in Blackheath, or the information centres in Glenbrook (p115) or Katoomba. All three sell a variety of walk pamphlets, maps and books.
>
> Note that the bush here is dense and that it can be easy to become lost – there have been deaths. Always leave your name and walk plan with the Katoomba police or at the national parks centre. The police and the national parks and information centres all offer free personal locator beacons and it's strongly suggested you take one with you, especially for longer hikes. Remember to carry lots of clean drinking water and plenty of food.
>
> The two most popular bushwalking areas are the Jamison Valley, south of Katoomba, and the Grose Valley, northeast of Katoomba and east of Blackheath. Top choices include the Golden Stairs Walk and the Grand Canyon Walk.
>
> One of the most rewarding long-distance walks is the 45km, three-day Six Foot Track from Katoomba along the Megalong Valley to Cox's River and on to the Jenolan Caves. It has camp sites along the way.

🛈 Information

Echo Point Visitors Centre (☑ 1300 653 408; www.bluemountainscitytourism.com.au; Echo Point; ⊘ 9am-5pm) A sizeable centre with can-do staff and a gift shop.

Blackheath

The crowds and commercial frenzy fizzle considerably 10km north of Katoomba in neat, petite Blackheath. The town measures up in the scenery stakes, and it's an excellent base for visiting the Grose and Megalong Valleys. There are several memorable lookouts around town, and trailheads for some top hikes.

◎ Sights & Activities

Evans Lookout VIEWPOINT
(Evans Lookout Rd) Signposted 4km from the highway in Blackheath, this lookout presents a magnificent perspective of sandstone cliffs dropping to the valley and canyon below. It's one of the most scenic of the Blue Mountains lookouts, and is also a trailhead for the majestic Grand Canyon bushwalk, perhaps the area's best half-day excursion.

★ Grand Canyon Walk HIKING
(Evans Lookout Rd) This spectacular 5km circuit plunges you from Evans Lookout into the valley for a memorable walk along the 'Grand Canyon' before looping back up to the road about 1.5km short of the lookout. Though strenuous on the descent and ascent, it's one of the area's shadier walks and takes most people around three hours.

🛏 Sleeping

★ Glenella Guesthouse GUESTHOUSE $$
(☑ 02-4787 8352; www.glenella.com.au; 56 Govetts Leap Rd; r $140-195, f $230-270; 🅿 🐾 ❄ 🛜) Gorgeous Glenella has been functioning as a guesthouse since 1912 and is now operated with enthusiasm and expertise by a young British couple who make guests feel welcome. There are seven comfortable bedrooms, an attractive lounge and a stunning dining room where a truly excellent breakfast (included in rates) is served. Marvellous period features include ceiling mouldings and lead lighting.

The owners also operate a **bunkhouse** (☑ 02-4787 6688; www.sportsbunkhouse.com.au; 60 Govetts Leap Rd; dm/s/d/tw $35/60/75/80; 🅿 😷 🛜) around the back.

Jemby-Rinjah Eco Lodge CABIN $$
(☑ 02-4787 7622; www.jemby.com.au; 336 Evans Lookout Rd; cabins $225-265; 🅿 😷 🛜) 🌱 Near Evans Lookout, these attractive, rustic eco-cabins are lodged so deeply in the gums and bottlebrush that it feels as though you're in very remote bushland, with just the rustle of leaves and the chirp of birds for company. All the one- and two-bedroom weatherboard cabins are equipped with kitchenette and crockery; the deluxe model has a Japanese hot tub.

🍴 Eating

Vesta BISTRO $$$
(☑ 02-4787 6899; www.vestablackheath.com.au; 33 Govetts Leap Rd; mains $29-38; ⊘ 5-10pm Wed-Fri, 12.30-3pm & 5-10pm Sat & Sun, closed

Wed summer;) Feeling the sting of a Blue Mountains cold snap? It's easy to warm up with Vesta's century-old wood-fired bakery oven roaring in the background, serving up hearty plates of roasted meats (all free range, grass fed and local), accompanied by share plates of homemade charcuterie and bottles of Aussie wine, to a boisterous local crowd.

Ashcrofts   MODERN AUSTRALIAN $$$
(02-4787 8297; www.ashcrofts.com; 18 Govetts Leap Rd; mains dinner $37-40, lunch $20-23; ⊗6-10pm Thu, 11.30am-2.30pm & 6-10pm Fri, 8am-2.30pm & 6-10pm Sat & Sun) This acclaimed restaurant is a long-time Blue Mountains favourite. The snug dining room is a charming spot to dip into the short but polished menu, which changes seasonally and favours creative pairings and delicious, generous textures. Weekend breakfasts are a great time to drop by, too.

❶ Information

Blue Mountains Heritage Centre (02-4787 8877; www.nationalparks.nsw.gov.au; ⊗9am-4.30pm) The helpful, official NPWS visitor centre has information about local walks and national parks. It's at the end of Govetts Leap Rd, near the Govetts Leap viewpoint, and has a small gallery attached.

Beyond Blackheath

Far from other Blue Mountains attractions, the limestone **Jenolan Caves** (02-6359 3911; www.jenolancaves.org.au; Jenolan Caves Rd, Jenolan; adult/child from $35/24; ⊗tours 9am-5pm) is one of the most extensive, accessible and complex systems in the world – a vast network that's still being explored. Several caves are open to the public, and tours cycle between them. There are various multi-tour packages and discounts.

Named Binoomea (Dark Places) by the Gundungurra tribe, the caves took shape 400 million years ago. White explorers first passed through in 1813 and the area was protected from 1866.

THE CENTRAL COAST

The largest town along the coast between Sydney and Newcastle is the transport and services hub of Gosford. Nearby, relaxed Avoca has a lovely beach and an old cinema, while Terrigal has a beautiful crescent-shaped

beach with good surf, a bustling town centre and a variety of top spots to refuel. A series of saltwater 'lakes' spreads north up the coast between Bateau Bay and Newcastle, including deep, placid Lake Macquarie.

⊙ Sights

Bouddi National Park   NATIONAL PARK
(02-4320 4200; www.nationalparks.nsw.gov.au; vehicle access $8) At this spectacular park, short walking trails lead to isolated beaches and dramatic lookouts from where you can experience the annual whale migration between June and November. There are camp sites ($24 to $33 for two people) at Little Beach, Putty Beach and Tallow Beach; book ahead. Only the Putty Beach site has drinkable water.

Australian Reptile Park   ZOO
(02-4340 1022; www.reptilepark.com.au; Pacific Hwy, Somersby; adult/child $35/19; ⊗9am-5pm) Get up close to koalas and pythons, and watch funnel-web spiders being milked (for the production of antivenin) and a Galapagos tortoise being fed. There are wonderful tours for kids. It's signposted off the M1 Pacific Motorway, or you could get a cab from Gosford station.

**Brisbane Water
National Park**   NATIONAL PARK
(02-4320 4200; www.nationalparks.nsw.gov.au; Woy Woy Rd, Kariong; vehicle access at Girrakool & Somersby Falls picnic areas $8) Bordering the Hawkesbury River, 9km southwest of Gosford, this park, despite its name, is mostly sandstone outcrops and forest, with only a short Brisbane Water frontage. It's famed for its explosions of spring wildflowers and Guringai stone engravings, the most impressive gallery of which is the Bulgandry Aboriginal Engraving Site, 3km south of the Pacific Hwy on Woy Woy Rd. A favourite retreat for Sydneysiders is the pretty village of Pearl Beach, on the southeastern edge of the park.

⨳ Sleeping

There are numerous holiday lets right up and down the coast, as well as a wide selection of hotel and motel accommodation. National parks offer rustic camping.

✕ Eating

Woy Woy Fishermen's Wharf   SEAFOOD $$
(02-4341 1171; www.woywoyfishermenswharf.com.au; The Boulevarde, Woy Woy; restaurant mains

$18-30; ⊙ takeaway 11am-4pm Sun-Wed, 11am-7pm Thu-Sat, restaurant 8-11am & noon-3pm Mon-Wed, 8-11am & noon-8.30pm Thu-Sat, noon-3pm Sun) 🖋 The Cregan family has been serving its outstanding fish and chips since 1974. Grab them takeaway and enjoy in the park (like the pelicans, who are fed daily at 3pm) or take a table at the smart restaurant, which dangles over the mangrove-y water. There's also a good fish shop here. It's just a couple of minutes from the train station.

Pearls on the Beach MODERN AUSTRALIAN $$$
(📞 02-4342 4400; www.pearlsonthebeach.com.au; 1 Tourmaline Ave, Pearl Beach; mains $41; ⊙ noon-2.30pm & 6-10pm Thu-Sun) Share tasty, unpretentious, flavoured Modern Australian dishes at this highly rated restaurant, housed in a comfortable whitewashed cottage right on the sand at idyllic little Pearl Beach. Save room for the very tempting dessert menu. Opening hours extend in January and reduce in winter.

ℹ Information

Central Coast Visitor Centre (📞 02-4343 4444; www.visitcentralcoast.com.au; 52 The Avenue, Kariong; ⊙ 9am-5pm Mon-Fri, 9.30am-3.30pm Sat, 10am-2pm Sun)

ℹ Getting There & Away

Driving from Sydney, you can choose to head straight up the M1 Pacific Motorway towards Newcastle (via various Central Coast exits) or meander along the coast.

Gosford is a stop on the Newcastle and Central Coast line, with frequent trains from Sydney and Newcastle (both: adult/child $8.30/4.15, 1½ hours). There are several other Central Coast stops, including Woy Woy. Trains also stop at Wondabyne within Brisbane Water National Park upon request (rear carriage only).

Local buses connecting the various towns and beaches are operated by **Busways** (📞 02-4368 2277; www.busways.com.au) and **Redbus** (📞 02-4332 8655; www.redbus.com.au).

THE HUNTER VALLEY

A filigree of narrow lanes criss-crosses this verdant valley, but a pleasant country drive isn't the main motivator for visitors – sheer decadence is. The Hunter is one big gorge fest: fine wine, gourmet restaurants, boutique beer, chocolate, cheese, olives, you name it. Bacchus would surely approve.

The Hunter wineries are welcoming to novices and refreshingly attitude-free. They nearly all have a cellar door with free or cheap tastings.

The Hunter Valley is exceedingly hot during summer, so – like its shiraz – it's best enjoyed in the cooler months.

⊙ Sights

Most attractions lie in an area bordered to the north by the New England Hwy and to the south by Wollombi/Maitland Rd, with the main cluster of wineries and restaurants in Pokolbin. For spectacular views and a more chilled-out pace, head to the vineyards northwest around Broke and Singleton.

Lake's Folly WINERY
(📞 02-4998 7507; www.lakesfolly.com.au; 2416 Broke Rd, Pokolbin; redeemable tasting fee $5; ⊙ 10am-4pm) Try the highly acclaimed cabernet blend and chardonnay, which are both grown, vintaged and bottled on the estate. These small-production wines tend to sell out, so the cellar door is closed for four to six months of the year, normally from mid-December. Call ahead.

First Creek Wines WINERY
(📞 02-4998 7293; www.firstcreekwines.com.au; 600 McDonalds Rd, Pokolbin; ⊙ 9.30am-5pm Mon-Sat, to 4pm Sun) Very centrally located, this winery has an exciting team of winemakers who produce elegant, age-worthy styles. The expertly crafted drops offer great value. Tastings are free and the staff is super friendly.

Petersons WINERY
(📞 02-4990 1704; www.petersonswines.com.au; 552 Mt View Rd, Mt View; ⊙ 9am-5pm Mon-Sat, 10am-5pm) Though this winery has a cellar door on the main road in Pokolbin, it's worth heading up to this location, where the ultra-friendly staff have more time for a chat and to guide you through the tasty, classically styled wines. It's a very welcoming experience. The Back Block shiraz is particularly delicious.

Small Winemakers Centre WINERY
(📞 02-4998 7668; www.smallwinemakers.com.au; 426 McDonalds Rd, Pokolbin; redeemable tasting fee $5; ⊙ 10am-5pm) With a sweet location by a little dam, this has a good attitude and showcases more than 30 varieties of wine from five great little estates, some of which don't have cellar doors. Generous tasting sessions.

Hunter Valley

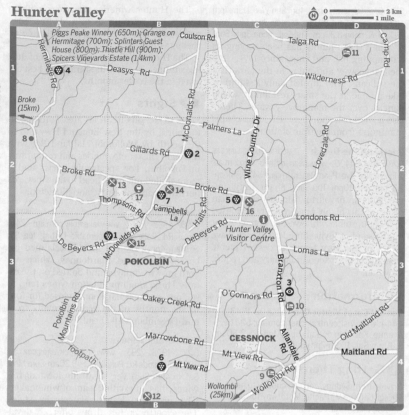

Hunter Valley

◉ Sights
1 Audrey Wilkinson Vineyard	B3
2 First Creek Wines	B2
3 Hunter Beer Co	C3
4 Keith Tulloch Winery	A1
5 Lake's Folly	C2
6 Petersons	B4
7 Small Winemakers Centre	B2

◉ Activities, Courses & Tours
8 Two Fat Blokes	A2

◉ Sleeping
9 Australia Hotel	C4
10 Hunter Valley YHA	C3

◉ Eating
11 Tonic	D1
12 Bistro Molines	B4
13 Enzo	B2
EXP.	(see 8)
14 Hunter Valley Smelly Cheese Shop	B2
15 Hunters Quarter	B3
Muse Kitchen	(see 4)
16 Muse Restaurant	C2

◉ Drinking & Nightlife
Goldfish Bar & Kitchen	(see 14)
17 Harrigan's	B2

Audrey Wilkinson Vineyard WINERY
(☎ 02-4998 1866; www.audreywilkinson.com.au; 750 DeBeyers Rd, Pokolbin; ☺ 10am-5pm) Enjoy the expansive views with a picnic at this hilltop cellar door. It's a sublime setting for one of the valley's oldest vineyards (first planted in 1866) and there's an interesting historic display. An extensive range of wines is available for tasting, with a free list, a $5 list and a $10 one. There are cottages here

(weekend rates $500 to $850) if you want to stay.

Piggs Peake Winery
WINERY
(✆02-6574 7000; www.piggspeake.com; 697 Hermitage Rd, Pokolbin; ⊙10am-5pm) Priding itself on nontraditional winemaking practices, this winery produces limited-edition, unwooded wines that are causing quite a stir in the viniculture world. The names of the wines come straight from the pig-pun: try the prosecco-style Prosciutto or, for those on a tight budget, the $10-a-bottle Swill.

Hunter Beer Co
BREWERY
(Potters Resort; ✆02-4991 7922; www.hunterbeerco.com; Wine Country Dr, Nulkaba; tours $10; ⊙10am-5pm, tours 4pm daily plus noon Sat & Sun) This is the Hunter's first microbrewery, just on the northern outskirts of Cessnock near the YHA. Join a tour to see how it all works and get three tastings. The tasting room has 10 beers on tap and the complex's pub also has the company's beers on draught.

🏃 Activities

Balloon Aloft
BALLOONING
(✆02-4990 9242; www.balloonaloft.com; $339) Take to the skies for a sunrise hot-air-balloon ride over the vineyards. The jaunt lasts for about an hour and is followed up with bubbles and breakfast at Peterson House Winery.

👉 Tours

If no one's volunteering to stay sober enough to drive, don't worry: there are plenty of winery tours available, ranging from minibuses that just do basic transport between wineries to full-on gourmet extravaganzas. Some operators will collect you in Sydney or Newcastle for a lengthy day trip. See www.winecountry.com.au.

★ Two Fat Blokes
FOOD, WINE
(✆0414 316 859; www.twofatblokes.com.au; 1616 Broke Rd, Pokolbin; half-day $69, full day $165-249) A barrel of fun and taste, these immersive gourmet experiences are a great way to discover the region. Upbeat guided tours take you to some excellent vineyards, but there's plenty more besides the wine, with cheese, beer, delicious lunches and plenty of entertaining background information. A standout.

Hunter Valley Boutique Wine Tours
WINE
(✆0419 419 931; www.huntervalleytours.com.au) Reliable and knowledgeable small-group

tours from $80 per person for a half-day (three cellars) and from $115 for a full day including lunch.

Kangarrific Tours
WINE
(✆0431 894 471; www.kangarrifictours.com; full-day $129) This small-group tour departs from Sydney and promises the Hunter's most diverse itinerary. Taste everything from wine to gelato and have morning tea with the eponymous roos.

★✲ Festivals & Events

Big international names (think Springsteen, Stones) regularly drop by for weekend concerts at the larger vineyards. If there's something special on, accommodation books up well in advance. Check for info at www.winecountry.com.au.

🛏 Sleeping

Numerous wineries offer accommodation, and there are lots of boutique self-catering places. Prices shoot up savagely on Friday and Saturday nights, when two-night minimum stays are common and weddings also put a strain on available accommodation. Many places don't accept children.

★ Hunter Valley YHA
HOSTEL $
(✆02-4991 3278; www.yha.com.au; 100 Wine Country Dr, Nulkaba; dm $35-37, r with/without bathroom $108/94; 🅿😊📶🏊) At the end of a long day's wine tasting or grape picking, there's plenty of bonhomie around the barbecue and pool at this attractive refurbished hostel. Dorms are four-berth and spotless, and there's a sweet verandah, as well as hire bikes and a nearby brewery-pub. Rooms can get hot. It's on the northern edge of Cessnock. HI discount applies.

Australia Hotel
PUB $
(✆02-4990 1256; www.australiahotel.com.au; 136 Wollombi Rd, Cessnock; s/tw with shared bathroom $45/60, r weekends $95; 🅿😊📶) The rooms above this local watering hole look a bit weary but are perfectly adequate for resting your woozy wine head. The sparkling new bathrooms will make you feel much better in the morning.

Grange on Hermitage
B&B $$
(✆02-4998 7388; www.thegrangeonhermitage.com.au; 820 Hermitage Rd, Pokolbin; r $195-260, cottages $390-460; 🅿😊❄📶) Spacious grounds, eucalypts and vines make this a most appealing place to relax. Rooms are enormous,

with modern amenities, kitchenette and spa bath, and there are lots of lovely touches by the friendly owners, like fresh flowers and just-baked muffins delivered to your door as part of breakfast. There are also two cottages sleeping four to six.

Thistle Hill
B&B $$

(☑02-6574 7217; www.thill.com.au; 591 Hermitage Rd, Pokolbin; r $285; P ❂ ❀ 🔊 ⊠) This idyllic 8-hectare property features rose gardens, a lime orchard, a vineyard, a self-contained cottage sleeping five and a luxurious guesthouse with six double rooms. Rooms and common areas have an elegant French provincial sensibility and are strikingly attractive. There's a great lounge and deck by the pool. Breakfast (continental midweek, cooked at weekends), wine and cheese are all supplied.

★ Tonic
BOUTIQUE HOTEL $$$

(☑02-4930 9999; www.tonichotel.com.au; 251 Talga Rd, Lovedale; d incl breakfast $270-350, apt $500-700; P ❂ ❀ 🔊 ⊠) The polished-concrete floors and urban minimalist style of this handsome complex work a treat in the vivid Hunter light. There's a lovely outlook over a dam into the sunset from the impressive rooms and two-bedroom apartment. Bathrooms and beds are great, breakfast supplies are placed in your room, and an excellent common area and genial host make for an exceptional experience.

No children under 15 years.

Splinters Guest House
B&B $$$

(☑02-6574 7118; www.splinters.com.au; 617 Hermitage Rd, Pokolbin; cottages $370-550; P ❂ ❀ 🔊 ⊠) These handsome cottages are some of the Hunter's best, with beautiful decor and smart furniture. The owners care for their guests very well, with a generous breakfast in the fridge plus wine and cheese, a dessert wine and other details. Cottages sleep six; some smaller ones were being built in late 2016.

✕ Eating

There's some excellent eating to be done in the Hunter, which has a reputation as a gourmet destination. Many restaurants don't open midweek. Bookings are essential. Many wineries have restaurants.

Hunter Valley Smelly Cheese Shop
DELI $

(☑02-4998 6713; www.smellycheese.net.au; Roche Estate, 2144 Broke Rd, Pokolbin; mains $12-18; ◷10am-5pm Sun-Thu, to 5.30pm Fri & Sat) Along with the great range of stinky desirables fill-

ing the cheese counter, there are deli platters, pizzas, burgers and baguettes to go, as well as a freezer of superb gelato. There are good daily specials and a cheery attitude despite the besieging hordes. There's another branch in Pokolbin Village.

Enzo
CAFE $$

(☑02-4998 7233; www.enzohuntervalley.com.au; cnr Broke & Ekerts Rds, Pokolbin; breakfast mains $16-31, lunch $23-37; ◷9am-4pm Mon-Fri, 8.30am-4pm Sat & Sun; 🔊) Claim a table by the fireside in winter or in the garden in summer to enjoy the rustic dishes served at this popular Italian-inflected cafe in a lovely setting. The food is reliably excellent, and David Hook winery is here, so you can add a tasting to your visit.

★ Muse Restaurant
MODERN AUSTRALIAN $$$

(☑02-4998 6777; www.musedining.com.au; 1 Broke Rd, Pokolbin; 2/3 courses $75/95; ◷noon-3pm Sat & Sun, 6.30-10pm Wed-Sat; 🍴) Inside the dramatic Hungerford Hill winery complex is the area's highest-rated restaurant, offering sensational contemporary fare and stellar service in an attractive modern space. Presentation is exquisite, especially for dishes on the degustation menu, which is compulsory on Saturday ($125, with wine $185). Vegetarians get their own menu (two/three courses $60/80).

★ Muse Kitchen
EUROPEAN $$$

(☑02-4998 7899; www.musedining.com.au; Keith Tulloch Winery, cnr Hermitage & Deasys Rds, Pokolbin; mains $34-36; ◷noon-3pm Wed-Sun, plus 6-9pm Sat; 🔊🍴) For a fabulous lunch, head to this relaxed incarnation of the Hunter's top restaurant, Muse (p124). Dine outside on a seasonal menu of European bistro food inspired by the vegetables, fruit and herbs grown up the road. Save room for the exquisite dessert selection and wine tasting at the Keith Tulloch (☑02-4998 7500; www.keithtullochwine.com.au; tastings $5; ◷10am-5pm) cellar door.

Hunters Quarter
MODERN AUSTRALIAN $$$

(☑02-4998 7776; www.huntersquarter.com; Cockfighter's Ghost, 576 De Beyers Rd, Pokolbin; mains $36-44; ◷6-11pm Mon, noon-3.30pm & 6-11pm Thu-Sat, noon-3.30pm Sun; 🔊) With a lovely outlook over the vines from the array of floor-to-ceiling windows, this place is bustling but intimate. Flavoursome dishes are produced from high-quality ingredients; the house-smoked salmon is a taste sensation. A good range of wines by the glass lets you taste your way around this and nearby vineyards. Monday is 'locals' night', when two/three courses are $60/75.

EXP.
MODERN AUSTRALIAN $$$

(☑02-4998 7264; www.exprestaurant.com.au; 1596 Broke Rd, Pokolbin; 5/8 courses $85/110; ⊙noon-2.30pm & 6-9pm Wed-Sat, noon-2.30pm Sun) Local lad Frank Fawkner had an impressive restaurant career in the region and elsewhere before opening his own place in Oakvale winery. His subtle, fresh, texture-rich degustation menus are wowing the Sydney food mafia, and with good reason. You'll need to book ahead.

Bistro Molines
FRENCH $$$

(☑02-4990 9553; www.bistromolines.com.au; Tallavera Grove, 749 Mt View Rd, Mt View; mains $38-44; ⊙noon-3pm Thu, Sun & Mon, noon-3pm & 7-9pm Fri & Sat) Set in the Tallavera Grove winery, this French restaurant run by the Hunter Valley's most storied chef has a carefully crafted, seasonally driven menu that is nearly as impressive as the vineyard views. There's lovely seating in the paved courtyard, and an elegant exterior. Daily specials supplement the menu.

🍷 Drinking & Nightlife

Wollombi Tavern
PUB

(☑02-4998 3261; www.wollombitavern.com.au; 2994 Great North Rd, Wollombi; ⊙10am-10pm Mon-Thu, 10am-midnight Fri, 9.30am-midnight Sat, 9am-10pm Sun) This fabulous little pub at the road junction in Wollombi is the home of Dr Jurd's Jungle Juice, a dangerous brew of port, brandy and wine. On weekends, the tavern is a favourite pit stop for motorbike clubs (the nonscary sort). You can camp for free in the meadow (no showers).

Goldfish Bar & Kitchen
BAR

(www.thegoldfish.com.au; Roche Estate, cnr Broke & McDonalds Rds, Pokolbin; ⊙noon-11pm Mon-Thu, to 1am Fri & Sat, to 10pm Sun; 🐾) All wined out? Try a classic cocktail on the spacious terrace or in the lounge of this popular bar, a great place to hang out. There's an impressive spirit selection and it also does a decent line in food. There's live music most Saturday nights.

Harrigan's
PUB

(☑02-4998 4300; www.harrigansirishpub.com. au; 2090 Broke Rd, Pokolbin; ⊙9am-10pm or later, bistro from 7am; 🐾) A comfortable Irish pub with beef-and-Guinness pies on the menu, a sprawling beer garden and live bands most weekends. Sitting on the deck here is a convivial Hunter Valley pleasure.

WORTH A TRIP

HAWKESBURY RIVER

Less than an hour from Sydney, the tranquil Hawkesbury River flows past honeycomb-coloured cliffs, historic townships and riverside hamlets into bays and inlets and between a series of national parks, including **Ku-ring-gai Chase** (p76) and **Brisbane Water** (p120).

Accessible by train, the riverside township of Brooklyn is a good place to hire a houseboat and explore the river. Further upstream, a narrow forested waterway diverts from the Hawkesbury and peters down to the chilled-out river town of Berowra Waters, where a handful of businesses, boat sheds and residences cluster around the free, 24-hour ferry across Berowra Creek.

Tinshed Brewery
MICROBREWERY

(www.facebook.com/tinshedbrewerydungog; 109 Dowling St, Dungog; ⊙11am-10pm Fri-Sun) This new craft brewery is run by an enthusiastic young local and features 44-gallon-drum tables and a series of delicious beers; let the staff talk you through what's on tap. Good sharing platters of cold meats are available to soak it all up. It's near the train station in handsome Dungog, which makes a good stop if you're heading north.

ℹ Information

Hunter Valley Visitor Centre (☑02-4993 6700; www.huntervalleyvisitorcentre.com.au; 455 Wine Country Dr, Pokolbin; ⊙9am-5pm Mon-Sat, to 4pm Sun; 🐾) Has a huge stock of leaflets and info on valley accommodation, attractions and dining.

ℹ Getting There & Away

BUS

Rover Coaches (☑02-4990 1699; www. rovercoaches.com.au) has five buses heading between Newcastle and Cessnock (1¼ hours) on weekdays and two on Saturday; no Sunday service. Other buses head to Cessnock from the train stations at Morisset (one hour, two daily) and Maitland (50 minutes, hourly or better Monday to Saturday, six Sunday).

CAR

From Sydney, you can head straight up the M1 motorway, then head to the valley via the exit near Gosford (which allows you to take the scenic route up through Wollombi), the Cessnock

DON'T MISS

HUNTER WINE TRAILS

Home to some of the oldest vines (dating from the 1860s) and biggest names in Australian wine, the Hunter is known for its semillon, shiraz and, increasingly, chardonnay.

The valley's 150-plus wineries range from small-scale, family-run affairs to massive commercial operations. Most offer free tastings, although some charge a small fee, usually redeemable against a purchase.

Grab a copy of the free Hunter Valley Official Map & Touring Guide from the visitor centre (p125) at Pokolbin and use its handy map to plot your course, or just follow your nose, hunting out the tucked-away small producers.

If you're buying cases, be prepared to negotiate a little. Thirteen for the price of 12 is common, as is throwing in a six-pack of a previous vintage. Most wineries offer significant discounts if you join their wine club, which means you have to buy another case or two in the next year.

DrinkWise Australia recommends that in order to comply with the breath-alcohol limit of 0.05, men who are driving should drink no more than two standard drinks in the first hour and then no more than one per hour after that (women, who tend to reach a higher blood-alcohol concentration faster than men, should drink only one standard drink in the first hour). Wineries usually offer 20mL tastes of wine – five equal one standard drink.

---

turn-off, or the Hunter Expressway (which begins near Newcastle).

TRAIN

Sydney Trains has a line heading through the Hunter Valley from Newcastle ($4.82, 50 minutes). Branxton is the closest station to the vineyards, although only Maitland has bus services to Cessnock.

🛈 Getting Around

There are several options for exploring without a car. The **YHA hostel** (p123) hires bikes, as do **Grapemobile** (☑ 02-4998 7660; www.grape mobile.com.au; 307 Palmers Lane, Pokolbin; per 8hr $45; ☉10am-6pm) and **Hunter Valley Cycling** (☑ 0418 281 480; www.hunter valleycycling.com.au; per 1/2 days $35/50). **Sutton Estate** (☑ 0448 600 288; www.sutton estateelectricbikehire.com; 381 Deasys Rd, Pokolbin; half/full day $50/65) rents electric bikes. The other choices are to take a tour (p123) or a **taxi** (☑ 02-6572 1133; www.taxi co.com.au).

Vineyard Shuttle (☑ 02-4991 3655; www.vine yardshuttle.com.au; ☉ 6pm-midnight Tue-Sat) Offers a door-to-door service between Pokolbin accommodation and restaurants.

NEWCASTLE

POP 308,300

The port city of Newcastle may be one-10th the size of Sydney, but Australia's second-oldest city punches well above its weight. Superb surf beaches, historical architecture and a sun-drenched climate are only part of its charm. Fine dining, hip bars, quirky boutiques, a diverse arts scene and a laid-back attitude combine to make it well worth a couple of days of your time.

Newcastle had a rough trot at the end of the 20th century, with a major earthquake and the closure of its steel and shipbuilding industries. Its other important industry, shipping coal, has a decidedly sketchy future too, but Novocastrians always seem to get by with creative entrepreneurship and a positive attitude.

◉ Sights

Newcastle has a constantly evolving and morphing small-gallery scene; check at the tourist office (p131) for the latest pop-up.

★ **Newcastle Maritime Museum** MUSEUM (☑ 02-4929 2588; www.maritimecentrenewcastle. org.au; Lee Wharf, 3 Honeysuckle Dr, Honeysuckle Precinct; adult/child $10/5; ☉10am-4pm Tue-Sun) Newcastle's nautical heritage is on show at this museum, appropriately located on the harbour. The intriguing exhibition provides an insight into the soul of the city, and there's a good dose of local history, covering shipwrecks (including the 2007 grounding of the *Pasha Bulker*, on which there's a film), lifeboats and the demise of the steelworks and shipbuilding industries. A quick intro by the staff is great for setting the scene.

★**Newcastle Art Gallery**   GALLERY
(🖉02-4974 5100; www.nag.org.au; 1 Laman St; ☺10am-5pm Tue-Sun) **FREE** Ignore the brutalist exterior, as inside this remarkable regional gallery are some wonderful works. There's no permanent exhibition; displays rotate the gallery's excellent collection, whose highlights include art by Newcastle-born William Dobell and John Olsen as well as Brett Whiteley and modernist Grace Cossington Smith.

Olsen's works, in particular, bring an explosive vibrancy to the gallery, with his generative organic swirls flamboyantly representing water-based Australian landscapes. Look out for his ceiling painting by the central stairwell and his brilliant *King Sun and the Hunter*, a tribute to the essence of his native city, painted at age 88 in 2016.

Newcastle Museum   MUSEUM
(🖉02-4974 1400; www.newcastlemuseum.com.au; 6 Workshop Way; ☺10am-5pm Tue-Sun, plus Mon school holidays; ⛟) **FREE** This attractive museum in the restored Honeysuckle rail workshops tells a tale of the city from its Indigenous Awabakal origins to its rough-and-tumble social history, shaped by a cast of convicts, coal miners and steelworkers. Exhibitions are interactive and engaging, ranging from geology to local icons like Silverchair and the Newcastle Knights. If you're travelling with kids, check out hands-on science centre Supernova and the hourly sound-and-light show on the steelmaking process. There's also a cafe.

Fort Scratchley   FORT
(🖉02-4974 5033; www.fortscratchley.com.au; Nobbys Rd; tunnel tour adult/child $12.50/6.50, full tour $16/8; ☺10am-4pm Wed-Mon, last tour 2.30pm) **FREE** Perched above Newcastle Harbour, this intriguing military site was constructed during the Crimean War to protect the city against a feared Russian invasion. During WWII the fort returned fire on a Japanese submarine, making it the only Australian fort to have engaged in a maritime attack. It's free to enter, but the guided tours are worth taking, as you venture into the fort's labyrinth of underground tunnels. Head to the shop for tickets or for a self-guided-tour brochure.

Nobby's Head   VIEWPOINT
Originally an island, this headland at the entrance to Newcastle's harbour was joined to the mainland by a stone breakwater built by convicts between 1818 and 1846; many of those poor souls were lost to the wild seas during construction. The walk along the spit towards the lighthouse and meteorological station is exhilarating.

King Edward Park   PARK
(Reserve Rd) This magnificently landscaped ocean-side park offers sweeping views, lots of grass and plenty of shady spots for lounging around. The best views are from the obelisk at the top.

★**Merewether Aquarium**   PUBLIC ART
(Henderson Pde, Merewether) Not an aquarium in the traditional sense, this pedestrian underpass has been charmingly transformed into a pop-art underwater world by local artist Trevor Dickinson. There are numerous quirky details, including the artist himself as a diver. Find it at the southern end of Merewether Beach, opposite the Surfhouse top entrance.

🏃 Activities

★**Bathers Way**   WALKING
(www.visitnewcastle.com.au) This scenic coastal path from Nobby's Beach to Glenrock Reserve winds past swathes of beach and fascinating historical sites including Fort Scratchley (p127) and the Convict Lumber Yard. Interpretative signs describing Indigenous, convict and natural history dot the 5km trail. North of Bar Beach, it connects with the high, swirling **Memorial Walk**, which offers magical sea views.

🛌 Sleeping

Newcastle has a good choice of midrange accommodation, from remodelled pub rooms to B&Bs and business hotels. Hostels and camping are also available.

Newcastle Beach YHA   HOSTEL $
(🖉02-4925 3544; www.yha.com.au; 30 Pacific St; dm/s/d $39/70/94; ⊜@⛉) It may have the look of a grand English mansion, but this sprawling, brick, heritage-listed YHA has the ambience of a laid-back beach bungalow, with great common spaces and airy, comfortable dorms. Just a minute away from the surf, it offers complimentary bodyboard use, surfboard hire, and BBQ nights and weekly pub meals for free. HI discount.

★**Junction Hotel**   BOUTIQUE HOTEL $$
(🖉02-4962 8888; www.junctionhotel.com.au; 204 Corlette St, The Junction; r $139-189;

Newcastle

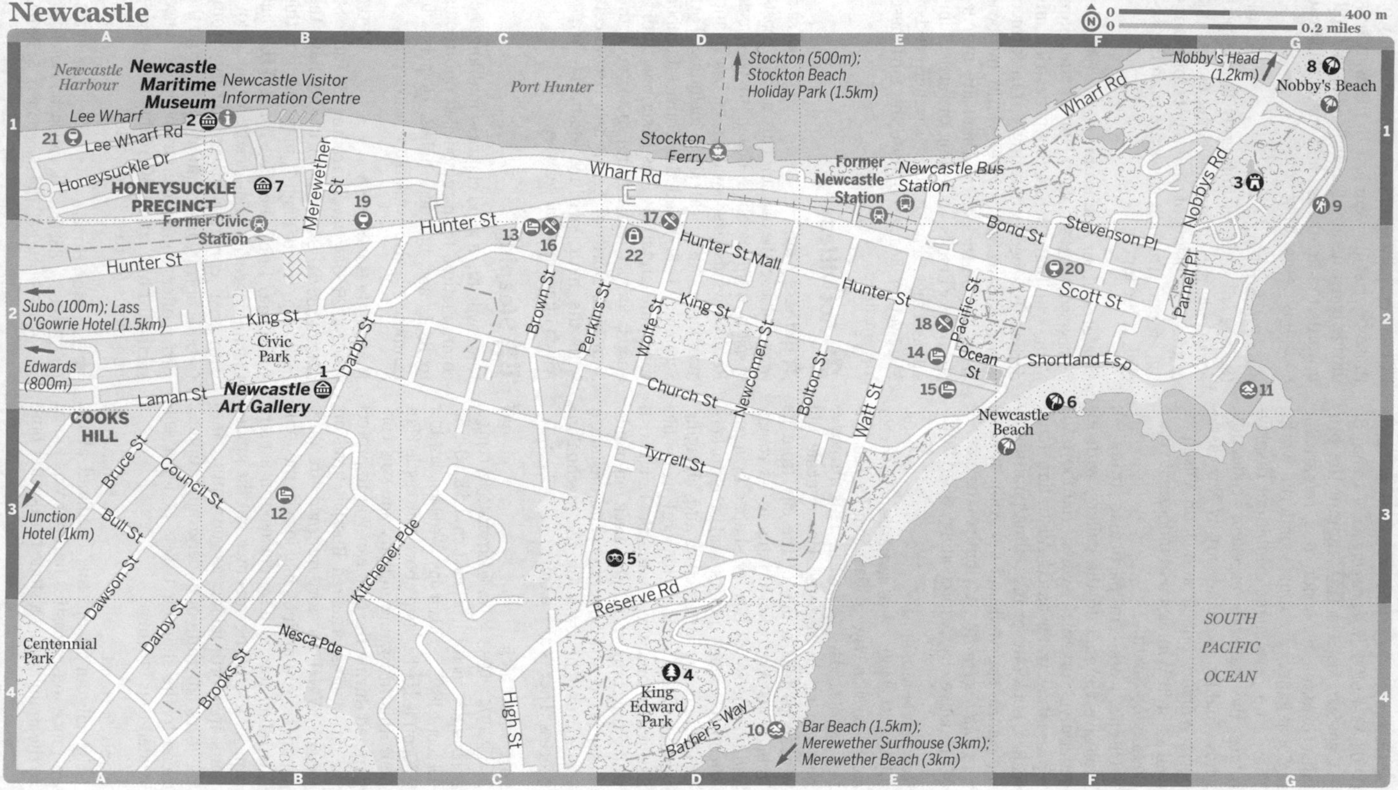

Newcastle Harbour

Port Hunter

SOUTH PACIFIC OCEAN

Newcastle Maritime Museum

Newcastle Visitor Information Centre

HONEYSUCKLE PRECINCT

Former Civic Station

Former Newcastle Station

Newcastle Bus Station

Stockton Ferry

Newcastle Art Gallery

Civic Park

COOKS HILL

Centennial Park

King Edward Park

Newcastle Beach

Nobby's Beach

Nobby's Head (1.2km)

Stockton (500m); Stockton Beach Holiday Park (1.5km)

Subo (100m); Lass O'Gowrie Hotel (1.5km)

Edwards (800m)

Junction Hotel (1km)

Bar Beach (1.5km); Merewether Surfhouse (3km); Merewether Beach (3km)

Street labels: Lee Wharf Rd, Honeysuckle Dr, Merewether St, Wharf Rd, Nobbys Rd, Parnell Pl, Stevenson Pl, Scott St, Bond St, Pacific St, Ocean St, Shortland Esp, Hunter St, Watt St, Bolton St, Newcomen St, Church St, King St, Wolfe St, Perkins St, Brown St, Darby St, Laman St, Council St, Bruce St, Bull St, Dawson St, Brooks St, High St, Reserve Rd, Tyrrell St, Kitchener Pde, Nesca Pde, Bathers Way, King Edward Park, Hunter St Mall, Hunter St

Map markers: 1, 2, 3, 4, 5, 6, 7, 8, 9, 10, 11, 12, 13, 14, 15, 16, 17, 18, 19, 20, 21, 22

0 400 m
0 0.2 miles

Newcastle

◉ ❊ 🛜) The upstairs of this suburban pub has been transformed with nine flamboyantly appointed rooms featuring African-animal themes and wacky colours. All have generous-sized beds and flashy bathrooms with disco lights and little privacy. Well located among the Junction's boutiques and cafes, it's just a 10-minute walk to the beach.

★ **Crown on Darby**   APARTMENT $$
(☑ 02-4941 6777; www.crownondarby.com.au; 101 Darby St; apt midweek $176-205, weekend $194-286; P ◉ ❊ 🛜) Close to cafes and restaurants, this excellent modern complex of 38 apartments is right on Newcastle's coolest street. Studios are reasonably sized and have kitchenettes. One-bedroom apartments are a worthwhile upgrade, with interconnecting options, full kitchens and huge living rooms; some have spa baths. Both open and closed balconies are available, so request your preference. Parking is a reasonable $15.

★ **Lucky Hotel**   BOUTIQUE HOTEL $$
(☑ 02-4925 8888; www.theluckyhotel.com.au; 237 Hunter St; r $145-180; ◉ ❊ 🛜) A slick but sympathetic revamp has turned this grand old 1880s dame into an upbeat, modern place to stay above a great pub. The 28 light-filled rooms are small but tastefully decorated, with mod touches like luxe bedding and toiletries, not to mention a hand-painted quote about luck in case you need the inspiration. Corridors showcase black-and-white photos of old Newcastle.

Novotel Newcastle Beach   HOTEL $$$
(☑ 02-4037 0000; www.novotelnewcastlebeach. com.au; 5 King St; r $279-334; P ◉ ❊ @ 🛜) Ideally situated for Newcastle Beach, this breezy hotel seamlessly checks out the business guests on Friday morning and welcomes families that afternoon. Rooms are moderately sized but stylishly furnished. It's worth the upgrade to the superior rooms, which offer floor-to-ceiling windows and better views. Accommodation and breakfast are free for under-16s. Wi-fi is free if you join the loyalty program.

✖ Eating

Newcastle has a thriving eating scene. Darby St is a local icon for cafes, Thai and Vietnamese restaurants and pizza, while the harbourfront has lots of options, particularly in the Honeysuckle Precinct near the tourist office. In Hamilton, eateries cluster along Beaumont St, and the beaches have plenty of nearby options too.

One Penny Black   CAFE $
(☑ 02-4929 3169; www.onepennyblack.com.au; 196 Hunter St; mains $14-18; ⊙ 6.30am-4.30pm; 🛜 ♪) It's perpetually popular for a reason – here you'll probably have to queue for an excellent espresso or filter coffee, served by staff who know their stuff. Devotees also rave about the toasties and fabulous breakfast platters.

★ **Edwards**   MODERN AUSTRALIAN $$
(☑ 02-4965 3845; www.theedwards.com.au; 148 Parry St; breakfast & lunch dishes $14-21, dinner

DON'T MISS

NEWCASTLE'S BEACHES

At the eastern end of town, surfers and swimmers adore **Newcastle Beach**; the **ocean baths** (www.newcastle.nsw.gov.au; Shortland Esplanade) `FREE` are a mellow alternative, encased in wonderful multicoloured art deco architecture. There's a shallow pool for toddlers and a backdrop of heaving ocean and chugging cargo ships. Surfers should goofy-foot it to **Nobby's Beach**, just north of the baths – the fast left-hander known as the Wedge is at its northern end.

South of Newcastle Beach, below King Edward Park, is Australia's oldest ocean bath, the convict-carved **Bogey Hole**. It's an atmospheric place to splash about in when the surf's crashing over its edge. The most popular surfing breaks are at **Bar Beach** and **Merewether Beach**, two ends of the same beach a bit further south.

The city's famous surfing festival, **Surfest** (www.surfest.com; Merewether Beach; ☺ Feb), takes place in February each year.

plates for 2 $41-60; ☺ 7am-midnight Tue-Sat, to 10pm Sun; ☎) If new Newcastle had a beating heart, it would be found at this happening West End bar-cafe-diner, stylishly flaunting its warehouse chic on this light-industrial street. It's the place to be at all hours, for delicious egg breakfasts, casual lunches, late-night bar snacks, great wines by the glass and succulent roast meats from the wood-fired oven.

Co-owned by Silverchair bass player Chris Joannou, this used to be a drive-through dry cleaners (you can still drop off your dirty clothes, or chuck them in the coin laundry). The complex also includes a motorcycle workshop and a music shop.

Momo CAFE $$
(☑ 02-4926 3310; www.facebook.com/momo wholefood.newcastle; 227 Hunter St; dishes $12-22; ☺ 7.30am-3pm; ☎ ☑) In a striking, high-ceilinged former bank building that at first seems too big for it, this friendly cafe specialises in wholefoods, offering mostly vegetarian and vegan choices. Textures, colours and flavours make the dishes very appealing, and influences range from Himalayan to local. The owners are considering opening some evenings.

Merewether Surfhouse CAFE, STEAK $$
(☑ 02-4918 0000; www.surfhouse.com.au; Henderson Pde, Merewether; mains cafe $15-20, bar $18-24, restaurant $32-39; ☺ cafe 7am-4pm, pizza 4-11pm Mon-Fri, 11.30am-11pm Sat & Sun, restaurant 11.30am-late Wed-Sat, to 4pm Sun) Watch the action on Merewether Beach from one of the many spaces in this architecturally notable complex. The swanky promenade cafe offers coffee and lazy breakfasts, and later in the day there's pizza and gelato. Head to the top-floor restaurant, which has floor-to-ceiling windows, and nails surf or turf at fine-dining prices; it's also a top spot for a sundowner.

★ **Subo** MODERN AUSTRALIAN $$$
(☑ 02-4023 4048; www.subo.com.au; 551d Hunter St; 5 courses $88; ☺ 6-10pm Wed-Sun; ☑) Book in advance for a table at tiny Subo, an innovative, highly lauded restaurant serving light, exquisite food with a contemporary French influence. The restaurant exclusively serves a five-course menu that changes seasonally.

Restaurant Mason MODERN AUSTRALIAN $$$
(☑ 02-4926 1014; www.restaurantmason.com; 3/35 Hunter St; set menus $80-125, mains $46; ☺ 6-9pm Tue & Wed, noon-3pm & 6-10pm Thu-Sat; ☑) There's a certain summery feel to this fine-dining restaurant, with tables placed under the plane trees outside and a dining space that opens to the elements. There's a modern-French feel to the menu, though a variety of other regional and avant-garde influences are present. Dishes make the most of fresh produce, including wild-foraged local herbs. There are separate tasting menus for vegetarians.

🍷 Drinking & Nightlife

★ **Coal & Cedar** COCKTAIL BAR
(☑ 0499 345 663; www.coalandcedar.com; 380-382 Hunter St; ☺ 4pm-midnight Mon-Sat, to 10pm Sun) Pull up a stool at the long wooden bar in this Prohibition-style speakeasy; early on it was so underground it didn't even publish the address. Now the secret's out, you'll find Newcastle's finest drinking old-fashioneds to the blues. The door can be tough to spot;

it's to the right of the stairs. If it's shut, text them to open up.

Lucky Hotel   PUB
(✐02-4925 8888; www.theluckyhotel.com.au; 237 Hunter St; ⊘11am-11pm Mon-Thu, to 1am Fri & Sat, to 10pm Sun; ☎) With a genuinely convivial vibe and a handsome interior of exposed brick and wooden fittings, this is a successfully characterful refurbishment of an old pub. On offer are a decent line in smoked meats, good drinks, pleasant outdoor high tables and comfy rooms upstairs.

Grain Store   BREWERY
(✐02-4023 2707; www.grainstorenewcastle.com. au; 64 Scott St; ⊘11am-10pm Tue-Thu, to 1am Fri & Sat, to 9.30pm Sun; ☎) Once the grain and keg store for the old Tooheys beer factory, this rustic brewery-cafe is an atmospheric place to refresh yourself with one of the 21 eclectic Australian-brewed craft beers on tap. There's all-day food, with pizzas, burgers and American-style meat dishes featuring prominently.

Honeysuckle Hotel   PUB
(✐02-4929 1499; www.honeysucklehotel.com. au; Lee Wharf, Honeysuckle Dr, Honeysuckle Precinct; ⊘10am-11pm Mon-Thu, to midnight Fri & Sat, to 10pm Sun; ☎) The deck at this waterfront place, located in a cavernous but cool converted warehouse looking across at the port, is a perfect spot for a sundowner. Sip Caribbean flavours under the rafters in the Rum Bar upstairs on Friday and Saturday, and there's usually live music at the weekends too.

☆ Entertainment

Newcastle Knights   SPECTATOR SPORT
(✐02-4028 9100; www.newcastleknights.com.au; McDonald Jones Stadium, Turton Rd, New Lambton) The pride of Newcastle, the Knights are the local rugby-league side. They've had a rough trot of late, but there's plenty of passion around them here, and going to a game is a great experience. In summer, the stadium is used by the Newcastle Jets A-league soccer team.

Lass O'Gowrie Hotel   LIVE MUSIC
(✐02-4962 1248; www.lassogowriehotel.com.au; 14 Railway St, Wickham; ☎) Built in 1877, this is the oldest pub in Newcastle and has been the heart of the local music scene for the last 15 years. See local original acts here from Wednesday to Sunday nights. It's just north of the new main train station at Wickham.

Shopping

Emporium   ARTS, FASHION
(www.renewnewcastle.org; 185 Hunter St; ⊘10am-4pm Wed & Sat, to 5pm Thu & Fri) 🖉 On the ground floor of the former David Jones department store are boutiques and galleries filled with a treasure trove of locally made art, fashion, furniture and design.

Newcastle City Farmers & Makers Market   MARKET
(✐02-4934 3013; www.newcastlecityfarmers market.com.au; Newcastle Showground, Griffiths Rd; ⊘8am-1pm Sun) A fabulous showcase of Hunter Valley gourmet produce, plus international delights like Tibetan dumplings and buttery French pastries.

ⓘ Information

Newcastle Visitor Information Centre
(✐02-4929 2588; www.visitnewcastle.com. au; Lee Wharf, 3 Honeysuckle Dr, Honeysuckle Precinct; ⊘10am-4pm Tue-Sun) Shares the Maritime Museum building by the water.

ⓘ Getting There & Away

AIR
Port Stephens Coaches (p132) has frequent buses stopping at the **airport** (NTL; ✐02-4928 9800; www.newcastleairport.com.au; 1 Williamtown Dr, Williamtown) en route between Newcastle (40 minutes) and Nelson Bay (one hour). A taxi from the airport to Newcastle city centre costs about $60. **Fogg's** (✐0410 581 452; www.foggsshuttle.com.au), **Hunter Valley Day Tours** (✐02-4951 4574; www. huntervalleydaytours.com.au) and **Newcastle Airport Transfers** (✐02-4928 9822; www. newcastleairport.com.au; 1/2/4 people $45/50/65) operate shuttles to Newcastle and the surrounding region.

Jetstar (✐13 15 38; www.jetstar.com) flies to/ from Melbourne, the Gold Coast and Brisbane; **Qantas** (✐13 13 13; www.qantas.com.au) flies to/from Brisbane; **Regional Express** (Rex; ✐13 17 13; www.rex.com.au) flies to/from Sydney and Taree; and **Virgin Australia** (✐13 67 89; www.virginaustralia.com) flies to/from Brisbane and Melbourne.

BUS
Nearly all long-distance buses stop at **Newcastle Bus Station**, at the eastern end of town, but most will only stop at the new **transport interchange** at Wickham once it opens in 2017.

Busways (📞02-4983 1560; www.busways. com.au) At least two buses daily to Tea Gardens ($20.50, 1½ hours), Hawks Nest ($20.90, 1¾ hours), Bluey's Beach ($28, two hours), Forster ($32, 3¼ hours) and Taree ($35, four hours).

Greyhound (📞1300 473 946; www.greyhound. com.au) Two to three daily coaches to/from Sydney ($32 to $35, 2¾ hours), Port Macquarie ($57 to $62, four hours), Coffs Harbour ($79 to $86, six to seven hours), Byron Bay ($140, 10½ hours) and Brisbane ($171, 13½ to 15 hours).

Port Stephens Coaches (📞02-4982 2940; www.pscoaches.com.au) Regular buses to Anna Bay (1¼ hours), Nelson Bay (1½ hours), Shoal Bay (1½ hours) and Fingal Bay (two hours).

Premier Motor Service (📞13 34 10; www. premierms.com.au) Daily coaches to/from Sydney ($34, three hours), Port Macquarie ($47, 3¾ hours), Coffs Harbour ($58, six hours), Byron Bay ($71, 11 hours) and Brisbane ($76, 14½ hours).

Rover Coaches (📞02-4990 1699; www.rover coaches.com.au) Four buses to/from Cessnock (1¼ hours) on weekdays and two on Saturday.

TRAIN

Sydney Trains (p111) will run regular services to Newcastle's new transport interchange at Wickham (scheduled to open in 2017) from Gosford ($8.30, 1½ hours) and Sydney ($8.30, 2¾ hours). Meanwhile, trains stop at Hamilton,

with connecting buses into the centre. A line also heads to the Hunter Valley; Branxton ($6.50, 50 minutes) is the closest stop to wine country.

Getting Around

BUS

Newcastle has an extensive network of **local buses** (📞13 15 00; www.newcastlebuses. info). There's a fare-free bus zone in the inner city between 7.30am and 6pm. Otherwise you need to tap on and off with an Opal card or pay the fare to the driver. The main depot is next to the former Newcastle train station in the east of the city.

FERRY

Stockton Ferry (www.transportnsw.info; adult/ child $2.60/1.30) Leaves every half-hour from Queens Wharf from 5.15am to about 11pm to the suburb of Stockton.

TRAIN

From mid-2017, all train services to Newcastle will terminate at the new station at Wickham. From here, shuttle bus 110 (in future, a light-rail service) runs into the centre, stopping at the former train stations of Civic and Newcastle. The shuttle bus is included in your rail fare. Until the Wickham station is finished, trains are stopping at Hamilton.

Byron Bay & North Coast New South Wales

Includes ➡

Why Go?

Lovely, lazy beach towns and pristine national parks leap-frog each other all the way up this stupendous stretch of coast. Inland, lush farmland and ancient tracts of World Heritage–listed rainforest do the same.

Providing a buffer between New South Wales' capital-city sprawl to the south and Queensland's Gold Coast strip up over the border, northern NSW offers an altogether simpler way of life. Farmers rub shoulders with big-city sea-changers and post-hippie alternative lifestylers here: if you're looking for stellar local produce, a single-origin coffee or a psychic reading, you won't be disappointed. And if you're searching for a surf break, rest assured there will be an awesome one, right around the next corner.

Best Places to Eat

➡ Fleet (p164)

➡ Three Blue Ducks at the Farm (p161)

➡ Paper Daisy (p164)

➡ Roadhouse (p162)

➡ Beachwood Cafe (p154)

➡ Bill's Fishhouse (p142)

Best Places to Sleep

➡ 28° Byron Bay (p160)

➡ Halcyon House (p164)

➡ Boogie Woogie Beach House (p139)

➡ Anchorage (p136)

➡ Sails Motel (p164)

When to Go
Byron Bay

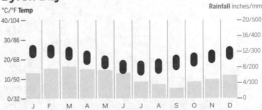

Jun & Jul Winter brings whales to the coast, lanterns to Lismore and big musos to Byron Bay.

Sep–Nov Returning whales, swimming weather and blooming jacarandas.

Dec–Apr Life's a beach; just book for it well ahead in January.

Byron Bay & Northern New South Wales Highlights

1 Myall Lakes National Park (p137) Laying claim to your own stretch of empty beach in coastal wilderness.

2 Dorrigo National Park (p148) Delving into the ancient World Heritage–listed Gondwana rainforest.

3 Worimi Conservation Lands (p135) Discovering the rich heritage of coastal Indigenous Australians.

4 Bellingen (p146) Enjoying the charm of a pretty, posh hinterland village.

5 Byron Bay (p157) Learning to surf amid spouting whales.

6 Fleet (p164) Discovering world-class dining at Brunswick Heads' Mod Oz restaurant.

7 Bangalow Market (p164) Feeling the love between the farmers, hippies and foodies.

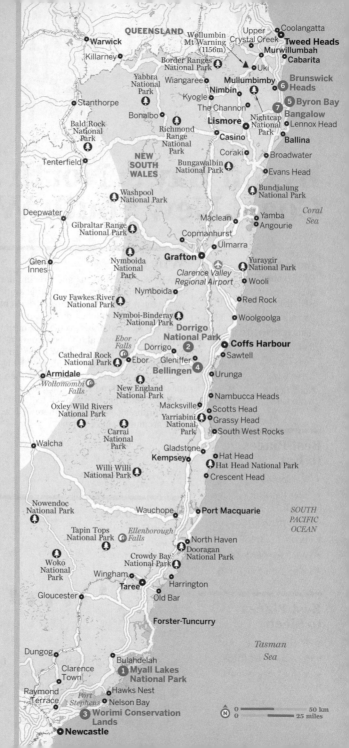

ℹ Getting There & Around

AIR

There are domestic airports at Taree, Port Macquarie, Coffs Harbour (great for Bellingen), Grafton, Ballina (Byron Bay) and Lismore. Additionally, Newcastle Airport is super handy for Port Stephens, and Gold Coast Airport is only 4km from Tweed Heads.

BUS

Greyhound (www.greyhound.com.au) and **Premier** (www.premierms.com.au) both have coach services linking Sydney and Brisbane via the Pacific Hwy. Other companies cover smaller stretches along the way.

TRAIN

NSW TrainLink (www.nswtrainlink.info) services between Sydney and Brisbane stop at Wingham, Taree, Nambucca Heads, Coffs Harbour and Grafton. There are coach connections to branch-line towns that are no longer serviced by rail.

Port Stephens

POP 69,730

An hour's drive north of Newcastle, the sheltered harbour of Port Stephens is blessed with near-deserted beaches, extraordinary national parks and a unique sand-dune system. The main centre, Nelson Bay, is home to both a fishing fleet and an armada of tourist vessels, the latter trading on the town's status as the 'dolphin capital of Australia'.

◉ Sights

Worimi Conservation Lands   NATURE RESERVE
(www.worimiconservationlands.com; 3-day entry permits $10) Located at Stockton Bight, these are the longest moving sand dunes in the southern hemisphere, stretching more than 35km. Thanks to the generosity of the Worimi people, the traditional owners who now manage the area, you're able to roam around and drive along the beach (4WD only, and always check conditions). Get your permits from the visitor centre or NPWS office in Nelson Bay, the Anna Bay BP service station, or the 24-hour Metro service station near the Lavis Lane entry.

Tomaree National Park   NATIONAL PARK
(www.nationalparks.nsw.gov.au/tomaree-national park) This wonderfully wild expanse offers beautiful hiking in an area that can feel far more remote than you actually are. The park harbours angophora forests as well as several threatened species, including the spotted-tailed quoll and powerful owl. You can spot outcrops of the rare volcanic rock rhyodacite. In spring, the Morna Point trail is strewn with wildflowers.

🏃 Activities

Just east of Nelson Bay is slightly smaller Shoal Bay, which has a long swimming beach; a short drive south is Fingal Bay, with another lovely beach on the fringes of Tomaree National Park. The park stretches west around the clothing-optional Samurai Beach, a popular surfing spot, and One Mile Beach, a gorgeous semicircle of the softest sand and bluest water.

Port Stephens Surf School   SURFING
(☑0411 419 576; www.portstephenssurfschool.com.au; 2hr group surf lessons $60 1hr group stand-up paddleboarding lessons $45) Offers both group and private surf and stand-up paddleboarding lessons at One Mile and Fingal Beaches. Board hire is also available (one/two hours $20/30).

☞ Tours

Port Stephens 4WD Tours   TOURS
(☑02-4984 4760; www.portstephens4wd.com.au; James Patterson St, Anna Bay) Offers a 1½-hour Beach & Dune tour (adult/child $52/31), a three-hour Sygna Shipwreck tour ($90/50) and a sandboarding experience ($28/20) out on the magnificent dunes of the Worimi Conservation Lands. You can stay as long as you like if sandboarding; just jump on the shuttle when you want to go home.

Port Stephens Paddlesports   KAYAKING
(☑0405 033 518; www.paddleportstephens.com.au; 35 Shoal Bay Rd, Shoal Bay; kayak/paddleboard hire per hr $25/30; ⊙Sep-May) Offers a range of kayak and stand-up-paddleboard hire as well as excursions, including 1½-hour sunset tours (adult/child $40/30) and 2½-hour discovery tours ($50/40).

🛏 Sleeping

Melaleuca Surfside Backpackers   HOSTEL $
(☑02-4981 9422; www.melaleucabackpackers.com.au; 2 Koala Pl, One Mile Beach; sites $20, dm per person $32-36, d tent/cabin $70/100; @ 🛜) Architect-designed cabins are set amid peaceful scrub inhabited by koalas, kookaburras and sugar gliders at this friendly, well-run place. You can also pitch your own tent among bushland (the whole site is blissfully car-free) or book one of the bed-equipped tents. There's a welcoming lounge

Port Stephens & the Great Lakes

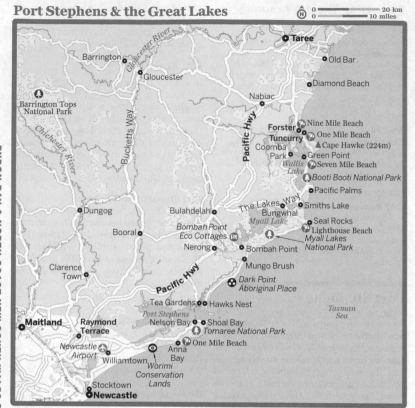

area and kitchen, and the owners offer sandboarding and other excursions.

Marty's at Little Beach HOTEL $$
(☑02-4984 9100; www.martys.net.au; cnr Gowrie Ave & Intrepid Close, Nelson Bay; r $120, apt $200-260; ☀🐾🛜🏊) This popular, low-key motel is an easy stroll to Little Beach and Shoal Bay, and has simple beach-house-inspired rooms and modern, self-contained apartments. Families with kids older than babes in cots are only accommodated in the two-bedroom executive suites.

O'Carrollyn's BUNGALOW $$
(☑02-4982 2801; www.theoasisonemile.com.au; 5 Koala Pl; bungalows $190-310; ☀🛜🏊) Nine two-bedroom, self-contained loft bungalows (two with Jacuzzis and some designed for families; all wheelchair-accessible) nestle around a billabong in 5 acres of landscaped garden. Guests also have use of garden BBQs

and outdoor dining tables. Various wellness therapists can be booked to come and give treatments in the on-site wellness area, which also has an infrared sauna.

★**Anchorage** RESORT $$$
(☑02-4984 2555; www.anchorageportstephens.com.au; Corlette Point Rd, Corlette; d $245-415; 🅿☀🛜🏊) Facing an expansive sweep of bay, this marina-fronted resort is Port Stephens' most stylish place to stay. Rooms have a crisp, coastal charm, with super-comfortable, relaxed interiors, and all have either a balcony or terrace. There are larger suites and apartments for those after the added luxury of space or for families.

The great pool area, excellent restaurant and Barbor spa will have you lingering. Come evening there's fine dining at Wild Herring and the cosy lure of a bay-window seat in the moody Hamptons-esque upstairs bar.

Bali at the Bay APARTMENT $$$
(☑02-4981 5556; www.baliatthebay.com.au; 1 Achilles St, Shoal Bay; apt $250-300; ✷) Two self-contained apartments (chock-full of flower-garlanded Buddhas and carved wood) do a good job of living up to the name here. It's the extras that make these private retreats really special: bathrooms are super luxe; there's complimentary sparkling wine and Bintang beer (naturally) in the fridge; and Nespresso machines. Spa treatments are also available.

🍴 Eating

Red Ned's Gourmet Pie Bar FAST FOOD $
(www.redneds.com.au; 17-19 Stockton St, Nelson Bay; pies $6; ☺6.30am-5pm) More than 50 varieties of weird and wonderful pies from crocodile in mushroom-and-white-wine sauce to macadamia-nut Thai satay chicken. There's also the absolute classic, savoury mince, or old-school lamb's fry and bacon. The beef is sourced from nearby Stroud and the chickens are free range.

Little Beach Boathouse SEAFOOD $$
(☑02-4984 9420; www.littlebeachboathouse. com.au; Little Beach Marina, 4 Victoria Pde; mains $28-38; ☺12-2pm & 5.30-9pm Tue-Sat, 11.30am-2.30pm Sun) In an airy but intimate dining room, right on the water, you can order fabulously fresh salads, local seafood share plates, and truffle and parmesan fries. It's hard to concentrate on the food when there are views of diving dolphins and majestic pelicans coming in to land.

Nice at Nelson Bay CAFE $$
(☑02-4981 3001; www.niceatnelsonbay.com.au; Nelson Towers Arcade, 71a Victoria Pde; breakfast mains $18.80; ☺8am-2pm) Breakfast heaven is hidden in an arcade near the waterfront, where this cafe serves up no less than six variations of eggs Benedict, a couple of groaning pancake dishes and thick-cut French toast served with savoury sides.

★Wild Herring SEAFOOD, MODERN AUSTRALIAN $$$
(☑02-4984 2555; www.anchorageportstephens. com.au; Corlette Point Rd, Corlette Point; mains $40-46; ☺6-10pm) The Anchorage resorts Galley Kitchen morphs into a resolutely fine-dining restaurant in the evening, but the simple waterfront space still vibes holiday calm. Dishes range from simply done kingfish with broccoli and vinaigrette made from a beautiful shellfish reduction, to more ambitious plates of langoustine and scallops

doused in sea-vegetable butter. Staff, attentive but chilled, can advise on the excellent wine list.

Point SEAFOOD $$$
(☑02-4984 7111; www.thepointrestaurant.com.au; Ridgeway Ave, Soldiers Point; mains $26-40, seafood platters $149; ☺noon-3pm Tue-Sun, 6-9pm Tue-Sat) The locals' favourite go-to restaurant for a romantic milestone, this marina spot has lovely views from the balcony and glassed-in dining room. It serves up loads of seafood choices, including oysters from local farm Holberts, plus steaks, duck and vegetarian options.

🍷 Drinking & Nightlife

★Swell CAFE, BAR
(☑02-4982 1378; www.swellkiosks.com.au; 10a Hannah Pde, One Mile; ☺6.30am-11pm) What every perfect beach needs: a year-round, all-day hangout. Come for the well-made flat-white coffee on the way to a dawn surf, for cheese toasties and milkshakes at lunch, and finish the day here with beers on tap and hand-cut hot chips. There's even live music on Sunday afternoons. Don't miss the prawn baguettes and 'bloke's burger' – an extra-large specimen with absolutely no salad or vegetable matter.

ℹ Information

Visitor Information Centre (☑1800 808 900; www.portstephens.org.au; 60 Victoria Pde, Nelson Bay; ☺9am-5pm) Has interesting displays about the marine park, lots of other information and a range of 'PS I love you' merchandise.

ℹ Getting There & Away

Port Stephens Coaches (☑02-4982 2940; www.pscoaches.com.au) zips around Port Stephens' townships heading to Newcastle and Newcastle Airport ($4.50, 50 minutes). A daily service runs to/from Sydney (one way/return $39/61, four hours) stopping at Anna Bay, Nelson Bay and Shoal Bay.

Port Stephens Ferry Service (☑0412 682 117; www.portstephensferryservice.com.au; adult/child return $24/13) and the **MV Wallamba** (☑0408 494 262; www.teagardens.nsw. au/index_files/wally.htm; adult/child return $20/10) chug from Nelson Bay to Tea Gardens (stopping at Hawks Nest) and back two to three times a day.

Myall Lakes National Park

On an extravagantly pretty section of the coast that feels deliciously remote, this large national park (p138) incorporates a patchwork of lakes, islands, dense littoral rainforest and beaches. **Seal Rocks**, a bush-clad hamlet hugging Sugarloaf Bay, is one of Australia's most epic surf destinations. Further south, the lakes support an incredible quantity and variety of bird life, including bowerbirds, white-bellied sea eagles and tawny frogmouths. The coastal rainforest is cut through with fire trails and beach tracks that lead to the beach dunes at **Mungo Brush**, perfect territory for spotting wildflowers and surprising dingoes.

◉ Sights

Seal Rocks
BEACH

(www.nationalparks.nsw.gov.au/myall-lakes-national-park; vehicles $8) This remarkably undeveloped town and its collection of beaches has long held mythic status among the global surfing community. There's plenty to enjoy even if you're not here for the idyllic, secluded breaks. Number One Beach has beautiful rock pools, usually mellow waves and beautiful sand. Or take the short walk to the Sugarloaf Point Lighthouse for epic ocean views, with a detour to lonely Lighthouse Beach, a popular surfing spot.

Broughton Island
BIRD SANCTUARY

(www.nationalparks.nsw.gov.au/myall-lakes-national-park) This island is uninhabited except for muttonbirds and little penguins, and its surrounding waters are home to an enormous diversity of fish. The diving is excellent, and the beaches are secluded.

Moonshadow (☑02-4984 9388; www.moonshadow.com.au; 35 Stockton St, Nelson Bay) ✈ runs full-day trips to the island from Nelson Bay on Sundays between October and Easter (more frequently over the summer school holidays), which include snorkelling and boom-net rides (adult/child $95/55). Basic camping (no power or water) at the island's Little Poverty Beach is operated by the NSW National Parks & Wildlife service, and must be prebooked online. If you have your own vessel (and have registered with Marine Rescue Port Stephens), you can arrange transfers – see the national parks website for current operators.

⌇ Sleeping

★ Treachery Camp
CAMPGROUND $

(☑02-4997 6138; www.treacherycamp.com.au; 166 Thomas Rd, Seal Rocks; sites adult $17-22, child $10-13 cabins $105-260) Tree-shaded free camping set behind the dunes and coastal scrub of Treachery Beach. Campers have access to a large amenities block for hot showers and cooking, as well as a great on-site cafe. Book well ahead for the cabins, which range from basic but pretty to architect designed.

Seal Rocks Holiday Park
CAMPGROUND $

(☑02-4997 6164; www.sealrocksholidaypark.com.au; Kinka Rd, Seal Rocks; sites $45, cabins $110-200; ☎) Offers a range of budget accommodation, including 14 cabins and grassed camping and caravan sites that are right on the water. Cabins sleep up to six and some include private bathrooms and overlook the sea.

NPWS Campgrounds
CAMPGROUND $

(☑1300 072 757; www.nationalparks.nsw.gov.au/myall-lakes-national-park; sites per 2 people $25-35) There are 19 basic camping grounds dotted around the park; only some have drinking water and flush toilets. All locations can be booked on website.

★ Bombah Point Eco Cottages
COTTAGE $$$

(☑02-4997 4401; www.bombah.com.au; 969 Bombah Point Rd, Bombah Point; cottages $275-325; ☎) ✈ In the heart of the national park, these architect-designed glass-fronted cottages sleep up to six guests. The 'eco' in the name is well deserved: sewage is treated on-site using a bio-reactor system; electricity comes courtesy of solar panels; and filtered rainwater tanks provide water. Cottages are quietly luxurious with huge rainwater spa baths and stylish cast-iron fireplaces.

Sugarloaf Point Lighthouse
COTTAGE $$$

(☑02-4997 6590; www.sealrockslighthouseaccommodation.com.au; cottages from $340; ☎) Watch the crashing waves and wandering wildlife from one of three fully renovated 19th-century lighthouse-keeper's cottages. Each is self-contained and has two or three bedrooms and a barbecue. Ceilings are high and the heritage-style interiors are mercifully unfussy. The location, as you might imagine, is extraordinary.

✗ Eating

This is self-catering country, with some great options for fresh seafood. Otherwise, head down to Port Stephens, up to Pacific Palms or inland for restaurants.

❶ Getting There & Away

From the town of Hawks Nest the scenic Mungo Brush Rd heads through the park to Bombah Broadwater, where the Bombah Point ferry makes the five-minute crossing every half-hour from 8am to 6pm ($6 per car). Continuing north,

DETOUR: OLD BAR TO LAKE CATHIE

Beyond the increasingly urban Forster, whose **visitor centre** (☑02-6554 8799; www. greatlakes.org.au; Little St, Forster; ☺9am-5pm) has info on this area, the coast reverts to a series of atmospheric little towns and long stretches of unspoilt beach and lush forest that are wonderful to explore.

Just back from the Pacific Hwy, Taree (population 17,800) is the rural centre that serves the fertile Manning Valley. Head a little west from here to the nearby town of Wingham for English-county cuteness with a rugged lumberjack history.

But the coast beckons. Old Bar, at the southern head of the Manning River, is a long-time surfing favourite but now has what might be the midcoast's first destination hotel, the marvellous **Boogie Woogie Beach House** (☑02-6557 4224; www.boogiewoogie beachhouse.com.au; 31 David St, Old Bar; d $189-280; ℗✴☏).

Further north, you can head east down the estuary to the sprawling beach town of **Harrington**, sheltered by a spectacular rocky breakwater and watched over by pelicans.

A short drive northeast of Harrington is Crowdy Head, a small fishing and surfing town at the edge of **Crowdy Bay National Park** (www.nationalparks.nsw.gov.au/crowdy-bay-national-park; vehicles $8). The views of deserted beaches and wilderness from the 1878 lighthouse are extraordinary. There are a number of beautifully remote campgrounds in the park. Little **Dooragan National Park** (www.nationalparks.nsw.gov.au/dooragan-national-park) **FREE** is immediately north of Crowdy Bay National Park, on the shores of Watson Taylor Lake, and is dominated by North Brother Mountain. A sealed road leads to the lookout at the top, which offers incredible views of the coast. Heading north you'll pass through Laurieton. Turn left here and cross the bridge to North Haven, an absolute blinder of a surf beach. Continuing north the road passes Lake Cathie (cateye), a shallow body of water that's perfect for kids to have a paddle in.

a 10km section of Bombah Point Rd heading to the Pacific Hwy at Bulahdelah is unsealed.

Port Macquarie

POP 44, 340

Making the most of its position at the entrance to the subtropical coast, Port, as it's commonly known, might be considered a mini-metropolis but it remains overwhelmingly holiday focused. A string of beautiful beaches fans out either side of town, all a short driving distance from the centre. Most are great for swimming and surfing, and they seldom get crowded.

⊙ Sights

Koala Hospital   WILDLIFE RESERVE
(www.koalahospital.org.au; Lord St; by donation; ☺8am-4.30pm) Chlamydia, traffic accidents and dog attacks are the biggest causes of illness and injury for koalas living near urban areas; about 250 end up in this shelter each year. You can walk around the open-air enclosures any time of the day, but you'll learn more on a tour (3pm). Signs detail the stories of some of the longer-term patients. Check the website for volunteer opportunities.

Sea Acres National Park   NATIONAL PARK
(☑02-6582 3355; www.nationalparks.nsw.gov.au/ sea-acres-national-park; 159 Pacific Dr; adult/child $8/4; ☺9am-4.30pm) This 72-hectare pocket of national park protects the state's largest and most diverse strand of coastal rainforest. It's alive with birds, goannas, brush turkeys and diamond pythons. The Rainforest Centre has an excellent **cafe** (☑02-6582 4444; www. rainforestcafe.com.au; mains breakfast $10-15, lunch $12-22; ☺9am-4pm; ☑) ♥ and audiovisual displays about the local Birpai people. The highlight is the wheelchair-accessible 1.3km-long boardwalk through the forest. Fascinating one-hour guided tours by knowledgeable volunteers are run during high season.

Glasshouse Regional Gallery   GALLERY
(☑02-65818888;www.glasshouse.org.au/regional-gallery; cnr Clarence & Hay Sts; ☺10am-4pm Tue-Sun) **FREE** This dynamic multilevel space provides an interesting overview of local creativity, and hosts regular touring exhibitions from Australia's top museums and galleries.

**Port Macquarie
Historical Museum**   MUSEUM
(☑02-6583 1108; www.port-macquarie-historical museum.org.au; 22 Clarence St; adult/child $5/2;

Port Macquarie

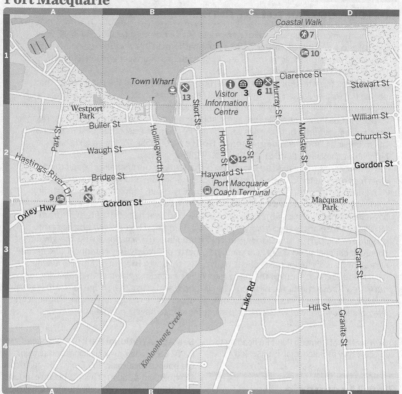

Port Macquarie

◎ Top Sights
1	Flynn's Beach	F4
2	Town Beach	E1

◎ Sights
3	Glasshouse Regional Gallery	C1
4	Koala Hospital	E4
5	Maritime Museum	E2
6	Port Macquarie Historical Museum	C1

⊕ Activities, Courses & Tours
7	Port Macquarie Coastal Walk	D1

⊜ Sleeping
8	Flynns on Surf	F4
9	Port Macquarie Backpackers	A2
10	Sundowner Breakwall Tourist Park	D1

✖ Eating
11	Bill's Fishhouse	C1
12	Fusion 7	C2
13	Latin Loafer	B1
14	Social Grounds	A2
15	Stunned Mullet	E2

⊙ 9.30am-4.30pm Mon-Sat) An 1836 house has been transformed into this surprisingly interesting little museum. Aboriginal and convict history are given due regard before more eclectic displays take over, including a 'street of shops' and a display of beautiful old clothes, which includes a whole section on underwear.

Maritime Museum MUSEUM
(www.maritimemuseumcottages.org.au; 6 William St; adult/child/family $5/2/12; ⊙ 10am-4pm) The old pilot station (1882) above Town

Beach has been converted into a small maritime museum, which is full of character. Allow a good hour to pore over its fascinating collection.

🏃 Activities

Surfing is particularly good at Town, Flynn's and Lighthouse beaches, all of which are patrolled in summer. The rainforest runs down to the sand at Shelly and Miners beaches, the latter of which is an unofficial nudist beach.

Whale season is from May to November; there are numerous vantage points around town, or you can get a closer look on a whale-watching cruise.

It's possible to walk all the way from the Town Wharf to Lighthouse Beach.

★ Port Macquarie Coastal Walk   WALKING

This wonderful coastal walk begins at Town Green foreshore and winds for about 9km

along the coast to **Tracking Point Lighthouse** (Lighthouse Rd) in Sea Acres National Park (p139). There are plenty of opportunities for swimming (it takes in eight beaches) and between May and November you can often view the whale migration. The walk can be divided into shorter 2km sections.

Soul Surfing   SURFING

(🏄 02-6582 0114; www.soulsurfing.com.au; classes from $50) A family-run school that is particularly good for nervous beginners. Also runs school-holiday intensives and day-long women's workshops that include yoga, relaxation and food along with the surf lessons.

🛏 Sleeping

Port Macquarie Backpackers   HOSTEL $

(🏄 02-6583 1791; www.portmacquariebackpackers.com.au; 2 Hastings River Dr; dm/s/d from $36/72/82; @ 🗢 ≋) This heritage-listed house has pressed-tin walls, colourful murals and a leafy backyard with a small pool. Traffic can be noisy, but the freebies (including wi-fi, bikes, beach shuttles and bodyboards) and a relaxed attitude more than compensate.

Sundowner Breakwall Tourist Park   HOSTEL $

(🏄 02-6583 2755; www.sundownerholidays.com; 1 Munster St; dm $28, sites per 2 people $38-45, cabins $98-310) With extensive facilities and a roomy feel, this quality place is right by the river mouth. There's a backpackers' area with a separate kitchen and lounge.

Flynns on Surf   VILLA $$

(🏄 02-6584 2244; www.flynns.com.au; 25 Surf St; 1-/2-/3-bedroom villas $180/240/300; P ❄ 🗢 ≋) These smart one-, two- and three-bedroom villas are set on their own private estate. Each has a gorgeous bush outlook and is fully self-contained, with extra comforts such as Nespresso machines and iPod docks. The surf is 200m away, and it's a three-minute walk into town.

Beachport   B&B $$

(🏄 0423 072 669; www.beachportbnb.com.au; 155 Pacific Dr; d $70-200; ❄ 🗢) At this excellent B&B the two downstairs rooms open onto private terraces, while the upstairs unit is more spacious. A basic do-it-yourself breakfast is provided, and Rainforest Cafe (p139) is just across the road. Prices include afternoon tea on arrival.

✗ Eating

Social Grounds
CAFE $

(151 Gordon St; mains $7-14; ⊘ 6am-2.30pm Mon-Fri, to noon Sat, 7am-noon Sun) Pull up a chair at the shared tables on the deck of this hip, super-stylish local hang-out. The wall menu wanders from eggs and bagels to towering Reuben sandwiches and gutsy salads. The coffee is dependably good.

★ Latin Loafer
TAPAS $$

(✆ 02-6583 9481; www.latinloafer.com.au; 74 Clarence St; dishes $10-20; ⊘ noon-3pm & 5-10pm Tue-Thu, noon-11pm Fri-Sun) Specialising in Spanish and South American wines, this fabulously atmospheric place has a spot overlooking the river. Salted-cod croquettes and beef empanadas make for good aperitivo snacks or combine with Peruvian spiced potatoes, kingfish ceviche and grilled octopus to make a meal.

★ Bill's Fishhouse
MODERN AUSTRALIAN $$

(✆ 02-6584 7228; www.billsfishhouse.com.au; 2/18-20 Clarence St; mains $22-32; ⊘ 6-10pm Tue-Sun & noon-2.30pm Fri-Sun) A super light and pretty space to escape the heat and eat the freshest of seafood (and lovely local poultry and beef, too). A brief menu – fish and chips, salmon with beets and greens, sirloin with bernaise – is augmented daily with the chef's pick from the fish market. The wine list is similarly tight. Bookings are advised at night.

★ Stunned Mullet
MODERN AUSTRALIAN $$$

(✆ 02-6584 7757; www.thestunnedmullet.com.au; 24 William St; mains $36-42; ⊘ noon-2.30pm & 6-10pm) This fresh, seaside spot is one serious dining destination. The inspired contemporary menu features classic dishes such as confit duck with truffled polenta, alongside exotic listings such as Patagonian toothfish. Note, all fish is wild caught. The extensive international wine list befits Port's best restaurant and there's a small but super-impressive wine-by-the-glass and half-bottle selection.

Fusion 7
FUSION $$$

(✆ 02-6584 1171; www.fusion7.com.au; 124 Horton St; mains $32-37; ⊘ 6-9pm Tue-Sat) Chef-owner Lindsey Schwab has worked in London with the father of fusion cuisine, Peter Gordon, and in some of Sydney's top restaurants. He now oversees a short but innovative menu where local produce features prominently and desserts are particularly wow-factor. Call ahead for bookings.

ⓘ Information

Visitor Information Centre (✆ 02-6581 8000; www.portmacquarieinfo.com.au; Glasshouse, cnr Hay & Clarence Sts; ⊘ 9am-5.30pm Mon-Fri, to 4pm Sat & Sun)

ⓘ Getting There & Away

AIR

Port Macquarie Airport (✆ 02-6581 8111; www.portmacquarieairport.com.au; Oliver Dr) is 5km from the centre of town; a taxi will cost $20 and it's served by regular local buses. Regular flights run to Sydney and Brisbane on **Qantaslink** (✆ 13 13 13; www.qantas.com.au) and **Virgin** (✆ 13 67 89; www.virginaustralia.com). **JetGo** (✆ 1300 328 000; www.jetgo.com) flies to Melbourne's Essendon Airport four times a week.

BUS

Regional buses depart from **Port Macquarie Coach Terminal** (Gordon St).

Busways (✆ 02-6583 2499; www.busways.com.au) Runs local bus services to Port Macquarie Airport ($5.50, 28 minutes) and Kempsey ($18, one hour).

Greyhound (✆ 1300 473 946; www.greyhound.com.au) Two daily buses head to/from Sydney (6½ hours), Newcastle (four hours), Coffs Harbour (2½ hours), Byron Bay (six hours) and Brisbane (10 hours).

Premier (✆ 13 34 10; www.premierms.com.au) Daily coaches to/from Sydney ($60, 6½ hours), Newcastle ($47, 3¾ hours), Coffs Harbour ($47, 2¼ hours), Byron Bay ($66, 7½ hours) and Brisbane ($67, 11 hours).

TRAIN

The closest train station is at Wauchope, 18km west of Port Macquarie. Buses connect with trains.

Crescent Head
POP 1070

This beachside hideaway has one of the best right-hand surf breaks in the country. Many come simply to watch the longboard riders surf the epic waves of **Little Nobby's Junction**. There's also good shortboard riding off Plomer Rd. Untrammelled **Killick Beach** stretches 14km north.

🛏 Sleeping

Surfari
HOSTEL, MOTEL $

(✆ 02-6566 0009; www.surfaris.com; 353 Loftus Rd; sites $20, dm/d $40/150; @ 🛜 🐾) Surfari started the original Sydney–Byron surf tours and now base themselves in Crescent Head because 'the surf is guaranteed every day'. The rooms are clean and comfortable, and surf-and-stay packages are a speciality. It's located 3.5km along the road to Gladstone.

Sun Worship Eco Apartments APARTMENT $$$
(☑1300 664 757; www.sunworship.com.au; 9 Belmore St; apt $230-320; ☎) ☕ Stay in guilt-mitigated luxury in one of five spacious rammed-earth villas featuring sustainable design, including flow-through ventilation, solar orientation and solar hot water. They're great, and have everything you need, but the decor doesn't quite live up to the excellence of the architecture.

ℹ Getting There & Away

Busways (☑02-6562 4724; www.busways. com.au) runs between Crescent Head and Kempsey ($10.50, 25 minutes) two to three times a day; no Sunday services.

Hat Head National Park

Covering almost the entire coast from Crescent Head to South West Rocks, this 74-sq-km **national park** (vehicle entry $8) protects scrubland, swamps and some amazing beaches, backed by one of the largest dune systems in NSW.

The isolated beachside village of Hat Head (population 325) sits at its centre. At the far end of town, behind the holiday park, a picturesque wooden footbridge crosses the Korogoro Creek estuary. The water is so clear you can see fish darting around.

Stop off at Gladstone's **Heritage Hotel** (www.heritagehotel.net.au; 21 Kinchela St, Gladstone; mains from $16; ☺10am-midnight Mon-Sat, to 9pm Sun), around a 20-minute drive inland and along the river.

The best views can be had from **Smoky Cape Lighthouse**, at the northern end of the park. During the annual whale migration it's a prime place from which to spot them.

Camp at **Hungry Gate** (www.nationalparks. nsw.gov.au/hat-head-national-park; sites per adult/ child $6/3.50), 5km south of Hat Head, for a beautifully back-to-basics holiday among native figs and paperbarks. The site operates on a first-in basis and does not take bookings; a ranger will come around and collect fees. There are nonflush toilets and a BBQ area, but you'll need to bring your own drinking water. Kangaroos provide entertainment.

South West Rocks

POP 4810

One of many pretty seaside towns on this stretch of coast, South West Rocks has spectacular beaches and enough interesting diversions for at least a night or two.

The lovely curve of **Trial Bay**, stretching east from the township, takes its name from the *Trial,* a boat that sank here during a storm in 1816 after being stolen by convicts fleeing Sydney. The eastern half of the bay is now protected by **Arakoon National Park**, centred on a headland that's popular with kangaroos, kookaburras and campers. On its eastern flank, **Little Bay Beach** is a small grin of sand sheltered from the surf by a rocky barricade. It's both a great place for a swim and also the starting point for some lovely walks.

◉ Sights

Trial Bay Gaol MUSEUM
(☑02-6566 6168; www.nationalparks.nsw.gov. au/arakoon-national-park; Cardwell St; adult/child $10/7; ☺9am-4.30pm) Occupying Trial Bay's eastern headland, this sandstone prison was built between 1877 and 1886 to house convicts brought in to build a breakwater. When nature had other ideas and the breakwater washed away, the imposing structure fell into disuse, aside from a brief, rather tragic, interlude in WWI when men of German and Austrian heritage were interned. Today it contains a museum devoted to its unusual history; even if you don't visit within, it's worth a detour for the views.

It's a pleasant 4km dawdle along the beach from South West Rocks.

⮕ Sleeping

Trial Bay Gaol Campground CAMPGROUND $
(☑02-6566 6168; www.nationalparks.nsw.gov.au/ arakoon-national-park; Cardwell St; sites $35, summer & school holidays $60) Behind the Trial Bay Gaol, this stunning NPWS camping ground affords generous beach views from most camp sites and hosts ever-present kangaroos. Amenities include drinking water and flush toilets, and coin-slot hot showers and gas BBQs. Online bookings for this camping ground must be made at least two days prior to your stay.

Smoky Cape Retreat B&B $$
(☑02-6566 7740; www.smokycaperetreat.com. au; 1 Cockatoo Pl, Arakoon; d $130-220; ☺❋☀) This cosy retreat in bushland near Arakoon has three private spa suites and rambling

gardens that house a saltwater pool and a tennis court. The owners run a charming cafe on their deck where they serve a complimentary hot breakfast.

★ **Smoky Cape Lighthouse B&B** B&B, COTTAGE **$$$**
(☑02-6566 6301; www.smokycapelighthouse. com; Lighthouse Rd; s/d $150/220, 3-bedroom cottages per 2 nights $500-580; ℗) Romantic evenings can be spent gazing out to sea while the wind whips around the historic lighthouse-keeper's residence and kangaroos come out to graze high up on the headland. Views are ridiculously beautiful; rooms are trad. Rates jump on weekends.

✕ Eating

★ **Malt & Honey** CAFE **$**
(☑02-6566 5200; 5-7 Livingstone St; mains $10-16; ⊙7.30am-4pm Tue-Sun) An urban sensibility combines with beach-town warmth and charm at this busy cafe. Pick up an early-morning latte (made with Toby's Estate beans) or grab a seat for crumpets with macadamia crumble, house-made muesli or the big breakfast of lamb chops, chorizo, eggs and bacon. Big salads and other healthy but satisfying options appear on the lunch menu.

❶ Information

Visitor Information Centre (☑02-6566 7099; www.macleayvalleycoast.com.au; 1 Ocean Ave; ⊙9am-4pm)

❶ Getting There & Away

Busways (☑02-6562 4724; www.busways. com.au) Runs two to four times a day to/from Kempsey from Monday to Saturday (adult/child $13.60/6.80, 46 minutes).

Nambucca Heads

POP 6220

Nambucca Heads is languidly strewn over a dramatically curling headland interlaced with the estuaries of the glorious Nambucca River. It's a quiet and rather unglamorous place, evoking sun-soaked holidays of the 1970s and '80s.

◉ Sights

Yarriabini National Park NATIONAL PARK
(www.nationalparks.nsw.gov.au/yarriabini-national-park) The highlight of this lush, rainforest-filled park is the dramatic coastal view from the summit of Mt Yarriabini, which is accessible via scenic Way Way Creek Rd.

Captain Cook Lookout VIEWPOINT
Of the area's numerous viewpoints, Captain Cook Lookout, set on a high bluff, is the best to ponder the swathe of beaches, and to look for whales during the migration season. A road here leads down to the tide pools of Shelly Beach.

V-Wall LANDMARK
For decades residents and holidaymakers have decorated the rocks of Nambucca's breakwater with vivacious multicoloured artwork, and with notes to lovers, families and new-found friends. Visitors are encouraged to paint their own messages, if they can find some space on the boulders.

🏃 Activities

Nambucca Boatshed BOATING
(Beachcomber Marine; ☑02-6568 6432; www. nambuccaboatshed.com.au/activities; Riverside Dr; boat hire per 2hr/day $80/220, kayak hire per hr $25; ⊙7am-4.45pm Mon-Sat, to 3pm Sun) Book online, or have the friendly staff rent you a motor boat, kayak or stand-up paddleboard and assist with local fishing advice. Conveniently, you can also stock up on lunch at the attached cafe.

🛏 Sleeping

White Albatross Holiday Park CAMPGROUND **$**
(☑02-6568 6468; www.whitealbatross.com. au; 52 Wellington Dr; sites $66, cabins $145-215; ❄🐕🏊🐾) Located near the river mouth, this large holiday park is laid out around a sheltered lagoon. The cabins are kept fastidiously clean and have full kitchens. There is a jolly on-site tavern with a great deck.

Riverview Boutique Hotel GUESTHOUSE **$$**
(☑02-6568 6386; www.riverviewlodgenambucca. com.au; 4 Wellington Dr; s $169 d $179-225; ℗❄🐕) This former pub, built in 1887, is a wooden, two-storey charmer with eight neat, smart rooms; all have private balconies and some rooms have views.

✕ Eating

★ **Taverna Six** GREEK **$$**
(☑02-6569 0000; www.facebook.com/Taverna Six; 405 Grassy Head Rd, Grassy Head; mains $22-28; ⊙6.30-9pm Thu-Sat, lunch from 11am Sun) Relax in the courtyard while an affable staff serves up generous helpings of mezze,

Nambucca Heads

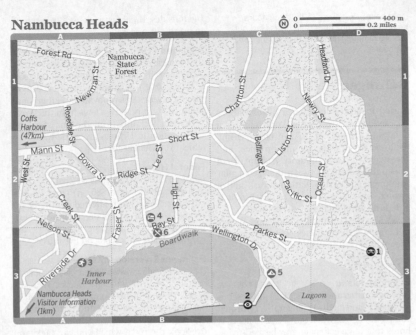

Nambucca Heads

◎ Sights
1 Captain Cook Lookout............................D3
2 V-Wall...C3

✪ Activities, Courses & Tours
3 Nambucca Boatshed..............................A3

🛏 Sleeping
4 Riverview Boutique Hotel.....................B2
5 White Albatross Holiday Park...............C3

✖ Eating
6 Matilda's...B3

---

herb-strewn salads, fresh seafood and local lamb. Fabulously authentic dishes utilise beautiful coastal produce along with some nice Greek imports, such as Peloponnese bottarga. Greek music plays and the surf rolls in across the road in a perfect Greek–Australian pairing.

Matilda's SEAFOOD $$$
(☑ 02-6568 6024; 6 Wellington Dr; mains $35; ⊘ 6-9pm Mon-Sat) This cute shack has spom old-fashioned beachfront character and serves up a menu of mostly seafood, including oysters. Locals rave about the cheesecake and pavlova desserts. BYO ($4 corkage).

ⓘ Information

Nambucca Heads Visitor Information Centre
(☑ 1800 646 587; www.nambuccatourism. com.au; cnr Riverside Dr & Pacific Hwy; ⊘ 9am-5pm)

ⓘ Getting There & Away

BUS
Long-distance buses stop at the visitor centre.
Busways (☑ 02-6568 3012; www.busways. com.au) Six buses to/from Bellingen ($9.70, 1¼ hours) and Coffs Harbour ($11.90, 1¼ hours) on weekdays, and one or two on Saturday.
Greyhound (☑ 1300 473 946; www.greyhound. com.au) Coaches run daily to/from Sydney ($100, eight hours), Port Macquarie ($22, 1¾ hours), Coffs Harbour ($13, 45 minutes), Byron Bay ($60, 4½ hours) and Brisbane ($106, 8¼ hours).
Premier (☑ 13 34 10; www.premierms.com. au) Daily coaches to/from Sydney ($63, eight hours), Port Macquarie ($38, 1¾ hours), Coffs Harbour ($34, 40 minutes), Byron Bay ($58, 5¾ hours) and Brisbane ($63, 9¼ hours).

TRAIN
NSW TrainLink (☑ 13 22 32; www.nswtrainlink. info) Three daily trains to/from Sydney ($66,

eight hours), Wingham ($25, three hours), Kempsey ($8, one hour) and Coffs Harbour ($5, 40 minutes), and two to Brisbane ($62, 6¼ hours).

Bellingen

POP 3040

Buried in deep foliage on a hillside above the Bellinger River, this gorgeous town dances to the beat of its own bongo drum. 'Bello' is flush with organic produce, and the switched-on community has an urban sensibility. Located between the spectacular rainforest of Dorrigo National Park and a spoiled-for-choice selection of beaches, it is a definite jewel on the east-coast route.

It's also the beginning of the iconic Waterfall Way, which continues past Dorrigo and then winds west to Armidale.

◉ Sights

Bellingen Island   WILDLIFE RESERVE
(www.bellingen.com/flyingfoxes) This little semi-attached island on the Bellinger River (it's only completely cut off when the river is in flood) is home to a huge colony of grey-headed flying foxes. For a closer look, take the steep path onto the island from Red Ledge Lane, on the northern bank. The best months to visit are from October to January, when the babies are being born and nursed. Wear long trousers and use inset repellent to ward off stinging nettles, leaches, ticks and mosquitoes.

At dusk the flying foxes fly out in their thousands to feed, though this impressive sight is best viewed from the bridge in the centre of town.

✼✥ Festivals & Events

Bellingen Readers & Writers Festival   LITERATURE
(www.bellingenwritersfestival.com.au) Established and emerging writers appear at talks, panels, readings, poetry slams and workshops over the Queen's Birthday long weekend in June.

Bello Winter Music   MUSIC
(www.bellowintermusic.com; ⊙ early Jul) A nicely chilled music festival with local and international folk, roots, blues, world, hip-hop and pop acts. There's great food, and both free and ticketed events.

🛏 Sleeping

Much of the region's accommodation is in small B&Bs and cottages scattered across the hillsides. Breakfast is generally included in overnight prices.

Bellingen YHA   HOSTEL $
(Belfry Guesthouse; ☑ 02-6655 1116; www.yha.com. au; 2 Short St; dm $30, r with/without bathroom $135/80; @ 🛜) A tranquil, homey atmosphere pervades this renovated weatherboard house, with impressive views from the broad verandah. Pick-ups from the bus stop and train station in Urunga are sometimes possible if you call ahead.

Federal Hotel   HOTEL $
(☑ 02-6655 1003; www.federalhotel.com.au; 77 Hyde St; d with shared bathroom $80; 🛜) This beautiful old country pub has renovated weatherboard rooms, some of which open onto a balcony facing the main street. Downstairs, the sprawling bars offer food and live music.

Bellingen Riverside Cottages   CABIN $$
(☑ 02-6655 9866; www.bellingenriversidecottages. com.au; 224 North Bank Rd; cottages $195-300; ✺ ✺) These polished mountain cabins have cosy interiors with country furnishings and big, sunny windows. Timber balconies overlook the river, which you can tackle on a complimentary kayak. Your first night includes a sizeable DIY breakfast hamper.

★ Lily Pily   B&B $$$
(☑ 02-6655 0522; www.lilypily.com.au; 54 Sunny Corner Rd; d $280; ✺ 🛜) Set on a knoll five minutes drive south of the centre, this beautiful architect-designed complex has three bedrooms overlooking the river. It's aesthetically undemanding but designed to pamper, with champagne and nibbles on arrival, lavish breakfasts served until noon, luxurious furnishings and more. It has a beautiful garden setting and mountain views.

★ Promised Land Retreat   CABIN $$$
(☑ 02-6655 9578; www.promisedlandretreat.com. au; 934 Promised Land Rd, Gleniffer; cabins $320; P ✺ 🛜) A 10-minute drive from town over the evocatively named Never Never River, these three stylish and private cottages feature open-plan living areas attached to decks with dramatic views to the Dorrigo escarpment. Facilities include a tennis court, a games room and complimentary mountain bikes.

✗ Eating

Eating in Bellingen is a pleasure: it has a large and ever-growing number of cafes and casual restaurants, most of which make use of local and organic produce.

DON'T MISS

WATERFALL WAY

Considered New South Wales' most scenic drive, the 190km Waterfall Way links a number of beautiful national parks between Coffs Harbour and Armidale, taking you through pristine subtropical rainforest, Edenic valleys, and, naturally, spectacular waterfalls. As you emerge into the tablelands, there is green countryside and wide plains. Bellingen is the natural starting point; even a short foray from Dorrigo will reward with stunning views.

➡ **Guy Fawkes River National Park** (www.nationalparks.nsw.gov.au/guy-fawkes-river-national-park) and the stunning Ebor Falls are 50km past Dorrigo.

➡ Make your way into the **Cathedral Rock National Park** (www.nationalparks.nsw.gov.au/cathedral-rock-national-park) or take a detour down Point Lookout Rd to **New England National Park** (www.nationalparks.nsw.gov.au/new-england-national-park), a section of the Gondwana Rainforests World Heritage Area.

➡ Further west **Oxley Wild Rivers National Park** (www.nationalparks.nsw.gov.au/oxley-wild-rivers-national-park) is home to the towering plunge waterfall beauty of Wollomombi Falls.

★ **Hearthfire Bakery**   BAKERY $
(☑ 02-6655 0767; www.hearthfire.com.au; 73 Hyde St; lunch mains $9-16; ⊙ 7am-5pm Mon-Fri, to 2pm Sat & Sun) Follow the smell of hot-from-the-woodfire organic sourdough and you'll find this outstanding country bakery and cafe. Try the famous macadamia fruit loaf or settle in with a coffee and a beautiful savoury pie. There is a full breakfast menu daily, and lunch dishes – including mezze plates, soups and salads – are served during the week.

Bellingen Gelato Bar   ICE CREAM $
(www.bellingengelato.com.au; 101 Hyde St; single/double scoops $4/6; ⊙ 10am-6pm daily Oct-Apr, closed Mon & Tue May-Sep) Robert Sebes, the former owner of a legendary inner-Sydney cafe, has been scooping out stellar gelato in Bellingen since 2006. It's all made from scratch, with minimal added sugar. Traditional Italian flavours, such as zabaglione and pistachio, are fabulously distinct, while Sebes' own creations – perhaps halva or spiced plum – are inventive but never faddish or overloaded.

Purple Carrot   CAFE $$
(☑ 02-6655 1847; 105 Hyde St; mains $15-18; ⊙ 8am-3pm) The breakfast-biased menu offers eggs galore alongside dishes such as brioche French toast, smoked trout on a potato rösti and creamy pesto mushrooms. Get in early for Sunday brunch.

Oak Street
Food & Wine   MODERN AUSTRALIAN $$$
(☑ 02-6655 9000; www.oakstreetfoodandwine.com.au; 2 Oak St; mains $30-37; ⊙ 6-10pm Wed-

Sat) This much-loved restaurant continues to turn out sophisticated, accessible dishes that make the most of the Bellinger Valley bounty in a beautifully atmospheric setting. A pre-dinner wine on the verandah is a quintessential hinterland experience.

🍷 Drinking & Nightlife

People of Coffee   CAFE
(☑ 1300 720 799; www.ameliafranklin.com.au; 3/44 Hyde St; ⊙ 6am-3pm Mon-Fri, to 2pm Sat) ✒ While there's no shortage of good coffee in Bellingen, Amelia Franklin roasts on-site with beans that are not only organic, but bird-friendly, rainforest-alliance and fair- and direct-trade certified. Come for top-quality coffee (espresso or cold drip). Her not-for-profit shopfront cafe also trains baristas. The toasties and healthy cakes are also delicious.

Bellingen Brewery & Co   MICROBREWERY
(3/5 Church St; ⊙ 5-11pm Wed-Fri, from noon Sat & Sun) From English-style bitters to a summer drinking ale, cider and an in-house 3.5% ginger beer. Excellent pub food, such as buffalo and barra burgers.

No 5 Church St   BAR
(www.5churchstreet.com; 5 Church St; mains $16-20; ⊙ 8am-8pm; 🛜) Morphing effortlessly from cafe to bar, this vibrant venue stages an eclectic roster of live music, movie nights and community gatherings. The menu, be it breakfast, lunch or dinner, comes with a directory of local growers who have produced the ingredients for the egg dishes, pizzas, salads and burgers.

🛍 Shopping

Bellingen Growers' Market   MARKET
(www.bellingengrowersmarket.com; Bellingen Showgrounds, cnr Hammond & Black Sts; ⊘8am-1pm 2nd & 4th Sat of month) Most of the produce here is organic and comes from surrounding farms. There are also plenty of secondhand clothes, as well as a cafe, a story-teller for the kids and roving musicians.

Bellingen Community Market   MARKET
(www.bellingenmarkets.com.au; Bellingen Park, Church St; ⊘9am-3pm 3rd Sat of the month) A regional sensation, with more than 250 stalls selling fresh produce, artisan food products, craft, clothing and plants.

ℹ Information

Waterfall Way Information Centre (☑ 02-6655 1522; www.visitnsw.com/visitor-information-centres/waterfall-way-visitor-centre-bellingen; 29-31 Hyde St; ⊘9am-5pm) Stocks brochures on scenic drives, walks and an arts trail.

ℹ Getting There & Away

Bellingen is a short drive inland from the coast along the spectacular Waterfall Way. Local **buses** (☑ 02-6655 7410; www.busways.com.au) service the town from Nambucca and Coffs, via Sawtell, and **coaches** (p149) run from Tamworth.

Dorrigo

POP 1070

Arrayed around the T-junction of two wider-than-wide streets, Dorrigo is a pretty little place. You get the sense that this might be the next Bellingen in terms of food and wine, but it hasn't quite happened yet. The winding roads that lead here from Armidale, Bellingen and Coffs Harbour, however, reveal rainforests, mountain passes and waterfalls – some of the most dramatic scenery in NSW.

◉ Sights

The town's main attraction is **Dangar Falls**, 1.2km north of town, which cascades over a series of rocky shelves before plummeting into a basin. You can swim if you have a yen for glacial bathing. A partly sealed road continues north past here and swings east into Coffs Harbour via beautiful winding rainforest roads and a huge tallow-wood tree, 56m high and more than 3m in diameter.

★ Dorrigo National Park   NATIONAL PARK

(☑ 02-6657 2309; www.nationalparks.nsw.gov.au; Dome Rd) This 119-sq-km park is part of the Gondwana Rainforests World Heritage Area and home to a huge diversity of vegetation and more than 120 species of bird. The **Rainforest Centre** (☑ 02-9513 6617; adult/child $2/1; ⊘9am-4.30pm; 🤖), at the park entrance, has displays and a film about the park's ecosystems, as well as information on walks. There's free wi-fi, a wonderful cafe, and a charging station for phones and cameras. The Skywalk platform juts out over the rainforest, providing wonderful views across the valleys below.

Starting from the Rainforest Centre, the Wonga Walk is a two-hour, 6.6km-return walk on a bitumen track through the depths of the rainforest. Along the way it passes a couple of very beautiful waterfalls, one of which you can walk behind.

🛏 Sleeping

★ Mossgrove   B&B $$
(☑ 02-6657 5388; www.mossgrove.com.au; 589 Old Coast Rd; d $225) Set on 2.5 hectares, 8km from Dorrigo, this lovely federation-era home has two traditionally furnished rooms, a cosy guest lounge and a private guest bathroom, all tastefully renovated while echoing the house's heyday. A continental breakfast is included.

★ Tallawarra Retreat B&B   B&B $$
(☑ 02-6657 2315; www.tallawalla.com; 113 Old Coramba Rd; s/d $130/160; 🐾) This peaceful B&B is set amid picturesque gardens and forest around 1km from Dorrigo town centre. The hosts are friendly and the four rooms are comfortable and blissfully quiet. The complimentary afternoon teas (homemade scones, jam and cream, and pots of tea or coffee) and the hearty, hot English breakfast, make for great value.

Lookout Mountain Retreat   B&B $$
(☑ 02-6657 2511; www.lookoutmountainretreat.com.au; 15 Maynards Plains Rd; d $140-190; P 🤖) Spectacular views and a blissfully quiet location make this 26-room place rather special. Exposed bricks and beams give the rooms a cosy feel, and they are spotless and surprisingly stylish. The suite has a kitchenette if you'd like to self-cater.

🍴 Eating

Dorrigo Wholefoods   CAFE $
(☑ 02-6657 1002; www.dorrigowholefoods.com.au; 28 Hickory St; mains with salad $14-16; ⊘6.30am-5pm Mon-Fri, 8am-2pm Sat) Head past the bulk

legumes and make up a plate from a cabinet of salads, cakes and savoury morsels such as lobster pot pie, Thai fish cakes and zucchini-ricotta fritters. The staff whips up super juice combinations, too.

Canopy Cafe CAFE $$
(☑ 02-6657 1541; www.canopycafedorrigo.com. au; Dome Rd; mains $13-22; ⊗ 9am-4.30pm) The food is as impressive as the view at this cafe within the Dorrigo National Park Rainforest Centre. The rather sophisticated menu runs from hearty breakfast dishes to spicy laksa and tasty open sandwiches, which can be eaten out on the sunny terrace.

ℹ️ Information

Dorrigo Information Centre (☑ 02-6657 2486; www.dorrigo.com; 36 Hickory St; ⊗ 10am-3pm Mon-Fri) Located in the middle of what passes for the main drag, this is run by volunteers who share a passion for the area. Pick up the useful scenic drives brochure ($1).

Rainforest Centre (p148) This park visitor centre, at the western entrance to Dorrigo National Park, has a shop, exhibits and a cafe.

ℹ️ Getting There & Away

Three **New England Coaches** (☑ 02-6732 1051; www.newenglandcoaches.com.au) per week head to Coffs Harbour ($48, 1½ hours)

Coffs Harbour

POP 71,800

Despite its inland city centre, Coffs has a string of fabulous beaches. Equally popular with families and backpackers, the town offers plenty of water-based activities, action sports and wildlife encounters, not to mention the kitsch yellow beacon that is the Big Banana. It also makes an easy base for exploring the quaint towns and beautiful drives of the hinterland.

◉ Sights

Park Beach is a long, lovely stretch of sand backed by dense shrubbery and sand dunes, which conceal the buildings beyond. **Jetty Beach** is somewhat more sheltered. **Diggers Beach**, reached by turning off the highway near the Big Banana, is popular with surfers, with swells averaging 1m to 1.5m. Naturists let it all hang out at **Little Diggers Beach**, just inside the northern headland.

★ **Muttonbird Island** ISLAND
(www.nationalparks.nsw.gov.au/muttonbird-island-nature-reserve) The Gumbaynggirr people knew this island as Giidany Miirlarl, meaning Place of the Moon. It was joined to Coffs Harbour by the northern breakwater in 1935. The walk to the top (quite steep at the end) provides sweeping vistas. From late August to early April this eco-treasure is occupied by some 12,000 pairs of wedge-tailed shearwaters, with their cute offspring visible in December and January.

Solitary Islands Aquarium AQUARIUM
(www.solitaryislandsaquarium.com; Bay Dr, Charlesworth Bay; adult/child $12/8; ⊗ 10am-4pm Sat & Sun, daily in school holidays) On weekends this small aquarium belonging to Southern Cross University's Marine Science Centre is open to the public. Touch-tanks and enthusiastic, well-qualified guides provide close encounters with fish, coral and an octopus (try visiting at feeding time) that frequent the waters of the Solitary Islands Marine Park.

Bunker Cartoon Gallery GALLERY
(www.bunkercartoongallery.com.au; John Champion Way; adult/child $3/2; ⊗ 10am-4pm) Displays rotating selections from its permanent collection of 18,000 cartoons in a WWII bunker.

Big Banana AMUSEMENT PARK
(www.bigbanana.com; 351 Pacific Hwy; ⊗ 9am-5pm) FREE Built in 1964, the Big Banana started the craze for 'Big Things' in Australia. Admission is free, with charges for associated attractions such as ice skating, toboggan rides, mini-golf, the waterpark, plantation tours and the irresistibly named 'World of Bananas Experience'. But beyond the kitsch appeal, there's really little to see.

🏃 Activities

Canoes, kayaks and stand-up paddleboards can be hired from Mangrove Jack's cafe (p152). Keen hikers should pick up a copy of the *Solitary Islands Coastal Walk* brochure ($2) from the visitor centre.

Coffs Creek Walk & Cycleway WALKING
A lovely 8km bush circuit links the central business district (CBD) with the harbour. We recommend starting at the Pet Porpoise Pool, Orlando St, or the Memorial Olympic Pool, Coffs St.

Coffs Harbour

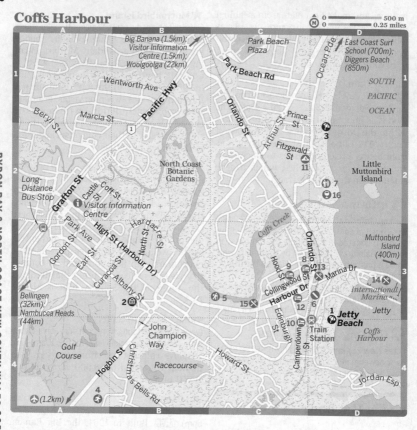

Coffs Harbour

Top Sights
1 Jetty Beach D4

Sights
2 Bunker Cartoon Gallery B3
3 Park Beach D2

Activities, Courses & Tours
4 Coffs City Skydivers A4
5 Coffs Creek Walk & Cycleway C3
6 Jetty Dive D3
7 Lee Winkler's Surf School D2

Sleeping
8 Coffs Harbour YHA C3

9 Coffs Jetty BnB C3
10 Observatory Apartments C4
11 Park Beach Holiday Park C2
12 Pier Hotel C3

Eating
13 Fiasco D3
14 Fishermen's Coop D3
Latitude 30 .... (see 14)
Lime Mexican .... (see 12)
15 Mangrove Jack's C3
Old John's .... (see 12)

Drinking & Nightlife
16 Surf Club Park Beach D2

East Coast Surf School SURFING
(☏ 02-6651 5515; www.eastcoastsurfschool.com.
au; Diggers Beach; lessons from $55) A particu-
larly female-friendly outfit run by former
pro surfer Helene Enevoldson.

Lee Winkler's Surf School SURFING
(☏ 02-6650 0050; www.leewinklerssurfschool.
com.au; Park Beach; from $55) One of the oldest
surf schools in Coffs.

Valery Trails　　　　HORSE RIDING
(☑02-6653 4301; www.valerytrails.com.au; 758 Valery Rd, Valery; 2hr rides adult/child $65/55) A stable of more than 75 horses and plenty of acreage to explore; located 15km northeast of town.

Coffs City Skydivers　　　　SKYDIVING
(☑02-6651 1167; www.coffsskydivers.com.au; Coffs Harbour Airport; tandem jumps $269-359) Throw yourself out of a plane from 4572m in the highest beach skydive in Australia.

Jetty Dive　　　　DIVING
(☑02-6651 1611; www.jettydive.com.au; 398 Harbour Dr) The Solitary Islands Marine Park is a meeting place of tropical waters and southern currents, making for a wonderful combination of corals, reef fish and seaweed. This dive shop offers spectacular diving and snorkelling trips (double boat dives $170), PADI certification ($445), and, from June to October, whale watching (adult/child $59/49).

🌟 Festivals & Events

Sawtell Chilli Festival　　　　FOOD & DRINK
(www.sawtellchillifestival.com.au; ⊙early Jul) The hottest food festival on the Coffs Coast draws thousands of visitors for spicy food, cooking demonstrations, street entertainment and dancing off the (mild) winter chill.

🛏 Sleeping

Coffs Harbour YHA　　　　HOSTEL $
(☑02-6652 6462; www.yha.com.au; 51 Collingwood St; dm $30-33, d $90-140; @🐾) A very friendly and nicely positioned hostel with spacious dorms. Private rooms have bathrooms, and the TV lounge and kitchen are clean and colourful. You can hire surfboards and bikes. A favourite with both families and young travellers on the fruit-picking circuit.

Park Beach Holiday Park　　　　CAMPGROUND $
(☑02-6648 4888; www.coffsholidays.com.au; Ocean Pde; camp sites $35-45, cabins $89-140; 🐾🐾) This holiday park is massive but has an ideal location at the beach. Kids are well catered for with a shaded jumping pillow and an action-packed pool featuring slides and fountains.

★ Coffs Jetty BnB　　　　B&B $$
(☑02-6651 4587; www.coffsjetty.com.au; 41a Collingwood St; d $130-170; 🐾🐾) A cut above your average B&B, this townhouse has private, tastefully decorated, spacious rooms with walk-in wardrobes and terrific bathrooms. Enjoy your breakfast on the balcony, then make the easy stroll to the beach and jetty restaurants. One of the suites has a kitchenette, while all have microwaves and fridges.

Pier Hotel　　　　PUB $$
(☑02-6652 2110; www.pierhotelcoffs.com.au; 356 Harbour Dr; s without bathroom $69-129, d $129-179, without bathroom $99-135; P🐾) The Pier reinvigorates the Australian tradition of the upstairs pub room. A mix of shared and en suite accommodation occupies the lovely, airy 1st floor, all of which is simple but smartly furnished and comfortable. Downstairs the pub has both an unreconstructed public bar as well as an atmospheric wine cellar that's open evenings. Complimentary airport pick-ups and drop-offs are a nice bonus.

Observatory Apartments　　　　APARTMENT $$
(☑02-6650 0462; www.theobservatory.com.au; 30-36 Camperdown St; apt $177-190; 🐾🐾🐾) The studio, two- and three-bedroom apartments in this attractive modern complex are bright and airy, with cook-up-friendly kitchens. All have balconies, with views to the ocean across the road and parkland, and some have spa baths.

🍴 Eating

Old John's　　　　CAFE $
(www.facebook.com/oldjohns; 360 Harbour Dr; mains $10-17; ⊙6.30am-3.30pm daily, 5.30-9pm Wed) Coffs' cool kid enclave, with the town's best coffee and a menu of healthy hipster favourites, from breakfast chia 'pud' and superfood bowls or lunch salads of salt-roasted beets, Bellingen greens and goat's curd. Wednesday, and occasionally other, evenings see live music, cocktails, sliders and pasta.

Fishermen's Coop　　　　FISH & CHIPS $
(☑02-6652 2811; www.coffsfishcoop.com.au; Marine Dr; mains $10-17; ⊙11am-7pm) Grab some excellent fish and chips and devour them right beside the fishing trawlers of Coffs' sizeable fleet. You can call ahead for takeaways, too.

★ Lime Mexican　　　　MEXICAN $$
(☑0421 573 570; www.limemexican.com.au; 366 Harbour Dr; dishes $14-18; ⊙5-10pm Tue-Sun; 🐾) Lime does modern Mexican tapas-style, designed to share. The taco line-up includes the usual favourites as well as grilled salmon, seared scallops and braised lamb, and there are big plates with pork belly on spic‑ rice, cheese-stuffed jalapeño peppers a‑ smoky paprika corn.

Mangrove Jack's CAFE $$

(☑ 02-6652 5517; www.mangrovejackscafe.com. au; Promenade Centre, Harbour Dr; mains breakfast $10-18, lunch $18-32, dinner $25-36; ☺ 7.30am-3pm daily, 5-9pm Fri & Sat; ☎) The attraction here is the wonderful location on a quiet bend of Coffs Creek and the balcony where you can enjoy a coffee or beer.

★**Fiasco** ITALIAN $$$

(☑ 02-6651 2006; www.fiascorestaurant.com. au; 22 Orlando St; pizzas $19-24, mains $29-39; ☺ 5-9pm Tue-Sat) Upmarket Italian fare is prepared in an open kitchen using produce from the best local suppliers and herbs from the restaurant's own garden. Expect authentic delights such as organic Angus beef with celeriac purée, homemade egg pasta with pesto and ricotta, and well-done pizzas from the simple margherita to those embellished with buffalo mozzarella or Roman-style pork belly.

You can also choose to sit at the bar for antipasti and a glass of Italian vermentino or barbera

Latitude 30 SEAFOOD $$$

(☑ 02-6651 6888; www.latitude30.com.au; 1 Marina Dr; mains $30-40; ☺ 8am-9pm) So much to choose from at this seafood spot on the Marina: will it be shared plates of Thai-style soft-shell crab, gravlax and braised octopus, or a main of fish pie or seafood paella? With a view of the charming working harbour to the jetty and Muttonbird Island, or across to Little Park Beach and the Pacific Ocean?

The deck makes a table here one of the most sought-after in town.

♟ Drinking & Nightlife

Surf Club Park Beach PUB

(☑ 02-6652 9870; www.surfclubparkbeach.com; 23 Surf Club Rd, Park Beach; ☺ 7am-11pm) A Sunday-afternoon session on the beach deck listening to local musicians is a top Coffs experience. Drinks can take you into a seafood or tapas dinner.

ⓘ Information

Visitor Information Centre (☑ 02-6651 1629; www.coffscoast.com.au; Coffs Central, 35-61 Harbour Dr; ☺ 9am-5pm)

ⓘ Getting There & Away

AIR

Qantas (☑ 13 13 13; www.qantas.com.au), **Virgin** (☑ 13 67 89; www.virginaustralia.com) and

Tigerair (☑ 02-8073 3421; www.tigerair.com. au) all fly to **Coffs Harbour Airport** (☑ 02-6648 4767; www.coffscoast.com.au/airport; Airport Dr), 3km southwest of town. There are Fly Corporate services to Brisbane.

BUS

Long-distance and regional buses operated by **Greyhound** (☑ 1300 473 946; www.greyhound. com.au), **Premier** (☑ 13 34 10; www.premierms. com.au) and **New England Coaches** (☑ 02-6732 1051; www.newenglandcoaches.com.au) leave from the **bus stop** on the corner of McLean St and the Pacific Hwy.

TRAIN

NSW CountryLink (☑ 13 22 32; www.nswtrain-link.info) runs three daily trains to Casino, which connect to Brisbane ($84.15, 5½ hours) by either train or coach, and south to Sydney ($95, nine hours).

North of Coffs Harbour

The Pacific Hwy runs near the coast – but not in sight of it – for 30km north of Coffs. Look for turn-offs to small beaches that are often quite uncrowded.

Around 25km north of Coffs, **Woolgoolga** (locally known as Woopi) is famous for its surf and its Sikh community. It's worth stopping by, particularly when the **Bollywood Beach Bazaar** (☑ 02-6654 7673; www.facebook.com/bollywoodmarket; ☺ 1st & 4th Sat of month) or **Curryfest** (www.curryfest.com.au; ☺ Sep) are on.

The village of Red Rock is set between a beautiful beach and a glorious fish-filled river inlet. **Yuraygir National Park** (www.nationalparks.nsw.gov.au/yuraygir-national-park; vehicle entry $8) is the state's longest stretch of undeveloped coastline, covering a 65km stretch of pristine coastal ecosystems stretching north from Red Rock. The isolated beaches are outstanding and there are bushwalking paths where you can view endangered coastal emus.

You can bush-camp at six basic camp sites (adult/child $10/5 per night).

Grafton

POP 18,700

The small city of Grafton on the Clarence River marks the start of the Northern Rivers region, which stretches all the way to the Queensland border. It's an area defined as much by its beaches and clement weather as it is by its three major waterways (the Richmond and Tweed Rivers are the others). Don't be fooled by the franchises along the highway – Grafton's grid of gracious streets has grand pubs and some splendid old houses.

◉ Sights

Victoria Street Precinct AREA
Victoria St is the city's main heritage precinct, with some fine examples of 19th-century architecture, including the **courthouse** (1862) at No 47, the **Anglican Cathedral** (commenced 1884) on the corner of Duke St and **Roches Family Hotel** (1871) at No 85.

✪✦ Festivals & Events

Jacaranda Festival CULTURAL
(www.jacarandafestival.org.au; ⊘late Oct) For two weeks from late October, Australia's longest-running floral festival paints the town mauve.

⌂ Sleeping & Eating

Annie's B&B B&B $$
(☑0421 914 295; www.anniesbnbgrafton.com; 13 Mary St; s/d $145/160; ❉☎❉) This beautiful Victorian house on a leafy corner has private rooms with an old-fashioned ambience, set apart from the rest of the family home. A continental breakfast is provided.

Heart & Soul Wholefood Cafe CAFE $
(☑02-6642 2166; 124a Prince St; mains $8-15; ⊘7.30am-5pm, to 2pm Sat, 8am-noon Sun; ☑) This beautifully styled cafe is the work of two couples who love plant-based eating. Expect ceramic bowls filled with warming Asian soups and stir fries, bright salads, and sweet treats such as the choc-mint 'cheese-fake'.

♟ Drinking & Nightlife

Roches Family Hotel PUB
(☑02-6642 2866; www.roches.com.au; 85 Victoria St; ⊘10am-11pm Mon-Thu, to midnight Fri & Sat, 11am-10pm Sun) Breaking the rule that states regional pubs must be cavernous and starkly lit, this historic corner hotel is a cosy spot for a drink or a reasonably priced bite. It's worth calling in just for a peek at the beer-can collection and the croc in the public bar.

ⓘ Information

Clarence River Visitor Information Centre
(☑02-6642 4677; www.clarencetourism.com; cnr Spring St & Pacific Hwy; ⊘9am-5pm; ☎) South of the river.

ⓘ Getting There & Away

AIR
Regional Express (Rex; ☑13 17 13; www.rex. com.au) flies to Sydney on weekdays from the **Clarence Valley Regional Airport** (GFN; ☑02-6643 0200; www.clarence.nsw.gov.au), 12km south of town.

BUS
Busways (☑02-6642 2954; www.busways. com.au) Runs local services including four to eight buses to Maclean (one hour), Yamba (1¼ hours) and Angourie (1½ hours) daily; all $12.30.

Greyhound (☑1300 473 946; www.greyhound. com.au) Coaches to/from Sydney (10½ hours, three daily), Nambucca Heads (2½ hours, two daily), Coffs Harbour (one hour, three daily), Byron Bay (three hours, three daily) and Brisbane (6½ hours, three daily).

Northern Rivers Buslines (☑02-6626 1499; www.nrbuslines.com.au) One bus to/from Maclean ($6, 43 minutes) and Lismore ($6, three hours) on weekdays.

Premier (☑13 34 10; www.premierms.com.au) Daily coaches to/from Sydney ($67, 9½ hours), Nambucca Heads ($34, 1¾ hours), Coffs Harbour ($34, one hour), Byron Bay ($47, 4¼ hours) and Brisbane ($52, 7½ hours).

Ryans Bus Service/Forest Coach Lines North (☑02-6652 3201; www.ryansbusservice. com.au) Weekday buses to/from Woolgoolga ($21, 1½ hours), Red Rock ($20, 50 minutes) and Coffs Harbour ($21.80, two hours).

TRAIN
There are good **train** (☑13 22 32; www. nswtrainlink.info) links to Sydney as well as Kempsey, Nambucca Heads, Coffs Harbour and also, less frequently, Brisbane.

Yamba & Angourie

At the mouth of the Clarence River, the fishing town of Yamba is rapidly growing in popularity thanks to its gently bohemian lifestyle, splendid beaches, and excellent cafes and restaurants. Oft heard descriptions such as 'Byron Bay 20 years ago' are not unfounded. Neighbour Angourie, 5km to the south, is a tiny, chilled-out place that has long been a draw for experienced surfers and was proudly one of Australia's first surf reserves.

◉ Sights

Angourie Blue Pools SPRING
(The Crescent) These springwater-fed waterholes south of Spooky Beach are the remains of the quarry used for the breakwater. Darin

folk climb the cliff faces and plunge to the depths. The saner can slip silently into the water, surrounded by bush, only metres from the surf.

Bundjalung National Park NATIONAL PARK
(www.nationalparks.nsw.gov.au/bundjalung-national-park; vehicle entry $8) Stretching for 25km along the coast north of the Clarence River to South Evans Head, this national park is largely untouched. Most of it is best explored with a 4WD. However, the southern reaches can be easily reached from Yamba via the passenger-only **Clarence River Ferries** (☑ 0408 664 556; www.clarence-riverferries.com.au; adult/child return $8.30/4.20; ⊙ 11am-3pm) to Iluka (at least four daily). This section of the park includes Iluka Nature Reserve, a stand of rainforest facing Iluka Beach, part of the Gondwana Rainforests World Heritage Area.

On the other side of Iluka Bluff the literally named Ten Mile Beach unfurls.

🏃 Activities

Yamba Kayak KAYAKING
(☑ 02-6646 0065; www.yambakayak.com; adult/child per 3hr $70/60, per 5hr $100/80) Half- and full-day kayaking adventures are the speciality, with forays into nearby wilderness areas. Hire also available.

Xtreme Cycle & Skate CYCLING
(☑ 02-6645 8879; www.facebook.com/Yamba CycleSkate; 34 Coldstream St, Yamba; bike hire per half-/full day $22/30; ⊙ 9.30am-4.30pm Mon-Fri, 9am-noon Sat, noon-2pm Sun) Great family-run shop that offers cycle hire (including dual-suspension mountain bikes), sales and repairs. Ask or check the Facebook page for details of its casual trail-ride convoy out in the state forest (they can of course rent you a bike if you don't have your own with you).

🛏 Sleeping

Pacific Hotel PUB $
(www.pacifichotelyamba.com.au/accommodation; 18 Pilot St, Yamba; dm $30-40, d with/without bathroom $130/80; 🅿 🛜) 'Motel-style' rooms in this lovely old pub have a lot of charm and satisfyingly clean lines. If you can put up with sharing a bathroom and manage to snare a corner cheapie, you've hit the view jackpot of a lighthouse out one window and the sea out the other. En suite rooms have balconies as well as fridges and TVs.

Yamba YHA HOSTEL $
(☑ 02-6646 3997; www.yha.com.au; 26 Coldstream St, Yamba; dm $32-36, d $95; @ 🛜 ⊛) This welcoming, family-run hostel has light-filled dorms, a popular bar and restaurant downstairs, and a barbecue area with a tiny pool on the roof.

Seascape Ocean Front Apartments APARTMENT $$
(☑ 0429 664 311; www.seascapeunits.com.au; 4 Ocean St, Yamba; apt $175-250; 🅿 🛜) Two ocean-view apartments, a small bungalow and a riverside cottage are all furnished in bright, contemporary nautical style. Apartment views are spectacular and each space has retained its '50s Australian coastal bones. As you can imagine, given the views, the location is the best. Prices are cheaper for mutiple-night stays.

🍴 Eating

★ Beachwood Cafe TURKISH $$
(☑ 02-6646 9781; www.beachwoodcafe.com.au; 22 High St, Yamba; mains breakfast $12-18, lunch $18-26; ⊙ 7am-2pm Tue-Sun) Cookbook author Sevtap Yüce steps out of the pages to deliver her bold *Turkish Flavours* to the plate at this wonderful little licensed cafe. Most of the tables are outside, where the grass verge has been commandeered for a kitchen garden. From the organic mandarin juice and passionfruit polenta cake to the Turkish-style sardines and dolmades for lunch, it's a surprising delight.

★ Leche Cafe CAFE $$
(☑ 0401 471 202; www.facebook.com/LecheCafe; 27 Coldstream St, Yamba; mains $14-25; ⊙ 6am-2pm) After some backyard yoga at Leche Cafe you might want to tuck into coconut bread and Byron Bay–based Marvell coffee. The sophisticated lunch menu is just as wholesome, with beetroot burgers, cauliflower curries and fish tacos. And it gets better: Leche hosts Saturday-night live gigs, DJs and parties, such as a midsummer Hawaiian luau.

🍷 Drinking & Nightlife

Pacific Hotel PUB
(☑ 02-6646 2466; www.pacifichotelyamba.com.au; 18 Pilot St, Yamba; ⊙ 10am-midnight Mon-Thu, to 1.30am Fri & Sat) Perched on the the cliffs overlooking Yamba Beach, this 1930-built hotel really does have some of the best pub views in Australia. There are regular live music and DJ nights, and the food's tasty, too.

ℹ Getting There & Away

Yamba is 15km east of the Pacific Hwy; turn off at the Yamba Rd intersection just south of the Clarence River. There are four to eight **Busways** buses (☑ 02-6645 8941; www.busways.com. au) from Yamba to Angourie ($3.40, nine minutes), Maclean ($9.30, 19 minutes) and Grafton ($12.30, 1¼ hours) daily. **Greyhound** (☑ 1300 473 946; www.greyhound.com.au) runs coach services up and down the coast to all the big towns and cities; **NSW Trainlink** (☑ 13 22 32; www.nswtrainlink.info) looks after the others.

Ballina

POP 14,070

At the mouth of the Richmond River, Ballina is spoilt for white sandy beaches and crystal-clear waters. In the late 19th century it was a rich lumber town; a scattering of gracious historic buildings can still be found on its backstreets. These days Ballina is popular with family holidaymakers and retirees, and home to the region's airport.

◎ Sights

For a good sampling of local history, stroll the length of Norton Street, which boasts a number of impressive late 19th-century buildings from Ballina's days as a rich lumber town.

Northern Rivers Community Gallery   GALLERY
(NRCG; ☑ 02-6681 6167; www.nrcgballina.com; 44 Cherry St) An excellent regional gallery representing the strong creative community that is an essential part of this region. Housed in the historic former Ballina Municipal Council Chambers, built in 1927, it hosts a rota of shows that showcase local artists and craftspeople, and also includes edgy, contemporary works and interesting events.

Big Prawn   LANDMARK
(Ballina Bunnings, 507 River St) Ballina's big prawn was nearly thrown on the BBQ in 2009, but no one had the stomach to dispatch it. After a 5000-signature pro-prawn petition and a $400,000 restoration in 2013, the 9m, 35-tonne, 30-year-old crustacean is looking as fetching as ever.

ᑕℱ Tours

Aboriginal Cultural Concepts   CULTURAL
(☑ 0405 654 280; www.aboriginalculturalconcepts. com; half-/full-day tours per person $80/160; ☉ Wed-Sat) Gain an Indigenous Australian perspective on the local area with heritage

tours exploring mythological sites along the Bundjalung coast. You can also do a self-drive tour meeting up with your guide at middens, former camping grounds, contact sites, fertility sites, fish traps and hunting areas along the way.

Kayak Ballina   KAYAKING
(☑ 02-6681 4000; www.kayakballina.com; tours $70) Kayak Ballina's beautiful waterways on these three-hour guided tours; you may pass dolphins and migratory birds.

⊨ Sleeping

Ballina Travellers Lodge   MOTEL $
(☑ 02-6686 6737; www.ballinatravellerslodge. com.au; 36-38 Tamar St; d without bathroom $75, with bathroom $115-125; ❄ ✳ 🛜 ☲) The motel rooms here are surprisingly plush, with feature walls, pretty bedside lamps and nice linen. Super-saver rooms (that is, the ones that share a bathroom) are a rung down in the decor stakes but represent good value.

Shaws Bay Holiday Park   CARAVAN PARK $
(☑ 02-6686 2326; www.northcoastholidayparks.com. au; 1 Brighton St; camp sites/cabins from $42/143; ✳ @ 🛜) Manicured and well positioned, this park is on the lagoon and an easy walk from the centre. The range of self-contained units includes three deluxe villas.

Ballina Palms Motor Inn   MOTEL $$
(☑ 02-6686 4477; www.ballinapalms.com; cnr Bentinck & Owen Sts; s $125, d $135-160; ✳ ✳ ☲) With its lush garden setting and carefully considered decor, this little place is a standout motel. The rooms aren't overly large, but they all have kitchenettes, floorboards, marble tops in the super-fresh bathrooms and high comfort levels.

Ballina Heritage Inn   MOTEL $$
(☑ 02-6686 0505; www.ballinaheritageinn.com. au; 229 River St; d $120-165; ✳ 🛜 ☲) Near the centre of town, this tidy inn has neat, bright and comfortable rooms that are a significant leap up in quality from most of the other motels on this strip.

✕ Eating

★ **Belle General**   CAFE $
(☑ 0411 361 453; www.bellegeneral.com; 12 Shelly Beach Rd; dishes $12-19; ☉ 8am-3pm) Eggs on kale; coconut and date loaf; blueberry hotcakes. Lamb burgers, paleo veggie lasagne, nasi goreng…everything is gluten-free, unle~ you're having something on sourdough to~

but even then you can sub in some quinoa loaf if you prefer.

Ballina Gallery Cafe
CAFE $$

(☑02-6681 3888; www.ballinagallerycafe.com.au; 46 Cherry St; mains breakfast $12-18, lunch $14-26; ⊙7.30am-3pm Wed-Sun) Ballina's 1920s former council chambers are home to the town's best cafe. Interesting breakfasts such as saganaki baked eggs and green fritters are offered with a side serve of contemporary art. Dine inside or outside on the verandah.

La Cucina di Vino
ITALIAN $$

(☑02-6618 1195; www.lacucinadivino.com; 2 Martin St; mains $24-35, pizzas $17-19; ⊙5-9pm Mon & Tue, 11am-3pm & 5-9pm Wed-Sun) Water views and carefully prepared dishes make this old-school Italian restaurant beneath the Ramada hotel a choice for a long lunch or dinner.

ℹ Information

Ballina Visitor Information Centre (☑02-6686 3484; www.discoverballina.com; 6 River St; ⊙9am-5pm)

ℹ Getting There & Away

AIR

Ballina Byron Gateway Airport (☑02-6681 1858; www.ballinabyronairport.com.au; Southern Cross Dr) is 5km north of the centre of town. Qantas flies from Sydney only, but **Jetstar** (☑13 15 38; www.jetstar.com.au) and **Virgin** (☑13 67 89; www.virginaustralia.com) also run services to/from Melbourne. A taxi to the centre of Ballina should cost roughly $12 to $15. There are regular buses and shuttle services and rental-car options for Ballina and beyond.

BUS

A number of bus lines service local towns and beyond, linking to Sydney and Brisbane, including NSW TrainLink buses that link to rail services in Casino.

Blanch's (☑02-6686 2144; www.blanchs. com.au)

Greyhound (☑1300 473 946; www.greyhound. com.au)

NSW TrainLink (☑13 22 32; www.nswtrainlink. info)

Premier (☑13 34 10; www.premierms.com.au)

Lennox Head
POP 7340

A protected National Surfing Reserve, Lennox Head's picturesque coastline has some of the best surf on the coast, with a world-class point break. Its village atmosphere and laid-back locals make it a mellow alternative to its boisterous and well-touristed neighbour, Byron, 17km north, and you can also get well-made coffee and a rather good feed.

◉ Sights

Seven Mile Beach
BEACH

Long and lovely Seven Mile Beach starts at the township and stretches north. It's accessible to 4WDs, but you will need a permit from the Caltex Service Station. The best place for a dip is near the surf club, at the northern end of town.

⬛ Sleeping

Lake Ainsworth Holiday Park
CAMPGROUND $

(☑02-6687 7249; www.northcoastholidayparks. com.au; Pacific Pde; camp sites $34-39, cabins $95-130; 🐾) By the lake and near the beach, this family-friendly holiday park has a wide range of units, from rustic cabins without bathrooms to a deluxe villa sleeping six. There are fresh amenities and a kitchen for campers.

Lennox Point Holiday Apartments
APARTMENT $$

(☑02-6687 5900; www.lennoxholidayapartments. com; 20-21 Pacific Pde; apt $195-250; 🅿🕸🐾) Gaze at the surf from your airy apartment in this new complex, then take a splash with a borrowed board from reception. The one-bedroom apartments are the same size as the two-bedrooms, so they feel somewhat more spacious.

✕ Eating

★Cafe Marius
LATIN AMERICAN $$

(☑02-6687 5897; www.cafemarius.com.au; 90-92 Ballina St; mains $16-24; ⊙7am-3.30pm Mon-Thu, to 9pm Fri & Sat, 8am-3.30pm Sun) Hip kids serve and consume a super-tasty selection of Latin American and Spanish dishes, excellent coffee and jugs of sangria from morning to late in this cool little licensed cafe, nestled down the back of an arcade. Fridays and Saturdays between 5pm and 7pm are 'lazy arvo' hours, when buckets of Corona beer go for $20.

Foam
MODERN AUSTRALIAN $$

(☑02-6687 7757; www.foamlennox.com; 41 Pacific Pde; mains lunch $18-24, dinner $28-38; ⊙noon-3pm & 6-10pm Wed-Fri, 7.30am-3pm & 6-10pm Sat, 7.30am-3pm Sun) With its Seven Mile Beach views and the atmosphere of a luxury beach house, the deck at Foam is the spot to fuel up over breakfast (even the bread is house-made) or a share a bottle of well-sourced wine over a long lunch. There's a Saturday dinner service with both à la carte and a five-course tasting menu ($85).

ⓘ Getting There & Away

Ballina airport is around 14km away and is serviced by local bus company **Blanch's** (☑ 02-6686 2144; www.blanchs.com.au) as well as local taxis.

Byron Bay

POP 4960

The intense popularity of Byron Bay can be, at first, a mystery. Sure, the beaches are sublime, but there are spectacular beaches all along this coast. Its locals have come to symbolise an Australian haute-boho lifestyle, yet much of the town is a squat, architectural mishmash and has a traffic problem. So why the legions of global fans? As they say in Byron, it's the vibe.

Come to surf epic breaks at dawn, paddle through hazy beach afternoons and sigh at the enchanting sunsets. Come to do reiki, refine your yoga practice, do a raw fast and hang with the fire-twirlers by the beach at sunset. Idle with the striped T-shirt set at the town's excellent restaurant tables, then kick on with backpackers, musicians, models, young entrepreneurs, ageing hippies and property developers at one of its beery, shouty pubs. Or, because it's Byron, do all of the above, then repeat.

◉ Sights

★ Cape Byron State Conservation Park
STATE PARK
(www.nationalparks.nsw.gov.au/cape-byron-state-conservation-area) Spectacular views reward those who climb up from the **Captain Cook Lookout** (Lighthouse Rd) on the **Cape Byron Walking Track**. Ribboning around the headland, the track dips and (mostly) soars its way to the lighthouse. Along the way, look out for dolphins (year-round) and migrating whales during their northern (June to July) and southern (September to November) migrations. You're also likely to encounter bold brush turkeys and shyer wallabies. Allow about two hours for the entire 3.7km loop.

You can also drive right up to the lighthouse (parking costs $7).

Cape Byron Lighthouse
LIGHTHOUSE
(www.nationalparks.nsw.gov.au; Lighthouse Rd; ⊙10am-4pm) FREE This 1901 lighthouse is Australia's most easterly and also its most powerful shipping beacon. Inside there are maritime and nature displays. If you want to venture to the top, you'll need to take one of the volunteer-run tours, which operate from 10am to 3pm (with gold-coin donation). There's also a cafe and self-contained accommodation in the lighthouse-keeper's cottages. Parking $7.

The Farm
FARM
(www.thefarmbyronbay.com.au; 11 Ewingsdale Rd, Ewingsdale; tours adult/child/family $10/5/25; ⊙7am-4pm) FREE A community of growers and producers share this impossibly photogenic, 80-acre green oasis just outside Byron, along with the Three Blue Ducks (p161) restaurant, a produce store, a bakery and a florist. The passionate dedication to traditional and sustainable practices here is both a working ethos and an educational mission. Feel free to roam and picnic between veggie plots and cattle-dotted fields. Tours happen twice daily (9am and 1pm) during January and mornings the rest of the year.

🏃 Activities

Adventure sports abound in Byron Bay and most operators offer a free pick-up service from local accommodation. Surfing and diving are the biggest draws.

Skydive Byron Bay
SKYDIVING
(☑02-6684 1323; www.skydivebyronbay.com; Tyagarah Airfield; tandem jumps $200-350) Hurtle to earth from 4267m with young, fun and well-trained instructors.

Be Salon & Spa
SPA
(☑0413 432 584; www.besalonspa.com.au; 14 Middleton St; 30min massages $60) Manicures, pedicures, facials and waxing are offered alongside 'metaphysical' healing, massage, re-balancing and naturopathy.

Go Sea Kayaks
KAYAKING
(☑0416 222 344; www.goseakayakbyron.com.au; adult/child $69/59) ⚓ Sea kayak tours in Cape Byron Marine Park led by a team of local surf lifesavers.

Byron Bay Ballooning
BALLOONING
(☑1300 889 660; www.byronbayballooning.com.au; Tyagarah Airfield; adult/child $350/175) One-hour sunrise flights including champagne breakfast; Byron's wonderful place to balloon over.

Surf & Bike Hire
CYCLING
(☑02-6680 7066; www.byronbaysurfandbikehire.com.au; 31 Lawson St; ⊙9am-5pm) Rents bik

Byron Bay

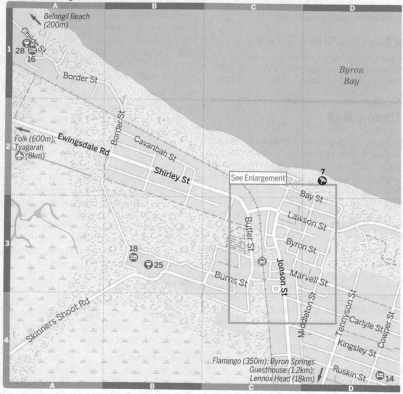

and surfboards (from $10 per day) plus other active gear.

Dive Byron Bay
DIVING

(☑ 02-6685 8333; www.byronbaydivecentre.com.au; 9 Marvell St; dives $60, snorkelling tours $69; ☺ 9am-5pm) Introductory ($165), freediving ($550) and Professional Association of Diving Instructors (PADI; from $1595) courses.

Black Dog Surfing
SURFING

(☑ 02-6680 9828; www.blackdogsurfing.com; 11 Byron St; 3½hr lessons $65) Intimate (seven people max) group lessons, including women's and kids' courses. Highly rated.

☞ Tours

★ Mountain Bike Tours
MOUNTAIN BIKING

(☑ 0429 122 504; www.mountainbiketours.com.au; half-/full-day tours $79/119) ✿ Environmentally aware bike tours into the rainforest and along the coast.

Aboriginal Cultural Concepts
CULTURAL

(☑ 0405 654 280; www.aboriginalculturalconcepts.com; half-/full-day tours $80/160; ☺ 10am-1pm Wed-Sat) Heritage tours exploring mythological sights along the Bundjalung coast. Includes bush-tucker tour.

✦ Festivals & Events

Byron Bay Writers' Festival
LITERATURE

(www.byronbaywritersfestival.com.au; ☺ early Aug) Gathers together big-name writers and literary followers from across Australia.

Splendour in the Grass
MUSIC

(www.splendourinthegrass.com; North Byron Parklands; ☺ late Jul) Three-day festival featuring big-name indie artists. Huge.

Byron Bay Bluesfest
MUSIC

(www.bluesfest.com.au; Tyagarah Tea Tree Farm; ☺ Easter; ☎) Held over Easter, this jam attracts high-calibre international performers

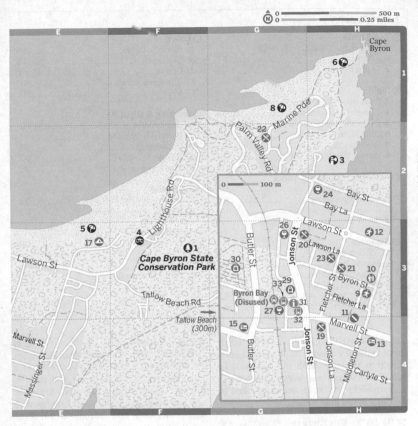

(Neil Young and Barry Gibb in recent years) and local heavyweights.

Sleeping

By any standards, Byron beds are expensive. Many locals rent out their own places, but even Airbnb and holiday lets are inflated. If you're in the market for 'barefoot luxury' – relaxed but stylish – you're in luck. Book well in advance for January, during festival time and school holidays. If you're not a teenager, avoid Schoolies Week (which actually runs for a few weeks from mid-November).

★ **Nomads Arts Factory Lodge**   HOSTEL $
(☎02-6685 7709;   www.nomadsworld.com/arts-factory; Skinners Shoot Rd; dm $35-43, d $85-115; ❋@�❋)   🍃 For an archetypal Byron experience, try this rambling mini-city next to a picturesque swamp, 15-minutes' walk from town. Choose from colourful six- to 10-bed dorms, a female-only lakeside cottage, or a tepee village. Couples can opt for aptly titled 'cube' rooms, island-retreat canvas huts or the pricier 'love shack' with bathroom.

Byron Beach Resort   HOSTEL $
(☎02-6685 7868;   www.byronbeachresort.com.au; 25 Childe St; dm $32-52, d $105-160, 2-bed cottages $260; P❋☎)   This fabulous, well-managed resort opposite Belongil Beach is a terrific and affordable alternative to staying in central Byron. Attractive dorms, cottages and self-contained apartments are scattered through the hammock-filled gardens. There's daily yoga, free bikes and the fun Treehouse (p162) pub next door. It's a 15-minute walk (or free shuttle ride) down Belongil Beach into town.

Clarkes Beach Holiday Park   CAMPGROUND
(☎02-6685 6496;   www.northcoastholidaypa
com.au; 1 Lighthouse Rd; camp sites $47-67, c

Byron Bay

$165-345; ❋ ☎) The cabins might be tightly packed but they, along with shady tent sites, sit within attractive bush in what must be one of the town's most spectacular settings, high up above the beach and overlooked by the Capy Byron lighthouse.

★ Barbara's Guesthouse GUESTHOUSE $$
(☑ 0401 580 899; www.byronbayvacancy.com; 5 Burns St; d $160-250; ☎) This pretty 1920s family home, in a quiet residential street, has four simple but elegant guest rooms. Lofty ceilings, smart beachy style and thoughtful hosts make this a great easy-going choice. There's a communal kitchen where breakfast supplies and a coffee machine greet you each morning, and there's an airy back deck for an early evening drink and catch up.

Flamingo GUESTHOUSE $$
(☑ 02-6680 9577; www.flamingobyronbay. au; 32 Bangalow Rd; ste $139-179, cottages $249-299; P ❋ ☎) The Flamingo offers a choice of suites, a super-stylish barn or a four-bedroom house. All feature polished timber floors, fully equipped kitchens, modern bathrooms and ~~large open verandahs, creating a perfect com-~~ ~~-nation of rustic Byron charm and on point~~ ~~ign.~~

Arcadia House B&B $$
(☑ 02-6680 8699; www.arcadiahousebyron. com.au; 48 Cowper St; d $145-375; ❋ ☎) Amid a large garden on a quiet street, this delightful old Queenslander has airy verandahs and six traditionally furnished rooms with four-poster beds and cushion-strewn sofas. It's about a 10-minute walk to the beach, or jump on a complimentary bike.

Byron Springs Guesthouse GUESTHOUSE $$
(☑ 0457 808 101; www.byronsprings.com.au; 2 Oodgeroo Garden; s without bathroom $95-125, d $175-235, d without bathroom $150-175; P ☎) Polished floorboards, crisp white linen, big verandahs and a leafy setting a couple of kilometres south of town make this a lovely choice if you like to be removed from the throng. A continental breakfast is included and there are complimentary bikes.

★ 28° Byron Bay BOUTIQUE HOTEL $$$
(☑ 02-6685 7775; www.28byronbay.com.au; 12 Marvell St; d from $460; P ❋ ☎ ❄) A perfect combination of absolute privacy and personal warmth make this a rare find. An effortless, relaxed luxury lends each of the four rooms a bolthole appeal (especially with their deep baths and individual plunge pools), but you're also just a short amble to

Byron's favourite upmarket eating options and, of course, the beach.

Elements
RESORT $$$

(📞02-6639 1500; www.elementsofbyron.com.au; 144 Bayshore Dr; 1-bedroom villa $380; 🅿❄🛜🏊) 🏊 Behind 2km of Belongil dunes, this is Byron's newest and most luxurious resort. One hundred or so private villas nestle in coastal bushland and, while there are no ocean views, the sound of the surf, and cicadas, is ever present. Split-level villas are spacious, tasteful and soothing. The main pavilion, pool and restaurant have a relaxed, almost ironic Australian glamour.

Byron Beach Abodes
VILLA $$$

(📞0419 490 010; www.byronbeachabodes.com. au; cottages & apt $295-995) A handpicked collection of Byron's best design-driven properties, Byron Beach Abodes attracts overseas guests, honeymooners and Sydney's fashion set. Each has its own unique style and is nestled in the town's most upmarket enclave. You're close to the beach, lighthouse walks and the coffee hub of Top Shop.

Our pick is the Chapel, the smallest and least expensive but with an eclectic allure (100-year-old exposed bricks, recycled timber beams) and a loft-like palette of black and white.

✕ Eating

Byron is a darling destination for food-focused travellers. This could well be the clean-eating capital of the country: golden lattes are ubiquitous; juices are always cold-pressed; and breakfast bowls are more common than bacon and eggs. Weekly markets overflow with farm-fresh produce. Plenty of upmarket restaurants serve climate-appropriate Modern Australian dishes, and more casual eateries do global favourites such as tacos, tapas and sushi. Ingredients are usually local and sourced from small, organic producers. Book ahead for dinner.

★ Bay Leaf Café
CAFE $

(www.facebook.com/bayleafcoffee; 2 Marvell St; mains $14-22; ☺7am-2pm) You might be tempted to snigger at the raft of Byron clichées on offer at this always busy cafe (golden lattes, coconut cold brew, tousle-haired locals of both sexes, kombucha, a '70s psych rock soundtrack etc), but that would mean missing out on food and drinks that are made with love and a remarkable attention to detail.

Chichuahua
MEXICAN $

(📞02-6685 6777; Feros Arcade, 25 Jonson St; tacos $6.50-7.50; ☺11am-8.30pm) Follow the holy Virgin to this arcade hole-in-the-wall taqueria that serves up Byron's most authentic and good-value Mexican. It's ripe for takeaway (and also delivers within central Byron), but you can eat in if there's a spare fold-out chair and table available. The slow-roast brisket and chilli-coconut prawn tacos are hard to go past.

Combi
CAFE $

(www.wearecombi.com.au; 21-25 Fletcher St; ☺7am-4pm) Melbourne clean-eating icons Combi have brought their signature raw, organic and highly Instagrammable drinks, cakes and breakfast and lunch bowls to Byron. House-made milk (coconut or almond milk) can be had in coffee, or made into fruit, matcha or turmeric lattes, and in matcha or raw cacao mylkshakes or superfood smoothies.

The raw extends to pizza, pad Thai and pasta, and there's slow-cooked soup or gluten-free sandwiches.

★ Three Blue Ducks at the Farm
FARM RESTAURANT $$

(📞02-6684 7888; www.thefarmbyronbay.com.au; 11 Ewingsdale Rd, Ewingsdale; ☺7.30am-3pm Mon-Sun, 5-10pm Fri-Sun) The legendary Sydney team behind Three Blue Ducks moved up north to showcase its paddock-to-plate food philosophy. Their rustic barn cafe and restaurant forms the beating heart of The Farm (p157). The breakfast menu does typical Byron healthy, but also surprises with 'spanner crab scramble' or black sausage and roast potatoes. Lunch and dinner menus are simple, but there's a gentle sophistication to the cooking.

★ St Elmo
SPANISH $$

(📞02-6680 7426; www.stelmodining.com; cnr Fletcher St & Lawson Lane; dishes $14.50-28; ☺5-11pm Mon-Sat, to 10pm Sun) Perch on a stool at this moody modern tapas restaurant, where rock-star bar staff create wicked cocktails or can pour you one of the better wines by the glass found in this part of the world (including natural and minimal intervention drops). The solidly Iberian menu is bold and broad, with traditional favourites mixing it up with contemporary flourishes.

★ Folk
CAFE

(www.folkbyronbay.com; 399 Ewingsdale Rd; ma $15-18; ☺7.30am-2.30pm) This deligh wooden-cottage cafe is located beside a caravan park but is a world unto itself. The barista may pause while making your organic cow, soy, macadamia, coconut or almond latte to wander out and flip over the James Taylor vinyl, and you'll settle in with the menu of incredibly pretty and super-healthy drinks, salads and gluten-free cakes.

Roadhouse MODERN AUSTRALIAN, CAFE $$
(✏0403 355 498; www.roadhousebyronbay.com; 6/142 Bangalow Rd; mains $14-29; ⊘6.30am-2.30pm & 6-10pm Tue-Sat, 6.30am-2.30pm Sun & Mon) A short trip out of town will find you at Byron's most atmospheric night spot. Rocking incredible, locally sourced wholefoods and coffee, Roadhouse also transforms into a dimly lit, blues-infused bar late into the night, with more than 500 types of whisky on the menu and fresh, pop-in-your-mouth cocktails.

Rae's Restaurant SEAFOOD $$$
(✏02-6685 5366; www.raesonwategos.com; 8 Marine Pde, Watego's Beach; mains $38-45; ⊘noon-3pm & 6-11.30pm) The sound of the surf perfectly sets off the excellent seafood, poultry and vegetarian dishes at this exclusive little retreat in Watego's. Dishes are simple, clear flavoured and use wonderful local produce. The seafood degustation ($115; or $175 with matched wines) is a super way to while away an afternoon or evening.

Byron at Byron Restaurant MODERN AUSTRALIAN $$$
(✏02-6639 2111; www.thebyronatbyron.com.au; 77-97 Broken Head Rd; mains $34-58; ⊘8am-9pm) With flickering candles and a rainforest backdrop 4km south of town, this intimate resort restaurant offers light, Mediterranean-style dishes created around the best of the Northern Rivers region produce, such as sweet Bangalow pork and Yamba prawns. If you don't want to commit to a long lunch or dinner, the casual snack menu from 3pm to 9pm uses the same stellar produce.

🍷 Drinking & Nightlife

★**Treehouse on Belongil** PUB
(✏02-6680 9452; www.treehouseonbelongil.com; 25 Childe St; ⊘7.30am-11pm) A homespun beach bar where wooden decks spill out among the trees, afternoons are for drinking, and live, original music is played all weekend. Most of the food comes from the wood-fired oven.

ron Bay Brewing Co BREWERY
(.byronbaybrewery.com.au; 1 Skinners Shoot ⊘11am-midnight) At this old piggery

turned booze barn you can drink frosty glasses of house pale lager in a light, louvred space by the brewing vats or outside in the tropical courtyard shaded by a giant fig tree.

Beach Hotel PUB
(www.beachhotel.com.au; cnr Jonson & Bay Sts; ⊘11am-late) Soak up the atmosphere and the views in the iconic beachfront beer garden. Surf movies are screened out the back, and even though the one-time owner, '70s comedy star Strop, has moved on, the original *Crocodile Dundee* hat adorns the bar.

Railway Friendly Bar PUB
(The Rails; ✏02-6685 7662; www.therailsbyron bay.com; 86 Jonson St; ⊘11am-late) 'The Rails' indoor-outdoor mayhem draws everyone from lobster-red British tourists to high-on-life earth mothers and babyboomer tourists. The front beer garden, conducive to long, beery afternoons, has live music. Excellent burgers, with variants including roo, fish and tofu.

Cocomangas CLUB
(www.cocomangas.com.au; 32 Jonson St; ⊘9pm-late Wed-Sat) Byron's longest-standing nightclub, with regular backpacker nights. No entry after 1.30am.

🛍 Shopping

★**Byron Farmers' Market** MARKET
(www.byronfarmersmarket.com.au; Butler Street Reserve; ⊘8-11am Thu) Both a market and a symbol of the strength of the local community, this weekly market has a wide variety of mainly organic stalls, with both fresh produce and all manner of local products. Come early and hang with the locals for great coffee and breakfast, then linger for live music.

Arts & Industry Estate ARTS & CRAFTS
(www.byronartstrail.com) A booming mini-city around 3km inland from Byron proper, the Arts & Industry Estate is home to Byron's ever-growing community of creative businesses. Check the website or grab the *Industry Trail* map available from the tourist office or your accommodation, and explore its many homewares, vintage, fashion, jewellery and gourmet businesses. There are also good cafes and a brewery for rest stops.

Byron Bay Artisan Market MARKET
(www.byronmarkets.com.au; Railway Park, Jonson St; ⊘4-9pm Sat Nov-Mar) Local artists and designers show their wares at this popular

DON'T MISS

BYRON BEACHES

West of the town centre, wild **Belongil Beach** with its high dunes avoids the worst of the crowds and is clothing-optional in parts. At its eastern end lies the **Wreck**, a powerful right-hand surf break.

Immediately in front of town, lifesaver-patrolled **Main Beach** is busy from sunrise to sunset with yoga classes, buskers and fire dancers. As it stretches east it merges into **Clarkes Beach**. The most popular surf break is at the **Pass** near the eastern headland.

Around the rocks is gorgeous **Watego's Beach**, a wide crescent of white sand surrounded by rainforest. A further 400m walk brings you to secluded **Little Watego's** (inaccessible by car), another lovely patch of sand directly under rocky Cape Byron. Head here at sunset for an impressive moonrise. Tucked under the south side of the Cape (entry via Tallow Beach Rd) is **Cosy Corner**, which offers a decent-sized wave and a sheltered beach when the northerlies are blowing elsewhere.

Tallow Beach is a deserted sandy stretch that extends for 7km south from Cape Byron. This is the place to flee the crowds. Much of the beach is backed by **Arakwal National Park**, but the suburb of **Suffolk Park** sprawls along the sand near its southern end. **Kings Beach** is a popular gay-friendly beach, just off Seven Mile Beach Rd past the Broken Head Holiday Park.

night market. Expect leather goods, jewellery and clothing, plus live entertainment.

ℹ Information

Byron Central Hospital (☎02-6639 9400; www.ncahs.nsw.gov.au; 54 Ewingsdale Rd; ⏰24hr)

Byron Visitor Centre (☎02-6680 8558; www.visitbyronbay.com; Old Stationmaster's Cottage, 80 Jonson St; ⏰9am-5pm) The place for accurate tourist information, and last-minute accommodation and bus bookings.

ℹ Getting There & Away

AIR

Byron Bay Shuttle (www.byronbayshuttle.com.au; adult/child $20/12) and **Xcede** (☎02-6620 9200; www.byronbay.xcede.com.au) serve both Coolangatta (Gold Coast) ($37) and Ballina ($18) airports. The former airport has more flights.

BUS

Coaches stop on **Jonson St** near the tourist office. Operators include **Premier** (☎13 34 10; www.premierms.com.au), **Greyhound** (☎1300 473 946; www.greyhound.com.au) and **NSW TrainLink** (☎13 22 32; www.nswtrainlink.info; Jonson St).

Blanch's (☎02-6686 2144; www.blanchs.com.au) Regular buses to/from Ballina Byron Gateway Airport ($9.60, one hour), Ballina ($9.60, 55 minutes), Lennox Head ($7.60, 35 minutes), Bangalow ($6.40, 20 minutes) and Mullumbimby ($6.60, 25 minutes).

Brisbane 2 Byron Express Bus (☎1800 626 222; www.brisbane2byron.com; one way/return

$38/76) Two daily buses to/from Brisbane ($38, two hours) and Brisbane Airport ($54, three hours); one service only on Sundays.

Byron Bay Express (www.byronbayexpress.com.au; one way/return $30/55) Five buses a day to/from Gold Coast Airport (1¾ hours) and Surfers Paradise (2¼ hours) for $30/55 one way/return.

Byron Easy Bus (☎02-6685 7447; www.byronbayshuttle.com.au) Minibus service to Ballina Byron Gateway Airport ($20, 40 minutes), Gold Coast Airport ($39, two hours), Brisbane ($40, 3½ hours) and Brisbane Airport ($54, four hours).

Northern Rivers Buslines (☎02-6626 1499; www.nrbuslines.com.au) Weekday buses to/from Lismore (1½ hours; $12), Bangalow (30 minutes) and Mullumbimby (20 minutes), both $9.70.

TRAIN

People still mourn the loss of the popular CountryLink train service that ran from Sydney. **CountryLink** (p152) now has buses connecting to trains at the Casino train station (70 minutes). Get full details from the rather forlorn former train station.

NORTH COAST HINTERLAND

Away from the coast, the lush scenery ganic markets and a large populatior embraces alternative lifestyles mal one of Australia's most alluring regic locals and visitors alike (real-este are now as common an overhear

BRUNSWICK HEADS & CABARITA BEACH

About 15km north of Byron Bay, Brunswick Heads is also home to a top restaurant. With a teeny-tiny and simple (if effortlessly stylish) shop front (entered from Fingal St) and most bookings snapped up on release, **Fleet** (✆02-6685 1363; www.fleet-restaurant.com.au; Shop 2/16 The Terrace; dishes $16-24, degustation $85; ◷3-10pm) might be Australia's most cultish dining destination. Josh Lewis (chef) and Astrid McCormack (front of house) pursue a purist but joyful passion for produce. Dishes utilise local, sometimes foraged ingredients, cuts and animals that other restaurants leave behind, and produce that farmers foist upon them on the day, say a bunch of wild amaranth. The series of small dishes that appear from the open kitchen, from cream of smoked mullet served with crisps of fish skin and potato or a 'schnitzel sandwich' of crumbed veal sweetbreads on a soft roll with anchovy mayo are punchy with flavour and pretty on the plate. If you've not booked, keep checking in, especially for 3pm late-lunch settings. Miracles do happen.

If you're thinking of staying overnight, try the **Sails Motel** (✆02-6685 1353; www.thesails motel.com.au; 26-28 Tweed St; d $125-175, 2-bedroom $195-245; P❈ᐧᔕ), a genteel 1960s motel that has been transformed. Its 22 rooms are light and simple with the occasional design piece, great eco toiletries, comfortable beds, and microwaves and pretty plates and cups for balcony picnics. Owners Amanda and Simon know everyone in town and can help you decide where to eat or swim or hike.

About 50km north of Byron Bay, Cabarita Beach is a deliciously undeveloped beach town with nature reserves to the north and west, which is renowned for its surf breaks.

It's home to **Halcyon House** (✆02-6676 1444; www.halcyonhouse.com.au; 21 Cypress Cr; d $500-900), one of east-coast Australia's most lauded new hotels. This is pure creative luxe, with lots of whimsy in the decor, free minibars stocked with local beers and treats, and organic toiletries. The location is idyllic, nestled just back from the beach in a sea of pandanus, but unlike resort hotels elsewhere, it still feels part of a happy coastal community. The ground floor is given over to its wonderful restaurant, **Paper Daisy** (2-/3-course lunch $75/95, 3-/4-course dinner $95/110; ◷7-9am, noon-3pm & 6-10pm). It's a busy, visual space with bistro chairs and lots of small oils hung salon-style. Dishes push boundaries, but gently and with a seductive finesse; think paper-bark grilled fish with fennel, seaweed and beach plants or a meringue with nectarine sorbet.

cleansing once was). Stay up here for deep relaxation, good food and access to numerous healing practitioners. Or day-trip from the coast, visiting beautiful towns such as Bangalow or hitting the hiking trails and swimming holes of one of the region's extraordinary national parks.

Bangalow

POP 2160

Surrounded by subtropical forest and rolling green farmland 14km from Byron, Bangalow (Bangers to friends) is home to a flourishing creative community, a dynamic, sustainable food scene and a range of urbane bouiques. A new arts precinct, which houses mmunity arts organisations plus a num of cute shops and a lovely cafe, is but ll up the hill on Station St. The little eaves during the monthly **Bangalow** (www.bangalowmarket.com.au; Bangalow ds; ◷9am-3pm 4th Sun of month), but

it's well worth making trip at any time for a dose of its languid sophistication.

🛏 Sleeping

Bungalow 3 GUESTHOUSE $$
(✆0401 441 582; www.messengerproperty.com. au/bungalow3; 3 Campbell St; studios $130-165, houses $230-320; ❈) This pretty weatherboard cottage in central Bangalow has two simply decorated white rooms, and French doors opening to the deck and edible garden. There is an additional one-bedroom studio; larger groups can hire out the whole place.

⭐**Bangalow Guesthouse** B&B $$$
(✆02-6687 1317; www.bangalowguesthouse.com. au; 99 Byron St; r $195-285; ᐧ) This stately old wooden villa sits on the river's edge, so guests can spot platypuses and oversized lizards as they enjoy breakfast. It's the stuff of B&B dreams, with spacious private rooms and elegant, soulful decor that works well with the original architecture.

✖ Eating

★ Woods CAFE $
(www.folkbyronbay.com; 10 Station St; mains $12-19; ⊙ 7.30am-3pm Tue-Sun) A hinterland outpost of Byron's Folk cafe, this place forms the heart of the arts precinct. It's as indie and folky as you might imagine, a lovely place of whitewash and wood that serves up good coffee, the healthiest of sweets, drinks, and beautiful lunches such as soba noodles or local spiced rice and quinoa with kale, pickles, watercress and toasted seeds.

Italian Diner ITALIAN $$
(www.theitaliandiner.com.au; 37-39 Byron St; mains $24-36, pizzas $20-26; ⊙ noon-3pm & 6-10pm) Sitting on the verandah of this buzzy bistro, enjoying a Campari and a bowl of *linguine gamberi* made with sweet local prawns, it's hard not to imagine that you're enjoying a long lunch somewhere by the Med. There are also fabulous wood-fired pizzas and luscious desserts.

Town Restaurant & Cafe MODERN AUSTRALIAN $$$
(☑ 02-6687 2555; www.townbangalow.com.au; 33 Byron St; cafe mains $16-24, restaurant degustation $85; ⊙ cafe 8am-3pm Mon-Sat, 9am-3pm Sun, restaurant 7-9.30pm Thu-Sat) Upstairs (Uptown, if you will) is one of northern NSW's perennially excellent restaurants, serving a six-course degustation menu carefully and imaginatively constructed from seasonal local produce. There's a vegetarian option too, and both menus can be had with matched wines (add $55). Head Downtown for simple but beautifully done cafe breakfasts, light lunches and a counter that's heavy with sweet baked things.

☕ Drinking & Nightlife

Bangalow Hotel PUB
(www.bangalowhotel.com.au; 1 Byron St; ⊙ 10am-midnight Mon-Sat, noon-10pm Sun) Sit on the deck of this much-loved and nicely preserved pub for a drink; listen to live music; and order gourmet burgers. Alternatively, reserve a table at its more-upmarket **Bangalow Dining Rooms** (☑ 02-6687 1144; www.bangalowdining.com; mains $20-34; ⊙ noon-3pm & 5.30-9pm).

🛍 Shopping

★ Little Peach ARTS & CRAFTS, ANTIQUES
(☑ 02-6687 1415; www.littlepeach.com.au; 17 Byron St; ⊙ 10am-5pm Mon-Fri, to 4pm Sat & Sun) This little piece of Japan has been a Bangalow favourite for years. Regular buying trips to Tokyo mean a never-ending stock of stunning wooden *kokeshi* dolls, kimonos and other beautiful pieces made from vintage Japanese silks, as well as beautifully chosen French accessories and globally sourced homewares.

Bangalow Farmers Market MARKET
(Bangalow Hotel Car Park, 1 Byron St; ⊙ 8-11am Sat) One of the most favoured of the farmers markets, because of its pretty setting.

ℹ Getting There & Away

Blanch's (☑ 02-6686 2144; www.blanchs.com.au) Weekday bus 640 goes to/from Byron Bay ($6.60, 20 minutes) and Ballina ($7.60, 30 minutes).

Byron Easy Bus (☑ 02-6685 7447; www.byronbayshuttle.com.au) Operates shuttles to/from Ballina Byron Gateway Airport.

Northern Rivers Buslines (☑ 02-6626 1499; www.nrbuslines.com.au; 📶) Weekday buses to/from Lismore (1¼ hours, $6).

NSW TrainLink (☑ 13 22 32; www.nswtrainlink.info) Daily coaches to/from Murwillumbah ($9.70, 1¼ hours), Tweed Heads ($11.30, two hours), Burleigh Heads ($13.70, 1½ hours) and Surfers Paradise ($15.30, two hours).

Lismore

POP 29,410

Lismore is the unassuming commercial centre of the Northern Rivers region, chock full of heritage buildings and possessing a country-town saunter. A vibrant community of creatives, the Southern Cross University student population and a larger than average gay and lesbian presence provide the town with an unexpected eclecticism. It's an interesting place to visit, though most travellers prefer to stay on the coast or venture deeper into the hinterland.

◉ Sights

Koala Care Centre WILDLIFE RESERVE
(☑ 02-6621 4664; www.friendsofthekoala.org; Rifle Range Rd; adult/family $5/10; ⊙ tours 10am & 2pm Mon-Fri, 10am Sat) This centre takes in sick, injured and orphaned koalas; visits are only possible by guided tour at the designated times. It's a great way to both meet koalas and to support this volunteer service that help's them. To see koalas in the wild head to **Robinson's Lookout** (Robinson Av, Girard's Hill), immediately south of the town centre.

Lismore Regional Gallery GALLERY
(www.lismoregallery.org; 131 Molesworth St; ⊙10am-4pm Tue, Wed & Fri, to 6pm Thu, to 2pm Sat & Sun) FREE Lismore's diminutive gallery has long been a cultural force in the town and a real centre of creative life in the region. At the end of 2017 it's set to relocate to a large new site on the corner of Keen and Magellan Sts, with more than five gallery spaces and exciting new programs in the works.

✺ Festivals & Events

Tropical Fruits LGBT
(www.tropicalfruits.org.au; ⊙31 Dec) This legendary New Year's bash is country NSW's biggest gay and lesbian event. There are also parties at Easter and on the Queen's Birthday holiday in June.

Lismore Lantern Parade PARADE
(www.lanternparade.com; ⊙Jun) More than 30,000 people line the streets to watch giant illuminated creatures glide past on the Saturday closest to the winter solstice.

🛏 Sleeping

Karinga MOTEL $
(☑02-6621 2787; www.karingamotel.com; 258 Molesworth St; d $120-145; ❋🕲❋) The pick of the litter, the Karinga has had a tasteful facelift: rooms have been fully refurbished and there's a good lap pool and spa.

★ Melville House B&B $$
(☑02-6621 5778; www.melvillehouselismore.com; 267 Ballina St; s $40-140, d $50-165; ❂❋❋❋) This grand country home was built in 1942 by the owner's grandfather and features the area's largest private swimming pool. The six rooms offer superb value and are decorated with local art, cut glass and antiques. Some have external bathrooms but even the small 'struggling writer's room' has its own. Breakfast is included for the larger rooms; otherwise it's $10 extra.

✕ Eating

★ Republic of Coffee CAFE $
(☑0403 570 503; www.facebook.com/republicof coffee; 98 Magellan St; ⊙6.30am-2pm Mon-Fri) The most serious-about-coffee cafe in town. You can also pick up good pies, donuts and other pastries. But you're here for the coffee, right?

★ Palate at the Gallery MODERN AUSTRALIAN $$
(☑02-6622 8830; www.palateatthegallery.com; 133 Molesworth St; breakfast $15-19, mains $16-32; ⊙11.30am-2.30pm Tue-Fri, 8am-2.30pm Sat & Sun, 6-10pm Wed-Sat; 🕲) This slick pavilion has French doors opening onto a sunny, shrub-lined terrace. It morphs seamlessly from a smart daytime cafe into one of Lismore's best night-time dining options, serving elegant dishes such as mussels in white wine and roast chicken in a tarragon and cream sauce.

🍷 Drinking & Nightlife

Deck BAR
(SCU Unibar; ☑02-6626 9602; www.unibarand cafe.scu.edu.au; 1 Military Rd; ⊙9am-midnight university term time) A university bar that has great gigs due to Southern Cross University's unique 'Bachelor of Rock'n'Roll' program. Upcoming gigs are listed on the website. It's a student bar, so can get messy.

🛍 Shopping

Farmers Market MARKET
(Lismore Showground; ⊙8-11am Sat) Lismore stages its farmers market at the showground, off Nimbin Rd.

ⓘ Information

Lismore Visitor Information Centre (☑02-6626 0100; www.visitlismore.com.au; 207 Molesworth St; ⊙9.30am-4pm)

ⓘ Getting There & Away

AIR

Lismore Regional Airport (☑02-6622 8296; www.lismore.nsw.gov.au; Bruxner Hwy) Three kilometres south of the city.

Regional Express (Rex; ☑13 17 13; www.regionalexpress.com.au) Flies to/from Sydney.

BUS

Buses stop at the **Lismore City Transit Centre** (cnr Molesworth & Magellan Sts).

Northern Rivers Buslines (☑02-6622 1499; www.nrbuslines.com.au) Local buses plus services to/from Grafton (three hours), Ballina (1¼ hours), Lennox Head (one hour), Bangalow (1¼ hours) and Byron Bay (1½ hours); all fares are $12.

NSW TrainLink (☑13 22 32; www.nswtrainlink.info) Coaches to/from Byron Bay ($9.25, one hour), Mullumbimby ($11.55, one hour), Brunswick Heads ($13.85, 1½ hours) and Brisbane ($40.35, three hours).

WORTH A TRIP

HINTERLAND NATIONAL PARKS

The spectacular waterfalls, the sheer cliff of solidified lava and the dense rainforest of 80-sq-km **Nightcap National Park** (www.nationalparks.nsw.gov.au/nightcap-national-park; vehicles $8), around 25km west of Mullumbimby, are perhaps to be expected in an area with the highest annual rainfall in NSW. It's part of the Gondwana Rainforests World Heritage Area and home to many native birds and protected creatures. From Nimbin, a 10km drive via Tuntable Falls Rd and Newton Dr leads to the edge of the park and then on to Mt Nardi (800m).

The **Historic Nightcap Track** (16km, 1½ days), which was stomped out by postal workers in the late 19th century, runs from Mt Nardi to **Rummery Park**, a picnic spot and camping ground. **Peate's Mountain Lookout**, just on from Rummery Park, offers a panoramic view all the way to Byron. The **Minyon Loop** (7.5km, four hours) is a terrific half-day hike around the spectacular Minyon Falls, which are good for an icy splash. A largely unsealed but very scenic road leads from the Channon to the Terania Creek Picnic Area, where an easy track heads to **Protestor Falls** (1.4km return).

The vast **Border Ranges National Park** (www.nationalparks.nsw.gov.au/border-ranges-national-park; vehicles $8) covers 317 sq km on the NSW side of the McPherson Range, which runs along the NSW–Queensland border. It's part of the Gondwana Rainforests World Heritage Area and it's estimated that representatives of a quarter of all bird species in Australia can be found here.

The eastern section of the park can be explored on the 44km **Tweed Range Scenic Drive** (gravel, and usable in dry weather), which loops through the park from Lillian Rock (midway between Uki and Kyogle) to Wiangaree (north of Kyogle on Summerland Way). The signposting on access roads isn't good (when in doubt take roads signposted to the national park), but it's well worth the effort.

The road runs through mountain rainforest, with steep hills and lookouts over the Tweed Valley to Wollumbin (Mt Warning) and the coast. The short walk out to the **Pinnacle Lookout** is a highlight and one of the best places to see the silhouette of Wollumbin against a rising sun. At **Antarctic Beech** there is a forest of 2000-year-old beech trees. From here, a walking track (about 5km) leads down to lush rainforest, swimming holes and a picnic area at **Brindle Creek**.

Northwest of Uki, 41-sq-km **Wollumbin National Park** (www.nationalparks.nsw.gov.au/wollumbin-national-park) surrounds Wollumbin (Mt Warning; 1156m), the most dramatic feature of the hinterland, towering over the valley. Its English name was given to it by James Cook in 1770 to warn seafarers of offshore reefs. Its far older Aboriginal name, Wollumbin, means 'cloud catcher', 'fighting chief of the mountain' or 'weather maker'.

The summit is the first part of mainland Australia to see sunlight each day, a drawcard that encourages many to make the trek to the top. You should be aware that, under the law of the local Bundjalung people, only certain people are allowed to climb the sacred mountain; they ask you not to climb it, out of respect for this law. Instead, you can get an artist's impression of the view from the 360-degree mural at the **Murwillumbah Visitor Information Centre** (☑ 1800 118 295, 02-6672 1340; www.tweedtourism.com.au; 271 Tweed Valley Way; ☺ 9am-4.30pm).

Wollumbin is part of the Gondwana Rainforests World Heritage Area. Keep an eye out for the Albert's lyrebird on the Lyrebird Track (300m return).

Waller's (☑ 02-6622 6266; www.wallersbus.com) Three buses weekdays to/from Nimbin ($9.50, 30 minutes).

Nimbin

POP 1670

Welcome to Australia's alternative-lifestyle capital, a little town set in an impossibly pretty valley that almost drowns under the weight of its own clichés. Once an unremarkable Northern Rivers dairy village, Nimbin was changed forever in May 197? Thousands of counter-culture kids a back-to-earth-movement types descen on the town for the Aquarius Festival. N stayed on and created new communi' the beautiful countryside around th hoping to continue the ideals expres ing the 10-day celebration.

Today the psychedelic murals of the rainbow-serpent Dreaming and marijuana bliss that line Nimbin's main street are fading, and the dreadlocked, beaded locals are weathered. While genuine remnants of the peace-and-love generation remain, the town has become much darker since the '80s. The brazen weed dealers who make a living from the bus tours that barrel up from Byron are known to also peddle harder drugs, and alcohol-fueled violence is on the rise. See it once, but you'll probably not come back.

◎ Sights

★ Djanbung Gardens GARDENS
(☑02-6689 1755; www.permaculture.com.au; 74 Cecil St; tours $5, with guide $20; ◉10.30am-4pm Wed-Sun, guided tours 11am Sat) FREE Nimbin has been at the forefront of the organic gardening movement and this world-renowned permaculture education centre, created out of a degraded cow pasture, is home to food forests, vegetable gardens, a drought-proof system of dams, ponds and furry farm animals. There's a range of short courses available and you can book ahead for guided tours on Saturday mornings ($20).

Hemp Embassy CULTURAL CENTRE
(☑02-6689 1842; www.hempembassy.net; 51 Cullen St; ◉9am-5pm) Part shop, part stronghold for minor political group the Hemp Party, this colourful place raises consciousness about impending marijuana legalisation, and provides all the tools and fashion items you'll need to attract police attention. The embassy organises the **MardiGrass festival** in May (www.nimbinmardigrass.com).

🛌 Sleeping

Nimbin Rox YHA HOSTEL $
(☑02-6689 0022; www.nimbinrox.com.au; 74 Thorburn St; sites/teepees/dm/d from $14/26/30/68; @🛜🐾) Escape the coastal crowds at this hostel and camping ground perched on a lush hill at the edge of town. You'll find plenty of spots to unwind, with hammocks strung among the trees, a lovely heated pool and a nearby swimming creek. Friendly managers go out of their way to please with

free pancake breakfasts and a regular shuttle run into town.

Grey Gum Lodge GUESTHOUSE $
(☑02-6689 1713; www.greygumlodge.com; 2 High St; d $85-135; @🛜) The valley views from the front verandah of this palm-draped wooden Queenslander-style house are gorgeous. All the rooms are comfortable, tastefully furnished and have their own bathrooms.

Black Sheep Farm GUESTHOUSE $$
(☑02-6689 1095; www.blacksheepfarm.com.au; 449a Gungas Rd; d $220; 🐾) Guests might struggle to leave this self-contained cabin with a saltwater pool and a Finnish sauna on the edge of a rainforest. It sleeps up to seven people ($20 per extra person). There's also a smaller and cheaper cottage available.

✕ Eating

Nimbin Hotel PUB FOOD $
(☑02-6689 1246; www.nimbinhotel.com.au; Cullen St; mains $11-22; ◉11am-10pm) This classic boozer has a vast back porch overlooking a verdant valley. The Hummingbird Bistro serves up everything from a 'treehugger's salad' to curries and grilled barramundi. There's live music most weekends, and backpacker rooms upstairs.

❶ Information

Nimbin Visitor Information Centre (☑02-6689 1388; www.visitnimbin.com.au; 46 Cullen St; ◉10am-4pm)

❶ Getting There & Away

Various operators offer day tours or shuttles to Nimbin from Byron Bay, sometimes with stops at surrounding sights. Most leave at 10am and return around 6pm.

Gosel's (☑02-6677 9394) Two buses on weekdays to Uki (40 minutes) and Murwillumbah (one hour).

Grasshoppers (☑0438 269 076; www.grasshoppers.com.au) Daily return bus trips from Byron ($55, including BBQ lunch).

Waller's (☑02-6622 6266; www.wallersbus.com) At least three buses on weekdays to/from Lismore (30 minutes).

Canberra & South Coast New South Wales

Includes ➡

Why Go?

There's something special about the New South Wales coast-line south of Sydney, something about the light, about the region's under-the-radar status, about the oysters, about the inlets, estuaries and national parks with marine mammals frolicking offshore.

While it can't compare weather-wise to the more visited North Coast its scenic beauty is staggering. Rough, rustic national parks and traditional fishing towns harbour some of the nation's most idyllic beaches, from the white sands and calm turquoise water of amazing Jervis Bay to big surf strands along the whole stretch from the Royal National Park to Eden.

Best Places to Eat

➡ Courgette (p177)

➡ Cupping Room (p177)

➡ Silos Restaurant (p186)

➡ Tallwood (p190)

➡ Wharf Rd (p187)

➡ Caveau (p181)

Best Places to Sleep

➡ Hotel Hotel (p176)

➡ Bannisters by the Sea (p190)

➡ Laurels B&B (p184)

➡ Mystery Bay Campground (p193)

➡ Crown & Anchor Inn (p199)

When to Go
Canberra

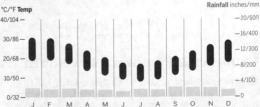

Mar
Good kayaking conditions and still a bit of warmth in the sea for swimming.

Oct
Peak whale- and seal-watching season, plus the Whale Festival in Eden.

Nov–Dec
Get down here before the school holidays start and have the beaches to yourself.

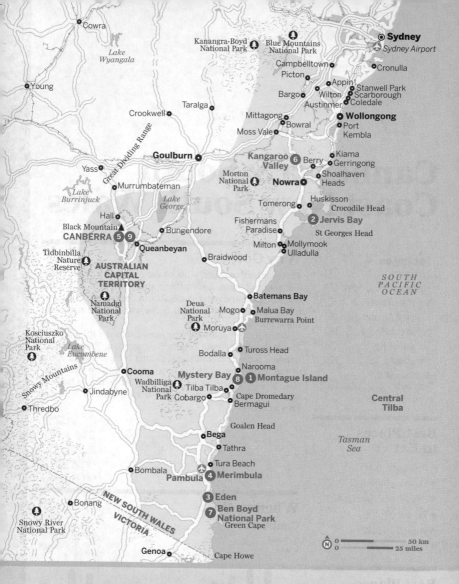

Canberra & Southern New South Wales Highlights

1 Montague Island (p193)
Encountering penguins and seals on this marvellous island sanctuary.

2 Jervis Bay (p187) Taking in white sands and crystal-clear waters at this paradisaical bay.

3 Whale watching (p198) Gasping in admiration at the bulk and grace of whales

4 Oyster eating (p198) Slurping the tastiest oysters in Merimbula and Pambula.

5 Parliament House (p173) Marvelling at the architectural splendour of Australia's seat of power.

6 Kangaroo Valley (p184) Contemplating a pastoral fantasy of rural Australia.

7 Ben Boyd National Park (p199) Hiking and wildlife-spotting in this excellent national park.

8 Mystery Bay (p193) Camping in rough comfort beside this idyllic beach.

9 National Museum of Australia (p175) Admiring the Australiana on display.

❶ Getting There & Around

AIR
Canberra Airport (p178) is within the city itself, only 7km southeast of Civic.

The only international flights are operated by **Singapore Airlines** (www.singaporeair.com), which flies to/from Singapore and Wellington.

BUS
Coaches run between Canberra and the capital cities, and from the capital cities along the coast.

CAR & MOTORCYCLE
The quickest route between Canberra and the coast is the Kings Hwy. The Princes Hwy winds its way from Wollongong in the north to Eden in the south and is the main route for exploring the coast.

TRAIN
Trains run between Canberra and Sydney; there are no direct trains between Melbourne and Canberra.

CANBERRA

Australians love to hate their capital, dismissing it as lacking in soul and being filled with politicians and bureaucrats. Don't let them put you off. Canberra is a wonderfully green little city, with a lively and sophisticated dining and bar scene, interesting architecture and a smorgasbord of major institutions to keep even the most avid culture vulture engrossed for days on end.

Laid out by visionary American architect Walter Burley Griffin and his wife Marion Mahony Griffin following an international design competition, Canberra features expansive open spaces, broad boulevards, aesthetics influenced by the 19th-century Arts and Crafts Movement, and a seamless alignment of built and natural elements.

During parliamentary sitting weeks the city hums with the buzz of national politics, but it can be a tad sleepy during university holidays, especially around Christmas and New Year.

History

The Ngunnawal people called this place Kanberra, believed to mean 'Meeting Place'. The name was probably derived from huge intertribal gatherings that happened annually when large numbers of bogong moths appeared in the city.

In 1901 Australia's separate colonies were federated and became states. The rivalry between Sydney and Melbourne meant neither could become the new nation's capital, so a location between the two cities was carved out of southern New South Wales (NSW) as a compromise. This new city was officially named Canberra in 1913, and became the national capital in 1927.

◉ Sights

★ **National Gallery of Australia** GALLERY
(🖉02-6240 6502; www.nga.gov.au; Parkes Pl, Parkes; costs vary for special exhibitions; ⊙10am-5pm) **FREE** The nation's extraordinary art collection is showcased in a suitably huge purpose-built gallery within the parliamentary precinct. Almost every big name you could think of from the world of Australian and international art, past and present, is represented. Famous works include one of Monet's *Waterlilies,* several of Sidney Nolan's *Ned Kelly* paintings, Salvador Dali's *Lobster Telephone,* an Andy Warhol *Elvis* print and a triptych by Francis Bacon.

Highlights include the extraordinary *Aboriginal Memorial* from Central Arnhem Land in the lobby, created for Australia's 1988 bicentenary. The work of 43 artists, this 'forest of souls' presents 200 hollow log coffins (one for every year of European settlement) and is part of an excellent collection of Aboriginal and Torres Strait Islander art. Most of the Australian art is on the 1st floor, alongside a fine collection of Asian and Pacific art.

Free guided tours are offered hourly from 10.30am to 2.30pm.

★ **National Portrait Gallery** GALLERY
(🖉02-6102 7000; www.portrait.gov.au; King Edward Tce, Parkes; ⊙10am-5pm) **FREE** Occupying a flash new purpose-built building, this wonderful gallery tells the story of Australia through its faces – from wax cameos of Indigenous Australians to colonial portraits of the nation's founding families, to Howard Arkley's DayGlo portrait of musician Nick Cave. There is a good cafe for post-exhibition coffee and reflection.

★ **Australian War Memorial** MUSEUM
(🖉02-6243 4211; www.awm.gov.au; Treloar Cres, Campbell; ⊙10am-5pm) **FREE** Canberra's glorious art deco war memorial is a highlight in a city filled with interesting architecture. Built to commemorate 'the war to end all wars', it opened its doors in 1941 when the next world

Central Canberra

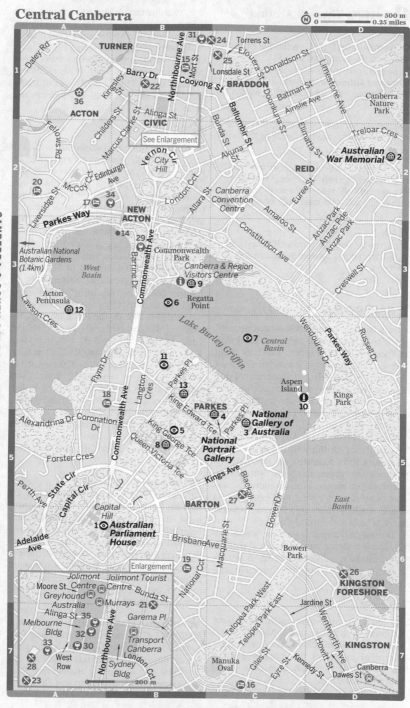

N

0 — 500 m
0 — 0.25 miles

TURNER

Daley Rd

31

24

Torrens St

15 Mort St

Elouera St

Donaldson St

Barry Dr

22

Cooyong St

Lonsdale St

25

BRADDON

Batman St

Ainslie Ave

Limestone Ave

Canberra Nature Park

36

ACTON

Kingsley St

Childers St

Marcus Clarke St

Alinga St

CIVIC

See Enlargement

Bunda St

Ballumbir St

Akuna St

Doonkuna St

Elmatta St

Treloar Cres

Australian War Memorial 2

Fellows Rd

20

McCoy Cct

Edinburgh Ave

Liversidge St

Vernon Cir

City Hill

London Cct

Allara St

Canberra Convention Centre

REID

Euree St

Amaroo St

Constitution Ave

Anzac Park

Anzac Pde

Anzac Park

17 34

Parkes Way

NEW ACTON

14

29

Commonwealth Ave

Commonwealth Park

Canberra & Region Visitors Centre

Creswell St

Australian National Botanic Gardens (1.4km)

West Basin

Barrine Dr

9

6

Regatta Point

Lake Burley Griffin

Wendouree Dr

Parkes Way

Russell Dr

Acton Peninsula

12

Lawson Cres

7

Central Basin

Aspen Island

10

Kings Park

11

Flynn Dr

Parkes Pl

18

13

PARKES

4

King Edward Tce

Parkes Pl

National Gallery of Australia 3

Langton Cres

5

King George Tce

8

Queen Victoria Tce

National Portrait Gallery

Kings Ave

Blackall St

Bowen Dr

East Basin

Alexandrina Dr

Coronation Dr

Commonwealth Ave

Forster Cres

BARTON

27

Perth Ave

State Cir

Capital Cir

Capital Hill

1

Australian Parliament House

Macquarie St

Brisbane Ave

Bowen Park

Adelaide Ave

19

National Cct

Bowen Dr

26

KINGSTON FORESHORE

Jardine St

Telopea Park West

Telopea Park East

Wentworth Ave

Howitt St

Enlargement

0 — 200 m

Jolimont Centre

Jolimont Tourist Centre

Moore St

Greyhound Australia

Bunda St

Murrays

21

Alinga St

35

Garema Pl

Melbourne Bldg

32

30

Transport Canberra

London Cct

33

West Row

Sydney Bldg

Northbourne Ave

Giles St

Eyre St

Kennedy St

Manuka Oval

16

Dawes St

KINGSTON

Canberra

28

23

war was already in full swing. Attached to it is a large, exceptionally well designed museum devoted to the nation's military history.

★ Australian Parliament House

NOTABLE BUILDING

(📞 02-6277 5399; www.aph.gov.au; ⏰ 9am-5pm) **FREE** Opened in 1988, Australia's national parliament building is a graceful and deeply symbolic piece of architecture. The building itself is embedded in the Australian soil, covered with a turf roof and topped by a spindly but soaring 81m-high flagpole. The same detailed thought has been applied to the interior and there's plenty to see inside, whether the politicians are haranguing each other in the chambers or not.

After passing through airport-style security, visitors are free to explore large sections of the building and watch parliamentary proceedings from the public galleries. The only time that tickets are required is for the high theatre of **Question Time** in the House of Representatives (2pm on sitting days); tickets are free but must be booked through the Sergeant at Arms. See the website for a calendar of sitting days.

After entering through the **Marble Foyer**, pop into the **Great Hall** to take a look at the vast tapestry, which took 13 weavers two years to complete. Upstairs in the corridors surrounding the hall, there are interesting displays including temporary exhibits from the Parliamentary art collection. Look out for a 1297 edition of the **Magna Carta** and the original of Michael Nelson Tjakamarra's *Possum & Wallaby Dreaming,* which features both on the $5 note and writ large as the mosaic you passed in Parliament's forecourt.

There are further displays in the **Members' Hall**, ringed with august portraits of former prime ministers. From the hall, corridors branch off towards the two debating chambers. Australia has a Westminster-style democracy and its chambers echo the colour scheme of the famous 'Mother of Parliaments' in London, with a subtle local twist. Rather than the bright red of the House of Lords and the deep green of the lower house, Australia's parliament house uses a dusky pink for its **Senate** and a muted green for the **House of Representatives**, inspired by the tones of the local eucalypts.

Lifts head up to the roof where there are lawns designed for people to walk on – a reminder to the politicians below that this is the 'people's house'. As the focal point of Canberra, this is the best place to get a perspective on Walter Burley Griffin's city design. Your eyes are drawn immediately along three axes, with the Australian War Memorial backed by Mt Ainslie directly ahead, the commercial centre

CANBERRA & SOUTH COAST NEW SOUTH WALES CANBERRA

Central Canberra

on an angle to the left and Duntroon (representing the military) on an angle to the right. Interestingly, the church is denied a prominent place in this very 20th-century design.

Free guided tours (30 minutes on sitting days, 45 minutes on nonsitting days) depart at 9.30am, 11am, 1pm, 2pm and 3.30pm.

Museum of Australian Democracy
MUSEUM

(☑ 02-6270 8222; www.moadoph.gov.au; Old Parliament House, 18 King George Tce, Parkes; adult/child/family $2/1/5; ☉ 9am-5pm) The seat of government from 1927 to 1988, this elegantly proportioned building offers visitors a whiff of the political past. Displays cover Australian prime ministers, the roots of democracy and the history of local protest movements. You can also visit the old Senate and House of Representative chambers, the parliamentary library and the prime minister's office. Kids will love the dress up and play rooms, while those with a thing for bling will enjoy the replica crown jewels.

Aboriginal Tent Embassy
HISTORIC SITE

(King George Tce, Parkes) First erected in 1972, this protest camp on the lawn in front of Old Parliament House came and went over the following 20 years but has been a constant presence since then, providing a continuing reminder of Indigenous dispossession for those visiting the symbolic heart of Australian democracy.

National Library of Australia
LIBRARY

(☑ 02-6262 1111; www.nla.gov.au; Parkes Pl, Parkes; ☉ gallery 10am-5pm) FREE This institution has accumulated more than 10 million items since being established in 1901 and has digitised more than nine billion files. Don't miss the **Treasures Gallery**, where artefacts such as Captain Cook's *Endeavour* journal and Captain Bligh's list of mutineers are among the regularly refreshed displays; free 30-minute tours are held at 11.30am daily.

WILDLIFE ON THE HOP

Canberra is one of the best cities in Australia for spotting wild kangaroos. Some of the best places include Weston Park on the shores of Lake Burley Griffin northwest of Parliament House, Government House, Mount Ainslie and Namadgi National Park.

Australian National Botanic Gardens
GARDENS

(☑ 02-6250 9588; www.nationalbotanicgardens.gov.au; Clunies Ross St, Acton; ☉ 8.30am-5pm) FREE On Black Mountain's lower slopes, these large gardens showcase Australian floral diversity over 35 hectares of cultivated garden and 50 hectares of remnant bushland. Various themed routes are marked out, with the best introduction being the 30-to-45 minute main path, which takes in the eucalypt lawn (70 species are represented), rock garden, rainforest gully and Sydney Region garden. A 3.2km bushland nature trail leads to the garden's higher reaches.

National Zoo & Aquarium
ZOO

(☑ 02-6287 8400; www.nationalzoo.com.au; 999 Lady Denman Dr, Weston Creek; adult/child $40/23; ☉ 9.30am-5pm) It's certainly not the biggest in Australia but Canberra's zoo is well laid out and animal friendly, with plenty of big cats and cute critters to keep the kids amused. It also offers various behind-the-scenes experiences where you can help to feed the sharks, lions, tigers and bears, and interact with rhinos and cheetahs.

National Arboretum
PARK

(☑ 02-6207 8484; www.nationalarboretum.act.gov.au; Forest Dr, Weston Creek; ☉ 6am-8.30pm Oct-Mar, 7am-5.30pm Apr-Sep) FREE Located on land previously affected by bush fires, Canberra's National Arboretum is an ever-developing showcase of trees from around the world. It is early days for many of the plantings, but it's still worth visiting for the spectacular visitor centre and the excellent views over the city. Regular guided tours are informative, and there is a brilliant adventure playground for kids.

To get here, catch bus 81 (weekdays) or bus 981 (weekends) from platform 10 at the Civic bus interchange.

Questacon
MUSEUM

(☑ 02-6270 2800; www.questacon.edu.au; King Edward Tce, Parkes; adult/child $23/18; ☉ 9am-5pm; ➕) This kid-friendly science centre has educational and fun interactive exhibits. Explore the physics of sport, athletics and fun parks; cause tsunamis; and take shelter from cyclones and earthquakes. Exciting science shows, presentations and puppet shows are all included.

National Museum of Australia   MUSEUM

(☑ 02-6208 5000; www.nma.gov.au; Lawson Cres, Acton Peninsula; tours adult/child $15/10; ☺ 9am-5pm) **FREE** As well as telling Australia's national story, this museum hosts blockbuster touring exhibitions. Don't miss the 12-minute introductory film, shown in the small rotating Circa Theatre before you dig in. The exhibition jam-packed with Aboriginal artefacts is a highlight. However, the disjointed layout of the displays means that the museum didn't quite gel in the way that Canberra's other national cultural institutions do.

National Capital Exhibition   MUSEUM

(☑ 02-6272 2902; www.nationalcapital.gov.au; Barrine Dr, Commonwealth Park; ☺ 9am-5pm) **FREE** This small but fascinating museum tells the story of how Canberra came to be Australia's capital. Displays include reproductions of the drawings entered in the international competition to design the city, including the exquisite watercolour renderings of the winning design created by Marion Mahony Griffin, the often overlooked wife and creative partner of Walter Burley Griffin.

Lake Burley Griffin   LAKE

This ornamental lake was created in 1963 when the 33m-high Scrivener Dam was erected on the Molonglo River. It's lined with important institutions and monuments, including the **National Carillon** (☑ 02-6257 1068; www.nationalcapital.gov.au; Aspen Island, Lake Burley Griffin) and **Captain Cook Memorial Water Jet** (Lake Burley Griffin). You can cycle the entire 28km perimeter in two hours or walk it in seven. Alternatively, you can split the route into smaller chunks by judicious use of the two main bridges.

Royal Australian Mint   MUSEUM

(☑ 02-6202 6999; www.ramint.gov.au; Denison St, Deakin; ☺ 8.30am-5pm Mon-Fri, 10am-4pm Sat & Sun) **FREE** The Royal Australian Mint is Australia's biggest money-making operation. Its gallery showcases the history of Australian coinage; here you can learn about the 1813 'holey dollar' and its enigmatic offspring, the 'dump'.

☞ Tours

Balloon Aloft   BALLOONING

(☑ 02-6249 8660; www.canberraballoons.com.au; 120 Commonwealth Ave, Yarralumla; adult/child from $330/240) Meet in the foyer of the Hyatt for a flight over Canberra – the ideal way to understand the city's unique design.

KIDS IN THE CAPITAL

Kids like Canberra because there's lots of cool stuff for them to do. Most of the museums and galleries have kids programs, and many offer dedicated tours and events – check websites for details.

For hands-on fun, visit **Questacon** (p174), the **National Museum of Australia** (p175) and the **Australian Institute of Sport** (AIS; ☑ 02-6214 1010; www.experienceais.com; Leverrier St, Bruce; adult/child $20/12; ☺ tours 10am, 11.30am, 1pm & 2.30pm). It's even possible to cuddle a cheetah and pat a red panda at the **National Zoo & Aquarium** (p174).

For fresh air and exercise, go for a bike ride around Lake Burley Griffin or head to the **Tidbinbilla Nature Reserve** (☑ 02-6205 1233; www.tidbinbilla.act.gov.au; Tidbinbilla Reserve Rd; entry per car $12; ☺ 7.30am-6pm Apr-Nov, to 8pm Oct-Mar, visitor centre 9am-5pm) or **Namadgi National Park** (☑ 02-6207 2900; www.environment.act.gov.au; Naas Rd, Tharwa; ☺ visitor centre 9am-4pm) **FREE**.

Lake Burley Griffin Cruises   CRUISE

(☑ 0419 418 846; www.lakecruises.com.au; Barrine Dr, Acton; adult/child $20/9; ☺ mid-Sep–May) Informative one-hour lake cruises.

✦✦ Festivals & Events

Enlighten   CULTURAL

(www.enlightencanberra.com.au; ☺ early Mar) For 10 days in early March various Canberra institutions are bathed in projections and keep their doors open late, while a night noodle market fills bellies and live music fills the air.

Floriade   FAIR

(www.floriadeaustralia.com; ☺ mid-Sep–mid-Oct) This elaborate display of spring flowers is one of the city's biggest events, drawing the crowds to Commonwealth Park from mid-September to mid-October.

🛏 Sleeping

Canberra's accommodation is at its busiest and most expensive during parliamentary sitting days. Hotels charge peak rates midweek, but reduced rates at weekends. Peak rates also apply during the Floriade festival in September and October.

★ **Blue & White Lodge** MOTEL $
(☎02-6248 0498; www.blueandwhitelodge.com.au; 524 Northbourne Ave, Downer; s/d $95/100; P✳🔹) On the main approach into Canberra from the north, this long-standing motel-style place and its indistinguishable sister, the Canberran Lodge, are reliable budget options in what can be a pricey city. It's a long walk into town but there's a bus stop nearby.

★ **Little National Hotel** HOTEL $$
(☎02-6188 3200; www.littlenationalhotel.com.au; 21 National Circuit, Barton; r from $119; P✳@🔹) Housed within a stark black-metal cube, this brilliant boutique hotel delivers affordable style by way of small but well designed rooms. Compensating for the lack of cat-swinging space is an appealing 'library' and a bar offering panoramic views of the city. Book early; advance bookings are a steal but prices can more than double when it's busy.

★ **East Hotel** HOTEL $$
(☎02-6295 6925; www.easthotel.com.au; 69 Canberra Ave, Kingston; apt from $220; P✳@🔹) Straddling the divide between boutique and business, East offers stylishly executed spaces and smile-inducing extras such as free lollies and design magazines for loan in the lobby. Even the studios have work desks, iPod docks, espresso machines and kitchenettes, and there are one- and two-bedroom suites if you need to spread out. Plus there's an exceedingly cool bar and a bookshop-restaurant downstairs.

Aria Hotel HOTEL $$
(☎02-6279 7000; www.ariahotel.com.au; 45 Dooring St, Dickson; r/apt from $159/191; P✳@🔹) The standard rooms aren't overly large in this new block but they have comfy beds, excellent rainfall showers, balconies and everything else you'd expect from a smart business hotel. There are some good deals to be had if you book ahead.

Avenue HOTEL $$
(☎02-6246 9500; www.avenuehotel.com.au; 80 Northbourne Ave, Braddon; r/apt from $143/219; P✳🔹) Raw concrete offset with angled glass provides a striking if somewhat brutal introduction to this large, contemporary hotel. Rooms are spacious and schmick; ask for one facing the central courtyard to avoid the traffic noise. Parking is free if you book directly.

University House HOTEL $$
(☎02-6125 5211; http://unihouse.anu.edu.au; 1 Balmain Cres, Acton; s/tw/d/apt from $101/135/150/195; P✳🔹) This 1950s-era building, with original custom-built furniture, resides in the bushy grounds of the Australian National University (ANU) and is favoured by research students, visiting academics and the occasional politician. The spacious rooms and two-bedroom apartments are unadorned but comfortable. There's also a peaceful central courtyard and a friendly little cafe downstairs.

★ **Hotel Hotel** HOTEL $$$
(☎02-6287 6287; www.hotel-hotel.com.au; 25 Edinburgh Ave, New Acton; r from $266; ✳🔹) Hotel Hotel's spectacular exterior translates to an equally hip interior. Rooms are quirkily decorated, and while the (very) subdued lighting isn't to everyone's taste, we're big fans of the hotel's audacious and dramatic ambience. Reception is filled with nooks, crannies and mini-libraries, and Hotel Hotel's **Monster Kitchen & Bar** (☎02-6287 6287; www.monsterkitchen.com.au; Hotel Hotel, 25 Edinburgh Ave, New Acton; breakfast $16-19, shared plates $20-35; ⊙6.30am-1am) is just as interesting.

★ **Hyatt Hotel Canberra** HOTEL $$$
(☎02-6270 1234; www.canberra.park.hyatt.com; 120 Commonwealth Ave, Yarralumla; r from $295, ste from $690; P✳@🔹🏊) Spotting visiting heads of state is a popular activity in the foyer of Canberra's most luxurious and historic hotel. More than 200 rooms, well used meeting spaces and a popular tea lounge mean that a constant stream of visitors passes through the building. Rooms are large and extremely well equipped, and facilities include an indoor pool, a spa, a sauna and a gym.

🍴 Eating

Canberra has a sophisticated dining scene, catering to political wheelers and dealers and locals alike. Established dining hubs include Civic, Kingston and Griffith, and there are good Asian eateries in Dickson. New Acton, the Kingston Foreshore development and Lonsdale St in Braddon are the hippest new areas.

Hamlet STREET FOOD $
(www.broddogs.com.au; 16 Lonsdale St, Braddon; mains $5-20; ⊙noon-late) Symptomatic of the enviable hipsterisation of Braddon, the Hamlet is a wonderfully ramshackle village of food trucks and hole-in-the-wall eateries, accompanied by a bar, a gallery and plenty of outdoor seating. Our current favourite

outlet is BrodDogs, a tasty offshoot of Kingston's Brodburger, which sells nothing but good-quality, tasty hot dogs. If that doesn't appeal, there's Italian, Greek, Vietnamese, Indian...

Two Before Ten
CAFE $

(www.twobeforeten.com.au; 1 Hobart Pl, Civic; mains $11-18; ⊙7am-4pm Mon-Fri, 8am-2pm Sat & Sun) Breaking from the Australian tradition that says good cafes should be bohemian and battered looking, this airy eatery brings a touch of Cape Cod to the centre of a city block. Serves are perhaps a little too fashionably petite but the coffee is excellent.

★ Cupping Room
CAFE $$

(⊉02-6257 6412; www.thecuppingroom.com.au; 1 University Ave, Civic; mains $11-24; ⊙7am-4pm; ☻) Queues often form outside this airy corner cafe, drawn by the prospect of Canberra's best coffee and an interesting menu, including vegetarian and vegan options. The seasonal chia pudding is extraordinary, but if you prefer something a little more familiar, the burgers are equally as epic. Choose your coffee blend from the tasting notes and prepare to be amazed.

★ Akiba
ASIAN $$

(⊉02-6162 0602; www.akiba.com.au; 40 Bunda St, Civic; noodle & rice dishes $12-15, share plates $18-33; ⊙11.30am-midnight Sun-Wed, to 2am Thu-Sat) A high-octane vibe pervades this super-slick pan-Asian eatery, fuelled by a hip young crew that effortlessly splashes together cocktails, dispenses food recommendations and juggles orders without breaking a sweat. A raw bar serves up delectable sashimi, freshly shucked oysters and zingy ceviche. Salt-and-Sichuan-pepper squid and pork-belly buns are crowd pleasers, and we love the Japanese-style eggplant.

★ Morks
THAI $$

(⊉02-6295 0112; www.morks.com.au; 19 Eastlake Pde, Kingston; mains $24-30; ⊙noon-2pm & 6-10pm Tue-Sat, noon-2pm Sun) Our favourite of the restaurants along the Kingston foreshore, Morks offers a contemporary spin on Thai cuisine, with Chinese and Malay elements added to the mix. Ask for a table outside to watch the passing promenade, and tuck into multiple serves of the starters; the sweet potato dumplings in Penang curry are staggeringly good.

Elk & Pea
LATIN AMERICAN $$

(⊉0436 355 732; www.elkandpea.com.au; 21 Lonsdale St, Braddon; breakfast & lunch $11-25, tacos $8, shared plates $39-45; ⊙7.30am-2.30pm Mon, to 11pm Tue-Sun) Mexican influences pervade the menu and cocktail list of this hip little anytime eatery, which includes spicy eggs for brekkie, burgers and wraps for lunch, and Canberra's best tacos for dinner. In the evening there's also a menu of substantial Latin American–influenced dishes designed to be split between two or three people.

★ Courgette
MODERN AUSTRALIAN $$$

(⊉02-6247 4042; www.courgette.com.au; 54 Marcus Clarke St, Civic; 3-course lunch $66, 4-course dinner $88; ⊙noon-3pm & 6.30-11pm Mon-Sat) With its crisp white linen, impeccable service and discreet but expensive ambience, Courgette is the kind of place to bring someone you want to impress, like a date or, perhaps the Finnish ambassador. The exacting standards continue with the precisely prepared, exquisitely plated and flavour-laden food.

★ Aubergine
MODERN AUSTRALIAN $$$

(⊉02-6260 8666; www.aubergine.com.au; 18 Barker St, Griffith; 4-course menu $90; ⊙6-10pm Mon-Sat) You'll need to travel out to the southern suburbs to find Canberra's top-rated restaurant. While the location may be unassuming, the same can't be said for the menu, which is exciting, innovative and seasonally driven. Although only a four-course menu is offered, you can choose between a handful of options for most courses. Service and presentation are assured.

Ottoman
TURKISH $$$

(⊉02-6273 6111; www.ottomancuisine.com.au; 9 Broughton St, Barton; mains $32-36; ⊙noon-2.30pm & 6-10pm Tue-Fri, 6-10pm Sat) Set in an elegant garden pavilion, Ottoman has long been a favourite dining destination for Canberra's power brokers. Familiar dishes (meze, dolma, kofte) are given subtle contemporary twists, but for the most part they're left deliciously traditional.

🍺 Drinking & Nightlife

Pubs and bars are concentrated in Civic and around Lonsdale and Mort Sts in Braddon. New Acton is also worth a look.

Aviary Rooftop
ROOFTOP BAR

(⊉0421 552 417; www.aviaryrooftop.com; 3 Barrine Dr, Acton; ⊙5pm-late Thu, noon-late Fri-Sun) Perched on top of a stack of shipping containers by the shore of Lake Burley Griffin, this large open-sided space offers drinks in plastic glasses and has regular DJ sets. I⁴ you're peckish, head to one of the food stalls downstairs by the popular basketball court.

Bar Rochford   WINE BAR

(☑02-6230 6222; www.barrochford.com; L1, 65 London Circuit, Civic; ☺5pm-late Tue-Thu, noon-1am Fri, 5pm-1am Sat) Bearded barmen concentrate earnestly on their cocktail constructions and wine recommendations at this sophisticated but unstuffy bar in the Melbourne Building. Dress up and hope for a table by one of the big arched windows.

Joe's Bar   COCKTAIL BAR

(☑02-6178 0050; www.joesateast.com; East Hotel, 69 Canberra Ave, Kingston; ☺noon-late) Colourful glass and draped metal beads add to the glitzy boho ambience at this attractive Italian food and wine bar attached to the East Hotel. The extensive cocktail list includes a whole page of speciality gin and tonics, and the bar staff really knows its Italian wines, too. Pace yourself with a serve of polenta chips, arancini balls or antipasti.

Molly's   COCKTAIL BAR

(www.molly.net.au; Rear, 37 London Circuit, Civic; ☺4pm-midnight Mon-Wed, to 2am Thu-Sat) The prohibition shtick is a now well worn trope but who doesn't love the thrill of wandering back lanes and discovering subterranean drinking dens? Molly's offers an eight-page whisky list, sorted by country (Indian whisky anyone?). To find it, turn off London Circuit at Gozleme Cafe, turn right and look for a lightbulb above an open wooden door.

Highball Express   COCKTAIL BAR

(www.highballexpress.com.au; L1, 82 Alinga St, Civic; ☺4pm-late Tue-Sat) There's no sign, so take a punt and climb the fire escape in the lane behind Smith's Alternative to this louche tropical take on a 1920s Cuban rum bar. The highball cocktails are excellent and often come served with banana chips.

BentSpoke Brewing Co   MICROBREWERY

(☑02-6257 5220; www.bentspokebrewing.com.au; 38 Mort St, Braddon; ☺11am-midnight) With 16 excellent beers and ciders on tap, BentSpoke is one of Australia's best craft brewers. Sit at the bike-themed bar or relax outside and kick things off with a tasting tray of four beers ($16). Our favourite is the Barley Griffin Ale, subtly tinged with a spicy Belgian yeast. Good pub food, too.

Smith's Alternative   BAR

(☑0401 084 773; www.smithsalternative.com; 76 Alinga St, Civic; ☺8am-midnight Mon-Thu, to 3am Fri & Sat, noon-midnight Sun) When the legendary Smith's Alternative Bookshop closed down, it turned out that the name worked just as well for its successor. The new Smith's is an artsy cafe-bar and performance space, with a makeshift stage in one corner and cakes in the cabinet. In the evenings, expect to be bemused by anything from live music to slam poetry to theatre.

Parlour Wine Room   WINE BAR

(☑02-6257 7325; www.parlour.net.au; 16 Kendall Lane, New Acton; ☺noon-late Tue-Sun) Modern banquettes share the polished wooden floor with well stuffed chesterfield lounges in this contemporary take on the Victorian smoking lounge. Views over the lake complement the list of local, Australian and international wines, and killer cocktails.

☆ Entertainment

ANU Bar   LIVE MUSIC

(☑02-6125 3660; www.anuunion.com.au; University Ave, Acton; gigs $5-20) The Uni Bar (on the Australian National University campus) has live gigs regularly during semester. Up-and-coming bands that have played here in the past include a little Seattle three-piece called Nirvana.

ℹ Information

Most of central Canberra is covered by a free wi-fi service.

Canberra & Region Visitors Centre (☑02-6205 0044; www.visitcanberra.com.au; Regatta Point, Barrine Dr, Commonwealth Park; ☺9am-4pm) Dispenses masses of information, including its own quarterly *Canberra Events* brochure.

ℹ Getting There & Away

AIR

Canberra Airport (☑02-6275 2222; www.canberraairport.com.au; 2 Brindabella Circuit) is within the city itself, only 7km southeast of Civic.

The only international flights are operated by Singapore Airlines (www.singaporeair.com), which flies to/from Singapore and Wellington.

Qantas (www.qantas.com) and associated QantasLink partners fly to/from Adelaide, Brisbane, Melbourne, Perth and Sydney. **Virgin Australia** (www.virginaustralia.com) flies to/from Adelaide, Brisbane, Gold Coast, Melbourne and Sydney. **Tigerair Australia** (www.tigerair.com.au) also heads to Melbourne, while **FlyPelican** (www.flypelican.com.au) services Newcastle and Dubbo.

BUS

The interstate bus terminal is at the **Jolimont Tourist Centre** (67 Northbourne Ave, Civic; ⊙ 5am-10.30pm), where you'll find booking desks for the major bus companies.

Greyhound Australia (✐ 02-6211 8545; www. greyhound.com.au; 65 Northbourne Ave; ⊙ 6am-6pm) Coaches to Sydney ($42, 3½ hours), Yass ($15, 55 minutes), Wagga Wagga ($40, three hours), Albury ($58, 4½ hours) and Melbourne ($88, eight hours), along with seasonal buses to the ski resorts.

Murrays (✐ 13 22 51; www.murrays.com.au; 65 Northbourne Ave; ⊙7am-7pm) Express services to Sydney ($45, 3½ hours), Wollongong ($49, 3¼ hours), Batemans Bay ($38, 2½ hours), Moruya ($41, 3¼ hours) and Narooma ($49, 4½ hours), as well as the ski fields.

NSW TrainLink (✐13 22 32; www.nswtrainlink. info) Coaches depart Canberra Railway Station on the Canberra–Cooma–Merimbula–Eden (daily) and Canberra–Cooma–Jindabyne (three per week) routes.

CAR & MOTORCYCLE

The Hume Hwy connects Sydney and Melbourne, passing 50km north of Canberra. The Federal Hwy runs north to connect with the Hume near Goulburn, and the Barton Hwy (Rte 25) meets the Hume near Yass. To the south, the Monaro Hwy connects Canberra with Cooma.

TRAIN

NSW TrainLink (p179) Services from Sydney ($56, four hours), Bowral ($34, 2½ hours), Bundanoon ($30, two hours) and Bungendore ($7, 40 minutes) pull into Kingston's **Canberra Railway Station** (Wentworth Ave, Kingston) three times daily.

V/Line (✐1800 800 007; www.vline.com.au) A daily service combines a train from Melbourne to Albury Wodonga with a bus to Canberra ($108, nine hours).

❶ Getting Around

TO/FROM THE AIRPORT

A taxi to the city centre costs from around $50 to $55.

Airport Express (✐1300 368 897; www. royalecoach.com.au; one way/return $12/20) runs between the airport and the city roughly hourly during the day.

Transport Canberra (p179) bus 11 runs between city platform 9 and Brindabella Business Park (right next to the airport) at least hourly between 6am and 6pm.

PUBLIC TRANSPORT

The bus network, operated by **Transport Canberra** (✐13 17 10; www.transport.act.gov.au; East Row, Civic; adult/child $4.70/2.30, day pass $9/4.50; ⊙ information centre 6.30am-10pm Mon-Sat, 8am-7pm Sun), will get you to most places of interest in the city. It recommends you use Google Maps as your travel planner, or call into the Civic office for maps and timetables.

A smart-card system operates, but if you're only here for a week or so, you're better off paying the driver in cash; a day pass costs less than two single tickets, so purchase one on your first journey of the day.

What is referred to as the city bus station is actually a set of 11 bus stops scattered along Northbourne Ave, Alinga St, East Row and Mort St.

At the time of writing, a new light rail track running north from Civic along Northbourne Ave, was under construction. The first stage is scheduled to be completed in late 2018.

WOLLONGONG & AROUND

POP 292,400

The 'Gong', 80km south of Sydney, has the laid-back ambience of a sizeable country town and is very likeable for just that reason. A small but enjoyable bar and restaurant scene adds to the charm of two excellent city beaches and a pretty harbour. The university gives it a youthful feel and the laid-back surfie lifestyle makes it easy to relax.

A spectacular forested sandstone escarpment runs south from the Royal National Park past Wollongong, overlooking a wonderful series of beaches, all with their own rail stop.

⊙ Sights

★**North Beach**   BEACH
Stretching north from the harbour, North Beach has breaks suitable for all visitors and is conveniently close to the city centre. It's the main centre of Wollongong beach action. For the most challenging waves head to the Acids Reef break near the rocks opposite Stuart Park. North Beach has lifesavers all year round at its southern end.

Wollongong City Beach   BEACH
The southern of Wollongong's two city beaches is a lovely stretch of whiteish sand with good swimming and, depending on the wind, surfing. Looking north it's a romantic vista of headland and lighthouse, but turn around and the view of the massive Port Kembla steelworks will banish any tropical island fantasies.

Wollongong

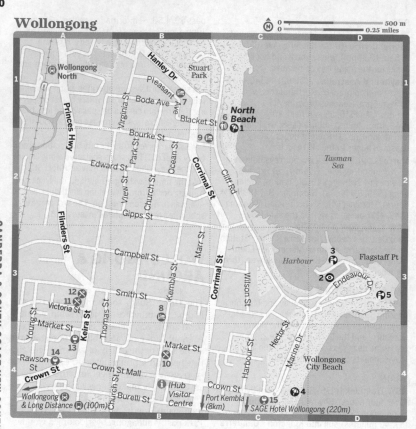

Wollongong

Wollongong Botanic Garden   GARDENS
(☎ 02-4227 7667; www.wollongong.nsw.gov.au/
botanicgarden; 61 Northfields Ave, Keiraville; ☺ 7am–
5pm Apr-Sep, 7am-6pm Mon-Fri, 7am-6.45pm Sat &
Sun Oct-Mar; ☐ 55A/55C) ✔ FREE Northwest
of the centre, but easily accessed on the
free 55 shuttle bus from the station, which
has a stop here, this has habitats including
tropical, temperate and woodland. It's a nice
break from the beach and a top spot for a
picnic lunch. In summer there's an outdoor
cinema (www.sunsetcinema.com.au).

Belmore Basin

HARBOUR

Wollongong's fishing fleet is based at this harbour's southern end. The basin was cut from solid rock in 1868. There's a fishing cooperative and the old **Breakwater Lighthouse** (built in 1872) on the point. Nearby, on the headland, is the newer **Wollongong Head Lighthouse** (Flagstaff Hill Lighthouse). The harbour beach is great for young children, with sand and gentle waves. Between here and North Beach there are both swimming pools and a swimmable rock pool.

Science Centre & Planetarium

MUSEUM

(📞02-4286 5000; www.sciencecentre.com.au; 60 Squires Way, North Wollongong; adult/child $14/10; ⊙10am-4pm Thu-Tue, daily Jan) Quizzical kids of all ages can indulge their senses here. The museum is operated by the University of Wollongong and covers everything from dinosaurs to electronics. Planetarium shows ($4.50, or $3 extra with an admission ticket) run throughout the day. You can get here on the free shuttle buses from Wollongong station (55A and 55C); they stops right outside.

Illawarra Escarpment State Conservation Area

PARK

(www.nationalparks.nsw.gov.au) Spectacular rainforest hugs the edge of the ever-eroding sandstone cliffs of the Illawarra escarpment that overlooks Wollongong and the coast north of it. It rises to 534m at Mt Kembla. For wonderful coastal views, drive up to the Mt Keira lookout (464m); take the freeway north and follow the signs. The train north from Wollongong also gives good rainforesty perspectives from down below.

🏃 Activities

Pines Surfing Academy

SURFING

(📞0410 645 981; www.pinessurfingacademy.com. au; 1a Cliff Rd, North Wollongong; 2hr lessons $50, 3-day course $120) Surf lessons at either City Beach or the Farm Beach.

HanggglideOz

ADVENTURE SPORTS

(📞0417 939 200; www.hanggglideoz.com.au; tandem flights midweek/weekends $245/295) A reliable hang-gliding operator offering tandem flights and courses from Bald Hill in Stanwell Park.

🛏 Sleeping

Keiraleagh

HOSTEL $

(📞02-4228 6765; www.backpack.net.au; 60 Kembla St; dm $25-38, s/d without bathroom $75/85, d $140; ⊖@🛜) This welcoming and rambling heritage house has a bohemian surf hippy vibe, basic cleanliness and a genuinely friendly atmosphere. The dorms could do with thicker mattresses, but it's the great garden and barbecue area that make it such a relaxing spot. It only takes cash.

SAGE Hotel Wollongong

HOTEL $$

(📞02-4201 2111; www.sagewollongong.com; 60-62 Harbour St; r $199-299; P ⊖ ❄ 🛜 ≋) Handy for the sports precinct and the city beach, this airy modern hotel has tastefully designed rooms and pretty good facilities. Rooms are a good size and come with coffee machine and other mod-cons. Try for one near the top of the building for ocean or golf-course views. The higher-grade rooms come with balcony. Good pubs and restaurants are a short walk away.

Beach Park Motel

MOTEL $$

(📞02-4226 1577; www.beachparkmotel.com.au; 10 Pleasant Ave, North Wollongong; r $125-210; P ⊖ ❄ 🛜) Just back from the beachfront park, this is a solid, friendly option. A variety of rooms have white brick walls, good space, colourful doors and comfortable facilities. Most look out onto parkland, the cheapest onto the carpark. It's a short walk from the beach and pretty good value.

Novotel Northbeach

HOTEL $$$

(📞02-4224 3111; www.novotelnorthbeach.com.au; 2-14 Cliff Rd, North Wollongong; r $299-379; P ⊖ ❄ @ 🛜 ≋) This renovated 200-roomer is right by the action at North Beach and is a great spot for a beach holiday, with bags of facilities and spacious and comfortable rooms, many featuring balconies with ocean or escarpment views. Prices soar on summer weekends – think $400 to $600 for a Saturday room.

🍴 Eating

Balinese Spice Magic

INDONESIAN $

(📞02-4227 1033; www.balinesespicemagic.com.au; 130 Keira St; lunch $10-18, dinner $17-26; ⊙5.30-9.30pm Tue & Wed, 11am-2.30pm & 5.30-9.30pm Thu, 11am-2.30pm & 5.30-11pm Fri, 5.30-11pm Sat; 🖉) Look forward to excellent Indonesian food and welcoming service from the friendly family owners. Thai and Vietnamese eateries also line Keira St, but this is our pick of the best flavours to remind you of your time drifting aimlessly around Southeast Asia. There are lots of vegan options.

★ Caveau

MODERN AUSTRALIAN $$$

(📞02-4226 4855; www.caveau.com.au; 122-124 Keira St; 7-course degustation menu $110, with wine $160; ⊙6-11pm Tue-Sat; 🖉) This lauded restaurant serves gourmet treats such as kingfish tartare and poached scampi. The menu changes seasonally and there's a three-course menu ($85) available from Tuesday to Thursday. There's a separate degustation for vegetarians. The ambience is Gong-casual with great spotty chairs and sleek dark decor.

★**Babyface** JAPANESE, AUSTRALIAN $$$
(🖉 02-4295 0903; www.burnsburyhospitality.com.au; 179 Keira St; mains $24-40; ⊘ 6-10pm Mon, 6-11pm Wed & Thu, noon-3pm & 6pm-midnight Fri & Sat, noon-3pm & 6-10pm Sun) Buzzy and loud, this relative Wollongong newcomer combines Japanese ideas with some wild Australian herbs and berries to create a blend of flavours. Salmon and kingfish are the backbones of the menu, which features a sashimi section, smaller plates and large ones. There are some very interesting wines by the glass and upbeat, friendly staff. Sit at the bar if no tables.

🍸 **Drinking & Nightlife**

★**His Boy Elroy** BAR
(🖉 02-4244 8221; www.hisboyelroy.com.au; 176 Keira St; burgers $12-19; ⊘ 5-10pm Mon & Tue, 11am-10pm Wed, Thu & Sun, 11am-midnight Fri & Sat) Recently re-opened in new premises, this excellent bar is now more burgers, cocktails and spirits than the cafe it began as. Offering outdoor seating, a revamped cocktail list and a great selection of interesting whiskies, it's great for a drink. The burgers are reliably excellent, and the new smoked meat choices should be great too.

Humber BAR
(🖉 02-4263 0355; www.humber.bar; 226 Crown St; ⊘ 6.30am-midnight Mon-Fri, 7.30am-midnight Sat, 7.30am-10pm Sun; 🛜) This relative newcomer occupies an unusually shaped building, once the Humber car dealership. Downstairs does coffees and lunches in the morning, then the place morphs into a stylish cocktail bar in the evening. The 1st-floor art deco–inspired bar is a beautiful space, while the rooftop feels like the deck of a yacht. Palms, parasols and fresh coconuts add to the carnival cruise feel.

Illawarra Brewery BAR
(🖉 02-4220 2854; www.thebrewery.net.au; cnr Crown & Harbour Sts; ⊘ 11am-11pm Mon-Thu, 10am-1am Fri & Sat, 10am-10pm Sun) This slick bar attached to the entertainment centre, with ocean views, has its own craft beers on tap, plus occasional seasonal brews. Guest beers from around Australia complete a happy and hoppy picture, and there's decent food on tap as well. The outdoor terrace is a great spot to sit. It's a popular one with sports fans too.

ℹ️ **Information**

IHub Visitor Centre (🖉 1800 240 737; www.visitwollongong.com.au; 93 Crown St; ⊘ 9am-5pm Mon-Sat, 10am-4pm Sun; 🛜) Bookings and information.

ℹ️ **Getting There & Away**

Trains (🖉 13 15 00; www.sydneytrains.info) on the **South Coast Line** run to/from Sydney's Central Station ($8.30, 90 minutes), and continue south as far as Nowra/Bomaderry via Kiama and Berry.

All long-distance buses leave from the eastern side of the railway station. **Premier** (🖉 13 34 10; www.premierms.com.au) has two daily buses to Sydney ($18, two hours) and Eden ($69, seven to eight hours). **Murrays** (🖉 13 22 51; www.murrays.com.au) has buses to Canberra ($48.40, 3¼ hours).

ℹ️ **Getting Around**

A free shuttle bus, the Gong Shuttle (routes 55A and 55C), runs every 10 to 20 minutes on a loop from the station to the university, and North Wollongong, useful for reaching North Beach, the Botanic Garden and Science Centre.

Royal National Park

This prime stretch of wilderness is at the city's doorstep, and encompasses secluded beaches, vertiginous cliffs, scrub, heath, rainforest, swamp wallabies, lyrebirds and raucous flocks of yellow-tailed black cockatoos.

This wonderful coastal park, protecting 15,091 hectares and stretching inland from 32km of beautiful coast, is the world's second-oldest national park (1879).

◎ **Sights**

Wattamolla Beach BEACH
(www.nationalparks.nsw.gov.au; Wattamolla Rd) About halfway along the coast, Wattamolla Beach is one of the park's favourite picnic spots and gets pretty busy in summer. It has the great advantage of having both a surf beach and a lagoon, allowing for safe swimming. There's also a waterfall; jumping is popular but strictly prohibited. The beach is 3.3km from the main road, accessed from very near the Bundeena turn-off.

Garie Beach
BEACH

(www.nationalparks.nsw.gov.au, Garie Beach Rd)
Three kilometres down a turn-off from the
main road, this excellent surf beach is a picturesque spot. Like all of the Royal National
Park surf beaches, swimming can be treacherous. There's a toilet block but no other facilities despite the large building complex,
though the beach is patrolled on summer
weekends.

🛏 Sleeping

Bonnie Vale Campground   CAMPGROUND $
(☑1300 072 757; www.nationalparks.nsw.gov.au;
Sea Breeze Lane, Bundeena; sites for 2 $33; P ⊜)
This campground is 1.5km west of central
Bundeena and has pleasant, flat, grassy sites.
It's right by the water, with both sheltered
bay beach and river estuary for swimming.
It is well equipped, with toilets, hot showers,
electric barbecues and picnic tables.

★ Beachhaven   B&B $$$
(☑02-9544 1333; www.beachhavenbnb.com.au; 13
Bundeena Dr, Bundeena; r $300-350; P ⊜❋☎)
Right on gorgeous Hordens Beach, this
classy B&B is run by a welcoming couple
who offer two fabulous rooms. Both have a
kitchenette, a king bed with plush fabrics,
and some fine antique furnishings, as well
as a generously stocked fridge and lovely pa-
tio area. Beach House is right by the sand,
while Tudor Cottage is tucked away in a little
subtropical garden.

Other highlights include a romantic out-
door spa bath overlooking the beach, kayak
and stand-up paddleboard on hand, and a
friendly tame possum family. Prices drop
markedly for multinight stays.

ℹ Information

Royal National Park Visitor Centre (☑02-
9542 0648; www.nationalparks.nsw.gov.
au; 2 Lady Carrington Dr, Audley; ⊗8.30am-
4.30pm) Entrance fees, camping permits,
maps and bushwalking information. The centre
is at Audley, 2km inside the park's northeastern
entrance, off the Princes Hwy. There's also a
cafe here with very pleasant verandah seating.

ℹ Getting There & Away

Cronulla Ferries (☑02-9523 2990; www.
cronullaferries.com.au; adult/child $6.40/3.20)
travels to **Bundeena** from Cronulla, accessible
by train from Sydney.

You can also get a train to Waterfall and hike
into the park from there.

KIAMA & AROUND

POP 12,800

Kiama's sculpted coastline includes numerous
beaches and crazy rock formations, including
a famous but often underwhelming blowhole.
The town is characterised by its likeably dag-
gy, laid-back vibe and magnificent mature
Norfolk pines. Inland are viewpoints and out-
door activities in the forested highlands.

◎ Sights

Kiama Blowhole   LANDMARK
Kiama's famous blowhole sits on the point
by the centre of town. It's fairly under-
whelming except when the surf's up and a
southeaster's blowing: then, water explodes
high up out of the fissure. It's floodlit at
night. The **Little Blowhole** (off Tingira Cres,
Marsden Head) along the coast to the south is
less impressive but much more regular.

**Minnamurra Rainforest
Centre**   NATURE RESERVE
(☑02-4236 0469; www.nationalparks.nsw.gov.
au; Minnamurra Falls Rd, via Jamberoo; car $12;
⊗9am-5pm, last entry 4pm) On the eastern
edge of **Budderoo National Park**, 15km in-
land from Kiama, this is a surprisingly lush
subtropical rainforest. A 2.6km loop walk
transits through the rainforest following a
cascading stream. Look out for water drag-
ons and lyrebirds. A secondary 1.6km walk
on a steepish track leads to the **Minnamur-
ra Falls**. The helpful visitor centre has park
and ecosystem information. There's a worth-
while cafe here, open 10am to 4pm at busy
times, 11.30am to 2.30pm on quieter days.

A weekday bus from Kiama station gets up
here, but there's six hours between arrivals.

★ Seven Mile Beach   BEACH
(www.nationalparks.nsw.gov.au) Backed by na-
tional park, this magnificent curved stretch
of white-ish sand lives up to its name (and
a bit more). It runs from Shoalhaven Heads
in the south to Gerroa in the north, and can
also be accessed via a series of turn-offs to
beachside national park picnic areas.

🛏 Sleeping & Eating

Bellevue Accommodation   APARTMENT $$
(☑02-4232 4000; www.bellevueaccommodation.
com.au; 21 Minnamurra St; r $150-250; P ❋☎)
This charming place hosts guests in modern
comfort within a two-storey 1890s heritage
manor. The apartments are equipped with
full kitchen, laundry facilities, lovely veran

space and ocean views. It's a short walk to the main street. There's usually a two-night minimum stay, but it's worth a call just in case.

★ **Kiama Harbour Cabins** CABIN $$$
(📞02-4232 2707; www.kiamacoast.com.au; Blowhole Point; cottages $300-400; 🅿😊✳🛜) In the best position in town, these cottages are neat as a pin and well equipped with barbecues on front verandahs overlooking the beach and the nearby ocean pool. Prices are for the January high season, when there's a seven-night minimum stay. At other times it's only two nights and rates are at least 25% lower.

Hungry Monkey CAFE $
(📞0403 397 353; http://thehungrymonkeyyy.com; 5/32 Collins St; dishes $12-20; ⊙6.30am-4pm Mon-Wed, 6.30am-9pm Thu-Sat, 7.30am-4pm Sun; 🛜🍴) One of a row of cute cottages housing craft shops and the like, this is a very likeable cafe doing burgers, wraps, salads and breakfast plates with great combos of ingredients and plenty of zing and taste. It serves food all day and is licensed too: a good all-rounder.

Kabari Bar BISTRO $$
(📞02-4233 0572; www.kabaribar.com; 78 Manning St; mains $18-30; ⊙food 8am-3pm Sun & Mon, to 10pm Wed-Sat) By the lively surf beach in town, this likeable shack has a takeaway kiosk that's busy all day but also puts on more sophisticated fare in its two-level restaurant section. It offers sweet water views and competently presented plates running from seafood to better meat dishes and pizzas. There's live music at the upstairs bar at weekends.

ℹ Information

Visitor Centre (📞02-4232 3322; www.kiama.com.au; Blowhole Point Rd; ⊙9am-5pm) On Blowhole Point. Helpful with finding accommodation.

ℹ Getting There & Away

Kiama is most easily reached by train, with frequent **Sydney Trains** (📞13 15 00; www.sydneytrains.info) departures to Wollongong, Sydney and Nowra (Bomaderry) via Berry. **Premier** (📞13 34 10; www.premierms.com.au) buses run twice daily to Eden ($69, 7½ hours) and Sydney ($25, 2½ hours). **Kiama Coaches** (📞02-4232 3466; www.kiamacoaches.com. au) runs to Gerroa, Gerringong and Minnamurra via Jamberoo).

If you're driving, take the beach detour via ~~r~~ingong and Gerroa and rejoin the highway ~~r~~ in Berry or just north of Nowra.

KANGAROO VALLEY

POP 300

From either Nowra or Berry, a shaded forested road meanders to pretty Kangaroo Valley. This lovely historic town is cradled by mountains, and the sleepy main street has cafes, craft shops, a historic sandstone bridge and a great pub. It's a sort of idealised rural Australia, with a vibrant palette of colours. Activities in the surrounding area include biking, hiking, canoeing and camping. See www.visitkangaroovalley.com.au for operators and B&B accommodation.

◉ Sights

★ **Cambewarra Lookout** VIEWPOINT
(⊙7.30am-9pm) Signposted off the Cambewarra Mountain between Kangaroo Valley and Nowra, this lookout offers a stupendous perspective over the winding Shoalhaven River and the alluvial agricultural lands far below, and right along the coast. There's a cafe here whose deck takes full advantage of the vista.

Fitzroy Falls WATERFALL
(www.nationalparks.nsw.gov.au; Morton National Park; per vehicle $4) Though the summers and reservoir requirements frequently reduce the actual torrent to a trickle, this 81m-high waterfall is worth a visit for the views alone. A spectacular outlook has views over forest-clad hills and juxtaposed with bare sandstone escarpment – a classic NSW scene. The **visitor centre** (📞02-4887 7270; www.nationalparks.nsw.gov.au; Nowra Rd, Fitzroy Falls; per vehicle $4; ⊙9am-5pm May-Aug, 9am-5.30pm Sep-Apr) here is the best resource for wildlife and walking information in the area and has a cafe. The falls are about 17km northwest of the bridge in Kangaroo Valley, up a steep mountain road.

🛏 Sleeping & Eating

Boutique B&Bs and farmstays cluster in and around town, and along the road to Berry. There are a couple of camping parks in the centre of the village; for a bush-camping experience head north out of town to Bendeela picnic spot. It's signed.

★ **Laurels B&B** B&B $$$
(📞02-4465 1693; www.thelaurelsbnb.com.au; 2501 Moss Vale Rd; r $265-295; 😊🛜) Five kilometres northwest of the bridge, this is a privileged spot to find yourself. Your delightful and cultured hosts offer a warmly personal welcome, and the four rooms in this lovely centenarian bungalow are sumptuous spaces with king

beds, elegant antique furniture and high comfort levels. Books, wine and cheese in the late afternoon, peaceful surrounding countryside: a delightfully civilised retreat.

Bistro One46
BISTRO $$
(☎02-4465 2820; www.bistro146.com.au; 146 Moss Vale Rd; mains $26-34; ⊙5.30-9pm Fri, 11am-3pm & 5.30-9pm Sat, 11am-3pm & 5.30-8.30pm Sun, 11am-2.30pm & 5.30-8.30pm Mon & Tue) In the centre of the village, this vine-swathed beauty has a pleasantly cosy interior and a sweet little verandah. The food is well presented, colourful and not overly complicated. It covers a range of bases, including kangaroo carpaccio, seafood and Italian, and it's all pretty tasty.

❶ Getting There & Away

Kennedy's (☎02-4421 7596; www.kennedystours.com.au) runs a few buses a week between Bomaderry train station and Kangaroo Valley.

SHOALHAVEN COAST

Well in weekender range from Sydney, this striking region features wonderful sandy beaches backed by a luscious green interior dotted with heritage towns, state forests and national parks. The white sands and turquoise waters of Jervis Bay are a highlight.

Berry
POP 1700

Berry, a slightly mannered but undeniably lovely heritage town, is a popular inland stop on the South Coast. Look forward to a smattering of antique and design stores, and a thriving foodie scene with good cafes and restaurants. Currently choked by its main-street highway traffic, Berry should become a much more tranquil, appealing place when the bypass is finished. At the time of writing, this was slated for 2018.

◉ Sights

The town's short main street features National Trust–classified buildings and there are good-quality vineyards in the rolling countryside around Berry.

★ Silos Estate
WINERY
(☎02-4448 6082; www.silosestate.com; B640 Princes Hwy, Jaspers Brush; ⊙tastings 11am-5pm) ✦ Beautifully set on a green hillside overlooking the pretty countryside between Berry and Nowra, this lovely winery is well worth a visit. It makes a range of tasty drops under two labels and also offers cheese and alpaca ham. There's an excellent restaurant here too, lots of forward-thinking environmental initiatives and four utterly relaxing boutique rooms ($205 to $275).

🛏 Sleeping

Conjuring up images of cosy wood fires, Berry is a popular weekender in winter as well as summer. There are lots of fairly upmarket choices across here and Kangaroo Valley.

Berry Hotel
HOTEL $
(☎02-4464 1011; www.berryhotel.com.au; 120 Queen St; s/d $80/110; ꟼ🐾🛜) This popular local watering hole has standard but large fan-cooled pub bedrooms with bathrooms down the hall. Mattresses could be firmer, but it's a pretty authentic place to stay, with its own style and plenty of value. There's a shared balcony space and, downstairs, decent food served in the pub's rear dining room and courtyard.

Berry Village Boutique Motel
MOTEL $$
(☎02-4464 3570; www.berrymotel.com.au; 72 Queen St; r $185-275; ꟼ🐾❄🛜🖲) On the main road, this is an exceedingly well run, upmarket place with a gourmet restaurant and large, comfortable rooms. They're modern and attractively carpeted with new king beds in some. Standard ones face the front, while those behind have a more tranquil park lookout. Higher-grade rooms have spa facilities. Constant improvements here are the sign of a quality establishment.

Bellawongarah at Berry
B&B $$$
(☎02-4464 1999; www.accommodation-berry.com.au; 869 Kangaroo Valley Rd, Bellawongarah; r $250-260; ꟼ🐾❄🛜) Rainforest surrounds this wonderful place, 8km from Berry on the mountain road to Kangaroo Valley. There are two rooms, one a sumptuous loft space in the main house, which features Asian art, a large spa bath overlooking the greenery, and a cosy lounge and sleeping area under the eaves. The other is a cute 1868 Wesleyan cottage-church with an airy, French provincial feel.

✕ Eating

Famous Berry Donut Van
CAFE $
(☎0435 297 530; 73 Princes Hwy; doughnuts $1.80; ⊙9am-6pm; 🅿) For generations now, parents driving the family down the South Coast for the holidays have bribed the kids

by promising a stop at this food truck if they were good along the way. The doughnuts are made fresh and, hot and sugary, are delicious. It also does coffee and other snacks.

★**Silos Restaurant**　MODERN AUSTRALIAN **$$**
(☑02-4448 6160; www.silos.com.au; B640 Princes Hwy, Jaspers Brush; 5-/8-course tasting menu $70/95; ⊙noon-2pm & 6-10pm Thu-Sat, noon-2pm Sun, open daily in Jan) The former grain silos that give this winery its name overlook this loveable restaurant, which has a sweet verandah space and dining room with dreamy views over the vineyard's grassy slopes. It's a sort of rural idyll but the cuisine would bear up in any urban gastro-street. Confident and innovative flavour combinations, local produce (including estate-farmed alpacas) and friendly staff make this a standout.

★**Hungry Duck**　ASIAN **$$**
(☑02-4464 2323; www.hungryduck.com.au; 85 Queen St; mains $16-35, 5-/9-course banquet $55/85; ⊙6-9.30pm Mon, Wed & Thu, noon-2pm & 6-9.30pm Fri-Sun; ☑) ✔ A contemporary Asian menu is served tapas-style, although larger mains are also available. There's a rear courtyard and kitchen garden where herbs are plucked for the plate. Fresh fish, meat and eggs are all sourced locally. Look for it near the BP station in the centre of town.

Berry Woodfired Sourdough　BAKERY, CAFE **$$**
(☑02-4464 1617; www.berrysourdoughcafe.com.au; cnr Prince Alfred & Princess Sts; pies $6.80, mains $16-26; ⊙8am-3pm Wed-Sun) Stock up on bread or dine in at this bakery that's beloved by foodies. Try the gourmet pies or go for a more substantial dish, with daily fish and meat specials adding to a short, quality menu. The owners also run **Milkwood Bakery** (☑02-4464 3033; www.berrysourdoughcafe.com.au; 109 Queen St; pies $6.80; ⊙6am-5.30pm Mon-Fri, 7am-5pm Sat & Sun) on Berry's main drag.

🛍 Shopping

Treat Factory　FOOD
(☑02-4464 1112; www.treatfactory.com.au; 6 Old Creamery Lane; ⊙9.30am-4.30pm Mon-Fri, 10am-4pm Sat & Sun) Well worth the short detour off the highway, this factory shop is an old-school place chock-full of nostalgic lollies such as rocky road and liquorice. It also does a nice line in pickles and sauces.

ℹ Getting There & Away

Trains run every hour or two to Nowra/Bomaderry ($3, 10 minutes) and to Kiama ($3.40, 30 minutes), where you change to trains heading north to Wollongong ($4.50, 1¼ hours) and Sydney ($6, 2¾ hours).

Premier (☑13 34 10; www.premierms.com. au) has buses to Sydney ($25, three hours, twice daily) via Kiama, and south to Eden via all coastal towns.

Nowra

POP 28,000

Nowra, around 17km from the coast, is the largest town in the Shoalhaven area. Although there are prettier South Coast towns, it's a solid, laid-back regional centre and can be a decent base for the surrounding attractions of Berry, Kangaroo Valley and Jervis Bay. Nowra's conjoined twin, Bomaderry, is the southern terminus of the South Coast rail line.

👁 Sights

Meroogal　MUSEUM
(☑02-4421 8150; www.sydneylivingmuseums.com. au; cnr West & Worrigee Sts; adult/child $12/8; ⊙10am-4pm Sat, plus Thu & Fri Jan & other school holidays) Intriguingly, this historic 1885 house contains the artefacts accumulated by four generations of women who have lived there. Entrance is by guided tour, which leaves on the hour (last tour 3pm). It's a lovely building in a tranquil setting near the oval some three blocks west of central Nowra.

Coolangatta Estate　WINERY
(☑02-4448 7131; www.coolangattaestate.com. au; 1335 Bolong Rd, Shoalhaven Heads; ⊙winery 10am-5pm) **FREE** On the north side of the estuary, 13km east of Bomaderry and just before Shoalhaven Heads, is this atmospheric and historic winery on an estate first established in 1822. There's cellar door tasting of its praiseworthy wines, a 'wine garden' and restaurant that makes a fine lunch spot, and tours of the estate on **Segways** (☑0402 000 222; www.segwaytourssouthcoast.com.au; tours $75-100) or in a large **'Bigfoot' vehicle** (☑0428 244 229; www.bishopsadventures.com.au; Coolangatta Estate, Shoalhaven Heads; adult/child $25/15) that takes you up the hill for tremendous views. The estate also offers excellent accommodation in convict-built buildings.

🛏 Sleeping & Eating

Coolangatta Estate　B&B **$$**
(☑02-4448 7131; www.coolangattaestate.com. au; 1335 Bolong Rd, Shoalhaven Heads; r $140-220; P☀️🛜🏊) Staying on this venerable wine-producing estate is a real treat. Rooms,

spread across different buildings, vary widely, from a cute convict-built timber cottage with a high bed and historic feel, to cosy rooms in the servants' quarters or separate lodge building. Room-only rates are available, and prices are significantly lower midweek. It's a popular wedding venue, so weekends are often booked out.

The estate is 13km east of the Bomaderry Princes Hwy junction.

Quest Nowra APARTMENT **$$**
(☑02-4421 9300; www.questnowra.com.au; 130 Kinghorne St; studio apt $189-216, 1-bedroom apt $209-236; P🅿️❄️🛜) A welcome addition to Nowra's somewhat limited accommodation scene, these modern apartments are run in an upbeat, amiable way in the centre of town. Studios have a big bed, a hotplate, a proper fridge and a microwave, while the apartments add a full kitchen and laundry. Space and facilities are excellent, and there's an on-site smokehouse cafe-restaurant. Rates can drop sharply off-season depending on demand.

★**Wharf Rd** MODERN AUSTRALIAN **$$**
(☑02-4422 6651; www.wharfrd.com.au; 10 Wharf Rd; small/large plates $17/32; ⊙noon-3pm & 6-10pm Wed-Sat, noon-3pm Sun, extended hours Dec & Jan) Right on the river, this restaurant is in Nowra's nicest corner, especially when the jacarandas are blooming alongside. Despite the roar of traffic, the dining room is a romantic venue for quality, cosmopolitan cuisine Shared plates include alpaca sirloin, blue-eye trevalla with chilli, or avocado and squid tacos. It's a likeable, unpretentious place that's easily the best restaurant in town.

🍷 **Drinking & Nightlife**

★**Hop Dog Beerworks** CRAFT BEER
(☑0428 293 132; www.hopdog.com.au; Unit 2, 175 Princes Hwy; ⊙tastings & sales 10am-4pm Tue-Thu & Sat, 10am-6pm Fri) In an industrial estate 4km south of central Nowra, Hop Dog's beautifully balanced hoppy brews have iconic status with beerhounds across the country. There's always something new on offer, and, despite the unromantic retail barn surrounds, it's great to drop by for a chat and a sip of something. Bottles and growlers are available to take away. It's near the big Bunnings Warehouse.

ℹ️ **Information**

Nowra Visitor Centre (☑1300 662 808; www.shoalhaven.nsw.gov.au; 42 Bridge Rd; ⊙9am-5pm Mon-Thu & Sat, 9am-6pm Fri, 10am-2pm

Sun) Just west of the Princes Hwy in a theatre complex.

ℹ️ **Getting There & Around**

Premier (☑13 34 10; www.premierms.com.au) has buses to Sydney ($25, three hours) and Eden ($57, five to six hours) via Ulladulla ($18, one hour) and other coastal towns.

Sydney Trains (☑13 15 00; www.sydneytrains.info) run from Sydney to Kiama, where you change to a train on the same platform for the onward connection to Nowra (Bomaderry) via Berry. The total journey takes around 2¾ hours. There's a train every hour or two.

Local buses connect Bomaderry station with the centre of town and run to Jervis Bay, Berry and surrounding towns.

Jervis Bay

This large, sheltered bay combines snow-white sand, crystalline waters, national parks and frolicking dolphins. Seasonal visitors include Sydney holidaymakers (summer and most weekends), and migrating whales (May to November).

In 1995 the Aboriginal community won a land claim in the Wreck Bay area and now jointly administers Booderee National Park at the southern end of the bay. By a strange quirk this area is actually part of the Australian Capital Territory, not NSW.

Most development is around Huskisson and Vincentia, and the northern shore has less tourist infrastructure. Beecroft Peninsula forms the northeastern side of Jervis Bay, ending in the dramatic sheer cliffs of Point Perpendicular. Most of the peninsula is navy land but is usually open to the public and harbours some beautiful, secluded beaches.

◉ **Sights & Activities**

Huskisson is the centre for most activities, which include whale watching, dolphin watching, kayaking and kitesurfing. South of Huskisson, the sand of gorgeous **Hyams Beach** is reputedly the world's whitest.

Jervis Bay Maritime Museum MUSEUM
(☑02-4441 5675; www.jervisbaymaritimemuseum.asn.au; Woollamia Rd, Huskisson; adult/child $10/free; ⊙10am-4pm) With a historic collection, the 1912 *Lady Denman* ferry and **Timbery's Aboriginal Arts & Crafts** gallery and sho⌐ There's a growers' market on the first Sat⌐ day of the month, and a visitor informa⌐ centre.

Jervis Bay Kayaks
KAYAKING

(☑ 02-4441 7157; www.jervisbaykayaks.com.au; 13 Hawke St, Huskisson; kayak hire 2hr/4hr/day $39/59/69, sea kayak hire 3hr/day $60/75, bike hire 2hr/day $29/50, tours $96-145) This friendly spot offers rentals of simple sit-on-top kayaks and stand-up paddleboards as well as of single and double sea kayaks on St Georges Basin or Jervis Bay (with experience). It can organise guided sea-kayaking trips, and self-guided camping and kayaking expeditions. It also hires bikes.

Dive Jervis Bay
DIVING, SNORKELLING

(☑ 02-4441 5255; www.divejervisbay.com; 64 Owen St, Huskisson; 2 dives $199) The marine park is popular with divers: the clear water offers good visibility, and there are lots of fruitful sites. Snorkellers can visit a nearby seal colony (May to October). This set-up offers PADI courses and guided dives, as well as equipment rental and bike hire.

ⓒ Tours

Jervis Bay Wild
WILDLIFE, BOATING

(☑ 02-4441 7002; www.jervisbaywild.com.au; 58 Owen St, Huskisson; trips $35-95) This operator offers 90-minute dolphin-watching trips and longer trips that offer whale watching in season and a circuit of the bay's beautiful beaches at other times. Another trip buses you to Currarong for a cruise back to Huskisson exploring the cliffscapes around the Beecroft Peninsula.

Dolphin Watch Cruises
WILDLIFE, BOATING

(☑ 02-4441 6311; www.dolphinwatch.com.au; 50 Owen St, Huskisson; ☺ dolphin-/whale-/seal-watching tour $35/65/85) This well-established set-up on the main street in Huskisson offers tours in a small, fast boat and a larger, more sedate triple-decker. Whale watching is great in season (September to November). It also has a 38ft catamaran available for sailing charters.

🛌 Sleeping

Prices increase on weekends and in January. Huskisson is the principal accommodation hub, but there are options in many of the settlements. Booderee National Park offers campsites, as does the Beecroft Peninsula.

Huskisson B&B
B&B $$

(☑ 02-4441 7551; www.huskissonbnb.com.au; 12 ̃merong St, Huskisson; r $225-255; P ☺ ❄ ☎ 🐾)
̃'s sweet centenarian timber cottage with ̃randah, near the entrance to town, of-

fers four bright, airy and colourful rooms containing comfy beds, stylish bathrooms with freestanding bathtubs and fluffy towels, and lots of little facilities that ease your stay. Breakfast is a quality affair that extends into cooked territory at weekends.

★ Paperbark Camp
LODGE $$$

(☑ 02-4441 6066; www.paperbarkcamp.com.au; 571 Woollamia Rd, Woollamia; d $395-620; P ☺ ☎)
🐾 Camp in ecofriendly style in these 12 super-luxurious safari tents with en suites and wraparound decks. It's set in dense bush 4km from Huskisson; borrow kayaks to paddle up the creek to the bay, or grab a bike for the ride into town. There's an excellent restaurant here exclusively for guests, and an impressive breakfast is included.

There's no power in the tents except for solar lighting, but there are chargers and a guest fridge in the reception complex.

🍴 Eating & Drinking

Huskisson is a trendy weekend spot for Sydneysiders and has a couple of excellent cafes, good pub food and a classy Asian fusion restaurant. Eating is much more limited in the Bay's other settlements, though there are options in Vincentia, Callala Bay and elsewhere.

5 Little Pigs
CAFE $

(☑ 02-4441 7056; www.5littlepigs.com.au; 64 Owen St, Huskisson; dishes $12-19; ☺ 7am-4pm Sun-Thu, to 5pm Fri & Sat; ☎ 🐾) Likeable and upbeat, this main-street cafe opens early and offers decent coffee and a range of excellent breakfasts and lunches. Blackboard specials add options and the friendly owners are good for a chat.

Wild Ginger
ASIAN $$

(☑ 02-4441 5577; www.wild-ginger.com.au; 42 Owen St, Huskisson; mains $31.50; ☺ 3-11pm Tue-Sun; ☎) By some distance Huskisson's most sophisticated restaurant, Wild Ginger is a relaxed showcase of flavours from Thailand, across Southeast Asia and Japan. Look forward to tasty local seafood featuring in delicately treated, aroma-packed dishes. It also does cocktails, which are only $10 until 6pm.

Huskisson Hotel
PUB

(Husky Pub; ☑ 02-4441 5001; www.thehuskisson.com.au; 73 Owen St, Huskisson; ☺ 11am-midnight Mon-Sat, to 10pm Sun; ☎) The social centre of Huskisson and indeed the whole Jervis Bay area is this light and airy pub that offers fabulous bay views and decent food, running from pizzas and burgers to fish and steak dishes, with daily specials in each category. The sizeable outside deck here packs out over summer and there's live music most weekends.

ⓘ Information

Jervis Bay Visitor Information Centre (Woollamia Rd, Huskisson; ⊗10am-4pm) Helpful tourist information within the Jervis Bay Maritime Museum building.

ⓘ Getting There & Away

Nowra Coaches (☑02-4423 5244; www.nowracoaches.com.au) runs buses around the Jervis Bay area, with connections to Nowra and the train station at Bomaderry.

Booderee National Park

Overlooking the crystal-clear waters of the southernmost part of Jervis Bay, this is a standout national park offering excellent beaches with adjacent camp sites, an interesting botanic garden, short walking trails and Indigenous heritage.

⊙ Sights

Booderee Botanic Gardens   GARDENS
(www.booderee.gov.au; ⊗8am-4pm) With enormous rhododendrons and coastal plant species once used for food and medicine by local Indigenous groups, these botanic gardens are within the park off the road to Cave Beach.

🛏 Sleeping

Bristol Point   CAMPGROUND $
(☑02-4443 0977; www.booderee.gov.au; camp sites $22, plus per adult/child $11/5; ℙ⊜) This sweet rustic national park camp site has forested sites with a short walking track down to a beach on Jervis Bay. It's for tents only and there's no power. It's a lot cheaper outside of school holidays. You can walk to the Green Patch beach and camp site at low tide.

Cave Beach   CAMPGROUND $
(☑02-4443 0977; www.booderee.gov.au; camp sites $22, plus per adult/child $11/5; ℙ) A grassy camping area near a majestic ocean beach means this is prime territory for surfers. There are toilets and cold-water showers. It's walk-in, so tents only. It's a 500m walk from the car park down to the sites, so don't leave valuables in your vehicle.

Green Patch   CAMPGROUND $
(☑02-4443 0977; www.booderee.gov.au; camp sites $22, plus per adult/child $11/5; ℙ) The largest of the Booderee campsites and the only one with campervans allowed, this is divided into two sections on either side of a lagoon. It's a short walk to the beach on Jervis Bay. There's no power but there's water, toilets, showers and barbecue facilities.

ⓘ Information

Booderee Visitor Centre (☑02-4443 0977; www.booderee.gov.au; Jervis Bay Rd; ⊗9.30am-3pm Sun-Thu, 9am-4pm Fri & Sat, 9am-4pm daily in Jan) Get maps and info from Booderee visitor centre at the Booderee National Park entrance.

ⓘ Getting There & Away

Buses get as far as Hyams Beach, but not to the park itself.

Ulladulla & Mollymook

POP 12,100

Ulladulla is a fishing-focused town with a picturesque coastal location. Adjoining it to the north, Mollymook has a gorgeous beach and is a favourite summer destination for Sydneysiders. There are some excellent places to stay and eat in town and other great beaches nearby.

⊙ Sights & Activities

Milton   VILLAGE
The characterful 19th-century town of Milton, 6km north of Ulladulla on the Princes Hwy, is a pleasant spot to visit, with craft shops, heritage buildings and an up-and-coming hipster vibe. There are good places to eat and stay here too.

Murramarang National Park   NATIONAL PARK
(www.nationalparks.nsw.gov.au; per car per day $8) Stretching along a secluded section of coastland, this scenic park offers excellent beaches, Indigenous heritage and plentiful animal and bird life. Surfing is good at several beaches and marked walking trails give scope for land-based activity.

★Pigeon House Mountain   HIKING
(Didthul) Some 33km west of Ulladulla by road, this iconic mountain in the Morton National Park section of the Budawang range is an excellent walk. It involves two climbs through bush separated by a flat phase, then an ascent up a series of ladders to a summit with magnificent views. It's 5.3km return from the car park; allow three to four hours.

🛏 Sleeping

Ulladulla Lodge
HOSTEL $

(☑02-4454 0500; www.ulladullalodge.com.au; 63 Princes Hwy, Ulladulla; dm $35, d $80-85; P😊) This guesthouse-style place has a surf vibe and laid-back feel. It's clean, comfy, and pretty close to the beach. The owners hire surfboards, wetsuits and kayaks. There's a common kitchen and barbecues, though limited wi-fi reception.

Mollymook Shores
MOTEL $$

(☑02-4455 5888; www.mollymookshores.com.au; 11 Golf Ave, Mollymook; r $145-235; P😊❄🕸) Right by the beachfront in Mollymook, this is more hotel than motel in style, with rooms arranged around a leafy courtyard. They've all been recently renovated and are spacious and well-equipped. Owners and staff are helpful and this makes an excellent coastal base. Seven different room types offers slightly different facilities. There's room-service breakfast but no restaurant.

★ Bannisters Pavilion
HOTEL $$$

(☑02-4455 3044; www.bannisters.com.au; 87 Tallwood Ave, Mollymook; r $275-430; P😊❄🕸🏊) Just back from Mollymook beach, this new hotel is visually striking but designed with great subtlety, blending in well with its surroundings. There's space to spare here, with wide hallways, plush, light rooms with pleasant woody outlooks and private patio or balcony space. The top deck is a lot of fun, with a bar, a heated pool and a restaurant creating a very casual-chic space.

★ Bannisters by the Sea
HOTEL $$$

(☑02-4455 3044; www.bannisters.com.au; 191 Mitchell Pde, Mollymook; r $365-510, ste $430-925; P😊❄🕸🏊) The bones of a 1970s motel provide the basis of this hip, unassumingly luxurious place. Rooms are effortlessly stylish, with light, appropriately beachy decor. Balconies with lovely coastal views and the sound of the rolling surf are highlights, as are the can-do staff and quality restaurant. Furled umbrellas outside every door are a nice touch: this is the South Coast, after all Breakfast is included in all rates.

🍴 Eating

Hayden's Pies
BAKERY $

(☑02-4455 7798; 166 Princes Hwy, Ulladulla; pies $4-7; ⊘6am-5pm Mon-Sat, 7am-5pm Sun) With traditional ones and a range of innovative gourmet pies – think Peking Duck or ⌐oat curry – this excellent bakery is awash with crusty goodness and delicious aromas. There's a daily pie special, gluten-free options and other home baking treats. Are these the South Coast's best pies? It's hard to think of a tastier one.

★ Tallwood
MODERN AUSTRALIAN, CAFE $$

(☑02-4455 5192; www.tallwoodeat.com.au; 2/85 Tallwood Ave, Mollymook; breakfast $12-26, dinner mains $28-36; ⊘6-10pm Wed-Fri & Mon, 8am-2.30pm & 6-10pm Sat & Sun, open for coffee at other times, longer hours Jan; 🖊) Tallwood kicks off the day with excellent coffee and delicious breakfasts such as ricotta hotcakes, before segueing into more innovative dishes at weekend brunches and dinner. Highlights to be enjoyed in the colourful and modern surroundings include Portuguese fish cakes with saffron mayo, Balinese-spiced duck, and *dukkah*-spiced eggplant. There are good vegetarian options, and Australian craft beers and wines are proudly featured.

★ Cupitt's Winery & Restaurant
MODERN AUSTRALIAN $$$

(☑02-4455 7888; www.cupitt.com.au; 58 Washburton Rd, Ulladulla; mains $30-40; ⊘food noon-2pm Wed-Sun & 6-8.30pm Fri & Sat, winery 10.30am-5pm Wed-Sun; 🕸) Enjoy respected cuisine and wine tasting in this restored 1851 creamery, 3km west of town and well signposted. It's a pleasantly rural location with relaxing views over a lake and cattle grazing in a green valley. There's boutique vineyard accommodation (one/two nights $330/575) and a craft brewery. The restaurant is focused on quality ingredients and slow food principles. Book ahead.

Rick Stein at Bannisters
SEAFOOD $$$

(☑02-4455 3044; www.bannisters.com.au; 191 Mitchell Pde, Mollymook; mains $36-48; ⊘12.30-3pm & 6-10pm Wed, Sat & Sun, 6-10pm Thu & Fri; 🕸) Elegantly situated on Bannister's Point, 1km north of town. Celebrity chef Rick Stein's excellently selected and presented seafood fare matches the fine views. There's a touch of French and a touch of Asian to the menu, which usually includes oysters, local snapper and seafood pie.

ℹ Information

Shoalhaven Visitor Centre (☑02-4444 8819; www.shoalhavenholidays.com.au; Princes Hwy, Ulladulla; ⊘9am-5pm Mon-Sat, 9am-4pm Sun) Bookings and information in the civic centre and library on the highway.

ℹ Getting There & Away

Premier (📞13 34 10; www.premierms.com.au) runs between Sydney ($35, 4¼ to five hours) and Eden ($50, four hours), via Batemans Bay ($14, 45 minutes) and Nowra ($18, one hour).

EUROBODALLA COAST

Meaning 'Land of Many Waters', this southern coastline celebrates all things blue. Swathes of green also punctuate the area's sprawling Eurobodalla National Park.

Batemans Bay

POP 11,300

Good nearby beaches and a sparkling estuary make this fishing port one of the South Coast's most popular holiday centres. The town sits at the point where the Clyde River becomes the sea and has a somewhat old-fashioned summer resort feel. Batemans Bay is a good base for watery activities.

◉ Sights & Activities

Closest to town is **Corrigans Beach**, and longer beaches north of the bridge lead into Murramarang National Park. Surfers flock to **Pink Rocks**, **Surf Beach**, **Malua Bay**, **McKenzies Beach** and **Bengello Beach**. **Broulee** has a wide crescent of sand, but there's a strong rip at the northern end.

Batemans Bay is a fine base for getting out on the water. Numerous operators offer lessons, hire and guided excursions with kayaks, surfboards, snorkels or stand-up paddleboards. Some are based in other towns but operate right along this section of coast.

Total Eco Adventures   WATER SPORTS
(📞02-4471 6969; www.totalecoadventures.com.au; 7/77 Coronation Dr, Broulee) This set-up offers kayaking, with various river excursions around the region, as well as hire. It also does snorkelling and stand-up paddling excursions and rents out surfboards.

Surf the Bay Surf School   SURFING
(📞0432 144 220; www.surfthebay.com.au; group/private lesson $40/90) This surfing and paddleboarding school operates at Batemans, Broulee and Narooma and has special courses for kids during school holidays. It also hires equipment.

Region X   KAYAKING
(📞1300 001 060; http://regionx.com.au; kayak rental 1hr $30, tours $75-95) Rent a kayak to explore nearby waterways or take one of several paddling tours around Batemans Bay and the coast to the south. It also offers cycle hire. The hire station is at Mossy Point, south of Batemans.

🛌 Sleeping

Zorba Waterfront Motel   MOTEL $$
(📞02-4472 4804; www.zorbamotel.com.au; Orient St; r $130-180; 🅿 ➡ ✳ 🛜) Handily located right by the string of bayside eateries, this is a friendly, family-run place that has been a solid option for years. The blue trim is true to its Greek name and rooms are spacious and comfortable, with balconies or terrace space. It's worth the small extra cost to get one with water views.

Bay Breeze   MOTEL $$
(📞02-4472 7222; www.baybreezemotel.com.au; 21 Beach Rd; r $175-300; 🅿 ➡ ✳ 🛜) Very centrally located, this upmarket motel has a super position overlooking the bay. It's very professionally run, and with just seven rooms, it has the attention to detail of a boutique hotel. There's a subtle Balinese theme in the attractive rooms, which are equipped with coffee machines and stylish bathrooms.

✕ Eating

Innes' Boatshed   FISH & CHIPS $
(📞02-4472 4052; 1 Clyde St; fish & chips $14, 6 oysters $9; ⊗9am-8pm Sun-Thu, 9am-8.30pm Fri & Sat) Since the 1950s this has been one of the South Coast's best-loved fish-and-chip and oyster joints. This is arguably the centre of the town. Head out to the spacious deck but mind the pelicans. It's cash only and there's no alcohol served or BYO arrangement.

Blank Canvas   CAFE $$
(📞02-4472 5016; Annetts Arcade, Orient St; dishes $14-32; ⊗8.30am-2pm & 5.30-8.30pm Wed-Mon Feb-Dec, 8.30am-9pm daily Jan; 🛜) Right on the water with a pleasant shady terrace, this cafe by day morphs into a more intimate Modern Australian dining experience in the evenings. It takes coffee seriously, with cold drip and various single origins available, making this the town's best stop for breakfast or brunch.

WORTH A TRIP

MOGO

Mogo is a historic strip of wooden houses with cafes and souvenir shops 9km south of Batemans Bay. It was originally a gold-rush town and **Gold Rush Colony** (02-4474 2123; www.goldrushcolony.com.au; 26 James St; adult/child $20/12; 10am-4pm) is a re-creation of a pioneer village of that era, complete with free gold panning and cabins for accommodation.

Mogo Zoo (02-4474 4930; www.mogozoo.com.au; 222 Tomakin Rd; adult/child $31/16; 9am-5pm), 2km east off the highway, is a small but interesting zoo with rare white lions and an enthralling troop of gorillas.

On the Pier SEAFOOD $$$
(02-4472 6405; www.onthepier.com.au; 2 Old Punt Rd; mains $29-35; 6-8.30pm Thu, noon-2pm & 6-8.30pm Fri & Sat, 9am-3pm Sun) With a lovely waterside location, this friendly Batemans favourite has magical views over the river and hills behind, especially at sunset. Local fish are a highlight, but it also does tasty meat dishes. Service is cheery and the ambience fairly casual. Opening hours vary somewhat through the year.

Information

Batemans Bay Visitor Centre (02-4472 6900; www.eurobodalla.com.au; cnr Princes Hwy & Beach Rd; 9am-5pm Sep-Apr, 9am-4pm May-Aug) Covering town and the wider Eurobodalla area.

Getting There & Away

The scenic Kings Hwy climbs the escarpment and heads to Canberra from just north of Batemans Bay.

Premier (13 34 10; www.premierms.com.au) runs buses to Sydney ($45, six hours) and Eden ($46, three to four hours) via Ulladulla ($16, 45 minutes) and Moruya ($11, 30 minutes).

Murrays (13 22 51; www.murrays.com.au) runs buses to Canberra ($37.60, 2½ hours), Moruya ($13.60, 40 minutes) and Narooma ($20.90, 1¾ hours).

V/Line (1800 800 007; www.vline.com.au) runs a bus-train combination to Melbourne via Bairnsdale ($60.60, 11½ hours) on Tuesdays, Fridays and Sundays.

Priors (02-4472 4040; www.priorsbus.com.au) runs regional services, including a bus to Broulee and Moruya via various surf beaches.

Moruya

POP 2500

Moruya ('black swan') has Victorian buildings gathered around a broad river. There's popular Saturday market and a couple of eat places for a bed and a meal.

Sleeping & Eating

★ **Post & Telegraph B&B** B&B $$
(02-4474 5745; www.postandtelegraphbb.blogspot.com; cnr Page & Campbell Sts; s/d incl breakfast $125/155; P ⊖ ☜) This 19th-century post and telegraph office is now an enchanting four-room B&B with great historical character. High ceilings, period features and antique furnishings and objects are allied with friendly, genuine hospitality and numerous thoughtful details. There's a shared verandah, decanters of sherry and port and an excellent common lounge. You couldn't ask for a lovelier spot.

The River MODERN AUSTRALIAN $$$
(02-4474 5505; www.therivermoruya.com.au; 16b Church St; mains $30-36, 5-course degustation $85, with matching wines $115; noon-2.30pm Wed-Sun, 6-9.30pm Wed-Sat; ❄) Perched right over the river in a position just west of the bridge in downtown Moruya, The River combines local and seasonal ingredients with international flavours. There's a short, quality Modern Australian menu with a five-course tasting menu option. Book ahead.

Getting There & Away

Moruya Airport (MYA; 0409 037 520; www.esc.nsw.gov.au; George Bass Dr) is 7km from town, near North Head. **Rex** (13 17 13; www.rex.com.au) flies from Merimbula and Sydney.

Murrays (13 22 51; www.murrays.com.au) buses head to Canberra ($40.80, 3½ hours), Batemans Bay ($13.30, 40 minutes) and Narooma ($14.80, 45 minutes).

Premier (p192) runs buses to Sydney ($49, six to seven hours) via Batemans Bay ($11, 30 minutes) and in the other direction to Eden ($46, 2½ to three hours) via all coastal towns.

Narooma

POP 2400

At the mouth of a tree-lined river estuary and flanked by surf beaches, Narooma is a pretty seaside town. It is also the jumping-off point for Montague Island, a very rewarding offshore excursion.

◉ Sights & Activities

★ Montague Island
(Baranguba)   NATURE RESERVE
(www.montagueisland.com.au) Nine kilometres offshore from Narooma, this small, pest-free island is home to seabirds and fur seals. Little penguins nest here, especially from September to February, while seals (and offshore whales) are most numerous from September to November. Various guided tours conducted by park rangers are number- and weather-dependent; book ahead through the visitor centre. The morning tours are longer and the evening tours wait for the penguins to come ashore. Boat operators can combine the island visit with snorkelling and whale watching.

You can stay at the island's beautifully renovated **lighthouse keepers' cottages** (☑02 4476 0800; www.nationalparks.nsw.gov.au; Montague Island; cottages $1200-1800; ⊜🔊) 🏄, but you'll need to book well ahead.

Narooma Marina   BOATING
(☑02-4476 2126; www.naroomamarina.com.au; 30 Riverside Dr; boat per hour/half-day/day $55/145/265, surfboard half-/full day $20/40, kayak $25 1st hour then $20 per hour) This friendly set-up on the river hires out canoes, kayaks, pedalos, fishing boats, surfboards and stand-up paddleboards. Basically, it's a one-stop shop for getting you out on the water. Note that you aren't allowed to land at Montague Island except on an approved tour.

Underwater Safaris   DIVING
(☑0415 805 479; www.underwatersafaris.com.au; 1/2 dives $80/120) This diving operator runs PADI courses and guided dives around Montague Island and elsewhere along the coast. It also runs snorkelling and whale-watching excursions.

⊂⊃ Tours

Montague Island
Nature Reserve Tours   WALKING, BOATING
(☑02-4476 2881; www.montagueisland.com.au; per person $90-125) A number of operators run boat trips to Montague Island, where you link up with a national parks guide to show you over the island, visiting the seal colonies, lighthouse and more. Evening tours in season let you watch the penguins march back onshore. Book via the visitor centres at Narooma (p194) or Batemans Bay.

🛌 Sleeping

Narooma Motel   HOSTEL, MOTEL $
(☑02-4476 3287; www.naroomamotel.com.au; 243 Princes Hwy; dm $35-40, d $100-130; 🅿⊜@🔊) Offering a genuine welcome and very fair prices, this motel is a likeable place that offers compact budget motel-style rooms and dormitory accommodation. There's a sizeable common kitchen, a lovely conservatory lounge and a peaceful garden area with barbecue. Heather and Les are kind hosts who go out of their way to make you feel welcome.

★ Whale Motor Inn   MOTEL $$
(☑02-4476 2411; www.whalemotorinn.com; 104 Wagonga St; d $143-231; 🅿⊜❄🔊❄🔊) 🏄 Excellently run by a friendly couple, this is a standout place to stop that offers a lot even in the lower categories: the Premier rooms are a real bargain, capacious and modern. The range of suites ramps it up another notch, with sophisticated facilities and lots of thoughtful extras. There's a small pool, a quality restaurant and a lovely panoramic outlook.

Anchors Aweigh   B&B $$
(☑02-4476 4000; www.anchorsaweigh.com.au; 5 Tilba St; s $105, d $149-225; 🅿⊜❄🔊) 🏄 Five very commodious and light rooms, two with spa bath and king-sized beds and one with a private verandah, make great South Coast bases at this cordially run B&B on a central side street. Public areas are great too; check out the teddy bear and other collections and the model train running through the breakfast room.

OFF THE BEATEN TRACK

MAGICAL MYSTERY BAY TOUR

South of Narooma, just before the turn-off to the Tilbas, take the road to gorgeously undeveloped **Mystery Bay** and the southernmost pocket of **Eurobodalla National Park**. At the southern end of the main surf beach, a rock formation has created an idyllic **natural swimming pool**. There's a council-run **campground** (☑0428 622 357; www.mysterybaycampground.com.au; Mystery Bay Rd, Mystery Bay; adult/child $16/4) under the trees. It's so close to the beach you could almost boil a billy with your tootsies in the sand.

Narooma

✕ Eating

Quarterdeck Marina CAFE $$
(☏02-4476 2723; www.quarterdecknarooma.com.au; 13 Riverside Dr; mains $15-29; ⊙10am-4pm Thu, 10am-8pm Fri, 10am-3pm & 6-8pm Sat, 8am-3pm Sun; 🛜) Enjoy excellent seafood lunches and Sunday breakfasts in this red shed under the gaze of dozens of tikis and autographed photos of 1950s TV stars. Great inlet views and regular live music. It's a real good-times Narooma hub.

Whale Restaurant MODERN AUSTRALIAN $$$
(☏02-4476 2411; www.whalemotorinn.com; 104 Wagonga St; mains $31-36; ⊙6-9pm Tue-Sat; 🛜) 🍽 The dining at this motel restaurant is as good as the dreamy coastal views. A philosophy of using quality local ingredients, some from its own vegetable garden, inspires a menu that showcases the magnificent local oysters, homemade pasta, foraged ingredients, Tilba cheeses, sustainable fish and aged beef. There's a pleasant lounge for a pre-dinner drink.

ℹ Information

Narooma Visitor Centre and Gallery (☏02-4476 2881; www.narooma.org.au; Princes Hwy; ⊙9am-5pm Oct-Easter, 10am-4pm Easter-Sep) This friendly volunteer-run visitor centre is great for local information and also includes a gallery stocked by the local arts and crafts society and a free historical museum. You can buy bus tickets here too.

ℹ Getting There & Away

Premier (☏13 34 10; www.premierms.com.au) runs buses to Eden ($41, 2½ hours) and Sydney ($58, seven hours) via Wollongong ($56, five hours).

V/Line (p192) runs a daily bus-train combination from Narooma to Melbourne ($60.60, 11 hours) via Bairnsdale.

Murrays (☑13 22 51; www.murrays.com.au) has daily buses to Moruya ($14.80, one hour), Batemans Bay ($20.90, two hours) and Canberra ($48.40, 4½ hours).

Local buses do circuits around the immediate Narooma area.

Tilba Tilba & Central Tilba

The coastal road north from Bermagui rejoins the Princes Hwy just before the loop road to these National Trust villages in the shadow of Gulaga. Tilba Tilba is tiny compared to its not-very-large neighbour, 2km down the road.

Central Tilba has remained virtually unchanged since it was a 19th-century goldmining boom town. Cafes and craft shops fill the heritage buildings along touristy Bate St. Behind the Dromedary pub, walk up to the water tower for terrific views of Gulaga (formerly called Mt Dromedary, hence the name).

◉ Sights

Foxglove Gardens GARDENS
(☑02-4473 7375; www.foxglovegardens.com; Corkhill Dr, Tilba Tilba; adult/child $9/2; ⊙9.30am-5pm Oct-Mar, 10am-4pm Apr-Sep) At the southern end of Tilba Tilba, this is a magical 3½-acre private garden. It offers a surprising and peaceful retreat into a secluded world of hidden avenues, a rose garden, bowers, a duck pond and other Victorian touches. The heritage cottage alongside was being prepped to offer B&B accommodation at time of research and should be well worth investigating.

⌂ Sleeping

★ Bryn at Tilba B&B $$
(☑02-4473 7385; www.thebrynattilba.com.au; 91 Punkalla-Tilba Rd, central Tilba; r $235-265; P ◒ ☎) Follow central Tilba's main street a kilometre out of town to this fabulous building that sits on a green-lawned hillside. It's a lovely, peaceful spot with wide-arching views from the rooms and wide verandah. Three rooms with hardwood floors, an airy feel and characterful bathrooms share sumptuous common spaces; there's also a separate self-contained cottage.

ⓘ Information

Bates Emporium (Bate St, Central Tilba; ⊙8am-5pm Mon-Fri, 8.30am-4.30pm Sat, 9am-4.30pm Sun; ☎) There's information and fuel at Bates Emporium, at the start of the main street of central Tilba.

ⓘ Getting There & Away

Premier (☑13 34 10; www.premierms.com.au) runs a daily bus to Sydney ($59, eight hours) via Narooma ($8, 25 minutes), and Eden ($36, two hours) via Merimbula ($28, 90 minutes).

SAPPHIRE COAST

The southernmost stretch of the NSW coast is one of its most memorable. Take virtually any road east of the Princes Hwy for mainly unblemished coast set amid rugged spectacular surroundings. Excellent national parks offer beaches, wildlife and rustic camping, the towns have an authentic feel and interesting heritage, and the whale watching from September to November is some of Australia's best. Another highlight is the local oysters, one of the world's great seafood treats.

Bermagui

POP 1500

South of bird-filled Wallaga Lake, Bermagui ('Bermie') is a laid-back fishing port with fisherfolk, surfers, alternative lifestylers and Indigenous Australians. Bermagui is off the highway, so it has a more tranquil vibe than some of the towns on it.

⌂ Sleeping & Eating

Harbourview Motel MOTEL $$
(☑02-6493 5213; www.harbourviewmotel.com.au; 56-58 Lamont St; s $160-185, d $180-205; P ◒ ❄ ☎) Run in very shipshape fashion, this motel has high-standard, spacious exemplary rooms that are kept spotless by the enthusiastic owner, who is a top source of local information. Each room has a private barbecue area, a full kitchenette and excellent facilities. There's an on-site Japanese restaurant and the place is very well located for the beach or Fishermen's Wharf.

Bermagui Motor Inn
MOTEL $$

(☑02-6493 4311; www.bermaguimotorinn.com.au; 38 Lamont St; s/d $120/130 deluxe d $165; P ❁❋✿) With an excellent location right at Bermagui's principal intersection, this is run by an amiable couple and has spacious, upgraded modern rooms with comfortable beds and decent facilities, including a laundry. Rooms in the budget category have just a double bed, while queen rooms offer more space and amenities.

★ Il Passaggio
ITALIAN $$

(☑02-6493 5753; www.ilpassaggio.com.au; Fishermen's Wharf, 73 Lamont St; pizzas $18-24, mains $26-36; ⊙6-9pm Wed & Thu, noon-2pm & 6-11pm Fri-Sun) Cheerfully located on the top deck of the building by the fishing harbour, Il Passagio has winning outdoor seating where you can look over the boats that brought your catch. Tasty proper-Italian pizzas are popular, and the short menu of quality mains, homemade pasta and antipasti bursts with flavour. Good wines and cheerful staff make this a winner.

🍷 Drinking & Nightlife

★ Horse & Camel Wine Bar
WINE BAR

(☑02-6493 3410; www.horseandcamel.com.au; Fishermen's Wharf, 73 Lamont St; ⊙3-10pm Thu-Sun Mar-Nov, 2pm-late Wed-Mon Dec-Feb) On the top level of the Fishermen's Wharf complex, this amiably run wine bar is a top spot to relax with a glass of something interesting while pondering the views over the boats from the balcony seating. Inside is cosy, and there's a pleasing array of deli share plates and chunky weekend pizzas ($17 to $26). Hours vary slightly according to demand.

❶ Information

Visitor Centre (☑02-6493 3054; www.visitbermagui.com.au; Bunga St; ⊙10am-4pm) The purpose-built information centre near the town's main intersection has a museum and discovery centre.

❶ Getting There & Away

Premier (☑13 34 10; www.premierms.com.au) runs daily between Sydney ($60, 8½ hours) and Eden ($31, 1¾ hours).

V/Line (p192) runs four coaches a week to Bairnsdale, Victoria, connecting with a train to Melbourne (total $60.60, 10½ hours)

Merimbula & Pambula
POP 7700

Arrayed along a long, golden beach and an appealing inlet, Merimbula hosts both holiday-makers and retirees. In summer, this is one of the few places on the far South Coast that gets crowded.

Merimbula and nearby Pambula are deservedly famous for their wonderful oysters – make sure you try some.

◉ Sights

Potoroo Palace
ZOO

(☑02-6494 9225; www.potoroopalace.com; 2372 Princes Hwy, Yellow Pinch; adult/child $20/12; ⊙10am-4pm; ⬧) Warmly run Potoroo Palace, a not-for-profit animal sanctuary, has echidnas, kangaroos, dingoes, koalas, potoroos and native birds. There's also a cafe here, with daily lunch specials. It's 9km northwest of Merimbula on the road to Bega.

Merimbula Aquarium
AQUARIUM

(☑02-6495 4446; www.merimbulawharf.com.au; Lake St; adult/child $22/15; ⊙10am-5pm) Right at the end of the road southeast of the centre, this is accessed through a restaurant with super views and has mostly local and tropical Australian fish species; there's also a turtle and some small sharks. Fish feeding sessions take place Monday, Wednesday and Friday at 11.30am. Entry usually includes a guided tour.

🏃 Activities

Cycle 'n' Surf
CYCLING, SURFING

(☑02-6495 2171; www.cyclensurf.com.au; 1b Marine Pde; bicycle hire per hr/half-day/full day $12/25/35) Reliable and friendly operator near the beach who specialises in bikes but also hires out bodyboards and surfboards.

Coastlife Adventures
SURFING, KAYAKING

(☑02-6494 1122; www.coastlife.com.au; Fishpen Rd; group/private surf lessons $65/120, kayak tours from $65, kayak & stand-up paddleboards rental per hour $25) Offer surfing and stand-up paddle-boarding lessons and hire, plus sea kayak tours and kayak hire. It also has bases at Pambula Beach and Tathra.

Merimbula Marina
WILDLIFE WATCHING

(☑02-6495 1686; www.merimbulamarina.com; Merimbula jetty, Market St) This operator runs popular whale-watching tours (adults $60 to $69) three times daily from September to November, as well as dolphin-watching cruises ($35)

Merimbula

and fishing trips ($90 for four hours). You can also hire a 'tinnie' boat and a rod and go for it yourself.

Merimbula Divers Lodge DIVING
(☑ 02-6495 3611; www.merimbuladiverslodge. com.au; 15 Park St; 1/2 boat dives $69/120, equipment for 1/2 dives $55/99) Offers basic instruction, PADI courses and snorkelling trips – good for beginners. It runs guided dives to nearby wrecks, which include the *Empire Gladstone*, which sank in 1950. There are accommodation packages available too.

🛏 Sleeping

NRMA Merimbula Beach Holiday Park CAMPGROUND $
(☑ 02-6499 8999; www.nrmaholidayparks.com.au; 2 Short Point Rd; camp sites $40-60, cabins & villas $150-360; P ☕ 🛜 🐾 🌊) A little away from the town centre but close to the surf action and vistas of Short Point Beach, this is a great spot with both powered and unpowered camp sites, some with clifftop views, and a range of cabins and villas, many of them upmarket.

Wandarrah Lodge HOSTEL $
(☑ 02-6495 3503; www.wandarrahlodge.com.au; 8 Marine Pde; dm/s/d $32/60/70; P ☕ 🛜) This clean, casual place, with friendly owners, a good kitchen and spacious shared areas, is near the surf beach and the bus stop. Rooms are simple, spotless and homey, with shared bathrooms, and there's a pool table, and kayak and surfboard hire. It was up for sale at time of research, so things may change.

Coast Resort APARTMENT $$$
(☑ 02-6495 4930; www.coastresort.com. au; 1 Elizabeth St; 1-/2-/3-bedroom apt $320/520/740; P ☕ ❄ 🛜 🌊) This huge, upmarket apartment-style complex is ultra-modern and commodious. Facilities are great and the two pools, tennis court and proximity to the beach are all very appealing. Prices halve outside the January high season.

✕ Eating

Dulcie's Cottage BURGERS $
(www.dulcies.com.au; 60 Main St; burgers $12-17; ⊙ noon-midnight Mon Sat, noon-10pm Sun; 🛜) Inner-city Sydney hipsterdom has arrived on the Sapphire Coast in the form of this bar and burger joint by the RSL club. A cute weatherboard cottage and casual outdoor seating makes a comfortable venue for convivial drinks and tasty burgers whipped up in a food truck out front (for licensing reasons apparently).

Merimbula Wharf SEAFOOD $$
(☑ 02-6495 4446; www.merimbulawharf.com.au; Lake St; mains $18-31; ⊙ 10am-5pm year-round plus 6-9pm some nights Dec-Apr; 🛜) The views over bay and beach are just stunning from the windows of this friendly restaurant that incorporates an aquarium at the wharf southeast of central Merimbula. Lunch fish dishes are uncomplicated and tasty; ring for summer dinner opening hours as they are a little variable.

★ **Wheelers** SEAFOOD $$$
(www.wheelersoysters.com.au; 162 Arthur Kaine Dr, Pambula; 12 oysters from shop $12-15, restaurant mains $34-42; ⊙ shop 10am-5pm Sun-Thu, 10am-6pm Fri & Sat, restaurant noon-2.30pm daily, 6pm-late Mon-Sat; 🖟) Come here on the way to Merimbula from Pambula, to enjoy totally delicious fresh oysters – either takeaway or from the shop or enjoyed in the relaxing restaurant. The menu features oysters prepared loads of ways and other great seafood and steak dishes. Tours showcasing some people's favourite bivalve depart at 11am Monday to Saturday ($12.50).

ℹ️ Information

Merimbula Visitor Information Centre (☑ 02-6495 1129; www.sapphirecoast.com.au; 4 Beach St; ⊙ 9am-5pm Mon-Fri, 9am-4pm Sat, 10am-4pm Sun) In the centre of town by the lake.

ℹ️ Getting There & Away

Merimbula Airport (MIM; ☑ 02-6495 4211; www.merimbulaairport.com.au; Arthur Kaine Dr) is 1km out of town on the road to Pambula. **Rex** (☑ 13 17 13; www.rex.com.au) flies daily to Melbourne and Sydney.

Premier (☑ 13 34 10; www.premierms.com.au) has two daily buses to Sydney and Eden. **NSW TrainLink** (☑ 13 22 32; www.nswtrainlink.info) runs a daily bus to Canberra ($40, four hours). Local **buses** (Market St) run Mondays to Fridays to Eden and Bega at schoolkid-friendly hours.

Eden

POP 3000

Eden's a sleepy, appealing place with real local character set on magnificent Twofold Bay. Often the only bustle is down at the harbour when the fishing boats – and, once the wharf is extended, cruise ships – come in. Around the surrounding area are stirring beaches, national parks and wilderness areas.

Eden's origins are as a whaling town; the activity began here as early as 1791. Now that the migrating humpback whales and southern right whales are left in peace, they pass so close to the coast that this is one of Australia's best whale-watching locations.

⊙ Sights

Killer Whale Museum MUSEUM
(☑ 02-6496 2094; www.killerwhalemuseum.com. au; 94 Imlay St; adult/child $10/2.50; ⊙ 9.15am-3.45pm Mon-Sat, 11.15am-3.45pm Sun) Established in 1931, the museum's main purpose is to preserve the skeleton of Old Tom, a killer whale and local legend. His is an extraordinary story: this cetacean Judas used to round up humpbacks for the local whaling fleet. A theatrette screens a cetacean documentary, while other exhibits include one on wartime – a surprising number of vessels were sunk by German mines around here.

Whale Lookout VIEWPOINT
A good spot to look for whales is at the base of Bass St. When whales are spotted, the Killer Whale Museum sounds a siren.

⌁ Tours

Ocean Wilderness KAYAKING
(☑ 0405 529 214; www.oceanwilderness.com.au; 4/6hr tours from $85/130) This professional set-up runs sea-kayaking trips through Twofold Bay and to Ben Boyd National Park, and a full-day excursion to Davidson Whaling Station.

Cat Balou Cruises WILDLIFE
(☑ 0427 962 027; www.catbalou.com.au; Main Wharf, 253 Imlay St; adult/child $85/65) This crew operates 3½-hour whale-spotting voyages from September to November; there are also shorter budget trips (adult/child $60/45). At other times of the year, dolphins and seals can usually be seen during the three-hour bay cruise (adult/child $75/50).

⚒ Festivals & Events

Whale Festival STREET CARNIVAL
(www.edenwhalefestival.com.au; ⊙ late Oct or early Nov) Eden comes alive in late October or early November for this festival, with a carnival, street parade and stalls plus guided whale watching and documentary screenings.

🛏 Sleeping

Great Southern Inn PUB $
(☑ 02-6496 1515; www.greatsoutherninn.com.au; 121 Imlay St; basic/standard r $40/100; ℗🖨🖨) The pub in the heart of town offers great value for its basic en suite rooms. The cheapest just has a bunk bed and a fan, but it's cheap.

Seahorse Inn BOUTIQUE HOTEL $$
(☑ 02-6496 1361; www.seahorseinnhotel.com. au; Boydtown Park Rd, Boydtown; r $205-349; ℗🖨✳🖨) At Boydtown, 8km south of Eden, the Seahorse Inn has a majestic waterside position with lawns running to the beach on Twofold Bay. It's a lavish boutique hotel with all the trimmings, and there's a good restaurant and garden bar open to nonguests. Rooms are modern and very amply proportioned, with king-sized beds in all. Most have

a balcony with water views. Rates include a continental breakfast.

★**Crown & Anchor Inn** B&B $$$
(☑02-6496 1017; www.crownandanchoreden.com.au; 239 Imlay St; r $190-230, multinight stay $160-190; ☺Sep-May; P☻☺☻) A real labour of love has gloriously restored this 1845 coaching inn, with period detail and original features throughout. It's a place of extraordinary character and historic authenticity. Rooms are small, cosy and delightful, with curious bathrooms hidden behind mirrors. There are lovely common areas too, including a back patio with a marvellous view over Twofold Bay. An excellent locally sourced breakfast is included.

The welcoming owners prefer guests to make reservations, and don't accept bookings that include young children.

 Eating

Sprout CAFE $
(☑02-6496 1511; www.sprouteden.com.au; 134 Imlay St; mains $12-18; ☺7.30am-4pm Mon-Fri, 8am-3pm Sat & Sun; ☻☻) ✔ On the main street, this shop and cafe showcases organic and sustainable produce, top-notch burgers and the best coffee in town. The back garden area is a pleasant spot in which to eat on a sunny day.

★**Wharfside Café** CAFE $$
(☑02-6496 1855; Main Wharf, 253 Imlay St; dishes $15-26, dinner mains $28-33; ☺8am-3pm daily year-round, plus 6-10pm Fri & Sat Nov-Mar; ☻) Decent breakfasts, tasty coffee and great outdoor tables by the harbour make this handsome, friendly cafe-restaurant a good way to start the day. Try some local seafood with a glass of wine for lunch; dinner options are more elaborate creations around fresh fish, big steaks and rich, tasty sauces. The main wharf is downhill from town.

ⓘ **Information**

Eden Visitor Centre (☑02-6496 1953; www.visiteden.com.au; Mitchell St; ☺9am-5pm Mon-Fri, 10am-4pm Sat & Sun) Bookings and information. By the main road roundabout in the centre. It also runs minibus tours to surrounding attractions.

ⓘ **Getting There & Away**

Premier (☑13 34 10; www.premierms.com.au) runs north to Sydney ($71, nine to 10 hours) twice daily via all major coastal towns. **NSW TrainLink** (☑13 22 32; www.nswtrainlink.info) runs a daily bus service to Canberra ($42, 4½ hours). For Melbourne ($51, 8¼ hours), **V/Line**

(p192) runs a bus and train combination via Bairnsdale.

Local buses have limited service to Merimbula and Bega on weekdays.

Ben Boyd National Park

With two sections either side of Eden, the 10,485-hectare **Ben Boyd National Park** (www.nationalparks.nsw.gov.au; vehicle in southern/northern section $8/free) is an excellent spot. The southern section has more to see, with some interesting heritage buildings, a long coastal walk and top wildlife-spotting opportunities. It is accessed by mainly gravel roads leading off sealed Edrom Rd, which leaves the Princes Hwy 19km south of Eden.

◉ **Sights & Activities**

Green Cape Lightstation LIGHTHOUSE
(☑02-6495 5000; www.nationalparks.nsw.gov.au; Green Cape Rd; 2-/4-person cottage $280/350) At the southern tip of the southern section of the Ben Boyd National Park, elegant 1883 Green Cape Lightstation offers awesome views. There are hour-long tours (available 10am to 2pm, adult/child $10/5) and three lavishly restored keepers' cottages. This is a great spot to see whales in season, and you may well see wombats in the late afternoon. On the way here, stop at the viewpoint for majestic vistas over Disaster Bay and Wonboyn Beach.

Boyd's Tower HISTORIC BUILDING
FREE At the end of Edrom Rd is the turn-off for Boyd's Tower, built in the late 1840s with Sydney sandstone. It was intended to be a lighthouse, but the government wouldn't give Boyd permission to operate it. It's an impressive structure, and one of the trailheads for the Light to Light walk.

★**Light to Light Walk** HIKING
This excellent 30km coastal walk links Boyd's wannabe lighthouse to the real one at Green Cape. There are camp sites along the route at Saltwater Creek and Bittangabee Bay.

🛏 **Sleeping**

Ben Boyd National Park Campgrounds CAMPGROUND $
(☑02-6495 5000; www.nationalparksnsw.gov.au; adult/child $12/6, minimum $24) If you are walking the 30km Light to Light Walk (p199), there are camp sites along the route at Saltwater Creek and Bittangabee Bay, which can be booked ahead online or by phone. They can also be accessed by road.

Melbourne & Coastal Victoria

Best Places to Eat

➡ Brae (p256)

➡ Attica (p227)

➡ IGNI (p247)

➡ Chris's Beacon Point Restaurant (p258)

➡ Fen (p264)

Best Places to Sleep

➡ Treasury on Collins (p217)

➡ Lighthouse Keepers' Cottages (p271)

➡ Beacon Point Ocean View Villas (p258)

➡ Drift House (p264)

➡ Great Ocean Ecolodge (p259)

Why Go?

From windswept beaches to cosmopolitan seaside towns and legendary surfing spots, Victoria's coastline has stunning vistas, cool-climate wineries and the culture-packed city of Melbourne. It's a diverse coast: fairy penguins march up and down beaches in the popular tourist destination of Phillip Island, while Victoria's west coast faces on to Bass Strait and attracts surfers and those searching for the iconic Twelve Apostles. Heading up the southeast coast from the hiking paradise of Wilsons Promontory is a long, cruisy expanse of beach that meets up with a popular, activity-filled lakes system around Lakes Entrance (Australia's largest inland waterway system). There are more stunning national parks on the approach to the Victoria–New South Wales border.

When to Go
Melbourne

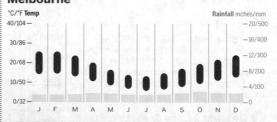

Dec & Jan
Beaches are packed during summer; book accomodation months ahead.

Feb & Mar
Quieter time; late summer weather can be particularly hot.

Apr–Nov
April has arguably the best weather, leading into cold nights and crisp winter days.

Melbourne & Coastal Victoria Highlights

1 Great Ocean Road (p244) Cruising by spectacular beaches and through inland rainforests.

2 Drinking & Dining Around Melbourne (p222) Seeking cool cafes, bars and restaurants.

3 Wilsons Prom Wilderness (p268) Strapping on your hiking boots to admire the beauty of this national park.

4 Penguin Parade, Phillip Island (p242) Watching the nightly parade of penguins waddling from the ocean to their sandy burrows.

5 Twelve Apostles (p259) Being mesmerised by majestic outlooks over these iconic limestone pillars.

6 Cape Otway (p258) Spying koalas in eucalyptus trees as you drive or hike through the lush rainforest en route to Cape Otway lighthouse

7 Mallacoota (p276) Hiring a boat and exploring the inlet, or visiting Gabo Island.

8 Ninety Mile Beach (p273) Camping in the dunes and fishing from the beach at this legendary stretch of sand.

MELBOURNE

POP 4,530,000

Stylish, arty Melbourne is both dynamic and cosmopolitan, and it's proud of its place as Australia's sporting and cultural capital. More than 230 laneways penetrate into the heart of the city blocks and it's here that the inner city's true nature resides, crammed into narrow lanes concealing world-beating restaurants, bars and street art. Melbourne is best experienced as a local would, with its character largely reliant upon its diverse collection of inner-city neighbourhoods. Despite a long-standing north–south divide (flashy South Yarra versus hipster Fitzroy), there's a coolness about its bars, cafes, restaurants, festivals and people that transcends the borders. Sport is a crucial part of the social fabric here, taking on something of a religious aspect. Melburnians are passionate about AFL football ('footy'), cricket and horse racing, while grand-slam tennis and Formula One car racing draw visitors in droves.

◉ Sights

◉ City Centre

★ Federation Square   SQUARE

(Map p208; www.fedsquare.com; cnr Flinders & Swanston Sts; ☒ Flinders St) While it's taken some time, Melburnians have come to embrace Federation Sq, accepting it as the congregation place it was meant to be – somewhere to celebrate, protest, watch major sporting events or hang out on its deckchairs. Occupying a prominent city block, 'Fed Square' is far from square: its undulating and patterned forecourt is paved with 460,000 hand-laid cobblestones from the Kimberley region in Western Australia, with sight lines to important Melbourne landmarks. Its buildings are clad in a fractal-patterned reptilian skin.

★ Ian Potter Centre:
NGV Australia   GALLERY

(Map p208; ☎ 03-8620 2222; www.ngv.vic.gov.au; Federation Sq; ⊙10am-5pm; ☒ Flinders St) FREE The National Gallery of Victoria's impressive Fed Sq offshoot was set up to showcase its extraordinary collection of Australian works. Set over three levels, it's a mix of permanent (free) and temporary (ticketed) exhibitions, comprising paintings, decorative arts, photography, prints, sculpture and fashion. Free tours are conducted daily at 11am, noon, 1pm and 2pm.

★ Hosier Lane   PUBLIC ART

(Map p208; ☒ Flinders St) Melbourne's most celebrated laneway for street art, Hosier Lane's cobbled length draws camera-wielding crowds snapping edgy graffiti, stencils and art installations. Subject matter runs to the mostly political and countercultural, spiced with irreverent humour; pieces change almost daily (not even a Banksy is safe here). Be sure to see Rutledge Lane (which horseshoes around Hosier), too.

Australian Centre for
the Moving Image   MUSEUM

(ACMI; Map p208; ☎ 03-8663 2200; www.acmi. net.au; Federation Sq; ⊙10am-5pm; ☒ Flinders St) FREE Managing to educate, enthral and entertain in equal parts, ACMI is a visual feast that pays homage to Australian cinema and TV, offering an insight into the modern-day Australian psyche perhaps as no other museum can. Its screens don't discriminate against age, with TV shows, games and movies on call, making it a great place to spend a day watching TV and not feel guilty about it. Free tours are conducted daily at 11am and 2.30pm.

Birrarung Marr   PARK

(Map p208; Batman Ave; ☒ Flinders St) Multiterraced Birrarung Marr is a welcome addition to Melbourne's patchwork of parks and gardens, featuring grassy knolls, river promenades, thoughtful planting of indigenous flora, and great viewpoints of the city and the river. There's also a scenic route to the MCG (p207) via the 'talking' William Barak Bridge – listen out for songs, words and sounds representing Melbourne's cultural diversity as you walk.

Flinders Street Station   HISTORIC BUILDING

(Map p208; cnr Flinders & Swanston Sts; ☒ Flinders St) If ever there were a true symbol of the city, Flinders St station would have to be it. Built in 1854, it was Melbourne's first railway station, and you'd be hard-pressed to find a Melburnian who hasn't uttered the phrase 'Meet me under the clocks' at one time or another (the popular rendezvous spot is located at the front entrance of the station). Stretching along the Yarra, it's a beautiful neoclassical building topped with a striking octagonal dome.

Parliament House   HISTORIC BUILDING

(Map p208; ☎ 03-9651 8568; www.parliament. vic.gov.au; Spring St; ⊙8.30am-5.30pm Mon-Fri; ☒ Parliament) FREE The grand steps of Victoria's parliament (1856) are often dotted with

WORTH A TRIP

HEIDE MUSEUM OF MODERN ART

The former home of John and Sunday Reed, **Heide** (☑03-9850 1500; www.heide.com.au; 7 Templestowe Rd, Bulleen; adult/child $22/18; ⊙10am-5pm Tue-Sun; ☑903, ☒Heidelberg) is a prestigious not-for-profit art gallery with a sculpture garden in its wonderful grounds. It holds regularly changing exhibitions, many of which include works by the famous artists that called Heide home, including Sir Sidney Nolan and Albert Tucker. The collection is spread over three buildings: a large purpose-built gallery, the Reeds' original farmhouse and the wonderful modernist house they built in 1963 as 'a gallery to be lived in'.

slow-moving, tulle-wearing brides smiling for the camera, or placard-holding protesters doing the same. On sitting days the public is welcome to view proceedings from the galleries. On nonsitting days, there are eight guided tours a day; times are posted online and on a sign by the door. Numbers are limited, so aim to arrive at least 15 minutes before time.

★**Chinatown**   AREA
(Map p208; www.chinatownmelbourne.com.au; Little Bourke St, btwn Swanston & Exhibition Sts; ☒Melbourne Central, Parliament) For more than 150 years this section of central Melbourne, now flanked by five traditional arches, has been the focal point for the city's Chinese community and it remains a vibrant neighbourhood of historic buildings filled with Chinese (and other Asian) restaurants. Come here for yum cha (dim sum) or to explore the attendant laneways for late-night dumplings or cocktails. Chinatown also hosts the city's **Chinese New Year** (www.chinesemelbourne.com.au; Little Bourke St; ⊙Jan or Feb) celebrations.

Chinese miners arrived in Victoria in search of the 'new gold mountain' in the 1850s and started to settle in this strip of Little Bourke St from the 1860s. To learn more about the Chinese Australian story, visit the excellent **Chinese Museum** (Map p208; ☑03-9662 2888; www.chinesemuseum.com.au; 22 Cohen Pl; adult/child $10/8.50; ⊙10am-4pm; ☒Parliament).

State Library of Victoria   LIBRARY
(Map p208; ☑03-8664 7002; www.slv.vic.gov.au; 328 Swanston St; ⊙10am-9pm Mon-Thu, to 6pm Fri-Sun, galleries 10am-5pm; ☒Melbourne Central) This grand neoclassical building has been at the forefront of Melbourne's literary scene since it opened in 1856. When its epicentre, the gorgeous octagonal **La Trobe Reading Room**, was completed in 1913, its reinforced-concrete dome was the largest of its kind in the world; its natural light illuminates the ornate plasterwork and the stu-

dious Melbourne writers who come here to pen their works. For visitors, the highlight is the fascinating collection showcased in the **Dome Galleries**.

Old Melbourne Gaol   HISTORIC BUILDING
(Map p208; ☑03-8663 7228; www.oldmelbournegaol.com.au; 337 Russell St; adult/child/family $25/14/55; ⊙9.30am-5pm; ☒Melbourne Central) Built in 1841, this forbidding bluestone prison was in operation until 1929. It's now one of Melbourne's most popular museums, where you can tour the tiny, bleak cells. Around 135 people were hanged here, including Ned Kelly, Australia's most infamous bushranger, in 1880; one of his death masks is on display. Visits include the Police Watch House Experience, where you get 'arrested' and thrown in the slammer (more fun than it sounds).

Queen Victoria Market   MARKET
(Map p208; www.qvm.com.au; 513 Elizabeth St; ⊙6am-2pm Tue & Thu, to 5pm Fri, to 3pm Sat, 9am-4pm Sun; ☒Flagstaff) With over 600 traders, the Vic Market is the largest open-air market in the southern hemisphere and attracts thousands of shoppers. It's where Melburnians sniff out fresh produce among the booming cries of spruiking fishmongers and fruit-and-veg vendors. The wonderful deli hall (with art-deco features) is lined with everything from soft cheeses, wines and Polish sausages to Greek dips, truffle oil and kangaroo biltong.

Koorie Heritage Trust   CULTURAL CENTRE
(Map p208; ☑03-8662 6300; www.koorieheritagetrust.com; Yarra Building, Federation Sq; tours adult/child $33/17; ⊙10am-5pm; ☒Flinders St) **FREE** Devoted to southeastern Aboriginal culture, this centre houses interesting artefacts and oral history. There's a shop and gallery downstairs while, upstairs, carefully preserved significant objects can be viewed in display cases and drawers. It also runs hourlong tours along the Yarra during summer, evoking the history and memories that lie beneath the modern city (book online).

Melbourne

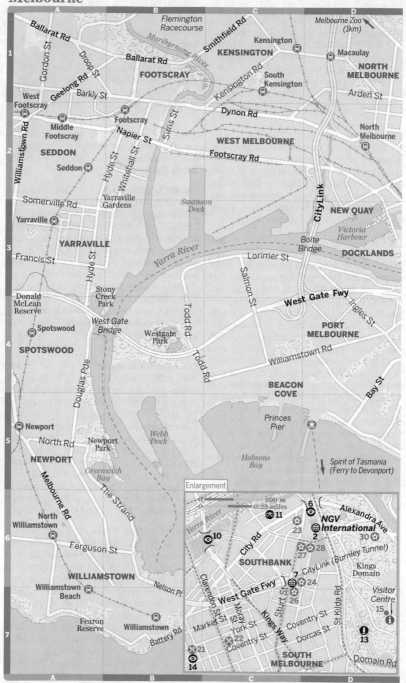

MELBOURNE & COASTAL VICTORIA

Ballarat Rd
Gordon St
Droop St
Geelong Rd
Barkly St
West Footscray
Middle Footscray
Williamstown Rd
SEDDON
Seddon
Somerville Rd
Hyde St
Yarraville
YARRAVILLE
Francis St
Hyde St
Donald McLean Reserve
Stony Creek Park
Spotswood
West Gate Bridge
SPOTSWOOD
Douglas Pde
Newport
North Rd
Newport Park
NEWPORT
Greenwich Bay
The Strand
Melbourne Rd
North Williamstown
Ferguson St
WILLIAMSTOWN
Williamstown Beach
Fearon Reserve
Nelson Pl
Williamstown
Battery Rd

Flemington Racecourse
Maribyrnong River
Smithfield Rd
Ballarat Rd
FOOTSCRAY
Footscray
Napier St
Sims St
Whitehall St
Yarraville Gardens
Swanson Dock
KENSINGTON
Kensington
South Kensington
Kensington Rd
Dynon Rd
WEST MELBOURNE
Footscray Rd
Yarra River
Melbourne Zoo (1km)
Macaulay
NORTH MELBOURNE
Arden St
North Melbourne
CityLink
NEW QUAY
Victoria Harbour
Bolte Bridge
DOCKLANDS
Lorimer St
Salmon St
Todd Rd
West Gate Fwy
Ingles St
PORT MELBOURNE
Westgate Park
Williamstown Rd
BEACON COVE
Bay St
Webb Dock
Princes Pier
Hobsons Bay
Spirit of Tasmania (Ferry to Devonport)

Enlargement

500 m
0.25 miles

Yarra River
11
10
City Rd
23
6
NGV International
2
SOUTHBANK
27
28
30
CityLink (Burnley Tunnel)
Kings Domain
Alexandra Ave
7
24
26
West Gate Fwy
Clarendon St
Market St
Moray St
York St
Sturt St
Kings Way
22
Coventry St
Coventry St
Dorcas St
St Kilda Rd
Visitor Centre
15
13
SOUTH MELBOURNE
Domain Rd
21
14

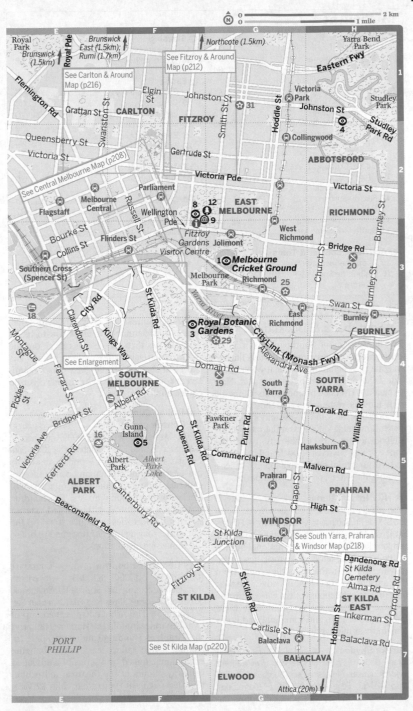

Melbourne

⊙ Southbank & Docklands

The reinvention of Southbank as a glitzy tourist precinct is so complete that it's hard to imagine that, before the 1980s, it was a gritty industrial zone supporting a major port. Now its pleasant riverside promenade is peppered with famous restaurants and hotels, while the presence of some of the city's top arts institutions makes it an essential part of any Melbourne itinerary. To the city's west, the once working wharves of Docklands have given birth to a mini city of apartments, offices, restaurants, plazas, public art and parks.

★ NGV International   GALLERY
(Map p204; ☑ 03-8662 1555; www.ngv.vic.gov.au; 180 St Kilda Rd, Southbank; ⊙ 10am-5pm; ℝ Flinders St) FREE Housed in a vast, brutally beautiful, bunkerlike building, the international branch of the National Gallery of Victoria has an expansive collection that runs the gamut from the ancient to the bleeding edge. Regular blockbuster exhibitions (prices vary) draw the crowds, and there are free 45-minute highlights tours at 11am and 1pm daily, and hourlong tours at midday and 2pm.

Eureka Skydeck   VIEWPOINT
(Map p204; ☑ 03-9693 8888; www.eureka skydeck.com.au; 7 Riverside Quay, Southbank; adult/child $20/12, Edge extra $12/8; ⊙ 10am-10pm; ℝ Flinders St) Melbourne's tallest building, the 297m-high Eureka Tower was built in 2006, and a wild elevator ride takes you to its 88 floors in less than 40 seconds (check out the photo on the elevator floor if there's time). The Edge – a slightly sadistic glass cube – cantilevers you out of the building; you've got no choice but to look down.

Australian Centre for Contemporary Art   GALLERY
(ACCA; Map p204; ☑ 03-9697 9999; www.accaon line.org.au; 111 Sturt St, Southbank; ⊙ 10am-5pm Tue-Sun; ⓐ 1) FREE ACCA is one of Australia's most exciting and challenging contemporary galleries, showcasing the work of a range of local and international artists. The building is, fittingly, sculptural, with a rusted exterior evoking the factories that once stood on the site, and a soaring interior designed to house often massive installations.

Arts Centre Melbourne   ARTS CENTRE
(Map p204; ☑ 1300 182 183; www.artscen tremelbourne.com.au; 100 St Kilda Rd, Southbank; ⊙ box office 9am-8.30pm Mon-Fri, 10am-5pm Sat; ℝ Flinders St) The Arts Centre is made up of two separate buildings, Hamer Hall and the Theatres Building (under the spire, including a free gallery space with changing exhibitions), linked by a series of landscaped walkways. Tours of the theatres and exhibitions leave daily at 11am (adult/child $20/15); the Sunday tour includes the backstage areas.

Richmond & East Melbourne

Melbourne is one of the world's great sporting cities, and Richmond and East Melbourne are the absolute nexus for all things sporting. The neighbourhood's southeastern skyline is dominated by the angular shapes of sporting stadia, none more hulking than the mighty Melbourne Cricket Ground. North from here are the genteel streets of East Melbourne, centred on pretty Fitzroy Gardens. Taking up the eastern flank, Richmond is a part-gentrified, part-gritty residential and commercial expanse peppered with interesting eateries, both budget and top end.

★**Melbourne Cricket Ground** STADIUM
(MCG; Map p204; ☑03-9657 8888; www.mcg.org.au; Brunton Ave, East Melbourne; tour adult/child/family $23/12/55, incl museum $32/16/70; ☺tours 10am-3pm; ⓡJolimont) With a capacity of 100,000 people, the 'G' is one of the world's great sporting venues, hosting cricket in summer and AFL (Australian Football League; Aussie rules) footy in winter. For many Australians it's considered hallowed ground. Make it to a game if you can (highly recommended), but otherwise you can still make your pilgrimage on nonmatch-day **tours** that take you through the stands, media and coaches' areas, change rooms and members' lounges. The MCG houses the state-of-the-art **National Sports Museum** (Map p204; ☑03-9657 8879; www.nsm.org.au; Gate 3, MCG, Brunton Ave, East Melbourne; adult/child/family $23/12/55; ☺10am-5pm; ⓡJolimont).

Fitzroy Gardens PARK
(Map p204; www.fitzroygardens.com; Wellington Pde, East Melbourne; ⓡJolimont) The city drops away suddenly just east of Spring St, giving way to Melbourne's beautiful backyard, Fitzroy Gardens. The park's stately avenues are lined with English elms, flowerbeds, expansive lawns, strange fountains and a creek. A highlight is **Cooks' Cottage** (Map p204; Fitzroy Gardens, Wellington Pde, East Melbourne; adult/child/family $6.50/3.50/18; ☺9am-5pm; ⓡJolimont), which belonged to the parents of navigator Captain James Cook. The cottage was shipped brick by brick from Yorkshire and reconstructed here in 1934. Nearby is a **visitor centre** (Map p204; ☑03-9658 9658; www.thatsmelbourne.com.au; ☺9am-5pm) with a cafe attached and the delightful 1930s **Conservatory** (Map p204; Fitzroy Gardens, Wellington Pde, East Melbourne; ☺9am-5pm).

Fitzroy, Collingwood & Abbotsford

A short tram ride from the city centre delivers you to the doorstep of some of the hippest enclaves in Melbourne, where up-to-the-minute eateries and midcentury furniture stores sit comfortably next to century-old classic pubs and divey live-music venues. Fitzroy, Melbourne's first suburb, and Collingwood have long had a reputation for vice and squalor and, despite ongoing gentrification, there's still enough grit holding these areas in check. Beyond Collingwood is largely industrial Abbotsford, bordered by a scenic stretch of the Yarra River, where more cafes and restaurants have started sprouting.

Abbotsford Convent HISTORIC SITE
(Map p204; ☑03-9415 3600; www.abbotsfordconvent.com.au; 1 St Heliers St, Abbotsford; tours $15; ☺7.30am-10pm; ⍰200, 207, ⓡVictoria Park) **FREE** The nuns are long gone at this former convent, which dates to 1861, but today its rambling collection of ecclesiastical architecture is home to a thriving arts community of galleries, studios, eateries (including the **Convent Bakery** (Map p204; ☑03-9419 9426; www.conventbakery.com; Abbotsford Convent, 1 St Heliers St, Abbotsford; mains $10-20; ☺7am-5pm; ⍰200, 207, ⓡVictoria Park) and vegetarian **Lentil as Anything** (Map p204; ☑03-9419 6444; www.lentilasanything.com; Abbotsford Convent, 1 St Heliers St, Abbotsford; by donation; ☺9am-9pm; ⏰; ⍰200, 207, ⓡVictoria Park)) and a bar, spread over nearly 7 hectares of riverside land. Tours of the complex run at 2pm Sunday.

Carlton & Brunswick

Home to Melbourne's Italian community and the University of Melbourne, Carlton dishes up a heady mix of intellectual activity, espresso and excellent food – the same things that lured bohemians to the area in the 1950s. You'll see the *tricolori* unfurled with characteristic passion come soccer finals and the Grand Prix.

Head west to multicultural-meets-hipster Brunswick to feast on Middle Eastern cuisine along Sydney Rd before bar-hopping home.

★**Melbourne Museum** MUSEUM
(Map p216; ☑13 11 02; www.museumvictoria.com.au; 11 Nicholson St, Carlton; adult $14, child & student free, exhibitions extra; ☺10am-5pm; ⍰Tourist Shuttle, ⓡCity Circle, 86, 96, ⓡParliament) This museum provides a grand

Central Melbourne

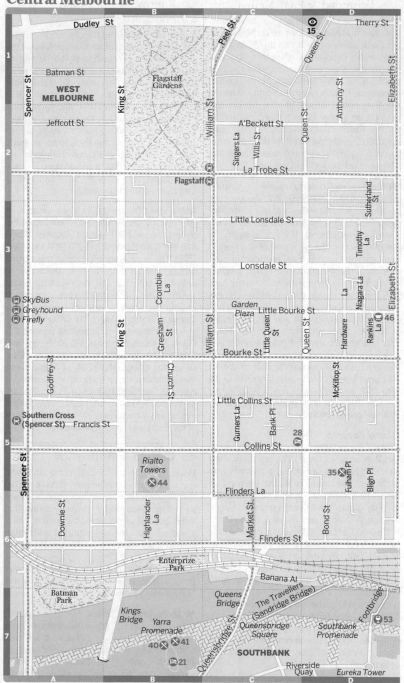

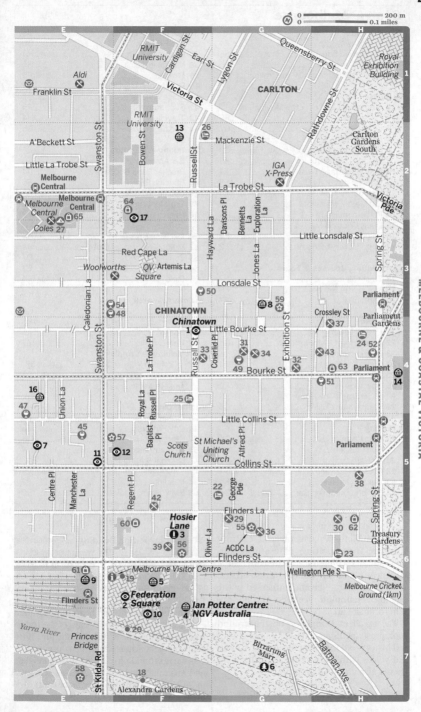

Central Melbourne

◉ Top Sights
1 Chinatown F4
2 Federation Square F6
3 Hosier Lane F6
4 Ian Potter Centre: NGV Australia F6

◉ Sights
5 Australian Centre for the Moving
   Image F6
6 Birrarung Marr G7
7 Block Arcade E5
8 Chinese Museum G3
9 Flinders Street Station E6
10 Koorie Heritage Trust F7
11 Manchester Unity Building E5
12 Melbourne Town Hall F5
13 Old Melbourne Gaol F2
14 Parliament House H4
15 Queen Victoria Market D1
16 Royal Arcade E4
17 State Library of Victoria F2

⊕ Activities, Courses & Tours
18 Kayak Melbourne F7
19 Melbourne By Foot F6
20 Rentabike F7

⊟ Sleeping
21 Crown Towers......................... B7
22 Grand Hyatt Melbourne G5
23 Hotel Lindrum......................... H6
24 Ovolo Laneways H4
25 QT Melbourne......................... F4
26 Space Hotel............................ F2
27 St Jerome's The Hotel E3
28 Treasury on Collins C5

✖ Eating
29 Chin Chin G6
30 Cumulus Inc H6
31 Flower Drum G4
32 Grossi Florentino G4
33 Hakata Gensuke F4
34 HuTong Dumpling Bar G4
35 Huxtaburger D5
36 Lee Ho Fook G6
37 Longrain H4
38 Mamasita H5
39 MoVida F6
40 Rockpool Bar & Grill B7
41 Spice Temple........................... B7
42 Supernormal F5
43 Traveller H4
44 Vue de Monde B5

⊙ Drinking & Nightlife
45 Bar Americano E5
46 Brother Baba Budan D4
47 Chuckle Park E5
48 Cookie E3
49 Croft Institute G4
50 Heartbreaker........................... F3
   Lui Bar ....(see 44)
51 Madame Brussels H4
52 Melbourne Supper Club............. H4
53 Ponyfish Island........................ D7
54 Rooftop Bar E3
   Siglo ....(see 52)

⊕ Entertainment
55 Cherry.................................... G6
56 Forum.................................... F6
57 Halftix.................................... E5
58 Hamer Hall............................. E7
   Melbourne Symphony
   Orchestra......................(see 58)
59 Ticketek................................. G3
   Ticketmaster..................(see 56)

⊟ Shopping
60 Alpha60.................................. F6
61 City Hatters............................ E6
62 Craft Victoria H6
63 Melbournalia........................... H4
   Original & Authentic
   Aboriginal Art ....(see 32)
64 Readings................................ F2
65 RM Williams............................ E2

sweep of Victoria's natural and cultural histories, incorporating dinosaur fossils, giant-squid specimens, a taxidermy hall, a 3D volcano and an open-air forest atrium of Victorian flora. Become immersed in the legend of champion racehorse and national hero Phar Lap.

The excellent **Bunjilaka**, on the ground floor, presents Indigenous Australian stories and history told through objects and Aboriginal voices with state-of-the-art technology. There's also an **IMAX cinema**.

★ **Royal Exhibition Building** HISTORIC BUILDING
(Map p216; ☑13 11 02; www.museumvictoria. com.au/reb; 9 Nicholson St, Carlton; tours adult/child $10/7; ☐ Tourist Shuttle, ☐ City Circle, 86, 96, ☐ Parliament) Built for the 1880 International Exhibition, and winning Unesco World Heritage status in 2004, this beautiful Victorian edifice symbolises the glory days of the Industrial Revolution, the British Empire and 19th-century Melbourne's economic supremacy. It was the first building to fly the Australian flag, and Australia's first parliament was held here in 1901. Tours of the building leave from Melbourne Museum (opposite) at 2pm.

North Melbourne & Parkville

This strip of central Melbourne stretches from the shabby railway yards and grid-locked thoroughfares of West Melbourne, through the surprisingly quiet Victorian neighbourhood of North Melbourne and into the ample green spaces of Parkville.

The big attraction here is the zoo, but it's also worth stopping by to sample the low-key neighbourhood pubs, eateries and shops of North Melbourne's Victoria, Errol and Queensberry Sts.

★Melbourne Zoo ZOO

(☎1300 966 784; www.zoo.org.au; Elliott Ave, Parkville; adult/child $33/17, child weekends & holidays free; ⏲8am-5pm; 👪; 🚆Royal Park) Established in 1861, this compact zoo is the oldest in Australia and the third oldest in the world. It remains one of the city's most popular attractions and it continues to innovate, recently becoming the world's first carbon-neutral zoo. Set in prettily landscaped gardens, the zoo's enclosures aim to simulate the animals' natural habitats and give them the option to hide if they want to (the gorillas and the tigers are particularly good at playing hard to get).

South Melbourne, Port Melbourne & Albert Park

The well-heeled trio of South Melbourne, Port Melbourne and Albert Park isn't short on lunching ladies, AFL stars and Porsche-steering Lotharios living it up in grandiose Victorian terraces and bayside condos. Leafy and generally sedate, the area boasts some of Melbourne's most beautiful heritage architecture, both civic and domestic. South Melbourne is the busiest neighbourhood, with a bustling market, cult-status cafes and sharply curated design stores. Albert Park offers culture in a former gasworks, while Port Melbourne's home to Station Pier, from where ferries shoot south to Tasmania.

South Melbourne Market MARKET

(Map p204; ☎03-9209 6295; www.southmelbournemarket.com.au; cnr Coventry & Cecil Sts, South Melbourne; ⏲8am-4pm Wed, Sat & Sun, to 5pm Fri; 🚋12, 96) Trading since 1864, this market is a neighbourhood institution, its labyrinthine guts packed with a brilliant collection of stalls selling everything from organic produce and deli treats to hipster specs, art and crafts. The place is famous for its dim sims (sold here since 1949), and there's no shortage of atmospheric eateries. From early January to late February, there's a lively night market on Thursday. The site is also home to a cooking school – see the website for details.

Albert Park Lake LAKE

(Map p204; btwn Queens Rd, Fitzroy St, Aughtie Dr & Albert Rd, Albert Park; 🚋96) Elegant black swans give their inimitable bottoms-up salute as you jog, cycle or walk the 5km perimeter of this constructed lake. Lakeside Dr was used as an international motor-racing circuit in the 1950s, and since 1996 the revamped track has been the venue for the **Australian Formula One Grand Prix** (☎1800 100 030; www.grandprix.com.au; Albert Park Lake, Albert Park; tickets from $55; ⏲Mar) each March. Also on the periphery is the Melbourne Sports & Aquatic Centre (p215), with an Olympic-size pool and child-delighting wave machine.

South Yarra, Prahran & Windsor

★Royal Botanic Gardens GARDENS

(Map p204; www.rbg.vic.gov.au; Birdwood Ave, South Yarra; ⏲7.30am-sunset; 🚌Tourist Shuttle, 🚋1, 3, 5, 6, 16, 64, 67, 72) FREE Melbourne's Royal Botanical Gardens are simply glorious. From the air, the 94-acre spread evokes a giant green lung in the middle of the city. Drawing over 1.5 million visitors annually, the gardens are considered one of the finest examples of Victorian-era landscaping in the world. You'll find a global selection of plantings and endemic Australian flora. Mini ecosystems, such as a cacti and succulents area, a herb garden and an indigenous rainforest, are set amid vast lawns.

Shrine of Remembrance MONUMENT

(Map p204; ☎03-9661 8100; www.shrine.org.au; Birdwood Ave, South Yarra; ⏲10am-5pm; 🚌Tourist Shuttle, 🚋3, 5, 6, 16, 64, 67, 72) FREE One of Melbourne's icons, the Shrine of Remembrance is a commanding memorial to Victorians killed in WWI. Built between 1928 and 1934, much of it with Depression-relief, or 'susso' (sustenance), labour, its stoic, classical design is partly based on the Mausoleum of Halicarnassus, one of the seven ancient wonders of the world. The shrine's upper balcony affords epic panoramic views of the Melbourne skyline and all the way up tram-studded Swanston St.

Fitzroy & Around

N 0 _____ 200 m
   0 _____ 0.1 miles

FITZROY NORTH

Queens Pde

Princes St

Alexandra Pde (Eastern Hwy)

CLIFTON HILL

Northcote (2km)

Cecil St

Westgarth St

Leicester St

CARLTON

Kay St

Rose St

Kerr St

Argyle St

Elgin St

Johnston St

Victoria St

Bell St

Moor St

King William St

Hanover St

Palmer St

Gertrude St

Victoria Pde

Nicholson St

Station St

Spring St

Mahoney St

John St

Fitzroy St

Brunswick St

Young St

Kent St

Napier St

George St

Gore St

Smith St

Napier St

Cecil St

Westgarth St

Rose St

Kerr St

Argyle St

Sackville St

Easey St

Keele St

Bedford St

Otter St

Stanley St

COLLINGWOOD

Little Oxford St

Oxford St

Cambridge St

Peel St

Langridge St

Mason St

Little Victoria St

Johnston St

Chapel St

FITZROY

Greeves St

St David St

Hodgson St

Condell St

Charles St

Webb St

Little George St

Little Gore St

Little Smith St

Atherton Reserve

Royal La

MELBOURNE & COASTAL VICTORIA MELBOURNE

1
28
15
12
29
19
5
17
21
16
13
14
9
22
4
20 8
30
27
7 18 6
23
24
26
11
10
25
2
3

Fitzroy & Around

★ **Justin Art House Museum** GALLERY
(JAHM; Map p218; ☑ 0411 158 967; www.jahm.com.
au; cnr Williams Rd & Lumley Ct, Prahran; adult/
child $25/free; ⊙ by appointment; ⛟ 5, 6, 64) The
geometric, zinc-clad home of Melbourne
art collectors Charles and Leah Justin doubles as the Justin Art House Museum. Book
ahead for a private tour of the couple's dynamic collection of contemporary art, con-
sisting of more than 250 pieces amassed
over four decades. There's a strong emphasis on video and digital art, with the works
rotated regularly. Guided tours take around
two hours. The house was designed by the
couple's daughter, Elisa.

⦿ St Kilda

St Kilda is Melbourne's slightly tattered bohemian heart, a place where a young Nick
Cave played gloriously chaotic gigs at the
George Hotel (formerly the Crystal Ball-
room) and a place featured in countless
songs, plays, novels, TV series and films.
Starting life as a 19th-century seaside resort,
the neighbourhood has played many roles:
post-war Jewish enclave, red-light district,
punk-rocker hub and real-estate hot spot. It's
a complex, hypnotic jumble of boom-style
Victorian mansions, raffish Spanish Moorish
apartments, seedy side streets, cosmopolitan
wine bars, crusty pubs, rickety roller coasters
and nostalgia-inducing theatres.

St Kilda Foreshore BEACH
(Map p220; Jacka Blvd, St Kilda; ⛟ 3, 12, 16, 96)
Despite the palm-fringed promenades and
golden stretch of sand, St Kilda's seaside appeal is more Brighton, England, than Venice,
LA. The kiosk at the end of **St Kilda Pier**
(Map p220; Jacka Blvd, St Kilda; ⛟ 3, 12, 16, 96) is
as much about the journey as the destination: the pier offers a knockout panorama of
the Melbourne skyline.

During summer **Port Phillip EcoCentre**
(Map p220; ☑ 03-9534 0670; www.ecocentre.com;
55a Blessington St, St Kilda) 🌿 runs a range of
tours, including urban wildlife walks and
coastal discovery walks, and offers information on the **little-penguin colony** that lives
in the breakwater behind the pier's kiosk.

Luna Park AMUSEMENT PARK
(Map p220; ☑ 03-9525 5033; www.lunapark.
com.au; 18 Lower Esplanade, St Kilda; single
ride adult/child $11/10, unlimited rides $50/40;
⊙ hours vary; ⛟ 3, 16, 96) Luna Park opened
in 1912 and still has the feel of an old-style
amusement park, with creepy Mr Moon's
gaping mouth swallowing you up as you
enter. There's a heritage-listed 'scenic railway' (the oldest operating roller coaster in
the world), a beautifully baroque carousel with hand-painted horses, swans and
chariots, as well as the full complement of
gut-churning rides.

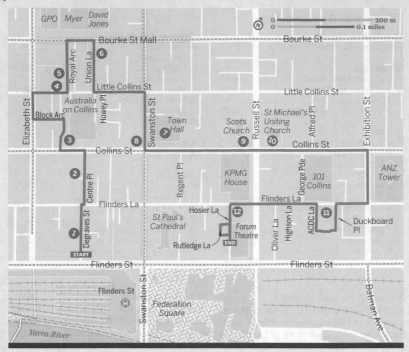

City Walk
Arcades & Laneways

START DEGRAVES ST
END MOVIDA
LENGTH 3KM; 2½ HOURS

Central Melbourne is a warren of 19th-century arcades and gritty-turned-hip cobbled bluestone laneways featuring street art, basement restaurants, boutiques and bars.

Start on ❶ **Degraves Street**, an archetypal Melbourne side street lined with interesting shops and cafes, then continue north, crossing over Flinders Lane to cafe-filled ❷ **Centre Place**, good for street art.

Cross Collins St, turn left and enter the ❸ **Block Arcade**; built in 1891 and featuring ornate plasterwork and mosaic floors, it's based on Milan's Galleria Vittorio Emanuele II arcade. Ogle the window display at the Hopetoun Tea Rooms before continuing through the arcade, turning left and exiting right onto Elizabeth St.

At the next corner cross the road and turn right into Little Collins St. ❹ **Chuckle Park**, then continue on and turn left into wonderfully ornate ❺ **Royal Arcade**; look out for

Gog and Magog, hammering away under the dome. Wander through to Bourke St Mall, then turn right and continue to street-art-covered ❻ **Union Lane** on the right.

Follow Union Lane to the end, turn left onto Little Collins St, then take a right on Swanston St. Walk past ❼ **Melbourne Town Hall**, on the other side of Swanston St, and pop into the 1932 ❽ **Manchester Unity Building** to snoop around its impressive foyer, then cross Swanston St and head up the hill to the 'Paris End' of Collins St. Along the way you'll pass the 1873 Gothic ❾ **Scots Church** (the first Presbyterian church in Victoria) and the 1866 ❿ **St Michael's Uniting Church**, built in Lombardic Romanesque style.

Turn right into Exhibition St, then right into Flinders Lane, and continue until you see ⓫ **Duckboard Place**. Head down the laneway and take your time to soak up the street art before horseshoeing around into AC/DC Lane, past rock 'n' roll dive bar Cherry.

Continue on down Flinders Lane to the street-art meccas of ⓬ **Hosier Ln** (p202) and Rutledge Lane before finishing with tapas and a hard-earned drink at MoVida.

♣ Activities

★ Kayak Melbourne KAYAKING
(Map p208; ☑0418 106 427; www.kayakmel
bourne.com.au; Alexandra Gardens, Boathouse Dr,
Southbank; tours $82-110; ☐11, 48) ✐ Ninety-
minute City Sights tours paddle past Southbank to Docklands, while two-hour River
to Sky tours include entry to the Eureka
Skydeck (p206). You can also start your day
saluting the sun on a two-hour Yoga Sunrise
tour, or end it with a 2½-hour Moonlight
tour starting from Docklands.

Fitzroy Swimming Pool SWIMMING
(Map p212; ☑03-9205 5180; 160 Alexandra Pde,
Fitzroy; adult/child/under 5yr $6.50/3.30/free;
⊙6am-9pm Mon-Thu, to 8pm Fri, 8am-6pm Sat &
Sun; ☐11) Between laps, locals love catching a
few rays up in the bleachers or on the lawn at
this local favourite; there's also a toddler pool.

Melbourne Sports & Aquatic Centre SWIMMING
(MSAC; Map p204; ☑03-9926 1555; www.msac.
com.au; Albert Rd, Albert Park; adult/child from
$8.20/5.60; ⊙5.30am-10pm Mon-Fri, 7am-8pm
Sat & Sun; ☐96, 112) Flanking Albert Park
Lake (p211), Melbourne's premier aquatic
centre was a venue for the 2006 Commonwealth Games. Facilities include indoor and
outdoor 50m pools, an indoor 25m pool, a
wave pool, water slides, a spa, sauna and
steam room, and spacious common areas.
Childcare is available.

Kite Republic KITESURFING
(Map p220; ☑03-9537 0644; www.kiterepublic.
com.au; St Kilda Sea Baths, 4/10-18 Jacka Blvd, St
Kilda; 1hr lesson $90; ⊙10am-6pm Mon-Fri, to 5pm
Sat & Sun; ☐96) Offers kiteboarding lessons,
tours and equipment; also a good source of
info. In winter it can arrange snow-kiting
at Mt Hotham. Also rents stand-up paddleboards (SUPs) and street SUPs.

Stand Up Paddle HQ WATER SPORTS
(Map p220; ☑0416 184 994; www.supb.com.au; St
Kilda Pier, St Kilda; hire per hr $30, 1½hr tour $99;
☐96) Arrange a lesson or hire SUP equipment
from St Kilda Pier, or join its Yarra River tour.

☞ Tours

Melbourne Street Tours WALKING
(☑03-9328 5556; www.melbournestreettours.
com; tours $69; ⊙city centre 1.30pm Tue, Thu &
Sat, Fitzroy 11am Sat) Three-hour tours exploring the street art of the city centre or Fitzroy.
The tour guides are street artists themselves,
so you'll get a good insight into this art form.

★ Rentabike CYCLING
(Map p208; ☑0417 339 203; www.rentabike.net.
au; Federation Wharf; rental per hr/day $15/40, 4hr
tour incl lunch adult/child $110/79; ⊙10am-5pm;
☐Flinders St) ✐ Rents bikes and runs **Real
Melbourne Bike Tours**, offering a local's insight into the city, with a foodie focus.

Melbourne By Foot WALKING
(Map p208; ☑1300 311 081; www.melbourneby
foot.com; departs Federation Sq; tours $40; ⊙1pm;
☐Flinders St) Take a few hours out and experience a mellow, informative three-hour
walking tour that covers laneway art, politics, Melbourne's history and diversity. Highly recommended; book online. There's also a
Beer Lovers tour ($85).

Aboriginal Heritage Walk CULTURAL
(Map p204; ☑03-9252 2429; www.rbg.vic.gov.au;
Royal Botanic Gardens, Birdwood Ave, South Yarra;
adult/child $31/12; ⊙11am Sun-Fri; ☐3, 5, 6, 8, 16,
64, 67, 72) ✐ The Royal Botanic Gardens is
on a traditional camping and meeting place
of the Kulin people, and this tour takes
you through their story – from songlines
to plant lore, all in 90 fascinating minutes.
The tour departs from the gardens' **visitor
centre** (Map p204; ☑03-9252 2429; www.rbg.
vic.gov.au; Observatory Gate, Birdwood Ave, South
Yarra; ⊙9am-5pm Mon-Fri, from 9.30am Sat & Sun;
☐Tourist Shuttle, ☐3, 5, 6, 8, 16, 64, 67, 72).

✦ Festivals & Events

Australian Open SPORTS
(www.australianopen.com; Melbourne Park, Olympic Blvd, Melbourne; ⊙Jan) The world's top tennis players and huge, merry-making crowds
descend for Australia's grand-slam tennis
championship.

AFL Grand Final SPORTS
(www.afl.com.au; MCG, Brunton Ave, East Melbourne; ⊙Sep) It's easier to kick a goal from
the boundary line than to pick up random
tickets to the Grand Final, usually held on
the final Saturday in September, but it's
not hard to get your share of finals fever
anywhere in Melbourne (particularly at
pubs).

Melbourne Cup SPORTS
(www.springracingcarnival.com.au; Flemington
Racecourse; ⊙Nov) Culminating in the prestigious Melbourne Cup, the Spring Racing Carnival is as much a social event as
a sporting one. The Cup, held on the first
Tuesday in November, is a public holiday in
Melbourne.

Carlton & Around

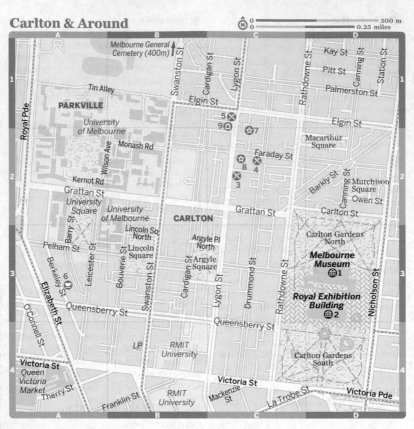

0 500 m
0 0.25 miles

Carlton & Around

⊙ Top Sights
1 Melbourne Museum	D3
2 Royal Exhibition Building	D3

⊗ Eating
D.O.C Delicatessen	(see 3)
3 D.O.C. Espresso	C2
4 D.O.C. Pizza & Mozzarella Bar	C2
5 Heartattack and Vine	C1

⊙ Drinking & Nightlife
6 Seven Seeds	A3

⊕ Entertainment
7 Cinema Nova	C2
8 La Mama	C2

⊡ Shopping
9 Readings	C1

Melbourne Festival PERFORMING ARTS
(www.melbournefestival.com.au; ⊙ Oct) Held at various venues around the city, this festival features a thought-provoking schedule of Australian and international theatre, opera, dance, visual art and music.

Melbourne International Film Festival FILM
(MIFF; www.miff.com.au; ⊙ Aug) Midwinter movie love-in that brings out black-skivvy-wearing cinephiles in droves.

MELBOURNE & COASTAL VICTORIA MELBOURNE

🛏 Sleeping

🛏 City Centre

Space Hotel
HOSTEL **$**

(Map p208; ☑03-9662 3888; www.spacehotel.
com.au; 380 Russell St; dm from $37, r with/with-
out bathroom from $100/89; ❋ 🛜; 🚇 Melbourne
Central) One of Melbourne's few genuine
flashpackers, this sleek place walks the
line between hostel and budget hotel. The
better private rooms have iPod docks and
flat-screen TVs, while dorms have thoughtful touches like large lockers equipped with
sensor lights and lockable adapters. Some
of the doubles have en suites and balconies.
The rooftop hot tub is another big tick.

Home @ The Mansion
HOSTEL **$**

(Map p212; ☑03-9663 4212; www.homeatthe
mansion.com; 80 Victoria Pde, East Melbourne;
dm/r from $33/80; @🛜; 🚇 Parliament) Located
within a castlelike former Salvation Army
building with grand double staircases, this is
one of Melbourne's few hostels with genuine
character. It has 92 dorm beds and a couple of double rooms; all rooms are light and
bright and have lovely high ceilings. There
are two small TV areas, a courtyard out the
front and a sunny kitchen.

★ Treasury on Collins
APARTMENT **$$**

(Map p208; ☑03-8535 8535; www.treasuryoncol
lins.com.au; 394 Collins St; apt from $198; ❋🛜;
🚊11, 12, 48, 109) This imposing stone neoclas-
sical building (1876) once housed a branch
of the Bank of Australia. An impressive bar
now fills the downstairs space, its impossi-
bly high ceiling supported by gilt-edged col-
umns. The apartments, on the other hand,
are modern and restrained, not to mention
chic and spacious. Winning extras include
coffee machines, laundries and free Netflix.

★ QT Melbourne
HOTEL **$$$**

(Map p208; ☑03-8636 8800; www.qtmelbourne.
com.au; 133 Russell St; r from $350; @🛜; 🚊86,
96) Rough concrete surfaces, brass trim, lifts
with tapestry light boxes that play house
music and say random stuff in a Russian
accent: this is one of Melbourne's newest,
quirkiest and best boutique hotels. The
rooms are beautifully kitted out and there's
a great plant-draped rooftop bar too.

★ Ovolo Laneways
BOUTIQUE HOTEL **$$$**

(Map p208; ☑03-8692 0777; www.ovolohotels.
com.au; 19 Little Bourke St; r from $219; ❋ @🛜;
🚇 Parliament) This boutique hotel mixes
hipster chic with a funky executive vibe.
It's friendly, fun and loaded with goodies –
there's a free self-service laundry, a free mini-
bar in each room, free booze downstairs at
the daily happy hour and a Nespresso ma-
chine in the lobby. It's just a shame about
the silly little sinks.

Hotel Lindrum
BOUTIQUE HOTEL **$$$**

(Map p208; ☑03-9668 1111; www.hotellindrum.
com.au; 26 Flinders St; r from $330; ❋🛜; 🚇 Par-
liament) One of the city's most attractive hotels, this was once the snooker hall of the
legendary and literally unbeatable Walter
Lindrum. Expect minimalist tones, subtle
lighting and tactile fabrics. Spring for a deluxe room and you'll snare either arch or bay
windows and marvellous Melbourne views.
And yes, there's a billiard table – one of Lindrum's originals, no less.

St Jerome's The Hotel
TENTED CAMP **$$$**

(Map p208; ☑0406 118 561; www.stjeromesthe
hotel.com.au; Melbourne Central rooftop, 3/300
Lonsdale St; tents $420-480; 🚇 Melbourne Cen-
tral) Each of the canvas glamping tents here
has a double or a queen bed with funky
bedspreads, reverse-cycle air-conditioners,
a complimentary cooler of craft beer and
cider, and free 10-pin bowling at Strike
next door. Come morning, there's an on-site
barista and brekky box. It's a great experi-
ence, but then it would need to be for these
prices.

Grand Hyatt Melbourne
HOTEL **$$$**

(Map p208; ☑03-9657 1234; www.melbourne.
grand.hyatt.com; 123 Collins St; r from $445;
❋ @🛜🏊; 🚇 Flinders St) Plenty grand enough
to warrant the name, this famous Collins
St five-star has over 500 rooms, with marble bathrooms, designated workspaces and
floor-to-ceiling windows looking out to the
city centre, Yarra River or MCG.

🛏 Southbank & Docklands

Hilton Melbourne South Wharf
HOTEL **$$**

(Map p204; ☑03-9027 2000; www.hiltonmel
bourne.com.au; 2 Convention Centre Pl, South Wharf;
r from $200; 🅿❋🛜; 🚊35, 70, 75) Polished
wood and natural fibres provide an earthy
feel in this luxurious hotel. Suites are huge
and some offer dazzling views along the river.
There's an in-house Aboriginal art gallery and
all of the art in reception is for sale – except
for the giant piece above the desk that ap-
pears to have been crafted from pot scourers.

South Yarra, Prahran & Windsor

MELBOURNE & COASTAL VICTORIA MELBOURNE

South Yarra, Prahran & Windsor

Crown Towers   HOTEL $$$
(Map p208; ☑ 03-9292 6868; www.crownhotels. com.au/crown-towers-melbourne; 8 Whiteman St, Southbank; r from $338; P ❄ 🛜 🏊; 🚇 55) Crown's flashest digs, this oversized hotel shrugs off the gaudy glitziness of its reception by the time you reach the quietly elegant rooms, many of which have extraordinary views. The large bathrooms have separate tubs and shower stalls, and the walk-in wardrobe is something you could easily get used to.

🛏 Fitzroy, Collingwood & Abbotsford

★ **Nunnery**   HOSTEL $
(Map p212; ☑ 1800 032 635; www.nunnery.com.au; 116 Nicholson St, Fitzroy; dm/s/d from $34/95/120; @ 🛜; 🚇 96) Built in 1888, the Nunnery oozes atmosphere, with sweeping staircases and many original features; the walls are dripping with religious works of art and ornate stained-glass windows. You'll be giving thanks for the big, comfortable lounges and communal areas. The next-door Nunnery Guesthouse has larger rooms in a private setting (from $130). It's popular, so book ahead. All rates include breakfast.

★ **Tyrian Serviced Apartments**   APARTMENT $$
(Map p212; ☑ 03-9415 1900; www.tyrian.com.au; 91 Johnston St, Fitzroy; apt from $188; P ❄ 🛜; 🚇 11) These spacious, self-contained modern apartments have a certain Fitzroy-celeb vibe. Big couches, flat-screen TVs, European laundries and balconies add to the appeal, and plenty of restaurants and bars are right at your door. It's rounded off with free wi-fi and parking. Rooms facing Johnston St can get noisy.

Brooklyn Arts Hotel   B&B $$
(Map p212; ☑ 03-9419 9328; www.brooklynart shotel.com.au; 48-50 George St, Fitzroy; s/d from $115/155; 🛜; 🚇 86) There are seven rooms in this character-filled hotel owned by filmmaker and artist Maggie Fooke. Set in a lovely terrace house, rooms vary in size but are all clean, quirky, colourful and beautifully decorated. Spacious upstairs rooms with high ceilings and balconies are the pick (from $220). Expect lively conversation at the included continental breakfast of local sourdough bread and homemade jams.

🛏 South Melbourne, Port Melbourne & Albert Park

★ **Coppersmith**   BOUTIQUE HOTEL $$
(Map p204; ☑ 03-8696 7777; http://coppersmith hotel.com.au; 435 Clarendon St, South Melbourne; r from $230; ❄ 🛜; 🚇 12) Low key, contemporary and elegantly restrained, the 15-room Coppersmith has every right to call itself a boutique property. Designer furniture, heavenly beds and fine woollen rugs set a seductive tone in the muted rooms, each with Nespresso machine, work desk, free wi-fi and recordable cable TV. On-site assets include a smart, locavore bistro-bar and a rooftop deck with skyline views.

St Kilda & Around

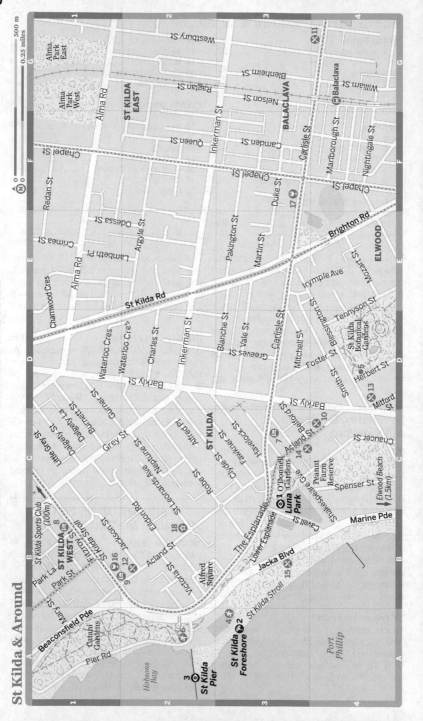

St Kilda & Around

🛏 South Yarra, Prahran & Windsor

Back of Chapel — HOSTEL $
(Map p218; ☑03-9521 5338; www.backofchap
el.com; 50 Green St, Windsor; dm $32-36, d $80;
☺reception 8.30am-5pm; @⑧⑤; ⬛6, 78, ⬛Wind
sor) Literally 20 steps from the cooler end
of Chapel St, Back of Chapel offers budget-
conscious slumber in an old Victorian terrace. A clean, laid-back spot with four- and
six-bed dorms, it also offers private twins,
doubles and triples. Facilities include communal kitchen, BBQ and coin-operated
laundry. It's especially popular with those on
a working holiday. All rates include breakfast.

Cullen — BOUTIQUE HOTEL $$
(Map p218; ☑03-9098 1555; www.artseriesho
tels.com.au/cullen; 164 Commercial Rd, Prahran; r
from $209; ✸@⑤; ⬛72, 78, 79, ⬛Prahran) The
work of late grunge painter Adam Cullen
drives the decor here: his vibrant and often
graphic art provides such visions as Ned Kelly shooting you from the opaque bedroom-
bathroom dividers. Rooms are stylish and
comfy, with handy kitchenettes, though the
standard studios are small. Rooms facing
north and west from level four and up offer
the best views.

Lyall — BOUTIQUE HOTEL $$$
(Map p218; ☑03-9868 8222, 1800 338 234;
www.thelyall.com; 16 Murphy St, South Yarra; r
from $255; ✸⑤; ⬛8, ⬛South Yarra) Just off
Toorak Rd, the 40-suite Lyall, with one- and
two-bedroom apartments, is all about the
good life: on-site spa and champagne bar,
original artwork by French-born Thierry B,
even a pillow menu. Suites are plush, if a little worn, with a seductive, textural palette of
shantung, taffeta, suede, velvet and brocade.
Regular guests include Melbourne-raised
singer Olivia Newton-John.

🛏 St Kilda

★ Base — HOSTEL $
(Map p220; ☑03-8598 6200; www.stayatbase.
com; 17 Carlisle St, St Kilda; dm/d from $34/145;
🅿✳@⑤; ⬛3, 16, 96) Well-run Base has
streamlined dorms (each with en suite) and
slick doubles. There's a floor – complete
with hair straighteners and champagne
deals – set aside for female travellers, and
a bar and live-music nights keep the good
times rolling.

Prince — HOTEL $$
(Map p220; ☑03-9536 1111; www.theprince.
au; 2 Acland St, St Kilda; r from $175; 🅿✳⑤✖;
⬛3, 12, 16, 96) The brooding, David Lynch–
esque lobby sets a sexy, stylish tone at this
fashionable favourite. Rooms are pared
back and chic, if a little tired. Also on-site
are the celebrated Prince Bandroom (p232;
be prepared for weekend noise) and the
Aurora Spa Retreat (Map p220; ☑03-9536
1130; www.auroraspatretreat.com; 2 Acland St, St
Kilda; 1hr massage $175; ☺10am-6pm Mon, Tue,
Thu & Fri, 11.30am-7.30pm Wed, 9am-5.30pm
Sat, 10am-3pm Sun; ⬛3, 12, 16, 96). Note that
the hotel's (unheated) pool is in a private-
function space and so isn't always accessible.

Hotel Tolarno
HOTEL **$$**

(Map p220; ☑03-9537 0200; www.tolarnoho
tel.com.au; 42 Fitzroy St, St Kilda; s/d/ste from
$109/119/169; ❄☎; ☐3, 12, 16, 96) Tolarno was once the site of art dealer Georges
Mora's seminal gallery, Tolarno. A range of
rooms are on offer and all come eclectically
furnished, with good beds, bright and bold
original artworks, Nespresso machine and
free wi-fi. Those at the front of the building
might get a bit noisy, but they compensate
with balconies and enormous windows
overlooking Fitzroy St.

🍴 Eating

🍴 City Centre

★ Hakata Gensuke
RAMEN **$**

(Map p208; ☑03-9663 6342; www.gensuke.com.
au; 168 Russell St; mains $13-14; ⊙11.30am-
2.45pm & 5-9.30pm Mon-Fri, noon-9.30pm Sat &
Sun; ☒Parliament) Gensuke is one of those
places that only does one thing and does
it extraordinarily well. In this case it's *ton-
kotsu* (pork broth) ramen. Choose from
three types (signature, sesame-infused
'black' or spicy 'god fire') and then order
extra toppings (marinated *cha-shu* pork,
egg, seaweed, black fungus). Inevitably
there will be a queue, but it's well worth
the wait.

★ Supernormal
ASIAN **$$**

(Map p208; ☑03-9650 8688; www.supernormal.
net.au; 180 Flinders Lane; dishes $16-39; ⊙11am-
11pm; ☒Flinders St) Drawing on his years
spent in Shanghai and Hong Kong, chef
Andrew McConnell presents a creative selection of pan-Asian sharing dishes, from
dumplings to raw seafood to slow-cooked
Sichuan lamb. Even if you don't dine in,
stop by for his now-famous takeaway New
England lobster roll. No dinner bookings,
so get here early to put your name on the
list.

★ Chin Chin
SOUTHEAST ASIAN **$$**

(Map p208; ☑03-8663 2000; www.chinchinres
taurant.com.au; 125 Flinders Lane; mains $20-39;
⊙11am-late; ☒Flinders St) Insanely popular,
and for good reason, chic Chin Chin serves
delicious Southeast Asian hawker-style food
designed as shared plates. It's housed in a
glammed-up old warehouse with a real New
York feel, and while there are no bookings,
you can fill in time at the **Go Go Bar** downstairs until there's space.

Mamasita
MEXICAN **$$**

(Map p208; ☑03-9650 3821; www.mamasita.
com.au; 1st fl, 11 Collins St; tacos $7, quesadillas
$15, shared plates $24-27; ⊙5-11pm Sun-Wed,
noon-midnight Thu-Sat; ☒Parliament) The restaurant responsible for kicking off Melbourne's obsession with authentic Mexican
street food, Mamasita is still one of the
very best. The chargrilled corn sprinkled
with cheese and chipotle mayo is a legendary starter, and there's a fantastic range of
corn-tortilla tacos and a mammoth selection
of tequila. It doesn't take reservations for
dinner, so prepare to wait.

MoVida
TAPAS **$$**

(Map p208; ☑03-9663 3038; www.movida.com.
au; 1 Hosier Lane; tapas $4-8, raciones $16-34;
⊙noon-late; ☒Flinders St) MoVida's location
in much-graffitied Hosier Lane is about as
Melbourne as it gets. Line up by the bar,
cluster around little window tables or, if
you've booked, take a seat in the dining area
for fantastic Spanish tapas and *raciones*.
MoVida Next Door – yes, right next door –
is the perfect place for preshow beers and
tapas.

Flower Drum
CHINESE **$$**

(Map p208; ☑03-9662 3655; www.flowerdrum.
melbourne; 1st fl, 17 Market Lane; mains $18-40;
⊙noon-3pm & 6-11pm Mon-Sat, 6-10.30pm Sun;
☎; ☒Parliament) Established in 1975, Flower Drum continues to be Melbourne's most
celebrated Chinese restaurant, imparting a
charmingly old-fashioned ambience through
its dark wood, lacquerwork and crisp white
linen. The sumptuous but ostensibly simple
Cantonese food (from a menu that changes
daily) is delivered with the top-notch service
you'd expect in such elegant surroundings.

HuTong Dumpling Bar
CHINESE **$$**

(Map p208; ☑03-9650 8128; www.hutong.com.
au; 14-16 Market Lane; mains $14-31; ⊙11.30am-
3pm & 5.30-10.30pm; ☒Parliament) HuTong's
reputation for divine *xiao long bao* means
getting a lunchtime seat anywhere in this
three-level building isn't easy. Downstairs,
watch chefs make the delicate dumplings,
then hope they don't watch you making a
mess eating them.

★ Lee Ho Fook
CHINESE **$$$**

(Map p208; ☑03-9077 6261; www.leehofook.com.
au; 11-15 Duckboard Pl; mains $32-42; ⊙noon-
2.30pm & 6-11pm Mon-Fri, 6-11pm Sat & Sun; ☒Parliament) Occupying an old brick warehouse
down a fabulously skungy laneway, Lee

Ho Fook is the epitome of modern Chinese culinary wizardry. The kitchen packs an extraordinary amount of flavour into signature dishes such as crispy eggplant with red vinegar, chicken crackling, liquorice wagyu beef, and crab and scallop rice with homemade XO sauce. The service is terrific too.

Cumulus Inc   MODERN AUSTRALIAN **$$$**
(Map p208; ☑03-9650 1445; www.cumulusinc.com.au; 45 Flinders Lane; breakfast $14-18, mains $36-44; ☺7am-11pm; ☑Parliament) This bustling informal eatery focuses on beautiful produce and simple but artful cooking, served at the long marble bar and at little round tables dotted about. Dinner reservations are only taken for groups, so expect to queue. Upstairs is the Cumulus Up wine bar.

Longrain   THAI **$$$**
(Map p208; ☑03-9671 3151; www.longrain.com; 44 Little Bourke St; mains $30-40; ☺6-10pm Mon-Thu, noon-3pm & 5.30pm-late Fri, 5.30pm-late Sat & Sun; ☑Parliament) Get in early or expect a long wait (sip a drink and relax, they suggest) before sampling Longrain's innovative Thai cuisine. The communal tables don't exactly work for a romantic date, but they're great for checking out everyone else's meals. Dishes are designed to be shared; try the pork-and-prawn eggnet, the amazing seafood dishes and the coconut sorbet.

Vue de Monde   MODERN AUSTRALIAN **$$$**
(Map p208; ☑03-9691 3888; www.vuedemonde.com.au; 55th fl, Rialto, 525 Collins St; set menu $230-275; ☺6-11pm Mon-Wed, noon-2pm & 6-11pm Thu-Sun; ☑Southern Cross) Surveying the world from the old observation deck of the Rialto tower, Melbourne's favoured spot for occasion dining has views to match its storied reputation. Visionary chef Shannon Bennett, when he's not mentoring on *MasterChef*, produces sophisticated set menus showcasing the very best Australian ingredients. Book well – months – ahead.

Grossi Florentino   ITALIAN **$$$**
(Map p208; ☑03-9662 1811; www.grossiflorentino.com; 1st fl, 80 Bourke St; 2-course lunch $65, 3-course dinner $140; ☺noon-2.30pm & 6pm-late Mon-Fri, 6pm-late Sat; ☑Parliament) Over-the-top gilded plasterwork, chandeliers and 1930s Florentine Renaissance murals engender a real sense of occasion at this top-notch Italian restaurant. Decadent set menus are accompanied by exquisite canapés and delicious bread, and the service is extremely slick. The Grill and Cellar Bar below offer more affordable options.

⊁ Southbank & Docklands

Crown (Map p204; ☑03-9292 8888; www.crown-melbourne.com.au; 8 Whiteman St, Southbank; ☐12, 55, 96, 109) has done a good job of luring people into its casino complex by installing some of Australia's most famous restaurateurs in glamorous riverside venues. While prices are steep, quality is high – unlike at some other eateries in this touristy stretch. South Wharf also has some interesting dining options right at the river's edge.

★Spice Temple   CHINESE **$$$**
(Map p208; ☑03-8679 1888; www.rockpool.com; Crown, Yarra Promenade, Southbank; mains $15-52; ☺6-11pm Mon-Wed, noon-3pm & 6-11pm Thu-Sun; ☒; ☐55) When he's not at **Rockpool** (Map p208; ☑03-8648 1900; www.rockpool.com; Crown, Yarra Promenade, Southbank; mains $35-70; ☺noon-2.30pm & 6-11pm Sun-Fri, 6-11pm Sat; ☐55) next door or in one of his Sydney restaurants, well-known chef Neil Perry pays homage to the spicy cuisines of China's central provinces at this excellent waterfront eatery. By day you can gaze at the river while you tuck into the $49 yum cha banquet. By night, descend to the atmospheric darkened tabernacle beneath.

⊁ Richmond

Minamishima   JAPANESE **$$$**
(Map p204; ☑03-9429 5180; www.minamishima.com.au; 4 Lord St, Richmond; per person $150; ☺6-10pm Tue-Sat; ☐48, 75) Hidden down a side street, Minamishima offers possibly the most unique Japanese dining experience this side of the equator. Sit at the bar seats and watch sushi master Koichi Minamishima prepare seafood with surgical precision and serve it one piece at a time. There's only a handful of seats, so book well in advance.

⊁ Fitzroy & Collingwood

★Lune Croissanterie   BAKERY **$**
(Map p212; www.lunecroissanterie.com; 119 Rose St, Fitzroy; pastries $5.50-12.50; ☺7.30am-3pm Mon, Thu & Fri, from 8am Sat & Sun; ☐11) The queues may have you turning on your heel, but good things come to those who wait, and here they come in the form of some of the best pastries you'll ever taste – from the lemon-curd cruffin to a classic almond croissant. In the

centre of this warehouse space sits a climate-controlled glass cube, the Lune Lab, where the magic happens.

★ Smith & Deli
DELI, VEGAN $

(Map p212; ☑ 03-9042 4117; www.smithand daughters.com; 111 Moor St, Fitzroy; sandwiches $10-15; ⊙ 8am-6pm Tue-Sat; ☑; ☐ 11) Full of '50s-NYC-deli charm with a vegan twist, this little takeaway creates what might be the closest vegetarians will get to eating meat – it's even been known to fool a few carnivores. Sandwiches are made to order and filled with all the favourites; try the Rubenstein, loaded with 'pastrami', sauerkraut and pickles, or opt for the Club Sandwiches Not Seals.

★ Gelato Messina
GELATO $

(Map p212; www.gelatomessina.com; 237 Smith St, Fitzroy; 1 scoop $4.80; ⊙ noon-11pm Sun-Thu, to 11.30pm Fri & Sat; ☐ 86) Messina is hyped as Melbourne's best ice-creamery and its popularity is evident in the queues of people in summer waiting to wrap their smackers around such smooth flavours as salted coconut and mango, poached figs in marsala, or blood-orange sorbet. You can watch the ice-cream makers at work through glass windows inside.

Huxtaburger
BURGERS $

(Map p212; ☑ 03-9417 6328; www.huxtaburger. com.au; 106 Smith St, Collingwood; burgers $10-14.50; ⊙ 11.30am-10pm Sun-Thu, to 11pm Fri & Sat; ☐ 86) This American-style burger joint is a hit for its crinkle-cut chips in old-school containers (go the spicy chipotle salt), tasty burgers (veg options available) on glazed brioche buns, and bottled craft beers. Other branches are in the city (Map p208; www. huxtaburger.com.au; Fulham Pl; burgers $7-14; ⊙ 11.30am-10pm; ☐ Flinders St) and Prahran (Map p218; www.huxtaburger.com.au; 203 High St, Prahran; burgers from $10; ⊙ 11.30am-10pm Sun-Thu, to 11pm Fri & Sat; ☐ 6, 78, ☐ Prahran).

Charcoal Lane
MODERN AUSTRALIAN $$

(Map p212; ☑ 03-9418 3400; www.charcoallane. com.au; 136 Gertrude St, Fitzroy; mains $19-31; ⊙ noon-3pm & 6-9pm Tue-Sat; ☐ 86) ✏ Housed in an old bluestone former bank, this training restaurant for Indigenous and disadvantaged young people is one of the best places to try native flora and fauna; menu items may include pan-seared emu fillet with lemon-myrtle risotto and wattleseed crème brûlée. The chef's native tasting plate for

two ($30) is a great place to start. Weekend bookings advised.

Belle's Hot Chicken
AMERICAN $$

(Map p212; ☑ 03-9077 0788; http://belles hotchicken.com; 150 Gertrude St, Fitzroy; chicken & a side from $17; ⊙ noon-10pm Sun-Thu, to 11pm Fri & Sat; ☐ 86) Chef Morgan McGlone knew he was onto a good thing while honing his kitchen skills in the States. But ever since he brought Nashville fried chicken back to Australia and paired it with natural wine, it's been a finger-lickin' revolution. Launch into tenders, drumsticks or wings with your preference of heat (note: 'Really F**kin Hot' is so named for good reason).

Vegie Bar
VEGETARIAN $$

(Map p212; ☑ 03-9417 6935; www.vegiebar.com.au; 380 Brunswick St, Fitzroy; mains $13-18; ⊙ 11am-10pm Sun-Thu, to 10.30pm Fri & Sat; ☎☑; ☐ 11) An oldie but a goodie, this cavernous warehouse eatery has been feeding droves of Melbourne's veggie-loving residents for over 20 years. Expect inventive fare and big servings from its menu of delicious thin-crust pizzas, tasty salads, burgers and curries, as well as great smoothies and fresh juices. Also has a fascinating selection of raw food dishes, and plenty of vegan choices.

★ Cutler & Co
MODERN AUSTRALIAN $$$

(Map p212; ☑ 03-9419 4888; www.cutlerandco. com.au; 55 Gertrude St, Fitzroy; mains $36-48; ⊙ 6pm-late Tue-Sun, lunch from noon Sun; ☐ 86) Hyped for all the right reasons, this is Andrew McConnell's flagship Melbourne restaurant and its attentive, informed staff and joy-inducing dishes have quickly made it one of Melbourne's top places for fine dining. The menu strives to incorporate the best seasonal produce across the à la carte offering, the degustation menu (from $150), and the casual Sunday lunch designed for sharing.

Saint Crispin
MODERN AUSTRALIAN $$$

(Map p212; ☑ 03-9419 2202; www.saintcrispin. com.au; 300 Smith St, Collingwood; 2/3 courses $50/65; ⊙ 6pm-late Tue-Thu, noon-late Fri-Sun; ☐ 86) The stylish interiors, light-filled space, prompt service and excellent food make this one of the best places for fine dining in the inner city. You can choose from two or three courses, or opt for the chef's tasting menu (from $100). The duo behind the restaurant spent time working together at Michelin-starred The Square in London.

Ides MODERN AUSTRALIAN **$$$**
(Map p212; ☑ 03-9939 9542; www.idesmelbourne.
com.au; 92 Smith St, Collingwood; 6-course de-
gustation $110; ⊘ from 6pm Wed-Sun; ☐ 86)
What started as a pop-up is now a perma-
nent restaurant in Smith St. Word spread
quickly that Attica (p227) sous chef Peter
Gunn had started his own establishment,
where he does the term 'creative' justice
with a contemporary take on fine dining.
It's a six-course, seasonal affair preceded
by hot bread with dangerously good house
peanut butter.

⅍ Carlton & Brunswick

Heartattack and Vine ITALIAN **$**
(Map p216; ☑ 03-9005 8674; www.heartattack
andvine.com.au; 329 Lygon St, Carlton; ⊘ 7am-
11pm Mon-Fri, from 8am Sat & Sun; 🛜; ☐ Tourist
Shuttle, ☐ 1,6) Heartattack and Vine is a re-
laxed space with a neighbourhood feel all
centred on a long wooden bar. Drop in for
a coffee morning or night, prop up at the
bar for an Aperol spritz or glass of wine,
grab a brekky pastry or prawn brioche roll
for lunch, or spend the evening sampling
the *cicchetti,* a Venetian take on tapas.

★ D.O.C. Espresso ITALIAN **$$**
(Map p216; ☑ 03-9347 8482; www.docgroup.net;
326 Lygon St, Carlton; mains $12-20; ⊘ 7.30am-
late Mon-Sat, 8am-late Sun; ☐ Tourist Shuttle,
☐ 1, 6) Run by third-generation Italian

Australians, authentic D.O.C. has breathed
new life into Lygon St. The espresso bar
features homemade pasta specials, Italian microbrewery beers and *aperitivo*
time (4pm to 7pm), when you can enjoy a
negroni with complimentary nibble board.

The affiliated **deli** (Map p216; ☑ 03-9347
8482; www.docgroup.net; 330 Lygon St, Carlton;
panini from $7; ⊘ 9am-7pm Mon-Sat, from 10am
Sun; ☐ Tourist Shuttle, ☐ 1, 8) next door does
great cheese boards and panini, while
around the corner is the original **pizzeria**
(Map p216; ☑ 03-9347 2998; www.docgroup.
net; 295 Drummond St, Carlton; pizzas $17-25;
⊘ 5pm-late Mon-Wed, noon-late Fri-Sun; ☐ Tourist Shuttle, ☐ 1, 6).

★ Rumi MIDDLE EASTERN **$$**
(☑ 03-9388 8255; www.rumirestaurant.com.au;
116 Lygon St, East Brunswick; dishes $13-28; ⊘ 6-
10pm; ☐ 1, 6) A fabulously well-considered
place that serves up a mix of traditional
Lebanese cooking and contemporary inter-
pretations of old Persian dishes. The *sigara
boregi* (cheese and pine-nut pastries) are a
local institution, and tasty mains from the
charcoal BBQ are balanced with a large and
interesting selection of vegetable dishes.

⅍ South Melbourne

St Ali CAFE **$**
(Map p204; ☑ 03-9686 2990; www.stali.com.
au; 12-18 Yarra Pl, South Melbourne; dishes $8-25;

MELBOURNE IN...

Two Days
Head over to check out the **Ian Potter Centre: NGV Australia** (p202) art collection
and have a look around **Federation Square** (p202) before joining a **walking tour**
(p215) to see Melbourne's street art. Enjoy lunch at MoVida (p222) then find a rooftop
bar (p229) to test the city's cocktails and take in the views before an evening **kayak
tour** (p215) down the Yarra River. Finish the night off dining at one of Melbourne's best
restaurants (p222). Start day two with a stroll along **Birrarung Marr** (p202) and
into the **Royal Botanic Gardens** (p211), then discover the gastronomic delights of the
Queen Victoria Market (p203). Catch a tram to **St Kilda** (p213) to wander along the
foreshore and pier before propping up at a bar in lively Acland Street for the evening.

One Week
Spend a couple of hours at the **Melbourne Museum** (p207) then head into Fitzroy to
boutique shop along Gertrude Street and grab lunch and coffee at **Proud Mary** (p229)
in Collingwood. Back in the city centre, wander through **Chinatown** (p203) and check
out Ned Kelly's armour at the **State Library** (p203) before grabbing some dumplings
at **HuTong** (p222) for dinner. Spend the rest of the week exploring the shopping and
cafe-hopping in hip Windsor and **Prahran** (p226), hitting the market in **South Melbourne** (p211) and heading out to the **Abbotsford Convent** (p207). Make sure to fit in
a meal at **Supernormal** (p222) and a drink at **Bar Americano** (p228).

⊕7am-6pm; 🖬12) A hideaway warehouse conversion where the coffee's carefully sourced and guaranteed to be good. If you can't decide between house blend, speciality, black or white, there's a six-coffee tasting 'adventure' ($20). The food menu covers all bases with competence and creativity, from virtuous vanilla-and-maple quinoa pudding with baby Thai basil to cult-status corn fritters with poached eggs and grilled halloumi.

Simply Spanish
SPANISH $$

(Map p204; ☑03-9682 6100; www.simplyspanish.com.au; South Melbourne Market, cnr Coventry & Cecil Sts, South Melbourne; gourmet paellas from $20.50, tapas $8-16; ⊕8am-9pm Wed-Sat, to 4pm Sun; 🖬12, 96) When a Melbourne restaurant wins the title of 'Best Paella Outside of Spain' in Valencia, you know you're on to a good thing. This casual market eatery is *the* place to go for paella, which is available here in numerous combos. While you wait, nibble on a tapas dish or two; the chilli-spiked garlic prawns are a top pick.

South Yarra & Prahran

★ Zumbo
DESSERTS $

(Map p218; ☑1800 858 611; http://zumbo.com.au; 14 Claremont St, South Yarra; macarons $2.80, cakes from $6; ⊕7am-7pm; 🖬58, 78, 🚊South Yarra) Aussie pâtissier Adriano Zumbo is hot property, famed for his outrageously creative, technically ambitious concoctions. Here, cheesecake might be made with yuzu-cream-cheese mousse and shaped like a Swiss cheese, and a tart might get spicy with churros-custard crème and Mexican-hot-chocolate crème. And then there's the '70s disco-chamber-like fit-out. Fine print: the coffee's better next door.

Two Birds One Stone
CAFE $

(Map p218; ☑03-9827 1228; www.twobirdsonestonecafe.com.au; 12 Claremont St, South Yarra; dishes $14-22.50; ⊕7am-3.30pm Mon-Fri, from 8am Sat & Sun; 🖬58, 78, 🚊South Yarra) Sandblasted oak stools, whitewashed timber and a wintry forest mural evoke Scandinavia at Two Birds One Stone, a crisp, contemporary cafe with smooth third-wave coffee and a smart, produce-driven menu. Find your happy place tucking into soul-nourishing dishes like ricotta pancakes with figs, marmalade syrup and pistachio cream, or pan-seared salmon with potato rösti, truffled cauliflower puree and poached eggs.

Gilson
MODERN AUSTRALIAN $$

(Map p204; ☑03-9866 3120; http://gilsonrestaurant.com.au; 171 Domain Rd, South Yarra; pizzas $18-25 , mains $24-34; ⊕6am-11pm Mon-Fri, from 7am Sat & Sun; 🖬58) Sassy new kid Gilson straddles the line between cafe and restaurant. Directly opposite the Botanic Gardens, it has a concrete and Italian-marble fit-out inspired by midcentury French modernism and contemporary, Italian-influenced food. Forgo the famous (and underwhelming) grilled cucumber for the outstanding pasta dishes and interesting wood-fired pizzas. Rounding things off are intriguing wines and cocktails, and attentive, knowledgeable staff.

Woodland House
MODERN AUSTRALIAN $$$

(Map p218; ☑03-9525 2178; www.woodlandhouse.com.au; 78 Williams Rd, Prahran; tasting menus from $125; ⊕6.30-9pm Tue, Wed & Sat, noon-3pm & 6.30-9pm Thu & Fri, noon-3pm Sun; 🖬6) In a glorious Victorian villa, Woodland House is home turf for young-gun chefs Thomas Woods and Hayden McFarland, former sous chefs for lauded Melbourne restaurateur Jacques Reymond. The menu spotlights quality local produce, cooked confidently and creatively in dishes like wood-roasted mussels with asparagus and salted yolk. Thursday and Friday offer a good-value three-course lunch with a glass of wine for $55.

Da Noi
ITALIAN $$$

(Map p218; ☑03-9866 5975; http://danoi.com.au; 95 Toorak Rd, South Yarra; mains $30-40, 4-course tasting menu $75-95; ⊕noon-10.30pm; 🖬58, 🚊South Yarra) Elegant Da Noi serves up beautiful dishes from Sardinia, the island home of owner-chef Pietro Porcu. Offerings change daily, with the chef's special reinterpreted several times a night on some occasions. For the full effect, opt for the four-course set menu, which sees the chef decide your dishes based on whatever's best that day. Bookings advised.

St Kilda

Glick's
BAGELS $

(Map p220; www.glicks.com.au; 330a Carlisle St, Balaclava; bagels from $4; ⊕6am-8pm Sun-Thu, 6am-30min before sunset Fri, 30min after sunset-midnight Sat; 🖬3, 16, 78, 🚊Balaclava) A staple for the local Jewish community, kosher bakery Glick's sells bagels baked and boiled in-house. Stick with the classics and try the 'New Yorker' with cream cheese and egg salad.

Monarch Cake Shop DESSERTS $
(Map p220; ☑03-9534 2972; www.monarch
cakes.com.au; 103 Acland St, St Kilda; slice of cake
from $5; ☺8am-9.30pm Sun-Thu, to 10pm Fri &
Sat; ☐96) Monarch is a favourite among St
Kilda's Eastern European cake shops, and
its *kugelhopf* (marble cake), plum cake and
Polish baked cheesecake can't be beaten. In
business since 1934, the shop doesn't seem
to have changed much, with a soft, old-time
atmosphere and wonderful buttery aromas.
It also does good coffee.

Lentil as Anything VEGETARIAN $
(Map p220; ☑0424 345 368; www.lentilasany
thing.com; 41 Blessington St, St Kilda; by donation; ☺noon-9pm; ☑; ☐3, 16, 96) Choosing
from the vegetarian menu is easy. Deciding what to pay can be hard. This unique
not-for-profit operation provides training
and educational opportunities for mar-
ginalised people, as well as tasty flesh-free
grub. Whatever you pay for your meal goes
towards helping new migrants, refugees,
people with disabilities and the long-term
unemployed. There are several branches, including one at Abbotsford Convent
(p207).

★**Attica** MODERN AUSTRALIAN $$$
(☑03-9530 0111; www.attica.com.au; 74 Glen
Eira Rd, Ripponlea; tasting menu $250; ☺6pm-
late Tue-Sat; ☐67, ☐Ripponlea) The only Aus-
tralian restaurant on the San Pellegrino
World's Top 50 Restaurants list, Attica is
home to prodigious Kiwi import Ben Sh-
ewry and his extraordinary culinary cre-
ations. Native ingredients shine in dishes
like bunya bunya with salted red kangaroo,
or bush-currant granité with lemon aspen
and rosella flower. Reservations accepted
three months ahead, on the first Wednes-
day of each month at 9am. Note that ta-
bles of two can go within a couple of hours,
especially for Friday and Saturday nights.
You'll have a better chance with a table
for four or more, or trying for dinner mid-
week. It's also worth emailing or calling to
check if availability isn't showing online. If
driving, follow Brighton Rd south and turn
left onto Glen Eira Rd.

Lau's Family Kitchen CHINESE $$$
(Map p220; ☑03-8598 9880; www.lauskitch
en.com.au; 4 Acland St, St Kilda; mains $26-45;
☺noon-3pm Mon-Fri, 12.30-3.30pm Sun, dinner
sittings 6pm & 8pm daily; ☐16, 96) This polished nosh spot serves beautiful, home-style

Cantonese with a few Sichuan surprises,
including a seductive braised eggplant with
spiced minced pork. Reserve for one of the
two dinner sittings, and check out the elegant wall panels, made from 1930s kimonos.

Stokehouse SEAFOOD $$$
(Map p220; ☑03-9525 5555; www.stokehouse.com.
au; 30 Jacka Blvd, St Kilda; mains $36-42; ☺noon-
3pm & 6pm-late; ☐3a, 16, 96) After a devastating
fire, the lauded Stokehouse is back, brighter
and better than ever. Striking contemporary
architecture and floor-to-ceiling bay views set
the right tone for fresh, modern, seafood-cen-
tric dishes, not to mention a stuff-of-legend
bombe Alaska. This is one of Melbourne's hot-
test restaurants, so always book ahead.

Cicciolina ITALIAN $$$
(Map p220; ☑03-9525 3333; www.cicciolinastkil
da.com.au; 130 Acland St, St Kilda; mains lunch
$18-30, dinner $27-45; ☺noon-10pm; ☐3, 16,
96) This hideaway of dark wood, subdued
lighting and pencil sketches is a St Kilda
institution. The menu is modern Italian,
with dishes that might see tortellini paired
beautifully with Persian feta, ricotta, pine
nuts, lime zest, asparagus and burnt sage
butter. Bookings only for lunch; for dinner,
eat very early or while away your wait in
the moody back bar.

🍸 Drinking & Nightlife

Melbourne's drinking scene is easily the best
in Australia and as good as any in the world.
There's a huge diversity of venues, ranging
from hip basement dives hidden down laneways to sophisticated cocktail bars perched
on rooftops. Many pubs have pulled up the
beer-stained carpet and polished the concrete, but don't dismiss the character-filled
oldies that still exist.

🍷 City Centre

★**Heartbreaker** BAR
(Map p208; ☑03-9041 0856; www.heartbreaker
bar.com.au; 234a Russell St; ☺5pm-3am Mon-
Sat, to 11pm Sun; ☐Melbourne Central) Black
walls, red lights, skeleton handles on the
beer taps, random taxidermy, craft beer, a
big selection of bourbon, rock and punk
on the sound system, and tough-looking
sweethearts behind the bar – all the pre-
requisites, in fact, for a hard-rocking good
time.

★ **Madame Brussels** ROOFTOP BAR
(Map p208; ☑ 03-9662 2775; www.madamebru
ssels.com; 3rd fl, 57-59 Bourke St; ⊘ noon-11pm
Sun-Wed, to 1am Thu-Sat; ☒ Parliament) Head up
to this wonderful rooftop terrace if you've
had it with Melbourne-moody and all that
dark wood. Although it's named for a famous 19th-century brothel owner, it feels
like a camp 1960s country club, with much
Astroturfery and wisteria, and staff dressed
for a spot of tennis.

★ **Croft Institute** BAR
(Map p208; www.thecroftinstitute.com.au; 21
Croft Alley; ⊘ 5pm-midnight Mon-Thu, 5pm-3am
Fri, 8pm-3am Sat; ☒ 86, 96) Hidden in a graf-
fitied laneway off a laneway, the slightly
creepy Croft is a laboratory-themed bar
downstairs, while upstairs at weekends the
1950s-themed gymnasium opens as a club.
There's a $5 cover charge for DJs Friday and
Saturday nights.

★ **Bar Americano** COCKTAIL BAR
(Map p208; www.baramericano.com.au; 20 Pres-
grave Pl; ⊘ 5pm-1am Mon-Sat; ☒ Flinders St) A
hideaway bar in a lane off Howey Pl, Bar
Americano is a teensy standing-room-on-
ly affair with black-and-white chequered
floors complemented by classic 'do not spit'
subway-tiled walls and a subtle air of speakeasy. Once it hits its 14-person max, the grille
gets pulled shut. The cocktails here don't
come cheap, but they do come superb.

★ **Siglo** ROOFTOP BAR
(Map p208; ☑ 03-9654 6631; www.siglobar.com.au;
2nd fl, 161 Spring St; ⊘ 5pm-3am; ☒ Parliament)
Siglo's sought-after terrace comes with Pa-
risian flair, wafting cigar smoke and serious
drinks. It fills with suits on Friday night,
which may lure or horrify you. Regardless,
pick a time to mull over a classic cocktail,
snack on upper-crust morsels and admire
the 19th-century vista over Parliament and St
Patrick's Cathedral. Entry is via the similarly
unsigned **Supper Club** (Map p208; ☑ 03-9654

GAY & LESBIAN MELBOURNE

Melbourne has a large gay and lesbian population, second in Australia only to Sydney,
and it's generally a very accepting city. Although same-sex marriage isn't legal, there's
equality in most other aspects of the law.

While there's still a handful of specifically gay venues scattered around the city, some
of the best hang-outs are weekly takeovers of mainstream bars (especially Sunday after-
noon at the **Railway Hotel** (Map p218; ☑ 03-9510 4050; www.therailway.com.au; 29 Chapel
St, Windsor; ⊘ noon-late; ☒ 5, 64, 78, ☒ Windsor) in Windsor, Sunday evening at the **Em-
erson** (Map p218; ☑ 03-9825 0900; www.theemerson.com.au; 143-145 Commercial Rd, South
Yarra; ⊘ 5pm-midnight Thu, noon-5am Fri & Sat, noon-3.30am Sun; ☒ 72, 78, ☒ Prahran) in
South Yarra and Thursday night at **Yah Yah's** (Map p212; http://yahyahs.com.au; 99 Smith
St, Fitzroy; ⊘ 5pm-5am Thu-Sat; ☒ 86) in Fitzroy.

Semiregular themed gay party nights are also popular, such as **Woof** (www.woofclub.
com), **DILF** (www.iwantadilf.com), **Closet** (www.facebook.com/closetpartyoz), **Fabuland**
(www.fabuland.com.au) and **Swagger** (www.facebook.com/swaggerparty). For lesbians,
there's **Fannys at Franny's** (www.francescasbar.com.au/fannys-frannys) and **Mother
Party** (www.facebook.com/sojuicysaturdays).

The big event on the queer calendar is the annual **Midsumma Festival** (www.mid
summa.org.au; ⊘ Jan/Feb). It has a diverse program of cultural, community and sporting
events, including the popular Midsumma Carnival at Alexandra Gardens, St Kilda's Pride
March and much more. Australia's largest GLBT film festival, the **Melbourne Queer
Film Festival** (www.melbournequeerfilm.com.au; ⊘ Mar), screens more than 100 films
from around the world.

For more local info, pick up a copy of the free magazines *Star Observer* (www.star
observer.com.au), *MCV* (www.gaynewsnetwork.com.au) and *Lesbians on the Loose*
(www.lotl.com). Gay and lesbian radio station JOY 94.9FM (www.joy.org.au) is another
important resource for visitors and locals. Useful associations and publications include
Gay & Lesbian Tourism Australia (www.galta.com.au), Star Observer (www.starobserver.
com.au), Gay News Network (www.gaynewsnetwork.com.au), Lesbians on the Loose
(www.lotl.com), DNA magazine (www.dnamagazine.com.au) and the Victorian AIDS
Council (www.vac.org.au).

6300; www.melbournesupperclub.com.au; 1st fl, 161 Spring St; ⊙5pm-4am Sun-Thu, to 6am Fri & Sat; ⋒Parliament).

Cookie
BAR

(Map p208; ⊿03-9663 7660; www.cookie.net.au; 1st fl, Curtin House, 252 Swanston St; ⊙noon-3am; ⋒Melbourne Central) Part bar, part Thai restaurant, this kooky-cool venue with grand bones is one of the more enduring rites of passage of the Melbourne night. The bar is unbelievably well stocked with fine whiskies, wines, and plenty of craft beers among the more than 200 brews on offer. The staff also know how to make a serious cocktail.

Rooftop Bar
ROOFTOP BAR

(Map p208; ⊿03-9654 5394; www.rooftopcin ema.com.au; 6th fl, Curtin House, 252 Swanston St; ⊙noon-1am; ⋒Melbourne Central) This bar sits at dizzying heights atop happening Curtin House. In summer it transforms into an outdoor cinema with striped deckchairs and a calendar of new and classic favourite flicks.

Lui Bar
COCKTAIL BAR

(Map p208; ⊿03-9691 3888; www.vuedemonde. com.au; 55th fl, Rialto, 525 Collins St; ⊙5.30pm-midnight Mon-Wed, 11.30am-1am Thu, 11.30am-3am Fri & Sat, 11.30am-midnight Sun; ⋒Southern Cross) Some people are happy to shell out $36 for the view from the 120m-high Melbourne Star, but we'd much rather spend $25 on a cocktail at this sophisticated bar perched 236m up the Rialto tower. Suits and jetsetters cram in most nights, so get there early (and nicely dressed) to claim your table.

⊕ Southbank & Docklands

Ponyfish Island
BAR

(Map p208; www.ponyfish.com.au; Southbank Pedestrian Bridge, Southbank; ⊙11am-late; ⋒Flinders St) Not content with hiding bars down laneways or on rooftops, Melburnians are finding ever more creative spots to do their drinking. Where better than a little open-air nook on the pylon of a bridge arcing over the Yarra? It's a surprisingly good spot to knock back beers while snacking on toasted sandwiches or cheese plates.

⊕ Fitzroy, Collingwood & Abbotsford

★Black Pearl
COCKTAIL BAR

(Map p212; ⊿03-9417 0455; www.blackpearlbar. com.au; 304 Brunswick St, Fitzroy; ⊙5pm-3am, Attic Bar 7pm-2am Thu-Sat; ⋒11) After 15 years

in the game, Black Pearl goes from strength to strength, winning awards and receiving global accolades along the way. Low lighting, leather banquettes and candles set the mood downstairs. Prop at the bar to study the extensive cocktail list or let the expert bartenders concoct something to your taste. Upstairs is the table-service Attic Bar; book ahead.

★Marion
WINE BAR

(Map p212; ⊿03-9419 6262; www.marionwine. com.au; 53 Gertrude St, Fitzroy; ⊙5-11pm Mon-Thu, noon-11pm Fri, 8am-11pm Sat & Sun; ⋒86) Melbourne's poster-boy chef, Andrew McConnell, knew what he was doing when he opened Marion. The wine list is one of the area's most impressive and the space – catering to both stop-ins and long, romantic chats – is a pleasure to be in. Food changes regularly, but expect charcuterie from McConnell's butcher Meatsmith and specials with a European bent (dishes $10 to $34).

★Everleigh
COCKTAIL BAR

(Map p212; www.theeverleigh.com; 150-156 Gertrude St, Fitzroy; ⊙5.30pm-1am; ⋒86) Sophistication and bartending standards are off the charts at this upstairs hidden nook. Settle into a leather booth in the intimate setting with a few friends for conversation, and exclaiming over classic 'golden era' cocktails like you've never tasted before.

★Naked for Satan
BAR

(Map p212; ⊿03-9416 2238; www.nakedfor satan.com.au; 285 Brunswick St, Fitzroy; ⊙noon-midnight Sun-Thu, to 1am Fri & Sat; ⋒11) Vibrant, loud and reviving an apparent Brunswick St legend (a man nicknamed Satan who would get down and dirty, naked because of the heat, in an illegal vodka distillery under the shop), this place packs a punch with its popular *pintxos* (Basque tapas; $1 to $2), huge range of beverages, and unbeatable roof terrace (Naked in the Sky) with wraparound balcony.

★Proud Mary
CAFE

(Map p212; ⊿03-9417 5930; 172 Oxford St, Collingwood; ⊙7.30am-4pm Mon-Fri, 8.30am-4pm Sat & Sun; ☎; ⋒86) A champion for direct-trade, single-origin coffee, this quintessential industrial Collingwood red-brick space takes its caffeine seriously. It's consistently packed, not only for the excellent brew but also for the equally top-notch food, such as ricotta hotcakes or free-range pork with fennel crackling.

Bar Liberty
BAR

(Map p212; http://barliberty.com; 234 Johnston St, Fitzroy; ⊙ 5pm-late Mon-Sat & from noon Sun; 🚆 86) From a team of hospitality heavy-weights, Bar Liberty is bringing carefully selected wines (over 300 on the list) and expertly crafted cocktails to Fitzroy minus any pretentiousness. The approach is laid-back, the atmosphere is relaxed and the dining focus is on bold, refined food. There are monthly wine dinners upstairs and a rear courtyard beer garden, Drinkwell.

Industry Beans
CAFE

(Map p212; ☑ 03-9417 1034; www.industrybeans. com; 3/62 Rose St, Fitzroy; ⊙ 7am-4pm Mon-Fri, 8am-4pm Sat & Sun; 🛜; 🚆 96, 11) It's all about coffee chemistry at this warehouse cafe tucked in a Fitzroy side street. The coffee guide takes you through the speciality styles on offer (roasted on-site), from Aer-oPress and pourover to cold drip and espresso, and helpful staff take the pressure off deciding. The food menu (brunch $12 to $35) is ambitious but doesn't always hit the mark.

Sircuit
GAY

(Map p212; www.sircuit.com.au; 103 Smith St, Fitzroy; ⊙ 7.30pm-late Wed-Sun; 🚆 86) Hugely popular with a big cross section of gay men, Sircuit is an old-school gay bar with pool tables, drag shows, a back room and, as the night progresses, a heaving dance floor.

Carlton

Seven Seeds
CAFE

(Map p216; ☑ 03-9347 8664; www.sevenseeds. com.au; 114 Berkeley St, Carlton; ⊙ 7am-5pm Mon-Sat, 8am-5pm Sun; 🚆 19, 59) The most spacious location in the Seven Seeds coffee empire, this rather out-of-the-way ware-house cafe has plenty of room to store your bike and sip a splendid coffee. Public cup-pings are held 9am Friday.

It also owns **Traveller** (Map p208; www. sevenseeds.com.au; 2/14 Crossley St; bagels $7-10; ⊙ 7am-5pm Mon-Fri; 🚆 86, 96) and **Broth-er Baba Budan** (Map p208; www.sevenseeds. com.au; 359 Little Bourke St; ⊙ 7am-5pm Mon-Sat, 9am-5pm Sun; 🛜; 🚆 Melbourne Central) cafes in the CBD.

 ## South Yarra, Prahran & Windsor

★Rufus
COCKTAIL BAR

(Map p218; ☑ 03-9525 2197; www.rufusbar.com. au; 1st fl, 143 Greville St, Prahran; ⊙ 4pm-late; 🚆 6, 72, 78, 🚆 Prahran) Hidden above Greville St, Rufus is deliciously posh and proper, dripping with chandeliers, tinted mirrors and swagged drapes. That the place is named after Sir Winston Churchill's belov-ed poodle is no coincidence: the late British prime minister is Rufus' muse, hence the emphasis on quality champagnes, martinis and whiskies, the standout Yorkshire-pud-ding roll, and your butlerlike waiter. Enter from the laneway.

Woods of Windsor
BAR

(Map p218; ☑ 03-9521 1900; www.woodsofwinds or.com.au; 108 Chapel St, Windsor; ⊙ 5.30pm-1am Tue-Sat; 🚆 78, 5, 6, 64, 🚆 Windsor) Dark timber, kooky taxidermy and a speakeasy vibe make the Woods a suitable place to hide on those brooding, rainy Melbourne nights. Bunker down for a standout selec-tion of whiskies (including rarer drops), or ditch them altogether for a little Italian subversion: the drinks list includes a string of variations on the classic negroni apéritif. *Cin cin!*

Market Lane Coffee
CAFE

(Map p218; ☑ 03-9804 7434; www.marketlane. com.au; Prahran Market, 163 Commercial Rd, South Yarra; ⊙ 7am-5pm Tue & Thu-Sat, to 4pm Wed, 8am-5pm Sun; 🚆 72, 78, 79, 🚆 Prahran) This is one of Melbourne's top speciality coffee roasters, hiding away at the back of Prahran Market. The beans here are strict-ly seasonal, producing cups of joe that are beautifully nuanced...and best paired with one of the scrumptious pastries. Free one-hour cuppings run at 10am on Saturday (get in by 9.30am to secure your place).

Yellow Bird
BAR

(Map p218; ☑ 03-9533 8983; www.yellowbird.com. au; 122 Chapel St, Windsor; ⊙ 7.30am-late Mon-Fri, from 8am Sat & Sun; 🚆 6, 78, 🚆 Windsor) This lit-tle bird keeps Windsor's cool kids happy with all-day drinks and diner-style food. It's owned by the drummer from Something for Kate, so the loud, dark rock 'n' roll ambience is genu-ine, with a passing cast of musos, a fantastic playlist of underground bands and one of the most outrageously kitsch bars in town.

Revolver Upstairs
CLUB

(Map p218; ☑03-9521 5985; www.revolverup stairs.com.au; 229 Chapel St, Prahran; ⊙5pm-4am Tue & Wed, 5pm-6am Thu, 5pm Fri to noon Sat, 24hr 5pm Sat-9am Mon; ☐6, 78, ☐Prahran) Rowdy Revolver can feel like an enormous version of your lounge room, but with 54 hours of nonstop music come the weekend, you're probably glad it's not. Live music, art exhibitions, not to mention interesting local, national and international DJs keep the mixed crowd wide awake.

St Kilda

★ Bar Di Stasio
WINE BAR

(Map p220; ☑03-9525 3999; http://distasio. com.au/about/bar-di-stasio; 31 Fitzroy St, St Kilda; ⊙11.30am-midnight; ☐3, 12. 16, 96) Within Pompidou-style scaffolding – the work of artist Callum Morton – lies this buzzing, grown-up bar, dominated by a floor-to-ceiling mural of Caravaggio's *Flagellation of Christ*. Behind the deep marble bar, waiters seemingly plucked from Venice's Caffè Florian mix perfect Campari *spritzes* while dishing out gorgeous bites, from lightly fried local seafood to elegant pastas (available until 11pm). Book: the place is extremely popular.

★ Pontoon
BAR

(Map p220; ☑03-9525 5445; http://pontoon stkildabeach.com.au; 30 Jacka Blvd, St Kilda; ⊙noon-midnight; ☐3, 16, 96) Beneath the fine-dining Stokehouse (p227) is its casual, buzzing bar-bistro, a light-soaked space with floor-to-ceiling windows and a deck looking right out at the beach and sunset. Slip on the shades and sip craft suds or a local prosecco while eyeing the crowd for the odd local celeb. A shared-plates menu delivers some decent bites, overpriced and undersized pizzas aside.

Local Taphouse
BAR

(Map p220; ☑03-9537 2633; www.thelocal.com. au; 184 Carlisle St, St Kilda; ⊙noon-late; ☐3, 16, 78, ☐Balaclava) Reminiscent of an old-school Brooklyn bar, the warm, wooden Local has a rotating cast of craft beers and an impressive bottle list. There's a beer garden upstairs, and a snug drawing-room mix of leather couches and open fires inside. Weekly events include live comedy (including well-established acts) on Monday, and live soul, funk, blues or reggae on Friday and Saturday.

☆ Entertainment

Cinemas

Moonlight Cinema
CINEMA

(Map p204; www.moonlight.com.au; Gate D, Royal Botanic Gardens, Birdwood Ave, South Yarra; ☐1, 3, 5, 6, 16, 64, 67, 72) Melbourne's original outdoor cinema hits the Royal Botanic Gardens from early December to early April, screening a mix of current mainstream releases and retro classics. Bring your own picnic hamper or buy light eats and booze at the venue; 'Gold Grass' tickets include waitstaff service and a reserved beanbag bed in the premium viewing area.

Astor
CINEMA

(Map p218; ☑03-9510 1414; www.astortheatre. net.au; cnr Chapel St & Dandenong Rd, Windsor; tickets $17; ☐5, 64, 78, ☐Windsor) This 1936 art-deco darling has had more ups and downs than a Hollywood diva. Recently saved from permanent closure, it's one of Melbourne's best-loved landmarks, with double features most nights and a mixed bag of recent releases, art-house films and cult classics. Discount tickets ($12 to $13) are available Monday, Wednesday and Thursday.

Cinema Nova
CINEMA

(Map p216; ☑03-9347 5331; www.cinemanova. com.au; 380 Lygon St, Carlton; ☐Tourist Shuttle, ☐1, 6) See the latest in art-house, docos and foreign films at this cinema, a locals' favourite. Cheap Monday screenings ($7 before 4pm, $9 after 4pm).

Live Music

There's a constant procession of big international acts hitting local stadiums, arenas and theatres, and many of Melbourne's smaller character-filled drinking dens and pubs double as live-music venues.

Check daily papers and street magazines **Beat** (www.beat.com.au) and **The Music** (www.themusic.com.au) for gig info. Radio station **3RRR** (102.7FM; www.rrr.org. au) broadcasts a gig guide at 7pm from Wednesday to Friday, and at 6pm on weekends. **Mess+Noise** (www.messandnoise. com) is an Australian-focused music website, with an informed, irreverent chat forum. FasterLouder (www.fasterlouder.com. au) also has a gig guide and music news.

The Tote
LIVE MUSIC

(Map p204; ☑03-9419 5320; www.thetotehotel. com; cnr Johnston & Wellington Sts, Collingwood;

TICKETS

Tickets for concerts, theatre, comedy, sports and other events are usually available from one of the following agencies:

Halftix (Map p208; www.halftixmelbourne.com; Melbourne Town Hall, 90-120 Swanston St; ⊘10am-2pm Mon, 11am-6pm Tue-Fri, 10am-4pm Sat; ⊠Flinders St) Discounted theatre tickets are sold on the day of performance.

Moshtix (www.moshtix.com.au)

Ticketek (Map p208; www.ticketek.com.au; 252 Exhibition St; ⊘9am-5pm Mon-Fri, 10am-3pm Sat)

Ticketmaster (Map p208; ⊠1300 111 011; www.ticketmaster.com.au; Forum, 150-152 Flinders St; ⊘9am-6pm Mon-Fri)

⊘4pm-late Wed-Sun; ⊠86) One of Melbourne's most iconic live-music venues, this divey Collingwood pub has a great roster of local and international punk and hardcore bands, and one of the best jukeboxes in the universe. Its temporary closure in 2010 brought Melbourne to a stop, literally: people protested on city-centre streets against the liquor-licensing laws that were blamed for the closure.

Cherry
LIVE MUSIC

(Map p208; www.cherrybar.com.au; AC/DC Lane; ⊘6pm-late Mon-Sat, 2pm-late Sun; ⊠Flinders St) Of course Melbourne's most legendary live-rock bar is located in a black-walled, neon-lit basement on AC/DC Lane. There's often a queue, but once you're inside a welcoming, slightly anarchic spirit prevails. Live music and DJs play seven nights a week, and there's a long-standing soul night on Thursday.

Forum
CONCERT VENUE

(Map p208; ⊠1300 111 011; www.forummelbourne.com.au; 150-152 Flinders St; ⊠Flinders St) One of the city's most atmospheric live-music venues, the Forum does double duty as a cinema during the Melbourne International Film Festival. The striking Moorish exterior (an over-the-top fantasia with minarets, domes and dragons) houses an equally interesting interior, with the southern night sky rendered on the domed ceiling.

Prince Bandroom
LIVE MUSIC

(Map p220; ⊠03-9536 1168; www.princebandroom.com.au; 29 Fitzroy St, St Kilda; ⊠12, 16, 96) The Prince is a legendary St Kilda venue, with a solid line-up of local and international acts spanning hip-hop, dance, rock and indie. It's an eclectic mix, with recent guests including UK rapper Tinie Tempah, American roots-rock trio Moreland & Arbuckle and Nordic hardcore-punk outfit Refused.

Corner
LIVE MUSIC

(Map p204; ⊠03-9427 7300; www.cornerhotel.com; 57 Swan St, Richmond; ⊘4pm-late Mon-Fri, noon-3am Sat, noon-1am Sun; ⊠Richmond) The band room here is one of Melbourne's most popular midsize venues, and it's seen plenty of loud and live action over the years, from Dinosaur Jr to the Buzzcocks. If your ears need a break, there's a friendly front bar. The rooftop has city views but gets packed, and often with a different crowd from the music fans below.

Theatre & Arts

Red Stitch Actors Theatre
THEATRE

(Map p218; ⊠03-9533 8082; www.redstitch.net; rear 2 Chapel St, Windsor; ⊠5, 64, 78, ⊠Windsor) Featuring prolific national talent, Red Stitch is one of Australia's most respected actors' ensembles, staging new international works that are often premieres in Australia. The company's intimate black-box theatre is located opposite the historic Astor cinema, down the end of a driveway.

Theatre Works
THEATRE

(Map p220; ⊠03-9534 3388; www.theatreworks.org.au; 14 Acland St, St Kilda; ⊠3, 16, 96) Theatre Works is one of Melbourne's veteran independent theatre companies. With award-winning creative director John Sheedy at the helm, the company's focus is firmly on new Australian works.

Melbourne Theatre Company
THEATRE

(MTC; Map p204; ⊠03-8688 0800; www.mtc.com.au; 140 Southbank Blvd, Southbank; ⊠1) Melbourne's major theatrical company stages around a dozen productions each year, ranging from contemporary (including many new Australian works) to Shakespeare and other classics. Performances take place in its award-winning Southbank Theatre, a striking black building enclosed within angular white tubing.

La Mama THEATRE
(Map p216; ☑03-9347 6948; www.lamama.com.au;
205 Faraday St, Carlton; tickets $10-25; ⊙box office
10.30am-5pm Mon-Fri, 2-3pm Sat & Sun; ☑Tourist
Shuttle, ☑1, 6) La Mama is significant in Melbourne's theatre scene. This tiny, intimate
forum produces new Australian works and
experimental theatre, and has a reputation for
developing emerging playwrights. It's a ramshackle building with an open-air bar. Shows
also run at its larger **Courthouse theatre** at
349 Drummond St, so check tickets carefully
for the correct location.

Classical Music

Melbourne Recital Centre CLASSICAL MUSIC
(Map p204; ☑03-9699 3333; www.melbourne
recital.com.au; 31 Sturt St, Southbank; ⊙box office
9am-5pm Mon-Fri; ☎; ☑1) This building may
look like a framed piece of giant honeycomb,
but it's actually the home (or hive?) where
the **Melbourne Chamber Orchestra** (www.
mco.org.au) and lots of other small ensembles regularly perform. Its two halls are said
to have some of the best acoustics in the
southern hemisphere. Performances range
from chamber music to contemporary classical, jazz, world music and dance.

**Melbourne Symphony
Orchestra** LIVE PERFORMANCE
(MSO; Map p208; ☑03-9929 9600; www.mso.
com.au; Hamer Hall, 100 St Kilda Rd, Southbank;
☑Flinders St) The MSO has a broad reach:
while not afraid to be populist (it's done
sell-out performances with Burt Bacharach
and Kiss), it usually performs classical sym-
phonic master works. It plays regularly at
its **Hamer Hall** (Map p208; ☑1300 182 183;
www.artscentremelbourne.com.au; 100 St Kilda
Rd, Southbank; ☑1, 3, 6, 16, 64, 67, 72, ☑Flinders
St) home, but it also has a summer series
of free concerts at the **Sidney Myer Music
Bowl** (Map p204; ☑1300 182 183; www.artscen
tremelbourne.com.au; Kings Domain, 21 Linlithgow
Ave, Southbank; ☑3, 5, 6, 8, 16, 64, 67, 72).

Dance

Australian Ballet BALLET
(Map p204; ☑1300 369 741; www.australian
ballet.com.au; 2 Kavanagh St, Southbank; ☑1) More
than 50 years old, the Melbourne-based Australian Ballet performs traditional and new
works in the Arts Centre and all around the
country. You can take an hour-long tour of the
Primrose Potter Australian Ballet Centre ($39,
bookings essential) that includes a visit to the
production and wardrobe departments and
watching the dancers practise in the studios.

Chunky Move DANCE
(Map p204; ☑03-9645 5188; www.chunkymove.
com.au; 111 Sturt St, Southbank; ☑1) This acclaimed contemporary-dance company performs mainly at the **Malthouse Theatre**
(Map p204; ☑03-9685 5111; www.malthousethe
atre.com.au; 113 Sturt St, Southbank; ☑1). It also
runs a variety of public dance classes; check
the website.

🔒 Shopping

🔒 City Centre

★**Craft Victoria** ARTS & CRAFTS
(Map p208; ☑03-9650 7775; www.craft.org.au;
31 Flinders Lane; ⊙11am-6pm Mon-Sat; ☑Parlia-
ment) This retail arm of Craft Victoria showcases handmade goods, mainly by Victorian
artists and artisans. Its range of jewellery,
textiles, accessories, glass and ceramics
bridges the art–craft divide and makes for
some wonderful mementos of Melbourne.
There are also a few galleries with changing
exhibitions; admission is free.

Alpha60 FASHION & ACCESSORIES
(Map p208; ☑03-9663 3002; www.alpha60.
com.au; 2nd fl, 209 Flinders Lane; ⊙10am-6pm;
☑Flinders St) Melbourne has a reputation
for top-notch retail spaces, but this place is
just showing off. Alpha60's signature store
is hidden within the Hogwartsian chapter
house of St Paul's Cathedral, where fresh,
casual women's clothing is displayed on a
phalanx of mannequins while giant projections of roosters keep watch. There's another
store below at ground level.

Melbournalia GIFTS & SOUVENIRS
(Map p208; ☑03-9663 3751; www.melbournalia.
com.au; 50 Bourke St; ⊙10am-7pm; ☑Parliament)
This is the place to stock up on interesting
souvenirs by more than 100 local designers
– prints featuring city icons, crazy socks and
great books on Melbourne.

Original & Authentic Aboriginal Art ART
(Map p208; ☑03-9663 5133; www.originaland
authenticaboriginalart.com; 90 Bourke St;
⊙10am-6pm; ☑Parliament) For over 20 years
this centrally located gallery has sourced
Indigenous art from the Central and Western Deserts, the Kimberleys and Arnhem
Land. It subscribes to the City of Melbourne's code of practice for Indigenous
art, ensuring authenticity and ethical deal-
ings with artists.

RM Williams CLOTHING
(Map p208; 03-9663 7126; www.rmwilliams.com; Melbourne Central, cnr La Trobe & Swanston Sts; 10am-7pm Sat-Wed, to 9pm Thu & Fri; Melbourne Central) An Aussie icon, even for city slickers, this brand will kit you out in stylish essentials for working the land, including a pair of its famous boots. The Melbourne Central branch occupies the historic brick shot tower at the centre of the complex and has a mini museum inside.

City Hatters HATS
(Map p208; 03-9614 3294; www.cityhatters.com.au; 211 Flinders St; 9am-5pm; Flinders St) Located beside the main entrance to Flinders St station, this evocatively old-fashioned store is the most convenient place to purchase an iconic Akubra hat, a kangaroo-leather sun hat or something a little more unique.

Fitzroy, Collingwood & Abbotsford

★**Third Drawer Down** HOMEWARES
(Map p212; www.thirddrawerdown.com; 93 George St, Fitzroy; 10am-6pm; 86) It all started with its signature tea-towel designs (now found in MoMA in New York) at this 'museum of art souvenirs'. It makes life beautifully unusual by stocking absurdist pieces with a sense of humour as well as high-end art by well-known designers. Giant watermelon stools sit next to Yayoi Kusama's ceramic plates and scarves by Ai Weiwei.

Mud Australia CERAMICS
(Map p212; 03-9419 5161; www.mudaustralia.com; 181 Gertrude St, Fitzroy; 10am-6pm Mon-Fri, to 5pm Sat, noon-5pm Sun; 86) You'll find some of the most aesthetically beautiful – as well as functional – porcelainware at Australian-designed Mud. Coffee mugs, milk pourers, salad bowls and serving plates come in muted pastel colours with a raw matte finish.

Polyester Records MUSIC
(Map p212; 03-9419 5137; www.polyesterrecords.com; 387 Brunswick St, Fitzroy; 10am-8pm Mon-Thu & Sat, to 9pm Fri, 11am-6pm Sun; 11) This popular record store has been selling Melburnians independent music from around the world for decades, and it also has a great range of local stuff. The knowledgeable staff will help you find what you're looking for and can offer great suggestions.

Aesop COSMETICS
(Map p212; 03-9419 8356; www.aesop.com; 242 Gertrude St, Fitzroy; 11am-5pm Sun & Mon, 10am-6pm Tue-Fri, 10am-5pm Sat; 86) This homegrown empire specialises in citrus- and botanical-based aromatic balms, hair masques, scents, cleansers and oils in beautifully simple packaging for both men and women. There are plenty of branches around town (and plenty of opportunities to sample the products in many of Melbourne's cafe bathrooms).

Rose Street Artists' Market MARKET
(Map p212; www.rosestmarket.com.au; 60 Rose St, Fitzroy; 11am-5pm Sat & Sun; 11) One of Melbourne's most popular art-and-craft markets (p234) showcases the best of local designers. Here you'll find up to 70 stalls selling matte silver jewellery, clothing, ceramics and iconic Melbourne screen prints. After shopping, head to the attached Young Blood's Diner (7am to 5pm Wednesday to Sunday) for rooftop cocktails or brunch, or both.

Crumpler FASHION & ACCESSORIES
(Map p212; 03-9417 5338; www.crumpler.com; 87 Smith St, Fitzroy; 10am-6pm Mon-Sat, to 5pm Sun; 86) Crumpler's bike-courier bags – designed by two former couriers looking for a bag they could hold their beer in while cycling home – are what started it all. The brand's durable, practical designs now extend to bags for cameras, laptops and iPads, and can be found around the world. The original messenger bags start at around $150.

Carlton

Readings BOOKS
(Map p216; www.readings.com.au; 309 Lygon St, Carlton; 9am-11pm Mon-Sat, 10am-9pm Sun; Tourist Shuttle, 1, 6) A potter around this defiantly prosperous indie bookshop can occupy an entire afternoon if you're so inclined. There's a dangerously loaded (and good-value) specials table and switched-on, helpful staff. Just next door is its speciality children's store.

Also in the **city centre** (Map p208; 03-8664 7540; www.readings.com.au; State Library, 328 Swanston St; 10am-6pm; Melbourne Central) and **St Kilda** (Map p220; 03-9525 3852; www.readings.com.au/st-kilda; 112 Acland St, St Kilda; 10am-9pm; 3, 16, 96).

South Yarra, Prahran & Windsor

ArtBoy Gallery ART
(Map p218; ☑03-9939 8993; http://artboy gallery.com; 99 Greville St, Prahran; ⊙10am-6pm Mon-Thu, to 5pm Sat, 11am-4pm Sun; ☒6, 72, 78, ☒Prahran) ArtBoy displays the talent of up-and-coming and established Melbourne artists. Artworks are affordable, unique and edgy, ranging from stencil to abstract, pop and photography. Even the gallery's rear roller door is a showcase for local creativity, with a feline-themed aerosol portrait by street artist Silly Sully. To see it, head around the corner onto Porter St and then into Brenchley Pl.

Lunar Store DESIGN
(Map p218; ☑03-9533 7668; www.lunarstore. com.au; 2/127 Greville St, Prahran; ⊙11am-5pm Mon-Wed, 10am-6pm Thu & Fri, 10am-5pm Sat, 11am-4pm Sun; ☒6, 72, 78, ☒Prahran) This adorable space belongs to Jules Unwin, who fills it up with her favourite things. It's a great place to score quirky, offbeat design objects by both local and foreign artisans. Snoop around and you might find anything from Danish earthenware pencil holders to Melbourne-made ceramic necklaces and pooch-themed pouches from LA. Fun, contemporary, yet strangely nostalgic.

Chapel Street Bazaar VINTAGE
(Map p218; ☑03-9529 1727; www.facebook.com/ ChapelStreetBazaar; 217-223 Chapel St, Prahran; ⊙10am-6pm; ☒6, 78, 79, ☒Prahran) Calling this a 'permanent undercover collection of market stalls' won't give you any clue as to what's tucked away here. Bluntly, this old arcade is a sprawling, retro-obsessive riot. Whether it's Italian art glass, modernist furniture, classic Hollywood posters or Noddy eggcups that float your boat, you'll find it here. Warning: prepare to lose all track of time.

Greville Records MUSIC
(Map p218; ☑03-9510 3012; www.greville records.com.au; 152 Greville St, Prahran; ⊙10am-6pm Mon-Thu & Sat, to 7pm Fri, 11am-5pm Sun; ☒78.79, ☒Prahran) One of the last bastions of the 'old' Greville St, this banging music shop has such a loyal following that the great Neil Young invited the owners on stage during a Melbourne concert. The forte here is vinyl, with no shortage of eclectic and limited-edition discs (a super-limited Bob Dylan

WORTH A TRIP

CAMBERWELL MARKET

Filled with secondhand and handcrafted goods, **Camberwell Sunday Market** (www.camberwellsundaymarket.org; Market Pl, Camberwell; ⊙6.30am-12.30pm Sun; ☒Camberwell) is where Melburnians come to offload their unwanted items and where antique hunters come to find them. It's great for discovering preloved (often rarely worn) items of clothing, restocking a bookcase and finding unusual curios.

Live in Sydney 1966 double vinyl has been discovered here...).

ℹ Information

DANGERS & ANNOYANCES
There are occasional reports of alcohol-fuelled violence in some parts of Melbourne's city centre late on weekend nights – particularly in King St.

INTERNET ACCESS
Free wi-fi is available at central city spots such as Federation Sq, Flinders St station, Crown Casino and the State Library. Free wi-fi is now the norm in most midrange accommodation, although you sometimes have to pay in both budget and top-end places. Many cafes also offer free wi-fi.

MEDIA
Key publications are the **Age** (www.theage.com. au) and the tabloid **Herald-Sun** (www.heraldsun. com.au).

MEDICAL SERVICES
If you've been bitten by a snake or spider or have consumed something you think might be poisonous, contact the **Victorian Poisons Information Centre** (☑13 11 26; www.austin.org.au/poisons) for advice.

Hospitals
Royal Children's Hospital (☑03-9345 5522; www.rch.org.au; 50 Flemington Rd, Parkville; ☒57)
Royal Melbourne Hospital (☑03-9342 7000; www.thermh.org.au; 300 Grattan St, Parkville; ☒19, 55, 59)

Medical Clinics
La Trobe St Medical (☑03-9650 0023; Melbourne Central, 211 La Trobe St; ⊙8.30am-5pm Mon-Fri; ☒Melbourne Central)

QV Medical Centre (📞03-9662 2256; www. qvmedical.com.au; L1 QV, 292 Swanston St; ⏱9am-5pm Mon-Sat, 10.30am-5.30pm Sun)

Travel Doctor (TVMC; 📞03-9935 8100; www. traveldoctor.com.au; L2, 393 Little Bourke St; ⏱9am-5pm Mon-Wed & Fri, to 8pm Thu, to 1pm Sat)

Pharmacies

Mulqueeny Midnight Pharmacy (📞03-9510 3977; www.mulqueenypharmacy.com.au/prah ran; 416 High St, Prahran; ⏱9am-midnight; 🚌6)

Priceline (📞03-9663 4747; www.priceline. com.au; Melbourne Central, 300 Lonsdale St; ⏱8am-7pm Mon-Wed, 8am-9pm Thu & Fri, 10am-7pm Sat & Sun)

Tambassis Pharmacy (📞03-9387 8830; cnr Brunswick & Sydney Rds, Brunswick; ⏱8am-midnight; 🚌19)

Victoria Market Pharmacy (📞03-9329 7703; www.victoriamarketpharmacy.com; 523 Elizabeth St; ⏱8am-5.30pm Mon-Fri, 8am-4pm Sat, 9.30am-3.30pm Sun)

POST

Australia Post offers a very reliable service; visit www.auspost.com.au for up-to-date postage rates and the location of post offices.

Melbourne GPO Post Shop (Map p208; 📞13 13 18; www.auspost.com.au; 250 Elizabeth St; ⏱8.30am-5.30pm Mon-Sat; 🚌19, 57, 59)

TOURIST INFORMATION

Melbourne Visitor Centre (Map p208; 📞03-9658 9658; https://whatson.melbourne. vic.gov.au; Federation Sq; ⏱9am-6pm; 📶; 🚊Flinders St) Comprehensive information on Melbourne and regional Victoria, resources for mobility-impaired travellers, and a travel desk for accommodation and tour bookings. There are power sockets for recharging phones too. There's a chance the centre might need to move sometime in 2017 due to construction work nearby.

❶ Getting There & Away

Most travellers to Melbourne arrive via Melbourne Airport, which is well connected to the city by shuttle bus and taxi. There are also interstate trains and buses, a direct boat from Tasmania, and two minor domestic airports nearby.

Flights, cars and tours can be booked online at lonelyplanet.com/bookings.

AIR

Melbourne Airport

Melbourne Airport (MEL; 📞03-9297 1600; www.melbourneairport.com.au; Departure Rd, Tullamarine) is the city's only international and main domestic airport, located 22km northwest of the city centre in Tullamarine. It has all of the facilities you'd expect from a major airport,

including **Baggage Storage** (📞03-9338 3119; www.baggagestorage.com.au; Terminal 2, International Arrivals, Melbourne Airport; per 24hr $16; ⏱5am-12.30am).

Dozens of airlines fly here from destinations in the South Pacific, Asia, the Middle East and the Americas. The main domestic airlines are **Qantas** (📞13 11 31; www.qantas.com), **Jetstar** (📞131 538; www.jetstar.com), **Virgin Australia** (📞13 67 89; www.virginaustralia.com), **Tigerair** (📞1300 174 266; www.tigerair.com) and **Regional Express** (Rex; 📞131 713; www. rex.com.au).

Avalon Airport

Jetstar (p236) flights to and from Sydney and Brisbane use **Avalon Airport** (📞03-5227 9100; www.avalonairport.com.au; 80 Beach Rd, Lara), around 55km southwest of Melbourne's city centre.

Essendon Airport

Once Melbourne's main international airport, **Essendon Airport** (MEB; 📞03-9948 9400; www.essendonairport.com.au; 7 English St, Essendon Fields; 🚌59) is only 11km north of the city centre. Now only small operators fly from here to domestic destinations.

Free Spirit Airlines (📞03-9379 6122; www. freespiritairlines.com.au) flies to/from Merimbula and Burnie.

Jetgo (📞1300 328 000; www.jetgo.com) flies to/from to Port Macquarie, Dubbo and Brisbane.

Sharp Airlines (📞1300 556 694; www.sharp airlines.com) flies to/from Flinders Island, King Island, Portland and Warrnambool.

BOAT

The **Spirit of Tasmania** (Map p204; 📞1800 634 906, 03-6419 9320; www.spiritoftasmania.com. au; Station Pier, Port Melbourne; adult/car 1 way from $99/188) ferry crosses Bass Strait from Melbourne to Devonport, Tasmania, at least nightly; there are also day sailings during peak season. The crossing takes 10 hours.

BUS

The main terminus for long-distance buses is within the northern half of Southern Cross station. Here you'll find counters for all the main bus companies, along with **luggage lockers** (📞03-9619 2588; www.southerncrossstation. net.au; Southern Cross station, 99 Spencer St; per 24hr $10-16; ⏱during train-service hours).

Firefly (Map p208; 📞1300 730 740; www. fireflyexpress.com.au; Southern Cross station, 99 Spencer St) Overnight coaches to/from Sydney ($65, 12 hours), Wagga Wagga ($65, 5¾ hours), Albury ($65, 3½ hours), Ballarat ($50, 1¾ hours) and Adelaide ($60, 9¾ hours).

Greyhound (Map p208; ☑1300 473 946; www. greyhound.com.au) Coaches to Albury ($55, 3½ hours), Wagga Wagga ($69, 6¼ hours), Gundagai ($75, 7¼ hours), Yass ($85, 8¼ hours) and Canberra ($88, eight hours).

V/Line (☑1800 800 007; www.vline.com.au) Services destinations within Victoria, including Korumburra ($15, two hours), Mansfield ($29, three hours) and Echuca ($29, three hours).

CAR & MOTORCYCLE

The most direct (and boring) route between Melbourne and Sydney is the Hume Hwy (870km). The Princes Hwy hugs the coast and is much more scenic but much longer (1040km). Likewise, the main route to/from Adelaide is the Western/Dukes Hwy (730km), but this misses out on the Great Ocean Road.

TRAIN

Southern Cross station is the terminus for inter-city and interstate trains.

Great Southern Rail (☑1800 703 357; www. greatsouthernrail.com.au) Runs the *Overland* between Melbourne and Adelaide ($149, 10½ hours, twice weekly).

NSW TrainLink (☑13 22 32; www.nswtrainlink. info) Twice-daily services to/from Sydney ($92, 11½ hours) via Benalla ($24, 2¼ hours), Wanga-ratta ($34, 2½ hours), Albury ($47, 3¼ hours) and Wagga Wagga ($63, 4½ hours).

V/Line (p237) Operates the Victorian train and bus networks; direct services include Geelong ($9, one hour), Warrnambool ($36, 3¾ hours), Ballarat ($15, 1½ hours), Bendigo ($22, two hours) and Albury ($38, four hours).

ⓘ Getting Around

TO/FROM THE AIRPORT

Melbourne Airport The **SkyBus** (Map p208; ☑1300 759 287; www.skybus.com.au; South-ern Cross station, 99 Spencer St; adult/child $18/9; ⓢ Southern Cross) departs regularly and connects the airport to Southern Cross station 24 hours a day. There are also services to other parts of Melbourne, including St Kilda.

Southern Cross station Long-distance trains and buses arrive at this large station on the Docklands side of the city centre. From here it's easy to connect to metropolitan trains, buses and trams.

Avalon Airport Near the neighbouring city of Geelong, but connected to Melbourne's South-ern Cross station by **Sita Coaches** (☑03-9689 7999; www.skybus.com.au; adult/child $22/10).

BICYCLE

➡ Cycling maps and information are available from the **Melbourne Visitor Centre** (p236)

and **Bicycle Network** (☑03-8376 8888; www. bv.com.au).

➡ Helmets are compulsory.

➡ Conventional bikes can be taken on trains (but not the first carriage), but only folding bikes are allowed on trams or buses. Front bike racks are being trialled on some bus routes.

➡ **Melbourne Bike Share** (☑1300 711 590; www.melbournebikeshare.com.au; subscription day/week $3/8) is an automated, self-service bike-share system; look out for the 52 bright-blue stations scattered around the city, central suburbs and St Kilda. They're ideal for short trips as the first half-hour of use is free once you pay for your subscription (which requires a credit card and $50 security deposit). Some but not all bikes have safety helmets left with them; otherwise helmets are available with a $5 subsidy from 7-Eleven, IGA and bike stores around the city.

➡ For bike hire, try **Humble Vintage** (☑0424 619 262; www.thehumblevintage.com; 2hr/day/week $25/35/90) or **Rentabike** (p215).

CAR & MOTORCYCLE

Driving in Melbourne presents its own set of challenges, due to the need to share the road with trams.

➡ Where the trams run along the centre of the road, drivers cannot pass them once they indicate that they're stopping, as passengers board and alight from the street.

➡ In the city centre many intersections are marked 'right turn from left only'. This is the counter-intuitive 'hook turn', devised so as not to block trams or other cars. Right-turning driv-ers are required to move into the far left of the intersection and then turn right once the lights on that side of the intersection turn green. See www.vicroads.vic.gov.au for further details.

Car Hire

Most car and campervan hire places have offices at Melbourne Airport and in the city or central suburbs.

Aussie Campervans (☑03-9317 4991; www. aussiecampervans.com)

Avis (☑03-8855 5333; www.avis.com.au)

Britz Australia (☑1300 738 087; www.britz. com.au)

Budget (☑1300 362 848; www.budget.com.au)

Europcar (☑1300 131 390; www.europcar. com.au)

Hertz (☑03-9663 6244; www.hertz.com.au)

Rent a Bomb (☑03-9428 0088; www.rent abomb.com.au; 452 Bridge Rd, Richmond; ☐48, 75)

Thrifty (☑1300 367 227; www.thrifty.com.au)

Travellers Autobarn (☑1800 674 374; www. travellers-autobarn.com.au) Hires and sells vehicles.

Car Sharing

Car-sharing companies that operate in Melbourne include **Flexi Car** (☑ 1300 363 780; www.flexicar. com.au), **Go Get** (☑ 1300 769 389; www.goget. com.au) and **Green Share Car** (☑ 1300 575 878; www.greensharecar.com.au). You rent the cars by the hour (from $9) or the day (from $55) and prices include petrol. Companies vary in terms of joining fees ($12 to $70) and how they charge (insurance fees, per hour and per kilometre). The cars are parked in and around the city centre and inner suburbs in designated 'car share' spots.

Parking

Parking inspectors are particularly vigilant in the city centre. Most of the street parking is metered and it's more likely than not that you'll be fined if you overstay your metered time. Also keep an eye out for 'clearway' zones (prohibited kerb-side parking indicated by signs), which can result in sizeable fines. There are plenty of parking garages in the city; rates vary. Motorcyclists are allowed to park on the footpath except in some parts of the city centre where there are signs.

Toll Roads

Both drivers and motorcyclists will need to purchase a Melbourne Pass ($5.50 start-up fee, plus tolls and a 75c vehicle-matching fee per trip) if they're planning on using one of the two toll roads: **CityLink** (☑ 13 26 29; www.citylink.com.au), from Tullamarine Airport to the city and eastern suburbs, or **EastLink** (☑ 03-9955 1400; www. eastlink.com.au), which runs from Ringwood to Frankston. Pay online or via phone – but pay within three days of using the toll road to avoid a fine.

Rental cars are sometimes set up for automatic toll payments; check when you hire.

PUBLIC TRANSPORT
Bus

Melbourne has an extensive bus network, with over 300 routes covering all the places that the trains and trams don't go. Most routes run from 6am to 9pm weekdays, 8am to 9pm Saturdays and 9am to 9pm Sundays. Night Bus services operate after midnight on weekends to many suburbs.

You'll need a myki card to use the buses; **PTV** has timetables, maps and a journey planner on its website.

Train

Flinders St station is the main city hub for Melbourne's 17 train lines. Trains start around 5am weekdays, run until midnight Sunday to Thursday, and all night on Friday and Saturday nights. Trains generally run every 10-20 minutes during the day and every 20-30 minutes in the evening.

Payment is via myki card; **PTV** has timetables, maps and a journey planner on its website.

Tram

Trams are intertwined with the Melbourne identity and an extensive network covers the city. They run roughly every 10 minutes during the day (more frequently in peak periods), and every 20 minutes in the evening. Services run until midnight Sunday to Thursday, 1am Friday and Saturday, and six lines run all night on weekends.

The entire city centre is a free tram zone. The zone is signposted on tram stops, with messages broadcast on board when you're nearing its edge to warn you that you should either hop off or pay with a myki card. Note that there's no need to 'touch off' your myki on the trams, as all zone 1 journeys are charged at the same rate – although it won't matter if you do.

PTV has timetables, maps and a journey planner on their website.

Tickets & Passes

Melbourne's buses, trams and trains use **myki**, a 'touch on, touch off' travel-pass system. It's not particularly convenient for short-term visitors as it requires you to purchase a $6 plastic myki card and then put credit on it before you travel.

Travellers should consider buying a **myki Explore**r ($15), which includes the card, one day's travel and discounts on various sights; it's available from SkyBus terminals, PTV hubs, the **Melbourne Visitor Centre** (p236) and some hotels. Otherwise, standard myki cards can be purchased at 7-Elevens or newsagents.

The myki can be topped up at 7-Eleven stores, machines at most train stations and at some tram stops in the city centre; online top-ups can take some time to process. You can either top up with pay-as-you-go **myki Money** or purchase a seven-day unlimited **myki Pass** ($41); if you're staying more than 28 days, longer passes are available.

For travel within metropolitan Melbourne (zones 1 and 2), the pay-as-you-go fare is $4.10 for two hours, or capped at $8.20 for the day ($6 on weekends). There are large fines for travelling without having touched on a valid myki card; ticket inspectors are vigilant and unforgiving.

For more information, see **PTV** (Public Transport Victoria; ☑ 1800 800 007; www.ptv.vic. gov.au).

TAXI

Melbourne's taxis are metered and require an estimated prepaid fare when hailed between 10pm and 5am (you may need to pay more or get a refund depending on the final fare). Toll charges are added to fares. Two of the largest taxi companies are **Silver Top** (☑ 131 008; www.silvertop.com.au) and **13 Cabs** (☑ 13 22 27; www.13cabs.com.au). **Uber** (www.uber. com) also operates in Melbourne.

MORNINGTON PENINSULA

The Mornington Peninsula – the boot-shaped area of land between Port Phillip Bay and Western Port Bay – has been Melbourne's summer playground since the 1870s, when paddle steamers ran down to Portsea. Today, much of the interior farming land has been replaced by vineyards and orchards – foodies love the peninsula, where a winery lunch is a real highlight – but it still retains lovely stands of native bushland.

The calm 'front beaches' are on the Port Phillip Bay side, where families holiday at bayside towns from Mornington to Sorrento. The rugged ocean 'back beaches' face Bass Strait and are easily reached from Portsea, Sorrento and Rye; there are stunning walks along this coastal strip, part of the Mornington Peninsula National Park.

The bay heads are so close that it's just a short hop by ferry across from Sorrento to Queenscliff on the Bellarine Peninsula.

ⓘ Information

Peninsula Visitor Information Centre
(☑1800 804 009, 03-5987 3078; www.visit morningtonpeninsula.org; 359h Nepean Hwy, Dromana; ☺9am-5pm) The visitor information centres along the peninsula can book accommodation and tours, and stock an abundance of brochures.

ⓘ Getting There & Away

The fastest way to the Mornington Peninsula is via the tollway Eastlink (M3) and exit at the Mornington Peninsula Fwy (M11) via Peninsula Link. The Point Nepean Rd (B110) also feeds into the Mornington Peninsula Fwy (M11), the main peninsula access. Alternately, exit the Moorooduc Hwy to Mornington and take the coast road around Port Phillip Bay.

Frequent Metlink trains run from Melbourne to Frankston, Hastings and Stony Point.

Inter Island Ferries (☑03-9585 5730; www.interislandferries.com.au; adult/child/bicycle return $26/12/8) Runs between Stony Point and Cowes via French Island.

Queenscliff–Sorrento Car & Passenger Ferries (☑03-5257 4500; www.searoad.com. au; foot passenger 1 way adult/child $11/8, driver & car 1 way/return $64/118; ☺hourly 7am-6pm, to 7pm Jan & long weekends) Sails between Sorrento and Queenscliff, enabling you to cross Port Phillip Bay by car or bicycle.

Ventura Bus Lines (☑03-9786 7088; www.venturabus.com.au) Offers public transport across the peninsula.

Sorrento & Portsea

Historic Sorrento is the standout town on the Mornington Peninsula for its beautiful limestone buildings, ocean and bay beaches, and buzzing seaside summer atmosphere. This was the site of Victoria's first official European settlement, established by an expedition of convicts, marines, civil officers and free settlers who arrived from England in 1803. The last village on the peninsula, posh Portsea is a bit like Victoria's equivalent of the Hamptons, where many of Melbourne's wealthiest families have built seaside mansions. Of most interest for tourists are the dive shops here offering a number of tours – from wreck dives and snorkelling to sea kayak trips to visit seals and dolphins – as well as nearby Point Nepean National Park.

◎ Sights & Activities

The calm bay beach is good for families and you can hire **paddle boards** on the foreshore. At low tide, the rock pool at the back beach is a safe spot for adults and children to swim and snorkel, and the surf beach is patrolled in summer. The 10-minute climb up to **Coppins Lookout** offers good views.

★**Bayplay**   DIVING, WATER SPORTS
(☑03-5984 0888; www.bayplay.com.au; 3755 Pt Nepean Rd; dives $68-130) A must for anyone wanting to get out on the water is this dive operator that offers PADI courses as well as guided diving and snorkelling trips to see a heap of marine life. However, it's most popular for its **sea-kayaking tours** (adult/child $99/88), where you can regularly spot dolphins and seals. They also do stand-up paddleboard tours (two hours $75), sailing trips (from $99) and hire out kayaks.

Moonraker Charters   WILDLIFE
(☑03-5984 4211; www.moonrakercharters.com.au; Esplanade Rd; sightseeing from $45, dolphin & seal swimming from $135) Operates dolphin- and seal-swimming tours from Sorrento Pier.

🛏 Sleeping

Sorrento Foreshore Camping Ground   CAMPGROUND $
(☑03-5950 1011; www.mornpen.vic.gov.au/activities/camping; Nepean Hwy; unpowered/powered sites $26/40, peak season $41/48; ☺Oct-May)

WORTH A TRIP

MORNINGTON PENINSULA REGIONAL GALLERY

The outstanding **Mornington Peninsula Regional Gallery** (MPRG; 03-5975 4395; http://mprg.mornpen. vic.gov.au; Dunns Rd; adult/child $4/free; 10am-5pm Tue-Sun) has changing exhibitions and a permanent collection of modern and contemporary Australian prints and paintings, representing the likes of Boyd, Tucker and Whiteley. There are free guided tours at 3pm on Wednesday, Saturday and Sunday.

Hilly, bush-clad sites between the bay beach and the main road into Sorrento.

Hotel Sorrento   HOTEL $$
(03-5984 8000; www.hotelsorrento.com.au; 5-15 Hotham Rd, Sorrento; r weekdays/weekends incl breakfast from $170/210;) The legendary Hotel Sorrento trades on its famous name and has a swag of accommodation. Its lovely 'On the Hill' double and family apartments have airy living spaces, spacious bathrooms and private balconies. Its pub has fabulous water views and is a good spot for a drink.

✕ Eating & Drinking

All Smiles   MODERN AUSTRALIAN $$
(03-5984 5551; www.allsmiles.com.au/morning ton-peninsula; 250 Ocean Beach Rd; mains $22-26; 9.30am-2.30pm Wed-Sun) Literally on the Sorrento back beach, the menu here is decent enough with pizza, fish and chips, and calamari salad, but it's really all about the view. The Sunday buffet breakfasts (adult/child $20/12) are a great way to treat yourself.

Acquolina Ristorante   ITALIAN $$
(03-5984 0811; 26 Ocean Beach Rd; mains $25-38; 6-10pm Wed-Mon Oct-Nov & Mar-May, daily in summer) Acquolina set the bar when it opened in Sorrento with its authentic northern-Italian fare. This is hearty, simple food – handmade pasta and ravioli dishes matched with wines sourced first-hand from Italy, grappa and homemade (utterly irresistible) tiramisu.

Cakes & Ale Bistro   FRENCH $$$
(03-5984 4995; www.cakes-and-ale.com.au; 100-102 Ocean Beach Rd; mains $29-45; noon-9pm Mon-Fri, 9am-9pm Sat & Sun) Offering some much needed class on Sorrento's main street is this smart restaurant doing seasonal produce sourced from around Victoria. Its attractive space is fitted out with plants, polished floors and distressed walls, and has a French-inspired menu of fisherman's pot pie, confit Milawa duck leg and roasted spatchcock. It does breakfasts on weekends, with quality coffee by **Little Rebel** (0418 121 467; www.littlerebel.com.au; 22 Collins Rd, Dromana; 8am-2pm Mon-Fri).

Portsea Hotel   PUB
(03-5984 2213; www.portseahotel.com.au; 3746 Point Nepean Rd;) Portsea's pulse is the sprawling, half-timber Portsea Hotel (c 1876), an enormous pub with a great lawn and terrace area looking out over the bay and historic pier. It's where the beautiful people come to be seen (especially come polo season), with regular events and DJs over summer. There's an excellent bistro (mains $24 to $27) and old-style **accommodation** (03-5984 2213; www.portsea hotel.com.au; 3746 Point Nepean Rd; s/d without bathroom from $75/145, s/d with bathroom from $135/180;).

ℹ Information

Sorrento Beach Visitors Centre (03 5984 1478; www.visitmorningtonpeninsula.org; cnr Ocean Beach Rd & George St; 10am-4pm) The visitors centre is on the main drag in town, with a whopping selection of brochures and an after-hours info touch screen.

ℹ Getting There & Away

Sorrento and Portsea are accessed from Melbourne, just under a two-hour drive, along Eastlink (M3) and Mornington Peninsula Freeway (M11). By public transport, from Melbourne take the train to Frankston station from where you can transfer to bus 788 to Sorrento and Portsea. Otherwise, the **ferry** (p239) is a great way to get across to Queenscliff, from where you can explore the Bellarine Peninsula and Great Ocean Road.

Point Nepean National Park

At the peninsula's western tip is the scenic **Point Nepean National Park** (13 19 63; www.parkweb.vic.gov.au; Point Nepean Rd; ⊘8am-5pm), a historic site that played an important role as Australia's defence site from the 1880s to 1945. Remarkably, it was from here where the first Allied shots were fired in both WWI and WWII.

The national park is known for its stunning coastal scenery and features a number of lovely walks and cycling paths. A large section of the park is a former range area and still out of bounds due to unexploded ordnance.

You can visit its **Fort Nepean**, as well at the fascinating historic **Quarantine Station precinct**. Dating from 1852, this complex was used to quarantine passengers right until 1979; today it's a museum with interesting displays detailing its history, along with some 50 heritage buildings to explore, including the Hospital and Wash House.

ℹ Information

Point Nepean Visitor Information Centre (⌂ 03-8427 2099; www.parkweb.vic.gov.au; Ochiltree Rd; ⊘10am-5pm) Will give you info on the park, hires bikes for $30.10 per day, as well as self-guided walking maps and iPod audio tours ($13.90). From Portsea you can walk or cycle to the point (12km return), or take the shuttle bus (adult/child return $10/7.50), a hop-on, hop-off bus service that departs the visitor centre every 30 minutes from 10.30am to 4pm.

ℹ Getting There & Away

Point Nepean National Park is at the far western tip of the Mornington Peninsula, facing directly across from Queenscliff and 112km from Melbourne. It's located about 2km west of Portsea.

To get to the national park by public transport take bus 788 from Frankston to the end of the line at Portsea, from where it's a 1km walk to the visitor centre.

MORNINGTON PENINSULA WINERIES

Most of the peninsula's wineries are in the hills between Red Hill and Merricks, and most have excellent cafes or restaurants attached. Several companies offer winery tours – ask at the visitor centre (p239). For an overview, check out **Mornington Peninsula Wineries & Region** (www.mpva.com.au). Wineries to consider include the following:

Montalto (⌂03-5989 8412; www.montalto.com.au; 33 Shoreham Rd, Red Hill South; ⊘cellar door & cafe 11am-5pm, restaurant noon-3pm, 6.30-11pm Fri & Sat) One of the Peninsula's best winery restaurants, renowned for its pinot noir and chardonnay. There's also the piazza and garden cafe for casual dining, as well as a beguiling sculpture garden.

Pier 10 (⌂03-5989 8849; www.pier10wine.com.au; 10 Shoreham Rd; mains $16-37; ⊘cellar door 11am-5pm, restaurant noon-2.30pm Thu-Sun, 6pm-late Fri & Sat) This scenic, boutique winery is within a converted tin shed that houses both its cellar door and bistro restaurant.

Port Phillip Estate (⌂03-5989 4444; www.portphillipestate.com.au; 263 Red Hill Rd, Red Hill South; 2-/3-course meal from $68/85, cellar door mains $15-22; ⊘cellar door 11am-5pm, restaurant noon-3pm Wed-Sun, 6.30-9pm Fri & Sat) A stunning winery inside a building that resembles a Bond villain's lair. It has one of the peninsula's best restaurants with stunning views, a gastronomic menu or lighter meals, and wine tastings ($5).

Red Hill Estate (⌂03-5931 0177; www.redhillestate.com.au; 53 Shoreham Rd, Red Hill South; ⊘cellar door 11am-5pm, restaurant noon-5pm, 6-9pm Sat) Sample maritime cool climate pinots and chardonnays or dine at the renowned Max's Restaurant, which in 2017 was about to undergo major redevelopment.

Ten Minutes By Tractor (⌂03-5989 6080; www.tenminutesbytractor.com.au; 1333 Mornington-Flinders Rd, Main Ridge; 5-/8-course tasting menu $114/144, 2-/3-course meal $69/92; ⊘cellar door 11am-5pm, restaurant noon-3pm Wed-Sun, 6.30-9pm Thu-Sat) This is one of regional Victoria's best restaurants and you won't find a better wine list on the Peninsula. The unusual name comes from the three vineyards, which are each 10 minutes apart by tractor.

T'Gallant (⌂03-5931 1300; www.tgallant.com.au; 1385 Mornington-Flinders Rd, Main Ridge; mains $16-32; ⊘cellar door 9am-5pm, restaurant 11.30am-3pm Mon-Fri, 11am-4pm Sat & Sun) A rustic trattoria with delicious wood-fired pizzas, pork sausages and homemade lasagne. Its cellar door offers free tastings of its luscious pinot gris and prosecco.

Mornington Peninsula National Park

Stretching from Portsea on the sliver of coastline to Cape Schanck and inland to the Greens Bush area, this national park showcases the peninsula's most beautiful and rugged ocean beaches. Along here are the cliffs, bluffs and crashing surf beaches of **Portsea, Sorrento, Blairgowrie, Rye, St Andrews, Gunnamatta** and **Cape Schanck**.

This is spectacular coastal scenery – well known to the surfers, hikers and fisherfolk who have their secret spots – and it's possible to walk all the way from Portsea to Cape Schanck (26km, eight hours).

Swimming and surfing is dangerous at these beaches: the undertow and rips can be severe, and drownings continue to occur. Swim only between the flags at Gunnamatta and Portsea during summer.

PHILLIP ISLAND

POP 9406

Famous for the Penguin Parade and Motorcycle Grand Prix racing circuit, Phillip Island attracts a curious mix of surfers, petrolheads and international tourists making a beeline for those little penguins.

At its heart, Phillip Island is still a farming community, but nature has conspired to turn it into one of Victoria's most popular tourist destinations. Apart from the nightly waddling of the penguins, there's a large seal colony, abundant bird life and fauna. The rugged south coast has some fabulous surf beaches, a swag of family attractions and plenty of accommodation. Visit in winter, though, and you'll find a very quiet place where the local population of farmers, surfers and hippies go about their business.

The Boonwurrung people are the traditional inhabitants of the island, though what they'd have made of coachloads of Penguin Parade tourists and biker gangs making their way over the San Remo bridge is anyone's guess.

◎ Sights

★**Nobbies Centre & Boardwalk** VIEWPOINT
(☑03-5951 2800; Summerlands) FREE At the island's southwestern tip is this dramatic viewpoint for the **Nobbies** offshore rock formations. Here the gigantic cafe and souvenir shop known as the **Nobbies Centre** has incredible ocean vistas and the multimedia Antarctic Journey. In front of the centre, a **boardwalk** winds down to vantage points of the formations, as well the blow hole, and beyond to the Seal Rocks – inhabited by Australia's largest fur-seal colony. There are coin-operated binoculars, but bring your own if you have them.

★**Penguin Parade** WILDLIFE RESERVE
(☑03-5951 2800; www.penguins.org.au; 1019 Ventnor Rd, Summerland Beach; admission from adult/child/family $25.10/12.50/62.70, underground viewing $60/30/150; ☺9.30am-dusk, penguins arrive at sunset) The Penguin Parade attracts more than half-a-million visitors annually to see the little penguins (*Eudyptula minor*), the world's smallest, and probably cutest of their kind. The main penguin complex includes concrete amphitheatres that hold up to 3800 spectators who come to see the little fellas just after sunset as they waddle from the sea to their land-based nests. There's also an underground viewing section, premium seats and VIP platforms for those wanting prime views; come summer book well in advance.

Antarctic Journey OBSERVATORY, THEATRE
(☑03-5951 2800; www.penguins.org.au/attractions/recreational-areas/the-nobbies; 1320 Ventnor Rd, Nobbies Centre, Summerlands; adult/child/family $18/9/45; ☺9am-5pm) On the southwest tip of the island is this cutting-edge multimedia exhibition space that spotlights the shared waters between here and Antarctica. Its interactive displays are highly informative, with cool augmented reality features. It's located in the Nobbies Centre (p242), a five-minute drive from the Penguin Parade, so aim to visit in mid afternoon if you're seeing the penguins.

Koala Conservation Centre ZOO
(☑03-5951 2800; www.penguins.org.au; 1810 Phillip Island Rd, Cowes; adult/child/family $12.50/6.25/31.25; ☺10am-5pm, extended hrs in summer) While in the wild there are only 20 to 30 of these furry marsupials left on the island, here at the Koala Conservation Centre you're guaranteed to see them. Whether from the treetop boardwalks or trails along the ground, you'll spot them chewing on eucalyptus leaves or dozing away – they sleep about 20 hours a day!

🏃 Activities

Phillip Island Grand
Prix Circuit
ADVENTURE SPORTS

(☑03-5952 9400; Back Beach Rd) Even when the motorbikes aren't racing, petrolheads love the Grand Prix Motor Racing Circuit. The visitor centre runs **guided circuit tours** (☑03-5952 9400; www.phillipislandcircuit.com.au; Back Beach Rd; 1hr tour adult/child/family $25/15/60; ⊙tours 2pm), or check out the **History of Motorsport Museum** (☑03-5952 9400; www.phillipislandcircuit.com.au; Back Beach Rd; adult/child/family $17.50/8.50/42; ⊙9am-5.30pm). The more adventurous can cut laps of the track with a racing driver in hotted-up V8s ($360; bookings essential). Drive yourself in a go-kart around a scale replica of the track with **Phillip Island Circuit Go Karts** (☑03-5952 9400; www.phillipislandcircuit.com.au; Back Beach Rd; per 10-/20-/30-min $35/60/80; ⊙9am-5.30pm, longer hr in summer).

👉 Tours

Wild Ocean Eco Boat
WILDLIFE WATCHING

(☑03-5951 2800; www.penguins.org.au; Cowes or Rhyll Jetty; per person adult/child/family Adventure Tour $85/65/235, Island Discovery $130/75/345, Shearwater Sunset $65/49/179; ⊙Adventure Tour 3pm, Island Discovery 11am Dec-Apr, Shearwater Sunset 7.15-8.30pm Nov-Apr) These boat tours give you the option of visiting various sights around the island: the Australian fur seal colony at Seal Rocks; the scenic coastline of dramatic rock formations; or sunset tours to see shearwaters return to their clifftop nests.

Go West
TOURS

(☑03-9485 5290; www.gowest.com.au; tour $135) One-day tour from Melbourne that includes entry to the Penguin Parade, lunch, wildlife encounters and wine-tasting. It has iPod commentary in several languages and wi-fi on the bus.

🎉 Festivals & Events

Australian Motorcycle Grand Prix
SPORTS

(☑1800 100 030; www.motogp.com.au) The island's biggest event is the Australian Motorcycle Grand Prix, one of the most scenic circuits on the MotoGP international calendar. Its three days of action are usually held in October, when the the island's population jumps from 8000 people to over 150,000.

🛏 Sleeping

⭐Island Accommodation YHA
HOSTEL $

(☑03-5956 6123; www.theislandaccommodation.com.au; 10-12 Phillip Island Rd, Newhaven; dm $27-50, d $99-155; @🛜) 🚲 This large purpose-built backpackers has huge identical living areas on each floor, complete with table tennis, PlayStations and cosy fireplaces for winter. Its rooftop deck has terrific views and its eco-credentials are excellent. Cheapest dorms sleep 12 and doubles are motel-standard. They have bike hire (per day $20), with the cycle path out front leading all the way to Cowes.

Cowes Caravan Park
CARAVAN PARK $

(☑03-5952 2211; www.cowescaravanpark.com.au; 164 Church St, Cowes; campsites from $40, cabins from $90-130; ❄🛜) The place for beach-side camping is this park that offers a range of campsites and en-suite cabins – the better ones have air-con and beach views. It's 1km from Cowes.

Phillip Island Glamping
TENTED CAMP $$

(☑0404 258 205; www.phillipislandglamping.com.au; d tent hire weekday/weekend from $120/140) A different kind of arrangement to the norm, here you book your camp site (choosing from any of the island's campgrounds), and the staff sets up your bell tent. It'll be ready to go upon your arrival, equipped with mattress, bedding, towels, heater, digital radio, table and chairs, esky and full cooking utensils. Once you're done, they'll clean it all up again – lazy camping at its best.

⭐Clifftop
BOUTIQUE HOTEL $$$

(☑03-5952 1033; www.clifftop.com.au; 1 Marlin St, Smiths Beach; d $235-290; ❄🛜) It's hard to imagine a better location for your island stay than perched above Smiths Beach. Of the seven luxurious suites here, the top four have ocean views and private balconies, while the downstairs rooms open onto gardens – all have fluffy beds and slick contemporary decor.

⭐Glen Isla House
BOUTIQUE HOTEL $$$

(☑03-5952 1882; www.glenisla.com; 230 Church St, Cowes; d/ste from $255/355; ❄🛜) This brilliant boutique hotel is one of the best addresses on the island. Ensconced in a renovated 1870 homestead and outbuildings, Glen Isla is all about understated, old-world luxury with modern touches such as huge plasma TVs. It has 2 acres of lovely gardens and is only a five-minute walk to the beach. No children under 12.

✖ Eating

BEANd
CAFE $

(☏ 0407 717 588; www.beand.com.au; 157 Marine Pde, Shop 4; breakfast $8-15; ⏱ 7am-4pm Thu-Tue) At the bridge heading into Phillip Island is this micro-coffee roaster that does a top-notch brew, using single-origin beans sourced from around Africa, Asia and Latin America. It's a vibrant, friendly little cafe, with all its coffee roasted onsite and prepared as pour overs, aeropress and espresso. All-day breakfasts and burgers for lunch.

Cape Kitchen
MODERN AUSTRALIAN $$

(☏ 03-5956 7200; www.thecapekitchen.com.au; 1215 Phillip Island Rd, Newhaven; breakfast from $19, lunch $27-48; ⏱ 8.30am-4.30pm Fri-Mon) Grab a window seat to take in all-encompassing ocean vistas while enjoying delicious breakfasts such as house-smoked salmon with scrambled eggs and sourdough. For lunch there's the likes of charcoal trout, red-curry Gippsland mussels or a roasted South Gippsland lamb shoulder to share.

❶ Information

Phillip Island Visitor Information Centre

(☏ 1300 366 422; www.visitphillipisland.com; 895 Phillip Island Tourist Rd, Newhaven; ⏱ 9am-5pm, to 6pm school holidays; 🛜) The main visitor centre on the island has a wall of brochures and maps. It sells tickets to the penguin parade, and sight packages that bring healthy discounts. It also offers a super-helpful accommodation booking service and has free wi-fi.

Cowes Visitor Information Centre (☏ 1300 366 422; www.visitphillipisland.com; cnr Thompson & Church Sts, Cowes; ⏱ 9am-5pm) An alternative to the info centre in Newhaven.

❶ Getting There & Away

About 140km from Melbourne by car, Phillip Island can only be accessed by crossing the bridge between San Remo and Newhaven. From Melbourne take the Monash Fwy (M1) and exit at Pakenham, joining the South Gippsland Hwy at Koo Wee Rup.

If you're on foot or bicycle, you can get here by ferry from Stony Point to Cowes.

Once on the island it's easy and quick to get around by car or bike – it's just a 15-minute drive from Cowes to the Penguin Parade or Grand Prix circuit.

By public transport you'll need to get a combination of train and bus to Phillip Island. V/Line runs around eight trips a day from Melbourne's Southern Cross Station to Cowes via Koo Wee Rup ($14.40, 2½ hours) or a longer journey via Dandenong (3½ hours).

Inter Island Ferries (www.interislandferries. com.au; Cowes Jetty; one-way adult/child $13/6; ⏱ departures 8.30am-8.15pm Mon-Thu, to 5.30pm Sat & Sun) Runs between Stony Point on the Mornington Peninsula and Cowes via French Island (45 minutes). There are three sailings Saturday to Thursday, and four on Fridays.

THE GREAT OCEAN ROAD

The Great Ocean Road (B100) is one of Australia's most famous road-touring routes. It takes travellers past world-class surfing breaks, through pockets of rainforest and calm seaside towns, and under koala-filled tree canopies. It shows off sheer limestone cliffs, dairy farms and heathlands, and gets you up close and personal with the crashing waves of the Southern Ocean.

WALKING THE GREAT OCEAN ROAD

The superb multiday **Great Ocean Walk** (www.greatoceanwalk.com.au) starts at Apollo Bay and runs all the way to the Twelve Apostles. It takes you through changing landscapes along spectacular clifftops, deserted beaches and forested Otway National Park.

It's possible to start at one point and arrange a pickup at another (public transport options are few and far between). You can do shorter walks or the whole 104km trek over eight days. Designated camp sites are spread along the Great Ocean Walk catering for registered walkers only; bring cooking equipment and tents (no fires allowed). Otherwise there are plenty of comfortable accommodation options from luxury lodges to caravan parks. Check out the helpful FAQ page on the website for all the info.

Walk 91 (☏ 03-5237 1189; www.walk91.com.au; 157-159 Great Ocean Rd, Apollo Bay; 3 day/4 night guided walks per person $800) can arrange your itinerary, transport and equipment hire, and can shuttle your backpack to your destination.

Hunt out the isolated beaches and lighthouses in between the towns and the thick eucalyptus forests in the Otway hinterlands to really escape the crowds. Rather than heading straight to the Great Ocean Road, a fork in the road at Geelong can take you the long, leisurely way there, through the Bellarine Peninsula with visits to charming Queenscliff and wineries en route.

Day-tripping tourists from Melbourne rush in and out of the area in less than 12 hours but, in a perfect world, you'd spend at least a week here.

Geelong

POP 210,875

As Victoria's second-largest city, Geelong is a proud town with an interesting history and pockets of charm. While Melburnians love to deride their little cousin as a boring backwater, in reality few of the knockers have veered off its main thoroughfare enough to really know what makes the town tick. Geelong's new bypass means travellers can skip the city and head straight to the Great Ocean Road; however, there are lots of reasons to make a stop here.

It's centred around the sparkling Corio Bay waterfront and the city centre, where heritage buildings from the boom days of the gold rush-era and thriving wool industry have now been converted into swanky restaurants and bars. It's also a footy-mad town, passionate about its home-town AFL team, the Cats.

◉ Sights

Geelong Waterfront   WATERFRONT
(Beach Rd) Geelong's sparkling revamped waterfront precinct is a great place to stroll, with plenty of restaurants set on scenic piers, plus historical landmarks, a 19th-century carousel, sculptures, grand homes, swimming areas, playgrounds and grassy sections ideal for picnics. In summer you can cool off at popular **Eastern Beach**, with an art-deco bathing pavilion complete with diving boards, sunbathing area and toddler pool. Jan Mitchell's 100-plus famous painted **Bay Walk Bollards** are scattered the length of the waterfront.

Geelong Art Gallery   GALLERY
(☑ 03-5229 3645; www.geelonggallery.org.au; 55 Little Malop St; ☺ 10am-5pm) FREE With over 6000 works in its collection, this excellent gallery has celebrated Australian paintings such as Eugene von Guérard's *View of Geelong* and Frederick McCubbin's 1890 *A Bush*

WORTH A TRIP

GREAT OCEAN ROAD CHOCOLATERIE & ICE CREAMERY

A sure way to placate those backseat nags of 'are we there yet?' is this roadside **chocolaterie** (☑ 03-5263 1588; www.gorci.com.au; 1200 Great Ocean Rd, Bellbrae; ☺ 9am-5pm), located 11km outside Anglesea. It's a massive site that makes all of its own truffles and chocolates (try its bush-tucker range), as well as 20 flavours of ice cream. There's an on-site cafe, and chocolate-making courses (from $40) most Saturdays; book online.

Burial. Also exhibits contemporary works and has free tours on Sundays at 2pm.

National Wool Museum   MUSEUM
(☑ 03-5272 4701; www.geelongaustralia.com.au/nwm; 26 Moorabool St; adult/child/family $9/5/30; ☺ 9.30am-5pm Mon-Fri, 10am-5pm Sat & Sun) More interesting than it may sound, this museum showcases the importance of the wool industry in shaping Geelong economically, socially and architecturally – many of the grand buildings in the area are former wool-store buildings, including the museum's 1872 bluestone building. There's a sock-making machine and a massive 1910 Axminster carpet loom that gets chugging at hourly intervals.

Old Geelong Gaol   HISTORIC BUILDING
(☑ 03-5221 8292; www.geelonggaol.org.au; cnr Myers & Swanston Sts; adult/child/family $10/5/22; ☺ 1-4pm Sat & Sun, daily school holidays) Built in 1849, HSM Prison Geelong may have closed its doors in 1991, but this old bluestone jail remains as terrifying as ever. You'll see its grim cells set over three levels, plus the shower block, watchtowers and gallows. Each exhibit is accompanied by audio, explaining anything from contraband of crude homemade weapons to former cellmates such as Chopper Read (cell 39). **Ghost tours** (☑ 1300 865 800; www.twistedhistory.net.au; adult/child $33/22) are also run here.

Boom Gallery   GALLERY
(☑ 0417 555 101; www.boomgallery.com.au; 11 Rutland St, Newtown; ☺ 9am-4pm Mon-Sat) FREE Down an industrial street off Pakington St, Boom's warehouse space in an old wool mill shows contemporary works by Melbourne and local artists. It sells great design objects and jewellery, and the attached cafe does fantastic coffee and seasonal food.

Great Ocean Road & Southwest Coast

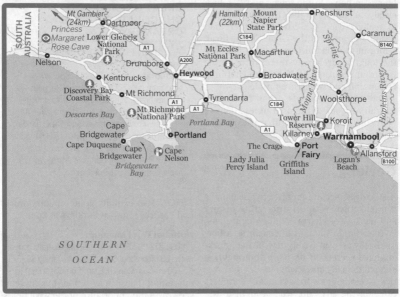

Narana Aboriginal Cultural Centre CULTURAL CENTRE

(☑ 03-5241 5700; www.narana.com.au; 410 Torquay Rd, Grovedale; ☺ 9am-5pm Mon-Fri, 10am-4pm Sat, cafe 8am-4pm Mon-Fri, to 3pm Sat, gallery Tue-Sat, by appointment Mon) **FREE** The Wathaurung people – the original inhabitants of Geelong – called the area Jillong, and this precinct in its outskirts offers a fascinating insight into their culture. There's a range of things going on: a **gallery** featuring Victoria's largest collection of indigenous art; a fusion **cafe** that offers contemporary dishes using indigenous ingredients; didgeridoo performances (or play it yourself); a boomerang-throwing gallery; and a native garden (by donation) which features emus, wallabies and koalas. Call ahead for daily tours.

🛏 Sleeping

Irish Murphy's HOSTEL $

(☑ 03-5221 4335; www.irishmurphysgeelong. com.au; 30 Aberdeen St, Geelong West; dm/s/d with shared bathroom $40/50/80, d with bathroom $60; [P] 🛜) Upstairs from an Irish pub, Geelong's only backpackers is a well-run affair with clean dorms, most of which only have two beds. Guests get 20% off meals in the lively pub downstairs, which also offers free haircuts on Thursdays if you buy a pint! It's a short walk from the city, Pakington St and Geelong station.

★**Devlin Apartments** APARTMENT $$

(☑ 03-5222 1560; www.devlinapartments.com.au; 312 Moorabool St; r $160-500; [✳] 🛜) Geelong's most stylish offerings are these boutique apartments, housed in a 1926 heritage-listed building (the former Gordon Tech school). Each of the apartments has themed designs including 'New Yorker' loft-style apartments with arched windows; 'Modernist', furnished with Danish designer chairs; and 'Industrial', featuring wrought iron, rustic wood and tiled brick bathrooms. There are motel-style rooms, too.

🍴 Eating

Hot Chicken Project AMERICAN $

(☑ 03-5221 9831; 84a Little Malop St; mains from $16; ☺ noon-10pm) Slotting in perfectly along Little Malop is this cosy, welcoming diner specialising in authentic Nashville chicken. Choose from a menu of wings, tenders or dark meats – or hot fish or tofu – in a spectrum of heat levels peaking at 'Evil Chicken', served with a side of slaw or turnip greens.

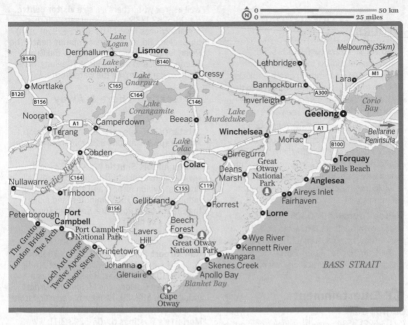

Tulip — MODERN AUSTRALIAN **$$**

(📞03-5229 6953; www.tuliprestaurant.com.au; 9/111 Pakington St, Geelong West; smaller/larger dishes from $18/22; ⊙noon-2.30pm Wed-Sat & 5.30-late Mon-Sat) One of only two hatted restaurants in Geelong, unassuming Tulip on 'Pako' St delivers a gastronomic experience with its mix of inventive small and large plates designed to share. Dishes may include native items such as kangaroo tartare with pepperberry oil, cured Spanish leg ham, whole lamb shoulder or poached ocean trout with grilled peas and mussels.

★**IGNI** — MODERN AUSTRALIAN **$$$**

(📞03-5222 2266; www.restaurantigni.com; Ryan Pl; 5-/8-courses $100/150; ⊙6-10pm Thu & Sun, noon-2.30pm & 6-10pm Fri & Sat) Creating a buzz among food lovers across Melbourne is this latest venture by well-lauded chef (and local boy) Aaron Turner. The set tasting menus change on a whim, incorporating a mix of indigenous and European flavours from saltbush to oyster leaf, or marron to squab, using a wood-fired grill fuelled by ironbark and red gum.

🍷 Drinking & Nightlife

★**Cartel Coffee Roaster** — COFFEE

(📞03-5222 6115; www.coffeecartel.com.au; 1-80 Little Malop St; single-origin coffee $4.50; ⊙7am-5pm Mon-Thu, to 5.30pm Fri, to 2pm Sat, 9am-2pm Sun) A big player in Australia's third-wave coffee movement is this single-origin roaster run by a passionate owner who personally forges relations with farmers across Africa, Asia and Latin America. The result is well-sourced beans, expertly roasted and prepared in its smart space on happening Little Malop.

★**Little Creatures & White Rabbit** — BREWERY

(📞Little Creatures 03-5202 4009, White Rabbit 03-5202 4050; www.littlecreatures.com.au; cnr Fyans & Swanston Sts; mains $16-28; ⊙11am-5pm Mon-Tue, 11am-9pm Wed-Fri, 8am-9pm Sat, 8am-5pm Sun; 🛜) Sharing space within the historic red-brick wool mill complex are these two separate, well-respected breweries that have come together to create a giant playground for beer lovers. **Little Creatures** is the bigger operation, a vast indoor/outdoor vibrant space, while **White Rabbit**, relocated from Healesville in 2015, is the more boutique offering, with a chic set-up among its brewing equipment.

ⓘ GREAT OCEAN ROAD TOURS

Go West Tours (☑03-9485 5290; www.gowest.com.au; tours $130) Melbourne-based company offering full-day tours taking in Bells Beach, koalas in the Otways, the Twelve Apostles, before returning to Melbourne. Free wi-fi on bus.

Otway Discovery Tour (☑03-9629 5844; www.greatoceanroadtour.com.au; 1/2/3-day tours $109/289/380) Very affordable Great Ocean Road tours. The two-day tours include Phillip Island, while the three-day version takes in the Grampians.

Ride Tours (☑1800 605 120, 0427 180 357; www.ridetours.com.au; tours $210) Two-day, one-night minibus trips along the Great Ocean Road. Rates include dorm accommodation and meals.

☆ Entertainment

Barwon Club   LIVE MUSIC
(☑03-5221 4584; www.barwonclub.com.au; 509 Moorabool St; ☺11am-late) The Barwon has long been Geelong's premier live music venue, and has spawned the likes of Magic Dirt, Bored! and Warped, seminal bands in the 'Geetroit' rock scene. As well as catching local and international bands, it's a great pub for a beer.

Kardinia Park   STADIUM
(Simonds Stadium; ☑03-5224 9111; www.kardiniapark.vic.gov.au; 370 Moorabool St, South Geelong; tickets from $25) Recently renovated and fitted with light towers, this AFL stadium is sacred ground for locals as the home of their beloved team, the Cats, who play here in winter.

ⓘ Information

INTERNET ACCESS

Geelong Library (www.grlc.vic.gov.au; 51 Little Malop St; ☺8.30am-5pm Mon-Fri; ☎) Geelong's modern new library is within a contemporary egg-shaped building with a good collection of books and 24-hour free wi-fi.

TOURIST INFORMATION

National Wool Museum Visitor Centre (www.visitgreatoceanroad.org.au; 26 Moorabool St; ☺9am-5pm; ☎) Geelong's main tourist information office has brochures on Geelong, the Bellarine Peninsula and the Otways, as well as free wi-fi. There's also a **visitor centre** (☑03-5283 1735; www.visitgreatoceanroad.org.au; Princes Hwy, Little River; ☺9am-5pm) on Geelong Rd, at the service station near Little River, for those heading directly to the Great Ocean Road, and a small **kiosk** (Geelong Waterfront; ☺9am-5pm) on the waterfront.

ⓘ Getting There & Away

AIR

Jetstar (p236) has services to/from **Avalon Airport** (p236), around a 20-minute drive from Geelong.

Avalon Airport Shuttle (☑03-5278 8788; www.avalonairportshuttle.com.au) meets all flights at Avalon Airport and goes to Geelong (adult/child $22/15, 35 minutes) and along the Great Ocean Road, starting from Torquay ($50/25, one hour).

BUS

Gull Airport Service (☑03-5222 4966; www.gull.com.au; 45 McKillop St; ☺office 9am-5pm Mon-Fri, 10am-noon Sat) Has 14 services a day between Geelong and Melbourne Airport (adult/child $32/20, 1¼ hours), departing from the city centre and Geelong station.

McHarry's Buslines (☑03-5223 2111; www.mcharrys.com.au) Runs frequent buses from Geelong station to Torquay and the Bellarine Peninsula ($3.20, 20 minutes).

V/Line (☑1800 800 007; www.vline.com.au; Gordon Ave, Geelong Train Station) Buses run from Geelong station to Apollo Bay ($19, 2½ hours, three daily) via Torquay ($3.20, 25 minutes), Anglesea ($6.40, 45 minutes), Lorne ($11.60, 1½ hours) and Wye River ($14.40, two hours). On Monday, Wednesday and Friday a bus continues to Port Campbell ($33.20, five hours) and Warrnambool ($37.60, 6½ hours), which involves a change at Apollo Bay. The train is a much quicker and cheaper option for those heading direct to Warrnambool ($25.80, 2½ hours), though you'll miss out on the Great Ocean Road experience. Heading inland, there's a bus to Ballarat ($10.20, 1½ hours).

CAR

The 25km Geelong Ring Road runs from Corio to Waurn Ponds, bypassing Geelong entirely. To get to Geelong city, be careful not to miss the Princes Hwy (M1) from the left lanes.

TRAIN

V/Line trains run frequently from **Geelong station** (☑03-5226 6525; www.vline.com.au; Gordon Ave) to Melbourne's Southern Cross station (from $8.80, one hour). Trains also head from Geelong to Warrnambool ($25.80, 2½ hours, three daily).

Bellarine Peninsula

Melburnians have been making the drive down the Princes Hwy (Geelong Rd) to the seaside villages along the Bellarine Peninsula for more than a century. It's known for its family and surf beaches, historic towns and its wonderful cool-climate wineries.

As well as linking up with the Great Ocean Road, it's just a short ferry trip from here over to the Mornington Peninsula.

 Activities

Bellarine Rail Trail CYCLING
(www.railtrail.com/au/vic/bellarine) Following the route of the historical train line, this 32.5km bike path links South Geelong station with Queenscliff. It's a mostly flat sealed surface that, other than a few crossings, avoids riding on the main roads, passing through Drysdale en route to Queenscliff.

ℹ Information

Bellarine Visitor Information Centre
(☑ 03-5250 6861, 1800 755 611; http://app. geelongbellarineovg.com; 1251 Bellarine Hwy, Wallington; ☺ 9am-5pm) Located within the premises of Flying Brick Cider Co., this tourist information centre has a heap of brochures and ideas on what to do in the area.

BELLARINE WINERIES & PRODUCE

The Bellarine/Geelong area has over 50 wineries, and is a region well known for its cool-climate pinot noir, chardonnay and shiraz. It's also an area famous for its local produce.

If you don't have your own wheels, consider a winery tour with **For the Love of Grape** (☑ 0408 388 332; www.fortheloveofgrape.com.au; half-/full-day tours from Geelong $75/139, from Melbourne $85/149), or visit during **Toast to the Coast** (www.toasttothecoast.com.au; tickets $45; ☺ early Nov) festival in November.

Most listings here are open daily during summer and on weekends; other times call ahead. For a full list of wineries, check out www.winegeelong.com.au.

Scotchmans Hill (☑ 03-5251 3176; www.scotchmans.com.au; 190 Scotchmans Rd, Drysdale; ☺ 10.30am-4.30pm) One of the Bellarine's first wineries remains one of its very best.

Jack Rabbit (☑ 03-5251 2223; www.jackrabbitvineyard.com.au; 85 McAdams Lane, Bellarine; ☺ noon-3pm daily, from 6pm Fri & Sat) Come to this boutique winery for stunning bay views enjoyed from its deck with a glass of its pinot and a bowl of mussels.

Flying Brick Cider Co. (☑ 03-5250 6577; www.flyingbrickciderco.com.au; 1251-1269 Bellarine Hwy, Wallington; tasting paddles $13; ☺ bar 10am-5pm Sun-Thu, 10am to late Fri & Sat, restaurant noon-3pm Mon-Thu, noon-3pm & 6-9pm Fri & Sat, noon-4pm Sun) A popular stop along the highway is this cider house that produces a range of quality apple and pear alcoholic ciders, enjoyed on its grassy outdoor area.

Basils Farm (☑ 03-5258 4280; www.basilsfarm.com.au; 43-53 Nye Rd, Swan Bay; ☺ 10am-5pm Fri-Sun, daily in Jan) Enjoy a bottle of *prosecco* (Italian sparkling white wine) and a produce platter while enjoying fabulous views of Swan Bay.

Terindah Estate (☑ 03-5251 5536; www.terindahestate.com; 90 McAdams Lane, Bellarine; mains $26-38; ☺ 10am-4pm) Another winery with incredible views, quality pinots and fine dining in its glasshouse shed.

Drysdale Cheeses (☑ 0437 816 374; www.drysdalecheeses.com; 2140 Portarlington Rd, Bellarine; ☺ 1-4pm 1st Sun of the month) Taste award-winning goats-milk cheese and yoghurts on the first Sunday of each month.

Manzanillo Olive Grove (☑ 03-5251 3621, 0438 513 621; www.manzanillogrove.com.au; 150 Whitcombes Rd, Drysdale; ☺ 11am-4.30pm Sat & Sun) Dunk bread into samples of cold-pressed extra virgin and chilli-infused olive oils.

Little Mussel Cafe (☑ 03-5259 1377; www.advancemussel.com.au; 230-250 Queenscliff Rd, Portarlington; mains $16-28; ☺ 10am-5pm Fri-Sun) The place to sample local mussels and oysters, served as chowder, in bowls of tomato and chilli, or on tasting plates.

Queenscliff

POP 1418

Historic Queenscliff is a charming seaside town that mixes a salty maritime character with one of Victoria's most picturesque streetscapes. Many of its heritage-listed 19th-century buildings have been converted into hotels, restaurants and art galleries. It's a great base from which to explore the nearby wineries and beaches, along with several historical sites and museums in town. The views across the Port Phillip Heads and Bass Strait are glorious.

◉ Sights

Fort Queenscliff   HISTORIC SITE
(☑ 03-5258 1488; www.fortqueenscliff.com.au; cnr Gellibrand & King Sts; 90-min tours adult/child/family $12/6/30; ◔11am, 1pm & 3pm daily school holidays, 11am Mon-Fri, 1pm & 3pm Sat & Sun nonpeak season) Queencliff's fort was first used as a coastal defence in 1882 to protect Melbourne from a feared Russian invasion. It remained a base until 1946, before being used as the Army Staff College until late 2012; today it functions as the defence archive centre. The 90-minute guided tours take in the military museum (not always accessible), the magazine, cells and its twin lighthouses. It's a defence area, so bring ID for entry. Cash only.

Queenscliff Maritime Museum   MUSEUM
(☑ 03-5258 3440; www.maritimequeenscliffe. org.au; 2 Wharf St; adult/child $8/5; ◔10.30am-4.30pm) Home to the last lifeboat to serve the Rip, this recommended museum has displays on the pilot boat process, shipwrecks, lighthouses and steamships. Don't miss the historic 1895 boat shed with its paintings that served as a record of passing ships in the bay.

⚡ Activities

Sea-All Dolphin Swims   WILDLIFE
(☑ 03-5258 3889; www.dolphinswims.com.au; Queenscliff Harbour; sightseeing tours adult/child $75/65, 3½hr snorkel $145/125; ◔8am & 1pm Oct-Apr) Offers sightseeing tours and swims with seals and dolphins in Port Phillip Heads Marine National Park. Seal sightings are guaranteed; dolphins aren't always seen, but there's a good chance. Snorkelling trips take in Pope's Eye (an unfinished military fort), which is home to abundant fish and an Australasian gannet

breeding colony, before visiting a permanent Australian fur seal colony at Chinaman's Hat.

Dive Victoria   DIVING
(Queenscliff Dive Centre; ☑ 03-5258 4188; www. divequeenscliff.com.au; Queenscliff Harbour; per dive with/without gear $140/65) Victoria's premier dive operator offers SSI dive courses and trips for all levels, from intro to technical. There are some 200 sites in the area, taking in rich marine life and shipwrecks from the past three centuries, including ex-HMAS *Canberra,* scuttled in 2009, and WWI submarines. Also does snorkel trips and dive lessons.

⚞ Festivals & Events

Queenscliff Music Festival   MUSIC
(☑ 03-5258 4816; www.qmf.net.au; ◔last weekend Nov) One of the coast's best festivals features big-name Australian and international musos with a folksy, bluesy bent. Held late November.

⛏ Sleeping

Queenscliff Dive Centre   HOSTEL $
(☑ 03-5258 4188; www.divevictoria.com.au; 37 Learmonth St; dm divers/nondivers $30/40, s/d $100/120; ☎⛊) While this hostel-style accommodation is primarily for divers, if there are rooms available it's a good option for budget travellers too. The modern shared kitchen and lounge facilities are bright and airy, while the simple rooms are out the back. It's BYO linen and towels ($15 to hire). It was built in 1864 when it was used as Cobb & Co horse stables.

Twomey's Cottage   B&B $$
(☑ 0400 265 877; www.classiccottages.com.au; 13 St Andrews St; d $110-140) Just the place to soak up Queenscliff's historical atmosphere, this heritage fisher's cottage is fantastic value. Its claim to fame is as the residence of Fred Williams when he painted his Queenscliff series, plus renowned recitalist Keith Humble composed music here, so creative vibes abound.

★ Vue Grand   HOTEL $$$
(☑ 03-5258 1544; www.vuegrand.com.au; 46 Hesse St; r incl breakfast $178-258; ✸☎) One of Queenscliff's most elegant historic buildings, the Vue has everything from standard pub rooms to its modern turret suite (boasting 360-degree views) and bay-view rooms (with freestanding baths in the lounge).

Athelstane House BOUTIQUE HOTEL **$$$**
(☑03-5258 1024; www.athelstane.com.au; 4 Hobson St; r incl breakfast $180-310; ❋☎) Dating back to 1860, double-storey Athelstane House is a beautifully kept historic building that's notable as Queenscliff's oldest guesthouse. Its rooms are spotless, and mix period touches with modern comforts such as corner spa baths, iPod docks, DVD players and fast wi-fi. Its front lounge is a good place to hang out, with a vintage record player and a stack of vinyl.

✕ Eating & Drinking

Shelter Shed CAFE **$$**
(☑03-5258 3604; www.sheltershedqueenscliff. com.au; 25 Hesse St; dishes $15-30; ⊙8am-3pm; ☎) Within a wonderful light-filled space with a glowing fire in winter, and an inviting garden courtyard for sunny days, this is a great choice for breakfast or lunch. It's popular for the Asian eggs on jasmine rice with abalone sauce, and its prawn watercress roll with dill mayo. There's plenty of grilled seafood and meat dishes too.

360 Q INTERNATIONAL **$$**
(☑03-5257 4200; www.360q.com.au; 2 Wharf St; breakfast from $15, lunch from $18, dinner $26-39; ⊙8am-4pm daily, 6-9pm Fri & Sat) Undoubtedly one of Queenscliff's best restaurants, 360 Q features wonderful views overlooking the picturesque marina. It does an original breakfast menu and some light lunch options such as a Vietnamese pork bánh mì, while for dinner try its fragrant chilli-tomato Portarlington mussels with crusty bread.

Vue Grand Dining Room MODERN AUSTRALIAN **$$$**
(☑03-5258 1544; www.vuegrand.com.au; 46 Hesse St; 2-/3-course meals $59/79, 5-course Bellarine tasting menu without/with wine or beers $95/149; ⊙6-9pm Wed-Sat) The grande dame of Queenscliff dining, Vue Grand's stately dining room serves up fabulous dishes such as lamb back strap with saffron, fennel, pomegranate and whipped feta, backed up by a splendid wine and beer menu. The Bellarine tasting menu is a fine journey around the peninsula, with local-produce-heavy dishes matched with local wine or beers.

Queenscliff Brewhouse PUB
(☑03-5258 1717; www.queenscliffbrewhouse.com. au; 2 Gellibrand St; ⊙11am-1am Mon-Sat, to 11pm Sun) Prickly Moses have set up their second brewhouse here in Queenscliff, branching out from their Otways base. Their full range is showcased on tap, as well as a selection of guest brewers, best enjoyed in the beer garden.

ⓘ Information

Queenscliff Visitor Centre (☑03-5258 4843; www.queenscliff.com.au; 55 Hesse St; ⊙9am-5pm; ☎) Plenty of brochures on the area. Also sells the self-guided walking tour map *Queenscliff – A Living Heritage*. Wi-fi and internet access next door at the library.

Torquay

POP 17,105

In the 1960s and '70s Torquay was just another sleepy seaside town. Back then, surfing in Australia was a decidedly countercultural pursuit, its devotees crusty hippy dropouts living in clapped-out Kombis, smoking pot and making off with your daughters. These days it's become unabashedly mainstream and the town's proximity to world-famous Bells Beach, and status as home of two iconic surf brands – Rip Curl and Quiksilver, both initially wetsuit makers – ensures Torquay's place as the undisputed capital of the Australian surf industry. It's one of Australia's fastest growing towns, experiencing a population increase of 67% between 2001 and 2013 that these days makes it feel almost like an outer suburb of Geelong.

⊙ Sights & Activities

Torquay's beaches lure everyone from kids in floaties to backpacker surf-school pupils. **Fisherman's Beach**, protected from ocean swells, is the family favourite. Ringed by shady pines and sloping lawns, the **Front Beach** beckons lazy bums, while surf life-savers patrol the frothing **Back Beach** during summer. Famous surf beaches nearby include Jan Juc, Winki Pop and, of course, **Bells Beach** (Great Ocean Rd).

★ Australian National Surfing Museum MUSEUM
(☑03-5261 4606; www.surfworld.com.au; 77 Beach Rd, Surf City Plaza; adult/child/family $12/8/25; ⊙9am-5pm) The perfect starting point for those embarking on a surfing safari is this well-curated museum that pays homage to Australian surfing. Here you'll see Simon Anderson's groundbreaking 1981 thruster, Mark Richard's awesome airbrushed board art collection and, most notably, Australia's

Surfing Hall of Fame. It's full of great memorabilia (including Duke Kahanamoku's wooden longboard), videos and displays on surf culture through the 1960s to the '80s.

Go Ride a Wave   SURFING
(☑03-5261 3616, 1300 132 441; www.gorideawave.com.au; 1/15 Bell St; 2hr lessons from adult/child $69/59) Offers lessons for surfing, SUP and kayaking, and hires boards, too. They run camps along the Great Ocean Road and Bellarine Peninsula. Rates are cheaper with advance booking.

Torquay Surf Academy   SURFING
(☑03-5261 2022; www.torquaysurf.com.au; 34a Bell St; 2hr group/private lessons $60/180) Offers surf lessons for groups or one-on-one. Also hires surfboards (from $25), SUPs (from $35), body-boards ($20) and wetsuits ($10), as well as bikes (from $20).

🛏 Sleeping

Bells Beach Backpackers   HOSTEL $
(☑03-5261 4029; www.bellsbeachbackpackers.com.au; 51-53 Surfcoast Hwy; van s/d $20/24, dm/d from $32/80; @🗗🛜) On the main highway in Torquay (not Bells Beach) is this friendly backpackers, which does a great job of fitting into the fabric of this surf town. It has a casual, homely atmosphere with basic rooms that are clean and in good nick, and a large kitchen that 'van packers' can also use.

Torquay Foreshore
Caravan Park   CAMPGROUND $
(☑03-5261 2496; www.torquaycaravanpark.com.au; 35 Bell St; powered sites $37-89, d cabins $109-295, 2-bedroom units $190-395; 🛜) Just behind the Back Beach is the largest camping ground on the Surf Coast. It has good facilities and premium-priced cabins with sea views. Wi-fi is in the camp kitchen only.

Beachside Accommodation   APARTMENT $$
(☑0419 587 445; www.beachsideaccommodation torquay.com.au; 24 Felix Cres; d $110-160; 🌸🛜) Only a five-minute stroll to the beach is this relaxed residential-style accommodation owned by a German-English couple, where you'll get a private patio with BBQ and an Aussie backyard atmosphere.

🍴 Eating & Drinking

Bottle of Milk   BURGERS $
(☑03-5264 8236; www.thebottleofmilk.com; 24 Bell St; burgers from $10; ⊘noon-9pm) Trading off the success of its **Lorne** (☑03-5289 2005; www.thebottleofmilk.com; 52 Mountjoy Pde;

burgers $11-18; ⊘8am-8pm) branch, Bottle of Milk's winning formula of burgers, beaches and beers makes it rightfully popular. Inside is decked out with booth seating, polished floorboards and tiled walls, or head out to its beer garden with an open fireplace. Good coffee, too.

★Bomboras Kiosk   CAFE $$
(www.bomboras.com.au; 48 The Esplanade, Fisherman's Beach; meals $5-22; ⊘7.30am-5pm) Right on the sand, this is just the place for hungry beachgoers to recharge with homemade sausage rolls, cakes, salads, milkshakes or locally roasted coffee. During the summer they open the rooftop bar with local brews, ciders, DJs and prime ocean views.

Fisho's   SEAFOOD $$
(☑0474 342 124; www.facebook.com/fishos torquay; 36 The Esplanade; mains from $19; ⊘noon-3pm & 5-8pm) Not your average fish and chip shop, instead this oceanfront joint does an original take on the classics such as tempura flake, zesty lime shark popcorn and sweet potato cakes. It's set up on the waterfront in an atmospheric weatherboard house with AstroTurf front seating, and local beers and cider on tap.

★Blackman's Brewery   MICROBREWERY
(☑03-5261 5310; www.blackmansbrewery.com.au; 26 Bell St; ⊘noon-10pm Wed-Sun, daily in summer) One of Vic's best microbreweries is this brewpub where you can taste all eight of Blackman's beers, which are produced on-site. Go the tasting paddle ($16) to enjoy its range of IPAs, unfiltered lager, pale ale and porters by a roaring fire or in the AstroTurf beer garden. They've also got a smoker for BBQ meats, pizzas and platters. Swing by at 4pm for a free brewery tour.

🛍 Shopping

Rip Curl Surf
Factory Outlet   FASHION & ACCESSORIES
(Baines Seconds; 16 Baines Cres; ⊘9am-5.30pm) Rips Curl's shiny main outlet is in the Surf City Plaza, but head round the back to the industrial estate for Rip Curl's factory outlet, where you'll get 30% off the price of last season's clothing and wetsuits. A big-name global brand these days, Rip Curl was founded here in Torquay in 1969.

ℹ Information

Torquay Visitor Information Centre (www.greatoceanroad.org; Surf City Plaza, Beach Rd;

⊘9am-5pm) The well-resourced tourist office next to the Australian National Surfing Museum makes a good starting point along the Great Ocean Road to fine tune your itinerary. There's free wi-fi and internet available at the library next door.

ⓘ Getting There & Away

Torquay is 15 minutes' drive south of Geelong on the B100.

McHarry's Buslines (p248) Runs an hourly bus (No 51) from 9am to 8pm (around 5pm weekends) from Geelong to Torquay ($3.20, 40 minutes). **V/Line** (p248) Buses run four times daily Monday to Friday (two on weekends) from Geelong to Torquay ($3.20, 25 minutes).

Torquay to Anglesea

The Great Ocean Road officially begins on the stretch between Torquay and Anglesea. A slight detour takes you to famous **Bells Beach**, the powerful point break that is part of international surfing folklore; it has hosted Australia's premier surfing event, the Bells Classic, since 1973. (It was here too, in name only, that Keanu Reeves and Patrick Swayze had their ultimate showdown in the film *Point Break*.

Around 3km away, on the outskirts of Torquay, is the surf town of **Jan Juc**, a local hang-out for surfers, with a mellow, sleepy vibe. Nine kilometres southwest of Torquay is the turn-off to spectacular **Point Addis**, a vast sweep of pristine clothing-optional beach that attracts surfers, nudists, hang-gliders and swimmers, as well as those embarking on the recommended Koorie Cultural Walk .

🏃 Activities

Koorie Cultural Walk   WALKING
A highly recommended detour signposted off the Great Ocean Road is the fantastic Koorie Cultural Walk, a 2km trail that details how the indigenous Wathaurung people lived here for millennia. It's a lovely bushwalk through the Great Otway National Park, with echidnas and wallabies, and spectacular coastal outlooks of dramatic cliffs and pristine beaches, including the lovely **Addiscott Beach**.

🎊 Festivals & Events

Rip Curl Pro   SURFING
(www.aspworldtour.com; ⊘Easter) Since 1973, Bells has hosted the Rip Curl Pro every East-

er long weekend. The world championship ASP tour event draws thousands to watch the world's best surfers carve up the big autumn swells, where waves have reached 5m during the contest! The Rip Curl Pro occasionally decamps to Johanna Beach, two hours west, when fickle Bells isn't working.

Anglesea

POP 2653

Mix sheer orange cliffs falling into the ocean with hilly, tree-filled 'burbs and a population that booms in summer and you've got Anglesea, where sharing fish and chips with seagulls by the Anglesea River is a decades-long family tradition for many.

🏃 Activities

Anglesea Golf Club   GOLF
(☎03-5263 1582; www.angleseagolfclub.com. au; Golf Links Rd; 20min kangroo tours adult/child $10/5, 9/18 holes from $25/45, club hire 9/18 holes $25/35; ⊘10am-4pm Mon-Fri) Here you can watch kangaroos graze on the fairways on an organised tour, or, even better, pair your sightings with a round of golf. If you don't want to do a tour, you'll be able to spot kangaroos from the road.

Go Ride a Wave   SURFING
(☎03-5263 2111, 1300 132 441; www.gorideawave. com.au; 143b Great Ocean Rd; 2hr lessons adult/child from $69/59, 2hr board hire from $25; ⊘9am-5pm) Long-established surf school that runs lessons and hires out boards, SUPs and kayaks.

🛏 Sleeping

Anglesea Backpackers   HOSTEL $
(☎03-5263 2664; www.angleseabackpackers.com; 40 Noble St; dm $30-35, d/f $115/150; @🖰) While most hostels like to cram 'em in, this simple, homely backpackers has just two dorm rooms and one double/triple, and is clean, bright and welcoming. In winter the fire glows warmly in the cosy living room. There are free bikes for guests and the owner can pick you up from town or as far away as Torquay.

Anglesea Beachfront Family Caravan Park   CAMPGROUND $
(☎03-5263 1583; www.angleseabeachfront.com.au; 35 Cameron Rd; powered sites $38-86, d cabins $110-271; @🖰🖳) Beach- and riverfront caravan park with a pool, wi-fi, two camp kitchens, a jumping pillow, an indoor spa and a games room. No, you probably won't get that book read.

✖️ Eating

Coffetti Gelato GELATO $
(📞0434 274 781; www.facebook.com/coffetti
gelato; Shop 4, 87-89 Great Ocean Rd, Anglesea
Shopping Village; cups from $4; ⏰8am-6pm, to
9.30pm in summer) Run by an Italian-Aussie
husband-wife team is this authentic gelat-
eria doing a range of delicious homemade
flavours as well as popsicles, granitas and
Ugandan coffee. It's just outside the entrance of the supermarket.

Maids Pantry CAFE $
(📞03-5263 1420; 119 Great Ocean Rd; breakfasts
& sandwiches from $8; ⏰7am-5pm) Across from
the Anglesea River is this bright, rustic cafe
that doubles as a provedore general store
stocking a good selection of local produce. It
has a wide selection of sandwiches, sliders,
pies and brunch specials, and has garden
seating round the back.

Captain Moonlite MODERN AUSTRALIAN $$
(📞03-5263 2454; www.captainmoonlite.com.au;
100 Great Ocean Rd; mains from $25; ⏰8am-10pm
Fri-Sun, 8am-4pm Mon, 5-10pm Thu) Sharing
space with the Anglesea Surf Life Saving
Club – with unbeatable views over the beach
– Captain Moonlite mixes unpretentious
decor with a quality, highly seasonal menu,
which it describes as 'coastal European'. Ex-
pect tasty breakfasts such as ocean trout and
soft-boiled egg on rye, mezze-style plates
and mains such as slow-roasted lamb and
fresh seafood.

ℹ️ Information

Anglesea Visitor Information Centre (www.
visitgreatoceanroad.org.au; Great Ocean Rd;
⏰9am-5pm; 📶) Located at the lake, this
information centre has a heap of brochures for
the area, including walks in the surrounding
national park.

ℹ️ Getting There & Away

Bus There are four to six daily V/Line buses to/
from Geelong to Anglesea ($6.40, 45 minutes)
on weekdays, and two departures on weekends.
Car The Geelong bypass has reduced the time
it takes to drive from Melbourne to Anglesea to
around 75 minutes.

Aireys Inlet & Around

POP 1071

Midway between Anglesea and Lorne,
Aireys Inlet is an attractive coastal hamlet
with a tight-knit community of locals and

sea-changers, plus plenty of holidaymakers.
It's home to a historic lighthouse which forms
the backdrop to glorious stretches of beach,
including **Fairhaven** and **Moggs Creek**. Ask
at the Anglesea visitor centre for brochures
on the great coastal walks around here.

⊙ Sights & Activities

★Split Point Lighthouse LIGHTHOUSE
(📞1800 174 045, 03-5263 1133; www.splitpoint
lighthouse.com.au; Federal St; 45min tours adult/
child/family $14/8/40; ⏰tours hourly 11am-2pm,
summer holidays 10am-5pm) Scale the 136 steps
to the top of the beautiful 'White Queen'
lighthouse for sensational 360-degree views.
Built in 1891, the 34m-high lighthouse is still
operational (though now fully automated).
During off-peak times a tour guide will ac-
company you to the top, whereas in summer
it's run as a self-guided tour with staff on
hand to answer questions.

Blazing Saddles HORSE RIDING
(📞0418 528 647, 03-5289 7322; www.blazingsad
dlestrailrides.com; Lot 1 Bimbadeen Dr; per person
1¼hr bush rides from $50, 2½hr beach & bush rides
$115) People come from around the world to
hop on a Blazing Saddles horse and head
along stunning Fairhaven Beach or into the
bush.

🛏️ Sleeping

Inlet Caravan Park CABIN $
(📞03-5289 6230; www.aicp.com.au; 19-25 Great
Ocean Rd; powered sites $39, cabins d $105-280;
@📶🏊) More cabin town than tent city,
this neat park is close to the township's few
shops.

★Cimarron B&B B&B $$
(📞03-5289 7044; www.cimarron.com.au; 105 Gil-
bert St; d $125-225; 📶) Built in 1979 from lo-
cal timbers and using only wooden pegs and
shiplap joins, Cimarron is an idyllic getaway
with views over Point Roadknight. The large
lounge area has book-lined walls and a cosy
fireplace, while upstairs are two unique, loft-
style doubles with vaulted timber ceilings;
otherwise there's a denlike apartment. Out
back, it's all state park and wildlife. Two-night
minimum stay. Gay friendly; but no kids.

Pole House RENTAL HOUSE $$$
(📞03-5220 0200; www.greatoceanroadholidays.
com.au; 60 Banool Rd, Fairhaven; from $470) One
of the most iconic houses along the Great
Ocean Road, the Pole House is a unique ar-
chitectural piece that, as the name suggests,

sits atop a pole, with extraordinary ocean views. Access to the house is via an external pedestrian bridge.

✗ Eating & Drinking

Willows Tea House   CAFE $
(☑03-5289 6830; 7 Federal St; scones $4, breakfast from $8; ⊙9am-5pm; 🖥) Soak up Aireys' seafaring atmosphere at this teahouse set up within a historic weatherboard cottage a few steps from the lighthouse. Stop by for morning or afternoon tea to indulge in homemade scones with jam and cream, enjoyed in its cosy interior or at outdoor tables.

★á la grecque   GREEK $$$
(☑03-5289 6922; www.alagrecque.com.au; 60 Great Ocean Rd; mains $28-40; ⊙noon-3pm & 6-9.30pm Wed-Sun Aug-Dec, noon-3pm & 6-9.30pm daily Dec-Apr, closed May-Jul) Be whisked away to the Mediterranean at this outstanding modern Greek taverna. Mezze such as seared scallops or braised cuttlefish with apple, celery and a lime dressing, and mains such as grilled pork shoulder, are sensational. So is the wine list.

★Aireys Pub   MICROBREWERY
(☑03-5289 6804; www.aireyspub.com.au; 45 Great Ocean Rd; pots from $5; ⊙11.30am-late; 🖥) Established in 1904, this pub is a survivor, twice burning to the ground before closing its doors in 2011, only to be revived by a bunch of locals chipping in to save it. Now it's better than ever, with an on-site brewery, Rogue Wave, to go with its fantastic kitchen (mains $20 to $34), meat smoker, roaring fire, live music and sprawling beer garden.

❶ Getting There & Away

Car From Melbourne count on around a 1¾-hour drive for the 123km trip to Aireys Inlet, and a bit longer if you're heading via Torquay (27km, 25 minutes).

Public Transport Departing from Geelong Station, V-Line has four to six daily buses (two on weekends) to Aireys Inlet ($8.80, one hour), which continue on to nearby stops at Fairhaven, Moggs Creek and Eastern View for the same fare.

Lorne

POP 1046

One of the Great Ocean Road's original resort towns, Lorne may be a tad overdeveloped these days but it still retains all the charms that have lured visitors here since the 19th century. Beyond its main strip it has an incredible natural beauty: tall old gum trees line its hilly streets, and Loutit Bay gleams irresistibly. It gets busy; in summer you'll be competing with day trippers for restaurant seats and lattes, but, thronged by tourists or not, it's a lovely place to hang out.

◉ Sights & Activities

★Qdos Art Gallery   GALLERY
(☑03-5289 1989; www.qdosarts.com; 35 Allenvale Rd; ⊙9am-5pm Thu-Mon, daily Jan) FREE Amid the lush forest that backs on to Lorne, Qdos always has something interesting showing at its contemporary gallery, to go with its open-air sculpture garden. There's also a lovely little cafe doing wood-fired pizzas and *ryokan*-style accommodation (p256).

Erskine Falls   WATERFALL
(Erskine Falls Access Rd) Head out of town to see this lovely waterfall. It's an easy walk to the viewing platform, or 250 (often slippery) steps down to its base, from where you can explore further or head back on up.

✸ Festivals & Events

Falls Festival   MUSIC
(www.fallsfestival.com; 2-/3-/4-day tickets $249/299/339; ⊙28 Dec – 1 Jan) A four-day knees-up over New Year's on a farm just out of town, this stellar music festival attracts a top line-up of international rock and indie groups. Past headliners include Iggy Pop, Kings of Leon and the Black Keys. Sells out fast (usually within an hour), and tickets include camping.

🛏 Sleeping

Big Hill Track   CAMPGROUND $
(☑13 1963; www.parkweb.vic.gov.au; 1265 Deans Marsh-Lorne Rd, Benwerrin) A good option for backpackers with tents or a van is this free camping ground located 15km north of Lorne, along the road heading to Birregurra. You'll need to chance your luck, however, as there are no bookings, with the 12 sites filled on a first-come, first-served basis.

Lorne Foreshore Caravan Park CAMPGROUND $
(☑03-5289 1382; www.lornecaravanpark.com.au; 2 Great Ocean Rd; unpowered sites $28-55, powered sites $37-89, d cabins $97-189; 🖥) Book at the Foreshore Caravan Park for all of Lorne's five caravan parks. Of the five, **Erskine River Caravan Park**, where the booking office is located, is the prettiest, though note there's no swimming in the river. It's on the left-

BRAE

Brae is regarded as one of Australia's best **restaurants** (☑03-5236 2226; www.brae restaurant.com; 4285 Cape Otway Rd, Birregurra; 8-course tasting plates per person $190-220, plus matched wines $125; ☺noon-3pm Fri-Mon & from 6pm Thu-Sat) 🍴. Owner-chef Dan Hunter mostly uses whatever is growing in its 30 acres of organic gardens to create some delightful gastronomic concoctions, all masterfully presented, and with plenty of surprises. For good reason it's a regular on the list of the World's Best 100 restaurants. Reservations are essential, and need to be made well in advance. It's located a 30-minute drive from Lorne in the picturesque town of Birregurra.

hand side as you enter Lorne, just before the bridge. Book well ahead for peak-season stays. Wi-fi in reception only.

★ **Qdos** RYOKAN $$$
(☑03-5289 1989; www.qdosarts.com; 35 Allenvale Rd; r incl breakfast from $300; 🐾) The perfect choice for those seeking a romantic getaway or forest retreat, Qdos' luxury Zen tree houses are fitted with tatami mats, rice-paper screens and no TV. Two-night minimum; no kids.

🍴 Eating

Swing Bridge Cafe & Boathouse CAFE $
(☑0423 814 770; 30 Great Ocean Rd; meals $10-16; ☺8am-2.30pm Fri-Mon, daily in summer) This tiny cafe overlooking the water at the historic swing bridge (c 1934) has an appealing retro beach vibe. It's the place for single-origin coffee, to go with its range of brioches filled with anything from pulled pork and beef brisket to jerk tofu with salsa verde. On summer evenings they do Argentinian-style charcoal barbecues or paella on the lawn.

★ **Lorne Beach Pavilion** MODERN AUSTRALIAN $$
(☑03-5289 2882; www.lornebeachpavilion.com. au; 81 Mountjoy Pde; breakfast $9-23, mains $19-45; ☺9am-5pm Mon-Thu, 9am-9pm Fri, 8am-9pm Sat & Sun) With its unbeatable location on the foreshore, life here is literally a beach, especially with a cold drink in hand. Cafe-style breakfasts and lunches hit the spot, while a more upmarket Modern Australian menu of seafood and rib-eye steaks is on for dinner. Come at happy hour for $7 pints, or otherwise swing by at sunset for a bottle of prosecco.

Ipsos GREEK $$
(☑03-5289 1883; www.ipsosrestaurant.com.au; 48 Mountjoy Pde; sharing plates $5-29; ☺noon-3pm & 6-10pm Thu-Mon, longer hours in summer) From the same family that ran Kosta (a Lorne institution that's relocated to Aireys Inlet) comes this smart, casual taverna that's opened in the exact same location where it all started in 1974. Run by the sons, the menu comprises mainly Greek-influenced sharing plates, or you can go its signature slow-roasted lamb shoulder ($66 for two).

ℹ Information

Lorne Visitor Centre (☑03-5289 1152, 1300 891 152; www.lovelorne.com.au; 15 Mountjoy Pde; ☺9am-5pm; 🛜) Stacks of information (including heaps of ideas for walks in the area), helpful staff, fishing licences, bus tickets and accommodation referrals. Also has a gift shop, internet access, free wi-fi and a charger out the front for electric cars.

ℹ Getting There & Away

Bus V/Line (p248) buses pass through daily from Geelong ($11.60,1½ hours) en route to Apollo Bay ($5, from one hour).
Car If driving from Melbourne allow just under two hours for the 143km journey.

Wye River
POP 140
The Great Ocean Road snakes spectacularly around the cliff-side from Cumberland River before reaching this little town with big ideas. Nestled discreetly in the pretty (steep) hillsides are some modest holiday houses and a few grander steel-and-glass pole-frame structures built on the 'challenging' housing sites. Unfortunatelyn on Christmas Day in 2015, major bushfires destroyed some 116 homes in the area, and the entire town was evacuated; fortunately, no deaths were recorded.

🛏 Sleeping & Eating

Big4 Wye River Holiday Park CAMPGROUND $
(www.big4wyeriver.com.au; 25 Great Ocean Rd; unpowered sites $30-45, powered sites $38-50, cabins $120-185, houses $310-395; 🌧@) Just back

from the beach is this popular caravan park, which sprawls over 10 hectares. Featuring an Otways forest backdrop, its grassy sites are great for camping, and there's a range of comfortable units.

★**Wye Beach Hotel**   PUB FOOD **$$**
(☑ 03-5289 0240; www.wyebeachhotel.com.au; 19 Great Ocean Rd; mains from $27; ⊙ 11.30am-11pm; ␗) Undoubtedly one of the best coastal pubs in Victoria, if not Australia – the ocean views just don't get much better than this. It has an unpretentious, local vibe and an all-regional craft-beer selection on tap – with brews from Forrest, Torquay and Aireys Inlet. There's pub food too, though it's a bit on the pricey side.

There are also comfortable motel-style double rooms ($130 to $160) with great views.

Wye General   CAFE **$$**
(☑ 03-5289 0247; www.thewyegeneral.com; 35 Great Ocean Rd; mains $15-26; ⊙ 8am-5pm Mon-Sat, to 4pm Sun) This well-loved general store does provisions and groceries; however it's most noteworthy for its smart indoor-outdoor cafe/bar. Polished concrete floors, timber features and a sophisticated retro ambience, it does old-fashioned cocktails, beer on tap and a menu of breakfasts, burgers and sourdough toasties made in-house.

❶ Getting There & Away

Bus There are several buses a day here from Geelong ($14.40, two hours).
Car Wye River is located 159km from Melbourne, around a 2½-hour drive. It's positioned approximately halfway between Lorne and Apollo Bay on the Great Ocean Road.

Kennett River

Located 25km east of Apollo Bay is Kennett River, which has some great **koala spotting** just behind the caravan park. There are also **glow worms** that shine at night up the same stretch of Grey River Rd (take a torch).

The friendly bush **Kennett River Holiday Park** (☑ 1300 664 417, 03-5289 0272; www.kennettriver.com; 1-13 Great Ocean Rd; unpowered sites $31-58, powered sites $37-68, d cabins from $115; ␗) is one of the best sites along the coast, equally popular with surfers, families, travellers and young couples. The beachview cabins have amazing vistas. There's free electric barbecues and a camp kitchen for cooking. Keep an eye out for koalas, which are regularly spotted here.

Kennett River is located directly on the Great Ocean Road, 165km from Melbourne. It's a 30-minute drive to Lorne. From Geelong there are three buses a day ($16, two hours).

Apollo Bay

POP 1095
One of the larger towns along the Great Ocean Road, Apollo Bay has a tight-knit community of fisherfolk, artists, musicians and sea changers. Rolling hills provide a postcard backdrop to the town, while broad, white-sand beaches dominate the foreground. It's also an ideal base for exploring magical Cape Otway (p258) and Otway National Park. It has some of the best restaurants along the coast and several lively pubs, and is one of the best towns on the Great Ocean Road for budget travellers, with numerous hostels and ready transport access.

◎ Sights & Activities

Mark's Walking Tours   WALKING
(☑ 0417 983 985; www.greatoceanwalk.asn.au/markstours; tours $50) Take a walk around the area with local Mark Brack, son of the Cape Otway lighthouse keeper. He knows this stretch of coast, its history and its ghosts better than anyone around. Daily tours include shipwreck tours, historical tours, glow-worm tours and Great Ocean Walk treks. Minimum two people – prices drop the more people on the tour.

Apollo Bay Surf & Kayak   ADVENTURE
(☑ 0405 495 909; www.apollobaysurfkayak.com.au; 157-159 Great Ocean Rd; 2hr kayak tours $70, 2hr surf lessons adult/child $65/60) Head out to an Australian fur seal colony in a double kayak. Tours (with full instructions for beginners) depart from Marengo Beach (to the south of the town centre). Also offers surf and SUP lessons, plus boards and mountain bikes (half-day $30) for hire.

🛏 Sleeping

YHA Eco Beach   HOSTEL **$**
(☑ 03-5237 7899; www.yha.com.au; 5 Pascoe St; dm/d/f from $29/75/112; @␗) ⌀ This multimillion-dollar, architect-designed hostel is an outstanding place to stay, with eco-credentials, great lounge areas, kitchens, a boules pit and rooftop terraces. Rooms are generic but spotless. It's a block behind the beach.

Pisces Big4 Apollo Bay
CAMPGROUND $

(📞 03-5237 6749; www.piscespark.com.au; 311 Great Ocean Rd; unpowered/powered sites from $34/42, cabins from $99; 🐾🏊) It's the unbeatable views from the oceanfront villas (from $190) that set this family-oriented park apart from the others.

★Beacon Point Ocean View Villas
VILLA $$$

(📞 03-5237 6218, 03-5237 6411; www.beaconpoint. com.au; 270 Skenes Creek Rd; r incl breakfast $200-350; 🅿🐾) With a commanding hill location among the trees, this wonderful collection of comfortable one- and two-bedroom villas is a luxurious yet affordable bush retreat. Most villas have sensational coast views, balcony and wood-fired heater. There's also a popular restaurant.

✖ Eating

★Chris's Beacon Point Restaurant
GREEK $$$

(📞 03-5237 6411; www.chriss.com.au; 280 Skenes Creek Rd; mains from $34; ⊙6pm-late daily, plus noon-2pm Sat & Sun; 🐾) Feast on memorable ocean views, deliciously fresh seafood and Greek-influenced dishes at Chris's hilltop fine-dining sanctuary among the treetops. Reservations recommended. You can also stay in its wonderful stilted villas. It's accessed via Skenes Creek.

La Bimba
MODERN AUSTRALIAN $$$

(📞 03-5237 7411; www.labimba.com.au; 125 Great Ocean Rd; mains $36-42; ⊙8.30am-3pm & 5.30-9.30pm Wed-Mon) This upstairs Mod Oz restaurant is worth the splurge. It's a warm, relaxed smart-casual restaurant with ocean views and a good wine list. Try the chilli Portarlington mussel hotpot, the local lamb or a kangaroo main.

🍷 Drinking & Nightlife

★Great Ocean Road Brewhouse
MICROBREWERY

(📞 03-5237 6240; www.greatoceanroadbrewhouse. com.au; 29 Great Ocean Rd; pots $5; ⊙pub 11am-11pm Mon-Thu, to 1am Fri & Sat, Tastes of the Region noon-8pm Mon-Thu, noon-9pm Fri, 10am-9pm Sat, 10am-8pm Sun) Set up by renowned Otways brewery Prickly Moses, this new taphouse pours an impressive range of ales. It's divided into two distinct entities: the front bar is more your classic pub and bistro with pool table; while through the back is their 'Taste of the Region' room, with 16 of their beers on tap to enjoy with local produce tasting platters.

Hello Coffee
COFFEE

(📞 0438 443 489; www.hellocoffee.com.au; 16 Oak Ave; ⊙7am-3pm Mon-Fri, 9am-2pm Sat; 🐾) Set up by a couple of local mates in a backstreet industrial estate is this roaster-cafe that does the best coffee in the region. They roast single-origin beans from around the world on-site, served as V60 pourovers, Chemex, nitro cold brew or classic espresso. It has a cosy lounge-room set up, and does good breakfasts and smoked pulled-pork rolls etc.

ℹ Information

Great Ocean Road Visitor Centre (📞 1300 689 297; www.visitapollobay.com; 100 Great Ocean Rd; ⊙9am-5pm; 🐾) Modern and professional tourist office with a heap of info for the area, and an 'eco-centre' with displays. It has free wi-fi and can book bus tickets, too.

ℹ Getting There & Away

Bus Apollo Bay is easily reached by public transport from Melbourne ($27.20, 3½ hours) via train to Geelong and transferring to a connecting bus. There are three daily services during the week, and twice on weekends; stops include Torquay ($15.40, two hours), Anglesea ($11.20, 1¾ hours) and Lorne ($5, one hour), among others.

Car From Melbourne the fastest route is inland via the Geelong bypass that leads through to Birregurra and Forrest, a 200km drive. If taking the scenic route along the Great Ocean Road (highly recommended) count on a 4½-hour drive.

Cape Otway

Cape Otway is the second-most-southerly point of mainland Australia (after Wilsons Promontory) and one of the wettest parts of the state. This coastline is particularly beautiful, rugged and historically treacherous for passing ships. The turn-off for Lighthouse Rd, which leads 12km down to the lighthouse, is 21km from Apollo Bay. It's a beautiful forested road with towering trees, which are home to a sizeable population of koalas.

◉ Sights

Cape Otway Lightstation
LIGHTHOUSE

(📞 03-5237 9240; www.lightstation.com; Lighthouse Rd; adult/child/family $19.50/7.50/49.50; ⊙9am-5pm) Cape Otway Lightstation is the oldest surviving lighthouse on mainland Australia and was built in 1848 by more than 40 stonemasons without mortar or cement. The **Telegraph Station** has fascinating displays on the 250km undersea telegraph cable link with Tasmania, laid in 1859. It's a sprawling complex with plenty to see, from Aboriginal cultural sites to WWII bunkers.

🛏 Sleeping

⭐ Bimbi Park   CARAVAN PARK $
(☑ 03-5237 9246; www.bimbipark.com.au; 90 Manna Gum Dr; unpowered sites $20-40, powered sites $25-45, dm $20, cabins $100-145; 🤖) 🏊 Down a dirt road 3km from the lighthouse is this character-filled caravan park with bush sites, cabins, dorms and old-school caravans. It's a fantastic option for families, and also for hikers on the Great Ocean Walk (p244). There's plenty of wildlife about, including koalas, plus horse rides (adult/child $65/55 per hour) and a rock-climbing wall. Good use of water-saving initiatives, too.

Blanket Bay   CAMPGROUND $
(☑ 13 19 63; www.parkweb.vic.gov.au; sites from $28.70) Blanket Bay is one of those 'secret' camping grounds that Melburnians love to lay claim to discovering. It's serene (depending on your neighbours) and the nearby beach is beautiful. It's not really a secret; in fact it's so popular during summer and Easter holidays that it regularly books out.

⭐ Great Ocean Ecolodge   LODGE $$$
(☑ 03-5237 9297; www.greatoceanecolodge.com; 635 Lighthouse Rd; r incl activities from $380; 🌿) 🏊 Reminiscent of a luxury African safari lodge, this mud-brick homestead stands in pastoral surrounds with plenty of wildlife. It's all solar-powered and rates go towards the on-site **Centre for Conservation Ecology** (www.conservationecologycentre.org). It also serves as an animal hospital for local fauna and has a captive tiger quoll breeding program, which you'll visit on its dusk wildlife walk with an ecologist.

Cape Otway Lightstation   B&B $$$
(☑ 03-5237 9240; www.lightstation.com; Lighthouse Rd; d incl entry to lighthouse $240-450) There's a range of options at this romantic and historic windswept spot (p258). You can book out the whole Head Lightkeeper's House (sleeps 16), or the smaller Manager's House (sleeps two). Prices are halved if you stay a second night.

Port Campbell National Park

East of the Otways, the Great Ocean Road levels out and enters narrow, flat scrubby escarpment lands that fall away to sheer, 70m-high cliffs along the coast between Princetown and Peterborough – a distinct change of scene. This is Port Campbell National Park, home to the Twelve Apostles, and the most famous and most photographed stretch of the Great Ocean Road.

None of the beaches along this stretch are suitable for swimming because of strong currents and undertows.

◉ Sights

⭐ Twelve Apostles   LANDMARK
(Great Ocean Rd) The most iconic sight and enduring image for most visitors to the Great Ocean Road, the Twelve Apostles provide a fitting climax to the journey. Jutting out from the ocean in spectacular fashion, these rocky stacks stand as if they've been abandoned to the ocean by the retreating headland. Today only seven 'apostles' can be seen from a network of viewing platforms connected by timber boardwalks around the clifftops.

There's pedestrian access to the viewing platforms from the car park at the **Twelve Apostles Visitor Centre** (⊙10am-5pm Sun-Fri, to 5.30pm Sat) – more a kiosk and toilets than an info centre – via a tunnel beneath the Great Ocean Road.

WORTH A TRIP

OTWAY FLY DETOUR

The popular **Otway Fly** (☑ 1800 300 477, 03-5235 9200; www.otwayfly.com; 360 Phillips Track; treetop walks adult/child $25/15, zipline tours $120/85; ⊙9am-5pm, last entry 4pm) is an elevated steel walkway suspended among the forest canopy, and includes a swaying lookout tower, 50m above the forest floor. Kids will enjoy the 'prehistoric path' loaded with dinosaurs, and everyone can test their bravery on the guided 2½-hour zipline tour – including a 120m run.

The best time to visit is sunset, not only for optimum photographic opportunities and to beat the tour buses, but also to see **little penguins** returning ashore. Sightings vary, but generally they arrive 20 to 40 minutes after sunset. You'll need binoculars, which can be borrowed from the Port Campbell Visitor Centre (p261).

Gibson Steps BEACH

These 86 steps, hacked by hand into the cliffs by 19th-century landowner Hugh Gibson (and more recently replaced by concrete steps), lead down to wild Gibson Beach. You can walk along the beach, but be careful not to get stranded by high tides.

Information

Twelve Apostles Visitor Centre Kiosk
(p259) Based across the road from the iconic Twelve Apostles is this tourist information building with a kiosk, interpretative panels and toilets. To access the Twelve Apostles you'll need to park here, from where you can access the site via a tunnel that passes under the road.

Port Campbell

POP 618

This small, laid-back coastal town was named after Scottish Captain Alexander Campbell, a whaler who took refuge here on trading voyages between Tasmania and Port Fairy. It's a friendly town with some nice little eateries and drinking spots, which make for an ideal place to debrief after visiting the Twelve Apostles. Its tiny bay has a lovely sandy beach, one of few safe places for swimming along this tempestuous stretch of coast.

Sleeping

Port Campbell Guesthouse Flashpackers GUESTHOUSE $

(☎0407 696 559; www.portcampbellguesthouse.com; 54 Lord St; s/d without bathroom $50/80, r with bathroom from $100; ❄📶) A place for budget, independent-minded travellers who aren't into the hostel scene. Instead this homely guesthouse feels more like going around to a mate's place. Set up within a historic cottage are four cosy rooms, a comfy lounge and a country kitchen with filter coffee.

Port Campbell Hostel HOSTEL $

(☎03-5598 6305; www.portcampbellhostel.com.au; 18 Tregea St; dm/s/d/tr/q from $38/80/130/175/240; @📶) This modern purpose-built double-storey backpackers has rooms with western views, a huge shared kitchen and an even bigger lounge area. There's a range of clean mixed dorms and private rooms with en suites. It's a short stroll to the beach, and there are pizzas in the evenings ($10) and mountain-bike hire. Wi-fi only in the lounge area.

The opening of its new brewery **Sow and Piglets** (☎03-5598 6305; 18 Tregea St; ⏲noon-late) is another reason to stay.

Sea Foam Villas APARTMENT $$

(☎03-5598 6413; www.seafoamvillas.com.au; 14 Lord St; r $185-570) Located directly across from the water, Sea Foam undoubtedly has the best views in town. It's only really worth it, however, if you can snag one of the bay-view apartments which are large, comfortable and luxurious.

HOW MANY APOSTLES?

The Twelve Apostles are not 12 in number and, from all records, never have been. From the viewing platform you can clearly count seven Apostles, but maybe some obscure others? We consulted widely with Parks Victoria officers, tourist-office staff and even the cleaner at the lookout, but it's still not clear. Locals tend to say, 'It depends where you look from', which really is true.

The Apostles are called 'stacks' in geologic parlance, and the rock formations were originally called the 'Sow and Piglets'. Someone in the 1960s (nobody can recall who) thought they might attract some tourists with a more venerable name, so they were renamed 'the Apostles'. Since apostles tend to come by the dozen, the number 12 was added sometime later. The two stacks on the eastern (Otway) side of the viewing platform are not technically Apostles – they're Gog and Magog.

The soft limestone cliffs are dynamic and changeable, with constant erosion from the unceasing waves – one 70m-high stack collapsed into the sea in July 2005 and the Island Archway lost its archway in June 2009.

TWELVE APOSTLES TRANSPORT & TOURS

Unless you're booked on a tour, having your own car is pretty much the only way to go in terms of exploring this area. The Apostles are located 15km from Port Campbell, with Loch Ard Gorge a little closer to town (around 12km).

Port Campbell Boat Charters (☑ 0428 986 366; www.portcampbellboatcharters.com. au; scenic tours/diving/fishing per person from $50/60/70) offers a unique way of viewing the Twelve Apostles, allowing you to see them from out on the water. Otherwise you can arrange a **scenic helicopter flight** (☑ 03-5598 8283; www.12apostleshelicopters.com.au; 15min flights $145) that'll take you over this dramatic stretch of coast.

From Port Campbell you can arrange a trip here with **Port Campbell Touring Company** (☑ 03-5598 6424, 0447 986 423; www.portcampbelltouring.com.au; half-day tours per person from $120, walks from $85). Otherwise the following tour operators make the trip here from Melbourne:

Go West Tours (p243)

Otway Discovery Tour (p243)

Ride Tours (p243)

✖ Eating

★ **Forage on the Foreshore**   CAFE **$$**
(☑ 03-5598 6202; 32 Cairns St; mains from $14; ☺ 9am-5pm; 🛜) In the old post office is this seafront cottage cafe with wooden floorboards, art on the walls, an open fireplace and a vintage record player spinning vinyl. There's an all-day breakfast menu, burgers and curries for lunch, and items featuring fresh crayfish and abalone.

ⓘ Information

Port Campbell Visitor Centre (☑ 1300 137 255; www.visit12apostles.com.au; 26 Morris St; ☺ 9am-5pm) Stacks of regional and accommodation information and interesting relics from various shipwrecks – the anchor from the *Loch Ard* is out the front. Offers free use of binoculars, stargazer telescopes, cameras, GPS equipment and scavenger hunts for kids.

ⓘ Getting There & Away

V/Line (p248) buses leave Geelong on Monday, Wednesday and Friday and travel through to Port Campbell ($32, five hours), but you'll need to transfer to a different bus in Apollo Bay ($11.20, two hours 15 minutes), which leaves a few hours later. There's also a bus to Warrnambool ($7.60, one hour 20 minutes).

Port Campbell to Warrnambool

Don't for a moment think that the Twelve Apostles are the end point of the Great Ocean Road, particularly given there's a whole string of iconic rock stacks on the road heading westward of Port Campbell. Some are arguably more scenic than the apostles themselves.

The drive continues through acres and acres of farming land here, passing through some laid-back towns. **Timboon**, about 16km inland from Peterborough, is best known for being surrounded by a number of wonderful places to sample local produce on the **12 Apostles Gourmet Trail** (www.12 apostlesfoodartisans.com). Here you'll be able to sample single-malt whiskeys, local homemade ice cream and chocolate, and fine wine and cheese.

⊙ Sights

London Bridge   LANDMARK
Just outside Port Campbell, en route to Peterborough, London Bridge has indeed fallen down. It was once a double-arched rock platform linked to the mainland, but in January 1990 the bridge collapsed leaving two terrified tourists marooned on the world's newest island – they were eventually rescued by helicopter. It remains a spectacular sight nevertheless. At dusk keep an eye out for penguins, who are often spotted on the beach.

Bay of Islands Coastal Park   VIEWPOINT
Past Peterborough (12km west of Port Campbell), the lesser-visited **Bay of Martyrs** and **Bay of Islands** both have spectacular lookout points of rock stacks and sweeping views comparable to the Twelve Apostles. Both have fantastic coastal walks, and there's a great beach at **Crofts Bay**.

MELBOURNE & COASTAL VICTORIA PORT CAMPBELL TO WARRNAMBOOL

The Arch
LANDMARK

Offshore from Point Hesse, the Arch is a rock formation worth stopping for. There's some good photo ops from the various viewing points looking down upon this intact bridgelike formation.

The Grotto
VIEWPOINT

A scenic stopover heading west from Port Campbell is the Grotto, where steep stairs lead down to a hollowed-out cavelike formation where waves crash through. It's approximately halfway between Port Campbell and Peterborough, a short drive from London Bridge (p261).

Warrnambool

POP 33,979

Once a whaling and sealing station, these days Warrnambool is booming as a major regional commercial and whale-watching centre. Overall it's an attractive city with heritage buildings, beaches, gardens and tree-lined streets; however, the major housing and commercial development around the fringes of the city looks much like city suburbs anywhere in Australia.

While it's the whales that Warrnambool is most famous for, it has some great art galleries and historical sights to visit. Plus its sizeable population of uni students gives the town some spark, and you'll find some cool bars and cafes about.

◉ Sights & Activities

★ Flagstaff Hill Maritime Village
HISTORIC SITE

(☑ 03-5559 4600; www.flagstaffhill.com; 89 Merri St; adult/child/family $18/8.50/48; ⊙ 9am-5pm, last entry 4pm) The world-class Flagstaff Hill precinct is of equal interest for its shipwreck museum, heritage-listed lighthouses and garrison as it is for its reproduction of a historical Victorian port town. It also has the nightly **Shipwrecked** (adult/child/family $26/14/67), an engaging 70-minute sound-and-laser show telling the story of the *Loch Ard*'s plunge.

The village is modelled on a pioneer-era Australian coastal port, with ye olde shoppes such as blacksmiths, candle makers and shipbuilders. If you're lucky the **Maremma dogs** (☑ 03-5559 4600; www.warrnamboolpenguins.com.au; adult/child $16/10) will be around for you to meet.

★ Warrnambool Art Gallery
GALLERY

(WAG; ☑ 03-5559 4949; www.thewag.com.au; 165 Timor St; ⊙ 10am-5pm Mon-Fri, noon-5pm Sat & Sun) **FREE** One of Australia's oldest art galleries (established in 1886), Warrnambool's collection of rotating permanent artworks showcases many prominent Australian painters. Its most famous piece is Eugene von Guérard's oil landscape *Tower Hill*, so detailed it was used by botanists as a historical record when regenerating the Tower Hill area to its original state. There's a contemporary component too, and several concurrent exhibitions on show.

Reel Addiction
WHALE WATCHING

(☑ 0468 964 150; www.boatcharterswarrnambool. com.au; whale-watching trips per person $65, half-day fishing per person from $180) Runs morning and afternoon trips to see the whales when they're in town – usually from June to September – or otherwise to see the seal colony on Lady Julia Percy Island. Fishing trips are their speciality.

🛏 Sleeping

Warrnambool Beach Backpackers
HOSTEL $

(☑ 03-5562 4874; www.beachbackpackers.com.au; 17 Stanley St; per person camping $12, dm $28-36, d $80-90; @ 🕾) A short stroll to the beach, this hostel has all backpackers' needs, with a huge living area, a kitchsy Aussie-themed bar, free wi-fi, and free pick-up service. Its rooms are basic, but clean. As well as campers, 'vanpackers' can stay here for $12 per person. It hires out bikes, surfboards, SUPs, wetsuits, kayaks and fishing equipment, plus offers free use of boogie boards.

Flagstaff Hill Lighthouse Lodge
GUESTHOUSE $$

(☑ 1800 556 111; www.lighthouselodge.com.au; Flagstaff Hill; d/house incl dinner from $155/375; 🕸 🕾) Once the former harbour master's residence, this charming weatherboard cottage can be rented as the entire house or separate rooms. It has a grassy area overlooking the Maritime Village and coastline. The rate includes entry to Flagstaff Hill Maritime Village, the Shipwrecked light show, dinner at Pippies restaurant and a bottle of wine, which makes it terrific value all up.

Hotel Warrnambool
PUB $$

(☑ 03-5562 2377; www.hotelwarrnambool.com. au; cnr Koroit & Kepler Sts; d incl breakfast without/ with bathroom from $110/140; 🕸 🕾) Renovations to this historic 1894 hotel have upgraded to boutique-scale, while keeping a classic pub-accommodation feel. Don't staying here at weekends if you want peace and quiet.

✕ Eating & Drinking

Kermond's Hamburgers BURGERS $
(☑ 03-5562 4854; www.facebook.com/kermonds
hamburgers; 151 Lava St; burgers $7.20-10; ☺ 9am-
9.30pm) Likely not much has changed at this
burger joint since it opened in 1949, with
Laminex tables, wood-panelled walls and
classic milkshakes served in stainless-steel
tumblers. Its burgers are an institution.

Standard Dave PIZZA $$
(☑ 03-5562 8659; 218 Timor St; pizza $15-24;
☺ 5pm-late Tue-Sun, noon-2pm Fri) Standard
Dave attracts a young indie crowd here for
awesome pizzas, a drink and decent music.
Its thin-crust pizzas use quality ingredi-
ents made from scratch or sourced locally.
Be sure to head through next door to **Dart
& Marlin** (216-218 Timor St; ☺ 5-11pm Wed-Fri,
2-11pm Sat & Sun).

Hotel Warrnambool PUB FOOD $$
(www.hotelwarrnambool.com.au; cnr Koroit &
Kepler Sts; lunch mains $12-27, dinner $28-34;
☺ noon-late; 🐾) One of Victoria's best coastal
pubs, Hotel Warrnambool mixes pub charm
with bohemian character and serves wood-
fired pizzas, among other gastro-pub fare.

Pickled Pig EUROPEAN $$$
(☑ 03-5561 3188; www.pickledpig.com.au; 78
Liebig St; dishes $17-37; ☺ 6-10pm Tue-Sat) War-
rnambool's place to dress up, the Pickled Pig
is smart dining with linen-clad tables and
chandeliers. The food is seasonal contempo-
rary European cuisine, which is best show-
cased in the chef's six-course tasting menu
(per person $85); bookings are advised.

Lucy BAR
(www.facebook.com/thelucybar; 2/167 Koroit St,
Ozone Walk; cocktails from $12; ☺ 3pm-late) A
cool new dive bar tucked down a graffiti-
splashed laneway. It's a tiny red-brick space,
with a cassette deck for tunes and a drinks
menu that specialises in local spirits pro-
duced by Victorian distilleries. They make
a mean single-origin espresso Martini, and
there are also gourmet jaffles, local wines,
beers and ciders.

ℹ Information

Warrnambool Visitor Centre (☑ 1800 637
725; www.visitwarrnambool.com.au; 89 Merri
St; ☺ 9am-5pm) For the latest on whale sight-
ings, local tours and accommodation bookings,
plus bike and walking trail maps.

ℹ Getting There & Away

BUS

There are three **V/Line** (☑ 1800 800 007, 03-
5562 9432; www.vline.com.au; Merri St) buses
a day along the Great Ocean Road to Apollo
Bay ($21, two hours), as well as five daily buses
to Port Fairy ($4.60, 35 minutes) and three to
Portland ($12.40, 1½ hours). There's also a bus
to Halls Gap ($27.20, three hours) four days a
week via Dunkeld ($18.20, two hours) en route
to Ararat ($32, three hours 40 minutes). There's
a coach to Melbourne too via Ballarat ($18.20,
two hours 50 minutes) departing Warrnambool
at 7.15am Monday to Friday. Buses are run by
Christian's Bus Co (☑ 03-5562 9432, 1300 734
441; www.christiansbus.com.au).

CAR

Warrnambool is an hour's drive west of Port
Campbell on the Great Ocean Road, and about
three-hour's drive from Melbourne on Princess
Hwy (A1).

TRAIN

V/Line trains run to Melbourne ($34.60, 3¼
hours, three or four daily) via Geelong ($24.80,
2½ hours).

Tower Hill Reserve

Tower Hill, 15km west of Warrnambool, is
a vast caldera born in a volcanic eruption
35,000 years ago. Aboriginal artefacts un-
earthed in the volcanic ash show that Indig-
enous people lived in the area at the time
and, today, the Worn Gundidj Aboriginal
Cooperative operates the **Tower Hill Nat-
ural History Centre** (☑ 03-5565 9202, 0448
509 522; www.worngundidj.org.au; walks adult/
child $22.95/10.65; ☺ 10am-4pm).

The centre is housed in a UFO-like
building designed by renowned Australian
architect Robin Boyd in 1962. **Bushwalks** led
by Indigenous guides depart daily at 11am
and 1pm and include boomerang-throwing
and bush-tucker demonstrations. **Spotlight-
ing night walks** (adult/child $28.95/14/65)
are available too, with 24-hours' advance
notice. The centre also sells handicrafts, art-
work and accessories designed by the local
Worn Gundidj community.

As well as the guided walks offered by the
Tower Hill Natural History Centre, there are
some other excellent walks, including the
steep 30-minute **Peak Climb** with spectac-
ular 360-degree views.

Port Fairy

POP 2835

Established as a whaling and sealing station in 1833, Port Fairy has retained its historic 19th-century maritime charm. Here it's all about heritage bluestone and sandstone buildings, whitewashed cottages, colourful fishing boats and wide, tree-lined streets. In 2012 it was voted the world's most liveable small community, and for most visitors, it's not hard to see why. There's also a number of nice beaches, surfing, fishing and plenty of wildlife to see.

◎ Sights

Wharf Area
PORT

Back in the 1850s Port Fairy's port was one of the busiest in Australia, serving as the main departure point for ships heading to England loaded up with wool, gold and wheat. Today there's still plenty going on at this charming marina, from the luxury yachts to the weatherworn fishing boats moored here.

Battery Hill
HISTORIC SITE

Located across the bridge from the picturesque harbour, Battery Hill is worthy of exploration, with cannons and fortifications positioned here in 1887 to protect the town from foreign warships. You'll also encounter resident black wallabies. It was originally used as a flagstaff, so the views are good.

★☆ Festivals & Events

★ Port Fairy Folk Festival
MUSIC

(www.portfairyfolkfestival.com; tickets $250-300; ⊙Mar) Australia's premier folk-music festival is held on the Labour Day long weekend in March. It includes an excellent mix of international and national acts, while the streets are abuzz with buskers. Accommodation can book out a year in advance.

🛏 Sleeping

Port Fairy YHA
HOSTEL $

(☑03-5568 2468; www.portfairyhostel.com.au; 8 Cox St; dm $26-30, s/tw/d from $41.50/70/75; @🛜) Easily the best budget option in town, in the rambling 1844 home of merchant William Rutledge, is this friendly, well-run hostel with a large kitchen, a pool table, free cable TV and peaceful gardens.

Merrijig Inn
HOTEL $$

(☑03-5568 2324; www.merrijiginn.com; 1 Campbell St; d from $120; 🛜) At the heritage-listed

Merrijig, one of Victoria's oldest inns, you can make your choice between the quaint doll's house 'attic' rooms upstairs, and roomier, more comfortable rooms downstairs. There's a wonderful back lawn with veggie garden and silkie bantam chickens, plus comfy lounges with fireplaces throughout.

★ Drift House
BOUTIQUE HOTEL $$$

(☑0417 782 495, 03-5568 3309; www.drifthouse.com.au; 98 Gipps St; d from $375; ❋🛜) An intriguing mix of 19th-century grandeur and 21st-century design, Drift House is a must for architecture lovers. Its grand frontage is the original 1860 double terrace, yet rooms open up to ultra-slick open-plan designs, decked out with boutique fittings. It's won a bunch of awards, and is undoubtedly *the* spot to treat yourself in town.

✗ Eating

Farmer's Wife
CAFE $

(☑03-5568 2843; www.facebook.com/farmerswifeportfairy; 47a Sackville St; mains $10-20; ⊙8am-2.30pm) Hidden down a walkway in a modern lot, Farmer's Wife doesn't need a heritage building to impress, and instead lets its food do the talking. Overseen by the chef previously from acclaimed Stag, the seasonal brunch menu features tempting items such as pork belly Benedict brioche, chilli fried eggs with pork quesadilla and salsa, and sourdough fruit toast.

★ Coffin Sally
PIZZA $$

(www.coffinsally.com.au; 33 Sackville St; pizzas $13-20; ⊙4-11pm) This historic building was once used as a coffin makers; today it's well regarded for traditional thin-crust pizzas, cooked in an open kitchen and wolfed down on streetside stools or in the dimly lit dining nooks out back next to an open fire. Its bar is also a good spot for a drink.

★ Fen
MODERN AUSTRALIAN $$$

(☑03-5568 3229; www.fenportfairy.com.au; 22 Sackville St; mains $39, 5-course degustation menu $110, tasting menu from $150; ⊙6-11pm Tue-Sat) One of coastal Vic's best restaurants, this husband-and-wife-run operation earned itself two chef's hats in 2017. Set up inside a heritage bluestone building, the decor is minimalist and relaxed, while the menu showcases seasonal local produce from southwestern Victoria. Expect local lamb, seafood and duck dishes, infused with indigenous flavours.

Merrijig Kitchen   MODERN AUSTRALIAN **$$$**
(📞03-5568 2324; www.merrijiginn.com; 1 Campbell
St; mains $28-38; ⏰6-9pm Thu-Mon; 📶) Here at
Port Fairy's most atmospheric restaurant you
can warm yourself by the open fire and enjoy
superb dining with a menu that changes daily
according to what's seasonal. It has a kitchen
garden, cures meats, smokes fish and features
an award-winning wine list. Delectable food
with great service.

ℹ Information

Port Fairy Visitor Centre (📞03-5568 2682;
www.portfairyaustralia.com.au; Bank St; ⏰9am-
5pm; 📶) Provides spot-on tourist information,
walking-tour brochures (20 cents), free wi-fi, V/
Line tickets, tourism brochures and publications.
There's also bike hire (half-/full day $15/25).

ℹ Getting There & Away

CAR

Port Fairy is 20-minutes' drive west of Warrnam-
bool on the A1. If coming from Melbourne it's
288km journey, with the most direct route being
along the B140 highway from Geelong.

PUBLIC TRANSPORT

Catch a train to Warrnambool, from where **V/
Line** (📞1800 800 007; www.vline.com.au) run
four to five buses a day to Port Fairy ($4.60,
35 minutes). The bus also heads to Tower Hill
($3.20) and Koroit ($3.20). There's also a bus
from Port Fairy to Portland ($8.60, 55 minutes).

Portland

POP 10,700

Portland's claim to fame is as Victoria's first
European settlement, founded as a whaling
and sealing base in the early 1800s. Despite
its colonial history, attractive architecture and
beaches, blue-collared Portland feels much
more like a regional hub than a tourist town.

Though with that said, there's a lot on offer.
The Great Southwest Walk is a big attraction,
as are seafood and fishing, whale-watching in
winter, plus some good surf breaks.

⊙ Sights

Historic Waterfront   WATERFRONT
(Cliff St) The grassy precinct overlooking the
harbour has several heritage bluestone build-
ings. **Customs House** (1850) is still a working
office, but you can ask to see its fascinating
display of confiscated booty in the cellar, in-
cluding a stuffed black bear among other ran-
dom items. Also here is the 1845 **courthouse**,
and the 1886 **Rocket Shed** with a display of
ship rescue equipment.

**Portland Maritime
Discovery Centre**   MUSEUM
(📞1800 035 567; Lee Breakwater Rd; adult/child
under 15yr $7.50/free; ⏰9am-5pm) Excellent
displays on shipwrecks and Portland's whal-
ing history, plus a sperm whale skeleton that
washed ashore and an original 1858 wooden
lifeboat. There's also a **cafe** (📞03-5521 7341;
mains from $17; ⏰9.30am-4.30pm) here with one
of the best views in town.

✗ Eating

Deegan Seafoods   FISH & CHIPS **$**
(📞03-5523 4749; 106 Percy St; fish from $6;
⏰9am-6pm Mon-Fri) This fish and chip shop
famously serves up the freshest fish in Victo-
ria. Whether you go the flake or the calamari
rings, you're in for a serious treat.

ℹ Information

Portland Visitor Centre (📞1800 035 567;
www.visitportland.com.au; Lee Breakwater Rd;
⏰9am-5pm) In a modern building on the wa-
terfront, this excellent information centre has a
stack of suggestions for things to do and see.

ℹ Getting There & Away

Bus V/Line buses connect Portland with Port
Fairy (from $8.60, 50 minutes) and Warrnam-
bool (from $12.40, one hour 40 minutes) three
times daily on weekdays, and once a day on
weekends. Buses depart from Henty St.

Car Portland is a one-hour drive west of Port
Fairy on the Princess Hwy (A1).

GREAT SOUTH WEST WALK

The 250km signposted loop that is the Great South West Walk begins and ends at Port-
land's visitor centre. It takes in some of the southwest's most stunning natural scenery:
from the remote, blustery coast, through the river system of the Lower Glenelg National
Park, and back through the hinterland to Portland. The whole loop would take at least 10
days, but it can be done in sections, and parts can be done as day walks or even a two-hour
loop. Maps are available from visitor centres in Portland and **Nelson** (p267). Visit www.
greatsouthwestwalk.com for all information, FAQs and registration details.

Nelson

POP 311

Tiny Nelson is the last vestige of civilisation before the South Australian border – just a general store, a pub and a handful of accommodation places. It's a popular holiday and fishing spot at the mouth of the Glenelg River, which flows through Lower Glenelg National Park. It's pretty much the halfway mark between Melbourne and Adelaide, and likes to think of itself as the beginning of the Great Ocean Road. Note that Nelson uses South Australia's 08 telephone area code.

🏃 Activities

Fishing and boating along the Glenelg River are the main activities that bring folk into Nelson; bream and estuary perch are the main catches.

★ Nelson Canoe Hire   CANOEING
(☑ 0409 104 798; www.nelsonboatandcanoehire. com.au; canoe hire per half-/full day $40/65, kayak hire per half-/full day $25/60) Exploring the 65km stretch of scenic river along Lower Glenelg National Park on a multiday canoe trip is one of Victoria's best hidden secrets. This outfit can rig you up for leisurely paddles or serious river-camping expeditions – three days including waterproof barrels. There's no office but they'll deliver you all the gear; BYO tent and supplies.

★ Nelson Boat Hire   BOATING
(☑ 0427 571 198, 08-8738 4048; www.nelson boatandcanoehire.com.au; dinghies per 4hr $115, motorboat per hr $55, houseboats per night $410-480; ⊙ Sep-Jul) Whether you head out for a few hours' fishing or hire a self-contained houseboat, cruising along the scenic waters of Lower Glenelg National Park will likely be the most relaxing time of your trip. The best bit is you don't need a boat licence. Houseboats, which sleep six, come with bathroom, fridge and kitchen, and have a two-night minimum hire period.

Nelson River Cruises   CRUISE
(☑ 0448 887 1225, 08-8738 4191; www.glenelgriver cruises.com.au; cruises adult/child $32.50/10; ⊙ Sep-Jun) These leisurely 3½-hour cruises head along the Glenelg River, departing Nelson at 1pm on Wednesday and Saturday, or daily during school holidays; check the website for the schedule. Tours include the impressive **Princess Margaret Rose Cave** (☑ 08-8738 4171; www.princessmargaretrosecave. com; Princess Margaret Rose Caves Rd, Mumbannar, Lower Glenelg National Park; adult/child/family $20/13/44; ⊙ tours depart 10am, 11am, noon, 1.30pm, 2.30pm, 3.30pm & 4.30pm, reduced hours winter), with its gleaming underground formations; tickets for the cave cost extra.

🛌 Sleeping

Kywong Caravan Park   CAMPGROUND $
(☑ 08-8738 4174; www.kywongcp.com; 92 North Nelson Rd; unpowered sites $23-28, powered sites $28-35, cabins d from $70; ❄ 🐾) Set 1km north of town, this 10 hectare park is next to the national park and Glenelg River, with plenty of wildlife (including bandicoots) and great birdwatching.

Nelson Cottage   COTTAGE $
(☑ 08-8738 4161; www.nelsoncottage.com.au; cnr Kellett & Sturt Sts; s/d with shared bathroom & breakfast $70/90; 🐾) This 1882 cottage, once used as a police station, has old-fashioned rooms with clean shared amenities. The owners are keen travellers so call ahead first to check if they're around.

🍷 Drinking & Nightlife

★ Nelson Hotel   PUB
(☑ 08-8738 4011; www.nelsonhotel.com.au; Kellett St; ⊙ 11am-late; 🐾) As real as outback pubs come, the Nelson Hotel (established in 1855) is an essential stop for a beer and a friendly yarn with locals. It's got a character-filled front bar, featuring a dusty stuffed pelican, and a bistro serving hearty meals (mains from $15). There are basic rooms too, which, while in need of a refurb, are perfectly fine for the night (single/double with shared bathroom $45/65).

DON'T MISS

CAPE BRIDGEWATER

Home to one of Australia's finest stretches of white-sand surf beach, Cape Bridgewater makes for an essential 21km detour off the Portland–Nelson Road. Its powdery white sands and turquoise waters resemble Queensland more than a remote Victorian beach. Though the beach is the main drawcard, there are also a number of walks featuring some dramatic scenery and an opportunity to swim with **Australian fur seals** (☑ 03-5526 7247; www.sealsbyseatours.com. au; Bridgewater Rd; 45min tours adult/child $40/25, cage dives $60/30; ⊙ Sep-May).

CAPE NELSON LIGHTHOUSE

Head up to the top of the still-operational (c 1884) **Cape Nelson lighthouse** (☑0428 131 253; www.capenelsonlighthouse.com.au; adult/child/family $15/10/40; ☉tours 11am & 2pm) for fantastic views overlooking the edge of the world. You'll also get shown around the premises while hearing tales of shipwrecks and the history of area. The **accommodation** (1-/2-bedroom cottages incl breakfast $200/270; ❋🛜) here is the perfect opportunity to indulge in that fantasy of living in a remote windswept lighthouse keeper's cottage. While the historic cottages have been refitted with modern comforts, they retain their maritime charm. You can book one or two rooms, with your pick of a sunrise or sunset view.

❶ Information

Nelson Visitor Centre (☑08-8738 4051; www.nelsonvictoria.com.au; ☉10am-12.30pm & 1.30-5pm; 🛜) Good info on both sides of the border; particularly helpful for the parks and the Great South West Walk. Also has wi-fi. During summer they have longer opening hours, otherwise they leave tourist packages for visitors after hours.

WILSONS PROMONTORY & GIPPSLAND

The Great Ocean Road may get the crowds, but Gippsland hides all the secrets. Gippsland is one region where it pays to avoid the cities – the towns along the Princes Hwy are barely worth a traveller's glance. But beyond the highway are some of the state's most absorbing, unspoiled and beautiful wilderness areas and beaches.

Along the coast there's Wilsons Promontory National Park, a fabulous destination for hikers and sightseers alike. This is only the start when it comes to stirring beaches. Epic Ninety Mile Beach yields to Cape Conran Coastal Park and Croajingolong National Park. Put them together and it's one of the wildest, most beautiful coastlines on Earth. Inland, the Buchan Caves are a must-see attraction, while the national parks at Snowy River and Errinundra are as deeply forested, remote and pristine as any in the country.

Koonwarra & Fish Creek

POP 385

Travellers in the know have been stopping for a bite to eat at Fish Creek on their way to the coast or the Prom for years. These days it has developed into a little bohemian artists community with craft shops, galleries, stu-

dios, bookshops and some great cafes. The Great Southern Rail Trail passes through.

Tucked away in rolling dairy country along the South Gippsland Hwy is the tiny township of Koonwarra that's built itself a reputation as something of a niche foodie destination.

◉ Sights

Celia Rosser Gallery   GALLERY
(☑03-5683 2628, 0455 777 334; www.celiarossergallery.com.au; Promontory Rd; ☉10am-4pm Fri-Sun) **FREE** A bright art space featuring the works of renowned botanical artist Celia Rosser who's most famous for her banksia watercolours. The *Banksia rosserae* was named after her; Queen Victoria is the only other woman to have a banksia in her name.

🛏 Sleeping

Fish Creek Hotel   PUB **$**
(☑03-5683 2404; www.fishcreekhotel.com.au; 1 Old Waratah Rd; mains $16-30, d with shared/private bathroom $85/100; ☉noon-2pm & 6-9pm) The striking art deco Fish Creek Hotel, universally known as the Fishy Pub, is not only an essential stop for a beer or bistro meal, but also serves as a handy base for trips into Wilsons Prom. There's a choice of upstairs comfortable pub rooms (no TV or kettle) with shared bathrooms, and self-contained motel accommodation at the back.

The Wine Farm   B&B **$$**
(☑03-5664 3204; www.thewinefarm.com.au; 370 Koonwarra–Inverloch Rd; d $150; ❋) Set on a 15-acre family-run boutique winery is this three-bedroom self-contained weatherboard cottage that's excellent value for couples and groups ($25 per extra person). It's a must for wine-lovers; South African vintner Neil Hawkins impresses with his range of 10 cool-climate varieties. Tastings at the cellar door can be arranged.

Wilsons Promontory & Gippsland

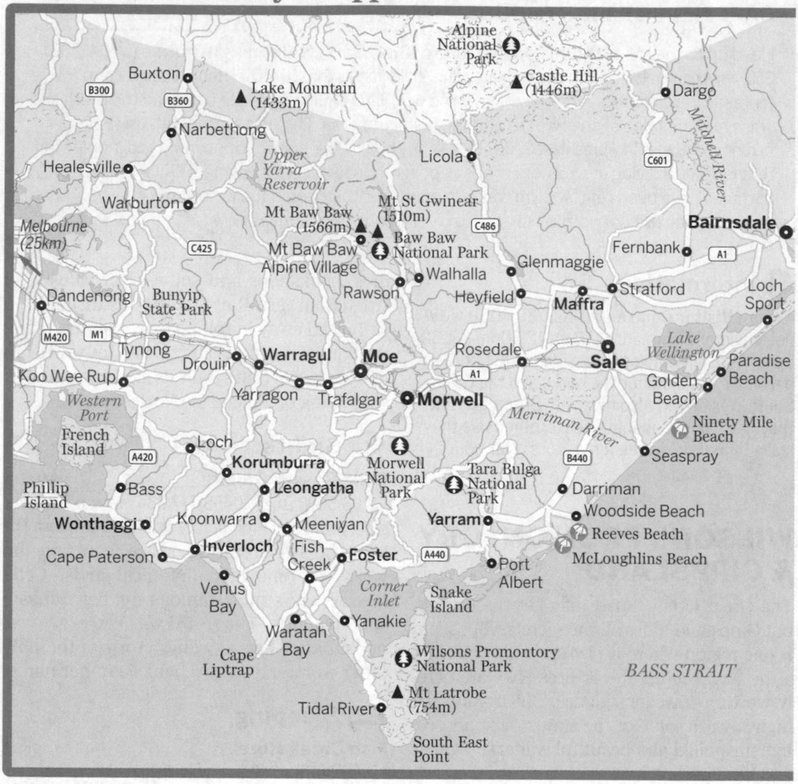

Eating

★Koonwarra Store CAFE $$

(☎03-5664 2285; www.koonwarrastore.com.au; 2 Koonwarra–Inverloch Rd; mains $12-26; ⏲8.30am-4pm; 📶) Local produce and wines are on sale in this renovated timber building. It's also a renowned cafe that serves simple food with flair, priding itself on using organic, low-impact suppliers and products – go the Koonie burger with all-Gippsland ingredients. Soak up the ambience in the wooded interior, or relax at a table in the gardens with local ice cream, regional wines and a cheese paddle.

Getting There & Away

By road Koonwarra is 32km southwest of Korumburra and 21km northeast of Inverloch. V/Line runs buses between Melbourne's Southern Cross and Koonwarra ($17.20, 2½ hours) three to four times a day. For Fish Creek, follow the signs off the South Gippsland Hwy at Foster (13km) or Meeniyan (28km). It's 24km (20 minutes) from Wilsons Promontory entrance gate. There are four direct daily buses from Melbourne's Southern Cross station ($20.40, 2¾ hours). It's also along the Korumburra–Foster bus line, with at least three departures daily.

Wilsons Promontory National Park

If you like wilderness bushwalking, stunning coastal scenery and secluded white-sand beaches, you'll absolutely love this place. The Prom, as it's affectionately known, is one of the most popular national parks in Australia. Hardly surprising, given its accessibility from Melbourne, its network of more than 80km of walking tracks, its swimming and surf beaches and the abundant wildlife. The southernmost part of mainland Australia, the Prom once formed part of a land bridge that allowed people to walk to Tasmania.

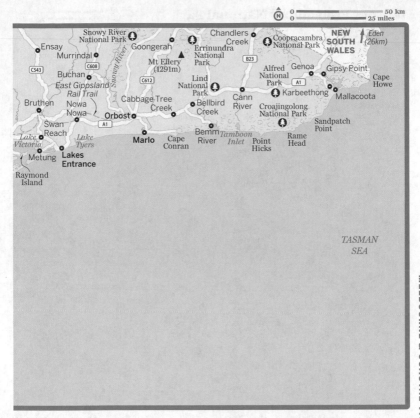

TASMAN
SEA

Tidal River, 30km from the park entrance, is the hub, although there's no fuel to be had here. It's home to the Parks Victoria office, a general store, a cafe and accommodation. The wildlife around Tidal River is incredibly tame, but to prevent disease do not feed the animals or birds.

◉ Sights

Norman Beach   BEACH
(Tidal River) The Prom's most popular beach is this beautiful stretch of golden sand, perfect for swimming and surfing, conveniently located at Tidal River campground.

Wilsons Promontory Lighthouse   LIGHTHOUSE
(Wilsons Promontory National Park) Close to being the southernmost tip of mainland Australia, this 19m granite lighthouse dates back to 1859. It's only accessibly on foot, a six-hour walk (18.3km) from Telegraph Saddle car park, hence most stay overnight at the Light-

house Keepers' Cottages (p271), or Roaring Meg campsite, 5.2km away.

🏃 Activities

Foster Kayak & Outdoor   OUTDOORS
(☑ 0475 473 211; www.facebook.com/foster kayakandoutdoor; 50 Main St, Foster; bike hire half/full day $35/70) Run by a Kiwi outdoor enthusiast, this adventure company hires out bikes for those wanting to tackle the **Great Southern Rail Trail** (www.railtrails.org.au) and surrounding mountain-bike trails; including 'fat' bikes and more genteel bicycles equipped with baskets stocked with local produce hampers. They also offer a range of innovative outdoor activities, where you can do anything from learning to free dive and kayak-fish to handplane bodysurfing.

Prom Country Scenic Flights   SCENIC FLIGHTS
(☑ 0488 555 123; www.promcountryflights.com. au; 3680 Meeniyan Promontory Rd, Yanakie; 45-min

Wilsons Promontory National Park

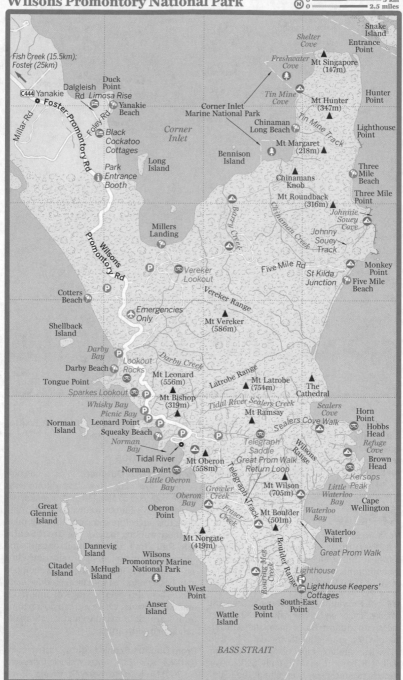

0 5 km
0 2.5 miles

Snake Island

Shelter Cove

Entrance Point

Freshwater Cove

Mt Singapore (147m)

Tin Mine Cove

Mt Hunter (347m)

Hunter Point

Fish Creek (15.5km); Foster (25km)

C444 Yanakie

Dalgleish Rd

Duck Point

Limosa Rise

Foley Rd

Yanakie Beach

Corner Inlet Marine National Park

Chinaman Long Beach

Mt Margaret (218m)

Lighthouse Point

Black Cockatoo Cottages

Corner Inlet

Bennison Island

Three Mile Beach

Park Entrance Booth

Long Island

Chinamans Knob

Mt Roundback (316m)

Three Mile Point

Millar Rd

Foster-Promontory Rd

Millers Landing

Barry Creek

Chinaman Creek

Johnnie Souey Cove

Johnny Souey Track

Wilsons Promontory Rd

Vereker Lookout

Vereker Range

Five Mile Rd

St Kilda Junction

Monkey Point

Five Mile Beach

Cotters Beach

Emergencies Only

Mt Vereker (586m)

Shellback Island

Darby Bay

Darby Creek

Latrobe Range

Mt Latrobe (754m)

The Cathedral

Lookout Rocks

Darby Beach

Mt Leonard (556m)

Tongue Point

Sparkes Lookout

Tidal River Sealers Creek

Mt Ramsay

Sealers Cove

Horn Point

Sealers Cove Walk

Hobbs Head

Whisky Bay

Picnic Bay

Mt Bishop (319m)

Refuge Cove

Norman Island

Leonard Point

Squeaky Beach

Telegraph Saddle

Wilsons Range

Brown Head

Norman Bay

Tidal River

Mt Oberon (558m)

Great Prom Walk Return Loop

Mt Wilson (705m)

Kersops Peak

Norman Point

Little Oberon Bay

Oberon Bay

Growler Creek

Telegraph Track

Mt Boulder (501m)

Little Waterloo Bay

Cape Wellington

Great Glennie Island

Oberon Point

Fraser Creek

Waterloo Bay

Dannevig Island

Wilsons Promontory Marine National Park

Mt Norgate (419m)

Waterloo Point

Great Prom Walk

Citadel Island

McHugh Island

South West Point

Boulder Range

Roaring Meg Creek

Lighthouse

Lighthouse Keepers' Cottages

Anser Island

Wattle Island

South Point

South-East Point

BASS STRAIT

flights adult/child under 10yr $210/100; ☺9am-5pm) Head to the skies for spectacular Prom views with these 45-minute flights over the coast, lighthouse and bushland. They're based just past the Yanakie General Store on the road into the park.

🛏 Sleeping

🛏 Tidal River

Situated on Norman Bay and a short walk to a stunning beach, Tidal River is incredibly popular. Book accommodation online well in advance through Parks Victoria (p272), especially for weekends and holidays.

Of Tidal River's 484 camp sites, only 20 are powered sites – so you'll need to book well in advance. For the Christmas school holiday period there's a ballot for sites (apply online by 30 June through Parks Victoria). There are also wooden huts with bunks and kitchenettes, comfortable self-contained units and spacious safari-style tented camping with en-suite bathrooms.

★Lighthouse Keepers' Cottages   COTTAGE $$$
(☑13 19 63, 03-5680 9555; www.parkweb.vic.gov.au; Wilsons Promontory National Park; d cottages $352-391, 12-bed cottages per person $127-141) These isolated, heritage-listed 1850s cottages, attached to a working light station on a pimple of land that juts out into the wild ocean, are a real getaway. Kick back after the 19km hike (around six hours) from Tidal River and watch ships or whales passing by. The cottages have thick granite walls and shared facilities, including a fully equipped kitchen.

Park Campsites – Tidal River CAMPGROUND $
(☑03-8427 2122, 13 1963; www.parkweb.vic.gov.au; Tidal River, Wilsons Promontory National Park; unpowered/powered sites $56.10/62.50) Camp sites sprawled across the precinct and along the foreshore within close assess to the beach. A maximum of eight campers are allowed at each site. There's access to hot showers, flush toilets, a dish-washing area, rubbish disposal points and gas barbecues. No camp fires permitted.

Park Cabins – Tidal River   CABIN $$
(☑13 1963, 03-8427 2122; www.parkstay.vic.gov. au; Tidal River, Wilsons Promontory National Park; 6-bed cabins from $234.50) These spacious and private self-contained cabins with fully equipped kitchen (but no TV) sleep up to six people. They have large, sliding-glass doors and a deck, and overlook the bush or river.

Wilderness Retreat
– Tidal River   TENTED CAMP $$$
(www.wildernessretreats.com.au; Tidal River, Wilsons Promontory National Park; d $318.50, extra person $26.20) Nestled in bushland at Tidal River, these large safari tents, each have their own deck, bathroom, queen-sized beds, fridge and heating, and there's a communal tent kitchen. Tents sleep up to four people and are pretty cool. It's like being on an African safari with a kookaburra soundtrack.

🛏 Yanakie & Foster

The tiny settlement of Yanakie offers the closest accommodation – from cabins and camping to luxury cottages – outside the park boundaries. Foster, the nearest main town, has a backpackers and several motels.

Black Cockatoo Cottages   COTTAGE $$
(☑03-5687 1306; www.blackcockatoo.com; 60 Foley Rd, Yanakie; d $150-250, 6-person houses $295-450) You can take in glorious views of the national park without leaving your comfortable bed – or breaking the bank – in these private, stylish, timber cottages. There are three modern cottages painted in a cool 'yellow-tailed black cockatoo' colour scheme, as well a 1970s-style brown-brick three-bedroom house.

★Limosa Rise   COTTAGE $$$
(☑03-5687 1135; www.limosarise.com.au; 40 Dalgleish Rd, Yanakie; d $295-400; ❄🐾) The views are stupendous from these luxury, self-contained cottages near the Prom entrance. The three tastefully appointed cottages (a studio, one bedroom and two bedroom) are fitted with wood-fire heaters, and full-length glass windows to take complete advantage of sweeping views across Corner Inlet, farmland and the Prom's mountains. Two-night minimum.

🍴 Eating

The **General Store** (☑03-5680 8520; Tidal River; mains $5-24; ☺9am-5pm Mon-Fri, to 6pm Sat, to 4pm Sun) in Tidal River stocks grocery items (but no alcohol), some camping equipment and a cafe. If you're hiking, or here for a while, it's cheaper to stock up in Foster. There's also a general store in Yanakie which is handy for food supplies, cold beer and Gippsland wines.

ℹ Information

Prom Country Visitor Information Centre
(cnr McDonald & Main St, Foster; ⊙ 9am-5pm)
Helpful info for those heading into Wilsons Prom,
as well as ideas for the surrounding region.
Tidal River Visitors Centre (✐ 03-5680 9555,
03-8427 2122, 13 19 63; www.parkweb.vic.gov.
au; ⊙ 8.30am-4.30pm, to 4pm in winter) The
helpful visitor centre at Tidal River books all park
accommodation (including permits for camping
away from Tidal River), and offers info for all
hiking options in the area.

ℹ Getting There & Away

Car Tidal River lies approximately 224km
southeast of Melbourne. There is no fuel here;
the closest petrol station is at Yanakie.
Public Transport There's no direct public
transport between Melbourne and the Prom. The
closest towns accessible by V/Line buses are
Fish Creek ($20.40, 2¾ hours) and Foster ($23,
three hours, four daily) via Dandenong and Koo
Wee Rup.

Lakes District

The Gippsland Lakes form the largest inland
waterway system in Australia, with the three
main interconnecting lakes – Wellington,
King and Victoria – stretching from Sale to
beyond Lakes Entrance. The lakes are actually saltwater lagoons, separated from the
ocean by the Gippsland Lakes Coastal Park
and the narrow coastal strip of sand dunes
known as Ninety Mile Beach. Apart from the
beach and taking to the water, the highlights
here involve hanging out at the pretty seaside
communities.

Sale

Gateway to the Lakes District, Sale is an important regional centre with little charm of
its own – but it has plenty of accommodation,
shops, restaurants and pubs, making it a convenient base from which to explore Ninety
Mile Beach.

TOP PROM WALKS

During school holidays and on weekends from Christmas to Easter, a free shuttle bus
operates between the Tidal River visitor car park and the **Telegraph Saddle car park** – a
nice way to start the Great Prom Walk. They run every 30 minutes from 8.30am to 5.45pm,
with a break for lunch at 1pm. For the overnight walks you'll need to arrange a hiking permit
beforehand, as well as payment for campsites and or other accommodation.

Great Prom Walk The most popular long-distance hike is a moderate 45km circuit
across to Sealers Cove from Tidal River, down to Refuge Cove, Waterloo Bay and the
lighthouse, returning to Tidal River via Oberon Bay. Allow three days and coordinate your
walk with tide times, as creek crossings can be hazardous. It's possible to visit or stay at
the lighthouse (p271) by prior arrangement with the parks office.

Sealers Cove Walk The best overnight hike, this two-day walk starts at Telegraph Saddle
and heads down Telegraph Track to stay overnight at beautiful Little Waterloo Bay (12km,
4½ hours). The next day, walk on to Sealers Cove via Refuge Cove and return to Telegraph Saddle (24km, 7½ hours).

Lilly Pilly Gully Nature Walk An easy 5km (two-hour) walk through heathland and eucalyptus forests, with lots of wildlife.

Mt Oberon Summit Starting from the Mt Oberon car park, this moderate-to-hard 7km
(2½-hour) walk is an ideal introduction to the Prom with panoramic views from the summit.
The free Mt Oberon shuttle bus can take you to the Telegraph Saddle car park and back.

Little Oberon Bay An easy-to-moderate 8km (three-hour) walk over sand dunes covered in coastal tea trees with beautiful views over Little Oberon Bay.

Squeaky Beach Nature Walk An easy 5km return stroll through coastal tea trees and
banksias to a sensational white-sand beach.

Prom Wildlife Walk This short 2.3km (45 minute) loop trail yields good kangaroo,
wallaby and emu sightings. It's located off the main road about 14km south of the park
entrance.

ℹ Information

Wellington Visitor Information Centre (📞 03-5144 1108; www.tourismwellington.com.au; 8 Foster St; ⏲ 9am-5pm; 🛜) A ton of brochures, wi-fi access and a free accommodation-booking service. From late 2017 they will be relocating to a new address at the Civic Centre, sharing space with the new Gippsland Art Gallery (📞 03-5142 3500; www.gippslandartgallery.com; 68 Foster St, Civic Centre; ⏲ 10am-5pm Mon-Fri, to 4pm Sat & Sun) and library.

Ninety Mile Beach

To paraphrase the immortal words of Crocodile Dundee...that's not a beach, *this* is a beach. Isolated Ninety Mile Beach is a narrow strip of sand backed by dunes, featuring lagoons and stretching unbroken for more or less 90 miles (150km) from near McLoughlins Beach to the channel at Lakes Entrance. The area is great for surf fishing, camping and long beach walks, though the crashing surf can be dangerous for swimming, except where patrolled at Seaspray, Woodside Beach and Lakes Entrance. The main access road to Ninety Mile Beach is the South Gippsland Hwy from Sale or Foster, turning off to Seaspray, Golden Beach and Loch Sport.

Metung

POP 1222

Curling around Bancroft Bay, little Metung is one of the prettiest towns in the Lakes District. Besotted locals call it the Gippsland Riviera, and with its absolute waterfront location and unhurried village charm, it's hard to argue.

⊙ Sights & Activities

Riviera Nautic   BOATING
(📞 03-5156 2243; www.rivieranautic.com.au; 185 Metung Rd; 2½hr tours adult/child/under 6yr $45/20/free, boat hire per 2hr/day $85/175, yachts & cruisers for 3 days from $1065; ⏲ tours 2.30pm Tue, Thu, Sat) Getting out on the water is easy in Metung, with Riviera Nautic hiring out boats and yachts for cruising, fishing and sailing on the Gippsland Lakes. There are also sightseeing cruises three times a week, with regular sightings of seals and dolphins. The liveaboard boats and motorised yachts offer a unique form of accommodation, and good value if you have a group. No boat licence required.

🛏 Sleeping

McMillans of Metung   RESORT $$
(📞 03-5156 2283; www.mcmillansofmetung.com.au; 155 Metung Rd; cottages/villas from $110/160;

❄ 🛜 🏊) This swish lakeside resort has won stacks of tourism awards for its complex of English country–style cottages set in 3 hectares of manicured gardens, as well its modern villas, private marina and spa centre.

Moorings at Metung   APARTMENT $$$
(📞 03-5156 2750; www.themoorings.com.au; 44 Metung Rd; apt $160-390; 🛜 🏊) At the end of the road in Metung, with water views to either Lake King or Bancroft Bay, this contemporary complex has a range of apartments from spacious studios to two-bedroom, split-level town houses. The complex has a tennis court, indoor and outdoor pools, a spa and a marina. Outside peak season it's good value.

✗ Eating

★**Nautica**   MODERN AUSTRALIAN $$
(📞 03-5156 2345; www.facebook.com/nautica metung; 50 Metung Rd; breakfasts from $10, mains from $19; ⏲ 8am-2pm & 6pm-late Wed-Sat, 8am-3pm Sun) A classy affair with polished wooden floorboards, open fire and views out to the water, Nautica is one not to miss. Start the day by treating yourself to a breakfast brioche roll filled with double bacon and Swiss cheese, while for lunch go the panko calamari or oysters. Dinner is anything from slow-cooked lamb shoulder to crispy-skin barramundi.

★**Metung Hotel**   PUB FOOD $$
(📞 03-5156 2206; www.metunghotel.com.au; 1 Kurnai Ave; mains $25-40; ⏲ kitchen noon-2pm & 6-8pm, pub 11am-late; 🛜) You can't beat the location overlooking Metung Wharf, and the big windows and outdoor timber decking make the most of the water views. The bistro serves top-notch pub food with a focus on fresh local seafood. The hotel also has the cheapest rooms in town ($85).

ℹ Information

Metung Visitor Centre (📞 03-5156 2969; www.metungtourism.com.au; 3/50 Metung Rd; ⏲ 9am-5pm) Accommodation-booking and boat-hire services. Also has a gift shop with local produce.

ℹ Getting There & Away

Metung lies south of the Princes Hwy along the C606; the turn-off is signposted at Swan Reach. The nearest major towns are Bairnsdale (28km) and Lakes Entrance (24km). The nearest inter-city rail services are at Bairnsdale.

Lakes Entrance

Lakes Entrance

POP 4569

With the shallow Cunninghame Arm waterway separating the town from the crashing ocean beaches, Lakes Entrance basks in an undeniably pretty location. In holiday season it's a packed-out tourist town with a graceless strip of motels, caravan parks, minigolf courses and souvenir shops lining The Esplanade. Still, the bobbing fishing boats, seafood, endless beaches and cruises out to Metung and Wyanga Park Winery should win you over.

🏃 Activities

Venture Out   ADVENTURE SPORTS
(📞 0427 731 441; www.ventureout.com.au; 347 The Esplanade; bike hire per hour/day $18/50, SUPs & kayaks per 2hr $25, tours from $45; ⊙ 10am-5pm, or call for bookings) Rents out bicycles, sea kayaks and stand-up paddleboards (SUPs), as well as running mountain-biking tours on single tracks through the surrounding forest.

Lonsdale Eco Cruises   CRUISE
(📞 0413 666 638; www.lonsdalecruises.com.au; Cunningham Quay; 3hr cruises adult/child/family $50/25/120; ⊙ 1pm Thu-Tue) 🛥 Scenic cruises out to Metung and Lake King on a former Queenscliff–Sorrento passenger ferry, with common dolphin sightings.

🛏 Sleeping

Eastern Beach Tourist Park   CARAVAN PARK $
(📞 03-5155 1581, 1800 761 762; www.easternbeach.com.au; 42 Eastern Beach Rd; unpowered sites $28-50, powered sites $35-69, cabins $118-285; @ 🛜 ⊠ 🐾) Most caravan parks in Lakes pack

'em in, but this one has space, grassy sites and a great location away from the hubbub of town in a bush setting back from Eastern Beach. A walking track takes you into town (30 minutes). New facilities are excellent, including a camp kitchen, barbecues and a kids' playground. Sells beers at reception, too.

Bellevue on the Lakes   HOTEL $$
(📞 03-5155 3055; www.bellevuelakes.com; 201 The Esplanade; d from $189, 2-bedroom apt from $249; ❄ 🛜 ⊠) Right in the heart of the Esplanade, Bellevue has neatly furnished rooms in earthy tones, most with water views. For extra luxury, go for the spacious spa suites or two-bedroom self-contained apartments.

🍴 Eating

★ **Ferryman's Seafood Cafe**   SEAFOOD $$
(📞 03-5155 3000; www.ferrymans.com.au; Middle Harbour, The Esplanade; mains lunch $18-24, dinner $21-45; ⊙ 10am-late) It's hard to beat the ambience of dining on the deck of this floating cafe-restaurant (an old Paynesville to Raymond Island passenger ferry), which will fill you to the gills with fish and seafood dishes. The fisherman's basket for lunch and seafood platter for dinner are popular orders. Downstairs you can buy fresh seafood.

Sparrows Nest   CAFE $$
(www.facebook.com/sparrowsnestlakesentrance; 581 The Esplanade; meals $11-21; ⊙ 7.30am-4pm; 🛜) Bringing a bit of urban style to Lakes Entrance is this cool spot doing single-origin coffees and house-made crumpets spread with Raymond Island honeycomb-butter speckled with bacon bits for breakfast. Lunches are good too, with the likes of pulled-pork

baguettes and craft beer by **Sailors Grave Brewing** (☐0466 331 936; www.sailorsgrave brewing.com; 7 Forest Rd; ⊙by appointment) in Marlo.

ⓘ Information

Lakes Entrance Visitor Centre (☐1800 637 060, 03-5155 1966; www.discovereastgippsland. com.au; cnr Princes Hwy & Marine Pde; ⊙9am-5pm; 🛜) Free accommodation- and tour-booking services. Also check out www.lakesentrance.com.

ⓘ Getting There & Away

Lakes Entrance lies 314km from Melbourne along the Princes Hwy.

V/Line (☐1800 800 007; www.vline.com.au) runs a train-bus service from Melbourne to Lakes Entrance via Bairnsdale ($39.80, 4½ hours, three daily).

East Gippsland & the Wilderness Coast

Beyond Lakes Entrance stretches a wilderness area of spectacular coastal national parks and old-growth forest. Much of this region has never been cleared for agriculture and it contains some of the most remote and pristine national parks in the state, making logging in these ancient forests a hot issue.

Buchan

POP 385

The sleepy town of Buchan, in the foothills of the Snowy Mountains, is famous for the spectacular and intricate limestone cave system at the Buchan Caves Reserve, open to visitors for almost a century. Underground rivers cutting through ancient limestone rock formed the caves and caverns, and they provided shelter for Aboriginal people as far back as 18,000 years ago. Buchan has huge potential as an outdoor adventure destination, with some 600 caves in the area – however only five remain open to the public. There are also swimming holes, mountain-biking trails, bushwalks and white-water rafting; see www.buchan.vic.au for more info.

⊙ Sights

★**Buchan Caves**   CAVE
(☐13 19 63; www.parks.vic.gov.au; tours adult/child/family $22/12.90/60.90, 2 caves $33/19.10/90.90; ⊙tours 10am, 11.15am, 1pm, 2.15pm & 3.30pm, hours vary seasonally) Since it was unveiled to Melburnians as a blockbuster sight in the early 1900s, the Buchan Caves has been dazzling visitors with its fantasy world of glistening calcite formations. Parks Victoria runs guided cave tours daily, alternating between **Royal** and **Fairy Caves**. They're both impressive: Royal has more colour, a higher chamber and dripping candle-like formations; Fairy has more delicate decorations and potential fairy sightings.

🛏 Sleeping

Buchan Caves Motel   LODGE **$$**
(☐03-5155 9419; www.buchanmotel.com.au; 67 Main Rd; d $130, tr & q $150) Enjoy views of the bucolic countryside from your balcony at this comfortable hilltop lodge with modern rooms featuring boutique touches. The friendly, young, enthusiastic owners are a wealth of knowledge on the area and have grand plans to capitalise on Buchan's tourism potential.

Buchan Caves Reserve   CAMPGROUND **$$**
(☐13 19 63; www.parks.vic.gov.au; unpowered/powered sites from $46/51, d cabins from $90, wilderness retreats d $191; ✱🖭) You can stay right by

the caves at this serene Parks Victoria camping ground edged by state forest. Though its campsites are exorbitantly priced, there are a couple of decent-value cabins, plus safari-style tents providing a 'luxury' wilderness experience, with comfortable queen-sized bed and air-conditioning. In summer there's a freshwater pool.

Drinking & Nightlife

Buchan Caves Hotel PUB
(☑ 03-5155 9203; www.facebook.com/buchancaves hotel; 49 Main Rd; ⊙ 11am-late) Rising from the ashes, the 125-year-old Buchan pub is back in business after burning to the ground in 2014. It came about via the world's first crowd-funding campaign to build a pub, with funds raised from around the globe. It reopened its doors in December 2016. Be sure to celebrate its return by stopping in for a chicken parma and a cold frothy.

ⓘ Getting There & Away

Buchan is an easy drive 56km north of Lakes Entrance. **Dyson's** (☑ 03-5152 1711) runs a bus service on Wednesday and Friday from Bairnsdale to Buchan ($16, two hours). It meets the train at Bairnsdale. At other times you'll need your own transport.

Cape Conran Coastal Park

This blissfully undeveloped part of the coast is one of Gippsland's most beautiful corners, with long stretches of remote white-sand beaches. The 19km coastal route from Marlo

> **WORTH A TRIP**
>
> ### KROWATHUNKOOLONG KEEPING PLACE
>
> A stirring and insightful Koorie cultural exhibition space, **Krowathunkoolong Keeping Place** (☑ 03-5152 1891, 03-5150 0737; www.batalukculturaltrail.com.au; 37-53 Dalmahoy St; adult/child $3.50/2.50; ⊙ 9am-5pm Mon-Fri) explores Kurnai life from the Dreaming until after European settlement. The exhibition traces the Kurnai clan from their Dreaming ancestors, Borun the pelican and his wife Tuk the musk duck, and covers life at Lake Tyers Mission, east of Lakes Entrance, now a trust privately owned by Aboriginal shareholders. The massacres of the Kurnai from 1839 to 1849 are also detailed.

to Cape Conran is particularly pretty, bordered by banksia trees, grass plains, sand dunes and the ocean.

🏃 Activities

Cape Conran is a fabulous spot for walking. One favourite is the nature trail that meets up with the East Cape Boardwalk, where signage gives you a glimpse into how Indigenous peoples lived in this area. Following an indigenous theme, take the West Cape Rd off Cape Conran Rd to **Salmon Rocks**, where there's an Aboriginal **shell midden** dated at more than 10,000 years old.

For some relaxed swimming, canoeing and fishing, head to the Yerrung River, which shadows the coast east of the cape and can be reached along Yerrung River Rd. There's good surfing at West Cape Beach, extending northwest from the cape and accessible from West Cape Rd. For qualified divers, Marlo-based **Cross Diving Services** (☑ 03-5154 8554, 0407 362 960; www.crossdiving.com.au; 20 Ricardo Dr; ⊙ shore dives with/without equipment hire $80/15, boat dives $100/150, 4-day open course $550) offers dives on most weekends.

🛏 Sleeping

Parks Victoria has three excellent privately managed accommodation options in Cape Conran Coastal Park – offering camping, **cabins** (☑ 03-5154 8438; www.conran.net.au; cabins $171.70-237.20) and **safari-style tented camping** (☑ 03-5154 8438; www.conran.net.au; d $191.20), which are all privately managed.

ⓘ Getting There & Away

Cape Conran Coastal Park lies south of the Princes Hwy, 405km from Melbourne. The well-signposted turn-off from the highway lies just east of the small settlement of Cabbage Tree. The park is around 15km south of the turn-off along Cabbage Tree-Conran Rd.

Mallacoota

POP 1032

One of Gippsland's, and indeed Victoria's, little gems, Mallacoota is the state's most easterly town, snuggled on the vast Mallacoota Inlet and surrounded by the tumbling hills and beachside dunes of beautiful Croajingolong National Park. Those prepared to come this far are treated to long, empty, ocean-surf beaches, tidal estuaries and swimming, fishing and boating on the inlet. It's a good place for wildlife too with plentiful kangaroos, as well as koalas and echidnas.

RAYMOND ISLAND

For one of the best places in Victoria to see koalas, drop down off the Princes Hwy to the relaxed lakeside town of Paynesville. Paynesville is the departure point for a five-minute ferry crossing to Raymond Island. There's a large colony of koalas here, mostly relocated from Phillip Island in the 1950s. Kangaroos and echidnas are also regularly spotted. The flat-bottom car-and-passenger ferry operates every 20 minutes from 6.40am to midnight and is free for pedestrians and cyclists. Cars cost $12 and motorcycles $5.

◉ Sights & Activities

The calm estuarine waters of Mallacoota Inlet have more than 300km of shoreline – hiring a boat is the best way to explore, and there are plenty of great walks along the water's edge.

For good surf, head to Bastion Point or Tip Beach. Get in touch with Surf Shack for board rental and surf classes. There's swimmable surf and some sheltered water at Betka Beach, which is patrolled during Christmas school holidays. There are also good swimming spots along the beaches of the foreshore reserve, at Bastion Point (patrolled by a surf life-saving club) and at Quarry Beach.

Gabo Island   ISLAND

On Gabo Island, 14km offshore from Mallacoota, the windswept 154-hectare **Gabo Island Lightstation Reserve** is home to seabirds and one of the world's largest colonies of little penguins, far outnumbering those on Phillip Island. Whales, dolphins and fur seals are regularly sighted offshore. The island has an operating **lighthouse**, built in 1862 and the tallest in the southern hemisphere – you can stay in the old keepers' cottages here.

Transport out here however is an issue, with boat access often restricted due to bad weather; **Wilderness Coast Ocean Charters** (☑0417 398 068, 03-5158 0701) and **Gabo Island Escapes** (☑0437 221 694, 03-5158 0605; per person $100) are your best bet.

Mallacoota Hire Boats   BOATING

(☑0438 447 558; www.mallacootahireboats.com; 10 Buckland Dr; motorboats per 2/8hr $70/160, kayaks 1/2 people per 2hr $30/50) Hires out kayaks, motorboats, pedal boats and fishing equipment. No boat licence required; cash only. They're based out of Mallacoota Foreshore Holiday Park.

🛏 Sleeping

Mallacoota Foreshore
Holiday Park   CARAVAN PARK $

(☑03-5158 0300; cnr Allan Dr & Maurice Ave; unpowered sites $16.60-33, powered sites $23.70-53;

🐾) Curling around the waterfront, the grassy sites here morph into one of Victoria's most sociable caravan parks, with sublime views of the inlet and its resident population of black swans and pelicans. No cabins, but the best of Mallacoota's many parks for campers. Reception is across the road in the same building as the visitor information centre.

★ Adobe Abodes   APARTMENT $$

(☑0499 777 968; www.adobeabodes.com.au; 17-19 Karbeethong Ave; d $95-145, extra person $15) 🐾 These unique mud-brick self-contained units in Karbeethong are something special. With an emphasis on recycling and eco-friendliness, the flats have solar hot water and guests are encouraged to compost their kitchen scraps. The array of whimsical apartments are comfortable and well equipped, and come with welcome baskets of wine and chocolate, and wonderful views.

★ Karbeethong Lodge   GUESTHOUSE $$

(☑03-5158 0411; www.karbeethonglodge.com.au; 16 Schnapper Point Dr; r incl breakfast $100-150) It's hard not to be overcome by a sense of serenity as you rest on the broad verandahs of this early 1900s timber guesthouse, which give uninterrupted views over Mallacoota Inlet and the expansive gardens. The large guest lounge and dining room have an open fire and period furnishings, there's a mammoth kitchen and the pastel-toned bedrooms are small but tastefully decorated.

Gabo Island Lighthouse   COTTAGE $$

(☑03-8427 2123, Parks Victoria 13 19 63; www.parkweb.vic.gov.au; up to 8 people $323.70-359.70) For a truly wild experience head out to stay at this remote lighthouse. Accommodation is available in the historic three-bedroom assistant lighthouse keeper's residence. There's a two-night minimum stay and a ballot for use during the Christmas and Easter holidays; take note there's no refunds if you're unable to reach the island (or get stranded there) during inclement weather.

✖ Eating & Drinking

★ **Lucy's**   ASIAN $$

(📞03-5158 0666; 64 Maurice Ave; mains $8-28; ⏱8am-8pm) Lucy's is popular for delicious and great-value homemade rice noodles with chicken, prawn or abalone, as well as dumplings stuffed with ingredients from the garden. It's also good for breakfast.

Mallacoota Hotel   PUB

(📞03-5158 0455; www.mallacootahotel.com.au; 51-55 Maurice Ave; ⏱noon-10pm) The local pub is a popular spot for a drink with a cosy indoor bar and a wonderful outdoor beer garden full of palm trees. Its bistro serves hearty meals (mains $20 to $40) from its varied menu, with reliable favourites being the chicken parma, Gippsland steak and pale ale fish and chips. Bands play regularly in summer. There's motel pub accommodation (single/double from $100/110) here, too.

ⓘ Information

Mallacoota Visitor Centre (📞03-5158 0800, 03-5158 0116, 0408 315 615; www.visitmallacoota.com.au; cnr Allan Dr & Maurice Ave; ⏱9am-5pm; 🖥) On the main strip across from the water is this extremely helpful tourist centre with a ton of info on the area and its walking trails, and a handy booklet on local sights ($1). Has wi-fi and internet access too.

ⓘ Getting There & Away

Mallacoota is 23km southeast of Genoa (on the Princes Hwy), which is 492km from Melbourne. Take the train to Bairnsdale (3¾ hours), then the V/Line bus to Genoa ($51.80, 3½ hours, one daily). The Mallacoota–Genoa bus meets the V/Line coach on Monday, Thursday and Friday, plus Sunday during school holidays, and runs to Mallacoota ($3.20, 30 minutes).

Croajingolong National Park

Croajingolong is one of Australia's finest coastal wilderness national parks, recognised by its listing as a World Biosphere Reserve by Unesco (one of 14 in Australia). The park covers 875 sq km, stretching for about 100km from the town of Bemm River to the NSW border. Magnificent, unspoiled beaches, inlets, estuaries and forests make it an ideal park for camping, walking, swimming and surfing.

◉ Sights & Activities

Point Hicks was the first part of Australia to be spotted by Captain Cook and the *Endeavour* crew in 1770, and was named after Lieutenant Zachary Hicks. There's a **lighthouse** (📞10am-3pm Mon-Fri 03-5158 4268; www.pointhicks.com.au; Lighthouse Track, Tamboon; adult/child/family $7/4/20; ⏱tours 1pm, Fri-Sun) here and accommodation in the old cottages (p278). You can still see remains of the SS *Saros*, which ran ashore in 1937, on a short walk from the lighthouse.

The five inlets, Sydenham, Tamboon, Mueller, Wingan and Mallacoota (the largest and most accessible), are popular canoeing and fishing spots. Two sections of the park have been declared wilderness areas (no vehicles, access to a limited number of walkers and permits required): the Cape Howe Wilderness Area, between Mallacoota Inlet and the NSW border, and the Sandpatch Wilderness Area, between Wingan Inlet and Shipwreck Creek.

🛌 Sleeping

Wingan Inlet   CAMPGROUND $

(📞13 19 63; www.parkweb.vic.gov.au; unpowered sites from $25.80) This serene and secluded camping ground has 24 sites among superb sandy beaches and great walks. The Wingan River Walk (5km, 2½ hours return) through rainforest has great waterholes for swimming. Bookings though Parks Victoria.

Point Hicks Lighthouse   COTTAGE $$

(📞03-5156 0432; www.pointhicks.com.au; bungalows $120-150, cottages $360-550) This remote lighthouse has two comfortable, heritage-listed cottages and one double bungalow, which originally housed the assistant lighthouse keepers. The cottages sleep six people, and have sensational ocean views and wood-burning fireplaces. Bring along your own bedding and towels, or you can hire it for $15 per person. To get here you'll need to walk 2.2km from the car park.

ⓘ Getting There & Away

Croajingolong National Park lies 492km east of Melbourne. Unsealed access roads of varying quality lead south off Princes Hwy and into the park from various points between Cann River and the NSW border. Among these are tracks leading to camping grounds at Wingan Inlet, Mueller Inlet, Thurra River and Shipwreck Creek.

Apart from Mallacoota Rd, all of the access roads are unsealed and can be very rough in winter, so check road conditions with Parks Victoria in **Cann River** (📞13 19 63, 03-5158 6351; www.parkweb.vic.gov.au; Cann River) or **Mallacoota** (📞13 19 63, 03-8427 2123; www.parkweb.vic.gov.au; Mallacoota) before venturing on, especially during or after rain.

Brisbane & Around

Best Places
to Eat

➡ Urbane (p299)

➡ Gauge (p300)

➡ Island Fruit Barn (p318)

➡ King Arthur Cafe (p301)

➡ Shouk Cafe (p304)

Best Places
to Sleep

➡ New Inchcolm Hotel &
Suites (p297)

➡ Next (p296)

➡ Spicers Balfour Hotel
(p298)

➡ Allure (p318)

➡ Bunk Backpackers (p297)

Why Go?

Sophisticated city galleries and rooftop bars, desolate subtropical beaches, cool-climate vineyards: the greater Brisbane
region deals in Queensland's most gasp-inducing contrasts.
Star of the show is Brisbane itself, a lush, sultry metropolis
with flourishing restaurant, bar and cultural scenes that at-
test to its coming of age. Lapping at the city's eastern fringe is
Moreton Bay, home to low-lying sandy isles – including Moreton Island – that beckon with their turquoise waves, sparkling
forests and passing parade of whales, turtles and dolphins.

Brisbanites are out on the streets: the weather is brilliant and so are the bodies. Fit-looking locals get up early
to go jogging, swimming, cycling, kayaking, rock climbing
or just to walk the dog. And when it's too hot outside, Brisbane's subcultural undercurrents run cool and deep, with
bookshops, globally inspired restaurants, cafes, bars and
live-music venues aplenty.

When to Go
Brisbane

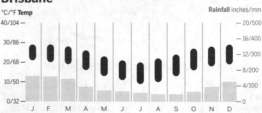

Jan Brisbane
swelters during
summer, making
it the perfect time
to cool off in the
surf.

May–Aug Cooler
temperatures
(bring a jacket)
and clear blue
skies.

Sep Spring has
sprung. Warmer
temperatures
and the hot-ticket
Brisbane and Big-
sound festivals.

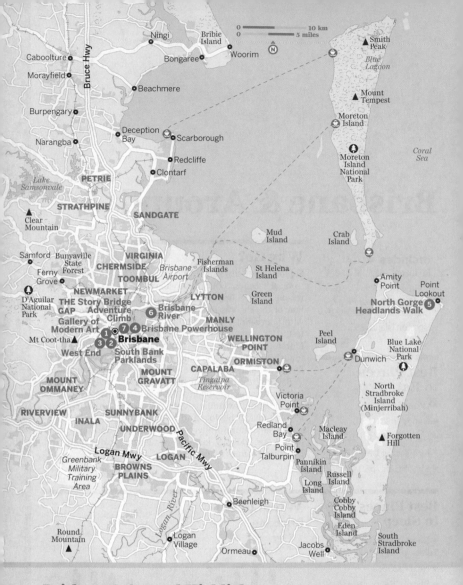

Brisbane & Around Highlights

① Gallery of Modern Art (p285) Finding your modern muse at one of Australia's hottest galleries of contemporary art.

② South Bank Parklands (p285) Picnicking, strolling or simply sunning by an inner-city beach at Brisbane's best-loved riverside hangout.

③ West End (p300) Roaming bookshops, microbreweries and band venues in Brisbane's boho heartland.

④ Brisbane Powerhouse (p289) Catching a show in a converted power station.

⑤ North Gorge Headlands Walk (p317) Experiencing one

of North Stradbroke Island's most beautiful walks.

⑥ Brisbane Riverwalk (p288) View the city skyline and the river on this illuminating path.

⑦ Story Bridge Adventure Climb (p291) Scale Brisbane's Story Bridge on this thrilling two-hour climb.

BRISBANE

POP 2.3 MILLION

No longer satisfied in the shadow of Sydney and Melbourne, Brisbane is subverting stereotypes and surprising the critics. Welcome to Australia's new subtropical 'It kid'. Brisbane's charms are evident: the arts, the cafes, the bars, the weather, the old Queenslander houses, the go-get-'em attitude. But it's the Brisbane River that gives the city its edge. The river's organic convolutions carve the city into a patchwork of urban villages, each with a distinct style and topography: bohemian, low-lying West End; hip, hilltop Paddington; exclusive, peninsular New Farm; prim, pointy Kangaroo Point. Move from village to village and experience Queensland's diverse, eccentric, happening capital.

◉ Sights

Most of Brisbane's major sights lie in the city centre (CBD) and South Bank directly across the river. While the former offers colonial history and architecture, the latter is home to Brisbane's major cultural institutions and the South Bank Parklands.

◉ Central Brisbane

★ City Hall   LANDMARK

(Map p286; ☑ 07-3339 0845; www.brisbane.qld. gov.au; King George Sq; ⊙ 8am-5pm Mon-Fri, 9am-5pm Sat & Sun, clock tower tours 10.15am-4.45pm, City Hall tours 10.30am, 11.30am, 1.30pm & 2.30pm; 🚇 Central) **FREE** Fronted by a row of sequoia-sized Corinthian columns, this sandstone behemoth was built between 1920 and 1930. The foyer's marble was sourced from the same Tuscan quarry as that used by Michelangelo to sculpt his *David*. The Rolling Stones played their first-ever Australian gig in the building's auditorium in 1965, a magnificent space complete with a 4300-pipe organ, mahogany and blue-gum floors and free concerts every Tuesday at noon. Free tours of the 85m-high clock tower run every 15 minutes; grab tickets from the excellent on-site Museum of Brisbane (p281).

★ Museum of Brisbane   MUSEUM

(Map p286; ☑ 07-3339 0800; www.museumof-brisbane.com.au; Level 3, Brisbane City Hall, King George Sq; ⊙ 10am-5pm; 🚇 Central) **FREE** Delve into Brisbane's highs and lows at this forward-thinking museum, tucked away inside City Hall. The current hero exhibition is 100% Brisbane. An innovative collaboration between the museum and Berlin-based theatre company Rimini Protokoll, the interactive project explores the lives of 100 current Brisbane residents, who together accurately reflect the city's population based on data from the Australian Bureau of Statistics (ABS). The result is a snapshot of a metropolis much more complex than you may have expected.

City Botanic Gardens   PARK

(Map p286; www.brisbane.qld.gov.au; Alice St; ⊙ 24hr; 🚌 QUT Gardens Point, 🚇 Central) **FREE** Originally a collection of food crops planted by convicts in 1825, this is Brisbane's favourite green space. Descending gently from the Queensland University of Technology campus to the river, its mass of lawns, tangled Moreton Bay figs, bunya pines, macadamia trees and tai chi troupes are a soothing elixir for frazzled urbanites. Free, one-hour guided tours leave the rotunda at 11am and 1pm daily, and the gardens host the popular Brisbane Riverside Markets (p313) on Sunday. Ditch the gardens' average cafe for a picnic.

Parliament House   HISTORIC BUILDING

(Map p286; www.parliament.qld.gov.au; cnr Alice & George Sts; ⊙ tours 1pm, 2pm, 3pm & 4pm nonsitting days; 🚌 QUT Gardens Point, 🚇 Central) **FREE** With a roof clad in Mt Isa copper, this lovely blanched-white stone, French Renaissance-style building dates from 1868 and overlooks the City Botanic Gardens. The only way to peek inside is on one of the free tours, which leave on demand at the listed times (2pm only when parliament is sitting). Arrive five minutes before tours begin; no need to book.

Roma Street Parkland   PARK

(Map p286; www.visitbrisbane.com.au/Roma-Street-Parkland-and-Spring-Hill; 1 Parkland Blvd; ⊙ 24hr; 🚇 Roma St) **FREE** This beautifully maintained, 16-hectare downtown park is one of the world's largest subtropical urban gardens. Formerly a market and a railway yard, the park opened in 2001 and is a showcase for native Queensland vegetation, complete with a rainforest and fern gully, waterfalls, skyline lookouts, a playground, barbecues and no shortage of frangipani. It's

BRISBANE & AROUND BRISBANE

Gallipoli Barracks
Military Area

Wardell St

ASHGROVE

Enoggera Creek

← D'Aguilar National
Park (3km)

Waterworks Rd

Coopers Camp Rd

Jubilee Tce

**KELVIN
GROVE**

16
Latrobe Tce

BARDON

Boundary St

PADDINGTON

See West End &
Petrie Terrace
Map (p290)

7

Mt Coot-tha
Reserve

Frederick St

AUCHENFLOWER

32 Milton

9
3

Sir Samuel Griffith Dr

MT COOT-THA

Western Fwy

M5

Milton Rd

Auchenflower

Coronation Dr

21 33

6

TOOWONG

Toowong

TARINGA

33

Moggill Rd

Taringa

Coronation Dr

**ST
LUCIA**

M5

Moggill Rd

20

**CHAPEL
HILL**

33

Coonan St

Indooroopilly

INDOOROOPILLY

St Lucia
Golf Links

Brisbane River

↓ Lone Pine Koala
Sanctuary (5km)

Chelmer

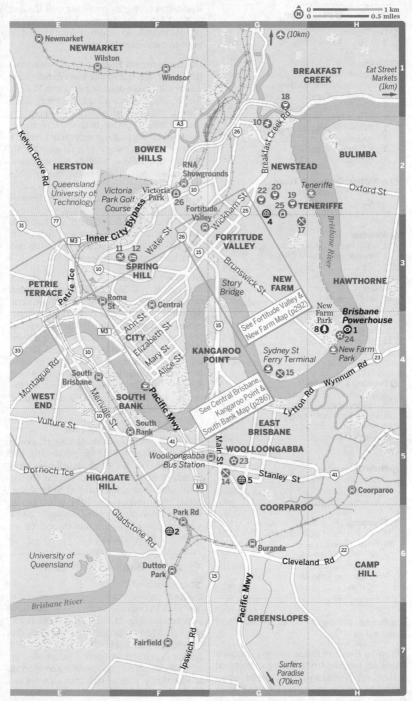

Greater Brisbane

something of a maze: easy to get into, hard to get out of.

Shrine of Remembrance LANDMARK
(Map p286; Anzac Sq, Ann St; ⊠Central) Designed in the Greek Revival style, this graceful monument honours the Australian men and women who have served in conflicts around the world. Its 18 columns symbolise 1918, the end of WWI, while the structure itself is made of prized Queensland sandstone from Helidon, a town to the west of Brisbane.

Old Government House HISTORIC BUILDING
(Map p286; ☑07-3138 8005; www.ogh.qut.edu.au; 2 George St; ⊙9am-4pm, 1hr guided tours 10.30am Tue-Thu; ⊠QUT Gardens Point, ⊠Central) FREE Hailed as Queensland's most important historic building, this 1862 showpiece was designed by estimable government architect Charles Tiffin as a plush residence for Sir George Bowen, Queensland's first governor. The lavish innards were restored in 2009 and the property now offers free podcast and guided tours; the latter must be booked by phone or email. The building also houses the William Robinson Gallery, dedicated to the Australian artist and home to an impressive collection of his works, including two Archibald Prize–winning paintings.

St John's Cathedral CHURCH
(Map p286; ☑07-3835 2222; www.stjohns cathedral.com.au; 373 Ann St; ⊙9.30am-4.30pm; ⊠Central) A magnificent fusion of stone, carved timber and stained glass just west of Fortitude Valley, St John's Cathedral is a beautiful example of 19th-century Gothic Revival architecture. The building is a true labour of love: construction began in 1906 and wasn't finished until 2009, making it one of the world's last cathedrals of this architectural style to be completed.

Commissariat Store Museum MUSEUM
(Map p286; www.queenslandhistory.org; 115 William St; adult/child/family $6/3/12; ⊙10am-4pm Tue-Fri; ⊠North Quay, ⊠Central) Built by convicts in 1829, this former government storehouse is the oldest occupied building in Brisbane. Inside is an immaculate little museum devoted to convict and colonial history. Don't miss the convict 'fingers' and the exhibit on Italians in Queensland.

◉ South Bank & West End

★**Queensland**
Cultural Centre CULTURAL CENTRE
(Map p286; Melbourne St, South Bank; ⊠South Bank Terminals 1 & 2, ⊠South Brisbane) On South Bank, just over Victoria Bridge from the CBD, the Queensland Cultural Centre is the epicentre of Brisbane's cultural confluence. Surrounded by subtropical gardens, the sprawling complex of architecturally notable buildings includes the Queensland Performing Arts Centre (p310),

the Queensland Museum & Sciencentre, the Queensland Art Gallery, the State Library of Queensland, and the particularly outstanding Gallery of Modern Art (GOMA).

★ **Gallery of Modern Art**   GALLERY
(GOMA; Map p286; www.qagoma.qld.gov.au; Stanley Pl, South Bank; ☉10am-5pm; ⛴ South Bank Terminals 1 & 2, ☒ South Brisbane) FREE All angular glass, concrete and black metal, must-see GOMA focuses on Australian art from the 1970s to today. Continually changing, and often confronting, exhibits range from painting, sculpture and photography to video, installation and film. There's also

an arty bookshop, children's activity rooms, a cafe (p300), a Modern Australian **restaurant** (Map p286; ☑07-3842 9916; mains $39-47; ☉noon-2pm Wed-Sun, plus 5.30-8pm Fri; ⛴ South Bank Terminals 1 & 2, ☒ South Brisbane), as well as free guided gallery tours at 11am, 1pm and 2pm.

South Bank Parklands   PARK
(Map p286; www.visitbrisbane.com.au; Grey St, South Bank; ☉dawn-dusk; ⛹; ⛴ South Bank Terminals 1, 2 & 3, ☒ South Brisbane, South Bank) FREE Should you sunbake on a sandy beach, chill in a rainforest, or eye-up a Nepalese peace pagoda? You can do all

---

BRISBANE'S GALLERY SCENE

While the Gallery of Modern Art, aka GOMA, and the **Queensland Art Gallery** (p287) might steal the show, Brisbane also has a growing array of smaller, private galleries and exhibition spaces where you can mull over both the mainstream and the cutting-edge.

The Pillars Project (Map p286; www.thepillarsproject.com; Merrivale St, South Brisbane; ☉24hr; ⛴198, ⛴ South Bank Terminals 1 & 2, ☒ South Brisbane) One of Brisbane's most unexpected art spaces. A series of pillars under the South Brisbane Rail Underpass have been transformed into arresting street-art murals by numerous artists. Among these is the internationally acclaimed, Brisbane-raised Fintan Magee.

Institute of Modern Art (IMA; Map p292; ☑07-3252 5750; www.ima.org.au; 420 Brunswick St, Fortitude Valley; ☉noon-6pm Tue, Wed, Fri & Sat, to 8pm Thu; ☒ Fortitude Valley) Located in the Judith Wright Centre of Contemporary Arts in Fortitude Valley is this excellent noncommercial gallery with an industrial vibe and regular showings by both local and international names working in mediums as diverse as installation art, photography and painting.

TW Fine Art (Map p292; ☑0437 348 755; www.twfineart.com; 181 Robertson St, Fortitude Valley; ☉10am-5pm Tue-Sat, to 3pm Sun; ⛴470, ☒ Fortitude Valley) Easy-to-miss, this Fortitude Valley gallery eschews the 'keep it local' mantra for intellectually robust, critically acclaimed contemporary art from around the world. It also runs an innovative online gallery of limited-edition prints, which you can browse at the gallery and have couriered straight to your home.

Fireworks Gallery (Map p282; ☑07-3216 1250; www.fireworksgallery.com.au; 52a Doggett St, Newstead; ☉10am-6pm Tue-Fri, to 4pm Sat; ⛴300, 302, 305, 306, 322, 393, 470) A fabulous warehouse space showcasing mainly painting and sculpture by both Indigenous and non-Indigenous contemporary Australian artists. It's just a short stroll from James St in Fortitude Valley.

Milani (Map p282; ☑07-3391 0455; www.milanigallery.com.au; 54 Logan Rd, Woolloongabba; ☉11am-6pm Tue-Sat; ⛴174, 175, 204) FREE A superb gallery with cutting-edge Aboriginal and confronting contemporary artwork. It's in an industrial corner of Woolloongabba, surrounded by car yards and hairdressing equipment suppliers – if it looks closed, simply turn the door handle.

Suzanne O'Connell Gallery (Map p292; ☑07-3358 5811; www.suzanneoconnell.com; 93 James St, New Farm; ☉11am-4pm Wed-Sat; ⛴470) FREE This New Farm gallery specialises in Indigenous art, with brilliant works from artists all across Australia. Check the website for regular exhibition openings.

Jan Murphy Gallery (Map p292; ☑07-3254 1855; www.janmurphygallery.com.au; 486 Brunswick St, Fortitude Valley; ☉10am-5pm Tue-Sat; ⛴195, 196, 199, ☒ Fortitude Valley) Fronted by a strip of Astroturf, this charcoal-grey gallery is another leading exhibition space for contemporary Australian talent in the thick of Fortitude Valley's gallery district.

Central Brisbane, Kangaroo Point & South Bank

Go Between Bridge

Pacific Mwy

Roma St

25

Roma St

11
Roma Street Parkland

SPRING HILL

51

29

Grey St

Makerston St

24

Herschel St

Roma St

Wickham Tce

Albert St

Upper Edward St

Wickham Park

King Edward Park

60

Central

Montague Rd

15

2
36

Gallery of Modern Art

Kurilpa Bridge
M3

Tank St

CityCat Ferry

Pacific Mwy

Turbot St

King George Square Bus Station

37

38 City Hall

Museum of Brisbane

Ann St

King George Square

1 18

66

Adelaide St

65

12

Anzac Square

Post Office Square

17

Peel St

Stanley Pl

4 Queensland Cultural Centre

NorthQuay

34

64

28

Burnett La

53

George St

Queen St Mall

68

23

Edward St

Elizabeth St

Market St

SOUTH BRISBANE

10

35

10 Queensland Cultural Centre

Melbourne St

Victoria Bridge

Melbourne St

26

Queen St Bus Station

42

Melbourne St

57

Brisbane River

Pacific Mwy

6

61

47

Stephens La

40

Charlotte St

Albert St

Mary St

56

43

Russell St

Merivale St

South Brisbane

Grey St

39
16

19

Stephens La

45

George St

Margaret St

49

30

13

54

South Bank Terminals 1 & 2

William St

M3

Alice St

62

Glenelg St

Little Stanley St

QUT Gardens Point

8

Cordelia St

10

59

69

22

67 63

ERNEST St

Grey St

SOUTH BANK

CityHopper Ferry

Queensland University of Technology (QUT)

7

City Botanic Gardens

5

Merivale St

Colchester St

Tribune St

South Bank Terminal 3

CityCat Ferry

CityHopper Ferry

41

Vulture St

South Bank

9

41

Goodwill Bridge

M3

58

Sidon St

Maritime Museum

Captain Cook Bridge

River Tce

River Tce

10

CT White Park

Vulture St

Pacific Mwy

River Tce

Llewellyn St

Main St

Stephens Rd

Stanley St

10

WOOLLOONGABBA

15

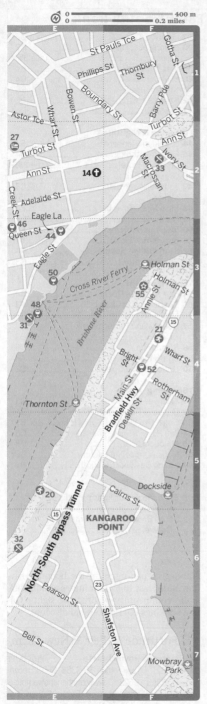

three in this 17.5-hectare park overlooking the city centre. Its canopied walkways lead to performance spaces, lush lawns, eateries and bars, public art and regular free events ranging from yoga sessions to film screenings. The star attractions are Streets Beach (p291), an artificial, lagoon-style swimming beach (packed on weekends); and the near-60m-high Wheel of Brisbane (p288), delivering 360-degree views on its 10-minute rides.

Queensland Art Gallery
GALLERY

(QAG; Map p286; www.qagoma.qld.gov.au; Melbourne St, South Bank; ⊘10am-5pm; ᛗSouth Bank Terminals 1 & 2, ᚏSouth Brisbane) **FREE** While current construction works (due for completion in September 2017) have temporarily limited its gallery space, QAG is home to a fine permanent collection of Australian and international works. Australian art dates from the 1840s to the 1970s: check out works by celebrated masters including Sir Sidney Nolan, Arthur Boyd, William Dobell and Albert Namatjira.

Queensland Museum & Sciencentre
MUSEUM

(Map p286; ☑07-3840 7555; www.southbank. qm.qld.gov.au; cnr Grey & Melbourne Sts, South Bank; Queensland Museum admission free, Sciencentre adult/child/family $14.50/11.50/44.50; ⊘9.30am-5pm; ᛗSouth Bank Terminals 1 & 2, ᚏSouth Brisbane) **FREE** Dig deeper into Queensland history at the state's main historical repository, where intriguing exhibits include a skeleton of the state's own dinosaur Muttaburrasaurus (aka 'Mutt'), and the *Avian Cirrus,* the tiny plane in which Queenslander Bert Hinkler made the first England-to-Australia solo flight in 1928. Also on-site is the Sciencentre, an educational fun house with a plethora of interactive exhibits delving into life science and technology. Expect long queues during school holidays.

Queensland Maritime Museum
MUSEUM

(Map p286; ☑07-3844 5361; www.maritime museum.com.au; Stanley St; adult/child/family $16/7/38; ⊘9.30am-4.30pm, last admission 3.30pm; ᛗMaritime Museum, ᚏSouth Bank) On the southern edge of the South Bank Parklands is this sea-salty museum, the highlight of which is the gigantic HMAS *Diamantina,* a restored WWII frigate that you can clamber aboard and explore.

Central Brisbane, Kangaroo Point & South Bank

Wheel of Brisbane   FERRIS WHEEL

(Map p286; ☏07-3844 3464; www.thewheel
ofbrisbane.com.au; Grey St, South Bank; adult/
child/family $19/13.50/55; ⊙10am-10pm Sun-
Thu, to 11pm Fri & Sat; ⊠South Bank Terminals 1
& 2, ⊠South Brisbane) Don't have wings but
pining for a lofty view of the city? Then consider a ride on the riverside Wheel, a few
steps from the Queensland Performing Arts
Centre (p310). The enclosed gondolas rise
to a height of nearly 60m, which, while not
spectacularly high, still offers a revealing,
360-degree panorama of the booming skyline. Rides last 10 to 12 minutes and include
audio commentary of Brisbane sights. Online bookings offer a nominal discount.

⦿ Fortitude Valley & New Farm

★ **Brisbane Powerhouse**   ARTS CENTRE
(Map p282; ☏box office 07-3358 8600, reception 07-3358 8622; www.brisbanepowerhouse.
org; 119 Lamington St, New Farm; ⊙9am-9pm
Tue-Sun; ⊠195, 196, ⊠New Farm Park) On the

eastern flank of New Farm Park stands the Powerhouse, a once-derelict power station superbly transformed into a contemporary arts centre. Its innards pimped with graffiti remnants, industrial machinery and old electrical transformers-turned-lights, the centre hosts a range of events, including art exhibitions, theatre, live music and comedy. You'll also find two buzzing riverside restaurants. Check the website to see what's on.

Brisbane Riverwalk   BRIDGE
(Map p292; 🚌195, 196, 🚢Sydney St) Jutting out over the city's big, brown waterway, the Brisbane Riverwalk offers a novel way of surveying the Brisbane skyline. The 870m-long path – divided into separate walking and cycling lanes – runs between New Farm and the Howard St Wharves, from where you can continue towards central Brisbane itself. The Riverwalk replaces the original floating walkway, sadly washed away in the floods of 2011.

Chinatown   AREA
(Map p292; Duncan St, Fortitude Valley; ⊘24hr; 🚇Fortitude Valley) Punctuated by a replica Tang dynasty archway at its western end, Duncan St is Brisbane's rather modest Chinatown. The pedestrianised strip (and the stretch of Ann St between Duncan St and Brunswick St Mall) is home to a handful of Chinatown staples, including glazed flat ducks hanging behind steamy windows, Asian grocery stores and the aromas of Thai, Chinese, Vietnamese and Japanese cooking. The area is at it most rambunctious during **Chinese New Year** (www.chinesenewyear. au; ⊘Jan/Feb) festivities.

New Farm Park   PARK
(Map p282; www.newfarmpark.com.au; Brunswick St, New Farm; ⊘24hr; 🚌195, 196, 🚢New Farm Park) On the tail end of Brunswick St by the river, New Farm Park will have you breathing deeply with its jacaranda trees, rose gardens and picnic areas. It's a perfect spot to spend a lazy afternoon, with gas barbecues and free wi-fi (near the rotunda at the river end of the park). Younger kids will especially love the playground – a Crusoe-esque series of platforms among vast Moreton Bay fig trees. **Jan Powers Farmers Market** (Map p282; www. janpowersfarmersmarkets.com.au; Brisbane Powerhouse, 119 Lamington St; ⊘6am-noon Sat) and the **Moonlight Cinema** (Map p282; www.moonlight.

com.au; Brisbane Powerhouse, 119 Lamington Rd, New Farm; adult/child $17/12.50; ⊘7pm Wed-Sun; 🚌195, 196, 🚢New Farm Park) happen here, too.

⊙ Greater Brisbane

Brisbane Botanic Gardens   GARDENS
(Map p282; ☑07-3403 2535; www.brisbane.qld.gov. au/botanicgardens; Mt Coot-tha Rd, Mt Coot-tha; ⊘8am-5.30pm, to 5pm Apr-Aug; 🚌471) **FREE** At the base of Mt Coot-tha, this 52-hectare garden houses a plethora of mini-ecologies, from cactus, bonsai and herb gardens, to rainforests and arid zones. Free guided walks are held at 11am and 1pm Monday and Saturday, and self-guided tours can be downloaded from the website. To get here via public transport, take bus 471 from Adelaide St in the city, opposite King George Sq ($4.60, 25 minutes).

Mt Coot-tha Reserve   NATURE RESERVE
(Map p282; www.brisbane.qld.gov.au; Mt Coot-tha Rd, Mt Coot-tha; ⊘24hr; 🚌471) **FREE** About a 15-minute drive or bus ride from the city, this huge bush reserve is topped by 287m Mt Coot-tha, Brisbane's highest point. On the hillsides you'll find the Brisbane Botanic Gardens, the **Sir Thomas Brisbane Planetarium** (Map p282; ☑07-3403 2578; www.brisbane.qld.gov.au/planetarium; admission free, shows adult/child/family/concession $15.80/9.60/43/13; ⊘10am-4pm Tue-Fri, 11am-8.15pm Sat, 11am-4pm Sun; 🚌471), walking trails and the eye-popping **Mt Coot-tha Lookout** (Map p282; ☑07-3369 9922; www. brisbanelookout.com; 1012 Sir Samuel Griffith Dr, Mt Coot-tha; ⊘24hr; 🚌471), the latter offering a bird's-eye view of the city skyline and greater metro area. On a clear day you'll even spot the Moreton Bay islands.

Lone Pine Koala Sanctuary   WILDLIFE RESERVE
(☑07-3378 1366; www.koala.net; 708 Jesmond Rd, Fig Tree Pocket; adult/child/family $36/22/85; ⊘9am-5pm; 🚌430) About 12km south of the city centre, Lone Pine Koala Sanctuary occupies a patch of parkland beside the river. It's home to over 130 koalas, plus kangaroos, possums, wombats, birds and other Aussie critters. The koalas are undeniably cute – most visitors readily cough up the $18 to have their picture snapped hugging one. There are animal presentations scheduled throughout the day.

BRISBANE & AROUND BRISBANE

West End & Petrie Terrace

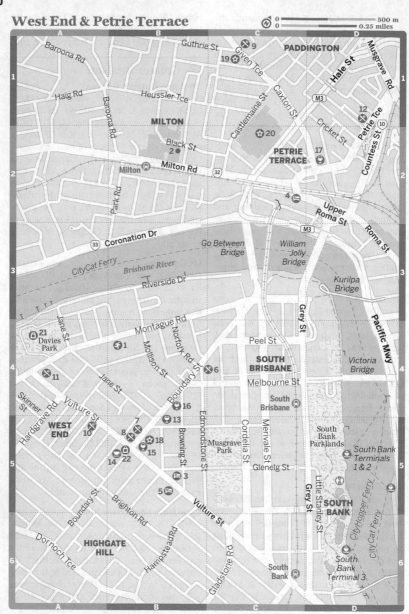

0 — 500 m
0 — 0.25 miles

BRISBANE & AROUND BRISBANE

Activities

You'll find a plethora of excellent art and heritage walking trails around town at www.brisbane.qld.gov.au/facilities-recreation/sports-leisure/walking/walking-trails.

CityCycle   CYCLING
(☏1300 229 253; www.citycycle.com.au; hire per hr/day $2.20/165, 1st 30min free; ⊗24hr) To use Brisbane's bike-share, subscribe via the website ($2/11 per day/week), then hire a bike (additional fee) from any of the 150 stations

West End & Petrie Terrace

around town. It's pricey to hire for more than an hour, so make use of the free first 30 minutes per bike and ride from station to station, swapping bikes as you go. Only a quarter of bikes include a helmet (compulsory to wear) so you may need to purchase one from shops such as Target or Kmart.

Spring Hill Baths   SWIMMING
(Map p282; ☎ 1300 332 583; www.cityaquatics andhealth.com.au; 14 Torrington St, Spring Hill; adult/child/family $5.40/3.90/16.40; ⊙ 6.30am-7pm Mon-Thu, to 6pm Fri, 8am-5pm Sat, 8am-1pm Sun; ☒ 30, 321) Opened in 1886, this quaint heated 25m pool was the city's first in-ground pool. Still encircled by its cute timber change rooms, it's one of the oldest public baths in the southern hemisphere.

Streets Beach   SWIMMING
(Map p286; ☎ 07-3156 6366; ⊙ daylight hours; ⛴ South Bank Terminals 1, 2 & 3, ☒ South Bank) A central spot for a quick (and free) dip is Australia's only artificial, inner-city beach at South Bank. Lifeguards, hollering kids, beach babes, strutting gym-junkies, palm trees, ice-cream carts – it's all here.

Urban Climb   CLIMBING
(Map p290; ☎ 07-3844 2544; www.urbanclimb. com.au; 2/220 Montague Rd, West End; adult/child $20/18, once-off registration fee $5; ⊙ noon-10pm Mon-Fri, 10am-6pm Sat & Sun; ☒ 60, 192, 198) A large indoor climbing wall with one of the largest bouldering walls in Australia. Suitable for both beginners and advanced climbing geeks.

Pinnacle Sports   CLIMBING
(☎ 07-3368 3335; www.pinnaclesports.com.au; 2hr abseiling from $80, 3hr climbing from $90) Climb the Kangaroo Point Cliffs or abseil down them: either way it's a lot of fun! Options include a two-hour sunset abseil, as well as full-day rock-climbing trips to the Glass House Mountains.

Story Bridge
Adventure Climb   ADVENTURE SPORTS
(Map p286; ☎ 1300 254 627; www.sbac.net.au; 170 Main St, Kangaroo Point; climb from $100; ☒ 234, ⛴ Thornton St, Holman St) Scaling Brisbane's most famous bridge is nothing short of thrilling, with unbeatable views of the city – morning, twilight or night. The two-hour climb scales the southern half of the structure, taking you 80m above the twisting, muddy Brisbane River below. Dawn climbs are run on the last Saturday of the month. Minimum age 10 years.

Riverlife   ADVENTURE SPORTS
(Map p286; ☎ 07-3891 5766; www.riverlife.com. au; Naval Stores, Kangaroo Point Bikeway, Kangaroo Point; hire bikes/in-line skates per 4hr $35/40, kayaks per 2hr $35; ⊙ 9am-5pm; ⛴ Thornton St) Based at the bottom of the Kangaroo Point Cliffs, Riverlife offers numerous active city thrills. Rock climb (from $55), abseil ($45) or opt for a kayak river trip (from $45). The latter includes a booze-and-food 'Paddle and Prawns' option ($85) on Friday and Saturday nights. Also rents out bikes, kayaks and in-line skates.

Fortitude Valley & New Farm

0 —————— 200 m
0 —————— 0.1 miles

Breakfast Creek Hotel (1.4km)

St Pauls Tce
Barry Pde
Alfred St
Wickham St
Brookes St
Constance St
East St
Fortitude Valley
Wickham St
CHINATOWN
Gipps St
FORTITUDE VALLEY
Warner St
Ballow St
Bakery La
Brunswick St Mall
Ann St
McLachlan St
Wandoo St
Chester St
Doggett St
Winn La
Winn St
Berwick St
Ann St
Duncan St (Chinatown Mall)
Robertson St
James St
Ivory St
Boundary St
Martin St
Arthur St
Bowen Tce
Brunswick St
Harcourt St
Story Bridge
Kent St
NEW FARM
Kent St
Terrace St
CT White Park
Story Bridge
Brisbane River
CityHopper Ferry
CityCat Ferry
Annie St
James St
Brisbane Powerhouse (1km);
Jan Powers Farmers Market (1km);
Watt (1km)
Barker St
Brunswick St
Browne St
Moray St
Villiers St
Moreton St
Merthyr Rd
Moreton St
Double Shot (200m)
New Farm Park (200m);
Moonlight Cinema (600m)

BRISBANE & AROUND

Fortitude Valley & New Farm

Q Academy   MASSAGE
(Map p292; ☎1300 204 080; www.qacademy.
com.au; 20 Chester St, Newstead; 1hr massage
$30; ☐300, 302, 305, 306, 322, 470) Q Acade-
my offers one of Brisbane's best bargains:
one-hour relaxation or remedial massage for
$30. Although the practitioners are massage
students at the accredited academy, all have
extensive theoretical training and enough
experience to leave you feeling a lot lighter.
It's a very popular spot, so book online at
least a week in advance.

Skydive Brisbane   SKYDIVING
(☎1300 663 634; www.skydive.com.au; from
$300) Offers tandem skydives over Brisbane,
landing on the beach in Redcliffe. See the
website for specials.

Fly Me to the Moon   BALLOONING
(☎07-3423 0400; www.brisbanehotairballooning.
com.au; adult/child incl transfers from $250/330)
One-hour hot-air balloon trips over the
hinterland. Flights are followed by a champagne breakfast at a vineyard in the Scenic
Rim region west of the Gold Coast. Return
transfers to Brisbane are available.

Tours

CityCat   BOATING
(☎13 12 30; www.translink.com.au; one way $5.60;
⊙5.25am-11.25pm) Ditch the car or bus and
catch a CityCat ferry along the Brisbane River for a calmer perspective. Ferries run every
15 to 30 minutes between the Northshore
Hamilton terminal northeast of the city to
the University of Queensland in the southwest, stopping at 16 terminals in between,
including Teneriffe, New Farm Park, North
Quay (for the CBD) and South Bank (also
handy for West End).

Brisbane Explorer   TOURS
(Map p286; ☎02-9567 8400; www.brisbane
cityexplorer.com.au; day tickets adult/child/f
amily $40/25/110; ⊙9am-5.15pm) This hop-
on, hop-off shuttle bus wheels past 15 Brisbane landmarks (in 1½ hours if you don't
jump off), including the CBD, Mt Coot-tha,

D'AGUILAR NATIONAL PARK

Suburban malaise? Slake your wilderness cravings at this 36,000-hectare **national park** (www.nprsr.qld.gov.au/parks/daguilar; 60 Mount Nebo Rd, The Gap), just 10km north-west of the city centre but worlds away (it's pronounced 'dee-ag-lar'). At the park's entrance, the **Walkabout Creek Visitor Information Centre** (☑07-3164 3600; www.walkaboutcreek.com.au; 60 Mount Nebo Rd, The Gap; wildlife centre adult/child/family $7.20/3.50/18.25; ☺9am-4.30pm) has maps. There's an on-site wildlife centre, home to a number of local critters, including reptiles and nocturnal marsupials.

Walking trails in the park range from a few hundred metres to a 24km-long loop. Among them is the 6km-return Morelia Track at the Manorina day-use area and the 4.3km Greenes Falls Track at Mt Glorious. Mountain biking and horse riding are also options. You can camp in the park too, in remote, walk-in bush **camp sites** (☑137 468; www.npsr.qld.gov.au/parks/daguilar/camping.html; per person/family $6.15/24.60). There are a couple of walks (1.5km and 5km return) kicking off from the visitor centre, but other walks are a fair distance away (so you'll need your own wheels).

To get here, catch bus 385 ($5.70, 25 minutes) from Roma St Station to The Gap Park 'n' Ride, then walk a few hundred metres up the road.

Chinatown, South Bank and Story Bridge. Tours depart every 45 minutes from Post Office Sq on Queen St. Buy tickets online or from the driver. A second, five-stop tour is also offered, taking in the Brisbane Botanic Gardens and Mt Coot-tha.

Brisbane Greeters   TOURS
(Map p286; ☑07-3156 6364; www.brisbane greeters.com.au; Brisbane City Hall, King George Sq; ☺10am) Free, small-group, hand-held intro-ductory tours of Brizzy with affable volun-teers. Book at least three days in advance, either online or by phone. Booking online allows you to opt for a 'Your Choice' tour, based on your personal interests and sched-ule. Note that 'Your Choice' tours should be booked at least five days in advance.

River City Cruises   CRUISE
(Map p286; ☑0428 278 473; www.rivercitycruises. com.au; South Bank Parklands Jetty A; adult/child/family $29/15/65) River City runs 1½-hour cruises with commentary from South Bank to New Farm and back. They depart from South Bank at 10.30am and 12.30pm (plus 2.30pm during summer).

XXXX Brewery Tour   TOURS
(Map p290; ☑07-3361 7597; www.xxxx.com.au; cnr Black & Paten Sts, Milton; adult/child $32/18; ☐375, 433, 475) Feel a XXXX coming on? This 1½-hour brewery tour includes a few humid-ity-beating ales (leave the car at home). Tours run four times daily Monday to Friday and nine times Saturday; check the website. Also on offer are combined brewery and Suncorp Stadium (p311) tours (adult/child $48/28) at 10.30am Thursday. Book tours in advance, and wear enclosed shoes. There's also an ale-house here if you feel like kicking on.

Brisbane Ghost Tours   TOURS
(☑07-3344 7265; www.brisbaneghosttours.com. au; walking tours adult/child/family $20/13/55, bus tours adult/child $50/40) 'Get creeped' on these 1½-hour guided walking tours or 2½-hour bus tours of Brisbane's haunted her-itage: murder scenes, cemeteries, eerie ar-cades and the infamous **Boggo Road Gaol** (Map p282; ☑07-3844 0059, 0411 111 903; www. boggoroadgaol.com; Annerley Rd, Dutton Park; his-tory tour adult/child/family $26.50/13.75/52, ghost tour adult/child over 12yr $45/30; ☺1½hr historical tours 11am Thu-Sun, plus 10am Sun, 2hr ghost tours 7.30pm Wed & Fri-Sun, also 8.30pm Fri; ☐112, 116, 202). Offers several tours a week; bookings essential.

Courses

Golden Pig Cooking
School & Cafe   COOKING
(Map p282; ☑07-3666 0884; www.goldenpig.com. au; 38 Ross St, Newstead; 4hr cooking class $165; ☺cafe 7.30am-noon Mon, to 2pm Tue-Fri; ☐300, 302, 305) In a warehouse on the edge of Newstead, chef Katrina Ryan runs a series of popular cooking classes, with themes rang-ing from modern Greek, Vietnamese and South American, to Middle Eastern, brunch and sourdough baking. Ryan's background is impressive, having worked at some of Australia's top restaurants. See the website for class times and types, which also include 'singles' classes for foodies sick of Tinder.

🎆 Festivals & Events

Brisbane International SPORTS
(www.brisbaneinternational.com.au; ☺ Jan) Running over eight days in early January, this pro tennis tournament is a prologue to Melbourne's Grand Slam Australian Open, held later in the month. Featuring the world's top players, it takes place at the Queensland Tennis Centre in the riverside suburb of Tennyson.

BrisAsia Festival CULTURAL
(www.brisbane.qld.gov.au; ☺ Jan/Feb) Running for three weeks in late January and February, the BrisAsia Festival celebrates both traditional and modern Asian cultures with over 80 events across the city. The festival program includes dance, music and theatre performances, film screenings, interactive community events and no shortage of Asian cuisines.

Brisbane Street Art Festival ART
(www.bsafest.com.au; ☺ Feb) The hiss of spray cans underscores this booming two-week festival, which sees local and international street artists transform city walls into arresting art works. Live mural art aside, the program includes exhibitions, music, theatre, light shows, workshops and street-art masterclasses.

Brisbane Comedy Festival COMEDY
(www.briscomfest.com; ☺ Feb/Mar) Feeling blue? Check yourself into this month-long laughfest, usually running from late February to March. Showcasing almost 70 comedy acts from Australia and beyond, festival gigs take place at the riverside Brisbane Powerhouse (p311) arts hub as well as at Brisbane City Hall (p281).

CMC Rocks Queensland MUSIC
(www.cmcrocks.com; ☺ Mar) The biggest country and roots festival in the southern hemisphere, taking place over three days and nights in March at Willowbank Raceway in the southwest outskirts of Brisbane. Expect big-name international acts like Dixie Chicks, Little Big Town and Kip Moore as well as home-grown country A-listers.

Anywhere Theatre Festival PERFORMING ARTS
(www.anywherefest.com; ☺ May) For over two weeks in May, all of Brisbane becomes a stage as hundreds of performances pop up across the city in the most unexpected places. Expect anything from theatre in laneways to cabaret in antique shops and bellowing sopranos in underground reservoirs.

Queensland Cabaret Festival PERFORMING ARTS
(www.queenslandcabaretfestival.com.au; ☺ Jun) Come June, the Brisbane Powerhouse (p311) cranks up the sass and subversion for the 10-day Queensland Cabaret Festival. Expect a mix of both local and international acts, with past performers including US actor and singer Molly Ringwald and British *chansonnière* Barb Jungr.

Queensland Music Festival MUSIC
(QMF; www.queenslandmusicfestival.org.au; ☺ Jul) Renowned singer-songwriter Katie Noonan is the current artistic director of this biennial statewide festival, which serves up an eclectic program of music ranging from classical to contemporary. Held over three weeks in July in odd-numbered years. Most events are free.

'Ekka' Royal Queensland Show CULTURAL
(www.ekka.com.au; ☺ Aug) Country and city collide at this epic 10-day event in August. Head in for fireworks, showbags, theme-park rides, concerts, shearing demonstrations and prize-winning livestock by the truckload. There's also a cooking stage, with demonstrations and the odd celebrity chef.

Bigsound Festival MUSIC
(www.bigsound.org.au; ☺ Sep) Held over three huge days in September, Australia's premier new music festival draws buyers, industry experts and fans of fresh Aussie music talent. With the Judith Wright Centre of Contemporary Arts (p310) as its heart, the fest features around 150 up-and-coming artists playing around 15 venues.

Brisbane Festival PERFORMING ARTS
(www.brisbanefestival.com.au; ☺ Sep) One of Australia's largest and most diverse arts festivals, running for three weeks in September and featuring an impressive schedule of concerts, plays, dance and fringe events. The festival ends with the spectacular 'Riverfire', an elaborate fireworks show over the Brisbane River.

Brisbane Pride Festival LGBT
(www.brisbanepride.org.au; ☺ Sep) Spread over four weeks in September, Australia's third-largest LGBT festival includes the popular Pride March and Fair Day, which sees thousands march from Fortitude Valley to New Farm Park in a celebration of diversity. Pride's fabulous Queen's Ball takes place in June.

Brisbane Writers Festival   LITERATURE
(BWF; www.uplit.com.au; ◈ Sep) Queensland's premier literary event has been running for over five decades. Expect a five-day program of readings, discussions and other thought-provoking events featuring both Australian and international writers and thinkers.

Oktoberfest   CULTURAL
(www.oktoberfestbrisbane.com.au; ◈ Oct) Brisbanites don their *lederhosen* and *dirndl* for Australia's biggest German shindig, held at the Brisbane Showgrounds over two weekends in October. It's a sud-soaked blast, with traditional German grub, yodellers, oompah bands and a dedicated 'Kinder Zone' with rides, Deutsch lessons and more for little aspiring Germans.

Park Sounds   MUSIC
(www.parksounds.com.au; ◈ Nov) Hip-hop rules at Brisbane's newest music festival, held at Pine Rivers Park in suburban Strathpine. The 2016 line-up included ARIA-winning A-listers Bliss n Eso, as well as other of-the-moment Aussie acts like Drapht and Pon Cho (of Thundamentals). Held over an afternoon in November.

Brisbane Asia Pacific Film Festival   FILM
(BAPFF; brisbaneasiapacificfilmfestival.com; ◈ Nov/Dec) A 16-day celebration of cinema from Oceania and Asia, with around 80 films from countries as diverse as Australia, New Zealand, China, Korea, the Philippines, Afghanistan, India, Russia and Iran. The program includes feature films, shorts and documentaries, as well as panel discussions and other special events.

🛏 Sleeping

Prices do not generally abide by any high- or low-season rules; wavering rates usually reflect demand. Rates are often higher midweek, as well as during major events and holiday periods.

🛏 Central Brisbane

Base Brisbane Embassy   HOSTEL $
(Map p286; ☑ 07-3014 1715; www.stayatbase.com; 214 Elizabeth St; dm/d/tw from $35/100/130; ✳ @ 🛜; 🚊 Central) A city branch of the Base chain, this spruced-up place is quieter than other hostels despite being just behind the bustling Queen St Mall. While it feels a little soulless, it does have its draws, among

them a large screening room for films, and a sun deck with barbecue and city views. Slurp craft beers at the **Embassy Hotel** (Map p286; www.embassybar.com.au; ◈ 11am-10pm Mon-Wed, to 11pm Thu, to late Fri, noon-late Sat) downstairs.

Base Brisbane Uptown   HOSTEL $
(Map p286; ☑ 07-3238 5888; www.stayatbase.com; 466 George St; dm/tw & d from $21/145; ✳ @ 🛜; 🚊 Roma St) This purpose-built hostel near Roma St Station flaunts its youth with mod interiors, decent facilities and overall cleanliness. Each room has air-con, a bathroom and individual lockers, and it's wheelchair-accessible. The bar downstairs is a party palace, with big-screen sports, DJs and open-mic nights.

Next   HOTEL $$
(Map p286; ☑ 07-3222 3222; www.snhotels.com/next/brisbane; 72 Queen St; r from $180; ✳ 🛜 ✳; 🚊 Central) Right above the Queen St Mall, Next delivers stylish, central, affordable accommodation. Rooms are generic though svelte and contemporary, with high-tech touchscreen technology and decent beds. The outdoor lap pool flanks a buzzing bar, itself adjacent to a handy traveller lounge (complete with massage chairs and showers) for guests who check-in early or want a place to relax before a late flight. There's an on-site gym too.

Ibis Styles   HOTEL $$
(Map p286; ☑ 07-3337 9000; www.ibisstyles brisbaneelizabeth.com.au; 40 Elizabeth St; d from $140; ✳ @ 🛜; 🚊 Central) Smart, contemporary, budget digs is what you get at the world's largest Ibis hotel. Multicoloured carpets and striking geometric shapes set a playful tone in the lobby, and while the standard rooms are smallish, all are comfortable and fresh, with fantastic mattresses, smart TVs and impressive river and South Bank views. Property perks include a small gym with quality equipment and guest laundry facilities.

Punthill Brisbane   HOTEL $$
(Map p286; ☑ 07-3055 5777, 1300 731 299; www.punthill.com.au/property/brisbane/punthill-brisbane; 40 Astor Tce, Spring Hill; 1-/2-bedroom apt from $150/185; 🅿 ✳ 🛜 ✳; 🚊 Central) Its lobby graced with retro bicycles (for hire), Punthill offers smart, contemporary suites in muted colours. Digs include comfy king beds, kitchenette or full kitchen, balcony and millennial details like flat-screen TV and iPod dock. On-site facilities include a small pool, gym and

guest laundry. A good all-round option, with competitive rates and a central location. Parking $25.

**New Inchcolm
Hotel & Suites** HISTORIC HOTEL **$$$**
(Map p286; 07-3226 8888; www.inchcolm. au; 73 Wickham Tce; d from $210; P ✲ 🕸; 🚇 Central) Built in the 1920s as doctors' suites, the heritage-listed Inchcolm (complete with oak-clad vintage elevator) is fabulously plush and intimate. Rooms in the newer wing have more space and light; in the heritage wing there's more character. All feature thoughtful touches, including coffee machines, Riedel stemware and minibars with locally sourced treats. There's also an in-house restaurant. Parking $40.

✕ 🏠 South Bank & West End

GoNow Family Backpacker HOSTEL **$**
(Map p290; 0434 727 570, 07-3472 7570; www. gonowfamily.com.au; 147 Vulture St, West End; dm $19-30, d $70; P ✲ 🕸; 🚇198, 199) These have to be the cheapest beds in Brisbane, and GoNow is doing a decent job of delivering a clean, respectful, secure hostel experience despite the bargain-basement pricing. It's not a party place: you'll be better off elsewhere if you're looking to launch into the night with drunken forays. The upstairs rooms have more ceiling height.

Brisbane Backpackers HOSTEL **$**
(Map p290; 1800 626 452, 07-3844 9956; www. brisbanebackpackers.com.au; 110 Vulture St, West End; dm $21-34, d/tw/tr from $100/110/135; P ✲ @ 🕸 🏊; 🚇198, 199) If you're looking to party, you're in the right place. This hulking hostel comes with a great pool and bar area, and while rooms are basic, they're generally well maintained. An easy walk from West End's buzzing eateries, bars and live-music venues.

Rydges South Bank HOTEL **$$**
(Map p286; 07-3364 0800; www.rydges.com; 9 Glenelg St, South Brisbane; r from $180; ✲ 🕸 🏊; 🚇 South Brisbane) Fresh from a recent refurbishment, this 12-floor winner is within walking distance of South Bank Parklands and major galleries. In rich hues of silver, grey and purple, standard rooms are large and inviting (try to get one facing the city), with sublimely comfortable beds, smart TVs, free wi-fi, motion-sensor air-con and small, but modern, bathrooms.

🏠 Fortitude Valley & New Farm

Bunk Backpackers HOSTEL **$**
(Map p292; 07-3257 3644, 1800 682 865; www. bunkbrisbane.com.au; 11-21 Gipps St, Fortitude Valley; dm from $25, s $60, tw/apt from $85/190; P ✲ @ 🕸 🏊; 🚇 Fortitude Valley) This old arts college was reborn as a backpackers over a decade ago – and the party hasn't stopped! It's a huge, five-level place with dozens of rooms (mostly eight-bed dorms), just staggering distance from the Valley nightlife. Facilities include a large communal kitchen, pool and jacuzzi, and in-house bar, **Birdees** (Map p292; 07-3852 5000; www.katarzyna.com. au/venues/birdees; 608 Ann St; ☺3pm-late Mon-Wed, noon-late Thu-Sun), as well as a few great five-bed apartments. Not for bed-by-10pm slumberers. Parking $12.

Bowen Terrace GUESTHOUSE **$**
(Map p292; 07-3254 0458; www.bowenterrace. com.au; 365 Bowen Tce, New Farm; dm from $34, s/d without bathroom from $70/80, d/f with bathroom from $95/145; P @ 🕸 🏊; 🚇196, 195, 199) In a restored, century-old Queenslander, Bowen Terrace offers modestly priced lodging in a real-estate hot spot. Simple rooms include TV, bar fridge, quality linen and lofty ceilings with fans (no air-con). There's a communal kitchen, as well as laundry facilities and a pool. Soundproofing between the rooms isn't great, but the place is good value for money, with more class than your average hostel.

Tryp BOUTIQUE HOTEL **$$**
(Map p292; 07-3319 7888; www.trypbrisbane. com; 14-20 Constance St, Fortitude Valley; r $160-340; ✲ 🕸; 🚇 Fortitude Valley) Fans of street art will appreciate this hip 65-room slumber pad, complete with a small gym, a rooftop bar and a glass-panelled elevator affording views of the graffiti-strewn shaft. Each of the hotel's four floors features work by a different Brisbane street artist, and while standard rooms are small, all are comfy and feature coffee machines and fab marshmallow beds.

Limes BOUTIQUE HOTEL **$$**
(Map p292; 07-3852 9000; www.limeshotel. com.au; 142 Constance St, Fortitude Valley; d from $180; P ✲ 🕸; 🚇 Fortitude Valley) Although the rooms at trendy Limes are tight, they do make good use of limited space, with plush bedding, kitchenette and work space. Thoughtful extras include coffee machines,

free wi-fi and gym passes. While we love the rooftop hot tub, bar and cinema, it can make for noisy nights; bring ear plugs if you're a light sleeper. Parking nearby for $20.

Spicers Balfour Hotel BOUTIQUE HOTEL $$$
(Map p292; ☑1300 163 054; www.spicers retreats.com/spicers-balfour-hotel; 37 Balfour St, New Farm; r from $280, ste from $430; ⓟ✳🛜; 🚌195, 196, 199) Sophisticated Spicers occupies two renovated heritage buildings on the same street. Slumber in one of the small, plush rooms in the old Queenlander or upgrade to a spacious, deco-inspired suite in the 1920s villa, four of which come with free-standing bath. All rooms and suites feature gorgeous beds, Bose sound system and free wi-fi. The hotel houses a reputable restaurant, and breakfast is included.

🛏 Greater Brisbane

Brisbane City YHA HOSTEL $
(Map p290; ☑07-3236 1004; www.yha.com.au; 392 Upper Roma St; dm from $34, tw & d with/ without bathroom from $125/107, f from $145; ⓟ✳@🛜🏊; 🚌375, 380, 🚆Roma St) This immaculate, well-run hostel has a rooftop pool and a sun deck with eye-popping river views. The maximum dorm size is six beds (not too big); most have bathrooms. Big on security, kitchen space (lots of fridges) and activities, the place runs film nights as well as weekly city walking tours and barbecues. That said, this is a YHA, not a nonstop party palace. Parking $12.

Brisbane City Backpackers HOSTEL $
(Map p286; ☑07-3211 3221, 1800 062 572; www. citybackpackers.com; 380 Upper Roma St; dm $19-33, d/tr from $80/105; ⓟ✳@🛜🏊; 🚌375, 380, 🚆Roma St) On the Upper Roma St hostel row, this hyperactive, low-frills party palace makes good use of its limited outdoor space, including a viewing tower and pool. The on-site bar has something happening every night: DJs, pool comps, quiz nights, karaoke... Free wi-fi, too. Cheaper rooms have no air-con. If you came to party, you're in the right place.

Newmarket Gardens Caravan Park CAMPGROUND $
(Map p282; ☑07-3356 1458; www.newmarket gardens.com.au; 199 Ashgrove Ave, Newmarket; powered/unpowered sites $43/41, on-site vans $57, budget r $68, cabins $135-160; ⓟ✳@🛜; 🚌390, 🚆Newmarket) Just 4km north of the city and dotted with mango trees, this place offers a row of five simple budget rooms (no air-con), five tidy cabins (with air-con) and a sea of van and tent sites. Not much in the way of distractions for kids. From central Brisbane, bus 390 stops around 200m east of the caravan park (alight at stop 20).

Art Series – The Johnson HOTEL $$
(Map p282; ☑07-3085 7200; www.artseries hotels.com.au/johnson; 477 Boundary St, Spring Hill; r from $165; ⓟ✳🛜🏊; 🚌301, 321, 411) Opened in 2016, this is Brisbane's first Art Series hotel. It's dedicated to abstract artist Michael Johnson, whose big, bold brushstrokes demand attention in the svelte lobby. Framed works by Johnson also grace the hotel's uncluttered contemporary rooms, each with heavenly AH Beard mattresses, designer lighting and free wi-fi. There's an on-site gym as well as a sleek 50m rooftop pool designed by Olympic gold-medallist Michael Klim.

🍴 Eating

Brisbane's food scene is flourishing – a fact not lost on the nation's food critics and switched-on gluttons. From Mod Oz degustations to curbside food trucks, the city offers an increasingly competent, confident array of culinary highs.

🍴 Central Brisbane

Miel Container BURGERS $
(Map p286; ☑07-3229 4883; www.facebook. com/mielcontainer; cnr Mary & Albert Sts; burgers from $12; ⊙11am-10pm Mon-Thu & Sat, to 11pm Fri; 🚆Central) Planted in a nook below Brisbane's skyscrapers, this rude-red shipping container flips outstanding burgers. Choose your bun, your burger, your veggies, cheese and sauces, then search for a spare seat by the footpath. If it's all too hard, opt for the classic Miel grass-fed-beef burger with onion jam, bacon and bush tomato. Succulent, meaty bliss.

Felix for Goodness CAFE $
(Map p286; ☑07-3161 7966; www.felixforgoodness. com; 50 Burnett Lane; mains lunch $12-22, dinner $23-24; ⊙7am-2.30pm Mon & Tue, to 9.30pm Wed-Fri, 8am-2pm Sat; 🛜🍴; 🚆Central) 🍴 Felix channels Melbourne with its arty laneway locale, industrial fit-out and effortlessly cool vibe. Sip espresso or chow down decent brunch grub such as spelt poppy-seed pikelets with vanilla cream, saffron cardamom

and poached pears, or pumpkin, ricotta and caramelised onion frittata. A short evening menu focuses on bar bites (best paired with a creative cocktail), with the odd pasta or risotto main.

Strauss
CAFE $

(Map p286; ☑07-3236 5232; www.straussfd.com; 189 Elizabeth St; dishes $6.50-13.50; ⊙6.30am-3pm Mon-Fri; 🔊; 🚇Central) Strauss bucks its corporate surrounds with low-key cool and a neighbourly vibe. Head in for pastries or a short, competent, locavore menu of creative salads, thick-cut toasted sandwiches (go for the pastrami, sauerkraut, cheese and pickle combo) and upgraded classics such as French toast paired with lemon curd and labne. The place takes its coffee seriously, with cold brew and rotating espresso and filtered options.

Govinda's
VEGETARIAN $

(Map p286; ☑07-3210 0255; www.brisbane govindas.com.au; 358 George St; all-you-can-eat $12.90; ⊙7am-8pm Mon-Fri, from 11am Sat; 🍴; 🚇Roma St) Grab a plate and pile it high with the likes of vegetarian curry, koftas (veggie puffs), salads, pappadams, chutneys and semolina fruit pudding at this no-frills budget eatery, run by the Hare Krishnas. You'll find another branch at **West End** (Map p290; ☑0404 173 027; 82 Vulture St, West End; all-you-can-eat $12; ⊙11am-3pm & 5-8pm Mon-Fri, 11am-3pm Sat; 🚇199).

Greenglass
FRENCH $$

(Map p286; www.facebook.com/greenglass336; 336 George St; lunch $12-30, dinner mains $18-35; ⊙7am-9pm Mon-Fri; 🚇Roma St) Up a flight of stairs wedged between a discount chemist and a topless bar is this pared-back, loft-style newcomer. Head up for novel breakfast items such as a charcoal bun filled with fried egg, avocado and thinly sliced pork belly, French-centric bistro lunch dishes and an enlightened wine list that favours small-batch Australian drops.

★Urbane
MODERN AUSTRALIAN $$$

(Map p286; ☑07-3229 2271; www.urbane restaurant.com; 181 Mary St; 5-course menu $110, 7-course menu $145; ⊙6-10.30pm Tue-Sat; 🍴; 🍽Eagle St Pier, 🚇Central) Argentinian chef Alejandro Cancino heads intimate Urbane, the apotheosis of Brisbane fine dining. If the budget permits, opt for the eight-course degustation, which does more justice to

Cancino's talents. Needless to say, dishes intrigue and delight, whether it's corn 'snow' (made by dropping corn mousse into liquid nitrogen) or pickled onion petals filled with tapioca pearls and regional macadamia nuts. The wine list is smashing.

Cha Cha Char
STEAK $$$

(Map p286; ☑07-3211 9944; www.chachachar.com. au; 5/1 Eagle St Pier; mains $35-90; ⊙noon-11pm Mon-Fri, 6-11pm Sat & Sun; 🍽Eagle St Pier, 🚇Central) Fastidious carnivores drool at the mere mention of this linen-tabled steakhouse, famed for its wood-fired slabs of premium Australian beef. Rib, rump and T-bone aside, the kitchen also offers first-rate seafood and roast game dishes including paperbark-smoked duck breast with roasted mushrooms, pomme fondant, grilled baby zucchinis and pomegranate jus. Part of the Eagle St Pier complex, the dining room's floor-to-ceiling windows come with river views.

✖ South Bank & West End

Plenty West End
CAFE $

(Map p290; ☑07-3255 3330; www.facebook.com/ plentywestend; 284 Montague Rd, West End; dishes $5.50-23.50; ⊙6.30am-3pm, kitchen closes 2.25pm; 🔊🍴; 🚍60, 192, 198) 🌿 In the far west of West End lies this graphics-factory-turned-cafe, a rustic, industrial backdrop for farm-to-table edibles. Scan the counter for freshly made panini and cakes, or the blackboard for headliners such as caramelised Brussels sprouts with pumpkin purée, feta, raisins and pumpkin seeds. Libations include fresh juices, kombucha on tap and fantastic, organic coffee. When you're done, pick up some pineapple hot sauce at the in-store providore.

Morning After
CAFE $

(Map p290; ☑07-3844 0500; www.morningafter. com.au; cnr Vulture & Cambridge Sts, West End; breakfast $9-19, lunch mains $15-21; ⊙7am-4pm; 🔊🍴; 🚍199) Decked out in contemporary blonde-wood furniture, gleaming subway tiles and bold green accents, this new-school West End cafe is crisper than an apple. Join the effortlessly cool for vibrant, revamped cafe fare such as zucchini fritters with fried eggs, carrot and ginger purée and Vietnamese salad, and bucatini pasta with kale pesto, spinach purée and pistachio. Alas, the coffee is a little less consistent.

Kiss the Berry
HEALTH FOOD $

(Map p286; ☑07-3846 6128; www.kisstheberry.
com; 65/114 Grey St, South Bank; bowls $10.50-
16; ⊗7am-5pm; ✐; ⛟South Bank Terminals 1 &
2, ⛴South Brisbane) Overlooking South Bank
Parklands is this youthful, upbeat açaí bar
serving fresh, tasty bowls of the organic
super-food in various combinations. Our
favourite is the naughty-but-nice Snickers
Delight (with banana, strawberries, raw cacao powder, peanut butter, coconut water,
almond milk, granola, raw cocoa nibs and
coconut yoghurt and flakes). For a liquid
açaí fix, opt for one of the meal-in-a-cup
smoothies.

★ Gauge
MODERN AUSTRALIAN $$

(Map p286; ☑07-3852 6734; www.gauge
brisbane.com.au; 77 Grey St, South Brisbane;
breakfast $12-19, mains $26-33; ⊗7am-3pm Mon-
Wed, 7am-3pm & 5.30-9pm Thu & Fri, 8am-3pm &
5.30-9pm Sat, 8am-3pm Sun; ⛟South Bank Termi-
nals 1 & 2, ⛴South Brisbane) All-day, cafe-style
Gauge is so hot right now. In a crisp, sparse
space punctuated by black-spun aluminium
lamps, native flora and a smashing wine
list, clean, contemporary dishes burst with
Australian confidence. Signatures include
a provocative 'blood taco' packed with
roasted bone marrow, mushroom and na-
tive thyme, and a brilliant twist on banana
bread – garlic bread with burnt vanilla and
brown butter.

Julius
ITALIAN $$

(Map p286; ☑07-3844 2655; www.juliuspizzeria.
com.au; 77 Grey St, South Brisbane; pizzas $21-
24.50; ⊗noon-9.30pm Sun, Tue & Wed, to 10pm
Thu, to 10.30pm Fri & Sat; ⛟South Bank Terminals
1 & 2, ⛴South Brisbane) Suited up in polished
concrete and the orange glow of Aperol, this
svelte Italian fires up superlative pizzas, divided into *pizze rosse* (with tomato sauce)
or *pizze bianche* (without). The former includes a simple, beautiful marinara, cooked
the proper Neapolitan way (sans seafood).
The pasta dishes are also solid, with *fritel-
le di ricotta* (fried ricotta dumplings filled
with custard) making a satisfying epilogue.

GOMA Cafe Bistro
CAFE $$

(Map p286; ☑07-3842 9906; www.qagoma.qld.gov.
au; Gallery of Modern Art, Stanley Pl, South Bank;
lunch $15-34; ⊗10am-3pm Mon-Fri, from 8.30am
Sat & Sun; ⛟South Bank Terminals 1 & 2, ⛴South
Brisbane) The casual, indoor-outdoor GOMA
Cafe Bistro serves high-quality burgers, sal-
ads and modern bistro mains, with both
breakfast and lunch served on the weekends.

Billykart West End
MODERN AUSTRALIAN $$

(Map p290; ☑07-3177 9477; www.billykart.com.au;
2 Edmondstone St, West End; breakfast $6-23.50,
dinner mains $26-36; ⊗restaurant 7am-2.30pm
Mon & Sun, 7am-9.30pm Tue-Sat, shop 11am-5pm
Mon, 11am-9pm Tue-Fri, 9am-9pm Sat, 9am-5pm
Sun; ⛴192, 196, 198, 199) Brisbane-based celeb
chef Ben O'Donoghue heads Billykart, a slick
yet casual eatery where billykart blueprints
and faux Queenslander veneers salute local
childhood memories. Dishes are beautifully
textured and flavoured, from the cult-status
breakfast Aussie-Asian eggs (tiger prawn,
bacon, deep-fried egg, oyster sauce, chilli
and shizu cress) to a smashing lunch-and-
dinner spanner crab spaghettini. Weekend
breakfast is especially popular; head in by
9am.

Sea Fuel
FISH & CHIPS $$

(Map p290; ☑07-3844 9473; www.facebook.com/
seafuel; 57 Vulture St, West End; meals $14-26;
⊗11.30am-8.30pm; ✎; ⛴199) The only thing
missing is a beach at Sea Fuel, one of Bris-
bane's best fish-and-chip peddlers. It's a pol-
ished, modern spot, with distressed timber
tabletops and blown-up photos of coastal
scenes. The fish is fresh and sustainably
caught in Australian and New Zealand wa-
ters, and the golden chips flawlessly crisp
and sprinkled with chicken salt. Alternatives
include fresh oysters, Thai fish cakes and
sprightly salads.

Chop Chop Chang's
ASIAN $$

(Map p290; ☑07-3846 7746; www.chopchop-
changs.com.au; 185 Boundary St, West End; mains
$18-32, banquet menus $38-55; ⊗11.30am-3pm
& 5.30-9.30pm; ⛴199) 'Happiness never de-
creases by being shared.' So said the Bud-
dha. And the hungry hordes at Chop Chop
Chang's seem to concur, passing around
bowls of flavour-packed, pan-Asian street
food like caramelised pork with tamarind,
star anise and cassia bark, Isaan-style *larb*
(ground-pork with pak chi farang, hot mint
and dry chilli) and cooling watermelon and
pomelo salad. Open later on Friday and Saturday nights.

★ Stokehouse Q
MODERN AUSTRALIAN $$$

(Map p286; ☑07-3020 0600; www.stokehouse.
com.au; River Quay, Sidon St, South Bank; mains
$36-42; ⊗noon-late Mon-Thu, 11am-late Fri-Sun;
⛟South Bank Terminal 3, ⛴South Bank) Sophis-
ticated Stokehouse guarantees a dizzying
high, its confident, locally sourced menu
paired with utterly gorgeous river and city
views. At crisp, linen-clad tables, urbanites

FOOD TRUCKS & NIGHT MARKETS

When it comes to food trucks and street food, Brisbane's crush has turned into a full-blown affair. There's an ever-growing number of food vans roaming city streets, serving up good-quality fast food, from tacos, ribs, wings and burgers, to wood-fired pizza, Brazilian hot dogs and Malaysian saté. You'll find a list of Brisbane food trucks (with respective menus) at www.bnefoodtrucks.com.au, a website that also includes a handy, interactive map showing the current location of food trucks across town.

From Tuesday to Sunday, Fish Lane (opposite the Queensland Museum & Sciencentre on Grey St) is the setting for **Eating at Wandering Cooks** (www.facebook.com/wandering cooks), a rotating mix of quality food trucks and stalls open for lunch and dinner.

Further east along the Brisbane River, in suburban Hamilton, is the hugely popular Eat Street Markets (p304). Easily reached on the CityCat (alight at Bretts Wharf), it's the city's hipsterish take on the night street-food market, with a maze of upcycled shipping containers pumping out everything from freshly shucked oysters to smoky American barbecue and Turkish gözleme, all to the sound of live, rocking bands.

toast to inspired creations such as chicken liver and Madeira brûlée with fruit toast, pear and native cranberry chutney. Next door, Stoke Bar offers similar views for a more casual (albeit pricey) drinking session.

✕ Fortitude Valley

★ King Arthur Cafe
MODERN AUSTRALIAN **$**

(Map p292; ☑07-3358 1670; www.kingarthur cafe.com; 164c Arthur St, Fortitude Valley; meals $11.50-21; ⊙7am-3pm Tue-Fri, to 2pm Sat-Mon; ⊚; ☐470, ☒Fortitude Valley) Just off James St, King Arthur is never short of eye-candy creatives, guzzling gorgeous coffee (including batch brew), nibbling on just-baked goods and tucking into revamped cafe classics like scrambled eggs with kale, broccoli, fermented chilli and goats curd, or warm smoked local fish with horseradish cream, potato hash and pickled seasonal veggies. Best of all, it's all made using local produce and ethically sourced meats.

Nodo Donuts
CAFE **$**

(Map p292; ☑07-3852 2230; www.nodo.com.au; 1 Ella St, Newstead; dishes $7.50-16; ⊙7am-3pm Tue-Fri, from 8am Sat & Sun; ⊚; ☐300, 302, 305, 306, 322, 470) Light-washed, hip-kid Nodo serves up Brisbane's poshest doughnuts (usually sold out by 2pm), with combos like blueberry and lemon and Valrhona chocolate with beetroot. They're baked (not fried), gluten-free and even include a raw variety, dehydrated for nine hours. The rest of the cafe menu is equally focused on natural, unrefined ingredients, from the green breakfast bowl to the activated almond-milk Magic Mushroom shake. Great coffee, too.

Ben's Burgers
BURGERS **$**

(Map p292; ☑07-3195 3094; www.bensburgers. com.au; Winn Lane, 5 Winn St; burgers $11; ⊙7am-late; ☒Fortitude Valley) Prime ingredients drive Ben's, a small, pumping joint in the Valley's coolest laneway. Roll out of bed for a breakfast Elvis (bacon, peanut butter, banana, maple syrup), or head in later for the trio of lunch and dinner burgers, among them a meat-free option. Sides are straightforward – fries or chilli-cheese fries – with brownies and pecan pie making for a fitting epilogue.

Thai Wi-Rat
THAI, LAOTIAN **$**

(Map p292; ☑07-3257 0884; 270-292 Brunswick St, Fortitude Valley; dishes $12-19; ⊙11am-3pm & 5-9.30pm Mon-Thu, to 10pm Fri-Sun; ☒Fortitude Valley) Under the watchful eyes of Thai royalty, locals sit at easy-wipe tables and tuck into chilli-heavy Thai and Laotian dishes at this lo-fi Chinatown eatery. Ditch the lunch specials for main-menu items like crunchy, tangy *som tum* (green paw paw salad) or classic *larb* (spicy minced-meat salad). The wines on offer aren't great, so consider bringing your own bottle of plonk. Takeaway available.

James Street Market
MARKET **$**

(Map p292; www.jamesst.com.au/james-st-market; 22 James St, Fortitude Valley; 8-piece sashimi $17, hot dishes $10-28; ⊙8.30am-7pm Mon-Fri, 8am-6pm Sat & Sun; ☐470, ☒Fortitude Valley) Local gourmands drop by this small, contemporary, lavishly stocked market for sophisticated fridge and pantry fare, including pesto-stuffed olives, stinky cheeses, dips, freshly baked bread, pastries and tubs of homemade gelato. If you're feeling a little peckish, the fresh-seafood counter serves good sushi, sashimi and warming dishes like Japanese noodle soup with Moreton Bay bugs.

★ Longtime
THAI $$

(Map p292; ☑ 07-3160 3123; www.longtime.com.au; 610 Ann St; mains $15-45; ☺ 5.30-10pm Tue-Thu & Sun, to 10.30pm Fri & Sat; ☎; ☐ Fortitude Valley) Blink and you'll miss the alley leading to this dim, kicking hot spot. The menu is designed for sharing, with a banging repertoire of sucker-punch, Thai-inspired dishes that include a must-try soft-shell-crab *bao* (steamed bun) with Asian slaw. Reservations are only accepted for 5.30pm, 6pm and 6.30pm sittings, after which it's walk-ins only (Tuesday and Sunday are the easiest nights to score a table).

Les Bubbles
STEAK $$

(Map p292; ☑ 07-3251 6500; www.lesbubbles.com.au; 144 Wickham St, Fortitude Valley; steak frites $30; ☺ noon-11pm Sun-Thu, to midnight Fri & Sat; ☐ Fortitude Valley) From the red-neon declaration – 'Quality meat has been served here since 1982' – to the photos of crooks and cops, this sassy steakhouse relishes its former brothel days. Today the only thing on the menu is superb steak frites, served with unlimited fries and salad. Simply choose your sauce (try the green peppercorn and cognac option) and your libation.

Tinderbox
ITALIAN $$

(Map p292; ☑ 07-3852 3744; www.thetinderbox.com.au; 7/31 James St, Fortitude Valley; pizzas $20-24, mains $28; ☺ 5pm-late Tue-Sun; ☐ 470, ☐ Fortitude Valley) Popular with on-point James St peeps, this modern, mosaic-clad bistro straddles a leafy laneway by the Palace Centro cinemas. The menu is a share-friendly, Italian affair, spanning spicy 'nduja (spreadable pork salumi) arancini and seared cuttlefish with chilli and rocket, to perfectly charred wood-fired pizzas including the standout *funghi* (porcini mushrooms, mozzarella and roasted onion). Wash it all down with an innovative cocktail.

★ E'cco
MODERN AUSTRALIAN $$$

(Map p286; ☑ 07-3831 8344; www.eccobistro.com.au; 100 Boundary St; mains $36-42, 5-course tasting menu $89; ☺ noon-2.30pm Tue-Fri, 6pm-late Tue-Sat; ☑; ☐ 174, 230, 300) Years on, E'cco remains one of the state's gastronomic highlights. Polished yet personable staff deliver beautifully balanced, visually arresting dishes, which might see cured ocean trout

flavoured with oyster emulsion or perfect suckling pig meet its match in smoked carrot purée, kimchi and spicy 'nduja (spreadable pork salumi). The kitchen offers a smaller, dedicated vegetarian menu (mains $30 to $38) as well as a highly recommended, good-value tasting menu for the full effect.

✖ New Farm

New Farm Confectionery
SWEETS $

(Map p292; ☑ 07-3139 0964; www.newfarmconfectionery.com.au; 14 Barker St, New Farm; sweets from $3; ☺ 10am-6pm Wed & Thu, to 9.30pm Fri & Sat; ☐ 195, 196, 199) For a locavore sugar rush, squeeze into this tiny confectioner, located on the side of the New Farm Six Cinemas. From the macadamia brittle and chocolate-coated Madagascan vanilla marshmallow, to the slabs of blackberry-infused white chocolate, all of the products are made using natural, top-tier ingredients. Nostalgic types shouldn't miss the sherbet powder, made with actual fruit and paired with lollipops for gleeful dipping.

Sourced Grocer
MODERN AUSTRALIAN $

(Map p282; ☑ 07-3852 6734; www.sourcedgrocer.com.au; 11 Florence St, Teneriffe; dishes $7-23; ☺ 7am-3pm Mon-Sat, 8am-3pm Sun, shop 7am-8pm Mon-Thu, to 7pm Fri, to 5pm Sat, to 4pm Sun; ☐ 199, 393, ☒ Teneriffe) You can have your avocado on sourdough (with smoked labna, naturally) *and* buy your local Bee One Third honey at Sourced Grocer, an understatedly cool warehouse turned cafe-providore. Decked out with cushioned milk crates, a vertical garden and native flora in recycled tins, its open kitchen smashes it with seasonal, locavore dishes like standout cabbage pancakes with crispy Brussels sprout leaves, soft egg and shaved goats-milk cheese.

Little Loco
CAFE $

(Map p292; ☑ 07-3358 5706; www.facebook.com/littlelococafe; 121 Merthyr Rd, New Farm; breakfast $8-17, lunch $14.50-17; ☺ 6am-3pm Mon-Fri, 6.30am-2.30pm Sat & Sun; ☑; ☐ 196, 199, 195) A white space speckled green with plants, this little New Farm local keeps peeps healthy with dishes such as the Green Bowl, a tasty, feel-great combo of kale, spinach, broccolini, feta, pomegranate seeds, avocado and dukkah. There's no shortage of vegetarian and paleo bites, as well as dairy- and gluten-free options. Such salubrious credentials make sense given that the cafe's owner is Brisbane soccer player Daniel Bowles.

Double Shot   CAFE $
(Map p282; 07-3358 6556; www.facebook.com/
doubleshotnewfarm; 125 Oxlade Dr, New Farm;
mains $11.50-19.50; 7am-3pm Wed, Thu & Sat,
to 9pm Fri, 8am-3pm Sun; 196, Sydney St)
With its button-cute wooden porch, manicured hedge and upbeat furniture, petite
Double Shot is a hit with brunching mums,
dog-walkers and polished, suit-clad realtors.
Join the New Farm crew for good coffee, coconut bread with whipped ricotta, Spanish
sardines on sourdough or refreshing green
papaya, coconut and chicken salad. Tapas
served from 3pm on Friday.

Chouquette   BAKERY $
(Map p292; 07-3358 6336; www.chouquette.
com.au; 19 Barker St, New Farm; items $2.50-11;
6.30am-4pm Wed-Sat, to 12.30pm Sun;
195, 196, 199) The best patisserie this side of
Toulouse? Something to think about as you
grab a nutty coffee and a bag of the name-
sake *chouquettes* (small choux pastries
topped with granulated sugar), a shiny slice
of *tarte au citron* (lemon tart), or a filled ba-
guette. Charming French-speaking staff are
the glacé cherry on the torte.

Balfour Kitchen   MODERN AUSTRALIAN $$
(Map p292; 1300 597 540; www.spicers
retreats.com/spicers-balfour-hotel/dining; Spicers
Balfour Hotel, 37 Balfour St, New Farm; breakfast
$14-25, dinner mains $32-38; 6.30-11am, noon-
2.30pm & 5.30-8.30pm Mon-Fri, from 7.30am Sat
& Sun; 195, 196, 199) Should you nosh in the
dining room, on the verandah or among the
frangipani in the courtyard? This polished
cafe-restaurant creates a very Queensland
conundrum. Wherever you may land a
linen-covered table, swoon over nuanced,
sophisticated dishes, from morning bri-
oche French toast with hazelnut, chocolate
ganache and sour cherries, to evening hot-
smoked barramundi paired with charred
cauliflower and pil-pil sauce. Live tunes
accompany Sunday lunch.

Himalayan Cafe   NEPALI $$
(Map p292; 07-3358 4015; 640 Brunswick St, New
Farm; mains $16-27; 5.30-9.30pm Tue-Thu & Sun,
to 10.30pm Fri & Sat; 195, 196, 199) Awash
with prayer flags, this free-spirited, kar-
ma-positive restaurant pulls in the punters
with authentic Tibetan and Nepalese dishes
such as tender *fhaiya deakau* (lamb with

veggies, coconut milk, sour cream and spices).
Repeat the house mantra: 'May positive forces
be with every single living thing that exists'.

Watt   MODERN AUSTRALIAN $$
(Map p282; 07-3358 5464; www.watt
brisbane.com.au; Brisbane Powerhouse, 119
Lamington St, New Farm; bar food $10-29, res-
taurant $25-34; 10.30am-6pm Mon, to 10pm
Tue-Fri, 8am-10pm Sat & Sun; 195, 196, New
Farm Park) On the riverbank level of the
Brisbane Powerhouse is Watt, a breezy,
contemporary space made for long, lazy
vino sessions and people watching. Keep it
casual with bar bites like Cuban fish tacos
and manchego croquettes, or book a table
in the restaurant for farm-to-table options
such as wild Bendigo rabbit pappardelle
with smoked speck, hazelnut, watercress
pesto and parmesan.

Bar Alto   ITALIAN $$$
(Map p282; 07-3358 1063; www.baralto.com.
au; Brisbane Powerhouse, 119 Lamington St, New
Farm; mains $27-33; restaurant 11.30am-9pm
Tue-Thu & Sun, to 10pm Fri & Sat, bar 9.30am-late
Tue-Sun; 195, 196, New Farm Park) At the
arts-pumping Brisbane Powerhouse, this
snappy upstairs bar-restaurant draws culture vultures and general bon vivants with
its enormous balcony, at the ready with
gorgeous river view. Local ingredients sing
in Italian-inspired dishes, such as spanner-
crab gnocchi, while the solid wine list includes a good number of interesting Italian drops. Book ahead if dining Friday to
Sunday (Sunday lunch can book out weeks
in advance in summer).

Kangaroo Point & Woolloongabba

Cliffs Cafe   CAFE $
(Map p286; 07-3391 7771; www.cliffscafe.com.
au; 29 River Tce, Kangaroo Point; dishes $6.50-
19.50; 7am-5pm; 234) Looking straight
out at the river, skyline and City Botanic
Gardens, lofty Cliffs offers what is arguably the best view of Brisbane. It's a casual,
open-air pavilion, serving big breakfasts,
panini, burgers, fish and chips, salads and
sweet treats. While the food won't necessarily blow your socks off, the unobstructed, postcard panorama will. Kick back with
a coffee or beer and count your blessings.

Pearl Cafe
CAFE $$

(Map p282; ☑ 07-3392 3300; www.facebook.com/pearl.cafe.brisbane; 28 Logan Rd, Woolloongabba; mains $16-34; ⏲ 7am-8pm Tue-Sat, to 3pm Sat & Sun; ☐ 125, 175, 204, 234) Channelling Melbourne and Paris with its Euro flair, Pearl is one of Brisbane's best-loved weekend brunch spots. There are freshly baked cakes on the counter, a sophisticated selection of spirits on the shelf, and beautiful cafe dishes on the menu. Snub the underwhelming avocado on toast for more inspiring options, among them the popular daytime pork cotoletta. Sandwiches are chunky and generously filled.

★1889 Enoteca
ITALIAN $$$

(Map p282; ☑ 07-3392 4315; www.1889enoteca.com.au; 10-12 Logan Rd, Woolloongabba; pasta $21-42, mains $32-49; ⏲ noon-2.30pm & 6-10pm Tue-Fri, 6-10pm Sat, noon-2.30pm Sun; ☐ 125, 175, 204, 234) Italian purists rightfully adore this moody, sophisticated bistro and wine store, where pasta is *not* served with a spoon (unless requested) and a Roman-centric menu delivers seductive dishes including *carciofi alla Giuda* (Jewish-Roman-style fried artichoke with parsley and lemon mascarpone) and melt-in-your-mouth gnocchi with pork and fennel sausage, parmesan cream and black-truffle tapenade. Superlative wines include drops from lauded, smaller Italian producers.

✗ Greater Brisbane

★Shouk Cafe
MIDDLE EASTERN $$

(Map p282; ☑ 07-3172 1655; www.shoukcafe.com.au; 14 Collingwood St, Paddington; dishes $15.50-22; ⏲ 7.30am-2.30pm; 🛜 🖊; ☐ 375) Shouk wins on many levels: affable staff, laid-back vibe, verdant views from the backroom and – most importantly – generous portions of fresh, gorgeous dishes inspired by the Middle East. Swoon over sardines on toasted rye with roasted capsicum, chopped olives, raisins, orange-pickled fennel and labna, or the beautiful *kusheri* (spiced brown rice with lentils, chickpeas and caramelised onion on a beetroot and tahini purée).

Eat Street Markets
STREET FOOD $

(☑ 07-3358 2500; www.eatstreetmarkets.com; 99 MacArthur Ave, Hamilton; admission adult/child $2.50/free, meals from $10; ⏲ 4-10pm Fri & Sat; 🛳 Bretts Wharf) What was once a container wharf has now become Brisbane's hugely popular take on the night food market. Its maze of shipping-containers-turned-kitchens

peddle anything from freshly shucked oysters to smoky American barbecue and Turkish gözleme. Add craft brews, festive lights and live music and you have one of Brisbane's coolest nights out. To get here, catch the CityCat ferry to Bretts Wharf.

Scout
CAFE $

(Map p290; ☑ 07-3367 2171; www.scoutcafe.com.au; 190 Petrie Tce, Petrie Terrace; mains $14-18; ⏲ 7am-3pm; ☐ 375, 380) This vintage neighbourhood shopfront was vacant for 17 years before Scout showed up and started selling bagels. The vibe is downbeat, affable and creative, with a short, clean menu of healthy salads and bagels stuffed with combos like roasted rosemary potatoes, gorgonzola, mozzarella and chilli jam.

Kettle & Tin
CAFE $$

(Map p290; ☑ 07-3369 3778; www.kettleandtin.com.au; 215 Given Tce, Paddington; mains $14-32; ⏲ 7am-4pm Mon & Sun, to 9pm Tue-Thu, to 10pm Fri & Sat; ☐ 375) Behind its picket fence, cute-as-a-button Kettle & Tin serves up solid, scrumptious cafe grub. Breakfast standouts include thick-cut Kassler bacon with sautéed kale, white beans, celeriac purée and roasted apple, while Paddo's lunching ladies fawn over the daikon and carrot salad with toasted sesame, nori seaweed and puffed rice. Come dinner, cross the Pacific with the ever-popular smoked-duck-breast fajitas.

Byblós
MIDDLE EASTERN $$$

(☑ 07-3268 2223; www.byblosbar.com.au; Portside Wharf, 39 Hercules St, Hamilton; mains $28-34, banquet per person $60; ⏲ 11.30am-late; 🛳 Bretts Wharf) A slice of contemporary Beirut by the Brisbane River, Byblós specialises in Lebanese and Mediterranean edibles. While service can be a little hit-and-miss, the menu delivers a solid selection of vibrant, mostly sharing-style dishes like *makanek* (homemade spiced sausages finished with roasted nuts), *shanklish* (soft aged cheese mixed with aniseed and chilli) and *salmon kebbi nayeh* (salmon minced with burghal and traditional spices).

🍷 Drinking & Nightlife

Brisbane's bar scene has evolved into a sophisticated entity, with sharp, competent drinking holes pouring everything from natural wines and locally made saisons, to G&Ts spiked with native ingredients. The city's live-music scene is equally robust, with cult-status venues in Fortitude Valley, West

LGBT BRISBANE

While Brisbane's LGBT scene is significantly smaller than its Sydney and Melbourne counterparts, the city has an out-and-proud queer presence.

Major events on the calendar include **Melt** (www.brisbanepowerhouse.org/festivals; ☉ Jan/Feb), a 12-day feast of queer theatre, cabaret, dance, comedy, circus acts and visual arts held at the Brisbane Powerhouse in January and February. In March, the Powerhouse also hosts the **Queer Film Festival** (www.brisbanepowerhouse.org/festivals/brisbane-queer-film-festival; ☉ Mar), a showcase for gay, lesbian, bisexual and transgender films. September heralds the **Brisbane Pride Festival** (p295), which peaks during Pride Fair Day, held at New Farm Park.

Fortitude Valley's **Wickham Hotel** (Map p292; ☑ 07-3852 1301; www.thewickham.com.au; 308 Wickham St; ☉ 6.30am-late Mon-Fri, 10am-late Sat & Sun; ☒ Fortitude Valley) attracts a mainly mixed crowd these days, though it remains a staunchly queer-friendly pub. The Valley is also home to gay-friendly clubs **Beat MegaClub** (Map p292; www.thebeatmegaclub.com.au; 677 Ann St, Fortitude Valley; ☉ 8pm-5am Mon-Sat, from 5pm Sun; ☒ Fortitude Valley) and the scenier **Family** (p307); on Sunday the latter hosts 'Fluffy', Brisbane's biggest gay dance party. Closer to the city centre, the **Sportsman Hotel** (Map p286; ☑ 07-3831 2892; www.sportsmanhotel.com.au; 130 Leichhardt St, Spring Hill; ☉ 1pm-1am Sun-Thu, to 2.30am Fri & Sat; ☒ Central) is another perennially busy gay venue: a blue-collar, orange-brick pub with pool tables, drag shows and a rather eclectic crowd. In general, you'll find a significant local gay presence in the inner suburbs of Fortitude Valley, New Farm, Newstead, West End and Paddington.

For current entertainment and events listings, interviews and articles, check out *Q News* (www.qnews.com.au) and *Blaze* (www.gaynewsnetwork.com.au). Tune in to *Queer Radio* (9pm to 11pm every Wednesday; www.4zzzfm.org.au), a radio show on 4ZZZ (aka FM102.1) – another source of Brisbane info. For lesbian news and views, *Dykes on Mykes* precedes it (7pm to 9pm Wednesday).

End and the city itself pumping out impressive local and international talent. Tip: always carry some photo ID.

☕ Central Brisbane

★ Super Whatnot
BAR

(Map p286; ☑ 07-3210 2343; www.superwhatnot.com; 48 Burnett Lane; ☉ 3-11pm Mon-Thu, noon-1am Fri, 3pm-1am Sat, 3-8pm Sun; ☒ Central) Trailblazing Super Whatnot remains one of Brisbane's coolest drinking holes, an industrial, split-level playpen in a former beauty school. Slip inside for cognoscenti craft beers, decent vino and crafty cocktails, served to a pleasure-seeking mix of indie kids and thirsty suits. Bar bites include cheeky hot dogs and nachos.

Coffee Anthology
CAFE

(Map p286; ☑ 07-3210 1881; www.facebook.com/coffeeanthology; 126 Margaret St; ☉ 7am-3.30pm Mon-Fri, to noon Sat; ☎; ☒ Central) True to its name, Coffee Anthology keeps caffeine geeks hyped with a rotating selection of specialist blends from cult-status roasters including Padre and Industry Beans. Tasting notes guide the indecisive, and you can even buy a bag or two if you like what's in your cup. Friendly, breezy and contemporary, the place also serves simple breakfast and lunch bites, from porridge and muffins to bagels.

Brooklyn Standard
BAR

(Map p286; ☑ 0405 414 131; www.facebook.com/brooklynstandardbar; Eagle Lane; ☉ 4pm-late Mon-Fri, 6pm-late Sat; ☒ Riverside, ☒ Central) The red neon sign sets the tone: 'If the music is too loud, you are too old'. And loud, live, nightly tunes are what you get in this rocking cellar bar, decked out in NYC paraphernalia and buzzing with a mixed-age crowd. Stay authentic with a Brooklyn lager or knock back a kooky cocktail (either way, the pretzels are on the house).

Gresham Bar
BAR

(Map p286; www.thegresham.com.au; 308 Queen St; ☉ 7am-3am Mon-Fri, 4pm-3am Sat & Sun; ☎; ☒ Central) Tucked into one corner of a noble, heritage-listed bank building, the Gresham evokes the old-school bars of New York; we're talking pressed-metal ceiling, Chesterfields and a glowing cascade of spirit bottles behind a handsome timber bar (complete with library-style ladder). It's a dark, buzzing, convivial spot, with an especially robust selection of whiskies and a snug side room you'll find difficult to leave.

John Mills Himself   CAFE, BAR
(Map p286; ☑ bar 0421 959 865, cafe 0434 064 349; www.johnmillshimself.com.au; 40 Charlotte St; ☺ cafe 6.30am-3.30pm Mon-Fri, bar 4-10pm Tue-Thu, to midnight Fri; ⊠ Central) No doubt Mr Mills would approve of this secret little coffee shop, occupying the very building in which he ran a printing business last century. Accessible from both Charlotte St and an alley off Elizabeth St, its marble bar and penny-tile floors set a very Brooklyn scene for top third-wave coffee. Later in the day, cafe becomes intimate bar, pouring craft Australian beers and spirits.

Mr & Mrs G Riverbar   BAR
(Map p286; ☑ 07-3221 7001; www.mrandmrsg. com.au; Eagle St Pier, 1 Eagle St; ☺ 3-10pm Mon & Tue, noon-11pm Wed & Thu, noon-midnight Fri & Sat, noon-10pm Sun; ☱ Eagle St Pier, ⊠ Central) Mr & Mrs G spoils guests with curving floor-to-ceiling windows overlooking the river, skyline and Story Bridge. It's a casually chic affair, with vibrantly coloured bar stools, cushy slipper chairs and hand-painted Moroccan side tables on which to rest your glass of chenin blanc. If you're feeling peckish, generous tapas dishes include succulent *keftethes* (Greek-style meatballs), cheese and charcuterie.

Riverbar & Kitchen   BAR
(Map p286; ☑ 07-3211 9020; www.riverbarand kitchen.com.au; 71 Eagle St; ☺ 7am-11.30pm; ☱ Riverside, ⊠ Central) A chilled-out spot for an afternoon ale or barrel-aged cocktail, Riverbar & Kitchen is true to its name, down by the muddy Brisbane River at the base of the Eagle St Pier complex. Decked-out like a boat shed, with coiled ropes, white-painted timber and booths, the vibe is casual, breezy and free-flowing. Decent food too, from morning staples to burgers, pizzas and surf-and-turf bistro mains.

☕ South Bank

Maker   COCKTAIL BAR
(Map p286; ☑ 0437 338 072; 9 Fish Lane, South Brisbane; ☺ 4pm-midnight Tue-Sun; ☱ South Bank Terminals 1 & 2, ⊠ South Brisbane) Intimate, black-clad and spliced by a sexy brass bar, Maker crafts seamless, seasonal cocktails

using house liqueurs, out-of-the-box ingredients and a splash of whimsy. Here, classic negronis are made with house-infused vermouth, while gin and tonics get Australian with native quandong and finger lime. Other fortes include a sharp edit of boutique wines by the glass and beautiful bar bites prepared with award-winning restaurant Gauge (p300).

Cobbler   BAR
(Map p290; www.cobblerbar.com; 7 Browning St, West End; ☺ 5pm-1am Mon, 4pm-1am Tue-Thu & Sun, 4pm-2am Fri & Sat; ☱ 60, 192, 198, 199) Whisky fans will weep tears of joy at the sight of Cobbler's imposing bar, graced with more than 400 whiskies from around the globe. Channelling a speakeasy vibe, this dimly lit West End wonder also pours a cognoscenti selection of rums, tequilas and liqueurs, not to mention a crafty selection of cocktails that add modern twists to the classics. Bottoms up!

Catchment Brewing Co   BREWERY
(Map p290; ☑ 07-3846 1701; www.catchment brewingco.com.au; 150 Boundary St, West End; ☺ 4-10pm Mon, 11am-10pm Tue-Thu & Sun, 11am-1am Fri & Sat; ☱ 199) Sink local suds at Catchment, a hip, two-level microbrewery with notable, seasonal nosh and live music in the courtyard. House brews include Pale Select, a nod to the signature beer of the defunct West End Brewery, while guest taps showcase other local beers. The best seats in the house are the two, tiny, 1st-floor balconies, serving up afternoon sun and Boundary St views.

Jungle   BAR
(Map p290; ☑ 0449 568 732; www.facebook. com/junglewestend; 76 Vulture St, West End; ☺ noon-midnight Thu-Sun; ☱ 199) Aloha and welcome to paradise... Well, at least to Brisbane's only proper tiki bar. An intimate, hand-built bamboo hideaway pimped with wood-carved stools, a green-glowing bar and DJ-spun Hawaiian tunes, it's an apt place to cool down with a tropical libation. Keep it classic with a rumalicious piña colada (served in a pineapple, naturally), or neck a Red Stripe lager from Jamaica.

Blackstar Coffee Roasters   CAFE
(Map p290; www.blackstarcoffee.com.au; 44 Thomas St, West End; ☺ 7am-5pm; ☎; ☱ 199) One of Brisbane's top coffee roasters, laid-back Blackstar is never short of West End hipsters, hippies and laptop-tapping creatives. Slurp a single-origin espresso or cool down with a

bottle of cold-pressed coffee. Food options (lunch dishes $10 to $17) include brownies, eggs and spanakopita, while its string of special events includes a ukulele night on the last Friday of the month.

Archive Beer Boutique BAR

(Map p290; ☑ 07-3844 3419; www.archivebeer boutique.com.au; 100 Boundary St, West End; ☺ 11am-late; 🚇 198, 199) A foaming juggernaut, Archive serves up a dizzying choice of craft suds. Whether you're hankering for a Brisbane chilli-choc porter, a Melbourne American IPA or a Sydney guava gose, chances are you'll find it pouring here. There are more than 20 rotating beers on tap, as well as hundreds of Aussie and imported bottled brews. Decent bar grub includes grilled meats, burgers and pizzas.

🍺 Fortitude Valley

★ Gerard's Bar WINE BAR

(Map p292; ☑ 07-3252 2606; www.gerardsbar. com.au; 13a/23 James St; ☺ 3-10pm Mon-Thu, noon-late Fri & Sat; 🚇 470, 🚇 Fortitude Valley) A stylish, grown-up bar that's one of Brisbane's best. Perch yourself at the polished concrete bar, chose an unexpected drop from the sharply curated wine list, and couple with standout bar snacks that include flawless croquettes and prized Jamón Iberico de Belotta. If you're craving a cocktail, try the signature 'Gerard the Drunk', an intriguing, climate-appropriate medley of vodka, passionfruit, pomegranate and rose water.

APO COCKTAIL BAR

(Map p292; ☑ 07-3252 2403; www.theapo.com. au; 690 Ann St; ☺ 3pm-1am Tue, noon-1am Wed, Thu & Sun, noon-3am Fri & Sat; 🚇 Fortitude Valley) A smart, quality-driven establishment, the APO was once an apothecary (hence the name). It's a dark, moody, two-level space, where Victorian brickwork contrasts with polished concrete floors and the odd marble feature wall. Drinks are sharp, sophisticated and include bottled single-batch cocktails such as a rhubarb-and-vanilla negroni. Topping it off is a smashing menu of French-Lebanese-inspired bites, including a not-to-be-missed Lebanese taco.

Eleven ROOFTOP BAR

(Map p292; ☑ 07-3067 7447; www.elevenrooftop bar.com.au; 757 Ann St; ☺ noon-midnight Tue-Thu & Sun, to 3am Fri & Sat; 🚇 Fortitude Valley) Slip into your slinkiest threads for Brisbane's finest rooftop retreat, its marble bar pouring a competent list of libations, including pickled-onion-pimped martinis and high-flying French champagnes. Drink in the multi-million-dollar view, which takes in the city skyline and Mt Coot-tha beyond, and schmooze to DJ-spun tunes later in the week. The dress code is especially strict on Friday and Saturday evenings; see the website.

Cloudland BAR

(Map p292; ☑ 07-3872 6600; www.katarzyna.com. au/venues/cloudland; 641 Ann St; ☺ 4pm-late Tue-Thu, 11.30am-late Fri-Sun; 🚇 Fortitude Valley) Jaws hit the floor at this opulent, multilevel bar, club and Pan-Asian restaurant. Named for a much-loved, long-demolished 1940s Brisbane dance hall, Cloudland has birdcage booths, lush foliage and vast chandeliers that are best described as enchanted forest meets sheikh palace meets Addams Family gothic. Free salsa lessons on Thursday from 9pm.

Family CLUB

(Map p292; ☑ 07-3852 5000; www.thefamily.com. au; 8 McLachlan St; ☺ 9pm-3.30am Fri-Sun; 🚇 Fortitude Valley) Queue up for one of Brisbane's biggest and mightiest clubs. The music here is phenomenal, pumping through four levels with myriad dance floors, bars, themed booths and elite DJs from home and away. Running on Sunday, the 'Fluffy' dance party is a big hit with Brisbane's younger, hotter, gay party peeps.

Holey Moley Golf Club COCKTAIL BAR

(Map p292; ☑ 1300 727 833; www.holeymoley.com. au; 25 Warner St; 9-hole minigolf game per person $16.50; ☺ noon-late Mon-Fri, 10am-late Sat & Sun; 🚇 Fortitude Valley) Minigolf, in a church, with cocktails is what awaits at Holey Moley (best booked ahead). Order a Putty Professor (rum, milk, chocolate sauce, peanut butter, Reese's Peanut Butter Cup, crushed Maltesers) and tee off on one of two courses. Each of the 18 holes is themed; the standout *Game of Thrones*–themed Iron Throne is by local artist Cezary Stulgis. Kids welcome until 5pm.

Bloodhound Corner Bar & Kitchen BAR

(Map p292; ☑ 07-3162 6402; www.bloodhound cornerbar.com.au; 454 Brunswick St; ☺ 3pm-late Mon-Wed, noon-late Thu-Sun; 🚇 Fortitude Valley) Starting life as a grocery store, this 19th-century pile is now a new-school Valley bar. Vintage brick walls, mottled floorboards and open fireplaces share the space with street art, a pinball machine and plenty of hipster beards. Guzzle international beers, well-mixed cocktails, or get experimental with one of the craft spirit flights. Decent bar snacks nod to South America, with live music upstairs on Saturday.

Woolly Mammoth Alehouse
BAR

(Map p292; ☑07-3257 4439; www.woolly mammoth.com.au; 633 Ann St; ⊙4pm-late Tue-Thu, from noon Fri-Sun; ☒Fortitude Valley) The combination of craft beer, giant Jenga and 4m shuffleboard table is not lost on Millennials, who stream into this big, polished playpen to let the good times roll. Brew types include IPAs, saisons and goses, most of which hail from Australian microbreweries. Check the website to see what's playing on the Mane Stage, which could be anything from comedy to UK hip-hop.

Elixir
ROOFTOP BAR

(Map p292; ☑07-3363 5599; www.elixirrooftop. com.au; 646 Ann St; ⊙4pm-late Wed-Fri, 1pm-late Sat & Sun; ☒Fortitude Valley) What rooftop Elixir lacks in views it makes up for in ambience. Hurry up the stairs for a sultry, tropical playpen of lush leaves, flickering tealights, DJ-spun beats and languid day beds. Refresh with craft beers or Elixir's Fresh Market martini, a twist on the classic using hand-picked market fruits. Check the website for weekly drinks and food promotions.

Press Club
COCKTAIL BAR

(Map p292; ☑07-3852 5000; www.pressclub.net. au; 339 Brunswick St; ⊙7pm-2.30am Tue-Thu, 6pm-3am Fri & Sat, 6pm-2am Sun; ☒Fortitude Valley) Looking more like a hang-out for aliens than journos (picture bar stools and glowing chandeliers), Press Club sets an offbeat scene for cocktails, ciders and smooth live tunes. Head in Tuesday and Saturday for R&B, Wednesday for jazz, Thursday for swing, or Friday for funk and soul. Tuesday nights are especially huge while Sunday's DJ sets are popular with local 'hospo' (hospitality) peeps.

New Farm

★Triffid
BAR

(Map p282; ☑07-3171 3001; www.thetriffid.com.au; 7-9 Stratton St, Newstead; ☒300, 302, 305, 306, 322, 393) Not only does the Triffid have an awesome beer garden (complete with shipping-container bars and a cassette-themed mural honouring Brisbane bands), it's also one of the city's top live-music venues. Music acts span local, Aussie and international talent, playing in a barrel-vaulted WWII hangar with killer acoustics. It's hardly surprising given that the place is owned by former Powderfinger bassist John Collins.

★Green Beacon Brewing Co
MICROBREWERY

(Map p282; ☑07-3252 8393; www.greenbeacon. com.au; 26 Helen St, Teneriffe; ⊙noon-late; ☎; ☒393, 470, ☒Teneriffe) In a cavernous warehouse in post-industrial Teneriffe, Green Beacon brews some of Brisbane's best beers. The liquid beauties ferment in vast stainless-steel vats behind the long bar before flowing through the taps and onto your grateful palate. Choose from six core beers or seasonal specials such as blood-orange IPA. Peckish? Decent bites include fresh local seafood, and there's always a guest food truck parked out front.

Newstead Brewing Co
MICROBREWERY

(Map p282; ☑07-3172 2488; www.newstead brewing.com.au; 85 Doggett St, Newstead; ⊙11am-midnight; ☒60, 393, 470, ☒Teneriffe) What was once a bus depot is now a pumping microbrewery, its 12 taps pouring six standard house brews, one cider and five seasonal beers (dubbed the 'fun stuff' by one staffer). For an enlightening overview, order the paddle board of four different brews. If beer doesn't rock your boat, knock back cocktails, craft spirits or wine from a small, engaging list of smaller producers.

On the food front, ditch the so-so pizzas for the deliciously spicy, tangy buffalo wings.

Death Before Decaf
COFFEE

(Map p292; 3/760 Brunswick St; ⊙24hr; ☒195, 196,199) Kick-ass speciality coffee, brewed all day and all through the night: this ink-loving, headbanging legend is a godsend for people craving a decent cup after 4pm. Death Before Decaf, we salute you.

Kangaroo Point & Woolloongabba

Canvas Club
COCKTAIL BAR

(Map p282; ☑07-3891 2111; www.canvasclub. com.au; 16b Logan Rd, Woolloongabba; ⊙noon-midnight Tue-Fri, from 10am Sat & Sun; ☒125, 175, 204, 234) Slap bang on Woolloongabba's main eating, drinking and shopping strip, Canvas sets a hip, arty scene for cheeky cocktail sessions. Debate the symbolism of the street-art mural while downing seasonal libations like the Don Pablo (rum, amaro and apple-and-cinnamon foam) or the silky smooth Bangarang (tequila, watermelon, chilli, coriander, lime and condensed milk). Smashing.

Story Bridge Hotel PUB
(Map p286; ☑07-3391 2266; www.storybridge hotel.com.au; 200 Main St, Kangaroo Point; ⊘6.30am-midnight Sun-Thu, to 1.30am Fri & Sat; ☐234, ☑Thornton St, Holman St) Beneath the bridge at Kangaroo Point, this beautiful 1886 pub and beer garden is perfect for a pint after a long day exploring. Regular live music (see the website for upcoming acts) and a good choice of drinking and eating areas.

☐ **Greater Brisbane**

★**Lefty's Old Time Music Hall** BAR
(Map p290; www.leftysoldtimemusichall.com; 15 Caxton St, Petrie Tce; ⊘5pm-late Tue-Sun; ☐375) Paint the town and the front porch too, there's a honky-tonk bar in Brisvegas! Tarted up in chandeliers and mounted moose heads (yep, those are bras hanging off the antlers), scarlet-hued Lefty's keeps the good times rolling with close to 200 whiskies and the sweet twang of live country and western. A short, star-spangled food menu includes chilli cheese fries and southern fried chicken.

Regatta Hotel PUB
(Map p282; ☑07-3871 9595; www.regattahotel. com.au; 543 Coronation Dr, Toowong; ⊘6.30am-1am; ☑Regatta) Dressed in iron lacework and prettier than a wedding cake, this 1874 pub is a Brisbane institution. Directly opposite the Regatta CityCat ferry terminal, its revamped drinking spaces include a polished, contemporary main bar, a chi-chi outdoor courtyard and a basement speakeasy called The Walrus Club (open 5pm to late Thursday to Saturday). Check the website for weekly events, which often include live music.

Breakfast Creek Hotel PUB
(Map p282; ☑07-3262 5988; www.breakfast creekhotel.com; 2 Kingsford Smith Dr, Albion; ⊘10am-late; ☐300, 302, 305) Built in 1889 and sporting an eclectic French-Renaissance style, the Breakfast Creek Hotel is a Brisbane icon. The pub offers various bars and dining areas, including a beer garden and an art-deco 'private bar' where the wooden kegs are spiked daily at noon. A converted electricity substation on-site is now home to

Substation No 41, an urbane bar with more than 400 rums in its inventory.

☆ **Entertainment**

Most big-ticket international bands have Brisbane on their radar, and the city regularly hosts top-tier DJ talent. World-class cultural venues offer a year-round program of theatre, dance, music and comedy.

Qtix (☑13 62 46; www.qtix.com.au) is a booking agency, usually for more high-brow entertainment.

Riverstage LIVE MUSIC
(Map p286; ☑07-3403 7921; www.brisbane.qld. gov.au/facilities-recreation/arts-and-culture/ riverstage; 59 Gardens Point Rd; ☑QUT Gardens Point, ☑Central) Evocatively set in the Botanic Gardens, this outdoor arena hosts no shortage of prolific national and international music acts. Past performers include U2, 5 Seconds of Summer, Ellie Goulding and Flume.

Lock 'n' Load LIVE MUSIC
(Map p290; ☑07-3844 0142; www.locknload bistro.com.au; 142 Boundary St, West End; ⊘3pm-late Mon-Thu, from noon Fri, from 7am Sat & Sun; ☎; ☐199) Ebullient and woody, this two-storey gastropub lures an upbeat crowd of music fans, here to watch jazz, acoustic, roots, blues and soul acts take to the small front stage. Catch a gig, then show up for breakfast or lunch the next day (the brekkie of craft-beer baked beans with fat bacon, sour cream, jalapeños and corn bread tames a hangover). Check the website for upcoming gigs.

Zoo LIVE MUSIC
(Map p292; ☑07-3854 1381; www.thezoo.com.au; 711 Ann St, Fortitude Valley; ⊘7pm-late Wed-Sun; ☑Fortitude Valley) Going strong since 1992, the Zoo has surrendered a bit of musical territory to Brightside, but it is still a grungy spot for indie rock, folk, acoustic, hip-hop, reggae and electronic acts, with no shortage of raw talent. Recent acts have included Gold Coast garage rockers Bleeding Knees Club and American indie pop artist Toro y Moi.

Underground Opera OPERA
(Map p286; ☑07-3389 0135, 0429 536 472; www. undergroundopera.com.au; Spring Hill Reservoir, Wickham Tce, Spring Hill; ⊘hours vary; ☐30, ☑Central) A professional, Brisbane-based performing-arts company running annual seasons of opera and Broadway musical recitals in the

OUTDOOR CINEMA

One of the best ways to spend a warm summer night in Brisbane is with a picnic basket and some friends at an outdoor cinema. **Moonlight Cinema** (p289) runs between December and early March at New Farm Park near the Brisbane Powerhouse. Films, which include current mainstream releases and the odd cult classic, screen from Wednesday to Sunday, flickering into life around 7pm.

A parallel option is **Ben & Jerry's Openair Cinemas** (Map p286; www.openair cinemas.com.au; Rainforest Green, South Bank Parklands, South Bank; adult/child online $17/12, at the gate $22/17; ⊙ from 5.30pm Tue-Sat, from 5pm Sun; 🚢 South Bank Terminals 1 & 2, 🚉 South Brisbane) at South Bank, where from late September to mid-November you can watch big-screen classics and recent releases under the stars (or clouds) at the Rainforest Green at South Bank Parklands. Hire a beanbag or deckchair, or bring a picnic rug. Note that most sessions sell out online prior to the night of the screening, so book in advance. Live music (which sometimes includes prolific Australian acts) runs beforehand.

subterranean Spring Hill Reservoir, built between 1871 and 1882. See the website for season dates and prices.

Brisbane Jazz Club   JAZZ
(Map p286; ☎ 07-3391 2006; www.brisbanejazz club.com.au; 1 Annie St, Kangaroo Point; adult/under 18yr $31/11; ⊙ 6.30-11pm Thu-Sat, 5.30-10pm Sun; 🚢 Holman St) Straight out of the bayou, this tiny riverside jazz shack has been Brisbane's jazz beacon since 1972. Anyone who's anyone in the scene plays here when they're in town.

South Bank Cineplex   CINEMA
(Map p286; ☎ 07-3829 7970; www.cineplex.com. au; cnr Grey & Ernest Sts, South Bank; adult/child from $6.50/4.50; ⊙ 10am-late; 🚢 South Bank Terminals 1, 2 & 3, 🚉 South Bank) The cheapest complex for mainstream releases: wade through a sea of popcorn aromas and teenagers.

New Farm Six Cinemas   CINEMA
(Map p292; ☎ 07-3358 4444; www.newfarm cinemas.com.au; 701 Brunswick St, New Farm; adult/child $16/10; ⊙ 10am-late; 🚌 195, 196, 199) When those subtropical heavens open up, take refuge at New Farm's historic movie palace. Recently remodelled and restored, its six, state-of-the-art screening rooms show mostly mainstream new releases. Tuesday is popular with penny-pinching film buffs, with all tickets a bargain $8.

Queensland Performing
Arts Centre   PERFORMING ARTS
(QPAC; Map p286; ☎ guided tours 07-3840 7444, tickets 136 246; www.qpac.com.au; Queensland Cultural Centre, cnr Grey & Melbourne Sts, South Bank; tours adult/child $15/10; ⊙ box office 9am-8.30pm Mon-Sat; 🚢 South Bank Terminals 1 & 2, 🚉 South Brisbane) Brisbane's main performing arts centre comprises four venues and a small exhibition space focused on aspects of the performing arts. The centre's busy calendar includes ballet, concerts, theatre and comedy, from both Australian and international acts. One-hour backstage tours run on Friday from 10.30am; book tickets by phone or email, or purchase them on the day from the QPAC cafe on the ground floor.

Metro Arts Centre   ARTS CENTRE
(Map p286; ☎ 07-3002 7100; www.metroarts.com. au; Level 2, 109 Edward St; ⊙ gallery 10am-4.30pm Mon-Fri, 2-4.30pm Sat, performance times vary; 🚢 Eagle St Pier, 🚉 Central) This downtown venue hosts community theatre, local dramatic pieces, dance and art shows. It's an effervescent spot for a taste of Brisbane's creative talent, be it offbeat, quirky, fringe, progressive or just downright weird. The on-site gallery hosts thought-provoking temporary art exhibitions and associated artist talks. See the website for upcoming exhibitions, performances and special events.

Judith Wright Centre
of Contemporary Arts   PERFORMING ARTS
(Map p292; ☎ 07-3872 9000; www.judithwright centre.com; 420 Brunswick St, Fortitude Valley; ⊙ box office 11am-4pm Mon-Fri; 🎵; 🚉 Fortitude Valley) Home to both a medium-sized and intimate performance space, this free-thinking arts incubator hosts an eclectic array of cultural treats, including contemporary dance, circus and visual arts. It's also the hub for

the hugely popular Bigsound Festival (p295), a three-day music fest. Scan the website for upcoming performances and exhibitions.

Brisbane Powerhouse PERFORMING ARTS
(Map p282; ☑box office 07-3358 8600; www.brisbanepowerhouse.org; 119 Lamington St, New Farm; ☐195, 196, ⚲New Farm Park) What was a 1920s power station is now a buzzing hub of nationally and internationally acclaimed theatre, music, comedy, dance and more. There are loads of happenings at the Powerhouse – some free – as well as popular in-house bars and restaurants with standout views over the Brisbane River. See the website for upcoming events.

Suncorp Stadium STADIUM
(Map p290; www.suncorpstadium.com.au; 40 Castlemaine St, Milton; ☐375, 379) In winter, rugby league is the big spectator sport here and local team the Brisbane Broncos call this stadium home.

Gabba STADIUM
(Brisbane Cricket Ground; Map p282; www.thegabba.com.au; 411 Vulture St, Woolloongabba; ☐174, 175, 184, 185, 200) You can cheer both AFL football and interstate and international cricket at the Gabba in Woolloongabba, south of Kangaroo Point. If you're new to cricket, try and get along to a Twenty20 match, which sees the game in its most explosive form. The cricket season runs from late September to March; the football from late March to September.

Paddo Tavern COMEDY
(Map p290; ☑07-3369 4466; www.standup.com.au; 186 Given Tce, Paddington; ☺pub 10am-late, comedy shows vary; ☐375) If a car wash married its supermarket cousin, their first-born would probably look like this ugly Paddington pub, which has incongruously adopted a pseudo Wild West theme inside. But it's one of the best places in Brisbane to see stand-up comedy: check the website for listings.

🔒 Shopping

Brisbane's retail landscape is deliciously eclectic, stretching from Vogue-indexed high-end handbags to weekend-market arts and crafts.

🔒 Central Brisbane

Noosa Chocolate Factory FOOD
(Map p286; www.noosachocolatefactory.com.au; 144 Adelaide St; ☺8am-7pm Mon-Thu, to 9pm Fri, 9am-6pm Sat, 10am-5pm Sun; ☐Central) 🍫 Don't delude yourself: the small-batch, artisanal chocolates from this Sunshine Coast Willy Wonka will override any self-control you have. Best sellers include generous, marshmallowy Rocky Road and a very Queensland concoction of unroasted macadamias covered in Bowen mango–flavoured chocolate. Best of all, the chocolate doesn't contain palm oil. A second branch at No 156 also serves speciality coffee and hot chocolate.

Maiocchi FASHION & ACCESSORIES
(Map p286; ☑07-3012 9640; www.maiocchi.com.au; Brisbane Arcade, 117 Adelaide St; ☺9am-5.30pm Mon-Thu, 8.30am-8pm Fri, 9am-4pm Sat, 11am-4pm Sun; ☐Central) Home-grown label Maiocchi is well known for its gorgeous, vintage-inspired frocks, simple in cut but rich in little details and quirks. Expect lots of custom prints, '50s silhouettes and the Japanese influences. Your next summery cocktail dress aside, the boutique also stocks tops, pants and shoes, as well as a thoughtfully curated selection of Australian-made jewellery, bags and homewares. You'll find it in the heritage-listed Brisbane Arcade.

Jan Powers Farmers Market MARKET
(Map p286; www.janpowersfarmersmarkets.com.au; Reddacliff Pl, George St; ☺8am-6pm Wed; ⚲North Quay, ☐Central) Central Brisbane lives out its bucolic village fantasies when local growers and artisans descend on Reddacliff Place to sell their prized goods. Fill your shopping bags with just-picked fruit and vegetables, meats and seafood, fresh pasta, fragrant breads, pastries and more. Stock up for a picnic in the City Botanic Gardens, or simply grab a coffee and a ready-to-eat, multiculti bite.

Archives Fine Books BOOKS
(Map p286; ☑07-3221 0491; www.archivesfinebooks.com.au; 40 Charlotte St; ☺9am-6pm Mon-Thu, to 7pm Fri, to 5pm Sat; ☐Central) Rickety bookshelves and squeaky floorboards set a nostalgic scene at this sprawling repository of pre-loved pages. While the true number of books on offer is a little less than the one

million claimed (our little secret), the place is a veritable sea of engaging titles. The oldest book on our last visit – by the canonised Roberto Francesco Romolo Bellarmino – dated back to 1630.

South Bank & West End

Where the Wild Things Are
BOOKS

(Map p290; ✆07-3255 3987; www.wherethe wildthingsare.com.au; 191 Boundary St, West End; ⊗8.30am-6pm Mon-Sat, to 5pm Sun; 🚕; 🚌199) Little brother to Avid Reader next door, Where the Wild Things Are stocks a whimsical collection of books for toddlers, older kids and teens. The bookshop also runs regular activities, from weekly storytime sessions to book launches, signings and crafty workshops covering topics such as book illustration. Scan the bookshop's website and Facebook page for upcoming events.

Jet Black Cat Music
MUSIC

(Map p290; ✆0419 571 299; www.facebook. com/jetblackcatmusic; 72 Vulture St, West End; ⊗10.30am-5pm Tue-Fri, 10am-4pm Sat; 🚌199) Serious music fans know all about Shannon Logan and her little West End record shop. She's usually behind the piano-cum-counter, chatting with a loyal fan base who drop in for an in-the-know, hard-to-find booty of indie vinyl and CDs. Logan only sells what she's passionate about, and the place also hosts occasional in-store gigs showcasing well-known local and international indie talent.

Junky Comics
BOOKS

(Map p290; ✆07-3846 5456; www.junkycomics-brisbane.com; 93 Vulture St, West End; ⊗10am-5.30pm Tue-Fri, to 5pm Sat, to 4pm Sun; 🚌199) Indie Junky stocks comics with cred, from classic DC, Dark Horse and Marvel titles, to female-, queer- and child-orientated works. You'll also find locally produced zines, graphic novels, art and prints, not to mention cool tees.

Fortitude Valley

Camilla
FASHION & ACCESSORIES

(Map p292; ✆07-3852 6030; www.camilla.com. au; 1/19 James St; ⊗9.30am-5pm Mon-Wed, Fri & Sat, to 7pm Thu, 10am-4pm Sun; 🚌470, 🚇Fortitude Valley) Fans of Camilla's statement-making silk kaftans include Beyoncé and Oprah Winfrey. While the label may be Bondi based, its wildly patterned, resort-style

creations – which also include frocks, tops, jumpsuits and swimwear – are just the ticket for languid lounging in chichi Brisbane restaurants and bars. Fierce and fabulous, these pieces aren't cheap, with kaftans starting from $500 and bikinis at around $300.

Libertine
PERFUME

(Map p292; ✆07-3216 0122; www.libertine parfumerie.com.au; 181 Robertson St; ⊗10am-5pm Mon-Fri, 9.30am-5pm Sat, 10am-4pm Sun; 🚌470, 🚇Fortitude Valley) While you won't stumble across any celeb-endorsed eau de toilettes at Libertine, you will discover some of the world's most coveted and hard-to-find perfume and skincare brands for women and men. Among them is Amouage (established for the Sultan of Oman), Santa Maria Novella and Creed, the latter's in-store offerings including the very fragrance created for Princess Grace on her wedding day.

Fallow
FASHION & ACCESSORIES

(Map p292; ✆07-3854 0155; www.fallow.com.au; Level 1, 354 Brunswick St; ⊗11am-5pm Mon-Fri, 10am-5pm Sat, 11am-4pm Sun; 🚇Fortitude Valley) Up a flight of stairs is this brooding chamber of avant-garde men's fashion. The focus is on sculptural, androgynous pieces from cult-status ateliers not usually stocked in Australia (think Germany's Pal Offner and Denmark's Aleksandr Manamis). Accessories include handmade fragrances from France's Mad et Len and an exquisite collection of handmade jewellery, including Gothic- and Edwardian-inspired pieces by Brisbane-based Luke Maninov.

Tym Guitars
MUSIC

(Map p292; ✆07-3161 5863; www.tym guitars.com.au; 5 Winn St; ⊗10am-5pm Tue-Thu & Sat, to 7pm Fri, 11am-4pm Sat; 🚇Fortitude Valley) Cult-status music store Tym stocks everything from vintage guitars and amps to handmade guitar pedals. (It's the kind of place where you might find a limited-edition pedal made by the likes of American alt-rocker J Mascis of Dinosaur Jr.) Tym's vinyl selection includes an especially notable collection of punk, stoner and psychedelic rock records, and the space hosts monthly alt-rock gigs.

Stock & Supply
FASHION & ACCESSORIES

(Map p292; ✆07-3061 7530; www.stockand supply.com.au; 4/694 Ann St; 🚇Fortitude Valley) Technically on Bakery Lane, just off Ann St, this youthful, unisex bolthole serves up a cool selection of smaller surf and streetwear brands. Pick up anything from graphic tees

TO MARKET, TO MARKET

Beyond the weekly farmers markets that feed the masses in **central Brisbane** (p311), **New Farm** (p289) and **West End** (p314) is a string of other fantastic local markets, peddling anything from handmade local fashion and bling, to art, skincare and out-of-the-box giftware. Hit the stalls at the following options.

Young Designers Market (Map p286; www.youngdesignersmarket.com.au; Little Stanley St, South Bank; ☺10am-4pm, 1st Sun of the month; ☒ South Bank Terminal 3, ☒ South Bank) Explore the work of up to 80 of the city's best emerging designers and artists, selling fashion and accessories, contemporary jewellery, art, furniture and homewares. Held beside South Bank Parklands, the market generally runs on the first Sunday of the month.

Collective Markets South Bank (Map p286; www.collectivemarkets.com.au; Stanley St Plaza; ☺5-9pm Fri, 10am-9pm Sat, 9am-4pm Sun; ☒ South Bank Terminal 3, ☒ South Bank) It might draw the tourist hordes, but this thrice-weekly event by South Bank Parklands peddles some great items, from artisan leather wallets and breezy summer frocks, to handmade jewellery, skincare, homewares and art.

Finders Keepers Markets A biannual market with over 100 art and design stalls held in a 19th-century museum that's now a concert hall in inner-suburban Bowen Hills. Complete with live music and food, it's a great spot to score high-quality, one-off fashion pieces, jewellery and more from local and interstate design talent.

Brisbane Riverside Markets (Map p286; ☏07-3870 2807; www.facebook.com/brisbane-riversidemarkets; City Botanic Gardens, Alice St; ☺8am-3pm Sun; ☒ QUT Gardens Point, ☒ Central) Come Sunday, chilled-out crowds gather at the northern end of the City Botanic Gardens for this weekly city-centre market. Scan the stalls for pretty, handmade frocks, scented candles, colourful ceramics and a plethora of street food from all corners of the globe. Live music keeps the mood festive and the peeps grooving.

to beachwear from the likes of skater outfit Crawling Death and surf-meets-art label The Critical Slide Society. The store also stocks wallets, jewellery, caps and footwear.

James Street   FASHION & ACCESSORIES
(Map p292; www.jamesst.com.au; James St; ☒470, ☒Fortitude Valley) Channelling LA with its low-slung architecture, sports cars and chic eateries is the Valley's glamtastic stretch of James St. Slip under its colonnade of fig trees for high-end boutiques, including celebrated Aussie fashion labels Scanlan & Theodore and Sass & Bide, home-grown designer Camilla Franks and Melbourne skincare brand Aesop.

Winn Lane   FASHION & ACCESSORIES
(Map p292; www.winnlane.com.au; Winn Lane; ☒Fortitude Valley) Duck behind Ann St (off Winn St) and discover this arty congregation of boutiques, bookshops, jewellers and casual eats. Spangled with street art, the lane has a vibe that is emerging and quirky. Don't miss **Miss Bond** (Map p292; ☏0410 526 082; www.facebook.com/missbond.com.au; 5g Winn Lane; ☺10am-4pm Wed-Sat, to 3pm Sun) for contemporary, locally designed jewellery,

Outpost (Map p292; ☏07-3666 0306; www.the-outpoststore.com.au; 5 Winn St; ☺10am-6pm Tue-Thu & Sat, to 8pm Fri, 9.30am-4.30pm Sun) for in-the-know men's labels and accessories and, just off Winn Lane, Tym Guitars, famed for its handmade guitar pedals, vintage guitars and punk-heavy vinyl collection.

New Farm

Commercial Road Antiques   ANTIQUES
(Map p282; ☏07-3852 2352; 85 Commercial Rd, Teneriffe; ☺10am-5pm; ☒393, 470, ☒ Teneriffe) Whether you're on the prowl for a Victorian dresser, a mid-century armchair or a '60s beatnik frock, chances are you'll find it in this warren of eclectic antiques and retro. It's especially great for vintage glassware, and there's usually a good selection of tribal and Asian decorative objects.

Greater Brisbane

Finders Keepers Markets   MARKET
(Map p282; www.thefinderskeepers.com/brisbane-markets; Old Museum, 480 Gregory Tce, Bowen Hills; adult/child $2/free; ☺hours vary; ☒370, 375,

Fortitude Valley) A biannual market with more than 100 art and design stalls held in a 19th-century museum that's now a concert hall in inner-suburban Bowen Hills. Complete with live music and food, it's a great spot to score high-quality, one-off fashion pieces, jewellery and more from local and interstate design talent.

Paddington Antique Centre ANTIQUES
(Map p282; ☑ 07-3369 8088; www.paddington antiquecentre.com.au; 167 Latrobe Tce, Paddington; ⊙10am-5pm Mon-Sat, to 4pm Sun; ☐375) Built in 1929, this former theatre is now a sprawling antiques emporium. Over 50 dealers sell all manner of treasure and trash under a peeling, midnight-blue ceiling, from flouncy English crockery, to retro fashion, lamps, toys, film posters, even the odd 17th-century Chinese vase. Take your time and pay attention – you never know what you might find.

Davies Park Market MARKET
(Map p290; www.daviesparkmarket.com.au; Davies Park, West End; ⊙6am-2pm Sat; ☐199, 192, 198) Under a grove of huge Moreton Bay fig trees, this popular, laid-back Saturday market heaves with fresh produce, not to mention a gut-rumbling booty of multicultural food stalls. Grab an organic coffee from the Gyspy Vardo, sip it on a milk crate, then scour the place for organic fruit and veggies, artisanal provisions, herbs, flowers, handmade jewellery and even the odd bonsai.

ⓘ Information

INTERNET ACCESS

Brisbane City Council offers free wi-fi access in much of central Brisbane (the CBD), and you will also find free wi-fi hot spots at South Bank Parklands, Roma Street Parkland, the State Library of Queensland, James St in Fortitude Valley and New Farm Park.

Brisbane Square Library (www.brisbane.qld. gov.au; 266 George St; ⊙9am-6pm Mon-Thu, to 7pm Fri, 10am-3pm Sat & Sun; ☎; ⓦ North Quay, ⓡ Central) Free wi-fi access.

MEDICAL SERVICES

CBD Medical Centre (☑ 07-3211 3611; www. cbdmedical.com.au; Level 1, 245 Albert St; ⊙7am-7pm Mon-Fri, 8.30am-5pm Sat, 9.30am-5pm Sun; ⓡ Central) General medical services and vaccinations.

Royal Brisbane & Women's Hospital (☑ 07-3646 8111; www.health.qld.gov.au/rbwh; Butterfield St, Herston; ☐370, 375, 333) Located 3km north of the city centre. Has a 24-hour casualty ward.

Travellers' Medical & Vaccination Centre (TMVC; ☑ 07-3815 6900; www.traveldoctor. com.au; 75a Astor Tce, Spring Hill; ⊙8.30am-4.30pm Mon-Fri; ⓡ Central) Travellers' medical services.

MONEY

American Express (☑1300 139 060; www. americanexpress.com; 261 Queen St; ⊙9am-5.30pm Mon-Fri; ⓡ Central) Foreign exchange bureau.

Travelex (☑ 07-3210 6325; www.travelex. com.au; Shop 149F, Myer Centre, Queen St Mall; ⊙8am-6pm Mon-Thu, to 8pm Fri, 9am-5pm Sat, 10am-4pm Sun; ⓡ Central) Money exchange.

POST

Main Post Office (GPO; Map p286; ☑13 13 18; www.auspost.com.au; 261 Queen St; ⊙7am-6pm Mon-Fri, 10am-1.30pm Sat; ⓡ Central) Brisbane's main post office.

TOURIST INFORMATION

Brisbane Visitor Information & Booking Centre (Map p286; ☑ 07-3006 6290; www. visitbrisbane.com.au; The Regent, 167 Queen St Mall; ⊙9am-5.30pm Mon-Thu, to 7pm Fri, to 5pm Sat, 10am-5pm Sun; ⓡ Central) Terrific one-stop info counter for all things Brisbane.

South Bank Visitor Information Centre (Map p286; ☑ 07-3156 6366; www.visitbrisbane.com.au; Stanley St Plaza, South Bank; ⊙9am-5pm; ⓦ South Bank Terminal 3, ⓡ South Bank) One of Brisbane's official tourist information hubs, with brochures, maps and festival guides, plus tour and accommodation bookings, and tickets to entertainment events.

ⓘ Getting There & Away

AIR

Sixteen kilometres northeast of the city centre, **Brisbane Airport** (www.bne.com.au; Airport Dr) is the third-busiest airport in Australia and the main international airport serving Brisbane and southeastern Queensland.

It has separate international and domestic terminals about 2km apart, linked by the **Airtrain** (☑1800 119 091; www.airtrain.com.au; adult one way/return $17.50/33), which runs every 15 to 30 minutes from 5am (6am on weekends) to 10pm (between terminals $5/free per adult/child).

It's a busy hub, with frequent domestic connections to other Australian capital cities and regional towns, as well as nonstop international flights to New Zealand, the Pacific islands, North America and Asia (with onward connections to Europe and Africa).

BUS

Brisbane's main bus terminus and booking office for long-distance buses is the **Brisbane Transit Centre** (Roma St Station; www.brisbanetransitcentre.com.au; Roma St), about 500m northwest of the city centre. It also incorporates Roma St train station, which services both long-distance and suburban trains.

Booking desks for **Greyhound** (☑1300 473 946, 07-4690 9850; www.greyhound.com.au) and **Premier Motor Service** (☑13 34 10; www.premierms.com.au) are here.

Long-haul routes include Cairns, Darwin and Sydney, though it's usually just as affordable to fly, not to mention a lot quicker.

CAR & MOTORCYCLE

Brisbane has an extensive network of motorways, tunnels and bridges (some of them tolled) run by **Transurban Queensland** (☑13 33 31; www.govianetwork.com.au). The Gateway Motorway (M1) runs through Brisbane's eastern suburbs, shooting north towards the Sunshine Coast and northern Queensland and south towards the Gold Coast and Sydney. See the Transurban Queensland website for toll details and fees.

Major car-rental companies have offices at Brisbane Airport and in the city. Smaller rental companies with branches near the airport (and shuttles to get you to/from there) include **Ace Rental Cars** (☑1800 620 408; www.acerentalcars.com.au; 330 Nudgee Rd, Hendra), **Apex Car Rentals** (☑1800 558 912; www.apexrentacar.com.au; 400 Nudgee Rd, Hendra) and **East Coast Car Rentals** (☑1800 327 826; www.eastcoastcarrentals.com.au; 504 Nudgee Rd, Hendra).

TRAIN

Brisbane's main station for long-distance trains is Roma St Station (essentially the same complex as the Brisbane Transit Centre). For reservations and information contact **Queensland Rail** (☑13 16 17; www.queenslandrail.com.au).

NSW TrainLink Brisbane to Sydney.

Spirit of Queensland Brisbane to Cairns.

Spirit of the Outback Brisbane to Longreach via Bundaberg, Gladstone and Rockhampton.

Tilt Train Brisbane to Rockhampton via Bundaberg and Gladstone.

Westlander Brisbane to Charleville.

ⓘ Getting Around

Brisbane's excellent public transport network – bus, train and ferry – is run by TransLink, which runs a Transit Information Centre at Roma St Station (Brisbane Transit Centre). The tourist offices in the **city centre** (p314) and **South Bank** (p314) can also help with public transport information. Complementing the network is a nifty network of bike paths.

TO/FROM THE AIRPORT

Airtrain (p314) services run every 15 to 30 minutes from 5am (6am on weekends) to 10pm, connecting Brisbane airport's two terminals to central Brisbane. Handy stops include Fortitude Valley, Central Station, Roma St Station (Brisbane Transit Centre), South Brisbane and South Bank (one-way/return $17.50/33). Trains continue to the Gold Coast (one-way from $33.70).

Con-X-ion (☑1300 370 471; www.con-x-ion.com) runs regular shuttle buses between the airport and hotels in the Brisbane city centre (one-way/return $20/36). It also connects Brisbane Airport to Gold Coast hotels and private residences (one-way/return $49/92), as well as to Sunshine Coast hotels and private residences (one-way/return from $52/96). Book tickets online.

A taxi to central Brisbane costs $50 to $60.

CAR & MOTORCYCLE

Ticketed two-hour parking is available on many streets in the CBD and the inner suburbs. Heed the signs: Brisbane's parking inspectors are pretty ruthless. During the day, parking is cheaper around South Bank and the West End than in the city centre, but it's free in the CBD in the evening from 6pm weekdays (from noon on Saturday). For more detailed information on parking, see www.visitbrisbane.com.au/parking.

PUBLIC TRANSPORT

Buses, trains and ferries operate on an eight-zone system: all of the inner-city suburbs are in Zone 1, which translates into a single fare of $4.60/2.30 per adult/child. If travelling into Zone 2, tickets are $5.70/2.85.

If you plan to use public transport for more than a few trips, you'll save money by purchasing a **Go Card** (www.translink.com.au/tickets-and-fares/go-card; starting balance adult/child $10/5). Purchase the card, add credit and then use it on city buses, trains and ferries, and you'll save more than 30% off individual fares. Go Cards are sold (and can be recharged) at transit stations, 7-Eleven convenience stores, newsagents, by phone or online. You can also top-up on CityCat ferry services (cash only).

Boat

CityCat (p293) catamarans service 18 ferry terminals between the University of Queensland in St Lucia and Northshore Hamilton. Handy stops include South Bank, the three CBD terminals, New Farm Park (for Brisbane Powerhouse) and

Bretts Wharf (for Eat Street Markets). Services run roughly every 15 minutes from 5.20am to around midnight. Tickets can be bought on board or, if you have one, use your Go Card.

Free **CityHopper ferries** zigzag back and forth across the water between North Quay, South Bank, the CBD, Kangaroo Point and Sydney St in New Farm. These additional services start around 6am and run till about 11pm.

TransLink also runs **Cross River Ferries**, connecting Kangaroo Point with the CBD, and New Farm Park with Norman Park on the adjacent shore (and also Teneriffe and Bulimba further north). Ferries run every 10 to 30 minutes from around 6am to around 11pm. Fares/zones apply as per all other Brisbane transport.

For more information, including timetables, see www.brisbaneferries.com.au.

Bus

Brisbane's bus network is extensive and especially handy for reaching West End, Kangaroo Point, Woolloongabba, Fortitude Valley, Newstead, as well as Paddington.

In the city centre, the main stops for local buses are the underground **Queen Street Bus Station** (Map p286) and **King George Square Bus Station** (Map p286). You can also pick up many buses from the stops along Adelaide St, between George and Edward Sts.

Buses generally run every 10 to 30 minutes, from around 5am (around 6am Saturday and Sunday) till about 11pm.

CityGlider and BUZ services are high-frequency services along busy routes. Note that tickets cannot be purchased on board CityGlider and BUZ services; use a Go Card (p315).

Free, hop-on, hop-off City Loop and Spring Hill Loop bus services circle the CBD and Spring Hill, stopping at key spots like QUT, Queen St Mall, City Botanic Gardens, Central Station and Roma Street Parkland. Buses run every 10 minutes on weekdays between 7am and 6pm.

Brisbane also runs dedicated nocturnal NightLink bus, train and fixed-rate taxi services (the latter from specified taxi ranks) from the city and Fortitude Valley. See translink.com.au for details.

Train

TransLink's **Citytrain network** has six main lines, which run as far north as Gympie on the Sunshine Coast and as far south as Varsity Lakes on the Gold Coast. All trains go through Roma St Station, Central Station and Fortitude Valley Station; there's also a handy South Bank Station.

The Airtrain (p314) service integrates with the Citytrain network in the city centre and along the Gold Coast line.

Trains run from around 4.30am, with the last train on each line leaving Central Station between 11.30pm and midnight (later on Friday and Saturday). On Sunday the last trains run at around 11pm or 11.30pm.

Single train tickets can be bought at train stations, or use your Go Card (p315).

For timetables and a network map, see www.translink.com.au.

TAXI

There are numerous taxi ranks in the city centre, including at Roma St Station, Treasury (corner of George and Queen Sts), Albert St (corner of Elizabeth St) and Edward St (near Elizabeth St). You might have a tough time hailing one late at night in Fortitude Valley: there's a rank near the corner of Brunswick St and Ann St, but expect long queues. The main taxi companies are **Black & White** (🕿13 32 22; www.blackandwhitecabs.com.au) and **Yellow Cab Co** (🕿13 19 24; www.yellowcab.com.au).

NightLink flat-fare taxis run on Friday and Saturday nights, with dedicated ranks at Elizabeth Street (corner of George St) in the city and on Warner St in Fortitude Valley.

AROUND BRISBANE

North Stradbroke Island

POP 2030

An easy 30-minute ferry chug from the Brisbane suburb of Cleveland, this unpretentious holiday isle is like Noosa and Byron Bay rolled into one. There's a string of glorious powdery white beaches, great surf and some quality places to stay and eat. It's also a hot spot for spying dolphins, turtles, manta rays and, between June and November, hundreds of humpback whales. 'Straddie' also offers freshwater lakes and 4WD tracks.

◎ Sights

**North Stradbroke Island
Historical Museum**   MUSEUM

(🕿07-3409 9699; www.stradbrokemuseum.com.au; 15-17 Welsby St, Dunwich; adult/child $5/1; ◷10am-2pm Tue-Sat, 11am-3pm Sun) describes shipwrecks and harrowing voyages, and gives an introduction to the island's rich Aboriginal history (the Quandamooka are the traditional owners of Minjerribah, aka Straddie).

Point Lookout

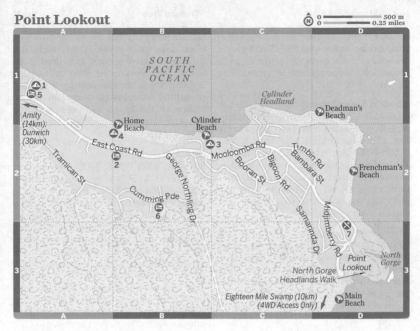

SOUTH
PACIFIC
OCEAN

Cylinder
Headland

Deadman's
Beach

Amity
(14km);
Dunwich
(30km)

Home
Beach

Cylinder
Beach

East Coast Rd

Tramican St

George Northling Dr

Mooloomba Rd

Booran St

Bigoon Rd

Timbin Rd

Bambara St

Frenchman's
Beach

Cumming Pde

Samarinda Dr

Midjimberry Rd

Point
Lookout

North
Gorge

North Gorge
Headlands Walk

Eighteen Mile Swamp (10km)
(4WD Access Only)

Main
Beach

🏃 Activities

At Point Lookout, the eye-popping **North Gorge Headlands Walk** is an absolute highlight. It's an easy 20-minute loop around the headland along boardwalks, with the thrum of cicadas as your soundtrack. Keep an eye out for turtles, dolphins and manta rays offshore. The view from the headland down Main Beach is a show-stopper.

About 8km east of Dunwich on Alfred Martin Way is the car park for **Naree Budjong Djara National Park** (www.nprsr.qld.gov.au/parks/naree-budjong-djara; Alfred Martin Way). From here, take the 2.6km walking track to Straddie's glittering centrepiece, Blue Lake (Kaboora): keep an eye out for forest birds, skittish lizards and swamp wallabies along the way. There's a wooden viewing platform at the lake, which is encircled by a forest of paperbarks, eucalypts and banksias. You can cool off in the water, if you don't mind the spooky unseen depths.

Point Lookout

🟢 Activities, Courses & Tours
  Manta Lodge & Scuba
  Centre...(see 5)

🛏 Sleeping
  1 Adder Rock Campground...................A1
  2 Allure...B2
  3 Cylinder Beach Campground............B2
  4 Home Beach Campground.................B2
  5 Manta Lodge YHA...............................A1
  6 Straddie Views..................................B2

✖ Eating
  7 Blue Room Cafe..................................D3

Manta Lodge & Scuba Centre   DIVING
(📞 07-3409 8888; www.mantalodge.com.au; 132 Dickson Way, Point Lookout; wetsuit/surfboard hire $20/30, diving course from $500) Based at the YHA (p318), Manta Scuba Centre offers a broad range of options. You can hire a wetsuit, mask, snorkel and fins ($25 for 24 hours) or a surfboard, or take the plunge with a diving course. Snorkelling trips (from $60) include a boat trip and all gear.

North Stradbroke Island Surf School SURFING
(☎07-3409 8342; www.northstradbrokeislandsurfschool.com.au; lessons from $50) Small-group, 1½-hour surf lessons in the warm Straddie waves. Solo lessons available if you're feeling bashful.

Straddie Super Sports CYCLING
(☎07-3409 9252; www.straddiesupersports.com.au; 18 Bingle Rd, Dunwich; hire per hr/day mountain bikes $10/50, kayaks $15/60, SUP board $10/50; ⏱8am-4.30pm Mon-Fri, to 3pm Sat, 9am-2pm Sun) A friendly shop hiring out mountain bikes, kayaks and stand up paddleboards, surfboards (per day $50) and bodyboards (per day $15). The place also sells fishing gear and camping accessories.

Straddie Adventures KAYAKING
(☎0433 171 477; www.straddieadventures.com.au; adult/child sea-kayaking trips from $75/40, sandboarding $35/30) Operated by the area's traditional Aboriginal owners, this outfit runs insightful sea-kayaking trips with an Indigenous cultural bent. Sandboarding sessions are also offered.

Sleeping

Straddie Camping CAMPGROUND $
(☎07-3409 9668; www.straddiecamping.com.au; 1 Junner St, Dunwich; 4WD sites from $16.55, powered/unpowered sites from $39/32, cabins from $120; ⏱booking office 8am-4pm Mon-Sat) There are eight island campgrounds operated by this outfit, including two 4WD-only foreshore sites (permits required – $43.75). The best of the bunch are grouped around Point Lookout: Cylinder Beach, Adder Rock and Home Beach all overlook the sand. Amity Point campground has new eco-cabins. Good weekly rates; book well in advance.

Manta Lodge YHA HOSTEL $
(☎07-3409 8888; www.mantalodge.com.au; 132 Dickson Way, Point Lookout; dm/d/tw/f from $35/90/90/115; @📶) This affable, three-storey hostel has clean (if unremarkable) rooms and a great beachside location. There's a communal firepit out the back, a curfew-free kitchen, cosy communal spaces, plus a dive school (p317) downstairs. Rental options include surfboards, bodyboards, stand-up paddleboards, bikes and snorkelling gear. Wi-fi is free in communal areas and $5 for 24 hours in the dorms.

Straddie Views B&B $$
(☎04-5950 2257; 26 Cumming Pde, Point Lookout; s/d from $125/150) There are two spacious downstairs suites at this B&B, run by friendly Straddie local Jan. Each is inviting and sophisticated, with queen-sized bed, private bathroom, earthy hues and thoughtful extras like chocolates on the bed and port in the decanter. Cooked breakfasts are served on the upstairs deck (the ocean views are free).

★ **Allure** APARTMENT $$$
(☎07-3415 0000, 1800 555 200; www.allurestradbroke.com.au; 43-57 East Coast Rd, Point Lookout; bungalows/villas from $175/250; ❄📶🏊) Set in a leafy compound with a pool, a gym and a kitchen garden for guests, Allure offers large, spotless, contemporary bungalows and villas. Bungalows are studio-style affairs with kitchenettes and mezzanine bedrooms, while villas offer full kitchens and separate bedrooms. All have private laundry facilities and outdoor deck with barbecues. While there isn't much space between the shacks, they're cleverly designed with privacy in mind. Cheaper rates for stays of more than one night.

Eating

★ **Island Fruit Barn** CAFE $
(☎07-3409 9125; 16 Bingle Rd, Dunwich; mains $10-16; ⏱7am-5pm Mon-Fri, to 4pm Sat, 8am-4pm Sun; 🌱) On the main road in Dunwich, Island Fruit Barn is a casual little congregation of tables with excellent breakfasts, smoothies, salads, sandwiches, winter soups and cakes, many gluten free or vegan, and all made using top-quality ingredients. Order the scrumptious spinach-and-feta roll, then stock up on fresh produce and gourmet condiments in the super-cute grocery section.

Blue Room Cafe CAFE $
(☎0438 281 666; 27 Mooloomba Rd, Point Lookout; dishes $10-18; ⏱7.30am-2.30pm, providore to 5.30pm Mon-Sat, to 2pm Sun; 🌱) A youthful, beach-shack-chic cafe, with a small alfresco terrace and fresh, feel-good dishes like red papaya filled with kiwi fruit and strawberries and topped with granola and cacao crunch; organic-egg omelette with spinach and goats-milk cheese; and generous fish tacos jammed with grilled fish and house-made Mexican black-bean corn salsa. Small bites include cookies and yummy vegan snacks. The adjoining providore is aptly named the Green Room.

ℹ Getting There & Away

The hub for ferries to North Stradbroke Island is the Brisbane seaside suburb of Cleveland. From here, **Stradbroke Ferries** (☑ 07-3488 5300; www.stradbrokeferries.com.au; return per vehicle incl passengers from $110, walk-on adult/child $10/5; ☺ 5.30am-8pm) offers passenger/vehicle services to Dunwich and back (45 minutes, 12 to 17 times daily). Cheaper online fares are available for vehicles. **Gold Cats Stradbroke Flyer** (☑ 07-3286 1964; www. flyer.com.au; Middle St, Cleveland; return adult/child/family $19/10/50; ☺ 5am-7.30pm) runs passenger-only trips daily between Cleveland and One Mile Jetty at Dunwich (30 minutes, 13 to 14 daily). A free Stradbroke Flyer courtesy bus picks up water-taxi passengers from the Cleveland train station 10 minutes prior to most water-taxi departures (see the website for exclusions).

Regular Citytrain (www.translink.com.au) services run from Brisbane's Central and Roma St Stations (as well as the inner-city stations of South Bank, South Brisbane and Fortitude Valley) to Cleveland station ($8.60, one hour). Buses to the ferry terminal meet the trains at Cleveland station (seven minutes).

ℹ Getting Around

Straddie is a big place: it's best to have your own wheels to explore it properly. If you plan to go off-road, you can get information and buy a 4WD permit ($43.75) from Straddie Camping.

Alternatively, **Stradbroke Island Buses** (☑ 07-3415 2417; www.stradbrokeislandbuses. com.au) meet the ferries at Dunwich and run to Amity and Point Lookout (one-way/return $4.70/9.40). Services run roughly every hour and the last bus to Dunwich leaves Point Lookout at 6.20pm. Cash only.

There's also the **Stradbroke Cab Service** (☑ 0408 193 685), which charges around $60 from Dunwich to Point Lookout.

Straddie Super Sports (p318) in Dunwich hires out mountain bikes (per hour/day $10/50).

Moreton Island

POP 300

If you're not going further north in Queensland but want a fix of tropical bliss, sail over to Moreton Island. Its prelapsarian beaches, dunes, bushland and lagoons are protected, with 95% of the isle comprising the **Moreton Island National Park & Recreation Area** (www.nprsr.qld. gov.au/parks/moreton-island). Apart from a few rocky headlands, it's all sand, with Mt Tempest, the highest coastal sand hill in the world, towering high at a lofty 280m. Off the west coast are the rusty, hulking Tangalooma Wrecks, which provide excellent snorkelling and diving.

The island has a rich history, from early Aboriginal settlements to the site of Queensland's first and only whaling station at Tangalooma, which operated between 1952 and 1962.

◉ Sights & Activities

Around half a dozen dolphins swim in from the ocean and take fish from the hands of volunteer feeders each evening. You have to be a guest of the Tangalooma Island Resort to participate, but onlookers are welcome. Also at the resort is the **Tangalooma Marine Education & Conservation Centre** (☑ 1300 652 250; www.tangalooma.com; Tangalooma Island Resort; ☺ 10am-noon & 1-4pm), which has a display on the diverse marine and bird life of Moreton Bay.

Island bushwalks include a desert trail (two hours) leaving from Tangalooma Island Resort, as well as the strenuous trek up Mt Tempest, 3km inland from Eagers Creek – worthwhile, but you'll need transport to reach the start.

Cape Moreton Lighthouse offers great views when the whales are passing by.

Moreton Bay Escapes (☑ 1300 559 355; www.moretonbayescapes.com.au; 1-day tour adult/child from $200/140, 2-day camping tours from $360/250) ⌀ runs informative one-, two- and three-day 4WD tours that will have you snorkelling or kayaking, sandboarding, watching marine wildlife and hiking. **Adventure Moreton Island** (☑ 07-3410 6927; www.adventuremoretonisland.com; 1-day tours from $145) runs a handful of day tours, among them an Island Adrenaline Tour ($189), allowing you to choose four activities from a list that includes quad-bike riding, sandboarding, and snorkelling at the Tangalooma Wrecks.

🛏 Sleeping

Tangalooma hosts the island's sole **resort** (☑ 1300 652 250, 07-3637 2000; www.tangalooma.com; Tangalooma; d from $210, 2-/3-/4-bedroom apt from $480/510/550; ❅ @ ☏ ⛱). There are also five national park **camping areas** (☑ 13 74 68; www.nprsr.qld.gov.au/experiences/camping; sites per person/family $6.15/24.60) on Moreton Island, all with

BRISBANE & AROUND MORETON ISLAND

water, toilets and cold showers. Be sure to book online or by phone before you get to the island.

ℹ️ Getting There & Away

Several ferries operate from the mainland. To explore once you get to the island, bring a 4WD or take a tour. Most tours are ex-Brisbane, and include ferry transfers.

Amity Trader (☑ 07-3820 6557; www.amity trader.com; 4WD/walk-on passengers return $270/40) Runs vehicle barges for 4WD vehicles and walk-on passengers from the Brisbane suburb of Victoria Point to Kooringal on Moreton Island several times monthly. See the website for the current timetable.

Micat (☑ 07-3909 3333; www.micat.com.au; Tangalooma; return adult/child from $52/35, standard 4WD incl 2 people $200-300) Vehicle ferry services from Port of Brisbane to Tangalooma around eight times weekly (75 to 90 minutes); see the website for directions to the ferry terminal.

Tangalooma Flyer (☑ 07-3637 2000; www. tangalooma.com; return adult/child $80/45) Fast passenger catamaran operated by Tangalooma Island Resort. It makes the 75-minute trip to the resort three to four times daily from Holt St Wharf in the Brisbane suburb of Pinkenba (see the website for directions).

The Gold Coast

Best Places to Eat

➡ Rick Shores (p332)

➡ Bstow (p333)

➡ Harry's Steak Bistro (p332)

➡ Glenelg Public House (p330)

➡ BSKT Cafe (p330)

Best Places to Sleep

➡ La Costa Motel (p335)

➡ Burleigh Break (p331)

➡ Island (p325)

➡ Sheraton Grand Mirage Resort (p327)

➡ QT (p325)

Why Go?

Built for pleasure and remaining a place utterly dedicated to sun, surf and the body beautiful, this strip of coast is possibly Australia's most iconic holiday destination. Its shimmering high-rises can, when glimpsed from afar, appear like a make-believe city, and its reputation for tackiness is occasionally deserved. But this is far outstripped by a booming, youthful spirit and startling physical beauty: some 52km of pristine sand and countless epic surf breaks, heartbreakingly hazy sunsets, blissful water temperatures and 300 sunny days a year.

While Surfers Paradise's malls and mega-clubs let the party-hard kids have their fun, the other neighbourhoods have a distinct charm of their own. Main Beach and Broadbeach corner coastal chic; Burleigh Heads, Mermaid and Palm Beach have a retro charm and booming culinary scene; while Coolangatta pleases with its pro-surfer vibe. Not to be overlooked is the lush, misty subtropical rainforest of the hinterland.

When to Go
Surfers Paradise

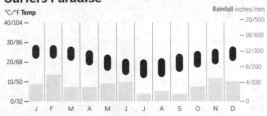

Dec–Feb Sunshine, high temperatures and busy beaches.

Jun–Aug Winter brings tourists from cooler climes, chasing the sun and still-swimmable water.

Oct & Nov Perfect weather, lower prices; time your visit to miss Schoolies week.

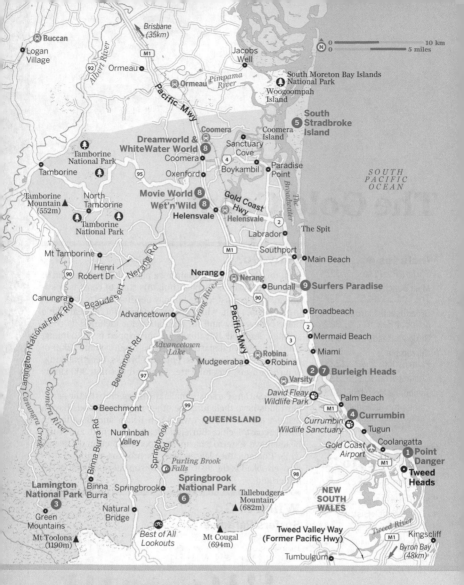

The Gold Coast Highlights

1 Point Danger (p334) Braving a dawn surf at this legendary break.

2 Burleigh Heads (p330) Eating your way around the young, fun and creative culinary scene.

3 Lamington National Park (p337) Bushwalking through craggy gorges and densely canopied rainforests.

4 **Balter** (p334) Talking beer and breaks with surfing legends at Currumbin's fabulous brewery.

5 South Stradbroke Island (p332) Retreating from the crowds to a long stretch of sand.

6 Springbrook National Park (p337) Taking in the view at the aptly named Best of All Lookout.

7 Burleigh Social (p332) Grabbing a 6am macadamia-milk latte before a soft-sand beach run to Miami.

8 Theme parks (p329) Testing your nerve (and your digestive system) on the Gold Coast's roller coasters.

9 Surfers Paradise (p323) Drinking, dancing and watching the sun come up at the beach.

ⓘ Getting There & Away

AIR

Gold Coast Airport (p303) is in Coolangatta, 25km south of Surfers Paradise. All the main Australian domestic airlines fly here. **Scoot** (www.flyscoot.com), **Air Asia** (☑1300 760 330; www.airasia.com) and **Air New Zealand** (☑13 24 76; www.airnewzealand.com.au) fly in from overseas.

Brisbane Airport (p303) is 16km northeast of Brisbane city centre and accessible by train. It is a useful arrival point for the Gold Coast, especially for international visitors.

BUS

Greyhound (www.greyhound.com.au) Has frequent services to/from Brisbane ($23, 1½ hours), Byron Bay ($35, 2½ hours) and beyond.

Premier Motor Service (☑13 34 10; www.premierms.com.au) A couple of daily services head to Brisbane (from $21, 1½ hours), Byron Bay (from $29, 2½ hours) and other coastal areas.

TRAIN

TransLink (☑13 12 30; https://translink.com.au) Citytrain services connect Brisbane with Nerang, Robina and Varsity Lakes stations on the Gold Coast (75 minutes) roughly every half hour. The same line extends north of Brisbane to Brisbane Airport.

ⓘ Getting Around

TO/FROM THE AIRPORT

Byron Bay Xcede (www.byronbay.xcede.com.au) Transfers from Gold Coast Airport to hotels and private addresses in Byron Bay; prebooking advised (adult/child $37/18.50).

Con-X-ion Airport Transfers (☑1300 266 946; www.con-x-ion.com) Transfers to/from Gold Coast Airport (one way adult/child from $22/13), Brisbane Airport (one way from adult/child $49/25) and Gold Coast theme parks.

Gold Coast Tourist Shuttle (☑1300 655 655, 07-5574 5111; www.gcshuttle.com.au; one way per adult/child $22/13) Meets flights into Gold Coast Airport and transfers to most Gold Coast accommodation. Also runs to Gold Coast theme parks.

BUS

Surfside Buslines (☑13 12 30; www.surfside.com.au), a subsidiary of Brisbane's main TransLink operation, runs regular buses up and down the Gold Coast, plus shuttles from the Gold Coast train stations into Surfers Paradise and beyond (including the theme parks).

Surfside, in conjunction with Gold Coast Tourist Shuttle also offers a Freedom Pass, which includes return Gold Coast Airport transfers, unlimited theme-park transfers and local bus travel for $78/39 per adult/child. It's valid for three days; five-, seven- and 10-day passes also available.

TRAM

G:link (Gold Coast Light Rail; ☑13 12 30; http://translink.com.au; tickets from $4.80, Go Explore day pass adult/child $10/5) is a handy if rather pricey light rail and tram service connecting Southport and Broadbeach with stops along the way. It's worth buying a Go Explore day pass (adult/child $10/5; available only from 7-Eleven shops) if you're doing more than one very short trip. Otherwise, you can buy single-trip tickets (from $4.80) from a machine on the tram platform.

Surfers Paradise

POP 22,150

Some may mumble that paradise has been lost, but there's no denying that Surfers' frenetic few blocks and its glorious strip of sand attracts a phenomenal number of visitors – 20,000 per day at peak. Party-hard teens and early-20-somethings come here for a heady dose of clubs, bars, malls and perhaps a bit of beachtime as a hangover remedy before it all starts again. Families like the ready availability of big apartments, loads of kid-friendly eating options and, yes, that beautiful beach.

⊙ Sights & Activities

SkyPoint Observation Deck VIEWPOINT
(www.skypoint.com.au; Level 77, Q1 Bldg, Hamilton Ave; adult/child/family $24/14/62; ⊗7.30am-8.30pm Sun-Thu, to 11.30pm Fri & Sat) Surfers Paradise's best sight is best observed from your beach towel, but for an eagle-eye view of the coast and hinterland, zip up to this 230m-high observation deck near the top of Q1, one of the world's notably tall buildings. You can also tackle the SkyPoint Climb up the spire to a height of 270m (adult/child from $74/54).

Cheyne Horan School of Surf SURFING
(☑1800 227 873; www.cheynehoran.com.au; 2hr lessons $49; ⊗10am & 2pm) Learn to carve up the waves at this school, run by former pro surfer Cheyne Horan. Multilesson packages reduce the cost.

Balloon Down Under BALLOONING
(☑07-5500 4797; www.balloondownunder.com; 1hr flights adult/child $279/225) Up, up and away on sunrise flights over the Gold Coast, ending with a champagne breakfast.

Surfers Paradise

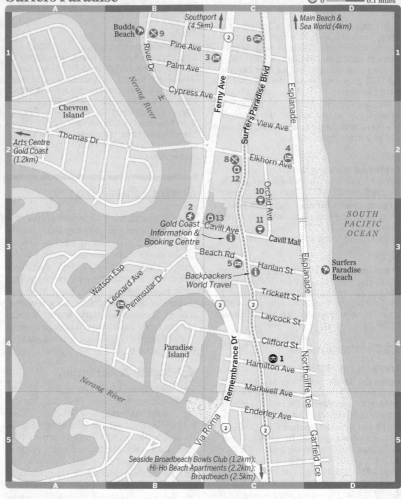

Surfers Paradise

THE GOLD COAST SURFERS PARADISE

Whales in Paradise   WHALE WATCHING
(☑07-5538 2111; www.whalesinparadise.com.
au; cnr Cavill & Ferny Aves; adult/child/family
$99/69/267; ⊘Jun-Nov) Leaves central Surf-
ers three times a day for 3½ hours of whale
watching.

✱ Festivals & Events

★**Bleach Festival**   CULTURAL
(www.bleachfestival.com.au; ⊘early Apr) Visual-art
shows, contemporary dance, music of all gen-
res, theatre and performances feature, held
in a variety of indoor and outdoor spaces.
There's a late-summer party vibe, with the occasional superstar performer heading the bill,
as well as some edgy and provocative work.

Gold Coast Film Festival   FILM
(www.gcfilmfestival.com; ⊘Apr) Mainstream
and art-house flicks from all over the world
feature in mid- to late April on outdoor
screens, including SIPFest, two nights of
short films screened right on the beach.

Gold Coast 600   SPORTS
(www.v8supercars.com.au; ⊘Oct) For three days
in October the streets of Surfers are transformed into a temporary race circuit for
high-speed racing cars.

🛏 Sleeping

Budds in Surfers   HOSTEL $
(☑07-5538 9661; www.buddsinsurfers.com.au; 6
Pine Ave; dm $32-34, d $95-110; @ 🛜 ⊛) Laid-
back Budds features tidy bathrooms, clean
tiles, a sociable bar and a nice pool, all just a
short hop from calm Budds Beach. Bike hire
available. Female-only dorms are available
on request and there's one double with en
suite.

Sleeping Inn Surfers   HOSTEL $
(☑07-5592 4455, 1800 817 832; www.sleepinginn.
com.au; 26 Peninsular Dr; dm $30-34, d $78-92;
@ 🛜 ⊛) This backpackers occupies an old
apartment block away from the centre, so,
as the name suggests, there's a chance you
may get to sleep in. Larger dorms come with
their own kitchen and bathroom and most
have a private living area. Note, no children
allowed, and guests in dorm rooms must
have an international passport. An adjoining apartment block offers some renovated
private rooms.

Chateau Beachside Resort   APARTMENT $
(☑07-5538 1022; www.chateaubeachside.com.au;
cnr Elkhorn Ave & Esplanade; studio/1-bedroom apt

ⓘ SCHOOLIES ON THE LOOSE

Every year in November, thousands of
teenagers flock to Surfers Paradise to
celebrate the end of their high-school
education in a three-week party known
as Schoolies Week. Although local
authorities have stepped in to regulate
excesses, boozed-up and drug-addled
teens are still the norm. It's not pretty.
For more info, see www.schoolies.com.

$99/119; ✴@🛜⊛) Less Loire Valley, more
Las Vegas, this seaside 'chateau' (actually
an 18-storey tower) has studios and apartments that are individually furnished, and
all but the very cheapest have ocean views.
The 18m pool is a bonus. Minimum two-
night stay.

★**Island**   HOTEL $$
(☑07-5538 8000; www.theislandgoldcoast.
com.au; 3128 Surfers Paradise Blvd; d $180-250;
P✴🛜⊛) The fabulously faded Islander
Hotel has been reborn as the Island and it's
indeed an island of contemporary style in
this corner of Surfers. Rooms have standard
low ceilings but their natural timber, white-
wash and monochromatic palette make for
a soothing bolt-hole. Plus they're spacious –
doubles are 27 sq metres, suites 45 sq metres
– and have king-sized beds.

★**QT**   HOTEL $$
(☑07-5584 1200; www.qtgoldcoast.com.au; 7
Staghorn Ave; d $185-280; ✴🛜⊛) Acapulco
chairs, retro bikes and preppy-styled staff
are a deliberate take on the mid-century-
design glory days of Surfers. The clever
transformation of what was yet another
bland '80s tower really does work, with an
airy lobby you'll be happy to hang about in.
Room interiors are less nostalgic, but have
plenty of colour pops.

Moorings on Cavill   APARTMENT $$
(☑07-5538 6711; www.mooringsoncavill.com.au;
63 Cavill Ave; 1-/2-bedroom apt from $135/185;
✴🛜⊛) This roomy 73-apartment tower at
the river end of Cavill Ave is great for fami-
lies: the vibe is quiet and respectful. The lo-
cation is hard to beat too: close to the beach,
shops and restaurants. Super-clean and
managed with a smile.

Q1 Resort
APARTMENT $$$

(☑07-5630 4500, 1300 792 008; www.q1.com.au; Hamilton Ave; 1-bedroom apt $189-259, 2-bedroom $276-375; ✳@🛜🏊) Spend a night in Australia's tallest residential tower, which features white-on-white interiors and fabulous wrap-around views. There's a lagoon-style pool and a fitness centre if the beach hasn't exhausted you. Prices fluctuate, with good specials for five-night, no-housekeeping stays.

🍴 Eating

Self-caterers will find supermarkets in the **Chevron Renaissance Shopping Centre** (www.chevronrenaissanceshoppingcentre.com.au; cnr Elkhorn Ave & Surfers Paradise Blvd; ⊙9am-5.30pm Mon-Sat, 10am-4pm Sun) and **Circle on Cavill** (www.circleoncavill.com.au; cnr Cavill & Ferny Aves; ⊙9am-5.30pm Mon-Sat, 10am-4pm Sun).

★ Bumbles Café
CAFE $$

(☑07-5538 6668; www.bumblescafe.com; 21 River Dr, Budds Beach; mains $14-24; ⊙7.30am-4pm) This gorgeous spot – a converted house (actually, at one stage, a brothel) – is the place for breakfast, sweet treats and coffee. It comprises a series of rooms, from the pink Princess Room (perfect for afternoon tea) to a library. Serves up some very desirable cakes.

Surfers Sandbar
MODERN AUSTRALIAN $$

(☑07-5526 9994; www.facebook.com/sandbargc; 52 Esplanade; mains $18-29; ⊙6.30am-midnight) After a staggering 19 years in beachside business, the owners here handed over the reins to their son. Back from serious hospitality work in Bali, he transformed Sandbar into a Riviera-meets-Canggu hot spot, full of intriguing interior details, happy locals and creative, globally inflected dishes.

Baritalia
ITALIAN $$

(☑07-5592 4700; www.baritaliagoldcoast.com.au; Shop 15, Chevron Renaissance Centre, cnr Elkhorn Ave & Surfers Paradise Blvd; pizzas $20-28, lunch specials $14-16, mains $20-38; ⊙8am-late; 🛜) A thoroughly Italian place with a fab outdoor terrace and friendly, European staff. Go for the Byron Bay slow-roasted pork belly, or excellent pastas, pizzas and risotto (including gluten-free choices). Decent Australian and Italian wines by the glass and good coffee.

🍸 Drinking & Nightlife

★ Elsewhere
CLUB

(☑07-5592 6880; www.elsewherebar.com; 23 Cavill Ave,; ⊙9pm-4am Thu-Sun) A Saturday Night Fever–style dance floor always bodes well for good times, and this little bar-to-club venue features DJs who know their electronica, including cracking live sets from the soon-to-be-famous. Crowds are cooler than elsewhere, but it's a friendly, conversation-filled place, until DJs seriously turn up the volume.

Black Coffee Lyrics
BAR, CAFE

(☑0402 189 437; www.facebook.com/black coffeelyrics; 40/3131 Surfers Paradise Blvd, Surfers Paradise; ⊙5pm-late Tue-Fri, from 8am Sat & Sun) Upstairs and hidden in an unexpected location – within a nondescript arcade – this is the antithesis to Surfers shiny. Filled with vintage furniture and bordering on grungy, it's a dark oasis where locals come for coffee and tapas-style dishes, for steaks, and for bourbon, boutique brews and espresso martinis until late. Weekend breakfasts are hearty and there's the option of beer or bloody Marys from 10am.

☆ Entertainment

Arts Centre Gold Coast
THEATRE, CINEMA

(☑07-5588 4000; www.theartscentregc.com.au; 135 Bundall Rd; ⊙box office 8am-9pm Mon-Fri, to 9pm Sat, 11am-7pm Sun) A bastion of culture and civility beside the Nerang River, the Arts Centre has two cinemas, a restaurant, a bar, the Gold Coast City Gallery and a 1200-seat theatre, which regularly hosts impressive productions (comedy, jazz, opera, kids' concerts etc).

ℹ Information

Backpackers World Travel (☑07-5561 0634; www.backpackerworldtravel.com; 3063 Surfers Paradise Blvd; ⊙10am-4pm; 🛜) Accommodation, tour and transport bookings and internet access.

Gold Coast Information & Booking Centre (☑1300 309 440, 07-5536 4709; www.visit-goldcoast.com; 2 Cavill Ave; ⊙8.30am-5pm Mon-Fri, 9am-6pm Sat, 9am-4pm Sun) The main Gold Coast tourist information booth; also sells theme-park tickets and has public transport info.

Surfers Paradise Day & Night Medical Centre (☑07-5592 2299; www.daynightmedical.com.au; 3221 Surfers Paradise Blvd; ⊙7am-11pm) General medical centre and pharmacy. Make an appointment, or just walk in.

Main Beach & The Spit

POP 3970

North of Surfers Paradise, the apartment towers are slightly less lofty and the pace eases up. Main Beach makes for a serene base if you're here for views, beach time and generally taking it easy. Tedder Ave may no longer possess place-to-be cache, but it still has a pleasantly village-like atmosphere, with enjoyable eating options alongside its chichi shops.

Further north the Spit separates the Southport Broadwater from the Pacific Ocean, stretching 5km to almost meet South Stradbroke Island. Its southern end is home to Marina Mirage, another upmarket shopping and eating zone, along with Mariner's Cove, a base for aquatic activities.

The beach up here, backed as it is with dunes and native parkland, has a startling sublimity. It also has some very uncrowded surf breaks that deliver when nothing else does.

◎ Sights & Activities

Main Beach Pavilion ARCHITECTURE
(Macarthur Pde; ⊘9am-5pm) FREE The lovely Spanish Mission–style Main Beach Pavilion (1934) is a remnant from pre-boom days. Inside are some fabulous old photos of the Gold Coast before the skyscrapers.

★Federation Walk WALKING
(www.federationwalk.org) This pretty 3.7km trail takes you through patches of fragrant littoral rainforest, flush with beautiful bird life, and runs parallel to one of the world's most beautiful strips of surf beach. Along the way, it connects to the Gold Coast Oceanway, which heads 36km to Coolangatta. Federation Walk begins and finishes at the entrance to Sea World, in the car park of Phillip Park.

Australian Kayaking Adventures KAYAKING
(⊋0412 940 135; www.australiankayakingadventures.com.au; half-day tours adult/child $85/75, sunset tours $55/45) Paddle out to underrated South Stradbroke Island, or take a dusk paddle around Chevron Island in the calm canals behind Surfers.

Island Adventures WHALE WATCHING
(⊋07-5532 2444; www.goldcoastadventures.com.au; Mariner's Cove, 60-70 Sea World Dr, Main Beach; cruises incl lunch adult/child $129/69) Alternatively, gawp at wildlife and the Broadwater's sprawling McMansions on this catamaran cruise that includes water sports and a BBQ lunch on McLaren's Landing Eco Resort.

🛏 Sleeping & Eating

Surfers Paradise YHA at Main Beach HOSTEL $
(⊋07-5571 1776; www.yha.com.au; 70 Sea World Dr, Main Beach; dm $33-36, d & tw $85; @🖥) Despite the Surfers Paradise of the name, this is a great 1st-floor position overlooking the marina. There's a free shuttle bus, BBQ nights every Friday, and the hostel is within wobbling distance of the Fisherman's Wharf Tavern. Sky-blue dorms; very well organised. Can also arrange tours and activities.

Main Beach Tourist Park CARAVAN PARK $
(⊋07-5667 2720; www.goldcoasttouristparks.com.au; 3600 Main Beach Pde, Main Beach; powered sites $62, cabins & villas from $165; P✳🖥🏊) Just across the road from the beach and surrounded by a phalanx of high-rise apartments, this caravan park is a family favourite. It's a tight fit between sites, but the facilities are good and the location is iconic.

Pacific Views APARTMENT $$
(⊋07-5527 0300; www.pacificviews.com.au; cnr Main Beach Pde & Woodroffe Ave, Main Beach; 1-bedroom apt $140-210; P✳🖥🏊) If you can cope with decor surprises, these individually owned and furnished apartments have amazing floor-to-ceiling views, living-room sized balconies and helpful staff. They're just one block back from the beach, and there's a cafe downstairs that will make you coffee at 5.30am if you're up for an early beach wander.

★Sheraton Grand Mirage Resort RESORT $$$
(⊋07-5577 0000; www.sheratongrandmiragegoldcoast.com; 71 Sea World Dr, Main Beach; d $280-400) This 270-room absolute-beachfront hotel recently received a light and lovely makeover. It has a relaxed glamour, and rooms are nicely low-slung and set among 6 hectares of tropical gardens. The large guest-only pool has a swim-up bar, and a delicious strip of Spit beach is accessible down a little path. The upstairs bar, open to nonguests, has ocean views.

Peter's Fish Market SEAFOOD $
(⊋07-5591 7747; www.petersfish.com.au; 120 Sea World Dr, Main Beach; meals $9-16; ⊘9am-7.30pm) A no-nonsense fish market–cum–fish and chip shop selling fresh and cooked seafood. It's fresh from the trawlers, in all shapes and sizes, and at great prices. Kitchen opens at noon.

Main Beach & The Spit

★ **Gourmet Farmers Market**   MARKET **$**
(☑ 07-5555 6400; www.facebook.com/Marina
MirageFarmersMarket; Marina Mirage, 74 Sea World
Dr, Main Beach; ☺ 7-11am Sat) On Saturday
mornings, the open spaces of the Marina
Mirage mall fill with stalls selling seasonal fruit and veg, baked goods, pickles, oils,
vinegars, seafood, pasta and more, all from
small-scale producers and makers.

★ **Pier**   MODERN AUSTRALIAN, PIZZA **$$**
(☑ 07-5527 0472; www.piermarinamirage.com.
au; Ground fl, Marina Mirage, Sea World Dr, Main
Beach; pizzas $18-24; ☺ noon-11.30pm) An easy
but super-stylish marina-side spot, with up-
stairs and downstairs seating, both perfect
for yachtie views. The mostly European staff
is winning and the menu is flexible. Wood-
fired pizzas can be combined with arancini
(which get their own menu), or there are
small and large dishes that tick a number of
culinary boxes without being faddish.

★ **Bar Chico**   MODERN AUSTRALIAN **$$**
(☑ 07-5532 9111; www.barchico.com.au; 26-30
Tedder Ave, Main Beach; dishes $12-22; ☺ 4pm-
midnight Mon-Wed, from noon Thu-Sun) A welcome addition to the Tedder strip, this dark
and moody European-style bar does fabulous cheese and charcuterie plates, fish or
meat tapas-style dishes and big, beguiling
salads. Displays a chef-like attention to detail, with in-house fermenting and curing,
and lots of high-end ingredients. Wine is
similarly thoughtful, with some particularly
nice Spanish drops.

Providore   CAFE **$$**
(☑ 07-5532 9390; www.providoremirage.com.au;
Marina Mirage, 74 Sea World Dr, Main Beach; mains
$16-29; ☺ 7am-6pm) Floor-to-ceiling windows
rimmed with Italian mineral-water bottles,
inverted desk lamps dangling from the ceil-
ing, good-looking Euro tourists, wines by
the glass, perfect patisserie goods, cheese
fridges, and baskets overflowing with fresh
produce: this excellent deli-cafe gets a lot of
things right.

🍸 Drinking & Nightlife

Southport Surf Lifesaving Club   CLUB
(www.sslsc.com.au; Macarthur Pde; ☺ 6.30am-mid-
night) This beautiful, airy pavilion-style club

GOLD COAST THEME PARKS

The gravity-defying rollercoasters and water slides at the Gold Coast's American-style parks offer some seriously dizzying action and, although recently beset with a number of accidents, still attract huge crowds. Discount tickets are sold in most of the tourist offices on the Gold Coast or can be bought **online** (☑ 13 33 86; www.themeparks.com.au). The Mega Pass ($110 per person for 14-day entry) grants unlimited entry to Sea World, Warner Bros Movie World, Wet'n'Wild and the little-kid-friendly farm-park Paradise Country (all owned by Village Roadshow). Dreamworld and WhiteWater World have a Summer Season Pass giving unlimited entry (adult/child $99/79).

A couple of tips: the parks can get insanely crowded, so arrive early or face a long walk from the far side of the car park. Also note that the parks don't let you bring your own food or drinks.

Dreamworld (☑ 07-5588 1111, 1800 073 300; www.dreamworld.com.au; Dreamworld Pkwy, Coomera; adult/child $65/55; ⊘ 10am-5pm) Touts itself as Australia's 'biggest' theme park. There are the 'Big 9 Thrill Rides', plus Wiggles World and the DreamWorks experience, both for younger kids. Other attractions include Tiger Island, and a range of interactive animal encounters. A one-day pass (adult/child $65/55) gives you entry to both Dreamworld and WhiteWater World.

Sea World (www.seaworld.com.au; adult/child $80/70; ⊘ 9.30am-5pm) Continues to attract controversy for its marine shows, where dolphins and sea lions perform tricks for the crowd. While Sea World claims the animals lead a good life, welfare groups argue that keeping such sensitive sea mammals in captivity is harmful, and is especially exacerbated when mixed with human interaction. The park also displays penguins and polar bears, and has water slides and rollercoasters.

Movie World (☑ 07-5573 3999, 13 33 86; www.movieworld.com.au; Pacific Hwy, Oxenford; adult/child $79/69; ⊘ 9.30am-5pm) Movie-themed shows, rides and attractions, including the Batwing Spaceshot, Justice League 3D Ride and Scooby-Doo Spooky Coaster. Batman, Austin Powers, Porky Pig et al roam through the crowds.

Wet'n'Wild (☑ 07-5556 1660, 13 33 86; www.wetnwild.com.au; Pacific Hwy, Oxenford; adult/child $79/69; ⊘ 10am-5pm) The ultimate water slide here is the Kamikaze, where you plunge down an 11m drop in a two-person tube at 50km/h. This vast water park also has pitch-black slides, white-water rapids and wave pools.

WhiteWater World (☑ 1800 073 300, 07-5588 1111; www.dreamworld.com.au/whitewaterworld; Dreamworld Pkwy, Coomera; adult/child $65/55; ⊘ 10am-4pm Mon-Fri, to 5pm Sat & Sun) This park features the Cave of Waves, Pipeline Plunge and more than 140 wet and watery activities and slides.

has spectacular views. The deck is open early for coffee, or head here for lazy beery afternoons. It's one of the only places open late north of Surfers.

Broadbeach, Mermaid Beach & Nobby Beach

POP 19,890

Directly south of Surfers Paradise, Broadbeach may be all about apartment towers and pedestrian malls, but it's decidedly more upmarket than its neighbour, with carefully landscaped streets and smart places to eat, drink and shop.

Miami Marketta (www.miamimarketta.com; 23 Hillcrest Pde, Miami; ⊘ cafe 6am-2pm Tue-Sat, street food 5-10pm Wed, Fri & Sat) is a permanent street market with food, fashion and live music, a smidge south of Mermaid in just-as-cool Miami.

🛏 Sleeping & Eating

Hi-Ho Beach Apartments   APARTMENT $$
(☑ 07-5538 2777; www.hihobeach.com.au; 2 Queensland Ave, Broadbeach; 1-/2-bedroom apt $175/275; P ✳ 🛜 🏊) A top choice for location, close to the beach and cafes. You're not paying for glitzy lobbies here, but rooms are comfortable and it's well managed, clean and quiet. And, hey, the Vegas-esque sign!

Peppers Broadbeach
APARTMENT $$$

(www.peppers.com.au/broadbeach; 21 Elizabeth Ave, Broadbeach; 1-/3-bedroom apt $500/800; ❀ 🛜 ⚎) When you want flawless, if unexciting, comfort, this Peppers apartment hotel is for you. Think marble dining tables, European kitchen appliances, wrap-around balconies, high-thread-count linen. The three bedroom 'sky homes' really take the luxury to town. The day spa has heated indoor and outdoor pools.

★Sparrow Eating House
MODERN AUSTRALIAN $

(✐07-5575 3330; www.sparroweatinghouse.com. au; 2/32 Lavarack Rd, Nobby Beach; sharing dishes $11-22; ⊙5pm-midnight Wed-Fri, from 7am Sat & Sun) This lovely, clean-lined monochrome industrial space with green accents has a low-key glamour and a kitchen that loves what it does. Come for a casual lunch of spring gnocchi with hazelnuts and herbs; enjoy a blood-orange margarita and some tequila prawns; or pop in for a glass of small-producer wine.

Cardamom Pod
VEGETARIAN $

(www.cardamompod.com.au; 1/2685 Gold Coast Hwy, Broadbeach; 1/2/3/4 dishes with rice $10/16/24/31; ⊙11.30am-9.30pm; ▣) ❂ Vegetarians rejoice! This magical Krishna-inspired, vegan-friendly eatery conjures up some of the best vegetarian cuisine around. Choose from curry, vegan bake or cheesy bake of the day. Finish off with a trademark dessert: raw, gluten- and sugar-free (and delicious). Everything is made from scratch on the premises.

★Glenelg Public House
STEAK $$

(✐07-5575 2284; www.theglenelgpublichouse.com. au; 2460 Gold Coast Hwy, Mermaid Beach; mains $22-32; ⊙5pm-midnight Mon-Thu, from noon Fri-Sun) This atmospheric little place uses premium produce and a sparing accompaniments. The epic steak list ($22 to $68, sharing $80 to $90) takes in local breeds, the best of New Zealand and New South Wales tablelands and both grass- and grain-fed cuts. There's also an 'early tea' dinner special before 6.30pm.

★BSKT Cafe
MODERN AUSTRALIAN $$

(✐07-5526 6565; www.bskt.com.au; 4 Lavarack Ave, Mermaid Beach; mains $10-27; ⊙7am-4pm Mon-Thu, to 10pm Fri & Sat, to 5pm Sun; ▣🖐) This satisfyingly industrial cafe is 100m from the beach, but that's far from its only charm: focused on organic produce, the dishes and service punch well above cafe level. Vegans and paleos will be at home here, as will kids, in the fenced play area, and yogis, in the upstairs yoga school.

🍷 Drinking & Nightlife

★Cambus Wallace
COCKTAIL BAR

(www.thecambuswallace.com.au; 4/2237 Gold Coast Hwy, Nobby Beach; ⊙5pm-midnight Tue-Thu, from 4pm Fri-Sun) Dark, moody, maritime-themed bar that attracts a good-looking but relaxed local crew. Settle in with something from its long, long list of bottled beer and cider, or try a Gold Coast take on cocktail classics (a coconut, lime and rum Maiden Voyage could not be better suited to the climate).

Seaside Broadbeach Bowls Club
CLUB

(✐07-5531 5913; www.broadbeachbowlsclub. com; 169 Surf Pde, Broadbeach; ⊙11.30am-8pm) Home to the best bowling greens in Australia – some say, the world. Far from a tired old space, this traditional club has had a modern makeover with its bars and restaurants bright, breezy and beachy. Come for a sunset beer on the huge terrace, and barefoot bowls.

Burleigh Heads
POP 9580

The super-chilled surfie enclave of Burleigh (drop the 'Heads', you're already fond friends, right?) has long been a family favourite, but is now having its moment in the sun. The town's retro vibe and youthful energy epitomise both the Gold Coast's timeless appeal and its new, increasingly interesting, spirit. You'll find some of the region's best cafes and restaurants here and, yes, that famous right-hand point break still pumps while the pine-backed beach charms everyone who lays eyes on it.

◉ Sights

Burleigh Head National Park
PARK

(www.npsr.qld.gov.au/parks/burleigh-head; Goodwin Tce, Burleigh Heads; ⊙24hr) FREE Walk the headland through this 27-hectare rainforest reserve, with its abundent bird life and walking trails. Great views of the Burleigh surf.

★Village Markets
MARKET

(✐0487 711 85Q; www.thevillagemarkets.co; Burleigh Heads State School, 1750 Gold Coast Hwy, Burleigh Heads; ⊙8.30am-1pm 1st & 3rd Sun of month) A long-running market that highlights local creators and collectors, with fashion and lifestyle stalls, live music and a strong local following.

David Fleay Wildlife Park
WILDLIFE RESERVE

(✐07-5576 2411; www.npsr.qld.gov.au/parks/david-fleay; cnr Loman Lane & West Burleigh Rd, West Burleigh; adult/child/family $22/10/55; ⊙9am-5pm) Opened by the doctor who first succeed-

Burleigh Heads

ed in breeding platypuses, this wildlife park has 4km of walking tracks through mangroves and rainforest, and plenty of informative native wildlife shows throughout the day. It's around 3km inland from Burleigh Heads.

Jellurgal Cultural Centre CULTURAL CENTRE
(☑ 07-5525 5955; www.jellurgal.com.au; 1711 Gold Coast Hwy, Burleigh Heads; ⊙ 8am-3pm Mon-Fri) ✔ FREE This Aboriginal cultural centre at the base of Burleigh's headland sheds some light on life here hundreds and thousands of years ago. There's a collection of artefacts and a number of different tours (various prices) available – all include walks to the headland (Jellurgal, the Dreaming Mountain), past middens and important Aboriginal sites.

🛏 Sleeping & Eating

Burleigh Break MOTEL **$**
(www.burleighbreak.com.au; 1935 Gold Coast Hwy, Burleigh Heads; d $120-160; ⓅⓈ) A progressive

Burleigh Heads

◎ **Top Sights**
1 Village Markets A1

◎ **Sights**
2 Burleigh Head National Park C3
3 Jellurgal Cultural Centre C3

🛏 **Sleeping**
4 Burleigh Beach Tourist Park.............. B2

🍴 **Eating**
5 Borough Barista B2
6 Finders Keepers B2
7 Harry's Steak Bistro........................... B2
8 Justin Lane Pizzeria & Bar B2
9 Rick Shores B2

renovation has seen one of the Gold Coast's beloved mid-century motels transformed into a friendly and great-value place to stay. Classic motel design means highway views,

SOUTH STRADBROKE ISLAND

This narrow, 21km-long sand island is largely undeveloped – the perfect antidote to the Gold Coast's busyness. At its northern end, the narrow channel separating it from North Stradbroke Island is a top fishing spot; at its southern end, where the Spit is only 200m away, you'll find breaks so good they have Gold Coast's surfers braving the swim over.

South Stradbroke was once attached to North Stradbroke, until a huge storm in 1896 blasted through the isthmus that joined them. South Stradbroke's isolation since has been a boon for its natural habitat. There are wallabies aplenty and pristine bush, sand and sea to explore. And, of course, no cars. If you don't wish to overnight (accommodation choices are limited), you can charter a boat or do a day tour with **Water'bout** (📞 0401 428 004; www.waterbout.com. au; Waterways Dr Boat Ramp, Proud Park, Main Beach; tours per adult $125).

Campers should head to North Currigee, South Currigee or Tipplers campgrounds.

but you're still just a minute's amble from the beach. Rooms have retained vintage features where possible, but otherwise are fresh and simple. Ask about long-stay discounts.

Burleigh Beach
Tourist Park   CARAVAN PARK $
(📞 07-5667 2750; www.goldcoasttouristparks.com. au; 36 Goodwin Tce, Burleigh Heads; powered sites $46-60, cabins $140-210; ❋ @ 🛜 🌊) This council-owned park is snug, but it's well run and in a great spot near the beach. Aim for one of the three blue cabins at the front of the park. There's a minimum two-night stay for cabins.

⭐ **Borough Barista**   CAFE $
(14 Esplanade, Burleigh Heads; mains $5-19; ⏰ 5.30am-2.30pm) It's all cool tunes and friendly vibes at this little open-walled espresso shack. Join local surfers for their dawn piccolo lattes and post-surf for a chia bowl or breakfast salad on a footpath bench. Lunches revolve around good proteins with burgers or big salads.

Paddock Bakery   BAKERY $
(📞 0419 652 221; www.paddockbakery.com; Hibiscus Haven, Miami; dishes $9-17; ⏰ 7.30am-2.30pm) An antique wood-fired oven sits in the heart of this beautiful old weatherboard cottage and turns out wonderful bread, croissants, granola and pastries. The semi-sourdough doughnuts have a devoted fan base, as do the Nutella doughboats – spherical shaped so as to fit more goo. There's a full breakfast and lunch menu, too, as well as top coffee and cold-pressed juices.

Burleigh Social   CAFE $
(2 Hibiscus Haven, Burleigh Heads; dishes $12-19; ⏰ 6am-2pm) This backstreet cafe has a party vibe from early morning at its picnic-table seating. There's paleo granola or the big paleo breakfast (salmon, bacon or ham with kale, eggs and avocado) or nicely done versions of Australian cafe staples such as smashed avocado, eggs on sourdough and bacon-and-egg rolls. Brisket subs and veggie burgers take it into lunch.

⭐ **Rick Shores**   MODERN ASIAN $$
(📞 07-5630 6611; www.rickshores.com.au; 43 Goodwin Tce, Burleigh Heads; mains $32-52; ⏰ noon-11pm Tue-Sun) Feet-in-the-sand dining can often play it safe, and while this Modern Asian newcomer sends out absolute crowd-pleasing dishes, it's also pleasingly inventive. The space is all about the view, the sound of the nearby waves, the salty breeze and communal-table conviviality. Serves are huge, which can allay the menu price if you're not dining solo and are into sharing.

⭐ **Harry's Steak Bistro**   STEAK $$
(📞 07-5576 8517; www.harryssteakbistro.com. au; 1744 Gold Coast Hwy, Burleigh Heads; mains $20-40; ⏰ 5-11pm Wed & Thu, noon-11pm Fri-Sun) Don't misread the menu – a mix and match steak-and-sauce affair, plus unlimited fries – as belonging to a chain restaurant. Harry's, a stylish, sparse paean to 'beef, booze and banter', is super-serious about its steaks, with each accredited the name of its farm and region.

⭐ **Justin Lane Pizzeria & Bar**   PIZZA $$
(📞 07-5576 8517; www.justinlane.com.au; 1708 Gold Coast Hwy, Burleigh Heads; pizzas $19-24; ⏰ 5pm-late) One of the seminal players in Burleigh's food and drinking scene, Justin Lane has now colonised most of an old shopping arcade. Yes, the fun stretches upstairs, downstairs and across the hall. Great pizzas, simple but flavour-packed pasta

dishes and possibly the coast's best regional Italian wine list make it a must, even if you're not here for the party vibe.

Finders Keepers   MODERN AUSTRALIAN **$$**
(☑07-5659 1643; www.finderskeepersbar.com.au; 49 James St; mains $16-29; ☺4-10pm Tue-Fri, 7am-11pm Sat & Sun) This dark, stylish restaurant feels like it's been transported from Sydney's Woollahra or Melbourne's South Yarra, but the friendly young staff is pure Burleigh. Similarly, the tapas-style dishes are a mix of sophistication (foie gras parfait and poached scallop mornay) and health-conscious coastal casual (ancient grain salad, and salmon on buckwheat and seasonal greens with a sea-vegetable butter sauce).

 Drinking & Nightlife

Black Hops Brewing   BREWERY
(www.blackhops.com.au; 15 Gardenia Grove, Burleigh Heads; ☺10am-6pm Mon-Fri, noon-4pm Sat) The Black Hops boys run a friendly and fun tap room where you can enjoy a paddle or whatever craft delight they've currently got on tap. There are eight poetically named beers – from the Bitter Fun pale ale to the Flash Bang white IPA – to choose from, or you can purchase whatever they have bottled.

Burleigh Brewing Company   BREWERY
(☑07-5593 6000; www.burleighbrewing.com.au; 17a Ern Harley Dr, Burleigh Heads; monthly tours $50; ☺3-6pm Wed & Thu, to 8.30pm Fri, 2-8pm Sun) Hang out in this light, woody and blokey space with fellow beer lovers. There's live music and local food trucks, not to mention a 24 tap line-up of Burleigh brews, including their main line and pilot project beers. Tours run on Wednesday nights mid-month and need to be booked through the website.

Currumbin & Palm Beach

POP 16,310

Around the point from Burleigh, Palm Beach has a particularly lovely stretch of sand, backed with a few old-style beach shacks. Its numbered streets are also home to some great coffee stops and dining ops. Further south again, Currumbin is a sleepy family-focused town, with a beautiful surf beach, safe swimming in Currumbin Creek and some evocative mid-century architecture worth clocking. It's also home to the iconic eponymous wildlife sanctuary.

◉ Sights & Activities

Kids will enjoy a summer swim at **Currumbin Rock Pools** (Currumbin Creek Rd, Currumbin Valley).

★**Currumbin Wildlife Sanctuary**   WILDLIFE RESERVE
(☑07-5534 1266, 1300 886 511; www.cws.org.au; 28 Tomewin St, Currumbin; adult/child/family $49/35/133; ☺8am-5pm) This nicely restrained, old-style operation includes Australia's biggest rainforest aviary, where you can hand-feed a technicolour blur of rainbow lorikeets. There's also kangaroo feeding, photo ops with koalas and crocodiles, reptile shows and Aboriginal dance displays. Entry is reduced after 3pm, and there's often an adults-at kids-prices special during school holidays.

✖ Eating & Drinking

Feather & Docks   CAFE **$**
(☑07-5659 1113; www.featheranddocks.com.au; 1099 Gold Coast Hwy, Palm Beach; dishes $12-18; ☺5.30am-3pm; ☑) Given the witness-the-fitness early-to-rise lifestyle round these parts, the notion of breakfast burgers and lunch that starts at 10.30am makes a lot of sense. That said, most things on the menu work for either breakfast or lunch, from the French toast to the brekky tortilla to the stacked pastrami melts.

★**Bstow**   MODERN AUSTRALIAN **$$**
(☑0410 033 380; www.bstow.com.au; 8th Ave Plaza, 1176 Gold Coast Hwy, Palm Beach; mains $18-24) Best-of-both-worlds Bstow is somewhere you'll want to hang with a drink – it does very special cocktails; think house-infused gin and freshly pressed, muddled or juiced mixers – but also warrants a leisurely dinner – the sharing-plate-style dishes are seriously considered, easy on the eye and a creative mix of tastes and textures.

Collective   MODERN AUSTRALIAN **$$**
(www.thecollectivepalmbeach.com.au; 1128 Gold Coast Hwy, Palm Beach; mains $17-24; ☺noon-9pm) Locals' favourites come together here, with five kitchens serving one great, rambling indoor-outdoor communal dining space, strung with fairy lights, flush with pot plants and packed with up to 300 happy eaters. There are two bars, one of them a balmy rooftop affair. Choose from burgers, pizza, tapas, Asian fusion, Mexican and Mod Oz share plates. You can even head here for a post-surf breakfast at 7am.

★ **Balter** BREWERY
(☑ 07-5525 6916; www.balter.com.au; 14 Traders Way, Currumbin; tasting paddles $12; ☺ 3-9pm Fri, 1-8pm Sat & Sun) Local surf star Mick Fanning (the man who punched a shark, right?) and his fellow circuit legends Joel Parkinson, Bede Durbidge and Josh Kerr are all partners in this wonderful new brewery, hidden away at the back of a Currumbin industrial estate. Come and sample the already sought-after Balter XPA or a special such as the German-style Keller pilsner.

Coolangatta

POP 5710

A down-to-earth beach town on Queensland's far southern border, 'Coolie' has quality surf beaches, including the legendary Superbank, and a tight-knit, very real community that makes it feel less touristy than it otherwise could. The legendary **Coolangatta Gold** (www.sls.com.au/coolangattagold; ☺ Oct) surf-life-saving comp happens here every October and the **Quiksilver & Roxy Pro** (www.aspworldtour.com; ☺ Mar) kicks off surfing's most prestigious world tour at Snapper Rocks each March. Follow the boardwalk north around Kirra Point for another beautiful long stretch of beach, sometimes challenging surf, and locally loved indie-atmosphere cafes and bars.

Point Danger Light, the lighthouse on the headland between Coolangatta and Tweed Heads, marks the border between Queensland and NSW and offers amazing views along the coast.

For local surfing lessons, try **Gold Coast Surfing Centre** (☑ 0417 191 629; www.goldcoastsurfingcentre.com; group lessons $45) or **Cooly Surf** (☑ 07-5536 1470; 25 Griffith St; 2hr surfing lessons $45; ☺ 9am-5pm).

🛏 Sleeping & Eating

Coolangatta Sands Backpackers HOSTEL $
(☑ 07-5536 7472; www.taphousegroup.com.au/coolangatta-sands-backpackers; cnr Griffith & McLean Sts, Coolangatta; dm $17-25, d $68-80; ✴@🛜) Above the boozy Coolangatta Sands Hotel, this hostel is a warren of rooms and corridors, but there's a fab wraparound balcony above the street (no booze allowed, unfortunately – go downstairs to the pub) and red chesterfields in the TV room for when it's raining.

Kirra Beach Tourist Park CARAVAN PARK $
(☑ 07-5667 2740; www.goldcoasttouristparks.com.au; 10 Charlotte St, Kirra; powered/unpowered sites $39/35, s/d $65/140, cabins $125-140; ✴@🛜🏊) A large council-run park with

Coolangatta

SOUTH PACIFIC OCEAN

Burleigh Heads (10km);
Surfers Paradise (25km)

Kirra Point

Coolangatta Beach

QUEENSLAND

Marine Pde

Coyne St
South St
Charlotte St
Coolangatta Rd

Musgrave St

Winston St

McLean St
Dutton St
Warner St

Griffith St

Lanham St

Greyhound

Miles St
Rutledge St
Garrick St

McLean St
Dutton St

Dixon St
Enid St

COOLANGATTA

Thompson St
Frances St

NEW SOUTH WALES

plenty of trees, wandering ibises and a camp kitchen and heated swimming pool. Good-value self-contained cabins (with or without bathroom), all a few hundred metres from the beach.

★**La Costa Motel**   MOTEL **$$**
(☑07-5599 2149; www.lacostamotel.com.au; 127 Golden Four Dr, Bilinga; d $130-185; ❄️🔉) One of the few motels of 1950s 'highway heritage', this mint-green weatherboard, located just off the Gold Coast Hwy, has stayed true to its roots on the outside, while the interiors are neat, comfortable and include kitchenettes. A lovely apartment with a private deck suits longer stays. Prices are significantly lower outside high season.

★**Hotel Komune**   HOTEL, HOSTEL **$$**
(☑07-5536 6764; www.komuneresorts.com; 146 Marine Pde, Coolangatta; dm $38-45, 1-bedroom apt $140-180, 2-bedroom apt $185-300; 🔉❄️) With a palm-laden pool area and an ultra laid-back vibe, this 10-storey converted apartment tower is the ultimate surf retreat. It has budget dorms, apartments and a hip penthouse begging for a party. That said, the party is usually to be found downstairs, at the on-site bar (well, nightclub) from around 9pm, with music Fridays to Sundays.

★**Black Sheep Espresso Baa**   CAFE **$**
(☑07-5536 9947; www.tbseb.com.au; 72-80 Marine Pde, Coolangatta; ◷5am-3pm) A passionate crew of coffee obsessives run this cute little cafe right in the heart of the Marine Pde shopping strip. Perfect espresso, filter coffee and that Gold Coast necessity, iced lattes, are joined by a small but creative breakfast and lunch menu.

Cafe Dbar   MODERN AUSTRALIAN **$$**
(☑07-5599 2031; www.cafedbar.com.au; 275 Boundary St, Coolangatta; mains $19-27; ◷11.15am-3pm Mon-Thu, to 8pm Fri-Sun) This lovely spot is perched above the cliffs of Point Danger, at the easternmost point of two states, almost on top of the NSW–Queensland border. You can deliberate on any number of fabulous breakfast options, grab a good takeaway coffee, or stay for share plates and salads. There's also a stylish little shop attached for a postprandial browse.

Bellakai   MODERN AUSTRALIAN **$$$**
(☑07-5599 5116; www.facebook.com/bellakai. coolangatta; 82 Marine Pde, Coolangatta; mains $30-40; ◷5am-9.30pm) From 5am (yes, 5am) until late, Bellakai plates up casual but spot-on dishes. The menu changes seasonally, but it will go something like this: fish of the day with red curry and wilted greens, or house-made parpadelle with prawns. Mornings mean coffee and Coolie locals catching up.

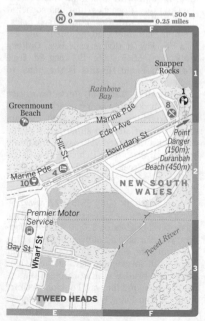

THE GOLD COAST TAMBOURINE MOUNTAIN

LOCAL KNOWLEDGE

GOLDIE'S BEST SURF BREAKS

The Gold Coast possesses some of the longest, hollowest and best waves in the world, and is lauded for its epic consistency. The creation of the 2km Superbank sand bar has made for a decade of even better waves, even more often.

Snapper Rocks A highly advanced point break at Coolangatta's far south; home to the Quiksilver Pro World Surfing League, and home break to Australian pro surfers Stephanie Gilmore and Joel Parkinson.

Duranbah Universally known as D-bah, this point and peaky beach break is good for those who like their waves technical and punchy.

Greenmount Classic beach break that benefits from a southerly swell.

Kirra Beautiful beach break that doesn't work that often, but, oh when it does.

Burleigh Heads Strong currents and boulders to watch out for, but a perfect break that's more often on than not.

The Spit One of north Goldie's stalwarts, this peaky beach break can work even when the surf is small.

Drinking & Nightlife

★ **Eddie's Grub House** BAR
(☏ 07-5599 2177; www.eddiesgrubhouse.com; 171 Griffith St, Coolangatta; ⊙ noon-10.30pm Tue-Thu & Sun, to midnight Fri & Sat) A totally old-school rock-and-roll bar, with dirty blues and best-of rock soundtrack, Eddie's is emblematic of the new Gold Coast: indie, ironic and really fun. Yes, there's grub to be had, and Eddie's 'dive bar comfort food' is exactly that. But this is a place for drinking, dancing, chatting and chilling (as they say themselves).

Coolangatta Hotel PUB
(www.thecoolyhotel.com.au; cnr Marine Pde & Warner St, Coolangatta; ⊙ 10am-late) The hub of Coolangatta's sometimes boisterous nocturnal scene, this huge pub, across from the beach, pumps with live bands (Grinspoon, The Rubens), sausage sizzles, pool comps, trivia nights, acoustic jam nights, surprisingly sophisticated pub-meal deals (pasta and rosé, anyone?) – basically, the works. Big Sunday sessions.

ℹ Getting There & Away

Greyhound (☏ 1300 473 946; www.greyhound.com.au) runs to Brisbane and beyond, while **Premier Motor Service** (☏ 13 34 10; www.premierms.com.au) heads as far north as Cairns. Coaches stop on Wharf St.

GOLD COAST HINTERLAND

Inland from the surf, sand and half-nakedness of the Gold Coast, the densely forested mountains of the McPherson Range feel a million miles away. There are some brilliant national parks here, with subtropical jungle, waterfalls, lookouts and rampant wildlife.

Tamborine Mountain

The squat, mountain-top rainforest community of Tamborine Mountain – comprising Eagle Heights, North Tamborine and Mt Tamborine – is 45km inland from the Gold Coast beaches, and has cornered the arts-and-craft, Germanic-kitsch, package-tour, chocolate-fudge-liqueur market in a big way. If this is your bag, **Gallery Walk** (☏ 07-5545 2006; 197 Long Rd, Eagle Heights) in Eagle Heights is the place to stock up.

Tamborine National Park (www.nprsr.qld.gov.au/parks/tamborine) comprises 13 sections stretching across the 8km plateau, offering waterfalls and super views of the Gold Coast. Accessed via easy-to-moderate walking trails are Witches Falls, Curtis Falls, Cedar Creek Falls and Cameron Falls. Pick up a map at the visitor centre in North Tamborine.

With **Skywalk** (☏ 07-5545 2222; www.rainforestskywalk.com.au; 333 Geissman Dr, North Tamborine; adult/child/family $20/10/49; ⊙ 9.30am-4pm) you can take a 1.5km walk descending down into the forest floor to pretty Cedar Creek, with spectacular elevated steel viewpoints and bridges cutting through the upper canopy along the way. Look out for rare Richmond birdwing butterflies en route.

🛏 Sleeping & Eating

⭐ **Songbirds Rainforest Retreat** HOTEL $$$
(📞 07-5545 2563; www.songbirds.com.au; Lot 10, Tamborine Mountain Rd, North Tamborine; villas $270-498; 🅿🛜) By far the classiest outfit on the hill. Each of the six Southeast Asian–inspired villas has a double spa with rainforest views; rates drop for stays of two nights or more. The award-winning restaurant, also on-site, is worth visiting for a long lunch.

⭐ **Long Road Bistro** MODERN AUSTRALIAN $$
(📞 07-5545 0826; www.witcheschasecheese.com.au/bistro; 165/185-187 Long Rd, Eagle Heights; mains $21-29; ⊙10am-4pm Mon-Fri, from 7am Sat & Sun) Pop in for a big Sunday roast (say, pork belly with a beetroot and green-apple relish) or grab a lentil burger or cookies-and-cream-pimped iced coffee. It's part of the **Witches Chase Cheese Company** (📞07-5545 2032; www.witcheschasecheese.com.au; 165 Long Rd, Eagle Heights; ⊙10am-4pm) so, as you might imagine, the cheese board is a winner. There's also live music and something of a party vibe on weekends.

Lamington National Park

Australia's largest remnant of subtropical rainforest cloaks the deep valleys and steep cliffs of the McPherson Range, reaching elevations of 1100m on the Lamington Plateau. Here, the 200-sq-km **Lamington National Park** (www.nprsr.qld.gov.au/parks/lamington) is a Unesco World Heritage Site and has more than 160km of walking trails.

The two most accessible sections of the park are Binna Burra and Green Mountains, both reached via long, narrow, winding roads from Canungra (not great for big campervans). Binna Burra can also be accessed from Nerang.

🛏 Sleeping & Eating

At the end of Lamington National Park Rd, **Green Mountains Campground** (📞13 74 68; www.nprsr.qld.gov.au/parks/lamington/camping.html; Green Mountains; site per person/family $6.15/24) is adjacent to the day-use visitor car park. There are plenty of spots for tents and caravans (and a toilet-and-shower block); book in advance.

Binna Burra Mountain Lodge (📞1300 246 622, 07-5533 3622; www.binnaburralodge.com.au; 1069 Binna Burra Rd, Beechmont;

powered/unpowered sites $35/28, safari tents $105, d with/without bathroom $290/175; 🅿) is an atmospheric mountain retreat; the closest thing to a ski lodge in the bush. You can stay in rustic log cabins, well-appointed apartments (known as 'sky lodges') with spectacular scenic rim views, or in a tent surrounded by forest. There's a good restaurant and teahouse.

The famous 1926 **O'Reilly's Rainforest Retreat** (📞07-5502 4911, 1800 688 722; www.oreillys.com.au; Lamington National Park Rd, Green Mountains; s $80-99, d $149-188, 1-bedroom villas $360-375; @🛜♨) has lost much of its original grandeur but retains a rustic charm – and sensational views! There are plenty of organised activities, plus a day spa, a cafe, a bar and a restaurant.

Springbrook National Park

About a 40-minute drive west of Burleigh Heads, **Springbrook National Park** (📞13 74 68; www.nprsr.qld.gov.au/parks/springbrook) is a steep remnant of the huge Tweed Shield volcano that centred on nearby Mt Warning in NSW more than 20 million years ago. It's a wonderland for hikers, with excellent trails through cool-temperate, subtropical and eucalypt forests offering a mosaic of gorges, cliffs and waterfalls.

Excellent viewpoints in the park include the appropriately named **Best of All Lookout** (Repeater Station Rd), **Canyon Lookout** (Canyon Pde), whch is also the start of a 4km circuit walk to Twin Falls and the superb lookout beside the 60m **Goomoolahra Falls** (Springbrook Rd), giving views across the plateau and all the way back to the coast.

🛏 Sleeping & Eating

There are 11 grassy sites at the pretty **Settlement Campground** (📞13 74 68; www.nprsr.qld.gov.au/parks/springbrook/camping.html; 52 Carricks Rd, Springbrook; sites per person/family $6/24), the only campground at Springbrook. There are toilets and gas BBQs but no showers. Book ahead.

Mouses House (📞07-5533 5192; www.mouseshouse.com.au; 2807 Springbrook Rd, Springbrook; d $270-320; ❄🛜) hides 12 cedar chalets, linked by softly lit boardwalks, in the magical misty woods. Each has a spa and a wood fire, and some are by a cascading stream.

Noosa & the Sunshine Coast

Best Places to Eat

➡ Spirit House (p359)
➡ Wasabi (p345)
➡ Noosa Beach House (p345)
➡ Embassy XO (p357)

Best Places to Sleep

➡ Oceans (p353)
➡ Monaco (p350)
➡ YHA Halse Lodge (p342)
➡ Glass House Mountains Ecolodge (p348)

Why Go?

The Sunshine Coast – the 100 golden kilometres stretching from the tip of Bribie Island to the Cooloola Coast – is aglow with perfect beaches, coveted surf and a laid-back, sun-kissed populace who will quickly tell you how lucky they are. Resort towns dot the coast, each with its own appeal and vibe, from upmarket, cosmopolitan Noosa to newly hip, evolving Caloundra.

Further inland is the lush, cool hinterland. It's here that you'll find the ethereal Glass House Mountains, looming over the land- and seascapes, and the iconic Australia Zoo. Further north, the Blackall Range offers a change of scenery with thick forests, lush pastures and quaint villages dotted with artisan food shops, cafes and crafty boutiques.

When to Go
Noosa

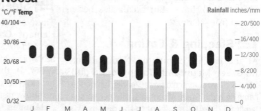

May Gourmands and gluttons nosh and slosh at the four-day Noosa Food & Wine.

Aug Postholiday lull means fewer crowds, solitary beach walks and warm, unsticky weather.

Sep Up-and-coming Caloundra draws music fans with its rocking surfside Caloundra Festival.

0 — 10 km
0 — 5 miles

Wolvi

Noosa River

Great Sandy National Park (Cooloola) ❸

Teewah Coloured Sand Cliffs

Fig Tree Point ⌂

Noosa Everglades

Kin Kin

Elanda Point

Lake Cootharaba

SOUTH PACIFIC OCEAN

Gympie (25km)

Cooran

Pinbarren

Boreen Point

Teewah Beach

Pomona

Bruce Hwy A1

Mount Tinbeerwah (265m) ▲

Tewantin **Noosa** ❷ ❶ **Noosa National Park**

Lake Cooroibah

Laguna Bay

Cooroy

Noosaville

Sunshine Beach

Eumarella Dr

Lake Weyba

6

12

70

Peregian Beach

Belli Park

Blackall Range

Bruce Hwy M1

Eumundi

Kenilworth (2km)

Yandina

Mapleton Falls National Park

Mt Coolum (208m) ▲

Coolum Beach

David Low Way

Point Perry

Yaroomba

11

Marcoola

Mapleton

Nambour

10

Bli Bli

Sunshine Coast Airport

Mudjimba Beach

Kondalilla National Park

Flaxton

Woombye

8

70

Maroochydore

Montville

Palmwoods

Buderim

Mooloolaba

Kawana Waters

Maleny

Mooloolah

Mooloolah River National Park

M1

6

❹ **Caloundra**

Landsborough

Australia Zoo

Peachester

6

Beerwah

Steve Irwin Way

Old Gympie Rd

❺ **Glass House Mountains**

Glass House Mountains Visitor and Interpretive Centre

Bribie Island

Woodford

Beerburrum

Bribie Island National Park

D'Aguilar

Bruce Hwy

Donnybrook

White Patch

D'Aguilar Hwy

60

Mt Mee

Caboolture Airfield

Toorbul

Ningi

Woorim

M1

85

Caboolture

Bongaree

Morayfield

Brisbane (45km)

ℹ Getting There & Around

AIR

Sunshine Coast Airport (p303) is at Marcoola, 10km north of Maroochydore and 26km south of Noosa. **Jetstar** (☑ 13 15 38; www.jetstar.com) and **Virgin Australia** (☑ 13 67 89; www.virginaustralia.com) have daily direct flights from Sydney and Melbourne; **Qantas** (☑ 13 13 13; www.qantas.com.au) flies direct from Sydney eight times weekly. Jetstar also runs direct flights from Adelaide three times weekly.

From July to October, **Air New Zealand** (www.airnewzealand.com) flies direct from Auckland three to four times weekly.

BUS

Greyhound Australia (☑ 1300 473 946; www.greyhound.com.au) has several daily services from Brisbane to Caloundra (from $19, two hours), Maroochydore (from $23, two hours) and Noosa (from $24, 2½ to 3¼ hours). **Premier Motor Service** (☑ 13 34 10; www.premierms.com.au) also runs buses to Maroochydore ($23, 1½ to 1¾ hours) and Noosa ($23, 2½ hours) from Brisbane.

Several companies offer transfers from Sunshine Coast Airport and Brisbane to points along the coast. Fares from Brisbane cost from around $40 to $60 and from Sunshine Coast Airport between $25 and $35. (Fares are around half-price for children.)

Con-X-ion (☑ 1300 370 471; www.con-x-ion.com) does airport transfers from the Sunshine Coast and Brisbane Airports.

Henry's (☑ 07-5474 0199; www.henrys.com.au) runs a door-to-door service from Sunshine Coast Airport to points north as far as Noosa Heads and Tewantin.

Sunbus (TransLink; ☑ 13 12 30; www.sunbus.com.au) is a local TransLink-operated bus that buzzes between Caloundra and Noosa, and from Noosa to the train station at Nambour ($8.60, 1¼ hours) via Eumundi.

Noosa

POP 39,380

Noosa is one of Australia's most fashionable resort towns, a salubrious hub backing onto crystalline waters and pristine subtropical rainforest. The town is located within the Noosa Biosphere Reserve, a Unesco-recognised area famous for its highly diverse ecosystem.

While the designer boutiques, polished restaurants and canal-side villas draw the beach-elite sophisticates, the beach and bush are free, leading to a healthy intermingling of urbane fashionistas and laid-back surfers

and beach bods. Noosa encompasses three main zones: upmarket Noosa Heads (around Laguna Bay and Hastings St), the more relaxed Noosaville (along the Noosa River) and the administrative hub of Noosa Junction.

On long weekends and school holidays, the main shopping and dining strip of Hastings St becomes a slow-moving file of traffic; the rest of the time, it's delightfully low(er) key.

◉ Sights & Activities

Covering the headland, **Noosa National Park** (www.noosanationalpark.com;) is one of Noosa's top sights; the most scenic way to reach it is to follow the boardwalk along the coast from town. The park's walking tracks lead to stunning coastal scenery, idyllic bays and great surfing. Pick up a walking-track map from the Noosa National Park Information Centre (p346) at the park's entrance.

For a panoramic view that takes in Noosa, its densely wooded national park, the ocean and distant hinterland, walk or drive up to **Laguna Lookout** (Map p341; Viewland Dr, Noosa Junction) from Viewland Dr.

Merrick's Learn to Surf　　SURFING
(☑ 0418 787 577; www.learntosurf.com.au; Beach Access 14, Noosa Main Beach, Noosa Heads; 2hr lessons $65; ◉ 9am & 1.30pm) Merrick's is one of the most popular surf schools on the Sunshine Coast, offering super-fun, two-hour group lessons twice daily, as well as the option of private tutorials. Kids aged seven and over are welcome, and the outfit runs special five-day kids' lessons during the school holidays, to boot. Lessons can be conducted in French, too – *très bien!*

Foam and Resin　　SURFING, WATER SPORTS
(Map p341; 53 Hastings St, Noosa Heads; surfboard rental 2hr/full-day $25/35, stand-up paddleboard rental 2hr $30; ◉ 9am-5pm) Owned and run by a Kiwi expat, this open-air surf rental kiosk sits opposite the visitor centre in Noosa Heads. It's generally cheaper than its competitor on the beach and offers good-quality equipment, including longboards and shortboards. Opening times can vary.

Adventure Sports Noosa　　KITESURFING, WATER SPORTS
(☑ 07-5455 6677; www.kitesurfaustralia.com.au; 136 Eumundi Noosa Rd, Noosaville; 2½hr kitesurfing lesson $275; ◉ 9am-5pm Mon-Fri, to 2pm Sat Aug-Apr, 10am-5pm Mon & Tue, 9am-5pm Thu & Fri, 9am-2pm Sat May-Jul) As well as running kitesurfing lessons, Adventure Sports hires out

Noosa Heads

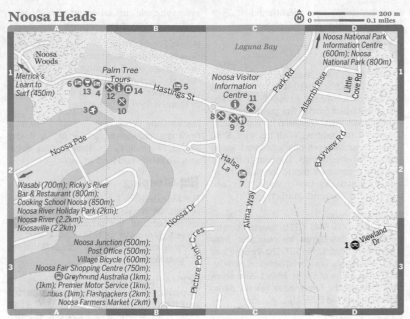

Noosa Heads

kayaks (half-day $35), bikes (two hours $19, full day $25) and stand-up paddle boards (half-day from $35, full day from $55).

Noosa Ocean Rider BOATING
(Map p343; ☑0438 386 255; www.facebook.com/NoosaOceanrider; Jetty 17, 248 Gympie Tce, Noosaville; 1hr per person/family $70/250) Thrills and spills on a very fast and powerful speedboat. Standard tours will have you zipping around the ocean side of Noosa National Park.

Kayak Noosa KAYAKING
(Map p343; ☑07-5455 5651; www.kayaknoosa.com; 194 Gympie Tce, Noosaville; 2hr sunset kayak adult/child $60/45) Tours around Noosa National Park. Also hires out kayaks (two hours from $25) and stand-up paddle boards (one/two hours $20/30).

Noosa Ferry CRUISE
(Map p341; ☑07-5449 8442; www.noosaferry.com) This excellent ferry service runs an informative hop-on, hop-off Classic Tour (all-day pass adult/child $25/7) between Tewantin and the Sofitel Noosa Pacific Resort jetty in Noosa Heads. It also offers an Eco Cruise (great for birdwatchers; adult/child $49/22.50) on Tuesdays and Thursdays, and a wonderful one-hour Sunset Cruise (BYO

alcoholic drinks; per adult/child $25/10) Tuesday to Saturday.

👉 Tours

Noosa Woody Hire
DRIVING
(📞 0475 587 385; www.noosawoodyhire.com; driving tour 1/2/4hr $190/290/590) Cruise around in an attention-stealing 1946 Ford Woody. Accommodating four to five passengers, the vehicle was lovingly restored by young, affable local Tim Crabtree. With his wife, Kim, the surfboard shaper offers tailored tours; all include refreshments. The four-hour tour includes a gourmet picnic lunch and can take in hinterland foodie stops; they can also visit the Eumundi Markets (p359).

Discovery Group
DRIVING
(Map p343; 📞 07-5449 0393; www.thediscovery group.com.au; 186 Gympie Tce, Noosaville; 1-day Fraser Island tour adult/child $175/120, 4hr Everglades tour $79/65) Runs wonderful one- and two-day 4WD truck tours of Fraser Island. Also offers trips through the Everglades (full-day guided canoe trip adult/child $129/90).

Bike On Australia
MOUNTAIN BIKING
(📞 07-5474 3322; www.bikeon.com.au; guided mountain-bike tours from $65, bike hire per day $25) Runs a variety of tours, including self-guided and adventurous eco-jaunts. The fun, half-day Off the Top Tour – downhill on a mountain bike – costs $79. Also rents out road bikes (three/seven days from $120/250).

🚴 Courses

Cooking School Noosa
COOKING
(📞 07-5449 2443; www.thecookingschoolnoosa.com; 2 Quamby Pl, Noosa Heads; ⏱ 5½hr session incl lesson, lunch & wine $250) Lauded restaurant Wasabi (p345) also runs hands-on cooking courses, helmed by in-house chefs as well as special guest chefs from around the country. Regular options include Japanese, Southeast Asian and French courses, all of which use seasonal local produce and conclude with lunch and sommelier-picked accompanying wines.

✨ Festivals & Events

Noosa Festival of Surfing
SURFING
(www.noosafestivalofsurfing.com; ⏱ Mar) A week of wave-riding action in March. There's a huge range of competition divisions, from invite-only pros to amateur competitions spanning all age brackets – there's even a dog surfing category! Water action aside, events include surf talks and workshops as well as film screenings and live music.

Noosa Food & Wine
FOOD & DRINK
(www.noosafoodandwine.com.au; ⏱ May) A four-day tribute to all manner of gastronomic delights, featuring prolific chefs, masterclasses, special lunches and dinners, as well as themed food and wine tours.

Noosa Long Weekend
CULTURAL
(www.noosalongweekend.com; ⏱ Jul) A 10-day festival of music, dance, theatre, film, visual arts, literature and food in July.

🛏 Sleeping

For an extensive list of short-term holiday rentals, try Noosa Visitor Information Centre (p346) and the privately run Accom Noosa (Map p341; 📞 07-5447 3444, 1800 072 078; www.accomnoosa.com.au; Shop 5/41 Hastings St, Noosa Heads).

★ YHA Halse Lodge
HOSTEL $
(Map p341; 📞 07-5447 3377; www.halselodge.com.au; 2 Halse Lane, Noosa Heads; dm $33.50, d $88; @ 🛜) This splendid, colonial-era Queenslander is a legendary backpacker stopover and well worth the clamber up its steep drive. There are four to six-bed dorms, twins, doubles and a lovely wide verandah. Popular with locals, the bar is a mix-and-meet bonanza, offering great meals (mains $16.50 to $26.50), cheap happy-hour beers, and live music on Thursdays. Close to the Main Beach action.

Flashpackers
HOSTEL $
(📞 07-5455 4088; www.flashpackersnoosa.com; 102 Pacific Ave, Sunshine Beach; mixed dm from $38, female dm $45, d from $100; ❄ 🛜 ☁) Flashpackers challenges the notion of hostels as flea-bitten dives. Thoughtful touches to its neat dorms include full-length mirrors, personal reading lights, ample wall sockets and the free use of surfboards and bodyboards.

Noosa River Holiday Park
CARAVAN PARK $
(Map p343; 📞 07-5449 7050; www.noosaholiday parks.com.au; 4 Russell St, Noosaville; unpowered/powered sites $38/46; 🛜) This park is especially appealing for its location on the banks of the Noosa River, right between Noosa Heads and Noosaville. The latter's eateries and bars are within walking distance and the site itself has lovely spots to take a dip in the river. It's a seriously popular place: reservations

Noosaville

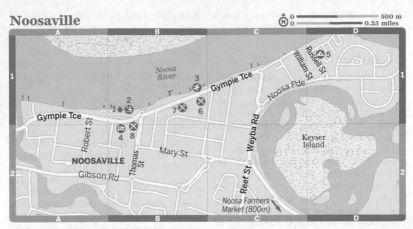

Noosaville

Activities, Courses & Tours
1 Discovery Group......................................B1
2 Kayak Noosa..B1
3 Noosa Ocean Rider................................B1

Sleeping
4 Islander Noosa Resort............................B2
5 Noosa River Holiday Park D1

Eating
6 Bordertown BBQ & Taqueria B1
7 Little Humid..B1
   Noosa Boathouse ....(see 2)
8 Thomas Corner B2

open nine months in advance and it usually books out soon after.

★ 10 Hastings
MOTEL **$$**

(Map p341; ☑ 07-5455 3350; www.10hastings street.com.au; 10 Hastings St, Noosa Heads; studio from $199, studio ste from $250, 2-bedroom apt from $400; ⓟ❋🛜🏊) A rarity along Noosa's central Hastings St, this renovated boutique motel is a refreshing alternative to the resorts. Clean, fresh, beach-chic rooms come as compact two-person studios and larger studio suites (sleeping two adults and two children). Larger still are the two-bedroom apartments (sleeping up to six). Perks include complimentary beach towels and mini-bar items. Check for minimum stays.

Hotel Laguna
APARTMENT **$$**

(Map p341; ☑ 07-5447 3077; www.hotellaguna.com. au; 6 Hastings St, Noosa Heads; studios/ste from $165/230; ⓟ❋🛜🏊) Neatly wedged between the river and Hastings St, Hotel Laguna consists of self-contained apartments and smaller studios. All apartments are privately owned and each is individually decorated, but all are smart and pleasant (if not always spotless). There's a communal guest laundry

and courtyard-style pool area. The location means you are only a roll-out-of-bed to the beach and a coffee whiff from great cafes.

Islander Noosa Resort
RESORT **$$**

(Map p343; ☑ 07-5440 9200; www.islandernoosa. com.au; 187 Gympie Tce, Noosaville; 2-/3-bedroom villas $220/270; ⓟ❋🛜🏊) Set on 1.6 hectares of tropical gardens, with a central lagoon-style pool area and wooden boardwalks meandering through the trees, this is a good family option in the heart of Noosaville. On-site facilities includes jacuzzis, saunas, gym and two tennis courts. Apartments are a little dated and not always as clean as they could be, but are comfy and pleasant.

★ Fairshore
APARTMENT **$$$**

(Map p341; ☑ 07-5449 4500; www.fairshore noosa.com.au; 41 Hastings St, Noosa Heads; 4-person apt from $495; ⓟ❋🛜🏊) A smart, family-friendly apartment resort with direct access to Noosa Main Beach and buzzing Hastings St, Fairshore comes with a magazine-worthy, palm-fringed pool area. Two-bedroom apartments offer one or two bathrooms; though each apartment varies in style, all have laundry facilities and most are airy and contemporary. There's also a small gym. Parking is free (vehicle height restriction 1.85m).

✖ Eating

Noosa prides itself on being a culinary destination, with global and local flavours on offer from fine restaurants to beachside takeaways. In Noosa Heads, eateries clutter Hastings St; in Noosaville, head to Thomas St and Gympie Tce.

Self-caterers can stock up on groceries at **Noosa Fair Shopping Centre** (☑07-5447 3788; www.noosafairshopping.com.au; 3 Lanyana Way, Noosa Junction; ⊙supermarket 8am-9pm Mon-Fri, to 5.30pm Sat, 9am-6pm Sun) in Noosa Junction. Altogether more atmospheric is the Sunday **Noosa Farmers Market** (☑0418 769 374; www.noosafarmersmarket.com.au; Noosa Australian Football Club Grounds, 155 Weyba Rd, Noosaville; ⊙7am-noon Sun).

Betty's Burgers & Concrete Co BURGERS $
(Map p341; ☑07-5455 4378; www.bettysburgers. com.au; 2/50 Hastings St, Noosa Heads; burgers $10-16; ⊙10am-9pm) Betty's has achieved cult status all the way down Australia's east coast, which explains the queues at its lush, semi-alfresco Noosa outlet – but the burgers are worth the wait for pillowy soft buns and flawlessly grilled, premium-meat patties (veggie option available). The perfect fries are wonderfully crispy and the more-ish concretes (frozen custard drinks) come in flavours like lemon-raspberry cheesecake. Bliss.

Bordertown BBQ & Taqueria AMERICAN, MEXICAN $
(Map p343; ☑07-5442 4242; www.facebook.com/ bordertownbarbeque; 1/253 Gympie Tce, Noosaville; burgers $12-17, tacos $7-9; ⊙8am-9pm Sun-Thu, to 10.30pm Fri & Sat; ☎☑) Pimped with murals by Queensland artists Mitch 13 and Thom Stuart, clued-in Bordertown rocks great burgers and succulent tacos (with authentic shells made by a Mexican family in Melbourne). Libations at the concrete bar include craft beers, creative cocktails and an alcoholic Bordertown Cola, made in-house using sassafras, vermouth and Fernet-Branca. Check their Facebook page for DJ sessions.

Hard Coffee CAFE $
(Map p341; ☑0410 673 377; 18 Hastings St, Noosa Heads; mains $10-16; ⊙7am-3pm) One of the cheaper options on Hastings St, super-casual

Hard Coffee lurks inside a nondescript food court. The food is simple but tasty, with options like smoked-salmon focaccia, steak sandwich BLAT, and a basic but satisfying avo smash for a bargain $10. Good coffee and no shortage of regulars chatting about the morning surf.

Tanglewood Organic Sourdough Bakery BAKERY $
(☑07-5473 0215; www.facebook.com/tanglewood organicsourdough; Belmondos Organic Market, 59 Rene St, Noosaville; pastries from $5; ⊙8am-5pm Mon-Fri, to 4pm Sat; ☎) Part of the upmarket Belmondos Organic Market, Tanglewood will have you oohing and aahing over its just-made, buttery pastries, artfully displayed on timber logs. If you can't make up your mind, opt for the standout pecan tart or their famous bread-and-butter pudding. Then there are the chocolate sea-salt cookies, not to mention those gorgeous loaves of artisan bread...

Massimo's GELATO $
(Map p341; 75 Hastings St, Noosa Heads; gelato from $5; ⊙9.30am-9.30pm Sun-Thu, to 10pm Fri & Sat) Both tourists and loyal locals queue here for Massimo's icy treats. Whether this is one of Queensland's best *gelaterias* is debatable, but there's no doubting the gelati's creamy texture and fresh, natural flavours. Cash only.

★Thomas Corner MODERN AUSTRALIAN $$
(Map p343; ☑07-5470 2224; www.thomas corner.com.au; cnr Thomas St & Gympie Tce, Noosaville; mains $16-33; ⊙11.30am-8pm Mon-Fri, 8am-8pm Sat & Sun; ☎) Lunching ladies rightfully adore this casually chic, alfresco nosh spot. It's run by locally renowned chef David Rayner, whose vibrant, beautifully plated creations might see locally smoked fish paired with endive, apple, labne and pancetta crumbs, or parmesan-and-sage gnocchi happily married with mushrooms, spinach, truffle paste and poached egg. The popular weekend breakfast menu is equally as inspired.

El Capitano PIZZA $$
(Map p341; ☑07-5474 9990; www.elcapitano.com. au; 52 Hastings St, Noosa Heads; pizzas $22-25; ⊙5-9.30pm) Down an easy-to-miss path and up a set of stairs is Noosa's best pizzeria, a hip, swinging hot spot with bar seating (good for solo diners), louvred windows and marine-themed street art. The light, fluffy pizzas here are gorgeous, made with sour-

dough bases and topped with artisan ingredients. Check the blackboard for pizza and cocktail specials – and always book ahead.

Noosa Boathouse MODERN AUSTRALIAN **$$**
(Map p343; ☑ 07-5440 5070; www.noosaboat house.com.au; 194 Gympie Tce, Noosaville; mains $20-38; ⊗ restaurant 11.30am-3pm & 5-8pm Tue-Sun, cafe 6am-6pm daily, rooftop bar 4.30-7pm Tue-Sun) This modern, floating nosh spot has numerous sections: cafe, fish-and-chip kiosk, rooftop bar (open for sunset drinks) and a Cape Cod–style restaurant. While the latter's menu – think Mod Oz with Italian and Asian touches – isn't quite as ambitious as it sounds, the place is a fantastic option for great-tasting food and killer views sans the eye-watering price tag.

Kaali INDIAN **$$**
(Map p341; ☑ 07-5474 8989; www.kaaligourmet indian.com; 2/2 Hastings St, Noosa Heads; mains $21-32.50; ⊗ 11am-9pm Mon-Fri, 5-10pm Sat & Sun; ☑) After all the Mod Oz cuisine on offer in Noosa Heads, this touch of India offers some spicy relief. At the western end of Hastings St, it's a casual spot, cooking up excellent curries and great tandoori breads.

★ **Noosa Beach House** MODERN AUSTRALIAN **$$$**
(Map p341; ☑ 07-5449 4754; www.noosabeach housepk.com.au; 16 Hastings St, Noosa Heads; mains $39-46, 6-course tasting menu $100; ⊗ 6.30-10.30am & 5.30-9.30pm daily, also noon-2.30pm Sat & Sun) An uncluttered mix of white walls, glass and timber, this effortlessly chic restaurant belongs to globe-trotting celebrity chef Peter Kuravita. Seasonal ingredients and fresh local seafood underscore a contemporary menu whose deeply seductive Sri Lankan snapper curry with tamarind and *aloo chop* (potato croquette) nods to Kuravita's heritage. Weekends see a good-value five-curry lunch, served family-style for $38 per person.

★ **Wasabi** JAPANESE **$$$**
(☑ 07-5449 2443; www.wasabisb.com; 2 Quamby Pl, Noosa Heads; 3 courses $80, 7-/9-course omakase menu $134/157; ⊗ 5-9.30pm Wed, Thu & Sat, noon-9.30pm Fri & Sun) An award-winning, waterside destination restaurant, Wasabi is on the lips of every local gourmand. Premium produce from the region and Wasabi's own farm sings in delicate yet thrilling dishes like handmade duck-egg noodles and fresh fish in burnt-onion broth with fish-crackling and legumes, or tempura-style spanner crab

and *yama imo* (mountain potato) dumpling with kombu salt and *yuzu* (a small citrus fruit) zest.

★ **Ricky's River Bar & Restaurant** MODERN AUSTRALIAN **$$$**
(☑ 07-5447 2455; www.rickys.com.au; Noosa Wharf, 2 Quamby Pl, Noosa Heads; mains $35-45, 6-course tasting menu $105, with matching wines $165; ⊗ noon-late) Perched on the Noosa River, elegant Ricky's is the darling of business folk discussing deals over long lunches. Reserve a table for lunch (the view is half the experience) and swoon over dishes like chargrilled calamari with almond cream, curry leaf, heirloom tomato and quinoa, or Coral Coast barramundi with cauliflower and macadamia *skordalia* (dip), preserved lemon, rhubarb and couscous.

Little Humid MODERN AUSTRALIAN **$$$**
(Map p343; ☑ 07-5449 9755; www.humid.com. au; 2/235 Gympie Tce, Noosaville; mains $27-42; ⊗ noon-2pm & 6-8.30pm Wed-Sun; ☑) This deservedly popular eatery serves up beautiful bistro fare with subtle twists: seasonal dishes like crispy-skin duck with liquorice and orange glaze; herb- and pine-nut-crusted ocean trout; and a decent range of vegetarian options, like creamed broccoli with caramelised fennel and baby spinach, field mushrooms and crushed kipfler potatoes. Book for dinner (up to a week ahead during holiday periods).

🍷 Drinking & Nightlife

★ **Clandestino Roasters** COFFEE
(☑ 1300 656 022; www.clandestino.com.au; Belmondos Organic Market, 59 Rene St, Noosaville; ⊗ 7am-4pm Mon-Fri, to 3pm Sat; ☎) It might be off the tourist radar, but this trendy warehouse microroastery packs in hipsters, surfers and suits, all here for Noosa's top coffee. Choose from two blends and eight single origins served a number of ways, including espresso-style, cold-drip, clover, V60 pourover and siphon. Communal tables and free wi-fi make it a popular spot with the laptop brigade.

★ **Village Bicycle** BAR
(☑ 07-5474 5343; 2/16 Sunshine Beach Rd, Noosa Junction; ⊗ 4pm-midnight Mon-Sat, from 12.30pm Sun) Noosa's coolest local drinking spot by far, Village Bicycle is run by young mates Luke and Trevor. Splashed with street art, it's a convivial space, packed nightly with loyal regulars here to knock back some

beers, tuck into quality bar grub – think tacos and burgers – and listen to live tunes.

Miss Moneypenny's COCKTAIL BAR
(Map p341; 07-5474 9999; www.missmoney pennys.com; 6 Hastings St, Noosa Heads; 11.30am-midnight;) Dashing, award-winning Miss Moneypenny's sets a sophisticated scene for languid toasts. Well-crafted cocktails fall into numerous categories, from Seasonals and Sours to tongue-in-cheek '80s Cruise Ship Drinks. Not that irony gets in the way of quality: even the piña colada is shaken with original Coco Lopez coconut cream. Nosh includes posh bar bites and pizzas ($16 to $30).

 Shopping

Noosa Longboards SPORTS & OUTDOORS
(Map p341; 07-5447 4776; www.noosalong boards.com; 20 Hastings St, Noosa Heads; 9am-5pm) Established in 1994, this iconic brand was one of the first to sell traditional-style longboards at the beginning of the long-board renaissance in Oz. Two decades on, it's famous for handcrafting them with a contemporary twist. Boards aside, the shop stocks its own beachwear label, threads from veteran Aussie label Okanui, as well as authentic, vintage Hawaiian shirts.

 Information

POST

Post Office (13 13 18; www.auspost.com. au; 91 Noosa Dr, Noosa Junction; 9am-5pm Mon-Fri, to 12.30pm Sat)

TOURIST INFORMATION

Noosa National Park Information Centre (07-5447 3522; 8.45am-4.15pm) At the entrance to Noosa National Park.

Noosa Visitor Information Centre (Map p341; 07-5430 5000; www.visitnoosa.com.au; 61 Hastings St, Noosa Heads; 9am-5pm;) Official tourist office.

Palm Tree Tours (Map p341; 07-5474 9166; www.palmtreetours.com.au; Bay Village Shopping Centre, 18 Hastings St, Noosa Heads; 9am-5pm) Long-standing tour desk.

 **Getting There & Away**

Long-distance bus services stop at the **Noosa Junction Bus Station** on Sunshine Beach Rd in Noosa Junction. **Greyhound Australia** (1300 473 946; www.greyhound.com.au) has several daily bus connections from Brisbane to Noosa (from $24, 2½ to 3¼ hours), while **Premier Motor Service** (p93) has one ($23, 2½ hours).

Most hostels have courtesy pick-ups.

Sunbus (TransLink; 13 12 30; www.sunbus. com.au) operates frequent services from Noosa to Maroochydore ($10.50, one hour to 1¼ hours) and Nambour train station ($10.50, 1¼ hours).

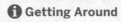 **Getting Around**

BICYCLE

Bike On Australia (p342) Rents out bicycles from several locations in Noosa, including **Flashpackers** (p342) in Sunshine Beach. Alternatively, bikes can be delivered to and from your door for $35 (or free if the booking is over $100).

BOAT

Noosa Ferry (p341) operates ferries between Noosa Heads and Tewantin several times a day (all-day pass adult/child $25/7). **Noosa Water Taxi** (0411 136 810; www.noosawatertaxi. com; one-way per person $10) operates a water-taxi service around Noosa Sound (Friday to Sunday), and is also available for private charters and water-taxi hire by appointment.

BUS

Sunbus has local services that link Noosa Heads, Noosaville, Noosa Junction and Tewantin.

CAR & MOTORCYCLE

All the major car-rental brands can be found in Noosa; rentals start at about $55 per day.
Noosa Car Rentals (0429 053 728; www. noosacarrentals.com.au)
Scooter Hire Noosa (07-5455 4096; www. scooterhirenoosa.com; 13 Noosa Dr, Noosa Heads; 4/24hr $39/59; 8.30am-5pm)

Bribie Island

POP 18,135

This slender island at the northern end of Moreton Bay is linked to the mainland by bridge and is popular with young families, retirees and those with a cool million (or three) to spend on a waterfront property. While it's far more developed than Stradbroke or Moreton Islands, there are still secluded spots to be found.

The **Abbey Museum** (07-5495 1652; www.abbeymuseum.com; 63 The Abbey Pl, off Old Toorbul Point Rd, Caboolture; adult/child $12/7, family from $19.80; 10am-4pm Mon-Sat) houses an extraordinary collection of art and archaeology, once the private collection of Englishman 'Reverend' John Ward. The Abbey Medieval Festival is held here in June or July.

The **Caboolture Warplane Museum** (☑ 07-5499 1144; www.cabooolturewarplanemuseum. com; Hangar 104, Caboolture Airfield, McNaught Rd, Caboolture; adult/child/family $10/5/30; ⊙ 9am-3pm) houses a booty of restored WWII planes, including a P51D Mustang, CAC Wirraway and Cessna Bird Dog.

Pick up maps and information at **Bribie Island Visitor Information Centre** (☑ 07-3408 9026; www.tourismbribie.com.au; Benabrow Ave, Bellara; ⊙ 9am-4pm).

🛏 Sleeping & Eating

Bribie Island National Park Camping   CAMPGROUND **$**
(☑ 13 74 68; www.npsr.qld.gov.au/parks/bribie island; camp sites per person/family $6.15/24.60) On the island's west coast, **Poverty Creek** is a large, grassy camping site. Facilities here include toilets, a portable toilet/waste disposal facility and screened cold showers. Just south, **Ocean Beach** offers similar facilities. On the east coast, the **Gallagher Point** camping area harbours a limited number of bush camping sites, with no toilets or other facilities. All three sites are accessible by 4WD.

On The Beach Resort   APARTMENT **$$$**
(☑ 07-3400 1400; www.onthebeachresort.com. au; 9 North St, Woorim; 2-/3-bedroom apt from $215/300; ❄❄) On The Beach out-luxes anything else on the island, with superb service and great facilities, including a saltwater pool and huge sun-deck. Apartments are modern, bright and breezy, with fully equipped kitchens and laundry facilities. There's a four-night minimum stay during the Christmas and Easter holiday periods.

Bribie Island SLSC   PUB FOOD **$$**
(☑ 07-3408 2141; www.thesurfclubbribieisland.com. au; First Ave, Woorim; mains $18-30; ⊙ 11.30am-2.30pm & 5.30pm-late) While the pub grub here won't blow you away, it's tasty enough and comes with a beachside deck for chilled wave-watching sessions. Expect all the surf-club staples, from garlic prawns and beer-battered barramundi to pasta dishes and golden schnitzel.

❶ Getting There & Away

There is no 4WD hire on Bribie, and you'll need a vehicle access permit ($46.25 per week) for the island's more off-track spots. Pick up one at **Gateway Bait & Tackle** (☑ 07-5497 5253; www.gatewaybaitandtackle.com.au; 1383 Bribie Island Rd, Ningi; ⊙ 5.30am-5pm Mon,

DON'T MISS

AUSTRALIA ZOO

Just north of Beerwah is one of Queensland's, if not Australia's, most famous tourist attractions. **Australia Zoo** (☑ 07-5436 2000; www.australiazoo. com.au; 1638 Steve Irwin Way, Beerwah; adult/child/family $59/35/172; ⊙ 9am-5pm) is a fitting homage to its founder, zany wildlife enthusiast Steve Irwin. The park has an amazing menagerie, with a Cambodian-style Tiger Temple, the famous Crocoseum and a dizzying array of critters, including native dingoes, Tasmanian devils and hairy-nosed wombats.

Various companies offer tours from Brisbane and the Sunshine Coast. The zoo operates a free bus to/from the Beerwah train station.

Tue, Thu & Fri, to 2pm Wed, 4.30am-5pm Sat, 4.30am-3pm Sun) or online (www.npsr.qld. gov.au).

Frequent Citytrain services run from Brisbane to Caboolture, from where **Bribie Island Coaches** (☑ 07-3408 2562; www.bribiecoaches.com. au) route 643 runs to Bribie Island via Ningi and Sandstone Point. Buses run roughly every hour, stopping in Bongaree and continuing through to Woorim. Regular Brisbane Translink fares apply (one-way from central Brisbane $11.40).

Glass House Mountains

The breathtaking volcanic plugs of the Glass House Mountains rise abruptly from the subtropical plains 20km northwest of Caboolture. In Dreaming legend, these curious rocky peaks belong to a family of mountain spirits. To British explorer James Cook, their shapes recalled the industrial, conical glass-making furnaces of his native Yorkshire. It's worth diverting off the Bruce Hwy onto the slower Old Gympie Rd to snake your way through dense bush, scattered with old Queenslander shacks and offering arresting views of these spectacular magma intrusions.

The Glass House Mountains National Park is broken into several sections (all within cooee of Beerwah), with picnic grounds and lookouts but no camping grounds. The peaks are reached by a series of sealed and unsealed roads that head inland from Steve Irwin Way, which itself is home to the blockbuster Australia Zoo, founded by the world-famous Crocodile Hunter himself.

Hikers are spoilt for choice here. A number of signposted walking tracks reach several of the peaks, but be prepared for some steep and rocky trails. A new track, the 6km Soldier Settlers Walk, has wonderful views and plants plus a crossing over a recently opened timber bridge. The moderate walk up Ngungun (253m) has sensational views, while Tibrogargan (364m) offers a challenging scramble. The steepish Beerburrum (278m) is also open. Note – at the time of research, the Tibrogargan walk was closed due to rock falls; contact the Glass House Mountains **tourist office** (☑07-5458 8848; www.visitsunshinecoast.com.au; cnr Bruce Pde & Reed St; ◷9am-4pm) for updates.

Rock climbers can usually be seen scaling Tibrogargan and Ngungun. Mt Coonowrin (aka 'crook-neck'), the most dramatic of the volcanic plugs, is closed to the public.

Glass House Mountains Ecolodge (☑07-5493 0008; www.glasshouseecolodge. com; 198 Barrs Rd; r $125-220; ❄🐾🛜) ✎, near Australia Zoo, offers a range of wonderful, good-value sleeping options, including cosy Orchard Rooms ($125), the reformed Church Loft ($220), and converted railway carriages. Mt Tibrogargan can be seen from the gorgeous garden.

The **Glasshouse Mountains Tavern** (www.glasshousemountainstavern.com.au; 10 Reed St; mains $14-32.50; ◷10am-9pm Sun-Thu, to midnight Fri, to 9.30pm Sat, kitchen closes around 8pm) cooks up tasty, no-nonsense pub nosh, including steaks, bangers (sausages), burgers and salads.

Caloundra

POP 77,600

Straddling a headland at the southern end of the Sunshine Coast, Caloundra has shaken off the quaint 'Valium Coast' clichés and reinvented itself as an unexpected centre of cool. Beyond its golden beaches, water sports and beautiful Coastal Pathway walking track is a burgeoning creative scene, spanning everything from top-notch speciality coffee shops and bars to impressive street art and a microbrewery, not to mention the coast's most sharply curated regional art galleries. The cherry on the proverbial cake is the Caloundra Music Festival (p350), one of Queensland's biggest, best-loved annual music events.

◉ Sights & Activities

On Sunday mornings, crowds flock to Bulcock St to browse the market stalls at **Caloundra Street Fair** (www.caloundrastreet fair.com.au; Bulcock St; ◷8am-1pm Sun).

Caloundra Regional Gallery   GALLERY
(☑07-5420 8299; http://gallery.sunshinecoast. qld.gov.au; 22 Omrah Ave; ◷10am-4pm Tue-Fri, to 2pm Sat & Sun) **FREE** When you're done with catching rays and waves, sidestep to this small, sophisticated gallery. Rotating exhibitions showcase quality local and national artists, with a number of outstanding Art Prize shows each year. The gallery stays up late for Friday[3]Live on the third Friday of the month, with music, talks, performances, drinks and bites.

Queensland Air Museum   MUSEUM
(☑07-5492 5930; www.qam.com.au; 7 Pathfinder Dr; adult/child/family $13/7/30; ◷10am-4pm) Occupying two hangars beside Caloundra Airport, the volunteer-run QAM houses circa 70 civilian and military aircraft, including a mid-century Douglas DC-3 (the world's first mass-produced all-metal airliner) and a supersonic F-111 fighter jet belonging to the Royal Australian Air Force. Displays shed light on various aspects of Australian and international aviation history, including wartime battles and women in aviation, and there's a small collection of fabulously retro brochures, cabin bags and in-flight crockery from Australian airlines past and present.

**Mind and Body
PT & Adventures**   HEALTH & FITNESS
(☑0401 286 200; www.mabpersonaltraining. com.au; tours per person (minimum 2) from $199) Sprightly personal trainer Melinda Bingley runs these pulse-racing fitness and adventure tours, which include hiking and kayaking excursions. Among them is a Glass House Mountains Discovery Adventure, which follows the expedition path of early English explorer Matthew Flinders. Running from Golden Beach in Caloundra to Mount Tibrogargan, the six-hour tour includes kayaking, bushwalking, driving and lunch.

Caloundra Surf School   SURFING
(☑0413 381 010; www.caloundrasurfschool.com. au; 1½hr lessons from $50) The pick of the local surf schools, with board hire also available.

Caloundra Jet Ski   OUTDOORS
(☑0434 330 660; www.caloundrajetski.com.au; cnr Esplanade & Otranto Ave) Affable, joke-cracking

Caloundra

N 0 —— 500 m
0 —— 0.25 miles

Caloundra

local Ken Jeffrey owns and operates these thrilling jet-ski tours of the Pumicestone Passage, the narrow waterway separating Caloundra and the northern tip of Bribie Island. Tours offer interesting insight into the area's ecosystem and are suitable for both novice and experienced jet-skiers (even the most nervous newbies will end up zipping across the blue like pros).

Deluxe Kombi Service DRIVING
(☑ 07-5491 5432, 0402 615 126; www.deluxekombi service.com.au; ☺ 1hr tour $77) What better way to explore the area than in a 1960s Kombi with a cool surfer dude? Local Michael Flocke has meticulously restored two rare vans (complete with sunroof and seating for eight), which he uses for insightful, anecdote-rich tours of the town and surrounding region. Book a one-hour town tour or longer, bespoke tours of the Sunshine Coast hinterland.

Sunshine Coast Skydivers SKYDIVING
(☑ 07-5437 0211; www.sunshinecoastskydivers. com.au; Caloundra Aerodrome, Pathfinder Dr; tandem jumps from $279) Send your adrenalin into overdrive as you scan Caloundra and the Pacific Ocean from a brain-squeezing 4570m up (or even just 2130m, if you prefer).

Blue Water Kayak Tours KAYAKING
(☑ 07-5494 7789; www.bluewaterkayaktours. com; half-day tours minimum 4 people $100, twilight tours $55; ☺ half-day tours 8.30am Tue-Sun, twilight tours Wed-Sun) Energetic kayak tours across the channel to the northern tip of

Bribie Island National Park; single and double kayaks are available. All tours must be booked in advance.

🎉 Festivals & Events

Caloundra Music Festival   MUSIC
(www.caloundramusicfestival.com; ⊘Sep-Oct) A four-day, family-friendly music festival held at Kings Beach, with 40,000-strong crowds and a diverse line-up of entertainment, featuring prolific current and veteran Australian rock and indie pop acts, as well as international guests.

🛏 Sleeping & Eating

Dicky Beach
Family Holiday Park   CARAVAN PARK $
(☑07-5491 3342; www.sunshinecoastholidayparks.com.au; 4 Beerburrum St; powered/unpowered site $46/41, cabins from $118; ❄🏵🐾) You can't get any closer to Dicky, one of Caloundra's most popular beaches. The brick cabins are as ordered and tidy as the grounds and there's a small swimming pool for the kids.

Caloundra Backpackers   HOSTEL $
(☑07-5499 7655; www.caloundrabackpackers.com.au; 84 Omrah Ave; dm from $26, d with/without bathroom from $75/60; 🐾) Caloundra's only hostel is a no-nonsense budget option with a sociable courtyard, book exchange, and weekly BBQ, pizza and wine-and-cheese nights. Dorms won't inspire, but they're clean and peaceful.

Monaco   APARTMENT $$
(☑07-5490 5490; www.monacocaloundra.com.au; 12 Otranto Ave; 1-/2-/3-bedroom apt from $159/240/329; 🅿❄🐾🏊) Modern, good-sized apartments one block from Bulcock Beach. Apartments are individually owned, so styles vary; the more expensive apartments offer full water vistas. Wi-fi is free but capped, and apartments are serviced every eight days. Property perks include a stylish, heated lap pool, separate kids' pool, spa, sauna, gym and games rooms. Minimum two-night stay, with cheaper rates for longer stays.

Rumba Resort   RESORT $$$
(☑07-5492 0555; www.rumbaresort.com.au; 10 Leeding Tce; r from $200; ❄🐾🏊) This sparkling, resort-white playground is the slickest slumber pad in town. Studio rooms are light, spacious and modern, each with two-person jacuzzi, home-theatre system and espresso machine. The pool area is worthy of a photo shoot and flanked by one of Caloundra's coolest new bars. Easy walking access to beachfront eateries, to boot.

★Baci Gelati   GELATO $
(49 Bulcock St; gelato from $4.50; ⊘9am-5pm Mon-Fri, 9.30am-5pm Sat, 10am-4pm Sun) Baci scoops out some of the best gelati in Queensland, made by an Italian expat, his Hungarian wife and a fellow Italian mate. The secret: top-quality ingredients, from fresh fruit and Bronte pistachios to Belgian chocolate and local Maleny milk. Creative flavours include ginger beer, chai, salted caramel and an extraordinary Sicilian hazelnut. Take-home packs are available (0.5/1L $12/23).

Stormie D's Cupcakery   BAKERY $
(☑07-5491 5812; www.stormiedscupcakery.com.au; 17a Bulcock St; mini/regular cupcakes $2.50/4.80; ⊘10am-4pm Mon-Fri, 9am-1pm Sat) Stormie Dutton could easily front an indie rock group, but she's too busy baking in her pink sugar temple. Her cupcakes are local legends, selling out quickly and offered in combos like strawberries and cream and orange with cranberry and pistachio. Be reckless and order the salted caramel milkshake, which comes with pretzels stuck to the rim with Nutella.

Green House Cafe   VEGETARIAN $
(☑07-5438 1647; www.greenhousecafe.com.au; 5/8 Orumuz Ave; mains $13-17; ⊘8am-3pm Mon-Fri, to 2pm Sat & Sun; 🌿) A showcase for local ingredients, this chilled, light-filled laneway spot serves up fresh, organic and filling vegetarian grub such as avocado on toast with cashew cheese, *shakshouka* (spiced, poached) eggs and *nasi goreng* (spiced fried rice). For a serious health kick, down a smoothie with kale and seasonal greens paired with banana, coconut-milk yoghurt, kiwi, chia seeds, coconut water and super-greens powder. Mama will approve.

Cptn   INTERNATIONAL $$
(☑07-5341 8475; www.cptnkingsbeach.com.au; 1/8 Levuka Ave, Kings Beach; mains lunch $18-29, dinner $26-29; ⊘6am-6pm Mon-Thu, to 9.30pm Fri-Sun, kitchen to 3pm Mon-Thu, to 8pm Fri-Sun; 🐾) Beachside Cptn beats the competition with its crisp, contemporary fit-out and beautiful, honest nosh. Don't expect culinary acrobatics, just well-executed, thoughtful dishes like barramundi fish and chips, grilled halloumi with roasted vegetables, or grilled chicken breast with mixed Mediterranean vegetables, roast potatoes, goats cheese and red-wine

jus. Good coffee, well-priced wines by the glass and a young, friendly team.

Drinking & Nightlife

Lamkin Lane Espresso Bar   CAFE
(www.facebook.com/lamkinlane; 31 Lamkin Lane; ☺6am-4pm Mon-Fri, 7am-noon Sat & Sun) The hearts of coffee snobs will sing at Lamkin Lane, where affable, knowledgeable baristas like nothing better than chatting about the week's pair of special blends and trio of single-origins. The team here have a strong relationship with their coffee farmers, which means your brew is as ethical as it is smooth and aromatic. Cash only.

**Moffat Beach
Brewing Company**   MICROBREWERY
(☑07-5491 4023; 12 Seaview Tce, Moffat Beach; ☺7am-4pm Mon & Tue, to late Wed-Sat, to 8pm Sun) Just up from hipster-staple Moffat Beach, this cafe-cum-microbrewery has both guest and house brews on tap (look out for the cult-status double IPA Iggy Hop). Bottled beers span Oz and the globe; the four-brew paddle ($20) will help the indecisive. Nod away to live tunes on Fridays from 5pm and on weekends from 3pm (the latter sessions are especially pumping).

26 Degrees   COCKTAIL BAR
(☑07-5492 0555; www.facebook.com/26degrees Bar; 10 Leeding Tce, Rumba Beach Resort; ☺10am-late; ☞) Twenty-six degrees is both the average temperature in Caloundra and the town's degree of latitude – it's now also one of Caloundra's most fashionable spots to imbibe. Located inside the Rumba Resort, the poolside bar is a beach-chic affair, with white louvres, whitewashed timber bar and lush green foliage. Dirty martini lovers will appreciate its funky version, made with marinated olives.

ⓘ Information

Sunshine Coast Visitor Centre (☑07-5458 8846; www.visitsunshinecoast.com; 7 Caloundra Rd; ☺9am-4pm Mon-Fri, to 3pm Sat & Sun; ☞) On the roundabout at the town's entrance; there's also a centrally located kiosk on **Bulcock Street** (☑07-5458 8847; www.visitsunshine coast.com; 77 Bulcock St; ☺9am-3pm; ☞). Both branches offer free wi-fi.

ⓘ Getting There & Away

Greyhound Australia (☑1300 473 946; www.greyhound.com.au) buses run one daily morning service from Brisbane to Noosa,

stopping in Caloundra (from $19, two hours) en route. There is also one morning service to Brisbane.

Sunbus (TransLink; ☑13 12 30; www.sunbus. com.au) has frequent services to Maroochydore ($5.70, one hour). Transfer in Maroochydore for buses to Noosa.

The **Caloundra Transit Centre** (23 Cooma Tce) is the main bus station for both long-distance and local buses, located a quick walk south of Bulcock St. (At the time of research the building itself was closed, though buses continue to stop here.)

Mooloolaba & Maroochydore

POP 12,550 & 18,300

Mooloolaba has seduced many with its sublime climate, golden beach and laid-back lifestyle. Eateries, boutiques and pockets of resorts and apartments have spread along Mooloolaba Esplanade, transforming this once-humble fishing village into one of Queensland's most popular destinations.

Further north, booming Maroochydore takes care of the business end, with a brandnew city centre under construction and a string of buzzing eateries, as well as its own stretch of sandy beachfront.

◉ Sights & Activities

Sea Life Sunshine Coast   AQUARIUM
(Map p352; ☑1800 618 021; www.underwaterworld.com.au; Wharf Marina, Parkyn Pde, Mooloolaba; adult/child/family $39/26/130; ☺9am-5pm) Kids will love this popular tropical oceanarium, complete with an 80m-long transparent underwater tunnel for close-up views of rays, reef fish and eight species of shark. There's a touch tank, live shows, presentations and – during school holidays – the option of sleeping at the aquarium overnight ($90 per person).

While visitors can also swim with seals and dive with sharks, it's worth considering that animal-welfare groups believe captivity is debilitating and stressful for marine animals and exacerbated by human interaction.

Wildlife HQ   ZOO
(☑0428 660 671; www.whqzoo.com; adult/child/family $29/15/79; ☺9am-4pm) Located at the **Big Pineapple** (www.bigpineapple.com.au; 76 Nambour Connection Rd, Woombye) FREE, this 8-hectare zoo houses native Australian, African, South American and rare Asian critters, among them red pandas and tahrs (Himalayan mountain goats).

Mooloolaba

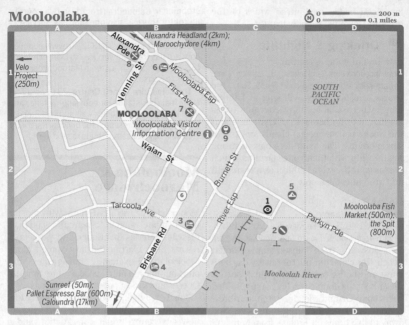

Sunreef DIVING
(Map p352; ☎ 07-5444 5656; www.sunreef.com.au; Wharf Marina, Parkyn Pde, Mooloolaba; dives from $165; ⊙ 8am-5pm Mon-Sat, to 4pm Sun) Offers two dives (from $165) on the wreck of sunken warship HMAS *Brisbane*. Also runs a day trip to Flinders Reef (from $229), including two dives, equipment, lunch and snacks. A PADI Open Water Diver course is $495.

Hire Hut WATER SPORTS
(Map p352; ☎ 07-5444 0366; www.hirehut.com.au; Wharf, Parkyn Pde, Mooloolaba) Hires out kayaks (two hours $25), giant stand-up paddle boards (two hours $350, up to 10 people per board), jet skis (one hour $180) and boats

(per hour/half-day from $42/75). Also hires out bicycles (two/four hours $19/25).

Robbie Sherwell's XL Surfing Academy SURFING
(☎ 07-5478 1337, 0423 039 505; www.xlsurfing academy.com; 1hr private/group lessons $95/45) Dip a toe into Aussie surf culture at this long-established school, which caters to all levels, from rookie to advanced.

☞ Tours

Coastal Cruises Mooloolaba CRUISE
(Map p352; ☎ 0419 704 797; www.cruisemooloolaba. com.au; Wharf Marina, Parkyn Pde, Mooloolaba) Sunset ($25) and seafood lunch cruises ($35)

through Mooloolaba Harbour, the river and canals.

Whale One
WILDLIFE

(Map p352; ☑1300 942 531; www.whaleone. com.au; Wharf Marina, Parkyn Pde, Mooloolaba; whale-watching tours adult/child/family $59/39/196) Between June and November, Whale One runs cruises that get you close to the spectacular acrobatic displays of humpback whales, which migrate north from Antarctica to mate and give birth.

✯✯ Festivals & Events

Big Pineapple Music Festival
MUSIC

(www.bigpineapplemusicfestival.com; ◎May) The one-day 'Piney Festival' is one of the region's top music events, with four stages showcasing titans of the current Aussie music scene. Past acts have included alternative rockers John Butler Trio and Birds of Tokyo, alt-electronica acts Rüfüs and Hermitude, and even Brisbane's own progressive-pop twins The Veronicas. Camp sites are available and sell out quickly.

Maroochy Music
& Visual Arts Festival
MUSIC

(www.mmvaf.com; ◎Sep; ☞) Headliners at this annual, one-day fest in Maroochydore have included of-the-moment Australian music acts Peking Duk and Matt Corby; alt-indie talent such as Boo Seeka, George Maple and Ngaiire have also taken the stage. The visual-arts side of the fest includes specially commissioned works from local and international artists.

🛏 Sleeping & Eating

Cotton Tree Holiday Park
CAMPGROUND $

(Map p354; ☑07-5459 9070; www.sunshinecoast holidayparks.com.au; Cotton Tree Pde, Cotton Tree, Maroochydore; powered/unpowered sites from $48/41, villas from $157) In Cotton Tree, a popular area of Maroochydore, this holiday park enjoys direct access to the beach and Maroochy River.

Mooloolaba Beach
Caravan Park
CARAVAN PARK $

(Map p352; ☑07-5444 1201; www.sunshinecoast holidayparks.com.au; Parkyn Pde, Mooloolaba; powered sites from $42) The park runs two sites: one fronting the lovely Mooloolaba Beach, and a smaller one at the northern end of the Esplanade, with the best location and views of any accommodation in town.

Mooloolaba Beach Backpackers
HOSTEL $

(Map p352; ☑07-5444 3399; www.mooloolaba backpackers.com; 75 Brisbane Rd, Mooloolaba; dm with/without bathroom $34/30, d $75; ☞❄☎) Some dorms have en suites, and although the rooms are a little drab, the number of freebies (bikes, surfboards, stand-up paddleboards and breakfast) more than compensates. Besides, it's only 500m from beachside activities and nightlife.

Dockside Apartments
APARTMENT $$

(Map p352; ☑07-5478 2044; www.dockside mooloolaba.com.au; 50 Burnett St, Mooloolaba; 2-/3-bedroom apt from $290/375; ☞❄☎☎) While the fully equipped apartments here are all different (all are privately owned and rented out), each is neat, clean and comfortable. The property sits in a quiet spot away from the hubbub, but is an easy walk from Mooloolaba's main restaurant and bar strip, surf club, beach and wharf precinct. Discounted rates for longer stays.

Maroochydore Beach Motel
MOTEL $$

(Map p354; ☑07-5443 7355; www.maroochydore beachmotel.com; 69 Sixth Ave, Maroochydore; s/d/f from $120/135/180; ☞❄☎☎) A quirky, spotless, themed motel with 18 different rooms, including the Elvis Room (naturally), the Egyptian Room, and the Aussie Room (complete with toy wombat). Although on a main road, it's less than a 200m walk to the beach.

★Oceans
RESORT $$$

(Map p352; ☑07-5444 5777; www.oceansmooloolaba. com.au; 101-105 Mooloolaba Esplanade, Mooloolaba; 2-bedroom apt from $500; ☞❄☎☎) Cascading water and contemporary art greet guests at this upmarket apartment resort directly across from the beach. Ocean views are de rigueur in the apartments, which are sleek and immaculately clean, with Nespresso machines, stand-alone spa and quality appliances. Apartments are serviced daily and there are also adults' and children's pools, a gym and a sauna. Parking and wi-fi are free.

★Velo Project
CAFE $

(☑07-5444 8693; www.theveloproject.com.au; 19 Careela St, Mooloolaba; dishes $6-22.50; ◎7am-2pm; ☞) In-the-know Velo sits on a Mooloolaba side street. A mishmash of recycled furniture and vintage ephemera, it's an easy, breezy affair, where locals play retro board games while munching on smashed avo with red onion, roasted garlic, corn and fresh herbs, or house-made toasted banana, macadamia and date bread with mascarpone and

Maroochydore

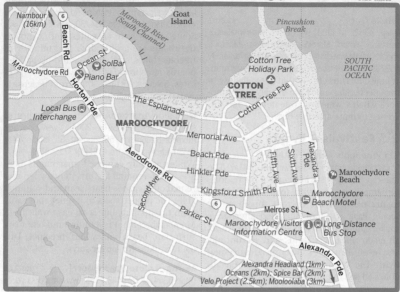

an orange-cardamom syrup. Great, locally roasted coffee, too.

Good Bar
AMERICAN $

(Map p352; ☑ 07-5477 6781; www.thegoodbar. com.au; 5/19-23 First Ave, Mooloolaba; burgers $12-20, hot dogs $12-16; ☺ 11am-late Tue-Sun, kitchen closes 10.30pm) Clad in concrete floors and red-and-black tiles, trendy Good Bar serves quality American grub, including succulent burgers and epic *haute dawgs* with combos like house-smoked Weiner with Asian slaw, peanuts, crispy noodles and *nam jim* (dipping sauce). Other standouts include a 20-hour smoked Cape Grim brisket. There's a French-Mex breakfast menu on weekends, plus craft spirits and beers behind the bar.

Piano Bar
MEDITERRANEAN $$

(Map p354; ☑ 0422 291 249; www.thepianobar. com.au; 22-24 Ocean St, Maroochydore; bar snacks $4-9, tapas $9-20; ☺ 5-10pm Mon & Tue, to 11pm Wed & Thu, noon-11pm Fri-Sun) Bohemian down to its tasselled lampshades, Liberace tomes and fedora-clad barkeeps, Piano Bar peddles generously sized, pan-Mediterranean tapas (order one or two at a time). The charred marinated octopus is pillow-soft, while the glazed beetroot with feta is beautifully textured. Less ubiquitous wine varietals and

live blues, funk or jazz Wednesday to Monday seal the deal.

★ Spice Bar
FUSION $$$

(Map p352; ☑ 07-5444 2022; www.spicebar.com. au; 1st fl, 123 Mooloolaba Esplanade, Mooloolaba; small plates $7-18, large plates $28-36; ☺ 6pm-late Tue, noon-3pm & 6pm-late Wed-Sun) Local gourmands swoon over this slick, contemporary eatery dishing up superb Asian-fusion fare. The menu is a share-plates affair, with options ranging from Hervey Bay scallops with a soy-ginger *sabayon* to butter-soft beef cheek *rendang* (curry) with sweet potato, snake beans and curry leaf. For the best experience, opt for one of the fantastic degustation menus (five/seven/10 courses $55/75/90).

Char
STEAK, SEAFOOD $$$

(Map p352; ☑ 07-5477 7205; www.charmooloolaba. com.au; 19 First Ave, Mooloolaba; mains $29-91; ☺ 5-9pm) Char is owned and proudly run by ex-Melburnian Brett Symons, who wanted to create a restaurant he would personally eat in. It's a smart yet relaxed space, with crisp white linen, tealights and a menu of simple yet elegant dishes. The secret? Top-tier produce, from ridiculously fresh Australian oysters to Wagyu beef from Cape Grim in northwest Tasmania. Book ahead.

Drinking & Nightlife

Pallet Espresso Bar   COFFEE
(☑ 0487 342 172; www.facebook.com/thepallet
espressobar; 2/161-163 Brisbane Rd, Mooloolaba;
☺ 6.30am-3pm Mon-Fri, to 1pm Sat) You'll find
(upcycled) pallets here, along with chatty
locals, a communal table and a couple of
soccer balls, in case you feel the urge to
have a kick on the lawn. Not a lot of food
options (think raisin toast and some sweet
baked treats), but what it does do well is
full-bodied, velvety, espresso-based coffee.
Just off Brisbane Rd.

Taps@Mooloolaba   BAR
(Map p352; ☑ 07-5477 7222; www.tapsaustralia.
com.au; cnr Esplanade & Brisbane Rd, Mooloolaba;
☺ noon-late) A beer fiend's nirvana, Taps lets
you pull your own suds. Seriously. It may
sound gimmicky, but it's serious business:
there are around 20 craft and other brews to
quench the most serious of post-surf thirsts.
Beer-friendly bites include cream-cheese-
stuffed jalapeños, burgers, loaded fries and
a taco salad.

SolBar   CLUB
(Map p354; ☑ 07-5443 9550; www.solbar.com.
au; 10/12-20 Ocean St, Maroochydore; ☺ 7.30am-
late) SolBar is a godsend for city-starved
indie fans. A constantly surprising line-up
takes to the stage here, and budding singer-
songwriters can try their own luck at the
open-mic night on Wednesdays. The venue
doubles as a swinging cafe-bar-restaurant,
serving everything from smashed avo,
pancakes and zucchini-and-corn fritters at
brekkie to lunch and dinner grub such as
burgers, pizzas and salads.

❶ Information

The **Mooloolaba Visitor Information Centre**
(Map p352; ☑ 07-5458 8844; www.visitsun
shinecoast.com.au; cnr Brisbane Rd & First
Ave, Mooloolaba; ☺ 9am-3pm; ☎) is located
a block away from the Esplande in the heart of
town. The **Maroochydore Visitor Information
Centre** (Map p354; ☑ 07-5458 8842; www.
visitsunshinecoast.com.au; cnr Sixth Ave &
Melrose St, Maroochydore; ☺ 9am-4pm Mon-
Fri, to 3pm Sat & Sun; ☎) also lies one block
from the beach.

Further north in Marcoola, Sunshine Coast
Airport also houses a **tourist information centre**
(☑ 07-5448 9088; www.visitsunshinecoast.com.

au; Sunshine Coast Airport, Friendship Dr, Mar-
coola; ☺ 9am-3pm).

❶ Getting There & Away

AIR

Sunshine Coast Airport (p303) Gateway
airport for the Sunshine Coast, with direct daily
flights to Sydney and Melbourne and thrice-
weekly direct flights to Adelaide. Seasonal
nonstop flights to Auckland, New Zealand.

BUS

Long-distance buses (Map p352) stop in front
of the Sunshine Coast Visitor Information Cen-
tre in Maroochydore and beside Underwater
World – Sea Life in Mooloolaba. **Greyhound**
(☑ 1300 473 946; www.greyhound.com.au)
buses stop in both Maroochydore and in Mool-
oolaba, running several times daily to Brisbane
(one-way departing Mooloolaba/Maroochydore
from $21/22, around two hours). **Premier
Motor Services** (☑ 13 34 10; www.premierms.
com.au) runs buses once daily to and from
Brisbane (one-way $23, 1½ to 1¾ hours).

Sunbus (TransLink; ☑ 13 12 30; www.sunbus.
com.au) has frequent services between Mool-
oolaba and Maroochydore ($4.60, 15 minutes)
and on to Noosa ($8.60, one to 1½ hours). The
local bus interchange (Map p352; Horton Pde,
Maroochydore) is at Sunshine Plaza shopping
centre.

Coolum

POP 7905

Rocky headlands create a number of seclud-
ed coves before spilling into the fabulously
long stretch of golden sand and rolling surf
of Coolum Beach. Like much of the coast
along here, the backdrop is spreading subur-
bia, but thanks to a reasonable cafe society
and easy access to the coast's hot spots, it's
a useful escape from the more popular and
overcrowded holiday scenes at Noosa, Mool-
oolaba and Maroochydore.

🏃 Activities

Skydive Ramblers (☑ 07-5448 8877; www.sky
diveforfun.com; Sunshine Coast Airport, Kittyhawk
Cl, Marcoola; jump from 1830/4570m $299/429)
will throw you out of a plane at a ridiculous
height. Soak up the coastal view before a
spectacular beach landing.

Coolum Surf School (☑ 0438 731 503; www.
coolumsurfschool.com.au; 2hr lesson $60, 5-lesson
package $225) will have you riding the waves in
no time with surfing lessons; it also hires out
surfboards/bodyboards ($50/25 for 24 hours).

🛏 Sleeping & Eating

Coolum Beach Caravan Park   CARAVAN PARK $
(📞 07-5446 1474; www.sunshinecoastholidayparks.com.au; 1827 David Low Way, Coolum Beach; powered sites $46, cabins from $157; 🐾) Location, location, location: the park not only has absolute beach frontage, but is also just across the road from Coolum's main strip.

Villa Coolum   MOTEL $
(📞 07-5446 1286; www.villacoolum.com; 102 Coolum Tce, Coolum Beach; 1-bedroom units $99-159, 2-bedroom units $129-180; 🐾❄️) Hidden behind a verandah, these good-value '70s-style units offer a warm, friendly welcome. While they show signs of wear and tear, they're spacious and upbeat, with tropical accents and comfy beds. Adding appeal is a pool, pleasant garden and walking distance to one of the area's in-the-know beaches, First Bay.

Element on Coolum Beach   APARTMENT $$$
(📞 07-5455 1777; www.elementoncoolumbeach.com.au; 1808 David Low Way, Coolum Beach; 1-2-3-bedroom apt from $224/230/359; P❄️🐾❄️) Coolum Beach's smartest slumber spot, with heated pool, central location and 49 huge, stylish apartments. Each apartment is individually owned, so interiors will vary. That said, you can expect spotless, fully equipped, contemporary digs in soothing neutral tones, with full-sized kitchens, tall windows and balconies. Rates come down for week-long stays.

The Caf   CAFE $
(📞 07-5446 3564; www.thecafcoolum.com; 21 Birtwill St, Coolum Beach; mains $14-19; ⊙ 6.30am-4pm; 🐾) Complete with cable-reel-turned-table, cockatoo wallpaper and laid-back vibe, this is arguably Coolum's coolest little cafe. The place whips up great gourmet salads and sandwiches, pies, fresh juices and feel-good smoothies.

Castro's Bar & Restaurant   ITALIAN, MODERN AUSTRALIAN $$
(📞 07-5471 7555; cnr Frank St & Beach Rd, Coolum Beach; pizzas $21-26, mains $24-34; ⊙ 5-8.30pm Mon-Thu, to 9pm Fri & Sat, to 8pm Sun) Not even vaguely Cuban, but this popular, casual spot does enjoy a Fidel-like longevity thanks to its mouth-watering menu. Tuck into satisfying wood-fired pizzas, gorgeous risottos (if it's available, order the sweetcorn, pumpkin, chicken and caramelised onion option), or surrender to Castro's smashing, slow-cooked confit duck, wood-fired and served with golden roast potatoes and poached pear stuffed with date chutney.

Peregian Beach & Sunshine Beach
POP 3530 & 2290

Fifteen kilometres of uncrowded, unobstructed beach stretch north from Coolum to Sunshine Beach and the rocky northeast headland of Noosa National Park.

Peregian is the place to indulge in long, solitary beach walks, surfing excellent breaks, and the not-so-uncommon spotting of whales breaking offshore. Locals will tell you that the place is popular with 'yummy mummies' catching up at breezy local cafes with strollers and yoga mats in tow.

A little further north, the laid-back-latte ethos of Sunshine Beach attracts Noosa locals and surfies escaping the summer hordes. Beach walks morph into bush trails over the headland; a stroll through the Noosa National Park takes an hour to reach Alexandria Bay and two hours to Noosa's Laguna Bay. Road access to the park is from McAnally Dr or Parkedge Rd.

🍴 Eating & Drinking

Le Bon Delice   CAFE $
(📞 07-5471 2200; www.lebondelice.com.au; cnr Heron St & David Low Way, Peregian Beach; cakes from $3, meals $9-14; ⊙ 7am-4pm Mon & Wed-Sat, to 3pm Sun) From the *mille feuille* (French vanilla slice), tarts and pillowy mousse cakes to the *dacquoises* (a dessert cake made with almond and hazlenut meringue) and eclairs, the calorific concoctions from French-born owner and *pâtissier* Jean Jacques at this corner patisserie are as beautiful to look at as they are to devour. If you're hankering for something savoury, nibble on the quiche. Also opens on Tuesdays during the school holidays.

Hand of Fatima   CAFE $$
(📞 0434 364 328; www.facebook.com/handoffatimacafe; 2/4 Kingfisher Dr, Peregian Beach; mains $17-18.50; ⊙ 5.30am-2.30pm) A friendly, lo-fi cafe where barefoot beach-goers banter with the staff while waiting for their impeccable macchiatos. In one corner is the tiny open kitchen, pumping out Middle Eastern–inspired dishes like breakfast Persian rice pudding with roasted fruits and nuts, or lunchtime braised *cotechino* (pork) sausage with lentils, caramelised onion and Turkish bread. Cash only.

★**Embassy XO**   CHINESE **$$$**
(☑ 07-5455 4460; www.embassyxo.com.au; 56 Duke St, Sunshine Beach; mains $29-42; ☺ restaurant 6-9pm Wed-Sun, also noon-2pm Fri & Sat, noon-3pm Sun, bar menu 3-6pm Wed-Sun) Smart, sophisticated Embassy XO is not your average suburban Chinese joint. Local produce drives smashing Asian dishes like Hinterland zucchini flowers stuffed with tofu and Sichuan chilli caramel and Moreton Bay bug wontons with *tobiko* (flying fish roe) and coconut miso bisque. Other options include gorgeous banquets (vegetarian/nonvegetarian $55/80), yum cha lunch Friday to Sunday and moreish bar snacks from 3pm to 6pm.

Pitchfork   MODERN AUSTRALIAN **$$$**
(☑ 07-5471 3697; www.pitchforkrestaurant.com. au; 5/4 Kingfisher Dr, Peregian Beach; mains $32-45; ☺ noon-2pm & 5pm-late Tue-Sun) The award-winning chefs at this bright, summery restaurant pump out a concise, contemporary menu where crispy soft-shell crab might get fresh peppercorn *nam jim* and green apple, or where roasted pork belly goes sultry in a smoked pork *jus*. Allow time for a meal here: sip on an Italian *soave* and soak up the action on the lush, green square.

Marble Bar Bistro   BAR
(☑ 07-5455 3200; www.marblebarbistro.com; 40 Duke St, Sunshine Beach; ☺ noon-9pm Sun-Thu, to midnight Fri & Sat; ☎) Kick back in a cushioned lounge or perch at one of the concrete bar tables at this sheltered, alfresco bar. Bites include hit-and-miss tapas ($8 to $22.50) and pizzas ($17.50 to $18.50), though the place is best for a toast rather than a memorable feed.

Cooloola Coast

Stretching for 50km between Noosa and Rainbow Beach, the Cooloola Coast is a remote strip of long sandy beach backed by the Cooloola Section of the Great Sandy National Park. Although it's undeveloped, the 4WD and tin-boat set flock here in droves, so it's not always as peaceful as you might imagine. If you head off on foot or by canoe along one of the many inlets or waterways, however, you'll soon escape the crowds. The coast is famous for the Teewah coloured sand cliffs, estimated to be about 40,000 years young.

Great Sandy National Park: Cooloola Section

Extending from Lake Cootharaba north to Rainbow Beach, this 54,000-hectare section of national park offers wide ocean beaches, soaring cliffs of richly coloured sands, pristine bushland, heathland, mangroves and rainforest, all of which are rich in bird life, including rarities such as the red goshawk and the grass owl. One of the most extraordinary experiences here is driving along the beach from Noosa North Shore to Double Island Point, around 50km to the north.

The route is only accessible to 4WDs with a vehicle permit (available from www. npsr.qld.gov.au) and forms part of the Great Beach Drive, a spectacular coastal touring route linking Noosa and Hervey Bay. At Double Island Point, a 1.1km-long walking trail leads up to spectacular ocean views and a lighthouse dating back to 1884. From June to October, it's also a prime place for spotting majestic humpback whales.

From the Double Island Point section of the beach, a 4WD track cuts across the point to the edge of a large tidal lake (perfect for kids and less-confident swimmers) and then along Rainbow Beach to the town of Rainbow Beach, passing along the way spectacular coloured cliffs made of ancient, richly oxidised sands in over 70 earthy shades. According to local Indigenous legend, the sands obtained their hues when Yiningie (a spirit represented by a rainbow) plunged into the cliffs after fighting an evil tribesman. The black sand is rutile, once locally mined to make titanium for American space technology.

    Great Beach Drive 4WD Tours (☑ 07-5486 3131; www.greatbeachdrive4wdtours.com; full-day tour adult/child/family $165/95/475) offers intimate, eco-centric 4WD tours of the spectacular Great Beach Drive from Noosa to Rainbow Beach. **Epic Ocean Adventures** (☑ 0408 738 192; www.epicoceanadventures.com. au; 1/6 Rainbow Beach Rd, Rainbow Beach; 3hr surfing/kayaking trip $65/75; ☺ shop 8am-5pm) runs adventure tours departing both Rainbow Beach and Noosa, and including dolphin- and turtle-spotting kayaking trips.

Hoof it along the beach with **Rainbow Beach Horse Rides** (☑ 0412 174 337; www. rainbowbeachhorserides.com.au; Clarkson Dr, Rainbow Beach; 90min beach ride $140), including an evocative, two-hour Full Moon Ride ($200).

WOODSTOCK DOWNUNDER

The famous **Woodford Folk Festival** (www.woodfordfolkfestival.com; ☉ Dec/Jan) features a huge diversity of over 2000 national and international performers playing folk, traditional Irish, Indigenous and world music, as well as buskers, belly dancers, craft markets, visual-arts performances, environmental talks and Tibetan monks. The festival is held on a property near the town of Woodford from 27 December to 1 January each year. Camping grounds are set up on-site with toilets, showers and a range of foodie marquees, but prepare for a mud bath if it rains. The festival is licensed, so leave your booze at home. Tickets cost $137 per day ($168 with camping) and can be bought online or at the gate. Check online for updated programs.

Woodford is 35km northwest of Caboolture. Shuttle buses run regularly from the Caboolture train station to and from the festival grounds.

The most popular (and best-equipped) **camping grounds** (☑13 74 68; www.npsr.qld. gov.au; sites per person/family $6.15/24.60) are Fig Tree Point (at the northern end of Lake Cootharaba), Harry's Hut (about 4km upstream) and Freshwater (about 6km south of Double Island Point) on the coast. You can also camp at designated zones on the beach if you're driving up to Rainbow Beach.

Rainbow Beach Ultimate Camping (☑07-5486 8633; www.rainbow-beach-hire-a-camp.com.au; 2-/3-/5-night camping experience for 1-4 people from $580/690/820) takes all the hard work out of camping by providing most of the equipment and setting it up for you, from the tent, mattresses, stretchers and crockery, to the dining table, BBQ, private toilet and shower.

For park information, contact the **QPWS Great Sandy Information Centre** (☑07-5449 7792; 240 Moorindil St, Tewantin; ☉8am-4pm).

Lake Cooroibah

A couple of kilometres north of Tewantin, the Noosa River widens into Lake Cooroibah. Surrounded by lush bushland, the glassy lake feels a world away from the bustle of Noosa and makes for a soothing day trip.

From the end of Moorindil St in Tewantin, cash-only **Noosa North Shore Ferries** (☑07-5447 1321; www.noosanorthshoreferries.com. au; one-way per pedestrian/car $1/7; ☉5.30am-10.20pm Sun-Thu, to 12.20am Fri & Sat) shuttles across the river to Noosa North Shore. Ferries depart roughly every 10 minutes.

The refreshingly feral **Gagaju Bush Camp** (☑07-5474 3522; http://gagaju.tripod.com; 118 Johns Rd, Cooroibah; dm $15; @) is a riverside eco-wilderness camp with basic dorms constructed out of recycled timber.

Noosa North Shore Retreat (☑07-5447 1225; www.noosanorthshoreretreat.com.au; Beach Rd, Noosa North Shore; powered/unpowered camp sites from $42/32, cottages/r from $170/220; ✳@✼) has everything from camping and vinyl 'village tents' to shiny motel rooms and cottages, and the Great Sandy Bar & Restaurant (mains $19 to $28).

Lake Cootharaba & Boreen Point

Cootharaba is the largest lake in the Cooloola Section of Great Sandy National Park, measuring about 5km across and 10km in length. On the western shores of the lake and at the southern edge of the national park, Boreen Point is a relaxed little community and home to one of Queensland's oldest and most atmospheric pubs. The lake is the gateway to the glassy Noosa Everglades, which lure with the offer of bushwalking, canoeing and bush camping.

From Boreen Point, a road leads another 5km to Elanda Point (unsealed for half the way).

Kanu Kapers (☑07-5485 3328; www.kanu kapersaustralia.com; 11 Toolara St, Boreen Point; guided tour adult/child from $155/80, 2-/3-day kayaking & camping tour $395/595) offers fantastic half-day and full-day guided tours of the Noosa Everglades, as well as two- and three-day kayaking and camping adventures to Cooloola National Park. Self-guided tours are also available.

On Lake Cootharaba, stunning little **Boreen Point Camping Ground** (☑07-5485 3244; www.noosaholidayparks.com.au; Esplanade, Boreen Point; powered/unpowered sites from $31/25) is crowd-free and provides your own secluded patch of lake-front, native bush.

Framed by palms, jacarandas, quandong trees and the odd bush turkey, the adorable

old **Apollonian Hotel** (☑07-5485 3100; www.
apollonianhotel.com.au; 19 Laguna St, Boreen Point;
mains $18-28; ⊙ kitchen 10am-8pm Sun-Thu, to
10pm Fri & Sat, bar 10am-10pm Sun-Thu, to midnight
Fri & Sat; 🐾) – complete with shady verandahs
and a beautifully preserved interior – dates
back to the late 19th century. It's famous for
its Sunday spit-roast lunch.

Eumundi

POP 3560

Adorable Eumundi is a quaint highland
village with a quirky New Age vibe that's
greatly amplified during its famous market
days. Fig trees, weatherboard pubs and tin-
roof cottages line its historic streetscape,
which is dotted with cafes, galleries, eclectic
boutiques and crafty folk.

Eumundi Markets (☑07-5442 7106; www.
eumundimarkets.com.au; 80 Memorial Dr; ⊙8am-
1.30pm Wed, 7am-2pm Sat) is one of Australia's
most famous and atmospheric artisan markets, attracting over 1.6 million visitors a year
to its 600-plus stalls. Dive into a leafy, bohemian wonderland of hand-crafted furniture,
jewellery, clothing and accessories, art, fresh
local produce, gourmet provisions and more.

The shamelessly charming **Majestic Theatre** (☑07-5485 2330; www.themajestictheatre.
com.au; 3 Factory St, Pomona; tickets adult/child
$14/7; ⊙screening 7.30pm Tue-Fri), in Pomona,
10km northwest of Eumundi, is Australia's
longest-running commercial theatre. The
venue screens films from the silent era
around four to 12 times a month.

Book lovers should check out **Berkelouw
Books** (☑07-5442 8366; www.facebook.com/
BerkelouwBooksEumundi; 87 Memorial Dr; ⊙9am-
5pm Mon, Tue, Thu & Fri, 8am-5pm Wed & Sat, 9am-
4pm Sun), packed with fascinating new, rare
and secondhand books.

Internationally renowned surfboard shap-
er **Tom Wegener** (www.tomwegenersurfboards.
com; Cooroy) offers homestays where you can
spend a day or two learning about the craft
of surfboard shaping. (You can also have him
make a board for you.) The homestay costs
$500 per day (excluding materials) and in-
cludes eight hours in the studio, plus meals
and surfing sessions.

🛏 Sleeping & Eating

Harmony Hill Station　　　　B&B $$
(☑0418 750 643, 07-5442 8685; www.harmony
hillaccom.com.au; 81 Seib Rd; carriages from $145,
lodge per night $550; 🐾) Perched on a hilltop

in a 5-hectare property, Harmony Hill will
have you slumbering in a restored, fully
self-contained 1912 railway carriage. Sleep-
ing up to four people, it's the perfect place
to relax or romance, with grazing kangaroos
and sunset-gazing from Lover's Leap. For
groups, there's also a beautifully appointed,
self-contained lodge with three queen-sized
bedrooms. Minimum stays apply.

Bohemian Bungalow　　　INTERNATIONAL $$
(☑07-5442 8679; www.bohemianbungalow.com.
au; 69 Memorial Dr; pizzas $19-25, mains $20-38;
⊙11.30am-9pm Wed-Fri, 8am-9pm Sat, 8am-
3pm Sun) The fare in this gorgeous white
Queenslander is outdone only by its whimsical interiors – postmodern bohemian
with peacocks, candles and ceramic horses on every ledge and corner. The menu is
equally mood-lifting, whether it's local eggs
with *vincotto*-roasted Noosa tomatoes or
banana-and-buckwheat pancakes or post-
brekkie items like smoked-salmon fish cakes
and gourmet sourdough pizzas.

Imperial Hotel　　　　PUB FOOD $$
(☑07-5442 8811; www.imperialhoteleumundi.
com.au; 1 Etheridge St, Eumundi; mains $18-34;
⊙10am-late) A gorgeous colonial-style pub
with kooky bohemian touches, the Imperial
is much-loved for its beer garden and live
music acts. The tasty menu covers all bases,
from fish tacos and Turkish-spiced zucchini
fritters to pasta dishes, burgers, surf-and-
turf mains and interesting salads.

⭐**Spirit House**　　　　THAI $$$
(☑07-5446 8994; www.spirithouse.com.au; 20
Nindery Rd, Yandina; share plates $14-49; ⊙noon-
3pm daily & 6-9pm Wed-Sat) One of Queensland's top dining destinations (book three
weeks ahead for weekends), Spirit House
evokes the deep jungles of Southeast Asia
with Thai flavours propelling confident
dishes like fried soft-shell crab with curry
powder and garlic, and braised duck leg
with fish sauce, watermelon, ginger and
mint. Also home to a cooking school (four-
hour classes are $150). It's 11km south of
Eumundi.

ℹ Information

Discover Eumundi Heritage & Visitor Centre
(☑07-5442 8762; www.discovereumundi.
com; 73 Memorial Dr, Eumundi; ⊙10am-3pm
Mon-Fri, to 2pm Sat, to 1pm Sun) Also houses
the town's modest **local history museum**
(admission free).

Sunshine Coast Hinterland

Inland from Nambour, the Blackall Range forms a stunning backdrop to the Sunshine Coast's beaches a short 50km away. A relaxed half- or full-day circuit drive from the coast follows a winding road along the razorback line of the escarpment, passing through quaint mountain villages and offering spectacular views of the coastal lowlands.

Maleny

POP 3440

Perched high in the rolling green hills of the Blackall Range, Maleny offers an intriguing melange of artists, musicians and other creative souls; ageing hippies; rural 'tree-changers' and co-op ventures. Its bohemian edge underscores a thriving commercial township that has moved on from its timber and dairy past without yielding to the tacky 'ye olde' tourist-trap developments of nearby mountain villages.

The stunning **Mary Cairncross Scenic Reserve** (☑07-5429 6122; www.mary-cairncross.com.au; 148 Mountain View Rd; by donation; ⊙7am-6pm) allows visitors to experience the subtropical rainforests that once blanketed the Blackall Range. Spread over 55 hectares southeast of central Maleny, the reserve includes walking tracks that snake through the rainforest, an oasis that's home to over 120 species of bird life, unbearably cute pademelons (rainforest wallabies) and fine examples of red cedar trees.

Maleny Botanic Gardens (☑07-5408 4110; www.malenybotanicgardens.com.au; 233 Maleny-Stanley River Rd; adult/child $16/free, incl aviary $26/7; ⊙9am-4.30pm) are a mind-clearing oasis of hedges, lawns and ponds, soaking up a natural tapestry of rare cycads, orchids, roses, azaleas and annuals, as well as a massive aviary.

🛏 Sleeping & Eating

Morning Star Motel   MOTEL $
(☑07-5494 2944; www.morningstarmotel.com; 2 Panorama Pl, Maleny; r $110-150; 🅿🕸) Run by

an affable couple, the rooms at this comfy motel have outstanding coastal views. The decor might be a little '80s but the bathrooms are immaculate and modern, and the rooms cosy and spotless. Deluxe suites even come with their own corner spa. Weekend prices are highest.

Sweets on Maple   SWEETS $
(☑07-5494 2118; www.sweetsonmaple.com.au; 39 Maple St, Maleny; homemade fudge 100g from $5; ⊙9.30am-4.30pm Mon-Fri, to 4pm Sat & Sun) There are many ye olde lolly shops in this neck of the woods, but Sweets on Maple licks them all. The old-fashioned sweets parlour lures in passers-by with the crazy-making smell of fresh-baking fudge, and keeps them there with flavours like chocolate chilli and Frangelico with lime. Succumb – your secret is safe with us.

🍷 Drinking & Nightlife

Brouhaha Brewery   MICROBREWERY
(☑07-5435 2018; www.brouhahabrewery.com.au; 6/39 Coral St, Maleny; ⊙10am-9pm Wed & Thu, to 11.30pm Fri & Sat, to 7pm Sun) Maleny is on the craft-beer radar thanks to this hip microbrewery sporting an industrial fit-out and outdoor deck. Its nine rotating brews include IPAs, stouts, saisons and sours, some made with local produce. Can't choose? Order the well-priced tasting paddle ($14). Quality grub (11am to 8pm) includes baked cob loaf with blue cheese and spinach, and Aussie bush–spiced squid.

Big Barrel   MICROBREWERY
(☑07-5429 6300; www.malenymountainwines.com.au; 787 Landsborough-Maleny Rd, Maleny; ⊙10am-5pm) Scotsman Ryan McLeod distilled whisky in Tasmania before buying this Maleny Mountain Wines cellar door and adding a microbrewery. Wines at Big Barrel include a smooth Maleny rosé (made using locally grown Chambourcin grapes), while the microbrewery uses local rainwater to produce some unusual drops, from malt-forward Scotch ale to a mango cider.

Fraser Island & the Fraser Coast

Best Places to Eat

➡ Coast (p367)
➡ Paolo's Pizza Bar (p367)
➡ Waterview Bistro (p369)
➡ Pop In (p371)
➡ Oodies Cafe (p375)
➡ Alowishus Delicious (p374)

Best Places to Sleep

➡ Eliza Fraser Lodge (p379)
➡ Debbie's Place (p369)
➡ Torquay Beachfront Tourist Park (p366)
➡ Colonial Lodge (p365)
➡ Standy's B&B (p371)
➡ Inglebrae (p374)

Why Go?

North of the much vaunted Sunshine Coast is this little pocket of quintessential Queensland which takes in World Heritage–listed Fraser Island and some mellow coastal communities, such as Hervey Bay and Rainbow Beach, the agricultural centre of Bundaberg, and numerous old-fashioned country towns never too far from the ocean.

Fraser is the world's largest sand island, home to ancient rainforests and luminous lakes, moody ocean swells and a beach shipwreck – few leave here unimpressed. Across the waters of the Great Sandy Strait, Hervey Bay appeals to retirees and young travellers alike, and from July to October, migrating humpback whales stream into the bay. Further south, tiny Rainbow Beach is a backpacker hot spot with decent surfing.

Bundaberg, the largest city in the region, is a friendly, sunny urban centre overlooking the sea of cane fields that fuels its eponymous rum, a fiery spirit guaranteed to scramble a few brain cells.

When to Go
Bundaberg

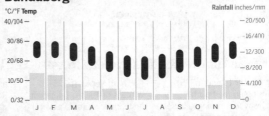

Aug Scoot your boots at the Gympie Music Muster.

Jul–Nov Watch humpback whales – optimal sighting time is August to October.

Nov–Mar Spy on turtles laying eggs in the sand at Mon Repos.

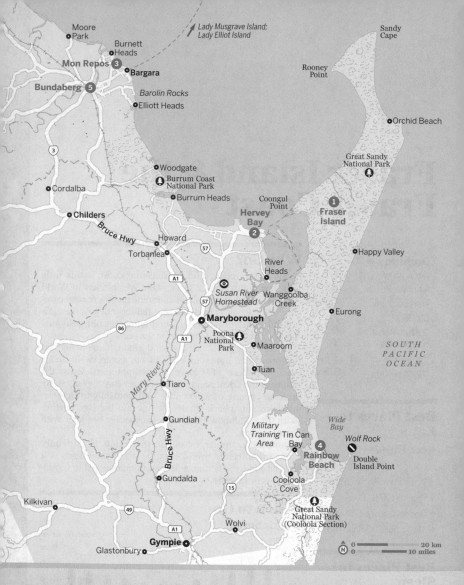

Fraser Island & the Fraser Coast Highlights

1 Fraser Island (p375)
Cruising up the beach
'highway', swimming in Lake
McKenzie and camping under
the stars.

2 Hervey Bay (p363)
Watching the whales play.

3 Mon Repos (p373)
Witnessing turtles take their
first flipper-stumble down the
beach.

4 Rainbow Beach (p368)
Gazing over the rainbow cliffs
from atop the Carlo Sandblow

and diving with sharks at Wolf
Rock.

**5 Bundaberg Rum
Distillery** (p373) Sampling
'liquid gold' at this distillery in
Bundaberg.

Hervey Bay

POP 52,288

Hervey Bay is an unassuming seaside community with an endless beachfront esplanade ideal for extensive lingering – Pialba, Torquay and Scarness all claim a section. Here patrons of beer gardens and cafes dust off their sandy feet after a dip in the warm, gentle waters surrounding the town. Young travellers with an eye on Fraser Island rub shoulders with grey nomads passing languidly through camp sites and serious fisherfolk recharging in pursuit of the one that got away. Throw in the chance to see majestic humpback whales frolicking in the water and the town's convenient access to the World Heritage–listed Fraser Island, and it's easy to understand how Hervey Bay has become an unflashy, yet undeniably appealing, tourist hot spot.

Fraser Island shelters Hervey Bay from the ocean surf and the sea here is shallow and completely flat – perfect for kiddies and summer holiday pics.

◉ Sights

Reef World
AQUARIUM

(☑ 07-4128 9828; Pulgul St, Urangan; adult/child $20/10, shark dives $55; ⊙ 9.30am-4pm) In operation since 1979, this small aquarium is popular with families for its interactive feeding sessions at 11am and 2.30pm. You can also take a dip with lemon, whaler and other nonpredatory sharks.

Fraser Coast Discovery Sphere
MUSEUM

(☑ 07-4191 2610; www.frasercoastdiscoverysphere. com.au; 166 Old Maryborough Rd, Pialba; gold-coin donation; ⊙ 10am-4pm) The stalwart of family-centred Hervey Bay tourism is a little tired, but still a very informative way to learn about the region's geography and marine life.

Wetside Water Park
PARK

(☑ 1300 79 49 29; www.frasercoast.qld.gov.au/ Wetside; The Esplanade, Scarness; ⊙ 10am-6pm Wed-Sun, daily during school holidays) On hot days, this wet spot on the foreshore can't be beaten. There's plenty of shade, fountains, tipping buckets and a boardwalk with water infotainment. Opening hours vary so check the website for updates.

🏃 Activities

Whale Watching

Whale-watching tours operate out of Hervey Bay every day (weather permitting) during the annual migrations between late July and early November. Sightings are guaranteed from August to the end of October (with a free subsequent trip if the whales don't show). Outside of the peak season, many boats offer dolphin-spotting tours. Boats cruise from Urangan Harbour out to Platypus Bay and then zip around from pod to pod to find the most active whales. Most vessels offer half-day tours for around $120 for adults and $60 for children, and most include lunch and/or morning or afternoon tea. Tour bookings can be made through your accommodation or the information centres.

Spirit of Hervey Bay
WHALE WATCHING

(☑ 1800 642 544; www.spiritofherveybay.com; Urangan Harbour; adult/child $120/60; ⊙ 8.30am & 1.30pm) The largest whale-watching vessel with the greatest number of passengers.

Freedom Whale Watch
WHALE WATCHING

(☑ 1300 879 960; www.freedomwhalewatch.com. au; Urangan Harbour) Watch the whales from three levels on a 58m catamaran (adult/child $130/90). This large business can also arrange well-regarded fishing charters and scuba-diving trips to Lady Elliot.

Blue Dolphin Marine Tours
WHALE WATCHING

(☑ 07-4124 9600; www.bluedolphintours.com. au; Urangan Harbour; adult/child $150/120) One of the more experienced outfits scouting for whale and whatever else the ocean can throw up in Hervey Bay. Smaller groups (24 maximum) aboard the speedy *Blue Dolphin* ensure an intimacy that is difficult to replicate on larger vessels.

Tasman Venture
WHALE WATCHING

(☑ 1800 620 322; www.tasmanventure.com.au; Urangan Harbour; whale-watching adult/child $115/60; ⊙ 8.30am & 1.30pm) One of the best, with underwater microphones and viewing windows. Sightings are guaranteed during the season; you get a free subsequent trip if the whales don't show. Throw in a Fraser Island day trip (adult/child $279/175) and you've knocked over 48 hours in style from the luxury of your Hervey Bay lodging.

Fishing

MV Princess II
FISHING

(☑ 07-4124 0400; adult/child $160/100) Wet your hook with an experienced crew who've been trolling these waters for more than two decades.

Hervey Bay

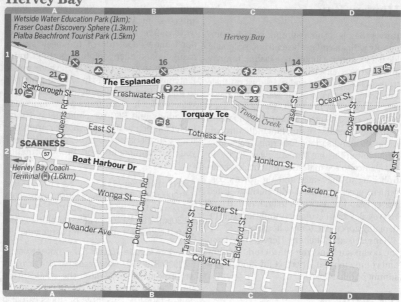

MV Fighting Whiting FISHING
(☎07-4124 3377; www.fightingwhiting.com.au; adult/child/family $70/35/175) Keep your catch on these calm-water tours. Sandwiches, bait and all fishing gear included.

Other Activities

Hervey Bay Ecomarine Tours CRUISE
(☎07-4124 0066; www.herveybayecomarinetours. com.au; Urangan Marina; 5hr tours adult/child $85/45) Cruise on a 12m glass-bottomed

boat, the only one in Hervey Bay. Includes snorkelling, coral viewing and an island barbecue. It's a wonderful day out with family or friends. The new owners also run peaceful 90-minute cruises at 7am and 5pm daily.

Air Fraser Island SCENIC FLIGHTS
(☎1300 172 706; www.airfraserisland.com.au) Air Fraser's 'Day Away' ($150) is terrific value for those looking to land on the island and explore a little on foot. Add a 4WD on arrival

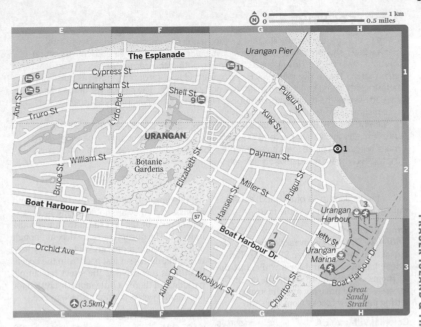

for another $100. Price includes return flight from Hervey Bay or Sunshine Coast.

Aquavue WATER SPORTS
(☑07-4125 5528; www.aquavue.com.au; 415a The Esplanade, Torquay) In the prime spot on the Torquay foreshore is this long-running aquatic-sports operator. They hire out paddle boards and kayaks ($20 per hour), catamarans ($50 per hour) and jet skis ($50 per 15 minutes). More adventurous souls who perhaps don't have time to visit Fraser properly can take a very fun 90-minute run to gorgeous Moon Point, which includes lunch ($260).

Susan River Homestead HORSE RIDING
(☑07-4121 6846; www.susanriver.com; Maryborough–Hervey Bay Rd) Horse-riding packages (adult/child $250/160) including accommodation, all meals and use of the on-site swimming pool and tennis courts. Day trippers can canter off on two-hour horse rides (adult/child $85/75).

Skydive Hervey Bay SKYDIVING
(☑0458 064 703; www.skydiveherveybay.com.au) Tandem skydives from $325 at 4270m, with up to 45 mouth-flapping seconds of free fall, the highest legal altitude in Australia. Or get a taste of the plummet from 1830m for $189.

🕝 Tours

Fraser Experience TOURS
(☑07-4124 4244; www.fraserexperience.com; adult/child from $180/130) Small group tours of Fraser Island; offers some freedom with the itinerary, though only one departure per day. Also available is a somewhat conspicuous Hummer tour.

Fraser Explorer Tours TOURS
(☑07-4194 9222; www.fraserexplorertours.com.au; 1-/2-day tours from $179/330) Very experienced drivers; lots of departures to Fraser Island.

🎊 Festivals & Events

Hervey Bay Ocean Festival CULTURAL
(www.herveybayoceanfestival.com.au; ⊙ Aug) The newly crowned Ocean Festival blesses boats and croons to the whales.

🛌 Sleeping

★ Colonial Lodge APARTMENT $
(☑07-4125 1073; www.herveybaycoloniallodge. com.au; 94 Cypress St, Torquay; 1-/2-bedroom apt $95/140; ❋ 🛜 ⊠) Only nine apartments at this hacienda-style lodge in the middle of Torquay mean that guests can hang out by the pool with a level of exclusivity. Staff are friendly and the apartments are bigger than average,

A WHALE OF A TIME

Every year, from July to early November, thousands of humpback whales cruise into Hervey Bay's sheltered waters for a few days before continuing their arduous migration south to the Antarctic. Having mated and given birth in the warmer waters off northeastern Australia, they arrive in Hervey Bay in groups of about a dozen (known as pulses), before splitting into smaller groups of two or three (pods). The new calves utilise the time to develop the thick layers of blubber necessary for survival in icy southern waters by consuming around 600L of milk daily.

Viewing these majestic creatures is simply awe-inspiring. You'll see these showy aqua-acrobats waving their pectoral fins, tail slapping, breaching or simply 'blowing', and many will roll up beside the whale-watching boats with one eye clear of the water…making those on board wonder who's actually watching whom.

with a lovely place to sit out front. It's a short walk to the shallows across the road.

Emeraldene Inn
INN $

(☑ 07-4124 5500; www.emeraldene.com.au; 166 Urraween Rd, Urraween; d from $110) The Emeraldene has been around for a while, but the 10 rooms deserve more attention given the very reasonable price tag and the lovely bush setting just a few blocks from the shore.

Colonial Village YHA
HOSTEL $

(☑ 07-4125 1844; www.yha.com.au; 820 Boat Harbour Dr, Urangan; dm/d/cabins from $22.50/52/81; ✳@☏☂) This excellent YHA is set on 8 hectares of tranquil bushland, close to the marina and only 50m from the beach. It's a lovely spot, thick with ambience, possums and parrots. Facilities include a pool, tennis and basketball courts, and a sociable bar-restaurant. All dorm rooms come with their own dining tables and desks, and stand-alone single beds.

Torquay Beachfront Tourist Park
CARAVAN PARK $

(☑ 07-4125 1578; www.beachfronttouristparks. com.au; The Esplanade, Torquay; unpowered/powered sites from $26/31; ☏) Fronting Hervey Bay's exquisitely long sandy beach, all of Beachfront's three shady parks live up to their name, with fantastic ocean views. This Torquay site is in the heart of the action. Other branches are at Pialba (☑ 07-4128 1399; The Esplanade, Pialba; unpowered/powered sites from $33.50/41; ☏) and Scarness (☑ 07-4128 1274; The Esplanade, Scarness; powered/unpowered sites from $41/34; ☏). Prices have jumped recently, but don't let that deter you; these are some of the East Coast's top sites.

Flashpackers
HOSTEL $

(☑ 07-4124 1366; www.flashpackersherveybay. com; 195 Torquay Tce, Torquay; dm $26-32, d $80; ✳☏☂) Very hospitable staff keep the guests happily engaged with activities, contests and movies when they are not lounging by the excellent pool, or fixing a snack from the walk-in fridge. The dorm rooms are decent enough and the en-suite rooms are quite posh by hostel standards. It's set just back from the beach, but this is a positive as the street has ample parking and there's a little more discretion for late-night revelers stumbling back to bed.

Mango Tourist Hostel
HOSTEL $

(☑ 07-4124 2832; www.mangohostel.com; 110 Torquay Rd, Scarness; dm/d $28/60; P✳☏) Small and discerning hostel run by knowledgeable local Phil, who communicates clearly and directly, and his lovely wife, who balances the act. Intimate and loaded with character (and geckos), the old Queenslander, set on a quiet street away from the beach, sleeps guests in a four-bed dorm room and two very homey doubles.

Shelly Bay Resort
APARTMENT $$

(☑ 07-4125 4533; www.shellybayresort.com. au; 466 The Esplanade, Torquay; 1-/2-bedroom units $139/170; ✳@☂) The bright, breezy beach-facing apartments at Shelly Bay Resort are some of the best value in town, especially the two-bedroom ones, which have prime corner locations overlooking the pool. Customer service is first class, whether staying for work or pleasure; there's a lot to like about this one.

Pier One
RESORT $$

(☑ 07-4125 4965; www.herveybaywaterfrontapts. com.au; 569 The Esplanade, Urangan; 1-/2-bedroom apt $189/259) The latest large-scale project on the Esplanade, Pier One sits alongside Pier Apartments and suits travellers looking for a view of the sea in the background and the pool in the foreground. The apartments are bigger than most, come with two bathrooms, Ikea furniture and a very reasonable price tag.

Arlia Sands Apartments
APARTMENT $$

(☑ 07-4125 4360; www.arliasands.com.au; 13 Ann St, Torquay; 1-/2-bedroom apt from $135/145; ❋ ☲) Excellent value, if a little less than stylish, these self-contained units have recently been upgraded just enough to make a difference. It's off the main drag yet close to the beach and shops and is très quiet.

Grange Resort
RESORT $$$

(☑ 07-4125 2195; www.thegrange-herveybay.com.au; 33 Elizabeth St, Urangan; 1-/2-bedroom villas from $235/305; ❋ 🛜 ☲) Reminiscent of a stylish desert resort with fancy split-level condos and filled with life's little luxuries, the Grange is thriving under new management and is close to the beach and to town. Pets are very welcome – a rarity in these parts – except in the fabulous pool bar where amphibious creatures sink beers until the sun goes down.

🍴 Eating

Bayaroma Cafe
CAFE $

(☑ 07-4125 1515; 428 The Esplanade, Torquay; breakfast $10-22, mains $9.50-20; ⊘ 6.30am-3.30pm; 🐾) Famous for its coffee, all-day breakfasts and people-watching position, Bayaroma has a jam-packed menu that truly has something for everyone – even vegetarians! Attentive, chirpy service is an added bonus.

Enzo's on the Beach
CAFE $

(www.enzosonthebeach.com.au; 351a The Esplanade, Scarness; mains $8-20; ⊘ 6.30am-5pm) This shabby-chic beachside cafe is the place to go to fill up on sandwiches, wraps, salads and coffees before working them off on a hired kayak or kitesurfing lesson.

Simply Wok
ASIAN $

(☑ 07-4125 2077; 417 The Esplanade, Torquay; mains $14-23; ⊘ 7am-10pm) Noodles, stir-fries, seafood and curries will satisfy any cravings for Asian cuisine, and there's a nightly (from 5pm to 9pm) all-you-can-eat hot buffet for $16.90. Surprisingly good breakfast.

★ Paolo's Pizza Bar
ITALIAN $$

(☑ 07-4125 3100; www.paolospizzabar.com.au; 2/446 The Esplanade, Torquay; mains $14-27; ⊘ 5-9pm) Hordes of locals come for a slice of Naples from the pizza oven or in the form of fine pasta (the spaghetti marinara at $22 was amazing), and relish the attentive family-run service. It's the best Italian in the region, but you can't book, so get here early to avoid the shoulder shrug.

★ Coast
FUSION $$

(☑ 07-4125 5454; 469 The Esplanade, Torquay; mains $21-60; ⊘ 5pm-late Tue & Wed, 11.30am-late Thu-Sun) A local restaurateur and a red-hot English chef have teamed up to deliver an outstanding Australian venture in the unlikely locale of Hervey Bay. Almost all meals are prepared to be shared, and span the Asian–Middle Eastern cuisine range. Not hungry? Share a cocktail pitcher (from $30) and nibble on bar snacks more akin to hors d'oeuvres.

Black Dog Café
MODERN AUSTRALIAN $$

(☑ 07-4124 3177; 381 The Esplanade, Torquay; mains $12-35; ⊘ lunch & dinner) Black Dog delivers a wide variety of contemporary Australian staples to all parts of Hervey Bay. Its relaxed diner down the Torquay end of the Esplanade serves up burgers, seafood, salads and the like without fuss and at very fair prices.

Eat at Dan & Steph's
CAFE $$

(449 The Esplanade, Torquay; Mains $16-24; ⊘ 6am-4pm Wed-Mon) Former TV cooking show winners Dan and Steph have kicked on from their public success with a popular restaurant with an informal vibe. Most meals take an interesting spin on familiar dishes. The smoked beef salad ($18) and the pumpkin and pomegranate black rice ($18) were both a big tick. Breakfast looks good, too.

🍸 Drinking & Nightlife

Beach House Hotel
PUB

(344 The Esplanade, Scarness) The Beach House has been reborn, thanks to a shed load of cash, a prime viewpoint on Scarness Beach and a willingness to give the people what they want: beer taps at every turn, gambling dens, a huge courtyard, decent food and accessible live music most nights of the week.

Hoolihan's
PUB

(382 The Esplanade, Scarness; ⊘ 11am-2am) Like all good Irish pubs, Hoolihan's is wildly popular, especially with the backpacker crowd. This one is pretty basic, but the kerbside seating is ideal for people-watching, or for being watched by people, whichever comes first.

Viper
CLUB

(410 The Esplanade, Torquay; ⊘ 10pm-3am Wed, Fri & Sat) Viper is the kind of club everyone rolls their eyes at when its name is mentioned early in the night, but you can't keep the dancers out come midnight, especially in summer. Music varies wildly between God-awful bad and actually pretty good.

❶ Information

Hervey Bay Visitor Information Centre
(📱1800 811 728; www.visitfrasercoast.com;
cnr Urraween & Maryborough Rds) Helpful and
well-stocked with brochures and information.
On the outskirts of town.

Marina Kiosk (📱07-4128 9800; Buccaneer Ave,
Urangan Boat Harbour, Urangan; ⊙6am-6pm)

❶ Getting There & Away

AIR

Hervey Bay airport is on Don Adams Dr, just off
Booral Rd. **Qantas** (📱13 13 13; www.qantas.
com.au) and **Virgin** (📱13 67 89; www.virginaus-
tralia.com.au) have daily flights to/from destinations around Australia.

BOAT

Boats to Fraser Island leave from River Heads,
about 10km south of town, and from Urangan
Marina. Most tours leave from Urangan Harbour.

BUS

Buses depart **Hervey Bay Coach Terminal**
(📱07-4124 4000; Central Ave, Pialba). **Greyhound** (📱1300 473 946; www.greyhound.com.
au) and **Premier Motor Service** (📱13 34 10;
www.premierms.com.au) have several services
daily to/from Brisbane ($72, 6½ hours), Ma-
roochydore ($91, six hours), Bundaberg ($29,
two hours) and Rockhampton ($92, six hours).

Tory's Tours (📱07-4128 6500; www.torys-
tours.com.au) has twice daily services to Brisbane airport (adult/child $80/68). **Wide Bay
Transit** (📱07-4121 3719; www.widebaytransit.
com.au) has hourly services from Urangan Marina (stopping along the Esplanade) to Maryborough ($8, one hour) every weekday, with fewer
services on weekends.

❶ Getting Around

Hervey Bay is the best place to hire a 4WD for
Fraser Island.

Aussie Trax (📱07-4124 4433; www.fraseris-
land4wd.com.au; 56 Boat Harbour Dr, Pialba)
Fraser Magic 4WD Hire (📱07-4125 6612; www.
fraser4wdhire.com.au; 5 Kruger Ct, Urangan)
Hervey Bay Rent A Car (📱07-4194 6626;
www.herveybayrentacar.com.au; 5 Cunningham
St, Torquay)
Safari 4WD Hire (📱07-4124 4244; www.safa-
ri4wdhire.com.au; 102 Boat Harbour Dr, Pialba)

Rainbow Beach

POP 1142
Rainbow Beach is an idyllic Australian beach
town at the base of the Inskip Peninsula,
which is best known for its colourful sand
cliffs and easy access by barge to Fraser
Island. It's a decidedly low-key place, half-
secret to non-4WD lovers who know little
of the dramatic approach possible along the
Cooloola Section of the Great Sandy National Park. It's a great place to try your hand
at different outdoor activities, tap into the
backpacker party scene, or just chill out with
family and friends.

🏃 Activities

Rainbow Paragliding   PARAGLIDING
(📱07-5486 3048, 0418 754 157; www.paragliding
rainbow.com; glides $200) If ever there was a
place worthy of leaping from, then the colourful cliffs of Rainbow Beach may just be it.
Jean Luc has been paragliding here with ex-
hilarated customers for 20 years. Better value than skydiving and a more mellow thrill.

Wolf Rock Dive Centre   DIVING
(📱07-5486 8004, 0438 740 811; www.wolfrockdive.
com.au; 20 Karoonda Rd; double dive charters from
$240) Wolf Rock, a congregation of volcanic
pinnacles off Double Island Point, is regarded as one of Queensland's best scuba-diving
sites. The endangered grey nurse shark is
found here all year.

Epic Ocean Adventures   SURFING
(📱0408 738 192; www.epicoceanadventures.com.
au; 3hr surf lessons $65, 3hr kayak tours $75) Rainbow Beach can throw up some challenging
breaks for beginners, but the instructors here
are first class. They also offer dolphin-spotting
sea-kayak tours.

Fraser's on Rainbow   ADVENTURE SPORTS
(📱07-5486 8885; www.frasersonrainbow.com)
Rainbow Beach is a smart alternative to
Hervey Bay as a gateway to Fraser Island.
These three-day tag-along tours cost $479
and are seriously fun.

Surf & Sand Safaris   ADVENTURE SPORTS
(📱07-5486 3131; www.surfandsandsafaris.com.
au; half-day tours adult/child $75/40) Half-day
4WD tours through the Great Sandy National Park and along the beach to the coloured
sands and lighthouse at Double Island Point.
Full-day trips can also be arranged through
a partner operator.

Skydive Ramblers   SKYDIVING
(📱0418 218 358; www.skydiveforfun.com.au;
10,000/14,000ft dives $350/399) Soft landings
on the beach; hard flying through the air.

Pippies Beach House   DRIVING
($\square$07-5486 8503; www.pippiesbeachhouse.com.
au) Departs Rainbow Beach; well-organised,
small convoys to Fraser Island ($417) with
high safety standards. Maximum of 34 guests
and highly recommended by the party set
filling out Pippies' dorm rooms.

🛏 Sleeping

Rainbow Beach Hire-a-Camp   CAMPGROUND $
($\square$0419 464 254, 07-5486 8633; all-inclusive
camping 4 people $145) Camping on the beach
is one of the best ways to experience this
part of the coast; if you don't have camping
gear, Rainbow Beach Hire-a-Camp can hire
out equipment, set up your tent, provide
food and cooking equipment and camp site,
organise camping permits and break camp
for you when you're done. Too easy!

Dingo's Backpacker's Resort   HOSTEL $
($\square$1800 111 126; www.dingosresort.com; 20 Spectrum St; dm $30; ❄@🛜🏊) This party hostel
with a busy public bar is not for those in
need of a good rest. It has loud music (live
or otherwise) and karaoke most nights, a
chill-out gazebo for a temporary escape, free
pancake breakfasts and cheap meals nightly.
Dorms are clean and adequate, while excellent tours can be arranged.

**Rainbow Beach
Holiday Village**   CARAVAN PARK $
($\square$07-5486 3222; www.rainbowbeachholiday
village.com; 13 Rainbow Beach Rd; powered/unpow-
ered sites from $43/36, villas from $120; ❄🛜🏊)
Popular beachfront park with a range of villas if you want the vibe but not the hassle.

Pippies Beach House   HOSTEL $
($\square$07-5486 8503; www.pippiesbeachhouse.com.
au; 22 Spectrum St; dm/d $24/65; ❄@🛜🏊)
This five-bedroom beach house has been
converted into a relaxed hostel – the party
is elsewhere in Rainbow – where you can
catch your breath between outdoor pursuits.
Free breakfast, wi-fi and boogie boards, and
lots of organised group activities, sweeten
the stay. Pippies has expanded, but insist on
staying in the main house if you can.

★ Debbie's Place   B&B $$
($\square$07-5486 3506; www.rainbowbeachaccom-
modation.com.au; 30 Kurana St; d/ste from
$150/180, 3-bedroom apt from $340; ❄🛜🏊)
Greenery abounds at Debbie's meticulously
kept Queenslander, which has become the
standard bearer for Rainbow Beach holiday
accommodation. The charming rooms are

fully self-contained, with private entrances
and verandahs. The effervescent Debbie is a
mine of information and makes this a cosy
home away from home. You can leave your
car here if taking a tour to Fraser.

Plantation Resort   RESORT $$$
($\square$07-5486 9600; www.plantationresortatrainbow.
com.au; 1 Rainbow Beach Rd; d from $250) The
high-end option in Rainbow is still shining
brightly enough to warrant the price tag.
Try to stretch the budget for an ocean-view
penthouse (from $380) to get the maximum
effect. Popular with conferences and out-of-
towners, the Plantation also has a smart bar-
restaurant, **Arcobaleno on the Beach** (pizzas $15-25; ⊘9am-10pm), where the beautiful
people gather for happy hour, live tunes and
audacious seafood delights.

🍴 Eating

Rainbow Fruit   CAFE $
($\square$07-5486 3126; 2 Rainbow Beach Rd; wraps from
$9; ⊘8am-5pm) Rainbow fresh fruit and
vegetables are sliced, diced and puréed for
a range of juices, wraps and salads at this
humble cafe on the main strip.

★ Waterview Bistro   MODERN AUSTRALIAN $$
($\square$07-5486 8344; Cooloola Dr; mains $26-35;
⊘11.30am-11.30pm Wed-Sat, to 6pm Sun) Sunset
drinks are a must at this swish restaurant
with sensational views of Fraser Island from
its hilltop perch. Get stuck into the signature
seafood chowder, steaks and seafood, or have
fun cooking your own meal over hot stones.

**Rainbow Beach
Surf Lifesaving Club**   PUB FOOD $$
($\square$07-5486 3249; Wide Bay Esplanade; mains from
$15; ⊘11am-10pm) The food is fairly standard
pub fare, served quickly, with huge slabs of
meat, pasta and sides of chips, but the view
and the accompanying beer are the reason
you come to places like Rainbow Beach in
the first place. The strong community spirit
is palpable, even if the odd resident boozer
makes for a sad mid-afternoon.

ℹ Information

Rainbow Beach Visitor Centre ($\square$07-5486
3227; www.rainbowbeachinfo.com.au; 8 Rainbow Beach Rd; ⊘7am-5.30pm) Despite the
posted hours, it's open sporadically.
Shell Tourist Centre (36 Rainbow Beach Rd;
⊘6am-6pm) At the Shell service station;
arranges tour bookings and barge tickets for
Fraser Island.

ⓘ Getting There & Away

Greyhound (☑1300 473 946; www.greyhound. com.au) has several daily services from Brisbane ($51, five hours), Noosa ($34, three hours) and Hervey Bay ($28, two hours). **Premier Motor Service** (☑13 34 10; www.premierms.com. au) has less expensive services. **Active Tours and Transfers** (☑07 5313 6631; www.active-transfers.com.au) runs a shuttle bus to Rainbow Beach from Brisbane Airport ($135, three hours) and Sunshine Coast Airport ($95, two hours).

Most 4WD-hire companies will also arrange permits and barge costs to Fraser Island ($100 per vehicle return), and hire out camping gear. Try **All Trax** (☑07-5486 8767; www.fraserisland4x4. com.au; Rainbow Beach Rd, Shell service station; per day from $165) or **Rainbow Beach Adventure Centre** (☑07-5486 3288; www.adventurecentre. com.au; 13 Spectrum St; per day from $180).

Maryborough

POP 23,113

Founded in 1847, Maryborough is one of Queensland's oldest towns, and its port saw the first shaky step ashore for thousands of 19th-century free settlers looking for a better life in the new country. Heritage and history are Maryborough's specialities; the pace of yesteryear is reflected in its beautifully restored colonial-era buildings and gracious Queenslander homes.

This charming old country town is also the birthplace of Pamela Lyndon (PL) Travers, creator of the umbrella-wielding Mary Poppins. The award-winning film *Saving Mr Banks* tells Travers' story, with early-1900s Maryborough in a starring role. There's a life-sized statue of Ms Poppins on the corner of Richmond and Wharf Sts. Mary Poppins groupies should schedule their trips for the Mary Poppins Festival in June/July.

◉ Sights

Brennan & Geraghty's Store   MUSEUM

(☑07-4121 2250; 64 Lennox St; adult/family $5.50/13.50; ◷10am-3pm) This National Trust–classified store traded for 100 years before closing its doors. The museum is crammed with tins, bottles and packets, including early Vegemite jars and curry powder from the 1890s. It's a nostalgic wonderland for Australian/British oldies and anyone interested in the tastes of times gone by.

Portside   HISTORIC SITE

(101 Wharf St; ◷10am-4pm Mon-Fri, to 1pm Sat & Sun) In the historic area beside the Mary Riv-er, Portside has 13 heritage-listed buildings, parkland and museums. The **Portside Centre** (☑07-4190 5730; cnr Wharf & Richmond Sts; ◷10am-4pm), located in the former Customs House, has interactive displays on Maryborough's history. Part of the centre, but a few doors down, the Bond Store Museum also highlights key periods in Maryborough's history. Downstairs is the original packed-earth floor and even some liquor barrels from 1864.

Maryborough Heritage City Markets   MARKET

(cnr Adelaide & Ellena Sts; ◷8am-1.30pm Thu) Market fun made all the more entertaining by the firing (1pm) of the historic Time Cannon, a town crier and rides on the *Mary Ann* steam loco (adult/child $3/2) through Queen's Park.

Heritage Centre   NOTABLE BUILDING

(☑07-4123 1842; cnr Wharf & Richmond Sts; ◷9am-4pm) If tracing your genealogical tree is a priority, head to the Heritage Centre where you'll find colonial immigration records from ships logs; and if dear old great-great-granddaddy arrived in Australia courtesy of Her Majesty's prison system, you'll find convict records as well.

Maryborough Military & Colonial Museum   MUSEUM

(☑07-4123 5900; www.maryboroughmuseum. org; 106 Wharf St; adult/couple/family $5/8/10; ◷9am-3pm) Check out the only surviving three-wheeler Girling car, originally built in London in 1911. There's also a replica Cobb & Co coach and one of the largest military libraries in Australia.

☞ Tours

Free **guided walks** (◷9am Mon-Sat) depart from the City Hall and take in the town's many sites.

Tea with Mary   TOURS

(☑1800 214 789; per person $20; ◷9.30am Thu & Fri) Tour of the historic precinct with a Mary Poppins–bedecked guide who spills the beans on the town's past; book through the visitor centre (p371).

Ghostly Tours & Tales   WALKING

(☑1800 811 728; tours incl dinner $75; ◷6pm last Saturday of the month) Get spooked on a torch-lit tour of the city's grisly murder sites, opium dens, haunted houses and cemetery. Tours begin from the Maryborough Post Office in Bazaar St.

✿ Festivals & Events

Mary Poppins Festival　　　　　CULTURAL
(www.marypoppinsfestival.com.au; ☺ Jun-Jul) A supercalifragilisticexpialidocious festival celebrating PL Travers and the famous Miss Poppins every June/July over the school holidays.

🛏 Sleeping & Eating

Ned Kelly's Motel　　　　　MOTEL **$**
(☑ 07-4121 0999; www.nedkellymotel.com.au; 150 Gympie Rd; s/d $45/75, cabins from $89; ❋ ❈) The fabled Victorian bushranger Ned Kelly never made it this far north, so his statue on the side of the road may hold you up momentarily. Don't be alarmed, it's just a budget motel bearing his name. Rooms are basic, but there's a pool and laundry. Very cheap rates.

★ Standy's B&B　　　　　B&B **$$**
(50 Ferry Rd; 1-/2-bedroom studios $150/180) Named after two retired Standardbred racehorses who now enjoy the lush riverside surrounds, this pristine new homestay on the outskirts of Maryborough offers an accessible piece of high-class rural living. The house itself is a white beauty on the banks of the Mary River and is set on 6 hectares of prime land. Guests can choose from two spacious, country-style studios, with white walls and polished floorboards. The food, service and surrounds are all excellent.

Eco Queenslander　　　BOUTIQUE HOTEL **$$**
(☑ 0438 195 443; www.ecoqueenslander.com; 15 Treasure St; per couple from $140) ✎ Lovely Cecile, the French adventurer who fell in love with Maryborough, is an enthusiastic host to the house she gleefully restored. The old Queenslander has a comfy lounge, full kitchen, laundry and cast-iron bathtub. Sustainable features include solar power, rainwater tanks, energy-efficient lighting and bikes for you to use. Minimum two-night stay.

★ Pop In　　　　　CAFE **$**
(203 Bazaar St; sandwiches $8.50; ☺ 7am-3pm Mon-Fri, to 1pm Sat) Very popular local cafe with a rotating fresh salad menu and a reputation for fine sandwiches and cakes. Service is efficient and friendly – it's the place to go for a quick meal if you're passing through Maryborough.

Toast　　　　　CAFE **$**
(☑ 07-4121 7222; 199 Bazaar St; dishes $6-12; ☺ 6am-4pm Mon-Sat, 6am-2.30pm Sun) Stainless-steel fittings, polished cement floors and coffee served in paper cups stamp the metro-chic seal on this groovy cafe. The best coffee we found for some distance.

❶ Information

Maryborough/Fraser Island Visitor Centre
(☑ 1800 214 789; www.visitfrasercoast.com; Kent St; ☺ 9am-5pm Mon-Fri, to 1pm Sat & Sun)

❶ Getting There & Away

Queensland Rail (☑ 1800 872 467; www.queenslandrail.com.au) has two services: the Spirit of Queensland($75, five hours) and the Tilt Train ($75, 3½ hours) connecting Brisbane with Maryborough West station. The station is 7km west of the centre, and is connected via a shuttle bus.

Greyhound (☑ 1300 473 946; www.greyhound.com.au) and **Premier Motor Service** (☑ 13 34 10; www.premierms.com.au) have buses to Gympie ($30, one hour), Bundaberg ($40, three hours) and Brisbane ($64, 4½ hours).

Wide Bay Transit (☑ 07-4121 4070; www.widebaytransit.com.au) has hourly services (fewer on weekends) between Maryborough and Hervey Bay ($8, one hour), departing from outside City Hall in Kent St.

Gympie

POP 18,359

Gympie is a pleasant former gold-rush town with some fine heritage architecture, lush parkland and a good ol' country feel. Come in August for the **Gympie Music Muster** (www.muster.com.au), one of the finest country music festivals in Australia.

The **Gympie Gold Mining & Historical Museum** (☑ 07-5482 3995; www.gympiegoldmuseum.com.au; 215 Brisbane Rd; adult/child/family $10/5/25; ☺ 9am-4pm) holds a diverse collection of mining equipment and steam engines, while the **Woodworks Forestry & Timber Museum** (☑ 07-5483 7691; www.woodworksmuseum .com.au; cnr Fraser Rd & Bruce Hwy; $5; ☺ 10am-4pm Mon-Sat) displays memorabilia and equipment from the region's old logging days.

If you can't muster up the energy to drive any further, the **Gympie Muster Inn** (☑ 07-5482 8666; www.gympiemusterinn.com.au; 21 Wickham St; d from $140) is a friendly motel.

Childers

POP 1570

Surrounded by lush green fields and rich red soil, Childers is a charming little town, its main street lined with tall, shady trees and lattice-trimmed historical buildings.

The lovely, 100-year-old Federal Hotel has swingin' saloon doors, while a bronze statue of two romping pig dogs sits outside the Grand Hotel. Backpackers flock to Childers for fruit-picking and farm work.

There's a moving memorial to the 15 backpackers who were tragically killed in a hostel fire in 2000, and fantastic art at the **Childers Palace Memorial & Art Gallery** ([☎]07-4130 4660; 72 Churchill St; ⊙9am-5pm Mon-Fri, to 3pm Sat & Sun) FREE.

The **Old Pharmacy** ([☎]0400 376 359; 90 Churchill St; adult/child $5/3; ⊙9am-3.30pm Mon-Fri, 9am-1pm Sat) was an operational apothecary's shop from 1894 to 1982, and also functioned as the town dentist, vet, optician and local photographer.

🛏 Sleeping & Eating

Sugarbowl Backpackers
CARAVAN PARK $

([☎]07-4126 1521; www.sugarbowlchilders.com; Bruce Hwy; powered site $29, cabin $90; [@][≋]) This proxy backpacker employment agency is well-maintained and welcoming for those seeking farm labour. A 10-minute walk out of town, Sugarbowl is a clean and green spot favoured by many seasonal pickers. Rates are for two people; prices drop for longer stays. Camping sites are also available.

Mango Hill B&B
B&B $$

([☎]1800 816 020, 0408 875 305; www.mangohill cottages.com; 8 Mango Hill Dr; d incl breakfast from $150; [≋]) For warm, country hospitality, the cute cane-cutter cottages at Mango Hill B&B, 4km south of town, are decorated with handmade wooden furniture, country decor and comfy beds that ooze charm and romance. There's an organic winery on-site called Hill of Promise. Perfect to break up your East Coast road trip, especially if you're travelling with a loved one.

Mammino's
ICE CREAM $

(115 Lucketts Rd; ice-cream cups $5; ⊙9am-5pm) On your way out of town, take a detour to Mammino's for wickedly delicious, homemade macadamia ice cream. Lucketts Rd is off the Bruce Hwy just south of Childers. Don't worry about the faded signs; this place is amazing.

Drunk Bean
CAFE $

([☎]07-4126 1118; Childers Shopping Centre, Bruce Hwy; mains $8-14; ⊙7am-4pm) Near the Woolworths supermarket is this excellent cafe that doubles as an arts-and-craft store. Breakfast, smoothies, light lunches and a stretch of the legs. Well worth pulling over for.

Federal Hotel
PUB FOOD $$

([☎]07-4126 1438; 71 Churchill St; mains from $17) This grand old federal-era pub is a ripper for hearty pub food and an ice-cold lager to wash it down. Take in a cross-section of Childers society over your parmigiana or steak.

🛈 Information

Childers Visitor Information Centre ([☎]07-4126 3886; 72 Churchill St; ⊙9am-4pm Mon-Fri, to 3pm Sat & Sun) Beneath the Childers Palace Memorial & Art Gallery.

🛈 Getting There & Away

Childers is 50km south of Bundaberg. **Greyhound Australia** ([☎]1300 473 946; www.greyhound.com.au) and **Premier Motor Service** ([☎]13 34 10; www.premierms.com.au) both stop at the Shell service station north of town and have daily services to/from Brisbane ($91, 6½ hours), Hervey Bay ($19, one hour) and Bundaberg ($27 1½ hours).

Burrum Coast National Park

Shifting between a lowland vegetation of stringybark trees, dense mangroves and flat coastal dunes, Burrum Coast National Park feels wonderfully remote. It's a popular spot for knowledgeable campers, birdwatchers, fishers, canoeists and hikers. The park covers two sections of coastline on either side of the little holiday community of Woodgate, 37km east of Childers. The Woodgate section of the park begins at the southern end of the Esplanade, and has attractive beaches and abundant fishing. The more isolated Kinkuna section of the park is thick bush and only for the serious explorer, but it does boast a fine, secluded beach with decent surf.

The **NPRSR camping ground** (www.nprsr.qld.gov.au; per person/family $6.75/24.60) at Burrum Point is reached by a 4WD-only track. Several walking tracks start at the camping ground or Acacia St in Woodgate.

Woodgate Beach Tourist Park ([☎]07-4126 8802; www.woodgatebeachtouristpark.com; 88 The Esplanade; unpowered/powered site $30/35, cabin $60-115, beachfront villa $140; [❋][@]) is right on the beach.

Bundaberg

POP 70,588

Bundaberg is the largest town in the Fraser Coast region and is known across the land more for its eponymous dark rum and fruit-farming backpackers than its coral-fringed beach hamlets. The town proper is an agricultural centre with some friendly pubs and a decent regional art gallery. However, in many people's eyes, the beach hamlets around Bundaberg are more attractive than the town itself. Some 25km north of the centre is Moore Park with wide, flat beaches. To the south is the very popular Elliott Heads with a nice beach, rocky foreshore and good fishing.

◉ Sights & Activities

★ **Bundaberg Rum Distillery**   DISTILLERY
(☑ 07-4131 2999; www.bundabergrum.com.au; Hills St; adult/child self-guided tours $19/9.5, guided tours $28.50/14.25; ☺10am-3pm Mon-Fri, to 2pm Sat & Sun) Bundaberg's biggest claim to fame is the iconic Bundaberg Rum: you'll see the Bundy Rum polar bear on billboards and bumper stickers all over town. Choose from either a self-guided tour through the museum, or a guided tour of the distillery – tours depart on the hour. Both include a tasting for the over-18-year-olds. Wear closed shoes.

Bundaberg Barrel   BREWERY
(☑ 07-4154 5480; www.bundaberg.com; 147 Bargara Rd; adult/child $12/5; ☺9am-4.30pm Mon-Sat, 10am-3pm Sun) Bundaberg's nonalcoholic ginger beer and other soft drinks aren't as famous as Bundy Rum, but they are very good. Visit the Barrel to take an audio tour of the small museum. Tastings are included and it's geared toward families.

Bundaberg Regional Arts Gallery   GALLERY
(☑ 07-4130 4750; www.bundabergregionalgalleries. com.au; 1 Barolin St; ☺10am-5pm Mon-Fri, 11am-3pm Sat & Sun) FREE This small (and vividly purple) gallery has surprisingly good exhibitions.

Hinkler Hall of Aviation   MUSEUM
(☑ 07-4130 4400; www.hinklerhallofaviation.com; Mt Perry Rd, Botanic Gardens; adult/child $18/10, family $28-40; ☺9am-4pm) This modern museum has multimedia exhibits, a flight simulator and informative displays chronicling the life of Bundaberg's famous son Bert Hinkler, who made the first solo flight between England and Australia in 1928.

TURTLE TOTS
....

Mon Repos, 15km northeast of Bundaberg, is one of Australia's most accessible turtle rookeries. From November to late March, female loggerheads lumber laboriously up the beach to lay eggs in the sand. About eight weeks later, the hatchlings dig their way to the surface, and, under cover of darkness, emerge en masse to scurry as quickly as their little flippers allow down to the water.

The Bundaberg Visitor Centre (p375) has information on turtle conservation and organises nightly tours (adult/child $12/6.25) from 7pm during the season. Bookings are mandatory and need to be made through the visitor centre or online at www.bundabergregion.org. The Bundaberg Visitor Centre also has reports of how many turtles have been seen through the season.

Alexandra Park & Zoo   PARK
(Quay St) FREE Lovely sprawling park with plenty of shady trees, flower beds and swaths of green lawn for a lazy picnic, right beside the Burnett River. There's also a small zoo for the littlies.

Anzac Park Pool   SWIMMING
(☑ 07-4151 5640; 19 Quay St; adult/child $4/3; ☺5.30am-6pm Mon-Thu, 5.30am-9pm Fri, 6am-6pm Sat, 9am-5pm Sun) This friendly public swimming pool is a Bundaberg institution on a lazy summer's day. Good management, yummy lolly (candy) selection and a glorious Olympic-sized pool.

Bundaberg Aqua Scuba   DIVING
(☑ 07-4153 5761; www.aquascuba.com.au; 239 Bourbong St; diving courses from $349) Leads dives to nearby sites around Innes Park.

★ **Lady Elliot Island**   TOURS
(☑ 07-5536 3644, toll-free 1800 072 200; www.lady elliot.com.au; adult/child $365/210) Fly to Lady Elliot Island, spend five hours on the Great Barrier Reef and use the resort's facilities.

Burnett River Cruises   CRUISE
(☑ 0427 099 009; www.burnettrivercruises.com.au; School Lane, East Bundaberg; 2½hr tours adult/child $26.50/10) The *Bundy Belle*, an old-fashioned ferry, chugs at a p]leasant pace to the mouth of the Burnett River. See website or call for tour times.

Bundaberg

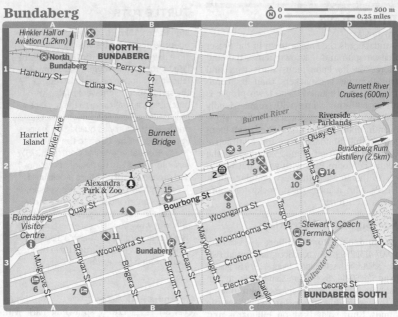

🛏 Sleeping & Eating

Bigfoot Backpackers HOSTEL $
(☑ 07-4152 3659; 66 Targo St; dm from $24; 🅿 ❋)
Pretty grim, bare-bones dorm rooms at this
central hostel, but it's an excellent place to
arrange fruit-picking jobs and to meet other
travellers in the spacious games-room area.

Bundaberg Spanish Motor Inn MOTEL $
(☑ 07-4152 5444; www.bundabergspanishmotorinn.
com; 134 Woongarra St; s/d $115/120; ❋ 🅿 🛜 ❋) A
Spanish hacienda-style motel doesn't feel out
of place in the Bundaberg climate, and this
old-fashioned motel in a quiet street off the
main drag is *muy bueno* (very good). Spotless
units are self-contained and all rooms overlook the central pool. Breakfast is *deliciosa*.

★ **Inglebrae** B&B $$
(☑ 07-4154 4003; www.inglebrae.com; 17 Branyan
St; r incl breakfast $130-150; ❋) For old-world
English charm in a glorious Queenslander,
this delightful B&B is just the ticket. Pol-
ished timber and stained glass seep from the
entrance into the rooms, which come with
high beds and small antiques.

★ **Alowishus Delicious** CAFE $
(☑ 07-4154 2233; 176 Bourbong St; coffees from $3,
mains $10-22; ⊙ 7am-5pm Mon-Wed, 7am-9pm Thu,
7am-11pm Fri, 8am-11pm Sat, 8am-5pm Sun) Final-
ly! A cafe open at night! This creative cater-
ing company is a great place to type that blog,
meet a friend for a late-night pastry, or bang
in a coffee between shifts picking mangoes.

Spicy Tonight   FUSION $
(☑ 07-4154 3320; 1 Targo St; dishes $12-20; ⊙ 11am-
2.30pm & 5-9pm Mon-Sat, 5-9pm Sun) What do
you get when you cross Thai and Indian? Spices you never knew could coexist. Bundaberg's
saucy little secret serves hot curries, vindaloo,
tandoori and a host of vegetarian dishes.

Indulge   CAFE $
(80 Bourbong St; dishes $9-18; ⊙ 8.30am-4.30pm
Mon-Fri, 7.30am-12.30pm Sat) Much of the local
Bundaberg sugar must go into the incredible cakes and pastries at this cafe, which
promotes local produce.

★ **Oodies Cafe**   CAFE $$
(☑ 07-4153 5340; www.oodies.com.au; 103 Gavin
St; ⊙ 6.30am-4pm) A double garage on the
edge of Bundaberg's CBD is the unlikely
venue for the town's coolest cafe. Oodies is
an oddity where you can lounge on leath-
er armchairs with the hipcats sipping chai
lattes, or dine from the healthy, well-priced
breakfast and lunch menus. Sandwiches,
burgers, cakes and more are served.

Cool Banana's Cafe   CAFE $$
(☑ 07-4198 1182; 91 Bourbong St; meals from $10;
⊙ 8am-8.30pm) Cheap and cheerful cafe run
by the same crowd as **Les Chefs** (☑ 07-4153
1770; 238 Bourbong St; mains $27; ⊙ lunch Tue-Fri,
dinner Mon-Sat). Daily specials include fish
and chips, kebabs and lamb roasts. Coffee
and breakfast is decent too.

🍷 Drinking & Nightlife

Spotted Dog Tavern   BAR
(☑ 07-4198 1044; 217 Bourbong St) Bundaberg's
most popular bar-restaurant is busy all day.
Food is nothing special – standard pub fare
without much fuss – but the music, live
sports, and air of permanent celebration on
the spacious patio make it a local favourite.

Bargara Brewing Company   CRAFT BEER
(☑ 07-4152 1675; 10 Tantitha St; ⊙ 11am-10pm
Wed-Sat, 5-10pm Sun) Bundaberg has a buzzing new rival to the rum monopoly in the
form of a craft brewery that serves fine platters of nibbles to accompany pints of Drunk
Fish, Great Barrier Beer and Hip Hop.

❶ Information

Bundaberg Visitor Centre (☑ 07-4153 8888,
1300 722 099; www.bundabergregion.org; 271
Bourbong St; ⊙ 9am-5pm) This reliable information centre serves the region admirably. Definitely stop by if you are driving through the area.

❶ Getting There & Away

AIR
Bundaberg is served daily by **Virgin** (☑ 13 67 89;
www.virginaustralia.com.au) and **Qantas** (☑ 13
13 13; www.qantas.com.au).

BUS
The **coach terminal** (☑ 07-4153 2646; 66 Targo
St) is on Targo St. Both **Greyhound** (☑ 1300 473
946; www.greyhound.com.au) and **Premier Motor
Service** (☑ 13 34 10; www.premierms.com.au)
have daily services connecting Bundaberg with
Brisbane ($94, seven hours), Hervey Bay ($29, two
hours) and Rockhampton ($54, five hours).

   Duffy's Coaches (☑ 1300 383 397) has numerous services every weekday to Bargara ($5,
35 minutes), leaving from the back of Target on
Woongarra St.

TRAIN
The **Queensland Rail** (p371) Tilt Train stops at
Bundaberg train station en route to Brisbane
($49, 4½ hours, Sunday to Friday). Queensland
Rail's Spirit of Queensland ($89, seven hours,
three weekly) also travels from Brisbane to Bun-
daberg on its route to Cairns and Rockhampton.

Bargara
POP 6893

16km east of Bundaberg, Bargara is a popular beachside holiday destination for Queenslanders due to its surf beach, long esplanade
and quiet, family-friendly atmosphere.

   Kacy's Bargara Beach Motel (☑ 07-4130
1100; www.bargaramotel.com.au; 63 Esplanade; d
from $139, 2-bedroom apt from $199; ❋ 🛜 ❄) has
a great location opposite the esplanade, and
a range of accommodation from pleasant
motel rooms to self-contained apartments.

   At **Windmill at Bargara** (☑ 07-4130 5906;
12 See St; mains from $13; ⊙ 6.30am-5pm; 🛜 🍴)
there's lots of space for the kids to play on
the grass and sip chai lattes while smiling
parents nibble on fresh gelato and bask in
the afternoon glow of exhaustion.

Fraser Island

The local Butchulla people call it K'Gari –
paradise – and for good reason. Sculpted
from wind, sand and surf, the striking blue
freshwater lakes, crystalline creeks, giant
dunes and lush rainforests of this gigantic
sandbar form an enigmatic island paradise
unlike anywhere else. Fraser Island is the
largest sand island in the world (measuring

Fraser Island

N 0 — 20 km
0 — 10 miles

Sandy Cape

CORAL SEA

Lake Marong

Rooney Point

Lake Wanhar

Marloo Bay

Hervey Bay Marine Park

Lake Carree

Lake Minker

Waddy Point Ranger Station

Platypus Bay

19

Orchid Beach

13

Middle Rocks

7

Indian Head

Hervey Bay

Triangle Cliff

Yathon Cliffs

Lake Gnarann

Arch Cliff

Lake Bowarrady

Bimjella Hill (174m)

Bowarrady (244m)

12

Dundubara Ranger Station

Coongul Point

9

Great Sandy National Park

Cathedral Beach

Moon Point

3

Point Vernon

5

See Hervey Bay Map (p364)

Blackfellow Point

2

Lake Garawongera

Hervey Bay Visitor Information Centre

1

Hervey Bay

14

Big Woody Island

15

Lake Garawongera

Happy Valley

6

Hervey Bay Coach Terminal

Kingfisher Bay

Rainbow Gorge

Poyungan Valley

Kingfisher Bay Ferry Terminal

16

Leading Hill (184m)

River Heads

Lake McKenzie

Poyungan Rocks

8

River Heads

Wanggoolba Creek Central Station

18

10

Lake Wabby

Eurong QPWS Information Centre

Eurong

Maryborough

4

Boomanjin Hill (211m)

17

Lake Benaroon

Lake Boomanjin

SOUTH PACIFIC OCEAN

Poona National Park

11

Dilli Village

Maaroom

Figtree Lake (Lake Goo Mboor)

Tuan

Great Sandy Strait

The Bluff (64m)

Tuan State Forest

Rainbow Beach (3km)

Fraser Island

120km by 15km), and is the only known place where rainforest grows on sand.

Inland, the vegetation varies from dense tropical rainforest and wild heath to wetlands and wallum scrub, with sandblows, mineral streams and freshwater lakes opening onto long sandy beaches. The island, most of which is protected as part of the Great Sandy National Park, is home to a profusion of bird life and wildlife, including the famous dingo, while offshore waters teem with dugong, dolphins, manta rays, sharks and migrating humpback whales.

◎ Sights & Activities

Starting at the island's southern tip, where the ferry leaves for Inskip Point on the mainland, a high-tide access track cuts inland, avoiding dangerous Hook Point, and leads to the entrance of the Eastern Beach's main thoroughfare. The first settlement is Dilli Village, the former sand-mining centre; Eurong, with shops, fuel and places to eat, is another 9km north. From here, an inland track crosses to Central Station and Wanggoolba Creek (for the ferry to River Heads).

Right in the middle of the island is the ranger centre at Central Station, the starting point for numerous walking trails. From here you can walk or drive to the beautiful McKenzie, Jennings, Birrabeen and Boomanjin Lakes. Lake McKenzie is spectacularly clear and ringed by white-sand beaches, making it a great place to swim; Lake Birrabeen sees fewer tour and backpacker groups.

About 4km north of Eurong along the beach, a signposted walking trail leads across sandblows to the beautiful Lake Wabby, the most accessible of Fraser's lakes. An easier route is from the Lake Wabby Lookout, off Cornwell's Break Rd from the inland side. Lake Wabby is surrounded on three sides by eucalyptus forest, while the fourth side is a massive sandblow that encroaches on the lake at a rate of about 3m a year. The lake is deceptively shallow and diving is very dangerous.

As you drive up the beach, during high tide you may have to detour inland to avoid Poyungan and Yidney Rocks, before reaching Happy Valley, which has places to stay, a shop and a bistro. About 10km further north is Eli Creek, a fast-moving, crystal-clear waterway that will carry you effortlessly downstream. About 2km from Eli Creek is the rotting hulk of the Maheno, a former passenger liner which was blown ashore by a cyclone in 1935 as it was being towed to a Japanese scrap yard.

Roughly 5km north of the Maheno you'll find the Pinnacles, an eroded section of coloured sand cliffs, and about 10km beyond, Dundubara, with a ranger station and an excellent camping ground. Then there's a 20km stretch of beach before you come to the rock outcrop of Indian Head. Sharks, manta rays, dolphins and (during the migration season) whales can often be seen from the top of this headland.

Between Indian Head and Waddy Point, the trail branches inland, passing Champagne Pools, which offers the only safe saltwater swimming on the island. There are good camping areas at Waddy Point and Orchid Beach, the last settlement on the island. Many tracks north of here are closed for environmental protection.

FRASER ISLAND & THE FRASER COAST FRASER ISLAND

SAND SAFARIS

The only way to explore Fraser Island (besides walking) is with a 4WD. For most travellers, there are three transport options: tag-along tours, organised tours or 4WD hire; the fourth option is to stay at one of the island's accommodations and take day tours from there. This is a fragile environment; bear in mind that the greater the number of individual vehicles driving on the island, the greater the environmental damage. With an average of 1000 people per day visiting the island, Fraser can sometimes feel like a giant sandpit with its own peak hour and congested beach highway.

Tag-Along Tours

Popular with backpackers, tag-along tours see groups of travellers pile into a 4WD convoy and follow a lead vehicle with an experienced guide and driver. Travellers take turns driving the other vehicles, which can be great fun, but has also led to accidents. Rates hover around $400 to $430; be sure to check if your tour includes food, fuel, alcohol etc. Accommodation is often in tents.

Advantages You can make new friends fast; driving the beaches is exhilarating.

Disadvantages If food isn't included you'll have to cook; groups can be even bigger than on bus tours.

Operators include the following:

Dropbear Adventures (☑1800 061 156; www.dropbearadventures.com.au) Lots of departures from Hervey Bay, Rainbow Beach and Noosa to Fraser Island; easy to get a spot.

Fraser's on Rainbow (p368) Departs from Rainbow Beach.

Pippies Beach House (p369) Departs Rainbow Beach; well-organised, small convoys with high safety standards.

Organised Tours

Most organised tours cover Fraser's hot spots: rainforests, Eli Creek, Lakes McKenzie and Wabby, the coloured Pinnacles and the *Maheno* shipwreck.

Advantages Expert commentary; decent food and comfortable accommodation; often the most economical choice.

Disadvantages Day-tour buses often arrive at the same place at the same time; less social.

Operators include the following:

Cool Dingo Tours (☑07-4120 3333; www.cooldingotour.com; 2-/3-day tours from $360/415) Overnight at lodges with the option to stay extra nights on the island. The party option.

Fraser Explorer Tours (p365) Very experienced drivers; lots of departures.

Fraser Experience (p365) Small group tours offer greater freedom with the itinerary.

Remote Fraser (☑07-4124 3222; www.tasmanventure.com.au; tours $150) Day tours to the less-visited west coast.

4WD Hire

You can hire a 4WD from Hervey Bay, Rainbow Beach or on Fraser Island itself. All companies require a hefty bond, usually in the form of a credit-card imprint, which you will lose if you drive in salt water – don't even think about running the waves!

When planning your trip, reckon on covering 20km an hour on the inland tracks and 40km an hour on the eastern beach. Most companies will help arrange ferries, permits and camping gear. Rates for multiday rentals start at around $185 a day.

Advantages Complete freedom to roam the island and escape the crowds.

Disadvantages You may encounter beach and track conditions that even experienced drivers find challenging; expensive.

There are rental companies in Hervey Bay (p368) and Rainbow Beach (p370). On the island, **Aussie Trax** (☑07-4124 4433; www.fraserisland4wd.com.au) hires out 4WDs from $283 per person, per day.

Air Fraser Island (p380) has a terrific-value 'Day Away' tour ($150) for those looking to land on the island and explore a little on foot. Depart from Hervey Bay or Sunshine Coast.

🛏 Sleeping

Camping permits are required in order to camp at NPSR camping grounds and any public areas (ie along the beach). The most developed **NPSR camping grounds** (☑13 74 68; www.npsr.qld.gov.au; per person/family $6.15/24.60), with coin-operated hot showers, toilets and BBQs, are at **Waddy Point** (☑13 74 68; www.nprsr.qld.gov.au; per person/family $6.15/24.60), **Dundubara** (www.nprsr.qld.gov.au; per person/family $6.15/24.60) and **Central Station** (☑13 74 68; www.nprsr.qld.gov.au; per person/family $6.15/24.60). Campers with vehicles can also use the smaller camping grounds with fewer facilities at **Lake Boomanjin** (☑13 74 68; www.nprsr.qld.gov.au; per person/family $6.15/24.60), and at **Ungowa** (☑13 74 68; www.nprsr.qld.gov.au; per person/family $6.15/24.60) and **Wathumba** (☑13 74 68; www.nprsr.qld.gov.au; per person/family $6.15/24.60) on the western coast.

Walkers' camps are set away from the main camping grounds, along the Fraser Island Great Walk trail. The trail map lists the camp sites and their facilities. Camping is permitted on designated stretches of the eastern beach, but there are no facilities. Fires are prohibited except in communal fire rings at Waddy Point and Dundubara – bring your own firewood in the form of untreated, milled timber.

Supplies on the island are limited and costly. Stock up well before arriving, and be prepared for mosquitoes and March flies.

Dilli Village Fraser Island   CAMPGROUND $
(☑07-4127 9130; www.usc.edu.au; sites per person $10, dm/cabins $50/120) Managed by the University of the Sunshine Coast, which uses this precinct as a base for research purposes, Dilli Village offers good sites on a softly sloping camping ground. Great value for the space.

Cathedrals on Fraser   CARAVAN PARK $
(☑07-4127 9177; www.cathedralsonfraser.com.au; Cathedral Beach; powered/unpowered sites $39/29, 2-bed cabins with/without bathroom $200/180; @) New owners have kept up the standard and lowered the prices at this spacious dingo-fenced park with abundant, flat, grassy sites. It's a hit with families.

★ Kingfisher Bay Resort   RESORT $$
(☑1800 072 555, 07-4194 9300; www.kingfisherbay.com; Kingfisher Bay; d from $178, 2-bedroom

DON'T MISS

FRASER ISLAND GREAT WALK

The Fraser Island Great Walk is a stunning way to experience this enigmatic island. The trail undulates through the island's interior for 90km from Dilli Village to Happy Valley. Broken up into seven sections of around 6km to 16km each, plus some side trails, it follows the pathways of Fraser Island's original inhabitants, the Butchulla people. En route, the walk passes underneath rainforest canopies, circles around some of the island's vivid lakes, and courses through shifting dunes.

It's imperative that you visit www.npsr.qld.gov.au for maps, detailed information and updates on the track, which can close when conditions are bad.

villas $329; ❄@≋) 🍃 This elegant eco-resort has hotel rooms with private balconies, and sophisticated two- and three-bedroom timber villas that are elevated to limit their environmental impact. There's a three-night minimum stay in high season. The Seabelle Restaurant is terrific (mains from $18), while the three bars are great fun in summer at sunset, especially the Dingo Bar.

Fraser Island Retreat   CABIN $$
(☑07-4127 9144; www.fraserisretreat.com.au; Happy Valley; d/apt from $140/200; @�≋) Located in the relatively remote Happy Valley, halfway along the east coast of the island, this retreat's nine timber cabins (each sleeping up to four people) are great for a comfortable nature experience. The cabins are airy, nestled in native foliage and close to the beach. On-site there's a camp kitchen, a licensed restaurant and a shop that sells fuel.

★ Eliza Fraser Lodge   LODGE $$$
(☑0418 981 610; www.elizafraserlodge.com.au; per person $375) Located at a stunning house up at Orchid Beach in the northeast of the island, Eliza Fraser is the finest lodging available by far. Serviced directly by Air Fraser (regular ferry transfers also available), the two-level house is exquisite for families or small groups. The hosts are expert guides and will organise fishing trips, nature hikes and 4WD adventures, or let you enjoy the run of the house and spectacular surrounds.

ℹ Information

You must purchase permits from **NPSR** (🖉 13 74 68; www.npsr.qld.gov.au) for vehicles (less than a month $48.25) and to camp in the NPSR camping grounds ($6.15/24.60 per person/family) before you arrive. Permits aren't required for private camping grounds or resorts. Buy permits online or check with visitor centres for up-to-date lists of where to buy them.

Eurong QPWS Information Centre (🖉 07-4127 9128) is the main ranger station. Others can be found at **Dundubara** (🖉 07-4127 9138) and **Waddy Point** (🖉 07-4127 9190). Offices are often unattended as the rangers are out on patrol.

ℹ Getting There & Away

Before crossing via ferry from either Rainbow Beach or Hervey Bay, ensure that your vehicle has suitably high clearance (if you're one of the few not visiting on a tour, that is) and, if camping, that you have adequate food, water and fuel.

AIR
Air Fraser Island (🖉 1300 172 706, 07-4125 3600; www.airfraserisland.com.au) charges from $150 for a return flight (30-minute round trip) to the island's eastern beach, departing Hervey Bay airport.

BOAT
Vehicle ferries connect Fraser Island with River Heads, about 10km south of Hervey Bay, or further south at Inskip Point, near Rainbow Beach. Ferries from Hervey Bay dock at Moon Point.

Fraser Venture Barge (🖉 1800 227 437, 07-4194 9300; www.fraserislandferry.com.au) Makes the crossing (pedestrian adult/child return $58/30, vehicle and four passengers

$175 return, 30 minutes) from River Heads to Wanggoolba Creek on the western coast of Fraser Island. It departs daily from River Heads at 8.30am, 10.15am and 4pm, and returns from the island at 9am, 3pm and 5pm.

Kingfisher Bay Ferry (🖉 1800 227 437, 07-4194 9300; www.fraserislandferry.com) Operates a daily vehicle and passenger ferry (pedestrian adult/child return $58/30, vehicle and four passengers return $175, 50 minutes) from River Heads to Kingfisher Bay, departing at 6.45am, 9am, 12.30pm, 3.30pm, 6.45pm and 9.30pm (Friday and Saturday only) and returning at 7.50am, 10.30am, 2pm, 5pm, 8.30pm and 11pm (Friday and Saturday only).

Manta Ray (🖉 07-5486 3935; www.mantaray-fraserislandbarge.com.au) Coming from Rainbow Beach, Manta Ray has two ferries making the 15-minute crossing from Inskip Point to Hook Point on Fraser Island, continuously from about 6am to 5.30pm daily (vehicle return $120).

ℹ Getting Around

A 4WD is necessary if you're driving on Fraser Island; you'll need a permit. Expensive fuel is available from stores at Cathedral Beach, Eurong, Kingfisher Bay, Happy Valley and Orchid Beach. If your vehicle breaks down, call the **tow-truck service** (🖉 0428 353 164, 07-4127 9449) in Eurong.

The 4WD **Fraser Island Taxi Service** (🖉 07-4127 9188; www.fraserservice.com.au) operates all over the island. Bookings are essential, as there's only one cab for the whole island!

If you want to hire a 4WD while on the island, Aussie Trax (p378) has a medium-sized fleet, from Suzuki Sierras to LandCruisers, available at the Kingfisher Bay Resort (p379).

ℹ DEALING WITH DINGOES

Despite its many natural attractions and opportunities for adventure, there's nothing on Fraser Island that gives a thrill comparable to your first glimpse of a dingo. Believed to be among the most genetically pure in the world, the dingoes of Fraser are sleek, spry and utterly beautiful. They're also wild beasts that can become aggressive at the drop of a hat (or a strong-smelling food sack). While attacks are rare, there are precautions that must be taken by every visitor to the island.

➡ However skinny they appear, or whatever woebegone look they give you, never feed dingoes. Dingoes that are human-fed quickly lose their shyness and can become combative and competitive. Feeding dingoes is illegal and carries heavy fines.

➡ Don't leave any food scraps lying around, and don't take food to the lakes: eating on the shore puts your food at 'dingo level', an easy target for scrounging scavengers.

➡ Stay in groups, and keep any children within arm's reach at all times.

➡ Teasing dingoes is not only cruel, but dangerous. Leave them alone, and they'll do same.

➡ Dingoes are best observed at a distance. Pack a zoom lens and practise some silence, and you'll come away with some brilliant photographs…and all your limbs intact.

Capricorn Coast & the Southern Reef Islands

Best Places to Eat

➡ Getaway Garden Café (p384)

➡ Ginger Mule (p389)

➡ Lightbox (p386)

➡ Megalomania (p391)

➡ Sol Foods (p384)

Best Places to Sleep

➡ Svendsen's Beach (p392)

➡ Cool Bananas (p383)

➡ Lady Elliot Island Eco Resort (p387)

➡ Takarakka Bush Resort (p394)

Why Go?

The stretch of coastline that straddles the tropic of Capricorn is one of the quietest and most lovely lengths of the east coast. While local families flock to the main beaches during school holidays, the scene is uncrowded for most of the year, and even in high season you needn't travel far to find a deserted beach.

Agnes Water and Town of 1770 are twin towns with a glowing reputation, and many travelers head from here for some of the world's best snorkelling and diving on the Southern Reef Islands. Opportunities for wildlife spotting are plentiful.

Great Keppel National Park is another tourism commercial in the making. The stunning powdery white sand and turquoise waters of the Capricorn Coast fit the holiday-brochure image perfectly. Unspoiled and windswept national parks such as Deepwater and Byfield can be found along the entire coastline, and are almost never busy.

Inland, you'll find bustling Rockhampton – Capricornia's economic hub and the capital of cattle country, with the steakhouses, rodeos and gigantic hats to prove it.

When to Go
Rockhampton

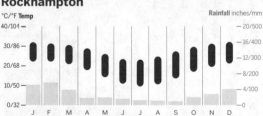

Feb The Agnes Blues & Roots Festival rocks the Discovery Coast.	**May–Sep** Warm winter temperatures are ideal for swimming and sunning.
Dec Nature puts on a stunning light show during the summer solstice at Capricorn Caves.	

Capricorn Coast & the Southern Reef Islands Highlights

1 **Heron Island** (p387) and **Lady Elliot Island** (p387) Diving the spectacular underwater coral gardens.

2 **Great Keppel Island** (p392) Claiming a tropical beach for the day.

3 **Agnes Water** (p383) Surfing and chilling at

4 **Carnarvon Gorge** (p393) Hiking to find aboriginal rock art.

5 **Rockhampton** (p388) Tucking into a huge steak in Australia's beef capital.

6 **Capricorn Caves** (p389) Crawling through black holes and tight tunnels.

7 **Gem Fields** (p394) Fossicking for a fortune-changing sapphire.

Queensland's most northerly surf beach.

Agnes Water & Town of 1770

POP 1650

Not so long ago the twin coastal towns of Agnes Water and Town of 1770 were tipped by property speculators as Australia's next Noosa or Gold Coast. Thankfully for visitors to this lovely outpost 70km south of Gladstone, hemmed in by national parks, hidden red rock coves and the Pacific Ocean, little has changed and the tourism boom was more like a fizz.

Agnes Water is the east coast's most northerly surf beach, a long, glorious point break rolling into an idyllic shoreline by a friendly strip of shops. A 6km jaunt down the road is the site of Captain Cook's first landing in Queensland in, you guessed it, 1770. The short bluff walks are outstanding, and the camping site is one of the most dreamy in the state, a launching point for kayaking and paddleboarding and fishing excursions around the inlets of the 'Discovery Coast'.

◉ Sights & Activities

Miriam Vale Historical Society Museum   MUSEUM
(☑07-4974 9511; www.agneswatermuseum.com; Springs Rd, near cnr Captain Cook Dr, Agnes Water; adult/child $3/free; ⊙1-4pm Mon & Wed-Sat, 10am-4pm Sun) The museum displays extracts from Cook's journal and the original telescope from the first lighthouse built on the Queensland coast.

★Scooter Roo Tours   ADVENTURE SPORTS
(☑07-4974 7697; www.scooterrootours.com; 2694 Round Hill Rd, Agnes Water; 3hr rides $85) You don't need to be a petrolhead to absolutely love this hilarious and informative 50km-tour of the Agnes Water area. Better yet, you only need a car licence to get low and dirty on a real 'chopper' bike. Wear long pants and closed-in shoes; they'll supply the tough-guy leather jackets (with flames, of course).

1770 SUP   WATER SPORTS
(☑0421 026 255; www.1770sup.com.au; 1½/2hr tours $45/50) Explore the calm waters and sandy banks of 1770 with a top-notch stand-up paddleboarding (SUP) instructor. Tours include an intro lesson, or rent your own board for $25/30 for one/two hours. The roving SUP trailer can often be found on the 1770 waterfront across from Tree Bar.

1770 Liquid Adventures   KAYAKING
(☑0428 956 630; www.1770liquidadventures.com.au) Paddle off on a spectacular twilight kayak tour. For $55 you ride the waves off 1770, before retiring to the beach for drinks and snacks as the sun sets – keep an eye out for dolphins. You can also rent kayaks (from $20/30 per one/two hours). Family tours ($30 per person) focus on bird and marine life and will appeal to any child who is comfortable paddling alone.

1770 Larc Tours   TOURS
(☑07-4974 9422; www.1770larctours.com.au; day trips adult/child $155/95) ✿ The ex-military Lighter Amphibious Resupply Cargo (LARC) vehicle makes a comfortable ride for exploring the natural joys of Bustard Head and Eurimbula National Park. Guides know their stuff and will entertain all ages. Aside from the signature seven-hour day trip (lunch included), they also run hour-long afternoon tours (adult/child $38/17) and sandboarding safaris ($120).

Hooked on 1770   BOATING
(☑07-4974 9794; www.1770tours.com; half-/full-day tours $175/250) Hooked on 1770 has full- and half-day fishing tours which come highly recommended by long-time locals and Australian repeat visitors alike.

✱✰ Festivals & Events

Agnes Blues & Roots Festival   MUSIC
(www.agnesbluesandroots.com.au; SES Grounds, Agnes Water; ⊙Feb) Top names and up-and-coming Aussie acts crank it up on the last weekend of February.

⌸ Sleeping

★Cool Bananas   HOSTEL $
(☑07-4974 7660, 1800 227 660; www.coolbananas.net.au; 2 Springs Rd, Agnes Water; dm $29; @🛜) The young and free go bananas for this funky, open-minded backpacker hangout, with a questionable colour scheme but an irresistible vibe cultivated by the friendly owners. Roomy six- and eight-bed dorms are functional, and management does not allow rooms to be locked in order to encourage mingling. Funnily enough, it works (smiles all round when we visited!). It's only a five-minute walk to the beach and shops.

Backpackers @ 1770   HOSTEL $
(☑0408 533 851; www.backpackers1770.com.au; 22 Grahame Colyer Dve, Agnes Water; dm/d

$26/60) The most established hostel in 1770 is a beauty. The upsides are obvious: easy interactions between staff and guests, spotless dorms, three smart doubles at a good price point and a lush communal garden where meals are taken and stories are shared. For many young travellers, this hostel is an east coast must.

1770 Camping Ground CARAVAN PARK $

(☑07-4974 9286; www.1770campingground.com.au; Captain Cook Dr, Town of 1770; powered/unpowered sites from $39/35, beachfront sites $44) This camping ground, 1770's favourite, must challenge for best location on the east coast. Fall into the shallow water from your tent strung among plenty of shady trees.

Workmans Beach Camping Area CAMPGROUND $

(Workmans Beach, Springs Rd, Agnes Water; sites per person $9) Workmans Beach is a council-run camping ground with spacious sites in gorgeous beachside surrounds. Facilities include cold-water showers, drop toilets and gas BBQs. If you're really smitten, you can stay up to 44 days. You can't book sites; just turn up, and good-humoured council staff will knock on your van/tent at an ungodly hour of the morning to sort out payment.

1770 Southern Cross Backpackers HOSTEL $

(☑07-4974 7225; www.1770southerncross.com; 2694 Round Hill Rd, Agnes Water; dm/d incl breakfast $25/85; @ 🕸🐾) The large eucalypt-forest retreat of Southern Cross is 2.5km out of town and will suit the more mellow backpacker (or one in search of time out!). There's plenty of space to lie about the pool, play games, cook a BBQ or sling a hammock. A courtesy bus takes revellers and beach-goers into the 'action' of Agnes, but most guests just roam between their bare four-bed dorms, pleasant double rooms and the Buddha Bar come nightfall.

The Lovely Cottages GUESTHOUSE $$

(☑07-4974 9554; www.thelovelycottages.com.au; 61 Bicentennial Dr, Agnes Water; cottages $155, 2 nights $300; P🌸🐾) New owners and a name change have boosted the creative energy at this eco-retreat and outdoor gallery, which is the epitome of Queensland casual bush chic. Each colourful cottage sleeps up to five people. There is an excellent lagoon-style pool, which makes for thrilling swimming in the bush scrub.

Agnes Water Beach Club APARTMENT $$

(☑07-4974 7355; www.agneswaterbeachclub.com.au; 3 Agnes St, Agnes Water; 1-/2-bedroom apt from $180/280; 🌸@🕸🐾) The Beach Club has the most convenient location for access to shops in Agnes and the patrolled beach. The apartments themselves are bright and comfortable, facing onto a good-sized pool. Very much a family atmosphere permeating the communal areas.

★1770 Getaway RESORT $$$

(☑07-4974 9323; www.1770getaway.com.au; 303 Bicentennial Dve, Agnes Water; d from $170; P🐾🕸🐾) The much-loved Getaway Garden Cafe (p384) has expanded its repertoire with a delightful series of villas running across 1.5 hectares acres of bush onto an empty stretch of beach. Each villa has an airy, open feel and luxury bathrooms. Breakfast by the pond can be included and there's a hip little boutique on-site.

✕ Eating

Sol Foods VEGAN $

(☑07-4974 9039; 1 Round Hill Rd, Agnes Water; salads from $10, cakes from $6; ⊙8am-4.30pm) This wholefoods grocer doubles as a cafe and an enlightened source of local knowledge. The vegan cakes are unbeatable and the salads are hearty and good value.

Agnes Water Bakery BAKERY $

(☑07-4974 9500; Round Hill Rd, Agnes Water; pies $5.50; ⊙6am-4pm Mon-Sat, to 2pm Sun) Don't dawdle if you want to get your mouth around one of this popular bakery's killer pies. Expect gourmet stuffings, including a couple of vegetarian selections. On the sweet side, the chocolate éclairs, jam scrolls and apple turnovers are usually gone by noon. Oh, and there's bread too.

★Getaway Garden Café MODERN AUSTRALIAN $$

(☑07-4974 9323; 303 Bicentennial Dr, Agnes Water; breakfast $7-19, lunch $10-22, dinner $20-25; ⊙8am-4pm Sun-Thu, & 5.30pm-late Wed & Sun) The region's most revered eatery continues to impress due to its culinary simplicity using only local ingredients, impeccable family-oriented service and natural, waterside setting. Breakfasts are healthy and accompanied by fine coffee and juices. Lunch features pizza, fish and burgers. The lamb spit roasts on Wednesday and Sunday nights are very popular with locals (book ahead). Stop in for cake and coffee outside of main meal times.

Tree Bar   MODERN AUSTRALIAN **$$**
(☑ 07-4974 7446; 576 Captain Cook Dr, Town of 1770; mains $16-34; ⊘ breakfast, lunch & dinner) This is the best outlook for a sundowner and a steak sandwich in 1770. This little salt-encrusted waterfront diner and bar is no award-winner, but it marvellously catches sea breezes from the beach through the trees. Prices are a little steep for the quality, but you couldn't paint a better view.

Agnes Water Tavern   PUB FOOD **$$**
(☑ 07-4974 9469; 1 Tavern Rd, Agnes Water; mains $15-30; ⊘ from 11.30am) A broad snapshot of Australian life is found in the huge tavern just outside town, where you can drink, gamble, play games, watch sport, party, eat, meet and enjoy the sunshine in the ample outdoor seating. The backpacker set keep it lively some nights. Lunch and dinner specials daily.

❶ Information

Agnes Water Visitors Centre (☑ 07-4902 1533; 71 Springs Rd, Town of 1770; ⊘ 9am-5pm Mon-Fri, to 4pm Sat & Sun) Staffed by above-and-beyond volunteers who even leave out information and brochures when it's closed, just in case a lost boat blows into town.

Discover 1770 (☑ 07-4974 7557; www. discover1770.com.au; next to Shell service station) With so many different operators plying the Discovery Coast – and often changing hands or merging businesses – the friendly folk at Discover 1770 can help to guide your decision making. At the time of research, it was the only outlet for arranging boats to Lady Musgrave Island.

❶ Getting There & Away

A handful of **Greyhound** (☑ 1300 473 946; www. greyhound.com.au) buses detour off the Bruce Hwy to Agnes Water; daily services include Bundaberg ($28, 1½ hours) and Cairns ($210, 21 hours). **Premier Motor Service** (☑ 13 34 10; www.premierms.com.au) also goes in and out of town.

Eurimbula & Deepwater National Parks

Eight kilometres south of Agnes Water is **Deepwater National Park** (www.nprsr.qld. gov.au/parks/deepwater), an unspoiled coastal landscape with long sandy beaches, walking trails, freshwater creeks, good fishing spots and two camping grounds accessible only by 4WD. It's also a major breeding ground for loggerhead turtles, which dig nests and lay eggs on the beaches between November and February; hatchlings emerge at night between January and April.

The 78-sq-km Eurimbula National Park, on the northern side of Round Hill Creek, has a landscape of dunes, mangroves and eucalypt forest. Both offer delightful beaches, hikes and splendid, relatively accessible isolation in the Australian bush.

Camping permits are available from the **NPRSR** (☑ 13 74 68; www.npsr.qld.gov.au; permit per person/family $6.15/24.60). Wreck Rock Campground has a sizeable picnic area, rain and bore water and composting toilets.

Gladstone

POP 37,941

Gladstone is a middle-sized town known nationwide, for better or worse, as a major port for the mining industry, and an industrial town with a power station and an incongruous outlook on the Great Barrier Reef. You might want to head straight for the marina (Bryan Jordan Dr), the main departure point for boats to the southern coral cay islands of Heron, Masthead and Wilson on the Great Barrier Reef. If there's anything happening in town, it's on at the port end of Gondoon St.

Lake Awoonga Boat Hire (☑ 07-4975 0930; tinnies half-day $80, kayaks per hour $15) is an unofficial tourist guide and friendly boat hire place, or you can charter the **MV Mikat** (☑ 0427 125 727; www.mikat.com.au).

CURTIS ISLAND

Curtis Island, just across the water from Gladstone, can't be confused with a resort island. Apart from swimming, fishing and lolling about on the dunes, its main drawcard is the annual appearance of rare flatback turtles on its eastern shores between October and January. Camping permits can be booked via **NPRSR** (☑ 13 74 68; www.nprsr.qld.gov.au; permit per person/family $5.45/21.80) or you can stay with the friendly folks at **Capricorn Lodge** (☑ 07-4972 0222; capricornlodge@ bigpond.com; lodgings from around $80). They have a corner store and a liquor licence. Curtis Ferry Services (p386) connects the island with Gladstone every day bar Tuesday and Thursday.

🛏 Sleeping

Gladstone Backpackers   HOSTEL $
(☑ 07-4972 5744; www.gladstonebackpackers.
com.au; 12 Rollo St; dm/tw $28/66; @ 🛜 ≋) Set
inside a big blue Queenslander down by the
marina, Gladstone Backpackers has under-
gone a makeover. There's a large communal
kitchen and shared bathrooms, while dorm
rooms and twins feel brand new. Grey
nomads, itinerant miners and European
wanderers like to sit on the airy verandah
and find common ground. There's free use
of bicycles and free pick-ups from the all
transport depots.

🍴 Eating & Drinking

Gladstone Yacht Club   PUB FOOD $$
(☑ 07-4972 2294; www.gyc.com.au; 1 Goondoon
St; mains from $22; ⊙ noon-2pm & 6-8.30pm
Mon-Thu, 11.30am-2.30pm & 5.30-9pm Fri & Sat,
11.30am-2pm & 6-8.30pm Sun) Clubs are a
mainstay of regional Australia. Hugely social
places where the beer flows, the yarns are
spun and the meals are generally massive
and good value. The Gladstone Yacht Club
is a welcoming place where burgers and sea-
food are the best bets. You can also eat on
the deck overlooking the water.

Tables on Flinders   SEAFOOD $$$
(☑ 07-4972 8322; 2 Oaka La; mains from $38;
⊙ lunch Tue-Fri, dinner Tue-Sat) If you feel like a
Gladstone splurge, this is the place to do it,
with exquisite local seafood including fresh
mudcrab, bugs and prawns dominating the
menu.

Lightbox   WINE BAR
(☑ 07-4972 2698; 56 Goondoon St; ⊙ 7am-late)
Indicative of Gladstone's maturing social
scene, this slick wine bar in the newly developed entertainment precinct also has a long
cocktail list and serves delicious charcuterie
(cured meat dishes). Breakfast and coffee
are also recommended.

❶ Information

Visitor Centre (☑ 07-4972 9000; Bryan Jordan
Dr; ⊙ 8.30am-4.30pm Mon-Fri, 9.30am-
4.30pm Sat & Sun) Located at the marina, the
departure point for boats to Heron Island, and
for free tours of the alumina refineries which
help drive the region's economy.

❶ Getting There & Away

AIR

Qantas (☑ 13 13 13; www.qantas.com.au) and
Virgin (☑ 13 67 89; www.virginaustralia.com)
operate flights to and from Gladstone Airport,
which is 7km from the city centre.

BOAT

Curtis Ferry Services (☑ 07-4972 6990; www.
curtisferryservices.com.au; return adult/child
$30/18, family from $84) has regular services
to Curtis Island on Monday, Wednesday, Friday,
Saturday and Sunday. The service leaves from
the Gladstone marina and stops at Farmers
Point on Facing Island en route. Transport
to other nearby islands can be arranged on
request.

You can also access the islands with various
charter operators.

If you've booked a stay on Heron Island, the
resort operates a launch (one-way adult/child
$50/25, two hours), which leaves the Gladstone
marina at 11am daily.

BUS

Greyhound Australia (☑ 1300 473 946; www.
greyhound.com.au) has several coach services
from Brisbane ($154, 10 hours), Bundaberg
($47, three hours) and Rockhampton ($24, 1½
hours). The terminal is at the BP service station

ART DETOUR

Cedar Galleries (☑ 07-4975 0444; www.cedargalleries.com.au; Bruce Hwy, Calliope; ⊙ 9am-
4pm Thu-Sat, 8am-4pm Sun) is a tranquil artists' bush retreat where you can watch painters
and sculptors at work in the rustic slab-hut studios. To unleash your creative genius you
can take art & craft classes with visiting artists (call ahead to book) or just browse the
gardens and the gallery. There's also a cafe, a beautiful handcrafted wedding chapel, kids'
jumping castle, a winery cellar door and a herd of friendly alpacas. The complex runs a
weekly farmers market every Sunday (from 8am to noon); the friendly bazaar is the ideal
spot for stocking up on gourmet goodies, freshly baked bread, local wines and handmade
gifts. Having too much fun to move on? Cedar Galleries has limited **farmstay accommodation** (studio $100 first night, $60 subsequent nights) available.

This old-school Aussie artists' colony (25km south of Gladstone) is signposted off the
Bruce Hwy, 7km southeast of Calliope.

on the Dawson Hwy, about 200m southwest of the centre.

TRAIN

Queensland Rail (☑ 07-3235 1122, 1800 872 467; www.queenslandrail.com.au) has frequent north- and southbound services passing through Gladstone daily. The Tilt Train stops in Gladstone from Brisbane (from $84, five hours) and Rockhampton (from $26, one hour).

Southern Reef Islands

While much fuss is made about the Great Barrier Reef's northern splendour, Southern Reef Island is the place of 'castaway' dreams: tiny coral atolls fringed with sugary white sand and turquoise-blue seas, and hardly anyone within flipper-flapping reach. From beautiful Lady Elliot Island, 80km northeast of Bundaberg, secluded and uninhabited coral reefs and atolls dot the ocean for about 140km up to Tryon Island. Lady Musgrave is essentially a blue lagoon in the middle of the ocean, while Heron Island is a discerning natural escape for adventurous families and world-class scuba diving.

Several cays in this part of the reef are excellent for snorkelling, diving and just getting back to nature – though reaching them is generally more expensive than reaching islands nearer the coast. Some of the islands are important breeding grounds for turtles and seabirds, and visitors should be aware of precautions to ensure the wildlife's protection.

Lady Elliot Island

Set on the southern rim of the Great Barrier Reef, Lady Elliot is a 40-hectare vegetated coral cay populated with nesting sea turtles and an impressive number of seabirds. It's considered to have the best snorkelling in the southern Great Barrier Reef and the diving is good too: explore an oceanbed of shipwrecks, coral gardens, bommies (coral pinnacles or outcroppings) and blowholes, and abundant marine life, including barracuda, giant manta rays and harmless leopard sharks.

Lady Elliot Island Eco Resort (☑ 1800 072 200; www.ladyelliot.com.au; r $175-420, child $95) has been around for a few decades now, but it has fortunately lost little of its ramshackle charm. The cabins are a great deal for groups of four on a budget, while the garden suites offer a little more protection from the wind and more space to stretch out at night.

Heron & Wilson Islands

Part of the smaller Capricornia Cays group, Heron Island is ranked among the finest scuba-diving regions in the world, particularly in terms of ease of access. Visitors to Heron generally know what they are coming for – underwater paradise – but the island's rugged beauty is reason enough to stay above the surface. A true coral cay, it is densely vegetated with pisonia trees and surrounded by 24 sq km of reef. There's a resort and research station on the northeastern third of the island; the remainder is national park. Note that 200,000 birds call the island home at different stages of the year, so there can be a lot of guano at times.

The island has excellent beaches, superb snorkelling and, during the season, turtle watching.

Heron Island Resort (☑ 1300 863 248; www.heronisland.com; d/ste from $330/572) is not particularly glamorous, despite the hefty price tag for a room, however the interaction with an incredible natural environment is difficult to find elsewhere in the world, and the resort itself should not be the reason you visit. Great deals are often available on its website. Meal packages are extra, and guests will pay $62/31 (one-way) per adult/child for launch transfer, $338 by seaplane from Gladstone.

The **Heron Islander** (☑ 1800 837 168; www.heronisland.com; adult/child one-way $62/31) departs Gladstone daily at 2pm (2½ hours).

For a more glamorous approach, take a **seaplane** (☑ 1300 863 248; www.heronisland.com; $338 one-way). Departures are daily subject to demand, and times can vary.

North West Island

North West is a spectacular 106-hectare coral cay, the second-biggest on the reef. Like much of the Capricornia Cays National Park, North West is a remote tropical haven, its walking and camping pedigree steadily growing in recent years. It is now an important site for nesting green turtles and birds; every October, hundreds of thousands of wedge-tailed shearwaters descend on the island to nest, squabble and scare the wits out of campers with their creepy nighttime howls. It's hard to imagine that North West was once a guano mine and home to a turtle-soup cannery. It really is paradise revisited.

Rockhampton & Around

POP 66,192

Welcome to Rockhampton ('Rocky' to its mates), where the hats, boots and utes are big...but the bulls are even bigger. With over 2.5 million cattle within a 250km radius of Rockhampton, it's called Australia's Beef Capital for a reason. This sprawling country town is the administrative and commercial centre of central Queensland, its wide streets and fine Victorian-era buildings (take a stroll down Quay St) reflecting the region's prosperous 19th-century heyday of gold and copper mining and beef-cattle industry.

Straddling the tropic of Capricorn, Rocky can be aptly scorching. It's 40km inland and lacks coastal sea breezes; summers are often unbearably humid. The town has a smattering of attractions but is best seen as a gateway to the coastal gems of Yeppoon and Great Keppel Island, and the Byfield National Park to the north.

◉ Sights

★ **Botanic Gardens** GARDENS
(☑ 07-4932 9000; Spencer St; ⊙ 6am-6pm) FREE Just south of town, these gardens are a beautiful oasis, with tropical and subtropical rainforest, landscaped gardens and lily-covered lagoons. The formal Japanese garden is a zone of tranquillity, there's a cafe (⊙ 8am to 5pm), and the small, well-kept zoo (⊙ 8.30am to 4.30pm, admission free) has koalas, wombats, dingoes, monkeys, a walk-through aviary and tonnes more.

Dreamtime Cultural Centre CULTURAL CENTRE
(☑ 07-4936 1655; www.dreamtimecentre.com. au; Bruce Hwy; adult/child $15.50/7.50; ⊙ 10am-3.30pm Mon-Fri, tours 10.30am & 1pm) The story of the local Dharumbal people is well conveyed in this easily accessible insight into Aboriginal and Torres Strait Islander heritage and history. The excellent 90-minute tours are hands on – throw your own boomerangs! – and appeal to all ages. It's about 7km north of the city centre.

Kershaw Gardens GARDENS
(☑ 07-4936 8254; via Charles St; ⊙ 6am-6pm) FREE Just north of the Fitzroy River, this excellent botanical park is devoted to Australian native plants. Its attractions include artificial rapids, a rainforest area, a fragrant garden and heritage architecture.

Mt Archer MOUNTAIN
This mountain (604m) has walking trails weaving through eucalypts and rainforest abundant in wildlife. A brochure to the park is available from the visitor centres.

Rockhampton Art Gallery GALLERY
(☑ 07-4936 8248; www.rockhamptonartgallery. com.au; 62 Victoria Pde; ⊙ 10am-4pm) FREE Boasting an impressive collection of Australian paintings, this gallery includes works by Sir Russell Drysdale and Sir Sidney Nolan. Contemporary Indigenous artists are also on display.

Archer Park Rail Museum MUSEUM
(☑ 07-4936 8191; www.rockhamptonregion.qld.gov. au; 51-87 Denison St; adult/child/family $8/5/26; ⊙ 10am-3pm Mon-Thu, 10am-1pm Sun) This museum is housed in a former train station built in 1899. Through photographs and displays it tells the station's story, and that of the unique Purrey steam tram. Take a ride on the restored tram – the only remaining one of its kind in the world! – every Sunday from 10am to 1pm.

Heritage Village MUSEUM
(☑ 07-4936 8688; www.heritagevillage.com.au; 296 Boundary Rd; adult/child/family $14/8.50/40; ⊙ 9am-4pm) A great place to break up a road trip, especially with kids, the Heritage Village is an active museum of replica historic buildings with townsfolk at work in period garb. The classrooms, garages and reconstructed shops will tickle all ages. There's also a visitor centre here. It's 10km north of the city centre, just off the Bruce Highway (A1).

🛏 Sleeping

Southside Holiday Village CARAVAN PARK $
(☑ 07-4927 3013; www.sshv.com.au; Lower Dawson Rd; powered/unpowered sites $38/30, cabins $93, villas $98-125; ❈ @ 🛜 ⛱) This is one of the city's best caravan parks, with neat, self-contained cabins and villas, large grassy camp sites and a good kitchen. Prices are for two people. It's about 3km south of the centre on a busy main road.

Rockhampton Backpackers HOSTEL $
(☑ 07-4927 5288; www.rockhamptonbackpackers .com.au; 60 MacFarlane St; dm/d $23.50/60; ❈ @ 🛜 ⛱) A very fluid, unpretentious YHA hostel that at times resembles an employment agency, Rocky Backpackers has an industrial-sized communal kitchen, open-plan living areas where travellers share

CAPRICORN CAVES

Capricorn Caves (07-4934 2883; www.capricorncaves.com.au; 30 Olsens Caves Rd; adult/child/family $30/15/75; 9am-5pm) are a rare acoustic and visual treat found deep beneath the Berserker Range 24km north of Rockhampton near the Caves township. The most popular one-hour tour includes a classical music recording and, around mid-morning, a sunlit refraction of stunning natural beauty. These ancient caves honeycomb a limestone ridge where you'll see cave coral, stalactites, dangling fig-tree roots and, less likely, little insectivorous bats.

In December, around the summer solstice (1 December to 14 January), sunlight beams directly through a 14m vertical shaft into Belfry Cave, creating an electrifying light show. If you stand directly below the beam, reflected sunlight colours the whole cavern with whatever colour you're wearing.

Daring spelunkers can book a two-hour 'adventure tour' ($75; reserve a day or more in advance) which takes you through tight spots with names such as 'Fat Man's Misery'. You must be at least 16 years old for this tour.

The Capricorn Caves complex has barbecue areas, a pool, a kiosk and accommodation (powered sites $35, cabins $150 to180).

information on cattle stations and fruit farms, and basic four-bed dorms. The pool is small but you'll take a cold puddle in Rocky's brutal summers.

Myella Farm Stay
FARMSTAY $$
(07-4998 1290; www.myella.weebly.com; Baralaba Rd; d/tr from $90/130, 2/3 days $250/390, powered sites $22;) Myella Farm Stay, 125km southwest of Rockhampton, gives you a taste of the outback on its 10.6-sq-km farm. Lots of options are available, including comfortable camping and bush meals ($10 to $20) for those who are just passing through. The best experience though is engaging in the many activities on offer in a package deal. The package includes bush explorations by horseback, motorcycle and 4WD, all meals, accommodation in a renovated homestead with polished timber floors and a wide verandah, farm clothes and free transfers from Rockhampton.

Criterion
HOTEL $$
(07-4922 1225; www.thecriterion.com.au; 150 Quay St; pub r $65-90, motel r $130-160;) The Criterion is Rockhampton's grandest old pub, with an elegant foyer, a friendly bar and a well-respected steakhouse. For travellers – or heavy drinkers – its top two storeys have dozens of dated period rooms, some in original heritage style, and all exceptional value for money. All rooms have showers, although the toilets are down the hall. If it's a little raw, or noisy, you can find a number of bland, though modern motel rooms next door.

Coffee House
MOTEL, APARTMENT $$
(07-4927 5722; www.coffeehouse.com.au; 51 William St; r $150-180;) The Coffee House features small, tiled motel rooms, self-contained apartments and spa suites, all thoughtfully decorated and including dark-wood writing desks. There's a popular and stylish cafe-restaurant–wine bar on-site.

★Denison Boutique Hotel
BOUTIQUE HOTEL $$$
(07-4923 7378; www.denisonboutiquehotel.com.au; 233 Denison St; d $200) The newest hotel in Rockhampton is also the finest: a gorgeous white building constructed in 1885. Surrounded by rose gardens and hedges, Denison rooms have king-sized four-poster beds, high ceilings and large plasma TVs. Discounts are available online, which make the experience very accessible.

✗ Eating & Drinking

Saigon Saigon
ASIAN $
(07-4927 0888; www.saigonbytheriver.com; Quay St; mains $12-28; lunch & dinner Wed-Mon;) This two-storey bamboo hut overlooks the Fitzroy River and serves delicious pan-Asian food with local ingredients like kangaroo and crocodile served in a sizzling steamboat. Not up for reptile? The menu is as intricate as the restaurant exterior's neon light display. Lots of vegetarian options, too.

Ginger Mule
STEAK $
(07-4927 7255; 8 William St; mains from $10; noon-midnight Tue-Thu, noon-2am Fri, 4pm-2am Sat) Rocky's coolest eatery bills itself as a

tapas bar, but everyone's here for one thing: steak! The steak sandwich ($11) has to be among the best bargain meals in Queensland, while the $12 sirloin flies out of the busy kitchen late into the night. Morphs into a cocktail bar late in the evening.

Pacino's ITALIAN **$$**
(☑07-4922 5833; cnr Fitzroy & George Sts; mains $25-40; ☺lunch & dinner) Run by the same family for 30 years, Pacino's is a riverside favourite and the best Italian for miles. Pricey, though consistently popular for enormous pasta dishes and many regional specialities. The lamb's brains and lobster ravioli are well above what you'd expect from such a small city, though avoid the pizza.

Restaurant 98 SEAFOOD **$$**
(☑07-4920 1000; www.98.com.au; 98 Victoria Pde; mains $18-46; ☺breakfast daily, lunch Mon-Fri, dinner Mon-Sat) Oysters, steak and flagons of fine red wine are the signature order at this licensed dining room attached to **Motel 98** (d from $124). Sit inside or on the terrace overlooking the Fitzroy River.

★ Great Western Hotel PUB
(☑07-4922 1862; www.greatwesternhotel.com.au; cnr Stanley & Denison Sts; ☺10am-2am) The GWH is part country pub, part concert venue, and part of Rockhampton's social fabric. Try to time your visit to Rocky for a Wednesday or Friday night when you can watch brave cattlefolk being tossed in the air by bucking bulls and broncos. The pub is a jocular place with enough memorabilia to stuff a B-grade Western. Touring bands occasionally rock here, alongside bouts of Ultimate Fighting and stand-up comedy; you can get tickets online. The food is all about great steak.

❶ Information

Tropic of Capricorn Visitor Centre (☑1800 676 701; Gladstone Rd; ☺9am-5pm) Helpful centre on the highway right beside the tropic of Capricorn marker, 3km south of the centre.

❶ Getting There & Away

AIR
Qantas (☑13 13 13; www.qantas.com.au) and **Virgin** (☑13 67 89; www.virginaustralia.com) connect Rockhampton with various cities. The airport is about 6km from the centre of town.

BUS
Greyhound (☑1300 473 946; www.greyhound.com.au) buses run from Rockhampton to Brisbane ($168, 12 hours) and Mackay ($65, four hours), among other destinations.

TRAIN
Queensland Rail (☑1800 872 467; www.queenslandrailtravel.com.au) runs a daily service to Brisbane ($135, 12 hours) and Gladstone ($39, three hours).

Yeppoon
POP 17,241
Yeppoon has slowly evolved from a tiny village known as a launching pad for trips to Great Keppel Island to today's more established seaside town. The long, beautiful beach serves as a holiday destination or residential highlight for many graziers, miners and other folk from nearby Rockhampton seeking to beat the heat. A hinterland of volcanic outcrops and pineapple patches and (a short drive north) the wonderful Byfield National Park, give Yeppoon a rich diversity often overlooked by travellers from other parts of Australia. The broad, quiet streets, sleepy motels and beachside cafes are the setting for a nightly migration of black-and-red flying foxes, which pass over the main beach and beyond in a startling sunset display.

🏃 Activities

Sail Capricornia CRUISE
(☑0402 102 373; www.sailcapricornia.com.au; full-day cruises incl lunch adult/child $115/75) Sail Capricornia offers snorkelling cruises on board the *Grace* catamaran, as well as sunset ($55) and three-day ($499) cruises.

Funtastic Cruises CRUISE
(☑0438 909 502; www.funtasticcruises.com; full-day cruises adult/child/family $98/80/350) Funtastic Cruises operates full-day snorkelling trips on board its 17m catamaran, with a two-hour stopover on Great Keppel Island, morning and afternoon tea, and all snorkelling equipment included. It can also organise camping drop-offs to islands en route.

🛏 Sleeping & Eating

Beachside Caravan Park CARAVAN PARK **$**
(☑07-4939 3738; Farnborough Rd; powered sites $31-34, unpowered sites $28) This basic, neat little camping ground, north of the town centre, commands a wonderful, totally beachfront location. It has good amenities and grassed

sites with some shade, but no cabins or on-site vans. Rates are for two people.

★ **Surfside Motel** MOTEL **$$**
(☑ 07-4939 1272; www.yeppoonsurfsidemotel.com.au; 30 Anzac Pde; r from $140; ❋ @ ☎ ✽) Location and service lift the Surfside to the top of the tree in Yeppoon. Across the road from the beach and close to town, this 1950s strip of lime-green motel units epitomises summer holidays at the beach. And it's terrific value – the rooms are spacious and unusually well equipped, complete with toaster, hair dryer and free wi-fi. Prices go down for three or more nights.

While Away B&B B&B **$$**
(☑ 07-4939 5719; www.whileawaybandb.com.au; 44 Todd Ave; s $115, d $140-155, incl breakfast; ❋) Perenially popular B&B, While Away has good-sized, immaculately clean rooms with wheelchair access and a quiet location back from the beach. The bubbly owners offer complimentary nibbles, tea, coffee, port and sherry as well as generous breakfasts.

Coral Inn Yeppoon HOSTEL **$$**
(☑ 07-4939 2925; www.coralinn.com.au; 14 Maple St; d/q from $129/149; ❋ ❋ @ ☎ ✽) Beautiful lawns and reef-bright colours in the rooms, all with bathrooms and mod-cons, make Coral Inn a great find, just back from the beach. Families and discerning groups in particular will enjoy the quad rooms, communal kitchen, and mini 'beach' area with hammocks and an inviting pool. Note that management does enforce a number of rules to deter rowdy backpackers.

Strand Hotel PUB FOOD **$**
(☑ 07-4939 1301; www.thestrandyeppoon.com.au; 2 Normanby St; mains from $16; ⊙ noon-2.30pm & 6-9pm Mon-Fri, 11.30am-2.30pm & 5.30-9pm Sat & Sun) There has been a welcome refurb in the form of glass frontage and faux-leather furniture at this grand old pub facing the sea. The food is dependable, ranging from pizzas ($16 to $24) to fantastic steaks ($29 to $42). There's live music most weekends, and the odd random weeknight.

★ **Megalomania** FUSION **$$$**
(☑ 07-4939 2333; www.megalomaniabarandbistro.com.au; cnr James & Arthur Sts; mains $26-40; ⊙ noon-2pm & 6pm-late Tue-Sat) An Oz-Asian fusion beast, with a stylish ambience that's hard to replicate anywhere, let alone a small coastal town, by head chef Callan Crigan. Panko-crumbed tiger prawns and red sea salt soft-shell crab were our starters ($18 each), and Byron Bay pork belly and white miso barramundi came in for mains ($36 each). You get the idea. Loll beneath the fig tree with your stiff cocktail, or clink silverware in the indoor woodsy surrounds.

ⓘ Information

Capricorn Coast Information Centre (☑ 1800 675 785; www.capricorncoast.com.au; Ross

---

WORTH A TRIP

BYFIELD

Byfield is a village in Byfield National Park, 40km north of Yepoon, a well-concealed landscape of rare diversity: empty sand dunes running up to rocky pinnacles, wetlands and semi-tropical rainforests. A 4WD will get you to remote hiking paths and isolated beaches beautiful enough to warrant a much longer stay.

Nob Creek Pottery (☑ 07-4935 1161; www.nobcreckpottery.com.au; 216 Arnolds Rd; ⊙ 10am-4pm Thu-Mon) **FREE** is a working pottery and gallery nestled in leafy rainforest. The gallery showcases hand-blown glass, woodwork and jewellery; the handmade ceramics are outstanding. Take a boat trip through the rainforest with **Waterpark Eco-Tours** (☑ 07-4935 1171; www.waterparkecotours.com; 201 Waterpark Creek Rd; 2-3hr tour $27.50, cabins $150), keeping an eye out for bright blue kingfishers, baby turtles and big daddy eels.

There are five **camping grounds** (☑ 13 74 68; www.nprsr.qld.gov.au; per person/family $6.15/24.60) to choose from (prebook). Nine Mile Beach and Five Rocks are on the beach and you'll need a 4WD to access them.

Set on 26 hectares of richly scented, cacophonous rainforest splendour, **Byfield Mountain Retreat** (☑ 07-4935 1161; www.byfieldmountainretreat.com; 216 Arnolds Rd; per night/week $250/1300) is only a short drive from Byfield village and will suit anyone looking for a deep nature experience.

Creek Roundabout; ⊙9am-5pm) Has plenty of information on the Capricorn Coast and Great Keppel Island, and can book accommodation and tours.

ⓘ Getting There & Away

Yeppoon is 43km northeast of Rockhampton. **Young's Bus Service** (☑ 07-4922 3813; www.youngsbusservice.com.au) runs frequent buses from Rockhampton ($6.70 one-way) to Yeppoon and down to the Rosslyn Bay Marina.

If you're driving, there's a free daytime car park at the marina. For longer, secure undercover parking, the **Great Keppel Island Security Car Park** (☑ 07-4933 6670; 422 Scenic Hwy; per day from $15) is on the Scenic Hwy south of Yeppoon, by the turn-off to the marina.

Keppel Konnections and Funtastic Cruises (p390) both leave from Yeppoon daily to Great Keppel Island and the Great Keppel National Park.

Great Keppel Island

This jewel of the Capricorn Coast is synonymous with deserted island fantasies of the urban travel set. Once home to one of Australia's most iconic resorts, the 4-sq-km island – natural bushland covering 90% of the interior – has a total of 17 beaches, all in the category of 'bloody beautiful'. A new mega-resort, environmental research centre and golf course are on the way, so get here soon if you prefer to do your islands in solitude.

⚡ Activities

Freedom Fast Cats　　　　　　　CRUISE
(☑ 07-4933 6888; www.freedomfastcats.com; Keppel Bay Marina, Rosslyn Bay; tours adult/child from $78/50) Operates a range of island tours, from glass-bottomed-boat reef-viewing to snorkelling and boom-netting.

Great Keppel Cruises　　　　　BOATING
(☑ 0401 053 666; www.greatkeppelcruises.com.au; half-/full-day trips $65/125) *Keppel Dreams* departs from Fisherman's Beach for snorkelling forays around the island. Departures are scheduled to fit in with Keppel Konnections arrival from Yeppoon.

Watersports Hut　　　　　WATER SPORTS
(☑ 0415 076 644; Putney Beach; ⊙Sat, Sun & school holidays) The Watersports Hut on the main beach hires out snorkelling equipment, kayaks and catamarans, and runs tube rides.

🛏 Sleeping & Eating

★**Svendsen's Beach**　　　　　CABIN $$
(☑ 07-4938 3717; www.svendsensbeach.com; d from $115) ⚑ The three-night minimum stays are barely enough at this secluded boutique retreat on the 'other' side of Great Keppel. Run by knowledgeable Carl and Lindy, the retreat is an ecofriendly operation, run on solar and wind power; there's even a bush-bucket shower. It's the perfect place for snorkelling, bushwalking and romantic getaways. Guests can choose from luxury tent-bungalows (doubles $115) on elevated timber decks, plus a colourful studio ($150) and house (from $220; sleeps up to four people), all within a turtle shuffle of the beach.

Great Keppel Island Hideaway　RESORT $$
(☑ 07-4939 2050; www.greatkeppelislandhideaway.com.au; safari tents $90 r $140-200, cabins $200-360) This hideaway is set across massive grounds on a sublime bend of Fisherman's Beach. The distance between the various cabins, houses and safari tents lends an air of rugged isolation to a family holiday. The reality is there's a beachfront restaurant (mains $12 to $25) nearby where guests compare their lodgings, sip on sundowners and half-contemplate a nature walk somewhere not too far away.

Keppel Lodge　　　　　GUESTHOUSE $$
(☑ 07-4939 4251; www.keppellodge.com.au; Fisherman's Beach; d per person $65-75, houses $520-600; @ 🖥) Keppel Lodge is terrific value and sandy stumbling distance to Fisherman's Beach. The pleasant open-plan house has four large bedrooms (with bathrooms) branching from a large communal lounge and kitchen. It's available in its entirety – ideal for a group booking – or as individual suites.

Island Pizza　　　　　　　PIZZA $
(☑ 07-4939 4699; The Esplanade; dishes $6-30; ⊙varies) You'll be doing better than us if you can figure out exactly when this incongruously located pizza house is open, but if you hang around long enough, someone will let you know. The pizzas are huge and delicious. Get anything with pineapple on it.

ⓘ Getting There & Away

Great Keppel is a 30-minute ferry trip from Roslyn Bay Marina in Yeppoon. **Keppel Konnections** (www.keppelkonnections.com.au)

Great Keppel Island

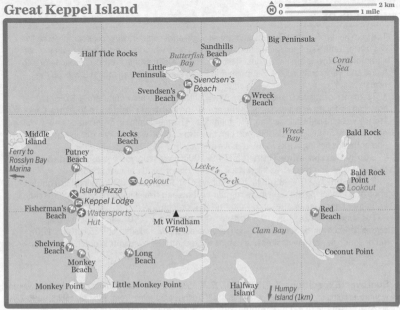

has twice-daily services to the island departing Yeppoon at 9am and 3pm and returning at 10am and 4pm. **Freedom Fast Cats** (📞 07-4933 6888; www.freedomfastcats.com; return adult/child/family $55/35/160) leave Yeppoon at 9.15am and return at 2.30pm or 3.45pm depending on the day and the season.

Capricorn Hinterland

The central highlands, west of Rockhampton, are home to two excellent national parks. Blackdown Tableland National Park is a brooding, powerful place, while visitors to Carnarvon National Park will be gobsmacked by the spectacular gorge.

At Emerald, 270km inland, try fossicking for gems in the heat and rubble – you'll be surrounded by the good people and vibe of the outback. Try to stick to the cooler months between April and November.

Carnarvon National Park

Carnarvon Gorge is a dramatic rendition of Australian natural beauty. The 30km-long, 200m-high gorge was carved out over millions of years by Carnarvon Creek and its tributaries twisting through soft sedimentary rock. What was left behind is a lush, other-worldly oasis, where life flourishes, shielded from the stark terrain. You'll find giant cycads, king ferns, river oaks, flooded gums, cabbage palms, deep pools, and platypuses in the creek. Escaped convicts often took refuge here among ancient rock paintings. The area was made a national park in 1932 after defeated farmers forfeited their pastoral lease.

For most people, Carnarvon Gorge *is* the Carnarvon National Park, because the other sections – including Mt Moffatt (where Indigenous groups lived some 19,000 years ago), Ka Ka Mundi and Salvator Rosa – have long been difficult to access.

Coming from Rolleston the road is bitumen for 75km and unsealed for 20km. From Roma via Injune and Wyseby homestead, the road is good bitumen for about 215km, then unsealed and fairly rough for the last 30km. After heavy rain, both these roads can become impassable.

The main walking track also starts here, following Carnarvon Creek through the gorge, with detours to various points of interest. These include the Moss Garden (3.6km from the picnic area), Ward's Canyon (4.8km), the Art Gallery (5.6km) and Cathedral Cave (9.3km). Allow at least a whole day for a visit.

GEM FIELDS

The gem fields of central Queensland are a tough landscape drawing prospectors who eke out a living until a jackpot (or sunstroke) arrives. Fossickers descend in winter – in the hot summers the towns are nearly deserted. Sapphires are the main haul, but zircons are also found and, very rarely, rubies. Sapphire and Rubyvale are two of the main towns on the fields.

To go fossicking you need a licence (www.dnrm.qld.gov.au; adult/family $7.75/11.15); they can be found at a few places in the area – the **Central Highlands Visitors Centre** (www.centralhighlands.com.au; 3 Clemont St,; ☉10am-4.30pm) in Emerald has a list – or online. If you just wish to dabble, you can buy a bucket of 'wash' (mine dirt in water) from one of the fossicking parks to hand-sieve and wash.

Bobby Dazzler Mine Tours (☎07- 4981 0000) will help you get your hands dirty in the right way, and throw in a fair whack of local history and colour to boot.

Pat's Gems (☎07-4985 4544; 1056 Rubyvale Rd, Sapphire; ☉8.30am-4pm) is a quirky shop and fossicking station where regular visitors and travelling prospectors can rent equipment and pick up tips on how to find that precious gem.

The super-clean and friendly **Sapphire Caravan Park** (☎07-4985 4281; www.sapphire caravanpark.com.au; 57 Sunrise Rd, Sapphire; powered/unpowered sites $29/25, cottages $115), set on four hilly acres with sites and cabins tucked into the eucalyptus forest, is great for fossickers.

Sunrover Expeditions (☎1800 353 717; www.sunrover.com.au; safaris per person incl all meals $940) runs a five-day camping safari into Carnarvon Gorge between August and October.

🛏 Sleeping

There are national park camp sites at **Big Bend** (☎13 74 68; www.qld.gov.au/camping; sites per person/family $6.15/24.60) and **Mt Moffat** (☎13 74 68; www.qld.gov.au/camping; sites per person/family $6.15/24.60), as well as the excellent **Takarakka Bush Resort** (☎07-4984 4535; www.takarakka.com.au; Wyseby Rd; powered/unpowered sites from $45/38, cabins $195-228), with safari tents, cottages and cabins.

Carnarvon Gorge Wilderness Lodge　　　　LODGE $$$
(☎1800 644 150; www.carnarvon-gorge.com; Wyseby Rd; d from $220; ☉closed Nov-Feb; ❄) Glampers can wake to kangaroos chewing grass outside their attractive tented chalets. This is outback chic set deep in the bush. Excellent guided tours are available, plus a full-board package (from $155 to $300 per person).

Whitsunday Coast

Best Places to Eat

➡ Mr Bones (p410)

➡ Fusion 128 (p399)

➡ Harry's Corner (p409)

➡ Jochheims Pies (p414)

➡ Paddock & Brew Company (p399)

Best Places to Sleep

➡ Qualia (p412)

➡ Kipara (p407)

➡ Stoney Creek Farmstay (p397)

➡ Riviera Mackay (p397)

➡ Platypus Bushcamp (p401)

Why Go?

Many travellers to Australia, especially those with a sailing pedigree, head straight for the Whitsunday Islands and barely leave. This white-fringed archipelago, a stunning feature of the Coral Sea coast, can be easily seen from shore. Opal-jade waters and pure-white beaches fringe the forested isles; around them, tropical fish swarm through the world's largest coral garden in the Great Barrier Reef Marine Park. The gateway to the islands, Airlie Beach, is a backpacker hub with a parade of tanned faces zinging between boats, beaches and nightclubs. This is as close to the islands as some budget travellers will get.

South of Airlie, Mackay is a typical coastal Queensland town with palm-lined streets framed by a jumble of art-deco buildings. It's a handy base for trips to Eungella National Park – a lush hinterland oasis where platypuses cavort in the wild. North of Airlie Beach is cute little Bowen, a low-key alternative for backpackers working through their holiday.

When to Go
Mackay

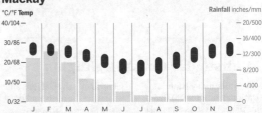

Jun–Oct The perfect time to enjoy sunny skies, calm days, mild weather and stinger-free seas.

Aug Sailing boats skim across the water and parties are held during Airlie Beach Race Week.

Sep & Oct Optimal conditions for kayaking around the islands.

Whitsunday Coast Highlights

1 Whitsunday Islands National Park (p405) Camping under the stars and making like an island castaway.

2 Whitsunday Islands (p403) Sailing through magnificent aquamarine waters.

3 Eungella National Park (p401) Waiting patiently for a

glimpse of a shy platypus and walking in the misty rainforest.

4 Airlie Beach (p405) Swilling beer and partying hard in fun-lovin' Airlie Beach.

5 Great Barrier Reef (p403) Diving and snorkelling the outer fringing reefs.

6 Hamilton Island (p412) Hiking the steep forest trails.

7 Whitehaven Beach (p413) Being dazzled by the bright-white silica sand.

8 Bowen (p414) Picking fruit or swimming in empty coves in this laid-back town.

9 Cape Hillsborough National Park (p402) Exploring where bush meets the beach at this semi-remote spot.

Mackay

POP 82,500

Once home to opera star Dame Nellie Melba, this workaday, midsized Queensland city puts tourism a distant second to the machinations of the sugar and agricultural industries, but there's nonetheless plenty to like about Mackay's tropical suburbia. For starters, it's an incongruously impressive art-deco destination, and even better is its location between protected mangroves and a smart, beachy marina. Mackay is a convenient base for excursions out of town, but when the backpacker shuffle and island-hopping overwhelms, its alfresco cafes provide a quick urban fix. It's only a 1½-hour drive to Airlie Beach and boats to the Whitsundays, and a scenic jaunt past the sugar-cane fields to Eungella National Park.

◉ Sights

Mackay's impressive art-deco architecture owes much to a devastating cyclone in 1918, which flattened many of the town's buildings. Enthusiasts should pick up a copy of *Art Deco in Mackay* from the visitor centre.

There are good views over the harbour from Rotary Lookout in North Mackay and over the beach at Lampert's Lookout.

Mackay Marina (Mackay Harbour) is worth the trip to wine and dine with a waterfront view, while the artificial **Bluewater Lagoon** (◷9am-5.45pm) FREE near Caneland Shopping Centre has water fountains, water slides, grassed picnic areas, free wi-fi and a cafe.

Mackay Regional Botanical Gardens
GARDENS

(Lagoon St) On 33 hectares, 3km south of the city centre, these gardens are a must-see for flora fans. Home to five themed gardens and the Lagoon cafe-restaurant (open Wednesday to Sunday).

Artspace Mackay
GALLERY

(☑07-4961 9722; www.artspacemackay.com.au; Gordon St; ◷10am-5pm Tue-Fri, 10am-3pm Sat & Sun) FREE Artspace Mackay is a welcoming regional art gallery showcasing works from local and visiting artists. Chew over the masterpieces at on-site noshery Foodspace (p399).

Beaches

Mackay has plenty of beaches, although not all are ideal for swimming. The best option near town is Harbour Beach, 6km north of the centre and just south of the Mackay Marina. The beach here is patrolled and there's a foreshore reserve with picnic tables and barbecues.

☞ Tours

Reeforest Adventure Tours
CULTURAL TOUR

(☑07-4959 8360, 1800 500 353; www.reeforest. com) The Mackay region's most experienced operator offers a wide range of junkets, including a platypus and rainforest eco-safari, two-day Eungella tours, and a Cape Hillsborough expedition in the footsteps of the Juipera mob. In the cane-crushing season (June to December), you can see how sugar cane is turned into sweet crystals with its two-hour tour of the Farleigh Sugar Mill (adult/child $28/14); long pants and enclosed shoes are required.

Heritage Walk
WALKING

(☑07-4944 5888; ◷8.45am Tue & Wed May-Sep) FREE Weekly wandering (1½ to two hours) that takes in the sights and secrets of ye olde Mackay. Leaves from Paxton's Warehouse on the corner of River and Carlyle Sts.

✦ Festivals & Events

Wintermoon Folk Festival
MUSIC

(www.wintermoonfestival.com; ◷Apr/May) Folk and world-music love-fest.

⌂ Sleeping

★ Stoney Creek Farmstay
FARMSTAY $

(☑07-4954 1177; www.stoneycreekfarmstay.com; Peak Downs Hwy; dm/stables/cottages $25/130/175) 🍃 This bush retreat 32km south of Mackay is a down 'n' dirty option in the best possible way. Stay in an endearingly ramshackle cottage, the rustic livery stable or the charismatic Dead Horse Hostel, and forget all about the mod-cons: this is dead-set bush livin'. Three-hour horse rides cost $105 per person and lots of other activities are available. Free dorm room if you ride for two consecutive days.

Mackay Marine Tourist Park
CARAVAN PARK $

(☑07 4955 1496, www.mmtp.com.au; 379 Harbour Rd; powered/unpowered sites $35/32, villas $110-180; ❄@🛜🐾🏖) A step up from the usual caravan parks: all cabins and villas come with private patios and widescreen TVs, and you've gotta love anywhere with a giant jumping pillow.

Riviera Mackay
APARTMENT $$

(☑07-4088 1459; www.rivieramackay.com.au; 5-7 Nelson St; 1-/2-bedroom apt $171/256) Mackay desperately need this light, stylish property, architecturally inspired by Palm Springs, and akin to a hip inner-city flat in a city further

Mackay

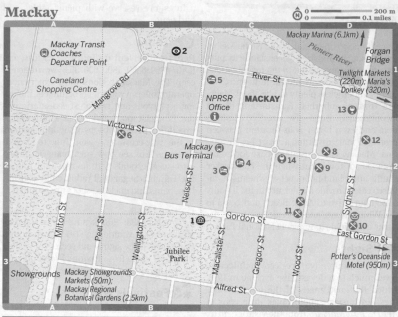

Mackay

⊙ Sights
1 Artspace Mackay	B3
2 Bluewater Lagoon	B1

🛏 Sleeping
3 Coral Sands Motel	C2
4 International Lodge Motel	C2
5 Riviera Mackay	C1

⊗ Eating
6 Austral Hotel	B2
7 Burp Eat Drink	D2

Foodspace	(see 1)
8 Fusion 128	D2
9 Kevin's Place	D2
10 Oscar's on Sydney	D3
11 Paddock & Brew Company	C2
12 Woodsman's Axe Coffee	D2

⊙ Drinking & Nightlife
13 Ambassador Hotel	D1
14 Cartel	C2

south. Very good value too in an expensive city for accommodation.

Coral Sands Motel MOTEL $$
(☑ 07-4951 1244; www.coralsandsmotel.com.au; 44 Macalister St; r from $115; ❀ 🛋 ☎ 🛆) One of Mackay's better midrange options, the Coral Sands boasts ultrafriendly management and large rooms in a central location. Popular with the transient workforce, it's a bit tropi-kitsch, but with the river, shops, pubs and cafes so close to your doorstep, you won't care. Great value.

Potter's Oceanside Motel MOTEL $$
(☑ 07-5689 0388; www.pottersoceansidemotel.com. au; 2c East Gordon St; d $149-169, f $269; ❀ 🛆 🛋) Near the unappealing Town Beach, Potter's is nonetheless an excellent temporary answer

to your travel woes. Very accommodating management will crack open a beer at check-in and point you to immaculate, modern rooms (some of which are wheelchair accessible) with garden views. The small restaurant does a pleasant breakfast; room service also available. Perfect for a dose of clean comfort if you've been taking the rough road too long.

International Lodge Motel MOTEL $$
(☑ 07-4951 1022; www.internationallodge.com.au; 40 Macalister St; r from $105; 🅿 ❀ 🛆) The ugly mustard building with a brown roof and a concrete garden is one of Mackay's better midrange motels. The rooms are clean, bright and cheerful, and your door is shouting distance from the city nightlife.

Clarion Hotel

Mackay Marina   LUXURY HOTEL $$$

(☑07-4955 9400; www.mackaymarinahotel.com; Mulherin Dr; d from $249; ❇@☎☎) This large chain hotel on the marina was the talk of the town when it opened, and it's still a professional operation and the pick for most corporate folk. There's an excellent on-site restaurant, kitchenettes, private balconies and an enormous swimming pool. It's located 6.5km northeast of the centre. To get there take Sydney St north across the Forgan Bridge. Online discounts make a mockery of the rack rates.

✗ Eating

Woodsman's Axe Coffee   CAFE $

(41 Sydney St; coffee from $4.30; ◷6am-2pm Mon-Fri, 7am-2pm Sat & Sun) The best coffee in town paired with light eats, from wraps to quiches to muffins.

Maria's Donkey   TAPAS $

(☑07-4957 6055; 8 River St; tapas $8-15; ◷noon-10pm Wed & Thu, to midnight Fri-Sun) Quirky, energetic riverfront joint dishing up tapas, jugs of sangria, occasional live music and general good times. Service is erratic, but somehow, that's part of the charm.

Fusion 128   MODERN AUSTRALIAN $$

(☑07-4999 9329; 128 Victoria St; mains $13.50-33; ◷11.30am-2pm & 5.30-10pm) Mackay is becoming quite the foodie destination. The latest instalment is Fusion 128, a superb, casual restaurant with a low-lit industrial design run by the effusive David Ming. It combines Asian flavours with Australian bush ingredients, and serves fine cocktails and desserts to match the mood.

Paddock & Brew Company   AMERICAN $$

(☑0487 222 880; 94 Wood St; mains $18-30) Mackay needed this upmarket, craft-beer-soaked, American home-style restaurant, which serves up amazing burgers ($25). Part of the new breed of north Queensland culinary creatives, the team at Paddock & Brew whiz between the wooden tables at this happening pre-party venue.

Oscar's on Sydney   FUSION $$

(☑07-4944 0173; cnr Sydney & Gordon Sts; mains $10-23; ◷7am-5pm Mon-Fri, to 4pm Sat, 8am-4pm Sun) The delicious *poffertjes* (Dutch pancakes with traditional toppings) are still going strong at this very popular corner cafe, but don't be afraid to give the other dishes a go. Top spot for breakfast.

Kevin's Place   ASIAN $$

(☑07-4953 5835; 79 Victoria St; mains $16-27; ◷11.30am-2pm & 5.30-8pm Mon-Fri, 5.30-8pm Sat) At Kevin's, housed in a marvellous deco building on Victoria St, large groups gather on round tables – square on the street – and share sizzling, spicy Singaporean dishes. Don't go past the classics such as mee goreng ($18). Lunch specials are a bargain from $12.

Austral Hotel   PUB FOOD $$

(☑07-4951 3288; www.theaustralhotel.com.au; 189 Victoria St; mains $19-36, steaks $24-47; ◷noon-2.30pm & 6-9pm) So many steaks, so little time. The Austral is a red-meat specialist, but it's also a knockabout Aussie pub with timber interiors, the horses on the telly and plenty of old, single men sipping pots of beer.

Foodspace   CAFE $$

(www.artspacemackay.com.au; Gordon St; mains $16-26; ◷9am-3pm Tue-Sun) You can graze on impressive salads, sandwiches and light meals prepared by beginning chefs at Foodspace, the licensed cafe inside Artspace Mackay (p397).

Burp Eat Drink   MODERN AUSTRALIAN $$$

(☑07-4951 3546; www.burp.net.au; 86 Wood St; mains from $33; ◷11.30am-3pm & 6pm-late Tue-Fri, 6pm-late Sat) Run by the enterprising NE Food mob, this swish Melbourne-style restaurant in the tropics has a small but tantalising menu. Sophisticated selections include pork belly with scallops, Kaffir-lime-crusted soft-shell crab, plus some serious steaks.

♚ Drinking & Nightlife

Cartel   CLUB

(99 Victoria St; ◷10pm-4am Thu-Sat) Frenetic dance club hosting a mix of resident and guest-star DJs. Changes name as fast as music trends.

Ambassador Hotel   BAR

(☑07-4953 3233; www.ambassadorhotel.net.au; 2 Sydney St; ◷5pm-late Thu, 4pm-late Fri-Sun) Both a social and historical landmark, the Ambassador is art deco outside, wild 'n' crazy inside. There's multilevel carousing on weekends, including Mackay's only rooftop bar. Remarkably, you will soon be able to sleep here in renovated dorms and double rooms.

🔒 Shopping

They like their markets in Mackay; try the **Mackay Showgrounds Markets** (Milton St; ◷6.30am-10am Sat), **Twilight Markets**

(Northern Beaches Bowls Club; ⊘5pm-9pm 1st Fri of the month) and the **Troppo Market** (Mt Pleasant Shopping Centre car park; ⊘from 7.30am 2nd Sun of the month).

ℹ Information

Mackay Visitor Centre (☑1300 130 001; www.mackayregion.com; 320 Nebo Rd; ⊘9am-5pm; 🛜) About 3km south of the centre. Internet access and wi-fi.

NPRSR Office (☑07-4944 7818; www.nprsr.qld.gov.au; Level 5, 44 Nelson St; ⊘8.30am-4.30pm Mon-Fri) For camping permits.

Post Office (69-71 Sydney St)

ℹ Getting There & Away

AIR

The airport is about 3km south of the centre of Mackay. **Jetstar** (☑13 15 38; www.jetstar.com.au), **Qantas** (☑13 13 13; www.qantas.com.au) and **Virgin** (☑13 67 89; www.virginaustralia.com) have flights to/from Brisbane.

BUS

Buses stop at the **Mackay Bus Terminal** (cnr Victoria & Macalister Sts), where tickets can also be booked. **Greyhound** (☑1300 473 946; www.greyhound.com.au) travels up and down the coast. Sample one-way adult fares and journey times: Airlie Beach ($33, two hours), Townsville ($72, 6½ hours), Cairns ($127, 13 hours) and Brisbane ($227, 17 hours).

Premier (☑13 34 10; www.premierms.com.au) is less expensive than Greyhound but has fewer services.

TRAIN

The Spirit of Queensland, operated by **Queensland Rail** (☑1800 872 467; www.queenslandrail.com.au), runs from Mackay to Brisbane ($199, 13 hours) and Cairns ($159, 14 hours). The train station is at Paget, 5km south of the city centre.

ℹ Getting Around

Major car-rental firms have desks at Mackay Airport; see www.mackayairport.com.au/travel/car-hire for listings. **NQ Car & Truck Rental** (☑07-4953 2353; www.nqcartruckrentals.com.au; 6 Malcolmson St, North Mackay) is a reliable local operator.

Mackay Transit Coaches (☑07-4957 3330; www.mackaytransit.com.au) has several services around the city, and connects the city with the harbour and northern beaches; pick up a timetable at the visitor centre or look online.

For a taxi, call **Mackay Taxis** (☑13 10 08).

Mackay's Northern Beaches

There's a lot of gorgeous, winding coastline and not a lot of people north of Mackay to the wilds of Cape Hillsborough. A series of headlands and bays shelter small residential communities that blossom in summer with local holidaymakers and year-round with romantic weekenders.

At Blacks Beach, the beach extends for 6km, so stretch those legs and claim a piece of Coral Sea coast for a day. **Blacks Beach Holiday Park** (☑07-4954 9334; www.mackayblacksbeachholidaypark.com.au; 16 Bourke St; unpowered/powered sites $30/35, villas $150-180; 🅿🕸🛜) has good beachfront facilities, while **Blue Pacific Resort** (☑07-4954 9090; www.bluepacificresort.com.au; 26 Bourke St; d $114-152, unit $209-220; 🕸🛜🛜) is also beautifully located.

North of Dolphin Heads is Eimeo, where the **Eimeo Pacific Hotel** (☑07-4954 6805; www.eimeohotel.com.au; Mango Ave; mains $18.50-32.50; ⊘10am-10pm) is a great place for a sunset drink. Bucasia is across Sunset Bay from Eimeo and Dolphin Heads. **Bucasia Beachfront Caravan Resort** (☑07-4954 6375; www.bucasiabeach.com.au; 2 The Esplanade; powered sites $30-45; 🕸🛜) has a selection of sites, some with absolute beachfront views.

Sarina
POP 5730

Sarina is a sugar heartland 34km south of Mackay. It's a quiet place to stop on the Bruce Hwy, however the nearby coastline is worth a longer detour, especially the area around Sarina Beach and Armstrong Beach, which buzzes on weekends.

The **Sarina Tourist Art & Craft Centre** (☑07-4956 2251; Railway Sq, Bruce Hwy; ⊘9am-5pm) showcases locally made handicrafts and assists with visitor information.

Sarina Sugar Shed (☑07-4943 2801; www.sarinasugarshed.com.au; Railway Sq; adult/child $21/11; ⊘9am-4pm, tours 9.30am, 11am, 12.30pm & 2pm Mon-Sat) is the only miniature sugar-processing mill and distillery of its kind in Australia. After the tour, enjoy a complimentary tipple at the distillery.

Armstrong Beach Caravan Park (☑07-4956 2425; www.caravanpark.wixsite.com/armstrong beach; 66 Melba St; powered site per couple $32) is a very laid-back place with spacious sites.

Whatever you order at **The Diner** (11 Central St; mains $5-12; ☺4am-6pm Mon-Fri, to 10am Sat), you'll get a plateful. Grills, sandwiches and burgers are popular; shakes, coffee and spiders wash it all down. Breakfast is popular with truck drivers.

Sarina Beach

On the shores of Sarina Inlet, this laid-back coastal village boasts a gorgeous, wide, long beach, a general store/service station and a boat ramp at the inlet. It's one of the best-looking beaches in the area with excellent opportunities for relaxing, fishing, beachcombing and spotting wildlife such as nesting marine turtles – but there are also warning signs for crocs.

Fernandos Hideaway (☑07-4956 6299; www.sarinabeachbb.com; 26 Captain Blackwood Dr; s/d/ste $130/140/160; ❄ ❅) is a hacienda-style B&B perched on a rugged headland near Sarina. It offers magnificent coastal views and absolute beachfront. In the living room there's a stuffed lion, a suit of armour and an eclectic assortment of souvenirs from the eccentric owners' global travels.

Eungella

Pretty little Eungella (*young*-gulluh; meaning 'land of clouds') sits perched 600m above sea level on the edge of the Pioneer Valley. It's the best-known town in the region and is synonymous with the magnificent Eungella National Park.

Lively markets are held on the first Sunday of each month (April to December) from 9am at the town hall.

The three, neat, self-contained wooden cabins at **Eungella Mountain Edge Escape** (☑07-4958 4590; www.mountainedgeescape.com. au; North St; 1-/2-bedroom cabin $120/140; ❄) form a wonderful vantage point for appreciating Eungella.

Eungella Chalet (☑07-4958 4509; www. eungellachalet.com.au; Chelmer St; r from $90, 1-/2-bedroom cabin $115/155; ❅) has a certain fading charm with basic hotel rooms and larger cabins out back. The pub food at the chalet **dining room** (mains $17-28; ☺12-2pm & 6-8pm) is satisfactory.

There's basic camping at the self-registration **Explorers' Haven** (☑07-4958 4750; 32 North St; unpowered/powered site $25/30; @ ☎).

Eungella National Park

Mystical, mountainous Eungella National Park covers nearly 500 sq km of the lofty Clarke Range, but is largely inaccessible except for the walking tracks around Broken River and Finch Hatton Gorge. The large tracts of tropical and subtropical vegetation have been isolated from other rainforest areas for thousands of years and now boast several unique species, including the orange-sided skink and the charming Eungella gastric-brooding frog, which incubates its eggs in its stomach and gives birth by spitting out the tadpoles.

Finch Hatton Gorge

Finch Hatton Gorge is a remarkable, prehistoric place set in a rugged subtropical rainforest. Hills of farmland disappear into a lush gorge dotted with volcanic boulders and buzzing with bird and insect life. It can feel like you've stepped through a geographical black hole into another physical dimension.

A gorgeous 1.6km walking trail leads to Araluen Falls, with its tumbling waterfalls and swimming holes, and a further 1km hike takes you to the Wheel of Fire Falls, another cascade with a deep swimming hole. Both these falls tend to be busy with locals on weekends.

Rainforest Scuba (☑0434 455 040; www. rainforestscuba.com; 55 Anzac Pde, Finch Hatton) claims the dubious title as the world's first rainforest dive operator; submerge in crystal-clear creeks where eels, platypus, turtles and fish share the habitat.

A brilliantly fun and informative way to explore the rainforest here is to glide through the canopy with **Forest Flying** (☑07-4958 3359; www.forestflying.com; $60). The sky-high guided tours see you harnessed to a 350m-long cable and suspended up to 25m above the ground; you control your speed via a pulley system.

Platypus Bushcamp (☑07-4958 3204; www.bushcamp.net; Finch Hatton Gorge; sites/dm/ huts $7.50/25/75; ❅) ✐ is a true-blue bush retreat hand-built by Wazza, the eccentric owner. The three basic huts are surrounded by rainforest. A creek with platypuses and great swimming holes runs next to the camp, and the big, open-air communal kitchen and eating area is the heart of the place.

For a peaceful sleep, stay at **Finch Hatton Gorge Cabins** (☑ 07-4958 3281; www.finchhattongorgecabins.com.au; cabins $155; ❄), set in enchanting subtropical surrounds, with a creek nearby.

Broken River

Cool and sometimes misty, Broken River is worth a detour inland from Mackay for its high-elevation rainforest where hilly cattle ranches house some very happy cows and prolific bird life. Broken River has some of the best walking tracks in the region and you may spot a few marsupials hiding in the brush.

Fern Flat Camping Ground (www.npsr.qld.gov.au/camping; sites per person/family $6.15/24.60) is a lovely place to camp, with shady sites adjacent to the river where the platypuses play. This is a walk-in camping ground and not vehicle accessible but it's an easy 500m past the information centre and kiosk. Register online.

Crediton Hall Camping Ground (www.npsr.qld.gov.au; sites per person/family $6.15/24.60), 3km after Broken River, is accessible to vehicles. Turn left into Crediton Loop Rd and turn right after the Wishing Pool circuit track entrance.

Non-campers should head to the **Broken River Mountain Resort** (☑ 07-4958 4000; www.brokenrivermr.com.au; d $140-200; ❄@☎☒), with cosy cedar cabins, ranging from small, motel-style units to a large self-contained lodge sleeping up to six. There's a cosy guest lounge with an open fire and the friendly **Possums Table Restaurant & Bar** (mains $25-35; ☺ breakfast & dinner).

ⓘ Getting There & Away

The park is 84km west of Mackay. There are no buses to Eungella or Finch Hatton, but **Reeforest Adventure Tours** (p397) runs day trips from Mackay and will drop off and pick up those who want to linger; however, tours don't run every day so your stay may wind up being longer than intended.

Cumberland Islands

There are about 70 islands in the Cumberland group, sometimes referred to as the southern Whitsundays. Almost all the islands are designated national parks. Brampton Island is well-known for its nature walks, and will soon be home to a 'seven-star' resort. Facilities on all islands, aside from Keswick Island, are very limited and access can be difficult unless you have your own boat or can afford to charter one (or a seaplane); ask for more info at the Mackay visitor centre (p400).

Keswick Island Campground (☑ 1300 889 290; unpowered sites from $20, ste from $80) has a number of unpowered sites within a very easy walking distance of pristine Basil Bay and is a real secret among the camping community.

The **Beach House** (☑ 1300 889 290; www.keswickisland.com.au; 6 Coral Passage Dr, Keswick Island; houses $275) is a good way to enjoy Keswick's beauty without any hassle. The modern, stylish property sleeps six comfortably and has direct beach access to Basil Bay.

Cape Hillsborough National Park

Cape Hillsborough National Park would be a must-visit in many parts of the world, but around these parts, nature lovers are spoiled for choice. Still, this semi-remote bush scrub falling into the sea some 50km north of Mackay is worthy of more serious attention. On the marvellous walking trails through the headlands, you may spot kangaroos, wallabies and sugar gliders. Turtles are common close to shore, and roos might be seen on the beach in the evening and early morning.

The park features rough cliffs, a broad beach, rocky headlands, sand dunes, mangroves, hoop pines and rainforest. There are also the remains of Aboriginal middens and stone fish traps, accessible by good walking tracks. On the approach to the foreshore area there's also an interesting boardwalk leading out through a tidal mangrove forest. Recent renovations have made it easier to negotiate the area on your own.

Smalleys Beach Campground (www.nprsr.qld.gov.au; site per person/family $6.15/24.60) is a small, pretty and grassed camping ground hugging the foreshore and absolutely jumping with kangaroos. There's no self-registration here; book permits online.

Cape Hillsborough Nature Resort (☑ 07-4959 0152; www.capehillsboroughresort.com.au; 51 Risley Pde; unpowered/powered site $29/34, cabin $80-265; ❄@☒) is popular with families from Mackay and grey nomads from way further south.

THE WHITSUNDAYS

Seen from above, the Whitsundays are like a stunning organism under the microscope. Indigo, aqua, yellow and bottle-green cellular blobs mesmerise the senses. Sheltered by the Great Barrier Reef, the waters are particularly perfect for sailing. Seen from afloat in the Coral Sea, any of the 74 islands will hypnotise on approach and leave you giddy with good fortune.

Some of the oldest archaeological sites on the east coast are found here and you can only imagine the displeasure of the Ngaro people at losing such land to sawmills and force.

Five of the islands have resorts but most are uninhabited, and several offer back-to-nature beach camping and bushwalking. Whitehaven Beach is the finest beach in the Whitsundays and, many claim, the world. Airlie Beach, on the mainland, is the coastal hub and major gateway to the islands, where you can book myriad tours and activities, or just party hard.

☘ Activities

Sailing & Cruising

Atlantic Clipper   BOATING
(www.atlanticclipper.com.au; 2-day, 2-night trips from $460) Young, beautiful and boozy crowd…and there's no escaping the antics. Snorkelling (or recovering) on Langford Island is a highlight.

Derwent Hunter   BOATING
(☑1800 334 773; www.tallshipadventures.com.au; day trips $195) A deservedly popular sailing safari on a beautiful timber gaff-rigged schooner. A good option for couples and those more keen on wildlife than the wild life.

SV Domino   BOATING
(www.aussieyachting.com; day trips $180) Takes a maximum of eight guests to Bali Hai Island, a little-visited 'secret' of the Whitsundays. Includes lunch and a good two-hour snorkel. The boat is also available for custom, private charters.

Prima Sailing   BOATING
(☑0447 377 150; www.primasailing.com.au; 2-day, 2-night tours from $390) Fun tours with a 12-person maximum. Ideal for couples chasing style and substance.

Whitehaven Xpress   BOATING
(☑07-4946 1585; www.whitehavenxpress.com.au; day trips $160) Various boat excursions, but best known for its daily trip to Whitehaven Beach.

Diving

Most dives in this area visit the easy-to-reach fringing reefs around the Whitsundays, but you can also dive further afield on the Great Barrier Reef.

Costs for open-water courses with several ocean dives start at around $900. **Whitsunday Diving Academy** (☑1300 348 464; www.whitsundaydivingacademy.com.au; 2579 Shute Harbour Rd, Jubilee Pocket) is a good place to start.

A number of sailing cruises include diving as an optional extra. Prices start from $95 for introductory or certified dives. Ferry operator Cruise Whitsundays (p407) offers dives (from $119) on day trips to its reef pontoon.

Most of the island resorts also have dive schools and free snorkelling gear.

Kayaking

Paddling with dolphins and turtles is one of the best ways to experience the Whitsundays. **Salty Dog Sea Kayaking** (☑07-4946 1388; www.saltydog.com.au; Shute Harbour; half-/full-day trips $80/130) offers guided tours and kayak rental ($50/80 per half-/full day), plus a brilliant six-day kayak and camping expedition ($1650) that's suitable for beginners.

TOP BEACHES

The Whitsundays boast some of the finest beaches in a country full of them. Our top picks:

Whitehaven Beach (p413) With azure-blue waters lapping the pure-white, silica sand, Whitehaven on Whitsunday Island is absolutely stunning.

Chalkies Beach Opposite Whitehaven Beach, on Haslewood Island, this is another idyllic, white-sand beach.

Langford Island At high tide, Langford is a thin strip of sand on the rim of a ludicrously picturesque coral-filled turquoise lagoon.

Butterfly Bay On the northern side of Hook Island is this protected bay, which flutters with butterfly song each winter.

Catseye Beach (p412) Hamilton Island's Catseye Beach is a busy-ish spot by Whitsunday standards, but its palm-shaded sand and turquoise waters are social-media ready.

Whitsunday Islands

0 — 10 km
0 — 5 miles

👉 Tours

Ocean Rafting
BOATING

(📞 07-4946 6848; www.oceanrafting.com.au; adult/child/family from $134/87/399) Visit the 'wild' side of the islands in a very fast, big yellow speedboat. Swim at Whitehaven Beach, regain your land legs with a guided national park walk, or snorkel the reef at Mantaray Bay and Border Island.

Ecojet Safari
TOURS

(📞 07-4948 2653; tours per person $195) Explore the islands, mangroves and marine life of the northern Whitsundays on these three-hour, small-group jet-ski safaris (two people per jet ski).

Big Fury
BOATING

(📞 07-4948 2201; www.magicwhitsundays.com; adult/child/family $130/70/350) Speed out to Whitehaven Beach on an open-air sports boat, and follow up with lunch and snorkelling at a secluded reef nearby. Great value and bookable through Airlie Beach travel agencies.

HeliReef
SCENIC FLIGHTS

(📞 07-4946 9102; www.helireef.com.au) Scenic helicopter flights from $135.

🛏 Sleeping

NPRSR (www.nprsr.qld.gov.au) manages the Whitsunday Islands National Park camping grounds on several islands for both independent campers as well as groups on commercial trips. Camping permits ($6.15/24.60 per person/family) are available online or at the **NPRSR booking office** (☑13 74 68; www.npsr.qld.gov.au; cnr Shute Harbour & Mandalay Rds; ⊙9am-4.30pm Mon-Fri) in Airlie Beach.

You must be self-sufficient and are advised to take 5L of water per person per day plus three days' extra supply in case you get stuck. You should also have a fuel stove as wood fires are banned on all islands.

Operated by **Whitsunday Island Camping Connections** (☑07-4946 6285; www.whitsundaycamping.com.au), the *Scamper* leaves from Shute Harbour and can drop you at South Molle, Denman or Planton Islands ($65 return); Whitsunday Island ($105 return); Whitehaven Beach ($155 return); and Hook Island ($160 return).

ℹ Getting There & Away

AIR

The two main airports for the Whitsundays are at Hamilton Island and Proserpine (Whitsunday Coast). Airlie Beach is home to the small Whitsunday Airport, about 6km from town.

Jetstar (☑13 15 38; www.jetstar.com.au) flies to Proserpine from Melbourne and Brisbane, while Virgin flies to/from Brisbane. Tiger runs from Sydney to Proserpine; **Qantas** (☑13 13 13; www.qantas.com.au), Jetstar and Virgin all service Hamilton Island from major Australian cities.

BUS

Greyhound (☑1300 473 946; www.greyhound.com.au) and **Premier** (☑13 34 10; www.premierms.com.au) detour off the Bruce Hwy to Airlie Beach. **Whitsunday Transit** (☑07-4946 1800; www.whitsundaytransit.com.au) connects Proserpine, Cannonvale, Abel Point, Airlie Beach and Shute Harbour.

Whitsundays 2 Everywhere (☑07-4946 4940; www.whitsundaytransfers.com) operates airport transfers from both Whitsunday Coast (Proserpine) and Mackay Airports to Airlie Beach.

Proserpine

POP 3875

There's no real reason to linger in this industrial sugar-mill town, which is the turn-off point for Airlie Beach and the Whitsundays. However, it's worth stopping at the helpful **Whitsundays Region Information Centre**

(☑1300 717 407; www.whitsundaytourism.com; ⊙10am-5pm) just south of town for information about the Whitsundays and surrounding region.

If you do find yourself in Proserpine with time to spare, head to **Colour Me Crazy** (☑07-4945 2698; 2b Dobbins Lane; ⊙8.30am-5.30pm Mon-Fri, to 3.30pm Sat, 9.30am-2.30pm Sun), an eye-popping labyrinth of out-there jewellery, clothing and homewares. Who knew there were so many uses for sequins?

Airlie Beach

POP 9165

Aside from being the obvious departure point for most trips to the unparalleled Whitsunday Islands, Airlie Beach has long been a destination par excellence on the east coast road-trip and binge-drink adventure trail. Its multiple hostels and massive beer gardens sit opposite a lawn-surrounded swimming lagoon where nothing much happens but the passing of carefree youth.

Sure, there's the relatively new Port of Airlie marina, with its faux-sophisticated hotel and restaurant complex, as well as the town's impressive sailing pedigree, but the heart of Airlie still beats to the rhythm of unskilled sailors, taking to the sparkling seas and jungle-clad isles with bleary-eyed wonder.

🏃 Activities

Lagoon SWIMMING
(Shute Harbour Rd) **FREE** Take a dip year-round in the stinger-croc-and-tropical-nasties-free lagoon in the centre of town.

Red Cat Adventures BOATING
(☑1300 653 100, 07-4940 2000; www.redcatadventures.com.au) Excellent family-owned operation with three distinct crafts and tours. Our pick is the Ride to Paradise ($569), a two-night adventure to a 'secret' resort, as well as many highlights of the Whitsundays.

Airlie Beach Skydivers SKYDIVING
(☑1300 759 348; www.airliebeachskydivers.com.au; 2/273 Shute Harbour Rd; 4270m jumps from $249) The only beach landing in Airlie Beach is provided by this passionate team with a shopfront on Shute Harbour Rd.

Skydive Airlie Beach SKYDIVING
(☑07-4946 9115; www.skydive.com.au/airlie-beach; skydives from $199) Jump out of a plane from 1830m, 2440m or 4270m and land in front of the cafe set on Airlie Beach. Fabulous group

Airlie Beach

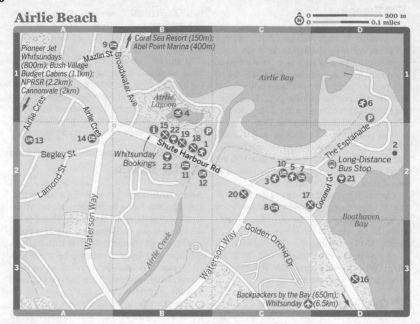

Airlie Beach

🅰 Activities, Courses & Tours
1 Airlie Beach Skydivers B2
2 Cruise Whitsundays D2
3 Explore Whitsundays C2
4 Lagoon B1
5 Whitsunday Sailing Adventures C2
6 Whitsunday Sailing Club D1

🛏 Sleeping
7 Airlie Beach Hotel C2
8 Airlie Beach YHA C2
9 Airlie Waterfront B&B B1
10 Airlie Waterfront Backpackers C2
11 Beaches Backpackers B2
Heart Hotel and Gallery .... (see 1)
12 Magnums Backpackers B2
13 Sunlit Waters A2
14 Waterview A2

🍴 Eating
15 Airlie Beach Treehouse B2
16 Denman Cellars Beer Cafe D3
17 Fish D'vine C2
18 Harry's Corner B2
19 Mr Bones B2
Village Cafe .... (see 12)
Wisdom Health Lab .... (see 18)
20 Woolworths Supermarket C2

🍷 Drinking & Nightlife
21 Just Wine & Cheese D2
22 Mama Africa B2
23 Paddy's Shenanigans B2

and there is not a more beautiful view in the world for a death-defying plummet.

Whitsunday Sailing Adventures BOATING
(☎ 07-4946 4999; www.whitsundayssailingadventures.com.au; The Esplanade) This well-connected agency can book seats on every sailing boat in town, plus a few decent dive operators.

Pioneer Jet Whitsundays BOATING
(☎ 1800 335 975; www.pioneerjet.com.au; Abel Point Marina; adult/child $69/49) The Ultimate

Bay Blast is a thunderous 30-minute spin in a jetboat. Fun and informative guides roundoff the experience. Expect to get very wet.

Just Tuk'n Around GUIDED TOUR
(www.justtuknaround.com.au; tours per person $30) Fun and informative 30-minute tours around the 'secrets' of Airlie Beach reveal more than you'd think possible in a small coastal town.

Lady Enid BOATING
(📞 0407 483 000; www.ladyenid.com.au; boat trips from $225) High-end bespoke sailing trips for couples aboard a heritage yacht.

Illusions BOATING
(📞 0455 142 021; www.illusion.net.au; day tours $125) A 12m catamaran that offers the least expensive, yet consistently good, sailing tours to the islands.

Solway Lass BOATING
(📞 1800 355 377; www.solwaylass.com; 3-day, 3-night trips from $589) You get a full three days and nights on this 28m tall ship – the only authentic tall ship in Airlie Beach. Popular with backpackers.

Whitsunday Sailing Club BOATING
(📞 07-4946 6138; www.whitsundaysailingclub.com.au; Airlie Point) The heart of the Airlie Beach Race Week is a family-friendly club and an authentic introduction to the town's nautical scene.

Explore Whitsundays SAILING
(📞 07-4946 5782; www.explorewhitsundays.com; 4 The Esplanade; 2-day, 1-night trips from $359) Inexpensive but well-run trips with a variety of options offered across a few vessels, each with its own ambience. Generally geared towards the backpacker set.

👉 Tours

Cruise Whitsundays CRUISE
(📞 07-4846 70602; www.cruisewhitsundays.com; Shingley Dr, Abel Point Marina; full-day cruises from $99) As well as operating a ferry to the Whitsunday Islands, Cruise Whitsundays offers trips to Hardy Reef, Whitehaven Beach and islands, including Daydream and Long. Or grab a daily Island Hopper pass (adult/child $125/65) and make your own itinerary. It also operates a popular day trip aboard the *Camira* ($195).

Air Whitsunday SCENIC FLIGHTS
(📞 07-4946 9111; www.airwhitsunday.com.au; Terminal 1, Whitsunday Airport) Offers a range of tours, including day trips to Whitehaven ($255) and scenic-flight-plus-snorkelling tours of the Great Barrier Reef ($375).

Whitsunday Crocodile Safari TOURS
(📞 07-4948 3310; www.crocodilesafari.com.au; adult/child $120/60) Spy on wild crocs, explore secret estuaries and eat real bush tucker.

🍃 Courses

Maritime & Sailing Training Centre BOATING
(📞 07-4946 6710; www.maritimetrainingcentre.com.au) Respected training provider offering sailing courses for those looking to explore further than the norm.

✨ Festivals & Events

Airlie Beach Race Week SAILING
(www.airlieraceweek.com; ⊘ Aug) The town's sailing pedigree is tested every August when sailors from across the world descend on Airlie for the town's annual regatta.

Airlie Beach Music Festival MUSIC
(www.airliebeachfestivalofmusic.com.au; ⊘ Nov) This festival has really taken off since its inception into the Whitsunday social calendar back in 2012. Party to three days of Australian and international rock, folk and electronic music, with plenty of local talent on show.

🛏️ Sleeping

Airlie Beach is a backpacker haven, but with so many hostels, standards vary and bedbugs are a common problem. There is also a remarkable variety of midrange accommodation particularly suitable for families. Not a lot at the very top end though.

⭐ Kipara RESORT $
(📞 07-4946 6483; www.kipara.com.au; 2614 Shute Harbour Rd; r/cabins/villas from $85/105/130; ❄️@🛜🏊) Tucked away in the lush, green environs of Jubilee Pocket, this budget resort makes it easy to forget you're only 2km from the frenzy of town (it's next to the bus stop so you don't need a car). It's mega-clean and offers outstanding value, with helpful staff, cooking facilities and regular wildlife visits – one of Airlie's best options. Huge discounts available online. There's a fab pool with surrounding deck.

⭐ Sunlit Waters APARTMENT $
(📞 07-4946 6352; www.sunlitwaters.com; 20 Airlie Cres; studios from $95, 1-bedroom apt $115; ❄️🛜🏊) Just so affordable for a tourist town like Airlie Beach! We expected the studio apartments to be tiny or rundown, but they are beautifully presented and have everything you need, including a self-contained kitchenette and stunning views from the long balconies. There's even a good swimming pool.

Flametree Tourist Village CARAVAN PARK $
(📞 07-4946 9388; www.flametreevillage.com.au; 2955 Shute Harbour Rd; powered/unpowered sites

$40/30, cabins from $109; ✳@✉✉) Our favourite camping ground and caravan park in the region has been thoroughly scrubbed up and is a top alternative to the chaos of Airlie Beach. Spacious sites are scattered through lovely, bird-filled gardens and there's a good camp kitchen and BBQ area. It's 6.5km west of Airlie.

Airlie Beach YHA   HOSTEL $

(☑07-4946 6312; www.yha.com.au; 394 Shute Harbour Rd; dm $33, d from $85; ✳@🛜✉) Trust YHA to provide a genuine alternative for young budget travellers to sordid hostels and inconvenient bush dumps. Central and reasonably quiet with a sparkling pool and great kitchen facilities, this is our favourite hostel in Airlie Beach, though the double rooms are pretty grim.

Airlie Waterfront Backpackers   HOSTEL $

(☑1800 089 000; www.airliewaterfront.com; 6 The Esplanade; dm/d from $22/74; ✳🛜) Basic hostel, with coveted ocean views and a very central location. A little less hectic than other downtown options.

Bush Village Budget Cabins   HOSTEL $

(☑07-4946 6177, 1800 809 256; www.bushvillage. com.au; 2 St Martins Rd; dm from $33, d with/without bathroom from $97/82; P✳@🛜✉) Not for those looking for a party, this budget place suits travellers who have their own vehicle and enjoy having a village to return to after a long day on the reef or a night on the tiles. The dorms and doubles are in a clutch of self-contained cabins and it's licensed so you can sit and drink a beer by the pool. It's a five-minute walk to Abel Point Marina and about a half-hour stroll to central Airlie Beach. Reception closes early so communicate clearly.

Beaches Backpackers   HOSTEL $

(☑07-4946 6244; www.beaches.com.au; 356 Shute Harbour Rd; dm/d from $20/85; ✳@🛜✉) The hostel scene in Airlie is pretty fickle, but Beaches is consistent in its bubbly customer service and unwavering desire to crank the party to maximum (and fair enough given the awesomeness of the open-air bar). Dorms are sufficient, but could be cleaner.

Note that the hostel sustained some damage from Cyclone Debbie; check ahead that they are taking guests.

Backpackers by the Bay   HOSTEL $

(☑07-4946 7267; www.backpackersbythebay.com; 12 Hermitage Dr; dm $27, d & tw $83; ✳@🛜✉) About a 10-minute walk from Airlie's centre,

this hostel is very quiet, which will suit those who like to keep their party and their sleep separate. The small rooms are cleaned every second day, and there are hammocks strung around a good-sized pool. You'll need to head into Airlie to arrange tours.

Waterview   APARTMENT $$

(☑07-4948 1748; www.waterviewairliebeach.com. au; 42 Airlie Cres; studios from $140, 1-bedroom units from $155; ✳🛜) Waterview's small units are an excellent choice for location and comfort. You can enjoy glimpses of the main street and gorgeous views of the bay. The rooms are modern, airy and spacious, and have kitchenettes for self-caterers. Top value for a couple in Airlie who can do without a pool.

Airlie Beach Hotel   HOTEL $$

(☑07-4964 1999; www.airliebeachhotel.com.au; cnr The Esplanade & Coconut Gr; motel r from $145, hotel r $195-295; ✳🛜✉) The ABH has seen it all in Airlie. The sea-facing hotel rooms are some of the best in town at this price point. With three restaurants and a bottle shop onsite and a perfect downtown location, you could do far worse than stay here.

The hotel was damaged during Cyclone Debbie and had to close temporarily: it is due to reopen in January 2018.

Coral Sea Resort   RESORT $$$

(☑07-4964 1300; www.coralsearesort.com; 25 Ocean View Ave; d from $275; ✳@🛜✉) Coral Sea Resort is an excellent option for families and older folk wanting quality service, spacious tiled rooms, and one of the best pool settings in Queensland. An easy stroll to the marina, it's located at the end of a low headland just west of the town centre. Many rooms have stunning views, but you'll save plenty of dosh by going for a garden view and then lingering poolside.

Airlie Waterfront B&B   B&B $$$

(☑07-4946 7631; http://airliewaterfrontbnb.com. au; cnr Broadwater Ave & Mazlin St; 1-/2-bedroom apt from $209/252; ✳@🛜✉) Karen and Malcolm are gregarious hosts at this misnamed property, which is more like a small resort. Views are superb from the position slightly above town, accessed by a five-minute stroll along the boardwalk. The two-bedroom apartments are the best value in town. Some rooms have a spa.

Heart Hotel and Gallery   BOUTIQUE HOTEL $$$

(☑1300 847 244; www.hearthotelwhitsundays. com.au; 277 Shute Harbour Rd; d $225-275, ste

SAILING THE WHITSUNDAYS

The Whitsundays are the place to skim across fantasy-blue waters on a tropical breeze. If you're flexible with dates, last-minute stand-by rates can considerably reduce the price and you'll have a better idea of weather conditions. Many travellers hang out in Airlie Beach for a few days for this exact purpose, although you may end up spending your savings in the pub!

Most vessels offer snorkelling on the fringing reefs, where the colourful soft corals are often more abundant than on the outer reef. Diving and other activities nearly always cost extra. Once you've decided, book at one of the many booking agencies in Airlie Beach.

Other than the superfast Camira, operated by Cruise Whitsundays (p407), sailing boats aren't able to make it all the way to destinations such as Whitehaven Beach on a day trip from Airlie Beach. Instead they usually go to the lovely Langford Reef and Hayman Island; check before booking.

Bareboat Sailing

Rent a boat without skipper, crew or provisions. You don't need formal qualifications, but you (or one of your party) have to prove that you can competently operate a vessel.

Expect to pay between $500 and $1000 a day in high season (September to January) for a yacht sleeping four to six people, plus a booking deposit and a security bond (refunded when the boat is returned undamaged). Most companies have a minimum hire period of five days.

There are a number of bareboat charter companies around Airlie Beach, including:

Charter Yachts Australia (☏1800 639 520; www.cya.com.au; Abel Point Marina; 4 people from $495)

Cumberland Charter Yachts (☏1800 075 101; www.ccy.com.au; Abel Point Marina)

Queensland Yacht Charters (☏1800 075 013; www.yachtcharters.com.au; Abel Point Marina)

Whitsunday Escape (☏1800 075 145; www.whitsundayescape.com; Abel Point Marina)

Whitsunday Rent A Yacht (☏1800 075 000; www.rentayacht.com.au; 6 Bay Tce, Shute Harbour)

Crewing

In return for a free bunk, meals and a sailing adventure, crewing will see you hoisting the mainsail and cleaning the head. Look for 'Crew Wanted' signs around the marina, and at restaurants and hotels. Your experience will depend on the vessel, skipper, other crew members (if any) and your own attitude. Be sure to let someone know where you're going, with whom and for how long. Aside from safety precautions, it may make them bitterly jealous.

$300-350) A brand-new luxury boutique hotel in the heart of Airlie. Architecturally inspired by early Queensland homes, the rooms are small but most are elegant. Good discounts online.

Eating

The strip facing the port at the new Port of Airlie is a good hunting ground for sophisticated, upmarket dining options, while downtown Airlie Beach has a mishmash of everything from cheap takeaway kebab shops to fancier restaurants with outdoor patios. There's a massive **Woolworths supermarket** (Shute Harbour Rd; ⊙8am-9pm) conveniently located in the centre of town for self-caterers.

Harry's Corner CAFE $
(☏07-4946 7459; 273 Shute Harbour Rd; mains $7-18; ⊙7am-3pm) Locals are wild about Harry's, which serves quaint European tea sets, Danish sandwiches, filled bagels and good-sized salads. The all-day breakfasts are a must for a hangover.

Wisdom Health Lab CAFE $
(1b/275 Shute Harbour Dr; toasties from $5.50, juices from $7; ⊙7.30am-3.30pm; ☏) Mostly a takeaway place, this rightfully busy corner cafe does have a few indoor and outdoor tables. It serves healthy toasties, sandwiches (including lots of vegetarian options such as a tasty lentil burger), and a huge array of fresh smoothies and juices.

★ Mr Bones
PIZZA **$$**

(🖉0413 017 331; Lagoon Plaza, 263 Shute Harbour Rd; shared plates $12-17, pizzas $15-23; ☺9am-9pm Tue-Sat) Carefully curated play lists and creative thin-based pizzas have made Mr Bones the coolest place to eat in Airlie since it opened six years ago. Overlooking the lagoon, the small, sunny restaurant also has an extensive 'not pizzas' menu of appetisers to play around with. Service is upbeat and interested. Great coffee, too.

Airlie Beach Treehouse
MODERN AUSTRALIAN **$$**

(🖉07-4946 5550; www.airlietreehouse.com; 6/263-265 Shute Harbour Rd; mains $18-36; ☺8.30am-9.30pm) This new restaurant by the lagoon is making ripples for its uncomplicated service and quality food in a shady setting.

Denman Cellars Beer Cafe
TAPAS **$$**

(🖉07-4948 1333; Shop 15, 33 Port Dr; tapas $10, mains $18-38; ☺11am-10pm Mon-Fri, 8am-11pm Sat & Sun) Regular live music and a convivial mood are found in this tapas bar that stocks more boutique beers – 700 brews! – than the rest of the town combined. The food – such as a shared seafood platter ($57), and 'beer bites' such as zucchini balls ($14) and duck pancakes ($17) – is decent. Larger meals are available.

Fish D'vine
SEAFOOD **$$**

(🖉07-4948 0088; 303 Shute Harbour Rd; mains $17-33; ☺5pm-late) Pirates were definitely onto something: this fish-and-rum bar is shiploads of fun, serving up all things nibbly from Neptune's realm and lashings and lashings of rum (over 200 kinds of the stuff). Yo-ho-ho! Sport eaters can take on the 'Seafood Indulgence', a mountain of shells and claws for a whopping $149.

Village Cafe
CAFE **$$**

(🖉07-4946 5745; 366 Shute Harbour Rd; mains $15-34; ☺7.30am-9.30pm) Interactive dining is a lot of fun at the very popular Village Cafe, where you sizzle your own meal on a volcanic slab. The massive breakfasts are popular with reef crews getting ready to set sail.

Drinking & Nightlife

It's said that Airlie Beach is a drinking town with a sailing problem. The bars at **Magnums** (🖉07-4964 1199, 1800 624 634; www.magnums.com.au; 366 Shute Harbour Rd; camp sites/van sites $24/26, dm/d from $24/56; ✳@⩔) and Beaches (p408), the two big backpackers in the centre of town, are always crowded, and are popular places to kick off a ribald evening.

Mama Africa
CLUB

(263 Shute Harbour Rd; ☺9pm-5am) Mama's is a jumping African-style safari nightclub throbbing with a beat that both hunter and prey find hard to resist. Themed nights and all kinds of promotions aimed at the backpacker party set ensure spontaneous all-nighters any day of the week.

Just Wine & Cheese
WINE BAR

(Shop 8, 33 Port Dr; wines by the glass $7-18; ☺3-10pm) Run by two astute wine aficionados, this glamorous bottle shop and bar serves fine examples of what it promises, with a view of the Port of Airlie marina.

Paddy's Shenanigans
IRISH PUB

(352 Shute Harbour Rd; ☺5pm-3am) Live music every night, but otherwise the usual sports-watching, hard-drinking venue.

ⓘ CYCLONE WARNING

In Queensland's far north, between November and April each year, cyclones – known in the northern hemisphere as hurricanes – are a part of life, with an average of four or five forming each season. It's rare for these cyclones to escalate into full-blown destructive storms; however, in March 2017 Severe Tropical Cyclone Debbie made landfall near Airlie Beach, causing significant damage and flooding in South East Queensland and the Northern Rivers area of New South Wales. Airlie Beach and Bowen were affected as well.

Bringing torrential rain, strong winds and ferocious seas, the storm killed at least twelve people in Australia, primarily as a result of extreme flooding. At the time of writing the clean-up was in full swing. We recommend checking ahead before you travel to ensure that accommodation is available and confirm the state of the beaches.

During the season, keep a sharp ear out for cyclone predictions and alerts. If a cyclone watch or warning is issued, stay tuned to local radio and monitor the Bureau of Meteorology website (www.bom.gov.au) for updates and advice. Locals tend to be complacent about cyclones, but will still buy out the bottle shop when a threat is imminent!

ℹ Information

Whitsunday Bookings (☑ 07-4948 2201; www.whitsundaybooking.com.au; 346 Shute Harbour Rd) Tina has been helping travellers book the right tour for years. For a while this office was even the default tourist information office, although now it looks like many of the other information booking centres along the strip.

Whitsundays Central Reservation Centre (☑ 1800 677 119; www.airliebeach.com; 259 Shute Harbour Rd) can take the hassle out of finding the right accommodation.

ℹ Getting There & Away

AIR

The closest major airports are Whitsunday Coast (Proserpine) and Hamilton Island.

Whitsunday Airport (☑ 07-4946 9180) is a small airfield 6km east of Airlie Beach, midway between Airlie Beach and Shute Harbour.

BOAT

Transfers between the **Port of Airlie** (www.portofairlie.com.au) and Hamilton, Daydream and Long Islands are provided by Cruise Whitsundays (p407).

BUS

Greyhound (☑ 1300 473 946; www.greyhound.com.au) and **Premier Motor Service** (☑ 13 34 10; www.premierms.com.au) buses detour off the Bruce Hwy to Airlie Beach. There are buses between Airlie Beach and all of the major centres along the coast, including Brisbane ($248, 19 hours), Mackay ($31, two hours), Townsville ($49, four hours) and Cairns ($100, nine hours).

Long-distance buses stop on the Esplanade, between the sailing club and the Airlie Beach Hotel.

Whitsunday Transit (☑ 07-4946 1800; www.whitsundaytransit.com.au) connects Proserpine (Whitsunday Airport), Cannonvale, Abel Point, Airlie Beach and Shute Harbour. There are several stops along Shute Harbour Rd.

Conway National Park

There's enough diverse beauty in Conway National Park to lure travellers to Airlie Beach away from the Whitsundays, deep into the rainforest hills and remote beaches that were once the hunting grounds of the Giru Dala. The mountains of this national park and the Whitsunday Islands are part of the same coastal mountain range. Rising sea levels following the last ice age flooded the lower valleys, leaving only the highest peaks as islands, now cut off from the mainland.

Several walking trails start from near the picnic and day-use area. Further along the main road, towards Coral Point and before Shute Harbour, there's a 1km track leading down to Coral Beach and the Beak lookout.

About 1km past the day-use area, there's a 2.4km walk up to the Mt Rooper lookout, with good views of the Whitsunday Passage and islands.

To reach the beautiful Cedar Creek Falls, turn off the Proserpine–Airlie Beach road on to Conway Rd, 18km southwest of Airlie Beach. It's then about 15km to the falls; the roads are well signposted.

Long Island

Long Island has secluded, pretty white beaches, lots of adorable wild rock wallabies and 13km of walking tracks.

Camp at Long Island's **Sandy Bay** (www.nprsr.qld.gov.au; sites per person/family $6.15/24.60).

Palm Bay Resort (☑ 1300 655 126; www.palmbayresort.com.au; villas/bures/bungalows from $229/249/329) is Long Island's luxury self-catering resort where guests can choose from a variety of secluded housing options. The pool is huge and the camaraderie between guests is understated given there is no dining area. The resort store sells gourmet groceries and a rustic bar provides the booze. If you want your own supplies delivered, contact **Whitsundays Provisions** (☑ 07-4946 7344; www.whitprov.com.au). This is a model for sustainable tourism that could have some legs.

Cruise Whitsundays (☑ 07-4946 4662; www.cruisewhitsundays.com) connects Palm Bay Resort to the Port of Airlie by frequent daily services ($48 each way).

Hook Island

The 53-sq-km Hook Island, the second-largest island in the Whitsundays group, is mostly national park and rises to 450m at Hook Peak. There are a number of good beaches dotted around the island, and some of the region's best diving and snorkelling locations.

There are national park **camping grounds** (www.npsr.qld.gov.au; sites per person/family $6.15/24.60) at Maureen Cove, Steen's Beach, Curlew Beach and Crayfish Beach. Although basic, they provide some wonderful back-to-nature opportunities.

South Molle Island

The largest of the Molle group of islands at 4 sq km, South Molle is virtually joined to Mid and North Molle Islands. Apart from the private residence area and golf course at Bauer Bay in the north, the island is all national park and is criss-crossed by 15km of walking tracks, with some superb lookout points.

There are national park **camping grounds** (☑13 74 68; www.npsr.qld.gov.au; sites per person/family $6.15/24.60) at Sandy Bay in the south, and at Paddle Bay near the resort.

Daydream Island

Daydream Island is the closest resort to the mainland and perfectly located to attract the tourist hordes. At just over 1km long and 200m wide, the island can be explored in an hour or two; one strength is its marine biology program, which allows visitors to encounter much of the region's wildlife in a short space of time. Unfortunately, it does feel overwhelming at times, more sterile than natural. Recently sold to an investment group that plans to make it a 'luxury' destination, it will likely retain its popularity as a day-trip destination and is suitable for everybody, especially busy families, or travellers with little time to explore the 'real' Whitsundays. Damage from Cyclone Debbie in early 2017 has meant the redevelopment has been brought forward. The resort is expected to reopen in 2018.

Daydream Island Resort & Spa (☑1800 075 040; www.daydreamisland.com; d from $245; ✳☎🖥☀) has a monopoly on the accommodation on the island, so you might expect some shoddy efforts but they know their clientele – families with kids, cautious international travellers and time-poor holiday-makers – and understand the buzz generated by the location alone. Rooms are reasonably priced and many face out to the glorious Coral Sea. Tennis courts, a gym, catamarans, windsurfing, three swimming pools and an open-air cinema are all included in the tariff. There's also a club with constant activities to keep children occupied.

Hamilton Island

POP 1346

Welcome to a little slice of resort paradise where the paved roads are plied with golf buggies, steep, rocky hills are criss-crossed by walking trails, and the white beaches are buzzing with water-sports action. Though it's not everyone's idea of a perfect getaway, it's hard not to be impressed by the selection of high-end accommodation, restaurants, bars and activities – if you've got the cash, there's something for everyone.

Day trippers can use some resort facilities – including tennis courts, a golf driving range and a minigolf course – and enjoy the island on a relatively economical budget.

A few shops by the harbour organise dives and certificate courses, and just about everyone can sign you up for a variety of cruises to other islands and the outer reef.

If you only have time for one walk, make it the clamber up to Passage Peak (239m) on the northeastern corner of the island.

🛏 Sleeping & Eating

★**Qualia** RESORT $$$
(☑1300 780 959; www.qualia.com.au; d from $1100; ✳@🖥☀) Stunning, ultraluxe Qualia is set on 30 secluded acres, with modern villas materialising like heavenly tree houses in the leafy hillside. The resort has a private beach, two restaurants, a spa and two swimming pools. It remains our favourite luxury resort for miles.

Reef View Hotel HOTEL $$$
(☑02-9007 0009; www.hamiltonisland.com.au/reef-view-hotel; d from $370; ✳@☀) Aptly named, this hilltop resort has spectacular views over the green hills out to turquoise seas. It's central and popular with families and groups. It's a slightly more manageable price for long-ish stays, and the mood is more low-key.

Whitsunday Holiday Homes APARTMENT $$$
(☑13 73 33; www.hihh.com.au; from $320; ✳@🖥☀) Private accommodation ranging from three-star apartments to family-friendly houses and five-star luxury digs. Rates include your own golf buggy for highbrow hooning. There's a four-night minimum stay in some properties.

Popeye's Fish n' Chips FISH & CHIPS $
(Front St; fish & chips $11.50; ☺10am-9pm Sun-Thu, 11.30am-9pm Fri & Sat) Massive boxes of fish and chips that can comfortably feed two people. Also sells burgers, chicken...and fishing bait.

Manta Ray Cafe CAFE $$
(☑07-4946 8213; Marina Village; mains $17-30; ☺10.30am-9pm) Wood-fired gourmet pizzas are a favourite here, but you can also settle in for an afternoon of drinks and oysters. It's popular with families and day visitors.

Romano's ITALIAN $$$

(07-4946 8212; Marina Village; mains $33-40; ⏱6pm-midnight Thu-Mon) Popular Italian restaurant with a large enclosed deck jutting out over the water.

🍷 Drinking & Nightlife

Marina Tavern PUB

(07-4946 8839; Marina Village; mains from $17.50; ⏱11am-midnight) The food is not the reason to come here. Stick with the beer and cocktails and indulge in some people-watchng.

ℹ Getting There & Away

AIR

Hamilton Island Airport is the main arrival centre for the Whitsundays, and is serviced by **Qantas** (☎13 13 13; www.qantas.com.au), **Jetstar** (☎13 15 38; www.jetstar.com.au) and **Virgin** (☎13 67 89; www.virginaustralia.com.au).

BOAT

Cruise Whitsundays (☎07-4946 4662; www. cruisewhitsundays.com) Connects Hamilton Island Airport and the marina with the Port of Airlie in Airlie Beach ($48).

Hayman Island

The most northern of the Whitsunday group, little Hayman is just 4 sq km in area and rises to 250m above sea level. It has forested hills, valleys and beaches, and a luxury five-star resort. Hayman Island has long been a stage for the lifestyles of the rich and famous. It is Australia's most celebrated island resort, first conceived by an airline magnate, and ever since then the enviable playground of celebrities and dignitaries of every stripe. Sadly, the average punter will have to settle for the other 73 islands; Hayman is for resort guests only.

An avenue of stately date palms leads to the entrance of **One&Only Hayman Island Resort** (☎07-4940 1838; www.hayman.com.au; r incl breakfast $730-12,300; ❇@🛜🏊) – one of the most gilded playgrounds on the Great Barrier Reef, with its hectare of swimming pools (open around the clock), landscaped gardens and exclusive boutiques. The rooms vary from well-appointed poolside cabins to deluxe three-bedroom suites and stand-alone villas; all are huge.

Resort guests must first fly to Hamilton Island Airport, before being escorted to Hayman's fleet of luxury cruisers for a pampered transfer to the resort.

Lindeman Island

Situated 15km southeast of the luxurious Hamilton Island, Lindeman was once a flashy resort but has since been returned to nature by liquidators. For the past decade, only nature photographers and hikers have provided any semblance of bustle, making independent treks for the varied island tree life and the sublime view from Mt Oldfield (210m). The mood is poised to change, however, as a $600 million redevelopment is set to commence in 2017. Lindeman is still mostly national park, with empty bays and 20km of impressive walking trails. Get here while you can.

Boat Port (sites per person/family $6.15/24.60) is an open camp site on a sandy beach area backed by rainforest. There are basic toilet and picnic facilities. It was once a bay used to clean sailing vessels, hence the name.

Whitsunday Island

Long proclaimed by talking heads of tourism as one of Australia's most beautiful beaches, Whitehaven Beach, on Whitsunday Island, is a pristine 7km-long stretch of blinding sand (at 98% pure silica, the sand is some of the whitest in the world), bounded by lush tropical vegetation and a brilliant blue sea. From Hill Inlet at the northern end of the beach, the swirling pattern of dazzling sand through the turquoise and aquamarine water paints a magical picture. There's excellent snorkelling from its southern end.

There are national park **camping grounds** (sites per person/family $6.15/24/60) at Dugong, Nari's and Joe's Beaches in the west; at Chance Bay in the south; at the southern end of Whitehaven Beach; and Peter Bay in the north.

Other Whitsunday Islands

The northern islands are undeveloped and seldom visited by cruise boats or water taxis. Several of these – Gloucester, Saddleback and Armit Islands – have national park camping grounds.

Bona Bay on Gloucester Island has the largest **campground** (☎13 74 68; www.npsr.qld.gov. au; sites per adult/family $6.15/24.60), with toilets, picnic tables and good shelter. Armit Island's basic campground has a toilet and picnic tables, while Saddleback's is modest, close to the mainland and has picnic tables.

Gateways to the Reef

There are numerous ways to approach Australia's massive undersea kingdom. You can head to a popular gateway town and join an organised tour, sign up for a multiday sailing or diving trip exploring less-travelled outer fringes of the reef, or fly out to a remote island, where you'll have the reef largely to yourself.

Southern Reef Islands

For an idyllic getaway off the beaten path, book a trip to one of several remote reef-fringed islands on the southern edge of the Great Barrier Reef. You'll find fantastic snorkelling and diving right off the island.

Port Douglas

An hour's drive north of Cairns, Port Douglas is a laid-back beach town with dive boats heading out to over a dozen sites, including more pristine outer reefs, such as Agincourt Reef.

The Whitsundays

Home to turquoise waters, coral gardens and palm-fringed beaches, the Whitsundays offer many options for reef-exploring: base yourself on an island, go sailing, or stay on Airlie Beach and island-hop on day trips.

Townsville

Australia's largest tropical city is far from the outer reef (2½ hours by boat) but has some exceptional draws: access to Australia's best wreck dive, an excellent aquarium, marine-themed museums, plus multiday liveaboard dive boats departing from here.

Cairns

The most popular gateway to the reef, Cairns has dozens of boat operators offering day trips with snorkelling, as well as multiday reef explorations on liveaboard vessels. For the uninitiated, Cairns is a good place to learn to dive.

SUPERJOSEPH / SHUTTERSTOCK ©

1. Clownfish **2.** Port Douglas (p463) **3.** Aerial view of the Great Barrier Reef **4.** Snorkellers near Cairns (p439)

GLENN VAN DER KNIJFF / GETTY IMAGES ©

Bowen

POP 9277

Bowen is a small coastal town set on a hill just north of Airlie Beach, and is famous for its mangoes – Bowen gets busy during fruit-picking season – but known locally for its secret bays and inlets. Its wide, quiet streets, wooden Queenslander houses and laid-back, friendly locals encourage a gentle pace of life. The foreshore, with its landscaped esplanade, picnic tables and BBQs, is a focal point, but there are some truly stunning – and little-visited – beaches and bays northeast of the town centre.

Keep an eye out for the 'Bowenwood' sign on the town's water tower; Baz Luhrmann's epic movie *Australia* was shot here in 2007 and the locals are still a little star-struck.

🛏 Sleeping & Eating

Bowen Backpackers   HOSTEL $

(☑ 07-4786 3433; www.bowenbackpackers.com. au; Herbert St; dm night/week from $40/190; ❄ @ 🗢) Located at the pretty beach end of Herbert St (past the Grandview Hotel), this is the place to stay if you're working in the surrounding fruit farms. New management has a stellar reputation around town. Rooms are neat and reasonably spacious.

Barnacles Backpackers   HOSTEL $

(☑ 07-4786 4400; www.barnaclesbackpackers. com; 18 Gordon St; dm from $30; 🗢) New management has taken over this 84-room hostel, which has close links to the fruit-picking industry. The communal areas have a clinical feel, but it's highly functional and quiet. Jury is out on the direction it will take, so listen to the backpacker grapevine for the latest.

Rose Bay Resort   RESORT $$

(☑ 07-4786 9000; www.rosebayresort.com.au; 2 Pandanus St; r $160-300; ❄ @ ⚊) Rose Bay is a seriously underrated beach, especially for snorkelling, and guests at this friendly resort have it pretty much all to themselves. Spacious studios and comfy units all sleep four guests comfortably. You'll need a car to reach the Bowen strip. Minimum two-night stay.

Jochheims Pies   BAKERY $

(49 George St; pies $5; ⊙ 5.30am-3.30pm Mon-Fri, to 12.30pm Sat) Jochheims has been keeping Bowen bellies full of homemade pies and baked treats since 1963. Try a Hugh Jackman (hunky beef) pie – the actor was a regular here during the filming of *Australia*.

Food Freaks   MODERN AUSTRALIAN $$

(☑ 07-4786 5133; mains $16-26; ⊙ lunch & dinner) Bowen is not the coolest place in Queensland and this restaurant is not the hippest place you will eat in, but that's the way they like it – and the way we like it – eating mod-Oz creations overlooking the marina. Fresh, fast and delicious.

Cove   CHINESE, MALAY $$

(☑ 07-4791 2050; Coral Cove Apartments, Horseshoe Bay Rd; mains $17-28.50; ⊙ lunch & dinner Tue-Sun) An unusually large Chinese and Thai restaurant with unbroken views of the Coral Sea from its timber deck. The menu features the usual Australian fusion entrees and mains; the service is excellent and there are extensive vegetarian and seafood dishes. Takeaway is available.

🍷 Drinking & Nightlife

Grand View Hotel   PUB

(☑ 07-4786 4022; www.grandviewhotelbowen. com; 5 Herbert St) Recently renovated but still high on the hill, the grand old Grand View is a ripping Aussie pub with a rocking beer garden and loads of memorabilia (including from Baz Lurhman's *Australia*). The restaurant looks promising, but it's very easy to forget to eat when you're nursing a pint in the late afternoon sunshine.

❶ Information

There's a friendly **information booth** (Santa Barbara Pde; ⊙ 10am-5pm Mon-Fri, hours vary Sat & Sun) in town and a **visitor centre** (☑ 07-4786 4222; www.tourismbowen.com. au; ⊙ 8.30am-5pm Mon-Fri, 10.30am-5pm Sat & Sun) 7km south of Bowen on the Bruce Hwy (look for the humongous mango). Both sell big scoops of Bowen mango sorbet.

❶ Getting There & Away

Greyhound (☑ 1300 473 946; www.greyhound. com.au) and **Premier** (☑ 13 34 10; www. premierms.com.au) are two companies that have frequent bus services running to/from Airlie Beach ($26, 1½ hours) and Townsville ($29, four hours).

Townsville to Mission Beach

Includes ➡

Best Places to Eat

➡ PepperVine (p435)

➡ Bingil Bay Cafe (p434)

➡ Oliveri's Continental Deli (p437)

➡ Longboard Bar & Grill (p422)

➡ Wayne & Adele's Garden of Eating (p423)

Best Places to Sleep

➡ Jackaroo Hostel (p433)

➡ Sejala on the Beach (p434)

➡ Civic Guest House (p421)

➡ Orpheus Island Lodge (p429)

➡ Base Backpackers (p426)

Why Go?

Spread out between the tourist darlings of Cairns and the Whitsunday Islands, this lesser-known, rainforested stretch of quiet, palm-edged beaches is where giant endangered cassowary graze for seeds, and koalas nap in gum trees on turquoise encircled islands. Oft-overlooked Townsville is the urban centre and offers pleasant, wide, modern streets, a landscaped seaside promenade, gracious 19th-century architecture, and a host of cultural venues and sporting events. It's also the jumping-off point for Magnetic Island, a great budget alternative to the Whitsundays and with far more wildlife – hand-feed wild wallabies, spot an incredible range of bird life on fantastic bushwalking trails, and look for koalas.

North of Townsville, beautiful Mission Beach is a laid-back village that ironically attracts thrill seekers by the busload, all eager to skydive over the reef and on to white-sand beaches, or go on an adrenalin-pumping white-water rafting trip along the Tully River.

When to Go
Townsville

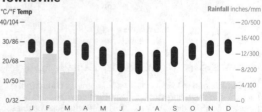

May–Oct Stinger-free seas make this the best time of year for water activities.

Aug Townsville shows off its cultural side during the Australian Festival of Chamber Music.

Sep Magnetic Island moves gently into second gear for the month-long Bay Dayz Festival.

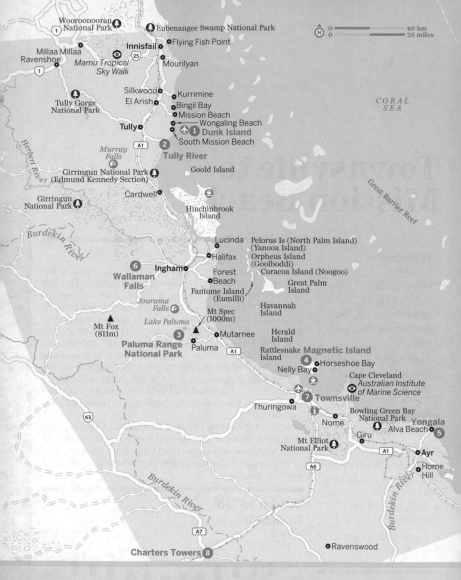

Map labels (from top):

Wooroonooran National Park
Eubenangee Swamp National Park
Flying Fish Point
Innisfail
Millaa Millaa
Ravenshoe
Mamu Tropical Sky Walk
Mourilyan
Silkwood
Kurrimine
El Arish
Bingil Bay
Mission Beach
Wongaling Beach
Dunk Island
South Mission Beach
Tully River
Tully
Murray Falls
Girringun National Park (Edmund Kennedy Section)
Goold Island
Cardwell
Girringun National Park
Hinchinbrook Island
Burdekin River
Lucinda
Pelorus Is (North Palm Island) (Yanooa Island)
Orpheus Island (Goolboddi)
Halifax
Wallaman Falls
Ingham
Forest Beach
Curacoa Island (Noogoo)
Fantome Island (Eumilli)
Great Palm Island
Jourama Falls
Mt Fox (811m)
Lake Paluma
Mt Spec (1000m)
Havannah Island
Paluma Range National Park
Mutarnee
Paluma
Herald Island
Rattlesnake Island
Magnetic Island
Horseshoe Bay
Nelly Bay
Cape Cleveland
Australian Institute of Marine Science
Townsville
Thuringowa
Nome
Bowling Green Bay National Park
Yongala
Alva Beach
Giru
Ayr
Mt Elliot National Park
Home Hill
Charters Towers
Ravenswood

CORAL SEA
Great Barrier Reef
Burdekin River

40 km
25 miles

Townsville to Mission Beach Highlights

1 Dunk Island (p436) Launching to this quintessential tropical Queensland escape.

2 Tully River (p430) Veering wildly around white-water bends.

3 Paluma Range National Park (p431) Searching for the shy platypus in the winding trails of this national park.

4 Magnetic Island (p424) Spotting dozing koalas or hand-feeding rock wallabies on this paradisiacal island.

5 Yongala (p423) Scuba diving at one of Australia's greatest wreck dives.

6 Wallaman Falls (p428) Admiring the view then schlepping down to the bottom of Australia's highest single-drop waterfall.

7 Townsville (p419) Cheering on the Cowboys, North Queensland's revered National Rugby League team.

8 Charters Towers (p425) Watching a *Ghosts After Dark* outdoor film screening in this outback gold-rush town.

Townsville

POP 174,797

Northern Queensland's less-visited major city is easy on the eye: at Townsville's heart is its handsome, endless esplanade, an ideal viewing platform to fabulous Magnetic Island offshore. It's a pedestrian-friendly city, and its grand, refurbished 19th-century buildings offer loads of landmarks. If in doubt, join the throngs of fit and fabulous marching up bright red Castle Hill to gaze across the city's dry environs.

Townsville has a lively, young populace, with thousands of students and armed forces members intermingling with old-school locals, fly-in-fly-out mine workers, and summer-seekers lapping up the average 320 days of sunshine per year. Needless to say, the nightlife is often full throttle.

◎ Sights

★ **Reef HQ Aquarium**   AQUARIUM
(www.reefhq.com.au; Flinders St E; adult/child $28/14; ⊙ 9.30am-5pm) A staggering 2.5 million litres of water flow through the coral-reef tank here, home to 130 coral and 120 fish species. Kids will love seeing, feeding and touching turtles at the turtle hospital. Talks and tours (included with admission) throughout the day focus on different aspects of the reef and the aquarium.

★ **Museum of
Tropical Queensland**   MUSEUM
(⌨ 07-4726 0600; www.mtq.qm.qld.gov.au; 70-102 Flinders St E; adult/child $15/8.80; ⊙ 9.30am-5pm) An absolute must for school-age children and grown-up science and history fans, the Museum of Tropical Queensland reconstructs scenes using detailed models with interactive displays. At 11am and 2.30pm you can load and fire a cannon, 1700s-style. Galleries include the kid-friendly MindZone science centre, and displays on North Queensland's history from the dinosaurs to the rainforest and reef.

**Australian Institute
of Marine Science**   RESEARCH INSTITUTE
(AIMS; ⌨ 07-4753 4444; www.aims.gov.au) 🌊 Scheduled to re-commence free two-hour tours (10am Fridays from March through November) in mid-2017 after extensive renovations, this marine-research facility at Cape Ferguson conducts crucial research into issues such as coral bleaching and management of the Great Barrier Reef, and how it relates to the community; advance bookings are essential. The turn-off from the Bruce Hwy is 35km southeast of Townsville.

Billabong Sanctuary   WILDLIFE RESERVE
(www.billabongsanctuary.com.au; Bruce Hwy; adult/child $35/22; ⊙ 9am-5pm) 🌊 Just 17km south of Townsville, this eco-certified wildlife park offers up-close-and-personal encounters with Australian wildlife – from dingoes to cassowaries – in their natural habitat. You could easily spend all day at the 11-hectare park, with feedings, shows and talks every half-hour or so.

Botanic Gardens   GARDENS
(⊙ sunrise-sunset) FREE Townsville's botanic gardens are spread across three locations: each has its own character, but all have tropical plants and are abundantly green. Closest to the centre, the formal, ornamental **Queens Gardens** (cnr Gregory & Paxton Sts; ⊙ sunrise-sunset) FREE are 1km northwest of town at the base of Castle Hill.

Castle Hill   VIEWPOINT
FREE Much of Townsville's fit and fabulous hoof it up this striking 286m-high red hill (an isolated pink granite monolith) that dominates Townsville's skyline for stunning views of the city and Cleveland Bay. Walk up via the rough 'goat track' (2km one-way) from Hillside Cres. Otherwise, drive via Gregory St up the narrow, winding 2.6km Castle Hill Rd. A signboard up top details short trails leading to various lookout points.

Cultural Centre   CULTURAL CENTRE
(⌨ 07-4772 7679; www.cctownsville.com.au; 2-68 Flinders St F; adult/child $5/2; ⊙ 9.30am-4.30pm) Showcases the history, traditions and customs of the local Wulgurukaba and Bindal peoples. Call for guided-tour times.

Maritime Museum of Townsville   MUSEUM
(⌨ 07-4721 5251; www.townsvillemaritimemuseum.org.au; 42-68 Palmer St; adult/child/family $6/3/15; ⊙ 10am-3pm Mon-Fri, noon-3pm Sat & Sun) One for the boat buffs, with a gallery dedicated to the wreck of the *Yongala* and exhibits on North Queensland's naval industries. Tours of decommissioned patrol boat HMAS *Townsville* are available.

⚡ Activities

Strand   SWIMMING
Stretching 2.2km, Townsville's waterfront is interspersed with parks, pools, cafes and playgrounds – with hundreds of palm trees

Townsville

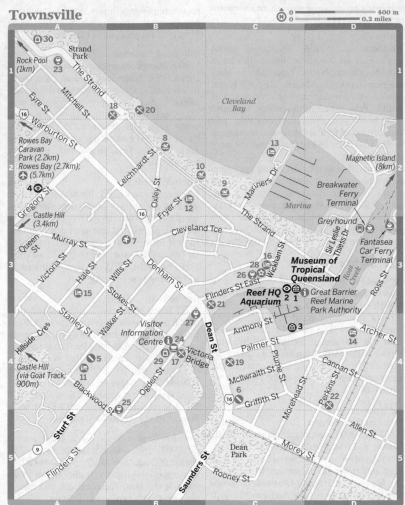

providing shade. Its sandy beach is patrolled and protected by two stinger enclosures.

At the northern tip is the **rock pool** (⊙24hr) **FREE**, an enormous artificial swimming pool surrounded by lawns and sandy beaches. Alternatively, head to the chlorinated safety of the heritage-listed, Olympic-sized swimming pool, **Tobruk Memorial Baths** (www.townsville.qld.gov.au; adult/child $5/3; ⊙5.30am-7pm Mon-Thu, to 6pm Fri, 7am-4pm Sat, 8am-5pm Sun). There's also a fantastic **water playground** (⊙10am-8pm Dec-Mar, to 6pm Sep-Nov, Apr & May, to 5pm Jun-Aug) **FREE** for the kids.

Skydive Townsville SKYDIVING
(☑07-4721 4721; www.skydivetownsville.com.au; 182 Denham St; 3050/4270m tandem dives from $395/445) Hurl yourself from a perfectly good plane and land right on the Strand, or over on Magnetic Island.

👉 Tours

Townsville History Walking Tour WALKING
(☑0400 560 471; www.townsvillehistorywalking tours.com.au; tours $20-80) New historical walking tours of Townsville are proving popular with locals and curious visitors. The City Day Tour ($50) and Palmer St

Townsville

Wine and Dine Tour ($80) are particularly recommended.

★ Festivals & Events

The city has a packed calendar of festivals and events, including the home games of its cherished North Queensland Cowboys (www.cowboys.com.au) National Rugby League team.

Townsville 500   SPORTS
(www.v8supercars.com.au; ◷ Jul) Racing cars roar through a purpose-built street circuit during the V8 Supercar Championship.

**Australian Festival
of Chamber Music**   MUSIC
(www.afcm.com.au; ◷ Aug) Townsville gets cultural during this internationally renowned festival at various venues across the city.

🛏 Sleeping

★ **Civic Guest House**   HOSTEL $
(☎ 07-4771 5381; www.civicguesthousetownsville.com.au; 262 Walker St; dm/d from $20/56; @ 🖰) This old-fashioned hostel respects the independent traveller's needs for cleanliness, comfort, security and easy company. The mustard-coloured, colonial-tinged Civic is a welcome change from the boisterous backpacker trend. Free transport to/from the ferry or bus station.

Orchid Guest House   GUESTHOUSE $
(☎ 07-4771 6683, 0418 738 867; www.orchidguesthouse.com.au; 34 Hale St; dm $28, d with/without bathroom $90/65; 🖰) The Orchid has really bloomed since our last visit. In a quiet hillside location within walking distance of town, the old suburban inner-city home is now wonderfully kept in that quaint Queensland fashion, with a peaceful flow of guests looking for a place to make plans for Magnetic Island or find temporary work.

Reef Lodge   HOSTEL $
(☎ 07-4721 1112; www.reeflodge.com.au; 4 Wickham St; dm $23-35, d with/without bathroom $80/62; 🖰@🖰) The only downtown hostel worth bothering with is a warren of room configurations, but the staff are very capable of creating a sense of community in the games room, chill-out zone and hammock-strewn garden area. Jobs can be found in the region here, if you've spent all your dough at the nearby nightclubs.

Rowes Bay Caravan Park   CARAVAN PARK $
(☎ 07-4771 3576; www.rowesbaycp.com.au; Heatley Pde; powered/unpowered sites $36/28, cabins with/without bathroom from $110/75, villas $115-140; 🖰@🖰🖰) Leafy park directly opposite Rowes Bay's beachfront. The villas are smaller than cabins, but spiffier.

GREAT BARRIER REEF TRIPS FROM TOWNSVILLE

The Great Barrier Reef lies further offshore from Townsville than it does from Cairns and Port Douglas; the extra fuel costs push up prices. On the upside, it's less crowded (and the reef suffers less from the effects of crowds). Trips from Townsville are generally dive-oriented; if you only want to snorkel, take a day trip that just goes to the reef – the *Yongala* wreck is for diving only. The *Yongala* is considerably closer to Alva Beach near Ayr than to Townsville, so if your main interest is wreck diving, you may want to consider a trip with Alva Beach–based Yongala Dive.

The visitor centre (p424) has a list of Townsville-based operators offering PADI-certified learn-to-dive courses with two days' training in the pool, plus at least two days and one night living aboard the boat. Prices start at $600, and you'll need to obtain a dive medical (around $60).

Operators include the following:

Adrenalin Dive (☑ 07-4724 0600; www.adrenalinedive.com.au; 252 Walker St) Day trips to the *Yongala* (from $264) and Lodestone Reef (from $229), both including two dives. Also offers liveaboard trips and dive-certification courses.

Remote Area Dive (RAD; ☑ 07-4721 4424; www.remoteareadive.com.au; 16 Dean St) Runs day trips (from $225) to Orpheus and Pelorus Islands. Also liveaboard trips and dive courses.

Historic Yongala Lodge Motel MOTEL $
(☑ 07-4772 4633; www.historicyongala.com.au; 11 Fryer St; motel r $79-139, 1/2-bedroom apt $115/159; ❋☀🛜☒) Built in 1884, this lovely historic building with gingerbread-house-style balustrades is but a short stroll from the Strand and city centre. The rooms and apartments are small but good value. Long-term 'tenants' and noisy party-goers can detract from the overall feel of the place, but there's enough variety and space to make it work.

Oaks M on Palmer BOUTIQUE HOTEL $$
(☑ 07-4753 2900; 81 Palmer St; d from $100; 🅿☀❋🛜☒) Perfect for an after-party or pre-dinner in-room drinks, Oaks M is right at the end of the Palmer St shuffle. The rooms are small, but stylish and bright. Popular with single professionals. Parking is free, service is discreet, and there's a small gym.

Mariners North APARTMENT $$$
(☑ 07-4722 0777; www.marinersnorth.com.au; 7 Mariners Dr; 2-/3-bedroom apt from $209/360; 🅿☀❋🛜☒) The pick for families in Townsville is Mariners North, located in the newer section of the marina, with a sandy stretch out front and a delightful pool. The apartments are very good, particularly the ground-floor ones with direct pool and garden access; others may prefer views over Cleveland Bay.

✗ Eating

Perpendicular to the Strand, Gregory St has a clutch of cafes and takeaway joints. The Palmer St dining strip offers a diverse range of cuisines: wander along and take your pick. Many of Townsville's bars and pubs also serve food.

Harold's Seafood SEAFOOD $
(cnr The Strand & Gregory St; meals $4-10; ⊗8am-9pm Mon-Thu, to 9.30pm Fri-Sun) The big fish-and-chip joint on the corner whips up fish burgers ($12) and large-sized barramundi and salad ($11).

★ Longboard Bar & Grill MODERN AUSTRALIAN $$
(☑ 07-4724 1234; www.longboardbarandgrill.com; The Strand, opp Gregory St; mains $15-37; ⊗11.30am-3pm & 5.30pm-late) The coolest place in Townsville for a light meal and a light party overlooking the water is this surf-themed pub-restaurant, which does terrific nightly specials including tacos and buffalo wings. The regular steak, seafood and pasta menu is very reliable. Orders are taken at the bar, but that's not a problem as the vibe is right most nights, and staff are fast and efficient.

Jam MODERN AUSTRALIAN $$
(☑ 07-4721 4900; 1 Palmer St; mains $15-30; ⊗7am-10pm) This neat midrange restaurant, on happening Palmer St, understands its

casual northern Queensland clientele and serves a wide menu with celebratory breakfasts and desserts.

Wayne & Adele's
Garden of Eating · MODERN AUSTRALIAN $$
(⊘07-4772 2984; 11 Allen St; mains from $19; ⊙6.30-10.30pm Mon, to 11pm Thu-Sat, noon-3pm Sun) Irreverence at every turn in this husband-and-wife-run gourmet restaurant situated in an Aussie backyard (well courtyard, at least). Those who like a side serving of quirky with their grub shouldn't miss mains including Safety Net (crocodile pattie with an eggnet Asian salad) or Bounce Back (tandoori kangaroo fillet with lime pickle yoghurt).

Summerie's Thai Cuisine · THAI $$
(⊘07-4420 1282; www.summeriesthaicuisine. com.au; 232 Flinders St; lunch specials $13, dinner mains from $17; ⊙11.30am-2.30pm & 5.30-10pm) A wildly successful local Thai restaurant with a prime downtown location and a new branch in the suburbs, Summerie's adapts traditional dishes to the Aussie palate and incorporates Coral Sea produce in dishes such as Barrier Reef (fish sauce, coriander and chilli-jam-spiced seafood), Heaven on Earth (slow-cooked coconut prawns with crunchy greens) and Summer Sunset (sweet-and-sour pineapple sauce).

A Touch of Salt · MODERN AUSTRALIAN $$$
(⊘07-4724 4441; www.atouchofsalt.com.au; 86-124 Ogden St; mains $35-37; ⊙noon-3pm & 6-11.30pm) Although the favoured high-end dining experience for Townsville's posh set doesn't look very stylish upon entry, the bar is slick, the service is fussy and the sophisticated Asian-fusion cuisine is ambitious (though can overreach at times).

🍷 Drinking & Nightlife

Townsville Brewery · BREWERY
(252 Flinders St; ⊙11.30am-midnight Mon-Sat) Brews are made on-site at this hopping, stunningly restored 1880s former post office. Soak up a Townsville Bitter or Bandito Loco.

Beach Bar · BAR
(Watermark Hotel, 72-74 The Strand) The place to be seen in Townsville. Well, if it's good enough for Missy Higgins and Silverchair, then it's good enough for the rest of us. Some serious Sunday sessions take place in the tavern bar with prime ocean views down the flash end of the Strand.

Coffee Dominion · CAFE
(www.coffeedominion.com.au; cnr Stokes & Ogden Sts; ⊙6am-5pm Mon-Fri, 7am-1pm Sat & Sun) 🍃 An eco-conscious establishment roasting beans sourced from the Atherton tablelands to Mombasa. If you don't find a blend you like, invent your own and they'll grind it fresh.

Grand Northern Hotel · PUB
(⊘07-4771 6191; 500 Flinders St) This historic 1901 pub in Townsville's bustling centre is not exactly a tranquil haven, but it's great for a beer at any time. For those who like to be in the thick of it all, the GN can't be beat.

Heritage Bar · BAR
(⊘07-4724 1374; www.theheritagetownsville.com; 137 Flinders St E; bar snacks from $11; ⊙5pm-2am Tue-Sat) A surprisingly chic craft bar. Suave 'mixologists' deliver creative cocktails ($18) to a cool crowd looking for something more than a beer-barn swillfest. Also has a sophisticated bar menu for meals (think BBQ bourbon pork, and scallop and chorizo gnocchi), as well as tipsy nibbles such as coconut prawns.

☆ Entertainment

Flynns · LIVE MUSIC
(www.flynnsirishbar.com; 101 Flinders St E; ⊙5pm-late Tue-Sun) A jolly Irish pub that doesn't try too hard to be Irish. Wildly popular for its live music every night except Wednesdays, when karaoke takes over.

🔒 Shopping

Check out the weekly **Cotters Market** (www. townsvillerotarymarkets.com.au; Flinders St Mall; ⊙8.30am-1pm Sun) or monthly **Strand Night Market** (www.townsvillerotarymarkets.com.au; The Strand; ⊙5-9.30pm 1st Fri of month May-Dec).

DIVING THE YONGALA WRECK

Yongala Dive (⊘07-4783 1519; www. yongaladive.com.au; 56 Narrah St, Alva Beach) offers dive trips ($259 including gear) out to the *Yongala* wreck from Alva Beach, 17km northeast of Ayr. It only takes 30 minutes to get out to the wreck from here, instead of a 2½-hour boat trip from Townsville. Book ahead for backpacker-style accommodation at its onshore **dive lodge** (dm/d $29/68; @), with free pick-ups from Ayr.

ⓘ Information

Great Barrier Reef Marine Park Authority
(☑ 07-4750 0700; www.gbrmpa.gov.au) National body overseeing the Great Barrier Reef.

Visitor Information Centre (☑ 07-4721 3660; www.townsvilleholidays.info; 280 Flinders St; ⊙ 9am-5pm) Extensive visitor information on Townsville, Magnetic Island and nearby national parks. There's another branch on the Bruce Hwy 10km south of the city.

ⓘ Getting There & Away

AIR

From **Townsville Airport** (www.townsvilleairport. com.au), **Virgin** (☑ 13 67 89; www.virginaustralia. com), **Qantas** (☑ 13 13 13; www.qantas.com.au), **Air North** (☑ 1800 627 474; www.airnorth.com. au) and **Jetstar** (☑ 13 15 38; www.jetstar.com.au) fly to Cairns, Brisbane, the Gold Coast, Sydney, Melbourne, Mackay and Rockhampton, with connections to other major cities.

BOAT

SeaLink (☑ 07-4726 0800; www.sealinkqld. com.au) runs an excellent ferry service to Magnetic Island from Breakwater in Townsville (return adult/child including all-day bus pass $35/17.50, 25 minutes). There's roughly one trip per hour between 5.30am and 11.30pm. All ferries arrive and depart Magnetic Island from the terminal at Nelly Bay.

BUS

Greyhound (☑ 1300 473 946; www.grey hound.com.au; The Breakwater, Sealink Travel Centre, Sir Leslie Thiess Dr) has three daily services to Brisbane ($249, 24 hours), Rockhampton ($129, 12 hours), Airlie Beach ($49, 4½ hours), Mission Beach ($44, 3¾ hours) and Cairns ($64, six hours). Buses pick up and drop off at the **Breakwater Ferry Terminal** (2/14 Sir Leslie Thiess Dr; lockers per day $4-6).

Premier Motor Service (☑ 13 34 10; www. premierms.com.au) has one service a day to/ from Brisbane ($184, 23 hours) and Cairns ($55, six hours), stopping in Townsville at the **Fantasea car ferry terminal** (Ross St, South Townsville).

TRAIN

Townsville's **train station** (Charters Towers Rd) is 1km south of the centre.

The Brisbane–Cairns Spirit of Queensland travels through Townsville five times a week. Journey time between Brisbane and Townsville is 25 hours (one-way from $189), while tickets to Cairns (6½ hours) start from $79. Contact **Queensland Rail** (☑ 1800 872 467; www. queenslandrail.com.au).

ⓘ Getting Around

TO/FROM THE AIRPORT

Townsville Airport is 5km northwest of the city centre in Garbutt. A taxi to the centre costs about $22.

BUS

Sunbus (☑ 07-4771 9800; www.sunbus.com. au) runs local bus services around Townsville. Route maps and timetables are available at the visitor information centre and online.

TAXI

Taxis congregate at ranks across town, or call **Townsville Taxis** (☑ 13 10 08; www.tsvtaxi. com.au).

Magnetic Island

POP 2500

Sitting within shouting distance of Townsville, Magnetic Island is a verdant island and one of Queensland's most laid-back residential addresses. The local population, who mostly commute to Townsville or cater for the tourist trade, must pinch themselves as they come home to the stunning coastal walking trails, gum trees full of dozing koalas (you're likely to spot some), and surrounding bright turquoise seas.

Over half of this triangular-shaped, mountainous island's 52 sq km is national park, with scenic walks and abundant wildlife, including a large (and adorable) rock wallaby population. Inviting beaches offer adrenalin-pumping water sports, and the chance to just bask in the sunshine. The granite boulders, hoop pines and eucalyptus are a fresh change from the clichéd tropical-island paradise.

◉ Sights

There's one main road across the island, which goes from Picnic Bay, past Nelly and Geoffrey Bays, to Horseshoe Bay. Local buses ply the route regularly. Walking trails through the bush also link the main towns. Maps are available at the ferry terminal ticket desk.

◉ Picnic Bay

Picnic Bay is one of the most low-key spots on the island, dominated more by a community of friendly locals than anything else. There's a stinger net during the season (November to May) and the swimming is superb. There's also a fine jetty if you like to throw in a line.

RAVENSWOOD & CHARTERS TOWERS

Detour inland from the coast to taste a bit of Queensland's outback character at these two old gold towns.

Ravenswood (population 160) is a tiny gold-mining town whose fortunes have fluctuated over the past century. It's now best known for its two grand hotels, one of which supposedly houses one of Queensland's most active resident ghosts.

Accommodation, food and, of course, drinks can be found in the town's two pubs, the **Imperial Hotel** (☑ 07-4770 2131; 23 Macrossan St; s/d $39/65; P ⊖ ❈ 🛜) and the **Railway Hotel** (☑ 07-4770 2144; 1 Barton St; s/tw/d $42/79/90; P ⊖ ❈ 🛜).

The 19th-century gold-rush settlement of Charters Towers (population 8500) is about 140km southwest of Townsville on the Flinders Hwy. William Skelton Ewbank Melbourne (WSEM) Charters was the gold commissioner during the rush, when the town was the second-largest, and wealthiest, in Queensland. The 'towers' are its surrounding tors (hills). With almost 100 mines, some 90 pubs and a stock exchange, the town became known simply as 'the World'. Today, a highlight of a visit to the Towers is strolling past its glorious facades and recalling the grandeur of those heady days.

The **Stock Exchange Arcade** (☑ 07-3223 6666; www.nationaltrust.org.au/places/stock-exchange-building-and-arcade; 76 Mosman St; ⊙ 9am-5pm), with its barrel-vaulted portico, was the commercial hub in the late 19th century. Today it features a breezy, sun-filtered cafe and a fine art gallery.

Come nightfall, panoramic Towers Hill, the site where gold was first discovered, is the atmospheric setting for an open-air cinema showing the 20-minute film *Ghosts After Dark* – check seasonal screening times and buy tickets ($10) at the visitor centre.

Staying at the atmospheric and friendly old **Royal Private Hotel** (☑ 07-4787 8688; www.royalprivate-hotel.com; 100 Mosman St; r from $60; ❈ 🛜) feels like something between time travel and visiting a museum. The creaky wooden beds and black-and-white-chequered bathroom tiles are charming or cheesy.

For those looking for a real-life cattle-station experience, contact friendly Rhonda at **Bluff Downs** (☑ 07-4770 4084; www.bluffdowns.com.au; dm $20, d $90-300, camp sites $20). The vast majority of guests are looking for medium-term employment, but passers-by are welcome. It's 110km northwest of Charters Towers.

Healthy Treat (☑ 07-4787 4218; 14 Gill St; meals $12-24) is an ever-popular eatery serving massive homemade burgers, sandwiches and meat dishes to a steady flow of families and professionals. The Mars Bar, Nutella and Salted Caramel thickshakes ($8) are intense.

The excellent **Charters Towers Visitor Centre** (☑ 07-4761 5533; www.charters towers.qld.gov.au; 74 Mosman St; ⊙ 9am-5pm) books all tours in town, including those to the reputedly haunted Venus Gold Battery, where gold-bearing ore was crushed and processed from 1872 to 1973.

◉ Nelly Bay

Magnetic Harbour in Nelly Bay is your first taste of life on the island. There's a wide range of busy but relaxing eating and sleeping options and a decent beach. There's also a children's playground towards the northern end of the beach, and good snorkelling on the fringing coral reef.

◉ Arcadia Bay

Arcadia village is a conglomerate of shops, eateries and accommodation. Its main beach, Geoffrey Bay, has a reef at its southern end (reef walking at low tide is discouraged). By far its prettiest beach is the cove at Alma Bay with huge boulders tumbling into the sea. There's plenty of shade here, along with picnic tables and a children's playground.

If you head to the end of the road at Bremner Point, between Geoffrey Bay and Alma Bay, at around 5pm you can have wild rock wallabies – accustomed to being fed at the same time each day – literally eating out of the palm of your hand. For those who make it out here, this can be a trip highlight.

⦿ Radical Bay & the Forts

Townsville was a supply base for the Pacific during WWII, and the forts were designed to protect the town from naval attack. If you're going to do just one walk, then the forts walk (2.8km, 1½ hours return) is a must. It starts near the Radical Bay turn-off, passing lots of ex-military sites, gun emplacements and false 'rocks'. At the top of the walk is the observation tower and command post, which have spectacular coastal views, and you'll almost certainly spot koalas lazing about in the treetops. Return the same way or continue along the connecting paths, which deposit you at Horseshoe Bay (you can catch the bus back).

Nearby Balding Bay is Maggie's unofficial nude beach.

⦿ Horseshoe Bay

Horseshoe Bay, on the north coast, is the best of Maggie's accessible beaches and attracts its share of young, hippie-ish nature lovers and older day trippers. You'll find water-sports gear for hire, a stinger net, a row of cafes and a fantastic pub. Bungalow Bay Koala Village has a **wildlife park** (☑07-4778 5577, 1800 285 577; www.bungalowbay.com.au; 40 Horseshoe Bay Rd; adult/child $29/13; ⊙2hr tours 10am, noon & 2.30pm), where you can cuddle crocs and koalas. Pick up local arts and crafts at Horseshoe Bay's **market** (⊙9am-2pm 2nd & last Sun of month), which sets up along the beachfront.

🏃 Activities

Big Mama Sailing   BOATING
(☑0437 206 360; www.bigmamasailing.com; full-day cruises adult/child $195/110) Hit the water on an 18m ketch with passionate boaties Stu, Lisa and Fletcher, who recently moved the Big Mama down from Mission Beach.

Pro Dive Magnetic   DIVING
(☑0424 822 450; www.prodivemagnetic.com; 43 Sooning St, Nelly Bay) This Nelly Bay dive school offers splashing Magnetic Island day trips for both snorkellers ($149) and scuba divers ($199). PADI courses cost $299.

Tropicana Tours   DRIVING
(☑07-4758 1800; www.tropicanatours.com.au; full day adult/child $198/99) Ziggy and Co run magnificent island tours that take in the island's best spots in their stretch 4WD. Prices include close encounters with wildlife, lunch

at a local cafe and a sunset cocktail. Shorter tours are also available, but the eight-hour version is a hit.

Horseshoe Bay Ranch   HORSE RIDING
(☑07-4778 5109; www.horseshoebayranch.com.au; 38 Gifford St; 2hr rides $120) Gallop dramatically into the not-so-crashing surf on this popular bushland-to-beach two-hour tour. Pony rides for littlies are available too (20 minutes, $20).

Magnetic Island Sea Kayaks   KAYAKING
(☑07-4778 5424; www.seakayak.com.au; 93 Horseshoe Bay Rd; morning/evening tours $85/60) 🏄 Magnetic Island is a perfect destination for sea kayaking, with plenty of launching points, secret beaches, marine life, and laid-back cafes to recharge in after your paddle. Join an eco-certified morning or sunset tour, or go it alone on a rented kayak (single/double per day $85/160).

Pleasure Divers   DIVING
(☑07-4778 5788; www.pleasuredivers.com.au; 10 Marine Pde, Arcadia; open-water courses per person from $300; ⊙8.30am-5pm) A snorkel tour with these guys based in Arcadia is a good-value way to get an appreciation of the ecology around Geoffrey Bay. Deep-water thinkers can do three-day PADI open-water courses to kick-start their scuba skills, as well as advanced courses and *Yongala* wreck dives for regular plungers.

🛏 Sleeping

For holiday cottages check out www.best ofmagnetic.com or www.magneticisland tourism.com.

⭐ **Base Backpackers**   HOSTEL $
(☑1800 242 273; www.stayatbase.com; 1 Nelly Bay Rd, Nelly Bay; camping per person $15, dm $32-37, d from $110; @�🌊) Away from any semblance of holidaymakers to disrupt your natural state, Base has to be one of the best-located hostels in Australia, situated between Nelly and Picnic Bays. It's famous for wild full-moon parties, and things can get raucous at any time at the infamous on-site Island Bar. Sleep, food and transport package deals are available.

Arcadia Beach Guest House   GUESTHOUSE $
(☑07-4778 5668; www.arcadiabeachguesthouse.com.au; 27 Marine Pde, Arcadia; dm from $35, safari tents $65, r with/without bathroom from $135/$75; ✱🗑🌊) Well-priced and staffed by effusive professionals, Arcadia Beach Guest House

does a lot right, including providing an enormous variety of sleeping quarters. Will you stay in a bright, beachy room (named after Magnetic Island's bays), a safari tent or a dorm? Go turtle-spotting from the balcony, rent a canoe, a Moke or a 4WD...or all of the above?

Magnetic Island B&B
B&B $$
(☑ 07-4758 1203; www.magneticislandbedand breakfast.com; 11 Dolphin Ct, Horseshoe Bay; d $150) The double rooms here book out quickly, but a new Bush Retreat ($190) sleeps four and is a great deal for some natural seclusion. Rooms are bright and breezy, and the hosts are astutely professional. There's a neat salt-water pool, and the inclusive breakfasts are wholesome and delicious. Minimum two-night stay applies.

Shambhala Retreat
BUNGALOW $$
(☑ 0448 160 580; www.shambhala-retreat-magnetic-island.com.au; 11 Barton St, Nelly Bay; d from $105; ❄☀) ✦ With some of the best-value, self-contained, tropical units on the island, Shambhala is a green-powered property with distinct Buddhist influences evident in the wall hangings and water features. Two units have outdoor courtyard showers; all have fully equipped kitchens, large bathrooms and laundry facilities. Local wildlife is often drawn to the patios. Minimum stay is two nights.

Arcadia Village Motel
HOTEL $$
(☑ 07-4778 5481; www.arcadiavillage.com.au; 7 Marine Pde, Arcadia; r from $120; ❄🛜☀) Situated down the quiet end of Marine Pde (which is saying something in a chilled-out place like Maggie), this family-friendly motel has an on-site bistro and bar, which can get a little rowdy on weekends. There are two awesome pools, and a great beach a short stroll across the street.

Island Leisure Resort
RESORT $$
(☑ 07-4778 5000; www.islandleisure.com.au; 4 Kelly St; burés d/f from $197/247; ❄🛜☀) Self-contained, Polynesian-style cabins (burés) give this by-the-beach spot an extra-tropical feel. Private patios allow guests to enjoy their own piece of paradise: a lagoon pool and BBQ area beckon social souls.

Magnetic Sunsets
APARTMENT $$
(☑ 07-4778 1900; www.magneticsunsets.com.au; 7 Pacific Dr; 1-/2-/3-bedroom apt $195/295/395, B&B s/d $115/159; ❄🛜☀) These great-value, self-contained apartments are just a literal stagger from the beach. Private balconies

overlook the bay; inside, they're cool, clean and welcoming. Smart, new B&B rooms are good alternatives.

Tropical Palms Inn
MOTEL $$
(☑ 07-4778 5076; www.tropicalpalmsinn.com.au; 34 Picnic St, Picnic Bay; s/d $120/130; ❄🛜☀) With a terrific little swimming pool right outside your front door and superbly friendly hosts, the simple, self-contained motel units here are bright and comfortable. Prices drop if you stay two or more nights, and you can also rent 4WDs here. Good discounts for longer stays.

✖ Eating & Drinking

★ Cafe Nourish
CAFE $
(☑ 07-4758 1885; 3/6 Pacific Dr, Horsehoe Bay; wraps from $9; ⊘ 8am-4pm) Horseshoe Bay has become the hip cafe strip and our favourite cafe on the island does the small things well: fresh, healthy wraps, breakfasts, smoothies and energy balls. And don't even get us started on the coffee. Service is energetic and heartfelt.

Arcadia Night Market
MARKET $
(RSL Hall, Hayles Ave, Arcadia; ⊘ 5.30-8pm Fri) Small but lively night market with licensed bar and plenty of cheap eats to chow through.

Noodies on the Beach
MEXICAN $
(☑ 07-4778 5786; 2/6 Pacific Dr, Horseshoe Bay; mains from $10; ⊘ 10am-10pm Mon-Wed & Fri, 8am-10pm Sat, 8am-3pm Sun; 🅿) An integral part of the Horseshoe Bay food scene, Noodies is an irreverent Mexican-themed cafe with a book exchange and a licence to serve killer margaritas.

Gilligan's Cafe
CAFE $$
(Arcadia Village; burgers $14-18; ⊘ 8am-4pm) Fun, licensed cafe in Arcadia that pumps out massive breakfasts and the finest burgers on Maggie. The owners have a *Gilligan's Island* thing going on. Get stranded while you enjoy the decent booze selection over lunch.

Marlin Bar
PUB FOOD $$
(☑ 07-4758 1588; 3 Pacific Dr, Horseshoe Bay; mains $16-24; ⊘ 11am-8pm) Marlin Bar is popular with sailing crews dropping anchor in Horseshoe Bay and locals looking for some live music in the evenings. Meals are on the large side and (surprise!) revolve around seafood. Dogs are welcome.

Picnic Bay Hotel
PUB FOOD **$$**

(☑ 07-4778 5166; www.picnicbayhotel.com.au; 1 The Esplanade, Picnic Bay; mains $11-26; ⊙ 9.30am-10pm) There are worse places to settle in at for a drink than the very quiet Picnic Bay, with Townsville's city lights sparkling across the bay. There's an all-day grazing menu and huge salads.

❶ Getting There & Away

SeaLink (☑ 07-4726 0800; www.sealinkqld.com.au) runs an excellent ferry service to Magnetic Island from Townsville (return adult/child including all-day bus pass $35/17.50, 25 minutes). There's roughly one trip per hour between 5.30am and 11.30pm. All ferries arrive and depart Maggie from the terminal at Nelly Bay. Car parking is available in Townsville.

Fantasea (☑ 07-4796 9300; www.magneticislandferry.com.au; Ross St, South Townsville) operates a car ferry crossing eight times daily (seven on weekends) from the south side of Ross Creek, taking 35 minutes. It costs $178 (return) for a car and up to three passengers, and $29/17 (adult/child return) for foot passengers only. Bookings are essential and bicycles are transported free.

❶ Getting Around

Sunbus (www.sunbus.com.au/sit_magnetic_island) ploughs between Picnic and Horseshoe Bays, meeting all ferries and stopping at major accommodation places. A day pass covering all zones is $7.20, or you can include it in your ferry ticket price. Be sure to talk to the bus drivers, who love chatting about everything Maggie.

Moke- ('topless' car) and scooter-rental places abound. You'll need to be over 21 years old, have a current driver's licence and leave a credit-card deposit. Scooter hire starts at around $40 per day, Mokes at about $75. Try **MI Wheels** (☑ 07-4758 1111; www.miwheels.com.au; 138 Sooning St, Nelly Bay) for a classic Moke, or **Roadrunner Scooter Hire** (☑ 07-4778 5222; 3/64 Kelly St, Nelly Bay) for scooters and trail bikes.

NORTH OF TOWNSVILLE

Heading north from Townsville, the scorched-brown landscape slowly gives way to sugar-cane plantations lining the highway and tropical rainforest shrouding the hillsides.

Waterfalls, national parks and small villages hide up in the hinterland, including Paluma Range National Park (part of the Wet Tropics World Heritage Area). Visitor centres in the area have leaflets outlining walking trails, swimming holes and camping grounds.

Ingham & Around
POP 4681

Ingham is a cane-cutting centre with a proud Italian heritage. It's also the guardian of the 120-hectare **Tyto Wetlands** (Tyto Wetlands Information Centre; ☑ 07-4776 4792; www.tyto.com.au; cnr Cooper St & Bruce Hwy; ⊙ 8.45am-5pm Mon-Fri, 9am-4pm Sat & Sun), which has 4km of walking trails and attracts around 230 species of birds, including far-flung guests from Siberia and Japan. The locals – hundreds of wallabies – love it too, converging at dawn and dusk. The town is the jumping-off point for the majestic Wallaman Falls; at 305m, it's the longest single-drop waterfall in Australia.

Mungalla Station (☑ 07-4777 8718; www.mungallaaboriginaltours.com.au; 2hr tours adult/child $70/35) ✐, 15km east of Ingham, runs insightful Aboriginal-led tours, including boomerang throwing and stories from the local Nywaigi culture, plus a traditional Kupmurri lunch. Minimum of 10 needed, so call ahead to check. Basic camping sites also available.

In August the **Australian Italian Festival** (www.australianitalianfestival.com.au) celebrates the fact that 60% of Ingham residents are of Italian descent. The motto is 'eat, drink and celebrate'.

You can camp at **Wallaman Falls Campground** (www.npsr.qld.gov.au; sites per person/family $6.15/24.60).

The poem that inspired the iconic Slim Dusty hit 'Pub With No Beer' (1957) was written in the **Lees Hotel** (☑ 07-4776 1577; www.leeshotel.com.au; 58 Lannercost St; s/d from $90/105, meals from $14; ⊙ lunch & dinner Mon-Sat; ✳ ⊚) by Ingham cane-cutter Dan Sheahan, after American soldiers drank the place dry. The en-suite rooms here are very comfortable, while the busy bistro does fine steak and pasta dishes. Oh, and there's plenty of beer.

The award-winning **Hinchinbrook Marine Cove Resort** (☑ 07-4777 8395; www.hinchinbrook-marine-cove-resort.com.au; 54 Dungeness Rd; d $135, bungalows $150; ✳ ✳) is terrific value given the bright, spacious bungalows sleep up to five, management are hands-on and there's easy access to Hinchinbrook Island.

WORTH A TRIP

ORPHEUS ISLAND

Orpheus is a heavenly 1300-hectare island 80km north of Townsville, with a protected national park and surrounding ocean that is part of the Great Barrier Reef Marine Park. Its dry sclerophyll forest is a geographical anomaly this far north, where bandicoots, green tree frogs, echidnas, ospreys and a peculiar number of goats roam free, the latter as part of a madcap 19th-century scheme to provide food for potential shipwreck survivors. Visitors gravitate towards the eucalypt-scented hiking trails and crystal-clear snorkelling.

Part of the Palm Islands group, Orpheus is surrounded by magnificent fringing reef that's home to a mind-blowing collection of fish (1100 species) and a mammoth variety of both hard and soft corals. While the island is great for snorkellers and divers year-round (pack a stinger suit in summer), seasonal treats such as manta-ray migration (August to November) and coral spawning (mid-November) make the trip out here all the more worthwhile.

Orpheus Island Lodge (07-4839 7937; www.orpheus.com.au; d incl meals from $1500) is arguably the finest five-star resort in Queensland, rivalling the more famous Hayman Island for sheer tropical splendour, food, service and prestige.

Nautilus Aviation (07-4034 9000; www.nautilusaviation.com.au; one way from Townsville $275) runs helicopters from Townsville at 2pm daily for $275 one-way. The spectacular trip takes 30 minutes. Otherwise, ask around the town of Lucinda to arrange a boat ride over.

Cardwell

POP 1300

It's no wonder the truck drivers make Cardwell a must-stop destination. Given the Bruce Hwy runs inland for most of the east coast, it's a rare blessing to see and hear the sea lapping right outside your vehicle window; the uninterrupted views of Hinchinbrook Island don't hurt either. Most travellers merely linger here for seasonal fruit picking (check at the backpackers if you're looking for work), but there are worse places in the world to slow down.

Cardwell Forest Drive is a scenic 26km round trip chock-a-block with lookouts, walking tracks and picnic areas signposted along the way. There are super swimming opportunities at Attie Creek Falls, as well as at the aptly named Spa Pool, where you can sit in a rock hollow as water gushes over you.

At **Girringun Aboriginal Art Centre** (www.art.girringun.com.au; 235 Victoria St; 8.30am-5pm Mon-Thu, to 2pm Fri) traditional woven baskets, paintings and colourful wooden sculptures are among the works for sale.

Sleeping & Eating

Cardwell Beachcomber Motel & Tourist Park CARAVAN PARK $
(07-4066 8550; www.cardwellbeachcomber. com.au; 43a Marine Pde; powered/unpowered sites $38/29, motel d $98-125, cabins & studios $120-130;) With a very sweet location across from the sea, the Beachcomber has a good variety of options, though the camping sites are a little tight. Cute studios and modern oceanview villas by the pool will take the heat off your east coast adventure. The small **Beachcomber restaurant** (mains from $25; breakfast daily, lunch & dinner Mon-Sat) serves light meals and can whip up a yummy breakfast.

Cardwell Central Backpackers HOSTEL $
(07-4066 8404; www.cardwellbackpackers. com.au; 6 Brasenose St; dm $24;) Good feedback from the banana farm workers suggests Cardwell Central can both arrange regular work and host in a heartfelt, secure way. They also accept overnighters. Free internet and pool table.

Seaview Cafe FAST FOOD $$
(87 Victoria St; mains $12-25; 24hr) The place with the giant crab on the roof, the cavernous Seaview is a famous stopover for hungry drivers. Trucker chefs dish up local flavours in the form of seafood sandwiches and a mammoth all-day breakfast ($17). It ain't fancy, but it gets the job done nicely.

Information

Rainforest & Reef Centre (07-4066 8601; www.greatgreenwaytourism.com; 142 Victoria St; 8.30am-5pm Mon-Fri, 9am-1pm Sat & Sun) The Rainforest & Reef Centre, next to Cardwell's jetty, has a truly brilliant interactive rainforest display, and detailed info on Hinchinbrook Island and other nearby national parks.

Hinchinbrook Island

Australia's largest island national park (399 sq km) is a holy grail for walkers, but it's not easy to get to and advance planning is essential. Granite mountains rise dramatically from the sea and wildlife creeps through the foliage. The mainland side is dense with lush tropical vegetation, while long sandy beaches and tangles of mangrove curve around the eastern shore.

Hinchinbrook Island Cruises (✆07-4066 8601; www.hinchinbrookislandcruises.com.au) runs a service from Cardwell's Port Hinchinbrook Marina to Hinchinbrook's Ramsay Bay boardwalk (per person one way $99, 1½ hours). It also operates a four-hour, two-island tour (adult/child $110/99) that includes a cruise between Goold and Garden Islands spotting dolphins, dugongs and turtles, before docking at Ramsay Bay boardwalk for a walk on the 9km-long beach and a picnic lunch.

NPRSR camp sites (✆13 74 68; www.npsr.qld.gov.au; sites per person $6.15) are interspersed along the wonderful 32km Thorsborne Trail (or East Coast Trail)

Tully

POP 2350

Though it may look like just another sleepy sugar-cane village, Tully is a burg with a boast, calling itself the 'wettest town in Australia'. A gigantic golden gumboot at Tully's entrance is as high as the waters rose (7.9m) in 1950: climb the spiral staircase to the viewing platform up top to get a sense of just how much that is! And while boggy Babinda challenges Tully's claim, the fact remains that all that rain ensures plenty of raftable rapids on the nearby Tully River, and shimmering fruit farms in need of travelling labour.

The Golden Gumboot Festival (☉May) celebrates the soak with a parade and lashings of entertainment.

Book at the visitor centre for 90-minute tours of Tully Sugar Mill (adult/child $17/11; ☉daily late Jun-early Nov).

🏃 Activities

Ingan Tours   TOUR
(✆07-4068 0189; www.ingan.com.au; 5 Blackman St) The Indigenous operators of Ingan Tours visit sacred story places on their full-day Spirit of the Rainforest tours (Tuesdays, Thursdays and Saturdays) and offer powerful, authentic insights into the lives of the area's first people and their relationship with the natural world. It's heady stuff and often the highlight of a trip to Australia for many visitors.

🛏️ Sleeping & Eating

Banana Barracks   HOSTEL $
(✆07-4068 0455; www.bananabarracks.com; 50 Butler St; 8-/4-bed dm weekly $135/165; @🛜🏊) Banana Barracks is the go-to backpackers for wannabe fruit pickers in the Tully region. The hostel is also the hub of Tully's nightlife, Rafters Bar, with an on-site nightclub.

Mount Tyson Hotel   PUB $
(✆07-4068 1088; www.mttysonhotel.com.au; s/d $60/105) This newly renovated pub is a bit bland in terms of ambience, but the motel rooms are fresh and clean, and provide good value for a short stay.

★**Redgates Steakhouse**   DINER $$
(✆0400 773 315; 99 Butler St) A top bloke runs this spacious diner on the way into town. The menu is long and changes often, but the mainstays are the burgers –

TULLY RIVER RAFTING

The Tully River provides thrilling white water year-round thanks to Tully's trademark bucket-downs and the river's hydroelectric floodgates. Rafting trips are timed to coincide with the daily release of the gates, resulting in Grade IV rapids foaming against a backdrop of stunning rainforest scenery.

Day trips with Raging Thunder Adventures (✆07-4030 7990; www.ragingthunder.com.au; full-day rafting $189) or R'n'R White Water Rafting (✆07-4041 9444; www.raft.com.au; full-day rafting from $179) include a BBQ lunch and transport from Tully or nearby Mission Beach.

WORTH A TRIP

PALUMA RANGE NATIONAL PARK

It's worth making time to venture off the Bruce Hwy via the Paluma Range National Park, southern gateway to the Wet Tropics World Heritage Area. The park is divided into two parts, the Mt Spec section and the northern Jourama Falls section, with both offering a variety of waterholes, inland beaches, hiking trails and a gentle entrée into tropical north Queensland. This glorious parallel universe, running alongside the Bruce Hwy from roughly Ingham to Townsville, is also prime platypus-spotting territory.

Mt Spec

The Mt Spec part of the park (61km north of Townsville or 40km south of Ingham) is a misty Eden of rainforest and eucalypt trees criss-crossed by a variety of walking tracks. This range of habitats houses an incredibly diverse population of birds, from golden bowerbirds to black cockatoos.

From the northern access route of the Bruce Hwy, take the 4km-long partially sealed Spiegelhauer Rd to Big Crystal Creek; from there, it's an easy 100m walk from the car park to Paradise Waterhole, a popular spot with a sandy beach and lofty mountain views.

The southern access route (Mt Spec Rd) is a sealed, albeit twisty, road that writhes up the mountains to Paluma Village. Beware: though you may have come up here 'just for a drive', the village's cool air and warm populace may change your mind.

En route to Paluma, be sure to stop off at Little Crystal Creek, a picturesque swimming hole with a cute stone bridge, picnic area and waterfalls.

In Paluma village the cool **Rainforest Inn** (☑07-4770 8688; www.rainforestinnpaluma. com; 1 Mt Spec Rd; d $125; ❄) has well-designed rooms and a nearby restaurant-bar.

Jourama Falls

Waterview Creek tumbles down these eponymous falls and other cascades past palms and umbrella trees, making this section a fine place for a picnic and a perambulation. It's a steep climb to the lookout; keep your eyes peeled for kingfishers, freshwater turtles and endangered mahogany gliders on the way up. The **NPSR camping ground** (www. npsr.qld.gov.au; sites per person/family $6.15/24.60) has cold showers, gas BBQs, water (treat before drinking) and composting toilets.

This part of the park is reached via a 6km sealed road (though the creek at the entrance can be impassable in the Wet), 91km north of Townsville and 24km south of Ingham. Be sure to fuel up before veering off the highway.

both the fish and beef ($12) get a massive thumbs up, while the thickshakes and coffee come in a close second. Wi-fi is fast and free.

ℹ Information

Tully Visitor & Heritage Centre (☑07-4068 2288; Bruce Hwy; ⊗8.30am-4.45pm Mon-Fri, 9am-2pm Sat & Sun) The Tully Visitor & Heritage Centre has a brochure outlining a self-guided heritage walk around town, with 17 interpretative panels (including one dedicated to Tully's UFO sightings), and walking-trail maps for the nearby national parks. The centre also has free internet and a book exchange.

ℹ Getting There & Away

Greyhound (☑1300 473 946; www.greyhound.com.au) and **Premier** (☑13 34 10; www.premierms.com.au) buses stop in town on the Brisbane–Cairns route; fares to Cairns/Townsville are $28/$43. Tully is also on **Queensland Rail's** (☑1800 872 467; www.traveltrain.com.au) Brisbane–Cairns train line.

Mission Beach

The rainforest meets the Coral Sea at Mission Beach, a tropical enclave of beach hamlets that has long threatened to take the Australian getaway circuit by storm. Yet this Coral Sea bolt-hole has maintained a beautiful balance between yoga living, backpacker bravado and eco-escape, plus it has Australia's highest density of cassowaries. Hidden among World Heritage rainforest, a short 30km detour from the Bruce Hwy, this 14km-long palm-fringed stretch of secluded

Mission Beach

N 0 ——— 500 m
0 ——— 0.25 miles

Mission Beach

inlets and wide, empty beaches is one of the closest access points to the Great Barrier Reef, and is the gateway to Dunk Island.

Collectively referred to as Mission Beach, or just 'Mission', the area comprises a sequence of individual, very small and laidback villages strung along the coast. Bingil Bay lies 4.8km north of Mission Beach proper (sometimes called North Mission). Wongaling Beach is 5km south; from here it's a further 5.5km south to South Mission Beach. Most amenities are in Mission proper and Wongaling Beach.

🏃 Activities

There's a stinger enclosure for swimming during stinger season (January through March).

Ingan Tours   WALKING
(☎1800 728 067; www.ingan.com.au; 4hr tours adult/child $130/70; ⊙Tue, Thu & Sat) Local

Aboriginal guides offer a unique insight into the ancient rainforest around Mission Beach. A fabulous new kayak tour along the Tully is also highly recommended (adult/child $100/65). Prices include pick-ups from Mission Beach and a light lunch.

Skydive Mission Beach SKYDIVING
(☎1300 800 840; www.skydivemissionbeach.com.au; 1 Wongaling Beach Rd; 1830/4270m tandem dives $199/334) Mission Beach is rightfully one of the most popular spots in Australia for skydiving, with views over gorgeous islands and blue water, and a soft landing on a white-sand beach. Skydive Australia, known locally as Skydive Mission Beach, runs several flights per day.

Altitude Skydivers SKYDIVING
(☎07-4088 6635; www.altitudeskydive.com.au; 4/46 Porter Promenade; 4270m $299) The new boys in town are a small, highly experienced and fun-loving jump team, with very competitive pricing.

Coral Sea Kayaking KAYAKING
(☎07-4068 9154; www.coralseakayaking.com; half-/full-day tours incl lunch $80/136) Knowledgeable full-day guided tours to Dunk Island; easygoing bob-arounds on the half-day option. Longer three-day journeys to the Barnard and Family Islands can be arranged.

Fishin' Mission FISHING
(☎0427 323 469; www.fishinmission.com.au; half-/full-day trips $160/260) Chilled-out reef-fishing charters with local pros. By far the most reputable operator in the area.

Sleeping

★Jackaroo Hostel HOSTEL $
(☎07-4068 7137; www.jackaroohostel.com; 13 Frizelle Rd; sites $12-15, dm/d incl breakfast from $25/58; P@🛜🏊) Oh to be young enough again to justify whiling away the days in a timber pole-frame retreat deep in the rainforest by a huge jungle pool overlooking the Coral Sea. Bugger it: just drive inland past Clump Mountain, find a quiet double room and wander around the communal areas granting silent, wise nods to those young rascals bronzing in the tropical sun.

Dunk Island View Caravan Park CARAVAN PARK $
(☎07-4068 8248; www.dunkislandviewcaravanpark.com; 21 Webb Rd; sites $30-32, 1-/2-bedroom units $105/135; ❄🛜🏊🐾) One of the best caravan parks we visited in northern Queensland; its views of Dunk Island are stupendous and the grounds are impeccably kept. The small pool is welcome in stinger season, and there's also an on-site cafe (fish and chips, $9).

Mission Beach Ecovillage CABIN $
(☎07-4068 7534; www.ecovillage.com.au; Clump Point Rd; d $119-150, 2-bedroom bungalows $180; ❄🛜🏊) With its own banana and lime trees scattered around its tropical gardens, and a direct path through the rainforest to the beach, this 'ecovillage' makes the most of its environment. Clustered around a rocky pool, the bungalows are a little worn, but there's a licensed restaurant and bubbly enough service to compensate.

Mission Beach Retreat HOSTEL $
(☎07-4088 6229; www.missionbeachretreat.com.au; 49 Porter Promenade; dm $22-25, d $56; ❄@🛜🏊) Bang in the centre of town, with the bonus of being beachfront, this is an easy, breezy backpacker spot that's hard not to like. YHA-accredited, it fills up quickly. Extras include a shuttle service to the supermarket and free wi-fi. Staff insist on friendly interaction with guests.

Rainforest Motel MOTEL $
(☎07-4088 6787; www.rainforestmotel.com; 9 Endeavour Ave; d/tw $95/105; ❄@🛜🏊) Though not about to gain plaudits for contemporary luxury, this hidden motel off Mission's humble main street is nonetheless great value and is very well serviced. Rooms are cool and clean, and the communal sitting areas near the tiny pool feel like you've been dropped in a rainforest garden. Free bikes available.

Sanctuary CABIN $
(☎1800 777 012, 07-4088 6064; www.sanctuaryatmission.com; 72 Holt Rd; dm $40, huts s/d from $75/80, cabins $185; ⏲mid-Apr–mid-Dec; @🛜🏊) 🍃 This popular group retreat centre is reached by a steep 600m-long rainforest walking track from the car park (4WD pick-up available). At Sanctuary you can sleep surrounded only by flyscreen on a platform in a simple hut, or opt for an en-suite cabin whose shower has floor-to-ceiling rainforest views. Yoga, night walks and massage are all available to guests at a cost.

Scotty's Mission Beach House HOSTEL $
(☎07-4068 8676, 1800 665 567; www.scottysbeachhouse.com.au; 167 Reid Rd; dm $24-29,

d $71; ✳@🤖🛜🖲) Dropped right on a quiet stretch of beach, Scotty's is a YHA hostel with modest rooms grouped around a grassy pool area. Management is tapped into the east coast circuit and is keen to help guests capitalise on their adventure. Out front, **Scotty's Bar & Grill** (mains $12-24; ⊙5pm-12am), open to nonguests, has something happening virtually every night, from fire-twirling shows to pool comps to live music.

Hibiscus Lodge B&B
B&B $$

(📞07-4068 9096; www.hibiscuslodge.com.au; 5 Kurrajong Cl; r from $145; 🛜) The main homestead of this charming Mission Beach property forms the backdrop for a local fauna roll-call. Hibiscus Lodge is a discerning choice; you can taste the self-satisfaction at the breakfast table. With only three (very private) rooms, bookings are essential. Generous online discounts are available. No kids.

Licuala Lodge
B&B $$

(📞07-4068 8194; www.licualalodge.com.au; 11 Mission Circle; d incl breakfast from $135; 🛜🖲) You'll need your own car and a willingness to sit still at this peaceful B&B located 1.5km from the beach and pretty much everything else. Guests alternate between the wonderful verandah, where breakfast can be taken overlooking landscaped gardens, and the swimming pool surrounded by a rock garden. Cassowaries pop by regularly to check out the scene.

Nautilus B&B
B&B $$

(1 Nautilus St; 2-bedroom apt from $180) While bookings are technically only available online, it's worth popping past Nautilus B&B and asking Dena if she can help you out. Two newly built, pristine white-tiled apartments sit side-by-side atop a hill overlooking the town, offering a smooth stay. The one large shared bathroom has a powerful shower, while each room has its own small courtyard.

The lounge and open-plan kitchen are great for enjoying your breakfast ($18 per person) and planning the day ahead. Look out for wallabies grazing nearby at sunset.

★ Sejala on the Beach
CABIN $$$

(📞07-4088 6699; www.sejala.com.au; 26 Pacific Pde; d $275; ✳🖲) Choose from 'Waves', 'Coral' and 'Beaches', three self-contained beach 'huts' within snoring sound of the coconut palms. Each one comes with rainforest shower, deck with private BBQ and loads of character. Perfect for hiding away with a partner.

Castaways Resort & Spa
RESORT $$$

(📞07-4068 7444; www.castaways.com.au; Pacific Pde; d $115-265 1-/2-bedroom units $290/360; ✳@🛜🖲) Stare longingly out to sea from your unit in this mainstay of the Mission Beach family holiday scene. Travellers on a budget can play it smart in a simple rainforest room ($115) and take advantage of the two elongated pools, a luxurious spa (www.driftspa.com.au; Pacific Pde) and stunning beach views from its tropical-style **bar-restaurant** (mains $12-32; ⊙breakfast, lunch & dinner). Come on Tuesdays for tropical high tea.

✖ Eating

Early Birds Cafe
CAFE $

(Shop 2, 46 Porter Promenade; mains $7-18; ⊙6am-3pm Thu-Tue; 🖊) The only joint open first thing in the morning, Early Birds wins return customers with its honest, cheap, cafe-style breakfasts (veggie $14) and famous, bigger-than-average fresh juices.

Fish Bar
SEAFOOD $

(📞07-4088 6419; Porter Promenade; mains $10-17; ⊙10am-midnight) Very affordable fish and other ocean creatures are served up in a casual atmosphere. A small courtyard has views of the sea. Takeaway available.

★ Bingil Bay Cafe
CAFE $$

(📞07-4068 7146; 29 Bingil Bay Rd; mains $14-23; ⊙6.30am-10pm; 🖊) Sunshine, rainbows, coffee and gourmet grub make up the experience at this lavender landmark with a great porch for watching the world drift by. Breakfast is a highlight, but it's open all day. Regular art displays and live music ensure a creative clientele.

Caffe Rustica
ITALIAN $$

(📞07-4068 9111; 24 Wongaling Beach Rd; mains $13-25, pizzas $10-25; ⊙5pm-late Wed-Sat, 10am-9pm Sun; 🖊) Traditional pizza and pasta are the staples at this evening haunt set inside a corrugated-iron beach shack; they also make their own gelato and sorbet. Bookings are encouraged as it's popular with locals year-round.

Garage Bar & Grill
MODERN AUSTRALIAN $$

(📞07-4088 6280; 41 Donkin Lane; meze plates $17; ⊙9am-late; ✳🖊) The hot spot in Mission with the twenty-something set, the Garage is famous for its delicious 'sliders' (mini

THE CASSOWARY: ENDANGERED NATIVE

Like something out of *Jurassic Park*, this flightless prehistoric bird struts through the rainforest. It's as tall as a grown man, has three razor-sharp, dagger-style clawed toes, a bright-blue head, red wattles (the lobes hanging from its neck), a helmet-like horn, and shaggy black feathers similar to an emu's. Meet the cassowary, an important link in the rainforest ecosystem. It's the only animal capable of dispersing the seeds of more than 70 species of trees whose fruit is too large for other rainforest animals to digest and pass (which acts as fertiliser). You're most likely to see cassowaries in the wild around Mission Beach, Etty Bay and the Cape Tribulation section of the Daintree National Park. They can be aggressive, particularly if they have chicks. Do not approach them; if one threatens you, don't run – give the bird right-of-way and try to keep something solid between you and it, preferably a tree.

It is estimated that there are 1000 or less cassowaries in the wild north of Queensland. An endangered species, the cassowary's biggest threat is loss of habitat, and most recently the cause has been natural. Tropical Cyclone Yasi stripped much of the rainforest around Mission Beach bare, threatening the struggling population with starvation. The cyclone also left the birds exposed to the elements, and more vulnerable to dog attacks and cars as they venture out in search of food.

Next to the Mission Beach visitor centre, there are cassowary conservation displays at the **Wet Tropics Environment Centre** (www.wettropics.gov.au), staffed by volunteers from the **Community for Cassowary & Coastal Conservation** (www.cassowary conservation.asn.au). Proceeds from gift-shop purchases go towards buying cassowary habitat. The website www.savethecassowary.org.au is also a good source of info.

burgers) and free-pour cocktails ($14). The hard-working chef mixes up the menu regularly and the management ensure there's a festive vibe in the beer garden with an eclectic playlist and tapas specials.

Millers Beach Bar & Grill   PUB FOOD $$
(207-4068 8177; www.millersbeachbar.com.au; 1 Banfield Pde; mains $14-38; ⊙3pm-late Tue-Fri, noon-late Sat & Sun) Wongaling Beach's evening star, Millers is so close to the beach you'll be picking sand out of your beer. It's a popular function space, but the occasional crowd only adds to the ambience, especially at sunset with Dunk Island calling in the distance. The fish burger ($18) was a hit when we visited.

Zenbah   INTERNATIONAL $$
(207-4088 6040; 39 Porter Promenade; mains $12-28; ⊙10am-1.30am Fri & Sat, to midnight Sun Thu) The colourful chairs on the pavement mark Zenbah as the vibrant little eatery/hang-out that it is. The food ranges from Middle Eastern to Asian all the way back to pizza, and you can digest it all against a backdrop of live tunes on Fridays and Saturdays.

Sealevel   SEAFOOD $$
(207-4088 6179; 42 Donkin Lane; mains $15-30; ⊙noon-9pm) The newest restaurant in Mission Beach village has the best location – beachfront and square – but is suffering a few teething problems due to poor layout

and an inconsistent menu. The line-caught jewfish was sensational ($17), but the barramundi ($18) was not fresh. A barren concrete area doubles as a beer garden. One to watch if they get it right.

★**PepperVine**   MODERN AUSTRALIAN $$$
(207-4088 6538; 2 David St; mains $16-32; ⊙4.30-11pm) On the Village Green, PepperVine is an uncomplicated contemporary restaurant borrowing from Italian, Spanish and Mod-Oz culinary influences, but nailing the atmosphere and service. Wood-fired pizza and a glass of Australian wine is the early evening staple, but the fine dining announces itself after sunset as the crowd descends.

🛍 Shopping

Between them, **Mission Beach Markets** (Porter Promenade; ⊙8am-1pm 1st & 3rd Sun of month) and **Mission Beach Rotary Monster Market** (Marcs Park, Cassowary Dr, Wongaling Beach; ⊙8am-12.30pm last Sun of month Apr-Dec) operate three Sundays a month.

ℹ Information

Mission Beach Visitor Centre (207-4068 7099; www.missionbeachtourism.com; Porters Promenade, Mission Beach; ⊙9am-4.45pm Mon-Sat, 10am-4pm Sun) The main visitor centre in town has reams of information in multiple languages.

WORTH A TRIP

PARONELLA PARK

Set beside a series of creeks and waterfalls 50km northwest of Mission Beach (with at least one resident croc), **Paronella Park** (✆ 07-4065 0000; www.paronellapark.com.au; Japoonvale Rd, Mena Creek; adult/child $44/23) is a whimsical tropical retreat and a romantic, Dali-esque escape from reality. Moss-covered steps, lush tropical foliage and huge palatial structures appear straight from some Victorian-Mayan movie set.

Self-made Spanish immigrant José Paronella built Paronella Park as a gift to his wife Margarita before opening it to the public. He died in 1948, and the park is now privately owned and National Trust listed.

Nearby camping and quaint on-site cabins ($90) are available.

Wet Tropics Environment Centre (✆ 07-4068 7197; www.wettropics.gov.au; Porter Promenade; ⊙ 10am-4pm) Next door to the Mission Beach Visitor Centre you'll find displays and movies about the local environment, including, of course, the cassowary.

❶ Getting There & Away

Greyhound (✆ 1300 473 946; www.greyhound.com.au) and **Premier** (✆ 13 34 10; www.premierms.com.au) buses stop in Wongaling Beach next to the 'big cassowary'. Fares with Greyhound/Premier are $25/19 to Cairns (two hours), $44/46 to Townsville (3½ hours).

Dunk Island

Dunk is known to the Djiru Aboriginal people as Coonanglebah (the island of peace and plenty). They're not wrong: this is pretty much your ideal tropical island, with lush jungle, white-sand beaches and impossibly blue water.

Walking trails criss-cross (and almost circumnavigate) Dunk: the circuit track (9.2km) is the best way to have a proper stickybeak at the island's interior and abundant wildlife. There's snorkelling over bommies (coral pinnacles or outcroppings) at Muggy Muggy and great swimming at truly beautiful Coconut Beach. On weekends in high season there are often special events

such as bongo lessons or a ukulele band – check with the Mission Beach Visitor Centre.

Dunk Island was hammered by Cyclone Yasi in 2011, but has since mostly recovered, although part of the old resort remains off limits and a veritable eyesore.

Mission Beach Charters (✆ 07-4068 7009; adult/child return $35/18; 3hr tour $50) runs a shuttle as well as a range of fishing, diving and camping trips, or you can stay at the **Dunk Island campground** (✆ 0417 873 390; per person/family $6.15/24.60).

Innisfail & Around

POP 7500

Innisfail is a handsome, unhurried North Queensland town known for river fishing, farming and a remarkable collection of art-deco edifices. Only 80km south of Cairns, but not a tourist in sight, here you can join the locals on the wide Johnstone River, dodge tractors along the pretty main street, or discuss the fortunes of the Cowboys rugby league team.

Relaxing, beachside Flying Fish Point is some 8km northeast of Innisfail's town centre, while national parks, including the fun Mamu Tropical Sky Walk (a 2.5km, wheelchair-accessible walking circuit through the canopy), are within a short drive. Turn-offs south of town lead to different beach communities including exquisite Etty Bay, with its wandering cassowaries, rocky headlands, rainforest, large stinger enclosure and a simple but superbly sited caravan park.

In March, the **Feast of the Senses** (www.feastofthesenses.com.au) is a highlight of the northern Queensland culinary calendar.

◉ Sights

Mamu Tropical Sky Walk VIEWPOINT (www.mamutropicalskywalk.com.au; Palmerston Hwy; adult/child/family $23/12/64; ⊙ 9.30am-5.30pm, last entry 4.30pm) ✐ About 27km along the Palmerston Hwy (signposted 4km northwest of Innisfail), this canopy-level rainforest walkway gives you eye-level views of the fruits, flowers and birds, and a bird's-eye perspective from its 100-step, 37m-high tower. Allow at least an hour to complete the 2.5km, wheelchair-accessible circuit.

The Palmerston Hwy continues west to Millaa Millaa, passing the entrance to the Waterfalls Circuit.

🛏 Sleeping & Eating

Backpackers Shack
HOSTEL $

(☑ 0499 042 446, 07-4061 7760; www.backpackers shack.com; 7 Ernest St; dm per week $195; P ⊛ @) Modest, dormitory-style accommodation awaits guests at the Shack, a locally operated, unofficial employment agency for seasonal fruit workers.

Flying Fish Tourist Park
CARAVAN PARK $

(☑ 07-4061 3131; www.ffpvanpark.com.au; 39 Elizabeth St, Flying Fish Point; powered sites $32-39, cabins $50-99, villa $119-125; ⊛ @ 🛜 ⊠) Travellers with their own wheels (or camping gear), will love this laid-back park from where you can fish right off the beach across the road, or organise boat rental through the friendly managers. The cabins are spacious and fragrant. Call ahead for directions.

⭐Barrier Reef Motel
MOTEL $$

(☑ 07-4061 4988; www.barrierreefmotel.com.au; Bruce Hwy; s/d from $135/145; ⊛ @ 🛜 ⊠) More than a road-trip stopover, the Barrier Reef Motel is almost reason enough to hang out an extra day or so in Innisfail. The Barrier Reef has exceptional motel-style rooms, with soothing tiled floors and large bathrooms, and assured customer service. It is right next to the visitor centre and the on-site **restaurant** (mains $28-30.50; ⊙ breakfast & dinner; 🍴) serves great 'surf and turf' (steak and seafood). The saltwater pool and bar give it an extra tick.

⭐Oliveri's Continental Deli
DELI $

(www.oliverisdeli.com.au; 41 Edith St; sandwiches $8.50-11; ⊙ 8.30am-5.15pm Mon-Fri, to 12.30pm Sat; 🍴) An Innisfail institution offering goodies including 60-plus varieties of European cheese, ham and salami, and scrumptious sandwiches. Fantastic coffee, too.

Innisfail Seafood
SEAFOOD $

(51 Fitzgerald Esplanade; ⊙ 8am-6pm Mon-Fri, 9am-4pm Sat, 10am-4pm Sun) Fresh-as-it-gets fish to throw on the barbecue and organic cooked prawns by the bagful ($18 to $20 per kilogram).

Flying Fish Point Cafe
SEAFOOD $

(9 Elizabeth St, Flying Fish Point; mains $12-25; ⊙ 7.30am-8pm) Regulars enjoy the idyllic, breezy seaside setting and the huge seafood baskets of battered and crumbed fish, barbecued calamari, wonton prawns, tempura scallops and more.

ℹ Information

NPRSR (www.nprsr.qld.gov.au) Has details of campgrounds and walking trails.

Visitor Information Centre (☑ 07-4061 2655; cnr Eslick St & Bruce Hwy; ⊙ 9am-4.30pm Mon-Fri, to 1pm Sat, to 12pm Sun) The helpful visitor centre gives out discount vouchers for many of the area's attractions and has a full list of accommodation options that can help with finding work.

ℹ Getting There & Away

Bus services operate once daily with **Premier** (☑ 13 34 10; www.premierms.com.au) and several times daily with **Greyhound** (☑ 1300 473 946; www.greyhound.com.au) between Innisfail and Townsville ($45 to $52, 4½ hours) and Cairns ($19 to $22, 1½ hours).

Innisfail is on the Cairns–Brisbane train line; contact **Queensland Rail** (☑ 1800 872 467; www.queenslandrail.com.au) for information.

Cairns & the Daintree Rainforest

Best Places to Eat

➡ Vivo (p457)

➡ Coco Mojo (p458)

➡ Ganbaranba (p449)

➡ Prawn Star (p451)

➡ On the Inlet (p469)

Best Places to Sleep

➡ Peppers Beach Club (p468)

➡ Cape Trib Beach House (p475)

➡ Cedar Park Rainforest Resort (p460)

➡ Coral Beach Lodge (p467)

➡ Sarayi (p457)

Why Go?

Tropical, touristy Cairns is an unmissable stop on any east coast traveller's itinerary. Experienced divers and first-time toe-dippers swarm to the steamy city for its easy access to the Great Barrier Reef, while those more interested in submerging themselves in boozy good times are well served by a barrage of bars and clubs. The Atherton Tablelands – home to cooler climes, volcanic craters, jungly waterfalls and gourmet food producers – are a short, scenic drive inland.

The winding road north of Cairns hugs ludicrously scenic sections of shoreline en route to ritzy Port Douglas; keep going and you'll meet the mighty Daintree River's vehicular ferry. From here, profuse, protected rainforest stretches up to Cape Tribulation and beyond, tumbling on to long swaths of white-sand beaches; don't be so awestruck that you forget to keep an eye out for crocs!

When to Go
Cairns

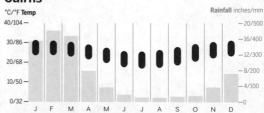

May Port Douglas pizazz at Carnivale. Stinger season ends.

Aug Milder temps and the Cairns Festival make this an ideal time to visit.

Nov Divers delight in the reef's annual coral spawning.

CAIRNS

POP 160,285

Cairns (pronounced 'cans') has come a long way since its beginnings as a boggy swamp and rollicking goldfields port. Heaving under the weight of countless resorts, tour agencies, souvenir shops and a million reminders of its proximity to the Great Barrier Reef, Cairns is unabashedly geared towards tourism.

Old salts claim Cairns has lost its soul, but it does have an infectious holiday vibe. The city centre is more boardshorts than briefcases, and you'll find yourself throwing away all notions of speed and schedules here, thanks to heady humidity and a hearty hospitality that can turn a short stroll into an impromptu social event. Fittingly, Cairns is awash with bars, clubs, eateries and cafes suiting all budgets. There's no beach in town, but the magnificent Esplanade Lagoon more than makes up for it; otherwise, the northern beaches are but a local bus ride or short drive away.

◉ Sights

Cairns' newest attraction, the state-of-the-art Cairns Aquarium (☑07-4044 7300; www. cairnsaquarium.com.au; 163 Abbott St; adult/child/family $42/28/126; ☉9am-5.30pm), was due to open in mid-2017.

★ Cairns Esplanade,
Boardwalk & Lagoon WATERFRONT
(www.cairns.qld.gov.au/esplanade; ☉lagoon 6am-9pm Thu-Tue, noon-9pm Wed; 🚻) FREE Sunseekers and fun-lovers flock to Cairns Esplanade's spectacular swimming lagoon on the city's reclaimed foreshore. The artificial, sandy-edged, 4800-sq-metre saltwater pool is lifeguard patrolled and illuminated nightly. The adjacent 3km foreshore boardwalk has picnic areas, birdwatching vantage points, free barbecues and fitness equipment. Follow the signposts for the excellent Muddy's (www. cairns.qld.gov.au/esplanade/facilities/playgrounds/muddys) FREE, which has playgrounds and water fun for little kids, and the skate ramp, beach volleyball courts, bouldering park and Fun Ship playground.

★ Flecker Botanic Gardens GARDENS
(☑07-4032 6650; www.cairns.qld.gov.au/cbg; 64 Collins Ave; ☉grounds 7.30am-5.30pm, visitor centre 9am-4.30pm Mon-Fri, 10am-2.30pm Sat & Sun) FREE These gorgeous gardens are an explosion of greenery and rainforest plants. Highlights include a section devoted to Aboriginal plant use, the Gondwana Heritage Garden, and an excellent conservatory filled with butterflies and exotic flowers. Staff at the made-of-mirrors visitor centre can advise on free guided garden walks (daily from 10am).

Follow the Rainforest Boardwalk to Saltwater Creek and Centenary Lakes, a birdwatcher's delight. Uphill from the gardens, Mt Whitfield Conservation Park (www.cairns.qld. gov.au/facilities-sport-leisure/sport-and-recreation/active-living/red-and-green-arrow-walking-tracks; Edge Hill) has walking tracks through the rainforest to city viewpoints.

★ Reef Teach CULTURAL CENTRE
(☑07-4031 7794; www.reefteach.com.au; 2nd fl, Mainstreet Arcade, 85 Lake St; adult/child/family $23/14/60; ☉lectures 6.30-8.30pm Tue-Sat) 🖉 Take your knowledge to new depths at this fun, informative centre, where marine experts explain how to identify specific species of fish and coral, and how to approach the reef respectfully.

CAIRNS GALLERIES

Cairns Regional Gallery (☑07-4046 4800; www.cairnsregionalgallery.com.au; cnr Abbott & Shields Sts; adult/child $5/free; ☉9am-5pm Mon-Fri, 10am-5pm Sat, 10am-2pm Sun) The permanent collection of this acclaimed gallery has an emphasis on local and Indigenous work.

Canopy Art Centre (☑07-4041 4678; www.canopyartcentre.com; 124 Grafton St; ☉10am-5pm Tue-Sat) Showcases prints, paintings, sculptures and weavings of Indigenous artists from Cairns and communities as far north as the Torres Strait.

Tanks Arts Centre (☑07-4032 6600; www.tanksartscentre.com; 46 Collins Ave; ☉9.30am-4.30pm Mon-Fri) Three gigantic, ex-WWII fuel-storage tanks have been transformed into art galleries; it's also an inspired performing-arts venue.

KickArts (www.kickarts.org.au; CoCA, 96 Abbott St; ☉10am-5pm Mon-Sat) FREE Showcases cutting-edge local and regional artworks, plus touring exhibitions.

Cairns & the Daintree Rainforest Highlights

1 Great Barrier Reef (p445) Diving, snorkelling and swimming among the fish, turtles and multicoloured corals.

2 Kuku-Yalanji Dreamtime Walks (p471) Walking alongside Mossman Gorge's crystal-clear waters.

3 Kuranda (p459) Riding the Skyrail above the rainforest to the markets, then returning to Cairns by the Kuranda Scenic Railway.

4 Palm Cove (p456) Indulging in the romantic restaurants and resorts of pristine Palm Cove.

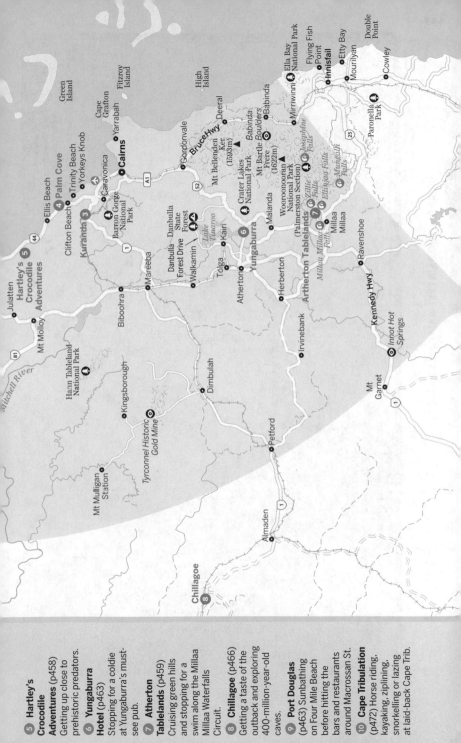

Cairns

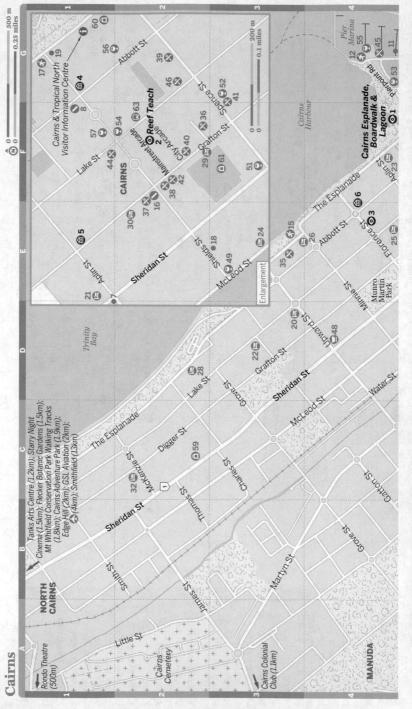

Mangrove Boardwalk NATURE RESERVE

(Airport Ave) FREE Explore the swampier side of Cairns on this revelatory wander into the wetlands. Eerie snap-crackle-slop noises provide a fitting soundtrack to the spooky surrounds, which are signposted with informative guides to the weird life forms scurrying in the mud below you. Slather yourself in mosquito repellent. The boardwalk (and its car park) is just before Cairns Airport (p303).

Tjapukai Aboriginal Cultural Park CULTURAL CENTRE

(☑ 07-4042 9999; www.tjapukai.com.au; Cairns Western Arterial Rd, Caravonica; adult/child/family $62/42/166; ⊙9am-5pm) This award-winning cultural extravaganza is managed by the area's original custodians and tells the story of creation using giant holograms and actors. There's a dance theatre, a gallery, boomerang- and spear-throwing demonstrations and turtle-spotting canoe rides. The Nightfire dinner-and-show package (adult/child/family $123/75/321, from 7pm to 9.30pm) culminates in a fireside corroboree.

Australian Armour & Artillery Museum MUSEUM

(☑ 07-4038 1665; www.ausarmour.com; 1145 Kamerunga Rd, Smithfield; adult/child/family $25/15/65; ⊙9.30am-4.30pm) Military and history buffs will enjoy this, the largest display of armoured vehicles and artillery in the southern hemisphere. Go for a ride in a tank (adult/child $15/10) or fire off bolt-action rifles (including a WWII British 303 and German Mauser) in the underground bunker (from $80).

Crystal Cascades WATERFALL

(via Redlynch) About 14km from Cairns, the Crystal Cascades are a series of beautiful waterfalls and idyllic, croc-free swimming holes that locals would rather keep to themselves. The area is accessed by a 1.2km (30-minute) pathway. Crystal Cascades is linked to Lake Morris (the city's reservoir) by a steep rainforest walking trail (allow three hours return); it starts near the picnic area.

There is no public transport to the pools. Drive to the suburb of Redlynch, then follow the signs.

🏃 Activities & Tours

Innumerable tour operators run adventure-based activities from Cairns, most offering transfers to/from your accommodation.

Cairs

An astounding 800-plus tours drive, chug, sail and fly out of Cairns daily, making the selection process almost overwhelming. We recommend operators with the benefit of years of experience, who cover the bases of what visitors are generally looking for, and then some.

★ **Cairns Zoom & Wildlife Dome**   ADVENTURE SPORTS, WILDLIFE
(☏ 07-4031 7250; www.cairnszoom.com.au; Wharf St; wildlife entry $24, wildlife & zoom $45; ☺ 9am-6pm) Cards, croupiers and...crocodiles? Sitting on top of the Reef Hotel Casino (p453), this unusual park brings

the best of Far North Queensland's outdoors inside, with a native-creatures zoo, aviary and recreated rainforest. The complex is criss-crossed with ziplines, swings, obstacle courses and more; the truly adventurous can even venture outside for a nerve-testing dome climb.

★ **Behana Days Canyoning** OUTDOORS
(☑0427 820 993; www.behanadays.com; tours $179) Give the salty stuff a break and join this fantastic freshwater expedition to beautiful Behana Gorge, a rainforest oasis of pools, waterfalls and canyons 45 minutes south of Cairns. The all-day tours include abseiling, ziplining, cliff jumping, snorkelling and swimming; you'll be shown the ropes (literally) on the day. Transfers and lunch included.

★ **Rapid Boarders** WATER SPORTS
(☑0427 364 311; www.rapidboarders.com.au; tours $235) If you'd rather ride in the rapids than on them, this utterly exhilarating full-day adventure is for you. Thrill seekers ride riverboards down the mighty Tully, taking on pumping Grade 3 rapids at eye level. It's the only tour of its kind in Australia. This is not for the water-shy; participants must be good swimmers and relatively fit.

★ **Aussie Drifterz** OUTDOORS
(☑0401 318 475; www.facebook.com/aussiedrifterz; adult/child $75/55) Scenic and serene (and virtually guaranteed to kick a hangover), a relaxing bob down the beautiful Behana Gorge on an inner tube is tough to beat. The crystal-clear river runs through natural tree tunnels, and you'll almost certainly catch glimpses of curious wildlife (don't fret; crocs not included).

Cairns Adventure Park ADVENTURE SPORTS
(☑07-4053 3726; www.cairnsadventurepark. com.au; 82 Aeroglen Dr, Aeroglen; packages from $39; ⊙9am-5pm) Zipline, rock climb or abseil in rainforest surrounds with views to the sea as breathtaking as the high-energy activities themselves. For something a little more sedate, Cairns Adventure Park also offers bushwalks and birdwatching. Contact the office about pick-ups from your accommodation; if you're driving, get there by taking the Aeroglen turn-off opposite Cairns Airport (p303).

Flyboard Cairns WATER SPORTS
(☑0439 386 955, 0487 921 714; www.flyboard cairns.com.au; 30/60min session $169/299) Billed as a combination of waterskiing, wakeboarding and snowboarding, flyboarding gives thrill seekers the chance to surf the sky while attached to a water jetpack – and cop some bird's-eye views while you're up there. It looks tricky, but the experienced instructors here guarantee even beginners will get airborne; no fly, no pay.

DIVE COURSES & TRIPS

Cairns, scuba-dive capital of the Great Barrier Reef, is a popular place to attain Professional Association of Diving Instructors (PADI) open-water certification. A staggering number of courses (many multilingual) are available; check inclusions thoroughly. All operators require you to have a dive medical certificate, which they can arrange (around $60). Reef taxes ($20 to $80) may apply.

Keen, certified divers should look for specialised dive opportunities such as night diving, annual coral spawning, and trips to Cod Hole, near Lizard Island, one of Australia's premier diving locations. Recommended dive schools and operators include the following:

Mike Ball Dive Expeditions (☑07-4053 0500; www.mikeball.com; 3 Abbott St; liveaboards from $1827, PADI courses from $395)

Cairns Dive Centre (CDC; ☑07-4051 0294; www.cairnsdive.com.au; 121 Abbott St; liveaboard 1-/2-nights from $435/555, day trips from $120, dive courses from $520)

Deep Sea Divers Den (☑07-4046 7333; www.diversden.com.au; 319 Draper St; day trips from $165)

Pro-Dive (☑07-4031 5255; www.prodivecairns.com.au; cnr Grafton & Shields Sts; day trips adult/child from $195/120, PADI courses from $765)

Tusa Dive (☑07-4047 9100; www.tusadive.com; cnr Shields St & Esplanade; adult/child day trips from $205/130) 🖉

AJ Hackett Bungy & Minjin ADVENTURE SPORTS
(☑07-4057 7188; www.ajhackett.com/cairns;
McGregor Rd, Smithfield; bungee $169, minjin $129,
combos from $259; ⊙from 10am) Bungee jump
from the 50m rainforest tower or drop 45m
and swing through the trees at 120km/h in
the Minjin harness swing. Pricing includes
return transfers from Cairns.

Scenic Flights

Great Barrier
Reef Helicopters SCENIC FLIGHTS
(☑07-4081 8888; www.gbrhelicopters.com.au;
Helipad, Pierpoint Rd; flights per person from
$175) Offers a range of scenic helicopter
flights, from a 10-minute soar above Cairns
city to an hour-long hover over the reef and
rainforest ($699).

GSL Aviation SCENIC FLIGHTS
(☑1300 475 000; www.gslaviation.com.au; 3 Tom
McDonald Dr, Aeroglen; 40min flights per person
from $179) Those wanting to see the reef from
above would do well to consider these scenic
flights; they are cheaper than chopper tours,
and offer more time in the air.

White-Water Rafting

Raging Thunder ADVENTURE SPORTS
(☑07-4030 7990; www.ragingthunder.com.au; 59-
63 Esplanade) These experienced folks offer
rafting, canyoning ($169) and hot-air balloon-
ing ($250) trips and tours. Foam-hounds can
choose between full-day Tully River rafting
trips (standard trip $209, 'xtreme' trip $250)
and half-day Barron trips ($133). They also
run transfers (adult/child/family $75/48/205)
to/from and activities on Fitzroy Island.

Foaming Fury RAFTING
(☑07-4031 3460; www.foamingfury.com.au; half-/
full-day trips from $138/200) Full-day trips on
the Russell River, and half-day trips down
the Barron. Prices include transfers. Family
rafting and multiday package options are
also available.

Ballooning & Skydiving

Hot Air Cairns BALLOONING
(☑07-4039 9900; www.hotair.com.au/cairns;
Reef Fleet Terminal; 30min flights adult/child from
$250/219) Balloons take off from Mareeba
to float through dawn over the Atherton
Tablelands. Prices include return transfers
from Cairns. These trips are worth the 4am
wake-up call.

Skydive Cairns ADVENTURE
(☑1300 663 634; www.skydive.com.au/cairns;
47 Shields St; tandem jumps from $334) Scream
from 4270m up at otherwise serene views of
the reef and rainforest.

City Tours

★Segway Tours OUTDOORS
(☑0451 972 997; www.cairnsninebottours.com;
tour $79; ⊙tours 9.30am & 3.30pm) Glide
through some of Cairns' most beautiful natural surrounds on an easy-to-master Segway.
The 90-minute tours start at the Esplanade
and run past mangroves, Centenary Lakes
and the Botanic Gardens; they're a peaceful
and immersive way to check out local flora
and fauna (including the ever-present possibility of a croc or two).

Cairns Discovery Tours TOURS
(☑07-4028 3567; www.cairnsdiscoverytours.com;
36 Aplin St; adult/child $75/40; ⊙Mon-Sat) Eye-
opening afternoon tours that take in the
sights of the city, Barron Gorge, the Botanic
Gardens (p439) (includes a horticultural-
ist-guided tour) and Palm Cove.

Fishing

Fishing Cairns FISHING
(☑0448 563 586; www.fishingcairns.com.au; half-
day trips from $95) Choose from a burley-bucket-
load of half- to multi-day fly, sports and game
fishing tours and charters, on calm or open
water. Prices vary accordingly.

Catcha Crab Tours FISHING
(☑07-4051 7992; www.cairnscatchacrab.com.au;
adult/child $95/75) These long-running tours
not only offer visitors the chance to catch
some tasty tucker, but are a simultaneously thrilling and relaxing way to take in the
mangroves and mudflats of Trinity Inlet. The
four-hour tours, which include morning or
afternoon tea plus a fresh crab lunch, depart
at 8.30am and 1pm. There are free pick-ups
if you're staying in the city centre.

⭐ Festivals & Events

Cairns Show CARNIVAL
(⊙Jul) Three days of carnival rides, agricultural exhibits, enthralling events (think
dancing diggers and wood-chopping competitions) and all the deep-fried delights you
can stomach. The last day of the Show is a
public holiday in Cairns.

Cairns Ukulele Festival MUSIC
(www.cairnsukulelefestival.net; ⊙late Aug) Uke
players from around the world descend on
Cairns every August to plinka-plinka in paradise. Events include workshops, jams and
parties.

SEX ON THE REEF

If you're a keen diver or just a romantic at heart, try to time your visit with the annual coral spawning, an all-in orgy in which reef corals simultaneously release millions of eggs and sperm into the water. The ejaculatory event has been described as looking like a psychedelic snowstorm, with trails of reproductive matter streaking the sea in rainbow colours visible from miles away.

The spawning occurs sometime in November or December; the exact date depends on factors including water temperature (must be 26°C or above), the date of the full moon, the stillness of the water and the perfect balance between light and dark (who doesn't appreciate a bit of mood lighting?). Most Cairns-based diving outfits offer special spawning night dives for those looking to get in on the action. Even if you're on land, you may notice an, um, 'amorous' aroma on the night of the mass love-in.

Cairns Festival FAIR
(www.cairns.qld.gov.au/festival; ☉end Aug-early Sep) The Cairns Festival takes over the city with a packed program of performing arts, visual arts, music and family events.

🛏 Sleeping

Cairns is a backpacker hot spot, with hostels ranging from intimate, converted houses to hangar-sized resorts. Holiday apartment complexes are dotted across the city. Dozens of nondescript, drive-in motels line Sheridan St.

Families and groups should check out **Cairns Holiday Homes** (☑07-4045 2143; www.cairnsholidayhomes.com.au). If you plan to stick around for a while, **Cairns Sharehouse** (☑07-4041 1875; www.cairns-sharehouse.com; 17 Scott St; per week from $120-260; ❋ 🛜 ❄) has around 200 long-stay rooms strewn across the city. The **Accommodation Centre** (☑1800 807 730, 07-4051 4066; www.accomcentre. com.au) has information on a wide range of sleeping options.

★**Bellview** HOSTEL $
(☑07-4031 4377; www.bellviewcairns.com.au; 85-87 Esplanade; dm/s/d $22/35/55, motel units $59-75; 🅿 ❋ 🛜 ❄) This low-key hostel has been on the radars of discerning backpackers since – seemingly – time eternal. There's little surprise it's lasted so long, thanks to a perfect position looming over the most bustling slice of the Esplanade, basic but well-maintained rooms and a staff that knows its stuff; the lovely pool helps too. Despite its central location, noise doesn't seem to travel to the rooms.

★**Cairns Coconut
Holiday Resort** CARAVAN PARK $
(☑07-4054 6644; www.coconut.com.au; cnr Bruce Hwy & Anderson Rd, Woree; powered sites/cabins/

units/villas/condos from $43/115/135/155/245; 🅿 ❋ 🛜 ❄) If you're travelling with kids and don't mind being a bit (8km) out of town, this holiday park is a destination unto itself. It's got a massive water park, two pools with slides, playgrounds, a humungous jumping pillow, tennis courts, minigolf, spas, an outdoor cinema and much more, all spread over 11 immaculate hectares. Accommodation choices are as varied as the facilities.

★**Cairns Plaza Hotel** HOTEL $
(☑07-4051 4688; www.cairnsplaza.com.au; 145 Esplanade; d/studios/ste from $124/150/170; 🅿 ❋ @ 🛜 ❄) One of Cairns' original high-rise hotels, the Plaza is – thanks to a full makeover and professional staff – one of the best. Rooms have crisp, clean decor, and functional kitchenettes; many enjoy stunning views over Trinity Bay. A guest laundry, friendly round-the-clock reception staff and great rates make it an excellent choice. Kids will be thrilled by its location, directly across from Muddy's (p439).

★**Travellers Oasis** HOSTEL $
(☑07-4052 1377; www.travellersoasis.com.au; 8 Scott St; dm/s/d from $28/57/68; 🅿 ❋ @ 🛜 ❄) Folks love this little hippie hostel, hidden away in a side street behind Cairns Central Shopping Centre. It's intimate, inviting and less party-centric than many of Cairns' other offerings. A range of room types – from three-, four- and six-bed dorms, to single, twin and deluxe double rooms – are available. Air conditioning is $1 for three hours.

★**Tropic Days** HOSTEL $
(☑07-4041 1521; www.tropicdays.com.au; 28 Bunting St, Bungalow; camping per person $14, tents $18, dm/d from $26/64; 🅿 ❋ @ 🛜 ❄) Tucked behind the showgrounds (with a

courtesy bus into town), this popular hostel has a tropical garden with hammocks, pool table, bunk-free dorms, fresh linen and towels, free wi-fi and a relaxed vibe. Its Monday night croc, emu and roo barbecues are legendary. Air conditioning is $1 for three hours.

Tropic Days and the equally awesome Travellers Oasis are sister hostels.

★ Gilligan's Backpacker's
Hotel & Resort
HOSTEL $

(☑07-4041 6566; www.gilligans.com.au; 57-89 Grafton St; dm/r from $24/120; ❋@🎧🏊) There's nothing quite like Gilligan's: a loud, proud, party-hardy flashpacker resort, where all rooms have bathrooms and most have balconies. Higher-priced rooms come with fridges and TVs. Guests get $4 dinners. The mammoth bar and adjacent lagoon pool is the place to be seen, and there's more nightly entertainment than you can poke a stick at. Pick-up central.

★ Lake Placid Tourist Park
CARAVAN PARK $

(☑07-4039 2509; www.lakeplacidtouristpark.com; Lake Placid Rd; powered sites from $37, bungalows from $60, en-suite cabins from $85, cottages from $110; ℗❋🎧🏊🐕) Just a 15-minute drive from the city centre, but far enough away to revel in rainforesty repose, this delightful spot overlooks the aptly named Lake Placid: it's an excellent alternative to staying downtown if you're driving. Camping and a variety of well-priced, tasteful accommodation options are available. It's within striking distance of a wide range of attractions and the northern beaches.

★ Northern Greenhouse
HOSTEL $

(☑07-4047 7200; www.northerngreenhouse. com.au; 117 Grafton St; dm/apt from $26/95; ℗❋🎧🏊) It fits into the budget category, but this friendly, relaxed place is a cut above, with tidy dorms and neat studio-style apartments with kitchens and balconies. The central deck, pool and games room are great for socialising. Free breakfast and Sunday BBQ seal the deal.

Cairns Central YHA
HOSTEL $

(☑07-4051 0772; www.yha.com.au; 20-26 McLeod St; dm/s/d from $27.50/59.50/71; ❋@🏊) Opposite Cairns Central Shopping Centre, this award-winning YHA is bright, spotlessly clean and professionally staffed. En-suite rooms are available and there are free pancakes for breakfast!

Floriana Guesthouse
GUESTHOUSE $

(☑07-4051 7886; www.florianaguesthouse.com; 183 Esplanade; s/d $79/89, studios $130-150; ❋@🎧🏊) The Cairns of old still exists at this quirky guesthouse, which retains its original polished floorboards and art-deco fittings. The swirling staircase leads to 10 individually decorated rooms; all have bathrooms.

Cairns Girls Hostel
HOSTEL $

(☑07-4051 2016; www.cairnsgirlshostel.com.au; 147 Lake St; dm/tw $20/48; 🎧) Sorry lads! This white-glove-test-clean, female-only hostel is one of the most accommodating budget stays in Cairns.

Cairns Colonial Club
RESORT $$

(☑07-4053 8800; www.cairnscolonialclub.com.au; 18-26 Cannon St, Manunda; r $95-175; ℗❋🎧🏊) A stalwart on the Cairns accommodation map since 1986, this Queenslander-style resort has a little something for everyone; families, businessfolk and solo travellers all love it here. Tucked away in a leafy suburb, the 11-acre complex boasts three pools, playgrounds, bars, a popular restaurant and gorgeous gardens. It's 4km from the centre of town; a shuttle bus runs regularly.

Bay Village Tropical Retreat
APARTMENT $$

(☑07-4051 4622; www.bayvillage.com.au; cnr Lake & Gatton Sts; d $135, apt $165-275; ℗❋🎧🏊) Sleek, shiny and ever-so-slightly removed from the Cairns hubbub, this complex offers large, cool apartments (one to three bedrooms) and spacious serviced rooms. It's a lovely place to hang your hat, and perhaps an even better spot for filling your stomach; it's attached to the award-winning Bayleaf Balinese Restaurant (p451).

Pacific Hotel
HOTEL $$

(☑07-4051 788; www.pacifichotelcairns.com; cnr Esplanade & Spence St; d from $144; ℗❋🎧🏊) In a prime location at the southern-end start of the Esplanade, this iconic hotel has been lovingly maintained and refurbished. There's a fun blend of original '70s features and woodwork, with fresh, modern amenities. All rooms have balconies. Friendly, helpful staff help to make this an excellent midrange choice. The fun **Bushfire Flame Grill** (☑07-4044 1879; www.bushfirecairns.com; steak from $38, churrasco per person $55; ⊙5.30pm-late) restaurant is attached.

Reef Palms
APARTMENT $$

(☑07-4051 2599; www.reefpalms.com.au; 41-47 Digger St; apt from $120; ℗❋@🎧🏊) Couples and families love the excellent value and friendly service at this quiet complex. The squeaky-clean apartments have cooking facilities and balconies or courtyards; larger apartments include a lounge area and spa.

★ 201 Lake Street   HOTEL $$$

(✆ 07-4053 0100, 1800 628 929; www.201lakestreet.com.au; 201 Lake St; r from $205, apt $270-340; ❈ ❋ ﹫ ❧) Lifted from the pages of a trendy magazine, this gorgeous apartment complex has a stellar pool and a whiff of exclusivity. Grecian white predominates and guests can choose from a smooth hotel room or contemporary apartments with an entertainment area, a plasma-screen TV and a balcony.

Harbour Lights   APARTMENT $$$

(✆ 07-4057 0800; www.cairnsharbourlightshotel.com.au; 1 Marlin Pde; apt $215-325; ᴾ ❈ ﹫ ❧) This collection of slick, self-contained apartments overlooks the marina from its prime position above the Reef Fleet Terminal (p454). Take in the splendid views from your balcony (request one facing the water) or the glorious saltwater pool. There's a collection of excellent restaurants just down the stairs (on the boardwalk).

Shangri-La   HOTEL $$$

(✆ 07-4031 1411; www.shangri-la.com/cairns; 1 Pierpoint Rd; d/ste from $235/395; ᴾ ❈ ﹫ ❧) Towering over the marina, this is one of Cairns' most swish hotels. All rooms and suites have private balconies and original local artworks on the walls; if you have cash to splash, consider a Horizon Club suite, with wraparound views of the water and 74 sq metres of designer space. Service is as attentive as you'd expect from this luxury chain.

✗ Eating

The **Night Markets** (www.nightmarkets.com.au; Esplanade; dishes $10-15; ⊙10am-11pm) have a cheap, busy Asian-style food court; despite the name, the eateries here are open all day.

For fresh fruit, veg and other local treats, hit Rusty's Markets (p453) on the weekend; for groceries, try **Cairns Central Shopping Centre** (✆ 07-4041 4111; www.cairnscentral.com.au; cnr McLeod & Spence Sts; ⊙9am-5.30pm Mon-Wed, Fri & Sat, to 9pm Thu, 10.30am-4pm Sun).

★ Ganbaranba   JAPANESE $

(✆ 07-4031 2522; 12 Spence St; mains $8-12; ⊙11.30am-2.30pm & 5-8.30pm) You'll recognise this tiny place by the queues outside, and the beatific faces of the customers

inside. This is a cult joint, and without a doubt the best place for ramen in Cairns. Slurpers can watch the chefs making noodles; if the view proves too tempting, you can ask for a refill for a mere $1.50. Absolutely worth the wait.

Cafe Fika   SWEDISH $

(✆ 07-4041 1150; www.swedishshop.com.au; 111-115 Grafton St; meals $9.50-15; ⊙7am-4pm Mon-Fri, 9am-2pm Sat) From meatballs with lingonberry jam to toast topped with *skagen* (prawn, dill and sour cream), this little Euro-haven serves up Swedish classics to hungry hordes of homesick Scandinavians and locals looking for something new. There's an excellent gourmet grocery store attached, stocked with treats from Sweden (of course), Germany, Hungary, Estonia, France and elsewhere.

Pineapple Cafe   HEALTH FOOD $

(www.facebook.com/pineapplecafecairns; 92 Lake St; mains $10-18; ⊙7am-3pm Mon-Sat) Healthy, fresh and creative cuisine is dished up by the ladleful at this adorable cafe; think acai and smoothie bowls, super-food salads, grass-fed beef burgers and all-day breakfasts that are actually good for you. The feel-good vibes don't end with what you put in your mouth: the cafe itself is adorned with happy-making murals and the staff always have a smile.

Bagus   INDONESIAN $

(✆ 07-4000 2051; www.baguscafe.info; 149 Esplanade; mains $10-20; ⊙6.45am-2.30pm & 5.30-8.30pm Mon, Tue, Thu & Sat, 6.45am-2.30pm Wed & Fri, noon-3pm & 5.30-8.30pm Sun) The heady aromas of traditional Indonesian street food waft from this friendly little hole in the wall; the nasi goreng could be straight from a beach cafe in Bali. Breakfasts ($4.50 to $11.50) are good value. Opposite Muddy's (p439) playground.

Tokyo Dumpling   JAPANESE $

(✆ 07-4041 2848; www.facebook.com/tokyodumpling46; 46 Lake St; dumplings from $4.50, bowls from $13.80; ⊙11.30am-9.30pm) Come to this spotless little takeaway for ludicrously moreish homemade dumplings and exceptional rice and noodle dishes. Lunch specials are between 11am and 2pm. We predict you won't be able to eat here just once.

Meldrum's Pies in Paradise   BAKERY $

(✆ 07-4051 8333; 97 Grafton St; pies $5.30-6.80; ⊙7am-4.30pm Mon-Fri, to 2.30pm Sat; ✉) Multi-award-winning Meldrum's deserves the

DAY TRIPS FROM CAIRNS

Cairns is a great base for day trips to many destinations in the region.

Great Barrier Reef

Reef trips generally include transport, lunch, stinger-suits and snorkelling gear. When choosing a tour, consider the vessel type, its capacity, inclusions and destination: outer reefs are more pristine but further afield; inner reefs can be patchy and show signs of decay.

Most boats depart from the Marlin Wharf around 8am, returning around 6pm. Check-in and booking facilities are located inside the Reef Fleet Terminal (p454). Smaller operators may check-in boat-side at their berth on the wharf itself; check with your operator.

Falla Reef Trips (☑ 0400 195 264; www.fallareeftrips.com.au; D-Finger, Marlin Marina; adult/child/family from $145/90/420, intro dives $85) Reach the reef in inimitable style on this graceful 1950s pearl lugger. The tours, which spend time at Coral Gardens and Upolu Cay, have an exclusive feel. There's a maximum of 22 guests (who can help with the sailing), personalised snorkel tours and the old-school boat is the polar opposite of the sleek fibreglass vessels bobbing elsewhere on the reef.

Reef Magic (☑ 07-4031 1588; www.reefmagiccruises.com; Reef Fleet Terminal; adult/child/family day trips from $210/105/525) A long-time family favourite, Reef Magic's high-speed catamaran sails to its all-weather Marine World pontoon moored on the edge of the outer reef. If you're water shy, try a glass-bottomed boat ride, chat with the marine biologist or have a massage!

Reef Encounter (☑ 07-4037 2700; http://reefencounter.com.au; 100 Abbott St; 2-day liveaboards from $450) If one day isn't enough, try an overnight 'reef sleep' with Reef Encounter. Twenty-seven air-conditioned en-suite cabins accommodate a maximum of 42 guests; you don't even have to snorkel or dive to appreciate this floating hotel. A wide range of programs, including meals and daily departures from Cairns, make this excellent value for those wanting something a little different.

Cape Tribulation & the Daintree

Active Tropics Explorer (☑ 07-4031 3460; www.capetribulationadventures.com.au; day tours from $159) These fun all-day trips take in the sights and cultural highlights of Mossman Gorge, the Daintree and Cape Trib; overnight tours and add-ons including horse riding, sea kayaking and 'jungle surfing' are also available.

Billy Tea Safaris (☑ 07-4032 0077; www.billytea.com.au; day trips adult/child/family $220/165/665) This reliable bunch offers exciting small-group day trips to Cape Trib in purpose-built 4WD vehicles. They also run multiday safaris heading as far north as Cape York and over to the islands of the Torres Strait.

Atherton Tablelands

Barefoot Tours (☑ 07-4032 4525; www.barefoottours.com.au; tours $105) Backpackers love this fun, full-day jaunt around the Tablelands, with swimming stops at waterfalls and a natural water slide. Free pick-ups from central accommodation from 7am; tours arrive back in town by 7pm to 8pm. Minimum age 13.

On the Wallaby (☑ 07-4033 6575; www.onthewallaby.com; day tours $99, overnight tours $139-189) Excellent activity-based tours of the Tablelands' rainforests and waterfalls including swimming, cycling, hiking and canoeing. Daily pick-ups from Cairns at 8am.

Uncle Brian's Tours (☑ 07-4033 6575; www.unclebrian.com.au; 1-/2-day tours $119/219; ☉ Mon-Sat) High-energy, small-group day and overnight trips taking in the Babinda Boulders, Josephine Falls, Millaa Millaa, Yungaburra, the Crater Lakes and more. Bring your togs!

Food Trail Tours (☑ 07-4041 1522; www.foodtrailtours.com.au; adult/child/family from $195/115/570) Taste your way around the Tablelands, visiting farms producing macadamias, tropical fruits, wine, cheese, chocolate and coffee. Tours run on Monday, Tuesday, Thursday and Saturday; accommodation transfers from Cairns and northern beaches are included.

accolades bestowed upon its seemingly innumerable renditions of the humble Aussie pie; it's been at it since 1972, an achievement that speaks volumes in a transient tourist town like Cairns. For something different, try the chicken and macadamia satay or tuna mornay with spinach pies; the many vegetarian options are delicious, and sell out quickly.

Lillipad CAFE **$**
(☏ 07-4051 9565; www.lillipadcafe.com; 72 Grafton St; dishes $12-22; ☺ 7am-3pm; ☝) With humongous feasts, from crêpes to wraps and a truckload of vegetarian options, this is one of the best-value options in town. It's a little bit hippie, and a whole lot busy: you'll probably have to wait a while. Don't miss the fresh juices.

★**Spicy Bite** INDIAN, FUSION **$$**
(☏ 07-4041 3700; www.spicybitecairns.com; cnr Shields St & Esplanade; mains $15.50-35; ☺ 5-10pm; ☝) Cairns has plenty of good Indian restaurants, but none are quite as innovative as this unassuming place, where fusion food has been turned into a write-home-about-it experience: where else on earth could you try crocodile masala or kangaroo tikka? The classic curries are divine, and there are loads of vegetarian and vegan options.

★**Prawn Star** SEAFOOD **$$**
(☏ 0456 421 172; www.facebook.com/prawn starcairns; E-Finger, Berth 31, Marlin Marina; seafood from $20; ☺ 10am-8pm) Trawler restaurant Prawn Star is tropical dining perfection: clamber aboard and fill yourself with prawns, mud crabs, oysters and whatever else was caught that day, while taking in equally delicious harbour views. A second boat – Prawn Star Too – was added to the eat-fleet in mid-2017, but seating is still limited and much in-demand: get there early. Why the Cairns waterfront isn't lined with restaurants like this is a mystery for the ages.

★**Bayleaf Balinese Restaurant** BALINESE **$$**
(☏ 07-4051 4622; www.bayvillage.com.au/bayleaf; Bay Village Tropical Retreat, cnr Lake & Gatton Sts; mains $14-25; ☺ noon-2pm Mon-Fri, 6pm-late nightly) One of Cairns' best restaurants isn't along the waterfront or in the lobby of a flash hotel, but rather, attached to a midrange apartment complex. It's completely unexceptional from the outside, but the Balinese food created inside by specialist chefs is outrageously good and wholly authentic. Order a ton of starters, go for the banquet or share a heap of mains.

★**Perrotta's at the Gallery** MEDITERRANEAN **$$**
(☏ 07-4031 5899; www.perrottasatg.com; 38 Abbott St; breakfast $7-23, mains $19-37; ☺ 6.30am-10pm; ☝) This unmissable eatery, connected to the Cairns Regional Gallery (p439), tempts you onto its covered deck with splendid gourmet breakfasts – until 3pm! – fresh juices, barista coffees and an inventive Mediterranean-inspired lunch and dinner menu. It's a chic spot with an interesting crowd and ideal people-watching perches.

Bobby's VIETNAMESE, CHINESE **$$**
(☏ 07-4051 8877; Oceana Walk Arcade, 62 Grafton St; mains from $12; ☺ 7am-10pm) Authentic Vietnamese and Chinese food are the go at Bobby's, beloved by locals and visitors that make the effort to find it. It's reputed to do the best *pho* in town; if you're after a midday filler, the marinated Vietnamese beef rolls will certainly hit the spot.

Fetta's Greek Taverna GREEK **$$**
(☏ 07-4051 6966; www.fettasgreektaverna.com.au; 99 Grafton St; mains $26.50-28.50, set menu $35; ☺ 11.30am-3pm Mon-Fri, 5.30pm-late daily) The white walls and blue-accented windows do a great job evoking Santorini, but it's the classic Greek dishes that are the star of the show here. The set menu goes the whole hog – dip, saganaki, moussaka, salad, grilled meats, calamari, baklava and coffee. Yes, you can break your plate.

Marinades INDIAN **$$**
(☏ 07-4041 1422; 43 Spence St; mains from $16, lunch thali from $10; ☺ 11.30am-2.30pm & 5.30-9.30pm Tue-Fri, 5.30-9.30pm Sat & Sun; ☝) One of Cairns' most popular Indian restaurants has a *long* menu of aromatic dishes, such as lobster marinated in cashew paste and Goan prawn curry. The lunch specials are great value.

★**Ochre** MODERN AUSTRALIAN **$$$**
(☏ 07-4051 0100; www.ochrerestaurant.com.au; Marlin Pde; mains $28-40; ☺ 11.30am-2.30pm & 5.30-9.30pm) The menu at this innovative waterfront restaurant utilises native Aussie fauna (such as croc with native pepper, or roo with quandong-chilli glaze) and flora (try wattle-seed damper loaf or Davidson plum mousse). It also cooks Tablelands steaks to perfection. Can't decide? Order a tasting plate.

Dundees SEAFOOD **$$$**
(☏ 07-4051 0399; www.dundees.com.au; Marlin Pde; mains $25-82; ☺ 11.30am-late) This tried-and-true waterfront restaurant comes up trumps

for ambience, generous portions and friendly service. The varied menu of appealing appetisers includes chunky seafood chowder, tempura soft-shell crab and lightly dusted calamari strips; main-meal highlights include barbecued lobster, wagyu eye fillets and enormous seafood platters.

🍷 Drinking & Nightlife

⭐ Three Wolves
BAR

(☑ 07-4031 8040; www.threewolves.com.au; Red Brick Laneway, 32 Abbott St; ⏱ 4pm-midnight Thu-Sat & Mon, 2-10pm Sun) Intimate, understated and bang on trend (think Edison bulbs, copper mugs and mixologists in old-timey barkeep aprons), this new laneway bar has delivered a very welcome dash of Melbourne. It's got an excellent selection of speciality spirits, cocktails and beers, plus a bar menu including hip faves like pulled-pork tortillas, sliders and New York–style hot dogs. Small but superb.

⭐ Green Ant Cantina
BAR

(☑ 07-4041 5061; www.greenantcantina.com; 183 Bunda St; ⏱ 4pm-late Tue-Sun) Behind the railway station (p454), this grungy, rockin' Tex-Mex bar is an ace and arty alternative hang-out. Smothered in bright murals and peopled by friendly folks, the Green Ant brews its own beers and hosts regular music events. It also does fab food, including pulled-pork quesadillas, jambalaya and the infamous, blistering Wings of Death.

⭐ Salt House
BAR

(☑ 07-4041 7733; www.salthouse.com.au; 6/2 Pierpoint Rd; ⏱ 11am-2am Mon-Fri, 7am-2am Sat & Sun) By the yacht club, Cairns' coolest, classiest bar caters to a hip and happy crowd. With killer cocktails, tremendous views, occasional live music and DJs, and a superb mod-Oz nibbles-and-mains menu, the Salt House is absolutely not to be missed.

⭐ Conservatory Bar
WINE BAR

(☑ 0467 466 980; www.theconservatorybar.com. au; 12-14 Lake St; ⏱ 4-10pm Wed-Thu, to midnight Fri & Sat, to 9pm Sun) Tucked away in a little room in a little laneway, this is Cairns' best wine bar, and one of the city's top places for a low-key tipple, whatever your flavour. It also makes fabulous cocktails and has loads of craft beers. It's relaxed, friendly and oozes a tropical sophistication all its own. The Conservatory regularly hosts exhibitions and live (mellow) music.

⭐ Lyquid Nightlife
CLUB

(☑ 07-4028 3773; www.lyquid.com.au; 33 Spence St; ⏱ 9pm-3am) Lyquid is the hottest ticket in town: dress to impress and party the night away with top DJs, professional bartenders and a happy, hyped-up young crowd.

⭐ Jack
PUB

(☑ 07-4051 2490; www.thejack.com.au; cnr Spence & Sheridan Sts; ⏱ 10am-late) The Jack is a kick-arse pub by any standards, housed in an unmissable heritage Queenslander with an enormous shaded beer garden. There are nightly events, including live music and DJs, killer pub grub, and an adjacent hostel (dorm from $26) for those who just can't tear themselves away.

Flying Monkey Cafe
CAFE

(☑ 0411 084 176; www.facebook.com/theflying monkeycafe; 154 Sheridan St; ⏱ 6.30am-3.30pm Mon-Fri, 7am-noon Sat) Fantastic coffee, ever-changing local art exhibitions, colourful buskers and a beyond-affable staff make the Monkey a must-do for caffeine-and-culture hounds.

Pier Bar
BAR

(☑ 07-4031 4677; www.thepierbar.com.au; Pier Shopping Centre, 1 Pierpoint Rd; ⏱ 11.30am-late) This local institution is much loved for its killer waterfront location and daily happy hour (5pm to 7pm). Its Sunday sessions are the place to see and be seen, with live music, food and drink specials and an always-happening crowd.

Grand Hotel
PUB

(☑ 07-4051 1007; www.grandhotelcairns.com; 34 McLeod St; ⏱ 10am-9pm Mon-Wed, to 11pm Thu, to midnight Fri & Sat, to 8pm Sun) Established in 1926, this laid-back haunt is worth visiting just to rest your beer on the bar – an 11m-long carved crocodile! There's usually live music on the weekend. It's a great place to loiter with the locals.

Woolshed
BAR

(☑ 07-4031 6304; www.thewoolshed.com.au; 24 Shields St; ⏱ 7pm-3am Sun-Thu, to 5am Fri & Sat) An eternal backpacker magnet and meat market, where young travellers, dive instructors and living-it-up locals get happily hammered and dance on tables. The classier Cotton Club speakeasy-style cocktail bar is downstairs.

PJ O'Briens
IRISH PUB

(www.pjobriens.com.au/cairns; cnr Lake & Shields Sts; ⏱ 11.30am-late) It has sticky carpets and reeks of stale Guinness, but Irish-themed PJs packs 'em in with party nights, pole dancing and dirt-cheap meals.

☆ Entertainment

Pop & Co Tapas & Music Bar   LIVE MUSIC
(☑07-4019 6132; 92 Abbott St; ☺5pm-late Wed-Sun) Live jazz, blues and croony tunes share the limelight with a good nibbles menu and some of the cheapest on-tap beers in town. It's a diminutive diamond, and its local popularity means it sometimes gets crowded. You'll find it next to the giant jelly babies at the Centre of Contemporary Arts as you head north down Abbott St.

Rondo Theatre   THEATRE
(☑1800 855 835; www.therondo.com.au; 46 Greenslopes St) Community plays and musicals hit the stage regularly at this small theatre opposite Centenary Lakes. It's 4.5km northwest of the city centre (take Sheridan St to Greenslopes St).

Starry Night Cinema   CINEMA
(www.starrynightcinema.com.au; Flecker Botanic Gardens, Collins Ave, Edge Hill; adult/child from $13/5) Enjoy classic films amid the foliage and finery of the Botanic Gardens (p439). Check the website for upcoming showings (there are usually one or two a month).

Reef Hotel Casino   CASINO
(☑07-4030 8888; www.reefcasino.com.au; 35-41 Wharf St; ☺9am-5am Fri & Sat, to 3am Sun-Thu) In addition to table games and pokies, Cairns' casino has four restaurants and four bars, including the enormous Casino Sports Arena bar.

Centre of Contemporary Arts   GALLERY, THEATRE
(CoCA; www.centre-of-contemporary-arts-cairns. com.au; 96 Abbott St; ☺10am-5pm Mon-Sat) CoCA houses the KickArts (p439) galleries of local contemporary visual art, as well as the JUTE Theatre (www.jute.com.au). Look for the jelly babies out the front.

🛍 Shopping

★ Rusty's Markets   MARKET
(☑07-4040 2705; www.rustysmarkets.com.au; 57-89 Grafton St; ☺5am-6pm Fri & Sat, to 3pm Sun) No weekend in Cairns is complete without a visit to this busy and vibrant multicultural market. Weave (and taste) your way through piles of seasonal tropical fruits, veggies and herbs, plus farm-fresh honey, locally grown flowers, excellent coffees, curries, cold drinks, antiques and more.

Doongal Aboriginal Art   ART
(☑07-4041 4249; www.doongal.com.au; 49 Esplanade; ☺9am-6pm) Authentic artworks, boomerangs, didgeridoos and other traditional artefacts by local and central Australian Indigenous artists. Worldwide shipping available.

Crackerbox Palace   VINTAGE
(☑07-4031 1216; www.crackerboxpalace.com. au; 228 Sheridan St; ☺10am-5pm Mon-Fri, to 3pm Sat) This treasure trove of all things vintage has been luring in the locals for over 20 years. It's crammed full of one-off clothes, furniture, records, knick-knacks and awesome oddities. Check your baggage weight allowances before stepping through the Palace doors; once you shop, it's hard to stop.

ℹ Information

MEDICAL SERVICES

Cairns 24 Hour Medical Centre (☑07-4052 1119; cnr Grafton & Florence Sts; ☺24hr) Centrally located medical centre; it also does dive medicals.

Cairns Base Hospital (☑07-4226 0000; 165 Esplanade) Largest hospital in Far North Queensland.

POST

Post Office (☑13 13 18; www.auspost.com. au; 38 Sheridan St; ☺8.30am-5.30pm Mon-Fri, 9am-12.30pm Sat)

TOURIST INFORMATION

Cairns & Tropical North Visitor Information Centre (☑07-4051 3588; www.tropicalnorth queensland.org.au; 51 Esplanade; ☺8.30am-6pm Mon-Fri, 10am-6pm Sat & Sun) This is the only government-run visitor information centre in town offering impartial advice. Hundreds of free brochures, maps and pamphlets are available. Friendly staff can help with booking accommodation and tours. Look for the yellow 'i' on the blue background.

ℹ Getting There & Away

AIR

Qantas (☑13 13 13; www.qantas.com.au), **Virgin Australia** (☑13 67 89; www.virginaustralia. com) and **Jetstar** (☑13 15 38; www.jetstar. com.au), and a handful of international carriers, arrive in and depart from Cairns Airport (p303), located approximately 6km from the city centre, with direct services to all Australian capital cities except Canberra and Hobart, and to regional centres including Townsville, Weipa and Horn Island. Direct international connections include Bali, Singapore, Manila, Tokyo and Port Moresby.

Hinterland Aviation (07-4040 1333; www.hinterlandaviation.com.au) has at least two flights daily from Cairns to Cooktown.

Skytrans (1300 759 872; www.skytrans.com.au) services Cape York communities and the Torres Strait islands.

BOAT

Almost all reef trips from Cairns depart the Marlin Wharf (sometimes called the Marlin Jetty), with booking and check-in facilities located inside the **Reef Fleet Terminal** (Pierpoint Rd). A handful of smaller operators may have their check-in facilities boat-side, on the wharf itself. Be sure to ask for the correct berth number.

International cruise ships and **SeaSwift** (1800 424 422, 07-4035 1234; www.seaswift.com.au; 41-45 Tingira St, Portsmith; one way/return from $650/1166) ferries to Seisia on Cape York dock at and depart from the **Cairns Cruise Terminal** (07-4052 3888; www.cairnscruiselinerterminal.com.au; cnr Wharf & Lake Sts).

BUS

Long-distance buses arrive at and depart from the **Interstate Coach Terminal** (Reef Fleet Terminal), Cairns Central Railway Station, the airport and the **Cairns Transit Mall** (Lake St). Operators include the following:

Cairns Cooktown Express (07-4059 1423; www.cairnsbuscharters.com/services/cairns-cooktown-express)

Greyhound Australia (1300 473 946; www.greyhound.com.au)

John's Kuranda Bus (0418 772 953)

Premier Motor Service (13 34 10; www.premierms.com.au)

Sun Palm (07-4087 2900; www.sunpalmtransport.com.au)

Tablelands Tours & Transfers (07-4045 1882; www.tablelandstoursandtransfers.com.au)

Trans North (07-4095 8644; www.transnorthbus.com; Cairns Central Railway Station)

CAR & MOTORCYCLE

Major car-rental companies have airport and downtown (usually on Sheridan St) branches. Daily rates start at around $40 for a compact auto and $80 for a 4WD. **Cruising Car Rental** (07-4041 4666; www.hirecarcairns.com; 196 Sheridan St; per day from $39) and **Rent-a-Bomb** (07-4031 4477; www.rentabomb.com.au; 144 Sheridan St; per day from $33) have cheap rates on older model vehicles. If you're looking for a cheap campervan, **Jucy**

(1800 150 850; www.jucy.com.au; 55 Dutton St, Portsmith; per day from $40), **Spaceships** (1300 132 469; www.spaceshipsrentals.com.au; 3/52 Fearnley St, Portsmith; per day from $40) and **Hippie Camper Hire** (1800 777 779; www.hippiecamper.com; 432 Sheridan St; per day from $44) have quality wheels at budget prices. **Bear Rentals** (1300 462 327; www.bearrentals.com.au; cars per day from $127) has top-notch Land Rover Defenders that make bush-bashing a breeze.

If you're in for the long haul, check hostels, www.gumtree.com.au and the big noticeboard on Abbott St for used campervans and ex-backpackers' cars.

If you prefer two wheels to four, try **Choppers Motorcycle Tours & Hire** (07-4051 6288; www.choppersmotorcycles.com.au; 150 Sheridan St; rental per day from $90) or **Cairns Scooter & Bicycle Hire** (07-4031 3444; www.cairnsbicyclehire.com.au; 47 Shields St; scooters/bikes per day from $87/11).

TRAIN

The Kuranda Scenic Railway (p460) runs daily; the Savannahlander (p309) offers a miscellany of rail journeys into the outback from **Cairns Central Railway Station** (Bunda St).

Queensland Rail (1300 131 722; www.queenslandrailtravel.com.au) operates services between Brisbane and Cairns.

🛈 Getting Around

TO/FROM THE AIRPORT

The airport is about 6km north of central Cairns; many hotels and hostels offer courtesy pick-up. **Sun Palm** (07-4087 2900; www.sunpalmtransport.com.au) meets all incoming flights and runs a shuttle (adult/child $15/7.50) directly to your accommodation; its **Airport Connect Shuttle** ($4) runs between the airport and a Sunbus stop on Sheridan St just north of town. **Cairns Airport Shuttle** (0432 488 783; www.cairnsairportshuttle.com.au) is a good option for groups; the more passengers, the cheaper the fare.

Taxis to the city centre are around $25 (plus $4 airport surcharge).

Some travellers choose to walk between the airport and town to save on bus or taxi fares, but keep in mind, these are busy roads: a pedestrian was hit by a car and killed in 2015. Also, crocodiles have been known to cross Airport Ave, which is bordered by mangrove swamps, so...

BICYCLE

Cairns is criss-crossed with cycling paths and circuits; some of the most popular routes take in the Esplanade, Botanic Gardens and Centenary Lakes. There's a detailed list of routes and maps at www.cairns.qld.gov.au/region/tour-ist-information/things-to-do/cycle.

Cairns Scooter & Bicycle Hire (☑ 07-4031 3444; www.cairnsbicyclehire.com.au; 47 Shields St; scooters/bikes per day from $87/11)

Pro Bike Rental (☑ 0438 381 749; www.pro bikerental.com.au; bikes per day from $120)

BUS

Sunbus (☑ 07-4057 7411; www.sunbus.com.au/cairns; single/daily/weekly ticket from $2.40/4.80/19.20)

TAXI

Cairns Taxis (☑ 13 10 08; www.cairnstaxis.com.au)

AROUND CAIRNS

Islands off Cairns

Green Island

Showing some of the scars that come with fame and popularity, this pretty coral cay (45 minutes from Cairns) nevertheless retains much of its beauty. The island has a rainforest interior with interpretive walks, a fringe of white-sand beach, and superb snorkelling just offshore; it's great for kids. You can walk around the island (which, along with its surrounding waters, is protected by national- and marine-park status) in about 30 minutes.

The star attraction at family-owned aquarium, **Marineland Crocodile Park** (☑ 07-4051 4032; www.greenislandcrocs.com.au; adult/child $19/9; ⊙ 9.30am-4pm), is Cassius, the world's largest croc in captivity at 5.5m. Believed to be over 110 years old, he's fed daily at 10.30am and 1.30pm.

If you don't want to get your hair wet, **Seawalker** (www.seawalker.com.au; per person $172) allows you to don a helmet and simply go for a (guided) stroll on the sea floor, 5m below the surface.

Luxurious **Green Island Resort** (☑ 07-4031 3300; www.greenislandresort.com.au; ste from $580; ❉ @ ☎) maintains a sense of privacy and exclusivity despite having sections opened to the general public, including restaurants, bars, an ice-cream parlour and water-sports facilities. Spacious split-level suites feature tropical themes, timber furnishings and inviting balconies.

Big Cat (☑ 07-4051 0444; www.greenisland.com.au; adult/child/family from $90/45/225) has transfers and day-return tours to Green Island.

Fitzroy Island

A steep mountaintop rising from the sea, fabulous Fitzroy Island has clinking coral beaches, giant boulders and rainforest walking tracks, one of which ends at a now-inactive lighthouse. It's a top spot for swimming and snorkelling; one of the best places to lay your towel is Nudey Beach, which, despite its name, is not officially clothing-optional.

The **Cairns Turtle Rehabilitation Centre** (www.saveourseaturtles.com.au; adult/child $8.80/5.50; ⊙ tours 1pm & 2pm) looks after sick and injured sea turtles before releasing them back into the wild. Daily educational tours (45 minutes, maximum 15 guests) take visitors through the turtle hospital to meet recovering residents. Bookings through the Fitzroy Island Resort are essential.

Fitzroy Island Resort (☑ 07-4044 6700; www.fitzroyisland.com; studios/cabins from $185/445, ste/apt from $300/350; ❉ 🛜 ☎) has tropi-cool accommodation ranging from sleek studios, suites and beachfront cabins through to luxurious apartments. The restaurant, bar and kiosk are open to day trippers. Budgeteers can book here for a site at the **Fitzroy Island Camping Ground** (sites $35).

Fast Cat (www.fitzroyisland.com/getting-here; adult/child/family $78/39/205) departs Cairns' Marlin Wharf (berth 20) at 8am, 11am and 1.30pm (bookings essential) and whisks you to Fitzroy Island in just 45 minutes. It returns to Cairns at 9.30am, 12.15pm and 5pm.

Frankland Islands

If the idea of hanging out on one of five uninhabited, coral-fringed islands with excellent snorkelling and stunning white-sand beaches appeals, cruise out to the Frankland Group National Park. These continental islands are made up of High Island to the north, and Normanby, Mabel, Round and Russell Islands to the south.

Frankland Islands Cruise & Dive (☑ 07-4031 6300; www.franklandislands.com.au; adult/child from $169/99) runs excellent day trips that include a cruise down the Mulgrave River, snorkelling gear, tuition and lunch.

Cairns' Northern Beaches

Despite what some brochures may infer, Cairns city is sans swimmable beach. But a 15-minute drive (or a local bus ticket) will get you out to a string of lovely beach communities, each with their own character: Yorkeys Knob is popular with sailors, Trinity is big with families, Holloways is loved by locals (and their dogs) and Palm Cove is a swanky honeymoon haven.

Once you're there, **Northern Beaches Bike Hire** (☑0417 361 012; www.cairnsbeaches bikehire.com; adult/child bikes per day from $20/14, per week $80/50) can deliver rental bikes to your digs, and collect them when you're done.

Yorkeys Knob

POP 2766

Yorkeys Knob is a laid-back beach community best known for its marina and **golf course** (☑07-4055 7933; www.halfmoonbaygolf. com.au; 9/18 holes $26/42, clubs hire $25), and the cheeky crocs that frequent it. The 'Knob' part of the name elicits chortles from easily amused locals; others wonder where the apostrophe went. Yorkeys has a stinger net in summer.

Blazing saddles (☑07-4055 7400; www. blazingsaddles.com.au; 154 Yorkeys Knob Rd; horse rides from $125) has half-day horse-riding tours that meander through rainforest, mangroves and sugar-cane fields.

For fresh seafood and delightful views of the marina's expensive floating toys from the expansive floating deck, **Yorkeys Knob Boating Club** (☑07-4055 7711; www.ykbc.com. au; 25-29 Buckley St; mains $18-30; ☺10am-midnight Mon-Thu, to 2am Fri & Sat, 8am-midnight Sun; ☑) is worth the trip from Cairns.

Trinity Beach

One of the region's better-kept secrets, Trinity Beach, with its gorgeous stretch of sheltered sand, pretty esplanade and sensibly priced dining and accommodation, has managed to stave off the tourism vibe, despite being a holiday hot spot and popular dining destination for locals in the know. There's not much to do here except eat, sleep and relax, but Trinity Beach's central position makes it easy to get out and about if you're feeling active.

One of the most handsome blocks on the beachfront, **Sea Point on Trinity Beach** (☑07-4057 9544; www.seapointontrinity beach.com; 63 Vasey Esplanade; apt $165-230; P❋❅☲) offers indoor-outdoor balconies, tiled floors and breezy outlooks.

Don't let the easy-breezy beach-shack vibe fool you into thinking the food at **Fratelli on Trinity** (☑07-4057 5775; www.fratelli.net.au; 47 Vasey Esplanade; mains $20-35; ☺7am-10pm Wed-Sun, from 5.30pm Mon & Tue) is anything less than top-class. Pastas are superb, and dishes like pistachio prawns and soft-shell crab with pomegranate and saffron aioli might even distract you from the million-dollar views.

Blue Moon Grill (☑07-4057 8957; www. bluemoongrill.com.au; Shop 6, 22-24 Trinity Beach Rd; mains $22-40; ☺4-10pm Mon-Thu, 7-11am & 4-10pm Fri-Sun) wows with a creative, original menu presented with passion. Where else can you try crocodile popcorn?

Palm Cove

POP 1215

The best known of Cairns' northern beaches, Palm Cove has grown into a destination in its own right. More intimate than Port Douglas and more upmarket than its southern neighbours, Palm Cove is a cloistered coastal community with a beautiful promenade along the paperbark-lined Williams Esplanade. Its gorgeous stretch of white-sand beach and its sprinkling of fancy restaurants do their best to lure young lovers from their luxury resorts; inevitably, they succeed.

If you can drag yourself off the beach or poolside, Palm Cove has some excellent water-sports operators including **Beach Fun Co** (☑0411 848 580; www.beachfunco.com; cnr Williams Esplanade & Harpa St), **Palm Cove Watersports** (☑0402 861 011; www.palmcovewatersports.com; 149 Williams Esplanade; kayak hire per hour from $20) and **Pacific Watersports** (☑0413 721 999; www.pacificwatersports.com.au; 41 Williams Esplanade), which offers turtle tours by SUP or kayak.

🛏 Sleeping & Eating

⭐**Cairns Beaches Flashpackers** HOSTEL $ (☑07-4055 3797; www.cairnsbeachesflash packers.com; 19 Veivers Rd; dm/d $45/120; P❋❅☲) Though technically a hostel – the first and only in Palm Cove – this splendid, spotless place 100m from the beach is more restful retreat than party palace. The bunk-free dorms are tidy and comfortable; the private rooms have bathrooms and sliding-door access to the pool. Cook in the immaculate communal kitchen, or scout for restaurants further afield on a Piaggio scooter.

Palm Cove Holiday Park CAMPGROUND $
(☑ 07-4055 3824; www.palmcovehp.com.au; 149 Williams Esplanade; powered/unpowered sites from $36/29; P ♠) For cheap, alfresco Palm Cove accommodation, stake out your spot at this modern, well-run beachfront camping ground near the jetty. It has tent and van sites, a new camp kitchen, a barbecue area and a laundry.

★**Sarayi** BOUTIQUE HOTEL $$
(☑ 07-4059 5600; www.sarayi.com.au; 95 Williams Esplanade; d $115-240; P ✴ ♠ ☒) White, bright and perfectly located among a grove of melaleucas across from the beach, Sarayi is a wonderful choice for couples, families and the growing number of visitors choosing to get married on its rooftop terrace. The name means 'palace' in Turkish, and it's an apt one: the laid-back but efficient management here does everything to ensure you're treated like royalty.

Reef Retreat APARTMENT $$
(☑ 07-4059 1744; www.reefretreat.com.au; 10-14 Harpa St; apt from $165; P ✴ ♠ ☒) This delightful property has a rightful reputation for excellent service. In a peaceful forested setting around a shaded pool, Reef Retreat's well-maintained one-, two- and three-bedroom apartments feature lots of rich timbers, durable high-quality furnishings, kitchenettes and wide, airy balconies.

★**Reef House**
Resort & Spa BOUTIQUE HOTEL $$$
(☑ 07-4080 2600; www.reefhouse.com.au; 99 Williams Esplanade; d from $300; P ✴ ♠ ☒) Once the private residence of an army brigadier, Reef House is more intimate and understated than most of Palm Cove's resorts. The whitewashed walls, wicker furniture and big beds romantically draped in muslin add to the air of refinement. The Brigadier's Bar works on an honesty system; complimentary punch is served by candlelight at twilight.

★**Chill Cafe** CAFE $$
(☑ 0439 361 122; www.chillcafepalmcove.com.au; 41 Williams Esplanade; mains from $19; ☺ 6am-late) The *primo* position on the corner of the waterfront Esplanade, combined with fun, friendly and attentive service, sexy tunes

and a huge airy deck are all great reasons to try the oversized, tasty treats (think fish tacos and chunky club sandwiches) offered by this hip cafe. You can also just soak up some sunshine with a juice or a beer.

Seafarer's Oyster Bar &
Restaurant SEAFOOD $$
(☑ 07-4059 2653; 45 Williams Esplanade; oysters per dozen from $20, mains from $19; ☺ noon-3pm & 5-8.30pm Mon-Thu, noon-8.30pm Fri-Sun) Come for the delicious oysters and the freshest seafood in town; stay for the beach breezes and social buzz.

★**Vivo** MODERN AUSTRALIAN $$$
(☑ 07-4059 0944; www.vivo.com.au; 49 Williams Esplanade; mains from $30; ☺ 7.30am-9pm) The most beautiful-looking restaurant on the Esplanade is also one of the finest. Menus (breakfast, lunch and dinner) are inventive and well-executed using fresh local ingredients, service is second to none, and the outlook is superb. Daily set menus are excellent value.

★**Beach Almond** SEAFOOD $$$
(☑ 07-4059 1908; www.beachalmond.com; 145 Williams Esplanade; mains from $27; ☺ 5-11pm Mon-Sat, noon-3pm & 5-11pm Sun) The rustic, ramshackle, beach-house-on-sticks exterior belies the exceptional fine-dining experience that awaits within. Black-pepper prawns, Singaporean mud crab and banana-leaf barramundi are among the fragrant innovations here, combining Asian flavours and spices.

Nu Nu MODERN AUSTRALIAN $$$
(☑ 07-4059 1880; www.nunu.com.au; 1 Veivers Rd; mains from $38, tasting menu per person from $70; ☺ 6.15am-late) Trendy Nu Nu uses fresh local produce to create Mod Oz masterpieces including poached prawns with candied bacon, apple, seed crumb and endive, and the stupendous wok-fried mud crab with sweet pork, chilli tamarind, ginger and market greens.

🍷 Drinking & Nightlife

Apres Beach Bar & Grill BAR
(☑ 07-4059 2000; www.apresbeachbar.com.au; 119 Williams Esplanade; ☺ 8am-11pm) The most happening place in Palm Cove, with a zany interior of old motorcycles, racing cars, and a biplane hanging from the ceiling, plus regular live music. Big on steaks of all sorts, too.

Surf Club Palm Cove BAR
(☑07-4059 1244; www.surfclubpalmcove.com.au;
135 Williams Esplanade; ⊗11am-10pm Mon & Tue, to
midnight Wed-Sat, 8am-midnight Sun) This local
hang-out is great for a drink in the sunny
garden bar, bargain-priced seafood and decent kids' meals.

Ellis Beach

Little Ellis Beach is the last – and arguably
the best – of Cairns' northern beaches and
the closest to the highway, which runs right
past it. The long sheltered bay is a stunner,
with a palm-fringed, patrolled swimming
beach, and a stinger net in summer. Cairns'
only (unofficial) clothing-optional beach,
Buchans Point, is at the southern end of Ellis; there's no stinger net here, so consider
your valuable assets before diving in in your
birthday suit.

North of Ellis Beach towards Port Douglas, **Hartley's Crocodile Adventures** (☑07-
4055 3576; www.crocodileadventures.com; Captain
Cook Hwy, Wangetti Beach; adult/child/family
$37/18.50/92.50; ⊗8.30am-5pm) 🐾 offers a
daily range of squeal-inducing events including croc farm tours, feedings, 'crocodile
attack' and snake shows, and croc-infested
lagoon cruises.

Ellis Beach Oceanfront Bungalows
(☑1800 637 036, 07-4055 3538; www.ellisbeach.
com; Captain Cook Hwy; powered/unpowered sites
from $41/34, cabins with shared bathroom from
$115, bungalow d from $170, oceanfront bungalows
from $190; ❀@❀) has camping, cabins and
contemporary bungalows, the best of which
have direct ocean views. Just try to drive
past **Ellis Beach Bar 'n' Grill** (☑07-4055
3534; www.ellisbeachbarandgrill.com.au; Captain

THE CAIRNS OF CAIRNS

As if the natural scenery on the road to
Port Douglas wasn't distracting enough,
the comely Captain Cook Hwy now has
another eye-catcher: hundreds upon
hundreds of mysterious, precariously
piled rocks. The stone stackers' identity
and mission has puzzled and delighted
locals: is it a play on 'cairns'? Conceptual
art? Whatever's going on, you'll want to
pull over for a peek and a ponder. You'll
find the cryptic collection just north of
Ellis Beach.

Cook Hwy; mains $10-30; ⊗8am-8pm) and not
stop for a beer and a burger.

Clifton Beach

Cute Clifton is very much a locals' beach,
with minimal development and long,
oft-deserted stretches of palm-lined sands
that run all the way to Palm Cove. If you're
after privacy or a place to let the little ones
run free, drop your bags.

Idyllic, private and hosted by a genuinely
welcoming couple, **South Pacific B&B** (☑07-
4059 0381; www.southpacificbnbcliftonbeach.com.
au; 18 Gibson Cl; s/d from $100/120; P❀❀🛜❀)
is everything a B&B should be with expansive, tropical rooms and cottages and exotic-
fruit-laden breakfasts.

Even if you're not staying at Clifton,
Coco Mojo (☑07-4059 1272; 14 Clifton Rd;
mains $23-40; ⊗5.30-11.30pm Mon & Tue, noon-
11.30pm Wed-Fri, 9am-11.30pm Sat & Sun) is
worth a special trip. The extensive menu
focuses on the wildly varying street foods
of the world, covering cuisines from Ni-
gerian to Texan, Indonesian to Lebanese;
somehow, the experienced international
chefs make it work.

South of Cairns

Babinda

Babinda is a small working-class town that
leads 7km inland to the Babinda Boulders,
where a photogenic creek rushes between
4m-high granite rocks. It's croc-free, but
here lurks an equal danger: highly treacherous waters. Aboriginal Dreaming stories
say that a young woman threw herself into
the then-still waters after being separated
from her love; her anguish caused the creek
to become the surging, swirling torrent it is
today. Almost 20 visitors have lost their lives
at the boulders. Swimming is permitted in
calm, well-marked parts of the creek, but
pay careful heed to all warning signs. Walking tracks give you safe access for obligatory
gasps and photographs.

There's free camping at Babinda Boulders
Camping Area.

Wooroonooran National Park

Part of the Wet Tropics World Heritage Area,
steamy, dreamy Wooroonooran National
Park brims with stunning natural spectacles,

including Queensland's highest peak (Mt Bartle Frere; 1622m), dramatic falls, tangled rainforest, unusual flora and fauna and blissfully cool swimming holes. It's heaven for hikers, or anyone looking to escape the (relative) rat race of bustling Cairns.

Contact **NPRSR** (☑13 74 68; www.nprsr. qld.gov.au/parks/wooroonooran; camping permits per person/family $6.15/24.60) about camping permits.

ATHERTON TABLELANDS

Climbing back from the coast between Innisfail and Cairns is the fertile food bowl of the far north, the Atherton Tablelands. Quaint country towns, eco-wilderness lodges and luxurious B&Bs dot greener-than-green hills between patchwork fields, pockets of rainforest, spectacular lakes, waterfalls, and Queensland's highest mountains, Bartle Frere (1622m) and Bellenden Ker (1593m).

The Tablelands make for a great getaway from the swelter of the coast; they're almost always a few degrees cooler than Cairns, and on winter nights things get downright chilly.

🛈 Getting There & Away

Trans North (p454) has regular bus services connecting Cairns with various spots on the Tablelands, including Kuranda ($6.70, 30 minutes), Mareeba ($19.60, one hour), Atherton ($25.30, 1¾ hours) and Herberton/Ravenshoe ($32/37.40, two/2½ hours, Monday, Wednesday, Friday).

Kuranda

POP 2966

Tucked away in thick rainforest, arty, alternative Kuranda is one of Cairns' most popular day trips. During the day, this hippie haven swarms with tourists soaking up the vibe, visiting animal sanctuaries and poking around its famous markets; come evening, you can almost hear the village sigh as the streets and pubs are reclaimed by mellow locals (and the occasional street-hopping wallaby).

Just getting here is an experience in itself: choose between driving a winding forest road, chugging up on a train or soaring over the treetops on Australia's longest gondola cableway (p460).

🔘 Sights & Activities

★ Kuranda Original Rainforest Markets   MARKET

(☑07-4093 9440; www.kurandaoriginalrainforest market.com.au; Therwine St; ⊗9.30am-3pm) Follow the clouds of incense down to these atmospheric, authentic village markets. Operating since 1978, they're still the best place to see artists at work and hippies at play. Pick up everything from avocado ice cream to organic lingerie and sample local produce such as honey and fruit wines.

BatReach   WILDLIFE RESERVE

(☑07-4093 8858; www.batreach.com; 13 Barang St; by donation; ⊗10.30am-2.30pm Tue, Wed, Thu & Sun) Visitors are welcome at this rescue and rehabilitation centre for injured and orphaned bats, possums and gliders. Passionate volunteers are more than happy to show folks around and explain the work they do. It's located next to the fire station.

Rainforestation   PARK

(☑07-4085 5008; www.rainforest.com.au; Kennedy Hwy; adult/child/family $47/23.50/117.50; ⊗9am-4pm) You'll need a full day to properly explore this enormous complex, divided into three sections: a koala and wildlife park, the interactive Pamagirri Aboriginal Experience, and a river and rainforest tour aboard the amphibious Army Duck boat-truck.

The park is 3km east of Kuranda. **Shuttles** (one-way/return adult $7/12, child $3.50/6) run every half-hour between the park and Kuranda village.

Rainforestation is included in the Capta 4 Park Pass (www.capta.com.au), which offers discounted entry to four Far North Queensland attractions.

Heritage Markets   MARKET

(☑07-4093 8060; www.kurandamarkets.com.au; Rob Veivers Dr; ⊗9.30am-3.30pm) This is Kuranda's more touristy market, hawking Australiana souvenirs – think emu oil, kangaroo-skin bow ties and Akubra hats – by the busload. It's also home to **Frogs** (www.frogsrestaurant.com.au; mains $12.40-35; ⊗9.30am-4pm; 🐾🅿) cafe and a handful of wildlife sanctuaries, including **Kuranda Koala Gardens** (☑07-4093 9953; www.koalagardens.com; adult/child $18/9, koala photos extra; ⊗9am-4pm), **Australian Butterfly Sanctuary** (☑07-4093 7575; www.australianbutter flies.com; adult/child/family $19.50/9.75/48.75; ⊗9.45am-4pm) and **Birdworld** (☑07-4093

9188; www.birdworldkuranda.com; adult/child $18/9; ☺9am-4pm).

Kuranda Riverboat
CRUISE

(☑07-4093 0082; www.kurandariverboat.com.au; adult/child/family $18/9/45; ☺hourly 10.45am-2.30pm) Hop aboard for a 45-minute calmwater cruise along the Barron River, or opt for an hour-long interpretive rainforest walk in a secluded spot accessible only by boat.

You'll find Kuranda Riverboat on the jetty behind the train station; buy tickets (cash only) for the cruise on board, or book online for the walk.

🍴 Sleeping & Eating

Kuranda Rainforest Park
CARAVAN PARK $

(☑07-4093 7316; www.kurandarainforestpark.com.au; 88 Kuranda Heights Rd; powered/unpowered sites $32/30, s/d without bathroom $35/70, cabins $90-110; ☐❋🛜🏊) This well-tended park lives up to its name, with grassy camp sites enveloped in rainforest. The basic but cosy 'backpacker rooms' open onto a tin-roofed timber deck, cabins come with poolside or garden views, and there's an excellent restaurant serving local produce on-site. It's a 10-minute walk from town via a forest trail.

Fairyland House
B&B $

(☑07-4093 9194; www.fairylandhouse.com.au; 13 Fairyland Rd; r per person from $60; ☐) With a vegan raw-food restaurant, tarot readings, yoga classes, abundant fruit garden and wellness workshops, this bush retreat is about as 'Kuranda' as they come. All rooms are airy and open onto the garden. It's a 4km walk to the village; no cooked or animal food products, cigarettes, alcohol, pets or drugs allowed.

⭐Cedar Park Rainforest Resort
RESORT $$

(☑07-4093 7892; www.cedarparkresort.com.au; 250 Cedar Park Rd, Koah; s/d incl breakfast from $165/175; ☐❋🛜) 🌿 Set deep in the bush (a 20-minute drive from Kuranda towards Mareeba), this unusual property is part Euro-castle, part Aussie-bush-retreat. In lieu of TV, visitors goggle at wallabies, peacocks and dozens of native birds; there are hammocks aplenty, creek access, a fireplace, and a gourmet restaurant with well-priced meals and free port.

German Tucker
GERMAN $

(www.germantucker.com; Therwine St; sausages $7.50-9; ☺10am-3pm) Fill up on classic *würste* or try the tasty emu and crocodile sausages at this amusing eatery, where they blast oompah music and splash out steins of top-notch German beer.

Petit Cafe
CRÊPES $

(www.petitcafe.com.au/kuranda; Original Kuranda Rainforest Markets, 7 Therwine St; crêpes $10-17; ☺8am-3pm) Duck out the back of the Kuranda Original Rainforest Markets (p459) for a mouth-watering range of crêpes with savoury or sweet fillings. Winning combinations such as macadamia pesto and feta cheese will entice *le* drool.

Annabel's Pantry
BAKERY $

(15 Therwine St; pies $4.50-6.50; ☺10am-3pm) Popular bakery offering around 25 pie varieties, including kangaroo and veggie.

⭐Kuranda Veranda
INTERNATIONAL $$

(www.kurandarainforestpark.com.au; Kuranda Rainforest Park, 88 Kuranda Heights Rd; mains $13-27; ☺5.30-9.30pm Mon, Tue & Thu-Sat, 11.30am-9.30pm Sun; ☑🍴) Hidden away in the foliage at the Kuranda Rainforest Park, this superb restaurant serves up massive portions of steaks, stir-fries and salads. Kids will have fun ticking off the ingredients for their very own 'create-a-tayta' (loaded baked potato) and the build-your-own sundaes. The restaurant has a no-phones rule, so put 'em away and enjoy the sound of real tweets for a change.

ℹ Information

Kuranda Visitor Information Centre (☑07-4093 9311; www.kuranda.org; Centenary Park; ☺10am-4pm) The knowledgeable staff at the unmissable, map-laden visitor centre in Centenary Park are happy to dish out advice.

ℹ Getting There & Away

Kuranda is as much about the journey (from Cairns) as the destination: choose between the **Skyrail Rainforest Cableway** (☑07-4038 5555; www.skyrail.com.au; cnr Cook Hwy & Cairns Western Arterial Rd, Smithfield; adult/child one way from $50/25, return $75/37.50; ☺9am-5.15pm) and the **Kuranda Scenic Railway** (☑07-4036 9333; www.ksr.com.au; adult/child one way from $50/25, return from $76/38), or do both with a combination return ticket (adult/child from $109.50/54.75). Fares to Kuranda from Cairns are $6.70 with Trans North (p454), $16 on the Cairns Cooktown Express (p454) and $5 with John's Kuranda Bus (p454).

Kuranda is a 25km drive up the Kuranda Range from Cairns.

Mareeba

POP 10,181

Mareeba revels in a Wild West atmosphere, with local merchants selling leather saddles, handcrafted bush hats and the oversized belt buckle of your bronco-bustin' dreams; unsurprisingly, it hosts one of Australia's biggest rodeos (www.mareebarodeo.com.au; ⊙ Jul).

Once the heart of the country's main tobacco-growing region, Mareeba has since turned its soil to more wholesome produce, with fruit orchards, coffee plantations and distilleries in abundance. There is also a handful of unusual natural attractions in the region that differ dramatically from those found in the higher-altitude central Tablelands.

Mareeba Tropical Savanna & Wetland Reserve (☑ 07-4093 2514; www.mareeba wetlands.org; adult/child/family $10/5/25; ⊙ 8.30am-4.30pm Apr-Dec) is a wonderful 20-sq-km reserve that includes woodlands, grasslands, swamps and the expansive Clancy's Lagoon, a birdwatchers' nirvana. **Granite Gorge Nature Park** (☑ 07-4093 2259; www.granitegorge.com.au; adult/child $10/3), 12km from Mareeba, occupies an alien landscape of humungous granite boulders, caves, turtle-inhabited swimming holes and wildlife galore.

Campers can use the **rodeo campgrounds** (☑ 07-4092 1654; www.mareebarodeo. com.au; Kerribee Park; powered/unpowered sites for 2 people $18/15) year-round.

Atherton

POP 7287

The largest settlement and unofficial capital of the same-named Tablelands, Atherton is a spirited country town that makes a decent base for exploring the region's highlights.

Many backpackers head up to the Tablelands for year-round fruit-picking work; the **Atherton Visitor Information Centre** (☑ 07-4091 4222; www.itablelands.com.au; cnr Main & Silo Sts; ⊙ 9am-5pm) can help with up-to-date work info.

Thousands of Chinese migrants came to the region in search of gold in the late 1800s. All that's left of Atherton's Chinatown now is corrugated-iron **Hou Wang Miau Temple** (☑ 07-4091 6945; www.hou-wang.org.au; 86 Herberton Rd; adult/child $10/5; ⊙ 11am-4pm Wed-Sun). Admission includes a guided tour.

DON'T MISS

TABLELANDS MARKETS

As is seemingly obligatory for any quaint country region, the tiny towns of the Tablelands host a miscellany of monthly markets. Kuranda's blockbuster bazaars are legendary, but for something a bit more down-home, check out the following:

Malanda Markets (Malanda Showgrounds; ⊙ 7am-noon 3rd Sat of month)

Yungaburra Markets (www.yungaburra markets.com; Gillies Hwy; ⊙ 7.30am-12.30pm 4th Sat of month)

Atherton Undercover Markets (Merriland Hall, Robert St; ⊙ 7am-noon 2nd Sun of month)

Tumoulin Country Markets (63 Grigg St; ⊙ 8am-noon 4th Sun of month)

Crystal Caves (☑ 07-4091 2365; www.cry stalcaves.com.au; 69 Main St; adult/child/family $22.50/10/55; ⊙ 9am-5pm Mon-Fri, to 4pm Sat & Sun; ⊛) is a gaudy mineralogical museum that houses the world's biggest amethyst geode (more than 3m high and weighing 2.7 tonnes).

Millaa Millaa

Evocatively nicknamed the 'Village in the Mist', charming Millaa Millaa is a small and gloriously green dairy community famous for its wonderful waterfalls. Surrounded by rolling farmland dotted with black-and-white cows, it's a picturesque spot to stop for lunch or to spend a few quaint and quiet nights.

There's accommodation at **Millaa Millaa Tourist Park** (☑ 07-4097 2290; www.millaa caravanpark.com.au; cnr Malanda Rd & Lodge Ave; powered/unpowered sites $29/24, cabins $65, with bathroom $75-110; P ⊛ ⊛ ⊛ ⊛) and the **Millaa Millaa Hotel** (☑ 07-4097 2212; www.millaa millaahotel.info; 15 Main St; s/d $85/95; P ⊛ ⊛). Stop in at the **Falls Teahouse** (☑ 07-4097 2237; www.fallsteahouse.com.au; 6 Theresa Creek Rd; meals from $10; ⊙ 9am-4pm, closed Wed) for a Devonshire tea.

Malanda & Around

Malanda has been a byword for 'milk' in north Queensland ever since 560 cattle made the 16-month overland journey from New

DON'T MISS

TABLELANDS FOR FOODIES

The Atherton Tablelands is a popular place for produce, foodie festivals and other gourmet treats. Some of the best:

Rainforest Bounty (☑07-4076 6544; www.rainforestbounty.com.au; 66 Lindsay Rd, Malanda; courses from $220) Riverside slow-cooking school using local ingredients in its one-day courses.

Cheesemaking & More (☑07-4095 2097; www.cheesemakingandmore.com.au; Quinlan Rd, Lake Eacham) Twice-monthly, two-day cheesemaking classes, and one-day courses on bread and butter making and hard cheese.

Gallo Dairyland (☑07-4095 2388; www.gallodairyland.com.au; Atherton-Malanda Rd; ⊙9.30am-4.30pm; ⓦ) Working farm outside Atherton with cheese factory and handmade chocolates.

Honey House (www.honeyhousekuranda.com; 7 Therwine St; ⊙9am-3pm; ⓦ) Kuranda institution with high-quality raw local honeys, hives and a resident beekeeper.

Tastes of the Tablelands (www.tastesofthetablelands.com; ⊙Oct) One-day festival showcasing the produce of the Tablelands with paddock-to-plate exhibitions, demonstrations and feasts.

Mt Uncle Distillery (☑07-4086 8008; www.mtuncle.com; 1819 Chewko Rd, Walkamin; ⊙10am-4.30pm; ⓦ) Whiskies, seasonal liqueurs and spirits distilled from local bananas, coffee, mulberries and lemons.

South Wales in 1908. There's still a working dairy here, at the **Malanda Dairy Centre** (☑07-4095 1234; www.malandadairycentre.com; 8 James St; ⊙9am-3pm Wed-Sun) **FREE**, which has a kid-friendly museum highlighting the region's bovine history.

Rainforest-shrouded Malanda and its surrounds – including the other-worldly Mt Hypipamee crater – are also home to shy, rare Lumholtz's tree-kangaroos; be sure to bring a low-wattage torch to enjoy an evening of spotlighting.

Spot a platypus or fish for barramundi at the **Australian Platypus Park & Tarzali Lakes Aquaculture Centre** (☑07-4097 2713; www.tarzalilakes.com; Millaa Millaa-Malanda Rd, Tarzali; ⊙10am-4pm; ⓦ).

Malanda Falls Visitor Centre (☑07-4096 6957; www.malandafalls.com; 132 Malanda-Atherton Rd; ⊙9.30am-4.30pm) has thoughtful displays and guided rainforest walks.

Yungaburra

Wee, winsome Yungaburra ticks every box on the country-cute checklist; within one lap of its tree-lined streets, you'll find 19 heritage-listed sites, a welcoming 1910 pub populated by local larrikins, boho-boutiques and cafes, and a dedicated platypus-watching platform. Its proximity to Lake Tinaroo and

some of the region's top natural attractions makes Yungaburra a contender for best base on the Tablelands.

The sacred, 500-year-old **Curtain Fig tree** (Fig Tree Rd, East Barron), signposted 3km out of town, is a must-see for its gigantic, other-worldly aerial roots that hang down to create an enormous 'curtain'. If you're very quiet, you might catch a glimpse of a timid monotreme at the **platypus-viewing platform** (Gillies Hwy) on Peterson Creek.

Explore the wilds around Yungaburra with **Alan's Wildlife Tours** (☑07-4095 3784; www.alanswildlifetours.com.au; day tours $90-500, multiday tours from $1790), led by a passionate local naturalist.

Tablelands Folk Festival (www.tablelands folkfestival.org.au; ⊙Oct) is a fabulous community event held in Yungaburra and neighbouring Herberton featuring music, workshops, performances and a market.

🛏 Sleeping & Eating

★**On the Wallaby**   HOSTEL **$**
(☑07-4095 2031; www.onthewallaby.com; 34 Eacham Rd; sites per person $15, dm/d with shared bathroom $25/60; 🛜) This cosy hostel features handmade timber furniture and mosaics, spotless rooms and no TV! Nature-based tours ($40) include night canoeing; tour packages and transfers are

available from Cairns. Cook for yourself in the communal kitchen, or indulge in the nightly barbecue ($12).

★**Yungaburra Hotel** PUB FOOD **$$**
(Lake Eacham Hotel; ☑07-4095 3515; www.yungaburrahotel.com.au; 6-8 Kehoe Pl; mains from $23; ⊙restaurant 11am-8pm, pub to 11pm) This wonderful, welcoming, original-timber country pub ranks as one of the best in the state, let alone on the Tablelands. It often hosts live jams and bands; even if there's nothing on, it's an ideal place to sink a schooner, meet the locals and soak up the old-school atmosphere. The restaurant does huge, wholesome meals.

ⓘ Information

Yungaburra Information Centre (☑07-4095 2416; www.yungaburra.com; Maud Kehoe Park; ⊙9am-5pm Mon-Sat, 10am-4pm Sun) The utterly delightful volunteers at this immaculate centre can help recommend accommodation, provide info on walks and tours and generally yarn about all things Yungaburra.

Lake Tinaroo

Lake Tinaroo, also known as Tinaroo Dam, was allegedly named when a prospector stumbled across a deposit of alluvial tin and, in a fit of excitement, shouted 'Tin! Hurroo!' The excitement hasn't died down since, with locals fleeing the swelter of the coast for boating, waterskiing and shore-line lolling. **Barramundi fishing** (☑0438 012 775; www.tinaroobarra.com; full-/half-day fishing $600/350) is permitted year-round, though if you're not joining a charter, you'll need to pick up a permit from local businesses.

The 28km Danbulla Forest Drive winds its way through rainforest and softwood plantations along the north side of the lake. The unsealed but well-maintained road passes the pretty Lake Euramoo and the boardwalk-encircled Cathedral Fig, a gigantic 500-year-old strangler fig similar to the Curtain Fig in nearby Yungaburra; it's also accessible via a signposted road off the Gillies Hwy.

There are five Queensland Parks **camping grounds** (☑13 74 68; www.npsr.qld.gov.au/parks/danbulla; camping permits per person/family $6.15/24.60) in the Danbulla State Forest. All have water, barbecues and toilets; advance bookings are essential.

Lake Tinaroo Holiday Park (☑07-4095 8232; www.laketinarooholidaypark.com.au; 3 Tinaroo Falls Dam Rd, Tinaroo Falls; powered/unpowered sites $37/27, cabins from $90; Ⓟ❄️🛜🏊) is a modern, well-equipped and shady camping ground with tinnies, canoes and kayaks for rent.

Crater Lakes National Park

Part of the Wet Tropics World Heritage Area, the two mirrorlike, rainforest-fringed croc-free volcanic crater lakes of Lake Eacham and Lake Barrine are popular for swimming.

There's info at the **Rainforest Display Centre** (McLeish Rd, Lake Eacham; ⊙9am-1pm Mon, Wed & Fri).

Spot water dragons and tortoises or simply relax and soak up the views on a 45-minute **cruise** (www.lakebarrine.com.au/cruises; adult/child/family $18/8/40; ⊙9.30am, 11.30am & 1.30pm) around Lake Barrine; book and board at the excellent **Lake Barrine Teahouse** (☑07-4095 3847; www.lakebarrine.com.au; Gillies Hwy; mains from $8.50; ⊙9am-3pm).

The pretty **Lake Eacham Tourist Park** (☑07-4095 3730; www.lakeeachamtouristpark.com; Lakes Dr; powered/unpowered sites $27/22, cabins $110-130; 📶🛜), 1km down from Lake Eacham, has shady sites, cosy cabins, a general store and a cafe.

PORT DOUGLAS

POP 3205

From its early days as a fishing village, Port Douglas has grown into a sophisticated and upmarket resort town that's quite a contrast to Cairns' hectic tourist scene. The outer Great Barrier Reef is less than an hour offshore, the Daintree Rainforest is practically in the backyard, and there are more resorts than you can poke a snorkel at: a growing number of flashpackers, cashed-up couples and fiscally flush families choose Port Douglas as their Far North base.

Apart from easy access to the reef and daily sunset cruises on the inlet, the town's main attraction is Four Mile Beach (p465), a broad strip of palm-fringed, white sand that begins at the eastern end of Macrossan St, the main drag for shopping, wining and dining. On the western end of Macrossan you'll find the picturesque Dickson Inlet and Reef Marina, where the rich and famous park their aquatic toys.

Port Douglas

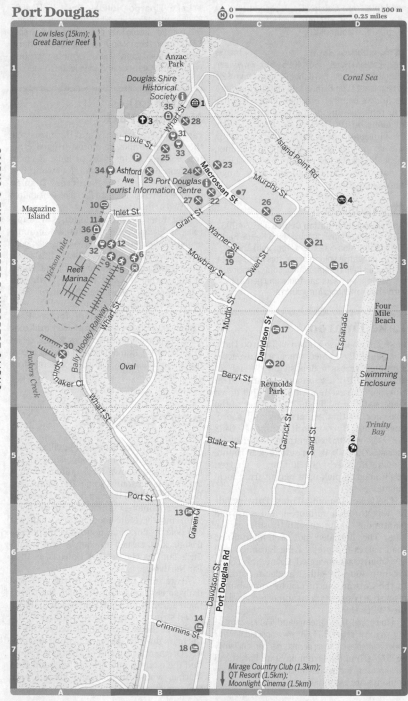

Port Douglas

◉ Sights

Four Mile Beach   BEACH
Fringed by lazy palms, this broad stretch of squeaky sand reaches as far as you can squint. There's a patrolled swimming area in front of the surf life-saving club (with a stinger net in summer) and sun loungers available for hire.

★**Wildlife Habitat Port Douglas**   ZOO
(☑07-4099 3235; www.wildlifehabitat.com.au; Port Douglas Rd; adult/child/family $34/17/85; ☺8am-5pm) This sanctuary endeavours to keep and showcase native animals in enclosures that mimic their natural environment, while allowing you to get up close to koalas, kangaroos, crocs, cassowaries and more. Tickets are valid for three days. For an extra special experience book for **Breakfast with the Birds** (adult/child/family breakfast incl admission $53/26.50/132.50; ☺8-10.30am) or **Lunch with the Lorikeets** (adult/child incl admission $56/28; ☺noon-2pm). It's 5km from town ($5 by shuttle bus).

Trinity Bay Lookout   VIEWPOINT
(Island Point Rd) Head up to Flagstaff Hill for absolutely sensational views over Four Mile Beach and the Coral Sea. Drive or walk up via Wharf St, or there's a walking path leading up from the north end of Four Mile Beach.

Court House Museum   MUSEUM
(☑07-4098 1284; www.douglashistory.org.au; Wharf St; adult/child $2/free; ☺10am-1pm Tue, Thu, Sat & Sun) The 1879 Court House contains historical exhibits, including the story of Ellen Thompson, who was tried for murder in 1887 and the only woman ever hanged in Queensland.

St Mary's by the Sea   CHURCH
(☑0418 456 880; 6 Dixie St) FREE Worth a little peek inside (when it's not overflowing with wedding parties), this quaint, non-denominational, white timber church was built in 1911.

✦ Activities

Port Douglas is best known for its smorgasbord of activities and tours, both on water and land. For golfers the **Mirage Country Club** (☑07-4099 5537; www.miragecountryclub.com.au; 9/18 holes $55/85) and **Palmer Sea Reef** (☑07-4087 2222; www.palmergolf.com.au; 9/18 holes with cart $85/145) are two of north Queensland's top resort courses.

Several companies offer PADI open-water certification as well as advanced dive certificates, including **Blue Dive** (☑0427 983 907; www.bluedive.com.au; 32 Macrossan St; reef intro diving courses from $300). For one-on-one instruction, learn with **Tech Dive Academy** (☑0422 016 517; www.tech-dive-academy.com; 4-day open-water courses from $1290).

WORTH A TRIP

CHILLAGOE

This charismatic former gold-rush town will fulfil your wildest, most romantic outback dreams. With a raw, unhurried quality, it's at the centre of an area that has impressive limestone caves, indigenous rock-art sites and the creepy-cool ruins of an early 20th-century **smelting plant** (www.nprsr.qld.gov.au/parks/chillagoe-caves). **Chillagoe Observatory** (☏ 07-4094 7155; www.coel.com.au; Hospital Ave; adult/child from 6 years $20/15; ☺ 7.30pm Easter-Oct) offers the chance to scan the clear outback skies through two huge telescopes.

Stop in at the **Hub** (www.qwe.com.au/chillagoe/the_hub.html; Queen St; ☺ 8am-5pm Mon-Fri, to 3pm Sat & Sun) for help with finding some of Chillagoe's more hidden highlights. The **Chillagoe–Mungana Caves National Park** (www.nprsr.qld.gov.au/parks/chillagoe-caves; 1-cave/2-cave/3-cave tours $26.30/41.75/52.45) website has information on walking tracks in the area.

Chillagoe's big annual events are the **rodeo** (www.chillagoerodeo.com.au; ☺ May) and **Great Wheelbarrow Race** (www.greatwheelbarrowrace.com; ☺ May).

★ **Wind Swell**   WATER SPORTS
(☏ 0427 498 042; www.windswell.com.au; Barrier St; lessons from $50) Kitesurfing and stand-up paddleboarding for everyone from beginners to high-flyers. Kitesurfing lessons and paddleboarding tours from the beach start at $50, but there are also plenty of advanced options. Find them in action at the southern end of Four Mile Beach (p465).

Port Douglas Yacht Club   BOATING
(☏ 07-4099 4386; www.portdouglasyachtclub. com.au; 1 Spinnaker Close; ☺ from 4pm Wed) Free sailing with club members every Wednesday afternoon: sign on from 4pm. Those chosen to go sailing are expected to stay for dinner and drinks in the club afterwards.

Aquarius Sunset Sailing   CRUISE
(☏ 07-4099 6999; www.tropicaljourneys.com; adult/child $60/50; ☺ cruises depart 4.45pm) Twilight sailing is practically de rigueur in Port Douglas. This 1½-hour catamaran cruise includes canapés, and BYO alcohol is allowed.

Ballyhooley Steam Railway   RAIL
(☏ 07-4099 1839; www.ballyhooley.com.au; 44 Wharf St; adult/child day pass $12/6; ☺ Sun; ⊞) Kids will get a kick out of this cute miniature steam train. Every Sunday (and some public holidays), it runs from the little station at Reef Marina to St Crispins Station four times between 10am and 4pm. A round trip takes about one hour; discounts are available for shorter sections.

Port Douglas Boat Hire   BOATING
(☏ 07-4099 6277; www.pdboathire.com.au; Berth C1, Reef Marina; rentals per hour $45; ☺ 8.30am-

5.30pm) Rents canopied, family friendly pontoon boats that can carry up to six people. An excellent way to explore the calm inland estuaries or go fishing.

☞ Tours

The outer reef is closer to Port Douglas than it is to Cairns, and the unrelenting surge of visitors has had a similar impact on its condition here. You will still see colourful corals and marine life, but it is patchy in parts.

Most day tours depart from Reef Marina. Tour prices usually include reef tax, snorkelling, transfers from your accommodation, lunch and refreshments.

★ **Quicksilver**   CRUISE
(☏ 07-4087 2100; www.quicksilver-cruises.com; Reef Marina; adult/child/family $238/119/535) Major operator with fast cruises to its own pontoon on Agincourt Reef. Try an 'ocean walk' helmet dive ($166) on a submerged platform or snorkelling with a marine biologist (from $60). Also offers 10-minute scenic helicopter flights ($175, minimum two passengers).

Reef Sprinter   SNORKELLING
(☏ 07-4099 6127; www.reefsprinter.com.au; Shop 3, Reef Marina; adult/child from $130/110) The fastest way to the reef, this 2¼-hour snorkelling trip gets to the Low Isles in just 15 minutes for one to 1½ hours in the water. Half-day outer reef trips are also available (from $200).

Poseidon   TOURS
(☏ 07-4087 2100; www.poseidon-cruises.com.au; Reef Marina; adult/child $240/171) This luxury

catamaran specialises in snorkelling trips to the Agincourt Ribbon Reefs, as well as scuba diving (one/two dives an additional $46/66).

Sail Tallarook BOATING
(☑ 07-4099 4070; www.sailtallarook.com.au; adult/child half-day sails $120/100) Morning and afternoon half-day sailing adventures on a historic 30m yacht. Also sunset and full-day sails.

Sailaway SAILING, SNORKELLING
(☑ 07-4099 4200; www.sailawayportdouglas.com; Shop 18, Reef Marina; adult/child $255/178; ⊕) Runs a popular catamaran sailing and snorkelling trip to the Low Isles that's great for families. The afternoon and sunset cruises are for adults only.

★ Tony's Tropical Tours TOURS
(☑ 07-4099 3230; www.tropicaltours.com.au; day tours from $185) This luxury, small-group (eight to 10 passengers) tour operator specialises in trips to out-of-the-way sections of the Mossman Gorge and Daintree Rainforest (adult/child $185/160), and Bloomfield Falls and Cape Trib (adults only $215 – good mobility required). A third tour heads south to the Tablelands. Highly recommended.

Bike N Hike CYCLING
(☑ 0477 774 443; www.bikenhiketours.com.au; tours $120-128) Mountain bike down the aptly named Bump Track on a cross-country bike tour, or take on an action-packed berserk night tour. Also does half-day cycling and hiking trips.

Back Country Bliss Adventures ADVENTURE
(☑ 07-4099 3677; www.backcountryblissadventures.com.au; tours $99-249) Go with the flow as you drift-snorkel down the Mossman River. Also small-group sea-kayaking, hiking and mountain-biking trips.

Lady Douglas BOATING
(☑ 0408 986 127; www.ladydouglas.com.au; Reef Marina, Wharf St; 1½hr cruises adult/child/family $35/15/90; ⊙ cruises 10.30am, 12.30pm, 2.30pm & 4.30pm) Lovely paddle steamer running four daily crocodile-spotting river tours (including a sunset cruise) along the Dickson Inlet.

★☆ Festivals & Events

Port Douglas Carnivale CARNIVAL
(www.carnivale.com.au; ⊙ May) Port Douglas is packed for this 10-day festival, which includes a colourful street parade featuring live music, and lashings of good food and wine.

Portoberfest BEER
(Reef Marina; ⊙ late Oct) The tropical take on Oktoberfest, with live music, German food and, *natürlich,* beer is held at Lure Restaurant in the Reef Marina.

🛏 Sleeping

Although it has a few backpacker resorts and caravan parks, Port Douglas isn't a true budget destination like Cairns – five-star resorts and boutique holiday apartments are more a part of the PD experience. Much of the accommodation is some distance from town off the 5km-long Port Douglas Rd, while most restaurants, bars, pubs and the marina are around the main drag, Macrossan St.

★ Coral Beach Lodge HOSTEL $
(☑ 07-4099 5422; www.coralbeachlodge.com; 1 Craven Close; dm $25-39, d $114; ❄ @ 🛜 ⊛) 🐾 A cut above most backpacker places, this fabulous, chilled-out hostel has well-equipped en-suite dorms (with four or five beds) and double or triple rooms that put many motels in the shade – flat-screen TVs, new bathrooms and comfy beds. Each room has an outdoor area with hammocks, and there's a lovely pool, games room, kitchen and the owners are helpful. Highly recommended.

Dougies HOSTEL $
(☑ 1800 996 200, 07-4099 6200; www.dougies.com.au; 111 Davidson St; tent s/tw $25/40, sites per person $25, dm/d $30/75; ❄ @ 🛜 ⊛) It's easy to hang about Dougies' sprawling grounds in a hammock by day and move to the bar at night. If you can summon the energy, bikes and fishing gear are available for rent and the beach is a 300m walk east. Free pick-up from Cairns on Monday, Wednesday and Saturday.

Port Douglas Backpackers HOSTEL $
(☑ 07-4099 5011; www.portdouglasbackpackers.com.au; 37 Warner St; dm $20-28, d $85; ❄ ⊛) For a cheap bed close to the centre of town, this brand-new place will suit travellers looking for action. There's a lively bar at the front, clean four- to eight-bed dorms, a few private rooms at the rear and a pool in-between. Free transfer to Cairns Tuesday, Thursday and Sunday.

Tropic Breeze Caravan Park   CARAVAN PARK **$**
(☏07-4099 5299; www.tropicbreeze.com.au; 24 Davidson St; powered/unpowered sites $48/37, cabins $120; ❄️🐾) This small park is beautifully located a short walk to the beach and town. Grassy sites, and units with kitchenette but no bathroom.

★**Pink Flamingo**   BOUTIQUE HOTEL **$$**
(☏07-4099 6622; www.pinkflamingo.com.au; 115 Davidson St; d $145-205; ❄️@🛜🏊) Flamboyantly painted rooms, private walled courtyards and a groovy alfresco pool-bar make the Pink Flamingo Port Douglas' hippest gay-friendly digs. With just two studios and 10 villas, it's an intimate stay in a sea of mega-resorts. Heated pool, a gym and bike rental are also on offer.

Mantra Aqueous on Port   APARTMENT **$$**
(☏07-4099 0000; www.mantraaqueousonport. com.au; 3-5 Davidson St; d from $180, 1-/2-bed apt from $280/415; ❄️🛜🏊) You can't beat the location of this unique resort with four individual pools. The pricier ground-floor rooms have swim-up balconies, and all rooms have outdoor Jacuzzi tubs! Studio and one- and two-bedroom apartments are available. Longer stays attract cheaper rates.

Birdsong Port Douglas   B&B **$$**
(☏07-4099 1288; www.portdouglasbnb.com; 6188 Captain Cook Hwy; d from $165; P❄️🛜🏊) Posh open-plan B&B set on sprawling tropical grounds back from the highway 5km from Port Douglas. Induce delusions of grandeur as you ogle the private helipad and gawp at the in-house movie theatre. Rates go down the longer you stay. Custom breakfasts to order and cooking classes available.

Martinique on Macrossan   APARTMENT **$$**
(☏07-4099 6222; www.martinique.com.au; 66 Macrossan St; apt $215; ❄️🛜🏊) Martinique is a terracotta boutique block that contains lovely tiled one-bedroom apartments, each with a small kitchen, a private balcony, colourful accents and plantation shutters. Wonderful hosts and an excellent mainstreet location near the beach seal the deal. The pool has six coves and is supervised by a lavish elephant and dolphin shrine. Good value.

★**Peppers Beach Club**   RESORT **$$$**
(☏1300 737 444; www.peppers.com.au/beachclub; 20-22 Davidson St; spa ste from $309, 1-/2-bedoom ste from $409/566; ❄️🛜🏊) A killer location and an exceptional, enormous, sandy lagoon pool, combined with luxurious, airy apartments with high-end furnishings and amenities, put Peppers right up there with Port Douglas' best. Some rooms have balcony spas, others swim-up decks or full kitchens. Family friendly, but recommended for young romantics.

Thala Beach Nature Reserve   RESORT **$$$**
(☏07-4098 5700; www.thalabeach.com.au; Captain Cook Hwy; d $255-668; ❄️🛜🏊) On a private coastal headland 15km south of Port Douglas, Thala Beach is an upmarket eco-retreat so relaxing that even locals come here to chill for the weekend. Luxurious treehouse-style bungalows are scattered throughout the jungle with easy access to a private stretch of beach, two pools, walking trails and a quality restaurant.

QT Resort   RESORT **$$$**
(☏07-4099 8900; www.qthotelsandresorts.com/port-douglas; 87-109 Port Douglas Rd; d $279-299, villas $329-439; ❄️@🛜🏊) Fresh, fun and funky, this one is aimed at a trendy, twenty- to thirty-something crowd. There's a lagoon pool and swim-up bar, retro-kitsch rooms with free wi-fi, chic staff, and DJs spinning lounge beats in Estilio, the cocktail bar. The breakfast buffet rates as one of the best in Port Douglas.

✗ Eating

Port Douglas' compact centre is awash with sophisticated cafes and restaurants, many with a tropical alfresco setting. All of the resorts also have restaurants.

Self-caterers can stock up on supplies at the large **Coles Supermarket** (11 Macrossan St; ⏰7am-6pm) in the Port Village shopping centre.

Cafe Fresq   CAFE **$**
(☏07-4099 6111; 27 Macrossan St; mains $6-19; ⏰7am-3pm) Cafe Fresq is always busy at breakfast with tables spilling out onto the footpath. Good coffee, gourmet breakfasts, pancakes and lunch items such as soft-shell crab burgers.

Cafe Ziva   FRENCH **$**
(20 Macrossan St; mains $7.50-22; ⏰12.30-10pm; 🛜) Ziva specialises in French-style pancakes with a range of savoury galettes (such as ham and cheese) and sweet crêpes, along with sandwiches, smoothies and fresh juice. The open-fronted cafe is good for people-watching.

Mocka's Pies BAKERY $
(☑ 07-4099 5295; 9 Grant St; pies $4.50-6; ⊙ 8am-4pm) Local institution serving classic Aussie pies with exotic fillings such as crocodile, kangaroo and barramundi.

★ **Yachty** MODERN AUSTRALIAN $$
(☑ 07-4099 4386; www.portdouglasyachtclub. com.au; 1 Spinnaker Close; mains $22-34; ⊙ noon-2.30pm & 5.30-8pm) One of the best-value nights out is the local yacht club, where well-crafted meals, from Moroccan spiced lamb to lobster tail, are served nightly with sunset views over Dickson Inlet. The lunch menu is similar but cheaper.

★ **On the Inlet** SEAFOOD $$
(☑ 07-4099 5255; www.ontheinlet.com.au; 3 Inlet St; mains $26-42; ⊙ noon-11.30pm) You'll feel like you're floating over Dickson Inlet here, with tables spread out along a huge deck from where you can await the 5pm arrival of George, the 250kg groper that comes to feed most days. Take up the bucket-of-prawns-and-a-drink deal ($18 from 3.30pm to 5.30pm) and enjoy watching the reef boats come in.

Seabean TAPAS $$
(☑ 07-4099 5558; www.seabean.com.au; 3/28 Wharf St; tapas $9-15, paella from $35; ⊙ 3-9pm Mon-Thu, noon-9pm Fri-Sun) This cool little tapas bar with bright red stools and attentive staff brings quality Spanish plates and paella to PD.

Little Larder CAFE $$
(☑ 07-4099 6450; Shop 2, 40 Macrossan St; mains $10-19; ⊙ 7.30am-3pm) Brekky until 11.30am then gourmet sandwiches and killer cocktails from noon. Good coffee, or try freshly brewed and super-healthy kombucha tea.

Beach Shack MODERN AUSTRALIAN $$
(☑ 07-4099 1100; www.the-beach-shack.com. au; 29 Barrier St; mains $26-31, pizza $21-26; ⊙ 4-10pm; ☑) It's quite a hike down to the southern end of Four Mile Beach (p465), but this locals' favourite is worth the trip for sublime pizzas, tapas and tasty dishes like macadamia-encrusted barramundi. The lantern-lit garden completes the beach theme with its sandy floor. Saturday is $20 pizza night.

★ **Harrisons Restaurant** MODERN AUSTRALIAN $$$
(☑ 07-4099 4011; www.harrisonsrestaurant. au; 22 Wharf St; lunch $19-26, dinner mains from $38; ⊙ noon-2pm & 5-10pm) Marco Pierre White–trained chef-owner Spencer Patrick whips up culinary gems that stand toe-to-toe with Australia's best. Fresh locally sourced produce is turned into dishes such as smoked duck breast and tamarind beef cheeks. Possibly the only place in Port where diners bother ditching their thongs for shoes.

Sassi Cucina e Bar ITALIAN $$$
(☑ 07-4099 6744; www.sassi.com.au; cnr Wharf & Macrossan Sts; mains $30-48; ⊙ noon-10pm) It's quite a splurge on an authentic Italian feast at this legendary local eatery but it remains a favourite in Port Douglas. The brainchild of owner-chef Tony Sassi, from Abruzzo, the spin on seafood and *spuntini* (small dishes) is world renowned: the balanced flavours of each dish should linger longer than your Four Mile Beach (p465) tan.

2 Fish Restaurant Port Douglas SEAFOOD $$$
(☑ 07-4099 6350; www.2fishrestaurant.com.au; Shop 11, 56 Macrossan St; mains $32-44; ⊙ noon-10pm) In a town where seafood is plentiful, 2 Fish stands out for its upmarket innovative dishes, over a dozen types of fish, from coral trout to red emperor and wild barramundi, along with locally caught oysters, prawns and sea scallops. Between lunch and dinner, tapas plates are available.

★ **Flames of the Forest** MODERN AUSTRALIAN $$$
(☑ 07-4099 3144; www.flamesoftheforest.com.au; Mowbray River Rd; dinner with show, drinks & transfers from $219; ⊙ Tue, Thu & Sat) This unique experience goes way beyond the traditional concept of 'dinner and a show', with diners escorted deep into the rainforest for a truly immersive night of theatre, culture and gourmet cuisine. Transport provided from Port Douglas or Cairns (no self-drive). Bookings essential.

🍷 Drinking & Entertainment

Pubs turn into clubs later in the night and Port has a **Moonlight Cinema** (www.moonlight.com.au/port-douglas; QT Resort, 87-109 Port Douglas Rd; adult/child $17.50/13; ⊙ Thu-Sun Jun-Oct) in season.

★ **Hemingway's** MICROBREWERY
(☑ 07-4099 6663; www.hemingwaysbrewery.com; Reef Marina, 44 Wharf St) Port Douglas deserves its own brewery and Hemingway's makes the most of a fabulous location on the Reef Marina with a broad deck, a long bar and

Dickson Inlet views. There are currently six brews on tap, including Hard Yards dark lager and Pitchfork Betty's pale ale. Naturally, food is available, but this is one for the beer connoisseurs.

Tin Shed
CLUB

(☏07-4099 5553; www.thetinshed-portdouglas.com.au; 7 Ashford Ave; mains $22-29; ⊗10am-10pm) Port Douglas' Combined Services Club (sign in as a guest member) has gone a bit fancy since its days of being dubbed the Tin Shed, but the over-water deck, good-value meals and reasonably priced drinks make this an inviting spot at any time of day.

Iron Bar
PUB

(☏07-4099 4776; www.ironbarportdouglas.com.au; 5 Macrossan St; ⊗11am-3am) Wacky outback meets Wild West decor of corrugated iron and old timber, setting the scene for a wild night out. Don't miss the nightly 8.30pm cane-toad races ($5).

Court House Hotel
PUB

(☏07-4099 5181; cnr Macrossan & Wharf Sts; ⊗9am-late) Elegant and unmissable, the old 'Courty' holds court on the street corner. It's a lively local, with live music on weekends and reasonable meals.

🛍 Shopping

The weekly **Reef Marina Sunset Market** (Reef Marina, Wharf St; ⊗noon-6.30pm Wed) and **Port Douglas Markets** (Anzac Park, Macrossan St; ⊗8am-2pm Sun) are both good for crafts, souvenirs and local produce.

ⓘ Information

There are many tour booking agents in PD masquerading as tourist information offices, but no official tourist office.

Douglas Shire Historical Society (☏07-4098 1284; www.douglashistory.org.au; Wharf St; ⊗10am-1pm Tue, Thu, Sat & Sun) Download do-it-yourself historical walks through Port Douglas, Mossman and Daintree, or chat with a local at the on-site Court House Museum (p465).

Port Douglas Tourist Information Centre (☏07-4099 5599; www.infoportdouglas.com.au; 23 Macrossan St; ⊗8am-6.30pm) Not a government tourist office, but a reliable private booking agency; pick up brochures here and book tours.

Post Office (☏07-4099 5210; 5 Owen St; ⊗8.30am-5pm Mon-Fri, 9am-noon Sat)

ⓘ Getting There & Away

Port Douglas Bus (☏070-4099 5665; www.portdouglasbus.com.au) and **Sun Palm** (☏07-4087 2900; www.sunpalmtransport.com.au; adult/child $35/17.50) operate daily between Port Douglas, Cairns and the airport.

Trans North (☏07-4095 8644; www.transnorthbus.com.au) picks up in Port Douglas on the coastal drive between Cairns and Cooktown.

ⓘ Getting Around

Hire bikes at the **Bicycle Centre** (☏07-4099 5799; www.portdouglasbikehire.com.au; 3 Warner St; half-/full-day from $16/20; ⊗8am-5pm).

Minibuses, such as those run by **Coral Reef Coaches** (☏07-4098 2800; www.coralreef-coaches.com.au), shuttle between town and the highway for around $5.

Major car-rental chains have branches here, or try **Comet Car Hire** (☏07-4099 6407; www.cometcarhire.com.au; 3/11 Warner St) and keep it local.

MOSSMAN
POP 1733

Surrounded by sugar-cane fields, the workaday town of Mossman, 20km north of Port Douglas, is best known for beautiful Mossman Gorge, part of Daintree National Park. The town itself is worth a stop to get a feel for a Far North Queensland working community and to stock up if you're heading further north.

◉ Sights & Activities

★ Mossman Gorge
GORGE

(www.mossmangorge.com.au) In the southeast corner of Daintree National Park, 5km west of Mossman town, Mossman Gorge forms part of the traditional lands of the Kuku Yalanji people. The gorge is a boulder-strewn valley where sparkling water washes over ancient rocks. It's 3km by road from the **visitor centre** (☏07-4099 7000; www.mossmangorge.com.au; ⊗8am-6pm) to a viewpoint and refreshing swimming hole – take care as the currents can be swift. You can walk the 3km but visitors are encouraged to take the **shuttle** (adult/child return $9.10/4.55, every 15 minutes).

There are several kilometres of walking trails on boardwalks and a picnic area at the gorge, but no camping.

★ **Kuku-Yalanji**
Dreamtime Walks   OUTDOORS
(adult/child $62/31; ⊙10am, 11am, noon, 1pm & 3pm) These unforgettable Indigenous-guided walks of Mossman Gorge last 1½ hours and include a smoking ceremony, bush tea and damper. Book through the Mossman Gorge Centre.

🛏 Sleeping & Eating

Mossman Motel Holiday Villas   VILLA $$
(☑07-4098 1299; www.mossmanmotel.com.au; 1-9 Alchera Dr; villas $140-200; P🅿️❄️@🛜💺) These great-value, spacious villas occupy lovely landscaped grounds complete with rock waterfall and pool.

★ **Silky Oaks Lodge**   RESORT $$$
(☑07-4098 1666; www.silkyoakslodge.com.au; Finlayvale Rd; treehouses $440-698; ste $898-998; ❄️@🛜💺) This international eco-resort on the Mossman River woos honeymooners and stressed-out execs with amazing architecturally designed treehouses, riverside lodge suites, luxury hammocks, rejuvenation treatments and polished-timber interiors and private spa baths. Activities include tennis courts, gym, yoga classes and canoeing. Its stunning **Treehouse Restaurant & Bar** (☑07-4098 1666; Finlayvale Rd; mains $36-50; ⊙7-10am, noon-2.30pm & 6-8.30pm) is open to interlopers with advance reservation.

THE DAINTREE

The Daintree represents many things: Unesco World Heritage–listed **rainforest** (www.daintreerainforest.com), a river, a reef, laid-back villages and the home of its traditional custodians, the Kuku Yalanji people. It encompasses the coastal lowland area between the Daintree and Bloomfield Rivers, where the rainforest tumbles right down to the coast. It's a fragile, ancient ecosystem, once threatened by logging, but now protected as a national park.

Part of the Wet Tropics World Heritage Area, the spectacular region from the Daintree River north to Cape Tribulation features ancient rainforest, sandy beaches and rugged mountains. North of the Daintree River, electricity is supplied by generators or, increasingly, solar power. Shops and services are limited, and mobile-phone reception is patchy at best. The **Daintree River Ferry** (www.douglas.qld.gov.au/community/daintree-ferry; car one-way/return $14/26, motorcycle $5/10, pedestrian & bicycle $1/2; ⊙6am-midnight) carries wanderers and their wheels across the river every 15 minutes or so.

Daintree Village

For wildlife lovers and birdwatchers, it's well worth taking the 20km each-way detour from the Mossman-Daintree Rd to tiny Daintree village, set on a plateau of farmland on the Upper Daintree River. Croc-spotting cruises are the main event. Try long-running **Crocodile Express** (☑07-4098 6120; www.crocodileexpress.com; 1hr cruises adult/child/family $28/14/65; ⊙cruises 8.30am); **Daintree River Wild Watch** (☑0447 734 933; www.daintreeriverwildwatch.com.au; 2hr cruises adult/child $60/35), which has informative sunrise birdwatching cruises and sunset photography

---

CONSERVATION, CONTROVERSY & CONTROL OF THE DAINTREE

The greater Daintree Rainforest is protected as part of Daintree National Park, but this protection is not without controversy. In 1983, despite conservationist blockades, what's now the Bloomfield Track was bulldozed through lowland rainforest from Cape Tribulation to the Bloomfield River. Ensuing publicity led to the federal government nominating Queensland's wet tropical rainforests for World Heritage listing, generating state government and timber industry opposition. In 1988 the area was inscribed on the World Heritage List and commercial logging here was banned.

Unesco World Heritage listing (www.whc.unesco.org) doesn't affect ownership rights or control. Since the 1990s the Queensland government and conservation agencies have attempted to buy back and rehabilitate freehold properties in the area, adding them to the Daintree National Park. Sealing the road to Cape Tribulation in 2002 triggered the buy back of even more land, which, coupled with development controls, now bears the fruits of forest regeneration. Check out **Rainforest Rescue** (www.rainforestrescue.org.au) for more information.

nature cruises; or **Daintree River Cruise Centre** (📞07-4098 6115; www.daintreeriver cruisecentre.com.au; 2914 Mossman-Daintree Rd; adult/child $28/14; ⏰9.30am-4pm).

The boutique 'banyans' (treehouses) of **Daintree Eco Lodge & Spa** (📞07-4777 7377; www.daintree-ecolodge.com.au; 3189 Mossman-Daintree Rd; treehouses $325-425; ✳@🔊🏊) 🍴 sit high in the rainforest a few kilometres south of the village. Nonguests are also welcome at its superb **Julaymba Restaurant** (📞07-4098 6100; www.daintree-ecolodge.com.au; 3189 Mossman-Daintree Rd; mains $28-32; ⏰dinner from 4.30pm), where the menu makes expert use of local produce.

In the village, **Big Barramundi Garden** (📞07-4098 6186; www.bigbarra.daintree.info; 12 Stewart St; mains $18-22, burgers from $9; ⏰10am-4pm) serves exotic burgers (barra, crocodile and kangaroo) and smoothies or fruit juices (black sapote, pawpaw) as well as Devonshire teas.

Cow Bay & Around

Tiny Cow Bay is the first community you reach after the Daintree ferry crossing. On the steep, winding road between Cape Kimberley and Cow Bay, the **Walu Wugirriga Lookout** (Alexandra Range Lookout) offers sweeping views beyond the Daintree River inlet; it's especially breathtaking at sunset.

The white-sand Cow Bay Beach, at the end of Buchanan Creek Rd, rivals any coastal paradise.

The award-winning **Daintree Discovery Centre** (📞07-4098 9171; www.discoverthedaintree.com; Tulip Oak Rd; adult/child/family $32/16/78; ⏰8.30am-5pm) features an aerial walkway leading you high into the forest canopy. A theatre screens films on cassowaries, crocodiles, conservation and climate change.

Get closer to nature on a boat trip with **Cape Tribulation Wilderness Cruises** (📞0457 731 000; www.capetribcruises.com; Cape Tribulation Rd; adult/child from $30/22) or a walking tour with **Cooper Creek Wilderness** (📞07-4098 9126; www.coopercreek.com.au; 2333 Cape Tribulation Rd; guided walks $60-170).

🛏 Sleeping & Eating

⭐**Epiphyte B&B**   B&B $
(📞07-4098 9039; www.rainforestbb.com; 22 Silkwood Rd; s/d/cabins from $80/110/150) This lovingly built, laid-back place is set on a lush

3.5-hectare property. Individually styled rooms are of varying sizes, but all have their own verandah. A spacious, private cabin features a patio, kitchenette and sunken bathroom. Minimum two-night stay.

Lync-Haven Rainforest Retreat   CAMPGROUND $
(📞07-4098 9155; www.lynchaven.com.au; Lot 44, Cape Tribulation Rd; camp sites per person $14, powered sites $32, d from $150; ✳) This family-friendly retreat is set on a 16-hectare property on the main road, about 5km north of Cow Bay, and has walking trails, hand-reared kangaroos, well-grassed sites and comfy en-suite rainforest cabins. The restaurant serves robust steaks, good pasta and fish.

⭐**Heritage Lodge & Spa**   LODGE $$$
(📞07-4098 9321; www.heritagelodge.net.au; Lot 236/R96 Turpentine Rd, Diwan; cabins $330; ✳🔊🏊) The friendly, accommodating owners of this wonderful retreat will do their best to make sure you feel at home. Their cute but comfortable renovated cabins are well spaced and ensconced in rainforest. A highlight is swimming in the crystal-clear waters of their gorgeous croc-free Cooper Creek swimming hole. On-site **dining** (mains $26-37; ⏰12-2pm & 5.30-9pm) and day spa are superb.

Daintree Ice Cream Company   ICE CREAM $
(📞07-4098 9114; www.daintreeicecream.com.au; Lot 100, Cape Tribulation Rd; ice creams $6.50; ⏰11am-5pm) We dare you to drive past this all-natural ice-cream producer with a palette of flavours that changes daily. You might get macadamia, black sapote and wattleseed – they're all delicious.

Cow Bay Hotel   PUB FOOD $$
(📞07-4098 9011; 1480 Cape Tribulation Rd; mains $18-24; ⏰noon-2pm & 6-8pm, bar 10am-10pm) If you're craving a decent counter meal, a coldie and that Aussie country pub atmosphere, the Cow Bay is the only real pub this side of the Daintree River.

Cape Tribulation
POP 330

Cape Trib is at the end of the winding sealed road from the Daintree River and, with its two magnificent beaches, laid-back vibe, rainforest walks and compact village, it's a little slice of paradise.

LIZARD ISLAND

The five islands of the Lizard Island Group are located 33km off the coast about 100km north of Cooktown. Lizard, the main island of the group, has rocky, mountainous terrain, glistening white beaches and spectacular fringing reefs for snorkelling and diving. Most of the island is national park and teeming with wildlife. Sumptuous accommodation and dining epitomise five-star luxury at the ultra-exclusive **Lizard Island Resort** (☎1300 863 248; www.lizardisland.com.au; Anchor Bay; d $1900-2900; ✴@❂✉), decimated by Cyclone Ita in April 2014 and exquisitely rebuilt and refurbished in 2015. There's limited bush camping at the island's **camp site** (☎13 74 68; www.npsr.qld.gov.au/parks/lizard-island/camping.html; Watsons Bay; per adult/family $6.15/24.60) ✐. There are no shops on the island. Book air transfers to/from Cairns through the resort.

Daintree Air Services (☎07-4034 9300; www.daintreeair.com.au; day tours from $740) offers spectacular full-day tours from Cairns including gourmet lunch, snorkelling gear, transfers and a local guide to take you to some of the most magnificent spots in this pristine ecosystem.

Despite the backpacker bars and tour operators (jungle surfing, anyone?), Cape Trib still retains a frontier quality, with road signs alerting drivers to cassowary crossings, and croc warnings making evening beach strolls a little less relaxing. The fact that there's no reliable mobile-phone reception or network internet adds to the remoteness – and freaks a few travellers out!

The rainforest skirts beautiful Myall and Cape Tribulation beaches, which are separated by a knobby cape. The village here marks the end of the sealed road: beyond, the strictly 4WD-only Bloomfield Track continues north to Wujal Wujal.

◉ Sights & Activities

Good access points for Cape Trib and Myall beaches are the signposted Kulki and Dubuji boardwalks, respectively.

Bat House   WILDLIFE RESERVE
(☎07-4098 0063; www.austrop.org.au; Cape Tribulation Rd; $5; ❂10.30am-3.30pm Tue-Sun) A nursery for injured or orphaned fruit bats (flying foxes), run by conservation organisation Austrop.

Mt Sorrow Ridge Walk   WALKING
Mt Sorrow is a demanding day hike for fit walkers. The ridge-walk trail starts about 150m north of the Kulki picnic area car park, just off the Bloomfield Rd. The strenuous walk (7km, five to six hours return, start no later than 10am), offers spectacular views over the rainforest and reef.

⌖ Tours

Most tours offer free pick-ups from local accommodation.

★Ocean Safari   TOURS
(☎07-4098 0006; www.oceansafari.com.au; Cape Tribulation Rd; adult/child/family $139/89/415; ❂8am & noon) Ocean Safari leads small groups (25 people maximum) on morning and afternoon snorkelling cruises to the Great Barrier Reef, just half an hour offshore. Wetsuit hire ($8) available.

Paddle Trek Kayak Tours   KAYAKING
(☎07-4098 1950; www.capetribpaddletrek.com.au; Lot 7, Rykers Rd; half-day guided trips $75-85) Guided sea-kayaking trips (morning/afternoon 2½/3½ hours) depart from Cape Trib Beach House (p475).

Mason's Tours   WALKING, DRIVING
(☎07-4098 0070; www.masonstours.com.au; Mason's Store, Cape Tribulation Rd) Long-timer Lawrence Mason conducts enlightening rainforest walks (groups of up to five people two hours/half day $300/500), including a night walk; 4WD tours up the Bloomfield Track to Cooktown are also available (groups up to five people half/full day $800/1250).

Jungle Surfing Canopy Tours   OUTDOORS
(☎07-4098 0043; www.junglesurfing.com.au; ziplines $95, night walks $45, combo $130; ❂7.45am-3.30pm, night walks 7.30pm) Get right up into the rainforest on an exhilarating two-hour flying-fox (zipline) surf

Cape Tribulation Area

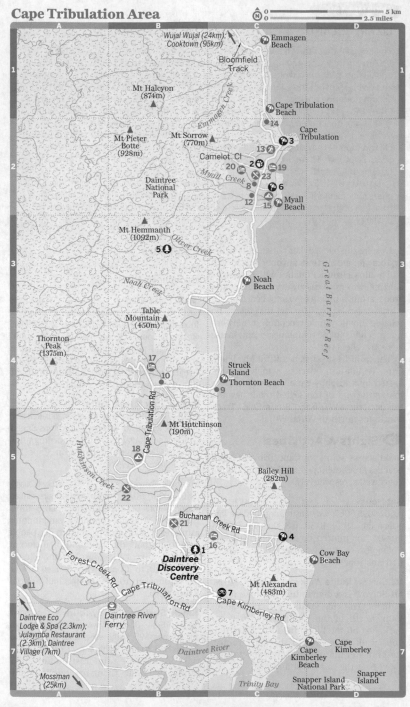

Cape Tribulation Area

through the canopy. Guided night walks follow biologist-guides who shed light on the dark jungle. Rates include pick-up from Cape Trib accommodation (self-drive not permitted).

D'Arcy of the Daintree DRIVING
(☑0402 849 249; www.darcyofdaintree.com. au; 116 Palm Rd, Diwan; tours adult/child from $146/108) Local Mike D'Arcy offers entertaining small-group 4WD trips up the Bloomfield Track to Wujal Wujal Falls (half day) and as far as Cooktown (full day).

Cape Trib Horse Rides HORSE RIDING
(☑07-4098 0043; www.capetribhorserides.com. au; rides per person from $99; ☉8am & 2.30pm) Leisurely morning and afternoon rides along the beach and into the forest.

🍴 Sleeping & Eating

Restaurants at Cape Trib's resorts are all open to nonguests. There's a **supermarket** (☑07-4098 0015; Cape Tribulation Rd; ☉8am-6pm) stocking basic supplies for self-caterers.

★ **Cape Trib Beach House** HOSTEL, RESORT $
(☑07-4098 0030; www.capetribbeach.com. au; 152 Rykers Rd; dm $29, cabins $150-180; ❄@☎️☎) The Beach House is everything that's great about Cape Trib – a secluded patch of rainforest facing a pristine beach and a friendly vibe that welcomes backpackers, couples and families. Clean dorms and romantic almost-beachfront cabins make the most of the location. The open-deck licensed **restaurant** (mains $18-30) and bar is so good many locals eat and drink here. HI affiliated.

Cape Tribulation Camping CAMPGROUND $
(☑07-4098 0077; www.capetribcamping.com.au; Lot 11, Cape Tribulation Rd; adult/child powered sites $20/10, unpowered sites $15/10) Myall Beach is just steps away from this lovely laid-back camping ground. Grassy sites are reasonably well spaced, facilities are good (unless you want a pool) and the Sand Bar is a sociable verandah restaurant serving Cape Trib's best wood-fired pizzas.

PK's Jungle Village HOSTEL $
(☑07-4098 0040; www.pksjunglevillage.com; Cape Tribulation Rd; unpowered sites per person $15, dm $25-32, cabin d $70-125; ❄@☎️☎) With the giant **Jungle Bar** (mains $11-25; ☉7.30am-10pm) restaurant-pool area, a boardwalk to Myall Beach and a range of budget accommodation, PK's has long been a favourite with backpackers. Camp sites and dorms are a little cramped but the place is well-maintained and sociable.

Rainforest Hideaway B&B $
(☑07-4098 0108; www.rainforesthideaway.com; 19 Camelot Close; d $135-149) 🍃 This colourful B&B, consisting of one room in the main house and a separate cabin, was single-handedly built by its owner, artist and sculptor 'Dutch Rob' – even the furniture and beds are handmade. A sculpture trail winds through the property.

★Whet   AUSTRALIAN $$
(☎07-4098 0007; www.whet.net.au; 1 Cape
Tribulation Rd; mains $16.50-33; ⊘11am-4pm &
6-8.30pm) Whet is regarded as Cape Trib's
most sophisticated place to eat, with a
loungy cocktail-bar feel and romantic, can-
dlelit, alfresco dining. Tempura wild barra-
mundi and house chicken-curry grace the
menu; all lunch dishes are under $20. You'll
often find locals at the bar.

★Mason's Store & Cafe   CAFE $$
(☎07-4098 0016; 3781 Cape Tribulation Rd; mains
$9-18, tasting plates from $29; ⊘10am-4pm)
Everyone calls into Mason's for tourist info,
the liquor store, or to dine out on exotic
meats. Pride of place on the menu at this
laid-back alfresco cafe goes to the croc burger, but you can also try camel, emu and kangaroo in burgers or tasting plates. A short
walk away is a crystal-clear, croc-free swimming hole ($1).

ℹ Information

Mason's Store (☎07-4098 0070; Cape
Tribulation Rd; ⊘8am-6pm) The best place
for regional info including Bloomfield Track
conditions.

Understand
East Coast
Australia

East Coast Australia Today

When most people think 'Australia', the east coast is what springs to mind: big cities, photogenic beaches, coral reefs and rolling surf. But in reality most of Australia – the 'outback' – is a vast desert. Turning its back on the sun-baked interior, the east coast is a celebration of life on the edge – a long, fertile strip of land where most Aussies live, work and play. In Australia, the east coast is most definitely where it's at.

Best on Film

Australia (Baz Luhrmann; 2008) Sweeping Aussie epic shot in NSW and Queensland.

Mad Max: Fury Road (George Miller; 2015) No Mel Gibson, but the fourth 'Mad Max' is a postapocalyptic stunner. Partly filmed in Sydney.

Dead Calm (Phillip Noyce; 1989) Yacht-bound Nicole Kidman gets nervous on the Great Barrier Reef.

Picnic at Hanging Rock (Peter Weir; 1975) Schoolgirls go missing in the disquieting Victorian landscape.

Two Hands (Gregor Jordan; 1999) Vicious humour in Sydney's criminal underworld.

Best in Print

The Bodysurfers (Robert Drewe; 1983) Sexy tales from Sydney's sandy suburbia.

He Died with a Felafel in his Hand (John Birmingham; 1994) Grungy share-house life in Brisbane and beyond.

The Secret River (Kate Grenville; 2005) Story of 19th-century convict life around Sydney.

Johnno (David Malouf; 1975) A coming-of-age tale set in 1940s Brisbane.

Mango Country (John Van Tiggelen; 2003) Gonzo, guffaw-inducing take on the far-out folks of Far North Queensland.

The Reef in Strife

Climate change remains a hot topic (no pun intended) along the east coast, particularly when it comes to Queensland's biggest tourist attraction, the Great Barrier Reef. In 2016 unusually elevated sea temperatures caused a disastrous 'bleaching' event, where sensitive corals failed to cope with the warmer environment and perished en masse. A second bleaching in 2017 struck at the worst time, before the coral had recovered. Similar bleaching events happened in 1998 and 2002, but never to this extent: over 50% of the reef has been affected, and parts of it may be beyond recovery.

If climate change continues at present rates and such bleaching events become more regular – especially in conjunction with the added threats of wave damage from more frequent cyclones, the continued scourge of the coral-eating crown-of-thorns starfish, and environmentally menacing port-expansion and dredging activities planned along the Queensland coast – some estimates suggest the reef's near-total devastation within the next 50 years. This destruction is unthinkable on many fronts, not least of which are the catastrophic economic consequences: the reef generates an estimated \$4 billion in annual tourism revenue for Australia.

Stability & Desirability

Australia has done comparatively well on the economic front of late. This commodities-powered nation was one of the only Organisation for Economic Co-operation and Development (OECD) nations to avoid recession during the 2008 Global Financial Crisis (GFC). Unemployment was expected to reach 8% to 10% during the GFC but didn't hit 6%. But when the economy in China (one of Australia's key export markets) stalled, the mining boom that kept Australia afloat during the GFC came to a screeching halt. A growing budget deficit now faces the conservative Liberal-National coalition federal government.

Despite these harsh fiscal conditions, Australia remains a hugely desirable destination for immigrants, and the nation boasts one of the world's highest living standards. In the UN's Human Development Index, Australia consistently appears in the world's top five countries for its high levels of education, health care, democratic freedoms, safety and security, and life expectancy. Australians enjoy a high per-capita income, with Melbourne, Sydney and Brisbane regularly topping the charts on 'World's Most Liveable Cities' lists.

Unreal Real Estate

Quality-of-living indexes aside, some Australians remain anxious about the future, particularly with regard to the real-estate sector.

When the GFC bit hard, economists and bankers across the Western world very sensibly said, 'Whoops! We've been lending people money they can't afford to pay back, and they've been blowing it on home loans that are too expensive' – and real estate prices tumbled. But not in Australia. The aforementioned mining boom was in full swing and nobody worried about ridiculous real-estate prices when there was always another chunk of Western Australia waiting to be exhumed and sold to China. Australians just kept on buying pricey houses, driving the market skywards.

Now, with the mining boom over and society having reached a tipping point where the median house price is more than five times the median annual household income, Australian real-estate prices are among the least affordable on the planet. Fears of a property 'bubble' about to burst are rife, but as long as interest rates remain low and the perception endures that Australia is the 'lucky country' and somehow immune to global strife, the national real-estate addiction will be hard to break.

This Sporting Life

Nowhere in Australia are sporting passions so divisive and heartfelt than along the east coast. This is a battleground, where sports fans must choose to align themselves either with the National Rugby League (NRL; www.nrl.com.au), the dominant code in Queensland, New South Wales (NSW) and the Australian Capital Territory (ACT), or the Australian Football League (AFL; www.afl.com.au), the Aussie Rules football comp dominant in Victoria and the rest of Australia. The mutual loathing between fans north and south of the Murray River divide is palpable.

Confusingly for everybody, in the AFL the Sydney Swans have been one of the more successful teams of late, winning the grand final in Melbourne in 2012 and being runner-up in 2014 and 2016. Meanwhile in the NRL, the Melbourne Storm won the 2012 grand final in Sydney and was runnerup in 2016. Strange days indeed...

POPULATION: **19,034,510**

AREA: **2,902,073 SQ KM**

GDP: **AUD$1.26 TRILLION**

UNEMPLOYMENT: **5.1%**

if East Coast Australia were 100 people

60 born in Australia   2 born in New Zealand
4 born in England   2 born in India
4 born in China   28 born elsewhere

belief systems
(% of population)

50 Christian   14 Agnostic   4 Buddhist

4 Muslim   2 Hindu   26 other

population per sq km

AUS   NZ   USA

≈ 3 people

History

Australia is an ancient continent. Rocks here have been dated back beyond the Archaean eon 3.8 billion years ago, and its Indigenous people have been here more than 50,000 years. Given this backdrop, 'history' as we describe it can seem somewhat fleeting...but it sure makes an interesting read!

First Australians

Before the coming of Europeans, culture was the common link for Indigenous peoples across Australia – through the many aspects common to all the Aboriginal nations they were able to interact with each other. In postcolonial Australia it is also the shared history that binds Aboriginal people.Many academics believe Indigenous Australians came here from somewhere else, with scientific evidence placing them on the continent at least 40,000 to 60,000 years ago. Aboriginal people, however, believe they have always inhabited the land.

At the time of European contact the Aboriginal population was grouped into 300 or more different nations, with distinct languages and land boundaries. Most Aboriginal people did not have permanent shelters and moved according to seasonal patterns of animal migration and plant availability. For thousands of years Aboriginal people lived within a complex kinship system that tied them to the natural environment. From the desert to the sea Aboriginal people shaped their lives according to their environments, developing different skills and a wide body of knowledge on their territory.

Intruders Arrive

In April 1770, Aboriginal people standing on a beach in southeastern Australia saw an astonishing spectacle out at sea. It was an English ship, the *Endeavour*, under the command of then-Lieutenant James Cook. His gentleman passengers were English scientists visiting the Pacific to make astronomical observations and to investigate 'new worlds'. As they sailed north along the edge of this new-found land, Cook began drawing the first British chart of Australia's east coast. This map heralded the beginning of conflicts between European settlers and Indigenous peoples.

Before Europeans arrived, Australia contained an estimated 750,000 Indigenous people, scattered among 300 or more Aboriginal nations. Among them, they spoke at least 300 Indigenous languages and dialects.

TIMELINE	60,000 BC	43,000 BC	3000 BC
	Although the exact start of human habitation in Australia is still uncertain, according to most experts this is when Aboriginal Australians first arrived on the continent.	A group of Indigenous Australians sits down in the Nepean Valley near current-day Sydney and makes some stone tools. Archaeological sites like this have been found across Australia.	The last known large immigration to the continent from Asia occurs. Over 300 languages are spoken among the myriad groups living in Australia.

A few days after that first sighting, Cook led a party of men ashore at a place known to the Aboriginal people as Kurnell. Though the Kurnell Aboriginal people were far from welcoming, the botanists of the *Endeavour* were delighted to discover that the woods were teeming with unfamiliar plants. To celebrate this profusion, Cook renamed the place Botany Bay. As his voyage northward continued, Cook strewed English names the entire length of the coastline. In Queensland, these included Hervey Bay (after an English admiral), Dunk Island (after an English duke), Cape Upstart, the Glass House Mountains and Wide Bay.

One night, in the seas off the great rainforests of the Kuku Yalanji Aboriginal people, in what is now known as Far North Queensland, the Endeavour was inching through the Great Barrier Reef when the crew heard the sound of ripping timbers. They had run aground near a cape which today is a tourist paradise. Cook was in a glowering mood: he named it Cape Tribulation, 'because here began all our troubles'. Seven days later Cook managed to beach the wounded ship in an Aboriginal harbour named Charco (Cook renamed it Endeavour), where his carpenters patched the hull.

Convict Beginnings

Eighteen years later, in 1788, the English were back to stay. They numbered 751 ragtag convicts and children, and around 250 soldiers, officials and their wives. This motley 'First Fleet' was under the command of a humane and diligent naval captain, Arthur Phillip. By a small cove, in the idyllic lands of the Eora people, Phillip established a British penal settlement. He renamed the place after the British Home Secretary, Lord Sydney.

Robert Hughes' bestseller *The Fatal Shore* (1987) depicts convict Australia as a terrifying 'Gulag' where Britain tormented rebels, vagrants and criminals. But other historians point out that powerful men in London saw transportation as a scheme for giving prisoners a new and useful life. Indeed, for many convicts their 'ticket of leave', was a kind of parole that gave them the freedom of the colony and the right to seek work.

However, the convict system could also be savage. Women (who were outnumbered five to one) lived under constant threat of sexual exploitation. Female convicts who offended their gaolers languished in the depressing 'female factories'. Male reoffenders were cruelly flogged, and could be hanged for minor crimes, such as stealing. In 1803 English officers established a second convict settlement at Hobart in Van Diemen's Land (later called Tasmania). Soon male reoffenders filled the grim prison at Port Arthur on the beautiful and wild coast. Others endured the senseless agonies of Norfolk Island in the remote Pacific. At first Sydney and these smaller colonies depended on supplies brought in by ship. Anxious to develop productive farms, the government granted land to soldiers, officers and emancipated convicts. After 30 years of trial and error, their farms began to flourish.

Reading Australian History

➤ *The Fatal Shore*, Robert Hughes (1986)

➤ *History of Queensland*, Raymond Evans (2007)

➤ *Burke's Soldier*, Alan Attwood (2003)

➤ *True History of the Kelly Gang*, Peter Carey (2000)

➤ *Birth of Melbourne*, Tim Flannery (2004)

AD 1607	1770	1776	1788
Spanish explorer Luis Torres manages to sail between Australia and New Guinea and not discover the rather large continent to the south. The strait bears his name today.	English captain James Cook maps Australia's east coast in the scientific ship *Endeavour*. He then runs aground on the Great Barrier Reef near a place he names Cape Tribulation.	The 13 British colonies in the US declare independence, leaving the King George III's government without a place to ship convicts. Authorities turn their attention to the vast Australian continent.	The Eora people of Bunnabi discover they have new neighbours; 11 ships arrive bearing soldiers and convicts, dropping anchor in what the new arrivals call Botany Bay.

On the Land

Each year settlers pushed deeper into the Aboriginal territories in search of pasture and water for their stock. These men became known as squatters (because they 'squatted' on Aboriginal lands) and many held this territory with a gun. In the USA the conflict between settlers and the indigenous people formed the basis for a rich mythology known as 'the Wild West', but in Australia the conflict has largely passed from white memory, so white historians now disagree about the extent of the violence. However, Aboriginal Australians still recount how their waterholes were poisoned and their people massacred. Some of the most bitter struggles occurred in the remote mining districts of central Queensland. In Tasmania the impact of settlement was so devastating that, today, no 'full blood' Tasmanian Aborigines survive; all of the island's Indigenous Australians are of mixed heritage.

On the mainland many of the squatters reached a truce with the defeated Indigenous people. In remote regions it became common for Aboriginal Australians to take low-paid jobs on farms, working on sheep and cattle stations as drovers, rouseabouts, shearers and domestics. Those lucky enough to be working on their traditional lands adapted their cultures to the changing circumstances. This arrangement continued in outback pastoral regions until after WWII.

The handsome blue-and-white Southern Cross flag flown at the Eureka stockade in 1854 has since become a symbol of union movements in Australia.

Gold & Rebellion

Transportation of convicts to eastern Australia ceased in the 1840s. This was just as well: in 1851 prospectors discovered gold in New South Wales (NSW) and central Victoria. The news hit the colonies with the force of a cyclone. From every social class, young men and some adventurous women headed for the diggings. Soon they were caught up in a great rush of prospectors, entertainers, publicans, sly-groggers, prostitutes and quacks from overseas. In Victoria the British governor was alarmed – both by the way the Victorian class system had been thrown into disarray, and by the need to finance law and order on the goldfields. His solution was to compel all miners to buy an expensive monthly licence, in the hope that the lower orders would return to their duties in town.

But the lure of gold was too great. In the reckless excitement of the goldfields, the miners initially endured the thuggish troopers who enforced the government licence. But after three years the easy gold at Ballarat was gone, and miners were toiling in deep, water-sodden shafts. They were now infuriated by a corrupt and brutal system of law that held them in contempt. Under the leadership of a charismatic Irishman named Peter Lalor, they raised the flag of the Southern Cross and swore to defend their rights and liberties. They armed themselves and gathered inside a rough stockade at Eureka, where they waited for the government to make its move.

Written in 1895 by AB 'Banjo' Paterson, 'Waltzing Matilda' is widely regarded as Australia's unofficial national anthem. Some say the song paid homage to striking sheep shearers during the 1890s labour uprisings.

1824	1835	1844–45	1871
The government establishes the brutal penal colony of Moreton Bay, a place of blood, sweat and tears. A second penal colony, Brisbane, follows two years later.	John Batman arranges the 'purchase' of 2500 sq km from Aboriginal Australians of the Dutigalla tribe for flour and trinkets. Melbourne is established on the north bank of the Yarra River.	The first guidebook to Australia is written in the form of a journal by Ludwig Leichhardt. It chronicles his party's exploration from Brisbane almost to Darwin. In 1848 he vanishes without a trace.	Aboriginal stockman Jupiter discovers gold in Queensland and the rush is on. Within 10 years Brisbane has made its fortune from both gold and wool.

In the predawn of Sunday 3 December 1854, a force of troopers attacked the stockade. In 15 terrifying minutes, they slaughtered 30 miners and lost five soldiers. The story of the Eureka stockade is often told as a battle for nationhood and democracy – as if a true nation must be born out of blood – but these killings were tragically unnecessary. The eastern colonies were already in the process of establishing democratic parliaments, with the full support of the British authorities. In the 1880s Lalor himself became Speaker of the Victorian parliament.

The gold rush also attracted boatloads of prospectors from China. The Chinese prospectors endured constant hostility from whites, and were the victims of ugly race riots on the goldfields at Lambing Flat (now called Young) in NSW in 1860–61. Chinese precincts developed in the backstreets of Sydney and Melbourne and, by the 1880s, popular literature indulged in tales of Chinese opium dens, dingy gambling parlours and oriental brothels. Many Chinese, however, went on to establish themselves in business and particularly in market gardening. Today, the busy Chinatowns of Sydney and

BURKE & WILLS

The Great Northern Expedition was an attempt to cross Australia from Melbourne to the Gulf of Carpentaria (on the northern coast of Australia), and was funded by the colonial government. Despite a sad lack of experience, Robert O'Hara Burke was chosen to lead the 19-man expedition with William 'Jack' Wills as his deputy. As 10,000 onlookers cheered them on, the group set off for the 3200km journey from Melbourne in August 1860. They were spectacularly unprepared, bringing with them such ephemera as heavy wooden tables, rockets, flags and a Chinese gong, as well as two years' worth of rations. All in all they brought more than 20 tonnes of supplies, loaded onto 26 camels, 23 horses and six wagons. Overburdened, they moved at a snail's pace, taking nearly two months to cover just 750km (the mail run took about 10 days), and the road was littered with discarded items. They also reached the hottest parts of Australia in the middle of summer. With temperatures soaring above 50°C, the group ran into serious troubles – equipment malfunctions, incessant quarrelling, resignations and dismissal of expedition members.

Growing frustrated, Burke split the group and made a dash for the coast with three others (Wills, Charles Gray and John King) in December. The main group stayed behind, ordered by Burke to wait three months before returning south. Burke calculated he could make it to the coast and back in two months. In fact it took over four months, and when they finally came near the coast, mangrove swamps prevented them from reaching the ocean. They returned to base camp (Gray died along the way), only to discover the group had packed up and headed south just hours earlier. The three then set off for a pastoral settlement near Mt Hopeless. Burke and Wills perished. King was rescued by Aboriginal Australians and nursed back to health. He was the only expedition member to make the full crossing and return alive.

1891	1901	1915	1918
A shearers' strike around Barcaldine, Queensland, establishes a labour legend; the confrontation leads to the birth of the Australian Labor Party.	The Australian colonies federate; a new national parliament meets in Melbourne. The White Australia policy is passed, which bans non-Europeans from immigrating.	In line with Australia's close ties to Britain, Australian and New Zealand Army Corps (the Anzacs) join the Allied invasion of Turkey at Gallipoli. The Anzac legend is born.	The Great War ends. From a country of 4.9 million, 320,000 were sent to war in Europe and almost 20% were killed. Cracks appear in Australian–British relations.

Melbourne, and the ubiquitous Chinese restaurants in country towns, are reminders of Chinese vigour.

Gold and wool brought immense investment and gusto to Melbourne, Sydney and a swath of Queensland. By the 1880s they were stylish modern cities, with gaslights in the streets, railways and that great new invention: the telegraph. In fact, the southern capital became known as 'Marvellous Melbourne', so opulent were its theatres, hotels, galleries and fashions.

Meanwhile, the huge expanses of Queensland were remote from the southern centres of political and business power. It was a tough, raw frontier colony, in which money was made by hard labour – in mines, in the forests and on cattle stations. In the coastal sugar industry, southern investors grew rich on a plantation economy that exploited tough Pacific Island labourers (known as 'Kanakas'), many of whom had been kidnapped.

Nationhood

On 1 January 1901 the six colonies of Australia became a federation of self-governing states – the Commonwealth of Australia. When the bewhiskered members of the new national parliament met in Melbourne, their first aim was to protect the identity and values of a European Australia from an influx of Asians and Pacific Islanders.

Their solution was what became known as the 'White Australia policy'. It was implemented mainly to restrict nonwhite immigration to Australia, but the policy also had a huge impact on Indigenous Australians. Assimilation into the broader society was encouraged by all sectors of government, with the intent to eventually 'fade out' the Aboriginal race. A policy of forcibly removing Aboriginal and Torres Strait Islander children from their families was official from 1909 to 1969, although the practice happened both before and after those years. Although accurate numbers will never be known, it is estimated that around 100,000 Indigenous children – or one in three – were taken from their families.

In 1902 white women won the right to vote in federal elections. In a series of radical innovations, the government introduced a broad social-welfare scheme and protected Australian wage levels with import tariffs. Its mixture of capitalist dynamism and socialist compassion became known as 'the Australian settlement'.

Revered by many as the great Australian novel, Patrick White's *Voss* (1957) was inspired by the story of the Prussian explorer Leichhardt. It's a psychological tale, a love story and an epic journey over the Australian desert.

War & the Great Depression

Living on the edge of this forbidding land, and isolated from the rest of the world, most Australians took comfort from the idea that they were still a part of the British Empire. When war broke out in Europe in 1914, thousands of Australian men rallied to the Empire's call. They had their first taste of death on 25 April 1915, when the Australian and New Zealand Army Corps (the Anzacs) joined British and French troops in an assault on the

1929	1937	1941	1956
The Great Depression: thousands go hungry as the economy crashes. Unemployment peaks at 28% in 1932 – one of the highest rates in the industrialised world (second only to Germany).	Cane toads are released into the wild to control pests damaging Queensland's sugar-cane fields. The action proves disastrous, creating a plague that spreads to other states.	The Japanese bomb Townsville. The war in the Pacific is on. Hundreds of thousands of Australian troops pour out to battlefields worldwide; thousands of American troops pour in and drink a lot of beer.	The summer Olympics are held in Melbourne – the first time the games are held in the southern hemisphere. Australia places third in the medal tally behind the USSR and the USA.

Gallipoli peninsula in Turkey. It was eight months before the British commanders acknowledged that the tactic had failed, but by then 8141 young Australians were dead. Soon the Australian Imperial Force was fighting in the killing fields of Europe. By the time the war ended, 60,000 Australian men had been slaughtered. Ever since, on 25 April, Australians have gathered at war memorials around the country and at Gallipoli for the sad and solemn services of Anzac Day.

Australia careered wildly through the 1920s, continuing to invest in immigration and growth, until the economy collapsed into the abyss of the Great Depression in 1929. Unemployment brought its shame and misery to one in three houses. For those who were wealthy – or who had jobs – the Depression was hardly noticed. In fact, the fall in prices actually meant that the purchasing power of their income was enhanced.

Heroes

In the midst of the hardship, sport brought escape to a nation in love with games and gambling. Champion racehorse Phar Lap won an effortless and graceful victory in the 1930 Melbourne Cup (the race that stops a nation). In 1932 the great horse travelled to the racetracks of America, where he mysteriously died. In Australia the gossips insisted that the horse had been poisoned by envious Americans. And the legend was established of a sporting hero cut down in his prime.

The year 1932 also saw accusations of treachery on the cricket field. The English team, under its aloof captain Douglas Jardine, employed a violent new bowling tactic known as Bodyline. Jardine's aim was to unnerve Australia's star batsman, the devastating Donald Bradman. The bitterness of the tour became part of the Australian legend, and Bradman batted on, achieving the unsurpassed career average of 99.94 runs.

WWII

In 1939, Australian servicemen sailed off to Europe for a new war. Though Japan was menacing, Australians took it for granted that the British navy would keep them safe. In December 1941 Japan bombed the US Fleet at Pearl Harbor. Weeks later the 'impregnable' British naval base in Singapore crumbled, and soon thousands of Australians and other Allied troops were enduring the savagery of Japan's prisoner-of-war camps.

As the Japanese swept through Southeast Asia and into Papua New Guinea, the British announced that they could not spare any resources to defend Australia. But the legendary US commander General Douglas MacArthur saw that Australia was the perfect base for American operations in the Pacific. In a series of savage battles on sea and land, Allied forces gradually turned back the Japanese advance. Importantly, it was the USA, not the British Empire, that came to Australia's aid. The days of the British alliance were numbered.

Best History Encounters

➡ The Rocks Discovery Museum (Sydney)

➡ Museum of Sydney (Sydney)

➡ Melbourne Museum (Melbourne)

➡ Queensland Museum (Brisbane)

➡ National Museum of Australia (Canberra)

The stuffed remains of the famous race horse Phar Lap are on show at the Melbourne Museum. The National Museum of Australia in Canberra has his heart; New Zealand (where he was foaled) has his skeleton.

1962	1969	1970s	1972
Indigenous Australians gain the right to vote in federal elections – but they have to wait until 1967 to receive full citizenship, which happens overwhelmingly in a nationwide referendum.	Setting the political scene in Queensland for the next 21 years, Joh Bjelke-Petersen becomes premier. His political agenda was widely described as 'development at any price'.	Inflation, soaring interest rates and rising unemployment bring the golden postwar days to an end. As house prices skyrocket, home ownership moves out of reach for many.	The Aboriginal Tent Embassy is erected on the lawns of Parliament House in Canberra. Over the next decades it serves as a reminder that Indigenous peoples have been denied sovereignty to their land.

Peace, Prosperity & Multiculturalism

As the war ended, a new slogan rang through the land: 'Populate or Perish!' The Australian government embarked on an ambitious scheme to attract thousands of immigrants. With government assistance, people flocked from Britain and from non-English-speaking countries. They included Greeks, Italians, Slavs, Serbs, Croatians, Dutch, Poles, Turks and Lebanese, among others. These 'new Australians' were expected to assimilate into a suburban stereotype known as 'the Australian way of life'.

This was the great era of the nuclear family in which Australians basked in the prosperity of a 'long boom'. Many migrants found jobs in manufacturing, where companies such as General Motors and Ford operated with generous tariff support. At the same time, there was growing world demand for Australia's primary products: metals, wool, meat and wheat. In time Australia even became a major exporter of rice to Japan.

This era of growth and prosperity was dominated by Robert Menzies, the founder of the modern Liberal Party and Australia's longest-serving prime minister. Menzies had an avuncular charm, but he was also a vigilant opponent of communism. As the Cold War intensified, Australia and New Zealand entered a formal military alliance with the USA – the 1951 Anzus security pact. And when the USA hurled its righteous fury into a civil war in Vietnam, Menzies committed Australian forces to the conflict. The following year Menzies retired, leaving his successors a bitter legacy. The antiwar movement split Australia.

There was a feeling among artists, intellectuals and the young that Menzies' Australia had become a dull, complacent country, more in love with American popular culture and British high arts than with its own talents and stories. Australia, they said, had 'an inferiority complex'. In an atmosphere of youth rebellion and newfound nationalism, Australians began to embrace their own history and culture. The arts blossomed. Universities flourished. A distinctive Australian film industry made iconic movies, mostly funded by government subsidies.

The most accessible version of the Anzac legend is Peter Weir's epic film *Gallipoli* (1981), with a cast that includes a fresh-faced Mel Gibson.

TERRA NULLIUS & MABO

In May 1982 Eddie Mabo led a group of Torres Strait Islanders in a court action to have traditional title to their land on Mer (Murray Island) recognised. Their argument challenged the legal principle of terra nullius (literally, 'land belonging to no one') and demonstrated their unbroken relationship with the land over a period of thousands of years. In June 1992 the High Court found in favour of Mabo and the Torres Strait Islanders, rejecting the principle of terra nullius – this became known as the Mabo decision. The result has had far-reaching implications in Australia ever since, including the introduction of the *Native Title Act* in 1993.

1975	1992	2000	2008
The Great Barrier Reef Marine Park is created. It later becomes a World Heritage Site, which angers Bjelke-Petersen, who intended to explore for oil on the reef.	After 10 years in the courts, the landmark Mabo decision is delivered by the High Court, effectively recognising Indigenous land rights across the country.	Sydney hosts the summer Olympics, which are a triumph of spectacle and goodwill. Aboriginal runner Cathy Freeman lights the flame at the opening ceremony and wins gold in the 400m event.	On behalf of parliament, Prime Minister Kevin Rudd delivers a moving apology to Aboriginal Australians for laws and policies that 'inflicted profound grief, suffering and loss'.

At the same time, increasing numbers of white Australians believed that Aboriginal Australians had endured a great wrong that needed to be put right – and from 1976 until 1992, Aboriginal Australians won major victories in their struggle for land rights. Australia's imports from China and Japan increased, and the White Australia policy became an embarrassment. It was officially abolished in the early 1970s, and Australia became a leader in the campaign against the racist 'apartheid' policies of white South Africa.

By the 1970s more than one million migrants had arrived from non-English-speaking countries, filling Australia with new languages, cultures, foods and ideas. At the same time, China and Japan began to outstrip Europe as Australia's major trading partners. As Asian immigration increased, Vietnamese communities became prominent in Sydney and Melbourne. In both those cities a new spirit of tolerance and diversity known as 'multiculturalism' became a particular source of pride.

New Challenges

In the 1970s the country began dismantling its protectionist scaffolding. New efficiency brought new prosperity. At the same time, wages and working conditions, which were once protected by an independent tribunal, became more vulnerable as egalitarianism gave way to competition. And after two centuries of development, the strain on the environment was starting to show – on water supplies, forests, soils, air quality and the oceans.

Under the conservative John Howard, Australia's second-longest-serving prime minister (1996–2007), the country grew closer than ever to the USA, joining the Americans in their war in Iraq. The government's treatment of asylum seekers, its refusal to acknowledge climate change, its anti-union reforms and the prime minister's seeming lack of empathy with Indigenous Australians dismayed more liberal-minded Australians. But Howard presided over a period of economic growth that emphasised the values of self-reliance and won him continuing support in middle Australia.

In 2007 Howard was defeated by the Labor Party's Kevin Rudd, an ex-diplomat who immediately issued a formal apology to Indigenous Australians for the injustices they had suffered over the past two centuries. Though it promised sweeping reforms in environment and education, the Rudd government found itself faced with a crisis when the world economy crashed in 2008; by June 2010 it had cost Rudd his position. New prime minister Julia Gillard, along with other world leaders, now faced three related challenges: climate change, a diminishing oil supply and a shrinking economy. These difficulties and dwindling party support for Gillard saw her ousted by a resurgent Rudd in 2013. Rudd's Labor subsequently lost the 2013 federal election, handing over the reins to Tony Abbott's right-wing Liberal–National Party coalition. With his own poll numbers slipping, Abbott fell to his Liberal Party colleague Malcolm Turnbull in 2015.

The 2000 Sydney Olympics were credited with being one of the most successful and smooth-running Olympiads ever, particularly for the Australian team, which finished in fourth place with 58 medals (16 gold).

2009	2011	2011	2016 & 2017
A record-breaking heatwave generates the catastrophic 'Black Saturday' bushfires in Victoria. Over 170 people die; property damage totals around $1 billion.	Powerful floods inundate vast areas of Queensland, including Brisbane, killing 35 people and causing billions of dollars of damage. Cyclone Yasi follows weeks later, devastating parts of north Queensland.	The Gold Coast in Queensland is announced as the successful bidder for the 2018 Commonwealth Games. Construction begins on massive infrastructure requirements, including a new tram line.	Two catastrophic 'bleaching' events, caused by warmer-than-usual water temperatures, have a severe impact on the Great Barrier Reef.

Climate Change & the Great Barrier Reef

The Great Barrier Reef (GBR) is one of the world's most diverse coral-reef ecosystems. It is also the world's largest, an archipelagic edifice so vast that it can be viewed from space. But, like coral reefs all around the world, the GBR is facing some big environmental challenges.

The Reef

The reef's ecosystem includes the sea-floor habitats between the reefs, hundreds of continental islands and coral cays, and coastal beaches, headlands and estuaries. The 2900 reefs (ranging from less than 1km to 26km in length) that make up the GBR system support truly astounding biological diversity, with over 1500 species of fish, over 400 species of reef-building coral, and hundreds of species of molluscs (clams, snails, octopuses), echinoderms (sea stars, bêches-de-mer, sea urchins), sponges, worms, crustaceans and seaweed. The GBR is also home to marine mammals (dolphins, whales, dugongs), dozens of species of birds and six of the planet's seven species of sea turtles. The GBR's 900-or-so islands range from ephemeral, unvegetated or sparsely vegetated sand cays to densely forested cays and continental islands.

At the Crossroads

These are tough times in which to be a coral reef. In the last three decades the GBR has endured more severe cyclones than in the whole of the last century, recurrent outbreaks of coral-devouring crown-of-thorns starfish, three major coral-bleaching events caused by unusually hot water temperatures, and record-breaking floods that washed huge volumes of fresh water, sediments, fertilisers and other farm chemicals into

GREAT BARRIER REEF MARINE PARK

Established in 1975, the 360,000-sq-km Great Barrier Reef Marine Park (about the same size as Italy) is one of the best-protected large marine systems on the planet. About 30% of the park is closed and the remainder is open to commercial and recreational fishing. There are a handful of coastal cities along the reef's southern half (notably Cairns, Townsville, Mackay and Gladstone), some with ports to service cattle and sugar export, and mineral export and import. Shipping lanes traverse its length and breadth, and ore carriers, cargo ships and cruise liners must use local marine pilots to reduce the risk of groundings and collisions.

Australia is internationally recognised for its leading management and protection of the Great Barrier Reef – the marine park is inscribed on the World Heritage List and has an envied program of management led by the Great Barrier Reef Marine Park Authority. But still, there is an aura of pessimism across the reef-science world. For comprehensive information and educational tools at all levels, see www.gbrmpa.gov.au and www.coral-watch.org.

the sea, triggering blooms of light-blocking plankton and disrupting the ecological relationships that keep coral reefs vibrant and resilient.

With all this going on, it's no surprise that a bit of web surfing could give the impression that the GBR is suffering more than other reefs around the world. But the plethora of information about risks to the reef simply reflects the amount of research, government investment and national commitment to tackling the challenge rather than pretending that everything is OK. It is an unfortunate reality that damaged reefs are easier to find now than they were 30 years ago, but the GBR is still one of the best places in the world to see coral reefs, especially if you have one of the hundreds of accredited tourism operators show you around. Like every reef around the world, the GBR is in trouble, but in this case scientists, reef managers, coastal residents and even visitors are joining forces to help the reef through the challenges of the century ahead.

Eroding the Foundation

Overshadowing the future of coral reefs is climate change. Global warming is a serious problem for these iconic ecosystems, even though they have evolved in warm water and thrive in clear, shallow seas along the equator and as far north and south as the Tropics of Cancer and Capricorn.

The main building blocks of coral reefs are 'stony' or 'hard' corals, and about 400 of the world's 700-or-so species occur on the GBR. The secret of their success as reef builders – and their Achilles heel in a warming world – is symbiosis between the coral and tiny single-celled plants called zooxanthellae that live within their tissues. Thanks to bright sunlight and warm waters, the zooxanthellae are photosynthetic powerhouses that produce sugars and other carbohydrates needed by the coral (a colony of polyps) to grow its tissues, produce sperm and eggs and build the colony's communal limestone skeletons. These skeletons, occupied by thousands of polyps and capable of growing several metres high and across in many different shapes, are an evolutionary bonanza in that they provide a rigid framework to orient the polyps to best utilise the sunlight and to use their stinging tentacles to catch passing pinhead-sized crustaceans that corals need nutritionally. Over thousands of years, the corals produce the reef framework, lagoon sands, coral beaches and coral islands that are the foundation for the entire coral-reef ecosystem. But now, as temperatures approach levels not seen for thousands of years, these foundations are at risk.

Changing Environments & Coral Bleaching

The idyllic symbiosis between coral and zooxanthellae evolved to perfectly match the environmental conditions of the past. But corals don't like change, and they are currently being hit with rates of change unparalleled for at least 400,000 years.

Bright sunlight and warm waters are required to support coral reefs, but it's a fine line between warm enough and too warm. Around the turn of the last century (1998 and 2002) and again in 2016, spikes in water temperature around the GBR caused the densely packed zooxanthellae to go into metabolic overdrive, producing free radicals and other chemicals that are toxic to the coral host. The corals' response was to expel their zooxanthellae, to rid themselves of the damaging toxins. Water temperatures must return to normal before the small numbers of remaining zooxanthellae start to reproduce and thus reinstate the corals' live-in food factory. But if the heat wave persists for more than a few weeks, the highly stressed corals succumb to disease and die, their skeletons soon becoming carpeted with fine, shaggy algal turfs. This is known as coral bleaching. The 2016 bleaching event was unprecedented and catastrophic, with coral mortality

REEF GEOLOGY

Unlike mainland Australia, today's Great Barrier Reef (GBR) is relatively young, geologically speaking. Its foundations formed around 500,000 years ago, with northern Australia by then surrounded by tropical waters as Australia drifted gradually northward from the massive South Pole land mass that was Gondwana. The GBR grew and receded several times in response to changing sea levels. Coastal plains that are now the sea floor were occupied by Indigenous Australians only 20,000 years ago, when the ice-age sea level was 130m lower than it is today. As the icecaps contracted, seas flooded continental shelves and stabilised near their current levels about 6000 to 8000 years ago. Corals settled atop high parts of the Queensland shelf, initiating the unique combination of biological and geological processes that have built the reef ecosystem we see today.

rates estimated at 67% in the far northern section of the reef (offshore reefs north of Cape Melville) and 26% in the northern section (inshore reefs north of Port Douglas). Critically, central and southern reef areas south of Cairns remained largely unaffected, with just 6% and 1% coral deaths reported.

An important reality is that these bleaching events aren't occurring in isolation: storm waves and outbreaks of the coral-eating crown-of-thorns starfish are also big killers of corals. The effects are cumulative, and with projections of an increase in the severity of cyclones and the frequency of coral-bleaching events, we are likely to see more incidents of broad-acre coral death under a changing climate.

It takes one to two decades for a healthy coral reef to bounce back after being wiped out. So far, damaged GBR sites have shown remarkable resilience to damaging events, but the future might not be so rosy, as more frequent events driven by climate change repeatedly decimate reefs before they can fully recover. In other parts of the world, some reefs have suffered the added insults of decades of pollution and overfishing. By those means, former coral areas have become persistent landscapes of rubble and seaweed.

Worry Globally, Act Locally

Floating in the warming waters of the GBR, feeling the immensity of the reef and the issues presented by a changing climate, it's easy to feel that action is futile. But science is showing that local efforts can make a difference. Reducing the amount of nutrients (from fertilisers) that enter GBR waters may increase the tolerance of corals to warmer seas, decrease crown-of-thorns outbreaks and help corals maintain dominance over seaweeds. State and federal governments are therefore working with farmers to improve practices and reduce the losses of chemicals and valuable soil into the reef, and their efforts have already begun to deliver encouraging results.

Science also suggests that those fishing practices that maintain abundant herbivorous fish on the reefs may also be vital in keeping corals in the ascendancy. Fishing is carefully regulated, making the GBR a rare example of a coral-reef system that maintains a healthy coral-seaweed balance while still delivering sustainable seafood. There is no commercial use of fish traps or spears, and responsible fishing practices adopted by most fishers in the GBR also mean that sharks are still a common sight (although more work needs to be done to secure the future of these important predators). Bottom trawling for prawns (shrimp) has been dramatically scaled back over recent decades, with associated improvements in the health of the soft-seabed communities between reef outcrops. Other issues on the radar for the GBR include ship groundings, dredging and port expansions, with several ports along the reef, including Abbot Point, Gladstone, Hay Point, Mackay and Townsville, slated for development.

The GBR tourism industry is a world leader in sustainable, ecofriendly and climate-friendly practices. Visiting the reef with an eco-accredited tourism business is not only a great way to experience the beauty and wonder of coral reefs, it's also one of the best things you can do to help the GBR, with a small part of your fare directly supporting reef research and management.

Beyond the Corals

Coral reefs are more than just corals – a multitude of critters call these ecosystems home. Green and loggerhead turtles bury their eggs at the back of coral-island beaches, where the warm sand incubates the developing embryos. The sex of the hatchlings is determined by the temperature the eggs experience: cooler temperatures cause eggs to develop into male hatchlings; warmer eggs become females. Turtle researchers are worried that a warmer world could create an imbalance in the sex ratio, putting extra strain on already depleted turtle populations. For turtles, the risks don't stop there. Rising sea levels (some predictions are as much as 1.1m higher by the end of this century) put many nesting areas at greater risk of deadly flooding. Turtles will need to find higher ground for nesting, but in many coastal areas natural barriers or urban development limit their options.

For coral-reef fish, sea-level change might not be a big issue, but changes in ocean temperature have the potential to affect the timing and success of important processes such as reproduction. There is also growing evidence that fish might be prone to the effects of ocean acidification, which is the direct result of increased absorption of carbon dioxide by the world's seas. The upside to this process is that it has kept the atmosphere from warming even faster. But the pH of seawater is important to a wide range of chemical and biological processes, including the ability of fish to find their home reef and to avoid predators.

Changing ocean currents also have the potential to make life difficult for animals that rely on the timing and location of water movements for their survival. Seabird chicks become vulnerable when their parents have to travel too far to find the schools of fish they need to feed their flightless young. Plankton, too, are vulnerable to changing chemistry and currents, with potential flow-on effects through entire food chains. Corals don't escape the effects of ocean acidification, either. More acidic water makes it more difficult for corals to build their skeletons, leading to slower growth or more fragile structures.

GET INVOLVED

You can help the reef in practical ways during your visit. You can report sightings of important reef creatures, or send in information about any problems you encounter directly to the Great Barrier Reef Marine Park Authority by contributing to the Eye on the Reef Program (go to www.gbrmpa.gov.au or get the free Eye on the Reef app). If you're around for long enough (or time your visit right), you could undertake some training and become a Reef Check volunteer (see www.reefcheckaustralia.org). If turtles are your passion, see www.seaturtlefoundation.org for opportunities to volunteer with them. If you're a resident, look out for www.seagrasswatch.org, and if you like fishing, combine your fishing with research at www.info-fish.net.

The Future

In the best traditions of good science, its practitioners are a sceptical lot, but most coral-reef experts agree that climate change is a serious issue. Where scientists may differ is about the rate at which and the extent to which reefs and their mind-boggling biodiversity may adjust or adapt.

You might have heard it said that 'the climate has changed before and we still have corals'. While this is true, previous episodes of rapid climate change caused mass extinctions from which the world took millions of years to recover. The solid body of science indicates that climate change is happening, and that coral reefs are right in the firing line. Energetic debate is required on the best ways of tackling this problem, with action at local, national and global levels needed if we are to give coral reefs a fighting chance of providing future generations with the wonderful experiences we can still enjoy.

If humans continue to pollute the atmosphere with greenhouse gases at present rates, we will likely overtax any realistic capacity of coral-reef ecosystems to cope. All around the world, coral reefs are proving themselves to be the 'canary in the coal mine' of climate change. The worldwide reduction in reef assets that occurred when heatwaves swept equatorial regions in 1998 provided a wake-up call to reef scientists, reef managers and the community at large about what the future holds, with the 2016 event providing further impetus for action. Like polar zones, coral reefs are sentinel systems that will continue to show us the impacts of climate change on the natural world (and the millions of humans who depend on these ecosystems). But the ending to the climate-change story is still being written. Any action to reduce sources of pressure on corals and other reef creatures buys coral reefs important time to adapt – and, hopefully, to cope – until society takes the necessary action to control its impacts on the climate.

Food & Drink

Australians once proudly survived on a diet of 'meat and three veg'. Fine fare was a Sunday roast; lasagne was exotic. Fortunately the country's cuisine has evolved, and these days Australian gastronomy is keen to break rules, backed up by top chefs, world-renowned wines, excellent coffee and a burgeoning craft-beer scene. All along the east coast you'll find incredible seafood, from humble fish-and-chippers to fine-dining restaurants overlooking the ocean, while fantastic food markets and hip cafe culture make for top-notch culinary exploring.

Modern Australian (Mod Oz)

The phrase Modern Australian (Mod Oz) has been coined to classify contemporary Australian cuisine: a melange of East and West; a swirl of Atlantic and Pacific Rim; a flourish of authentic French and Italian.

Immigration has been the key to this culinary concoction. An influx of immigrants since WWII, from Europe, Asia, the Middle East and Africa, introduced new ingredients and new ways to use staples. Vietnam, Japan, Fiji – no matter where the food is from, there are expat communities and interested locals keen to cook and eat it. You'll find Jamaicans using Scotch bonnet peppers and Tunisians making *tajine*.

As the Australian appetite for diversity and invention grows, so does the food culture surrounding it. Cookbooks and foodie magazines are bestsellers and Australian celebrity chefs – highly sought overseas – reflect Australia's multiculturalism in their backgrounds and dishes.

If all this sounds overwhelming, never fear. The range of food in Australia is a true asset. You'll find that dishes are characterised by bold and interesting flavours and fresh ingredients. All palates are catered for along the east coast: the chilli meter spans gentle to extreme, seafood is plentiful, meats are full flavoured and vegetarian needs are considered (especially in the cities).

Local Delicacies

Australia's size and diverse climate – from the tropical north to the temperate south – mean that there's an enormous variety of produce on offer.

Seafood connoisseurs prize Sydney rock oysters – the best are from the New South Wales (NSW) south coast – and scallops from Queensland. Rock lobsters (aka crayfish) are fantastic and fantastically expensive; mud crabs, despite the name, are a sweet treat. Another odd-sounding delicacy is 'bugs' – like shovel-nosed lobsters without a lobster's price tag; try the Balmain and Moreton Bay varieties. Aussie prawns are also superb, particularly the school prawns or the eastern king (Yamba) prawns found along the northern NSW coast.

Aussies love their seafood, but they've not lost their yen for a hefty chunk of steak. Rockhampton is the beef capital of Australia, while lamb from Victoria's lush Gippsland is also highly prized.

Queensland's fertile fields are dappled with banana and mango plantations, orchards and vast seas of sugar cane. In summer mangoes are so plentiful that Queenslanders actually get sick of them. The macadamia,

The total at the bottom of a restaurant bill is all you really need to pay in Australia. Tipping isn't mandatory here, but is appreciated when service has been provided with a smile. Around 10% is the norm (perhaps more if your kids have trashed the dining room).

a buttery native nut, grows throughout southeastern Queensland – you'll find them tossed in salads, crushed in ice cream and petrified in sticky cakes.

There's a small but brilliant farmhouse-cheese movement in Australia, hampered by the fact that all the milk must be pasteurized. Despite this, the results can be spectacular.

Coffee Culture

Coffee has become an Australian addiction. There are Italian-style espresso machines in every cafe, boutique roasters are all the rage and, in urban areas, the qualified barista is ever-present (there are even barista-staffed cafes attached to petrol stations). Sydney and Melbourne have given rise to a whole generation of coffee snobs, with the two cities duking it out for bragging rights as Australia's coffee capital. The cafe scene in Melbourne is particularly artsy, and the best way to immerse yourself in it is by wandering the city centre's cafe-lined laneways. Beyond the big cities, you'll be able to find a decent coffee in most towns, but you might still struggle in rural areas.

Foodie Touring Hot Spots

The vine-covered Hunter Valley (a few hours north of Sydney) produces far more than just wine. Among the rolling hillsides, you'll find farmhouse cheeses, smoked fish and meats, seasonal produce (figs, citrus, peaches, avocados), Belgian-style chocolate, boutique beer, olives and much more. For a memorable assemble-your-own picnic, it doesn't get much better than this.

In the Atherton Tableland in north Queensland, you can get a first-hand look at the nation's best coffee-growing plantations. Even better, you'll get to sample the good stuff, plus coffee liqueur and dark-chocolate-coated coffee beans.

Farmers Markets

Local farmers markets are terrific places to sample the culinary riches of the region, support local growers and enjoy the affable airs (live music, friendly banter, free food sampling). You'll find fruit, veggies, seafood, nuts, meat, bread and pastries, liqueurs, beer, wine, coffee and much more in markets all along the east coast. For locations, check the website of the **Australian Farmers Market Association** (www.farmers markets.org.au).

Wine Country

South Australia may be the nation's wine-production behemoth, but dating from the 1820s, the Hunter Valley is Australia's oldest wine region. The Hunter is home to more than 120 wineries, with a mix of boutique, family-run outfits and large-scale commercial vintners. The Lower Hunter is known for shiraz and unwooded semillon. Upper Hunter wineries specialise in cabernet sauvignon and shiraz, with forays into verdelho

---

Vegemite: you'll either love it or hate it. For reference, Barack Obama diplomatically called it 'horrible'. It's certainly an acquired taste, but Australians consume more than 22 million jars of the stuff each year.

Best Markets

Sydney Fish Market

Prahran Market (Melbourne)

Noosa Farmers Market

Byron Farmers' Market

Jan Power's Farmers Market (Brisbane)

Koonwarra Farmers Market (South Gippsland)

THE AUSSIE BBQ

The iconic Australian barbecue (BBQ, or barbie) is a near-mandatory cultural experience. In summer locals invite their mates around in the late afternoon and fire up the barbie, grilling burgers, sausages (snags), steaks, seafood, and vegie, meat or seafood skewers – if you're invited, bring some meat and cold beer. Year-round the BBQ is wheeled out at weekends for quick-fire lunches. There are also coin-operated and free BBQs in parks around the country – a terrific, traveller-friendly option.

> **BYO**
>
> If a restaurant is 'BYO', it means you can bring your own alcohol. If the eatery also sells alcohol, you can usually only bring your own bottled wine (no beer, no cask wine) and a 'corkage' charge is added to your bill. The cost is either per person or per bottle, and can be up to $20 per bottle in fine-dining places.

and chardonnay. The area around Canberra also sustains a growing number of excellent wineries.

To the south, Victoria has more than 500 wineries. Just northeast of Melbourne, the Yarra Valley is a patchwork of vines producing fine pinot noir, peachy chardonnay and crisp sparkling. Further south, the hills and valleys of the Mornington Peninsula and Bellarine Peninsula produce beautiful cool-climate reds and whites – most famously pinot noir, subtle, honeyed chardonnay, pinot gris and pinot grigio. Gippsland is also gaining a reputation as a wine-growing region with its maritime-climate pinots and chardonnays.

There's even a wine region in Queensland – the Granite Belt, two hours southwest of Brisbane – which has been carving out a name for itself in recent years. The neighbouring towns of Stanthorpe and Ballandean are gateways to this understated region.

Most wineries are open to visitors, with free tastings, though some keep limited hours (opening only on weekends).

Beer, Breweries & Bundaberg

As the Australian public develops a more sophisticated palate, local beers are rising to the occasion, with a growing wealth of microbrews available. The default options (Carlton, VB, XXXX and Tooheys) are passable if you're dry on a hot day, but for something more flavourful, look for some of the following labels:

Balter Brewery (www.balter.com.au) Surfside beers from Currumbin in Queensland, aimed at putting a 'grin on your head'.

Burkes Brewing Company (www.burkesbrewingco.com) Best known for its Hemp Premium Ale, a sweet golden beer brewed (legally, apparently) through hemp filters. From Brisbane.

Burleigh Brewery Co (www.burleighbrewing.com.au) Stalwart craft brewer at Burleigh Heads on the Gold Coast: 'balance, character and soul'.

Grifter Brewing Co (www.thegrifter.com.au) Excellent ales (red, pale, IPA), pilsner and stout, straight outta Marrickville in Sydney.

Mountain Goat (www.goatbeer.com.au) Brewed in the Melbourne suburb of Richmond (not particularly mountainous); the English-style Hightale Ale makes a perfect pint. Almost mainstream these days.

Fortitude Brewing Co (www.fortitudebrewing.com.au) Some of Queensland's best craft brews (also under the Noisy Minor label).

Piss (www.pi55.com.au) Once you're past the puns, it's an excellent, rich lager. From Victoria.

Young Henrys (www.younghenrys.com) Ballsy brews from Newtown in Sydney's inner west. And a distillery!

You'll also encounter Bundaberg Rum (www.bundabergrum.com.au) almost everywhere on the east coast. It's a plentiful potion from Bundaberg in Queensland, bottles of which are incongruously emblazoned with a polar bear.

Top Foodie Sites

www.dimmi.com.au (Sydney, Canberra and Brisbane)

www.broadsheet.com.au (Melbourne)

www.grabyourfork.blogspot.com (Sydney)

www.melbourne-gastronome.com (Melbourne)

www.eating brisbane.com (Brisbane)

www.lifestylefood.com.au

Sport

Whether they're filling stadiums, glued to the big screen at the pub, or on the couch in front of the TV, Australians invest heavily in sport – both fiscally and emotionally. The federal government kicks in more than $300 million every year – enough cash for the nation to hold its own against formidable international sporting opponents. Despite slipping to 10th place at the 2016 Rio Olympics (down from 58 medals and fourth place in Sydney in 2000), expectations are always high.

Sporting Obsessions

All three east-coast states can stake legitimate claims to the title of Australia's sporting mecca (even Canberra has pro teams and more than its fair share of sports-mad residents). The object of passion, however, varies from state to state. In New South Wales (NSW) and Queensland it's the gladiatorial arena of rugby league, while down south, Victoria is a smouldering cauldron of Australian Football League (AFL). Cricket unifies everyone and is a nationwide obsession in summer.

But these sports are hardly the only games in town. Australians love all sport, from basketball and car racing (the Aussie Formula One Grand Prix happens in Melbourne every March) to tennis, soccer, horse racing, netball, surfing, even bull riding. When competition is afoot, the roaring crowds will appear (case in point: Brisbane's Australia Day Cockroach Races attract upwards of 7000 cheering fans each year).

'Footy' in Australia can mean a number of things: in NSW and Queensland it's usually rugby league, but the term is also used for AFL, rugby union and soccer.

AFL

Australia's most attended sport, and one of the two most watched, is Australian Rules football (Aussie Rules). While traditionally embedded in the Victorian culture and identity, the Australian Football League (www.afl.com.au) has expanded its popularity across the country, including rugby-dominated NSW and Queensland. Long kicks, high marks and brutal collisions whip crowds into frenzies, and the roar of 50,000-plus fans yelling 'Baaall!!!' upsets dogs in suburban backyards for kilometres around.

During the season (March to September) Australians go footy mad, entering tipping competitions, discussing groin and hamstring strains and savouring the latest in loutish behaviour (on and off the field). It all culminates on the last Saturday in September, when Melbourne hosts the AFL grand final – the whole city goes berserk. Around 100,000 fans pack into the Melbourne Cricket Ground and millions more watch on TV.

Some teams – notably Essendon, Richmond and Port Adelaide – run Indigenous programs designed to promote the sport in Aboriginal communities across the country, and all teams recruit Indigenous players, praising their unique vision (eg kicking the ball into a space for a teammate to run into) and silky skills.

An oft-repeated quote is 'Rugby [union] is a hooligans' game played by gentlemen. Football [soccer] is a gentlemen's game played by hooligans.' Others have added that 'Rugby league is a hooligans' game played by hooligans'.

Rugby

While Melburnians refuse to acknowledge it (or do so with a scowl akin to that directed at an unfaithful spouse), there are other versions of 'footy' in Australia. The **National Rugby League** (NRL; www.nrl.com)

is the most popular sporting competition north of the Murray River. The competition, which parallels the AFL season from March to September, features 16 teams – 10 from NSW, three from Queensland, and one each from Australian Capital Territory (ACT), New Zealand and Victoria. To witness an NRL game is to appreciate all of Newton's laws of motion – bone-crunching!

One of the most anticipated events in the league calendar (apart from the grand final in September) is the State of Origin series held in June or July, when all-star players from Queensland take on their counterparts from NSW in explosive state-against-state combat. At the time of writing the NSW Blues were poorly out of form, having beaten their Queensland arch-rivals, the Maroons, just once since 2006 – a momentary rebellion in 2014, quickly snuffed out in 2015 and 2016.

Rugby Union (www.rugby.com.au) is almost as popular as rugby league. Historically, union was an amateur sport played by upper-class gents from prestigious British public-school systems, while league was associated with working-class communities of northern England. The ideological divide carried over to Australia, where it has remained to a large degree over the past century.

The national union team, the Wallabies, won the Rugby World Cup in 1991 and 1999 and were runners-up in 2003 and 2015. In between world cups, annual Bledisloe Cup matches between Australia and arch-rival New Zealand (the world-beating All Blacks) draw huge crowds. Bledisloe matches form part of the annual southern-hemisphere **Rugby Championship** (www.sanzarrugby.com/therugbychampionship) played between Australia, New Zealand, South Africa and Argentina.

Teams from Australia, South Africa, Argentina, Japan and New Zealand also field rugby union teams in the super-popular **Super Rugby** (www.superxv.com) competition, which includes five Australian teams: the Waratahs (Sydney), the Reds (Brisbane), the Brumbies (ACT), the Force (Perth) and the Rebels (Melbourne).

Cricket

The Aussies dominated both test and one-day cricket for much of the noughties, holding the number-one world ranking for most of the decade. But the subsequent retirement of once-in-a-lifetime players such as Shane Warne and Ricky Ponting has sent the team into an extended 'rebuilding' phase. Losses in the biennial Ashes series against arch-enemy England came in 2009, 2011, 2013 and 2015, despite momentary redemption in an unusual 2014 series (usually only held in odd-numbered years) when Australia demoralised England 5-0. The Ashes trophy is a tiny terracotta urn containing the ashen remnants of an 1882 cricket bail (the perfect Australian BBQ conversation opener: ask a local what a 'bail' is).

Despite the Australian cricket team's bad rep for sledging (verbally dressing down one's opponent on the field), cricket is still a gentleman's game. Take the time to watch a match if you never have – such tactical cut and thrust, such nuance, such grace... For current cricketing info, see www.espncricinfo.com.

Soccer

The most played sport by Aussie kids, round-ball football has a strong following in the nation, with strong interest in overseas leagues and increasing passion for the local competition.

Australia's national soccer team, the **Socceroos** (www.socceroos.com.au), qualified for the 2006, 2010 and 2014 World Cups after a long history of almost-but-not-quite getting there. Results have been mixed, from advancing to the second knockout stage of the comp in 2006 to a straight-sets elimination in 2014.

It's said by some cynics that more Australians know cricket legend Don Bradman's test batting average (99.94) than know the year Captain Cook first bobbed around the coast (1770).

The first Australian cricket team to tour England was 100% Victorian Aboriginal – in 1868. The subsequent 'whiteness' of the sport in Australia meant that this achievement was unheralded until quite recently.

SURF'S UP!

Australia has been synonymous with surfing ever since the Beach Boys enthused about 'Australia's Narrabeen', one of Sydney's northern beaches, in *Surfin' USA*. Other east-coast surfing hot spots, such as Bells Beach, the Pass at Byron Bay, and Burleigh Heads on the Gold Coast, resonate similarly with international wave addicts. Ironman and surf-lifesaving competitions are also held on beaches around the country, attracting dedicated fans to the sand.

Quite a few Australian surfers have attained world-champion status. Legendary names in the men's comp include Mark Richards, Tom Carroll, Joel Parkinson and three-time champ Mick Fanning; and in the women's comp there's Wendy Botha, seven-time champion Layne Beachley, six-time winner Stephanie Gilmore and 2016 champion Tyler Wright.

The national **A-League** (www.a-league.com.au) has enjoyed increased popularity in recent years, successfully luring a few big-name international players to bolster the home-grown talent pool. The women's **W-League** (www.w-league.com.au) is growing strongly too. To avoid competition with the rugby and AFL, the season runs through the Australian summer, with the grand final played in early May.

Tennis

Every January in Melbourne, the **Australian Open** (www.australianopen. com) attracts more people to Australia than any other sporting event. The men's competition was last won by an Australian, Mark Edmondson, back in 1976 – and after former world number-one Lleyton Hewitt retired in 2016, the mantle has been passed to the unpopular but talented Nick Kyrgios and Bernard Tomic. An Australian last won the women's comp in 1978, when Chris O'Neil took home the cup. Veteran Queenslander Sam Stosur is still Australia's best hope, having won the US Open in 2011 and hovering around the top-20 player rankings ever since.

Actor Russell Crowe spent part of his childhood in Sydney. Today he's part-owner of the 100-year-old South Sydney Rabbitohs team in the National Rugby League.

Swimming

Australia is girt by sea and pockmarked with pools: Australians know how to swim. Australia's greatest female swimmer, Dawn Fraser, won the 100m freestyle gold at three successive Olympics (1956–64), plus the 4 x 100m freestyle relay in 1956. Australia's greatest male swimmer, Ian Thorpe (aka Thorpie or the Thorpedo), retired in 2006 aged 24, with five Olympic golds swinging from his neck. In early 2011 Thorpe announced his comeback, with his eye fixed on the 2012 London Olympics – but he failed to make the team in the selection trials and clambered out of the pool again to finish his autobiography.

Horse Racing

Australian's love to bet on the 'nags' – in fact, betting on horse racing is so mainstream and accessible that it's almost a national hobby!

Australia's biggest race – the 'race that stops a nation' – is the **Melbourne Cup** (www.flemington.com.au/melbourne-cup-carnival), which occurs on the first Tuesday in November. The most famous Melbourne Cup winner was the New Zealand–born Phar Lap, who won in 1930 before dying of a mystery illness (suspected arsenic poisoning) in America. Phar Lap is now a prize exhibit in the Melbourne Museum. The British-bred (but Australian trained) Makybe Diva is a more recent star, winning three cups in a row before retiring in 2005.

Survival
Guide

Deadly & Dangerous

If you're the pessimistic type, you might focus on the things that can bite, sting, burn or drown you in Australia: bushfires, treacherous surf, blazing heat, jellyfish, snakes, spiders, sharks, crocodiles, ticks... But chances are the worst you'll encounter are a few pesky flies and mosquitoes. So splash on some insect repellent and boldly venture forth!

OUT & ABOUT

At the Beach

Around 80 people per year drown on Australia's beaches, where pounding surf and rips (strong currents) can create serious hazards. If you happen to get caught in a rip and are being taken out to sea, swim parallel to the shore until you're out of the rip, then head for the beach – *don't* try to swim back against the rip; you'll only tire yourself.

Bushfires

Bushfires happen regularly in Australia. In hot, dry and windy weather and on total-fire-ban days, be extremely careful with naked flames (including cigarette butts) and don't use camping stoves, campfires or barbecues. Bushwalkers should delay trips until things cool down. If you're out in the bush and you see smoke,

take it seriously: find the nearest open space (downhill if possible). Forested ridges are dangerous places to be. Always heed the advice of authorities.

Coral Cuts

Coral can be extremely sharp; you can cut yourself by merely brushing against the stuff. Thoroughly clean cuts and douse with antiseptic to avoid infection.

Heat Sickness

Hot weather is the norm across much of east-coast Australia and can lead to heat exhaustion or more severe heatstroke (resulting from extreme fluid depletion). When arriving from a temperate or cold climate, remember that it takes two weeks to acclimatise.

Unprepared travellers die from dehydration each year in remote areas. Always carry sufficient water for any trip (driving or hiking), and let someone know where you're going and when you expect to arrive. Carry communications equipment and if in trouble, stay with your vehicle rather than walking for help.

Sun Exposure

Australia has one of the highest rates of skin cancer in the world. Monitor exposure

to direct sunlight closely. Ultraviolet (UV) radiation is greatest between 10am and 4pm, so avoid skin exposure during these times. Wear a wide-brimmed hat and a long-sleeved shirt with a collar. Always use SPF 30+ sunscreen; apply it 30 minutes before exposure and reapply regularly to minimise sun damage.

THINGS THAT BITE & STING

Crocodiles

The risk of a crocodile attack in tropical Far North Queensland is real, but with some common sense it is entirely avoidable. 'Salties' are estuarine crocodiles that can grow to 7m. They inhabit coastal waters and are mostly seen in the tidal reaches of rivers, though on occasion they're spotted on beaches and in freshwater lagoons. Always heed any advice, such as crocodile warning signs, that you might come across. Don't assume it's safe to swim if there are no signs: if you're not sure, don't swim.

If you're away from popular beaches anywhere north of Rockhampton, avoid swimming in rivers, waterholes and in the sea near river outlets. Don't clean fish or prepare food near the water's edge, and camp at least 50m away from waterways. Crocodiles are particularly mobile and dangerous during the breeding season (October to March).

Jellyfish

Jellyfish – including the potentially deadly box jellyfish and irukandji – occur in Queensland's tropical waters. It's unwise to swim north of Agnes Water between November and May unless there's a stinger net. 'Stinger suits' (full-body Lycra swimsuits) prevent stinging, as do wetsuits. Swimming and snorkelling are usually safe around Queensland's reef islands throughout the year; however, the rare (and tiny) irukandji has been recorded on the outer reef and islands.

Wash stings with vinegar to prevent further discharge of remaining stinging cells, followed by rapid transfer to a hospital. Don't attempt to remove the tentacles.

Marine Animals

Marine spikes and poisonous spines – such as those found on sea urchins, catfish, stingrays, scorpionfish and stonefish – can cause severe local pain. If you're stung, immediately immerse the affected area in hot water (as hot as can be tolerated) and seek medical care.

Contact with blue-ringed octopuses and Barrier Reef cone shells can be fatal, so don't pick them up. If someone is stung, apply a pressure bandage, monitor breathing carefully and conduct mouth-to-mouth resuscitation if breathing stops. Seek immediate medical care.

Mosquitoes

'Mozzies' can be a problem just about anywhere in the region. Malaria isn't present, but dengue fever is a danger in the north of Queensland, particularly during the wet season (November to April).

Most people recover in a few days, but more severe forms of the disease can occur.

To minimise bites:

➡ Wear loose, long-sleeved clothing.

➡ Apply repellent with minimum 30% DEET on exposed skin.

➡ Use mosquito coils.

➡ Sleep under fast-spinning ceiling fans.

Sharks

Despite extensive media coverage, the risk of shark attack in Australia is no greater than in other countries with extensive coastlines. Check with surf life-saving groups about local risks.

Snakes

There's no denying it: Australia has plenty of venomous snakes. Few species are aggressive: unless you are messing with or accidentally stand on one, you're unlikely to be bitten. About 80% of bites occur on the lower limbs: wear protective clothing (such as gaiters) when bushwalking.

If bitten, apply an elastic bandage (or improvise with a T-shirt). Wrap firmly around the entire limb – but not so tightly that you cut off the circulation – and immobilise with a splint or sling; then seek medical attention. Don't use a tourniquet, and don't try to suck out the poison.

Spiders

Australia has poisonous spiders, although deaths are extremely rare. Common species:

➡ Funnel-web: a deadly spider found in New South Wales (including Sydney). Apply pressure to bites and immobilise before transferring to hospital.

➡ Redback: live throughout Australia. Bites cause

DEADLY & DANGEROUS JELLYFISH

A BIT OF PERSPECTIVE

Australia's plethora of poisonous and biting critters is impressive, but don't let it put you off. There's approximately one shark-attack and one croc-attack fatality per year here. Blue-ringed-octopus deaths are rarer – only two in the last century. Jellyfish do better – about two deaths annually – but you're still more than 100 times more likely to drown. Spiders haven't killed anyone in the last 20 years. Snake bites kill one or two people per year, as do bee stings, but you're about a thousand times more likely to perish on the nation's roads.

increasing pain followed by profuse sweating. Apply ice and transfer to hospital.

➡ Whitetail: blamed for causing slow-healing ulcers. If bitten, clean bite and seek medical assistance.

➡ Huntsman: a disturbingly large spider that's basically harmless, though seeing one can affect your blood pressure (and/or underpants).

Ticks

Common bush ticks can be dangerous if lodged in the skin and undetected. When walking in tick-prone areas, check your body every night (and those of children and dogs). Remove a tick by dousing with methylated spirits or kerosene and levering it out intact. See a doctor if bites become infected (tick typhus cases have been reported in Queensland).

Directory A–Z

Accommodation

The east coast is a well-trodden route with plenty of accommodation for all budgets, but you still need to book ahead – especially through summer, over Easter and during school holidays.

Reviews are listed in budget order and then by preference.

Bed & Breakfasts

East-coast B&B options include restored miners' cottages, converted barns, rambling old houses, up-market country manors, beachside bungalows and simple bedrooms in family homes. Tariffs are typically in the midrange bracket ($150 to $250 per night, including breakfast), but can be much higher. Some B&B hosts may also cook dinner for guests (usually 24 hours' notice is required).

Local tourist offices can usually give you a list of options. Good online information:

B&B and Farmstay Far North Queensland (www.bnbnq.com.au)

B&B and Farmstay NSW & ACT (www.bedandbreakfastnsw.com.au)

Bed & Breakfast Site (www.babs.com.au)

Hosted Accommodation Australia (www.australianbedandbreakfast.com.au)

OZ Bed and Breakfast (www.ozbedandbreakfast.com)

Booking Services

Useful websites:

Couchsurfing (www.couchsurfing.com) Find a bed on the fly.

Flatmates (https://flatmates.com.au) For longer-term share-house stays.

Lonely Planet (www.lonelyplanet.com/australia/hotels) Recommendations and bookings.

Camping & Holiday Parks

If you want to explore the east coast on a shoestring, camping is the way to go. Better yet, book a campervan you can sleep in and explore this long shore. Caravan parks are often close to the beach and town centres, and are great bang for your family-friendly buck. Campsites in national parks are even more affordable.

PRICES

Camping in national parks can cost from nothing to $15 per person – nights spent around a campfire under the stars are unforgettable. Tent sites at private camping and caravan parks usually cost between $22 and $32 per couple per night (slightly more with electricity). Many of these places also hire out cabins with kitchenettes, running from $70 to $170 per night, sleeping one to six people.

NATIONAL PARKS

Camping areas within national parks are administered state by state, with bookings usually handled online.

New South Wales (www.environment.nsw.gov.au/nationalparks)

Queensland (www.nprsr.qld.gov.au)

Victoria (www.parkweb.vic.gov.au)

SLEEPING PRICE RANGES

The following price ranges refer to a double room with bathroom in high season (December to February down south, June to September up north):

$ less than $130

$$ $130 to $250

$$$ more than $250

Expect to pay $20 to $50 more in expensive areas – notably Sydney – and during school and public holidays.

MAJOR CHAINS

If you intend to do a lot of caravanning or camping, joining a major chain will save you some money:

Big 4 (www.big4.com.au)

Discovery Holiday Parks (www.discoveryholidayparks.com.au)

Top Tourist Parks (www.toptouristparks.com.au)

Farmstays

Many coastal and hinterland farms offer a bed for the night and the chance to see rural Australia at work. At some you sit back and watch other people raise a sweat, while others like to get you involved in day-to-day activities. Check out B&B Australia (www.babs.com.au, under family holidays/farmstays) and Willing Workers on Organic Farms (www.wwoof.com.au). Regional and town tourist offices should also be able to tell you what's available in their area.

Hostels

Backpacker hostels are highly social, low-cost fixtures on the east coast. There are staggering numbers of them, ranging from family-run places in converted houses to huge, custom-built resorts replete with bars, nightclubs and party propensity. Standards range from outstanding to awful, and management from friendly to scary.

Dorm beds typically cost $28 to $35, with single rooms sometimes available (around $70) and doubles costing $80 to $110. Chain organisations include the following:

Base Backpackers (www.stayatbase.com)

Global Backpackers (www.globalbackpackers.com.au)

Nomads (www.nomadsworld.com)

VIP Backpackers (www.vipbackpackers.com)

YHA (www.yha.com.au) YHA offers dorms, twin and double rooms, and cooking and laundry facilities. The vibe is generally less 'party' than in independent hostels...but there's always plenty of cutlery. Nightly charges start at $27 for members; hostels also take non-YHA members for an extra $3. Australian residents can become YHA members for $25 for one year, $45 for two. Join online or at any YHA hostel. Families can also join: just pay the adult price, then kids under 18 can join for free. The YHA is part of Hostelling International (www.hihostels.com); if you already have HI membership in your own country, you're entitled to YHA rates in Australian hostels.

Hotels

Hotels along the east coast are often the business or luxury-chain variety (midrange to top end): comfortable, anonymous, mod-con-filled rooms in multistorey blocks. Expect to pay more than $150 a night per double, though significant discounts can be offered when business is quiet.

More interestingly (and more expensively), boutique hotels offer quirky, luxurious experiences and are often brilliantly located (central big-city laneways, remote tropical peninsulas). Expect to pay upwards of $250 per night, but you definitely get what you pay for.

Motels

Drive-up motels offer comfortable midrange accommodation and are found all over the east coast. They rarely offer a cheaper rate for singles, so are better value for couples or small families. You'll mostly pay between $100 and $150 for a simple room with kettle, fridge, TV, air-con and bathroom...and that inexplicably romantic on-the-road motel vibe.

BOOK YOUR STAY ONLINE

For more accommodation reviews by Lonely Planet authors, check out http://lonelyplanet.com/australia/east-coast-australia/hotels. You'll find independent reviews, as well as recommendations on the best places to stay. Best of all, you can book online.

Pubs

Traditional hotels that serve beer are more commonly known as pubs (from the term 'public house'). Generally, rooms are small and weathered, with a long amble down the hall to the bathroom. They're usually central and cheap – singles/doubles with shared facilities cost from $60/80, more if you want a private bathroom – but if you're a light sleeper, avoid booking a room above the bar and check whether a band is playing downstairs that night.

Rental Accommodation

If you're on the east coast for a while, or just want to base yourself in a city for a week or two, then a rental apartment will be an economical option – particularly if you're travelling with kids, a group of mates or just want to cook dinner once in a while. Expect to pay upwards of $150 a night. Beachside and country cottages are pricier, starting at around $200 per night, but often include breakfast.

Resorts

There are plenty of islands in Queensland, and plenty of them have resorts. Here's your chance to either ditch the kids and sleep for a week (with the odd dip in the pool and cocktail), or bring the family along for a fun-filled tropical holiday full of activities (snorkelling, kayaking, bushwalking, windsurfing, swimming, sailing...). Most resorts are at the pricey end of the scale – at least $250 a night, often a *lot* more – but some offer good family rates, particularly out of peak season.

Children

If you can survive the long-haul distances, travelling Australia's east coast with the kids can be a real delight. Attitudes towards children are tolerant, and there's oodles of interesting stuff to see and do, both indoors and outdoors: beaches, theme parks, museums, wildlife parks, national parks, playgrounds, bike paths...

Lonely Planet's *Travel with Children* contains plenty of useful information, or look for the excellent (and free) *Melbourne's Child*, *Sydney's Child*, *Brisbane's Child* or *Canberra's Child* magazines (www.childmags.com.au), loaded with region-specific info.

Practicalities

Accommodation Most motels supply cots; many also have playgrounds and swimming pools, as well as child-minding services. Many B&Bs, on the other hand, market themselves as child-free sanctuaries.

Change Rooms & Breastfeeding All cities and major towns have public rooms where parents can breastfeed or change nappies (diapers). Most Australians have a relaxed attitude about breastfeeding or nappy changing in public.

Child Care If you want to leave Junior behind for a few hours, try Babysitters R Us (www.babysittersrus.com.au), Busy Bees Babysitting (www.busybeesbabysitting.com.au) or Dial-an-Angel (www.dialanangel.com).

Child Safety Seats Under national laws, safety restraints are compulsory for all children up to seven years of age. Major hire-car companies will supply and fit child safety seats, charging a one-off fee of around $25. Phone taxi companies in advance to organise child safety seats.

Concessions Discounts for children apply for such things as accommodation, admission fees, and air, bus and train transport, with some discounts as high as 50% of the adult rate. However, the definition of 'child' can vary from under 12 to under 18 years.

Eating Out Dedicated menus are common, but selections are usually uninspiring (ham-and-pineapple pizza, fish fingers, chicken nuggets etc). If a restaurant doesn't have a kids menu, find something on the regular menu and ask the kitchen to adapt it. It's usually fine to bring toddler food in with you. Many places can supply high chairs.

Health Care Australia has high-standard medical services and facilities, and items such as baby formula and disposable nappies are widely available.

Customs Regulations

Entering Australia you can bring in most articles free of duty, provided the **Australian Customs Service** (☏1300 363 263; www.border.gov.au) is satisfied they're for personal use and that you'll be taking them with you when you leave.

➡ There's a duty-free quota per person of 2.25L of alcohol (if you're over 18), 50 cigarettes (yes, you read that right) and dutiable goods up to the value of $900 ($450 if you're under 18).

➡ Amounts of more than A$10,000 cash (or its equivalent) must be declared.

➡ Authorities take biosecurity very seriously, and are vigilant in their efforts to prevent introduced pests getting into the country. Be sure to declare all goods of animal or vegetable origin. Dispose of any fresh food and flowers. If you've recently visited farmland or rural areas, it's best to scrub your shoes before you get to the airport; you'll also need to declare them to Customs.

➡ Weapons and firearms are either prohibited or require a permit and safety testing. Other restricted goods include products made from protected wildlife species, nonapproved telecommunications devices and live animals.

➡ When you leave, don't take any protected flora or fauna with you. Customs comes down hard on smugglers.

Discount Cards

Senior Cards Travellers over 60 with some form of identification (eg a Seniors Card: www.australia.gov.au/content/seniors-card) are often eligible for concession prices. Most Australian states and territories

---

PRACTICALITIES

Newspapers Leaf through the daily *Sydney Morning Herald*, Melbourne's *Age*, Brisbane's *Courier-Mail* or national *The Australian*.

Radio Tune in to ABC radio; at www.abc.net.au/radio.

Smoking Illegal in pubs, bars, restaurants, offices, shops, theatres etc, and within certain signposted distances of public-facility doorways (airports, bus depots, cinemas etc).

TV The main free-to-air TV channels are the government-sponsored ABC, multicultural SBS and the three commercial networks – Seven, Nine and Ten – plus numerous additional channels from these main players.

Weights and Measures Australia uses the metric system.

issue their own versions of these, which can be used Australia-wide.

Student & Youth Cards The internationally recognised International Student Identity Card (www.isic.org) is available to full-time students aged 12 and over. The card gives the bearer discounts on accommodation, transport and admission to various attractions. The same organisation also produces the International Youth Travel Card (IYTC), issued to people under 26 years of age and not full-time students. It has benefits equivalent to the ISIC. Also similar is the International Teacher Identity Card (ITIC), available to teaching professionals. All three cards are available online or from student travel companies ($30).

Electricity

Type I
240V/50Hz

Embassies & Consulates

Canberra has a full suite of foreign embassies, while many countries also maintain consulates in Sydney and/or Melbourne, some in Brisbane and a couple in Cairns. See protocol.dfat. gov.au.

Food & Drink

For more on eating and drinking, see p493.

Health

Although there are plenty of hazards in Australia, few travellers should experience anything worse than sunburn or a hangover. If you do fall ill, health-care standards are high.

Health Insurance

Health insurance is essential for all travellers. You may prefer a policy that pays doctors or hospitals directly rather than requiring you to pay on the spot and claim later. If you have to claim later make sure you keep all documentation. Check that the policy covers ambulances and emergency medical evacuations by air.

Availability & Cost of Health Care

The Medicare system covers Australian residents for some health-care costs. Visitors from countries with which Australia has a reciprocal health-care agreement are eligible for benefits specified under the Medicare program. Agreements are currently in place with Belgium, Finland, Italy, Malta, the Netherlands, New Zealand, Ireland, Norway, Slovenia, Sweden and the UK; check the details before departing these countries. For further details, visit www.humanservices.gov.au/customer/subjects/medicare-services. But even if you're not covered by Medicare, a short consultation with a local GP will usually only set you back $60 or $70.

PHARMACEUTICALS

Painkillers, antihistamines for allergies, and skincare products are widely available at chemists (pharmacies) throughout Australia. You may find that medications readily available over the

counter in some countries are only available in Australia by prescription. These include the oral contraceptive pill, some medications for asthma and all antibiotics.

Insurance

A good travel-insurance policy covering theft, loss and medical problems is essential. Some policies specifically exclude designated 'dangerous activities' such as scuba diving, white-water rafting and even bushwalking. Make sure the policy you choose fully covers you for your activity of choice, and covers ambulances and emergency medical evacuations by air.

Worldwide travel insurance is available at www.lonelyplanet.com/travel-insurance. You can buy, extend and claim online anytime – even if you're already on the road.

Internet Access

➡ By far the easiest way to access the internet is to buy a local prepaid SIM card, pop it in your (unlocked) phone and sign up for a data package. Expect to pay around $2 for the SIM, then $30 to $50 for a month of calls, texts and data.

➡ Nearly all hotels and hostels provide wi-fi connections, although many, especially top-end places, charge for the service, or make the free service so slow that you are virtually forced to pay for 'premium' access.

➡ Many cafes and bars offer free wi-fi. Most public

TAP WATER

Tap water in Australia is generally safe to drink. Water taken from streams, rivers and lakes should be treated before drinking.

EATING PRICE RANGES

The following price ranges refer to a main course:

$ less than $15

$$ $15 to $30

$$$ more than $30

libraries and shopping centres also offer it.

➡ Pay-as-you-go wi-fi hot spots are common in busy areas such as airports.

➡ Because of the greater access to free connections, internet cafes are thin on the ground these days.

Legal Matters

➡ Australia is very strict when it comes to driving under the influence of alcohol or illegal drugs. There is a significant police presence on the roads, and they have the power to stop your car and see your licence (you're required to carry it), check your vehicle for roadworthiness and insist that you take a breath test for alcohol. The legal limit is 0.05 blood alcohol concentration (measured as grams per 100mL, equivalent to what many other countries would call 0.5). If you're over, you face a hefty fine and other sanctions.

➡ First offenders caught with small amounts of illegal drugs are likely to receive a fine rather than go to jail, but a conviction may affect your visa status.

➡ If you remain in Australia after your visa expires, you will officially be an 'overstayer' and could face detention and expulsion, and then be prevented from returning to Australia for up to three years.

LGBT Travellers

Australia's east coast – Sydney especially – is a popular destination for gay and lesbian travellers. The legendary annual **Sydney Gay & Lesbian**

Mardi Gras (www.mardigras. org.au; ⊙Feb-Mar) draws huge numbers of visitors, as does Melbourne's **Midsumma Festival** (www.midsumma.org. au; ⊙Jan/Feb).

In general, Australians are open-minded about same-sex relationships, but the further out of the cities you get, the more likely you are to run into homophobia. Same-sex acts are legal in all states, but the age of consent varies.

Gay and lesbian magazines include *DNA*, *Lesbians on the Loose (LOTL)* and the Sydney-based *SX*. In Melbourne look for *MCV*; in Queensland look for *Queensland Pride*.

Resources

Gay & Lesbian Tourism Australia (www.galta.com.au)

Gay News Network (www.gaynewsnetwork.com.au)

Same Same (www.samesame.com.au)

Maps

You'll find plenty of maps available when you arrive in Australia. Visitor centres usually have free maps of the region and towns, although quality varies. Automobile associations are a good source of reliable road maps. City street directories, such as those produced by Ausway, Gregory's and UBD, are very useful but they're expensive, bulky and usually only worth getting if you intend to do a lot of driving in one city.

For bushwalking and other activities that require large-scale maps, the topographic sheets put out by Geoscience Australia (www.ga.gov.au) are the ones to get. Many of the more popular maps are usual-

ly available over the counter at outdoor-equipment shops.

Money

There are ATMs everywhere and major credit cards are widely accepted, though there's often a surcharge.

ATMs & Eftpos

ATMs ATMs proliferate in east-coast cities, but don't expect to find them everywhere, certainly not off the beaten track or in small towns. Most ATMs accept cards issued by other banks (for a fee) and are linked to international networks.

Eftpos Most service stations, supermarkets, restaurants, cafes and shops have Electronic Funds Transfer at Point of Sale (Eftpos) facilities, allowing you to make purchases (with your credit or debit card) and even withdraw cash (with your debit card).

Fees Remember that withdrawing cash through ATMs or Eftpos may incur significant fees – check the costs with your bank first.

Credit & Debit Cards

Credit cards such as MasterCard and Visa are widely accepted for most accommodation and services, and a credit card is essential (in lieu of a fat wad of cash) to hire a car. They can also be used to get cash advances over the counter at banks and from many ATMs, depending on the card – but be aware that these withdrawals incur immediate interest. Diners Club and American Express cards are not as widely accepted.

For lost credit cards contact the following:

American Express (☑1300 132 639; www.americanexpress.com.au)

Diners Club (☑1300 360 060; www.dinersclub.com.au)

MasterCard (☑1800 120 113; www.mastercard.com.au)

Visa (☑1800 450 346; www.visa.com.au)

Currency
The Australian dollar comprises 100 cents. There are 5c, 10c, 20c, 50c, $1 and $2 coins, and $5, $10, $20, $50 and $100 notes.

Money Changers
Changing foreign currency is usually no problem at banks throughout Australia, or at licensed money changers such as Travelex or AmEx in airports and cities. Expect substantial fees.

Taxes & Refunds
There's a 10% goods and services tax (GST) automatically added to almost everything you buy, Australia-wide. If you purchase goods with a total minimum value of $300 from any one store within 60 days of departure from Australia, the Tourist Refund Scheme entitles you to a refund of any GST paid.

Keep your receipts and carry the items on board your flight as hand luggage (or get them checked before you check them in); you can get a refund at the designated booth located at international airports (see www.border.gov.au for more information).

Tipping
Tipping isn't traditionally part of Australian etiquette, but it's increasingly the norm to tip around 10% for good service in restaurants, and a few dollars for porters (bell-hops) and taxi drivers.

Opening Hours
Business hours vary from state to state, but use the following as a guide:

Banks 9.30am–4pm Monday to Thursday, to 5pm Friday

Bars 4pm–late

Cafes 7am–5pm

Nightclubs 10pm–4am Thursday to Saturday

Post Offices 9am–5pm Monday to Friday; some also 9am–noon Saturday

Pubs 11am–midnight

Restaurants Noon–2.30pm and 6pm–9pm

Shops 9am–5pm Monday to Saturday

Supermarkets 7am–8pm

Post
Australia Post (www.auspost.com.au) is the nationwide provider. Most substantial towns have a post office, or an Australia Post desk within a bank. Services are reliable, but slower than they used to be (recent cost-saving cut-backs are to blame). Express Post delivers a parcel or envelope interstate within Australia by the next business day; otherwise, allow four days for urban deliveries, and longer for country areas.

Public Holidays
Public holidays vary from state to state (and sometimes year to year). The following is a list of the main national and state public holidays; check locally for precise dates.

National
New Year's Day 1 January

Australia Day 26 January

Easter (Good Friday to Easter Monday inclusive) Late March or early April

Anzac Day 25 April

Queen's Birthday Second Monday in June

Christmas Day 25 December

Boxing Day 26 December

Australian Capital Territory
Canberra Day Second Monday in March

Bank Holiday First Monday in August

Labour Day First Monday in October

New South Wales
Bank Holiday First Monday in August

Labour Day First Monday in October

Queensland
Labour Day First Monday in May

Royal Queensland Show Day (Brisbane) Second or third Wednesday in August

Victoria
Labour Day Second Monday in March

Melbourne Cup Day First Tuesday in November

School Holidays
Key times when prices are highest and much accommodation is booked out in advance:

➡ Christmas holiday season (mid-December to late January)

➡ Easter (March–April)

➡ Shorter (two-week) school-holiday periods generally fall in mid-April, late June to mid-July, and late September to mid-October.

Telephone
Emergency & Important Numbers

Australia's country code	☎61
International access code	☎0011
Ambulance, fire, police	☎000
Centres Against Sexual Assault	☎1800 806 292
Translating & Interpreting Service	☎131 450

Mobile Phones
Connections To get connected, buy a starter kit, which may include a phone or, if you have your own phone, a SIM card (usually $2) and some call/data credit. Pick up starter kits and SIM cards at airport mobile-phone shops or

outlets in the big cities. Purchase recharge vouchers at convenience stores and newsagents. Expect a calls-plus-data package to cost around $30 a month for around 3GB–5GB.

Numbers Local numbers with the prefix 04xx belong to mobile phones.

Reception The east coast generally gets good mobile-phone reception, but service can be haphazard or nonexistent in the interior and far north (eg the Daintree Rainforest).

Local Calls

➡ Local calls from private phones cost 30c and are untimed.

➡ Local calls from public phones cost 50c and are untimed.

➡ Calls to mobile phones attract higher rates and are timed.

International Calls

➡ When calling overseas you need to dial the international access code from Australia (✆0011), the country code then the area code (without the initial ✆0).

➡ If calling Australia from overseas the country code is ✆61 and you need to drop the ✆0 in the state/territory area codes.

Long Distance Calls & Area Codes

➡ STD (long-distance) calls can be made from private phones, mobile phones and virtually any public phone and are cheaper during off-peak hours (7pm to 7am).

➡ When calling from one area to another area within the same area code, there's no need to dial the area code before the local number. If these calls are long-distance (more than 50km away), they're charged at long-distance rates, even though they have the same area code.

➡ Area codes on the east coast:

State/ Territory	Area Code
ACT	✆02
NSW	✆02
Queensland	✆07
Victoria	✆03

Information & Toll-Free Calls

➡ Toll-free numbers (prefix 1800) can be called free of charge, though they may not be accessible from certain areas or from mobile phones.

➡ Calls to numbers beginning with ✆13 or ✆1300 are charged at the rate of a local call.

➡ To make a reverse-charge (collect) call within Australia, dial 1800-REVERSE (✆1800 738 3773) from any public or private phone.

➡ Telephone numbers beginning with either ✆1800, ✆13 or ✆1300 cannot be dialled from outside Australia.

Phonecards

A variety of phonecards can be bought at newsagents, hostels and post offices for a fixed dollar value (usually $10, $20 etc) and can be used with any public or private phone. Shop around.

Most public phones use phonecards; some also accept credit cards. Old-fashioned coin-operated public phones are becoming increasingly rare (and if you do find one, chances are the coin slot will be gummed up or vandalised beyond function).

Time

Australia is divided into three time zones:

Eastern Standard Time (GMT 10 hours) Queensland, New South Wales (NSW), Australian Capital Territory (ACT), Victoria and Tasmania.

Central Standard Time (half-hour behind Eastern Standard Time) Northern Territory, South Australia.

Western Standard Time (two hours behind Eastern Standard Time) Western Australia.

Note that Queensland remains on Eastern Standard Time all year, while most of the rest of Australia switches to daylight-saving time over the summer (October to early April), when clocks are wound forwards one hour.

Tourist Information

Tourist information is provided in Australia by various regional and local offices – often info centres staffed by volunteers (chatty retirees) in key tourist spots. Each state also has a government-run tourist organisation ready to inundate you with information:

New South Wales (www. visitnsw.com)

Queensland (www.queensland-holidays.com.au)

Victoria (www.visitvictoria.com)

The Australian Tourist Commission (www.australia. com) is the countrywide government body charged with luring foreign visitors.

Travellers with Disabilities

Disability awareness in Australia is reasonably high. Legislation requires that new accommodation must meet accessibility standards and tourist operators must not discriminate. Facilities for wheelchairs are improving in accommodation, but there are still many older establishments where the necessary upgrades haven't been made: call ahead to confirm.

Download Lonely Planet's free Accessible Travel guide from http://lptravel.to/ AccessibleTravel.

Resources

Australian Tourist Commission (www.australia.com) Publishes detailed, downloadable information for people with disabilities, including travel and transport tips and contact addresses of organisations in each state.

Deaf Australia (www.deafau.org.au)

National Disability Service (☑02-6283 3200; www.nds.org.au) The national industry association for disability services.

National Information Communication & Awareness Network (Nican; ☑1300 655 535, 02 6241 1220; www.nican.com.au) Australia-wide directory providing information on access, accommodation, sports and recreational activities, transport and specialist tour operators.

Vision Australia (☑1300 847 466; www.visionaustralia.org.au)

Visas

All visitors to Australia need a visa. New Zealand visitors are granted a visa on arrival. All other passport holders must apply for a visa. Apply online through the **Department of Immigration and Border Protection** (☑1300 363 263, 02-6275 6666; www.border.gov.au).

eVisitor (651)

➡ Many European passport holders are eligible for a free eVisitor visa, allowing stays in Australia for up to three months within a 12-month period.

➡ eVisitor visas must be applied for online. They are electronically stored and linked to individual passport numbers, so no stamp in your passport is required.

➡ It's advisable to apply at least 14 days prior to the proposed date of travel to Australia.

Electronic Travel Authority (ETA; 601)

➡ Passport holders from the European countries eligible for eVisitor visas, plus passport holders from Brunei, Canada, Hong Kong, Japan, Malaysia, Singapore, South Korea and the USA, can apply for either a visitor ETA or business ETA.

➡ ETAs are valid for 12 months, with stays of up to three months on each visit.

➡ ETA visas cost $20.

Visitor (600)

➡ Short-term Visitor visas have largely been replaced by the eVisitor and ETA. However, if you're from a country not covered by either, or you want to stay longer than three months, you'll need to apply for a Visitor visa.

➡ Standard Visitor visas allow one entry for a stay of up to three, six or 12 months, and are valid for use within 12 months of issue.

➡ Visitor visas cost from $130 to $1000.

Work & Holiday (462)

➡ Nationals from Argentina, Bangladesh, Chile, China, Indonesia, Israel, Malaysia, Poland, Portugal, the Slovak Republic, Slovenia, Spain, Thailand, Turkey, Uruguay and the USA aged between 18 and 30 can apply for a Work and Holiday visa prior to entry to Australia.

➡ Once granted, this visa allows the holder to enter Australia within three months of issue, stay for up to 12 months, leave and re-enter Australia any number of times within those 12 months, undertake temporary employment to supplement a trip, and study for up to four months.

➡ Application fee $440.

Working Holiday (417)

➡ Young (aged 18 to 30) visitors from Belgium, Canada, Cyprus, Denmark, Estonia, Finland, France, Germany, Hong Kong, Ireland, Italy, Japan, the Republic of Korea, Malta, the Netherlands, Norway, Sweden, Taiwan and the UK are eligible for a Working Holiday visa, which allows you to visit for up to 12 months and gain casual employment.

➡ Holders can leave and re-enter Australia any number of times within those 12 months.

➡ Holders can only work for any one employer for a maximum of six months.

➡ Apply prior to entry to Australia (up to a year in advance); you can't change from another tourist visa to a Working Holiday visa once you're in Australia.

➡ Conditions include having a return air ticket or sufficient funds ($5000) for a return or onward fare.

➡ Application fee $440.

➡ Second Working Holiday visas can be applied for once you're in Australia, subject to certain conditions.

Visa Extensions

If you want to stay in Australia for longer than your visa allows, you'll need to apply for a new visa (usually a Visitor visa 600). Apply online at least two or three weeks before your visa expires.

Volunteering

Lonely Planet's *Volunteer: A Traveller's Guide to Making a Difference Around the World* provides useful information about volunteering.

Resources

Conservation Volunteers Australia (www.conservationvolunteers.com.au) Nonprofit organisation involved in tree planting, walking-track construction, and flora and fauna surveys.

Go Volunteer (www.govolunteer.com.au) National website listing volunteer opportunities.

Greening Australia (www.greeningaustralia.org.au) Helps volunteers get involved with environmental projects in the bush or in plant nurseries.

Reef Check (www.reefcheckaustralia.org) Train to monitor the health of the Great Barrier Reef (not so healthy of late...).

Sea Turtle Foundation (www.seaturtlefoundation.org) Volunteer opportunities in sea-turtle conservation.

Volunteering Australia (www.volunteeringaustralia.org) Support, advice and volunteer training.

Volunteering Qld (www.volunteeringqld.org.au) Volunteering info and advice across Queensland.

Willing Workers on Organic Farms (www.wwoof.com.au) WWOOFing is where you do a few hours' work each day on a farm in return for bed and board. Most hosts are concerned to some extent with alternative lifestyles, and have a minimum stay of two nights. Join online for $70. You'll get a membership number and a booklet listing participating enterprises ($5 overseas postage). There's also an app available ($20).

Women Travellers

The east coast is generally a safe place for women travellers, although the usual sensible precautions apply. Sexual harassment is rare, though some macho Aussie males still slip – particularly in rural areas when they've been drinking. Hitchhiking isn't such a great idea anywhere in Australia these days, even when travelling in pairs.

Work

If you come to Australia on a tourist visa then you're not allowed to work for pay. You'll need either a Work and Holiday (462; p509) or Working Holiday (417; p509) visa; see www.border.gov.au for details.

Finding Work

It's easy to find bar and hospitality work in the major cities, as well as during peak season in tourist hubs such as Cairns, the Gold Coast and resort towns along the Queensland coast.

To serve alcohol in Australia, you need to do an online Responsible Service of Alcohol (RSA) course. It's very easy and fast to do online but, frustratingly, there's a different one for each state. The NSW one is quite a bit more expensive (around $110) than the Victorian or Queensland ones.

Seasonal fruit picking (harvesting) relies on casual labour, and there is something to be picked, pruned or farmed somewhere in Australia year-round (just don't expect to make a fortune).

People with computer, secretarial, nursing and teaching skills can find work temping in the major cities (via employment agencies).

Resources

Backpacker noticeboards and local newspapers are good resources for local work opportunities.

Australian JobSearch (www.jobsearch.gov.au) Myriad jobs across the country.

Career One (www.careerone.com.au) General employment site; good for metropolitan areas.

Gumtree (www.gumtree.com.au) Great for finding casual jobs quickly.

Harvest Trail (www.harvesttrail.gov.au) Harvest job specialists.

National Harvest Telephone Information Service (☏1800 062 332) Advice on when and where you're likely to pick up harvest work.

Seek (www.seek.com.au) General employment site; good for metropolitan areas.

Travellers at Work (www.taw.com.au) Excellent site for working travellers in Australia.

Workabout Australia (www.workaboutaustralia.com.au) Gives a state-by-state breakdown of seasonal work opportunities.

Income Tax

If you're earning money in Australia, you'll be paying tax in Australia and will have to lodge a tax return. See the website of the Australian Taxation Office (www.ato.gov.au) for info on how to do this, including getting a payment summary from your employer, timing and dates for lodging returns, and receiving your notice of assessment.

As part of this process you'll need to apply for a Tax File Number (TFN) to give your employer. Without it, tax will be deducted at the maximum rate from your wages. Apply online via the Australian Taxation Office; it takes up to four weeks to be issued.

Transport

GETTING THERE & AWAY

Australia's east coast is a long way from just about everywhere (including Australia's west coast) – getting here usually means a long-haul flight. Flights, tours and rail tickets can be booked online at lonelyplanet.com/bookings.

Entering the Country

If you're arriving on the east coast on an international flight, the process is usually straightforward and efficient, with the usual passport checks and customs declarations.

Air

High season (with the highest prices) for flights into Australia is roughly over the country's summer (December to February); low season generally tallies with the winter months (June to August), though this is actually peak season in the tropical north.

Airports & Airlines

On the east coast, most international flights head to Sydney, Melbourne or Brisbane, though Cairns and the Gold Coast (and now even Canberra!) also receive the occasional international flight.

Brisbane Airport (www.bne.com.au; Airport Dr)

Cairns Airport (☑07-4080 6703; www.cairnsairport.com; Airport Ave)

Canberra Airport (☑02-6275 2222; www.canberraairport.com.au; 2 Brindabella Circuit)

Gold Coast Airport (www.goldcoastairport.com.au; Longa Ave, Bilinga)

Melbourne Airport (MEL;☑03-9297 1600; www.melbourneairport.com.au; Departure Rd, Tullamarine)

Sydney Airport (☑02-9667 9111; www.sydneyairport.com.au; Airport Dr, Mascot)

Australia's international carrier is Qantas (www.qantas.com.au), which has an outstanding safety record (...as Dustin Hoffman said in *Rainman*, 'Qantas never crashed'). Qantas offers a discount-fare Walkabout Pass for passengers flying into Australia from overseas with Qantas or American Airlines. The pass allows you to link up around 80 domestic Australian destinations for less than you'd pay booking flights individually. See www.qantas.com.au for more information.

Land

If you're exploring all of Australia, travelling overland to the east coast from elsewhere in this wide brown land may well be how you arrive.

Bus

Aside from bus routes linking the states along the east coast, long-distance buses truck into Queensland from the Northern Territory, and

---

CLIMATE CHANGE & TRAVEL

Every form of transport that relies on carbon-based fuel generates CO_2, the main cause of human-induced climate change. Modern travel is dependent on aeroplanes, which might use less fuel per kilometre per person than most cars but travel much greater distances. The altitude at which aircraft emit gases (including CO_2) and particles also contributes to their climate change impact. Many websites offer 'carbon calculators' that allow people to estimate the carbon emissions generated by their journey and, for those who wish to do so, to offset the impact of the greenhouse gases emitted with contributions to portfolios of climate-friendly initiatives throughout the world. Lonely Planet offsets the carbon footprint of all staff and author travel.

DEPARTURE TAX

Departure tax is included in the price of a ticket.

into Victoria and New South Wales from South Australia. Greyhound (www.greyhound.com.au) is the main interstate player.

Car & Motorcycle

The highways rolling into Victoria, New South Wales and Queensland from South Australia and the Northern Territory are in good shape and well trafficked.

Train

Trains from Adelaide roll into Melbourne, and into Sydney from as far off as Perth; **Great Southern Rail** (www.greatsouthernrail.com.au) is the operator.

Sea

Cruise & Cargo Ship

Numerous companies operate holiday cruises to east-coast Australia from all over the world. Shorter cruises are also available between Brisbane, Melbourne or Sydney and destinations in New Zealand and the Pacific.

Alternatively, some freighter ships allow passengers to travel on board as they ship cargo to/from Australia: see websites such as www.freighterexpeditions.com.au and www.freighter cruises.com for options.

Yacht

It is possible (if not straightforward) to travel between Australia and Papua New Guinea, Indonesia, New Zealand and the Pacific islands by hitching rides or crewing on yachts – usually you have to at least contribute towards food. Ask around at marinas and sailing clubs in places such as Coffs Harbour, Great Keppel Island, Airlie Beach, the Whitsundays and Cairns.

April is a good time to look for a berth in the Sydney area.

GETTING AROUND

Air

East-coast Australia is well serviced by airlines big and small.

Hinterland Aviation (www.hinterlandaviation.com.au) Flies between Cairns and Cooktown.

Jetgo (www.jetgo.com) Flights between Essendon Airport in Melbourne's northern suburbs and Brisbane and Port Macquarie, and between the Gold Coast, Rockhampton and Townsville.

Jetstar (www.jetstar.com.au) Budget offshoot of Qantas; has extensive services.

Qantas (www.qantas.com.au) Australia's main player; extensive services.

Regional Express (www.regionalexpress.com.au) Connects Melbourne, Sydney, Brisbane, Cairns and Townsville with small regional airports.

Skytrans (www.skytrans.com.au) Serves northern Queensland and the Torres Strait, flying from Cairns to Bamaga (tip of Australia) among other obscure locations.

Tiger Airways (www.tigerair.com) Budget offshoot of Singapore Airlines. Serves multiple east-coast destinations from Melbourne to Cairns.

Virgin Australia (www.virginaustralia.com.au) Services throughout Australia.

Bicycle

Whether you're hiring a bike to ride around a city or wearing out your sprockets on a long-distance haul, the east coast is ideal for cycling. There are bike paths in most cities, and in the country you'll find thousands of kilometres of good (and not too hilly) roads. Many touring cyclists carry camping

equipment, but it's feasible to travel from town to town staying in hostels, hotels or caravan parks.

Legalities Bicycle helmets are compulsory, as are white front lights and red rear lights for riding at night.

Weather The Aussie summer cooks! Always carry plenty of water. Wear a helmet with a peak (or a cap under your helmet), use sunscreen and avoid cycling in the middle of the day. Beware summer northerlies that can make a northbound cyclist's life hell. It can get very cold in Victoria and inland New South Wales, so pack appropriate clothing.

Bicycle Hire

Rates charged by most rental outfits for road or mountain bikes range from $10 to $15 per hour and $25 to $50 per day. Security deposits can range from $50 to $200, depending on the rental period.

Buying a Bike

For a new road or mountain bike in Australia, your bottom starting price will be around $600. With all the requisite on-the-road equipment (panniers, helmet, lights etc) you're looking at upwards of $1700.

To sell your bike (or buy a secondhand one), try hostel noticeboards or online at Trading Post (www.tradingpost.com.au), Gumtree (www.gumtree.com.au) or Bike Exchange (www.bikeexchange.com.au).

Resources

Each state and territory has a cycling organisation that can help with local information and put you in touch with touring clubs:

Bicycle Network Victoria (www.bicyclenetwork.com.au)

Bicycle NSW (www.bicyclensw.org.au)

Bicycle Queensland (www.bq.org.au)

Pedal Power ACT (www.pedalpower.org.au)

Boat

There are no formal east-coast ferry services, but sailing up and down the coast in a yacht is a possibility. Ask around at marinas in Coffs Harbour, Great Keppel Island, Airlie Beach, the Whitsundays, Sydney and Cairns.

Bus

East-coast Australia's bus network is reliable, but not the cheapest for long hauls. Most buses have air-con and toilets; all are smoke-free. There are no separate classes on buses (very democratic). Book seats at least a day ahead (a week or two during summer). Small towns eschew formal bus terminals for an informal drop-off/pick-up point, usually outside a post office or shop.

Bus Companies

Long-distance bus route operators include the following:

Con-x-ion (www.coachtrans online.com.au) Connects Sydney, Melbourne, Brisbane, Gold Coast and Sunshine Coast airports with surrounding areas.

Firefly Express (www.firefly express.com.au) Runs between Sydney, Canberra, Melbourne and Adelaide.

Greyhound Australia (www. greyhound.com.au) The main player, with an extensive nationwide network.

NSW TrainLink (www.nswtrain link.info) Coach and train services in New South Wales.

Premier Motor Service (www. premierms.com.au) Greyhound's main competitor on the east coast. Has fewer daily services but usually costs a little less.

Trans North (www.transnorth bus.com.au) Cairns to Cooktown via the inland route (Kuranda, Mareeba) or the coast (Port Douglas, Daintree).

V/Line (www.vline.com.au) Bus connections complementing Victorian regional train services.

ROUTE	FARE ($)	TIME (HR)
Brisbane–Airlie Beach	247	20
Brisbane–Airlie Beach	344	32
Melbourne–Canberra	88	8
Melbourne–Sydney	133	12
Sydney–Brisbane	188	17
Sydney–Byron Bay	157	12
Townsville–Cairns	65	5½

Costs

Following are typical, non-discounted, one-way bus fares for some popular east-coast routes:

Reservations

During summer, school holidays and public holidays, you should book well ahead, especially on intercity services. At other times you should have few problems getting onto your preferred service.

Reserve at least a day in advance if you're using a travel pass.

Bus Passes

Bus passes are a good option if you plan on multiple stopovers. Book online or phone at least a day ahead to reserve a seat.

Greyhound offers myriad money-saving passes; check the website for comprehensive info. The main options:

Hop-On/Hop-Off Passes Up to 90 days of one-direction travel along eight popular long-haul routes – including Cairns to Melbourne ($529) and Brisbane to Cairns ($345) – stopping as often as you like.

Kilometre Pass Gives you go-anywhere flexibility, plus the choice to backtrack. Choose from 1000km ($189) up to 25,000km ($2675). Valid for 12 months.

Short-Hop Passes Set shorter hop-on/off routes, including

Sydney to Melbourne ($105), Sydney to Byron Bay ($115) and Sydney to Brisbane ($139). Valid for six months.

Premier Motor Service offers several passes for one-way travel along the east coast, including a six-month pass between Sydney and Cairns ($350) and a three-month pass between Sydney and Brisbane ($100).

Car & Motorcycle

The best way to see the east coast is by car – it's certainly the only way to access interesting out-of-the-way places without taking a tour.

Motorcycles are popular, as the climate is ideal for bikes for much of the year. A fuel range of 350km will easily cover fuel stops along the coast. The long, open roads here are really made for large capacity machines (750cc and up).

Driving Licences

To drive in Australia you'll need to hold a current driving licence issued in English from your home country. If the licence isn't in English, you'll also need to carry an International Driving Permit, issued in your home country.

Fuel

Diesel and unleaded petrol are available from service stations. LPG (gas) is also available in populated areas, but not always at more remote service stations. On main east-coast highways there's usually a small town or petrol station every 50km or so.

Prices vary from place to place, but at the time of writing unleaded was hovering between $1.40 and $1.60 in the cities. Out in the country, prices soar – in outback Queensland you can pay as much as $2.20 per litre.

Automobile Associations

The national **Australian Automobile Association**

Sydney to Melbourne via the Princes Hwy

Total Distance = 1041km

93 Distance (km) between towns

SYDNEY
93
[1]
Wollongong
28
Kiama
47
Nowra
68
Canberra (144km)
Ulladulla
48
[52]
Batemans Bay
69
Narooma
Cooma (101km)
77
[18]
Bega
35
Pambula — Merimbula
Eden
19
57
NSW
VICTORIA Genoa
Bombala (85km) [B23]
47 — Mallacoota (23km)
Cann River
Bemm River (23km)
75
Orbost
Marlo (15km) & Cape Conran (34km)
59
Lakes Entrance
Metung (10km)
Omeo (120km) [B500] 36
Bairnsdale
69
[A1]
Sale [A440]
Yarram (72km)
49
Traralgon [C482]
Yarram (60km)
31
Moe [B460]
28
Leongatha (56km)
Warragul
72
Dandenong
34
MELBOURNE

(AAA; ☎02-6247 7311; www.aaa.asn.au) is the umbrella organisation for the various state associations.

The state organisations have reciprocal arrangements with other states and with similar organisations overseas, including AAA in the USA and RAC or AA in the UK. Bring proof of membership with you.

NRMA (☎13 11 22; www.mynrma.com.au) Covers NSW and the Australian Capital Territory (ACT).

RACQ (☎13 19 05; www.racq.com.au) Covers Queensland.

RACV (☎13 72 28; www.racv.com.au) Covers Victoria.

Hire

There are plenty of car-rental companies, big and small, ready to put you behind the wheel. The main thing to remember is distance – if you want to travel far, you'll need unlimited kilometres.

Larger car-rental companies have drop-offs in major cities and towns. Smaller local firms are sometimes cheaper but may have restrictions. The big firms sometimes offer one-way rentals, which may not cost any extra. Most companies require drivers to be over the age of 21, though in some cases it's 18 and in others it's 25. Typical rates are from $40/60/80 per day for a small/medium/large car.

The usual big international companies (Avis, Budget, Europcar, Hertz, Thrifty) all operate in Australia. The following websites offer rate comparisons and last-minute discounts:

Carhire.com (www.carhire.com.au)

Drive Now (www.drivenow.com.au)

Webjet (www.webjet.com.au)

CAMPERVANS

Companies for campervan hire – with rates from around $90 (two berths) or $150 (four berths) per day, usually with minimum five-day hire and unlimited kilometres – include the following:

Apollo (☎1800 777 779; www.apollocamper.com)

Britz (☎1300 738 087; www.britz.com.au)

Hippie Camper (☎1800 777 779; www.hippie camper.com)

Jucy Rentals (☎1800 150 850; www.jucy.com.au)

Maui (☎1800 827 821; www.maui.com.au)

Mighty Campers (☎1800 821 824; www. mightycampers.com.au)

Spaceships (☎1300 132 469; www.spaceships rentals.com.au)

Travelwheels (☎0412 766 616; www.travel wheels.com.au)

FOUR-WHEEL DRIVES

Having a 4WD enables you to get right off the beaten track and revel in the natural splendour that many travellers miss. Something midsized like a Nissan X-Trail costs around $100 to $150 per day; for a Toyota Land-Cruiser you're looking at around $150 up to $200, which should include unlimited kilometres. Check insurance conditions carefully, especially the excess, as they can be onerous.

The major car-hire companies have 4WD rentals, or try Apollo or Britz.

ONE-WAY RELOCATIONS

Relocations are usually cheap deals, although they don't allow much time flexibility. Most of the large hire companies offer deals, or try the following operators:

Drive Now (www.drivenow.com.au)

imoova (www.imoova.com)

Relocations2Go (www.facebook.com/relocations2go)

Transfercar (www.transfercar.com.au)

Insurance

Third-Party Insurance In Australia, third-party personal-injury insurance is included in the vehicle-registration cost, ensuring that every registered vehicle carries at least minimum insurance. We recommend extending that minimum to at least third-party property insurance – minor collisions can be amazingly expensive.

Rental Vehicles When it comes to hire cars, understand your liability in the event of an accident. You can pay an additional daily amount to the rental company that will reduce your liability in the event of an accident from upwards of $3000 to a few hundred dollars.

Exclusions Be aware that if you're driving on dirt roads you may not be covered by insurance (even if you have a 4WD): if you have an accident you'll be liable for all costs. Also, many insurance policies don't cover damage to windscreens or tyres – always read the small print.

Purchase

If you plan to stay several months and do plenty of driving, buying a car will probably work out to be cheaper than renting one. You can buy from a car dealer, a private seller or from the dedicated travellers' car markets in Sydney.

REGISTRATION & LEGALITIES

When you buy a vehicle in Australia, you need to transfer the registration into your own name within 14 days. Each state has slightly different requirements and different organisations that do this. Similarly, when selling a vehicle you need to advise the state or territory road transport authority of the sale and change of name.

Sydney to Brisbane via the Pacific Hwy

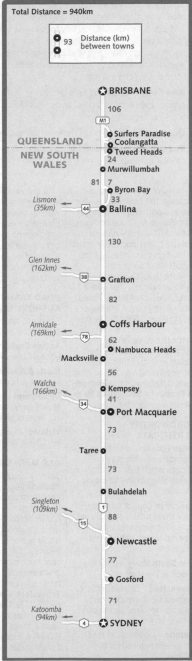

TOLL ROADS

There are a handful of toll roads on the east coast – mostly on major freeways around Melbourne, Sydney and Brisbane. Ensure you pay tolls online or you'll face hefty fines – whether you're travelling in your own vehicle or in a rental. Unless you've organised a toll pass ahead of time, you usually have two or three days to pay after driving the toll road.

New South Wales Pay tolls by signing up for a pass online: www.roam.com.au, www.myRTA.com or www.roamexpress.com.au.

Queensland Pay tolls online: www.govia.com.au.

Victoria Pay tolls by signing up for a pass online: www.citylink.com.au.

In NSW, Queensland and Victoria, the buyer and seller need to complete and sign a transfer-of-registration form. In the ACT there's no form, but the buyer and seller need to co-sign the reverse of the registration certificate.

Note that it's much easier to sell a car in the same state in which it's registered, otherwise you (or the buyer) must re-register it in the new state, which can be a hassle.

It's the buyer's responsibility to ensure the car isn't stolen and that there's no money owing on it; check the car's details with the **Personal Property Securities Register** (www.ppsr.gov.au).

ROADWORTHY CERTIFICATE

Sellers are required to provide a roadworthy certificate when transferring registration in the following situations:

Australian Capital Territory – Once the vehicle is six years old; annual inspection record also required for vehicles running on gas.

New South Wales – Once the vehicle is five years old.

Queensland – Safety Certificate required for all vehicles; certificate also required for vehicles running on gas.

Victoria – Certificate of roadworthiness required for all vehicles.

If the vehicle you're considering doesn't have a roadworthy certificate, it's worth having a roadworthiness check done by a mechanic before you buy it. The state automobile associations have lists of licenced vehicle testers.

ROAD TRANSPORT AUTHORITIES

For more information about processes and costs:

Access Canberra (www.rego.act.gov.au) Covers ACT.

Roads & Maritime (www.rta.nsw.gov.au) Covers NSW.

Department of Transport & Main Roads (www.tmr.qld.gov.au) Covers Queensland.

VicRoads (www.vicroads.vic.gov.au) Covers Victoria.

CAR MARKETS

Sydney and Cairns are particularly good places to buy cars from backpackers who have finished their trips: try hostel noticeboards. There are also a couple of big backpacker car markets in Sydney. It's possible these cars have been around Australia several times, so it can be a risky option. Try **Sydney Travellers Car Market** (02-9331 4361; www.sydney travellerscarmarket.com.au; Level 2, Kings Cross Car Park, Ward Ave, Kings Cross; 10am-5pm Mon-Sat; Kings Cross).

Road Hazards

Fatigue Be wary of the weary; driving long distances (particularly in hot weather) can be utterly exhausting. Falling asleep at the wheel is not uncommon. On a long haul, stop and rest every two hours or so – do some exercise, change drivers or have a coffee.

Roadkill A huge problem in Australia. Many Australians avoid travelling once the sun drops because of the risks posed by nocturnal animals on the roads.

Two-Lane Roads East Coast Australia has few multilane highways, although there are stretches of divided road (four or six lanes) in busy areas such as the toll roads in Sydney, Melbourne and Brisbane. Two-lane roads, however, are the only option for many routes.

Unsealed Roads Conditions vary wildly and cars perform differently when braking and turning on dirt. Don't exceed 80km/h on dirt roads; if you go faster you won't have time to respond to a sharp turn, stock on the road or an unmarked gate or cattle grid. If you're in a rental car, check your contract to ensure you're covered for driving on unsealed roads.

Road Rules

Australians drive on the left-hand side of the road; all cars are right-hand drive.

Drink-Driving Random breath tests are common. If you're caught with a blood alcohol concentration of more than 0.05 grams per 100ml, expect a court appearance, a fine and the loss of your licence. Police can randomly pull any driver over for a breathalyser or drug test.

Give Way If an intersection is unmarked (unusual) and at roundabouts, you must give way to vehicles entering the intersection from your right.

Mobile Phones Using a mobile phone while driving is illegal (excluding hands-free technology).

Seatbelts & Car Seats Seatbelt usage is compulsory. Children up to the age of seven must be belted into an approved safety seat.

Speed Limits The general speed limit in built-up and residential areas is 50km/h (sometimes 60km/h). Near schools the limit is usually 25km/h around school drop-off and pick-up times. On the highway it's 100km/h or 110km/h. Police have speed radar guns and cameras and are fond of using them in strategic locations.

Parking

One of the big problems with driving around big cities like Sydney, Brisbane and Melbourne (or popular tourist towns like Byron Bay) is finding somewhere to park. Even if you do find a spot there's likely to be a time restriction, a meter (or ticket machine) or both. Parking fines range from about $50 to $120 and if you park in a clearway your car will be towed away or clamped – check the signs.

In the cities there are large car parks where you can park all day for $20 to $40.

Hitching & Ride-Sharing

Hitching is never entirely safe in any country in the world, and we don't recommend it. Travellers who decide to hitch should understand that they are taking a small but potentially serious risk. People who do choose to hitch will be safer if they travel in pairs and let someone know where they are planning to go.

Ride-sharing is a good way to split costs and environmental impact with other travellers. As with hitching, there are potential risks: meet in a public place before hitting the road, and if anything seems off, don't hesitate to back out. Hostel noticeboards are good places to find ads; also check the following online classifieds:

Catch a Lift (www.catchalift.com)

Coseats (www.coseats.com)

HopHop Ride (www.hophopride. com.au)

Share Ur Ride (www.shareur ride.com.au)

Local Transport

Brisbane, Melbourne and Sydney have public-transport systems utilising buses, trains, ferries and/or trams. Larger regional towns and cities have their own local bus systems. Sizeable towns also have taxis.

The new G:link (Gold Coast Light Rail; www.gold linq.com.au) is now operational, linking 16 stops over 13km between Southport and Broadbeach.

Train

Train travel is a comfortable option for short- or long-haul sectors along the east coast, but it's also a few dollars more than travelling by bus and it may take a few hours longer.

Rail services within each state (and sometimes extending interstate) are run by that state's rail body:

NSW TrainLink (☎13 22 32; www.nswtrainlink.info) Operates from Sydney south to Canberra and Melbourne, and along the coast north to Brisbane (but not Byron Bay).

Queensland Rail Travel (☎1300 131 722; www. queenslandrailtravel.com. au) Connects Brisbane with the Gold Coast and Sunshine Coast, extending to Cairns with offshoots to Charleville, Mt Isa and Longreach.

Sydney Trains (☎13 15 00; www.sydneytrains.info) Connects Sydney with the Blue Mountains, South Coast and Central Coast.

V/Line (☎1800 800 007; www. vline.com.au) Connects Victoria with NSW, South Australia and the ACT.

Costs

Children, students and backpackers can generally secure a discount on standard fares. If you can stretch your budget to a sleeper cabin, we highly recommend it (sleeping upright in a seat surrounded by the snoring proletariat isn't always a great way to travel). Note that cheaper fares are generally nonrefundable with no changes permitted. Some typical fares:

Brisbane–Cairns Adult/child seated from $369/185; in a cabin from $519/311

Sydney–Brisbane Adult/child seated $92/46; cabin $216/180

Sydney–Canberra Adult/child seated $40/20

Sydney–Melbourne Adult/child seated $92/46; cabin $216/180

Reservations

During national holidays, school holidays and weekends, book your seat a week or two in advance if possible. Many discount fares require you to reserve well in advance.

Rail Passes

Coverage of the east coast by rail isn't bad, and several useful passes are sold.

Discovery Pass Allows travel with unlimited stops in any direction on the NSW TrainLink regional train and coach network, including extensions to Melbourne, Brisbane and Canberra; available for 14 days ($232), one month ($275), three months ($298) or six months ($420). Routes must be prebooked.

Queensland Coastal Pass Available only to international visitors; allows one month ($209) or two months ($289) of one-direction travel on the main Queensland Rail Travel trains, between the Gold Coast and Cairns.

Queensland Explorer Pass Available only to international visitors; allows one month ($299) or two months ($389) of travel in any direction on the whole Queensland Rail Travel network.

Behind the Scenes

SEND US YOUR FEEDBACK

We love to hear from travellers – your comments keep us on our toes and help make our books better. Our well-travelled team reads every word on what you loved or loathed about this book. Although we cannot reply individually to your submissions, we always guarantee that your feedback goes straight to the appropriate authors, in time for the next edition. Each person who sends us information is thanked in the next edition – the most useful submissions are rewarded with a selection of digital PDF chapters.

Visit **lonelyplanet.com/contact** to submit your updates and suggestions or to ask for help. Our award-winning website also features inspirational travel stories, news and discussions.

Note: We may edit, reproduce and incorporate your comments in Lonely Planet products such as guidebooks, websites and digital products, so let us know if you don't want your comments reproduced or your name acknowledged. For a copy of our privacy policy visit lonelyplanet.com/privacy.

OUR READERS

Many thanks to the travellers who used the last edition and wrote to us with helpful hints, useful advice and interesting anecdotes: Chris Senior, Helen Snazell, Jack and Deidre Evans, Jane Edwards, Jenny Williams, Jerry Palmer, Kay Blaha, Nadine Kleeman, Sain Alizada, Sebastian Hochradner, Sergio Estevao, Steve Walker

WRITER THANKS

Andy Symington

As a prodigal Sydneysider returned for this project, I've had so much invaluable advice and help from friends, about what's going on in town, that I can't possibly thank them all. Tourist offices and more were helpful across the region. Particular gratitude, however, goes to Stephen Freiberg, Kate McGuinness, Hugh O'Keefe, Ben Hamilton, Matthew Beech, Iain and Amanda Ashley, Tasmin Waby and the LP team. And also, as ever, to my family.

Kate Armstrong

Particular thanks to Jacqui Loftus-Hills, Visit Victoria; Wendy Jones, Goulburn River Valley Tourism; Sue Couttie, Tourism Northeast; Marie Glasson, Greater Shepparton City Council; Fran Martin, Echuca Visitor Information Centre. Finally, to my dear friends Sue Mulligan, Lou Bull and Emmo – with thanks.

Cristian Bonetto

First and foremost, an epic thankyou to Drew Westbrook for his hospitality and generosity. Sincere thanks also to Craig Bradbery, Tim Crabtree, Amy Ratcliffe, Leanne Layfield, Terese Finegan, Michael Flocke, Simon Betteridge, Annabel Sullivan, Garry Judd and the many locals who offered insight and insider knowledge along the way. At Lonely Planet, a huge thanks to Tasmin Waby for her support and encouragement.

Peter Dragicevich

Researching this guidebook was an absolute pleasure, especially because of the wonderful company that I had on the road. Special thanks go to Braith Bamkin, Peter van Gaalen, Marg Toohey and Jo Stafford for all their practical assistance in Melbourne, and to David Mills and Barry Sawtell for the Canberra Morrissey safari. And cheers to all my eating and drinking buddies along the way, especially Errol Hunt, Kim Shearman, Cristian Bonetto and Maryanne Netto.

Paul Harding

Thanks to all those travellers and locals who helped with company and advice on my journey through Queensland's most remote corners, especially the helpful guys who got me out of vehicular trouble at Elliot Falls. Thanks to Tamara for coffee and a chat in Cairns, and to Tasmin at LP. But mostly to Hannah and Layla for being there.

BEHIND THE SCENES

Trent Holden

First up a massive thanks to Tasmin Waby for commissioning me to update the bulk of regional Victoria. Was an absolute honour to cover my home state. Totally blown away how much cool stuff there is to visit out here. Thanks to all the tourist visitor centres across the state, who are staffed by a fantastic team of volunteers who are doing a sensational job. Cheers to everyone else for giving me the time of day for a chat, and helping me put together this new edition. As per always lots of love to my family, particularly my partner Kate, who I had the great fortune of having accompany me around this time round.

Kate Morgan

Big thanks to Destination Editor, Tasmin Waby, for the opportunity to basically eat and drink my way around Melbourne's best neighbourhoods! Thank you to Caro Cooper for suggestions and being a drinking partner on occasion, and to my partner Trent for all your help and support.

Charles Rawlings-Way

Huge thanks to Tasmin for the gig, and to all the helpful souls I met and friends I reconnected with on the road who flew through my questions with the greatest of ease. Biggest thanks of all to Meg, who held the increasingly chaotic fort while I was busy scooting around in the sunshine ('Where's daddy?') – and made sure that Ione, Remy, Liv and Reuben were fed, watered, schooled, tucked in and read to.

Tamara Sheward

Sweaty Cairns hugs and hearty thanks to my friends, family, local experts and random ring ins who helped me delve ever deeper into the wonders of my hometown and surrounds; it's always an eye-opener being a traveller/travel writer in one's own backyard. At LP, mega-thanks to Tasmin Waby for the gig, and for your eternal encouragement; and to chapter co-author Paul Harding. The biggest clink of the coconuts goes, as ever, to my favourite FNQers: my crazy crocodiles Dušan and Masha.

Tom Spurling

To Goose for riding shotgun to Rockhampton and making me go for a jog. To Lucy for sleeping in the backseat and showing no interest in cryptic crosswords. To the bar staff in Ravenswood for reminding me why I wanted this job in the first place. To The Whitsundays for being discovered. To the Town of 1770 for providing so many openings at dinner parties ('A number? Really?'). To my children for not missing me very much (I will never forget that slight, O and P).

Donna Wheeler

Love and gratitude to Juliette Claire for her inspiration and incredible regional knowledge. Thanks to ex-locals Peter Maclaine and Debbie Wheeler, especially for Pete's surfing expertise. Thanks to Harry in Broadbeach, to the Byron skydivers and to Amanda and Simon in Brunswick Heads for great hospo insights. Thanks also to Nic Wrathall for your company during some long research days and Brigid Healy and Andrew King, Kate Dale, Darryn Devlin for Sydney homecoming love. Finally thanks to Joe Guario. for everything.

ACKNOWLEDGEMENTS

Climate map data adapted from Peel MC, Finlayson BL & McMahon TA (2007) 'Updated World Map of the Köppen-Geiger Climate Classification', Hydrology and Earth System Sciences, 11, 163344.

Cover photograph: Surfing near Noosa, Queensland, Nick Rains/Getty Images ©

THIS BOOK

This 6th edition of Lonely Planet's *East Coast Australia* guidebook was researched and written by Andy Symington, Kate Armstrong, Cristian Bonetto, Peter Dragicevich, Paul Harding, Trent Holden, Kate Morgan, Charles Rawlings-Way, Tamara Sheward, Tom Spurling and Donna Wheeler. The previous edition was coordinated by Charles Rawlings-Way. This guidebook was produced by the following:

Destination Editor
Tasmin Waby

Product Editor Jessica Ryan, Catherine Naghten

Senior Cartographer
Julie Sheridan

Book Designer
Nicholas Colicchia

Assisting Editors
Andrew Bain, Sarah Bailey, Imogen Bannister, Michelle Bennett, Laura Crawford, Melanie Dankel, Andrea Dobbin, Gabrielle Innes, Ali Lemer, Jodie Martire, Rosie Nicholson, Lauren O'Connell, Charlotte Orr, Susan Paterson, Chris Pitts, Gabrielle Stefanos, Saralinda Turner, Simon Williamson

Cartographer
Rachel Imeson

Cover Researcher
Campbell McKenzie

Thanks to Jennifer Carey, Heather Champion, Daniel Corbett, Megan Eaves, Sandie Kestell, Claire Naylor, Karyn Noble, MaSovaida Morgan, Lauren O'Connell, Rachel Rawling, Vicky Smith, Angela Tinson, Clifton Wilkinson

Index

Map Legend

Sights

- Beach
- Bird Sanctuary
- Buddhist
- Castle/Palace
- Christian
- Confucian
- Hindu
- Islamic
- Jain
- Jewish
- Monument
- Museum/Gallery/Historic Building
- Ruin
- Shinto
- Sikh
- Taoist
- Winery/Vineyard
- Zoo/Wildlife Sanctuary
- Other Sight

Activities, Courses & Tours

- Bodysurfing
- Diving
- Canoeing/Kayaking
- Course/Tour
- Sento Hot Baths/Onsen
- Skiing
- Snorkelling
- Surfing
- Swimming/Pool
- Walking
- Windsurfing
- Other Activity

Sleeping

- Sleeping
- Camping

Eating

- Eating

Drinking & Nightlife

- Drinking & Nightlife
- Cafe

Entertainment

- Entertainment

Shopping

- Shopping

Information

- Bank
- Embassy/Consulate
- Hospital/Medical
- Internet
- Police
- Post Office
- Telephone
- Toilet
- Tourist Information
- Other Information

Geographic

- Beach
- Gate
- Hut/Shelter
- Lighthouse
- Lookout
- Mountain/Volcano
- Oasis
- Park
- Pass
- Picnic Area
- Waterfall

Population

- Capital (National)
- Capital (State/Province)
- City/Large Town
- Town/Village

Transport

- Airport
- Border crossing
- Bus
- Cable car/Funicular
- Cycling
- Ferry
- Metro station
- Monorail
- Parking
- Petrol station
- Subway station
- Taxi
- Train station/Railway
- Tram
- Underground station
- Other Transport

Note: Not all symbols displayed above appear on the maps in this book

Routes

- Tollway
- Freeway
- Primary
- Secondary
- Tertiary
- Lane
- Unsealed road
- Road under construction
- Plaza/Mall
- Steps
- Tunnel
- Pedestrian overpass
- Walking Tour
- Walking Tour detour
- Path/Walking Trail

Boundaries

- International
- State/Province
- Disputed
- Regional/Suburb
- Marine Park
- Cliff
- Wall

Hydrography

- River, Creek
- Intermittent River
- Canal
- Water
- Dry/Salt/Intermittent Lake
- Reef

Areas

- Airport/Runway
- Beach/Desert
- Cemetery (Christian)
- Cemetery (Other)
- Glacier
- Mudflat
- Park/Forest
- Sight (Building)
- Sportsground
- Swamp/Mangrove